Dear Readers,

Through its first three editions, *Succeeding with Technology* has made its way into the hands of tens of thousands of instructors and students at dozens of colleges, universities, and technical schools across the country and around the world. A lot has changed in the world of technology since the publication of the last edition; we have created *Succeeding with Technology, Fourth Edition* to encompass the latest technology and trends, and to take *Succeeding with Technology* to the next level in terms of quality and relevance.

The original approach and philosophy of our book remains consistent in this new edition: to prepare students for success in their careers and personal lives through the use of technology, to provide coverage beyond PCs to all digital technologies, and to cut through the jargon to focus on technology concepts that truly provide value.

In our second edition, we worked hard to fine-tune the organization and balance of the book based on feedback from teachers and students. In the third edition we made minor adjustments to organization, and focused on improving the overall quality and relevance of the content. According to feedback from teachers and students, along with our own experience using the book in our classes, we believe that we have been successful in evolving *Succeeding with Technology* to a balance and depth of coverage that best suits student and teacher needs.

Since the third edition of *Succeeding with Technology* , technological advances have continued at exponential rates, fundamentally altering the way we live our lives and providing new tools to leverage for success. Online social networks and Web 2.0 technologies provide individuals with new ways to communicate, and collaborate. This, combined with revolutionary smart phones like the iPhone, Google Android, Palm Pre, and dozens of others, have students and professionals engaged online for major portions of each day. Web development frameworks like Drupal, Joomla, WordPress, and many others allow nearly anyone to create professional-grade Web sites for themselves or their businesses. New software continues to empower users to be more creative, effective, efficient, and productive than ever before. This digital power is becoming increasingly available anywhere, anytime due to the move toward cloud computing.

While technological advances provide amazing new opportunities for success, they also provide new ethical dilemmas and threats. Governments are heavily invested in cyber-espionage, cyber-attacks, and cyber-defenses. Botnet armies comprised of millions of compromised PCs spew spam and attack individual, business, and government information systems. Scams, fraud, identity theft, piracy, and other criminal activities are fueled by the increasing power of computers.

In this, our fourth edition of *Succeeding with Technology*, the focus is on updating the content to reflect recent shifts in the use and application of digital technologies. This edition retains coverage of important core fundamental concepts, while adding new technologies and applications and eliminating content that is no longer relevant. Great care is taken to create a textbook that truly reflects the most important and relevant uses of technology as applied toward success in careers and life. The secondary goal of this new edition is to expand

and improve elements of the textbook that engage the reader, including real-life examples with citations, photos, screenshots, figures, tables and other visual elements, and the current issues, events and case studies provided in chapter boxes.

Additionally, *Succeeding with Technology, Fourth Edition* provides a new and revolutionary integrated set of learning tools that reinforce students' understanding and retention of course material. Chapter highlights, key term definitions, and practice quiz questions and flash-card drills are accessible in the book, on the Web from PCs and mobile phones, and in audio format to access on an iPod or other MP3 player. A feature called *In the News* provides RSS feeds of the latest news stories related to chapter content. All new high-quality and engaging PowerPoint presentations are provided for each chapter and are accessible on the Web from PC and mobile phones. *Student Edition Labs* and useful links to related content on the Web are provided to allow students to extend their learning beyond the textbook content.

We sincerely appreciate the instructors and students who are using *Succeeding with Technology* in their classes. We remain committed to developing the best textbook and accompanying materials possible. We maintain high standards that are continually tested through the use of this book by our own students. We are proud of this new edition and hope you enjoy it!

Ken Baldauf
Ralph Stair

For Mom and Dad, who have always served as examples of the person I strive to be
—KJB

For Lila and Leslie
—RMS

Succeeding with Technology

COMPUTER CONCEPTS FOR YOUR LIFE.

FOURTH EDITION

KENNETH J. **Baldauf**
RALPH M. **Stair**

Australia • Brazil • Japan • Korea • Mexico • Singapore • Spain • United Kingdom • United States

Succeeding with Technology, 4th Edition
by Ken Baldauf and Ralph Stair

Vice President, Publisher: Nicole Jones Pinard

Executive Editor: Marie Lee

Associate Acquisitions Editor: Brandi Shailer

Senior Product Manager: Kathleen Finnegan

Product Manager: Leigh Hefferon

Associate Product Manager: Julia Leroux-Lindsey

Editorial Assistant: Zina Kresin

Developmental Editor: Deb Kaufmann

Marketing Manager: Ryan DeGrote

Marketing Coordinator: Kristen Panciocco

Content Product Manager: Jennifer Feltri

Art Director: Marissa Falco

Designer: GEX Publishing Services

Cover Designer: Nancy Goulet

Front cover, large image: © Terry Vine/ Blend Images/Corbis

Front cover, three small images: © Shutterstock

Background image (front/back cover): Don Bishop/Photodisc/Getty Images

Back cover, large image: flashfilm/Photodisc/ Getty Images

Proofreader: Christine Clark

Indexer: Sharon Hilgenberg

Compositor: GEX Publishing Services

Library of Congress Control Number: 2009940056

ISBN-13: 978-0-538-74578-9
ISBN-10: 0-538-74578-9

Course Technology
20 Channel Center Street
Boston, MA 02210
USA

Cengage Learning is a leading provider of customized learning solutions with office locations around the globe, including Singapore, the United Kingdom, Australia, Mexico, Brazil, and Japan. Locate your office at:
International.cengage.com/region

Cengage Learning products are represented in Canada by Nelson Education, Ltd.

For your lifelong learning solutions, visit **course.cengage.com**

Visit our corporate website at **www.cengage.com**

Purchase any of our products at your local college store or at our preferred online store **www.CengageBrain.com**

Printed in the United States of America
1 2 3 4 5 6 7 8 9 14 13 12 11 10

Brief Contents

Contents

1 Why Study Computers and Digital Technologies? 2

5 Telecommunications, Wireless Technologies, and Computer Networks 270

6 Digital Media for Work and Leisure 324

7 Database Systems 384

8 E-Commerce 432

11 Computer Crime and Information Security 554

12 Digital Society, Ethics, and Globalization 620

Preface

You know technology...

Now what are you going to do with it?

Most students entering college have already had years of exposure to computers and other digital technologies. Elementary and high school students use computers to write papers, create presentations, communicate with each other, conduct research, and entertain themselves. Cell phones, digital cameras, and iPods are standard equipment for teens. Students understand the basics of computers and technology, and how to use them for day-to-day activities. But today's technological world requires much more. *Succeeding with Technology* teaches students what they need to know about technology and how to apply it to life situations to achieve success.

The creation of *Succeeding with Technology* was guided by the philosophy that for students to prosper, they must grasp underlying principles of the technologies that have an impact on our lives and understand how those principles are related to real-world activities. No one is capable of gaining true understanding by memorizing long lists of technical terms. This textbook won't overwhelm you with descriptions of numerous inconsequential devices. Instead, *Succeeding with Technology* provides straightforward explanations of the principles that guide technological development, without overwhelming the reader with too much detail. An understanding of the concepts provided in this book will translate into a practical understanding of the specific devices and practices in use today and in years to come.

The authors understand that technology in and of itself is not interesting to most people. What most people do find interesting are the exciting ways that technology is being used to improve our day-to-day lives, our professional productivity, society, and the world. *Succeeding with Technology* invests as much effort in showing how technology is used as it does in explaining how technology works. Every concept is backed up with practical examples of how it is making an impact on everyday life.

We are proud of the fourth edition of this unique textbook that takes readers beyond traditional computer competence and fluency, to a deeper understanding of not only how digital technology works, but more importantly, how it can be harnessed to improve your life.

Welcome to the 4th Edition of *Succeeding with Technology: Computer concepts for your life.*

Approach

Succeeding with Technology employs a different approach from many of the other computer concepts books on the market. It is a direct outgrowth of the trends that are causing the introductory computer course to change. From its high-impact graphic design to its content, the unique approach of this textbook is sure to engage and excite readers.

- **Focus on careers**. This textbook contains a wealth of examples of how technology systems are used in different disciplines. Starting with Chapter 1, almost every page of this textbook contains exciting, current examples of how real people and organizations have used technology to achieve success. Through reading the examples, students can evaluate what careers and fields match their interests and talents.
- **Beyond PCs.** We go beyond desktop PCs to provide coverage of the wide variety of computers, computer systems, and digital technologies that are in use today. From cell phones to servers, from wireless networks to virtual private networks, we cover the latest technology that students are likely to encounter at home and at work.
- **Speaks to students with varied skill levels.** Although this textbook assumes that the reader has used a computer, the material is presented in a manner that is sure not to leave anyone behind, while engaging even the most experienced computer user.
- **Less jargon and fewer key terms.** We include everything readers need to know and nothing they don't. Only important terms that students are likely to encounter in the real world appear in bold as key terms.
- **Important social issues explored.** This textbook confronts important controversial issues head on with complete coverage from all perspectives. P2P file sharing, the digital divide, students and plagiarism, globalization, Net neutrality, artificial intelligence, and many other current issues are explored, providing an excellent launching pad for class discussion.

New to the 4th Edition

A LOT has changed in the world of technology since the release of the third edition of this book. People are more engaged with technology than ever before. Web 2.0 technologies such as social networks have college students connecting to the Internet many times every day. People are applying new technologies in new ways to obtain success in their lives. *Succeeding with Technology, Fourth Edition* presents the latest ways to get ahead and lead a successful, fulfilling life with technology. It focuses on the latest trends that are impacting the way we live, while including just the right amount of foundational concepts to provide a thorough understanding.

In this fourth edition there have been three overarching goals:

1. To raise the overall quality and visual appeal of the book,
2. To update the currency of the material to reflect the trends and technologies of importance today, and
3. To increase the value and usability of our online content.

In order to raise the overall quality and visual appeal of the book, the authors and editors have invested time in several areas:

- **New and engaging photographs** have been acquired to provide a glimpse into how technology is being used, and to allow the reader to evaluate today's amazing devices. We realize that providing impressive photos in a textbook has an impact on keeping readers engaged. The visuals in this edition are designed to draw the reader into the content and lead the reader through each chapter page by page.
- **Dozens of new screenshots** are provided to show readers software and online content that they probably haven't seen before but will want to run out and try.
- **Balanced coverage of all platforms and types of digital devices**. From Windows 7 to Mac OS X Snow Leopard to Ubuntu Linux, from powerhouse desktops to ultra-compact netbooks to the iPhone and iPhone challengers, dozens of today's most useful and exciting devices are introduced and examined.
- **Wealth of new diagrams and tables** provide visual interest and allow the reader to absorb important concepts effortlessly.

The currency of the material has been updated in several areas:

- **Coverage has been shifted to reflect current use of technologies.** For example, four years ago, instant messaging, Web portals, and news Webcasts were new and exciting. Two years ago, the hot technologies included online social networks, Web 2.0, and podcasts, to name a few. Today, while the focus continues to be on social networking and user-generated content, new trends have arisen including cloud computing, green computing, botnets, and others. Content in this fourth edition has been adjusted to give each technology the amount of coverage it deserves, depending on its importance in society today. Unlike many computer concepts books that simply grow and grow over each edition to become a catalog of all technologies that ever existed, overwhelming the reader, *Succeeding with Technology* has removed content that is no longer relevant, diminished content on technologies that are becoming antiquated, and added content on the latest technologies.
- **Key Term and Glossary definitions have been updated** to sync with current trends and usage.
- **All outdated examples have been removed, and replaced with new and engaging examples.** Adopters of *Succeeding with Technology* in its earlier versions are well aware of the abundant use of pertinent real-life examples embedded throughout the content. Most examples are cited to their original source in the news. An effort has been made to balance examples with content to provide the most insight without overwhelming the reader with too many examples. Rather than providing several short examples for a concept, one example is selected that is most thorough and interesting.
- **All Community Technology and Job Technology boxes have been updated with new and thought-provoking articles**. Many of the Technology 360 stories (and end-of-chapter Action Plans) have been refreshed or rewritten to keep them current.
- **All new TechEdge news tidbits** have been sprinkled in each chapter to generate more interest.

- **End-of-chapter questions and projects have been updated** to match the new content and to provide additional exercises for variety across multiple semesters.

Last but not least, our online content has had a makeover so that it provides considerably more value to the overall *Succeeding with Technology* product:

- **Redesigned Useful Links section** provides hundreds of links to the latest information on important chapter concepts. Teachers and students alike will find these links a valuable resource for digging deeper into chapter topics.
- **New In the News section** is updated each week with references to current online articles related to chapter topics. Teachers will find these useful for generating in-class discussions and assigning research projects.
- **Downloadable audio review** gives students a portable means to review key terms, hear a chapter overview and summary, and test themselves with audio flash cards on a chapter-by-chapter basis.
- **Expand Your Knowledge Student Edition Labs** help students review and extend their knowledge of over 30 chapter concepts through hands-on simulations and review exercises.
- **Online practice tests** for students to test themselves in each chapter
- **Updated learning objectives and key terms**
- **Updated lab demonstrations correlate to chapters throughout the book**

We believe that through these improvements, you will find that *Succeeding with Technology, Fourth Edition* targets your needs and provides a high-quality and engaging read.

FEATURES

Succeeding with Technology has a set of features designed to engage interest, show how to solve problems, and demonstrate what people can accomplish with computers.

Chapter Content

Learning Objectives and **Chapter Contents** show you exactly what subjects will be covered in each chapter. Read this before you dive in so that you know what to expect.

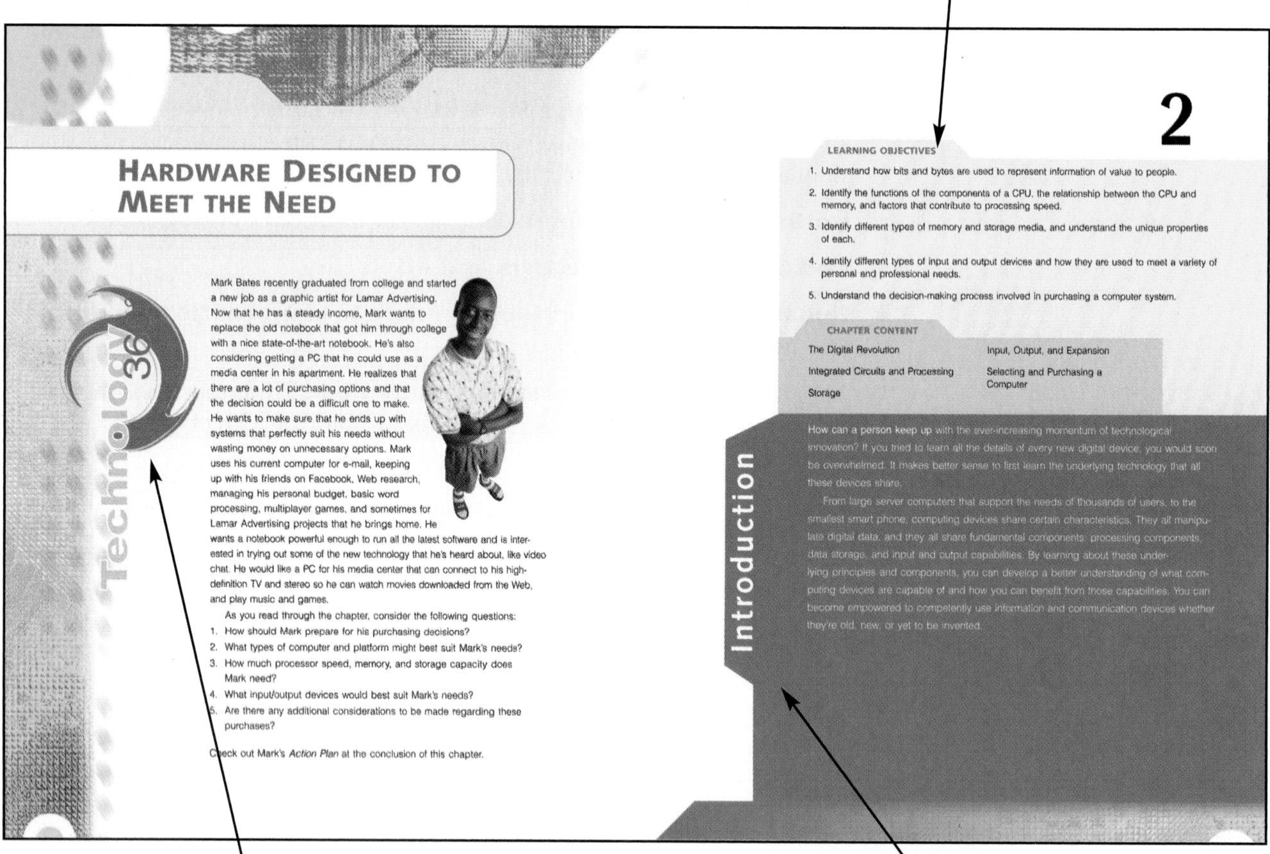

HARDWARE DESIGNED TO MEET THE NEED

Technology 360

Mark Bates recently graduated from college and started a new job as a graphic artist for Lamar Advertising. Now that he has a steady income, Mark wants to replace the old notebook that got him through college with a nice state-of-the-art notebook. He's also considering getting a PC that he could use as a media center in his apartment. He realizes that there are a lot of purchasing options and that the decision could be a difficult one to make. He wants to make sure that he ends up with systems that perfectly suit his needs without wasting money on unnecessary options. Mark uses his current computer for e-mail, keeping up with his friends on Facebook, Web research, managing his personal budget, basic word processing, multiplayer games, and sometimes for Lamar Advertising projects that he brings home. He wants a notebook powerful enough to run all the latest software and is interested in trying out some of the new technology that he's heard about, like video chat. He would like a PC for his media center that can connect to his high-definition TV and stereo so he can watch movies downloaded from the Web, and play music and games.

As you read through the chapter, consider the following questions:

1. How should Mark prepare for his purchasing decisions?
2. What types of computer and platform might best suit Mark's needs?
3. How much processor speed, memory, and storage capacity does Mark need?
4. What input/output devices would best suit Mark's needs?
5. Are there any additional considerations to be made regarding these purchases?

Check out Mark's *Action Plan* at the conclusion of this chapter.

2

LEARNING OBJECTIVES

1. Understand how bits and bytes are used to represent information of value to people.
2. Identify the functions of the components of a CPU, the relationship between the CPU and memory, and factors that contribute to processing speed.
3. Identify different types of memory and storage media, and understand the unique properties of each.
4. Identify different types of input and output devices and how they are used to meet a variety of personal and professional needs.
5. Understand the decision-making process involved in purchasing a computer system.

CHAPTER CONTENT

The Digital Revolution
Integrated Circuits and Processing
Storage
Input, Output, and Expansion
Selecting and Purchasing a Computer

Introduction

How can a person keep up with the ever-increasing momentum of technological innovation? If you tried to learn all the details of every new digital device, you would soon be overwhelmed. It makes better sense to first learn the underlying technology that all these devices share.

From large server computers that support the needs of thousands of users, to the smallest smart phone, computing devices share certain characteristics. They all manipulate digital data, and they all share fundamental components: processing components, data storage, and input and output capabilities. By learning about these underlying principles and components, you can develop a better understanding of what computing devices are capable of and how you can benefit from those capabilities. You can become empowered to competently use information and communication devices whether they're old, new, or yet to be invented.

Technology 360 scenario discusses people like you who face problems that can be solved with the help of technology. You will learn how they solve their problems using concepts presented in the chapter.

The **Chapter Introduction** welcomes you to the chapter. Learn what is most important in each chapter before you start reading.

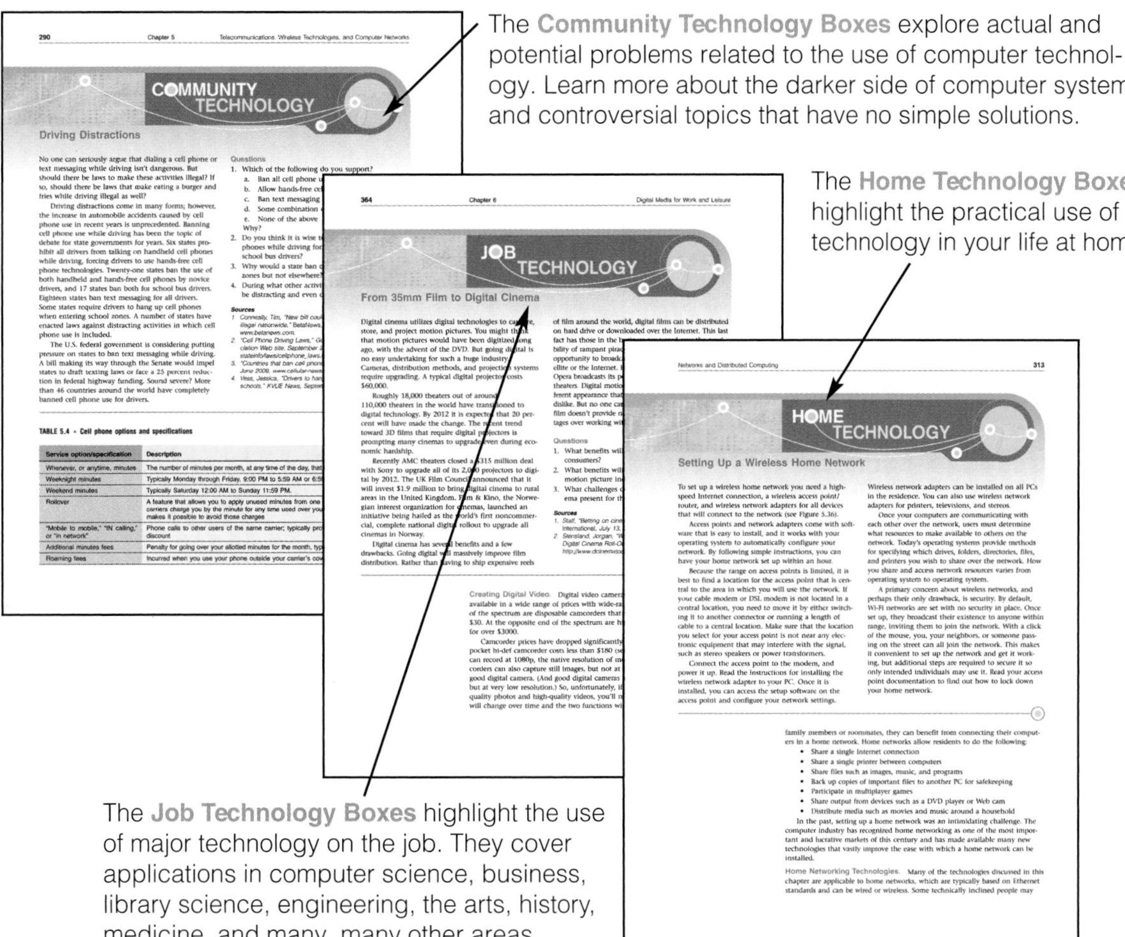

The **Community Technology Boxes** explore actual and potential problems related to the use of computer technology. Learn more about the darker side of computer systems and controversial topics that have no simple solutions.

The **Home Technology Boxes** highlight the practical use of major technology in your life at home.

The **Job Technology Boxes** highlight the use of major technology on the job. They cover applications in computer science, business, library science, engineering, the arts, history, medicine, and many, many other areas.

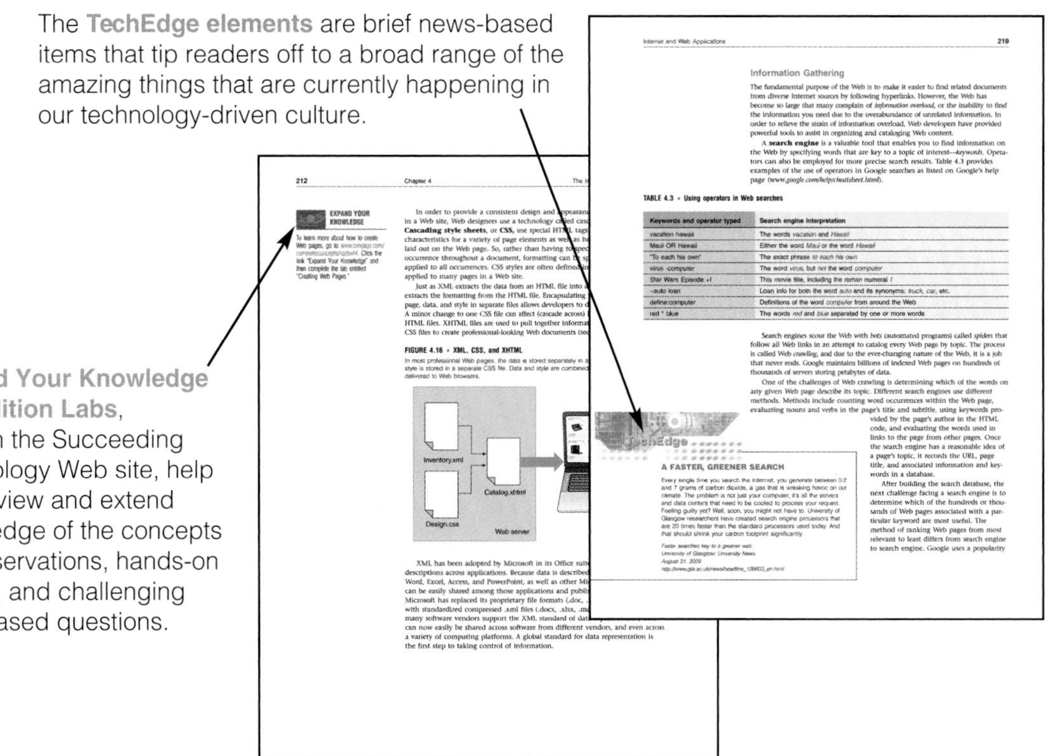

The **TechEdge elements** are brief news-based items that tip readers off to a broad range of the amazing things that are currently happening in our technology-driven culture.

The **Expand Your Knowledge Student Edition Labs**, available on the Succeeding with Technology Web site, help students review and extend their knowledge of the concepts through observations, hands-on simulations, and challenging objective-based questions.

End-of-Chapter

A wealth of end-chapter material helps students retain concepts and use them beyond the course.

In the **Technology 360 Action Plans** that appear at the end of each chapter, you will see how to use the chapter's concepts to solve the problems or answer the questions presented in the Technology 360 scenarios appearing at the beginning of the chapter.

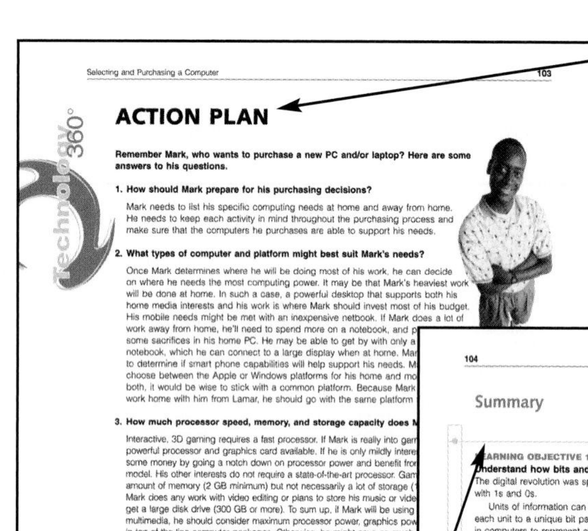

Selecting and Purchasing a Computer 103

ACTION PLAN

Remember Mark, who wants to purchase a new PC and/or laptop? Here are some answers to his questions.

1. How should Mark prepare for his purchasing decisions?

Mark needs to list his specific computing needs at home and away from home. He needs to keep each activity in mind throughout the purchasing process and make sure that the computers he purchases are able to support his needs.

2. What types of computer and platform might best suit Mark's needs?

Once Mark determines where he will be doing most of his work, he can decide on where he needs the most computing power. It may be that Mark's heaviest work will be done at home. In such a case, a powerful desktop that supports both his home media interests and his work is where Mark should invest most of his budget. His mobile needs might be met with an inexpensive netbook. If Mark does a lot of work away from home, he'll need to spend more on a notebook, and p some sacrifices in his home PC. He may be able to get by with only a notebook, which he can connect to a large display when at home. Mar to determine if smart phone capabilities will help support his needs. M choose between the Apple or Windows platforms for his home and mo both, it would be wise to stick with a common platform. Because Mark work home with him from Lamar, he should go with the same platform

3. How much processor speed, memory, and storage capacity does M

Interactive, 3D gaming requires a fast processor. If Mark is really into gam powerful processor and graphics card available. If he is only mildly intere some money by going a notch down on processor power and benefit fro model. His other interests do not require a state-of-the-art processor. Gam amount of memory (2 GB minimum) but not necessarily a lot of storage (Mark does any work with video editing or plans to store his music or vide get a large disk drive (300 GB or more). To sum up, if Mark will be using multimedia, he should consider maximum processor power, graphics pow in top-of-the-line computer packages. Otherwise, he might save as much basic package. Mark should keep in mind that powerful desktop PCs are notebooks.

4. What input/output devices would best suit Mark's needs?

As a gamer and artist, Mark wants a large display, a color printer, a ga and a flatbed scanner. He plans to check with his employer to see wh tablets are recommended, and then he will configure his home comput work as possible. He should also purchase an upgraded video card w memory to smoothly run the gaming animation.

5. Are there additional considerations to be made regarding these pu

Since Mark is new to video conferencing, he needs to do some research required. For video communication over the Internet, he needs a broadba webcam. Mark also needs to check the video connections on his HDTV t and adapter may be required to connect his PC.

104 Chapter 2 Hardware Designed to Meet the Need

Summary

LEARNING OBJECTIVE 1

Understand how bits and bytes are used to represent information of value to humans.

The digital revolution was sparked by the computer's ability to represent and manipulate information digitally, with 1s and 0s.

Units of information can be represented with bits in a standardized code by assigning each unit to a unique bit pattern using a look-up chart. ASCII is a standardized code used in computers to represent character data. Bits can also be used to store values by using the binary number system. The binary number system uses two digits, 0 and 1. Binary numbers are used for calculations, to represent color intensities in images, and to represent the amplitude of sound waves used to store digital music and sound. There are many methods of decoding and interpreting a byte. Each method boils down to either the look-up table approach or binary numbers. By implementing standards, bytes can have consistent meaning across common applications. Because all different types of data are represented with 1s and 0s, digital convergence is producing devices that can handle all types of data.

Figure 2.1—p. 58

LEARNING OBJECTIVE 2

Identify the functions of the components of a CPU, the relationship between the CPU and memory, and the factors that contribute to processing speed.

The CPU processes the data into information that is meaningful to people. The CPU's primary components are the control unit that fetches and interprets instructions, the arithmetic/logic unit that carries out the instructions, and registers that store the bytes being processed. The CPU uses RAM as its primary storage. RAM provides the CPU with a working storage area for program instructions and data. Data flows back and forth between the CPU and RAM across the system bus.

The control unit in the CPU uses the four-step machine cycle to carry out program instructions: fetch instruction, decode instruction, execute instruction, and store results. Each processor has an instruction set, a finite number of instructions that it is designed to carry out. Clock speed, wordlength, and bus speed all have an impact on the speed of processing. All activity in the system takes place in time with a processor's system clock. Clock speeds are measured in megahertz (MHz) and gigahertz (GHz). The number of bits the CPU can process at any one time is called its wordlength. Clock speed, wordlength, and several other system components all affect the processor's performance.

Moore's Law states that in silicon-based processors, transistor densities in an integrated circuit will double every two years.

Figure 2.8—p. 64

LEARNING OBJECTIVE 3

Identify different types of memory and storage media, and understand t

RAM is volatile and temporarily stores data as long as there is an electrical cu more permanent storage that has its instructions hardwired into its circuitry. RO boot process that runs when the computer is powered up.

Magnetic, optical, and solid-state storage are three types of secondary sto store data and programs more permanently. Magnetic storage includes disks (access) and tapes (sequential access). Optical storage includes CDs, DVDs,

The **Summary**, organized by learning objectives, offers a balanced review of major topics and includes tables, figures, and photos to help you integrate and remember the material.

45555_02 10/27/2009 13:51:53 Page 105

Test Yourself 105

discs, which are available in read-only discs and writable discs. Solid-state storage includes flash memory devices such as solid-state drives, USB thumb drives, and media cards.

LEARNING OBJECTIVE 4

Identify different types of input and output devices and how they are used to meet a variety of personal and professional needs.

People use input devices to provide data and instructions to the computer, and they use output devices to receive results from the computer. General-purpose input devices include the keyboard and mouse for desktop computers, the touch pad for notebook computers, and the touch screen and stylus for tablet PCs. Scanners are used in a variety of industries to avoid data-entry errors by capturing data close to its source. Special-purpose input devices include game controllers, tablets and pens, and webcams

Printers, plotters, and displays are the primary forms of output devices. Displays are selected by size and resolution. LCD flat panel displays are the most popular type. Color ink-jet and non-color laser printers are popular for home and small business use, although color laser printer prices are becoming more affordable.

Figure 2.38—p. 96

LEARNING OBJECTIVE 5

Understand the decision-making process involved in purchasing a computer system.

When selecting a computer system, you must first analyze your specific computing needs at home, school, work, or on the road. Select a computer type and platform that supports those needs. Options include desktop computers, notebook computers, tablet PCs, netbooks, and smart phones. Select options that provide for more than the minimum requirements of the applications you want to run.

Test Yourself

LEARNING OBJECTIVE 1: **Understand how bits and bytes are used to represent information of value to humans.**

1. Most computers use ______________ to represent character data using bytes.
   a. hexadecimal
   b. kilobytes
   c. decimal notation
   d. ASCII code
2. True or False: Digital music is stored using binary numbers.
3. The ______________ number system is ideal for digital systems because it has only two digits, 1 and 0.
4. True or False: All software interprets a byte such as 11110000 the same way.
5. ______________ refers to the ability of one device to handle several different types of digital information, such as voice communications, character data, and music.
   a. Digital revolution
   b. Digital convergence
   c. Digital communications
   d. Digital economy

LEARNING OBJECTIVE 2: **Identify the functions of the components of a CPU, the relationship between the CPU and memory, and the factors that contribute to processing speed.**

6. A(n) ______________ processor incorporates four CPUs on one chip.
7. True or False: A faster system clock means a faster, more powerful processor.

Use the **Test Yourself** assessment tests and answers appearing immediately after the Summary to test your knowledge and understanding of the chapter's key concepts.

The **Key Terms** list presents the most important technical terms used in the chapter with definitions and page references.

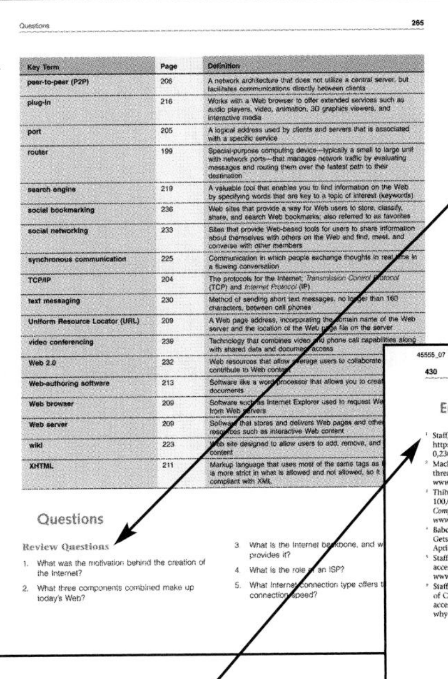
Questions 265

Key Term	Page	Definition
peer-to-peer (P2P)	206	A network architecture that does not utilize a central server, but facilitates communications directly between clients
plug-in	216	Works with a Web browser to offer extended services such as audio players, video, animation, 3D graphics viewers, and interactive media
port	205	A logical address used by clients and servers that is associated with a specific service
router	199	Special-purpose computing device—typically a small to large unit with network ports—that manages network traffic by evaluating messages and routing them over the fastest path to their destination
search engine	219	A valuable tool that enables you to find information on the Web by specifying words that are key to a topic of interest (keywords)
social bookmarking	236	Web sites that provide a way for Web users to store, classify, share, and search Web bookmarks; also referred to as favorites
social networking	233	Sites that provide Web-based tools for users to share information about themselves with others on the Web and find, meet, and converse with other members
synchronous communication	225	Communication in which people exchange thoughts in real time in a flowing conversation
TCP/IP	204	The protocols for the Internet; *Transmission Control Protocol* (TCP) and *Internet Protocol* (IP)
text messaging	230	Method of sending short text messages, no longer than 160 characters, between cell phones
Uniform Resource Locator (URL)	209	A Web page address, incorporating the domain name of the Web server and the location of the Web page file on the server
video conferencing	239	Technology that combines video and phone call capabilities along with shared data and document access
Web 2.0	232	Web resources that allow average users to collaborate [illegible] contribute to Web content
Web-authoring software	213	Software like a word processor that allows you to creat[illegible] documents
Web browser	209	Software such as Internet Explorer used to request We[illegible] from Web servers
Web server	209	Software that stores and delivers Web pages and othe[illegible] resources such as interactive Web content
wiki	223	Web site designed to allow users to add, remove, and [illegible] content
XHTML	211	Markup language that uses most of the same tags as [illegible] is more strict in what is allowed and not allowed, so it [illegible] compliant with XML

Questions

Review Questions

1. What was the motivation behind the creation of the Internet?
2. What three components combined make up today's Web?
3. What is the Internet backbone, and w[illegible] provides it?
4. What is the role of an ISP?
5. What Internet connection type offers t[illegible] connection speed?

By studying the **Review Questions**, you can reinforce your understanding of the topics and terms covered in the chapter.The **Discussion Questions** provide an opportunity to gain an understanding of the broader issues.

45555_07 11/4/2009 9:3:41 Page 430

430 Chapter 7 Database Systems

Endnotes

1. Staff, UPS Fact Sheet, accessed June 10, 2009, http://www.pressroom.ups.com/mediakits/factsheet/0,2305,866,00.html?mkname=companyinfo.
2. Maclean, William. "UK must pry on data to block threats: ex-spy boss," Reuters, March 25, 2009, www.reuters.com.
3. Thibodeau, Patric, "White House set to unleash 100,000 federal data sources via data.gov," *Computerworld*, June 4, 2009, www.computerworld.com.
4. Babcock, Charles, "In Database Market, Oracle Gets Bigger, Others Hang On," *InformationWeek*, April 25, 2008, www.informationweek.com.
5. Staff, "MySQL Market Share," MySQL Web site, accessed June 12, 2009, www.mysql.com/why-mysql/marketshare.
6. Staff, "craigslist Relies on MySQL to Serve Millions of Classified Ads," *Behind the Scenes with MySQL*, accessed June 12, 2009, http://www.mysql.com/why-mysql/case-studies/mysql-craigslist-casestudy.pdf.
7. Staff, "MySQL Powers Transaction-Heavy News Delivery System for the Associated Press," *Behind the Scenes with MySQL*, accessed June 12, 2009, http://www.mysql.com/why-mysql/case-studies/mysql-ap-casestudy.pdf.
8. Hoover, Nicholas, "DHS Disaster Recovery Plans Lacking, Report Finds," *InformationWeek*, May 14, 2009, www.informationweek.com.
9. Staff, "Life Fitness Improves Product Insight and Decision Making with Dashboard-Based Business Intelligence," *Oracle Customer Snapshot*, accessed June 12, 2009, http://www.oracle.com/customers/snapshots/life-fitness-bi-snapshot.pdf.
10. Staff, "Yangtze Power Improves Business Intelligence with Integrated Database and Analysis Tools," Oracle Customer Case Study, accessed June 12, 2009, http://www.oracle.com/customers/snapshots/yangtze-power-case-study.pdf.
11. Mearian, Lucas, "E-health data collection key to tracking swine flu spread," *Computerworld*, April 29, 2009, www. computerworld.com.

Real-life examples in the text are documented with **Endnotes** references, which allow students to delve deeper into the issues and topics raised in the text.

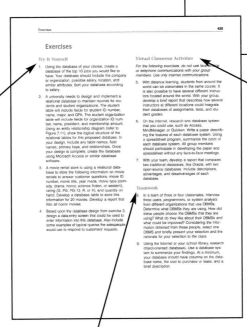

Exercises 429

Exercises

Try It Yourself

1. Using the database of your choice, create a database of the top 10 jobs you would like to have. Your database should include the company or organization, possible salary, location, and similar attributes. Sort your database according to salary.
2. A university needs to design and implement a relational database to maintain records for students and student organizations. The student table will include fields for student ID number, name, major, and GPA. The student organization table will include fields for organization ID number, name, president, and membership amount. Using an entity relationship diagram (refer to Figure 7.11), show the logical structure of the relational tables for this proposed database. In your design, include any table names, field names, primary keys, and relationships. Once your design is complete, create the database using Microsoft Access or similar database software.
3. A movie rental store is using a relational database to store the following information on movie rentals to answer customer questions: movie ID number, movie title, year made, movie type (comedy, drama, horror, science fiction, or western), rating (G, PG, PG-13, R, or X), and quantity on hand. Develop a database table to store this information for 20 movies. Develop a report that lists all horror movies.
4. Based upon the database design from exercise 3, design a data-entry screen that could be used to enter information into this database. Also include some examples of typical queries the salespeople would use to respond to customers' requests.

Virtual Classroom Activities

For the following exercises, do not use face-to-face or telephone communications with your group members. Use only Internet communications.

5. With distance learning, students from around the world can be classmates in the same course. It is also possible to have several different instructors located around the world. With your group, develop a brief report that describes how several instructors at different locations could integrate their databases of assignments, tests, and student grades.
6. On the Internet, research one database system that you could use, such as Access, MindManager, or Quicken. Write a paper describing the features of each database system. Using a spreadsheet program, summarize the costs of each database system. All group members should participate in developing the paper and spreadsheet without any face-to-face meetings.
7. With your team, develop a report that compares two traditional databases, like Oracle, with two open-source databases. Include descriptions, advantages, and disadvantages of each database.

Teamwork

8. In a team of three or four classmates, interview three users, programmers, or system analysts from different organizations that use DBMSs. Determine what DBMSs they are using. How did these people choose the DBMSs that they are using? What do they like about their DBMSs and what could be improved? Considering the information obtained from these people, select one DBMS and briefly present your selection and the rationale for your selection to the class.
9. Using the Internet or your school library, research object-oriented databases. Use a database system to summarize your findings. At a minimum, your database should have columns on the database name, the cost to purchase or lease, and a brief description.

The **Try It Yourself** exercises are designed to work with your skills in software and application tools. Some help you explore a topic or concept using word processing, spreadsheet, database, and graphics applications; others involve using the Internet to find information and answers to important questions in different fields.

The **Virtual Classroom Activities** require that you interact with other students and the instructor without face-to-face meetings. Using Internet communications, you can develop joint projects with other students. These activities are valuable for courses that use a virtual classroom or distance learning approach and for traditional courses.

Use the **Teamwork** exercises to learn how to be an effective team member by working with classmates to accomplish a task using material covered in the chapter and usually a software application or the Internet.

STUDENT ONLINE COMPANION

The student online companion will help you learn and practice new concepts for every chapter in this book. Visit *www.cengage.com/computerconcepts/np/swt4* to access the online companion.

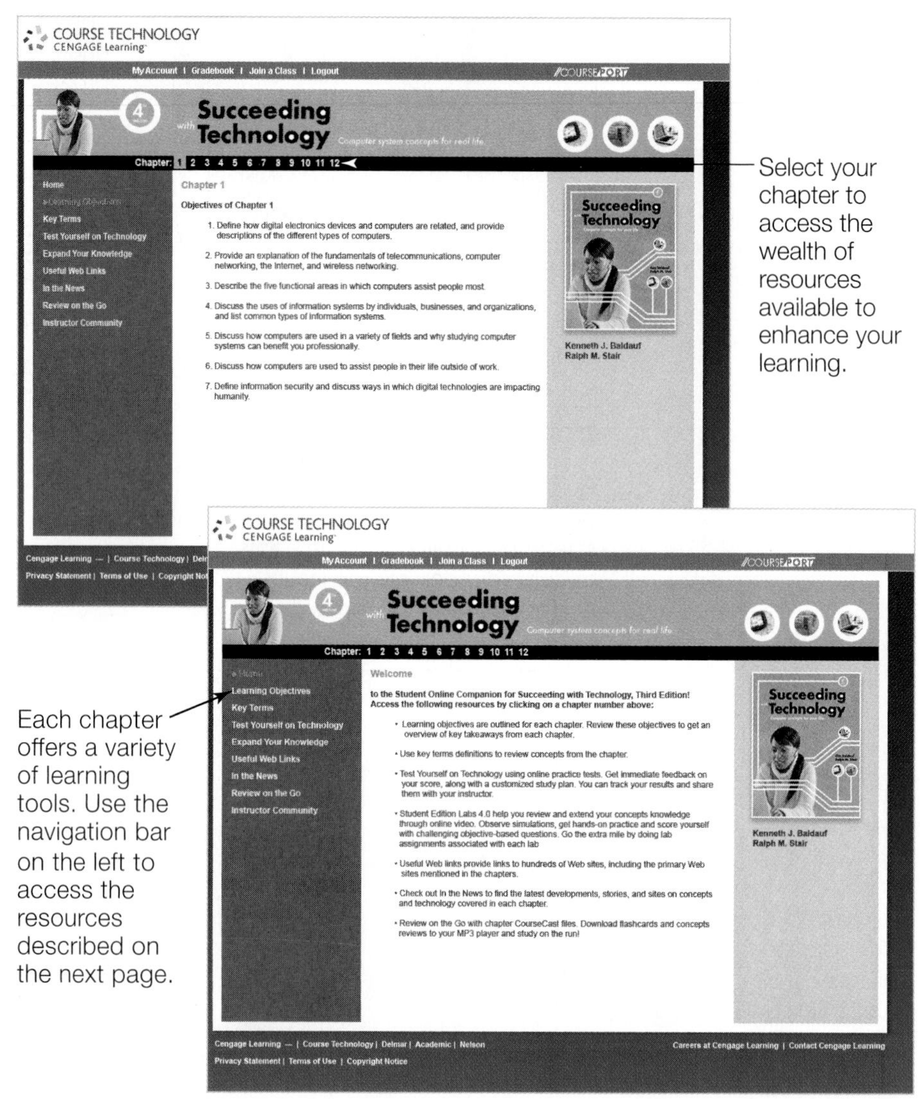

COURSE TECHNOLOGY
CENGAGE Learning
Succeeding with Technology
Chapter 1
Objectives of Chapter 1
Select your chapter to access the wealth of resources available to enhance your learning.
Welcome
Each chapter offers a variety of learning tools. Use the navigation bar on the left to access the resources described on the next page.

The Succeeding with Technology Student Online Companion contains the following features:

- Detailed **learning objectives** for each chapter. Review these to get an overview of what is covered.
- Chapter **key terms** are provided along with their definitions; use these to review and study concepts from the chapter.
- **Test Yourself on Technology** are Practice Tests that will allow you to test yourself on the content in each chapter and immediately get feedback on what you got right and wrong along with a customized study plan. You can also track your results and share your results with your instructor.
- **Useful Web Links** provide you access to the primary Web sites mentioned in the chapters, technology-related career information, and more!
- Download **Audio Review** files to your MP3 player and study on the go! Downloadable review files offer you valuable audio study tools.
- The **Expand Your Knowledge Student Edition Labs** help you review and extend your knowledge of chapter concepts through observations, hands-on simulations, and challenging objective-based questions.

INSTRUCTOR RESOURCES

Just as *Succeeding with Technology* goes beyond computer literacy and fluency to provide students with the information they need to be successful with technology, we also take the instructor resources to the next level. The package includes:

Instructor's Manual

The Instructor's Manual provides materials to help instructors make their classes informative and interesting. The manual offers several approaches to teaching the material with a sample syllabus and comments on different components. It also suggests alternative course outlines and ideas for projects. For each chapter, the manual includes learning objectives, lecture notes, classroom and lab activities and quizzes, teaching tips, and key terms.

ExamView® Test Bank

This objective-based test generator lets the instructor create paper- LAN- or Web-based tests from test banks specifically designed for this text. Test banks include true/false, multiple choice, completion, and essay questions, and integrate both figures and critical thinking into a number of questions. Use the exams as is, or modify to create your own unique tests for your course.

PowerPoint Presentations

Microsoft® Office PowerPoint® slides are provided for each chapter. Instructors can use the slides as teaching aids during classroom presentations or as printed handouts for classroom distribution. Presentations are fully customizable, allowing instructors to add their own slides for additional topics introduced in class.

Solutions

Solutions for all of the end-of-chapter questions and activities can be found on the Instructor Resources CD or at *www.cengage.com/coursetechnology*.

Figure Files

Figure files for all images used in the textbook are provided on the Instructor Resources CD. Instructors can use these files to create presentations or customize the presentations that accompany the book.

DISTANCE LEARNING CONTENT

WebTUTOR

Content for Online Learning

Course Technology has partnered with the leading distance learning solution providers and class-management platforms today. To access this material, Instructors will visit our password-protected instructor resources available at *www.cengage.com/coursetechnology*. Instructor resources include the following: additional case projects, sample syllabi, PowerPoint presentations per chapter, and more. For additional information or for an instructor username and password, please contact your sales representative. For students to access this material, they must have purchased a WebTutor PIN-code specific to this title and your campus platform. The resources for students may include (based on instructor preferences), but not limited to: topic review, review questions and practice tests.

SAM COMPUTER CONCEPTS

Skills Assessment Manager

SAM 2007 is designed to help bring students from the classroom to the real world. It allows students to train and test on important computer skills in an active, hands-on environment.

SAM's easy-to-use system includes powerful interactive exams, training and projects on the most commonly used Microsoft® Office applications. SAM simulates the Office 2007 application environment, allowing students to demonstrate their knowledge and think through the skills by performing real-world tasks such as bolding word text or setting up slide transitions. Add in live-in-the-application projects and students are on their way to truly learning and applying skills to business-centric document.

Designed to be used with the New Perspectives Series, SAM includes handy page references, so students can print helpful study guides that match the New Perspectives Series textbooks used in class. For instructors, SAM also includes robust scheduling and reporting features.

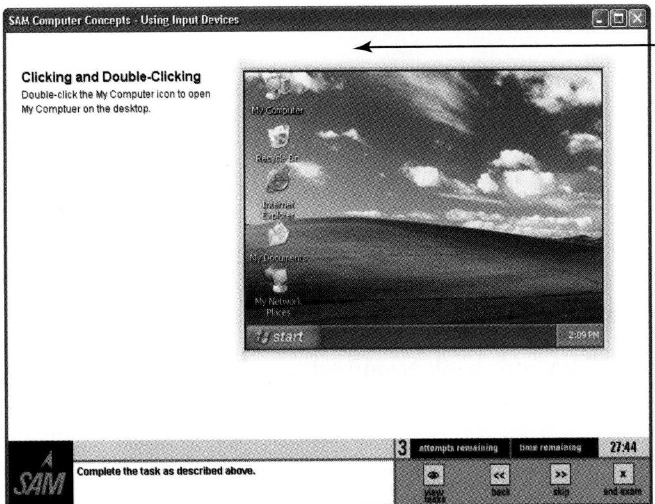

Hands-on tasks allow you to demonstrate your understanding of important computer concepts and applications

CourseCasts – Learning on the Go. Always available... always relevant.

Want to keep up with the latest technology trends relevant to you? Visit our site to find a library of podcasts, CourseCasts, featuring a "CourseCast of the Week," and download them to your mp3 player at *http://coursecasts.course.com*.

Our fast-paced world is driven by technology. You know because you're an active participant—always on the go, always keeping up with technological trends, and always learning new ways to embrace technology to power your life.

Ken Baldauf, host of CourseCasts and one of the authors of this text, is a faculty member of the Florida State University Computer Science Department where, as Director of the Program in Interdisciplinary Computing, he has taught computing and technology classes to tens of thousands of FSU students. Ken is an expert in the latest technology trends; he gathers and sorts through the most pertinent news and information for CourseCasts so your students can spend their time enjoying technology, rather than trying to figure it out. Open or close your lecture with a discussion based on the latest CourseCast.

Visit us at *http://coursecasts.course.com* to learn on the go!

ACKNOWLEDGMENTS

Developing any book is a difficult undertaking. We would like to thank our teammates at Cengage Learning for their dedication and hard work. Special thanks to Leigh Hefferon, Product Manager, and Marie Lee, Executive Editor. We would also like to thank Nicole Pinard, Vice President, Computing Technology and Information Systems. We would like to acknowledge and thank Deb Kaufmann, our Developmental Editor. She deserves special recognition for her tireless effort and help in all stages of this project. Jennifer Feltri at Course Technology and Louise Capulli and Marisa Taylor at GEX, Inc. guided the book through the production process. Abby Reip helped with the photos and illustrations. We would also like to thank Naomi Friedman, who researched and wrote the TechEdge elements that appear in the margins of every chapter.

We greatly appreciate the perceptive feedback from all the reviewers who worked so hard to assist us on the First, Second, Third, and Fourth editions, including:

Lancie Affonso, College of Charleston
Gregg W. Asher, Minnesota State University, Mankato
Jim P. Borden, Villanova University
Joseph DeLibero, Arizona State University
Nichol W. Free, Computer Learning Network
Alla Grinberg, Montgomery College
J. Scott Hilberg, Towson University
Martha Lindberg, Minnesota State University, Mankato
Bill Littlefield, Indiana University—Kelley School of Business
Joan Lumpkin, Wright State University
Cathy Radziemski, Arizona State University
Kristin A. Roberts, Grand Rapids Community College
Richard Schwartz, Macomb Community College
Elizabeth Spooner, Holmes Community College
DeLyse Totten, Portland Community College
Therese Viscelli, Georgia State University
Amy B. Woszczynski, Kennesaw State University

Ken Baldauf would like to thank Florida State University for its support of this project, and his family for their support and patience throughout the writing process.

Ralph Stair would like to thank the faculty and staff of the College of Business Administration at Florida State University for their support and encouragement. He would also like to thank his family, Lila and Leslie, for their support.

We are committed to listening to our adopters and readers and to developing creative solutions to meet their needs. We strongly encourage your participation in helping us provide the freshest, most relevant information possible. We welcome your input and feedback. If you have any questions or comments, please contact us through Course Technology or your local representative, via e-mail at *course.succeeding@cengage.com*, via the Internet at *www.cengage.com/coursetechnology*, or address your comments, criticisms, suggestions, and ideas to:

Ken Baldauf
Ralph Stair
Cengage Course Technology
20 Channel Center Street
Boston, MA 02210

THE AUTHOR TEAM

Succeeding with Technology benefits from the author team of Ken Baldauf and Ralph Stair. Ralph has his roots in business management information systems, while Ken has his roots in computer science. The combination provides a balanced blend of the two perspectives of technology and its uses.

Having taught more than 50,000 students in computer fluency, digital media, and Web development courses over the past 12 years, **Ken Baldauf** brings practical experience and insight to *Succeeding with Technology*. With a background in teaching computer science, Ken started out teaching computer programming and Web development classes. He developed an interest in the impact of technology on society and the world; in particular, how technology supports individuals in leading more productive and fulfilling lives. This interest led Ken to head the Computer Literacy program at Florida State University, where he was instrumental in guiding computer literacy standards. In 2008 Ken became the Director of FSU's new Program in Interdisciplinary Computing, where he works with academic units to develop computing courses that meet discipline-specific needs. Ken is also the creator and host of Course Technology's *Coursecast of the Week*—a technology podcast for college students, and author and developer of *Emerge with Computers*, a new online learning framework from Course Technology that teaches Concepts, Issues, and Skills related to computer fluency.

Ralph Stair is Professor Emeritus in the College of Business at Florida State University, and has spent about 20 years teaching introductory computer courses. While at Florida State University, he developed market-leading information systems textbooks (*Principles of Information Systems* and *Fundamentals of Information Systems*) that were among the first to bring important upper-level information systems content to the introductory computer course used primarily in business schools. These popular textbooks are used around the world. Ralph Stair enjoys listening to people who use his textbooks and developing the best textbooks possible. The success of these textbooks allowed him to retire early from Florida State University to devote more time to research and writing. *Succeeding with Technology* is an outgrowth of his devotion to showing students how they can succeed with technology.

WHY STUDY COMPUTERS AND DIGITAL TECHNOLOGIES?

Tonya Roberts faced the same dilemma as many college freshmen: she had no idea what major to pursue. A fellow student told Tonya about the career center at the university and Tonya decided to check it out. She tossed her notebook PC into her backpack, donned her headphones, cranked up her favorite music on her iPhone, and took off for the career center. At the center, a career counselor showed Tonya how to use computerized questionnaires to relate her aptitudes, interests, and work environment preferences to various careers. Tonya was able to generate lists of potential careers, including what the job involved, salaries earned, education required, and other important information. Tonya connected her thumb drive to the computer's USB port, saved the information, pocketed the thumb drive, and headed to the student union.

At a quiet spot at the student union, she connected her notebook to the school's wireless network, plugged in her thumb drive, called up the files from the career center, and studied her possible futures. The career center's Web site provided links to several online career and job placement services. Before long she became accustomed to the job search tools and the language of the job market. She learned that there are all kinds of jobs out there for individuals with the right credentials and found several that captured her interest. The job postings she found acted as an incentive throughout her college education.

In her senior year, Tonya revisited the career center, this time to arrange for job interviews. The career center maintained a large database of potential employers and applicants. Tonya added her name to the list and left her cell phone number and e-mail address so that they could quickly contact her when an employer was interviewing.

As you read through this chapter, consider the following questions:

1. What types of computers and digital devices played a role in Tonya's search for the ideal career and job?
2. How did telecommunications, the Internet, and computer networks assist Tonya in her quest?
3. What types of computer-based information systems might have been used by Tonya and the career center in looking for a career and job?
4. Why are computers and digital technologies important to Tonya's career and personal life?
5. What security and ethical issues might be involved in the use of databases at the career center?

Check out Tonya's *Action Plan* at the conclusion of this chapter.

1

Introduction

LEARNING OBJECTIVES

1. Define how digital electronics devices and computers are related, and provide descriptions of the different types of computers.
2. Provide an explanation of the fundamentals of telecommunications, computer networking, the Internet, and wireless networking.
3. Describe the five functional areas in which computers assist people most.
4. Discuss the uses of information systems by individuals, businesses, and organizations, and list common types of information systems.
5. Discuss how computers are used in a variety of fields and why studying computer systems can benefit you professionally.
6. Discuss how computers are used to assist people in their life outside of work.
7. Define information security and discuss ways in which digital technologies are impacting humanity.

CHAPTER CONTENT

Why study computers and digital technologies? As you will see throughout this book, understanding computers and digital technologies can help you achieve your personal and professional goals. You can use computers to obtain and play the latest music, keep track of your expenses and develop a monthly budget, and obtain information about almost any topic. Today, computers are used in all career areas from anthropology to zoology. Computers and digital technologies are indispensable in business, engineering, science, the fine arts, the military, and all other fields. In this book, you will see hundreds of examples of how individuals and organizations have used computers to achieve their goals.

This book introduces you to essential concepts in digital technologies that every student should know prior to starting a career. To realize the vast potential of computer and information systems, you will learn the latest about hardware, software, and the Internet. You will also learn about telecommunications and network systems, databases, electronic commerce and transaction processing, and information and decision support systems. Important information on information security, systems development, multimedia, and ethical and societal issues will show you how computer and information systems can be acquired and controlled to maximize their potential.

This society thrives on information. People depend on computer-based systems to create, store, process, access, and distribute information. Information is knowledge, and knowledge is power! This is true for all ages in all walks of life. Students use computers to research homework topics, communicate with friends, and acquire the latest music; investors use computers to make multimillion-dollar decisions; financial institutions employ computers to transfer billions of dollars around the world instantaneously; and chemical engineers use computers to store and process information about chemical reaction rates to design biodegradable products.

Employers expect graduating college students to be as fluent with computers and digital technology as they are with the English language. Meanwhile, the number of jobs in technical fields is growing by leaps and bounds. Table 1.1 illustrates how many job ads, even in nontechnical fields, specify computer skills. Employers advertising professional positions that require a bachelor's degree assume that applicants will have a thorough understanding of digital technologies and their uses. Applicants who don't are simply squeezed out of the running. The more you know about computers and technology, the more marketable you are—no matter what your career. Employers recognize that computers can assist in acquiring important job skills and knowledge, communicating effectively, and working efficiently. Whatever your career area, you must excel not only in your area of expertise but also in digital information technologies in order to be successful. A *knowledge worker* is a professional who makes use of information and knowledge (see Figure 1.1). Will your future career require you to be a knowledge worker? You should certainly hope so; otherwise, your work may not be very challenging or fulfilling.

TABLE 1.1 • Monster.com job ads

Today's employers expect applicants to have a thorough understanding of digital technologies and their uses.

Employer	Position	Computer skills requirements
Nike	*Visual merchandising specialist*	"Computer skills, including Microsoft Word, Excel, and Outlook"
Levi Strauss & Co.	*Manager, graphic design*	"Current knowledge of industry trends, graphic design technology, and innovative printing techniques"
GE Healthcare	*Human resources administrative assistant*	"Experience with MS Word, Excel, PowerPoint, and a database is required"
Skyhawks Sports Academy	*Professional coach*	"Internet and computer skills are a must!"
Walt Disney World Resort	*Designer*	"Minimum 2 years experience working with Microsoft applications (Word, Excel, PowerPoint, and Outlook), Minimum 3 years AutoCAD (latest version) experience/proficiency"

Computer literacy is a working understanding of the fundamentals of computers and their uses. Originally, computer literacy was focused on desktop computer skills. Today typical computing experience extends far beyond the desktop to numerous mobile and networked devices. Rather than accessing digital information and services through one desktop location, today people interact with a wide range of digital devices from many locations (see Figure 1.2). This increased interaction with and reliance on digital technologies has made understanding them all the more important. Today you need much more than just a fundamental understanding; you need to become a master of technology.

Some technology educators feel that the phrase *computer literacy* isn't sufficient to describe the mastery of technology that is required today. Other titles

FIGURE 1.1 • Knowledge worker
Today's workers employ many different types of digital electronics devices for maximum productivity.

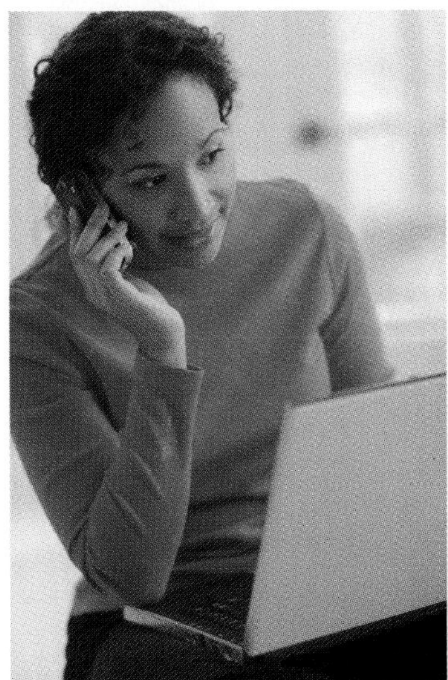

have been suggested, such as *information technology literacy, computer competency, computer fluency,* even *information and communications technology literacy*. Whatever you call it, everyone agrees that a deep and broad understanding of digital technologies and their use is a valuable asset for success in careers and life. Knowing how to use certain software applications is not enough; you need to understand how to apply your knowledge of computers and digital technology to real-life problems. This textbook provides computer literacy by examining all types of digital technologies and showing how they are being used by individuals to enhance their professional and personal lives.

Digital technologies have forever changed society, businesses, organizations, and personal lives. This chapter provides some fundamental concepts and presents a framework for understanding computers and digital technologies. This understanding will set the stage for future chapters and help you unlock the potential of computers to achieve your personal and professional goals.

WHAT IS A COMPUTER?

What is a computer? This may seem like a silly question in today's computer-saturated world, but if you think about it, there are so many different types of digital devices in use today that it has become difficult to define what is and isn't a computer! Although it might be safe to assume that most devices that have a keyboard and mouse are considered computers, what about other digital devices like the Wii, cell phone, and digital camera? Here's a brief definition: a **computer** is a digital electronics device that combines hardware and software to accept the input of data, process and store the data, and produce some useful output. To understand this definition, and to help define what is and is not a computer, you must first understand the basics of digital technology and the general functions of a computer.

FIGURE 1.2 • The digital world
Digital technologies are an integral part of everyone's lives and require a high degree of understanding and knowledge.

Digital Technology

The purpose of this textbook, summed up by its title, is to provide information that can help students succeed in reaching their personal and professional goals by using the strengths of technology. **Technology** refers to tools, materials, and processes that help solve human problems. Many of today's technologies fall under the classification of digital electronics. These are the technologies that you will study. Today's well-equipped knowledge worker makes use of many digital technologies. Each technology serves a specific function that meets a unique need in a particular environment. Personal computers, cell phones, digital cameras, and digital music players are all considered digital electronics devices. What does it mean to be digital?

Digital refers to technologies and devices based on digits (numbers). A **digital electronics device** is any device that stores and processes *bits* electronically. A **bit** (short for *binary digit*) represents data using technologies that can be set to one of two states, such as on or off, charged or not charged. Each state is assigned a 1 or a 0, the only two possible values for binary digits. For example, *on* might be assigned a 1, and *off* a 0. A string of bits could be notated as 10011011. This is the essence of a digital device—the ability to represent, process, transfer, and store data and information as 1s and 0s.

A group of eight bits is called a **byte**. Bytes can represent all types of useful data and information, such as characters, values, colors, or sounds. Bytes can be grouped together to create an electronic **file,** a named collection of instructions

Digital "Snail Mail"

With everything in the world seemingly being digitized, it's hard to believe that people are still going to their mailboxes each day and opening envelopes to read printed type on paper sent across the country via airplanes and trucks and delivered by human postal carriers. "How long will this 'snail mail' system last?" you might ask. Well, alternatives are beginning to present themselves, and no, the solution isn't exactly e-mail.

It would be nice if postal mail could evolve overnight into e-mail, but traditional systems as entrenched as government postal services change v-e-r-y s-l-o-w-l-y (at a snail's pace, you might say). In the meantime, there is Earth Class Mail. You can have your postal mail forwarded to Earth Class Mail, and the company will digitize it and send it to you over the Internet.

The digitization process involves first scanning the envelope without opening it. The scanned envelope is sent as a PDF file in a secure, encrypted fashion to your e-mail inbox for your visual inspection. You then choose to either have Earth Class Mail throw it out without opening it (junk mail), forward the unopened letter to your postal mailbox, or open the letter, scan it, and send images of the content to your e-mail inbox. The company says that roughly 90 percent of the mail they handle is categorized by clients as junk and is thrown out unopened.

This type of mail-handling service is catching on globally. The Swiss Postal Service has opened a version of Earth Class Mail for Swiss, German, Austrian, French, and Italian citizens. Digital mail forwarding costs around $20 per month for up to 50 letters. If this service catches on, it may mean the beginning of the end for snail mail and a mass reduction in the use of paper and fossil-fuel-burning delivery systems, which would benefit the environment.

Questions

1. What benefits does snail (postal) mail offer over e-mail? Would any such benefits prevent snail mail from eventually evolving into digital mail?
2. Might a new type of digital mail, different from e-mail, be required to handle the types of communication that utilize snail mail?
3. If an Earth Class Mail system were free for use, would you subscribe to it? How much might you be willing to pay for such a service?

Sources

1. *Cheng, Jacqui, "Swiss Postal Service lets users check snail mail online,"* Ars Technica, *July 13, 2009, www.arstechnica.com.*
2. *Earth Class Mail Web site, accessed July 21, 2009, www.earthclassmail.com.*
3. *O'Rourke, Ciara, "Delivering Letters to Your Inbox,"* The New York Times, *July 12, 2009, www.nytimes.com.*

or data stored in the computer or digital device. **Data** refers to the items stored on a digital electronics device, including numbers (values), characters (letters), sounds (such as your voice over a cell phone network), music (CDs and MP3s), or graphics (photos, drawings, and movies). Anything that can be expressed and recorded can be represented as 1s and 0s and stored as files in digital devices. The process of transforming nondigital information such as things you experience with your senses—written or spoken words, music, artwork, photographs, movies, even tastes and fragrances—to 1s and 0s is called **digitization**.

When the bits and bytes are processed to a format that is useful to people—statistics in a graph, the results of a Web search, music in your headphones, photos on a display—it is called information. **Information** is data organized and presented in a manner that has additional value beyond the value of the data itself. The primary purpose of digital electronics devices is to process digital data (such as sales figures) into information (such as a graph comparing sales by month).

At the heart of all digital electronics devices is a microprocessor. A **microprocessor**, sometimes called a *chip* or just a *processor*, combines microscopic electronic components on a single integrated circuit that processes bits according to software instructions.

Computers, computer networks, and other digital electronics devices store, transfer, and process bits and bytes in vast quantities. It is typical to refer to the power of digital technologies in terms of thousands, millions, billions, even trillions of bits and bytes. For example, today's typical PC can store millions of bytes on a CD and billions of bytes on a hard drive. High-speed Internet connections are able to send and receive billions of bits per second. Table 1.2 shows common prefixes used to express multiples of bits, bytes, and other digital metrics, and Table 1.3 shows the size in bytes of some common digital items. Bytes are typically represented with an uppercase *B* and bits with a lowercase *b*. For example, *KB* stands for kilobyte and *Kb* for kilobit. These are important metrics to understand if you want to measure the power and effectiveness of digital technologies.

TABLE 1.2 • Prefixes for digital technology metrics

Prefix	Value	
Kilo	1,000	Thousand
Mega	1,000,000	Million
Giga	1,000,000,000	Billion
Tera	1,000,000,000,000	Trillion
Peta	1,000,000,000,000,000	Quadrillion
Exa	1,000,000,000,000,000,000	Quintillion

TABLE 1.3 • Storage capacity examples

Example storage sizes	
Text file	1 KB
Spreadsheet file	50 KB
High-resolution digital photo	1.2 MB
MP3 digital music file	5 MB
Music file on CD	64 MB
Microsoft Office software	640 MB
A typical motion picture	7.38 GB
Sears inventory and customer database	55 TB
CERN database (nuclear and particle physics research)	20 PB
Google database	30 PB

Computer Functions

Now that you understand what a digital electronics device is, what about the rest of the definition of a computer? Recall that a computer is a digital electronics device that combines hardware and software to accept the input of data, process and store the data, and produce some useful output (Figure 1.3). **Hardware** refers to the tangible components of a computer system or digital device. **Software** comprises the electronic instructions that govern the computer system's functioning.

FIGURE 1.3 • Computer functions

A computer is used to input, process, and store data and provide useful output.

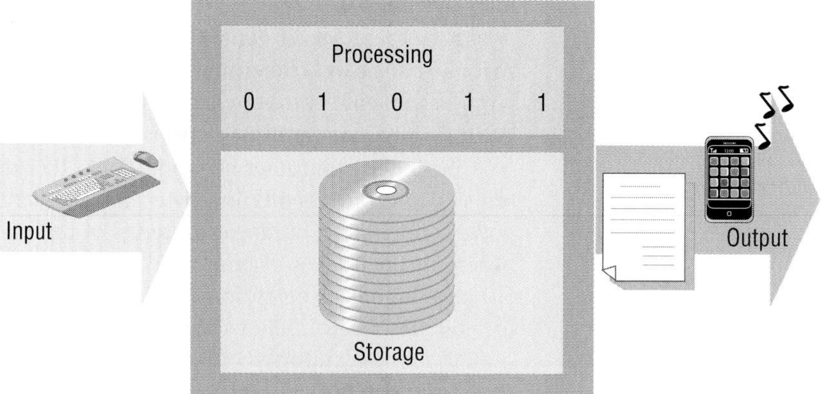

Strictly speaking, this definition covers not only desktop, notebook, and handheld computers, but also today's popular digital electronics devices. Cell phones, digital cameras, handheld gaming devices, and digital music players all process input into some form of output—voice, photos, video, music—based on program instructions or software. So, although nearly all digital electronics devices fall under the definition of a computer, in casual conversation the term *computer* is generally used to refer to *general-purpose computers,* those that can run any of hundreds of different software applications. Computers designed for one particular function are called *special-purpose computers* and are typically referred to by the type of computing they perform: digital music player, digital video recorder, digital camera, motion detector, controller, blood pressure monitor, and so on.

Types of Computers

Computers are becoming increasingly pervasive. As you walk across campus you are bound to see some students working on notebook computers, others talking or sending text messages on their cell phones, and still others walking to the beat of their favorite music playing on an iPod. You may pass an ATM or two or kiosks that provide special services such as campus maps or access to college records. You might play a quick round of your favorite video game on your cell phone during a break. Computers of one sort or another are within reach wherever you go.

FIGURE 1.4 • Dell desktop PC

Dell's STUDIO One 19 desktop PC includes an all-in-one design with a touch screen.

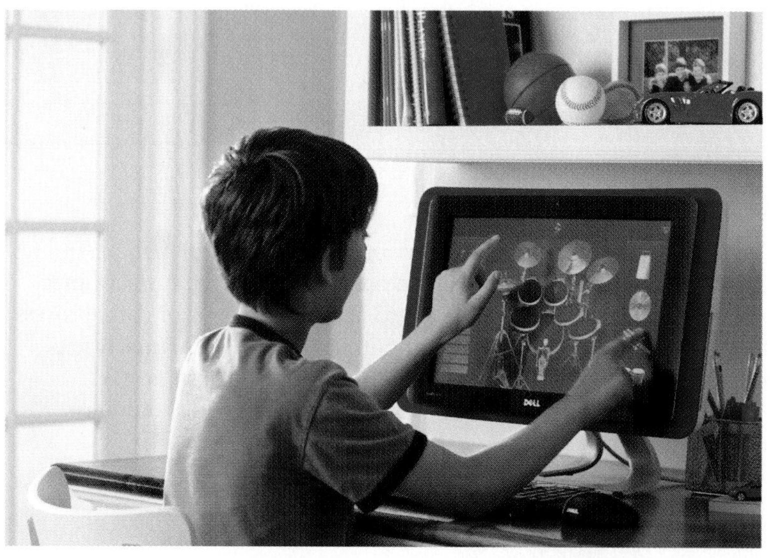

Personal Computers. The type of digital device that most people associate with the word *computer* is called a personal computer. A **personal computer**, or **PC**, is a general-purpose computer designed to accommodate the many needs of an individual. Personal computers come in a wide variety of types and styles from a wide variety of manufacturers. The most traditional and powerful type of PC is the desktop computer (Figure 1.4). *Desktop computers,* such as the Dell Dimension or

Apple iMac, are designed to be stationary and used at a desk. They typically include a tower case (also called the system unit) that houses the circuitry, a display, keyboard, mouse, speakers, and a printer. Some "all-in-one" PCs sandwich the system unit and display into one case to save desktop space.

FIGURE 1.5 • Netbook computer

Netbooks are ultramobile, inexpensive notebook computers designed for light mobile computing on "the Net."

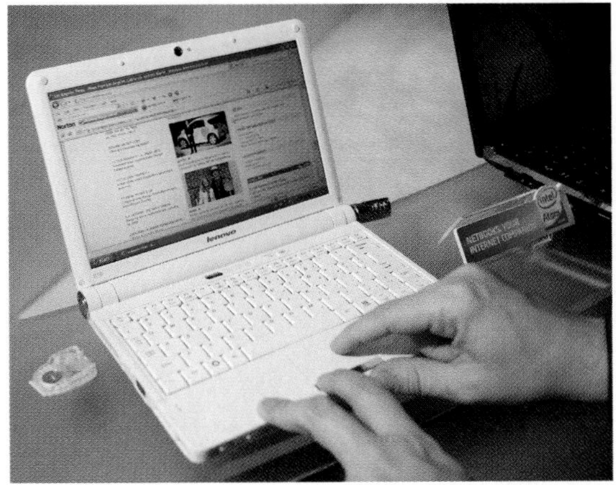

Notebook computers, also called *laptop computers*, such as the Lenovo Thinkpad or Apple MacBook, are also considered personal computers and provide desktop or near-desktop power in a portable case. Notebooks come in a variety of sizes to cater to different environments. *Netbooks* are small, inexpensive, ultraportable notebooks designed primarily for Web applications and lightweight productivity applications. With small 10" displays, netbooks are perfect for travel, but don't typically include the power and storage required for digital media applications (Figure 1.5). On the other end of the spectrum is Apple's MacBook Pro. With display sizes up to 17 inches and processing power that rivals high-end desktops, the MacBook Pro can handle professional media applications without trouble.

World-renowned nature photographer Ben Horton has traveled the world with his cameras and MacBook Pro. He uses his MacBook Pro to edit photos onsite, allowing for the possibility of reshooting images when necessary. Portable computing power has allowed Ben to become more efficient with his time while getting the best photographic results.[1] Examples such as this illustrate the portable power of a notebook computer combined with valued computer skills.

FIGURE 1.6 • Tablet PC

Tablet PCs allow you to write or draw on the screen, and are useful for making handwritten notes and digital art.

Tablet PCs are portable personal computers, similar to a notebook computer in size, that provide a touch-sensitive display on which you can write and draw (see Figure 1.6). A special electronic stylus is used to write or draw on the screen, as well as to select menu items and manipulate the cursor. All that is written and drawn on the display is interpreted, processed, and stored digitally. Tablet PCs are useful in environments where you have to access your computer while on the go and on your feet.

The *convertible model tablet PC* converts between notebook PC and tablet by allowing the display to be opened, rotated, and then closed so that the display is on the outside. Convertible tablets are useful in that they provide both keyboard and stylus methods of input. A *slate model tablet PC* does not provide a keyboard. Slates are lighter than convertible models and allow you to connect to a larger display, keyboard, and mouse through a docking station.

Handheld computers, also called *PDAs* (for personal digital assistant), are personal computers that are only slightly larger than traditional cell phones. Like tablet PCs, handheld computers use a touch-sensitive display and stylus for input. Handwriting-recognition software translates written characters to editable word-processing characters. Handhelds have traditionally been used for personal information management (PIM) such as maintaining to-do lists, storing appointments on a personal calendar, and storing contacts in an address book. PDAs evolved to provide hundreds of computer applications. Eventually, they evolved to include cellular and Internet communication, morphing into today's smart phones. While there are still PDAs available without cell phone capabilities, they are losing market share to smart phones.

Smart phones combine PC, Internet, media, and cell phone capabilities in a single handset. Typical smart phone applications are listed in Table 1.4. However, for some smart phone platforms there are literally thousands of useful software applications available for download. For example, the Apple iPhone has over 65,000 applications available created by developers using software development tools provided by Apple.

FIGURE 1.7 • Smart phone

Smart phones such as the Palm Pre offer mobility and compact computing.

TABLE 1.4 • Typical smart phone applications

Smart phone applications
• Phone
• Music player
• Video player
• Web browser
• Camera
• Photo viewer
• Text messaging
• Maps and GPS
• Voice recorder
• Notes
• Calendar
• To-do list
• Stock market
• Weather
• YouTube viewer
• Calculator
• Custom personal and business apps

The data stored on a smart phone is typically synchronized with the data stored on a desktop or notebook PC. When you **synchronize** or **sync** two digital devices, you update the files shared between the devices so that both copies are up-to-date and identical. A smart phone typically connects to a PC through a *docking station* or *cradle,* a small stand for a handheld device that is used to recharge its battery and to connect to a PC. Upon connecting, synchronization software automatically transfers and updates files. Synchronization can also take place without the cradle using wireless networking.

Synchronization has become a standard routine for mobile device users. iPod users are familiar with the process of synchronizing playlists between an iPod and the iTunes software on their PCs. Users of smart phones are familiar with connecting to a PC to synchronize calendars, to-do lists, photos, music, videos, and sometimes other types of data files. For example, if you run into a friend, make a date to go out, and note it on your smart phone, when you get home and connect your phone to your PC, that appointment will be transferred to the calendar on your PC.

Increasingly, synchronization is being managed over the Internet. Calendars, to-do lists, contacts, e-mail, and other information is being stored on Web servers owned by companies like Google, Microsoft, and Apple, or private businesses. Internet-connected smart phones, notebooks, and desktop PCs retrieve the information from the server when needed, and update the information on the server whenever it is changed. It is likely that most or all of our data will be soon stored on servers and accessed in this manner.

If you work for a mid- to large-size corporation, there is a strong likelihood that you will be using a smart phone like the BlackBerry to connect to the corporate network. Employees using smart phones wirelessly connected to corporate servers are able to access centrally stored database records, files, calendar appointments, contacts, and other information just as though they were sitting at their office PC. For example, mobile sales reps at Adidas, the athletic gear corporation, depend on their BlackBerries when they call on retailers.[2] Custom software installed on the device allows sales reps to access up-to-the-minute inventory data stored in the corporate database. Tim Oligmueller, sales force automation manager for Adidas, says their customers are "totally impressed." "They love that our sales reps can pull out their BlackBerry devices and, while sitting right in front of them, can pull up the data without having to make a phone call or follow up later." The sales reps are also able to check their e-mail, keep track of appointments and personal notes, access mission-critical applications such as workload management software, and make phone calls, all with a device that fits in a pocket.

Different types of PCs cater to different needs and environments. It is important for professionals to take advantage of the unique capabilities of each type of PC, from powerful desktops to notebooks and netbooks, to tablets and smart phones.

Computer Platforms. A computer's type, processor, and operating system define its **platform**. When describing a computer's platform in terms of hardware, one would list the type of computer—handheld PC, desktop PC, server, and so on—along with a description of the unique hardware features that make up the computer, including processor type and other internal component specifications. Because operating systems are designed for a specific type of hardware platform, the operating system itself is often used to define a computing platform. The platform is important for two reasons: (1) it defines the user's experience and interaction with the computer, and (2) it provides specifications for software developers. Typically, software is written to run on one particular platform. The two most popular personal computer platforms are IBM-compatible, commonly referred to as Windows, and Apple. Hundreds of manufacturers make Windows computers. Only one company makes Apple computers. Smart phone platforms include Symbian and Microsoft Mobile (see Figure 1.8).

FIGURE 1.8 • Three smart phone platforms

Smart phones running operating systems from Palm, Google, and Apple provide different features and experiences for the user.

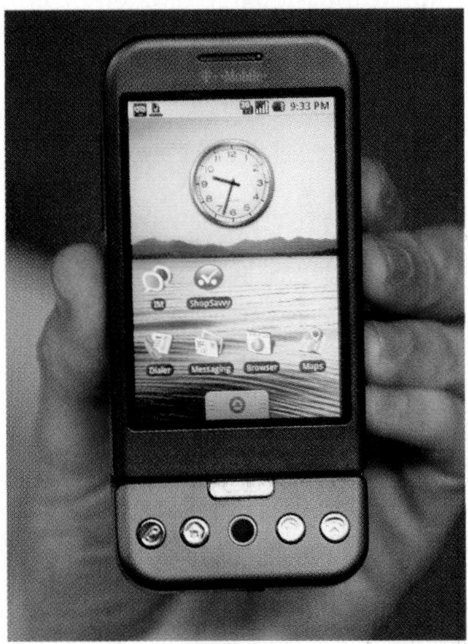

Servers. The larger computers that power today's network and Internet services are called servers. **Servers** are powerful general-purpose computers that

FIGURE 1.9 • Modular data center

A modular data center design, patented by Google, utilizes shipping containers to hold hundreds of servers each.

provide information services to numerous users over a computer network. Servers often have multiple processors and large amounts of storage to support many simultaneous users. In most cases, servers run 24 hours a day, 365 days a year, in order to provide uninterrupted service. Although servers are general-purpose computers that can run a variety of software applications, most are dedicated to specific duties. For example, a *Web server* is responsible for serving up Web pages over the Internet. When you access your school's Web site, the files that make up the Web site are delivered to your computer by one or perhaps a few Web servers designed to satisfy tens of thousands such requests each day. When you request a video from YouTube, you are drawing on resources distributed over tens of thousand of servers satisfying hundreds of millions of requests each day. A *file server* may store and deliver files to employees' desktop computers over a company's private network. An *e-mail server* handles sending and receiving e-mail messages. A *print server* manages the printing requests for a printer shared by multiple users on a network. Large businesses and organizations typically have many types of servers providing a wide assortment of services to their employees and the public.

Servers come in a wide variety of sizes with varying capacities, from serving dozens to thousands of users at once (see Figure 1.9). A *midrange server* has the capacity to service dozens or even hundreds of users at a time. Baylor College of Medicine uses three IBM midrange servers at the core of its information system. The servers manage business operations, college records, and patient records for the college and associated hospital.[3]

A *mainframe server* can service hundreds or thousands of users at a time over a computer network. Mainframe servers, often simply called *mainframes*, have been used in companies and organizations since the late 1950s. Prior to the introduction of PCs in the early 1980s, employees used *terminals*, desktop computers with a keyboard and display but little else, to connect to a mainframe and access data. Many mainframes have been retired in favor of smaller, faster, and more efficient servers, but they are still required for the large data environments found in government institutions and large corporations. For example, employees and management at Whirlpool Corporation run applications and access corporate data from one central mainframe computer. Whirlpool runs its global business processes on mainframe computers designed to support its 73,000 employees at more than 70 manufacturing and research centers around the world.[4]

SUPERCOMPUTERS SPUR A NEW RACE AMONG SUPERPOWERS

Or, rather, among the *former* superpowers. Racing to regain his country's prominent international position, Russian President Dmitry Medvedev issued an urgent call to invest in supercomputers. How can Russian businesses hope to compete in international markets when products, such as aircraft, were developed on paper while the United States and other countries used supercomputers? The president pointed out that 476 of the 500 best supercomputers in the world were produced in the United States, and it was high time that Russia began to catch up.

U.S. Supercomputing Lead Rings Sputnik-Like Alarm for Russia
Patrick Thibodeau
Computerworld
July 28, 2009
http://www.computerworld.com/s/article/9136005/U.S._supercomputing_lead_rings_Sputnik_like_alarm_for_Russia

Supercomputers. **Supercomputers**, the most powerful computers manufactured, harness the strength of hundreds or even thousands of processors simultaneously to accomplish very difficult tasks. IBM's Roadrunner computer, shown in Figure 1.10, with over 20,000 processors, is being used to solve problems at the U.S. Department of Energy's National Nuclear Security Administration.[5] The Earth Simulator (*www.jamstec.go.jp/es/en*) uses 5120 processors to simulate the Earth's climate in an effort to determine what steps are necessary to ensure a healthy future for the planet and its inhabitants. Disney uses a supercomputer with 900 processors to create its feature animations.

FIGURE 1.10 • Supercomputer: IBM Roadrunner

Roadrunner was the world's fastest supercomputer in 2008 and 2009, with over 20,000 processors delivering a peak performance of 1.7 petaflops.

Supercomputers have helped to answer many of life's most perplexing questions and solve some important problems. The human genome (the structure of human DNA) was decoded using supercomputers. Many of today's most useful pharmaceuticals were developed with the assistance of supercomputers. Supercomputers, through highly advanced simulations, put an end to nuclear testing in developed countries. There are still many difficult questions and problems that may be solved only by using future generations of supercomputers.

Special-Purpose Computers.

Special-purpose computers are manufactured to serve a specific purpose, such as game consoles, e-book readers, digital media players, digital cameras, and smart home appliances.

The Amazon.com Kindle e-book reader is a special-purpose computer designed to access and view electronic books (Figure 1.11). The processor and operating system used in the Kindle allow users to connect to the Kindle store, where books, magazines, newspapers, and blogs are available to download for a fee. The Kindle displays pages of text on a unique display that provides a paper-like viewing quality. Some publishers are formatting textbooks to distribute for the Kindle.

FIGURE 1.11 • Special-purpose computer: Amazon Kindle

The Kindle is designed to allow users to purchase and view digital books, magazines, newspapers, and blogs.

You may have noticed an increasing number of public-access computers, called kiosks, in public areas and stores. A **kiosk** is a computer station that provides the public with specific and useful information and services. Usually equipped with a touch screen, kiosks provide everything from online store catalogs, such as at JCPenney and Staples, to maps and exhibit information, such as in cities, on campuses, and in museums. The ATM where you can withdraw money from your bank account is a kiosk. Kiosks that allow customers to print photos from their digital cameras have become very popular. There are church kiosks that accept donations and respond with a blessing, and airport check-in kiosks that produce boarding passes.

Special-purpose computers also work behind the scenes in the devices that support professionals and control the automated equipment that is increasingly prevalent in everyone's daily life. **Embedded computers**, sometimes called *microcontrollers*, are special-purpose computers (typically an entire computer on one chip) that are embedded in electrical and mechanical devices in order

FIGURE 1.12 • Embedded computer: magnetic resonance imaging (MRI)
Embedded computers are used in a multitude of special-purpose devices used by professionals, such as this MRI device.

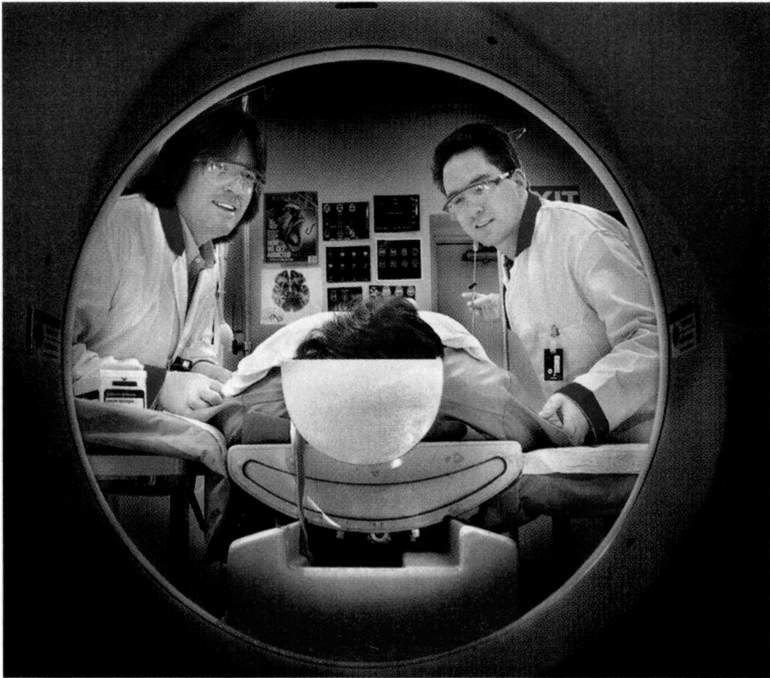

to control them. Automatic doors; washing machines; elevators; automobile systems such as fuel injection, braking, and airbag deployment; microwave ovens; copy machines; telephones; and numerous other gadgets encountered every day are controlled by embedded computers. In fact, there are many more embedded computers in use today than general-purpose computers. A home may have only one or two PCs, but it probably contains dozens of embedded computers.

Embedded computers control special-purpose devices used in nearly all professions. Embedded computers can be found at the heart of systems used by security experts, such as airport screening devices, metal detectors, and bomb detection devices, as well as the radar guns used to catch speeders. The manufacturing industry makes use of all types of automated systems controlled by embedded computers to manufacture products. Embedded computers are essential to the specialized tools used by doctors, nurses, and medical technicians to examine and diagnose patients, such as the MRI device shown in Figure 1.12.

Mobile Digital Devices

The largest area of growth in technology has been in mobile devices. Today, people are doing their work on the go more than ever before. Working life has been transformed from one in which individuals work independently at a desk, to one in which teamwork and mobility are the norm. The "desk" has to be wherever you are. The trend of digital electronic devices to become smaller and increasingly powerful has fully supported the move to an increasingly mobile workforce. The power of a 1990s computer that filled an entire desktop now fits in a 6-ounce handheld computer.

Mobile Computing. Among the types of computers defined in the previous section are several different mobile computers: notebooks, tablets, netbooks, and smart phones. Over the past few years, notebook PC sales have overtaken desktop PC sales. Consumers love the freedom that mobile computing provides. As wireless networks grow to cover larger areas, you can expect to see continuing increases in mobile computer sales. Many colleges have wireless campuses where students can use mobile computers to access the school network and the Internet from anywhere on campus.

NEW SOFTWARE MAY ACTUALLY PREVENT CRASHES

You're getting sleepy, very sleepy. Your eyes are closing. But, uh-oh, you're at the wheel of a car—and you're going to crash! Or maybe not. A team of computer scientists from the United States and India are developing software that uses an in-car camera and image processing to detect when drivers yawn and issue a warning. The algorithm they have developed can distinguish between talking, smiling, singing, and yawning, that telltale sign of fatigue. The warning could possibly prevent up to 100,000 crashes in the United States alone.

Yawn Alert for Weary Drivers
ScienceDaily
July 29, 2009
http://www.sciencedaily.com/releases/2009/07/090727102042.htm

FIGURE 1.13 • It's a cell world after all

Cell phone communications are changing the way people relate with each other.

Many cities are working to provide free wireless Internet access in business districts and airports. Services such as Boingo provide subscribers with wireless Internet access at thousands of locations around the world. The phenomenal rate of growth in mobile computing is driven by wireless network technologies.

Mobile Communications. Cell phones and cell phone services are among the fastest-growing digital markets (Figure 1.13). The ability to phone from almost any location has transformed society. Online communications and associations are beginning to supersede here-and-now communications and associations. Today's cell phones, however, do far more than provide mobile voice communications. *Text messaging,* also known as *Short Message Service (SMS)* and *texting,* involves using a cell phone to send short text messages to other cell phone users. Due to its relatively low price and convenience, texting has become as popular a use of cell phones as voice communications.

Cell phone handsets are available in a wide range of styles with varying levels of capabilities. The most powerful cell phones (referred to earlier as smart phones) double as handheld computers and media players. *Third-generation (3G) cell phones* offer high-speed Internet access. Some cell phone services allow cell phones to be used to connect PCs to the Internet. Through a process called *tethering,* cell phone Internet subscriptions can be shared with notebook computers.

Mobile Media. Recent years have witnessed an explosion of handheld media devices. The launch of the Apple iPod in 2003 brought portable digital music into the mainstream. While portable *MP3 players*—handheld devices that play music stored in the digital MP3 format—have been available for some time, it was the iPod's slick design and marketing that brought it to the attention of the general public. In 2004, several companies, such as Creative and Samsung, hoped to take advantage of public enthusiasm for mobile media by introducing *portable media center* devices that play digital movies as well as music. Movies, television shows, and other video clips can be downloaded from the Web or transferred from DVD to the devices and displayed on the 3.8-inch screen. In 2005, the introduction of Sony's PlayStation Portable (PSP) brought handheld gaming to a new level with a high-quality widescreen display for realistic interactive 3-D graphics. In 2006, Apple introduced a video iPod and added video distribution to its popular iTunes store. In 2007, select cell phone carriers began offering a television programming service for subscribers. Table 1.5 provides some of the milestones in mobile technologies over the past two decades.

TABLE 1.5 • Evolution of mobile technologies

Year	Events
1983	• First personal digital assistant (PDA) introduced by Casio • First consumer camcorder introduced
1984	• Cell phone technology introduced (**1st generation**)
1988	• First digital camera introduced by Sony
1989	• Nintendo Game Boy handheld gaming device released
1991	• First *digital* cellular service introduced in Finland (**2nd generation**)
1992	• Cell phones evolve from car phones to mobile hand sets
1993	• SMS texting on cell phones arrives first in Finland
1995	• Global Positioning System (GPS) technology becomes fully operational • First *digital* camcorders introduced • First digital camera with LCD from Casio • First digital camera to record video
1996	• PalmPilot PDA introduced with handwritten character recognition
1997	• First integrated cell phone and camera
1998	• First digital audio music players hit the market with 32 MB flash memory
1999	• First Internet access over cell phone in Japan
2001	• Apple introduced iPod music player with 5 GB microdrive and the slogan, "1,000 songs in your pocket." • First high-speed Internet available over cellular service in Japan (**3rd generation**)
2002	• First commercial camera phones arrive in the United States
2002	• Archos introduces portable media player for music, photos, and video (20 GB microdrive) • Birth of smart phones: Palm Treo and RIM BlackBerry
2003	• First music phones arrive in South Korea
2004	• Nintendo DS portable gaming device released
2005	• Sony Playstation Portable • iPod 5 supports video playback
2006	• First GPS applications made available on some cell phones
2007	• Apple introduces iPhone, supporting voice communications, computing, gaming, GPS, and media
2009	• Google Android-based phones and the Palm Pre are introduced to compete with the iPhone
2010	• Very high-speed Internet over cell phone grows across the United States (**4th generation**)

Digital Convergence. The past decade has witnessed a major convergence of numerous mobile technologies. Table 1.5 shows landmark developments in mobile technologies. The introduction of the iPhone in 2007 was a culmination of advances in several mobile technologies integrated extremely effectively into one small handheld device. While media players, PDAs, digital cameras, handheld games, and GPS handsets still exist, they are gradually being replaced by multifunction smart phones. Figure 1.14 illustrates how the paths of major technologies merged as they became integrated into smart phones.

FIGURE 1.14 • Mobile device integration

The iPhone and similar smart phones include the functionality of at least six devices in one small handset.

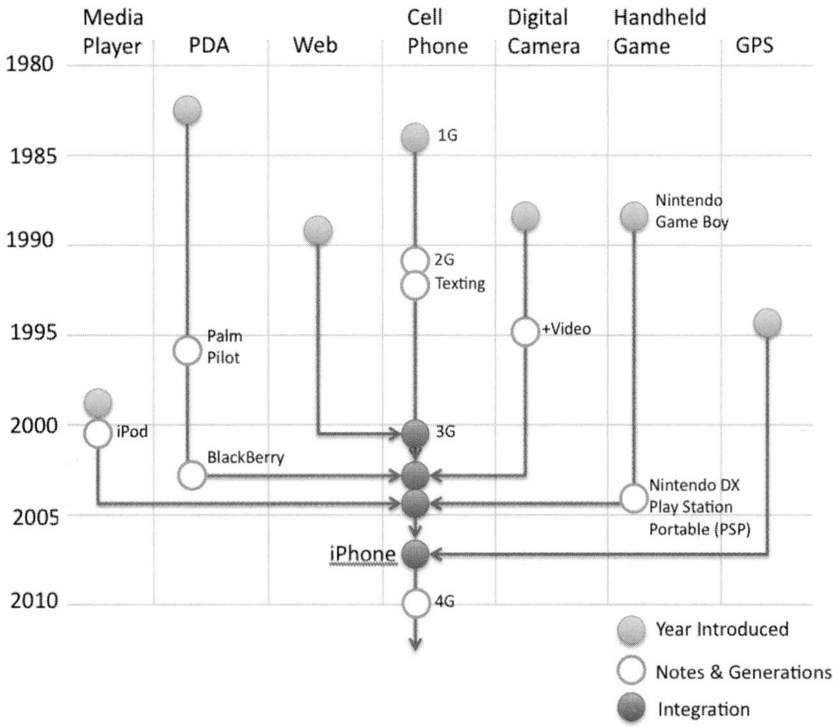

It should be noted that advances in cellular technologies through three generations to high-speed Internet access made it possible for the iPhone and other smart phones to succeed. As cellular networks evolve to fourth generation very-high-speed networks, the services provided by cellular handsets will be even more useful.

In answer to the question "What is a computer?" you have learned that all digital electronics devices can be classified as computers. Some are general-purpose computers and others are special-purpose computers. Throughout this text you will learn about all different types of computers and digital devices and how they are used at home, at work, and on the road. From supercomputers to desktop computers, from servers to cell phones, from kiosks to handheld games, you will see how computers provide digital services for every environment and need. You will see that the ability to connect to information sources, individuals, and services from any location is of particular value and importance.

THE POWER OF CONNECTIONS

It is commonly understood that people are able to accomplish more and produce better solutions when they work together rather than individually. "There is strength in numbers," "Two heads are better than one," and other common expressions underscore this widely held belief. Today's businesses and organizations put great emphasis on teamwork. Today's digital networks provide the technical foundation to support the communication that is at the heart of teamwork.

Telecommunications

Telecommunications are communications that take place electronically over a distance. Forms of telecommunication include telephone systems, radio, television, and computer networks. Telecommunications components include a transmitter that sends a signal over a medium, such as fiber-optic cables or the air, to a receiver (Figure 1.15).

FIGURE 1.15 • Telecommunications

Telecommunications involves a transmitter sending a signal electronically over a medium to a receiver.

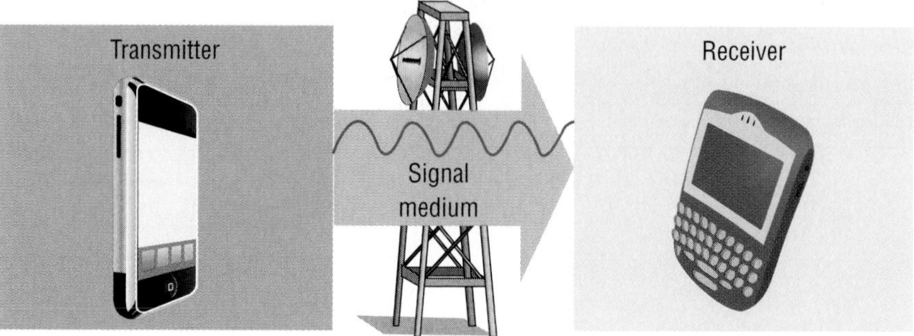

The *telecommunications industry*, often called the *telecom industry*, focuses on electronic voice and data communications. Telecom giants such as Sprint and Verizon offer voice, data, and Internet services for residential customers and businesses. Telecom companies maintain the large networks over which telephone and Internet communications travel (see Figure 1.16).

FIGURE 1.16 • A telecom company's global network

Global telecommunication networks span the United States and the world, providing voice and data communications and carrying Internet traffic.

A **computer network** is a telecommunications network that connects two or more computers for the purpose of sharing data, hardware, and software resources. Computer networks can range in size from two computers to thousands of computers or, in the case of the Internet, over a billion computers. For computers to communicate—to send and receive data—they must follow the same set of communication rules called protocols. **Protocols** are rules that allow two or more computers to communicate over a network.

The Internet

Multiple computer networks joined together to form larger networks are called *internetworks*. In 1969, research commenced to build what would eventually become the largest internetwork in the world. That research provided the protocols and technologies that govern today's Internet. The **Internet** is the world's largest public computer network: a network of networks that provides a vast array of services to individuals, businesses, and organizations around the world. The Internet population is rapidly approaching two billion. People rely on the Internet for news and information, communication, education, entertainment, commerce, travel arrangements, job hunting, and many other important activities.

The *Web*, short for **World Wide Web**, is an Internet service that provides convenient access to information through hyperlinks. A *hyperlink* is an object in a Web document that can be clicked to access related information. Developed and released to the public in the early 1990s, the Web opened the Internet to the general public. Because of its ingenious and easy-to-use design, the Web has become the primary tool for accessing most Internet information and services.

Wireless Networking

Wireless is the technology buzzword of the decade. **Wireless networking** uses radio signals rather than cables to connect computers and digital devices to computer networks and often through those networks to the Internet. The increasingly mobile workforce is benefiting greatly from wireless networking technologies that allow workers to remain connected to business networks and the Internet while on the go. Just as the cell phone expanded people's telephone capabilities, wireless networking is expanding their computing capabilities.

Wireless networks are being installed in businesses and homes and on campuses in order to allow individuals within range to access information and services stored on networks. **Wi-Fi**, short for *wireless fidelity*, is a popular wireless networking standard that connects computers to other computers, computer networks, and the Internet (see Figure 1.17). When you see wireless Internet access advertised in coffee shops, restaurants, bookstores, hotels, airports, and other public places, chances are they are using Wi-Fi. Most notebook computers come equipped with Wi-Fi capability. Wi-Fi is popular in homes, where it allows residents to share an Internet connection, printers, and files between several computers. It is also being used in homes to transmit music and movies between computers and televisions and stereos. Wi-Fi is popular in businesses as it is easy to install and provides employees with the ability to take their computers with them anywhere on the premises without losing a network connection.

FIGURE 1.17 • Wi-Fi

Wi-Fi wireless networking technology is used at many colleges to give students access to the Internet anywhere on campus.

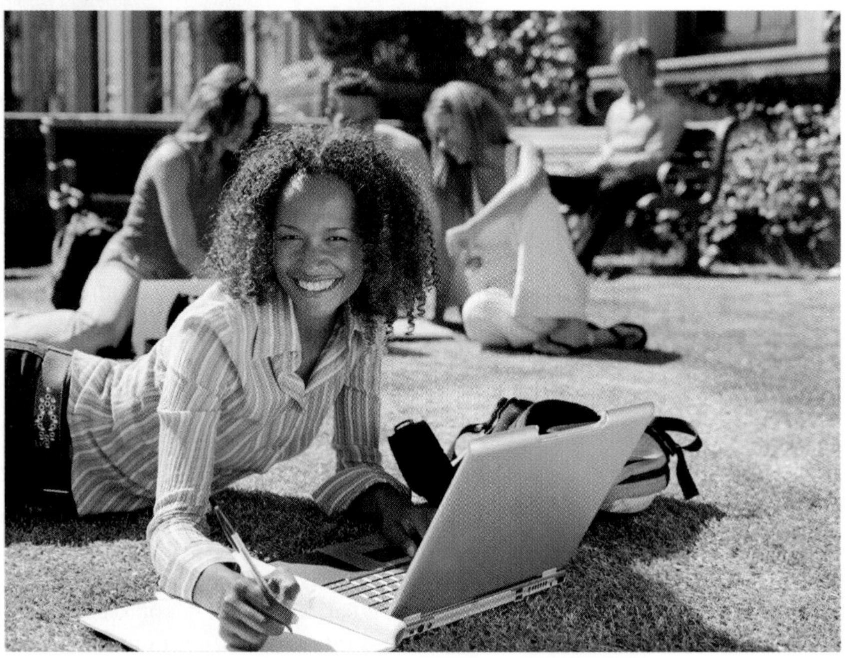

Wireless technologies, telecommunications, the Internet, and the Web are all important factors in using technology to succeed. You will find examples throughout this book showing how people in various careers are using the power of connections to accomplish their personal and professional goals.

WHAT CAN COMPUTERS DO?

Although computers and digital electronics devices seem to provide almost limitless services, there are some activities in which they excel and others for which they are ill suited. For example, computers are excellent at carrying out well-defined, repetitive tasks accurately and quickly. Computers have no problem carrying out long complicated calculations at lightning speed. A computer can sort through millions or billions of data records in a matter of seconds to find those that match a keyword or some other criteria, a task that might take a human a lifetime. Fortunately, the things that computers do well—working with large amounts of data and repetitive tasks—are things that people find difficult and monotonous; the creative and interpersonal endeavors that people find most engaging, computers are ill suited to perform. For example, a computer could write a poem or compose a song, but such would be found lacking in substance. Designing a new marketing campaign, choosing an employee for promotion, listening to the complaints of a patient and interpreting their meaning, and many other professional activities require human creativity and intuition; however, often they can be accomplished much more effectively when supported by computers. It is helpful for computer users to consider the areas in which computers can assist people most: computation, automation, communications, digital media and entertainment, and information management (see Figure 1.18).

FIGURE 1.18 • Computer strengths
Computers are used most effectively in these five areas.

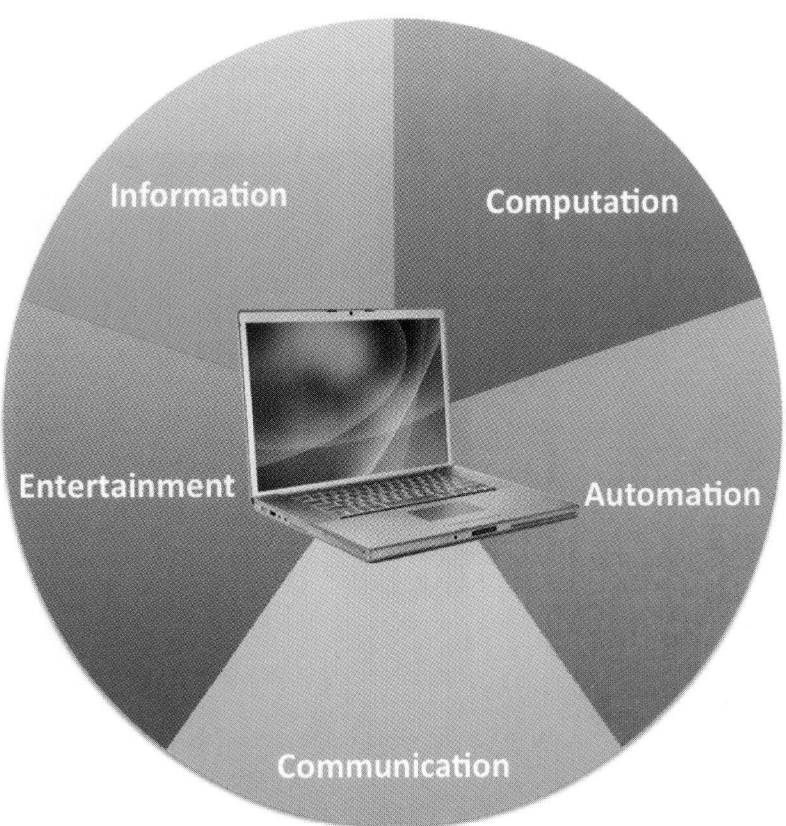

Computation

Computers were invented to compute. While the word *compute* can be interpreted in different ways, it is used here to mean calculating a solution to a mathematical problem. This is the number-crunching aspect of computers. Early computers calculated missile trajectories during World War II. After the war, they were put to work for the U.S. government calculating census data and in private industry calculating financial data. Over the years, computation has remained paramount in the value that computers provide. Computers can crunch endless streams of numbers in a fraction of the time humans can without ever tiring. And they do it faster and better every year. With each newer and faster supercomputer, new answers to age-old questions are discovered. For example, in a project they call Folding @ home, Stanford University scientists are enlisting the assistance of thousands of Internet-connected PCs to help run simulations and unravel the mysteries of protein folding to find cures to numerous diseases. Anyone can join the effort by installing software on their PC available at*http://folding.stanford.edu.*

Computational science is an area of computer science that applies the combined power of computer hardware and software to solving difficult problems in various scientific disciplines. One of the world's fastest supercomputers, IBM's BlueGene/P, was named for its computational scientific purpose: to study biomolecular (genetic) phenomena; the blue is added simply because it is IBM's favorite color. Another example is Virginia Tech's powerful supercomputer System X. System X was created by linking together 1100 dual-processor Apple computers (see Figure 1.19). Meteorologists are using the supercomputer to crunch numbers and simulate the structure of tornadoes so they can better understand them. Biologists are using the supercomputer to examine the many roles water plays in the human body. Scientists in all areas rely on computers to do the mathematical grunt work and simulate natural phenomena that are difficult or impossible to study in real life.

FIGURE 1.19 • Virginia Tech's System X

Supercomputers like System X carry out calculations and simulations that would otherwise be beyond human capabilities.

People rely on computers to find solutions to problems that are beyond the abilities of the human brain, and yet the human brain functions in a manner that computers find difficult if not impossible to duplicate. If the speed of the human brain were measured and represented as a processor speed, it has been estimated that it can carry out 100 trillion operations (thoughts) per second. The world's fastest supercomputer, IBM's Roadrunner, has a theoretical peak performance of 1.7 quadrillion (million billion) operations per second. Still, no one has suggested that this machine can think like a human, though it may be only a matter of time before researchers are able to model the functioning of the human brain in a supercomputer.

Artificial intelligence (**AI**) is an area of computer science that deals with simulating human thought and behavior in computers. Most AI experts are not interested in creating computers that think like humans. People already know how to make more humans; who would want to make computers into humans? It makes more sense to use those things that computers do best to complement human intelligence, to extend natural human abilities, and to take over and automate activities that people find tedious, dangerous, and difficult.

Automation

Automation involves utilizing computers to control otherwise human actions and activities. For example, an area of AI called *computer vision* uses video cameras as eyes for a computer system that can tirelessly "watch" objects or areas and accurately interpret what it is "seeing." Vision systems are used in security applications and quality control. *Expert systems*, another branch of AI, automates tasks that are carried out by human experts—tasks that can be well defined and are typically tedious, monotonous, or hazardous to the human expert. *Natural language processing* is a branch of AI that empowers computers with the ability to understand spoken words and provides more convenient ways for people to interact with computers.

Another area in which computers are helpful is through the automation of physical tasks. *Robotics* is a branch of AI that empowers computers to control mechanical devices to perform tasks that require a high degree of precision or are otherwise tedious, monotonous, or hazardous for humans. Robotics is mostly known for its use in the manufacturing process, such as robotic arms that perform welding on an assembly line. However, closer examination makes clear that robotics is an increasing presence in people's everyday lives. The Roomba is a well-known robotic vacuum cleaner that finds its way around every square inch of floor, sucking up the dirt as it goes. The same company that manufactures the Roomba, iRobot Corporation, has much more complex robots assisting U.S. military troops with surveillance, reconnaissance, and bomb disposal. The latest design is armed with a Taser electroshock weapon to assist law enforcement officers in dangerous situations.

At Sonoma State University, the Jean and Charles Schulz Information and Technology Center uses an automated storage and retrieval system (ASRS) to retrieve books from the library shelves. Increasingly, such systems are being used to store and retrieve warehouse inventory (see Figure 1.20). In New York, fully automated trains are being used on a 24-station line connecting Manhattan and Brooklyn. A lone train operator sits in the front car watching the controls.

FIGURE 1.20 • Automated storage and retrieval

Automated storage and retrieval systems are able to store and retrieve inventory with the press of a button.

Automation allows people to exceed their natural abilities and empowers those with disabilities. New *smart homes* allow residents to open and close curtains, turn on sprinkler systems, control media throughout the house, and adjust environmental controls from any Internet-connected computer or wall-mounted display.

Communication

Computer systems control, support, or provide many forms of communication. Obvious examples are computer-based forms of communication such as e-mail, instant messaging, and Web logs, more commonly known as *blogs*. *Social networking* has attracted even more individuals to the Web. An online social network provides Web-based tools for users to share information about themselves and to find, meet, and converse with others in the social network (see Figure 1.21). MySpace and Facebook are social networks that allow members to create Web pages that include all types of information about themselves and their interests.

FIGURE 1.21 • Social network: Facebook

Social networks like Facebook allow members to use communications tools to create and maintain relationships with like-minded people.

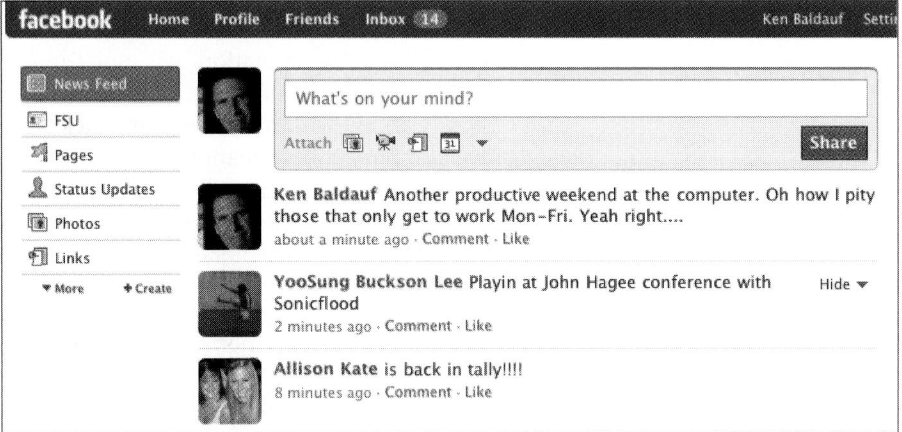

What may be less apparent is that computers and computer networks are increasingly supporting phone-based voice communications as well. Most phone networks are phasing out traditional phone technologies in favor of digital computer technologies. In 2003, Sprint began moving its entire phone network to the digital technologies used by the Internet.

Businesses and individuals are also exploring using digital phone services to save money and enjoy better service. **Voice over Internet Protocol**, more commonly known as **VoIP** (pronounced *voip*) is a popular technology that allows phone conversations to travel over the Internet or other data networks.

Residential VoIP services, sometimes referred to as *broadband phones*, are becoming popular with home users who are interested in low phone bills and added features such as receiving voice mail alerts via e-mail. Residential VoIP subscribers must have a high-speed Internet connection in their home. They connect their standard phone to a device that digitizes the signal to travel over the Internet. Residential VoIP customers can accept calls made to their phone number and make calls from any Internet-connected location to any phone number (Figure 1.22).

FIGURE 1.22 • Comcast Triple Play

Digital cable TV, high-speed Internet, and phone service are all offered over one digital cable.

New models of cell phones are making use of Wi-Fi networks for faster and cheaper communications. A Wi-Fi phone uses the cell network just like all cell phones, but when a Wi-Fi network is available, it jumps onto the Internet for a better connection that doesn't add to your monthly minutes. T-Mobile offers a Wi-Fi phone service that provides subscribers with a Wi-Fi access point to set up at home, or access from tens of thousands of T-Mobile wireless hotspots around the world.

Phone networks and data networks are steadily merging into a single entity that utilizes the efficient technology of the Internet. Google Voice allows users to route phone calls to different or multiple numbers and manage calls and voice mail on the Web. Voice communication is destined to become fully integrated with Internet communication, offering increased control over recordkeeping and availability.

Other forms of communication such as radio and television are transforming into computer-driven digital media as well. Digital cable and digital radio services offer audiences an increased variety of programming with crystal clear connections. Books, magazines, and newspapers are gradually migrating from paper to bits and bytes on devices like Amazon's Kindle, smart phones, and of course, the Web. More people read *The New York Times* online than the printed version of the paper. People are increasingly experiencing the world through computers and interacting with each other through digital connections. Communication is definitely one of today's most important uses of computers and digital technologies.

Entertainment

Digital media refers to music, video, photographs, graphic art, animation, and 3D graphics stored and processed in a digital format. Digital technologies have vastly expanded the creative toolkits of artists of every genre. Music is recorded in a manner that is truer to the quality of the original performance. Three-dimensional animation provides more fuel for the imagination than traditional 2D cartoons. Game consoles like the Xbox 360, PlayStation 3, and the Wii feature 3D graphics that provide players with a more lifelike experience as they maneuver within virtual environments.

Digital technologies not only enrich people's entertainment experiences but also have revolutionized entertainment distribution (see Figure 1.23). The Internet has opened new marketing and delivery mechanisms that make media easier than ever to acquire. Portable digital media devices and smart phones have made it possible to enjoy music, photos, and entertainment wherever you go. Digital technologies have improved the quality and increased the quantity of creative works in this connected society. The improved circulation of media products can only be considered a positive influence on society from both provider and consumer points of view. Suppliers and distributors of media are working to develop new business models that allow for the free flow of media content while financially supporting those that create and manage the media.

Information

Perhaps the greatest impact of computers on the society is in information storage, management, retrieval, and distribution. As documents, expressive and creative works, and other forms of information have been digitized, the resulting amount of stored information has become overwhelming.

FIGURE 1.23 • Online entertainment: Hulu.com

Television, movies, and video entertainment are migrating online through Web sites like hulu.com.

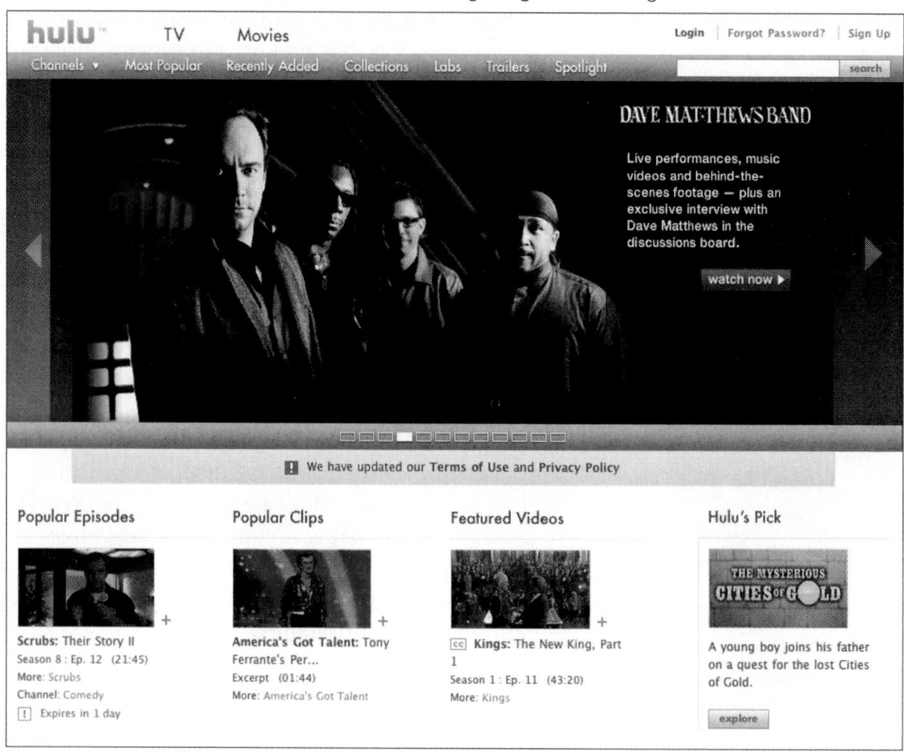

FIGURE 1.24 • Components of a computer-based information system

The six components of a CBIS work together to assist us in managing information.

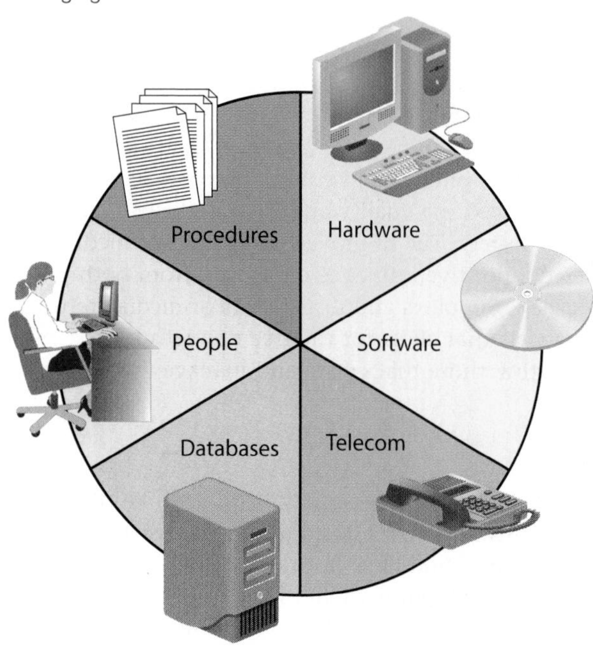

Information overload is the common term used to describe a state in which the amount of information available overpowers one's ability to manage and use it. An information system, or more specifically a **computer-based information system** (**CBIS**), makes use of computer hardware and software, databases, telecommunications, people, and procedures to manage and distribute digital information (see Figure 1.24). A **database** is a collection of data stored on a computer, organized to meet users' needs. Databases are a key component to managing information, and information systems are the primary defense against information overload.

Individuals use information systems to manage their contacts, e-mail, and online documents. Businesses use information systems to analyze business data to determine courses of action that might provide greater profits. The Web might be considered the world's largest information system, providing a convenient framework for publishing and finding information on the Internet. Consider how Facebook.com, the corporation, makes use of the six components of a computer-based information system:

- Hardware: Web servers on which to store user pages, PCs and printers for Facebook employees to use.
- Software: Web browsers on user PCs, and Web server software to deliver Facebook pages to users.
- Databases: Storage for user profiles, photos, statuses, and relationships.

- Telecommunications: Routers and cables to connect servers to the Internet and manage incoming Web page requests.
- People: Managers, system engineers, support operators, designers, programmers, and many other Facebook employees.
- Procedures: Web protocols that govern the transfer of information over the Web, and human protocols for conducting business.

Information management plays such a crucial role in the interactions with computers that the next section of this chapter looks at it in more detail.

Consider how *you* use computers. You will discover that all of your uses of computers fall under one of the above categories: computation, automation, communication, entertainment, or information. To maximize your success in your chosen career and personal endeavors, you must consider how to best use computers in these five areas and work to ensure that you are taking advantage of the latest and greatest technologies. This book is created to do exactly that.

INFORMATION SYSTEMS

The term *information system* covers a wide variety of computer applications. It is helpful to pause and consider some of the common terminology associated with information technology. The expression *computer system* is typically used to describe multiple computers working together over a network toward a common goal. A computer-based information system was formally defined in the previous section and can be considered more simply as a computer system designed to manage information. The expression **information technology** (**IT**) can be defined as issues related to the components of a computer-based information system. Table 1.6 is provided to assist you in understanding the subtle differences among these commonly used expressions.

TABLE 1.6 • Important distinctions among technical terminologies

Term	Definition
Digital electronics device	Any device that stores and processes bits electronically
Computer	A digital electronics device that utilizes hardware to accept the input of data, and software, or a computer program, to process and store the data and produce some useful output
Computer system	Multiple computers working together over a network toward a common goal
Information system	A computer system that makes use of hardware, software, databases, telecommunications, people, and procedures to manage and distribute digital information
Information technology (IT)	Issues related to the components of an information system

If you think about it, information management is the most common use of personal computers. A word processor assists people in managing the information in a document. E-mail systems, to-do lists, address books, and the Web are all information management systems. Music, movies, and photographs can be considered information, so any application used to catalog and play these media files can be considered information management software. When it comes down to personal computer use, a computer's information management abilities are typically used much more than its computational abilities.

The use of information systems escalates vastly in businesses and the workplace. No matter what the apparent purpose of any particular business or career, you can be sure that information management plays a large role in its daily activities.

NASA uses information systems to analyze data retrieved from the Mars Rovers (see Figure 1.25). In the real estate industry, huge databases manage information on available properties. Scientists share research data stored and managed by information systems accessible over the Internet. Photographers make use of information systems to store and catalog digital photographs. Whatever profession you name, you can find an information system that assists those professionals in managing their information and in being more efficient and effective in their work.

FIGURE 1.25 • Information systems at NASA

NASA scientists use management information systems to examine the data sent from Mars Rovers.

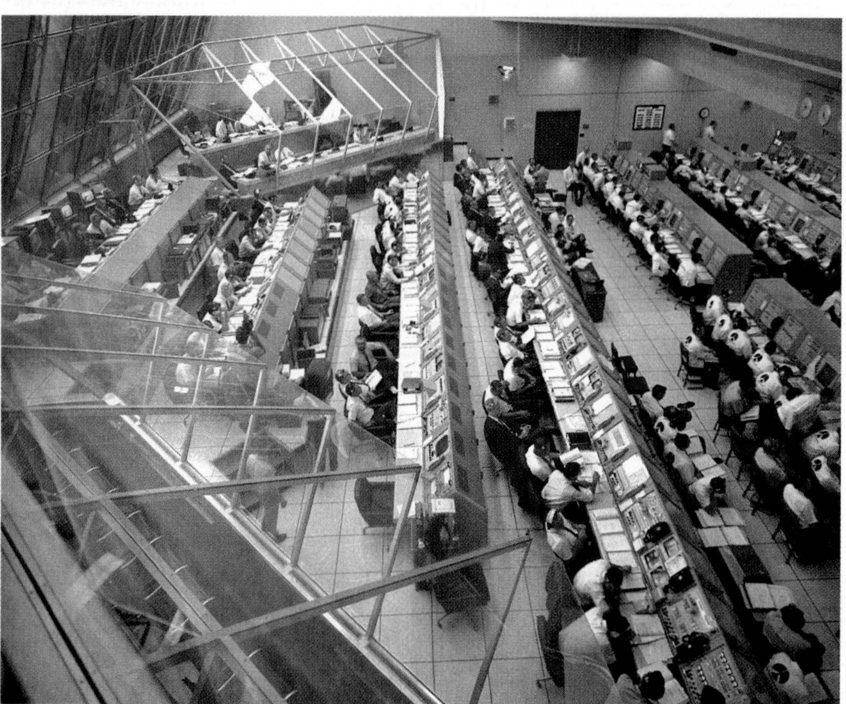

The information systems that people use every day at work and at home are not haphazardly designed and created. **Systems development** is the activity of creating new systems or modifying existing ones. *Systems analysts* are information professionals responsible for designing information systems. There are specific and formal types of information systems with which all students should be familiar prior to beginning a professional life.

Types of Information Systems

There are many formally defined information systems that people and businesses use to manage information. The most basic systems simply record useful data, and the most advanced serve as intelligent advisors. Table 1.7 introduces you to the most common types of information systems from the most basic to the most intelligent.

TABLE 1.7 • Common types of information systems

IS	Use
Transaction Processing System (TPS)	An information system used to support and record transactions such as a customer purchasing a product or a business paying an employee
E-commerce	Information systems that support online transactions, such as a customer purchasing music at eMusic.com or a bank transferring funds between accounts
Management Information System (MIS)	An information system used to provide useful information to decision makers, usually in the form of a report such as a quarterly report of investment earnings or a grade report for your classes this semester
Decision Support System	An information system used to support problem-specific decision making, such as an online dating service's list of compatible partners or an investment firm's supercomputer system for analyzing stock performance
Expert System	An information system that can make suggestions and draw conclusions in one particular area of expertise much the same way that a human expert can, such as a medical expert system that makes recommendations based on a patient's symptoms

USING DIGITAL TECHNOLOGIES TO SUCCEED IN YOUR CAREER

As you will see throughout this book, people and organizations use digital technologies to succeed in the workplace and in life. As you read about the use of technology in various fields, think of how you can use these examples to help you achieve your own personal goals and career aspirations. You will find that an example of how computers are used in one field can often be directly applied in other fields.

Of course, it would be impossible to cover every career or industry. This section gives you a sampling of what is possible, beginning with the obvious: computer-based professions.

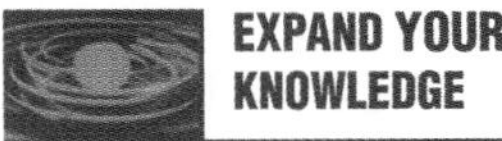

EXPAND YOUR KNOWLEDGE

To learn more about careers and technology, go to www.cengage.com/computerconcepts/np/swt4. Click the link "Expand Your Knowledge" and then complete the lab entitled "Careers and Technology."

Computer-Based Professions

As computing has grown to become an important part of all industries, the demand for computer professionals has increased. People who work in a computer-based profession are involved in designing, building, and maintaining hardware, software, database systems, telecommunications, and Internet systems. *Software engineers*, for example, design and develop new software applications to meet a wide variety of needs. *Computer scientists* conduct state-of-the-art research into computing topics such as artificial intelligence, robotics, computer networks, and operating systems. Electrical and computer engineers research and design processors and electrical circuits that could profoundly change people's lives in the future (Figure 1.26).

FIGURE 1.26 • Computer science and engineering

Computer scientists and electrical engineers conduct research to improve all aspects of computer systems.

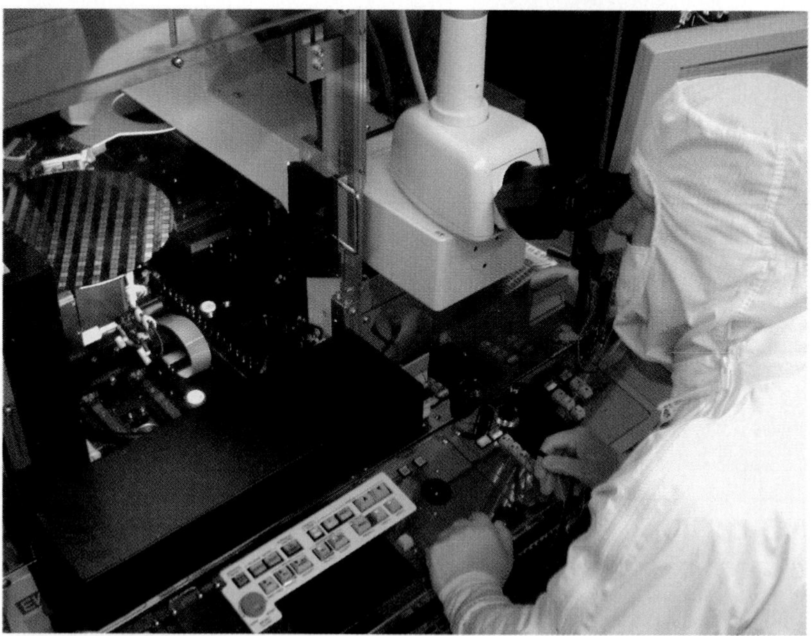

Inside the computer industry, computer professionals work in areas such as design, manufacturing, sales, and services, often with a specific major product line. From a wide array of products, computer systems professionals may choose to specialize in equipment designed for use within certain areas such as networks and telecommunications, multimedia systems, expert systems, or imaging technology. Others may choose to work in certain industry segments such as education, manufacturing, business, laboratories, engineering, and many other areas.

In businesses, computer personnel typically work in a computer department that employs a chief information officer (CIO), computer programmers, systems analysts, computer operators, and a number of other computer personnel. Computer personnel have a variety of job titles and responsibilities. The chief technology officer (CTO), for example, typically works under a CIO and specializes in hardware and related equipment and technology. In addition to technical skills, computer personnel also need skills in written and verbal communication, an understanding of organizations and how they operate, and the ability to work with people (users).

College students interested in a computer-based profession should choose to earn a degree in computer science, management information systems, or electrical and computer engineering. Many universities also have developed degree programs in information technology to meet the high demand for professionals in this field. For example, your school might have a College of Information that teaches IT skills.

Business and Communications

A variety of career opportunities exist in business and communications, marketing, sales, accounting, finance, organizational behavior, human resources, leisure and hospitality, and information systems. Computers are essential in producing business documents and reports, including payroll checks, inventory reports, tax documents, and many others. Computers are used to support the entire supply chain from manufacturing to sales (see Figure 1.27).

FIGURE 1.27 • Computers in business

Computers are an essential element in most businesses.

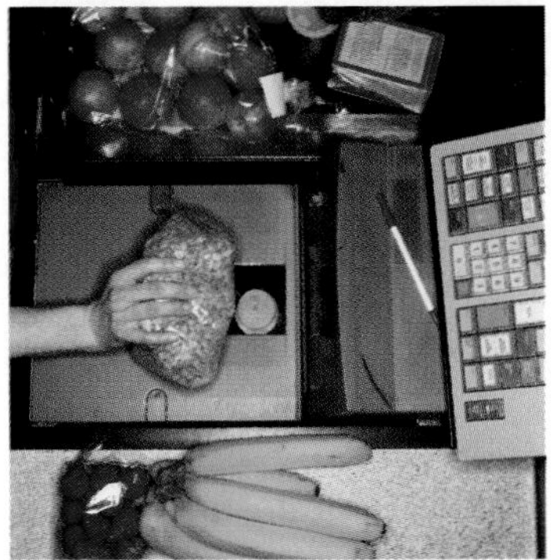

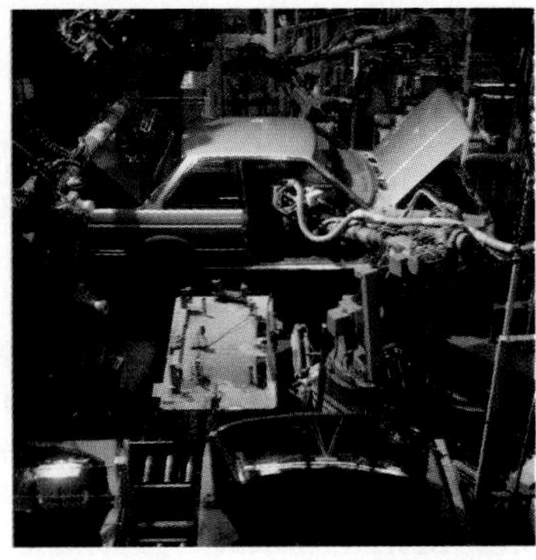

Most businesses succeed in using technology to increase revenues or reduce costs. Here are just a few examples. In factories, computers are being used to design and manufacture products, using *computer-assisted design (CAD)* and *computer-assisted manufacturing (CAM)*. For example, Toyota uses a CAM system that allows the company to build almost any type of vehicle in any of its plants.

In banking, computers are used to instantly move billions of dollars from one institution to another, using *electronic funds transfer (EFT)*. Computers are used in all aspects of retail. Products usually have *Universal Product Codes (UPCs)* on them that can be read by scanners. Computer systems are also used to check for customer credit, handle returns, and provide a vast array of reports to managers. Marketing and advertising companies use computers to collect and analyze vast stores of consumer data. The information is used to provide high-quality products and services to customers. Shopping carts at Bloom grocery stores, on the east coast of the United States, are equipped with the CONCIERGE computer system, and connect wirelessly to the stores' information systems to provide personalized recommendations and promotions to customers based on their purchasing history.[6]

Science and Mathematics

Chemistry, biology, mathematics, statistics, astronomy, physics, meteorology, environmental sciences, oceanography, sports science, and military science are just a few fields in science where computers are used. Computers are used to analyze geological samples collected on Mars. Scientists are using computers to analyze string theory equations. String theory attempts to explain both large-scale physics and the physics of subatomic particles, in which a particle's location in space is not certain at any point in time, but is based on mathematical probability instead.

COMPUTER-BASED PRIMORDIAL SOUP

Scientists continue to argue about whether life originated on the ocean's surface, around undersea vents, or in outer space. One technological wizard—along with a team of international consultants—is creating a computer program, the "Evo-grid," that simulates conditions present on Earth four billion years ago. Researchers are waiting to see what virtual molecules will emerge from this primordial soup.

'Toy Universe' Could Solve Life's Origins
Leslie Mullen
Astrobiology Magazine
July 2, 2009
http://www.space.com/scienceastronomy/090702-am-evogrid-evolution.html

Cell Networks Help Save African Farms

Computing and digital technologies play an important role in all professions. Professionals using digital technologies can also have a big impact on cultures, countries, and the world. Such is the case with professionals working on a new initiative to bring badly needed weather and climate data to farmers in Africa.

Around 700 million Africans depend on the land to make their living, and three-fifths of these depend on the food they grow to feed themselves and their families. Often, unexpected weather causes devastation to crops and to those dependent on them. Some 300,000 deaths each year and $100 billion in economic losses are blamed on weather-related devastation for which farmers are ill prepared.

One problem is that there are only a couple hundred weather-monitoring stations in Africa, one-eighth the amount recommended by the World Meteorological Society. But the spread of cellular technology in Africa is beginning to open lines of communication that keep farmers better informed. One initiative designed to assist Africans, sponsored by the Global Humanitarian Forum, Ericsson, the World Meteorological Organization, and mobile operator Zain, will deploy 5,000 new automated weather stations at existing cellular base stations across Africa.

Automated sensors of several kinds will collect data from the weather stations to begin creating a database that will inform researchers of weather conditions and patterns over time. The sponsors of the "Weather Info for All" initiative claim that the new systems will "provide a massive increase in crucial information to predict and manage climate shocks."

If this initiative is successful, it paves the way for many other technologies that will collect regional data and use cellular networks to transmit it to a central computer system. There is talk of tracking water levels, smoke particles, wildlife, and vegetation. Not only could such systems aid Africans, but they could also provide valuable information for efforts to control global warming.

Questions

1. What is an unexpected benefit of installing cell phone towers across Africa?
2. What does this story convey about the value of a technological infrastructure to developing countries?
3. How can computing and information technologies assist developing countries to better engage with the digital global economy?

Sources

1. *Banks, Ken, "Weather stations will use mobile infrastructure,"* Computerworld, *July 20, 2009, www.computerworld.com.*
2. *Ericsson Staff, "Mobile Communications to Revolutionize African Weather Monitoring," Ericsson Press Release, June 18, 2009, www.ericsson.com.*

Scientists are also using computers to forecast weather, hunt for hurricanes, analyze the environmental impact of forest fires, and make detailed maps using *geographic information systems (GISs)*. Scientific visualization uses computers to produce 2D and 3D images and video of scientific phenomena which cannot otherwise be witnessed (Figure 1.28). By inputting large quanties of data that describe a phenomenon, scientists are able to create visual models to examine the phenomenon to discover new qualities and relationships.

FIGURE 1.28 • Computers in science

Visualization software and two supercomputers were used to render this image of the gravitational effects caused by the collision of two black holes.

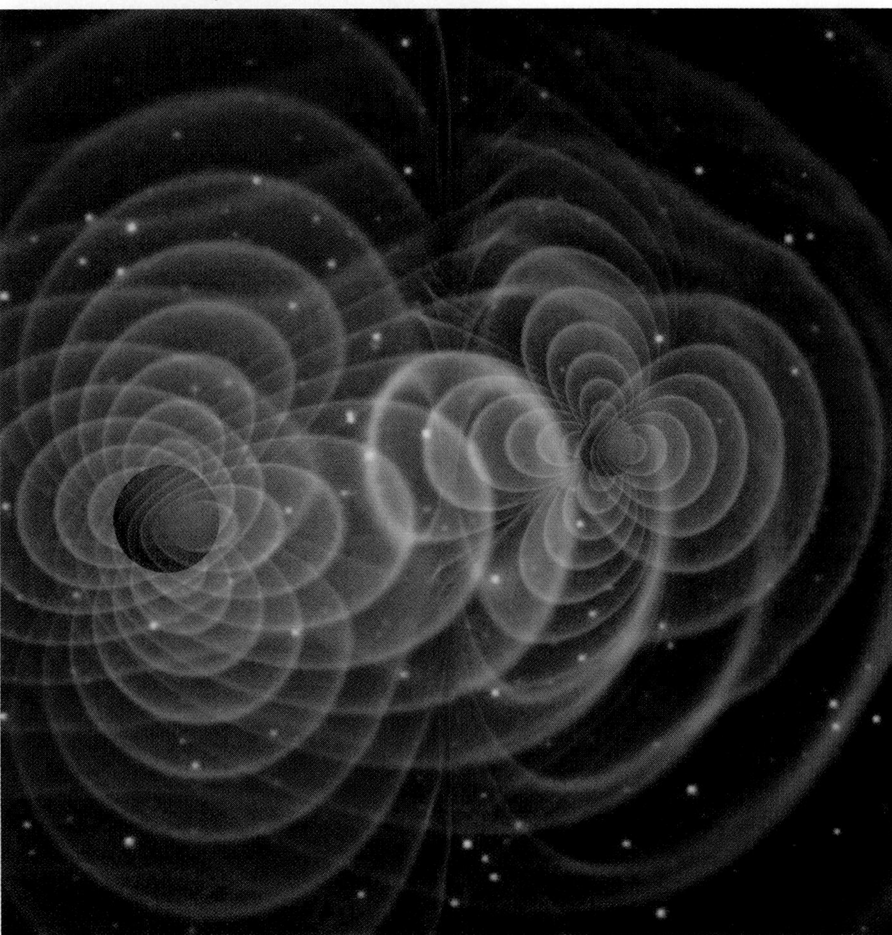

Advanced machines and computers have enabled medical research scientists to use protein sequencers and synthesizers to map the entire human genome. Scientists have used computers to advance their knowledge so rapidly that people have a hard time keeping up. New technology moves from theory to truth in every area every day.

Engineering

Engineering careers include aeronautical, mechanical, electrical, chemical, civil, industrial, and environmental engineering. Engineers use computers in design and operations (see Figure 1.29). In chemical engineering, for example, engineers use computers to design petroleum refinery operations to produce a variety of gasoline and diesel fuels using minimal energy requirements. Computers are used to design new aircraft and space vehicles. Computers are also used to make complex thermodynamics, power consumption, circuits and signal, and reactor design calculations, to name a few.

FIGURE 1.29 • Computers in engineering

The design of bridges and highways is enhanced through the use of computers.

Social Sciences

The social sciences include economics, geography, psychology, political science, sociology, and urban planning. In economics, computers are used to determine leading economic indicators, the Consumer Price Index used to monitor inflation, and a number of other indicators to monitor and control the economy. In geography, computers are used to map geographic areas. In political science, computers are used in a wide variety of areas. The results of political surveys and polls are reported in the popular news almost daily. Computers are used in public elections, where they have caused great debate. The vulnerability of computer systems to hackers, viruses, and other forms of corruption have kept most countries and states from wholly relying on computers for tallying votes.

Fine Arts

The use of computers in the arts surprises many people. Professionals in fine arts that might appear to be beyond the use of computers are making use of computers as much as other professionals. Artists use computers to experiment with design and color, sometimes using 3D graphics software. Computers eliminate the cost of having to experiment using actual materials such as paint and clay by providing virtual artistic materials. Some artists have moved completely to digital media, creating their artwork on computers to be viewed and appreciated in its computer-generated form (see Figure 1.30). Film studies, visual arts, theater, literature, dance, photography, and music all benefit from computers.

FIGURE 1.30 • Computers in fine arts

Software such as Adobe Creative Suite empowers graphic artists to create effective images efficiently.

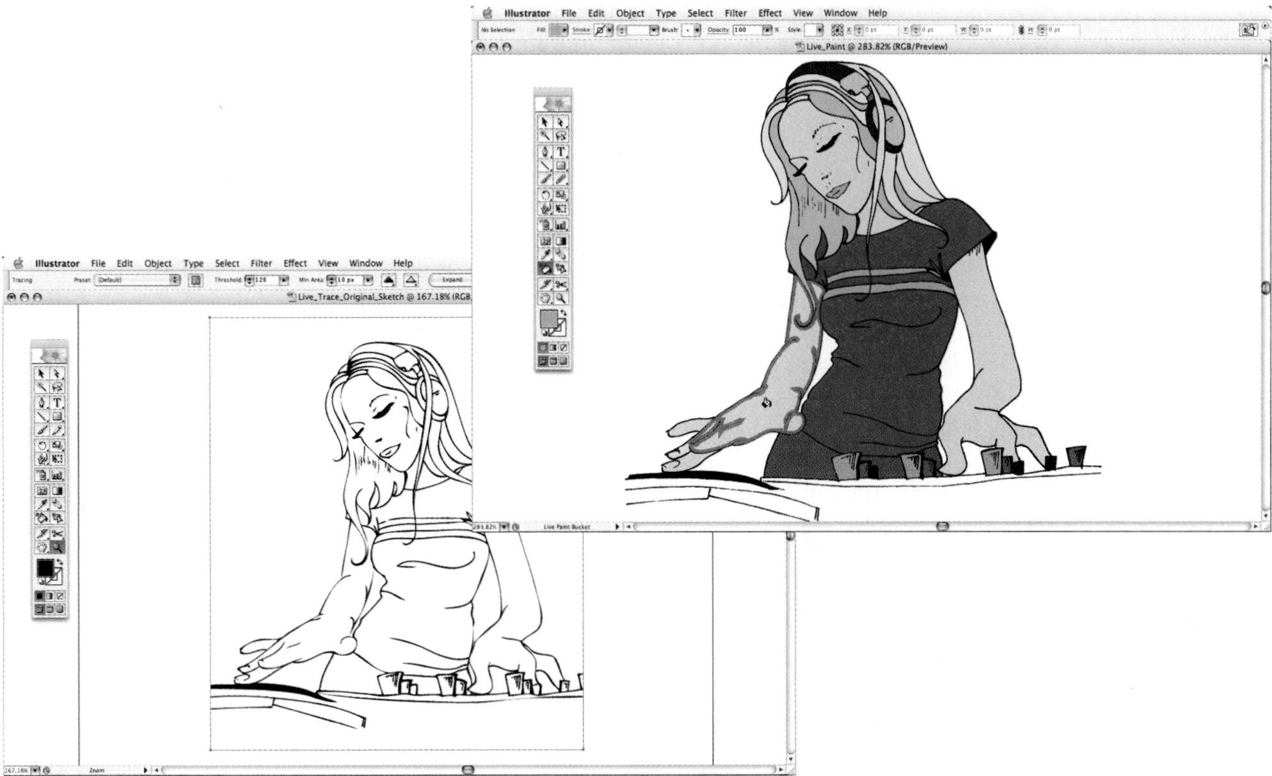

Computers have been widely used for producing music using *Musical Instrument Digital Interface (MIDI)*, special effects in most films produced, digital photography, and the ever-popular video games. Computers have empowered photo and video editors to alter images to improve their quality or content without leaving any trace of their work. In this way it has become impossible to tell the difference between fact and fiction when viewing photos and film. In dance, computers are used to capture motion and choreograph complex dance movements. In graphic arts, sophisticated software such as Adobe Creative Suite can be used to design, develop, print, and place beautiful advertising, brochures, posters, prints, and videos on the Internet.

Sports, Nutrition, and Exercise

Computers have been used in many aspects of sports, nutrition, and exercise. National Football League teams, for example, use computers to provide instant feedback. Computers are programmed to diagram and analyze offensive and defensive plays of teams and their opponents. The computer analyzes an opposing team's play from the past few games and predicts what the opponent will do in specific situations. The computer has also been used to design football equipment that reduces the chance of permanent paralysis or brain damage to players by analyzing films during which an injury takes place and producing graphs showing the force in pounds absorbed at points of the player's body at certain moments in time. Yet another use of the computer in sports is biomechanics, a familiar concept in Russian and East German athletics since the early 1960s. It has been used in the United States as well to coach its Olympic athletes. A computer programmed to watch athletes draws attention to factors too subtle to be detected by the human coach and shows athletes how to improve their techniques. Garmin designed a GPS unit for cyclists that clips to the bike and analyzes distance, direction, elevation, and speed of the cyclist to determine athletic progress.[7] Diet and nutrition for athletes and others can be analyzed by software to reduce weight and improve performance.

Government and Law

Since the 1950s computers have been used in compiling the U.S. Census (Figure 1.31). Massive databases are part of most of the government's operations, such as the Internal Revenue Service. Other governmental agencies, including the United States Postal Service (USPS), the Census Bureau, the Department of Homeland Security, and a variety of state and local agencies would have difficulty operating without computers. Space programs worldwide would still be in the realm of science fiction without computers.

FIGURE 1.31 • Computers in government

A census taker for the U.S. Census Bureau uses a handheld computer to collect census data.

Computer technology is improving legal practice in several major areas. The software company Autonomy developed WorkSite to provide document management as well as collaboration with others using a private network and the Internet. WorkSite presents relevant information on each client, such as word-processing documents, e-mail, billing information, and images in a single view accessible to everyone on the team. Millions of publications and records of interest to legal professionals and researchers are becoming increasingly digitized and available over the Internet through services such as LexisNexis. Computers are also used in the courtroom for evidence presentation and courtroom communications. Support services such as document imaging and management, graphics and animation for litigation, and electronic evidence management are all possible using the computer.

Medicine and Health Care

Careers in medicine and health care include nursing, nutrition, exercise physiology, social work, psychology, family therapy, and medicine. Computers produce medical records and reports to hospital administrators, insurance companies, and government agencies. Electronic health records (EHRs) can improve health care and reduce health care costs by billions of dollars annually. President Obama has made EHRs a priority in his efforts to reform U.S. health care.[8]

One of the biggest challenges of implementing EHRs is digitizing, storing, and manipulating X-rays and other medical images. (Figure 1.32) Such systems can cost a hospital millions of dollars, but hospitals that can afford the systems are finding tremendous value. The Picture Archiving and communications system (PACS) at Pittsburgh Medical Center allows doctors and hospital staff to access and view medical images from their large desktop displays or on their BlackBerry smart phones.[9]

FIGURE 1.32 • Computers in medicine

Computers have revolutionized gathering, displaying, and communicating medical information and visual data.

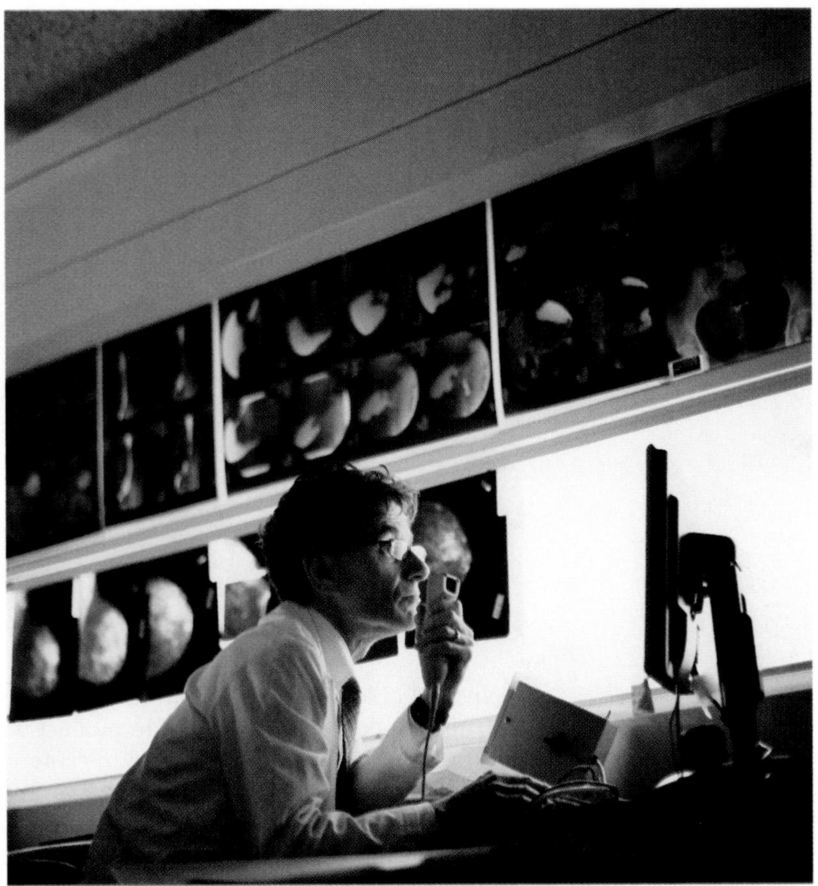

Some medical computers help doctors diagnose diseases and prescribe treatment. Specialized medical expert systems, software that is programmed to act like a team of expert doctors, can convert a patient's symptoms and problems into likely diseases and estimate the chances that the patient has each disease. Some medical expert systems also have the ability to suggest treatment options. In some cases, expert systems software explores possible diseases and treatments that might have been overlooked by even the best doctor.

Magnetic resonance imaging (MRI) machines are used in most hospitals today. Surgeons use the three-dimensional images produced by computer graphics to help them operate. They also use software to locate and remove some of the causes of seizures. Tests that detect cancer or measure chemical levels are performed using microchip-loaded probes that are threaded into the body via a catheter.

Criminology, Law Enforcement, and Security

Computers are used extensively in criminology, law enforcement, and security (Figure 1.33). Computers provide crime fighters with invaluable information on criminals, stolen vehicles, and missing persons. The Missing Child Act authorized the creation of a database to help local and state law enforcement authorities locate and identify the thousands of children reported missing each year. The creation of a database of unidentified dead bodies has helped eliminate the uselessness of a family spending its life savings to search for a missing child whose body had already turned up in another state.

FIGURE 1.33 • Computers in law enforcement

Law enforcement officers depend on computers to store and research criminal records and "connect the dots" in tough cases.

Instead of a polygraph, computers can be used to "read" a voice, to detect the stress produced by lying, and to produce a voiceprint, which is as unique as fingerprints. Computers can be used to capture facial thermograms (systems of blood vessels), which, like fingerprints, are unique in each individual, and can be read using an infrared camera, a computer, and a database. Responding to 911 calls, helping find missing children, locating missing motor vehicles, and analyzing crime scene information are just a few additional applications of computers.

With the increase in breaches of computer security, there are new and exciting careers in security and fraud detection and prevention. The University of Denver, for example, offers a master's program in cybersecurity.

Education and Training

Computers are used in most aspects of education and training. Computer-aided instruction (CAI) can deliver course content and measure student performance. Distance learning is used to deliver courses and instruction to and from remote locations; instructors and students can be located around the world. The Internet is increasingly being used for training and assessment. People with vision disabilities can use special hardware and computer monitors. Many software packages have built-in help facilities and educational tools.

USING DIGITAL TECHNOLOGIES TO ACHIEVE PERSONAL GOALS

A successful career can be rewarding in many ways. It makes you feel valuable and gives a boost to your self-esteem, improving your general view of the world. If you are fortunate, it may also give a boost to your bank account. Most people would agree that life is also full of many successes that may have nothing to do with one's career or monetary rewards. Many of the best things in life occur outside the workplace. Computers and digital technologies are playing an increasing role in assisting people to achieve personal goals and lead more rewarding, productive, and fulfilling lives outside of work.

Personal Finance

Personal finance software such as Quicken can assist individuals with living within a budget, saving for the future, and investing. Web sites such as The Motley Fool (*www.fool.com*) provide practical advice and tutorials on topics such as getting out of debt and investing wisely. Spreadsheet software and online tools allow users to run what-if scenarios to determine how changes in their budget today will influence their wealth in the future.

Personal Information Management

PIM software is the "Swiss army knife" of personal use software. It provides a personal calendar to keep track of where you need to be and when. You can set an alarm to remind you of an appointment. PIM also stores your personal to-do lists and address book. Some PIM software comes with personal journal software so that you can record brilliant ideas or your life story. PIM software is especially valuable when accessible from a smart phone anywhere, anytime (Figure 1.34).

FIGURE 1.34 • Personal information management

PIM software on mobile phones helps users keep their lives and plans well organized.

Personal Research

The Web is increasingly used as the first and primary information source for personal questions and needs. People are relying more heavily on the Internet to provide information during important life changes—pivotal points in their lives such as starting a new career, planning a marriage, buying a home, or having a baby (see Figure 1.35). The Web helps to uncover options and learn strategies for choosing the correct path.

FIGURE 1.35 • Personal research

More than ever, people are using the Internet to help them research important events in their lives.

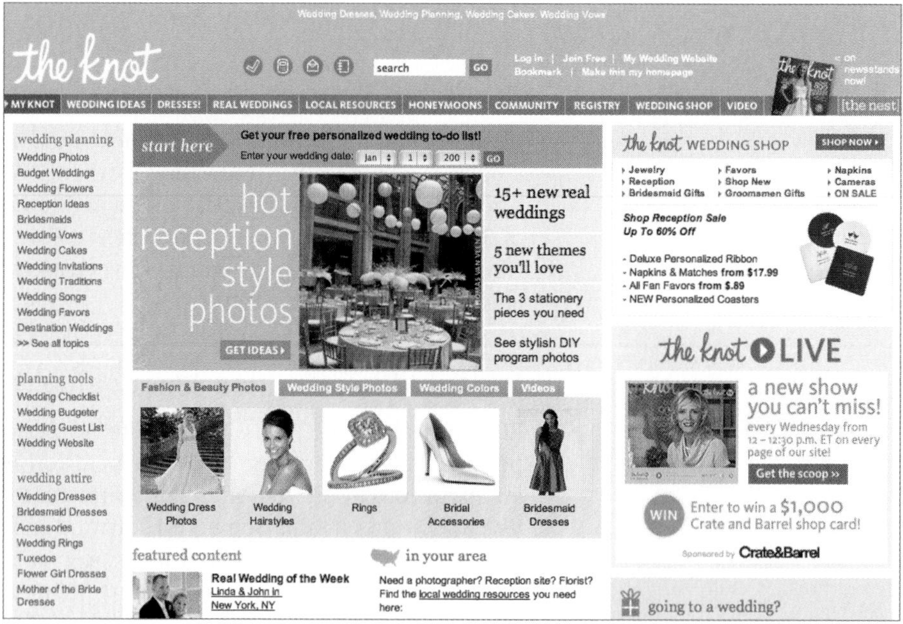

The Web also provides information from experts in areas of personal interest. You may be interested in learning more about Einstein or finding out what it takes to earn a pilot's license. It is hard to come up with a topic that won't draw a thousand hits in a search engine. However, it is important to develop the skills for distinguishing valuable information published by credible experts from rubbish and misinformation published by self-proclaimed experts.

Digital technologies have made personal research so much more convenient than it used to be. In so doing they have empowered people in many ways. In the pre-PC days, a person struck by an idea or question would need to go to the library to gain more information on the topic. Perhaps the person would have been fortunate enough to have a set of encyclopedias at home. In either case, most ideas and questions would probably evaporate by the time the person gained access to more information on the topic. Today, when you are struck by an idea or question, you can simply look up information online.

Handheld and other computing devices are making it possible to research topics whenever and wherever a thought may strike. Consider the power of this spontaneous information access. For the first time, you can progress from a germ of an idea, to research, to new discovery—wherever the idea strikes, with no time wasted. How many brilliant inventions, theorems, and discoveries may be hastened by humankind's ability to research information spontaneously? How many potentially brilliant discoveries have fallen by the wayside in the past due to the delay in the flow of information?

Personal Relations

Many people are turning to the Web to make new friends and look up old friends. Facebook and other social networks are popular ways to renew old friendships and meet new friends with similar interests. Online matchmaker eHarmony.com claims to have created matches that have resulted in thousands of marriages that are going strong (see Figure 1.36). Classmates.com maintains lists and contact information of millions of individuals based on the school they went to and the year they graduated, making it easy to get in touch with old friends. Genealogy.com can map your family tree if you provide your parents' names. Digital technology is making it easier than ever before to create personal connections.

FIGURE 1.36 • eHarmony.com

Online matchmakers like eHarmony can pair up couples based on detailed personality profiles.

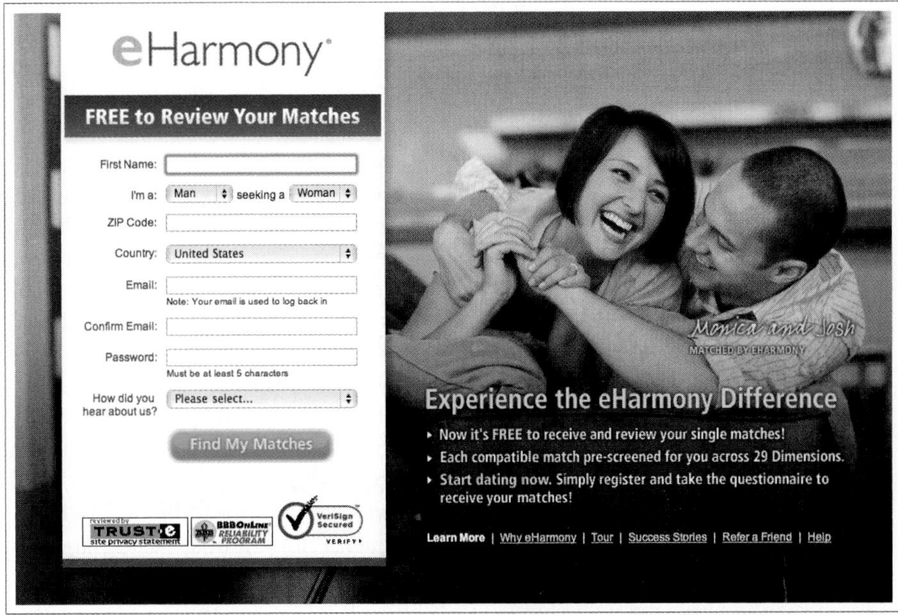

Other Personal Computing

There is a wide assortment of other personal software applications that include recipe management software, health and nutrition software, home inventory software, kids and parenting software, and assorted packages that support varying hobbies and interests.

A new market in media management software is emerging to assist individuals in managing personal digital photos, music collections, and video. Some of this new software is designed to run on PCs that connect to entertainment systems to control digital television and stereo systems.

INFORMATION SECURITY AND THE SOCIAL IMPACT OF DIGITAL TECHNOLOGIES

Digital technologies help people to be more productive and successful. Nearly everyone agrees that technology has raised the standard of living and will continue to provide increasing benefits. But as it is with all major social changes, there are negative and even dangerous effects of technology. Our increasing dependence on digital technology makes society more vulnerable should that technology fail. There are many ways in which digital lifestyles are vulnerable and open to abuse. This section provides an overview and some fundamental concepts on this topic.

Information Security

Information security refers to the protection of information systems and the information they manage against unauthorized access, use, manipulation, or destruction, and against the denial of service to authorized users. Information security is a growing concern as increasing amounts of important and private information is stored digitally on systems connected to public networks and wireless private networks. From bank account and credit account access codes, to personal medical records, to secret business strategies, to national defense initiatives, to e-mail sent to a friend, people trust information systems to keep their most valuable and secret information safe and secure. Unfortunately, there are active forces determined to steal and corrupt that information.

FIGURE 1.37 • Busted!

Kevin Mitnick spent five years behind bars for hacking into private corporate networks and stealing proprietary information.

The word "hacker" traditionally meant a particularly brilliant computer expert. Over time the meaning has changed considerably. Today, according to popular media usage, a **hacker** is an individual who subverts computer security without authorization. This term is used broadly in the news media to label individuals who use technology for terrorism, vandalism, credit card fraud, identity theft, intellectual property theft, and many other forms of crime (see Figure 1.36). Some hackers use their talents to make political statements. For example, the United Nations Web site was hacked and a message was posted: "HACKED BY KEREM125 M0STED AND GSY THAT IS CYBERPROTEST HEY ÝSRAIL AND USA DONT KILL CHILDREN AND OTHER PEOPLE PEACE FOR EVER NO WAR." It should be noted that many computer experts consider themselves to be hackers even though they do not break or attempt to break any laws. Some prefer to use the term cracker, for criminal hacker, and attacker, or intruder, to identify hackers who break the law.

Hackers are able to access supposedly secure networks and computers, often using Internet connections, by taking advantage of vulnerabilities in software. Hackers can also intercept information as it travels over a network or the Internet. Wireless networks are especially vulnerable to hackers as no physical connection is required to access the network.

Computers and computer systems are also vulnerable to viruses and spyware, software developed by hackers that can be inadvertently contracted from e-mail attachments, Web sites, or files downloaded over the Internet. Viruses and spyware can corrupt your computer files, causing your computer to malfunction. They can open "back door" access to your system to be used by hackers to exploit your system resources. They can access your private data and deliver it to others over the Internet. They can also turn your computer into a "zombie" computer that spreads viruses, spyware, and spam to others over the Internet without you suspecting a thing. Zombie computers are often assembled into botnet armies, placing thousands of compromised computers at the disposal of a hacker who can harness their combined power for attacks on Internet servers and other resources—or just to send out a whole lot of spam.

Hackers, viruses, and spyware can mean big trouble to businesses that depend on a healthy technology infrastructure. A company such as Amazon.com or eBay could lose millions if its servers were brought down for even a short time.

Keeping networks and the information they store secure takes effort on many levels. Important safeguards must be implemented by individuals, businesses, and governments in order to achieve a secure information infrastructure. Information security is so important that recently the United Nations has taken an interest in managing it. Information security is also a high priority for the U.S. Department of

Homeland Security (DHS). The *National Strategy to Secure Cyberspace* was developed as a framework for protecting cyberspace (the Internet and associated networking infrastructures), which is recognized as essential to the U.S. economy, security, and way of life. The document states that its purpose is to "engage and empower Americans to secure the portions of cyberspace that they own, operate, control, or with which they interact. Securing cyberspace is a difficult strategic challenge that requires coordinated and focused effort from our entire society: the federal government, state and local governments, the private sector, and the American people." President Obama is taking cybersecurity very seriously, and has created a top-level position to coordinate government efforts to protect a "strategic national asset": the digital networks that handle phone calls, e-mail, government and military data, and also control power grids, nuclear plants, and airplane traffic.[10] The U.S. Department of Defense has created a new command for defending military cyberspace as well.[11]

The Impact of Digital Technologies on the World

To *pervade* means to become diffused throughout every part of something. Society is entering the age of pervasive computing. *Pervasive computing* implies that computing and information technologies are diffused throughout every part of the environment. Rather than being obvious and "in your face," the pervasive computing environment is ubiquitous. *Ubiquitous computing* suggests that technology is becoming so much a part of the environment that people don't even notice it. Mark Weiser, who coined the expression *ubiquitous computing,* refers to this as the age of "calm technology," when technology "recedes into the background of our lives."[12] A pervasive and ubiquitous computing environment is one in which you can access digital information and media at any time and in any place with very little effort (see Figure 1.38).

FIGURE 1.38 • Pervasive computing

Increasingly, environments support access to information and media at any time and any place with little effort.

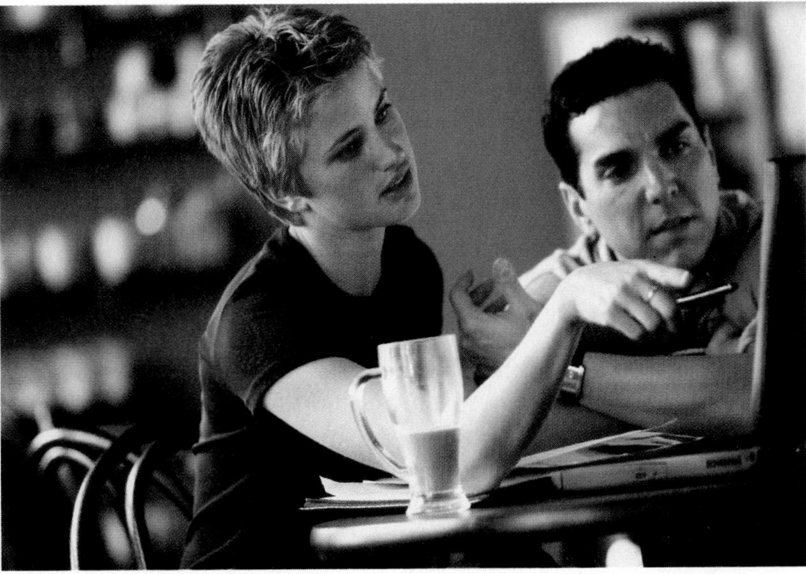

Although this is true in much of the developed world, there are societies and portions of societies that, due to poverty, geographical isolation, or lack of technical infrastructure, have been unable to enjoy the benefits of digital technologies. The **digital divide** is a title used for the social and economic gap between those who have access to computers and information technologies and those who do not. Access to information is empowering. It provides individuals, businesses, and cultures with a distinct advantage over those that do not have it. The digital divide is an issue between developed countries and third-world countries. It is also an issue between wealthy and poor populations within a country. These social divisions often run along lines of race, class, and culture.

Much work has been done in recent years to narrow the digital divide within the United States. Portions of the No Child Left Behind Act[13] and programs such as National Educational Technology Standards (NETS, *http://cnets.iste.org*) have brought Internet connections to 99 percent of U.S. public schools with an average student-to-computer ratio of 5:1. Numerous programs have been established to help narrow the divide between varying income classes, races, and international communities (see Figure 1.39).

FIGURE 1.39 • The digital divide

Efforts are under way to widen access to computers and technology in the United States as well as in other less developed countries.

Those who enjoy the benefits of technology are being confronted by many technology-related ethical issues. For example, the Internet empowers freedom of expression by providing a means to distribute and access digital information and media, such as art, photographs, music, and movies, worldwide with little effort. This has led to rampant violations of copyright laws that protect the intellectual properties of the creator and/or owners of the media and information. The Internet population is left confused as to what is ethically right and wrong when it comes to sharing intellectual property. In the meantime, the recording industry and motion picture industry are pushing to implement technologies that would control what could be shared over the Internet, but these could also dramatically reduce freedom of expression, impede the development of culture, and stifle the free flow of information.

Ethical questions are also raised over what information should be restricted on the Internet. Should hate groups be allowed to promote their philosophies? Should scientific research that provides information that could pose a danger to national or international security be available online? How can parents protect children from viewing adult content? Who should decide what content is *adult*? These are only a few of the issues with which governments are grappling, sometimes reaching differing conclusions.

Technology provides convenience and valuable services, but these often come at a price of some degree of lost privacy. The more that an information system knows about you, the better it can provide customized services that meet your unique needs. In many cases you provide information about yourself in order to enjoy the benefits of the service. But much of the information about you is collected and stored without your knowledge. This *invisible information gathering* makes some people nervous and concerned about their rights to privacy.

Most commercial Web sites track your movement within the pages of the Web site to determine which topics or products are of most interest to you. The next time you visit, those items may be the first thing you see. If you provide the company with information by filling out an online form, you may start receiving e-mail about the items that the company feels interest you most. Many businesses sell customer information to other interested parties.

Digital information is easy to collect, distribute, combine, and analyze. Some companies are in the business of aggregating information from numerous public and private databases to develop profiles of individuals that can be quite revealing. A company by the name of CheckPoint, for example, combines data from credit bureaus; local, state, and federal agencies; telephone records; private corporations; and other sources to build a detailed account of a person's life. CheckPoint has billions of records in its system that it sells to marketing companies, businesses, and government agencies.

Technology-influenced social change is occurring at a frantic pace. In many ways it is like riding a runaway roller coaster. There is no turning back, and at times it feels as though individuals have little or no control over their technological future. But there is much at stake, and it is important that those involved have a say in what they find acceptable and unacceptable.

This chapter has introduced the basic concepts and terms that are necessary for you to understand in order to move forward in learning about computers, information systems, and other topics in digital electronics. This chapter has also provided an overview of the topics that are covered in the chapters that follow so that they will not seem brand new as you begin each chapter. Take some time to review the keywords for this chapter and work through the exercises that follow so that you have a basic understanding on which to build.

ACTION PLAN

Remember Tonya Roberts from the beginning of this chapter? She was the student who was having difficulty deciding on a major. Here are answers to the questions asked about Tonya's situation.

1. **What types of computers and digital devices played a role in Tonya's search for the ideal career and job?**

   Tonya's thumb drive provided portable storage so that she could transfer files from the career center's system to her own notebook PC. Her PC provided her access to the career center files and Web resources for researching careers and job ads. Tonya's iPhone provided a way for the career center to contact her when an interview slot was available (and provided music for Tonya's entertainment).

   The career center used PCs running special career center software for students to use.

   The career center probably also used a server on which it could maintain a database of companies and applicants. The career center used a Web server to provide additional career information to students over the Web.

2. **How did telecommunications, the Internet, and computer networks assist Tonya in her quest?**

   It is likely that the career center maintained a network of computers from which students accessed career information from a central server. The Internet provided Tonya with information from several Web resources. A digital cell phone network provided a means for the career center to contact Tonya at any time.

3. **What types of computer-based information systems might have been used by Tonya and the career center in looking for a career and job?**

   Depending on the complexity of the software, either a decision support system or expert system was used to analyze Tonya's personality profile and suggest careers. A management information system is used to manage the database of employer and applicant information.

4. **Why are computers and digital technologies important to Tonya's career and personal life?**

   Because most information is or is becoming digital, the more Tonya knows about the systems that manage digital information, the more she can take advantage of information to obtain knowledge and enjoy entertainment and services that provide a more successful and fulfilling life.

5. **What security and ethical issues could be involved in the use of databases at the career center?**

   The information in the database contains personal student information. Individuals in the career center need to judge with whom they can safely share this information within and outside the career center. Students should be made aware of who has access to the information. The career center must also take all possible actions to protect their network and database from hackers, viruses, and spyware.

Summary

LEARNING OBJECTIVE 1

Define how digital electronics devices and computers are related, and provide descriptions of the different types of computers.

A digital electronics device is one that stores and processes data as bits, 1s and 0s. A computer is a digital electronics device that combines hardware and software to accept the input of data, process and store the data, and produce some useful information as output. There are general-purpose computers, such as PCs, servers, and supercomputers and there are special-purpose computers such as MP3 players, digital cameras, and scores of other digital devices custom-designed to carry out a particular task. Personal computers include desktop, notebook, netbook, tablet, and handheld computers. Mobile digital devices, such as mobile computers, cell phones, and smart phones and media devices, are ideal for the increasingly mobile workforce and population.

Figure 1.4—p. 8

LEARNING OBJECTIVE 2

Provide an explanation of the fundamentals of telecommunications, computer networking, the Internet, and wireless networking.

Telecommunications are forms of communication that take place electronically over a distance. Forms of telecommunication include telephone systems, radio, television, and computer networks. A computer network is a telecommunications network that connects two or more computers for the purpose of sharing data, hardware, and software resources. The Internet is the world's largest public computer network; it is a network of networks that provides a vast array of services to individuals, businesses, and organizations around the world. The Web is an application that makes use of the Internet to deliver information and services through a convenient interface that utilizes hyperlinks. Wireless networking is very popular because it uses radio signals rather than cables to connect computers and digital devices to computer networks and the Internet.

Figure 1.17—p. 20

LEARNING OBJECTIVE 3

Describe the five functional areas in which computers assist people most.

The things that computers do well—working with large amounts of data and repetitive tasks—are things that people find difficult and monotonous. The things that people find most engaging—creative endeavors—computers are ill suited to perform. Computers excel in five functional areas: computation, automation, communications, entertainment, and information management. Computers are good at computing, that is to say, they calculate solutions to mathematical problems. Computers provide automation services such as those involved in robotics systems. Computers support most of today's electronic forms of communication. Much of today's entertainment is provided by computers in the form of digital music, movies, and interactive games. Finally, perhaps the most useful of a computer's skills is managing massive amounts of digital information.

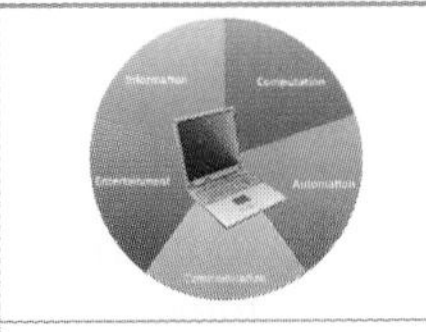

Figure 1.18—p. 21

LEARNING OBJECTIVE 4

Discuss the uses of information systems by individuals, businesses, and organizations, and list common types of information systems.

The four primary types of information systems are transaction processing systems (TPS), management information systems (MIS), decision support systems (DSS), and expert systems (ES). A transaction processing system is an information system used to support and record transactions such as paying for products or paying an employee. Transactions carried out electronically online, over the Internet, or using other telecommunications and network systems are called e-commerce. A management information system is an information system used to provide useful information to decision makers, usually in the form of a report. A decision support system is an information system used to support problem-specific decision making. An expert system (ES) is an information system that can make suggestions and reach conclusions in one particular area of expertise, much the same way that a human expert can.

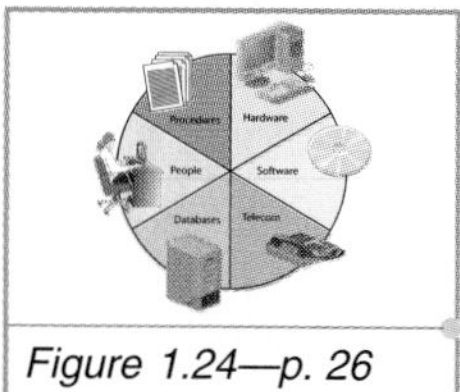

Figure 1.24—p. 26

LEARNING OBJECTIVE 5

Discuss how computers are used in a variety of fields and why studying computer systems can benefit you professionally.

Computers play an important role in all professions, including those in business, communications, science, math, engineering, social sciences, fine arts, sports, nutrition, government, law, health care, criminology, law enforcement, security, education, and training.

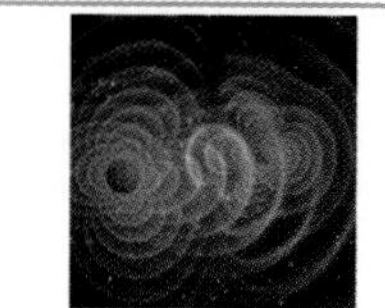

Figure 1.28—p. 33

LEARNING OBJECTIVE 6

Discuss how computers are used to assist people in their life outside of work.

Computers and digital technologies are playing an increasing role in assisting people to achieve personal goals and lead more rewarding, productive, and fulfilling lives outside of work. Applications of particular usefulness include personal finance, personal information management, personal research, personal relations, personal media, and entertainment.

Figure 1.35—p. 40

LEARNING OBJECTIVE 7

Define information security and discuss ways in which digital technologies are impacting humanity.

Information security refers to the protection of information systems and the information they manage against unauthorized access, use, manipulation, or destruction, and against the denial of service to authorized users. Information security has become a growing concern as increasing amounts of important and private information is stored digitally on systems connected to public networks and wireless private networks. A hacker is an individual who subverts computer security without authorization. Computers and computer systems are also vulnerable to viruses

Figure 1.39—p. 44

and spyware that can be inadvertently contracted from e-mail attachments, Web sites, or files downloaded over the Internet. Keeping networks and the information they store secure takes effort on many levels. Important safeguards must be implemented by individuals, businesses, and governments in order to achieve a secure information infrastructure.

You live in an increasingly pervasive and ubiquitous computing environment, one in which you can access digital information and media at any time and in any place with little effort. The digital divide refers to the social and economic gap between those who have access to computers and information technologies and those who do not. Access to information is power. Those who enjoy the benefits of technology are being confronted by many technology-related ethical issues. Pervasive digital communications are influencing the manner in which relationships and communities are defined, established, and maintained. Convenience and valuable services often come at a price of some degree of privacy. Much of the information collected and stored about individuals is done without their knowledge.

Test Yourself

LEARNING OBJECTIVE 1: Define how digital electronics devices and computers are related, and provide descriptions of the different types of computers.

1. ________________ is the working understanding of the fundamentals of computers and their uses.
   a. Information management
   b. Computer literacy
   c. Digital technology
   d. Digitization
2. ________________ is data organized and presented in a manner that has additional value beyond the value of the data itself.
   a. Software
   b. Input
   c. Information
   d. A database
3. The four activities that define a computer are ________________ .
4. Which of the following is not considered a PC?
   a. notebook computer
   b. netbook computer
   c. smart phone
   d. Kindle eBook reader
5. True or False: Words, music, artwork, photographs, movies, tastes, and fragrances can be digitized.

LEARNING OBJECTIVE 2: Provide an explanation of the fundamentals of telecommunications, computer networking, the Internet, and wireless networking.

6. Communications that take place electronically over a distance are called ________________ .
7. ________________ are rules that are implemented in network software and hardware to establish connections between two or more computers to allow them to communicate.
   a. Network architectures
   b. Internetworks
   c. Access points
   d. Protocols
8. If a coffee shop advertises free wireless Internet, chances are it is provided through ________________ technology.
   a. kiosk
   b. smart phone
   c. Wi-Fi
   d. server
9. True or False: The Internet and the Web are essentially the same thing.

LEARNING OBJECTIVE 3: Describe the five functional areas in which computers assist people most.

10. The five areas in which computers can assist people most are ________________ .
11. True or False: People are better than computers at working with large amounts of data.
12. ________________ technology provides the ability to make phone calls over a high-speed Internet connection.

13. A(n)________________ combines hardware, of software, telecom, database, people, and procedures to assist in managing information.
    a. AI
    b. CBIS
    c. VoIP
    d. network

LEARNING OBJECTIVE 4: Discuss the uses of information systems by individuals, businesses, and organizations, and list common types of information systems.

14. A(n) ________________ is an information system used to support problem-specific decision making.
    a. transaction processing system (TPS)
    b. management information system (MIS)
    c. decision support system (DSS)
    d. expert system (ES)
15. The process of creating new or modifying existing systems is called ________________ .
16. A(n) ________________ is an information system that can make suggestions and reach conclusions in one particular area of expertise much the same way that a human expert can.
    a. transaction processing system (TPS)
    b. management information system (MIS)
    c. decision support system (DSS)
    d. expert system (ES)
17. A(n) ________________ is an information system used to provide useful information to decision makers usually in the form of a report.
    a. transaction processing system (TPS)
    b. management information system (MIS)
    c. decision support system (DSS)
    d. expert system (ES)
18. ________________ are information professionals responsible for designing information systems.

LEARNING OBJECTIVE 5: Discuss how computers are used in a variety of fields and why studying computer systems can benefit you professionally.

19. In businesses, computer personnel typically work in a computer department that may employ all the following, except a ________________ .
    a. chief information officer (CIO)
    b. chief executive officer (CEO)
    c. systems analyst
    d. computer operator
20. True or False: Scientific virtualization assists scientists in viewing phenomena that are ordinarily unable to be seen.
21. True or False: The uses of computer systems in almost every field are almost limitless.

LEARNING OBJECTIVE 6: Discuss how computers are used to assist people in their life outside of work.

22. True or False: For important life decisions, people generally turn to the Web first for information.
23. Individuals typically depend on ________________ software to support their personal needs.
    a. custom-designed
    b. expensive
    c. off-the-shelf
    d. client/server
24. ________________ software typically includes a personal calendar, to-do list, and an address book.

LEARNING OBJECTIVE 7: Define information security and discuss ways in which digital technologies are impacting humanity.

25. ________________ refers to the protection of information systems and the information they manage against unauthorized access, use, manipulation, or destruction, and against the denial of service to authorized users.
26. Which of the following can be accomplished by a spyware program?
    a. corrupt your computer files
    b. crash your hard drive
    c. block access to hackers
    d. fry your motherboard
27. A ________________ is an individual who subverts computer security without authorization.
28. The ________________ is a title used for the social and economic gap between those who have access to computers and information technologies and those who do not.
29. A ________________ is a collection of zombie computers simultaneously controlled to attack servers and other Internet resources or to send a lot of spam.

Test Yourself Solutions **1.** b. Computer literacy, **2.** c. Information, **3.** input, processing, storage, output, **4.** d. Kindle eBook reader, **5.** True, **6.** telecommunications, **7.** d. Protocols, **8.** c. Wi-Fi, **9.** False, **10.** computation, automation, communications, digital media and entertainment, and information management, **11.** False, **12.** Voice over IP or VoIP, **13.** b. CBIS, **14.** c. decision support system (DSS), **15.** systems development, **16.** d. expert system (ES), **17.** b. management information system (MIS), **18.** Systems analysts, **19.** b. chief executive officer (CEO), **20.** False, **21.** True, **22.** True, **23.** c. off-the-shelf, **24.** Personal information management (PIM), **25.** Information security, **26.** a. corrupt your computer files, **27.** hacker, **28.** digital divide, **29.** botnet.

Key Terms

Key Term	Page	Definition
artificial intelligence (AI)	22	An area of computer science that deals with simulating human thought and behavior in computers
bit	5	Represents data using technologies that can be set to one of two states, such as on or off, charged or not charged
byte	5	A group of eight bits used to represent all types of useful data and information, such as characters, words, or sounds
computer	5	A digital electronics device that combines hardware and software to accept the input of data, process and store the data, and produce some useful output
computer literacy	4	A working understanding of the fundamentals of computers and their uses
computer network	19	A telecommunications network that connects two or more computers for the purpose of sharing data, hardware, and software resources
computer-based information system (CBIS)	26	Makes use of computer hardware and software, databases, telecommunications, people, and procedures to manage and distribute digital information
data	6	The items stored on a digital electronics device, including numbers, characters, sounds, music, or graphics
database	26	A collection of data stored on a computer, organized to meet users' needs
digital	5	Refers to technologies and devices based on digits (numbers)
digital divide	43	The social and economic gap between those who have access to computers and information technologies and those who do not
digital electronics device	5	Any device that stores and processes bits electronically
digitization	6	The process of transforming nondigital information, such as things you experience with your senses, to 1s and 0s
embedded computer	13	Sometimes called microcontrollers; special-purpose computers (typically an entire computer on one chip) that are embedded in electrical and mechanical devices in order to control them
file	5	Bytes combined to represent a named collection of instructions or data stored in the computer or digital device
hacker	42	An individual who subverts computer security without authorization
hardware	7	The tangible components of a computer system or digital device
information	6	Data organized and presented in a manner that has additional value beyond the value of the data itself

Key Term	Page	Definition
information security	42	Issues related to the protection of the components of an information system
information technology	27	Issues related to the components of a computer-based information system
Internet	19	The world's largest public computer network; a network of networks that provides a vast array of services to individuals, businesses, and organizations around the world
kiosk	13	A computer station that provides the public with specific and useful information and services
microprocessor	7	Sometimes called a chip or just a processor; combines microscopic electronic components on a single integrated circuit that processes bits according to software instructions
personal computer (PC)	8	A general-purpose computer designed to accommodate the many needs of an individual
platform	11	A computer's type, processor, and operating system
protocols	19	Rules that allow two or more computers to communicate over a network
server	11	A powerful general-purpose computer that provides information services to numerous users over a computer network
smart phone	9	A handheld computer that includes cell phone capabilities, or a cell phone that includes handheld computer capabilities including Internet access
software	7	The electronic instructions that govern the computer system's functioning
supercomputer	12	The most powerful type of computer, using hundreds or even thousands of processors simultaneously to accomplish very difficult tasks
synchronize or **sync**	10	To update the files shared between devices so that all copies are up to date and identical
systems development	28	The activity of creating new or modifying existing systems
technology	5	Tools, materials, and processes that help solve human problems
telecommunications	18	Communications that take place electronically over a distance
Voice over Internet Protocol (VoIP)	24	Allows phone conversations to travel over the Internet or other data networks
Wi-Fi	20	A popular wireless networking standard that connects computers to other computers, computer networks, and the Internet
wireless networking	19	Networking that uses radio signals rather than cables to connect computers and digital devices to computer networks and often through those networks to the Internet
World Wide Web	19	An Internet service that provides convenient access to information through hyperlinks

Questions

Review Questions

1. What is a knowledge worker?
2. How many bits are in a byte?
3. How many megabytes are in a terabyte?
4. List the six prefixes for digital technology metrics in order starting with *kilo*.
5. How does information differ from data?
6. What is a computer?
7. List four different types of PCs.
8. Name three types of servers.
9. What type of wireless technology is used to provide wireless Internet access on college campuses?
10. Describe how five career areas can benefit from computer systems.
11. List four examples of computer kiosks.
12. Name six devices that been integrated into the iPhone and other similar smart phones.
13. List the five things that computers are good at, and give examples of each.
14. Provide an example of a computer's computational power.
15. What is an information system? Describe the components of an information system.
16. What are the components of a computer-based information system (CBIS)?
17. What is the difference between a transaction processing system and a management information system?
18. What is the difference between a decision support system and an expert system?
19. Why is it important to study information systems?
20. Name three threats to information security that may endanger Internet users.

Discussion Questions

21. What are the benefits of digitizing information such as documents, music, and images? Consider the difference between a traditional library and a digital library.
22. List the digital devices that you own and use and describe what essential valuable service each one provides. How much do these devices affect your life?
23. Describe an information system provided by your school that is frequently used by students. What benefits does it provide to students and the school? Do you consider it well designed? Why or why not?
24. What career area or field is of interest to you? Describe how you could use one or more computer systems to advance your career in this area or field.
25. If you own a computer, what tools and techniques have you implemented to protect it from hackers, viruses, and spyware?
26. What social and ethical issues about computers and digital technology concern you the most? Which one is the most dangerous to you and society?
27. Do you feel that you are "computer fluent"? What computer skills do you feel you should acquire?
28. Is an iPhone a computer? Why?
29. What is your impression of reading books on a device like the Kindle? If given the chance, would you download your class textbooks to a Kindle rather than purchasing them in the bookstore? Should e-books be priced differently than bound books? Why?
30. What computer platform do you use for your PC? Why did you select that platform? Would you consider changing?
31. What is the most valued service that your cell phone provides other than communication?
32. How has wireless technology impacted student life?
33. How would you answer the question posed in the title of this chapter: Why Study Computers and Digital Technology?

Exercises

Try It Yourself

1. Think about yesterday and the day before. Consider your activities. List all the computers and digital devices you came in contact with, including items such as ATMs and digital cable television. Compare your list to others in your class. List five overall benefits that digital technologies have provided you and the businesses that run them.
2. Stand near a busy part of campus during a between-class rush and calculate the percentage of students using cell phones. Discuss how the use of cell phones is changing the social environment of your campus.
3. List the top 10 ways you use computers and categorize them into the five functional areas of computer use: computation, automation, communication, entertainment, and information management. What area of computer functionality do you use most?
4. Visit an online technology store such as Best Buy and pick five digital technology devices that you would like to own. Why do you find these items desirable?
5. Prepare a USB thumb drive to use for the lab and Web exercises throughout the text. Create one folder for each chapter in the textbook (you should have 12 folders when you are done). As you work through the Try It Yourself exercises and complete other work using the computer, save your assignments for each chapter in the appropriate folder. Add a text file to the root directory of the disk or drive that includes your name and contact information. Name the file OWNER_INFO.
6. At one or more local or online computer stores, research your ideal personal computer system, including all hardware, software, and so on. Using a spreadsheet, list the cost of each item and compute the total cost for the entire computer system.
7. Using the Internet, research a career area that interests you. (You can use a search engine, such as Yahoo.com or Google.com or an employment service such as Monster.com.) Using your word processor, prepare a report describing the number and types of computer-related occupations that are available in that career area. In addition, note how many other occupations require some computer systems technology and skills.
8. Visit *download.cnet.com* and select five software programs that would be valuable to you for personal use. Type a word-processing document that lists the applications, what they do, and why you find them interesting.

Virtual Classroom Activities

For the following exercises, do not use face-to-face or telephone communications with your group members. Use only Internet communications.

9. Use any form of online interactive forum to discuss digital devices with your group. Each member can share what devices they have or would like to have. Determine what three devices are most popular with your group and post your results on the Web.
10. Use the Internet to research distance learning. What are the advantages of distance learning for a student? What are the disadvantages?
11. With a group or team, investigate invasion of privacy issues, including identity theft. What can you do to avoid invasion of your privacy? What new laws should be passed to protect people from the invasion of privacy?

Teamwork

12. Your first task is this: One member of the group must send an e-mail message to a second member of the group, giving an opinion on a current event. The second person should state an opinion in response and forward that message, including the first message, to the third member of the group. Continue with this process until the last member of the group forwards the entire string of messages back to its originator. Print this final message and submit it to your instructor. It should contain the names and comments of each member of the group.
13. Within your team, brainstorm about the characteristics of a good group or team member. Develop a contract to be used by your team to ensure that all members of the team will work hard to complete all teamwork assignments. Note that you can revisit this document and modify it if necessary. If you do, have all members initial the changes.

14. Your team should explore how a computer system can be used to obtain a competitive advantage in two or more career areas. You can use the Internet to search for ideas. Use your word-processing program to write a report on what you found.

Endnotes

[1] Taub, Eric, "Ben Horton: Photos from the Edge," *Apple Pro Profiles*, August 15, 2008, www.apple.com/pro/profiles.

[2] RIM Staff, "Adidas America," *Blackberry Case Studies*, http://na.blackberry.com/eng/newsroom/success/adidas.jsp.

[3] IBM Staff, "Baylor College of Medicine finds new IT muscle with an IBM Power Systems solution," IBM Case Studies, January 28, 2009, http://www-01.ibm.com/software/success/cssdb.nsf/CS/DLAS-7NQNNH?OpenDocument&Site=powersystems&cty=en_us.

[4] IBM Staff, "Whirlpool Corporation focuses on operational excellence as global growth shifts into high gear," IBM Case Studies, December 23, 2008, http://www-01.ibm.com/software/success/cssdb.nsf/CS/JSTS-7MGRLY?OpenDocument&Site=eserverzseries&cty=en_us.

[5] IBM Staff, "The Supercomputer at Los Alamos," IBM Web Site, accessed July 19, 2009, http://www-03.ibm.com/systems/deepcomputing/rr/.

[6] Press Release, "Smart Carts Transform Shopping Experience," Springboard, Nov 13, 2008, http://springboardnetworks.com/index.php?action=news,press.

[7] Garmin Web site, accessed July 21, 2009, https://buy.garmin.com/shop/shop.do?cID=160&pID=10885.

[8] Goldman, David, "Obama's big idea: Digital health records," *CNNMoney*, January 12, 2009, http://money.cnn.com.

[9] Wolfe, Alexander, "Pittsburgh Medical Center CIO On Smartphones As Notebook Replacements," *InformationWeek*, November 5, 2008, www.informationweek.com.

[10] Krebs, Brian, and Ellen Nakashima, "Obama Says He Will Name National Cybersecurity Adviser," *The Washington Post*, May 30, 2009, http://www.washingtonpost.com/wp-dyn/content/article/2009/05/29/AR2009052900350.html.

[11] Jackson, William, "New DOD Cyber Command to defend military cyberspace," *Washington Technology*, Jun 24, 2009, www.washingtontechnology.com.

[12] Ubiquitous Computing Web site, accessed July 21, 2009, www.ubiq.com/hypertext/weiser/UbiHome.html.

[13] No Child Left Behind, Part B Grants for Education Technology, accessed July 21, 2009, http://www.ed.gov/nclb/landing.jhtml.

HARDWARE DESIGNED TO MEET THE NEED

Mark Bates recently graduated from college and started a new job as a graphic artist for Lamar Advertising. Now that he has a steady income, Mark wants to replace the old notebook that got him through college with a nice state-of-the-art notebook. He's also considering getting a PC that he could use as a media center in his apartment. He realizes that there are a lot of purchasing options and that the decision could be a difficult one to make. He wants to make sure that he ends up with systems that perfectly suit his needs without wasting money on unnecessary options. Mark uses his current computer for e-mail, keeping up with his friends on Facebook, Web research, managing his personal budget, basic word processing, multiplayer games, and sometimes for Lamar Advertising projects that he brings home. He wants a notebook powerful enough to run all the latest software and is interested in trying out some of the new technology that he's heard about, like video chat. He would like a PC for his media center that can connect to his high-definition TV and stereo so he can watch movies downloaded from the Web, and play music and games.

As you read through the chapter, consider the following questions:

1. How should Mark prepare for his purchasing decisions?
2. What types of computer and platform might best suit Mark's needs?
3. How much processor speed, memory, and storage capacity does Mark need?
4. What input/output devices would best suit Mark's needs?
5. Are there any additional considerations to be made regarding these purchases?

Check out Mark's *Action Plan* at the conclusion of this chapter.

2

LEARNING OBJECTIVES

1. Understand how bits and bytes are used to represent information of value to people.
2. Identify the functions of the components of a CPU, the relationship between the CPU and memory, and factors that contribute to processing speed.
3. Identify different types of memory and storage media, and understand the unique properties of each.
4. Identify different types of input and output devices and how they are used to meet a variety of personal and professional needs.
5. Understand the decision-making process involved in purchasing a computer system.

CHAPTER CONTENT

Introduction

How can a person keep up with the ever-increasing momentum of technological innovation? If you tried to learn all the details of every new digital device, you would soon be overwhelmed. It makes better sense to first learn the underlying technology that all these devices share.

From large server computers that support the needs of thousands of users, to the smallest smart phone, computing devices share certain characteristics. They all manipulate digital data, and they all share fundamental components: processing components, data storage, and input and output capabilities. By learning about these underlying principles and components, you can develop a better understanding of what computing devices are capable of and how you can benefit from those capabilities. You can become empowered to competently use information and communication devices whether they're old, new, or yet to be invented.

In Chapter 1 you learned that a computer is a digital electronics device that supports four activities:

- Input: Capturing and gathering raw data
- Processing: Converting or changing raw data into useful outputs
- Storage: Maintaining data within the system on a temporary or permanent basis
- Output: Producing the results of the processing in a manner that is discernable to human senses or used as input for another system

Although it is easy to see how PCs and other types of computers fit this definition, you might sometimes overlook other electronics devices that also meet these criteria. For example, a basic cell phone accepts your voice and keypad entry as input; stores and processes sound-related data, phone numbers, and other data; and outputs an electronic signal and text to the display. Other examples of computers include special-purpose devices such as video game consoles, digital music players, and high-definition camcorders.

This chapter looks in detail at hardware that supports the four activities of computer systems, starting with the most elementary concepts that are shared by all computing devices.

THE DIGITAL REVOLUTION

The world is in the midst of a digital revolution (Figure 2.1), and most experts agree that we have seen only the tip of the iceberg. It is impossible to guess how your life will be affected by advances in digital technologies over the next five or ten years. By understanding the underlying principles of digital electronics, you can be better prepared to thrive in that future. To understand the importance of digitization, it is essential to learn more about how computers of all types use bytes to represent data and information.

FIGURE 2.1 • Digital electronics

Notebook computers, MP3 players, cell phones, and a wide array of other devices are all based on the same digital technology.

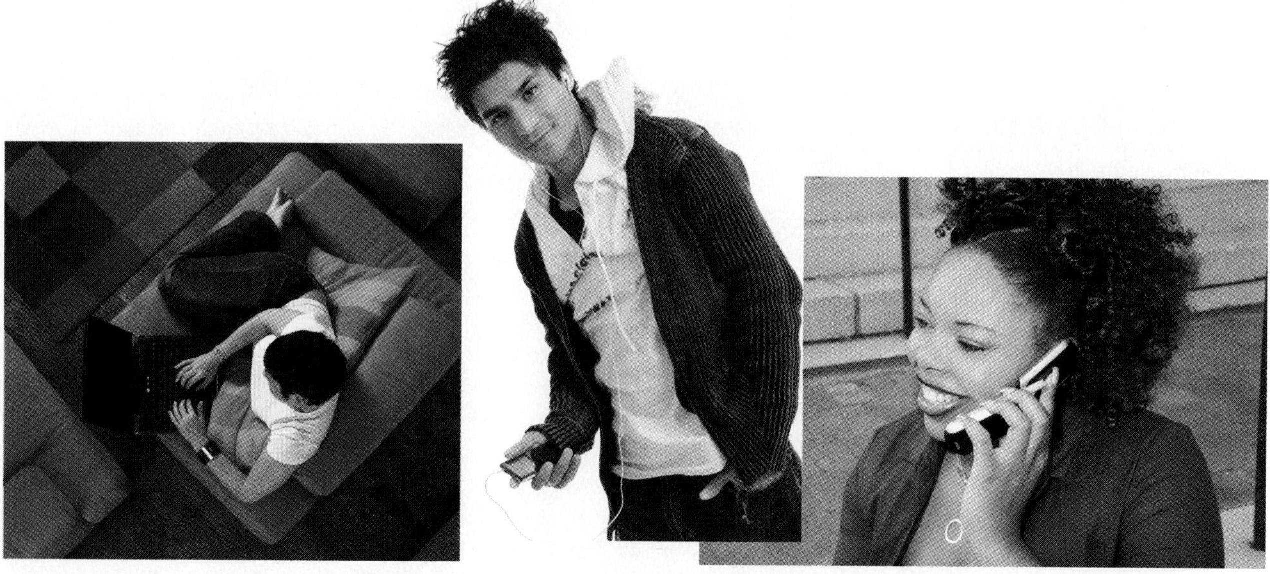

Representing Characters and Values with Bytes

In Chapter 1 you learned that digital devices store and process data as *bits* and that in order to be useful, bits are typically organized into groups of eight called *bytes*. Bytes are treated differently depending on their purpose, just as characters are treated differently depending on how they are used. For example, when you see the symbols 322-2413 you treat them differently depending on whether it is a friend's phone number or a math problem of subtracting one value from another.

The same is true with bytes. When bytes are used to represent a finite set of data such as the letters in the alphabet, the 52 cards in a deck, or the model numbers of vehicles manufactured by Ford, a table can be used to associate each unit of data with a unique bit pattern. This approach to data representation can be considered a "look-up table" approach. For example, in an alphabet look-up table, you might look up 01000111 to find that it represents the uppercase letter G. A playing card look-up table might show that 01000111 is the queen of hearts. Computer programmers can assign bytes to represent anything by designing a look-up table. Bit patterns representing the characters on computer keyboards have been defined in this manner. In the early days of computing, the computer industry agreed on a code for representing keyboard text characters and named it the *American Standard Code for Information Interchange (ASCII)*. Figure 2.2 shows a portion of the ASCII chart.

FIGURE 2.2 • Look-up table

Look-up tables such as the ASCII chart are used to associate data with bytes.

ASCII Chart			
A	01000001	P	01010000
B	01000010	Q	01010001
C	01000011	R	01010010
D	01000100	S	01010011
E	01000101	T	01010100
F	01000110	U	01010101
G	01000111	V	01010110
H	01001000	W	01010111
I	01001001	X	01011000
J	01001010	Y	01011001
K	01001011	Z	01011010
L	01001100		
M	01001101		
N	01001110		
O	01001111		

The look-up table approach to data representation has become standardized for various applications. A *standard* is an agreed-upon way of doing something within an industry. Standards are very important to digital technologies because they allow devices from different manufacturers to work together, share data, and function in essentially the same way. The ASCII standard allows digital devices to share keyboard-entered data. The MP3 standard allows a digitized song to be played on numerous different devices. There are standards for every popular look-up table data representation scheme.

The **binary number system** uses only two values, 0 and 1, and is used by computers and digital devices to represent and process data. There are infinitely many number systems, all equal in power, and all supporting the same mathematical operations as our decimal number system. Table 2.1 shows the decimal number 238 as it is represented by four popular number systems. The decimal number system, also called base 10, was adopted by humans because of its ease of use for our 10-fingered species. The binary, or base 2, system was adopted for computer use because of its ease of use in a machine that uses two-state bits.

TABLE 2.1 • Number systems

Decimal (base 10)	Binary (base 2)	Octal (base 8)	Hexadecimal (base 16)
238	11101110	356	EE

The octal and hexadecimal number systems are used in computer science as a shorthand method of notating bytes. Graphic artists use hexadecimal numbers to represent color codes in graphics software.

Because bytes can be used to represent values with binary numbers, computers are able to do some very useful things. Besides their use in performing mathematical calculations, binary numbers are the key ingredient for digitizing sound, music, photographs, drawings, paintings, animation, and movies. Your favorite movie on DVD and songs on a CD or MP3 are nothing more than long lists of binary numbers interpreted by your media player as colors to display or sound waves to play.

EXPAND YOUR KNOWLEDGE

To learn more about binary numbers, go to www.cengage.com/computerconcepts/np/swt4. Click the link "Expand Your Knowledge" and then complete the lab entitled "Binary Numbers."

As you can see, there are many methods of decoding and interpreting a byte. One particular bit pattern, say 11110000, could be interpreted differently by a digital camera, a digital music player, or a tablet computer (see Figure 2.3). On a PC, a byte can be interpreted differently by an e-mail program, spreadsheet software, a photo-editing program, and media player software. Each method boils down to either the look-up table approach or binary numbers. By implementing standards, bytes can have consistent meaning across common applications.

FIGURE 2.3 • Digital data representation

The same byte can represent different things to different software and digital devices.

1 1 1 1 0 0 0 0

Bits, Bytes, and People

Digitization is the great equalizer of information. Whether the information is headline news, a text message, music, photos, videos, or voice, it is all just a bunch of bits to the machine. This is the underlying principle behind digital convergence. **Digital convergence** is the trend to merge multiple digital services into one device. At home, a PC used as a media center provides access to audio and video entertainment, computing, information, and voice, video, and text communications. At work, many businesses are combining phone networks with data networks to carry voice, video, and text communications and information over the same network lines. On the road, digital convergence takes the form of smart phones and other multipurpose handheld devices that merge cell phone, PDA (personal digital assistant), MP3 player, digital video player, and digital camera functionality into a single portable device, as shown in Figure 2.4.

The digitization of information grants users power over that information. Learning the basic principles of digitization and binary data representation allows you to move beyond just knowing what buttons to push, to a deeper understanding of what is happening inside the machine and in your culture.

FIGURE 2.4 • Digital convergence in your hand

The HTC Touch Cruise combines a digital cell phone, GPS navigation, digital camera, digital music and video player, and smart phone applications with Internet access in one device.

Working from a Smart Phone

Successful realtors have little time to sit at a desk. Most of their work entails driving and communicating with clients from the car. Jim Soda is an award-winning realtor for Prudential in Sarasota, Florida. When it came time for Jim to select a computer that best served his needs, it was clear that he would need a mobile device.

Realizing that many of his customers preferred e-mail communication over phone communication, Jim needed a computer that could give him anywhere, anytime access to e-mail. He also required access to home-listing software, which utilizes the Internet to search databases of information on homes that are on the market. And he needed an electronic calendar application to keep track of client meetings and other business activities.

Jim chose the BlackBerry smart phone from RIM. The BlackBerry allows Jim to respond to client e-mails within minutes no matter where he is. The BlackBerry also provides Mobile Listing Advantage software that allows Jim to quickly access detailed information on any house—no need to pull out a notebook, or drive back to the office. With the BlackBerry calendar application, Jim doesn't need to worry about missing any important meetings.

Since switching from a desktop PC to the BlackBerry, Jim's client contact has increased dramatically. His clients are also impressed at Jim's ability to provide information within minutes.

Questions

1. What benefits does Jim's BlackBerry provide him over his competitors who rely on a desktop PC?
2. What other professions would benefit from the use of a BlackBerry or other smart phone?
3. Do you think Jim requires any other type of PC in addition to his BlackBerry? Why?

Sources

1. *RIM Staff, "Realtor Uses BlackBerry and Mobile Listing Advantage to Increase Efficiency, Effectiveness and Win Over Customers," BlackBerry Success Story, accessed September 4, 2009, http://www.blackberry.com/.*

INTEGRATED CIRCUITS AND PROCESSING

The ability to digitize information is at the heart of the digital revolution; however, digitized information is valueless without the ability to process it into useful forms (see Figure 2.5). Processors are important components of all digital devices. CD and MP3 players process digitized music into analog sound, a digital cell phone processes voice sound waves into digital signals and back again, a digital cable TV receiver processes digital video data into images on your television screen, and, of course, computers process data into useful information and services.

FIGURE 2.5 • Neuroimaging on a Mac

Dr. Nouchine Hadjikhani finds the processing power of the Apple Mac G5 essential for viewing MRI images of the brain to unravel the mystery of migraines.

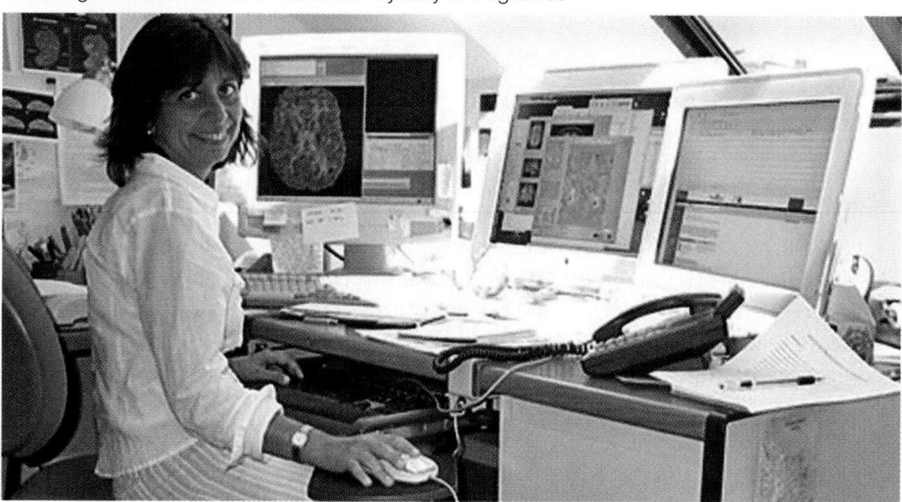

The quality of a digital electronics device is typically a reflection of the speed of its processor. This is especially true in computers: increasing processor speeds provide faster and more robust services. At home, faster processors support increased media applications such as flight simulators and 3D interactive gaming. In the professional world, faster processors are allowing graphic artists to reach new heights in visual effects, while accountants and financial analysts are able to run calculations on increasing amounts of data in decreasing amounts of time. Faster processors are providing additional features in all types of digital devices. Many cell phones now have the processing power to provide speech recognition features that allow you to speak a name rather than dial the number. Handwriting recognition is becoming increasingly reliable in tablet PCs because of more powerful processors (see Figure 2.6). Smaller, faster processors are providing capabilities in small mobile devices that rival those of desktop computers.

FIGURE 2.6 • Processor power

Increases in processor power are providing higher-quality services such as handwriting recognition.

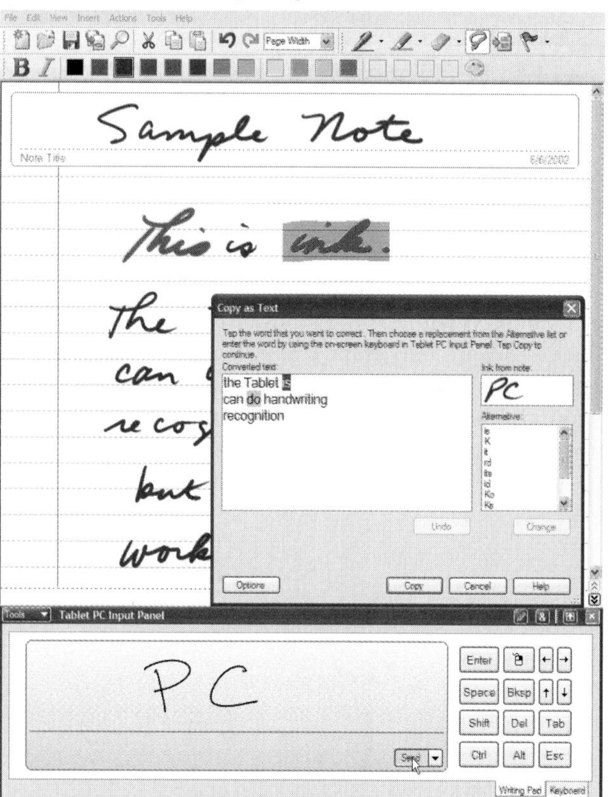

This section provides a look at the technology used in today's processors, as well as how to measure the quality of a processor in order to make wise purchasing decisions.

Integrated Circuits

Computers use digital switches not only to store bits and bytes but also to process them. Chapter 1 showed how any object having two distinct states can be used as a digital switch. Over the years, computers have used different devices as digital switches, progressing from physical switches and relays, to vacuum tubes, to transistors. The **transistor** is an electronics component, composed typically of silicon, that opens or closes a circuit to alter the flow of electricity to store and manipulate bits. Invented in 1947 at Bell Labs, transistors have become the key ingredient of all digital circuits, including those used in computers. When electricity is flowing through a transistor it represents a 1; when it is not flowing it represents a 0. By combining transistors and using the output from one or more transistors as the input to others, computers control the flow of electricity in a manner that represents mathematical and logical operations.

In the late 1950s, Jack Kilby of Texas Instruments and Robert Noyce of Fairchild Semiconductor developed a method to integrate multiple transistors into a single module called an **integrated circuit**. Integrated circuits, also called *chips*, are used to store and process bits and bytes in today's computers. A group of integrated circuits that work together to perform the processing in a computer system is called the **central processing unit (CPU)**. Today's technology is able to pack all the CPU circuits onto a single module smaller than the size of your smallest fingernail, called a *microprocessor*. The microprocessor and other supportive chips are housed on circuit boards where embedded pathways electronically join the chips together. The primary circuit board of a computing device is called the **motherboard** and the pathways are called *buses* (see Figure 2.7).

FIGURE 2.7 • Motherboard

The motherboard from an iPhone 3G S is packed with integrated processing, networking, and memory chips.

The Central Processing Unit and Random Access Memory

Processing is the act of manipulating data in a manner defined by programmed instructions. Computer programs contain lists of instructions for the processor to carry out. A processor is engineered to carry out specific instructions called its *instruction set*. When a computer runs a program, the processor progresses through the program's sequence of instructions, carrying out each instruction with specially designed circuitry (Figure 2.8), and jumping to various subsets of instructions as a user interacts with the program.

COPPER WIRES OUT, NANOTUBES IN

Researchers at Massachusetts Institute of Technology (MIT) have discovered a way to replace old-fashioned copper wire with carbon nanotubes, and the result is a smaller, faster computer chip. As computer chips get smaller, the copper wires cannot sustain the electrical current sufficiently and the chip doesn't work well. Nanotubes are tubes made of lattices that are only a single atom deep. So, size is no longer a problem.

MIT Creates Nanotube Process That Could Shrink, Speed Chips
Sharon Gaudin
Computerworld
September 16, 2009
http://www.computerworld.com/s/article/9138114/MIT_creates_nanotube_process_that_could_shrink_speed_chips

FIGURE 2.8 • Processor complexity

The Intel processor on the left contains more complexity than the high-resolution satellite image of Chicago on the right.

EXPAND YOUR KNOWLEDGE

To learn more about the motherboard and its components, go to www.cengage.com/computerconcepts/np/swt4. Click the link "Expand Your Knowledge" and then complete the lab entitled "Understanding the Motherboard."

A CPU consists of three primary components: the arithmetic/logic unit, the control unit, and registers. The **arithmetic/logic unit (ALU)** contains the circuitry to carry out instructions, such as mathematical and logical operations. The **control unit** sequentially accesses program instructions, decodes them, and coordinates the flow of data in and out of the ALU, the registers, RAM (random access memory), and other system components such as secondary storage, input, and output devices. *Registers* hold the bytes currently being processed.

The latest technique in chip design is referred to as *multicore technology* and refers to housing more than one CPU on a chip. Intel, AMD, and other manufacturers are manufacturing *dual-core processors* and *quad-core processors* that use two and four CPUs on one chip that work together to provide twice and four times the speed of traditional single-core chips (see Figure 2.9). Intel and AMD have recently released six-core processors with plans to go higher.[1] Intel has built a prototype 80-core processor, containing 100 million transistors, slated for delivery by 2011. The challenge of incorporating the chip into systems will be in connecting it to memory and getting software engineers to write software in a new way.[2]

FIGURE 2.9 • Dual-core processors

A researcher displays a wafer that contains over a hundred of Intel's dual-core processors.

The CPU works closely with random access memory. **Random access memory (RAM)** is temporary, or *volatile*, memory that stores bytes of data and program instructions for the processor to access. RAM capacities in today's new PCs typically range from 1 GB in low-end PCs and netbooks, to 6 GB in powerful desktop PCs. Data flows back and forth between the CPU and RAM across the front side bus. The *front side bus (FSB)* consists of electronic pathways between the

CPU and RAM capable of transporting several bytes at once. Typically the FSB connects to a *chipset* that ties together several bus systems sending and receiving bytes from memory, input and output devices, storage, networks, and other motherboard components. Figure 2.10 shows how the system bus connects the CPU to the chipset, and through it to RAM and other components on the motherboard.

FIGURE 2.10 • CPU, chipset, front side bus, and RAM

Instructions and data flow back and forth between the CPU and RAM over the FSB controlled by a bridge in the chipset.

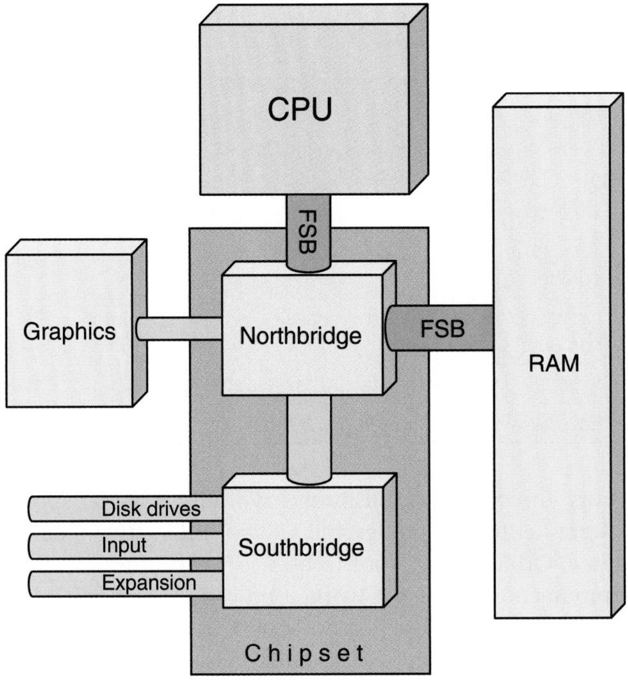

FIGURE 2.11 • Execution of an instruction

The machine cycle consists of four steps: fetch, decode, execute, and store.

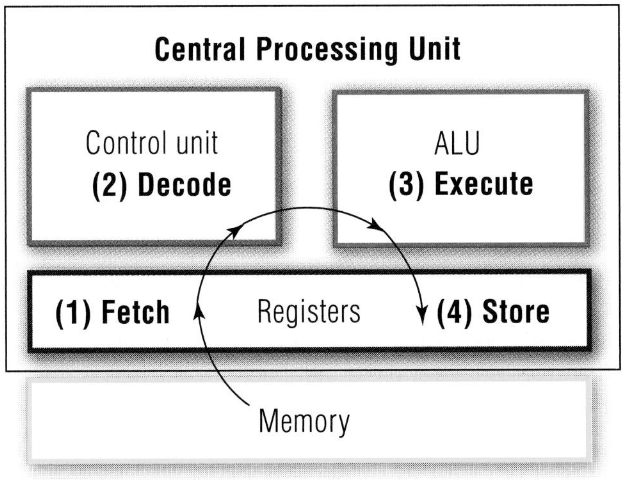

To understand the function of processing and the interplay between the CPU and RAM, you need to examine the way a typical computer executes a program instruction.

The Machine Cycle. The execution of an instruction is a step-by-step process that involves two phases: the instruction phase and the execution phase. These two phases together make up the *machine cycle*. Figure 2.11 shows the four steps in the machine cycle.

Instruction Phase

In the instruction phase of the machine cycle, the computer carries out the following steps:

Step 1: Fetch instruction. The instruction to be executed is accessed from RAM by the control unit. The control unit stores the RAM address of the currently executing instruction.

Step 2: Decode instruction. The instruction is decoded, relevant data is moved from RAM to the CPU registers, and the stored address of the current instruction is incremented to prepare for the next fetch.

Execution Phase

In the execution phase of the machine cycle, the computer carries out Steps 3 and 4:

Step 3: Execute the instruction. The ALU does what it is instructed to do. This could involve making either an arithmetic computation or a logical comparison.

Step 4: Store results. The results are stored in registers or RAM.

Processors perform a variety of instructions on different types of data. For example, the processor in an iPod reads bytes of digitized sound from a digital music file and processes the digits into a form you can listen to—music. A digital camera accepts input from a sensor in a camera lens and outputs a list of color codes to a file. An e-mail program translates keyboard data into ASCII characters and forwards the collection of characters to an e-mail server for processing. The efficiency of the manner in which a processor makes use of the machine cycle directly impacts the quality of performance of a digital device.

CPU Characteristics. The first consideration in selecting a computer is typically its speed: how quickly it can carry out such tasks as loading a program, opening a file, and writing to a CD. Processor manufacturers design a variety of processors to meet numerous needs and budgets (see Table 2.2).

TABLE 2.2 • Varying processors for varying needs

Processor family	Computer type	Description
Intel Celeron AMD Sempron	Desktop PCs	Manufactured for users on a limited budget; doesn't support high-end graphics applications
Intel Pentium AMD Athlon, AMD Phenom	Desktop PCs	Moderate multiuse processors for a variety of computer types
Intel Core 2 AMD Athlon X2	Desktop PCs and notebooks	Dual-core and quad-core processors for advanced graphics and high-speed processing
AMD Turion X2	Notebook PCs	Dual-core high performance, low power for long battery life
Intel Itanium AMD Opteron	Servers	Designed for multiple processor computing
Intel Xeon	Workstations	Designed for high-speed processing on special-purpose computers
Intel Core i7	Desktop PCs	Includes "intelligent multi-core for extreme gaming"
Intel Atom	Netbooks and mobile devices	Low power, fast performance, longer battery life

When selecting processors for computers, businesses typically consider speed and power consumption. Terra Reilly, co-founder and CEO of interactive media and marketing agency Captive Orbit, didn't want to be tied to an office all day. She uses two notebook computers for all of her work: a powerful notebook for CPU-intensive graphics editing, and a small, light netbook that she takes everywhere for Web research and communication. The mobility and power provided by her two different mobile computers allow her to pursue her interests in travel, skiing, and rock climbing, while growing her business from any location.[3]

One component that contributes to the speed at which a processor can carry out an instruction is the system clock. Each CPU contains a *system clock* that produces a series of electronic pulses at a predetermined rate called the **clock speed**. These pulses are used to synchronize processing activities. Just as a person's heartbeat circulates blood through the body, the system clock distributes bits and bytes through the components of a computer system. Clock speeds in today's digital devices are measured in **megahertz (MHz)**, millions of cycles per second, or **gigahertz (GHz)**, billions of cycles per second. Faster clock speeds generate more heat in a device and require larger cooling systems. For this reason, you'll find that smaller devices generally have a lower maximum available clock speed.

Although clock speed has a direct effect on overall system performance, it is not the only contributing factor. In fact, clock speeds can be deceptive. Some older computers might have faster clock speeds but perform much slower than today's computers. This is because today's smarter architectures, such as multi-core architectures, are able to do much more with each cycle of the system clock. In today's computers, it is not so much how fast the system clock ticks, but how much the processor can do with each tick of its clock.

Rather than emphasizing clock speed when marketing its processors, Intel uses *processor numbers*. For example, one model of the Intel Core2 Extreme processor is processor number QX6800. The processor number represents performance specifications that contribute to system performance. Table 2.3 lists these factors.

TABLE 2.3 • Computer performance factors

Architecture	Basic design of a microprocessor; may include process technology and/or other architectural enhancements
Cache (MB/KB)	A temporary storage area for frequently accessed or recently accessed data; having certain data stored in a cache speeds up the operation of the computer. Cache size is measured in megabytes (MB) or kilobytes (KB).
Clock speed (GHz/MHz)	Speed of the processor's internal clock, which dictates how fast the processor can process data; clock speed is usually measured in GHz (gigahertz, or billions of pulses per second)
Front side bus (GHz/MHz)	The connecting path between the processor and other key components such as the memory controller hub; FSB speed is measured in GHz or MHz

Cache (pronounced cash) *memory* is a type of high-speed memory that a processor can access more rapidly than RAM. Cache memory functions somewhat like a notebook used to record phone numbers. Although a person's private notebook may contain only 1 percent of all the numbers in the local phone directory, the chance that the person's next call will be to a number in his or her notebook is high. Cache memory works on the same principle: a cache controller makes "intelligent guesses" as to what program instructions and data are needed next and stores them in the nearby cache for quick retrieval.

Three levels of cache are used in today's personal computers: L1, L2, and L3. The levels indicate the cache's closeness to the CPU. L1 is stored on the same chip as the microprocessor; L2 and L3 are on separate chips. Considerably more expensive than RAM, cache memory is provided in much smaller capacities. Cache sizes vary from processor to processor. The larger the cache, the faster the processing.

Another important factor that affects a computer's performance is the processor's wordlength. *Wordlength* is the number of bits that a CPU can process at once. A processor with a 32-bit wordlength has the capacity to be twice as fast as a processor with a 16-bit wordlength. Today's personal computers typically use wordlengths of 32 or 64 bits. Intel Pentium 4 processors have a 32-bit wordlength; AMD Athlon 64 processors have a wordlength of 64 bits. The benefits of 64-bit wordlength are only experienced if the operating system and software are designed to take advantage of the processor's 64-bit capabilities. While Intel processors and both Windows and Mac OS X have evolved to 64-bit architectures, software developers have been slower to migrate their applications from 32-bit to 64-bit. That is likely to change as 64-bit processors become the norm.

By now you've gathered that judging a computer's quality and speed by its specifications can be complicated. The truest measure of a processor's performance is the amount of time it takes to execute an instruction. This measure is called *MIPS,* for millions of instructions per second; a more precise measurement is called *FLOPS,* for floating-point operations per second. Today's personal computers carry out billions of instructions per second, or operate in the *gigaflop* range. Supercomputers run in the *teraflop* (trillion) and *peta flop* (quadrillion) range. For example, IBM's ASCI White computer assists the U.S. government in simulating a nuclear detonation at 12.3 teraflops—12.3 trillion floating-point operations per second. It has been estimated that a human brain's probable processing power is around 100 teraflops, roughly 100 trillion calculations per second. The fastest supercomputer in 2009, according to the "top 500" ranking (*www.top500.com*), was the IBM Roadrunner, which was clocked at 1.1 petaflops. The next-generation IBM Sequoia is being designed to run at 20 petaflops.[4]

Multiprocessing and Parallel Processing. Some computing tasks require more powerful computers. Individuals pursuing careers in motion picture special effects, animation, or other demanding graphics production areas can look forward to working on workstations with multiple processors to assist in graphic imaging. Scientists running experiments with large quantities of data also require extra processing power. In Chapter 1, you learned about midrange and mainframe servers that support the computing needs of an entire organization. These computers also use multiprocessing.

As the name implies, *multiprocessing* is processing that occurs using more than one processing unit. The purpose: to increase productivity and performance. One form of multiprocessing involves using coprocessors. Typically used in larger workstations, *coprocessors* are special-purpose processors that speed processing by executing specific types of instructions while the CPU works on another processing activity. Each type of coprocessor performs a specific function. For example, today's PCs typically include a **graphics processing unit (GPU)**, a powerful processor that handles advanced graphics rendering for demanding graphics applications such as the 3D environments of games. Sometimes a PhysX processor is used for calculating the physics of objects in 3D virtual environments. While most PCs aren't considered multiprocessing systems, many do use coprocessors.

Toyota employs multiprocessor systems to provide race car drivers with simulated race conditions (Figure 2.12). The system controls a full-size race car rigged with hydraulic controllers that shake and shudder the car as though driving on an actual track. Car movement combined with an immersive virtual environment allow drivers to practice on a specific track as many times as needed.[5]

FIGURE 2.12 • Multiprocessor systems: race simulation

Toyota employs multiprocessor systems to create a virtual reality simulation for driver training.

Another form of multiprocessing is called *parallel processing,* which speeds processing by linking several microprocessors to operate at the same time, or in parallel. The challenge of multiprocessing is not in connecting the processors but in making them work effectively as a unified set. Accomplishing this difficult task requires special software that can allocate, monitor, and control multiple processing jobs at the same time. A technique called *grid computing* or *clustering* allows processors from different computers to work together over a network on complex problems. Some businesses form large parallel processing grids out of the networked PCs that remain behind when the employees go home for the evening. Other organizations such as SETI (*www.seti.org*) allow Internet users to donate their PC's processor power to problems too large for supercomputers, such as scanning the heavens for extraterrestrial life (*http://setiathome.ssl.berkeley.edu*).

Massively parallel processing (MPP), used in supercomputers, involves using hundreds or thousands of processors operating together. For example, NASA's most powerful supercomputer, named Columbia (see Figure 2.13), is revitalizing the aerospace agency's high-end computing infrastructure by applying the power of 10,160 processors to make breakthrough scientific discoveries that support agency missions.

FIGURE 2.13 • Massively parallel processing

NASA's Columbia MPP supercomputer uses 10,160 processors to assist NASA scientists in making breakthrough scientific discoveries.

Physical Characteristics of the CPU. CPU speed is also limited by physical constraints. Most CPUs are collections of digital circuits imprinted on silicon wafers, or chips, each no bigger than the tip of a pencil eraser. To turn a digital circuit within the CPU on or off, electrical current must flow through a medium (usually silicon) from point A to point B. The time it takes for the current to travel between points can be decreased by reducing the distance between the points.

Gordon Moore, cofounder of Intel, observed in 1965 that the continued advances in technological innovation made it possible to reduce the size of transistors, doubling their density on the chip every two years. He predicted that this trend would continue. This prediction has come to be known as **Moore's Law**, and over the years it has proved true (see Figure 2.14). There has been controversy over whether Gordon Moore originally claimed two years or 18 months for his law, but both Intel and Mr. Moore currently state it as two years.

FIGURE 2.14 • Moore's Law

Moore's Law predicts that transistor densities in new silicon-based chips will double every two years.

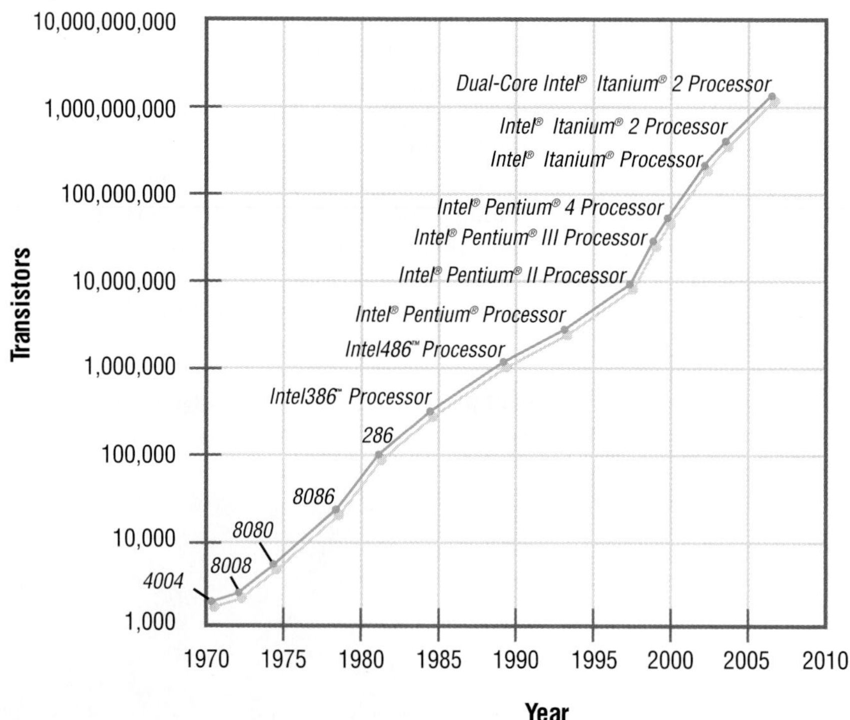

The importance of Moore's Law lies in the fact that when transistor densities increase, so does the speed of the processor, since the electrons have shorter distances to travel. One interpretation of Moore's Law assumes that if transistor densities double, processor speeds will also double every two years. This has also proven true. This is helpful information, as it allows you to predict how fast computers will be in years to come. In recent years, Intel has changed its focus to processor technologies that support powerful computing in small mobile devices. The company has also been working to refine processor architecture by refining key technologies into fewer chips.[6] Because of these diversions, Moore's law has not been met in recent years; rather, transistor numbers have actually decreased as the transistors are working smarter and more efficiently.

It is anticipated that Moore's Law will continue to hold true for the next decade; however, at some point Moore's Law will fail due to the inherent physical limitations of silicon. The high-tech industry is researching alternatives to the silicon-based chip in order to keep processor speeds increasing over time. Table 2.4 lists some active areas of research in processing technologies. It is likely that one or more of these areas of research will lead to a breakthrough that elevates computing to a much higher level, with processing speeds thousands of time faster than today's silicon-based processors.

TABLE 2.4 • Some active areas of research in processing technologies

Technology	Description
High-k materials	The use of materials with a high dielectric constant (k), such as hafnium and zirconium, creates smaller transistors than silicon can support.
Optical computing	Some companies are experimenting with chips called *optical processors* that use light waves instead of electrical current. The primary advantage of optical processors is their speed. It has been estimated that optical processors have the potential to be 500 times faster than traditional electronic circuits.
Three-dimensional processing	Currently, processing takes place in two dimensions on a thin wafer. Stacking wafers into 3D arrays could speed processing by allowing processing to occur horizontally and vertically.
Quantum computing	Quantum computing proposes the manipulation of quantum states to perform computations far faster than is possible on any conventional computer. A quantum computer doesn't use bits, but instead uses a fundamental unit of information called a quantum bit or *qubit*. The qubit displays properties in adherence to the laws of quantum mechanics, which differ radically from the laws of classical physics.
DNA computing	DNA computing, or molecular computing, is a promising new technology emerging from nanotechnology and based on DNA. Israeli scientists built the first "programmable molecular computing machine," composed of enzymes and DNA molecules, that can perform 330 trillion operations per second—more than 100,000 times the speed of the fastest PC.

STORAGE

There have been tremendous developments in storage technologies in recent years. People are able to store more data in smaller devices and media for considerably less money than ever before. The large quantities of data that used to be chained to desktop computers can now be easily taken anywhere or copied and shared with others. Chances are you are carrying gigabytes of data with you on a flash drive. Storage technologies are affecting our personal and professional lives and society in general. The use of CD-Rs to store music has had a tremendous impact on the music industry. Recordable DVDs are having the same impact on the motion picture industry. Being aware of the storage options available provides opportunities that can improve your quality of life.

Storage has been defined as the ability to maintain data within the system temporarily or permanently. The previous section discussed one form of temporary storage called RAM, sometimes called *memory* or *primary storage*. This section provides a more detailed look at the physical form of RAM, along with other storage used by computer systems. This section also looks at *secondary storage devices* that are used to store data more permanently than RAM, such as when the computer is turned off.

CAN YOU SAY "TERABIT"?

You've probably seen it at the movies or on TV: some magical personality reaches into her tiny handbag and pulls out everything you could ever want or need. Neat trick? South Korean engineers have figured out how to do exactly that with data storage. They've created superdense data-storage systems that cram in 125 gigabytes (a.k.a., a terabit) in one square inch! Such dense storage used to hog energy, but engineers have created a material that bends as pressure rises, so that these devices may become the next lean, green storage machines.

Super-Dense Data Stores Cool Down
Colin Barras
New Scientist
September 16, 2009
http://www.newscientist.com/article/dn17802-superdense-data-stores-cool-down.html

System Storage

System storage is storage that is used by a computer system for standard operations. There are several forms of system storage, including RAM, cache, video RAM, ROM, and CMOS. Of these, RAM has the largest capacity. The following section looks at the physical circuit boards that make up RAM. You should find this information helpful when and if you decide to upgrade the memory on your computer.

RAM SIMMs and DIMMs. You have seen how RAM works hand in hand with the CPU to carry out program instructions. RAM exists as a set of chips grouped together on a circuit board called a *single in-line memory module (SIMM)*, or a *dual in-line memory module (DIMM)*. Most of today's PCs use DIMMs that have a 64-bit data path, twice that of a SIMM. RAM DIMMs are inserted into slots in the motherboard near the processor (see Figure 2.15). A new computer typically comes with two or four RAM slots, half of which are occupied with DIMMs, and half left available for future expansion.

FIGURE 2.15 • Motherboard RAM

RAM DIMMs are inserted into slots in the motherboard near the processor.

There are many different types of RAM: DRAM, SDRAM, RD-RAM, DDR-SDRAM, FPMRAM, EDO-RAM, BEDO-RAM—the list goes on and on. Each type of RAM reflects a manufacturer's effort to use a new technology to get data to the processor more quickly. Today's desktop and notebook PCs typically use either DDR-SDRAM or DDR-II SDRAM. DDR-II doubles the speed of DDR, which makes it an ideal partner for today's fastest processors. When upgrading RAM, you should consult your computer documentation or contact the manufacturer to find out what type of RAM your computer uses.

In advertisements for new computers, processor specifications are typically listed first, and then RAM specifications (see Figure 2.16). Most new computers come with 1 to 4 GB of RAM. Memory prices are continuously dropping. At the time this book was published, 2 GB of memory cost around $50. Besides processor and RAM specifications, a computer shopper is likely to run into another confusing specification: graphics memory. The following section describes how graphics memory affects system performance.

FIGURE 2.16 • Computer ad

Computer ads typically list processor, storage, and display specifications.

Sony VAIO VGN-NW180J/S - Core 2 Duo P7350 2 GHz - 15.5" TFT

NW180J/S - Core 2 Duo P7350 / 2 GHz - Centrino 2 - RAM 4 GB - HDD 400 GB - DVD±RW (±R DL) / DVD-RAM / BD-ROM - Mobility Radeon HD 4570 - Gigabit Ethernet - WLAN : 802.11 a/b/g/n (draft) - Vista Home Premium 64-bit - 15.5" Widescreen TFT 1366 x 768 (WXGA) - camera - silver rattan

HP Compaq Business Notebook 6510b - Core 2 Duo T8100 2.1 GHz - 14.1" TFT

Core 2 Duo T8100 / 2.1 GHz - RAM 1 GB - HDD 120 GB - DVD±RW (+R DL) / DVD-RAM - GMA X3100 Dynamic Video Memory Technology 4.0 - Gigabit Ethernet - WLAN : 802.11a/b/g - TPM - fingerprint reader - Vista Business / XP Pro downgrade - 14.1" Widescreen TFT 1280 x 800 (WXGA) BrightView - Smart Buy

Apple MacBook Core 2 Duo 2.13 GHz - 13.3" TFT

Core 2 Duo 2.13 GHz - RAM 2 GB - HDD 160 GB - DVD±RW (±R DL) - GF 9400M shared video memory (UMA) - Gigabit Ethernet - WLAN : 802.11 a/b/g/n (draft), Bluetooth 2.1 EDR - MacOS X - 13.3" Widescreen TFT 1280 x 800 (WXGA) - camera - white

ASUS F70SL A1 - Core 2 Duo T6400 2 GHz - 17.3" TFT

Core 2 Duo T6400 / 2 GHz - RAM 4 GB - HDD 320 GB - DVD±RW (±R DL) / DVD-RAM - GF 9300M GS - WLAN : 802.11b/g/n (draft), Bluetooth 2.1 EDR - Vista Home Premium 64-bit - 17.3" Widescreen TFT 1600 x 900 Color Shine - camera - Microsoft Office Ready

Graphics Memory. *Graphics memory*, sometimes called *video RAM* or *VRAM*, is used to store image data for a computer display in order to speed the processing and display of video images. Graphics memory acts as a *buffer* or intermediate storage area between the microprocessor and the display. When images are sent to the display, they are first read by the processor from RAM and then written to video RAM. From video RAM, the data is converted to signals that are sent to the display. Most of today's PCs come equipped with at least 256 MB of graphics memory and may include a GPU to process the graphics and take the load off the CPU. Support for special 3D processing in high resolution and highly detailed colors and shading may also be included. For example, Windows Vista Premium and Windows 7 require support for DirectX 9 graphics with a WDDM driver, at least 128 MB of graphics memory, Pixel Shader 2.0, and 32 bits per pixel. While this vocabulary is foreign to most casual computer users, Microsoft has made it required learning. If your computer does not have these graphics capabilities, you won't be able to enjoy the best features of these operating systems.

Desktop systems often use a graphics circuit board called a *graphics card* or *video card* (Figure 2.17) that contains the graphics memory, GPU, and other graphics hardware and is plugged into the motherboard. On notebook systems, the graphics hardware is typically integrated on the motherboard. Graphics memory and processing have become a very important component of personal computers because of their support for 3D graphics animations and video games that many users enjoy. Graphics support specifications are often listed third in computer ads after processor and memory—that's how important it is. A top-of-the-line graphics card can make a computer come to life!

FIGURE 2.17 • Video card

Today's video cards are computers themselves that include a graphics processor, graphics memory, and other graphics circuitry.

Graphics hardware, memory, and GPU not only are important for gaming but also empower useful applications for professionals. The 3D effects that we enjoy in movies would not be possible if the producers didn't have powerful graphics hardware. Designers use this hardware to design products using computer-assisted design (CAD) software. Scientists and physicians use 3D graphics hardware and visualization software to examine phenomena not viewable to the naked eye.

ROM. You won't see ROM listed in a desktop or notebook computer advertisement, but it is vitally important to the functioning of a computer. **Read-only memory (ROM)** provides permanent storage for data and instructions that do not change, such as programs and data from the computer manufacturer, including the boot process used to start the computer. Because both the processor and RAM require electricity to store data, both are empty when a computer is initially powered up. The computer requires a place to permanently store the instructions needed to start up the computer and load the operating system into RAM. ROM fulfills this purpose.

In ROM, the combination of circuit states is fixed, and therefore the data represented by this combination is not lost if the power is removed. ROM stores a program called the BIOS (basic input/output system). The BIOS stores information about your hardware configuration along with the boot program. The boot program contains the instructions needed to start up the computer. After running some system diagnostics, the boot program loads part of the operating system into memory and turns over control of the processor to the operating system. Many of today's computers use *flash BIOS,* which means that the BIOS has been recorded on a flash memory chip rather than a ROM chip. Flash memory (covered later in this chapter) is intended to store data permanently, like ROM, but can be updated with revisions when they become available.

Because smart phones typically don't include a hard disk drive, they use ROM to not only store the BIOS but also store the operating system and applications that are included with the device.

CMOS Memory. *CMOS memory* (pronounced *see-moss*, short for complementary metal-oxide semiconductor) provides semipermanent storage for system configuration information that may change. CMOS is unique in that it uses a battery to stay powered up. CMOS is the reason that a PC is able to maintain the correct time and date even when it is powered down. In addition to keeping time, CMOS stores information about a computer system's disk drive configuration, startup procedures, and low-level operating system settings. On PCs that run Windows, you can view CMOS settings by pressing a designated key such as F2 during the startup procedure when prompted. CMOS provides a service somewhere between RAM and ROM in that it is permanent like ROM and doesn't go away when the computer is turned off, but its contents can be changed like RAM.

Secondary-Storage Technologies

In addition to the system storage used in the operation of the computer system, there is also *secondary storage,* used to store data and software more permanently without the need for electricity. Hard drives, CDs, DVDs, and flash drives are all forms of secondary storage.

It is not unusual for students to carry billions of bytes of data on USB drives dangling from key chains and on MP3 players or cell phones. At the same time, Internet storage facilities store gigabytes of data for you to access over any Internet-connected device. Soon, as wireless networks become more pervasive, you may not need to tote data around at all.

Even with all the storage options available to us, we are barely able to keep up with the rapidly growing demand for storage space. A good example is the Internet Archive. The Internet Archive has been storing snapshots of the entire Web each year since 1996. By going to the Internet Archive Web site (*www.archive.org*) and using the "Wayback Machine" you can call up any Web site and see its contents at any time since 1996. The archive's total collection of Web sites in 2003 was around 100 terabytes (that's 100,000 gigabytes) of data. In 2009 the Archive was at around 3 petabytes (3 million gigabytes) and growing at a rate of 100 terabytes per month.[7] Table 2.5 lists some other examples of the high storage demands of business and research.[8]

The National Energy Research Scientific Computing Center (NERSC) in Berkeley, California, supports a great deal of research done for the U.S. Department of Energy. As one of the largest facilities in the world devoted to providing computational resources and expertise for scientific research, NERSC includes a large supercomputer and a huge amount of storage. Its High Performance Storage System (HPSS) stores 8.8 petabytes of scientific data. The system uses thousands of tape cartridges retrieved by a robotic arm (see Figure 2.18). From huge data banks to tiny USB flash drives, secondary storage affects everyone on personal and societal levels.

TABLE 2.5 • High storage demands of business and research

Database	Storage requirements
Yahoo	2 PB
IRS	150 TB
eBay	6 PB
National Energy Research Scientific Computing Center	8.8 PB
World Data Centre for Climate	6 PB

FIGURE 2.18 • The High Performance Storage System (HPSS) at NERSC

One of the storage silo robots in NERSC's 8.8-petabyte High Performance Storage System.

In discussions of secondary storage, the term *storage device* refers to the device itself, the drive or circuitry that reads and writes data. *Storage media* refers to the objects that hold the data, such as disks. Some storage devices, such as flash memory drives, combine the device and media in one module. The *storage capacity* of a storage medium is the maximum amount of bytes that it can hold. *Access time* refers to the amount of time it takes for a request for data to be fulfilled by the device. When selecting storage devices and media, you should examine the portability, storage capacity, and access time associated with the media and match them to the task at hand, preferably at the least cost.

EXPAND YOUR KNOWLEDGE

To learn more about how to take care of your hard drive, go to www.cengage.com/computerconcepts/np/swt4. Click the link "Expand Your Knowledge" and then complete the lab entitled "Maintaining a Hard Drive."

Magnetic Media: Disks and Tapes. **Magnetic storage** devices use the magnetic properties of iron oxide particles to store bits and bytes more permanently than RAM. No physical storage medium can be genuinely permanent. It can be destroyed in any number of ways: fire, flood, sledgehammer. But if not abused, magnetically stored data lasts years, even decades, before deteriorating. In magnetic storage, a surface is coated with a layer of particles that are organized into addressable regions (formatted). In the process of reading and writing data, a read/write head passes over the particles to determine, or set, the magnetic state of a given region. Two types of media use magnetic storage: disks and tapes. You can see a hard disk's storage surface and read/write heads in Figure 2.19.

FIGURE 2.19 • Hard disk drive

Hard disk drives store data on multiple stacked disks called platters that are read by read/write heads.

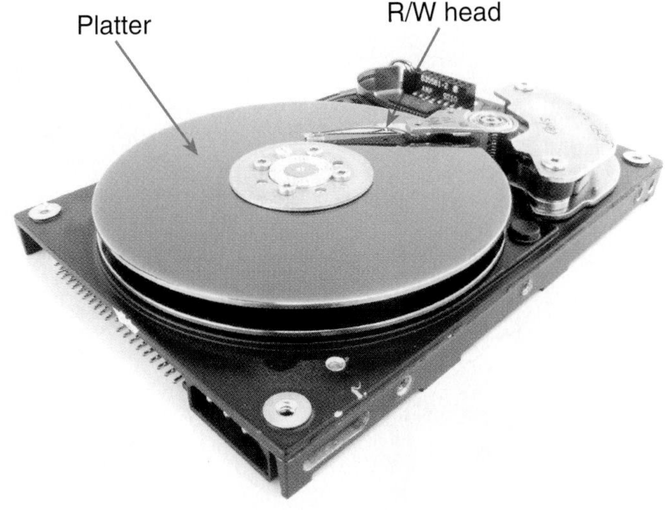

Magnetic disks can be thin steel platters (hard disks) or Mylar plastic film (floppy disks). When reading data from or writing data onto a disk, the computer can go directly to the desired piece of data by positioning the read/write head over the proper track of the revolving disk. Thus, the disk is called a *direct access* storage medium.

Magnetic disk storage varies widely in capacity and portability, starting at around 200 GB for small netbooks, and ranging up to a terabyte or more on high-powered gaming PCs. Since hard drives provide high capacity and fast data access speeds, personal computers rely on them as the main secondary-storage medium.

Microdrives, tiny hard drives that can store gigabytes of data on a disk one or two inches in size, have transformed handheld devices. Microdrives that can hold several gigabytes (see Figure 2.20) have been available as add-ons for portable devices. Some cell phones and handheld computers are offered with hard drives built in. These devices traditionally have been limited to 32, 64, or 128 MB of storage. Boosting the storage up to the gigabyte range provides these devices with the capability to store hours of music, video (TV shows, movies, or personal video), hundreds of photos, data files, and software. Adding a hard drive is a major step in bringing full desktop capabilities to handheld devices. The 20 GB and 40 GB Toshiba microdrives are what made the first iPods so popular. Two 60 GB microdrives enable the current iPod Classic to store up to 30,000 songs.

FIGURE 2.20 • Microdrive

This tiny 6 GB microdrive can hold about 1200 MP3 songs or several full-length motion pictures.

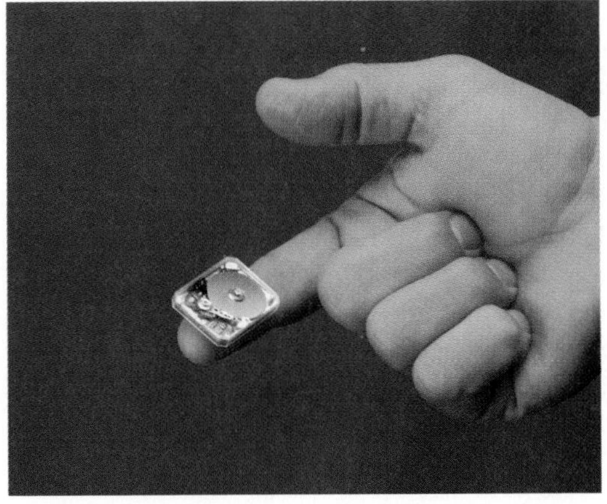

Magnetic tape is a storage medium used by businesses and organizations that need to store and back up large quantities of data (Figure 2.21). Similar to the kind of tape found in audio or video cassettes, magnetic tape is Mylar film coated with iron oxide particles. Magnetic tape is an example of a *sequential access* storage medium because data is written and read in sequential order from the beginning of the tape to the end. Although access is slower, magnetic tape is usually less expensive than disk storage. For applications that require access to very large amounts of data in a set order, for example, for archiving old data, sequential access is ideal. Government agencies, such as the U.S. Census Bureau, and large insurance corporations store large quantities of data on tape.

FIGURE 2.21 • Magnetic tape storage

Frank Elliott, IBM vice president for tape storage, holds IBM's 1 terabyte tape cartridge that holds the equivalent of the 1500 CDs that surround him.

Businesses and organizations often provide large quantities of storage to employees over a network. Server computers can provide a central store for important corporate data for employees to share. Arrays of disks can be formed and used in groups to handle terabytes and even petabytes of data. A technology called a *storage area network* or *SAN* links together many storage devices over a network and treats them as one large disk. Hackensack University Medical Center, in Hackensack, New Jersey, used a SAN to assist in going fully digital—paperless and filmless. The hospital stores digital images of X-rays, ultrasounds, and MRIs, prescription medicine orders, medical test results, patient medical histories, medical references, and, of course, patient billing and other business-related data, all on a huge, high-speed, SAN that interconnects different kinds of data storage devices with associated data servers.

In order to safeguard the valuable data stored on their computer systems, some businesses implement RAID. *RAID* or *redundant array of independent disks* uses a second system of disks to maintain a backup copy of the data stored on the primary disks. If the original drives or data become damaged, the secondary disks can take over with little loss of time or work. RAID can turn a tragedy into only a momentary inconvenience and safeguards companies from the risk of down time.

Optical Storage

Optical storage media, such as CDs, DVDs, and Blu-ray, store bits by using an optical laser to burn pits into the surface of a highly reflective disc surface. A pit represents a 0, and the lack of a pit represents a 1. The 1s and 0s are read from the disc surface by using a low-power laser that measures the difference in reflected light caused by the pits (or lack thereof) on the disc. Audio CDs that store music, data CDs that store software, and DVDs and Blu-ray discs that store motion pictures all use the same fundamental technology.

The first optical media to be mass-marketed to the general public was the CD-ROM. A **compact disc read-only memory (CD-ROM)**, commonly referred to as a CD, is an optical medium that stores up to 700 MB of data. Just like the ROM on your motherboard, once data has been recorded on a CD, it cannot be modified—the disc is read-only. Originally designed to store music, the CD soon replaced the cassette tape as the most popular form of music distribution and migrated to more general data storage uses in the computer marketplace. The CD ideally satisfied the increasing storage demands of large software programs.

A **digital video disc read-only memory (DVD-ROM)** stores over 4.7 GB of data in a fashion similar to CDs except that DVDs are able to write and read much smaller pits on the disc surface (see Figure 2.22) and can sometimes write to and read from multiple disc layers. Unlike CDs, DVDs can store an entire digitized motion picture. An additional benefit of DVD drives is that they are backward compatible with CD-ROMs, meaning that they can play CDs as well as DVDs. *Backward compatible* is an expression used to indicate that a new version of some technology still supports the specifications of the old version.

FIGURE 2.22 • CD, DVD, and Blu-ray

CDs, DVDs, and Blu-ray discs all use optical technologies with varying levels of precision to store increasing amounts of data in the same amount of space.

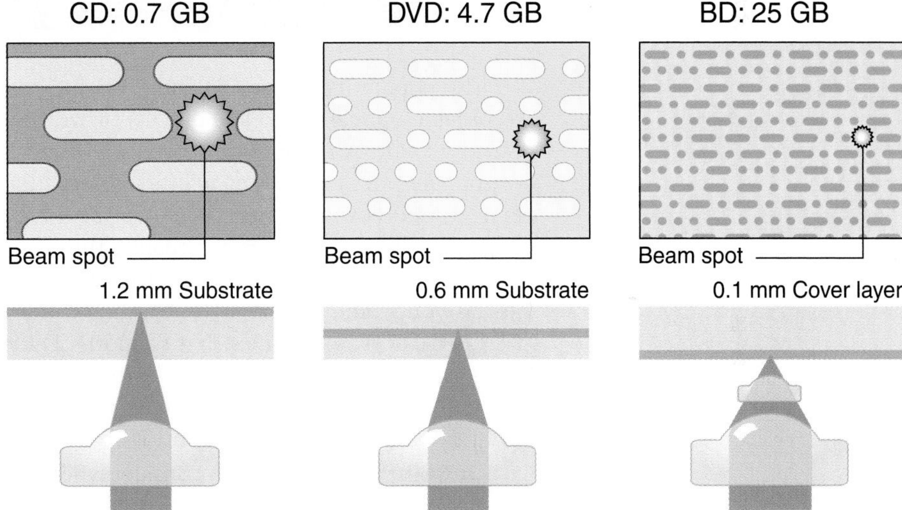

Blu-ray makes use of the shorter wavelength of blue light to read and write even smaller pits on the optical disc surface for higher capacity. A single-layer Blu-ray disc (25 GB) can hold a 135-minute high-definition movie and still have room for two hours of bonus material in standard definition (see Figure 2.23). Two-layer discs storing 50 GB are available, and experiments with 20-layer discs have produced a 400 GB capacity.[9] Blu-ray's high capacity makes it the perfect media for distributing high-definition movies, which are too large to fit on a standard DVD.

FIGURE 2.23 • Blu-ray disc

High-definition movies are distributed on Blu-ray discs.

The popularity of the CD and DVD has soared since the introduction of recordable optical discs. The process of writing to an optical disc is sometimes called *burning*. A number of different CD and DVD burners are available today at reasonable prices. Different manufacturers support different standards and formats in efforts to win customers over to their products. Manufacturers use *R* to indicate that a medium is recordable; that is, it can be written to only once. *RW*, for rewritable, is used to indicate that a disc can be rewritten numerous times, just as you would a hard drive. Currently, the most popular format for writable CDs is **CD-RW,** and drives that support CD-RW are referred to simply as CD burners. The most popular DVD burners support the two most popular DVD standards, +RW and –RW. Most new PCs come with a combination drive that can read and write both CDs and DVDs.

One other specification to consider when purchasing a CD or DVD burner is the time it takes to read and write data from and to the disc. Specifications for a typical DVD burner are either 8X or 16X. The *X* stands for "times the original transfer rate" of a disc. A 16X drive would burn a disc twice as fast as an 8X drive.

Solid-State Secondary Storage

A **solid-state storage** device stores data using transistors. RAM is considered volatile solid-state storage, which means if the computer's power is turned off the data stored is lost. This section deals with nonvolatile, or secondary, solid-state storage, which stores data more permanently without the need for electricity. **Flash memory** is a form of solid-state storage that updates (flashes) the data it holds in large blocks. Unlike other secondary storage such as magnetic disks and tapes, and optical CDs and DVDs, flash memory requires no moving parts to read and write data. It is therefore much faster and much quieter, requires less power, and produces less heat. Because of these significant benefits, solid-state storage is becoming very popular. The high price of the technology is the only thing holding it back from replacing other forms of secondary storage; however, the price is rapidly dropping. Solid-state storage devices include flash memory cards, USB flash drives, solid-state disks, and hybrid disks.

A *flash memory card* is a chip that, unlike RAM, is nonvolatile and keeps its memory when the power is shut off. Flash chips are small and can be easily modified and reprogrammed, which makes them popular in computers, cellular phones, digital cameras, and other products. When used in media devices such as digital cameras, camcorders, and portable MP3 players, flash memory cards are sometimes referred to as *media cards*. Secure Digital (SD) cards, Mini SD, and Micro SD cards are popular flash memory cards for cell phones, digital cameras, and other devices that need to store a lot of data in a tiny package (see Figure 2.24). Micro SD cards range in capacity from megabytes to 16 GB.

FIGURE 2.24 • Micro SD card

A micro SD card is smaller than a coin.

A **flash drive**, also called a *USB drive*, or *thumb drive*, is a small flash memory module about the size of your thumb or smaller, shown in Figure 2.25, that conveniently plugs into the USB port of a PC or other digital electronics device to provide convenient, portable, high-capacity storage. **Universal Serial Bus (USB)** is a standard that allows a wide array of devices to connect to a computer through a common port. Although they are called drives, they contain no moving parts as do magnetic or optical drives. They use solid-state technology to store anywhere from 1 GB to 128 GB of data, ranging in price from $8 to over $400.

FIGURE 2.25 • Flash drives

Flash drives attach to a USB port and come in a variety of shapes and styles. Some can store several gigabytes of data.

When connected to a PC, a USB drive is recognized by the operating system and is given a drive letter, such as the G: drive. Saving a file to the G: drive stores it on the USB flash drive. When you are done, you simply eject and remove the flash drive from the PC and take it with you. USB drives can easily be used on any computer equipped with a USB port, making them the portable storage media of choice for many computer users. Although USB flash drives do not come close to CD-RWs and DVD+RWs in terms of cost per MB, the convenience they offer makes them well worth the expense.

As flash drives grow in capacity and capability, they are threatening the future of magnetic hard drives as the first choice for secondary storage in PCs. Many companies are now producing *solid-state disks (SSD)* using flash technology to replace the traditional magnetic hard drive in PCs. An SSD reads data 300 percent faster and writes data 150 percent faster than traditional hard drives. It boots up a computer much faster, is lighter and more durable, uses less power, and runs cooler and quieter than a hard drive (in fact, it is silent). SSDs are being used in small, light subnotebook PCs designed for business travelers. For example, the MacBook Air offers a 128 GB SSD option. Since it is a relatively new technology, SSD drives are unable to provide the capacity of traditional hard drives, and cost considerably more.

A *hybrid drive* combines the best features of flash memory and magnetic storage. Up to a gigabyte of flash memory is used as a buffer to cache data that is needed during normal operations. A magnetic hard drive is used to store data as usual. A hybrid drive computer boots very quickly, and spins and accesses the hard drive only a small percentage of the time, so it runs very quietly. It provides most of the advantages of an SSD, with the added advantage of providing hundreds of gigabytes of storage that is currently unavailable with SSDs.

A notebook with an SSD is called a *solid-state notebook* and contains no moving parts save for the optical drive (see Figure 2.26). Prices for solid-state notebooks are currently high, but they are falling. As SSDs become faster and cheaper, there is little doubt that they will become common in mobile PCs.[10]

FIGURE 2.26 • Solid-state notebook

This Sony VAIO SR includes an option for a 256 GB SSD for an additional $660.

Evaluating Storage Media: Access Method, Capacity, and Portability

As with other computer system components, the access methods, storage capacities, and portability you require of secondary-storage media are determined by your objectives. An objective of a credit card company's computer system, for example, might be to rapidly retrieve stored customer data in order to approve customer purchases. A fast access method is critical to the success of the system. In a hospital setting, physicians evaluating patients might find portability, capacity, and privacy to be major considerations in selecting and using secondary-storage media and devices.

Storage media that provide faster access methods are generally more expensive than media that provide slower access. For example, a 4 GB flash drive costs 30 times as much as a 4.7 GB DVD-RW disc. This may be worth the cost to someone who needs to use the device to store and read data from several different PCs, since all PCs have a USB port, but not all have a DVD burner. In general, optical and magnetic storage is very inexpensive—pennies per GB. Solid-state storage is relatively expensive—dollars per GB for SSDs. The characteristics of these media make each appropriate for different needs.

INPUT, OUTPUT, AND EXPANSION

EXPAND YOUR KNOWLEDGE

To learn more about input devices, go to www.cengage.com/computerconcepts/np/swt4. Click the link "Expand Your Knowledge" and then complete the lab entitled "Using Input Devices."

Users interact with computers through input and output (I/O) devices. Of all the computer hardware components, I/O devices have the most direct impact on a user's computing experience. To accommodate a wide variety of data and the many environments in which data is processed, there are literally hundreds of different input devices on the market. By learning about input devices, you also learn what computers are capable of. Output devices connect directly with our senses. Although most output from a computer is visual, much is auditory, and some exotic devices even affect our other senses. This section explores input and output and the different peripheral devices that users add to their computers to expand their functionality.

Input and Output Concepts

An **input device** assists in capturing and entering raw data into the computer system. Successful input devices must be easy to learn to use and effortless to manipulate. An **output device** allows you to observe the results of computer processing with one or more of your senses. Personal computers typically use only a handful of I/O devices. You have likely used a keyboard, mouse, display monitor, and printer for much of your life. Using these devices is second nature to many people. New personal computing devices and product designs can present new and challenging methods of input. The touch screen keyboard on an iPhone may take some getting used to, as does texting with a phone's numeric keypad or a tiny QWERTY keyboard. Touch pads on notebook computers are easy to become accustomed to. Touch screens, using a stylus, and handwriting recognition may be a bit more challenging on tablet PCs. These basic I/O devices are a small subset of all the specially designed input devices available. From drawing tablets used by graphic artists to magnetic ink character readers used by banks to bar-code readers at the supermarket, a variety of input devices have been designed to accommodate the unique needs of professionals. The goal behind the design of such devices is always speed and functionality.

FIGURE 2.27 • UPS signature device

UPS drivers collect customers' signatures by having them sign an electronic pad that stores the signature electronically.

Speed and Functionality. Rapidly and accurately getting data into a computer system is the goal of most input devices. Some activities have very specific needs for output and input, requiring devices that perform specific functions. For example, many reporters use input devices that record and transcribe human speech to ease the stress of typing late-breaking stories. The more specialized the application, the more specialized the associated I/O device. UPS had special electronic pads created for its drivers to use to collect customer signatures (see Figure 2.27). The pads improved the efficiency of recordkeeping for UPS.

The Nature of Data. *Human-readable data* can be directly read and understood by humans. A sheet of paper containing lists of customers is an example of human-readable data. By contrast, *machine-readable data* is read by computer devices. Customer data that is stored on a disk is an example of machine-readable data. Note that it is possible for data to be both human-readable and machine-readable. For example, both human beings and computer system input devices can read the magnetic ink on bank checks.

Source Data Automation. Regardless of how data gets into the computer, it is important that it be captured near its source. *Source data automation* involves automating data entry where the data is created, thus ensuring accuracy and timeliness. Source-data automation is used by librarians who use scanners to check out and check in library materials. The moment a book is scanned at checkout, its status changes in the online card catalog to "checked out." Some rental-car companies use automated scanners that scan vehicles as they exit and enter the rental lot. The scanner collects data on the vehicle, including the mileage and gas gauge data, date, and time, and prepares a customer invoice before the customer returns to the counter.

As you enter into the era of pervasive computing, everyday objects may serve as I/O devices. Microsoft researchers are working on technologies that turn any surface into a touch-sensitive display (Figure 2.28). Imagine checking text messages on your kitchen table as you eat breakfast, and viewing your photo album on the kitchen wall!

FIGURE 2.28 • New forms of I/O

The Microsoft surface computing project uses combinations of sensors, cameras, and projectors to turn various surfaces, such as tables, desks, counters, or walls, into computing interfaces.

Input Devices

Input devices can be classified as either general purpose or special purpose. A *general-purpose I/O device* is designed for use in a variety of environments. This category of I/O devices includes keyboards and displays. A *special-purpose I/O device* is designed for one unique purpose. An example of a special-purpose I/O device is the pill-sized camera from Given Imaging that, when swallowed, records images of the stomach and the small intestine as it passes through the digestive system. Another example of a special-purpose input device is the iPod's patented Click Wheel that is used to navigate its menu system. The ability to "shake to shuffle" the song order on the iPod is also a form of input.

Personal Computer Input Devices. Today's PCs are multimedia devices that can input (and output) many kinds of data, such as text, audio, and video. Various input devices are used to capture these types of data, including keyboards, mice, microphones, digital cameras, and scanners.

A computer keyboard and a computer mouse are the most common input devices, used for entering data such as characters, text, and basic commands. A number of companies are developing new keyboards that are more comfortable, adjustable, and faster to use. For example, the Microsoft *ergonomic keyboard* is designed in such a way as to reduce the stress on your wrists common with traditional keyboards.

A computer mouse is used to direct the computer's activities by selecting and manipulating symbols, icons, menus, or commands on the screen. Different types of mice are available, including corded and cordless, one-, two-, or three-button, with scroll wheel and without. Some users prefer a trackball over a mouse. A *trackball* sits stationary and allows you to control the mouse pointer by rolling a mounted ball. If you've ever tried to draw pictures using a mouse, you know how frustrating it can be. *Graphics tablets* allow you to draw with a penlike device on a tablet to create drawings on your display (Figure 2.29).

FIGURE 2.29 • Graphics tablet

Graphic artists and photographers use graphics tablets for maximum control of a digital brush, pen, or pencil.

Mobil Input Devices. Other methods for entering data are tailored for mobile computing. Notebook computers integrate the mouse as a touch-sensitive pad below the Spacebar called a *touch pad*. By moving your finger across the pad you direct the mouse cursor on the screen. Multitouch pads allow the use of two or three fingers to manipulate objects on the display. Most touch pads can also be tapped to click.

Smaller mobile devices are doing away with the keyboard and mouse altogether. Handheld computers, some smart phones, and tablet PCs use a **touch screen** that allows you to select items on the screen by touching them with your finger or a *stylus*—a short penlike device without ink. These devices translate characters written on the screen with a stylus into ASCII characters that can be stored and edited in a word-processing document. There are different handwriting recognition systems that make use of varying styles of writing. Some require the user to use a specific alphabet of characters that the system can recognize. Apple decided that a stylus is too cumbersome and designed the iPhone's touch screen for fingertip use. A keyboard is displayed on the touch screen for typing with your fingertips (see Figure 2.30), and a small cloth is provided to wipe off fingerprints. Keyboards implemented via software on a touch-sensitive display are called *soft keyboards*.

FIGURE 2.30 • The iPhone keyboard

The iPhone's keyboard is displayed on the touch-sensitive display, programmed to display keys useful for the given task and to assist with typographical mistakes.

Microphone Input Devices. Microphones can take human speech as input, digitize the sound waves, and use *speech recognition software* to translate the input into dictated text that appears on the screen or into commands. On the factory floor, equipment operators can use speech recognition to give basic commands to machines while using their hands to perform other operations. Speech recognition software can be used to take dictation, translating spoken words into ASCII text. *Voice recognition*, a similar technology, can be used by security systems to allow only authorized personnel into restricted areas.

Gaming Devices. Gamers enjoy specialized input devices that let them quickly react to game action. Most gamers prefer to use a **game controller** device to control game characters and objects; some games, such as flight simulators, are easier to navigate using a *joystick*, a device resembling a stick shift.

Digital Cameras. Many people are switching from film to digits as they discover the convenience of digital photography. A *digital camera* captures images through the camera's lens and stores them digitally rather than on film. The quality of a digital camera is typically judged on how many megapixels (millions of pixels) can be captured in an image. A *pixel* is one of many tiny dots that make up a picture in the computer's memory. A traditional inexpensive film-based camera produces 1.2-megapixel images. Today, most cell phones come with a 1.2- to 3-megapixel camera. You can buy a 10-megapixel digital camera for under $100. As with most technology, prices in the digital camera market are rapidly dropping. Most cameras capture images on a flash memory card that you can download to your PC using a USB cable or a wireless connection. Some computers and printers have flash memory card readers that allow you to download pictures directly to your PC or printer.

Many digital cameras, in addition to taking still images, allow you to capture short video recordings. If you are interested in longer video, you can purchase a camcorder. A bit more costly, *digital camcorders* allow you to take full-length digital video that you can watch on your TV, download to your computer, or transfer to CD, DVD, or VCR tape. Many camcorders record direct to DVD, while others have high-definition capabilities. *Webcams* provide a lower-priced video camera for use as a computer input device. They are ideal for video conferencing over the Web, as shown in Figure 2.31.

FIGURE 2.31 • Webcam

Webcams, like the ones built into most notebook displays, connect to your computer for video conferencing over the Internet.

EXPAND YOUR KNOWLEDGE

To learn more about other input and output devices, go to www.cengage.com/computerconcepts/np/swt4. Click the link "Expand Your Knowledge" and then complete the lab entitled "Peripheral Devices."

Scanning Devices. You can input both image and character data using a scanning device. Both *page scanners* and *handheld scanners* can convert monochrome or color pictures, forms, text, and other images into digital images. It has been estimated that U.S. enterprises generate over one billion pieces of paper daily. To cut down on the high cost of using and processing paper, many companies look to scanning devices to help them manage their documents. Combined with *character recognition software*, a scanner can transform document images into editable word-processing documents.

A 3D scanner is used to capture the characteristics of 3D objects into a computer. A 3D scanner typically uses lasers to measure an object on all sides. Once captured, the object can be virtually manipulated using 3D graphics software. 3D scanners are useful tools for 3D animators and designers.

The field of biometrics uses a variety of scanning devices. *Biometrics* is the study of measurable biological characteristics. Biometrics is becoming increasingly useful in the area of security as a tool for confirming a person's identity. Scanners and software can verify an individual's identity by examining biological traits, such as retinal or iris patterns, fingerprints, or facial features. First Financial Credit Union is using one such device to verify customer identity. The bank has installed kiosks at remote locations where customers are able to access all the services that a branch office has to offer, including applications for new accounts and loans. The kiosks save the bank the cost of opening new branches. Fingerprint scans assure the bank that the customers making the transactions are who they say they are.

Businesses and organizations use a number of special-purpose scanners and optical readers to collect data. A *magnetic ink character recognition* (*MICR*) device reads special magnetic-ink characters such as those written on the bottom of checks. *Optical mark recognition* (*OMR*) readers read "bubbled-in" forms commonly used in examinations and polling. *Optical character recognition* (*OCR*) readers read hand-printed characters. *Point-of-sale (POS) devices* are terminals, or I/O devices connected to larger systems, with scanners that read codes on retail items and enter the item number into a computer system.

Output Devices

Computer output consists of the results of processing produced in a manner that is observable by human senses or that can be used as input into another system. Output can be visual (on a display or printed page) or audio (through speakers); in the case of virtual reality systems, output can even be tactile and olfactory to re-create real environments. Output from one system can be fed into another system as input. For example, consider the system that controls natural gas distribution throughout the United Kingdom. One computer system monitors the pressure in the natural gas pipes that crisscross the country. The output from that system is fed into the computer system that regulates the flow of gas to maintain consistent and safe levels.

Display Technologies. Remarkable progress has been made with display technologies, including those used with personal computers. With today's wide selection of monitors and displays, price and overall quality can vary tremendously.

USE YOUR BRAIN!

What if you could open a door, turn on the lights, change the TV channel—with only your mind? Recently, researchers from around the world have teamed up to create the first brain-computer interface technology. Electrodes attached to your scalp transmit the brain's electrical activity to electroencephalogram (EEG) equipment. In addition to using the system to control a virtual house, potential real-world uses include teaching people with disabilities to use prosthetic limbs or control electric wheelchairs.

Virtual Smart Home Controlled By Your Thoughts
ScienceDaily
May 26, 2009
http://www.sciencedaily.com/releases/2009/05/090511091733.htm

The first consideration when selecting a display is typically size. Display size is measured diagonally and ranges from 10 inches for netbooks to 12–17 inches for notebooks, up to 24 inches and higher for desktop PCs (see Figure 2.32). You could even connect a PC to a huge 65" high-definition TV for life-size gaming action and media. If you use a lot of graphics applications, games, video, or artwork, or like to multitask with many windows open on the screen at once, you probably want to go with a larger display size. If you mostly deal in text, e-mail, and Web pages, and want to conserve desktop space or go mobile, a smaller display size should suit your needs. Wide-screen displays have become popular both on notebook computers and desktops as increasing numbers of users are viewing movies on their PCs.

FIGURE 2.32 • Curved display

This 43" curved display wraps your computer's output around you.

The quality of a screen is often measured in pixels. **Display resolution** is a measure, in width by height, of the number of pixels on the screen. *Dot pitch* refers to the measure of space between pixels. The lower the dot pitch, the better the image quality. The higher the resolution, the higher the level of detail and image quality. A screen with a 1024 × 768 resolution (786,432 pixels) has a higher level of sharpness than one with a resolution of 640 × 350 (224,000 pixels). The higher the resolution, the smaller the pixels and images they create. If you want to fit more on your display, you could do so by choosing a higher resolution. On the other hand, if you found that the font or images on your display are too small to see clearly, you could choose a lower resolution that would increase the size of the objects on the display.

Knowledge of display technology has become useful when shopping for televisions. Today's display technologies offer many options for televisions as well as computers. *High-definition TV* (HDTV) uses a resolution that is twice that of traditional television displays for sharper, crisper images. HDTV uses a wide-screen format, which means it uses the same height and width ratio used in movie theaters. Standard television displays and traditional computer displays use a 4:3 ratio representing 4 inches of width for every 3 inches of height. Wide-screen displays use a ratio of 16:9. As PCs and entertainment media continue to merge, it becomes useful to understand the display options of both.

A **liquid crystal display (LCD)** is a thin, flat display that uses liquid crystals—an organic, oil-like material—placed between two pieces of glass to form characters and graphic images on a backlit screen. Once used primarily as a laptop display, LCD displays are quickly displacing the old-style CRT (cathode-ray tube) displays for desktop systems. The two primary choices in LCD screens are passive-matrix and active-matrix LCD displays. Passive-matrix displays are typically dimmer, slower, but less expensive. Active-matrix displays are bright, clear, and have wider viewing angles than passive-matrix displays.

You have probably heard of plasma display televisions. A *plasma display* is a flat panel display that uses plasma gas between two flat panels to excite phosphors and create light. The use of plasma in displays became popular in the late 1990s because it could be used to create large, flat, thin televisions at a reasonable cost. LCD has lower limits on size and, at the time, was more expensive to manufacture. Over time, as LCD production has become less costly, and as LCD displays have increased in size, they have overtaken plasma television technology in popularity.

Light-emitting diode (LED) displays are a relatively new technology that has become popular in notebook PCs and is expanding to desktop displays and televisions. LED displays use LEDs to provide the backlight in thin displays rather than the fluorescent light used in traditional LCDs. Using LED backlighting requires 12 percent less power than traditional LCDs and provides a more even distribution of light and truer colors. It is also a greener technology, since it does not require the use of mercury that is used in traditional LCDs. LCD, plasma, and LED displays are all types of *flat panel displays*.

Touch displays have become more popular on desktop computers. Windows 7, the latest version of the Windows OS, provides robust support for touch screen navigation and applications.[11] Touch displays are perfectly suited for meeting the light computing demands of *nettop PCs*—desktop PCs designed primarily for Web-based applications.

Electronic paper, or e-paper, is a display technology designed to look like printed characters on paper. Unlike other displays, e-paper does not use a backlight to illuminate pixels. Instead, e-paper technologies manipulate pigment particles between glass plates or plastic sheets to create points of varying shades of gray. The result is what appears to be a printed page that can be easily viewed from any angle, even in bright outdoor light.

E-paper is primarily used in e-book readers (see Figure 2.33), providing black and white text and images. Philips and other companies are racing to produce color e-paper.[12]

FIGURE 2.33 • E-paper

E-books, like this one from Plastic Logic, provide a book-like presentation using e-paper.

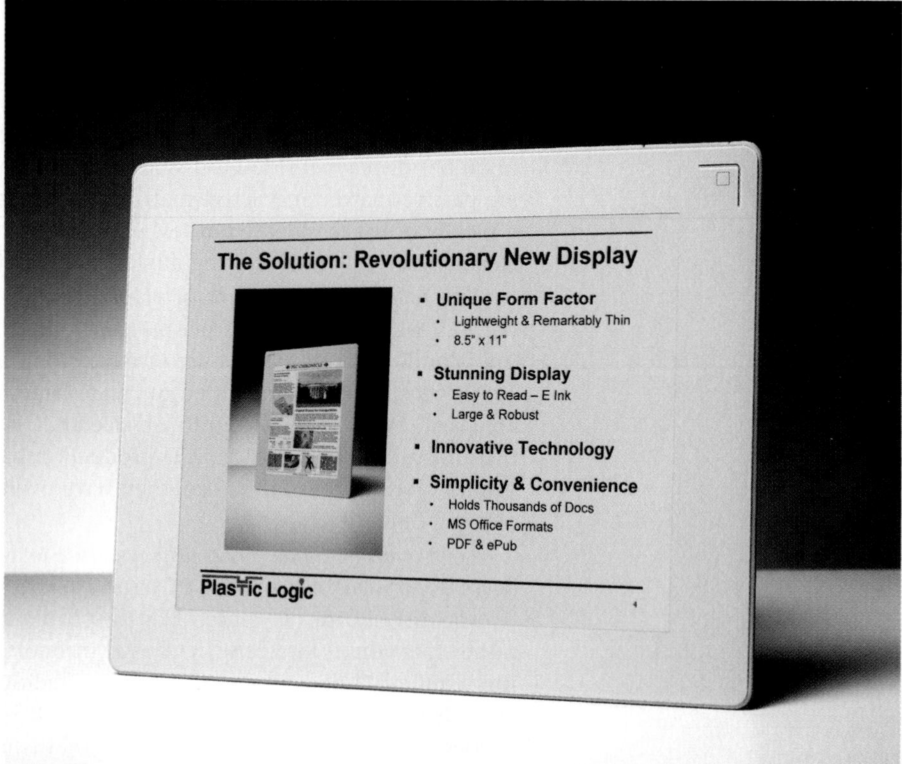

E-paper research is closely related to the development of displays that use materials other than glass. In 2004, Philips Electronics unveiled one of the first ultra-thin flexible plastic displays. A *flexible display* uses polymer-based semiconductors to create a flexible plastic display that can be rolled, folded, dropped, and mangled with no damage to the material. Building electronics out of conductive polymers, or plastics, is an area of research called *organic electronics* because the molecules in these materials are carbon based. Recently, two companies, the Dutch firm Polymer Vision, and Cambridge University startup Plastic Logic, have been working to bring flexible displays to the market.

Consider the benefits of plastic displays. More rigid plastic can be used to create lightweight, unbreakable displays for mobile devices. Flexible plastic can be used to create large displays that can be rolled up into a small package, or small wristband displays. It has even been suggested that displays can be shaped into contact lenses.

LCD projectors are designed for projecting presentations from your computer onto a larger screen. These small portable devices are a must-have item for people in businesses that require them to make presentations to large audiences. LCD projectors can interface with most desktop and notebook computers. *Pico Projectors* are designed for ultra portability to display images from smart phones or other pocket-sized devices. There are even projectors that display navagation maps, vehicle speed, and other useful information on car windshields (Figure 2.34).

FIGURE 2.34 • Vehicle projector from Microvision

Projecting useful information on vehicle windshields may be safer than dashboard displays.

Printers and Plotters. Another form of output is referred to as *hard copy*, paper output from a printer. A variety of printers with different speeds, features, and capabilities are available. The two most popular types of printers are color ink-jet printers and laser printers. A *laser printer* uses techniques similar to those of photocopiers to provide the highest-quality printed output. Color laser printers are rather expensive, so many home users settle for either a less expensive, monochrome laser or a color ink-jet printer. An *ink-jet printer* sprays droplets from ink cartridges onto paper to create pixels. Although ink-jet printers create good-looking hard copy, it is not quite as polished as what laser printers provide. Also, ink may run if it gets wet, so use care when printing addresses onto envelopes and hope they aren't delivered on a rainy day. Table 2.6 lists the various types of printer technologies.

The latest trend in home printers is the photo printer (Figure 2.35). Sparked by low-price digital cameras, *photo printers* have become a popular method for printing photo-quality images on special photo-quality paper. Some photo printers don't require a PC. Just connect your digital camera or media card directly to the printer, use the onboard display to edit the photo, if necessary, and print it directly to professional-grade photo paper.

FIGURE 2.35 • Photo printer

Some photo printers allow you to print directly from the camera or media card without the need for a PC.

TABLE 2.6 • Printer technologies

Technology	Description
Laser (B & W and color)	Utilizes lasers to scan images across the printer's photoreceptor for clean and clear results; popular with businesses and professionals
Direct thermal	Utilizes heat to create print on special paper; no need for toner or ink; used for industrial printers such as those at filling station pumps and cash registers
Ink-jet	Creates images by spraying variable-sized droplets of colored ink on paper; popular for home use
Dot-matrix	Also called an impact printer since it strikes a print head against an ink ribbon to create characters and images; becoming outdated but still in use in some industries
Dye sublimation	Similar to ink-jet but uses an ink ribbon rather than spray; popular for photo printing
Thermal transfer	Similar in function and use to direct thermal, but applies heat to a print ribbon to transfer ink to paper, rather than directly to special paper
LED	Works like a laser printer but replaces lasers with light-emitting diodes (LEDs); a newer green technology that requires little maintenance
Solid ink	Utilizes solid blocks of ink rather than liquid ink for brighter, deeper colors and environmentally friendly printing

Small business owners or people who work from home can benefit from multifunction printers. *Multifunction printers* combine the functionality of a printer, fax machine, copy machine, and digital scanner in one device—digital convergence applied to printing technologies. Although you would expect such a device to be very expensive, many can be purchased for less than $200.

The speed of a printer is typically measured by the number of *pages printed per minute* (*ppm*). The quality of resolution of printers is similar to the resolution of display screens. A printer's output resolution depends on the number of dots printed per inch. A printer with a 600 *dots-per-inch* (*dpi*) resolution prints more clearly than one with a 300 dpi resolution. When shopping for a printer, consider the quality of the output (judged by resolution specs and personal evaluation of printed copy), speed of the printer (ppm), price of the printer, and how quickly the printer consumes toner or ink along with the price of refills. The initial investment in a printer can end up paling in comparison to the price of toner or ink cartridge refills over time.

Plotters are a type of hard-copy output device used for printing large graphic designs. Businesses typically use plotters to generate paper or acetate blueprints and schematics, or print drawings of buildings or new products onto paper or transparencies.

3D printers use CAD blueprints as input, and they output an actual 3D color scale prototype model in a matter of hours. This activity is sometimes referred to as rapid prototyping. Zcorporation (*www.zcorp.com*) is the leading manufacturer of 3D printers and markets them for a wide variety of applications, from product design, production prototypes, and architectural concepts to education, health care, and the arts. Figure 2.36 shows a gargoyle that has been scanned into a computer using a 3D scanner, and the results of that object being printed using a 3D printer.

FIGURE 2.36 • 3D scanning and printing

The object on the left was scanned into the computer using a 3D scanner, and then reproduced with a 3D printer, creating the object on the right.

Computer Sound Systems. Most of today's desktop personal computer systems include at least low-quality speakers to output sound. Sound is used by the computer operating system and other software to cue the user to certain events, like the flourish of music that plays when Microsoft Windows starts up and shuts down. Other event-driven sounds are included to draw the user's attention to important information: for example, the beep that sounds when a warning dialog box is displayed.

Sound systems also support entertainment applications such as CD/MP3 music players and DVD movie players. The sound systems on most notebook and handheld computers are not of sufficient quality to do justice to such media; so users of such systems typically turn to headphones for higher-quality sound.

Multimedia and gaming enthusiasts often purchase more expensive sound systems for their computers. For example, a surround sound system with a subwoofer can provide additional realism to games in a virtual reality simulation.

A computer's ability to output sound is particularly important to individuals who have limited vision. Screen-reader programs such as JAWS®, by the Freedom Scientific Corporation, read aloud the text displayed on the screen.

Other I/O Devices

Many special-purpose input/output devices are designed to support scientific and medical research. For example, a new type of digital movie camera that uses ultrafast laser pulses is able to record things faster and smaller than ever. It is providing scientists with striking 3D color movies of atoms, molecules, and living cells in action. Neurobiologists use the camera to watch the brain think, develop, age, and deal with disease. They can see neurons grow inside the living brain. Such close examination of the workings of the brain is leading to new understandings about how the brain functions.

Chemists are using another new input device to track the motions of the particles—electrons, protons, and neutrons—that make up an atom. To do so, they use an advanced laser strobe light that slices time into the shortest bit yet achieved—an *attosecond*—a billionth of a billionth of a second.

Computer scientists and musicians at the MIT Media Lab are experimenting with special input devices that allow children to compose and perform music without any musical instrument skills. The input devices include a drawing pad that plays music based on children's drawings; soft, squeezable, colorful instruments that let kids mold, transform, and explore musical material; and a variety of other devices that release the creativity in children.

Haptic output is a type of computer output that the user feels. Vibration in a game controller as a race car rolls over gravel is an example of haptic output. Researchers are experimenting with new ways that haptics can assist users in all types of computing devices (see the Community Technology box).

The area of virtual reality has produced a number of unique and interesting I/O devices. For example, the *virtual reality headset* can project output in the form of three-dimensional color images. Spatial sensors in the headset act as input devices, and when you move your head, images and sounds in your headset change. Virtual reality devices already allow architects to design and "walk through" buildings before they begin construction. They allow physicians to practice surgery though virtual operations and pilots to simulate flights without ever leaving the ground.

High-Fidelity Haptics

Microsoft and Apple are both investing heavily in touch screen technologies. Windows 7 has robust support for touch screen devices, and it's a safe bet that Apple PCs will have touch screens very soon. One related technology that is looming large on the horizon is haptics. Haptics provides the ability to feel computer output. You may have experienced haptics in game controllers that vibrate and shake when game action takes you over a bumpy road. Cell phones include haptic feedback that vibrates the device to communicate various messages, such as when your phone rings.

Haptics is about to move to a new level of sophistication. Immersion Corporation has developed a technology it calls "high-fidelity haptics." In a demonstration of the technology, a volunteer was asked to play pinball on a haptic-equipped tablet PC. The volunteer claimed that she was able to feel the ball roll across the hard surface of the virtual pinball machine. She could feel the ball hit bumpers and paddles. She could feel all of the motion of the game, just as if she had her hands on an actual pinball machine. Without the haptics, she found the game cold and lifeless.

Microsoft and Apple are looking to haptics to help users adjust to interacting with a computer through a touch-sensitive display rather than with a keyboard and mouse. Through haptics, a displayed (soft) keyboard might provide many of the tactile cues that a physical keyboard provides. Far beyond current haptic technologies, high-fidelity haptics will provide thousands of different sensations that will carry important tactile cues and information to bring the virtual reality of computing a little closer to physical reality.

Questions

1. What types of computer applications might haptics assist? How?
2. Is there any possible down side to expanding haptics in computing?
3. Looking to the future, what types of haptics devices might be developed to create realistic virtual reality environments?

Source

1. *Elgan, Mike, "Haptics: The feel-good technology of the year,"* Computerworld, *July 24, 2009, http://www.computerworld.com/.*

Wearable PCs have small system units that can clip to a belt or fit in a pack, head-mounted displays, and hands-free or one-handed input devices. They are used by individuals who need to have access to data while doing physical work such as repairing a jet engine or inspecting a city's underground utility tunnels. Figure 2.37 shows a research scientist using a wearable PC designed for use underwater.

FIGURE 2.37 • Wearable PC

Wearable PCs such as this one for divers often use head-mounted displays (attached here to the diving mask) and special hands-free or one-handed input devices.

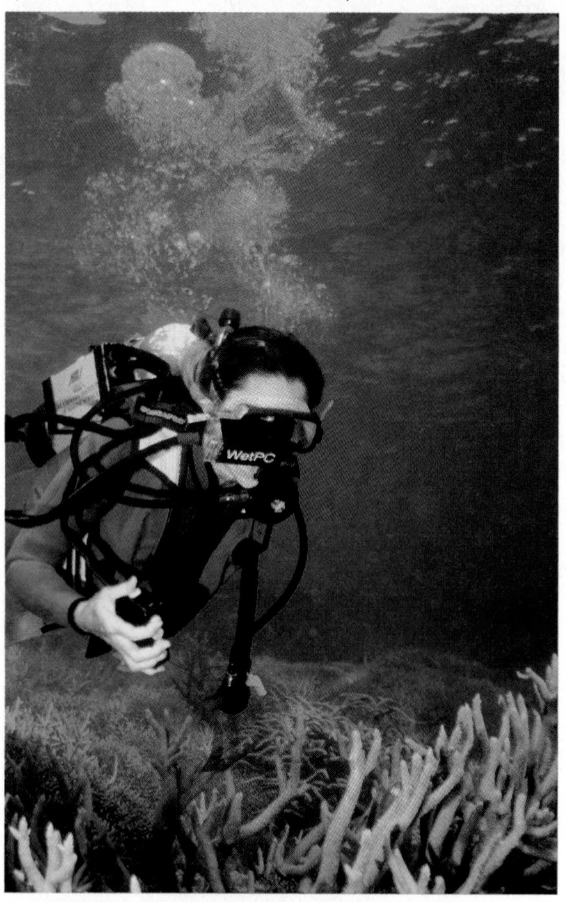

Expansion

Most computers provide users with the means to add devices and expand their computers' functionality. A desktop computer user might want to add a scanner, a notebook user might want to add a webcam for video conferencing, and a smart phone user might want to add a GPS device. This section describes the most common methods of expanding a computer system.

Desktop Computer Expansion. One fact that has traditionally complicated system expansion is that peripheral devices use a variety of cables and connectors. Desktop computers provide standard *ports* (sockets) for display, keyboard, printer, and mouse connectors, but have not easily accommodated the many other special-purpose cables and connectors. Those days are over. Today's computers come with a number of USB ports and all kinds of devices that use them (see Figure 2.38). It is not unusual to find six or more USB ports on a new computer, into which you can plug the keyboard, mouse, and additional devices of your choice, such as handheld computers, digital cameras, portable MP3 players, network devices, joysticks, memory modules, and many others, all using a common connector design. USB provides not only a connection to the computer for data transfer but also a power line that can be used to power a number of useful and entertaining gadgets.

FIGURE 2.38 • Universal Serial Bus

Many of today's peripheral devices connect to a computer using the USB port.

More-specialized peripheral devices may come with their own circuit board, called an *expansion board* or *expansion card*, to be installed in a desktop computer. Installation of these devices is not as convenient as simply plugging in a USB connector, but typically it is easy enough for most computer users to handle. The method of installing them varies from machine to machine, so users should consult their owner's manual for specific instructions. After removing the cover from a desktop computer, you see a bank of *expansion slots* at the rear of the computer's motherboard (see Figure 2.39); some slots may already contain cards. By viewing the width of the card you want to install, you can determine which slot can accommodate the card. After installing the card according to instructions, the port on the card is exposed at the back of the computer for use.

FIGURE 2.39 • Expansion slots

More-specialized peripheral devices may come with an expansion card to be installed in the expansion slots on the motherboard of your computer.

FireWire (also known as IEEE 1394) competes with USB as a standard for connecting devices to PCs. FireWire was developed by Apple in the 1990s but now can also be found on Windows PCs. Videographers, musicians, and media hobbyists appreciate the speed at which FireWire transfers data between the computer and devices such as video cameras, digital music players, recording equipment, and other peripheral devices. Although FireWire typically outperforms the original USB standard, USB 2 competes more closely with FireWire in terms of data transfer speed. The recently released USB 3 is 10 times faster than USB 2.

Mobile Computer Expansion. Like desktop PCs, notebook computers include USB ports for convenient expansion. Most peripherals are designed to use USB. However, notebook computers also provide *PCMCIA slots* that accept *PCMCIA cards*, usually called *PC Cards*. PC Cards support a number of devices. For example, wireless network adapters and additional storage devices can be purchased as PC Cards for notebook computers. Notebook computers also include ports to add a standard keyboard, mouse, printer, and display or LCD projector.

Smart phones can also accommodate additional devices. For instance, you can connect a global positioning system (GPS) to some smart phones, which when combined with GPS software can display your location on a map. Other options for smart phones include webcams and LCD projectors. The iPhone supports numerous types of addtional devices, including a variety of medical monitoring devices that connect with special iPhone Apps.

SELECTING AND PURCHASING A COMPUTER

Putting together a complete computer system is more involved than simply connecting computer devices. Take a moment to think about how car manufacturers build a car. They match the components to the intended use of the vehicle. Racing cars, for example, require special types of engines, transmissions, and tires. To select the right transmission for a racing car, you must consider not only how much of the engine's power can be delivered to the wheels, but the cost of the transmission, how reliable it is, and how many gears it has. Similarly, you must assemble the components of a computer system based on its intended use. You must choose a specific type of computer (desktop, notebook, tablet, smart phone, or netbook) and ensure that the processor, RAM, graphics memory, secondary storage, and input and output devices, when combined, will serve your needs.

You should always base a computer system purchase on a careful study of the needs that it will address. Wyndham Resorts had issues with getting customers through the check-in and checkout process efficiently. To address the problem, they equipped their hospitality staff with handheld computers (see Figure 2.40) and sent them out to check customers in at the curb or even when they arrived at the airport. Other resorts have installed kiosks that allow customers to check in and out without the assistance of staff. Kiosks and handheld computers ideally address the specified problem: checking customers in and out as quickly and accurately as possible.

FIGURE 2.40 • Handheld computers in action

Wyndham Resorts decided that handheld computers were the best way to improve its check-in process.

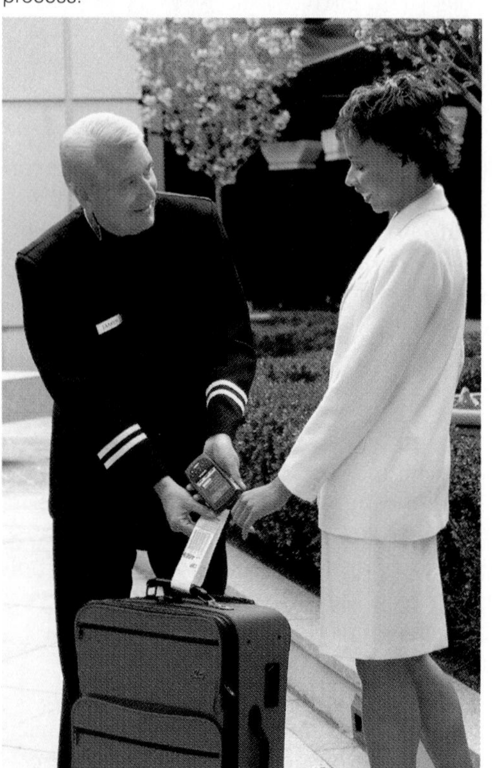

Researching a Computer Purchase

Businesses such as Wyndham Resorts employ IT (information technology) professionals to select and purchase computer systems to meet their business needs. For your own computer purchases *you* need to function as the IT professional. IT professionals typically begin the process of designing a computer system by studying the needs of the organization. You, too, should begin by considering the ways in which you plan to use your computer. Make a list of your typical computing activities and the software that you use. Include software that you are interested in using in the future at work and at home.

Check the minimum system requirements for the software you want to use. You'll find that software that incorporates more graphics requires faster processors, more advanced graphics hardware, and more memory. Table 2.7 provides examples of system requirements for various types of software. At a minimum, the computer you purchase should meet the system requirements of the software you want to use. However, minimum requirements are what is needed to barely get the software to work. To run the software most fluidly, you should purchase a computer that satisfies more than the minimum requirements.

TABLE 2.7 • Minimum system requirements for popular software

Software that relies on graphics and 3D graphics requires more powerful computers.

Software	Operating system	Processor	RAM	Hard drive	Video card
Microsoft Office	Microsoft Windows XP (SP2)	500 MHz	256 MB	1.5 GB	N/A
Adobe Photoshop	Windows 2000 or Mac OS 10.2	Intel Pentium III, or PowerPC G3	320 MB	750 MB	16-bit
Halo 3 (PC game)	Windows Vista	2 GHz	1 GB	7 GB	DX9, NVIDIA 6000, or ATI x700
Windows 7	N/A	1 GHz	1 GB	16 GB	DX9, WDDM 1.0 driver

This chapter has provided you with the technical knowledge that is required for making a wise computer purchase. Even armed with this understanding, purchasing a new computer system requires a considerable amount of research. The computer market changes so rapidly that no matter how much you know about computers, it takes some time to catch up with the current state of technology and the market. Fortunately, many free resources are available to assist you in learning as much as you need to know.

Web sites such as *www.cnet.com* and *www.zdnet.com* can help you decide on a computer type and platform. Browsing around your local computer store is another method of investigating the market. Shopping online can give you a good idea of the state of the market in terms of PC specifications and price. Magazines such as *Computer Shopper* and *MacWorld* can provide additional information. Many computer industry magazines have information online as well.

Computer Vendors

Computer systems can be purchased online, over the phone, or in a local computer store. They can be purchased new or used, leased, or paid for in installments. The method you use to purchase a computer depends on your personal preferences and financial situation.

Online Vendors. Apple and many of the Windows PC manufacturers provide online stores that allow customers to configure and purchase computers (see Figure 2.41). Buying directly from the manufacturer can sometimes save you money. The main benefit, though, is that it allows you to custom configure your PC. Online customers can choose processor, memory capacity, hard disk capacity, secondary-storage devices, display type and size, and numerous other options. PCs purchased directly from the manufacturer are usually delivered in under two weeks. Users can choose service options that provide in-home service should any trouble occur with the PC. Some vendors provide overnight pickup and delivery service that supports repairs by mail for notebook PCs in two working days.

FIGURE 2.41 • Sony Vaio Advisor

Sony provides a useful tool to assist shoppers with finding a model that best suits their needs.

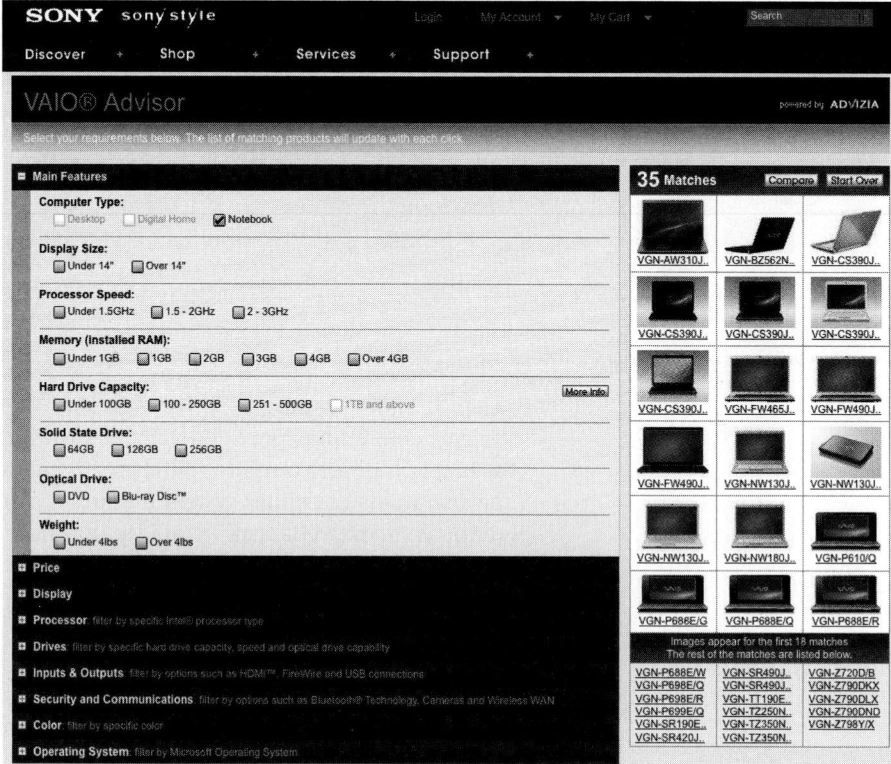

Online computer retailers sell computers from varying manufacturers. Online merchants allow you to compare packages from varying manufacturers to find the best configuration and price. Often these sites provide filters that allow you to sort by price, processor speed, popularity, and other specifications. Since these computers are already configured and ready to go, they offer little in the way of customization but very speedy delivery. Computers are covered by the manufacturer's warranty. Online computer retailers provide a good way to scout out computer manufacturers, compare prices, and narrow the field. Some online merchants, like CompUSA and Best Buy, also have brick-and-mortar retail stores but offer many more products online. Table 2.8 lists some online computer manufacturers and retailers.

TABLE 2.8 • Online vendors

You can buy computers online directly from the manufacturer or from an online retailer.

Buy direct from manufacturer	Buy from online retailers
www.alienware.com	www.bestbuy.com
www.apple.com	www.buy.com
www.dell.com	www.cdw.com
www.fujitsu.com/us/services/computing	www.compusa.com
www.gateway.com	www.jr.com
www.hp.com	www.newegg.com
www.lenovo.com	www.pcconnection.com
www.samsung.com/us/	www.tigerdirect.com
www.sonystyle.com	www.walmart.com
www.toshiba.com	

Auction sites such as eBay provide yet another option for online computer shopping. Secondhand computers and other bargains found on eBay typically do not include a warranty and thus incur a risk. Because computers lose value quickly, any computer older than four years is probably not worth anything on the market. Before purchasing a used computer, compare it in price and quality to new PCs. With PC prices dropping dramatically every year, there is little market for used computers.

Local Vendors. Your local computer store offers you the advantage of being able to try out the PC you are considering. You may also benefit from the advice of a qualified salesperson. What's more, if you get your computer home and find some trouble with it, you may be able to return it to the store for another one. Local stores may also provide special sale prices, package deals, or other incentives that make this option worth your while. Local merchants understand that there are good deals online and often try to match them. For this reason, it is a good idea to shop online prior to visiting a store.

The downside of purchasing locally is that you have little or no opportunity to customize your PC—what you see is what you get. One should also be sure that you are not sold a PC that the store is trying to get rid of, but doesn't really match your needs.

Payment Options. Once you have decided on the PC you want, you may be faced with a variety of payment options. Online or in the store, you can find vendors willing to take cash or credit. Many have partnerships with banks and can arrange a computer loan for your purchase. Some vendors provide methods of trading in your PC after two years for a new one at a discounted price.

The Home Technology feature provides strategies to use when purchasing a computer. It outlines the important considerations involved in a purchase and provides ways in which to apply the knowledge you have acquired from this chapter.

Strategies for Computer Shopping

Purchasing a new computer, whether it is a desktop, notebook, tablet, smart phone, or netbook, requires an organized process to ensure that you get a computer that is well suited to your needs.

1. **Choose a type of computer: notebook, desktop, tablet, smart phone, or netbook.** With computers, portability is gained through sacrifices in power. The smaller the computer, the fewer activities it supports. This is true not only in terms of processor power, memory, and storage capacities, but also in terms of display size, mode of input (keyboard versus stylus), and ability to connect to networks and the Internet. Consider the ways in which you use a computer as they relate to these features. Remember that full-size displays, keyboards, and mice can be connected to portable computers. Then weigh the limitations of portable devices against the benefits that portability provides.
2. **Choose a platform.** Once you've decided on desktop, notebook, tablet, netbook, or smart phone, you should turn your focus to platform. If you are purchasing a desktop or notebook, you need to choose between Windows or Mac (or Linux for those more technically inclined). Tablet PCs are currently available only for Windows. Smart phone choices depend on the phones designed for your service provider. You should choose the platform that best supports your use. Consider the platform choice of friends and others in your field and seek out impartial online reviews.
3. **Choose a manufacturer.** Once you've selected a platform, you are faced with choosing from manufacturers that support the platform. Of course there is only one manufacturer for Apple computers, but all other platforms provide many manufacturers from which to choose. Many find it wise to go with a manufacturer with a long-standing reputation. This way you are assured that the manufacturer will be around to support your equipment. In choosing a manufacturer, consult professional reviews and get the advice of respected friends and associates.
4. **Choose a model.** Once you've decided on a platform and manufacturer, you need to decide on a model based on your needs and budget. Different models and prices reflect differences in components such as processor, memory capacity, hard drive capacity, graphics card, and display size and technology. Typically some trade-offs must be negotiated to keep your computer selection within budget. Keep in mind that the cheapest models support only the most basic needs, and the most expensive models reflect state-of-the-art technologies that are typically released to the market at an inflated price.
5. **Select add-ons.** Often you have options for additional equipment, features, and services. Of these add-ons, the most critical is the warranty. Mobile computers are subject to damage, so it is wise to purchase a warranty that covers the length of time that you plan to use the device. Because desktop computers are seldom moved, they are less prone to damage, and you might be able to get by with a shorter warranty. Other add-ons such as printers, external drives, and software should be compared in price to other vendors. If they are less expensive packaged with your new computer, then they should be considered.

ACTION PLAN

Remember Mark, who wants to purchase a new PC and/or laptop? Here are some answers to his questions.

1. **How should Mark prepare for his purchasing decisions?**

   Mark needs to list his specific computing needs at home and away from home. He needs to keep each activity in mind throughout the purchasing process and make sure that the computers he purchases are able to support his needs.

2. **What types of computer and platform might best suit Mark's needs?**

   Once Mark determines where he will be doing most of his work, he can decide on where he needs the most computing power. It may be that Mark's heaviest work will be done at home. In such a case, a powerful desktop that supports both his home media interests and his work is where Mark should invest most of his budget. His mobile needs might be met with an inexpensive netbook. If Mark does a lot of work away from home, he'll need to spend more on a notebook, and perhaps make some sacrifices in his home PC. He may be able to get by with only a high-powered notebook, which he can connect to a large display when at home. Mark will also need to determine if smart phone capabilities will help support his needs. Mark will need to choose between the Apple or Windows platforms for his home and mobile computer(s). If purchasing both, it would be wise to stick with a common platform. Because Mark will be bringing some of his work home with him from Lamar, he should go with the same platform that is used at his work.

3. **How much processor speed, memory, and storage capacity does Mark need?**

   Interactive, 3D gaming requires a fast processor. If Mark is really into gaming, he should go with the most powerful processor and graphics card available. If he is only mildly interested in gaming, he could save some money by going a notch down on processor power and benefit from a good deal on last year's model. His other interests do not require a state-of-the-art processor. Gaming also requires a significant amount of memory (2 GB minimum) but not necessarily a lot of storage (100 GB would suffice). However, if Mark does any work with video editing or plans to store his music or video files on his computer, he should get a large disk drive (300 GB or more). To sum up, if Mark will be using his computer for gaming and multimedia, he should consider maximum processor power, graphics power, memory, and storage offered in top-of-the-line computer packages. Otherwise, he might save as much as $800 by going for a more basic package. Mark should keep in mind that powerful desktop PCs are half the price of equally powerful notebooks.

4. **What input/output devices would best suit Mark's needs?**

   As a gamer and artist, Mark wants a large display, a color printer, a game controller, a drawing tablet, and a flatbed scanner. He plans to check with his employer to see what types of displays and drawing tablets are recommended, and then he will configure his home computer to be as similar as the one at work as possible. He should also purchase an upgraded video card with a significant amount of memory to smoothly run the gaming animation.

5. **Are there additional considerations to be made regarding these purchases?**

   Since Mark is new to video conferencing, he needs to do some research to find out what hardware is required. For video communication over the Internet, he needs a broadband Internet connection and a webcam. Mark also needs to check the video connections on his HDTV to determine what kind of cable and adapter may be required to connect his PC.

Summary

LEARNING OBJECTIVE 1

Understand how bits and bytes are used to represent information of value to humans.

The digital revolution was sparked by the computer's ability to represent and manipulate information digitally, with 1s and 0s.

Units of information can be represented with bits in a standardized code by assigning each unit to a unique bit pattern using a look-up chart. ASCII is a standardized code used in computers to represent character data. Bits can also be used to store values by using the binary number system. The binary number system uses two digits, 0 and 1. Binary numbers are used for calculations, to represent color intensities in images, and to represent the amplitude of sound waves used to store digital music and sound. There are many methods of decoding and interpreting a byte. Each method boils down to either the look-up table approach or binary numbers. By implementing standards, bytes can have consistent meaning across common applications. Because all different types of data are represented with 1s and 0s, digital convergence is producing devices that can handle all types of data.

Figure 2.1 —p. 58

LEARNING OBJECTIVE 2

Identify the functions of the components of a CPU, the relationship between the CPU and memory, and the factors that contribute to processing speed.

The CPU processes the data into information that is meaningful to people. The CPU's primary components are the control unit that fetches and interprets instructions, the arithmetic/logic unit that carries out the instructions, and registers that store the bytes being processed. The CPU uses RAM as its primary storage. RAM provides the CPU with a working storage area for program instructions and data. Data flows back and forth between the CPU and RAM across the system bus.

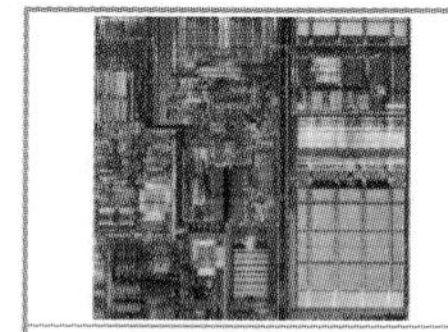

Figure 2.8 —p. 64

The control unit in the CPU uses the four-step machine cycle to carry out program instructions: fetch instruction, decode instruction, execute instruction, and store results. Each processor has an instruction set, a finite number of instructions that it is designed to carry out. Clock speed, wordlength, and bus speed all have an impact on the speed of processing. All activity in the system takes place in time with a processor's system clock. Clock speeds are measured in megahertz (MHz) and gigahertz (GHz). The number of bits the CPU can process at any one time is called its wordlength. Clock speed, wordlength, and several other system components all affect the processor's performance.

Moore's Law states that in silicon-based processors, transistor densities in an integrated circuit will double every two years.

LEARNING OBJECTIVE 3

Identify different types of memory and storage media, and understand the unique properties of each.

RAM is volatile and temporarily stores data as long as there is an electrical current. ROM is more permanent storage that has its instructions hardwired into its circuitry. ROM stores the boot process that runs when the computer is powered up.

Magnetic, optical, and solid-state storage are three types of secondary storage used to store data and programs more permanently. Magnetic storage includes disks (random access) and tapes (sequential access). Optical storage includes CDs, DVDs, and Blu-ray

Figure 2.19 —p. 77

discs, which are available in read-only discs and writable discs. Solid-state storage includes flash memory devices such as solid-state drives, USB thumb drives, and media cards.

LEARNING OBJECTIVE 4

Identify different types of input and output devices and how they are used to meet a variety of personal and professional needs.

People use input devices to provide data and instructions to the computer, and they use output devices to receive results from the computer. General-purpose input devices include the keyboard and mouse for desktop computers, the touch pad for notebook computers, and the touch screen and stylus for tablet PCs. Scanners are used in a variety of industries to avoid data-entry errors by capturing data close to its source. Special-purpose input devices include game controllers, tablets and pens, and webcams.

Figure 2.38 —p. 96

Printers, plotters, and displays are the primary forms of output devices. Displays are selected by size and resolution. LCD flat panel displays are the most popular type. Color ink-jet and non-color laser printers are popular for home and small business use, although color laser printer prices are becoming more affordable.

LEARNING OBJECTIVE 5

Understand the decision-making process involved in purchasing a computer system.

When selecting a computer system, you must first analyze your specific computing needs at home, school, work, or on the road. Select a computer type and platform that supports those needs. Options include desktop computers, notebook computers, tablet PCs, netbooks, and smart phones. Select options that provide for more than the minimum requirements of the applications you want to run.

Test Yourself

LEARNING OBJECTIVE 1: Understand how bits and bytes are used to represent information of value to humans.

1. Most computers use ________________ to represent character data using bytes.
   a. hexadecimal
   b. kilobytes
   c. decimal notation
   d. ASCII code
2. True or False: Digital music is stored using binary numbers.
3. The ________________ number system is ideal for digital systems because it has only two digits, 1 and 0.
4. True or False: All software interprets a byte such as 11110000 the same way.
5. ________________ refers to the ability of one device to handle several different types of digital information, such as voice communications, character data, and music.
   a. Digital revolution
   b. Digital convergence
   c. Digital communications
   d. Digital economy

LEARNING OBJECTIVE 2: Identify the functions of the components of a CPU, the relationship between the CPU and memory, and the factors that contribute to processing speed.

6. A(n) ________________ processor incorporates four CPUs on one chip.
7. True or False: A faster system clock means a faster, more powerful processor.

8. The process for executing a program instruction is called the ________________ .
   a. machine cycle
   b. clock speed
   c. cache
   d. execution cycle

LEARNING OBJECTIVE 3: Identify different types of memory and storage media, and understand the unique properties of each.

9. When a computer is first powered on, the processor is fed instructions from ________________ .
   a. register storage
   b. RAM
   c. ROM
   d. secondary storage
10. True or False: Solid-state storage is currently the least expensive type of storage.
11. A(n) ________________ port can be used to attach a wide variety of peripherals to a computer.

LEARNING OBJECTIVE 4: Identify different types of input and output devices and how they are used to meet a variety of personal and professional needs.

12. ________________ involves automating data entry where the data is created, thus ensuring accuracy and timeliness.
    a. Keyboard input
    b. Source data automation
    c. Secure data entry
    d. Special-purpose device input
13. A QWERTY keyboard displayed for use on a touch-sensitive display is called a(n) ________________ keyboard.
14. True or False: LCD displays provide a higher-quality image than LED displays.

LEARNING OBJECTIVE 5: Understand the decision-making process involved in purchasing a computer system.

15. What is the first thing you should do when considering a computer for purchase?
    a. Choose a manufacturer.
    b. Consider a platform.
    c. Decide between a desktop, notebook, tablet, smart phone, or netbook.
    d. Examine your usage and needs.
16. True or False: In general, desktop computers are less powerful and less expensive than notebook computers.
17. The first consideration in selecting a computer system is ________________ .
    a. platform
    b. processor
    c. portability
    d. manufacturer

Test Yourself Solutions: **1.** d. ASCII code, **2.** True, **3.** binary, **4.** False, **5.** b. Digital convergence, **6.** quad-core, **7.** False, **8.** a. machine cycle, **9.** c. ROM, **10.** False, **11.** USB, **12.** b. Source data automation, **13.** soft, **14.** False, **15.** d. Examine your usage and needs. **16.** False, **17.** c. portability.

Key Terms

Key Term	Page	Definition
arithmetic/logic unit (ALU)	64	A component of the CPU that contains the circuitry to carry out instructions, such as mathematical and logical operations
binary number system	59	A number system that uses only two values, 0 and 1, and is used by computers and digital devices to represent and process data
CD-RW	80	Rewritable CD; a CD that can be rewritten numerous times just as you would a hard drive
central processing unit (CPU)	63	A group of integrated circuits that work together to perform the processing in a computer system
clock speed	66	A series of electronic pulses at a predetermined rate used to synchronize processing activities

Key Term	Page	Definition
compact disc read-only memory (CD-ROM)	79	Optical media that stores up to 700 MB of data
control unit	64	Part of the CPU that accesses and decodes program instructions, and coordinates the flow of data among various system components.
digital convergence	60	The trend to merge multiple digital services into one device
digital video disc read-only memory (DVD-ROM)	79	Optical media that stores over 4.7 GB of data
display resolution	88	A measure, in width by height, of the number of pixels on the screen
flash drive	81	A small flash memory module, about the size of your thumb or smaller, that conveniently plugs into the USB port of a PC or other digital electronics device to provide convenient, portable, high-capacity storage
flash memory	80	Form of solid-state storage that updates (flashes) the data it holds in large blocks
game controller	85	Used to control game characters and objects
gigahertz (GHz)	66	Billions of cycles per second
graphics processing unit (GPU)	68	A powerful processor that handles advanced graphics rendering for demanding graphics applications such as the 3D environments of games
input device	83	Assists in capturing and entering raw data into the computer system
integrated circuit	63	Also called *chips*; multiple transistors integrated into a single module used to store and process bits and bytes in today's computers
liquid crystal display (LCD)	89	A thin, flat display that uses liquid crystals—an organic, oil-like material—placed between two pieces of glass to form characters and graphic images on a backlit screen
magnetic storage	76	Uses magnetic properties of iron oxide particles to store bits and bytes more permanently than RAM
megahertz (MHz)	66	Millions of cycles per second
Moore's Law	69	Continuing advances in technological innovation will make it possible to reduce the size of transistors, doubling their density on a processor chip every two years
motherboard	63	The primary circuit board of a computing device
optical storage	78	Stores bits by using an optical laser to burn pits into the surface of a highly reflective disc surface
output device	83	Device that allows you to observe the results of computer processing with one or more of your senses
random access memory (RAM)	64	Temporary, or *volatile*, memory that stores bytes of data and program instructions for the processor to access
read-only memory (ROM)	74	A type of system memory that provides permanent storage for data and instructions that do not change, such as programs and data from the computer manufacturer, including the boot process used to start the computer
solid-state storage	80	Stores data using transistors; can be volatile (as with RAM), or nonvolatile (as with flash memory)
touch screen	85	Allows you to select items on the screen by touching them with your finger or a stylus

Key Term	Page	Definition
transistor	62	An electronics component composed typically of silicon; opens or closes a circuit to alter the flow of electricity to store and manipulate bits
Universal Serial Bus (USB)	81	Standard that allows a wide array of devices to connect to a computer through a common port

Questions

Review Questions

1. Explain how the bytes that represent keyboard characters are decoded.
2. Why do computers use the binary number system?
3. Describe the components of a machine cycle.
4. What is *digital convergence*?
5. What is the FSB and how does it affect processing speed?
6. What factors affect processing speed?
7. What are the two most popular personal computer platforms? How do they differ?
8. Describe the various types of memory.
9. What is the purpose of graphics memory and a GPU?
10. Describe various types of secondary-storage media in terms of access method, capacity, and portability.
11. What are the benefits of using a hybrid drive rather than a traditional hard disk drive?
12. What factors determine the appropriate system output and input devices?
13. Discuss the speed and functionality of common input and output devices.
14. What benefits does USB provide for desktop and notebook computers?
15. What are the advantages and disadvantages of shopping for a computer online?
16. Describe the six steps of selecting and purchasing a computer.

Discussion Questions

17. Smart phones allow you to make phone calls, take pictures, listen to digital music, and access data, such as your calendar and address book. What other functionality would you like to see provided by a handy, all-in-one portable device? How can such a function be incorporated digitally?
18. Paper is difficult and expensive to organize, manipulate, and store over extended periods of time. In light of paper's drawbacks, discuss the impact(s) of various input and storage devices on organizations.
19. Contrast magnetic storage devices, optical storage devices, and solid-state storage devices. What are the advantages and disadvantages of each in terms of cost, convenience, and capacity?
20. Consider and discuss strategies for storing data for long periods of time. For example, if you store all of your personal photos and music on your hard drive, what storage strategy might you use to ensure that your great-grandchildren's children will be able to enjoy them 100 years from now?
21. Discuss how the hardware needs of a small law firm might differ from the needs of the office of a registrar for a university.
22. List the activities that you do, or would do if you were able to, on computers both at your desk and away. What computer device(s) would best support your needs (desktop, notebook, tablet PC, smart phone)? What are your needs in terms of processor speed, memory capacity, and storage capacity? Provide your rationale.

Exercises

Try It Yourself

1. Use a spreadsheet to convert decimal into binary, octal, and hexadecimal number systems. Most spreadsheet applications have a function that automatically does this conversion for you. For example, Microsoft Excel includes functions named DEC2BIN, DEC2OCT, and DEC2HEX. Create a chart that looks like this:

Decimal	Binary
1	1
2	10
3	11
4	100
5	101
6	110
7	111
8	1000
9	1001
10	1010

Example of function usage:

Decimal	Binary
1	=DEC2BIN(A2)
2	=DEC2BIN(A3)

Recall that the binary number system has only two digits (0 and 1). Create a second table in your spreadsheet that converts binary numbers to decimal (BIN2DEC). Type in binary values 1 through 10100 and use either a function or your brain to do the conversions. Use your tables to experiment with these number systems for better understanding.

2. Use a spreadsheet to create a table that lists the system requirements of the top five software programs that you use. Be sure to include any software you use that you think is most demanding. Use the sort command to list the software applications in order, from most to least demanding.

3. You and two friends have decided to start your own business. You have secured a small business loan from the bank and leased some office space. Your partners have placed you in charge of purchasing desktop computers for the six employees of your company—the three owners and three clerical employees. None of the employees needs a really fast processor, but the partners need larger amounts of memory and storage. The employees need the ability to archive data on a DVD. All employees need a lot of work room on their desks, so whatever you buy has to take up as little desktop space as possible.

   Your budget is $10,000. You have already selected a vendor; now you need to decide what should be included in each of the two types of systems: the owners' systems and the employees' systems. Visit *www.dell.com* to shop for computers. Create a spreadsheet to find the best solution. Add a short memo explaining the rationale for your solution. Include the price of your owners' computers and your employees' computers and what components each includes. Also include the minimum and maximum price possible for each computer system.

4. Visit *www.cnet.com* and find the reviews for peripherals. In a word-processing document, list the subcategories of input/output devices that you find under peripherals.

   View the pages for each of the types of peripherals. Sort the products by Editor's rating, and read the review of the top-ranked item. Write a short paragraph for the top-ranked item in each category, and explain why you might or might not want to purchase the device.

5. Using common Web search engines, such as *www.ask.com* and *www.google.com*, find the name of the fastest supercomputer in existence. What is its name, who made it, how fast is it, and what is it used for? Do the same for the second-fastest supercomputer. What is the difference between the two in speed and in age? Do these two computers support Moore's Law?

6. Consider the computing needs of your present or future career. Are there any special or unique hardware requirements? Use the Web to research

this topic. Rank the following in order of importance for your professional computer system (most important being 1):

_______________ Portability

_______________ Network/Internet connection

_______________ Large high-quality display

_______________ Fast processor

_______________ Large amount of memory

_______________ Large-capacity hard disk drive

_______________ Large-capacity portable storage

_______________ High-quality printer

_______________ Flatbed scanner

_______________ Digital camera

_______________ Special-purpose input device (provide description, if applicable)

Virtual Classroom Activities

To complete the following exercises, do not use face-to-face or telephone communications with your group members. Use only Internet communications.

7. Assume that you are partners in a new business. Decide what business you are in. Assign each group member a role within the business. One member should act as company president and group leader, chosen by casting electronic ballots. Each group member should then decide what type of computer he or she needs to perform his or her job. Use the chapter content to decide what type of computer(s) best suit your needs. Include processor speed, memory and storage types and capacities, along with I/O devices—the options discussed in this chapter. Justify your choices.

8. Each group member should go shopping on the Web to find the lowest-priced computer that meets each user's personal computing needs. All members should submit their computer specifications and price to the group leader. Have an online discussion about the differences among the users' choice of PCs and see if you can decide which user is getting the best deal. Also consider who is spending the least and the most and whether their computing needs support the amount they would spend. The group leader should compile the data and submit the results.

Teamwork

9. Identify the public and department-run computer labs on your campus. Divide them equally between team members. Each team member should visit his or her assigned labs and, either by observation or contact with the lab administrator, list the type of equipment used in the lab. Include processor speeds, memory capacity, storage types used on the computers, and manufacturer's name for all devices, including scanners, printers, and other peripherals. Find out how often computers are replaced, and what happens to the old computers. Reconvene and decide which lab on campus best meets students' needs. Discuss your school's policies and procedures for computer replacement and see if you can improve upon them. Write a report that summarizes your findings.

10. Assign each group member a particular computer component to research: processor, memory, storage, input device, or output device. Search the Web, periodicals, or computer stores for unique examples of such devices that were not included in this chapter. Compile your data to create a unique computer. The group with the most bizarre computer wins.

Endnotes

[1] Mick, Jason, "AMD Heats up Server War With Low Power 40 W Six-core Opterons," *Daily Tech*, September 1, 2009, http://www.dailytech.com/.

[2] Persons, Mark, "Multiple challenges for multicore processors," *International Science Grid This Week*, August 19, 2009, http://www.isgtw.org/.

[3] Reilly, Terra, "Doing More... with a netbook," *Inside Intel*, April 2009, http://inside.intel.com/.

[4] Madrigal, Alexis, "I See Your Petaflop and Raise You 19 More," *Wired*, February 2, 2009, http://www.wire.com/.

[5] Munro, Jim, "Toyota turn to virtual reality," *The Sun*, September 2, 2009, http://www.thesun.co.uk/.

[6] Crothers, Brooke, "Moore's Law expressed as fewer chips," *Cnet*, September 13, 2009, http://news.cnet.com.

[7] Mearian, Lucas, "Internet Archive to unveil massive Wayback Machine data center," *Computerworld*, March 19, 2009, www.computerworld.com.

[8] Lai, Eric, "Size matters: Yahoo claims 2-petabyte database is world's biggest, busiest," *Computerworld*, May 22, 2008, http://www.computerworld.com/.

[9] Beavis, Gareth, "Pioneer Reveals 400GB Blu-ray Disc," *TechRadar*, July 7, 2008, http://www.techradar.com/.

[10] Perenson, Melissa, "Solid-State Drives Go Mainstream," *Computerworld*, August 28, 2009, http://www.computerworld.com/.

[11] Lai, Eric, "Windows 7: The OS that launches a thousand touch-screen PCs?", *Computerworld*, August 20, 2009, http://www.computerworld.com/.

[12] Loftus, Jack, "Color E-Paper From Philips That Could Replace Monitors, the Real Thing," *Gizmodo*, May 10, 2009, http://www.gizmodo.com/.

Software Solutions for Personal and Professional Gain

Alexandra Pollack is a second-semester freshman in college and working part-time to help pay her expenses. Her roommate just purchased a new computer and told Alex she can have her old PC. It's a good notebook computer, only a year and a half old. There is one drawback: a virus ravished the notebook and all the software, including the operating system, has been removed. Alex must purchase and install all new software. She sets out to make a list of the software she will need for work, school, and fun. She's on a tight budget and will have to work hard to get as much useful software as possible for under $200.

Alex is majoring in political science and is interested in going to law school after she graduates. She is currently working as a clerk at a local law firm. The firm allows her to do some of her work from her dorm room, which is convenient for Alex. Working from her dorm room saves her a 25-minute drive and the cost of the expensive clothes she would need to work at the law firm's office. The law firm told her that she needs Microsoft Office to do her work from home. Besides needing an operating system and the latest version of Microsoft Office, Alex also needs a Web browser, a media player, and software to assist her in organizing her life.

As you read through the chapter, consider the following questions:

1. What is the best operating system for Alex to load on her used notebook?
2. Which productivity software will best suit Alex's needs?
3. What other software can assist Alex with her interests?

Check out Alex's *Action Plan* at the conclusion of this chapter.

3

LEARNING OBJECTIVES

1. Explain how software is created, distributed, installed, and maintained.
2. Describe the functions of system software and operating systems, and provide examples of operating systems for PCs, larger computer systems, and mobile devices.
3. Describe different types of productivity software and explain how application software assists people at home, at work, and in between.
4. List areas of research in artificial intelligence and tell how AI is being used in everyday applications.

CHAPTER CONTENT

Software from Conception to Installation and Beyond

System Software

Application Software

Smart Software: Artificial Intelligence

Introduction

Software is the key to unlocking the potential of any computer system and developing effective computer applications. Without software, the fastest, most powerful computer is useless. It can do nothing without instructions to follow and programs to execute. With software, people and organizations can accomplish more in less time.

All software is developed using a programming language. Programming languages have gone through a number of generations, and with today's languages, writing computer programs is easier and faster than ever. Programming languages are used to develop two basic types of software: system software and application software. System software makes computers run more efficiently, whereas application software helps people, groups, and organizations achieve their goals. Both types of software are discussed in this chapter, as well as issues related to the acquisition, installation, and maintenance of all kinds of software.

Both system and application software continue to become more powerful and more intelligent. This chapter concludes with a section on "smart software," that is, artificial intelligence: what it is and how it is changing the way technology supports our needs.

In the early days of computing, when computer hardware was expensive, software costs were a comparatively small percentage of total computer system costs. The situation has dramatically changed. Today, software can be 75 percent or more of the total cost of a particular computer system. This is certainly true for big business systems, but also for personal computers. It is more difficult to see in PC prices since software is often included in the price of the PC. Without the software, PC prices would be considerably lower. Table 3.1 illustrates the value of PC hardware as it compares to software when purchased separately. Because PC manufacturers purchase software in large quantities, they receive discounts and are able to include $1000 worth of software by adding a few hundred dollars to the price of the PC.

TABLE 3.1 • PC costs: hardware versus software

Hardware only	Software only
$400 Notebook computer	$220 Operating system $120 Office suite $ 80 Security software $100 Photo-editing software $400 Miscellaneous software
Total: $400	Total: $920

Software has become more expensive than hardware for several reasons:

- Advances in hardware technology have resulted in dramatically reduced hardware costs.
- Increasingly complex software requires more time to develop, hence, it is more costly.
- Salaries for individuals who develop software have increased because of the increased demand for their skills.

SOFTWARE FROM CONCEPTION TO INSTALLATION AND BEYOND

As you learned in Chapter 1, *software* consists of the electronic instructions and programs that govern a computer system's functioning and control the workings of the computer hardware. Computer programs are sets of instructions or statements to the computer. Ultimately, these statements direct the circuitry within the hardware to operate in a certain fashion. A **software engineer** is a professional who writes sets of instructions using programming languages and programming logic to create useful software.

System and Application Software

There are two basic types of software: system software and application software. **System software** is the set of programs that coordinates the activities of the hardware and various computer programs. System software includes operating systems like Windows 7 and Mac OS X that are essential for a computer to operate. Other system software such as disk management tools and virus scan software is designed to keep the computer running smoothly and effectively. System software, especially the operating system, is written for a specific set of hardware and CPU. As explained in Chapter 1, the hardware configuration of the computer system combined with the particular operating system in use is known as the *computer platform.*

Application software consists of programs written to perform tasks or solve problems for people, groups, and organizations. Some application software, like word processors, spreadsheets, and database management software, assists people and organizations to be more productive. Other application software, like media players and games, helps people to have fun.

In short, system software assists computer hardware with the work it is designed to do, while application software assists people with work and activities that people do. To determine whether software is system software or application software, simply ask whether the software fundamentally helps the computer or people.

How Software Works

Software usually consists of a number of files, ranging from a few to dozens or more. Files can have an extension at the end of the filename. An *extension* identifies the type of file and is placed after the filename, following a period. At least one of the files associated with a program is an executable program file with an .exe extension (see Figure 3.1). Other files can store data and supportive tools for the executable file. A text file typically has a .txt extension. Many word processing files have a .doc or .docx extension. For example, the .doc extension in the file Report1.doc indicates that the Report1 file is a Microsoft Word document; Word 2007 and Word 2010 use .docx for an extension, and a .wpd extension indicates a WordPerfect document. Microsoft Windows is typically set to hide the filename extensions from the user. You can enable visible filename extensions in Windows Folder Options.

FIGURE 3.1 • The files that make up software

The Firefox Web browser software is composed of multiple files and folders, displayed here in Windows 7. The firefox.exe file contains the machine instructions for running Firefox.

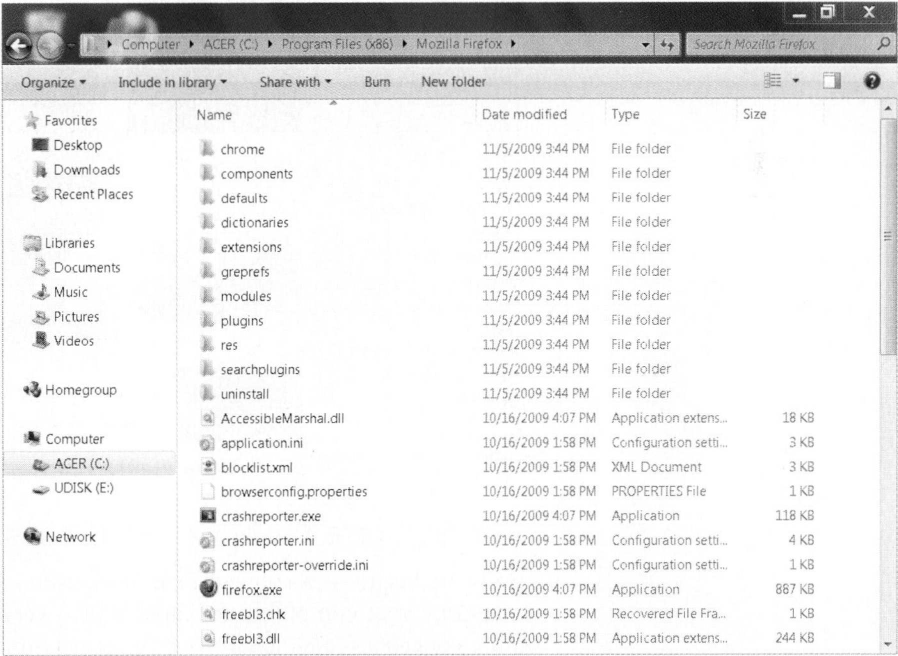

There are many ways to start or run executable files. The most common ways are to click an icon on the desktop, in the Windows Start menu, or on the Mac Dock or in Finder. When a program such as a word processor is started, machine-level program instructions are copied from the computer's disk drive, where they are permanently stored, into the computer's memory. Once in memory, the instructions are transferred to the processor and executed. As you create a document—for example, a newsletter including text in columns, images, and other features—the word processing software carries out the commands you specify and formats the document as you wish (see Figure 3.2). When you are finished, you can close the program and stop it from running in memory in a variety of ways, such as clicking the close button or selecting Quit from a menu. When you close the program, it is removed from the computer's memory. The computer's memory also contains part of the operating system and data that may be needed by the program.

FIGURE 3.2 • Using word-processing software

Software, like Microsoft Word shown here, is stored on the hard drive, runs in the computer's memory, and allows users to create, edit, print, and save documents.

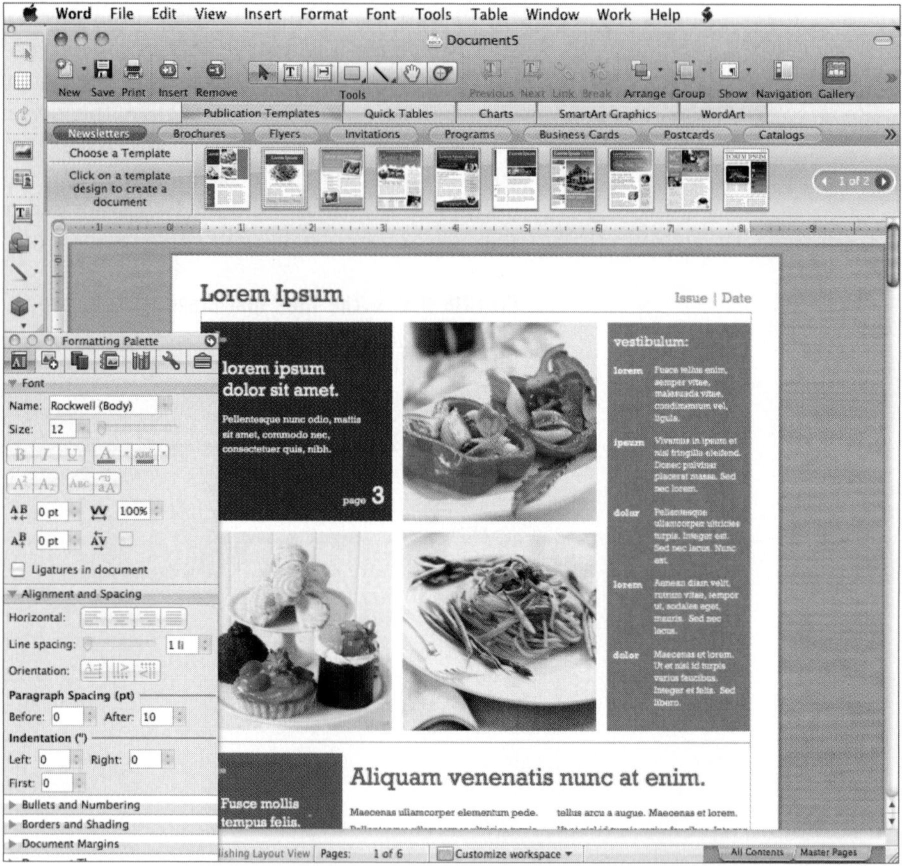

The Software Development Process

Software begins as a concept or idea for some new computer application. Understanding what computers are capable of is very useful in determining if a software concept is feasible. Software engineers understand how the processor carries out instructions and can follow that logic to develop a design for the software.

There are several tools that software engineers use to map out the logical design of software. When the engineer has developed a refined design for the software it is time to code it using instructions that the computer can follow. All software, both system software and application software, is written in coding schemes called programming languages. A **programming language**, the primary tool of software engineers, provides commands for writing software that are translated to the detailed step-by-step instructions executed by the processor to achieve an objective or solve a problem.

In the very early years of computing, writing computer programs was quite complex. The various switches and circuits that composed the computer hardware had to be manually set; that is, data was represented by physically switching various circuits on or off. In modern computers, however, the CPU works in conjunction with various software programs to control the digital circuitry. For this to occur, the CPU must receive signals from the computer program that it can convert into actions (the switching of the circuits on and off). Since these signals are not the actions themselves, but merely instructions that these actions should occur, they are called program code. *Program code* is the set of instructions that signal the CPU to perform circuit-switching operations. In the simplest coding schemes, a line of code typically contains a single instruction such as "Retrieve the data in memory address X." As discussed in Chapter 2, the instruction is then decoded during the instruction phase of the machine cycle.

A programming language includes sets of symbols and rules used to write program code. Like writing a report or a paper in English, writing a computer program in a programming language requires that the programmer follow a set of rules. Each programming language uses a set of symbols that have special meanings, much as English uses the Roman alphabet. Each language also has its own set of rules for how the symbols should be combined into statements capable of conveying meaningful instructions to the CPU. Programming involves translating what a user wants to accomplish into a logic that the computer can understand and execute.

Using a programming language, programmers create a *source code* file that is translated into an *object code* file that contains the machine-level instructions that the processor carries out. Most software is developed using a software tool called a compiler. A *compiler* takes source code, a program written in a programming language, and produces object code, with an executable file and supportive files, as output. Compilers are written to interpret specific programming languages. Figure 3.3 illustrates the compiling process for a simple password program written using the C++ programming language.

FIGURE 3.3 • Compiling code from source to object

A compiler takes source code (in this case, written in the C++ programming language) as input and outputs an executable file.

```
void main()
{
    char password[20] = "opensaysme";
    char input[20];
    while(strcmp(password, input)) {
        clrscr();
        cout << "\nPlease Enter The Password:";
        cin >> input;
    }
    cout << "\nWelcome, Oh Great One!\n";
    exit(1);
}
```

Source code file: Password.cpp

```
01000101001010100101010010010100111101
01001001010101001001000101001001001010
01001001001010100100101001010010100101
01010101010101010101010101010010100101
01001010101010101010010100101010010101
01010101010101010101010100101010100100
10101010101001010101010010101010010101
01010101010101001010101010010100101010
```

Object code file: Password.exe

Some programming languages use an *interpreter* rather than a compiler to create object code. An interpreter translates source code to object code one command at a time, while the software is executing. This technique is used in many of the programs that run in a Web browser and is the trademark of programs written with the Java programming language. Compiled programs typically run faster than interpreted programs. Most software sold commercially is compiled rather than interpreted.

Programming Languages

Programming languages have evolved since the early days of computing, and they continue to evolve. As shown in Table 3.2, the evolution of programming languages can be thought of in terms of generations of languages.

Although programming languages have evolved beyond four generations, most software is developed using variations of third-level languages. Fourth-generation languages are used primarily for database manipulation and queries. Fifth-generation languages, sometimes called artificial intelligence languages, are not yet advanced enough to provide programmers with the power and control of third-generation languages.

Thousands of large books have been written about programming languages and software engineering; the subject area is immense. In this section, you will be introduced to the most fundamental and important concepts in only a few paragraphs. The following are a few tools and approaches that have become widely adopted by software engineers and are changing the way software is developed and improving the resulting products.

TABLE 3.2 • The evolution of programming languages

Generation	Language	Introduced	Sample statement or action
First	Machine language	1940s	00010101
Second	Assembly language	1950s	MVC
Third	High-level languages such as Pascal, COBOL, C, C++, and Java	1960s	balance = balance + deposit;
Fourth	Query and database languages such as SQL, FOCUS, and NATURAL	1970s	PRINT EMPLOYEE NUMBER IF GROSS PAY > 1000
Beyond fourth	Natural and intelligent languages such as Prolog, OPS5, and Mercury	1980s	IF certain medical conditions exist, THEN a specific diagnosis is made

Visual Programming. *Visual programming* uses a graphical or "visual" interface for software development combined with programming language text-based commands. Prior to visual programming, programmers were required to describe the windows, buttons, text boxes, and menus that they were creating for an application by using only text-based programming language commands. With visual programming, the software engineer drags and drops graphical objects such as buttons and menus onto the application form. Then, using a programming language, the programmer defines the capabilities of those objects in a separate code window. *Visual Basic* was one of the first visual programming interfaces. Today software engineers use Visual Basic .NET, Visual C++, Visual C# (# is pronounced "sharp" as in music), Visual J#, and other visual programming tools.

EXPAND YOUR KNOWLEDGE

To learn more about visual programming, go to www.cengage.com/computerconcepts/np/swt4. Click the link "Expand Your Knowledge" and then complete the lab entitled "Visual Programming."

Many people refer to visual programming interfaces such as Visual C# as visual programming "languages." This is fine for casual references, but in truth there is a lesser-known category of programming language that claims the title "visual." A true *visual programming language* allows programmers to create software by only manipulating programming elements graphically without the use of any text-based programming language commands. Examples include Alice, Mindscript, and Microsoft Visual Programming Language used for programming robotics. Visual programming languages are ideal for teaching novices the basics about programming without the need to memorize programming language syntax.

Integrated Programming Environments. The majority of software used today is created using an integrated development environment. An *integrated development environment*, or *IDE*, combines all the tools required for software engineering into one package. For example, the popular IDE Microsoft Visual Studio includes an editor that supports several visual programming interfaces and languages, a compiler and interpreter, programming automation tools, a debugger—a tool for assisting the software engineer in finding errors in the code—and other tools that provide convenience to the developer (see Figure 3.4).

FIGURE 3.4 • A Microsoft Visual Studio project

Microsoft Visual Studio is a popular IDE for creating today's software.

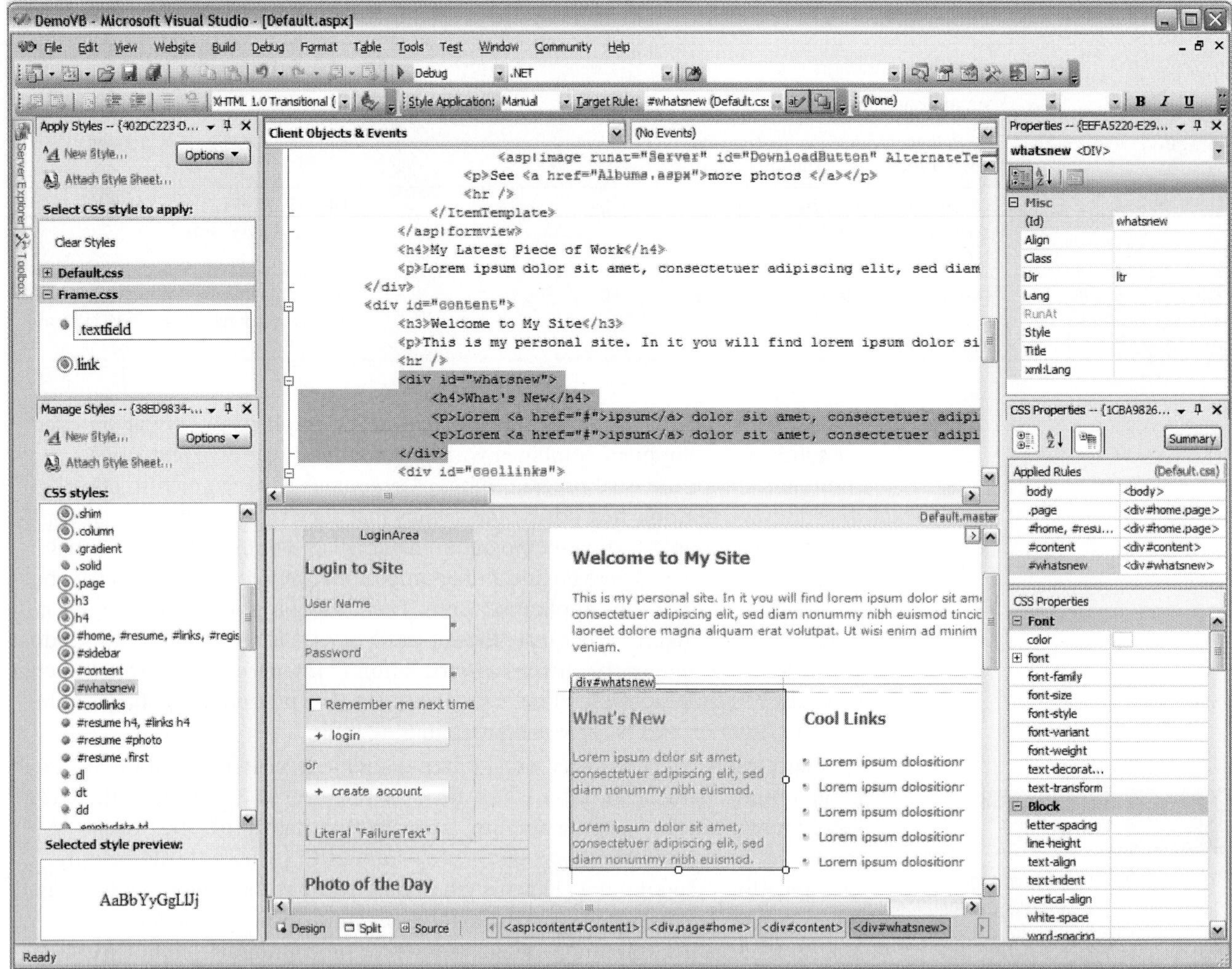

Object-Oriented Programming. *Object-oriented programming languages* are based on the creation and interaction of reusable programming objects. Examples include Visual Basic .NET, C++, C#, Java, Perl, and Python. In object-oriented programming, data, instructions, and other programming procedures are grouped together, or encapsuluated, in reusable *objects*. Objects are linked together in a manner that creates a useful program: one object's output serves as another object's input.

Object-oriented programming has become the dominant programming paradigm. Programs are developed by breaking down solutions into a series of steps for which objects are created. Unlike traditional procedural programming where software development starts on a blank page, object-oriented development begins with the engineer collecting objects from object libraries, arranging them, and filling in gaps with new objects, to create a new and unique program (see Figure 3.5). Object-oriented programming is so popular because of the time it saves.

FIGURE 3.5 • Object-oriented programming

By combining existing program objects with new ones, programmers can quickly and easily develop new object-oriented programs.

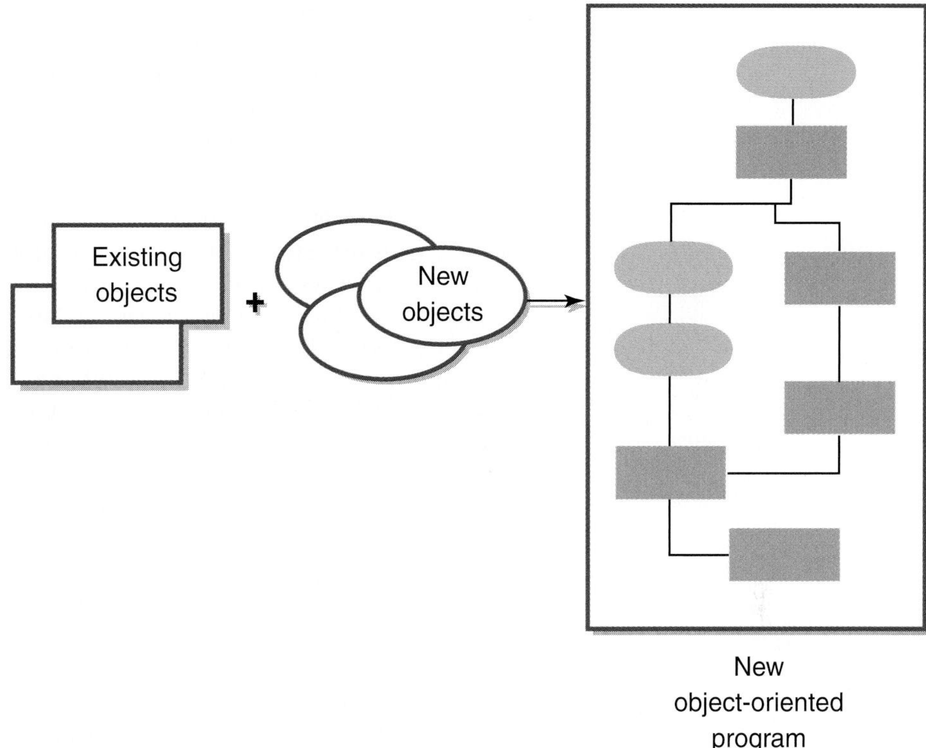

Web Services. You've probably observed that much of the software that you interact with is accessed through a Web browser. Increasingly, software engineers are developing software to run over the Internet rather than on a stand-alone PC. Web Services is the technology of choice for developing such software.

A **Web service** is a software system that automates tasks by controlling communication between computers over the Internet. Through Web services, software developers are able to provide tools to automate trivial or repetitive tasks that traditionally require human interaction. For example, Microsoft has developed a calendar service that allows users to share their appointment books with others on the Web. Using this service, you could easily make appointments with your dentist, hairstylist, or mechanic through your Web browser without the need to speak with a receptionist (see Figure 3.6).

FIGURE 3.6 • Web services

A calendar Web service running on your home PC could interact with the calendar Web service installed on a computer in the dentist's office to allow you to make an appointment without the need to speak to a receptionist.

Web services are becoming increasingly important in online transactions because they are ideal for automating the exchange of information between computer systems. For example, a manufacturer could use a Web service to order materials from a supplier. The Web service on the supplier's system could then notify the manufacturer of whether the item is in stock and when to expect delivery.

Web services have, in no small manner, contributed to the distribution of work subprocesses across different locations, which has in turn contributed to outsourcing and the rise of the global workforce. Thanks to the Internet and Web services, companies are able to outsource portions of their work processes to the lowest bidder, which may be located anywhere in the world. Using Web services, a project can be managed from the home location while contributors around the world work together as though they were in the same room. Everyone involved in the production process has access to common resources through Internet connections and Web services.

Application Programming Interface (API). An **application programming interface (API)** is a set of programming tools provided to access an operating system or online service in order to create software based on that operating system or online service. The use of an API opens up a system or device so that others besides the manufacturer can develop software to run on the system or device. Without APIs, only Microsoft would develop software for Windows computers, only Apple would develop software for the Mac and iPhone, and only Sony would develop software for the Wii. APIs provide users with a rich variety of software.

An API might be restricted to one particular programming language, or it could support many languages. For example, Facebook designed its API for the PHP scripting language. Microsoft Windows, however, supports the use of many programming languages that can manipulate the Windows environment using the programming tools provided by the Windows API.

Some APIs are combined with an SDK. A *software development kit*, or *SDK*, is a programming environment designed to write software for a particular platform. Facebook, the iPhone, Google Maps, and Google Android all provide SDKs for creating software. The iPhone SDK is shown in Figure 3.7. Notice that the SDK provides an iPhone simulator that allows developers to test code.

APIs may be made publicly available or licensed to specific software developers. For example, the Wii API is available only to software companies that Sony has approved for developing software for its gaming console.

FIGURE 3.7 • Web services and distributed work processes

The iPhone software development kit provides convenient tools to develop and test iPhone applications.

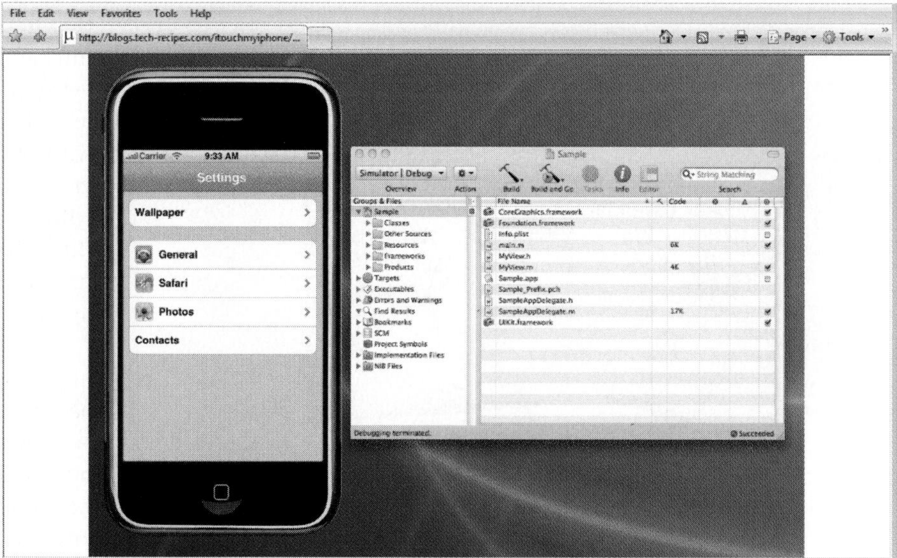

Software Copyrights and Licenses

Once created, software is considered the intellectual property of those who created it or paid to have it created. Like a book or song, software does not have a physical existence except for the media that holds it. It exists in digital form and can be easily copied and distributed. In order to control the use and distribution of software, most creators of software protect it with copyrights and licensing provisions.

A **copyright** defines exclusive rights legally granted to the owner. A **software license** defines the permissions, rights, and restrictions provided to the person who purchases a copy of the software. The two are legally tied together in that the copyright certifies certain rights to the owner and the license informs the buyer of what he or she can legally do with the software according to the copyright.

When you purchase software, in most cases, you don't actually own the software; rather, you are licensed to use the software on your computer. This is called a single-user license (see Figure 3.8). A **single-user license** permits the user to install the software on one computer, or sometimes two computers, used by one person. A single-user license does not allow you to copy and share the software with others. Table 3.3 describes different types of software licenses. Licenses that accommodate multiple users are usually provided at a discounted price.

FIGURE 3.8 • Single-user license

Most PC software will not allow the user to install the software without first clicking "I accept the terms in the License Agreement."

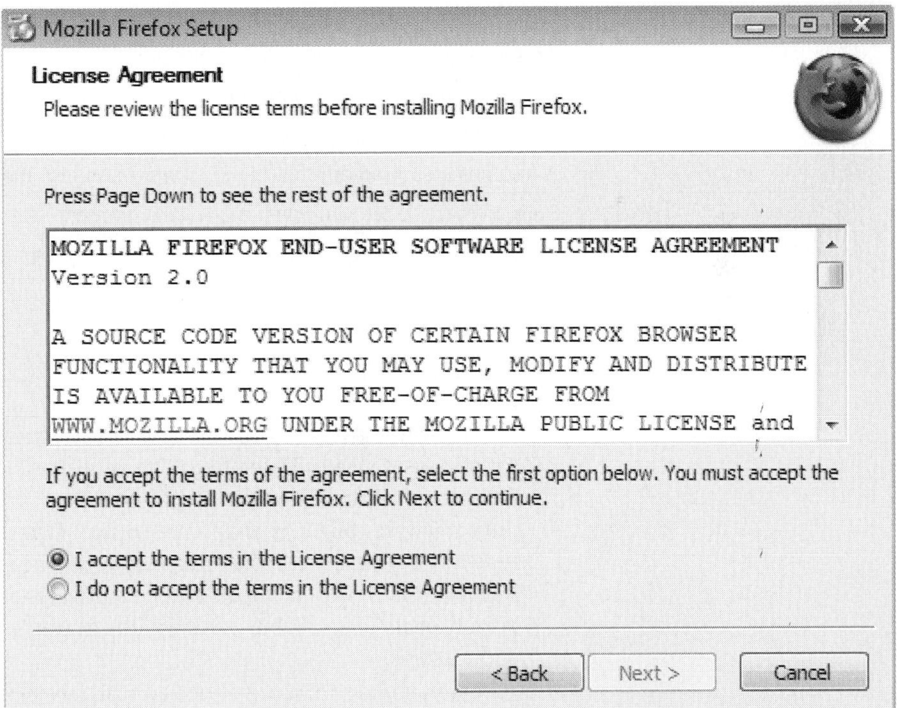

Freeware, Open-Source Software, and Alternative Licensing

Some software developers are less interested in profiting from their intellectual property and have developed alternative copyrights and licensing agreements. *Freeware* is software that is made available to the public for free. There are a number of reasons software developers might give away their product. Some wish to

TABLE 3.3 • Software licenses

License	Description
Single-user license	Permits the user to install the software on one computer, or sometimes two computers, used by one person
Multiuser license	Specifies the number of users allowed to use the software and can be installed on each user's computer; for example, a 20-user license can be installed on 20 computers for 20 users
Concurrent-user license	Designed for network-distributed software; allows any number of users to use the software but only a specific number of users to use it concurrently (at the same time)
Site license	Permits the software to be used anywhere on a particular site, such as a college campus, for everyone on the site

build customer interest and name recognition. Others simply don't need the money and wish to make a valuable donation to society. Still others, such as those associated with the Free Software Foundation (*www.fsf.org*), believe that all software should be free. Some freeware is placed in the *public domain* where anyone can use the software free of charge. Creative works that reach the end of their term of copyright revert to the public domain. Table 3.4 shows some examples of freeware.

TABLE 3.4 • Examples of freeware

Software	Description
Thunderbird	An e-mail and newsgroup software program
Pidgin	An instant messaging software program that runs on Windows and Linux operating systems
Adobe Reader	A free program used to read Adobe PDF files
AVG Anti-Virus	A free antivirus program that requires registration on the *www.stop-sign.com* Web site
WinPatrol	Free software to tell you when a spyware program tries to install itself on your computer
OpenOffice.org	A free and open-source suite of word processing, spreadsheet, presentation, and database programs
IrfanView	A free photo editor
Free games	Download free games at *www.download-free-games.com*

Freeware differs slightly from free software. Freeware simply implies that the software is distributed for free. The term *free software* was coined by Richard Stallman and the Free Software Foundation, and implies that the software is not only freeware, but it is also open source. **Open-source software** is distributed, typically for free, with the source code so that it can be studied, changed, and improved by its users. Open-source software evolves from the combined contribution of its users. Table 3.5 provides examples of popular open-source software applications.

Open-source software is not completely devoid of restrictions. Much of the popular free software in use today is protected by the *GNU General Public License (GPL)*. The GPL grants users the right to do the following:

- Run the program for any purpose
- Study how the program works and adapt it to your needs
- Redistribute copies so you can help the neighborhood
- Improve the program, and release improvements to the public

TABLE 3.5 • Examples of open-source software

Software type	Open-source example
Operating system	Linux
Application software	OpenOffice.org
Database software	MySQL
Internet browser	Mozilla Firefox
Instant messaging	Jabber
Internet TV viewer	Miro
Graphics	GIMP

Software under the GPL is typically protected by a copyleft (a play on the word copyright), which requires that any copies of the work retain the same license. A copylefted work cannot be owned by any one person, and no one is allowed to profit from its distribution. The Free Software Directory (*http://directory.fsf.org*) lists over 5000 software titles in 22 categories licensed under the GPL.

One other type of alternative license is the Creative Commons license (*http://creativecommons.org*). The **Creative Commons license** is designed to allow the creators of intellectual property to specify the terms of the license in order to grant certain freedoms to users, while still providing the owner with some control of the property and the ability to profit from distribution of the work. For example, the Creative Commons license requires that the original creator be given credit in any copies of the work. The owner of the property can select to allow or disallow any free commercial use of the work, or modifications to the work. The Creative Commons approach falls somewhere between traditional licensing that doesn't allow any copying or altering, and the GPL that allows any amount of copying and altering. Artists who use Creative Commons like it because it allows them to earn a living from the distribution of their works, while encouraging others to build on their creativity.

Wired magazine and Flavorpill.net hosted a concert in New York City to raise money for Creative Commons. The sold-out show featured Girl Talk, DJ Diplo, Peeping Tom, Missing Pieces, and other artists who use and support the Creative Commons form of licensing. Many musicians use Creative Commons licensing for their music (Figure 3.9), some of which is distributed each year on a free Creative Commons promotional CD.

FIGURE 3.9 • Creative Commons

David Byrne from the Talking Heads performs at the Creative Commons benefit concert.

Creative Commons is the brainchild of Stanford University law professor Lawrence Lessig, who is concerned that traditional forms of copyright and licensing are strangling creativity in modern culture. Dr. Lessig's book *Free Culture* has started a movement, especially popular with college students, called the Free Culture Movement. Students for Free Culture (*freeculture.org*) is an organization that "promotes the public interest in intellectual property and information & communications technology policy."

Acquiring Software

Personal computer users are accustomed to downloading or purchasing software in a store. This type of software is called *off-the-shelf software*; it is mass-produced for general public use. Businesses may find it necessary to have *custom software* developed to meet their unique and specific needs. It is also possible to modify some off-the-shelf software for the best of both worlds.

Off-the-Shelf Software. Most essential software comes preinstalled on a PC when you purchase it. New PCs come with an operating system, a Web browser, media software, a word processor, security software, assorted accessory software, and perhaps more. Many users enjoy other unique software that does not come preloaded and that they must purchase and install themselves. Businesses and organizations typically buy bare-bones systems on which they add their own software. Over the life of a PC many programs are added and removed according to the needs and whims of the user.

Off-the-shelf software gets its name from being available on store shelves. Stores like Best Buy, Staples, and Wal-Mart provide dozens of software titles in their stores (see Figure 3.10). These stores and many others stock thousands of titles in their online stores. Software, like books, is a perfect product for selling online; since it isn't something you have to physically handle in order to decide to buy it. Many software applications can be downloaded directly from the distributor and put immediately to use, saving the shopper the need to drive to a store. You can also easily comparison shop and find the best price online. All of these reasons contribute to the increasing trend of purchasing software online rather than from a brick-and-mortar store.

FIGURE 3.10 • Off-the-shelf software

Stores like Best Buy and Staples stock dozens of software titles, but many more are available online.

When you acquire PC software, it is wise to check the software documentation to make sure that your computer meets the storage, processor, and memory requirements to run the software. This information, often called *system requirements*, is usually printed on the outside of the box that contains the software or on the Web page from which you download the software. Be warned! With almost all store-bought software, once you open the box, you cannot return it for a refund.

Some software manufacturers take advantage of the ability to distribute software online by offering free samples. **Shareware** is a marketing method for distributing software that allows customers to use software free of charge for a limited time in order to evaluate the software and decide if they wish to purchase it. Sometimes called the "try before you buy" marketing model, shareware typically gives the user 30 days to use and evaluate the software for free. After 30 days, a registration fee is required for continued use of the product. Most shareware software is relatively inexpensive, with registration fees in the range of $15 to $80. Some fairly expensive software is distributed as shareware as well. For example, Adobe Photoshop can be downloaded and used for free for 30 days, but costs $999.99 to register. One good source for shareware is *www.shareware.com*.

A new model for software distributions is the *subscription model*. Rather than purchasing the software with a one-time fee, with a software subscription you pay an annual fee for as long as you wish to use the software. This model is ideal for software such as virus protection that requires continuous updates. For example, McAfee VirusScan Plus for Microsoft Windows has a yearly subscription rate of $44.99 to protect up to three PCs. Each time your PC connects to the Internet your virus protection is updated, and any software upgrades are automatically installed. Some believe that the subscription model, and more generally, a pay-per-use model, may be the trend of the future. For someone who uses presentation software only a couple of times a year, paying $10 to download and use PowerPoint for a week just prior to a big presentation would mean big savings over having to purchase and own the software for $198.

As Web development tools become more powerful and network speeds increase, you may not need to install any application software on your computer;

you can just run it from your Web browser. Consider Google Docs, which allows users to create, edit, and share word-processing documents, spreadsheets, and presentations through a Web-based interface (see Figure 3.11). While Google Docs is not as powerful as full-blown products like Microsoft Word and Excel, it is a simple and convenient way to access and share basic documents over the Internet.

FIGURE 3.11 • Web-based software: Google Docs, Spreadsheets, and Presentation

Google Docs, Spreadsheets, and Presentation are free Web-based applications that provide all the tools needed to create basic documents without having to install software on your own PC.

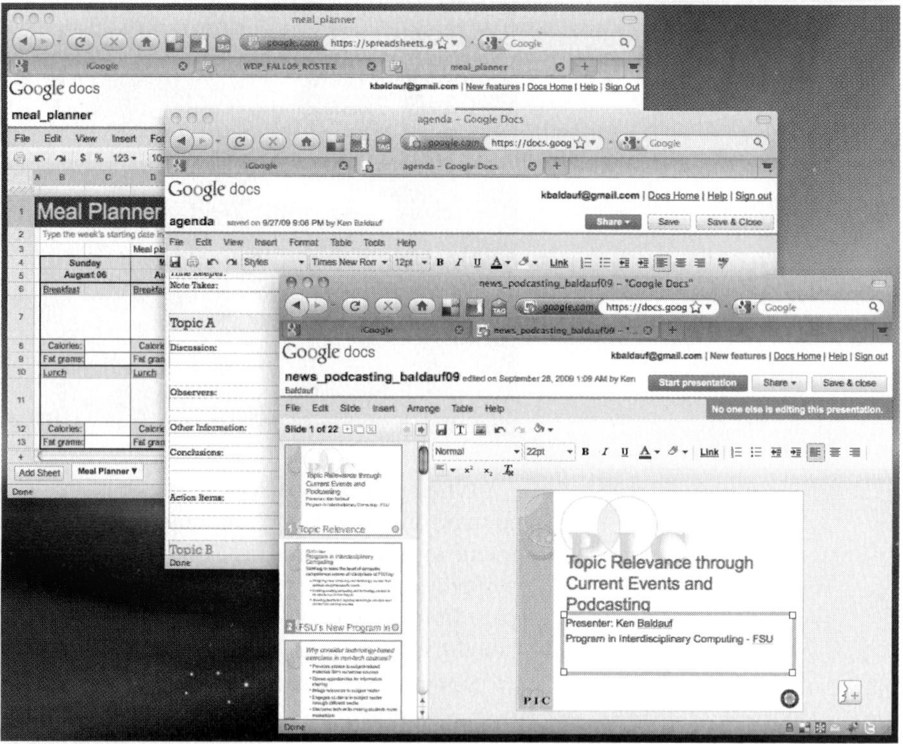

Applications delivered using a Web interface are sometimes referred to as *rich Internet applications* or *RIAs*. Many companies, including Microsoft, are moving to deliver RIAs. Microsoft Office Web Apps were released in 2009 to support online sharing and editing of Microsoft Office documents. Table 3.6 lists several popular RIAs.

TABLE 3.6 • Rich Internet Application (RIA) examples

RIA	Use
Google Docs: *docs.google.com*	Word processing, spreadsheets, presentations, online forms
Google Calendar: *www.google.com/calendar*	Calendaring, scheduling
37signals: *37signals.com*	Project management, customer relationship management (CRM), personal information management (PIM)
Zoho: *www.zoho.com*	Productivity apps, project management, CRM, PIM, and more
SlideRocket: *www.sliderocket.com*	High-end presentations (for fee)
Adobe Buzzword: *buzzword.acrobat.com*	Word processing
Nozbe: *www.nozbe.com*	To-do list manager
Adobe Photoshop Express: *www.photoshop.com*	Photo editing
Aviary: *aviary.com*	Image and audio/music editing

Safelite Goes Paperless and Wireless

If you've ever had a cracked windshield, you've probably heard of the Safelite AutoGlass corporation. The company has 1,800 technicians that make "house calls" to repair and replace millions of automobile windows annually. Until recently, Safelite was a paper-driven company. Technicians picked up paperwork from Safelite offices, and submitted completed work orders with associated paperwork at the end of the day for financial processing. In between, Safelite technicians were continuously checking in with the office, providing schedule updates, ordering glass, and checking credit card validity.

Safelite VP of IT Rod Ghani convinced Safelite to replace the paperwork with wireless technologies and sophisticated software. Ghani equipped each technician with a BlackBerry smart phone and a mobile card scanner/printer. Over the course of six months, Ghani's IT department developed automated systems for dispersing job orders to technicians, processing and collecting transaction data, and tracking technicians using GPS. Ghani's team combined the BlackBerry's proprietary software with their own custom software to create the ideal tool for Safelite technicians and managers.

Today, Safelite technicians begin each day by checking their customer itinerary on their BlackBerry calendar. Technician progress is tracked throughout the day, and customers are contacted by the call center in the event that a technician falls behind schedule. As the technician completes each job, the customer's credit card is swiped, the transaction is wirelessly transferred to the Safelite office, and a receipt is provided. Orders for glass and parts can be placed directly into the Safelite inventory system using custom software on the BlackBerry. The BlackBerry provides several modes of communication, including voice and e-mail, but there is rarely a need for a technician to phone the office anymore. This valuable software solution has reduced paperwork and phone calls at Safelite, increased productivity, streamlined administration, and made for happier customers.

Questions

1. What challenges do you imagine Safelite's VP of IT faced in selling company management and technicians on the totally new way of doing business?
2. What role did software play in providing valuable services to Safelite technicians?
3. It is difficult to implement software solutions without facing equally challenging hardware considerations. What hardware was necessary to empower the software used in Safelite's new systems?

Sources

1. *Blackberry Staff, "Safelite Autoglass," Blackberry Customer Success, accessed September 28, 2009, http://na.blackberry.com/eng/newsroom/success/safelite.jsp.*
2. *Safelite Web site, accessed September 28, 2009, www.safelite.com.*

One problem with online applications is they are unavailable if the user is unable to connect to the Internet. To counter this problem, Google created a technology called Google Gears that allows its online apps to run on PCs even if they are disconnected from the Internet. Copies of files are synched between the PC and Google servers to provide continuous access to files and services. Microsoft Office Web Apps work hand-in-hand with Office Apps installed on the user's PC.

Some developers are working on moving the entire experience online. With a *Web-based operating system,* also called a *WebOS,* your operating system, software, and data files all reside on a Web server. The device you use to access your computing environment (formerly called a PC) contains only software to connect to the WebOS. Using such a system would allow you to access your computing environment from any Internet-connected device. While this form of computing has promise, it depends on pervasive and fast Internet connections. Two Web OSs free for use are icloud (*icloud.com*) and EyeOS (*eyeos.org*). These online operating systems come with a number of applications including file management, word processing, calendar, contacts, Web browser, calculator, notepad, and games, with many other applications being developed for the open-source platform.

Custom Software. For common computing activities such as word processing, listening to music, watching videos, and crunching numbers, users benefit from purchasing off-the-shelf software. The popular word processors, media players, and spreadsheet software being marketed today have years of development behind them and the input of dozens or even hundreds of software engineers. However, when a company discovers that there is no off-the-shelf software available to meet a particular need, it must invest time and money in developing custom software. New custom software does not benefit from years of testing but is an essential component in a business's competitive strategy.

A publishing company, for example, might want to develop customized software to deliver course material over the Internet. In some cases, this leads to in-house software development, during which the organization's software engineers are responsible for all aspects of developing the necessary programs. In other cases, customized software can be obtained from external vendors. For example, a third-party software firm, sometimes called a *value-added software vendor*, may develop or modify a software program to meet the needs of a particular industry or company. A specific software program developed for a particular company or organization is called *contract software*. See Figure 3.12.

FIGURE 3.12 • Custom software

Custom software was designed to provide this online practice test on the material in this chapter at the textbook Web site.

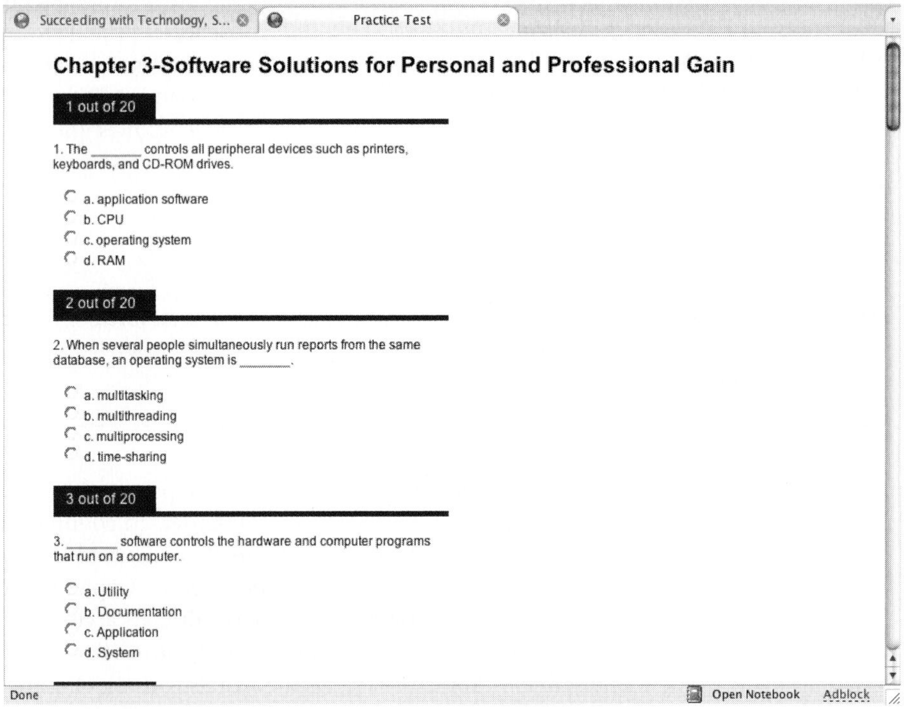

For many businesses and organizations, software acquisition involves a combination of purchasing off-the-shelf software, altering some off-the-shelf software, and creating some custom software. A case in point is an online collaboration system developed for MTV Networks. MTV Networks employs 7000 people around the world. Until recently, the company utilized paper-based systems for processing new employees, financial auditing, project updates, and other business systems. MTV Networks decided to go paperless with these systems by purchasing and customizing Microsoft SharePoint, a popular business intelligence document management system. MTV's own software engineers customized SharePoint to deliver MTV-specific services to its locations around the world. The result is much reduced time and effort for company employees, and increased savings for the company.[1]

EXPAND YOUR KNOWLEDGE

To learn more about installing and uninstalling software, go to www.cengage.com/computerconcepts/np/swt4. Click the link "Expand Your Knowledge" and then complete the lab entitled "Installing and Uninstalling Software."

Installing New Software, Handling Bugs, and Removing Old or Unwanted Software

In order to enjoy the benefits of software and maintain a healthy system, three activities are typically required: installing the software, dealing with bugs, and removing the software. This section provides an overview of these activities.

Installing New Software. Installing new software is usually straightforward (see Figure 3.13). Software for personal computers typically comes on CDs or is downloaded as a compressed file from the Web. Table 3.7 provides the steps of a typical installation process.

FIGURE 3.13 • Installing new software

These screens show four points in the typical process of installing new software on a Windows PC.

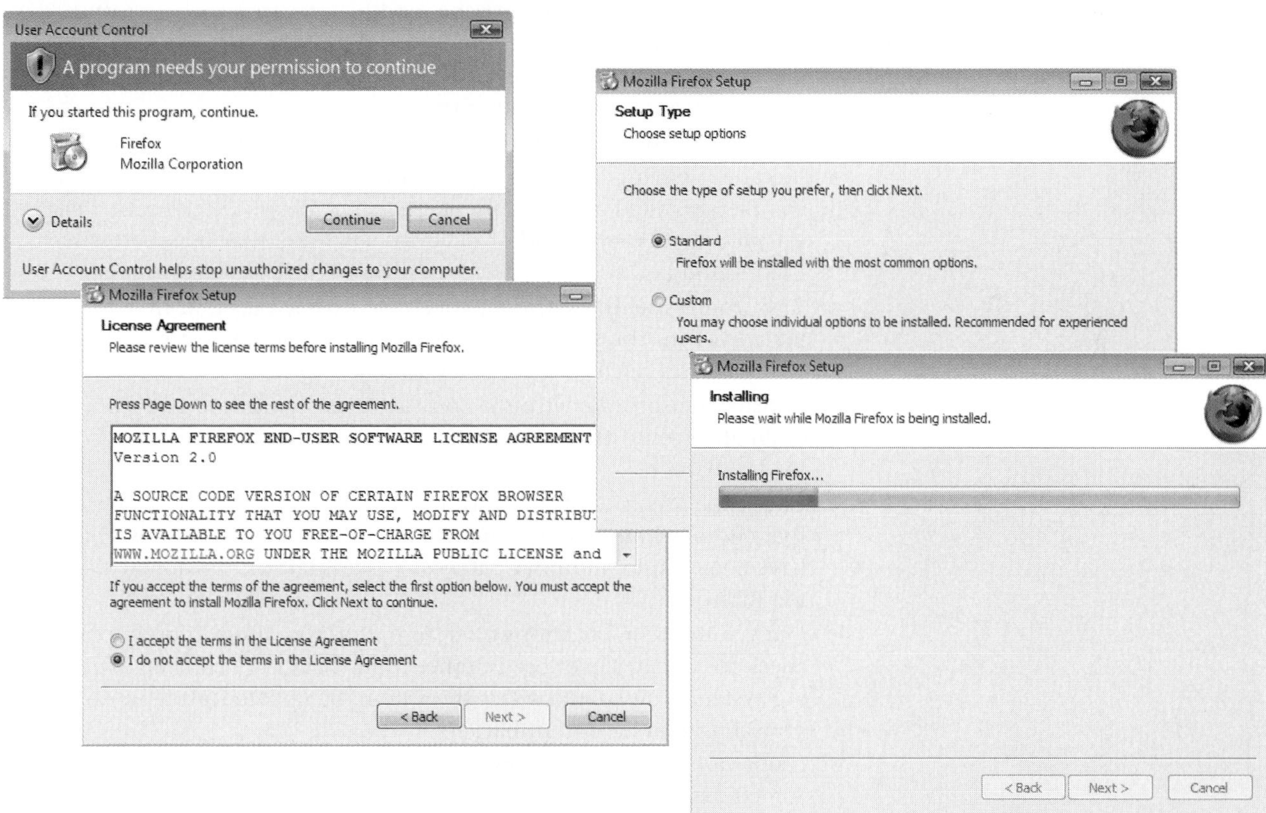

Once the software is installed, you will find launch icons to start the software on either your desktop, start menu, or wherever your particular operating system stores its applications.

Handling Software Bugs. **Software bugs** consist of one or more defects or problems that prevent the software from working as intended or working at all. Software can contain thousands or millions of lines of computer code, so it can

TABLE 3.7 • Installing software

1. Run the installation file	Place the CD that contains the software in the computer's CD drive, or double-click the installation file that you downloaded. In most cases, the software installation process will start immediately. If not, the instructions that come with the software will lead you through what is needed, depending on your computer and its operating system. Software that is downloaded from the Web will include instructions for installation at the Web site or in an associated README text file.
2. Interact with the installation wizard	Once the installation process has begun, follow the instructions as they appear on the screen. You will likely be given choices during the installation. Most software products have recommended default installation settings. *Default settings* are those chosen in advance for you as typical settings.
3. Agree to license	You will probably be asked to agree to the terms of the software license. You have no choice if you wish to install the software; you cannot progress without agreeing.
4. Select install location	You may be asked where on your hard drive you wish to install the software. Unless you have an unusual system, the default choice is best.
5. Choose standard or custom	You may be asked whether you wish Standard installation or Custom installation. Standard installation installs the most commonly used components of the software, or perhaps all of it. Custom installation allows you to select which components of the software you wish to install.
6. Register and/or activate the software	Once the software is installed, you might have to register or activate the software before it can be used. This is usually done over the Internet.

be very difficult to remove all bugs before it is made available to the public. Software companies often provide patches and updates to overcome software bugs. For example, bugs and security holes are found in Microsoft Windows fairly frequently and Microsoft issues **software patches**, software updates that are designed to correct them each month.

Here are some things you can do to overcome pesky software bugs:

- Be careful buying or acquiring the latest software before it has been completely tested and used by others. Some people would rather get software that is a year old or older to make sure that most errors have been found and fixed.
- After you install the software, check the *readme* files that may be included with the software. These files often contain last-minute updates or disclosures, including bugs and how to deal with them.
- Register the software with the software maker. Software companies will often alert you if there is a problem or bug and give you steps to follow to eliminate it.
- Check the Web site of the software vendor often. There can be updates that eliminate any known bugs. In addition, vendors often list bugs that have been found and offer patches or fixes that can be downloaded over the Internet.
- Many software applications offer an option to manually or automatically check for updates over the Internet from within the software. For operating systems you should select the automatic update feature in order to protect your system from hackers.
- If software is malfunctioning, try running the setup program again. Sometimes it contains a utility to fix software problems. If it doesn't have such an option, you can try uninstalling and reinstalling the software.
- Check with popular online technology news services such as *cnet.com*, which often have articles on software bugs and possible solutions.
- If all else fails, carefully document exactly what happened when you found the bug and then contact the software vendor for a solution.

Removing (Uninstalling) Software. Operating systems provide a method for safely and completely removing software from the system. In Microsoft Windows, you use the "Uninstall a program" feature to assist you in removing software (see Figure 3.14). In Mac OS, you simply drag the program icon from the Applications window to the trashcan. Since software maintains a presence in many areas of a system, it is important to use proper procedures in order to remove all components. Sometimes even with proper procedures, software does not uninstall correctly, creating system problems. This is especially a problem for Windows users and is addressed by a number of system utilities. Norton SystemWorks and McAfee QuickClean are examples of utilities that help eliminate unwanted elements of software you have removed to help your system run smoothly.

FIGURE 3.14 • Removing software

Operating systems provide a method to safely and completely remove software from the system.

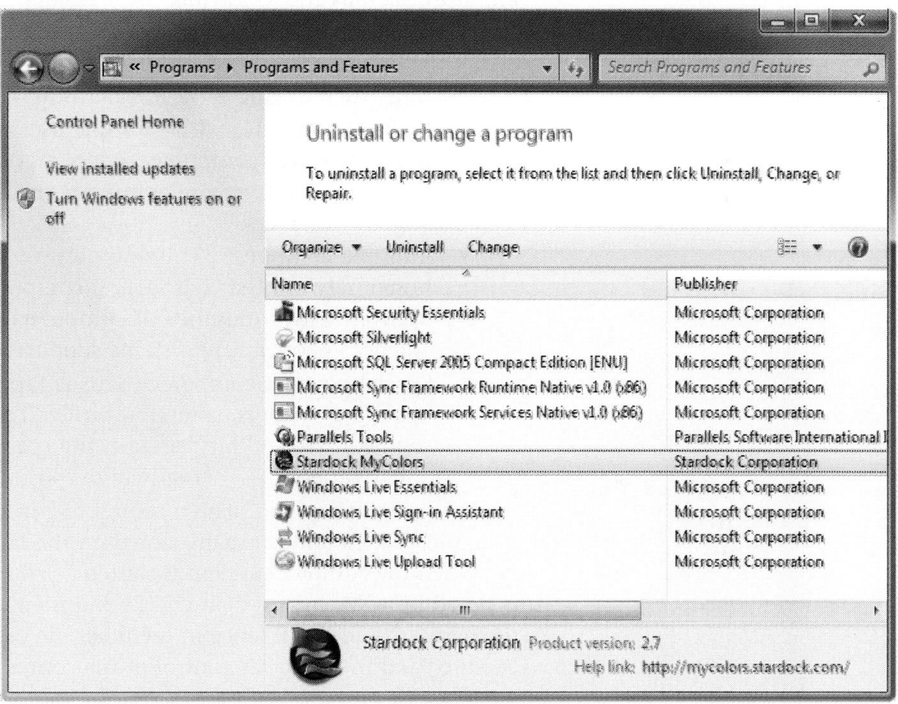

SYSTEM SOFTWARE

Controlling the operations of computer hardware is one of the most critical functions of system software. System software includes operating systems and utility programs that interact with the computer hardware and application software programs, creating a layer of insulation between the two.

Operating Systems

An **operating system (OS)** is a set of computer programs that runs or controls the computer hardware and acts as an interface with both application programs and users (see Figure 3.15). Operating systems can control one computer or multiple computers, or they can allow multiple users to interact with one computer.

FIGURE 3.15 • Operating systems

An operating system (OS) is a set of computer programs that runs or controls the computer hardware and acts as an interface with both application programs and users.

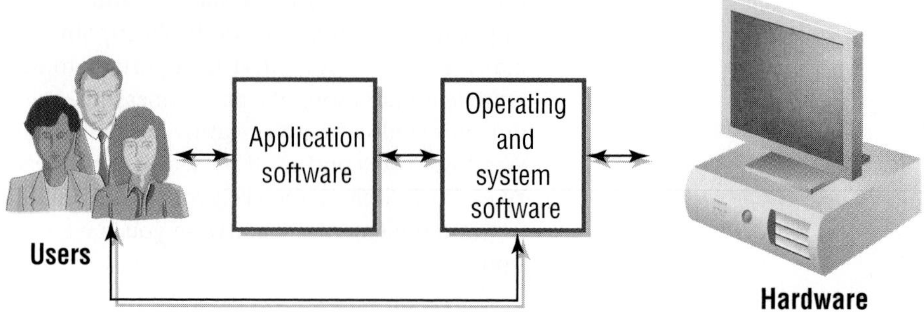

Operating systems are designed to support a variety of computer platforms and uses, such as the following:

- A single computer with a single user: This is typical of a personal computer (desktop, notebook, or smart phone) that supports one user at a time, such as Apple OS X, Microsoft Windows, or Google Android.
- A single computer with multiple users: This is typical of larger mainframe or server computers that can accommodate hundreds or thousands of people, all using the computer at the same time, such as z/OS for large IBM servers.
- Multiple computers: This is typical of a network of computers, such as a home network that has several computers attached or a large computer network with thousands of computers attached around the world. Today's PC operating systems support such networks.
- Special-purpose computers: This is typical of a number of special-purpose operating systems, sometimes called embedded systems, that control sophisticated military aircraft, the space shuttle, some home appliances, and a variety of other special-purpose computers.

The operating system plays a central role in the functioning of the complete computer system and is usually stored on the hard drive. In a desktop or notebook PC, when the computer system is started a process called the **boot process,** which is stored in ROM, runs system checks and then transfers the operating system from the hard drive to RAM. Once in memory, the operating system instructions are executed and the OS takes control of the computer. This is called *booting* the computer, and it can take several minutes. In handheld computers and smart phones, the operating system is stored in ROM. This combined with the smaller size of the operating system allows handheld devices to boot almost instantaneously.

Although it is most common to run just one operating system on a computer, it is possible to have two or more operating systems stored on a single computer by *partitioning* a hard disk to contain different operating systems. This can be useful when you need to run different programs or applications that require different operating systems on the same computer. When the computer starts, you are given the opportunity to choose which operating system to use. For example, a Windows PC might give you the option to boot into Ubuntu Linux, or a Mac might utilize Apple's Bootcamp software to provide an option to launch Windows 7 rather than Mac OS X. These scenarios are referred to as *dual booting* because you can boot into one of two operating systems.

Another option for utilizing multiple operating systems is virtualization. *Virtualization software,* also referred to as *virtual machine (VM) software,* allows one operating system to run on top of another by creating a virtual machine on which the guest operating system can run. For example, VirtualBox software from Sun allows Linux to run in a window while the computer is running Windows or Mac OS. It can allow Windows to run on a Mac, and practically any OS to run on any other. Figure 3.16 shows Windows running on a Mac desktop using Parallels Desktop VM software.

FIGURE 3.16 • Virtual machine software

Virtual machine software allows this Mac computer to run Microsoft Windows in a window running on Mac OS.

Because of the tremendous amount of resources required by two operating systems running simultaneously, VM software is most successful when run on more powerful PCs. Virtualization is also used on servers in order to make more efficient use of server resources.

Whichever and however many operating systems you choose to use, all operating systems perform certain similar tasks, such as controlling computer hardware, managing memory, managing the processor(s), controlling input and output devices, storing and manipulating files, and providing a user interface. Most operating systems today also provide networking features.

Providing a User Interface. One of the most important functions of any operating system is providing a user interface. A user interface allows one or more people to have access to and command of the computer system. The first user interfaces for mainframe and personal computer systems were command based (see Figure 3.17). A **command-based user interface** requires that text commands be typed at a prompt in order to perform basic tasks. For example, the command ERASE FILE1 would cause the computer to erase or delete a file named FILE1. RENAME and COPY are other examples of commands used to rename or copy files from one location to another. Most operating systems provide access to a *command prompt* to allow system administrators and advanced users to interact with the operating system through specific commands. However, the default user interface today is the graphical user interface.

FIGURE 3.17 • Command-based interface

A command-based user interface uses text commands to get the computer to perform basic or administrative activities.

```
Command Prompt
Copyright (c) 2006 Microsoft Corporation.  All rights reserved.

C:\Users\tyler>dir
 Volume in drive C is HP_PAVILION
 Volume Serial Number is 3443-D383

 Directory of C:\Users\tyler

05/19/2007  01:10 PM    <DIR>          .
05/19/2007  01:10 PM    <DIR>          ..
05/16/2007  04:56 PM    <DIR>          Contacts
05/28/2007  01:35 PM    <DIR>          Desktop
05/28/2007  01:02 PM    <DIR>          Documents
05/27/2007  05:52 PM    <DIR>          Downloads
05/27/2007  01:11 PM    <DIR>          Favorites
05/16/2007  04:56 PM    <DIR>          Links
05/19/2007  11:50 AM    <DIR>          Music
05/28/2007  01:28 PM    <DIR>          Pictures
05/16/2007  04:56 PM    <DIR>          Saved Games
05/16/2007  04:56 PM    <DIR>          Searches
05/20/2007  07:54 PM    <DIR>          Videos
               0 File(s)              0 bytes
              13 Dir(s)  138,327,076,864 bytes free

C:\Users\tyler>
```

A **graphical user interface (GUI)** makes use of a keyboard and mouse to manipulate graphics images on the display to issue commands to the computer system. A graphical user interface offers many advantages over a command-based user interface. For example, a GUI is very intuitive and easy to use. Often you can simply explore to figure out how to perform some task, and if you can't figure it out, help menus and wizards can assist you. A GUI allows you to view several applications at once and copy data between applications.

The most popular graphical user interfaces all include the same or similar features and functionality; however, the style of those features may differ from OS to OS (see Figure 3.18). For example, all current and popular PC GUI operating systems (Microsoft Windows, Mac OS, and Linux Desktop) include:

- Icons: Small pictures that can be clicked to issue a command
- A desktop: The main area of the display where work is done; may be decorated with attractive images (wallpaper or background) and icons for opening frequently used programs and documents
- Windows: Rectangular areas on the display that contain the running programs; can be moved, maximized, sized, and minimized
- Menus and dialog boxes: Devices for specifying parameters and issuing commands
- Information bar: Location on the desktop used to show which programs are currently running and to allow the user to switch between applications; typically associated with other functions as well (in Windows, called the Taskbar; in Mac, the Dock; in Linux, Panels)
- Program launch area: Where to go to launch applications (in Windows, called the Start Menu; in Mac, the Applications window and the Dock; in Linux, the Applications menu)

SMARTER STACK SEARCHES

Library users used to have to search paper-based card catalogs. Then computers arrived, and libraries begrudgingly transitioned to software that operated on the same old principles: look under C for cars, find nothing, look under A for automobiles, still nothing, and finally, as you tear out the last of your hair, there it is under V for vehicles. Universities are finally stepping up to the plate and developing smart software that will sort results by relevance, ask you questions like "Did you mean...", and even employ an indexing system that works a lot like Google.

After Losing Users in Catalogs, Libraries Find Better Search Software
Marc Parry
Chronicle of Higher Education
September 28, 2009
http://chronicle.com/article/After-Losing-Users-in-Catal/48588/

- File viewer and organizer: A place to view and organize your files, typically organized as Documents, Music, Videos, etc.
- System viewer: A place to view information about the computer and its resources (in Windows Vista and Linux, called Computer; in Mac, Finder)
- System settings: An interface for changing and customizing system settings like display resolution, wallpaper, screen saver, sound, security, users, etc.; (in Windows, the Control Panel; in Mac OS, System Preferences; in Linux, System)
- Network resources: A tool for viewing resources (other computers, printers, storage, etc.) on the network, if you are connected
- Gadgets or widgets (sometimes): Small programs such as clock, calculator, weather report, or stock ticker that are displayed on the desktop

FIGURE 3.18 • Microsoft Windows and Mac OS X

Microsoft Windows, Mac OS X, and other operating systems all include tools for launching applications, manipulating files, viewing system resources, and adjusting system settings.

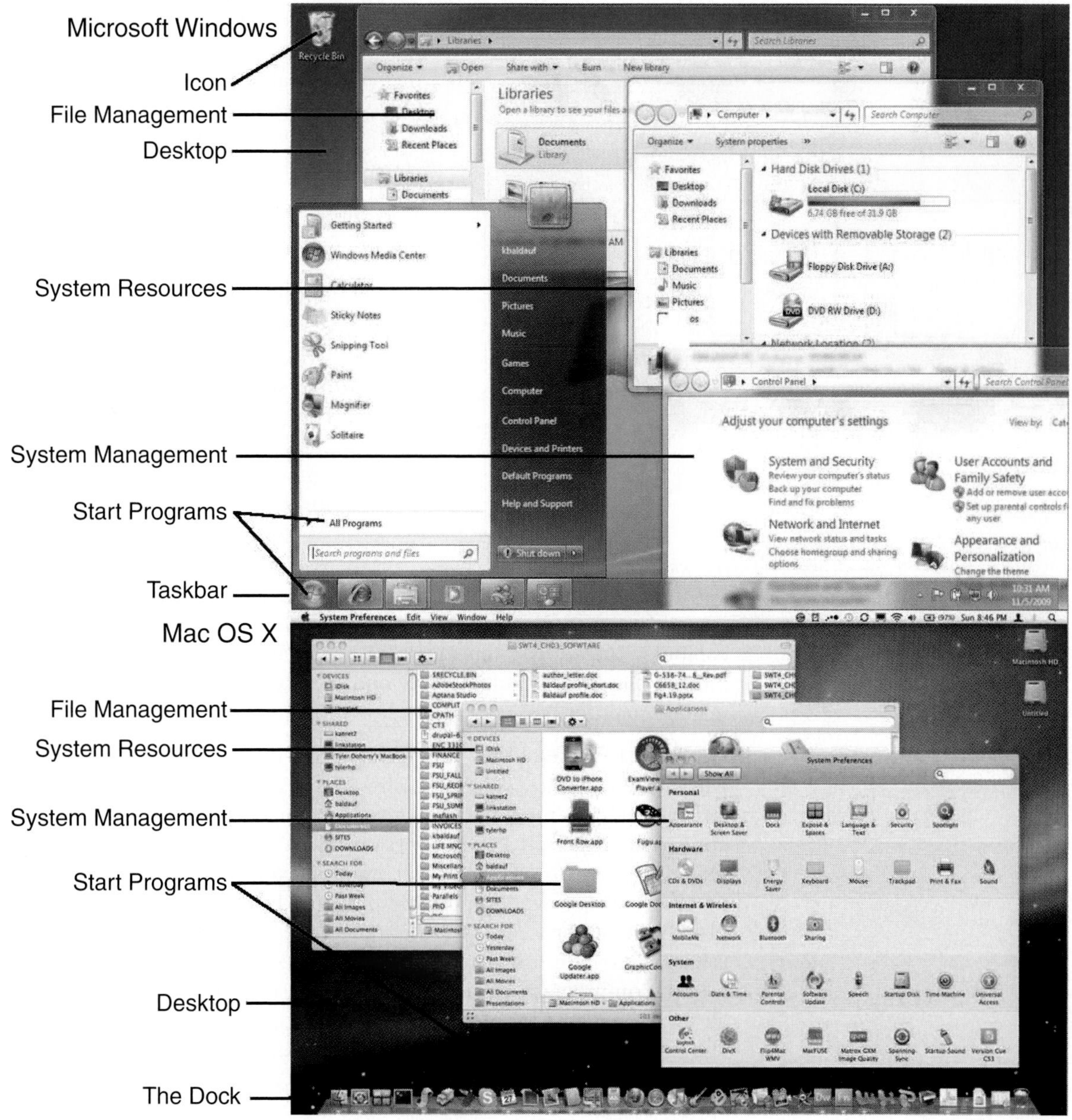

The user interface dictated by the OS makes it easy for users to learn new applications on one OS. But stylistic differences between operating systems can make it challenging for a user to switch from one OS to another. For example, a Windows user will be thrown off by Mac's interface that has maximize, minimize, and Close buttons on the left side rather than the right, and the fact that the Close button does not quit the application. Such challenges can be overcome with a little guidance and practice.

Controlling Common Computer Hardware Functions. Operating systems control many common hardware functions such as capturing user input and providing output; managing the processor, memory, and storage; formatting disks; and communicating with peripheral devices. Operating systems are designed to work with specific types of computers and processors. Application software is written to operate on a particular type of operating system, not on a particular type of computer (see Figure 3.19).

FIGURE 3.19 • System layers

The operating system interfaces with the hardware, controlling processing, storage, and I/O, and the application software interfaces with the operating system.

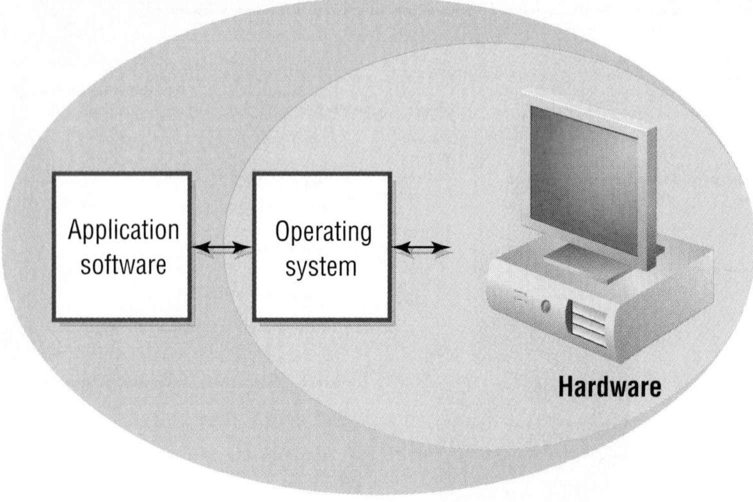

If a computer manufacturer creates a computer model with new and faster processor technologies, the operating system will need to be modified to control the new hardware; the application software is not affected. Having an OS layer that adapts to new and varied hardware allows software engineers to design many thousands of applications that can function on different types of hardware. This is sometimes referred to as *hardware independence*.

Managing Memory. Operating systems control how memory is accessed and work to maximize the use of memory and storage. These functions allow the computer to efficiently and effectively store and retrieve data and instructions and supply them to the CPU, thus speeding processing.

Many operating systems use *virtual memory*, or *virtual storage*, which allows users to store and retrieve more data without physically increasing the actual storage capacity of memory. Virtual memory extends standard memory by treating a portion of the disk drive as memory. Most computer operating systems make use of virtual memory to allow users to run more applications simultaneously and to maximize the efficiency of memory management for best performance.

Managing Processors. The OS controls the operation of all processors within the computer system. As discussed in Chapter 2, the processor must retrieve each instruction, decode it, and then execute it. In addition, most operating systems permit several programs to be running at the same time, each requiring processor resources. For example, you may be entering text through a keyboard using a word-processing program, be connected to the Internet and playing the latest songs by using a media player, have your appointments and calendar program open and running, and be printing the results from a tax preparation program, all at the same time. The operating system makes sure that all these programs access the computer's processor(s) in an efficient and effective manner. The operating system also makes sure that one program doesn't interfere with the operation of another program.

The ability of the OS to run several programs or tasks at the same time is called **multitasking** (see Figure 3.20). Some operating systems allow several users to use the same computer at the same time, which is called *time sharing*. Multitasking and time sharing work by assigning each of the billions of cycles per second of the system clock to different tasks or users. The speed at which the processor switches attention between multiple tasks or users makes it appear as though there are several processors, each devoted to a specific job.

FIGURE 3.20 • Multitasking

Today's operating systems support multitasking—running multiple applications simultaneously.

Managing Storage. The operating system keeps track of files stored on disk and manages all storage devices within and attached to the system. When you save a file to your hard drive or flash drive, or burn it to a CD or DVD, the operating system finds space on the device to store the file in an efficient manner and records the location so the file may be accessed later.

The storage-management portion of an OS converts a logical request for data into the physical location where the data is stored. A *logical view* of data is the way a user thinks about data; for example, C:/Documents/Homework/report.doc. With a logical view, the user doesn't have to know where the data is physically stored in the computer system. However, a computer is able to translate the logical view of data into the *physical view* of data; for example, hard disk, track 1, sector 3.

The operating system performs this task through the use of a *file system*, a way of organizing how data and files are physically stored and how they are logically manipulated. For example, older Windows operating systems used the *file allocation table (FAT)* file system, and newer and current Windows operating systems use *New Technology File System (NTFS)*. NTFS is a more secure and stable file system than FAT and supports better data recovery if there are problems. The Linux and UNIX operating systems use several different file systems such as ext3 or ufs.

Managing Input, Output, and Peripherals. Just as the OS manages the hardware inside the computer, it also manages and coordinates the use of input and output devices and other peripheral equipment. Today's computers usually have keyboards, pointing devices, printers, and display screens. Some users have other peripheral devices that can be attached as well, like game controllers, Webcams, and iPods. The operating system must manage all of these devices.

Any device that connects to a computer includes associated software called the **device driver** that must be installed in order for the operating system to recognize and communicate with the device (see Figure 3.21). For example, suppose you get a fancy new wireless mouse with extra buttons for controlling the volume on your media player. In order for the operating system to understand the unique controls that this mouse has, the device driver must be installed. The device driver is designed by the company that manufactures the peripheral device and is written for a particular operating system. For example, if you upgrade from one version of Windows to another, you may find that you need to download new device drivers for some of your devices in order for them to be recognized by the new OS. Device drivers can typically be found and downloaded at the Web site of the manufacturer. As with other software, it is useful to download and install upgrades for your device drivers when and if they become available.

FIGURE 3.21 • Devices and drivers

Windows provides a tool for viewing all the devices on the computer and updating their drivers.

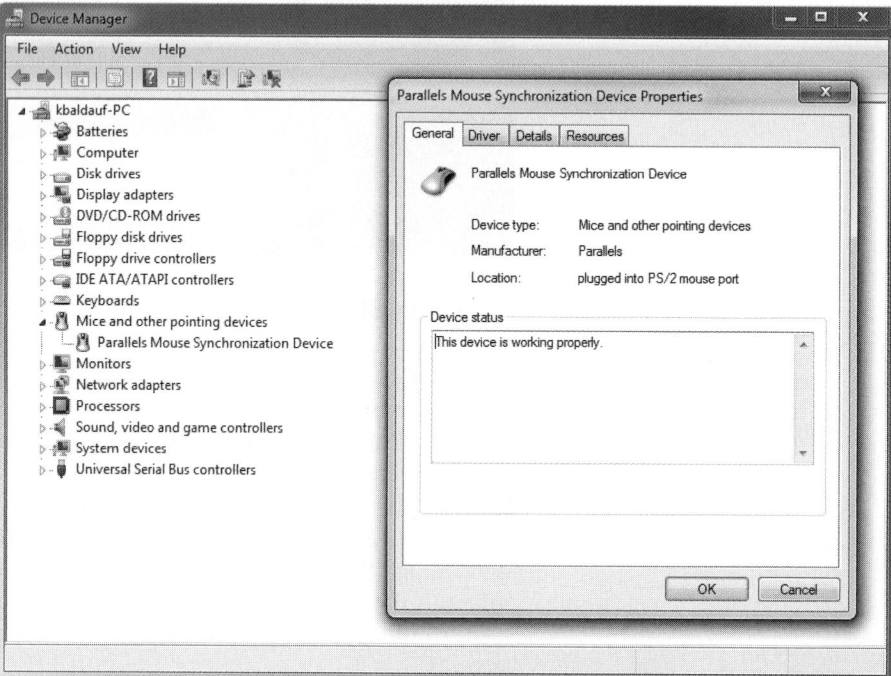

Managing Files. Operating systems provide tools and mechanisms for managing files on a computer (see Figure 3.22). Windows users make use of a program named Documents to manage their files, while Mac users use Finder. All computers store and manipulate files that can contain data, instructions, or both. Operating systems allow you to organize files into folders, sometimes referred to as directories. Folders can hold one or more files. Organizing files into folders or subfolders makes it much easier to locate files, compared to having all files in one large folder or directory. Lists of files on a computer can be viewed alphabetically, by size, by type, or even by the date they were created or last modified. In addition, operating systems allow files to be copied from hard disks to portable media such as USB drives and CD-Rs. This feature is essential for keeping accurate and current backup files. File management can protect certain files from unwanted users; one approach is to use secure passwords and identification numbers. OS file-management features also allow you to search for files in various folders or directories using keywords or even partial words.

FIGURE 3.22 • File management: Microsoft Windows

Microsoft Windows provides many options for viewing lists of files, including thumbnail images for photographs.

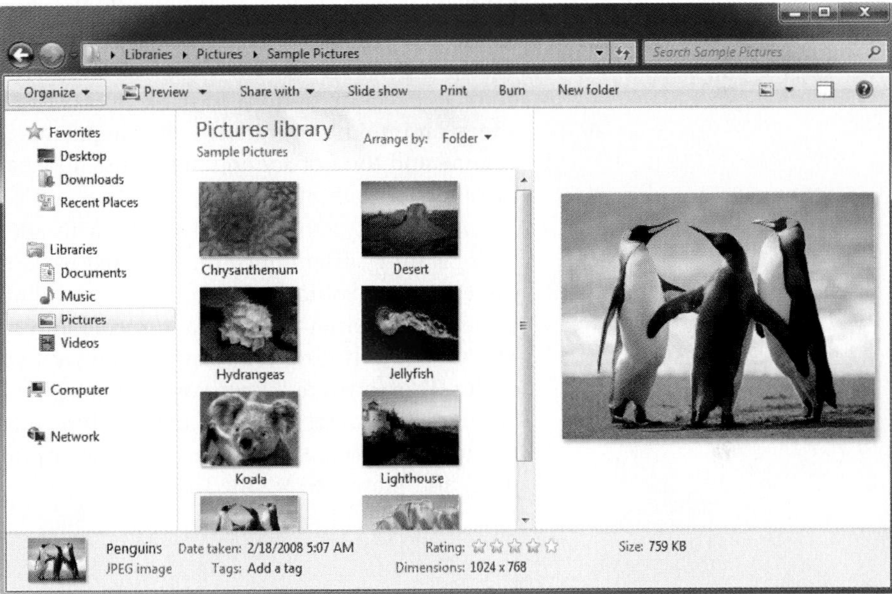

Each OS file system has conventions that specify how files can be named and organized (see Table 3.8). In Windows, for example, filenames can be 256 characters long, both numbers and spaces can be included in the filename, and uppercase and lowercase letters can be used. Linux doesn't permit spaces in filenames, and certain characters, such as \, *, >, and <, cannot be used. File systems also specify how files can be organized in folders or subfolders.

TABLE 3.8 • Conventions or rules for filenames

Convention (Rule)	Windows	Macintosh	Linux
Length in characters	256	256	255
Case sensitive?	No	Yes	Yes
Can numbers be used?	Yes	Yes	Yes
Can spaces be used?	Yes	Yes	No

Managing Network Functions. Many of today's operating systems, including ones for personal computers, allow multiple computers to be connected together, sharing disk space, printers, and other computer resources. From personal computers to huge networks of large mainframe computers, network management features of today's operating systems allow computers to work efficiently and effectively together. In Microsoft Windows or Mac OS X, you simply click the Network icon to view resources available on your current network.

Today's personal computer operating systems also include wireless networking capabilities. Most notebooks are equipped with wireless network adapters and antennas that let you know when a public wireless network is within range and then assist you in connecting.

Other Operating System Functions. Operating systems perform a number of other important functions. Windows operating systems store important information about hardware devices, software settings, and user preferences in a database called the *Registry*. The Registry is automatically updated when new hardware or software is installed, or user preferences are entered. The Registry can also be manually changed by skilled computer technicians. Because changes to the Registry can dramatically alter or damage how a computer operates, manual changes by unskilled users are not advised.

You can also modify operating systems to make them more user friendly. For example, people with visual or physical disabilities can use the Microsoft Windows accessibility options to make it easier to use the computer. You can alter screen and mouse operations, change printer and modem operations, change the volume and tone of sound, and adjust how battery power is managed and used by notebook computers.

Operating systems typically come with additional software that is not part of the operating system, including limited word processors, graphics programs, and games such as Solitaire, Minesweeper, and Pinball. Some operating systems also come with Internet browsers and media players. Windows Media Center and Mac OS X Front Row, for example, can turn your PC into a media control center. This software allows you to manage television programming, digital video, digital music files, and digital photos. It includes a television tuner, a digital video recorder, a digital music player, a photo album and slide show software, and more (see Figure 3.23).

FIGURE 3.23 • Windows Media Center

Windows Media Center software transforms your PC into a media controller that manages and presents television, movies, music, and photos.

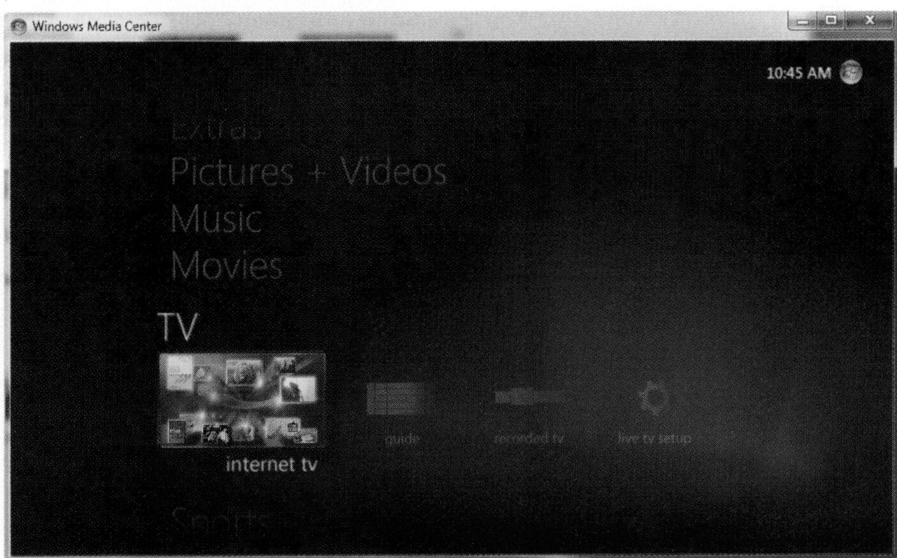

PC Operating Systems Today

In 1983 Apple computer released the first personal computer with a graphical user interface and dramatically changed the way people thought about computers. The first version of Microsoft Windows was released in 1985. With the power of IBM behind it, and a more open architecture than Apple, Microsoft Windows went on to become the dominant operating system for personal computers. Today 88 percent of personal computers run some version of Microsoft Windows, while 10 percent run Mac OS, and 2 percent run Linux (see Figure 3.24).[2] While Microsoft has the lion's share of the market, it has been struggling to maintain its monopoly against the increasing popularity of Mac OS and Linux with some populations, notably young adults. All three of the top operating systems have features in common, and each one has unique qualities that inspire its users to believe that it is better than the others. This section will introduce you to the three most popular personal computer operating systems, starting with the one that is by far most popular.

FIGURE 3.24 • PC operating system market share

As of August 2009, Microsoft maintained monopoly power in the PC operating system market.

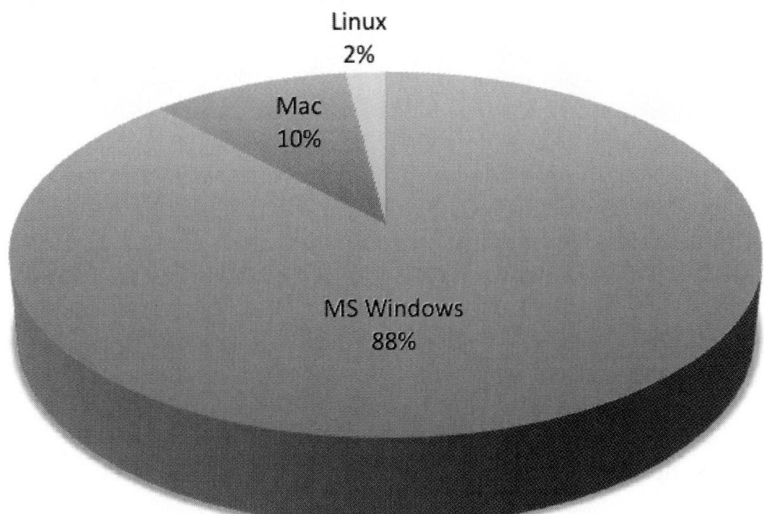

Microsoft Windows. **Microsoft Windows** is the most popular operating system for personal computers. Over the years there have been many versions of Microsoft Windows, such as Windows NT, Me, 2000, XP, and Vista, each adding features and improvements over previous editions, for example, new graphical interfaces and networking capabilities. The most recent version is Windows 7 (Figure 3.25), released in 2009 with features intended to make the user experience simpler and the operating system easier to use.

FIGURE 3.25 • The Windows 7 desktop

Windows 7 features multitouch support, a streamlined user interface, and improved performance.

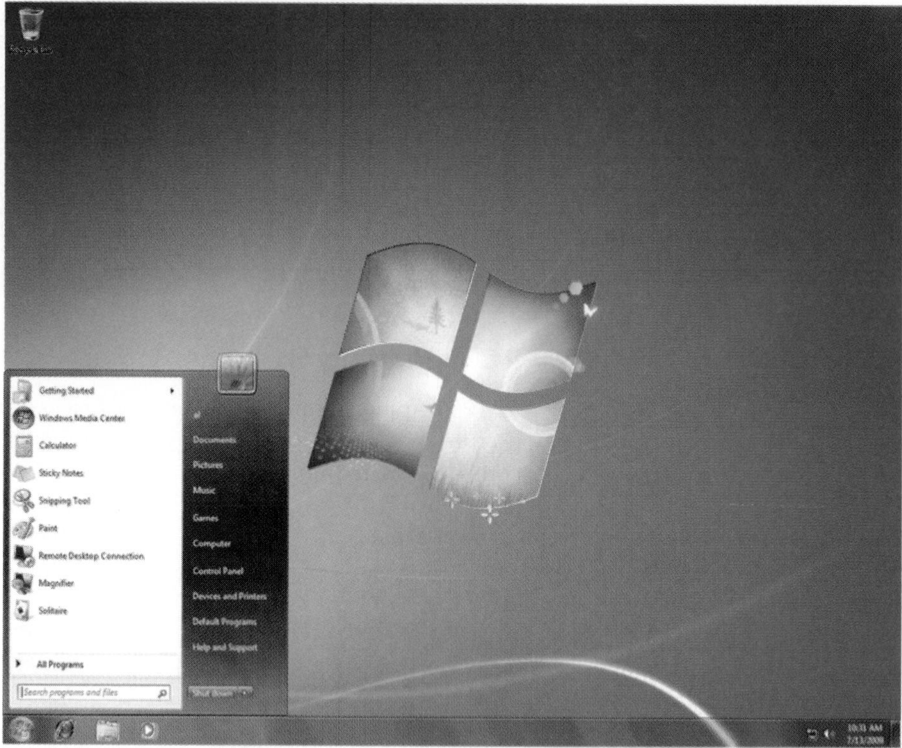

There are several editions of Windows 7 for varying computing environments:

- Windows 7 Starter: A "lite" version of Windows designed for netbook PCs—"less waiting, less clicking, less hassle."
- Windows 7 Home Premium: Designed for home and personal applications, including digital media, TV integration, and home networking.
- Windows 7 Professional: Includes all the features of Home Premium plus business features such as a Windows XP Mode to run older applications, and support for convenient backups and tighter security.
- Windows 7 Ultimate: Includes all the features of Professional plus BitLocker encryption technology for high levels of security and support for 35 languages.

Windows 7 has been referred to by many reviewers as Windows Vista done right. The previous version of Windows, Windows Vista, included major changes to the operating system, some of which may not have been implemented perfectly. Among the improvements to Windows that Vista brought were the Aero design. Aero provides high-resolution graphics that incorporate translucent window effects and 3D graphics functions.

EXPAND YOUR KNOWLEDGE

To learn more about the Windows operating system, go to www.cengage.com/computerconcepts/np/swt4. Click the link "Expand Your Knowledge" and then complete the lab entitled "Using Windows."

One of the less noticeable but perhaps more important improvements implemented in Windows Vista is security. Since Windows is the number one target of hackers, viruses, and spyware, Microsoft worked hard to provide safeguards for Vista. Vista includes robust backup and restore tools, encryption technology for files stored on the hard drive, and diagnostic utilities for tuning the system. Microsoft recommends its Windows Security Essentials software (sold separately) for protecting Vista from hackers, viruses, and spyware.

New features in Windows 7 include:

- An improved taskbar, previews, bigger icons, and personalization features
- Easier home network setup
- Shortcuts to your favorite resources utilizing "jump lists"
- New window sizing and arranging tools called Aero Snap, Shake, and Peek
- Windows Search allows users to search their PC in the same manner that they search the Web
- Performance improvements allow Windows 7 to perform more quickly and consume fewer resources
- Windows Touch enables Windows 7 to be operated using a touch-sensitive display

This last feature is expected to have an impact on the way users interact with their PC. Many PC manufacturers have PC models featuring touch-sensitive displays. Some are designed for casual home use for quick information access in the kitchen, hallway, or living room. Such PCs are sometimes referred to as *nettops* rather than desktops, since their primary function is to access the Internet.

The Center for the Study of the Presidency and Congress upgraded to Windows 7 as soon as it was possible, eager to experience its benefits. The center is a nonprofit government policy think tank that researches political issues and works to propose well-thought-out, bipartisan solutions. Members of the center utilize a large collection of historic and current documents in their deliberations. Windows 7 provides several tools that allow the group to manage documents more easily. For example, the HomeGroup feature allows members of the center to quickly wirelessly network their notebook PCs to pass documents back and forth. The Federated Search feature allows the group to execute searches for topics or documents that span the local PC, local network, and the Internet. The group also finds that they are less bothered by system problems since system tools like the Problem Steps Recorder and Action Center make troubleshooting less time-consuming and manage fixes without interrupting workflow.[3]

Apple Computer Operating Systems. **Mac OS** is the native operating system for Apple PCs. Like Windows, Apple operating systems have gone through revisions and changes to make them more useful. Easy-to-use graphical user interfaces have always been a hallmark of Apple systems. The latest versions of Mac OS continue to be easy to learn and use. Simplicity does not mean that Apple's latest operating system is not powerful, however. Macintosh operating systems offer many outstanding graphics capabilities and are very popular with professionals working in art, photography, motion picture, animation, and music industries (see Figure 3.26). Because high-end Macs offer powerful processing architectures, they are also popular with mathematicians and scientists.

FIGURE 3.26 • The Mac OS X operating system

Mac OS X Snow Leopard features refinements to the user interface, and faster 64-bit processing.

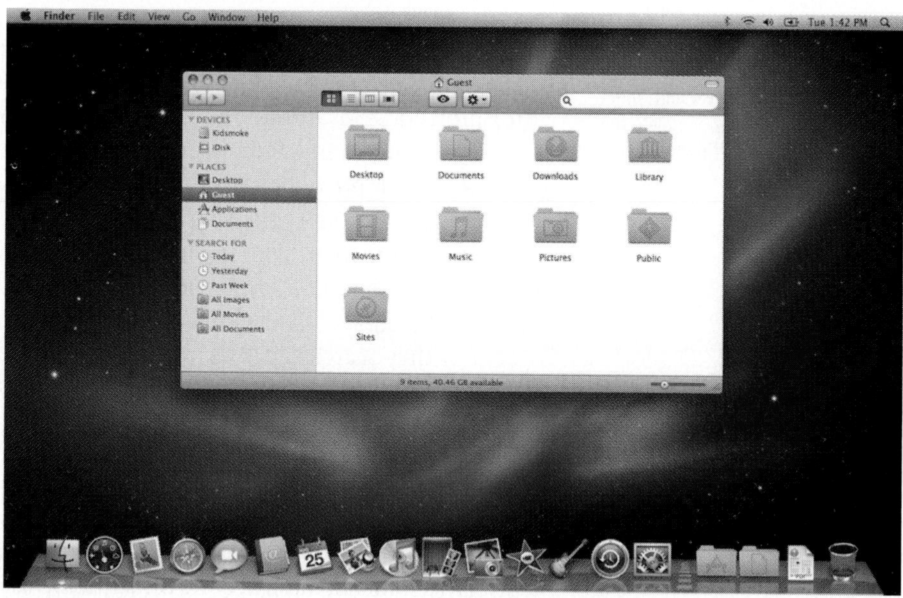

The most recent Mac OS, named X (ten), is built on the UNIX operating system, an industrial-strength OS originally developed for mainframe systems and renowned for its stability and security. Mac OS X has undergone several updates, each named after large cats: Puma (10.1 in 2001), Jaguar (10.2 in 2002), Panther (10.3 in 2003), Tiger (10.4 in 2005), Leopard (10.5 in 2007), and Snow Leopard (10.6 in 2009). Each update has implemented improvements and expanded features over its predecessor.

As with the most recent version of Microsoft Windows, Mac OS X Snow Leopard has provided refinements and tweaks to the previous version of Mac OS rather than major new design and features. The improvements include:

- Runs faster using fewer system resources (7 GB less hard drive space)
- Improved features added to the Dock for file previewing and application swapping
- Faster backups, wake-ups, and shutdowns
- 64-bit application support
- Improved native applications that make use of the 64-bit architecture
- Grand Central Dispatch, a technology for developers that will allow more powerful applications to be developed

Mac users often rely on Apple for their application software needs. Safari is Apple's Web browser, Mail is the Mac e-mail program, Address Book stores contacts, and iChat is for instant messaging with or without video. These and many other useful software tools are provided free with Mac OS X. The Mac iLife suite of applications (sold separately) includes iChat, iPhoto, iMovie HD, iDVD, iTunes, iWeb, and GarageBand. Mac iWork software (also sold separately) includes the Pages word processor, Numbers spreadsheet, and Keynote presentation software. Many Mac users also use Microsoft Office for Mac for their productivity software. By doing so, they can share files and interact with Windows users without fear of compatibility issues.

Because Apple makes both the hardware and the operating system for its computers, and because Mac OS X is built on UNIX technology, Macs have a reputation of being more stable and secure than Microsoft Windows PCs. Mac users also do not face as large a threat from viruses and spyware as do Windows users, although that may change over time. Very few Mac users feel it necessary to invest in antivirus and antispyware protection, and very few have ever been infected. However, Mac OS X does provide file encryption, password protection, and a firewall to keep hackers off your machine and out of your files. The latest version of Mac OS X also includes antivirus tools.

While Microsoft Windows has dominated the business desktop market, Macs are beginning to make inroads. Macs are especially popular with "techies" and technology companies. The popular business-focused social network, LinkedIn, provides all of its engineers with Mac Pros that feature dual quad-core CPUs. LinkedIn uses Macs as an enticement for top-of-the-line engineers. LinkedIn engineers enjoy using the Mac's video conferencing tools to brainstorm and share documents. The company's other personnel, from product managers to executives, can choose to use either Microsoft Windows PCs or Macs, but 70 percent choose Macs (see Figure 3.27). The company IT department has no problem providing services to all employees over the dual platform integrated network.[4]

FIGURE 3.27 • Macs in business

Most LinkedIn employees prefer working on Macs.

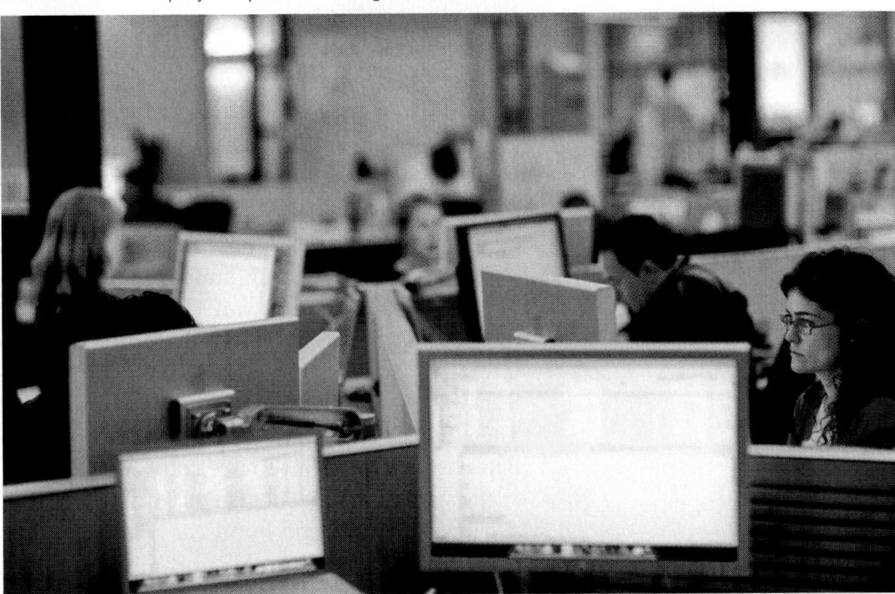

Linux. **Linux** is a free, open-source operating system for PCs. The Linux operating system was developed by Linus Torvalds in 1991. Linux was designed to provide a powerful, free, UNIX-like operating system that would run on desktop PCs. As with UNIX, Linux can be used as a command-line operating system or through a desktop interface such as GNOME (see Figure 3.28). Today, it is being used on computers from small personal computers to large mainframe systems. Unlike many other operating systems, Linux is open source; you'll recall that means that users have access to the source code. The operating system is available free to users under a General Public License (GPL) arrangement. Some vendors also offer commercial (not free) versions of Linux that include more features and offer user support.

FIGURE 3.28 • Linux Ubuntu with GNOME

Ubuntu, with the GNOME user interface, is a popular version of Linux that also includes free open-source software for common computing activities.

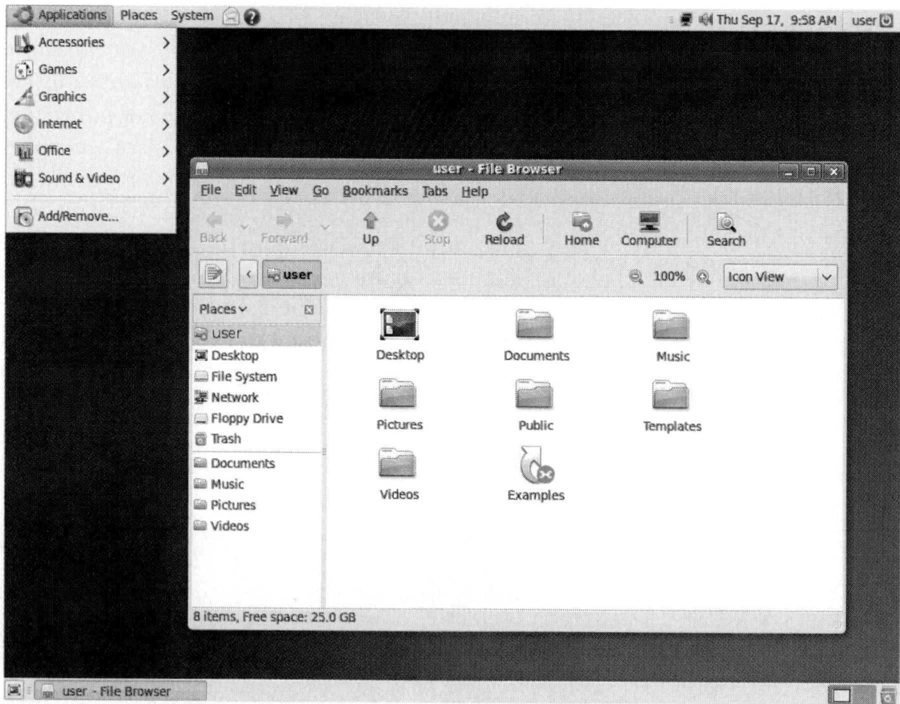

There are many versions, called distributions, of Linux that have been designed by the user community. Distributions based on Debian Linux feature free, unencumbered software and have a reputation for being very stable; Ubuntu falls under this category. Red Hat Enterprise–based distributions are designed for large corporate systems and servers, with a free community version called Fedora. Slackware-based distributions are highly customizable and are favored by techies. There are specialized distributions created for specific devices like smart phones. Because Linux is open-source software, there are many more customized and stable versions than Microsoft Windows or Mac OS. There are literally hundreds of versions of Linux, and hundreds of thousands of unique Linux setups.

Linux has a big advantage compared to other operating systems such as Windows and Mac OS X: people not only can get copies of Linux free of charge or at low cost, but they also can develop utilities, applications, and enhancements to the operating system. Besides including all the standard OS functionality, settings, and support, Linux Ubuntu comes loaded with free open-source applications. Ubuntu includes the software listed in Table 3.9 plus several accessories and over a dozen games. Considering that Ubuntu and all of this software is free to download from *www.ubuntu.com*, it becomes easy to understand why Linux users think it's the best OS.

Oxford Archaeology decided to switch from Microsoft Windows to Linux Ubuntu for its workforce. The over 300 archaeologists and specialists employed by the company are dedicated to recording, protecting, and preserving archaeological artifacts for the betterment of humanity. The company's information systems manager decided that, over the long term, the open-source alternative would save the company money, and give it more flexibility than a closed and proprietary system such as Microsoft Windows. Ubuntu has provided an excellent platform for the GIS, mapping, and geospacial systems on which Oxford Archaeology depends.[5]

TABLE 3.9 • Software included with Linux Ubuntu

Graphics	Internet	Office	Sound and Video
• F-Spot Photo Manager • GIMP Image Editor • gThumb Image Viewer • XSane Image Scanner	• Ekiga Softphone • Evolution Mail • Firefox Web Browser • Gairn Internet Messenger • Terminal Server Client	• OpenOffice Database • OpenOffice Presentation • OpenOffice Spreadsheet • OpenOffice Word Processor	• Movie Player • Rhythmbox Music Player • Serpentine Audio CD Creator • Sound Juicer CD Extractor • Sound Recorder

Operating Systems for Servers, Networks, and Large Mainframe Computer Systems

Some operating systems are designed specifically for larger computer systems or computer systems that require a server. These systems operate over a network, so network management functions are an important element. Windows Server 2008, Linux, Novell NetWare, and Sun Microsystems Solaris are examples of network operating systems.

Solaris, by Sun Microsystems, is the most popular version of the UNIX operating system for industry (see Figure 3.29). The online marketplace eBay uses Sun Microsystems servers, software, storage, and services to run its operations.[6] Solaris is the operating system that manages eBay's database servers, Web servers, tape libraries, and identity management systems, to name a few. The online auction company found that when it switched to Sun and Solaris, system performance increased by 20 percent. Using the right OS can make a big difference to the bottom line for businesses. The Idaho National Laboratory uses the same operating system, Solaris, to conduct research in its work to design more efficient and safe nuclear reactors.[7]

FIGURE 3.29 • Sun Solaris (UNIX) in industry

Even powerful industrial operating systems are often accessed through a GUI interface, but you are more likely to find users accessing the command line or coding windows.

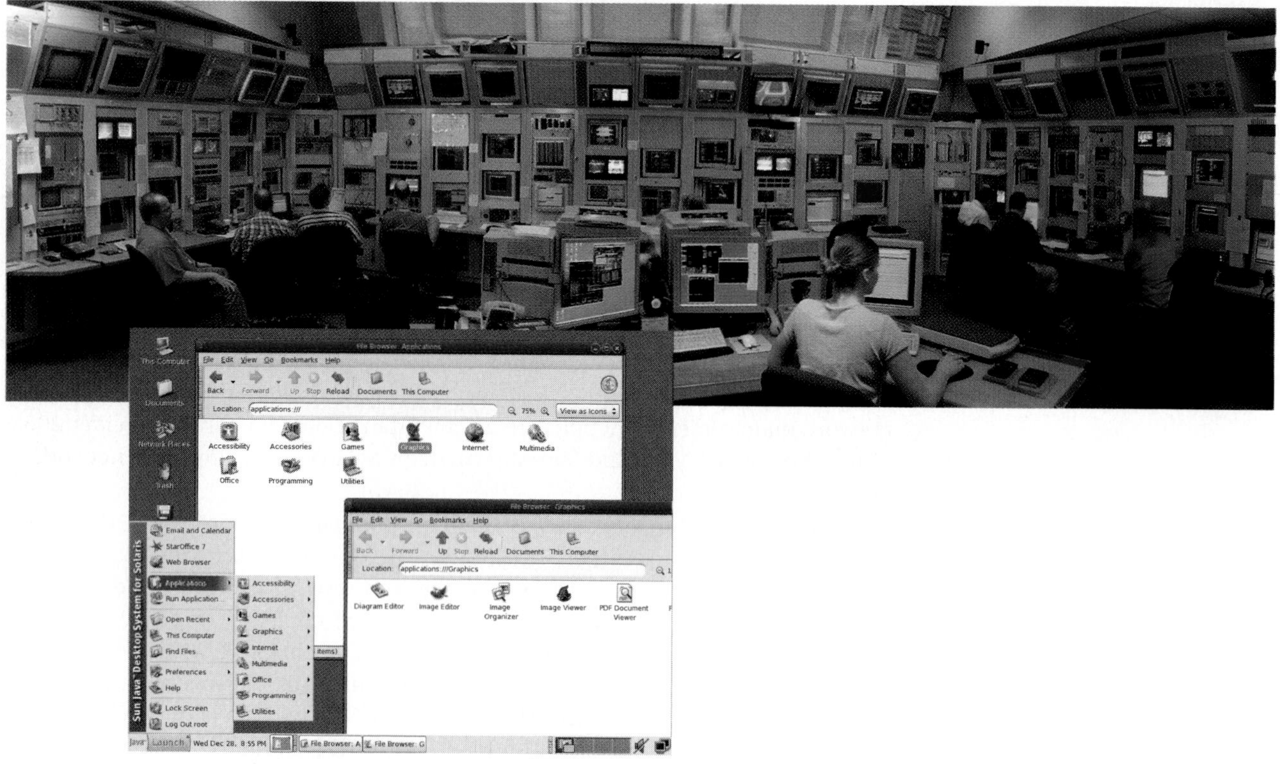

Large mainframe computer manufacturers typically provide proprietary operating systems with their specific hardware, such as z/OS, a 64-bit operating system for IBM's large mainframe computers. MPE/iX is an operating system used by Hewlett-Packard's mainframe computers. Enterprise Systems Architecture/370 (ESA/370) and Multiple Virtual Storage/Enterprise Systems Architecture (MVS/ESA) are older operating systems used on IBM mainframe computers.

Operating Systems for Handheld Computers and Special-Purpose Devices

Operating systems for handheld devices and other small devices that contain computers are called *embedded operating systems* because they are typically embedded in a computer chip. The original handheld computer, the Palm Pilot, ran the Palm OS. Palm recently retired Palm OS after 13 years of use, in favor of a new operating system Palm calls Web OS. Web OS is better suited for smart phones, with an interface designed to compete against the iPhone. The iPhone uses a streamlined version of Apple's Mac OS X. Today's very popular BlackBerry handheld communication device uses the BlackBerry OS, specifically designed for the BlackBerry. When an OS is designed for a particular device and is the only OS available for that device, it is considered a proprietary OS. Operating systems that can be used on many different devices, like Microsoft Windows Mobile, are called portable operating systems. Windows Mobile can be found on smart phones from AT&T, HP, Motorola, and others. Symbian makes operating systems for many of today's popular cell phones. Figure 3.30 shows a number of smart phone operating systems.

FIGURE 3.30 • Smart phone operating systems

Apple iPhone OS, Palm Web OS, Microsoft Mobile, and BlackBerry OS are popular smart phone operating systems.

Many other small mobile devices also use embedded operating systems. The iPod and other digital music players have embedded operating systems. In fact, all computing devices—special purpose and general purpose—have operating systems: the Mars Rover (see Figure 3.31), military weapons, and home appliances. Microsoft makes embedded operating systems for industrial devices, ATMs, set-top boxes, medical devices, and in-dash automobile devices. Windows Automotive operating system is designed to provide services to drivers and passengers. For example, the SYNC feature in some Ford vehicles is powered by Microsoft Auto, a version of Windows Automotive designed for communications and media, and provides hands-free communications and wireless connections with popular media devices through an in-dash console.

FIGURE 3.31 • The Mars Rover

The Mars Rover uses an OS created by the Windriver company.

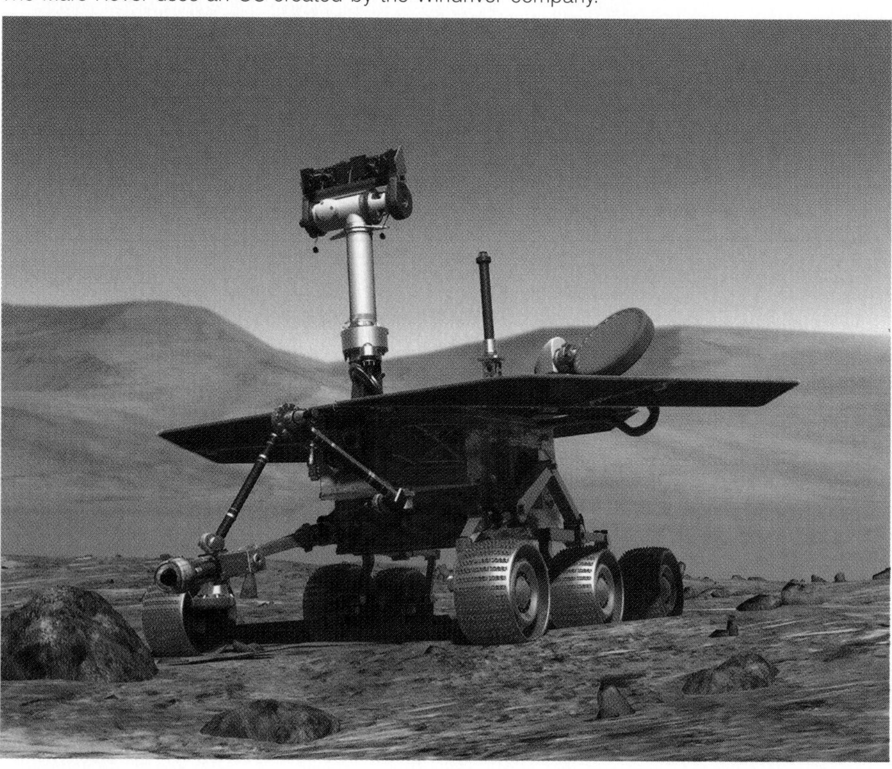

Utility Programs

Another type of system software, besides the operating system, is the utility program. A **utility program** is any system software besides the OS that assists in maintaining, managing, and protecting computer system resources. In fact, as operating systems have developed, they have incorporated features that were originally found in separate utility programs, such as disk maintenance utilities. Utilities are used to merge and sort sets of data, keep track of computer jobs being run, and perform other important routine tasks. Utility programs often come installed on computer systems; a number of utility programs can also be purchased.

BIG BROTHER IS FILTERING YOU

You've heard about antiviral and parental control software, but how would you feel if your government controlled which Web sites you could visit? In 2009, the Chinese government required all personal computers to be equipped with Green Dam Youth Escort. They claimed that the software only blocked sites featuring pornography and violence, but users discovered that the software also barred entrance to Web sites of dissident groups. However, China quickly reversed its policy amidst widespread criticism from a growing anti-censorship movement.

Alexa Olesen
China Backpedals on Filtering Software Order
Associated Press
June 17, 2009
http://www.physorg.com/news164423969.html

The following are common utilities that protect computer systems and keep them running smoothly:

- Defragmentation and disk utilities: Maintain files on disk and arrange them in a manner that allows for fast access
- Backup utilities: Safeguard files by creating backup copies
- Security software: Search for and remove viruses and spyware from computers, and guard against attacks; must be updated frequently (see Figure 3.32)

- Spam and pop-up blockers: Save users time by eliminating unwanted junk mail and ads
- Windows cleaners: Remove unwanted programs and leftover traces of programs from the system, and maintain the Windows Registry for smoother OS operation
- Parental controls: Filter Internet content and place restrictions on computer use for the safety of minors

FIGURE 3.32 • Parental controls on Mac

Parental control utilities allow parents to control what content and applications can be accessed by children.

A number of utilities are designed to assist users in managing and transferring files:

- File management utilities: Provide tools for copying, deleting, renaming, and organizing files
- File compression utilities: Allow files to be bundled together into one compressed file to save storage space and allow for easier transfer
- CD/DVD burners: Copy and store files on CDs and DVDs
- File transfer utilities: Move and share files across networks
- Search utilities: Find files (see Figure 3.33)

FIGURE 3.33 • Windows 7 Search

Windows 7 Search utility allows users to search their PC and local network just as they search the Web.

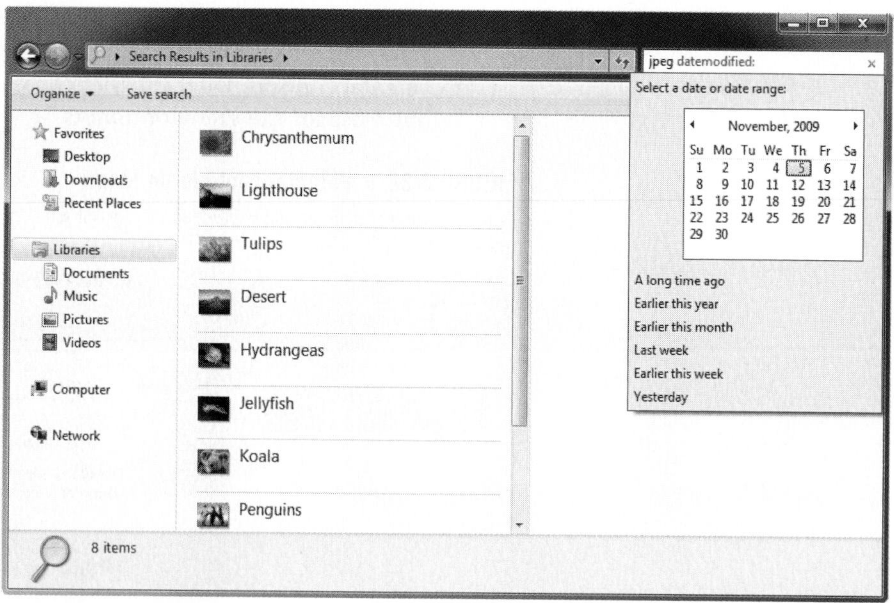

APPLICATION SOFTWARE

As discussed earlier in this chapter, the primary function of *application software* is to apply the power of the computer to give people, groups, and organizations the ability to solve problems and perform specific activities or tasks. While system software supports the computer's functions, application software supports people's functions. Individuals can use application software to advance their career, to communicate with others, to access a vast array of knowledge, or to serve up entertainment. Groups and organizations use application software to help people make better decisions, reduce costs, improve service, or increase revenues.

Productivity Software

Productivity software is any software designed to help individuals be more productive. Over the years this category of software has included the most popular personal computer applications: word processors, spreadsheets, database-management systems, presentation software, and personal information management software. Productivity software is used at home for personal tasks and at work for professional tasks. For example, a spreadsheet application might be used at home to set up a personal budget or in a business to design a corporate budget.

Word-Processing Software. Word processing is perhaps the most highly used application software for individuals. **Word-processing software** allows users to create formatted text documents varying in complexity from simple to-do lists to professional magazine layouts. Microsoft Word is the most popular word-processing program and is available for both PCs and Macintosh computers (see Figure 3.34). Apple Pages, Corel WordPerfect, Lotus WordPro, and Sun Microsystems Write are other examples of word processors. Google Docs, Adobe Buzzword, and Zoho Writer are free Web-based word processors. Writer from OpenOffice.org is an open-source word-processing software option.

FIGURE 3.34 • Word-processing software

Powerful word-processing applications like Microsoft Word allow novices to create professional-looking documents.

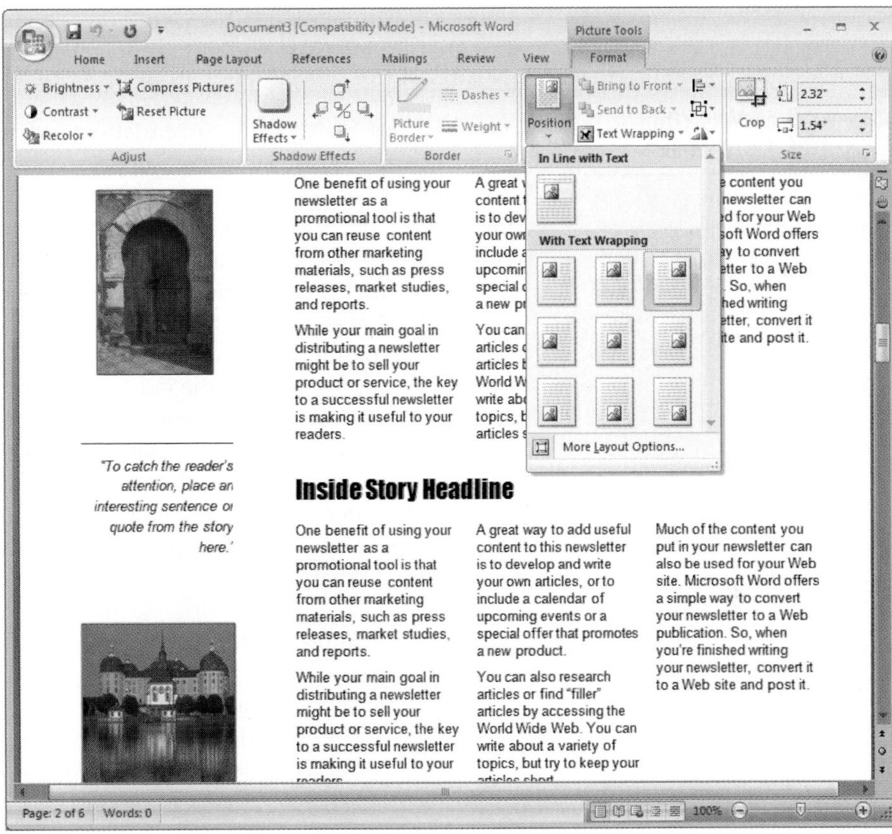

EXPAND YOUR KNOWLEDGE

To learn how to get the most out of your word-processing application, go to www.cengage.com/computerconcepts/np/swt4. Click the link "Expand Your Knowledge" and then complete the lab entitled "Word Processing."

The features available on today's word processors are stunning. All of the common features you would expect are included, such as easy text entry and formatting, and the capability to develop attractive tables, check spelling and grammar, and generate footnotes and endnotes. You can create automatically numbered or bulleted lists and insert photos, graphics, and drawings. Today's word-processing programs also have sophisticated document-processing features such as generating a table of contents at the beginning of the text and an index at the end. Word 2007 and Word 2010 include intuitive features that provide easily accessible tools for a variety of document styles. New features in Word 2010 include a navigation pane that provides a birds-eye view of a document, a powerful document search tool, and impressive graphics tools for creating SmartArt graphs and visualizations and image and font effects.

JoAnna Minneci is a renowned professional chef in Los Angeles, California, who runs her own catering and in-home cooking services. She caters to some Hollywood stars and believes in treating her nonstar customers as though they are stars. Ms. Minneci uses Word for Mac to design colorful and artistic menus and gift certificates. The cross-platform compatibility of Microsoft Office for Mac allows her to deliver materials such as menus, contracts, and budgets to clients working on Macintoshes or Windows-based PCs.

Word-processing programs can be used with a team or group of people collaborating on a project. The authors and editors who developed this book, for example, used the Track Changes and Reviewing features of Microsoft Word to track and make changes to chapter files without overwriting each other's work.

You can insert comments in or make revisions to a document that a coworker can review and either accept or reject. Microsoft Office Web Apps, Google Docs, and other online word processors provide an excellent environment for collaboration, allowing individuals to work on the same document simultaneously. Software that functions to support group collaboration is sometimes referred to as *groupware*.

EXPAND YOUR KNOWLEDGE

To learn how to get the most out of your spreadsheet application, go to www.cengage.com/computerconcepts/np/swt4. Click the link "Expand Your Knowledge" and then complete the lab entitled "Spreadsheets."

Spreadsheet Software. **Spreadsheet software**, like Microsoft Excel, Apple Numbers, and Corel Quattro Pro, supports complicated numerical analysis and calculations and allows users to perform *"what-if" analysis* on financial and other numeric data. A spreadsheet contains rows that are numbered and columns that are lettered. Cell D10, for example, is found at the intersection of row 10 and column D. You can enter text, numbers, or complex formulas into a spreadsheet cell (see Figure 3.35). For example, you can have a spreadsheet automatically get the total or average of a column or row of numbers. If you have a budget spreadsheet containing your actual expenses for the last several months, you can change one number and immediately see the impact on your average monthly expenditures, your total for the month, and any other calculations that you have entered into your spreadsheet. In general, if you change a value in a spreadsheet, all the formulas based on the value are changed immediately and automatically. The authors and publisher used a spreadsheet to plan and monitor important deadlines to publish this book in a timely fashion.

FIGURE 3.35 • Spreadsheet software

Spreadsheet software like Microsoft Excel is excellent for making complicated calculations, creating "what-if" scenarios, and creating graphs.

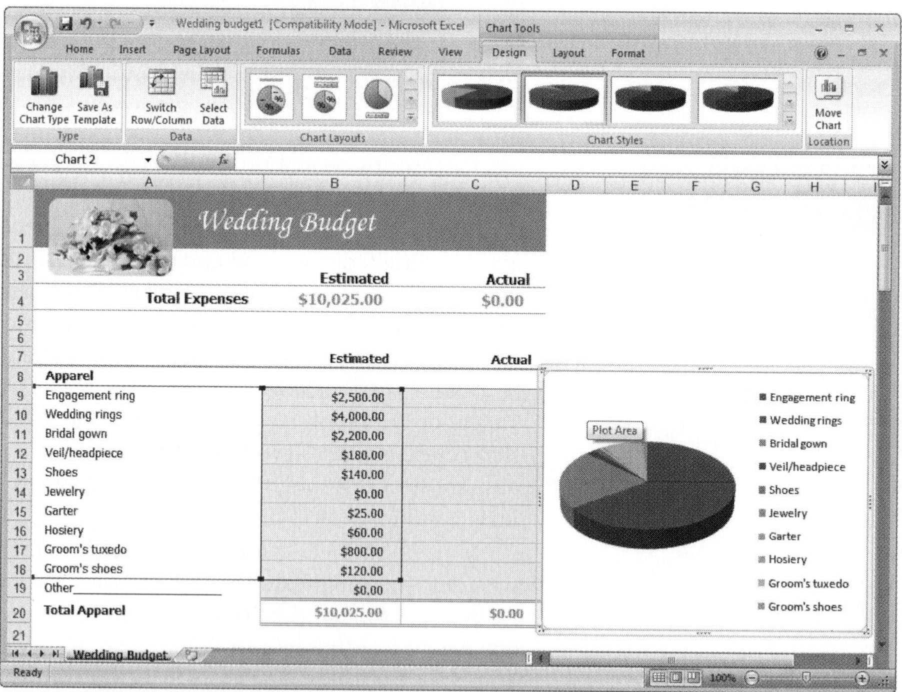

Spreadsheet programs have many built-in functions for science and engineering, statistics, and business. The science and engineering functions include sine, cosine, tangent, degrees, maximum, minimum, logarithms, radians, square root, and exponents. The statistical functions include correlation, statistical testing, probability, variance, frequency, mean, median, mode, and much more. The business functions include depreciation, present value, internal rate of return,

EXPAND YOUR KNOWLEDGE

To learn more about advanced spreadsheet features, go to www.cengage.com/computerconcepts/np/swt4. Click the link "Expand Your Knowledge" and then complete the lab entitled "Advanced Spreadsheets."

and the monthly payment on a loan, to name a few. Spreadsheets also provide methods of displaying data in an attractive and meaningful way. Microsoft Excel provides dozens of types and styles of graphs that can illustrate numeric information visually. It also provides automated tools for formatting numeric information in any one of a wide variety of attractive tables.

Spreadsheets include many of the tools associated with word processing, including the ability to format fonts and text alignment, insert images, and check spelling. Microsoft Excel 2010 also includes the group collaboration tools provided in Word 2010.

Optimization is another powerful feature of many spreadsheet programs. *Optimization* allows the spreadsheet to maximize or minimize a quantity subject to certain constraints. For example, a company that produces dog food might want to minimize its costs while meeting certain nutritional standards. Minimizing costs becomes the objective and the nutritional standards are the constraints. An optimization feature can determine the blend of dog food ingredients that minimizes costs and meets the nutritional requirements. This is just one of many examples of the use of optimization in spreadsheets. Because of the power and popularity of spreadsheet optimization, some colleges and universities offer complete courses based on Solver in the Microsoft Excel spreadsheet. Most of these courses are in engineering and business schools.

Presentation Software. **Presentation software** supports formal presentations by providing "slides" that can be used to accompany and embellish a live presentation or to present the material without the use of a human speaker. Presentation software is extremely useful for transmitting information to professional groups and audiences that can vary from a few people to thousands (see Figure 3.36). Physicians and medical personnel use presentation software to show the results of medical research at conferences. Forest service consultants use presentation software to describe new forest management programs, and businesses almost always use presentation software to present financial results or new initiatives to executives and managers. Because of its established use in most professions, many colleges and departments require students to become proficient with presentation software.

FIGURE 3.36 • Presentation software

Presentation software like Microsoft PowerPoint is essential for making professional presentations to large and small audiences.

Most presentations created with presentation software, such as Microsoft PowerPoint, Apple Keynote, Freelance Graphics, and Harvard Graphics, consist of a series of slides. Each slide can be displayed on a computer screen, printed as a handout, or (more commonly) projected onto a large viewing screen for audiences. Powerful built-in features allow you to develop attractive slides and complete presentations. Slides typically include visual aids such as graphs and images that allow an audience to better understand the topic being presented. Slides may be animated with moving objects and transitions, and may include music and video. You can select a template for a type of presentation, such as recommending a strategy for managers, communicating bad news to a sales force, giving a training presentation, or facilitating a brainstorming session. The presentation software takes you through the presentation step by step, including applying color and attractive formatting. Of course, you can also custom design your own presentation.

Electronic presentations are increasingly being used to provide training over the Web and to provide information at kiosks in public areas and industry trade shows. Online presentation tools such as Google Presentation, Slide Rocket, and BrainShark allow for online presentation development and delivery. Individuals can progress through the presentation themselves by clicking icons on-screen, or the presentation can be set to progress automatically at specified time intervals.

EXPAND YOUR KNOWLEDGE

To learn how to get the most out of your presentation graphics application, go to www.cengage.com/computerconcepts/np/swt4. Click the link "Expand Your Knowledge" and then complete the lab entitled "Presentation Software."

Database-Management Software. **Database-management software** is used to store, manipulate, and manage data in order to find and present useful information. Databases can be used to store large tables of information (see Figure 3.37). Each table can be related. For example, a company can create and store tables that contain customer information, inventory information, employee information, and much more. Assume a customer decides to place an order for two flash drives, one for herself and one for a friend, by calling a sales rep with whom she has worked in the past. The sales rep can record the customer number, the item number for the flash drive, and the quantity, two in this case. The database-management software does the rest. First, the program takes the customer number and goes to the customer table to retrieve the name, address, and credit card information. With the employee number of the sales rep from the customer table, the database-management software goes to the employee table to determine any sales commissions that should be paid to the sales rep. Next, the database-management system takes the item number for the flash drive and goes to the inventory table to get all the information about the flash drive and make sure that there are at least two in stock. Once all of this is done, the order can be processed and the two flash drives sent to the customer. All of this is done as a result of giving the customer number, item number, and quantity to the database-management software. Before database-management software existed, processing an order was done manually, requiring a lot of time and potentially making many mistakes.

FIGURE 3.37 • Database-management software

Database-management software like Microsoft Access can be used to store large tables of information and produce important documents and reports.

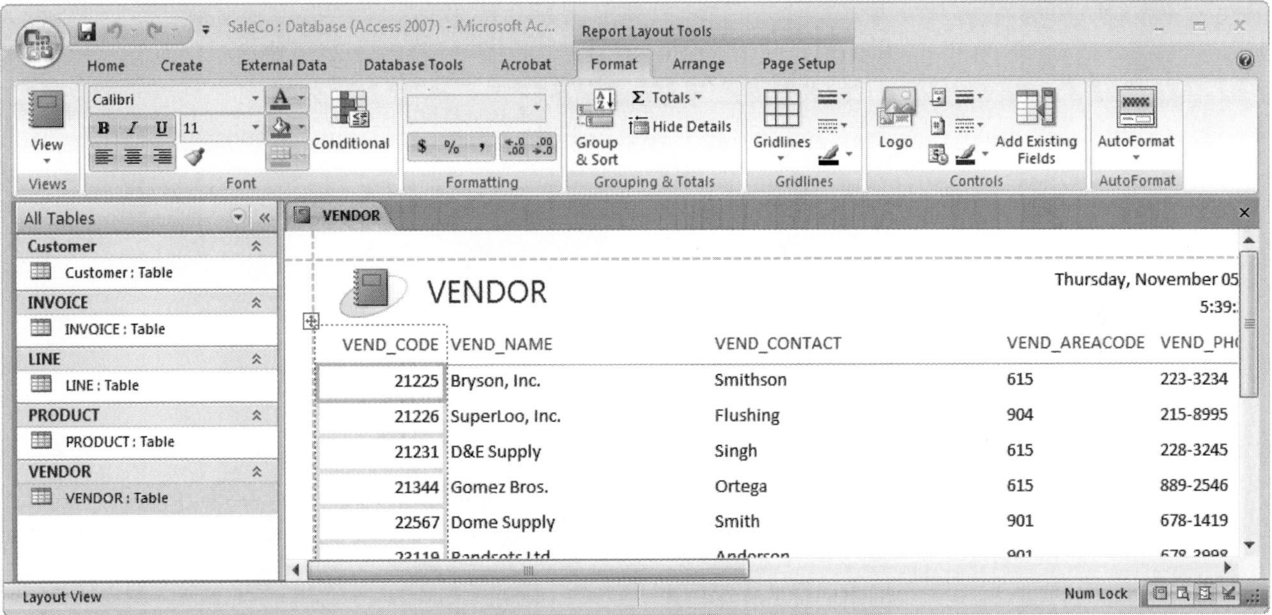

In addition to order processing, database-management software can be used to perform many of the business functions for a small business, including payroll, inventory control, order processing, bill paying, and producing tax returns. Database-management systems can also be used to track and analyze stock and bond prices, analyze weather data to make forecasts for the next several days, and summarize medical research results. At home, you can use database-management software to keep a record of expenses, a list of what is in your apartment or home, or a list of the members of a student government organization.

Microsoft Access is designed to support the small databases used at home or in a small business. Larger corporations rely on large database systems, such as Microsoft SQL Server or Oracle, for the millions of records they maintain and manipulate.

Personal Information Management. **Personal information management (PIM) software** helps individuals store useful information, such as to-do lists, appointment calendars, and contact lists. In addition, information in a PIM can be linked. For example, you can link an appointment with a sales manager that appears in the calendar with information on the sales manager in the address book. When you click the appointment in the calendar, information from the address book is automatically opened and displayed on the computer screen.

Personal information managers, such as Microsoft Outlook, can be used on handheld computers, laptops, or large-scale computers (see Figure 3.38). Smart phones can sync with a corporate PIM system over the cell phone network or the Internet. Microsoft Exchange Server is popular messaging and collaborative software installed on the servers of many businesses to provide PIM services to employees over the corporate network, and sometimes wirelessly to smart phones like the BlackBerry and iPhone.

FIGURE 3.38 • Personal information management software

PIM software like Microsoft Outlook assists individuals, groups, and organizations in storing and managing information such as e-mail, to-do lists, calendars, and contact information.

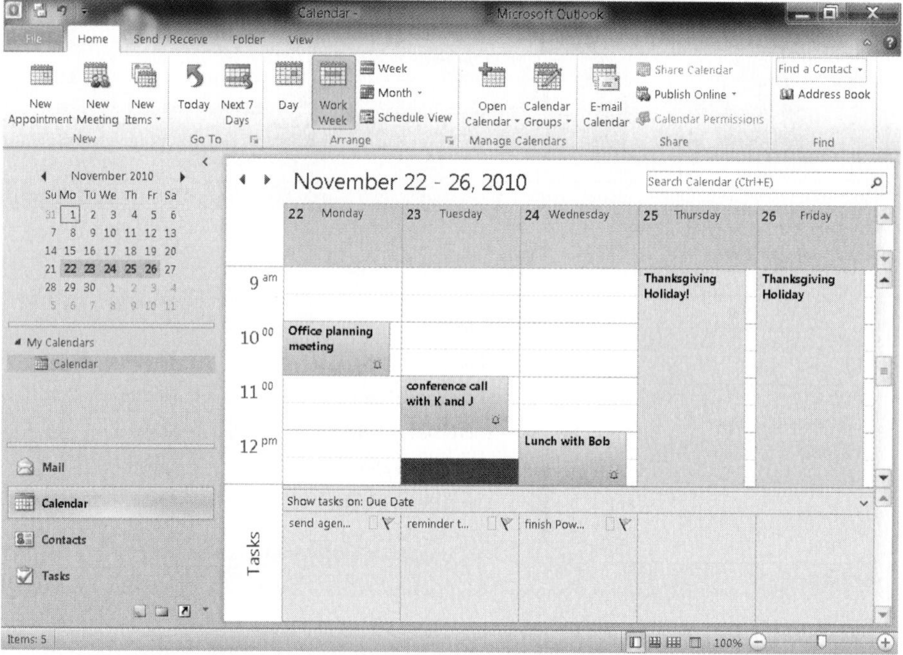

Many companies use Microsoft Outlook, Apple iCal, Google Calendar, and other calendaring applications to schedule group meetings. For example, meeting organizers can schedule Web conferences directly using Microsoft Office Outlook Calendar. E-mail is automatically distributed to specified meeting participants who receive meeting requests to attend the Web conferences, and click to accept the invitation. The meeting time is then automatically added to each participant's calendar. When it is time for a meeting, all participants click a URL from the meeting request and the link takes them to the Web-conferencing area.

Digital Note Taking. Microsoft OneNote is software designed for tablet PCs that takes advantage of the tablet's pen-and-paper style interface (see Figure 3.39). OneNote is a productivity tool that allows users to combine handwritten notes, diagrams, and other images with typed notes on the same page. You can save the pages and easily search for information within the pages. For instance, a search for *Becky* might bring up a handwritten note you made to yourself to meet Becky at the mall, an e-mail you sent to Becky last week, and a photo of Becky. OneNote is being marketed to college students as a useful tool for taking class notes. Using your tablet PC, you can take handwritten notes in class, make an audio recording of the lecture, and copy and paste passages and images from the Web right into your notes.

FIGURE 3.39 • Mobile productivity tools

People on the go can be productive with tablet PCs and software like Microsoft OneNote.

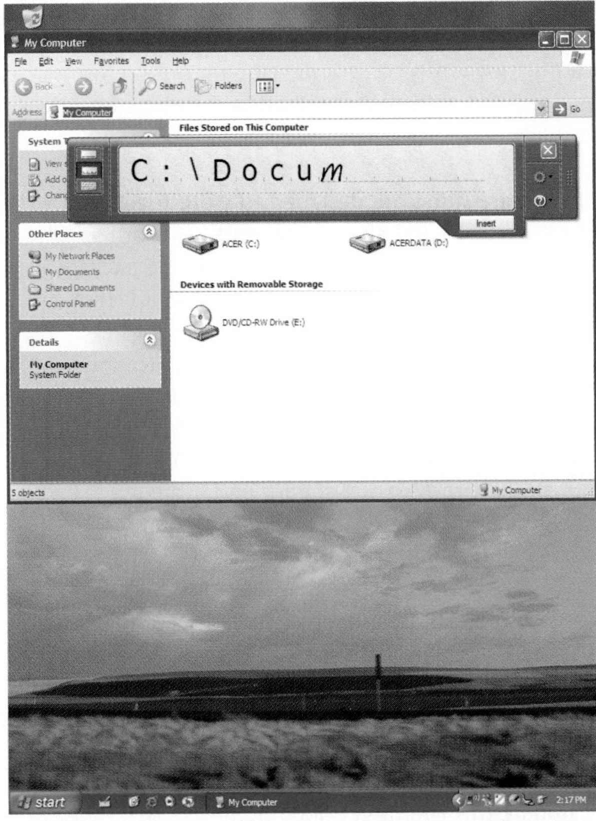

Software Suites. A **software suite** is a collection of application software packages sold together. Software suites can include word processors, spreadsheets, presentation software, database-management systems, personal information managers, and more (see Figure 3.40). It is even possible to select which software packages are part of the suite.

FIGURE 3.40 • Software suite

Software suites like Apple's iWork can include a word processor, spreadsheet, presentation software, and sometimes other applications.

Microsoft Office is by far the most popular suite of productivity software. The latest version, Microsoft Office 2010, is available in several configurations: Home and Student, Standard, Home and Business, Professional, and Professional Plus. Each configuration includes different software to meet varying needs. All versions include Word, Excel, PowerPoint, and OneNote.

Most versions include Outlook and some include Access. Other software provided in some versions of Office 2010 includes Publisher for creating publications, Web Apps for creating and sharing documents online, Communicator for advanced digital communications tools, InfoPath for developing online forms, SharePoint for group collaboration, and advanced integration solutions for larger enterprises such as content management, information rights, and policy capabilities.

Different versions of most software suites are designed to work together. In other words, you can work in Office 2010 and share your work with others who are using an older version of Office. Often, a newer version of a software package can automatically read files from an older version of the same software, a feature called *backward compatibility*.

Although Microsoft Office is by far the most popular suite of applications, it isn't the only game in town. Competitors to Microsoft Office include Corel WordPerfect Office, IBM Lotus SmartSuite, Apple iWork, and Sun Microsystems StarOffice. There is also a free open-source office suite called OpenOffice.org (*www.openoffice.org*) that is compatible with Microsoft Office and available for Microsoft Windows, Solaris, Linux, and Mac OS X. Zoho Office Suite (*www.zoho.com*) is a free Web-based suite of applications that includes Writer, Sheet, Show, Wiki, Notebook, Projects, CRM, Creator, Planner, and Chat.

Using a software suite has a number of advantages. The software has been designed to work similarly, so that once you learn the basics for one application, the other applications are easier to learn and use. You can also easily share data between applications in the suite. For example, with a technology Microsoft calls object linking and embedding (OLE), Office users copy and paste data between office applications and link the data so that when it is changed in the source document it is automatically updated in the target document.

Buying software in a bundled suite is cost effective: together the programs usually sell for less money than they would cost if purchased individually. However, since not all the applications may be needed or desired, some people prefer to buy the applications individually.

Integrated Software Packages. Rather than bundling separate programs into a suite, *integrated software packages* provide the functionality of different types of software all in one program. For example, Microsoft Works provides basic word processing, spreadsheet, database, address book, and other applications features all in one program. Although each application is not as powerful as stand-alone software or comparable applications in software suites, integrated software packages offer basic capabilities for less money. In fact, NeoOffice, an integrated package for Mac, is free! See Figure 3.41.

FIGURE 3.41 • Integrated software

NeoOffice is free integrated office software for Macs that includes a word processor, spreadsheet, presentation tool, drawing tool, and database.

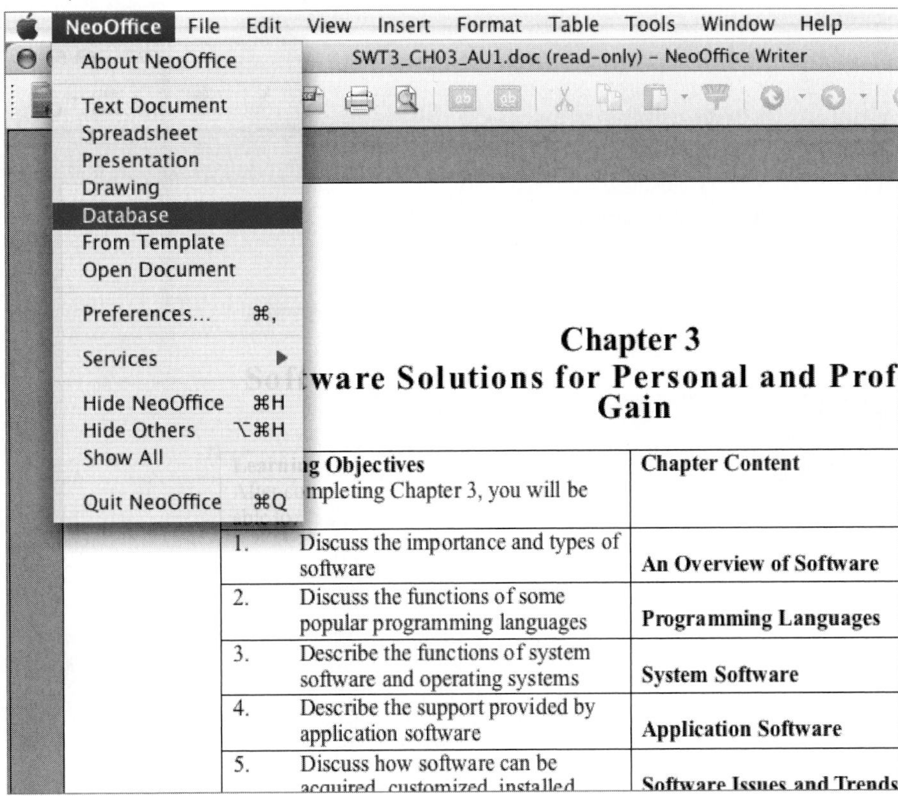

Mobile Software Packages. Cell phones, smart phones, tablets, and netbooks are typically sold with software already installed that takes advantage of the device's unique features. For example, cell phones come with limited PIM software, games, and sometimes media software. Smart phones include additional Internet software. Netbooks, designed for online applications, focus on Web browsing and mobile applications. Beyond the software provided by the manufacturer, most devices allow users to download additional software developed by third parties. Apps stores have become popular for finding unique applications to add to smart phones.

Additional Application Software for Individuals

There are a number of other interesting and powerful application software tools for individuals. In some cases, the features and capabilities of these application software tools can more than justify the cost of an entire computer system. Some of these programs are listed in Table 3.10, and you can see examples of some of them in Figure 3.42.

FIGURE 3.42 • Additional application software

Examples of specific software applications—video editing, music, and statistical software—are shown here.

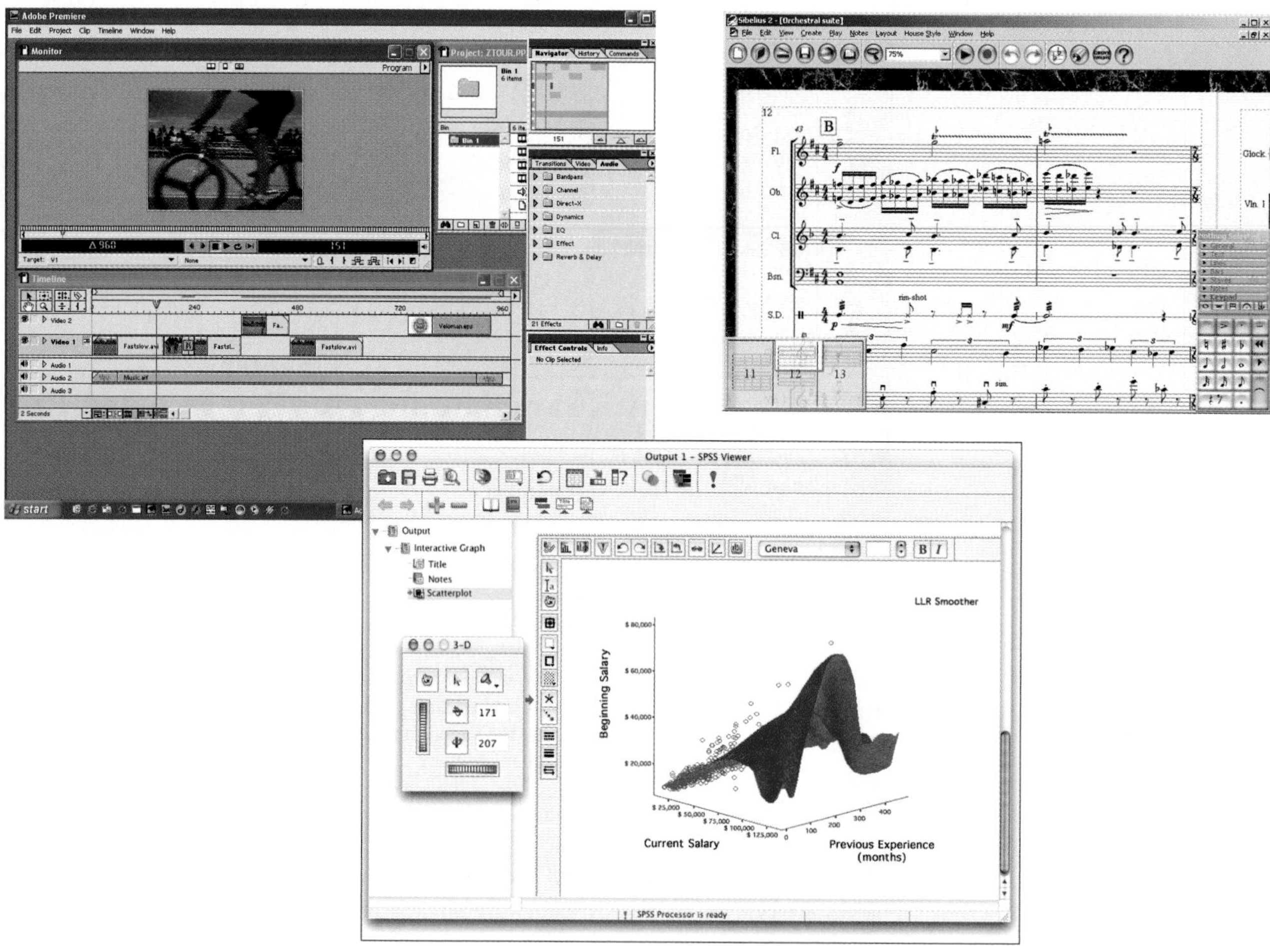

TABLE 3.10 • Examples of additional application software

Type of software	Explanation
Project management	Used to plan, schedule, allocate, and control people and resources (money, time, and technology) needed to complete a project according to a schedule. Project by Microsoft is an example of a project-management software package.
Financial management and tax preparation	Provides income and expense tracking and reporting to monitor and plan budgets; some programs have features to manage investment portfolios. Tax-preparation software allows you to prepare federal and state returns. Quicken and Money are examples of financial-management packages.
Web authoring	Used to create attractive Web pages and links. Dreamweaver and Microsoft Expression Web are examples of Web-authoring tools.
Music	Creates, stores, and compresses music; Apple's GarageBand lets amateurs create professional-sounding recordings. Sibelius is a score-writing software product available on PCs and Apple Macintosh computers and used around the world by music teachers. Starclass is another music-teaching software package that includes 180 lesson plans.
Photo and video editing	Used to store, edit, and manipulate digital photographs and video clips; for example, Moving Picture is a film-editing program that has been used by ABC, CBS, FOX, NBC, PBS, A&E, and other broadcasters. Adobe Premiere has a variety of editing tools, audio filters, and over 300 video templates that can be customized. Other video-editing software includes Pinnacle Edition DV and Video Toaster.

TABLE 3.10 • Examples of additional application software (continued)

Type of software	Explanation
Educational and reference	Developed for training and distance learning because many university professors believe that colleges and universities must invest in distance learning for their students. Some universities offer complete degree programs using this type of software over the Internet. Blackboard software helps instructors deliver and administer courses over the Internet.
Desktop publishing	Used to create high-quality printed output, including text and graphics; various styles of pages can be laid out. Art and text files from other programs can also be integrated into published pages. A number of the programs in Adobe Creative Suite can be used in desktop publishing.
Computer-aided design (CAD)	Used by engineers, architects, and designers to design and develop buildings, electrical systems, plumbing systems, and more; examples are Autosketch, CorelCAD, and AutoCad.
Statistical	Performs a wide array of statistical tests; two popular applications in the social sciences are SPSS and SAS. Colleges and universities often have a number of courses in statistics that use this type of application software.
Entertainment, games, and leisure	Can be used alone or with other people while connected to the Internet. Games include adventure, sports, simulation, and strategy

Application Software for Businesses and Organizations

Application software is not only useful for individuals, it is indispensable to businesses and organizations in helping them to achieve goals. Application software can be used to process routine transactions (see Figure 3.43), provide information to help people make better decisions, and perform a number of specialized functions to handle unique but important tasks.

FIGURE 3.43 • Order processing in a call center

Call center employees use order entry software to access product information and place orders.

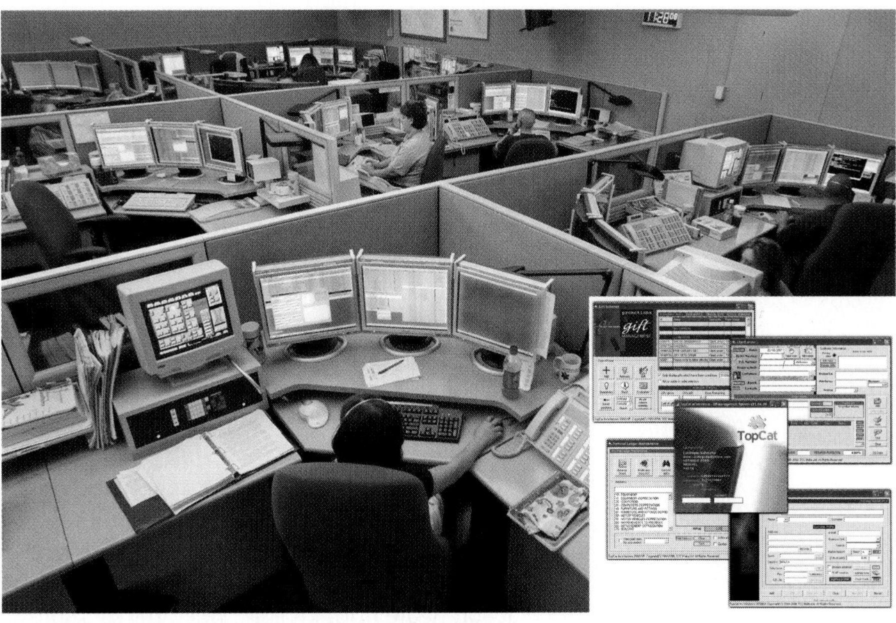

Routine Transaction Processing Software. Software that performs routine functions that benefit the entire organization can be developed or purchased. One

Governing from the Cloud

The U.S. government now has its own App Store! In an effort to reduce its $75 billion annual IT budget, the Fed is encouraging agencies to embrace "cloud computing," delivering information and computing services including software, business systems, and data storage, over the Internet. A new Web site at Apps.Gov provides access to federally approved cloud computing services for Business, IT Services, Productivity, and Social Media. By moving to Internet-delivered services, the federal agencies can reduce their own IT infrastructure and costs. Since cloud computing will enable the government to close and consolidate its own data centers, the move will be good for the environment as well.

Google is designing a version of its cloud applications, including Google Docs, specifically for U.S. government agencies. The applications are being designed to meet regulatory requirements as Google works to achieve the U.S. government's Federal Information Security Management Act (FISMA) certification. The certification is necessary to assure the government that its documents would be safe, secure, and private when managed on Google servers.

Questions

1. How would the U.S. government's use of cloud computing benefit the environment?
2. What dangers to privacy and security are involved with moving from federal data centers to cloud computing data centers?
3. Do you favor the government's move to cloud computing? Why or why not?

Sources

1. *Helft, Miguel, "Now, Even the Government Has an App Store,"* The New York Times, *September 15, 2009, www.nytimes.com.*
2. *Morphy, Erika, "Apps.Gov to Bring Cloud Efficiencies to Federal Agencies,"* E-Commerce Times, *September 16, 2009, www.ecommercetimes.com.*
3. *McMillan, Robert, "Google to deliver 'government cloud' to feds in 2010,"* Computerworld, *September 15, 2009, www.computerworld.com.*

of the first transaction processing software packages was a payroll program for Lyons Bakeries in England, developed in 1954. A fast-food chain might develop a materials ordering and distribution program to make sure that each fast-food franchise gets the necessary raw materials and supplies during the week. This materials ordering and distribution program can be developed internally using staff and resources in the company's Information Technology (IT) department or purchased from an external software company. Local, state, and national governments also need routine transaction processing software. A European lottery, for example, allows the sale of lottery tickets on the Internet and using mobile phones.

As discussed in Chapter 1, transaction processing software is often a component of larger systems called *transaction processing systems (TPSs)*. A few examples are shown in Table 3.11. Some computer vendors, such as SAP, package these important applications into a unified package called *enterprise resource planning (ERP)* packages.

Transaction processing software is also used by organizations to provide valuable services to individuals. One of the world's most popular Web sites, eBay, owes its success to transaction processing software that supports online transactions between individuals. When an eBay buyer purchases an item such as a Spiderman collectable action figure from an eBay seller, the TPS software transfers funds from the buyer's bank account to the seller's.

TABLE 3.11 • Examples of application software for routine business activities

Accounts payable
Accounts receivable
Asset management
Billing
Cash-flow analysis
Check processing
General ledger
Human resources management
Inventory control
Invoicing
Order entry
Payroll
Purchasing
Receiving
Sales ordering
Scheduling
Shipping

Application Software for Information, Decision Support, and Specialized Purposes

As discussed in Chapter 1, routine transaction activities can store and generate a vast amount of data that can be transformed into useful information to help people or groups make better decisions (see Figure 3.44). Although these systems are popular in businesses and corporations, they are also used in many other areas. Voice stress software is being developed to help detect fraud in the insurance industry. Pilot programs have been very successful in detecting people who try to make false claims and in detecting scam insurance companies.

Physicians also use software to make better decisions. Cancer is a major killer, second only to heart attacks for some age groups. People diagnosed with cancer each year undergo radiation, where X-ray beams are shot into the body to kill the cancer cells. Sophisticated software is now being used to increase the cure rate. This type of software analyzes hundreds of scans of the cancerous tumor to create

FIGURE 3.44 • Decision support

Managers and executives depend on application software to assist them with important organizational decisions.

a 3D view of the tumor. The program can then consider thousands of angles and doses of radiation to determine the best radiation program. The software analysis takes only minutes, but the results can save years or decades of life for the patient.

Table 3.12 presents some additional examples of applications for information, decision support, and specialized purposes.

TABLE 3.12 • Examples of application software for information, decision support, and specialized purposes

Application	Description
Management reporting software	A variety of reports can be produced from the data generated and stored from routine processing, including reports that are produced on a schedule, reports of exceptional or critical situations requiring immediate attention, and reports that are produced only when requested or demanded.
Groupware	Groupware can support a team of managers working on the same production problem, letting them share their ideas and work via connected computer systems. Lotus Notes is a popular group software product by IBM that helps people in distant locations work together by sharing schedules, notes, discussions, documents, and actual work on projects. Other examples include Microsoft Exchange and Novell GroupWise.
Decision support software	Special decision support systems (DSSs) can be developed to perform sophisticated qualitative and quantitative analysis for individual decision makers and managers. Software to help decision makers determine the best location for a new warehouse is an example.
Executive support software	Executive support software is designed to support top-level executives and decision makers, such as generals in the military or presidents of companies.
Expert systems software	Expert systems software is programmed to act like an expert in a field such as medicine. Expert system software can be used to diagnose complex medical conditions in patients.

SMART SOFTWARE: ARTIFICIAL INTELLIGENCE

At a Dartmouth College conference in 1956, John McCarthy proposed the term *artificial intelligence* to describe computers with the ability to simulate human thought and behavior. Many AI pioneers attended that first AI conference; a few predicted that computers would be as "smart" as people by the 1960s. That prediction has not yet materialized, but many benefits of artificial intelligence research can be seen in software applications today.

We are entering the era of smart machines, when computers are able to process information as fast as or faster than the human brain. Comparing processors to brains is a bit like comparing apples to oranges. Brains process in a massively parallel manner using 100 billion processors (neurons) that work together to form our thoughts. Neurons are slow compared to today's computers, but because they function simultaneously, our fastest supercomputers are only just now approaching brain-level processing power. Processing power is only one step in building a thinking machine. The tricky part is in the software.

The "Blue Brain" project is a bold attempt to simulate a human brain at a molecular level in software running on the world's fastest supercomputer, IBM's Blue Gene. The project has succeeded in simulating the functioning brain of a mouse. It has been estimated that we will have effective software models of the human brain by the mid-2020s. It has been further speculated that by 2060 one computer will be smarter than the entire human race.

Some refer to the time when computers exceed human intelligence as the *technological singularity*. This singularity is expected to spur an intelligence explosion where computers take their training and development into their own "hands" and rapidly accelerate their own advancement and hopefully the advancement of humankind. In his book *The Singularity Is Near,* Ray Kurzweil (Figure 3.45) takes an optimistic view of the near future and the impending singularity. He states that "the Singularity will allow us to transcend these limitations of our biological bodies and brains. We will gain power over our fates. Our mortality will be in our own hands.... We will fully understand human thinking and will vastly extend and expand its reach."[8]

FIGURE 3.45 • The Singularity Is Near

AI expert and author Ray Kurzweil believes that the boundary between man and machine is disappearing, and that the days ahead will be the "most transforming and thrilling period in history."

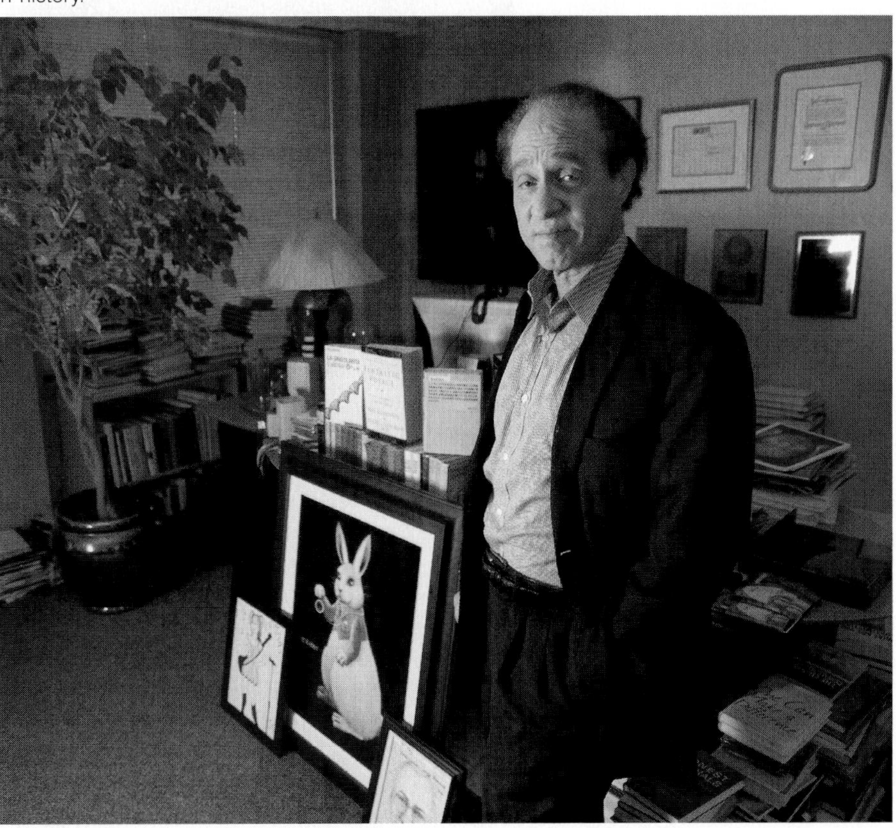

While the future of humanity with regard to the technological singularity is unclear, progress in many areas of artificial intelligence is clearly affecting our daily lives in many areas. AI techniques are being implemented in both system software and application software to make our lives easier and to support us in our work.

An Overview of Artificial Intelligence

Science fiction novels and popular movies have featured scenarios of computer systems and intelligent machines taking over the world (see Figure 3.46). From the 1927 movie *Metropolis* to 1968's *2001: A Space Odyssey* to the more recent *The Matrix* trilogy, *A.I.*, and *I Robot*, storytellers have entertained and thrilled the public by pitting humans against intelligent machines. While intellectually superior computers taking over the world is a scary idea, the reality is that artificial intelligence has so far been a very useful tool.

FIGURE 3.46 • Artificial intelligence in movies

In *I, Robot*, set in 2035, robots begin acting independently, perpetrating crimes and potentially threatening the survival of the human race.

Artificial intelligence (AI) refers to the science and engineering of creating computer systems that simulate human thought and behavior. AI is of interest to many professionals, including computer scientists, psychologists, philosophers, neuroscientists, and engineers, who often collaborate on research. While some researchers are working to create computers that can think like humans, most are focused on developing software that can automate specific tasks that require a subset of human intelligence. As with all computer software, the overall purpose of artificial intelligence applications is to help individuals and organizations achieve their goals.

Before exploring the field of artificial intelligence, it is useful to first consider what defines human intelligence. What makes us intelligent beings? This is an area of study known as *cognition*—the manner in which our brain processes information that allows us to acquire knowledge and understanding. One attribute of intelligence is the ability to learn, or acquire knowledge. How do we do this? Often we acquire knowledge through observation. Observation requires sensory input, so our senses are an important component in acquiring knowledge. Here's some food for thought (no pun intended): could an individual without any senses acquire knowledge?

If you think about this very deeply you will no doubt end up pondering some deep philosophical questions such as "when does human life begin?" and "what is a soul?" Conversations about human versus artificial intelligence seem to inevitably lead to metaphysical and philosophical questions. When and if computers acquire intelligence equal to or beyond that of humans, there will no doubt be great philosophical debates as to whether an intelligent computer has a soul. For the purpose of our discussion we will stick to a scientific understanding of intelligence.

Biologically speaking, we acquire information through our senses, which stimulates neural activity in our brains. Chemical synapses create junctions between neurons that carry signals from neuron to neuron. These synapses allow neurons to form interconnected neural circuits, which are the basis for human thought. As we repeatedly observe phenomena around us, the neural circuits in our brain become stronger to represent knowledge and beliefs. For example, if we observe geese flying south prior to winter one year, we may not make much of it. But as we observe the same phenomenon year after year, we begin to recognize the pattern as being a seasonal occurrence.

In order to imbue computers with intelligence, we must be able to recognize the traits of intelligent behavior so that we can recognize them in computers. Certainly our ability to use our senses to observe the world around us and store knowledge (remember) are important elements of intelligence. Another important element is our ability to reach conclusions and establish new understandings by combining information in new ways. For example, if you notice that your friend is especially grumpy, and you know your friend had an exam in the previous class, you might assume that the exam didn't go well. The word *assume* is another intelligent capability: drawing conclusions when not all of the necessary information is known. Another important element in exhibiting intelligence is our ability to communicate and use language.

Communication and language are key elements in the Turing Test. Alan Turing was an English mathematician, logician, and cryptographer who is well known for his belief that computers would someday be as intelligent as humans. In his 1950 paper titled "Computing machinery and intelligence," Turing proposed a test, now known widely as the **Turing Test**, that he claimed would be able to determine if a computer exhibited human intelligence. The Turing Test proceeds as follows: "A human judge engages in a natural language conversation with two other parties, one a human and the other a machine; if the judge cannot reliably tell which is which, then the machine is said to pass the test." Turing believed that if a machine could pass his test, it would have to be considered intelligent. Many AI researchers have challenged Turing's assumption, claiming that clever use of language does not necessarily imply intelligence.

While no machine is said to have passed the Turing Test, many are getting better at impersonating humans. Artificial Life, Inc. manufactures virtual people and puts them to work on the Web and on cell phones. The company offers virtual hosts to greet visitors at corporate Web sites. Using a chat window, the virtual host is programmed to participate in friendly banter with the visitor and answer questions about the company. If the visitor's questions get too difficult, the virtual host turns it over to a human customer support agent. People who use the system say that they are unable to detect whether they are chatting with a virtual or human agent. Artificial Life's latest and most popular products are virtual girlfriend and virtual boyfriend software. Tired of dealing with your human boyfriend or girlfriend? Download v-girl or v-boy to your cell phone and develop an AI relationship through chat and video (Figure 3.47). Watch out, though; v-relationships can be as complex and difficult as real ones!

FIGURE 3.47 • Virtual boyfriend

Artificial Life's v-boy and v-girl software for cell phones provides virtual relationships that can develop or fall apart.

Today, there are profound differences between human and artificial intelligence, but the differences are declining in number, as shown in Table 3.13. One of the driving forces behind AI research is an attempt to understand how human beings actually reason and think. It is believed that the ability to create machines that can reason will be possible only once the human processes for doing so are fully understood. Experts in the AI field are continuously learning about human intelligence as they create artificial intelligence.

TABLE 3.13 • A comparison of natural and artificial intelligence

Attributes	Natural intelligence (human)	Artificial intelligence (machine)
Acquire a large amount of external information	High	Low
Use sensors (eyes, ears, touch, smell)	High	Low
Be creative and imaginative	High	Low
Learn from experience	High	Low
Be forgetful	High	Low
Make complex calculations	Low	High
Be adaptive	High	Low
Use a variety of information sources	High	Low
Transfer information	Low	High

Teaching Computers to Think

There are many uses for intelligent software. AI software assists us with evaluating and interpreting large amounts of data. AI software can act as an informed advisor with difficult decisions. AI software can provide a challenging game opponent in a virtual reality computer-generated world or in a game of chess. In order for software to be able to perform any of these functions well, it requires a few useful components:

- A set of logical rules to apply to the input to produce useful output; all software has this ability
- Instructions for how to handle unexpected input and still produce useful output; this would be the ability for the software to "wing it" when its set of rules no longer exactly fits the scenario
- The ability to learn with experience to become better at what it is designed to do; this ability is referred to as *machine learning*.

A number of formal methods are used to create intelligent software that has these abilities. They fall under two categories: **conventional AI** methodologies such as expert systems, case-based reasoning, Bayesian networks, and behavior-based AI that rely on the programmer to instill the software with logical functionality to solve problems, and **computational intelligence** methodologies such as neural networks, fuzzy systems, and evolutionary computation that set up a system whereby the software can develop intelligence through an iterative process. Figure 3.48 illustrates the hierarchical organization of AI methodologies. It is often the case that AI developers combine methods from different methodologies to achieve their goals.

FIGURE 3.48 • AI methodologies

AI research is divided into two types of methodologies: conventional AI and computational intelligence.

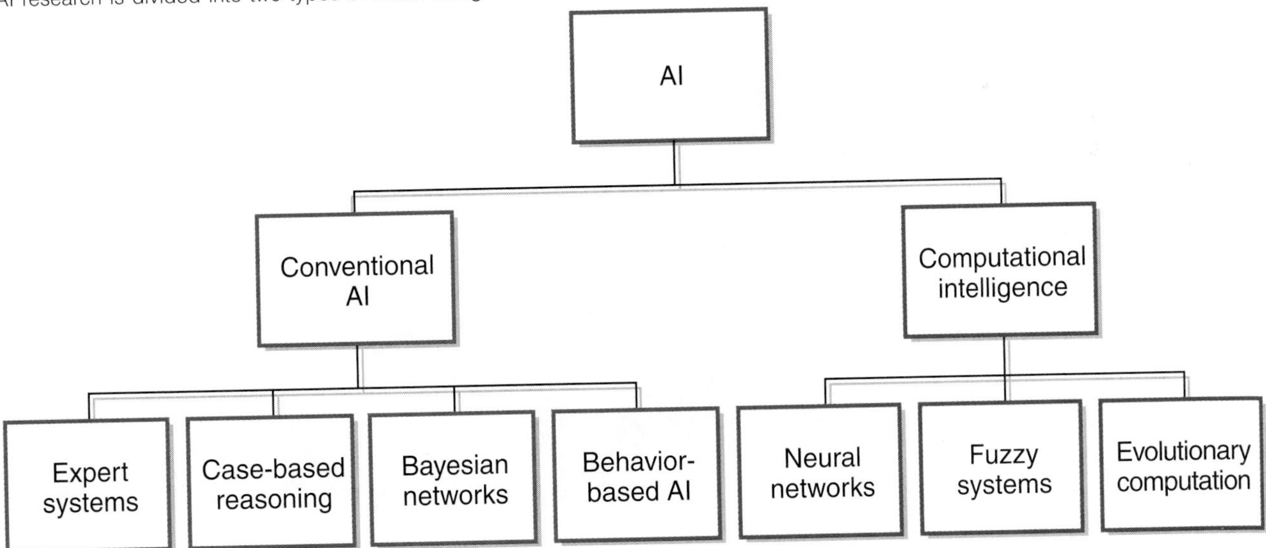

Expert Systems. An **expert system (ES)** is software that functions like a human expert in a particular field or area. Expert systems are created with the assistance of a human expert who provides subject-specific knowledge. The rules applied by the expert to perform some activity are programmed into the expert system software. Charles Bailey, one of the original members of the Library and Information Technology Association, developed one of the first expert systems in the mid-1980s to search the University of Houston's library to retrieve requested resources and citations.

Like human experts, computerized expert systems use heuristics, or "rules of thumb," to arrive at conclusions or make suggestions. A *heuristic* provides a solution to a problem that can't necessarily be proven as correct but usually produces a good result. The biggest challenge in designing an expert system is in capturing knowledge and relationships that are not precise or exact. Heuristics help in this regard.

Many expert systems are used in various professions every day. Computerized expert systems have been developed to diagnose diseases when given a patient's symptoms (see Figure 3.49), suggest the cause of a mechanical failure of an engine, predict future weather events, and assist in designing new products and systems. FocalPoint, by TriPath Imaging (*www.tripathimaging.com*), is an expert system that examines Pap smears for signs of cervical cancer. The FDA has approved FocalPoint for primary cancer screening. Expert systems are also used in the automotive industry to solve hard-to-diagnose problems. An expert system was used to determine the best way to distribute weight in a ferryboat to reduce the risk of capsizing or sinking. Expert systems can also be used to spot defective welds during the manufacturing process. The expert system analyzes radiographic images and suggests which welds could be flawed. The CIA is testing such software to see whether it can be used to detect possible terrorists when they make hotel or airline reservations.

FIGURE 3.49 • Expert systems

Medical expert systems help diagnose patients and suggest treatments.

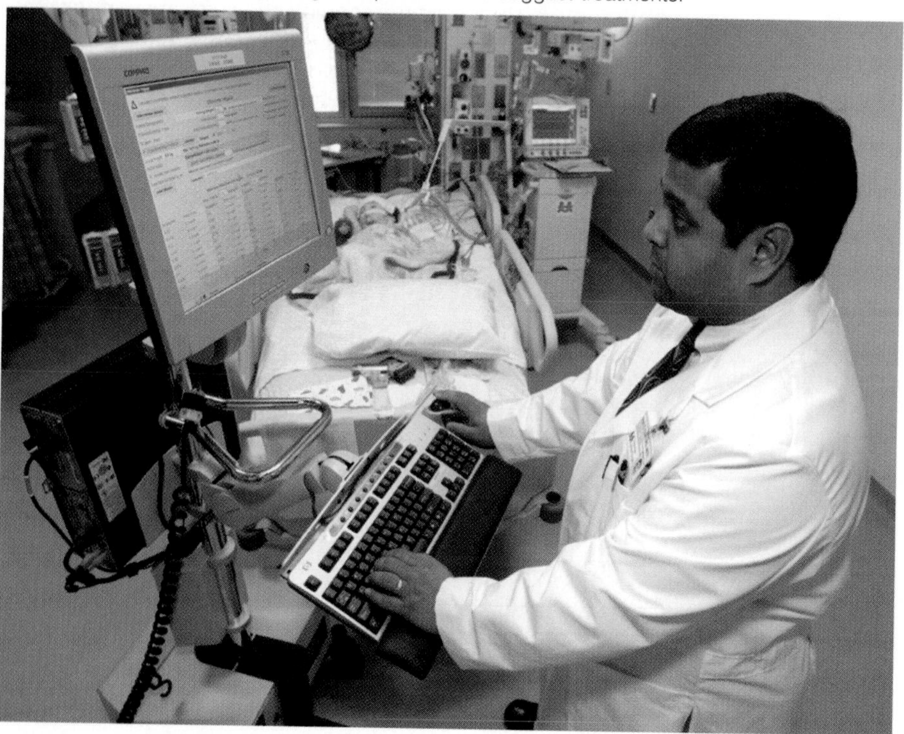

Case-Based Reasoning. In *case-based reasoning*, the AI software maintains a library of problem cases and solutions and, when confronted by a new problem, adjusts and applies a relevant previous solution to the new problem. Case-based reasoning relies on the four Rs for solving new problems:

- Retrieve: Find cases in the case library relevant to the new problem.
- Reuse: Map the solutions from a previous case or cases to the variables of the new problem, adjusting where necessary.
- Revise: Test the solution and revise if necessary.
- Retain: Store the new problem and its newly acquired successful solution as a case in the library.

AI software built on case-based reasoning is useful for help-desk support, medical diagnosis, and other situations where there are many similar cases to diagnose. Customer support agents can make use of case-based reasoning systems to help them with assisting customers. The system looks up similar previous customer cases and provides previous solutions.

Bayesian Networks. A *Bayesian network*, sometimes called a belief network, is a graphical model that represents a set of variables and their relationships and dependencies. For example, a Bayesian network could be designed to represent the variables in a person's behavior, physical chemistry, and family history to determine the likeliness that the person suffers from depression. A Bayesian network provides a model of a real-life scenario that can be incorporated into software to create intelligence. Bayesian networks are used in medical software, engineering, document classification, image processing, military applications (see Figure 3.50), and other activities.

FIGURE 3.50 • Bayesian network: Combat Air Identification Fusion Algorithm (CAIFA)

This Bayesian network is used in missile defense software and draws on multiple, diverse sources of ID evidence to determine the allegiance, nationality, platform type, and intention of targeted aircraft.

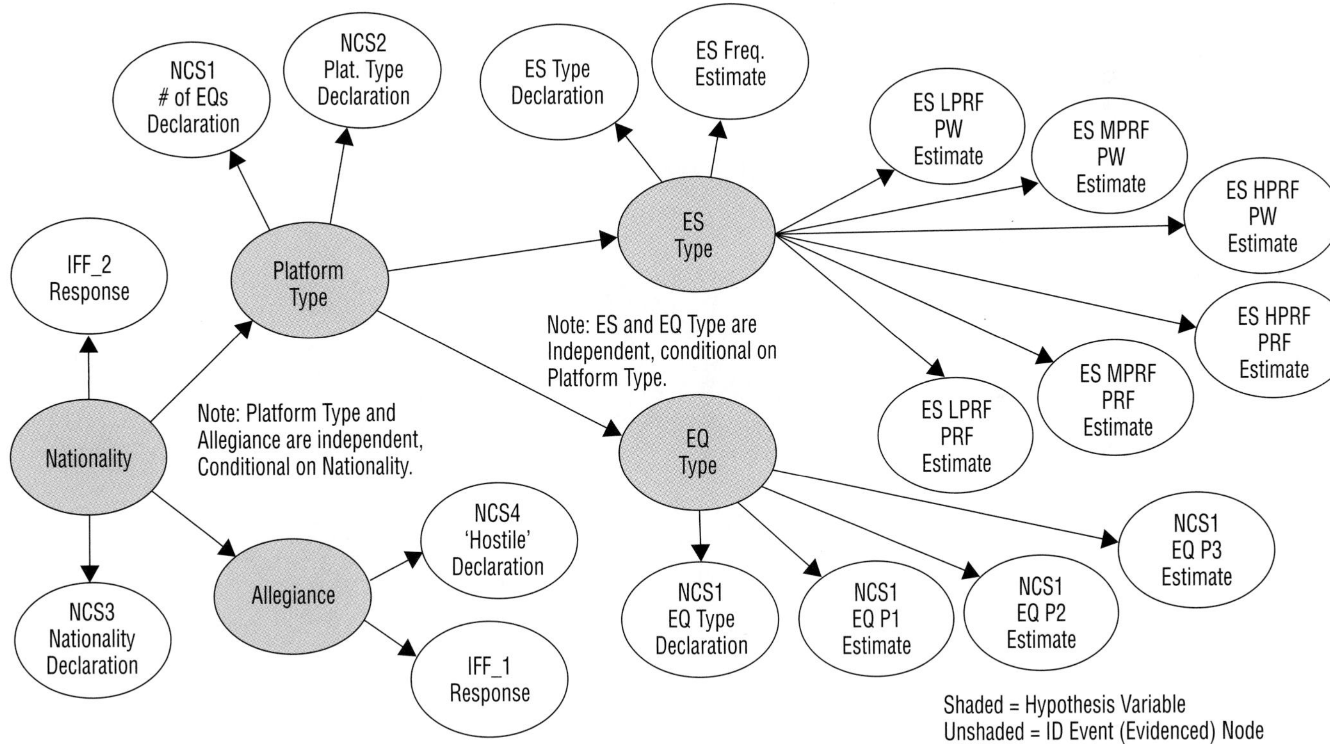

Behavior-Based AI. *Behavior-based AI* is very popular in the programming of robots. It is a methodology that simulates intelligence by combining many semi-autonomous modules. Each module has a specific activity for which it is responsible. By combining these simple modules, the resulting system exhibits intelligent behavior; it becomes smarter than the sum of its parts. You may have met Robosapien (Figure 3.51). Robosapien and other such robotic toys are controlled by behavior-based AI software.

FIGURE 3.51 • Behavor-based AI: Robosapien

Behavior-based AI techniques are used in the software that makes Robosapien sensitive to the surrounding world.

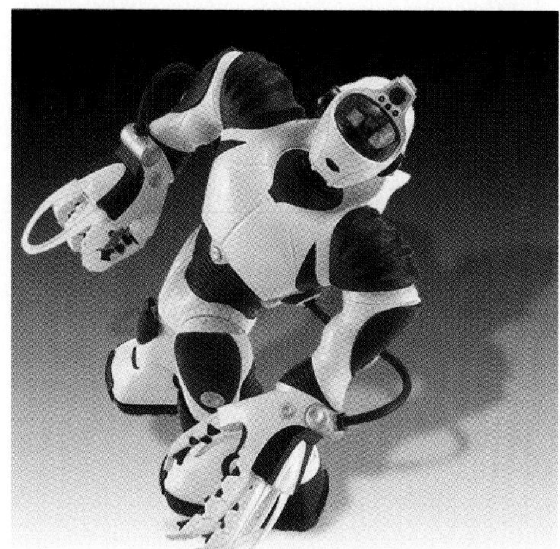

Neural Networks. An increasingly important aspect of AI involves neural networks. A **neural network** simulates the functioning of the neurons in a human brain in software (see Figure 3.52). Initially a neural network is loaded with a random program, and the output is measured against a desired output, which positively or negatively affects the pathways between neurons. When the neural net begins getting closer to the desired output, the positive effects on the system begin to create circuits that become trained to produce the correct output. Similar to a child's learning, a neural net discovers its own rules. For example, a neural net can be trained to recognize the characteristics of a male face and, once trained, may be able to accurately identify faces in photos as male or female.

FIGURE 3.52 • Natural and artificial neural networks

AI neural networks use software to simulate the processing that takes place between neurons in our brain.

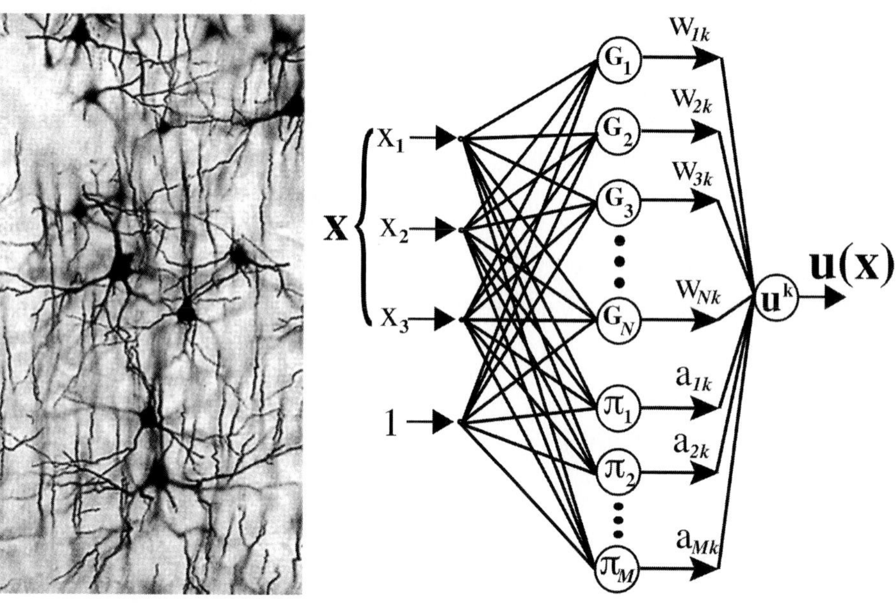

Once a neural net is trained, it can process many pieces of data at once with impressive results. Some of the specific features of neural networks include:

- The ability to retrieve information even if some of the neural nodes fail
- Fast modification of stored data as a result of new information
- The ability to discover relationships and trends in large databases
- The ability to solve complex problems for which all of the information is not present

Neural networks can help us understand how our own brains work. Altering the rules of interaction between "neurons" can lead to interesting and educational results. Neuroscientists study and tinker with neural nets to better understand emergent behavior in the brain.

Neural networks excel at pattern recognition, and this ability can be used in a wide array of applications including voice recognition, visual pattern recognition, robotic control, symbol manipulation, and decision making. Neural nets can be used to help prevent terrorism by analyzing and matching images from multiple cameras focusing on people or locations. Sandia Laboratories has developed a neural network system to give soldiers in a military conflict real-time advice on strategy and tactics. Neural network software designed for investors looks for stock market patterns and advises brokers when to buy or sell. Some hospitals use neural networks to determine a patient's likelihood of contracting cancer or other diseases. Companies making robots can use neural networks to improve motor coordination and movement in robots. The neural network software can give the robot a smooth walk and allows it to get up if it falls.

Fuzzy Systems. Computers typically work with numerical certainty; certain input values always result in the same output. However, in the real world, as you know from experience, certainty is not always the case. To handle this dilemma, a specialty research area in computer science, called fuzzy systems, based on fuzzy logic, has been developed. **Fuzzy logic** is derived from fuzzy set theory, which deals with reasoning that is approximate rather than precise. A simple example of fuzzy logic might be one in which cumulative probabilities do not add up to 100 percent, a state that occurs frequently in medical diagnosis. Another example of fuzzy logic involves unclear terms, such as *tall* or *many*. Fuzzy logic deals with ambiguous criteria or probabilities and events that are not mutually exclusive. Fuzzy systems based on fuzzy logic allow people to incorporate interpretations and relationships that are not completely precise or known.

A *fuzzy control system* is based on fuzzy logic and is typically used to control machines. For example, the microcontroller that controls the antilock brakes in your car uses fuzzy logic, based on varying road conditions, to apply just enough brakes to stop quickly while avoiding a skid.

Evolutionary Computation. *Evolutionary computation* includes areas of AI that derive intelligence by attempting many solutions and throwing away the ones that don't work: a "survival of the fittest" approach. A **genetic algorithm** is a form of evolutionary computation that is used to solve large, complex problems where a number of algorithms or models change and evolve until the best one emerges. The approach is based on the theory of evolution, which requires variation and natural selection. The first step in developing a genetic algorithm solution is to change or vary a number of competing solutions to a problem. This can be done by changing the parts of a program or combining different program segments into a new program. If you think of program segments as building blocks similar to genetic material, this process is similar to the evolution of species, where the genetic makeup of a plant or animal mutates or changes over time (see Figure 3.53).

FIGURE 3.53 • Genetic algorithms

The process of a genetic algorithm is similar to the evolution of species, where the genetic makeup of a plant or animal mutates over time.

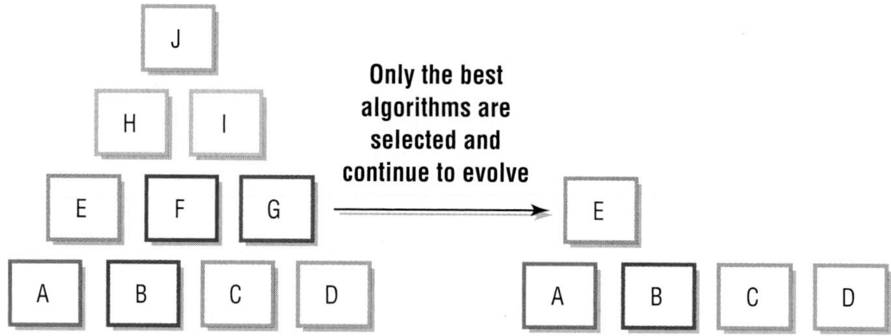

The second step is to select only the best models or algorithms, which then continue to evolve. Programs or program segments that are not as good as others are discarded. This part of the process is similar to natural selection, where only the best or fittest members of a species survive and continue to evolve. This process of variation and natural selection continues until the genetic algorithm yields the best possible solution to the original problem. For example, some investment firms use genetic algorithms to help select the best stocks or bonds. Genetic algorithms are also used in computer science and mathematics.

AI Applications

Artificial intelligence has many and varied applications. AI techniques can be integrated into systems and applications to make them more intuitive. AI software is used to automate various types of logic used to make decisions. AI software can be connected to sensors and mechanical apparatus to create a variety of forms of robots. This section explores some of the common uses for AI.

Robotics. **Robotics** involves developing mechanical or computer devices to perform tasks that require a high degree of precision or are tedious or hazardous for humans. In recent years, robots have also become a form of entertainment in toys for children and adults. Contemporary robotics combines both high-precision machine capabilities and sophisticated controlling software. The controlling software in robots is what is most important in terms of AI.

There are many applications of robots, and research into these unique devices continues. For many businesses, robots are used to do the three Ds—dull, dirty, and dangerous jobs. Manufacturers use robots to assemble and paint products. The U.S. Army is involved in developing medical robotics to allow doctors to perform surgery in combat areas via remote control. Not only does this technique make it safer for doctors in combat situations, it allows them to "be" in several places at once. A surgical system, for example, can allow doctors to operate using a robotic arm. Sitting at a console, the surgeon can replace a heart valve or remove a tumor. The robotic

IT'S A BIRD... IT'S A PLANE... IT'S AN INSECT ROBOT

Sound like science fiction? Well, Japanese scientists are working to make it a reality. They hope to create robot-moths to detect drugs and robot-bees to locate earthquake survivors. Already researchers have attached a device similar to a toy car to a male moth and used female moth pheromones to motivate the insect to turn the device right or left. Researchers hope soon to construct an entire artificial insect brain.

Japanese scientists aim to create robot-insects
Miwa Suzuki
AFP
July 13, 2009
http://www.google.com/hostednews/afp/article/ALeqM5i1yofjORtZ9Oo5LHEfRTNHlsLppg

arm can be accurately controlled and requires only a small incision in the patient, making surgery more precise and the recovery easier. Some surgical robots cost more than $1 million and have multiple surgical arms and sophisticated vision systems.

FIGURE 3.54 • DARPA Grand Challenge

This robotic vehicle maneuvers itself over the rough terrain of the DARPA Grand Challenge.

The DARPA Grand Challenge is the ultimate robotic test. Sponsored by the U.S. Defense Department's Advanced Research Projects Agency (DARPA), the event offers $2 million for the winning entry of a robotic vehicle that can navigate a challenging course autonomously, without any communication with humans (Figure 3.54). DARPA hopes that the annual event will spur advances in robotics technology for use by the military.

Computer Vision. Another application of AI involves computer vision. **Computer vision** combines hardware (cameras and scanners) and AI software that permit computers to capture, store, and interpret visual images and pictures. A California wine bottle manufacturer, for example, can use a computerized vision system to inspect wine bottles for flaws. The vision system can save the bottle producer both time and money.

Vision systems can be used to give robots "sight" (see Figure 3.55). Generally, robots with vision systems can recognize black and white and some shades of gray, but they do not have good color or three-dimensional vision. Other systems concentrate on only a few key features in an image, ignoring the rest. It may take years before a robot or other computer system can "see" in full color and draw conclusions from what it sees, the way humans do.

FIGURE 3.55 • ASIMO (advanced step in innovative mobility)

Honda's ASIMO robot has eyes and a vision system sophisticated enough that it can use light switches, turn doorknobs and work at tables.

Computer vision systems are also being developed to assist in human sight. Researchers at MIT have developed a microchip that could return vision to the blind. The microchip, when implanted and connected to the optic nerve, receives wireless signals from a camera mounted in a pair of eyeglasses. The result could provide enough vision to allow formerly blind individuals to navigate down a street and recognize faces.[9]

Natural Language Processing. **Natural language processing** uses AI techniques to enable computers to generate and understand natural human languages, such as English. One area of natural language processing that is evident in today's software and business systems is speech recognition. **Speech recognition** allows a computer to understand and react to spoken statements and commands (Figure 3.56). With speech recognition, it is possible to speak into a microphone connected to a computer and have the computer convert the electrical impulses generated from the voice into typed words and sentences or program commands. Both Microsoft Windows and Mac OS X have utilities that allow you to speak commands to the computer. Microsoft Word has a speech utility that allows you to dictate to the computer instead of typing. Speech recognition is not to be confused with voice recognition, which is a different technology used in the security field to identify an individual by the sound of his or her voice.

FIGURE 3.56 • Speech recognition technology

Speech recognition technology has advanced enough that many computer users are considering it as an alternative to typing.

Speech recognition had to overcome some difficult obstacles before it was ready for market:

- Speech segmentation: If you listen to a person speak from a computer's perspective, you would notice that there is roughly the same length of pause between syllables in words as there is between words in the sentence (roughly none). How is the computer to determine where one word ends and the next begins?
- Ambiguity: There is no difference between the sound of the words *their, there,* and *they're.* When spoken, how is the computer to know which one is intended? Also, consider the sentence "Time flies like an arrow." As a human you can understand the meaning of this sentence, but a computer would have to choose between several interpretations. Perhaps it would consider that this is a command to measure the speed (time) of an insect (a fly) as an arrow would.
- Voice variety: Everyone speaks differently. It would be difficult for one program to understand both Arnold Schwarzenegger and Paris Hilton.

The only way to overcome these obstacles is with AI techniques. The computer must learn a dictionary of words to determine how to parse a sentence into individual words. It must also learn grammatical rules in order to overcome the problem of ambiguity. It must also have some insight into human thinking to understand a sentence such as "Time flies like an arrow." Finally, speech recognition must be able to learn the individual speaking quirks of the user. For this reason, speech recognition software gets better the longer it is trained to an individual user.

Perhaps you've encountered speech recognition when using directory assistance or making collect or calling card calls. Some brokerage firms have search engines that use natural language processing to allow customers to get their questions answered through the brokerage firm's call center.

Other natural-language-processing applications include foreign language interpreting and text-to-speech processing.

Handwriting Recognition. In the same vein as speech recognition, handwriting recognition provides an alternative form of input for computer systems. *Handwriting recognition* uses AI techniques in software that is able to translate handwritten characters or words into computer-readable data. *Graffiti* is handwriting recognition technology developed for the Palm Pilot that allows users to write one character at a time using a custom-designed alphabet. Microsoft uses stronger AI technology in its handwriting recognition software that allows OneNote users to write out full words and sentences anywhere on the touch-sensitive screen with printed characters or in cursive.

Face Recognition. Face recognition is a hot area of AI research for governments working to secure their borders. Face recognition is a form of computer vision that uses cameras and AI software to identify individuals by unique facial characteristics (Figure 3.57). Face recognition is used in authentication—verifying the identity of a person—for access to secure areas or systems, and in surveillance to catch criminals.

FIGURE 3.57 • Face recognition software

Face recognition software uses computer vision to capture images of an individual's face and match them against facial images in a database.

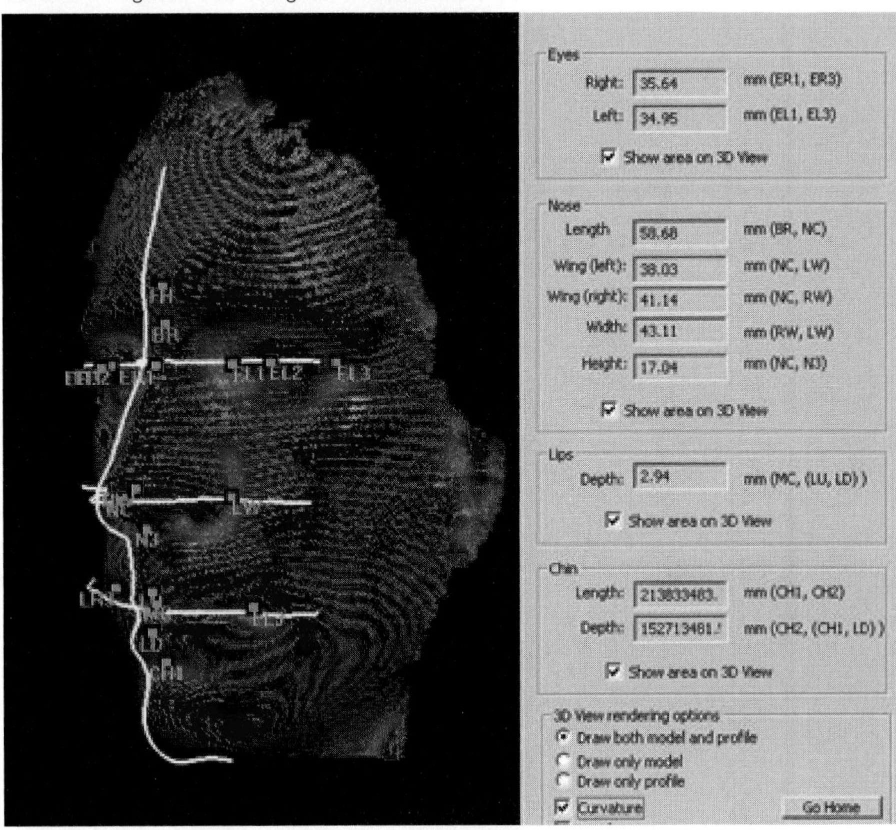

Australian travelers flying into or out of Australia are learning about face recognition. The Australian SmartGate system uses facial-scan technology to compare the traveler's face against the scan encoded in a microchip contained in the traveler's ePassport.[10] Security agencies are hesitant to rely too heavily on face recognition technology to identify individuals in a crowd, since the technology can be easily fooled by disguises. Australia's approach of matching a scan against a previous scan is one that should be more trustworthy.

Speech recognition, handwriting recognition, and face recognition all fall under the general AI category of pattern recognition.

Intelligent Agents. An **intelligent agent** (also called an intelligent robot or *bot*, an abbreviation for robot) consists of programs and a knowledge base used to perform a specific task for a person, a process, or another program. Like an agent who searches for the best endorsement deals for a top athlete, an intelligent agent often searches to find the best price, the best schedule, or the best solution to a problem. Often used to search the vast resources of the Internet, intelligent agents can help people find information on an important topic or the best price for a new digital camera. Intelligent agents have been used by the U.S. Army to route security clearance information for soldiers to the correct departments and individuals. What used to take days when done manually now takes hours. Intelligent agents can also be used to make travel arrangements, monitor incoming e-mail for viruses or junk mail, and coordinate the meetings and schedules of busy executives. Some companies use intelligent agents to find job candidates by searching millions of resumes in a database by title, company, gender, and other factors to find the best job candidates.

Artificial Creativity. *Artificial creativity* is a branch of AI that works to program computers to express themselves through art, music, poetry, and other expressive outlets. Some AI software has become quite talented at creating emotionally moving works of art. The most useful output, however, is the insight it gives us into the workings of human creativity.

Harold Cohen was an English painter with an established international reputation before he joined and eventually directed the Center for Research in Computing and the Arts (CRCA) at the University of California, San Diego. The mission of the CRCA is to facilitate the invention of new art forms that arise out of the developments of digital technologies. Harold Cohen created an AI artist named AARON that independently paints large impressive works of art with paintbrush and canvas (see Figure 3.58).

FIGURE 3.58 • A painting by a machine

This painting was created by a painting robot named AARON who was created by Harold Cohen. Who should get the credit?

AI expert Ray Kurzweil has created an AI program he calls the Cybernetic Poet that is able to create poetry in the style of human poets. The software "reads" poem samples from one or more human poets, then creates one of its own in the same style. Here is a haiku written by the Cybernetic Poet after reading the poetry of John Keats and Wendy Dennis:

You broke my soul
The juice of eternity,
The spirit of my lips.

British jazz saxophonist Paul Hodgson has written a music program called Improviser that is able to create songs on a synthesizer in styles ranging from Bach to jazz great Charlie Parker. The software has earned the respect of many musicians.

Virtual Reality

Virtual reality is a computer-simulated environment that can be manipulated by a user. Virtual reality is often linked to artificial intelligence because it leans on AI technologies in its development and also because, like AI, it is artificial, a simulation created in a computer. In fact, another name for virtual reality is artificial reality.

Immersive virtual reality refers to a simulation in which the user becomes fully immersed in an artificial, three-dimensional world that is completely generated by a computer (see Figure 3.59). By using a special headset with a computer-simulated view and stereo sound, you could become immersed in the computer simulation as if it were the real world. As you turn your head, the virtual world pans around before your eyes. Special gloves could allow you to manipulate objects in the virtual world. A treadmill could allow you to walk around the virtual landscape. Headphones and 3D stereo could create the illusion of sound from various locations in the virtual space. Such technology is useful for playing realistic games, training on the battlefield, or taking a tour of a building.

FIGURE 3.59 • Virtual reality systems

Virtual reality systems use computers to simulate an environment or event.

A virtual reality CAVE (Cave Automatic Virtual Environment) allows the user to experience a virtual environment without the headset. CAVE technology projects images to four, five, or six surfaces of a room, transforming the room into a virtual landscape. If you have ever seen the Holodeck on the television show *Star Trek*, you have a good idea of what CAVE technology has as its goal.

Lighter forms of virtual reality are used on the Web and home PC that do not require any special hardware. Developmental tools allow developers to create 3D environments that can be manipulated with your mouse. You are probably familiar with Web sites that provide a 360-degree view of a product like an iPhone or a car. At Toyota.com you can use such a tool to sit in the driver's seat and look around. Other Web sites allow you to take a tour of a home or condo anywhere around the world, see inside the human body, or be on stage with a rock band.

PC software in general has recently taken a turn toward virtual reality. The latest operating systems from Microsoft and Apple make heavy use of high-end 3D graphics processors that transform your computing experience into a virtual world of its own. Icons, taskbars, and windows zoom in and out of the 3D space that is your display. The PC desktop has become a 3D virtual space with translucent and reflective objects, and a look and feel that simulates depth. Microsoft and Apple have provided programming tools to allow other companies to create 3D animated software to run on their platforms. It is easy to foresee a computing future where our PCs become alternative virtual worlds that we enter to work and play.

ACTION PLAN

Remember Alex from the beginning of the chapter, who wants to know what software she should get for her used notebook? Here are answers to her questions.

1. What is the best operating system for Alex to load on her used notebook?

Since the PC that Alex was given is not a Mac, Alex will have to choose between Windows and Linux. With only a $200 budget, Alex will not be able to afford Windows 7 and Microsoft Office 2010. Alex's best option is to go with Linux and save her money until she can afford a new Windows computer or Mac. Of course, it's possible that Alex will learn to prefer Linux over the other two platforms. Alex downloads and installs Ubuntu on her notebook.

2. Which productivity software will best suit Alex's needs?

Ubuntu comes with many software applications. The productivity suite OpenOffice.org is able to read and write Microsoft Office–formatted documents, so she should be able to work on documents for her job. In order to make sure that this is okay, Alex should talk with the system administrator at the law firm. Also, Alex has access to lots of free productivity software available on the Web, like Google Docs.

3. What other software can assist Alex with her interests?

Alex can visit *http://directory.fsf.org* to find more free software for her Linux PC. It might be a good idea to find PIM software to assist with managing her schedule, or Alex could make use of Web-based PIM like Google Calendar. Alex may have challenges getting her Ubuntu notebook to do all the things a Windows PC can do. For example, iTunes is not available for Ubuntu. However, a quick Google search turns up solutions for transferring music between her iPod and Ubuntu notebook.

Summary

LEARNING OBJECTIVE 1

Explain how software is created, distributed, installed, and maintained.

Software consists of the electronic instructions and programs that govern a computer system's functioning and that control the workings of the computer hardware. System software is the set of programs that coordinates the activities of the hardware and various computer programs. Application software consists of programs written to perform tasks or solve problems for people, groups, and organizations. Software usually consists of a number of files, ranging from a few to dozens or more.

Figure 3.10—p. 127

All software, both system software and application software, is written in coding schemes called programming languages. A programming language, the primary tool of computer programmers, provides commands for writing software that are translated to the detailed step-by-step instructions executed by the processor to achieve an objective or solve a problem. Using a programming language, programmers create a source code file that is translated into an object code file containing the machine-level instructions that the processor carries out. Most software is developed using a software tool called a compiler. Programming APIs and developer toolkits provide convenient tools for developing software for specific platforms such as Facebook, the iPhone, and Google Android.

A copyright defines exclusive rights legally granted to the owner. A software license defines the permissions, rights, and restrictions provided to the person who purchases a copy of the software. A single-user license permits the user to install the software on one computer, or sometimes two computers, used by one person. Open-source software is distributed, typically for free, with the source code so that it can be studied, changed, and improved by its users.

Off-the-shelf software is mass-produced for general public use. Businesses find it necessary to have custom software developed to meet their unique and specific needs. Shareware is a marketing method for distributing software that allows customers to use software free of charge for a limited time in order to evaluate the software and decide if they wish to purchase it. Software often has bugs consisting of one or more defects or problems that prevent the software from working as intended. Software companies often provide patches and updates to overcome software bugs.

LEARNING OBJECTIVE 2

Describe the functions of system software and operating systems, and provide examples of operating systems for PCs, larger computer systems, and mobile devices.

An operating system (OS) is a set of computer programs that runs or controls the computer hardware and acts as an interface with both application programs and users. In a desktop or notebook PC, when the computer system is started, a process called the boot process, which is stored in ROM, runs system checks and then transfers the operating system from the hard drive to RAM. One of the most important functions of any operating system is providing a user interface. Operating systems control many common hardware functions such as capturing user input and providing output; managing the processor, memory, and storage; formatting disks; and communicating with peripheral devices. Today's popular PC operating systems include Microsoft Windows, Mac OS, and Linux. Another type of system software, besides the operating system, is a utility program. A utility program is any system software besides the OS that assists in maintaining, managing, and protecting computer system resources.

Figure 3.25—p. 144

LEARNING OBJECTIVE 3

Describe different types of productivity software and explain how application software assists people at home, at work, and in between.

Word-processing software allows users to create formatted text documents varying in complexity from simple to-do lists to professional magazine layouts. Spreadsheet software, like Microsoft Excel and Corel Quattro Pro, supports complicated numerical analysis and calculations and allows users to perform "what-if" analysis on financial and other numeric data. Presentation software supports formal presentations by providing "slides" that can be used to accompany and embellish a live presentation or to present the material without the use of a human presenter. Database-management software is used to store, manipulate, and manage data in order to find and present useful information. Personal information management (PIM) software helps individuals store useful information, such as to-do lists, appointment calendars, and contact lists. A software suite is a collection of application software packages sold together. Software suites can include word processors, spreadsheets, presentation software, database-management systems, personal information managers, and more. There are a number of other interesting and powerful application software tools for individuals. Application software is not only useful for individuals but is indispensable to businesses and organizations in helping them to achieve goals.

Figure 3.36—p. 158

LEARNING OBJECTIVE 4

List areas of research in artificial intelligence and tell how AI is being used in everyday applications.

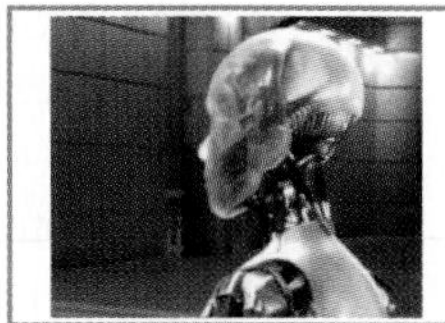
Figure 3.46—p. 170

Artificial intelligence (AI) refers to the science and engineering of creating computer systems that simulate human thought and behavior. Conventional AI methodologies such as expert systems, case-based reasoning, Bayesian networks, and behavior-based AI rely on the programmer to instill the software with logical functionality to solve problems. Computational intelligence methodologies such as neural networks, fuzzy systems, and evolutionary computation set up a system whereby the software can develop intelligence through an iterative process. An expert system (ES) is software that functions like a human expert in a particular field or area. A neural network simulates the functioning of the neurons in a human brain in software. Computers typically work with numerical certainty; certain input values always result in the same output. However, in the real world, certainty is not always the case. To handle this dilemma, a specialty research area in computer science called fuzzy systems, based on fuzzy logic, has been developed. A genetic algorithm is a form of evolutionary computation that is used to solve large, complex problems where a number of algorithms or models change and evolve until the best one emerges.

Artificial intelligence has many and varied applications. Robotics involves developing mechanical or computer devices to perform tasks that require a high degree of precision or are tedious or hazardous for humans. Computer vision combines hardware (cameras and scanners) and AI software that permit computers to capture, store, and interpret visual images and pictures. Natural language processing uses AI techniques to enable computers to generate and understand natural human languages, such as English. Speech recognition allows a computer to understand and react to spoken statements and commands. Handwriting recognition uses AI techniques to translate handwritten characters or words into computer-readable data. An intelligent agent (also called an intelligent robot or bot) consists of programs and a knowledge base used to perform a specific task for a person, a process, or another program. Virtual reality is a computer-simulated environment which can be manipulated by a user.

Test Yourself

LEARNING OBJECTIVE 1: Explain how software is created, distributed, installed, and maintained.

1. A(n) ________________ is the primary tool of computer programmers.
2. A(n) ________________ takes source code, a program written in a programming language, and produces object code, executable files, and supportive files, as output.
   a. software patch
   b. software bug
   c. interpreter
   d. compiler
3. True or False: A calendar program is an example of application software.
4. True or False: Most popular software is protected by copyright law or licensing provisions.
5. ________________ software makes the source code available to users.
6. Which of the following types of license is designed to provide freedom to owners of intellectual property and consumers?
   a. single-user license
   b. Creative Commons license
   c. site license
   d. concurrent license

LEARNING OBJECTIVE 2: Describe the functions of system software and operating systems, and provide examples of operating systems for PCs, larger computer systems, and mobile devices.

7. The _______________ is a collection of programs that interact with the computer and application hardware, creating a layer of insulation between the two.
8. _______________ is the most popular operating system for PCs.
9. Which of the following is not a typical function of an operating system?
   a. control multiple processors
   b. control special-purpose computers
   c. manage the word-processing function
   d. manage the memory function
10. True or False: Multitasking involves running more than one processor at the same time.
11. _______________ allows more than one person to use a computer system at the same time.
12. Windows is an example of _______________ .
   a. a graphical user interface
   b. a command-based operating system
   c. a proprietary operating system
   d. a language translator

LEARNING OBJECTIVE 3: Describe different types of productivity software and explain how application software assists people at home, at work, and in between.

13. True or False: Database programs can contain optimization features to minimize or maximize a quantity subject to constraints.
14. What type of application software would an anthropologist use to catalog numerous artifacts in a manner that allows easy sorting and filtering?
   a. word processing
   b. spreadsheet
   c. database
   d. presentation software
15. _______________ software helps individuals, groups, and organizations store useful information, including a list of tasks to complete, a list of names and addresses, and an appointment calendar.
16. Google Docs, Zoho, Adobe Buzzword, and Nozbe are all examples of _______________ .
   a. utilities
   b. personal information management software
   c. shareware
   d. rich Internet applications

LEARNING OBJECTIVE 4: List areas of research in artificial intelligence and tell how AI is being used in everyday applications.

17. _______________ combines hardware (cameras and scanners) and AI software that permit computers to capture, store, and interpret visual images and pictures.
18. What type of artificial intelligence is used to simulate or act like the physical functioning of the human brain?
   a. fuzzy logic
   b. expert systems
   c. neural networks
   d. genetic algorithms
19. True or False: Face recognition is a reliable and widely used method of identifying individuals in a crowd.
20. A(n) _______________ acts like a human expert in a field or area.

Test Yourself Solutions **1.** programming language, **2.** d. compiler, **3.** True, **4.** True, **5.** Open-source, **6.** b. Creative Commons license, **7.** operating system, **8.** Microsoft Windows, **9.** c. manage the word-processing function, **10.** False, **11.** Time-sharing, **12.** a. a graphical user interface, **13.** False, **14.** c. database, **15.** Personal Information Management (PIM), **16.** d. rich Internet applications, **17.** Computer vision, **18.** c. neural networks, **19.** False, **20.** expert system.

Key Terms

Key Term	Page	Definition
application programming interface (API)	122	A set of programming tools provided to access an operating system or online service in order to create software based on that operating system or online service
application software	115	Programs written to perform tasks or solve problems for people, groups, and organizations
artificial intelligence (AI)	170	Refers to the science and engineering of creating computer systems that simulate human thought and behavior
boot process	134	Stored in ROM; when the computer is powered up, it runs system checks, then transfers the operating system from the hard drive to RAM
command-based user interface	135	Requires that text commands be typed at a prompt in order to perform basic tasks
computational intelligence	173	Artificial intelligence methodologies such as neural networks, fuzzy systems, and evolutionary computation that set up a system whereby the software can develop intelligence through an iterative process
computer vision	179	Combines hardware (cameras and scanners) and AI software that permit computers to capture, store, and interpret visual images and pictures
conventional AI	173	Artificial intelligence methodologies such as expert systems, case-based reasoning, Bayesian networks, and behavior-based AI that rely on the programmer to instill the software with logical functionality to solve problems
copyright	123	Defines exclusive rights legally granted to the owner
Creative Commons license	125	Designed to allow the creators of intellectual property to specify the terms of the license in order to grant certain freedoms to users, while still providing the owner with some control of the property
database-management software	158	Used to store, manipulate, and manage data in order to find and present useful information
device driver	140	Software that interfaces with an operating system to control an input or output device such as a printer
expert system (ES)	173	Software that functions like a human expert in a particular field or area; created with the assistance of a human expert who provides subject-specific knowledge
fuzzy logic	177	Derived from fuzzy set theory, which deals with reasoning that is approximate rather than precise
genetic algorithm	177	A form of evolutionary computation that is used to solve large, complex problems where a number of algorithms or models change and evolve until the best one emerges
graphical user interface (GUI)	136	Makes use of a keyboard and mouse to manipulate graphics images on the display to issue commands to the computer system
intelligent agent	181	Also called an intelligent robot or *bot*, an abbreviation for robot; consists of programs and a knowledge base used to perform a specific task for a person, a process, or another program
Linux	147	A free, open-source operating system for PCs

Key Term	Page	Definition
Mac OS	145	The native operating system for Apple PCs
Microsoft Windows	144	The most popular operating system for personal computers
multitasking	139	The ability of the OS to run several programs or tasks at the same time
natural language processing	179	Uses AI techniques to enable computers to generate and understand natural human languages, such as English
neural network	176	Simulates the functioning of the neurons in a human brain in software
open-source software	124	Distributed, typically for free, with the source code so that it can be studied, changed, and improved by its users
operating system (OS)	133	A set of computer programs that runs or controls the computer hardware and acts as an interface with both application programs and users
personal information management (PIM) software	160	Helps individuals store useful information, such as to-do lists, appointment calendars, and contact lists
presentation software	157	Supports formal presentations by providing "slides" that can be used to accompany and embellish a live presentation or to present the material without the use of a human presenter
programming language	117	The primary tool of computer programmers; provides commands for writing software that is translated to the detailed step-by-step instructions executed by the processor to achieve an objective or solve a problem
robotics	178	Involves developing mechanical or computer devices to perform tasks that require a high degree of precision or are tedious or hazardous for humans
shareware	127	A marketing method for distributing software that allows customers to use software free of charge for a limited time in order to evaluate the software and decide if they wish to purchase it
single-user license	123	Permits the user to install the software on one computer, or sometimes two computers, used by one person
software bug	131	One or more defects or problems that prevent the software from working as intended or working at all
software engineer	114	A professional who writes sets of instructions using programming language and programming logic to create useful software
software license	123	Defines the permissions, rights, and restrictions provided to the person who purchases a copy of the software
software patch	132	Corrections to software code designed to fix software bugs
software suite	161	A collection of application software packages sold together; can include word processors, spreadsheets, presentation software, database-management systems, personal information managers, and more
speech recognition	179	Allows a computer to understand and react to spoken statements and commands

Key Term	Page	Definition
spreadsheet software	156	Supports complicated numerical analysis and calculations and allows users to perform *"what-if" analysis* on financial and other numeric data
system software	114	The set of programs that coordinates the activities of the hardware and various computer programs
Turing Test	171	A test designed by Alan Turing to determine if a computer exhibits human intelligence
utility program	152	Any system software besides the OS that assists in maintaining, managing, and protecting computer system resources
virtual reality	183	A computer-simulated environment that can be manipulated by a user
Web service	121	A software system that automates tasks by controlling communication between computers over the Internet
word-processing software	154	Allows users to create formatted text documents varying in complexity from simple to-do lists to professional magazine layouts

Questions

Review Questions

1. Why does software represent such a significant amount of the total cost of a computer system?
2. Explain the difference between system software and application software.
3. Draw a diagram that outlines the relationship among hardware, system software, and application software.
4. What is open-source software?
5. What are object-oriented programming languages? Why have they become popular?
6. What is a software license?
7. What steps would you take to find and eliminate a software bug or error?
8. What is an operating system? List five services it provides.
9. What are the advantages of using a graphical user interface (GUI)? Why do some technicians use a command-line interface?
10. What is a compiler? What is an interpreter?
11. Describe four utility programs. How might each be used?
12. What is a software suite? What is an integrated software package?
13. What benefits does a Creative Commons license offer those that use it?
14. What are the two branches of artificial intelligence?
15. What is the difference between artificial and natural intelligence?
16. Describe three new developments in artificial intelligence and explain why they are important.
17. What is robotics? What are neural networks?
18. What are the capabilities of an expert system?
19. What is virtual reality?

Discussion Questions

20. What are the benefits and drawbacks of the three most popular PC operating systems? Which do you prefer and why?
21. Why do you think new technologies such as Facebook and the iPhone provide software development kits (SDKs) for developers? How do SDKs benefit developers and the companies that provide the SDK?
22. What are the benefits of open-source software for users and the computing community in general? Is it possible for software companies to make money through open-source development? Why or why not?
23. Discuss the advantages and disadvantages of customized software versus off-the-shelf software.
24. Pick a career you would like to pursue. What types of application software might you find useful?
25. What are the characteristics of intelligent behavior?
26. How could robots be used in the military or law enforcement?
27. Give an example of how expert systems can be used in a field of interest to you.
28. What type of college or university courses might benefit from virtual reality? Why?

Exercises

Try It Yourself

1. Using a word-processing program, create a document that describes the top five application software packages for a career area of your choice. Give a brief description of each application software package and a description of how it might benefit you professionally.
2. Describe the types of software you would like to use at home for entertainment. Use a database program to develop a table listing different operating systems that would be most appropriate for this software (this may involve some online research), along with their benefits, disadvantages, and costs.
3. Visit *http://developers.facebook.com/get_started.php?tab=principles* and read about the Guiding Principles of Facebook application development. Choose a Facebook App and explain how it meets or fails to meet the Guiding Principles.
4. Use the Internet to explore the decisions that are required for your chosen career area or field. Also use the Internet to explore expert systems. Using your word-processing program, describe how you could develop an expert system for your career area or field. Develop five heuristics, or "rules of thumb," that show how your expert system could make decisions given certain conditions or situations.
5. Use the Internet or your online university library to search for new artificial intelligence applications. Write a two-page report describing two of your most interesting findings.

Virtual Classroom Activities

For the following exercises, do not use face-to-face or telephone communications with your group members. Use only Internet communications.

6. Software is a key component of any distance learning system. What software applications do you use for online learning, research, collaboration, and communications in your class? Are any of the applications integrated into a larger system or software suite? Are they rich Internet applications or installed on your computer? How effective are these software tools? How might they be improved?
7. What software is available on your cell phone or smart phone? Which do you find most useful? What software is not available that you would like to use?
8. Interview a campus system administrator and ask what the policy is regarding updating your school's application and system software. Are there any procedures for teachers or students to request additional software for use in campus computer labs?

Teamwork

9. In a group of three or four classmates, interview three programmers or programmer/analysts from different businesses to determine what programming languages they are using to develop applications. How did these software developers choose the languages they are using? What do they like about their own language and what could be improved? Which language would the programmers choose for software development if the decision were completely their own choice? It is possible that the programmers may each choose a different language. Considering the information obtained from the programmers, select one of these languages and briefly present your selection and the rationale for the selection to the class.
10. Open-source software is popular with many people. Have each team member investigate an open-source software product, such as a word processor, operating system, photo editor, or spreadsheet program. Each team member should write a brief description of the software, including the features of the software versus the features of a commercial software package. The team should then write a description of the advantages and disadvantages of open-source software compared to commercial software.
11. Have your team determine what types of embedded software packages are being used by classmates, friends, and family members.
12. Your team should brainstorm at least five ideas for expert systems that would be useful on campus. Try to develop rules you might use to make decisions (say, to choose classes for a semester). This exercise will show the difficulty of using multiple experts to build a knowledge base and the difficulty in defining rules for a knowledge base.

Endnotes

[1] Microsoft Staff, "Case Study: MTV Networks International (MTV)," Microsoft Case Studies, Accessed September 22, 2009, *http://download.microsoft.com/download/6/1/f/61f4b191-6cdb-4a44-9d28-e7040544f576/MTV.pdf.*

[2] Keizer, Gregg, "Windows market share dives again as Mac nears 10%," *Computerworld*, January 2, 2009, *www.computerworld.com.*

[3] Microsoft Staff, "Workflow Speeds Up for Government Policy Think Tank," Microsoft Case Study, June 23, 2009, *www.microsoft.com/casestudies.*

[4] "LinkedIn. Not Just Your Ordinary Network," Apple Business Profiles, Accessed October 12, 2009, *www.apple.com/business/profiles/linkedin.*

[5] Ubuntu Staff, "Ubuntu is the open source platform of choice for Oxford Archaeology," Ubuntu Case Studies, accessed September 22, 2009, *www.ubuntu.com/products/casestudies/oxford-archaeology.*

[6] Sun Staff, "eBay Inc," Sun Customer Snapshot, accessed September 22, 2009, *www.sun.com/customers/servers/ebay.xml.*

[7] Sun Staff, "Idaho National Lab," Sun Customer Snapshot, accessed September 22, 2009, *www.sun.com/customers/servers/inl.xml.*

[8] Kurzweil, Ray, *The Singularity Is Near*, Penguin Books, 2005, p. 9.

[9] Gaudin, Sharon, "MIT creating microchip that could restore vision," *Computerworld*, September 24, 2009, *www.computerworld.com.*

[10] Australian government Smartgate page, accessed September 27, 2009, *www.customs.gov.au/site/page.cfm?u=5552.*

The Internet and World Wide Web

Josh Greene has been using e-mail and the Web for as long as he can remember. His Web activities are so predictable that he imagines he has worn ruts in the online paths he repeatedly travels. While the Web provides great resources for keeping up with friends and looking up information, Josh feels like he's tapped into only a small portion of what's available. Some of his friends are into online multiplayer gaming, and torrenting movies and music, but that's all foreign to Josh; he doesn't even know where to begin. He's also heard that these activities can be hazardous and perhaps illegal. His school is really cracking down on file sharing, and he is concerned about picking up a virus. Besides, Josh's computer takes f-o-r-e-v-e-r to download movie files. Josh knows that the Web and Internet are evolving quickly and wonders how to keep up with what is new and exciting. Come to think of it, Josh isn't even sure about what the difference is between the Internet and the Web.

A number of Josh's friends have gotten new cell phones with all kinds of cool features. They send each other messages throughout the day. They always talk about cool stuff they found online and spend some evenings partying—on their computers! Josh's roommate is traveling to visit an online friend over the weekend. Josh is feeling a bit left out. Like it or not, Josh will be spending *his* evening online, as he has a big research project due tomorrow. He is unable to get to the library so he plans on doing his research on the Internet, but isn't sure where to start.

As you read through the chapter, consider the following questions:

1. What online activities can Josh use to enrich his quality of life?
2. Which online activities are legal and safe, and which are not?
3. How should Josh conduct his research on his computer?

Check out Josh's *Action Plan* at the conclusion of this chapter.

4

LEARNING OBJECTIVES

1. Describe how the Internet developed and how hardware, protocols, and software work together to create the Internet.
2. Explain the underlying structure of the Web and the technologies that support it.
3. Define the categories of information and services that the Internet and Web provide and the forms of communication they support.
4. Explain what Internet2 and Web 3.0 are and the types of applications they may provide in the future.

CHAPTER CONTENT

Introduction

You've learned how hardware and software work together to assist people in achieving their goals. This in itself is highly valuable. However, the true power of computing lies in connecting computing devices and users through the interconnected networks that make up the Internet. The Internet connects people on a global scale and provides a host of communication platforms, information, and services.

The Web is an Internet service that provides a user-friendly interface to resources on the Internet. It organizes and presents information on the Internet in a manner that is easy to navigate. More than any other technology, the Web has empowered individuals by providing a public forum to share ideas. The Internet has leveled the playing field between small and large organizations and provided opportunities for some organizations that would otherwise never stand a chance of competing. The Web, at any given time, can be viewed as a snapshot of the human condition. Anything of personal or professional interest to any person is represented here: the good, the bad, and the ugly. Thus, it has its share of controversy.

For students and professionals, the Web has become a primary source of information in support of scholarly research. Because of the vast amount of information and the lack of quality control, researchers must learn unique methods for finding valuable and verifiable information in the midst of millions of pages that provide just the opposite. This chapter addresses all of these issues and much more!

The Internet provides a platform on which hundreds of millions of people combine and share knowledge and views. If two heads are better than one, hundreds of millions of heads sharing knowledge and unique perceptions are powerful indeed. The Internet brings the power of global community to computing.

Internet technology and the physical connections between devices support many applications, the most popular of which are e-mail and the Web. E-mail provides a convenient and low-cost form of communication over the Internet, while the Web provides a convenient method of sharing information and services. The terms "Web" and "Internet" are often used interchangeably, but they are actually two different sets of technologies. The Internet provides the technological infrastructure on which the Web and other Internet-based services depend. The Web provides a convenient platform for delivering information and services using the Internet. People are using the Web as a resource for communicating, sharing, learning, finding entertainment, and making new friends. The Web has become a major platform for building online communities (see Figure 4.1). It is rapidly becoming a primary platform for delivering software applications like word processing, spreadsheet, presentation, navigation, and games. Businesses invest in the Web to leverage competitive advantages. Products are marketed and sold over the Web. Great works of creativity are published and distributed over the Web. The Web is highly regarded and a part of daily life for many of us, but what exactly is it?

FIGURE 4.1 • Video conferencing from 36,000 feet above the Pacific Ocean

A CalTech researcher participates in a video/audio collaborative session over the Internet with colleagues in Slovakia and Switzerland.

INTERNET TECHNOLOGY

The many services provided on the Web are made possible through the underlying network connections that make up the Internet. The Internet is relatively young and still in its early stages of development. New ways of using the Internet are being developed and introduced every day. This section provides a brief overview of the origins of the Internet so that you can observe how it has come to be so influential. This section also teaches principles that govern the Internet so that you can be more knowledgeable about its capabilities and limitations.

A Brief History of the Internet

As defined in Chapter 1, the Internet is a global, public network of computer networks. A *computer network* is a collection of computing devices connected to share resources such as files, software, processors, storage, and printers. There are millions of privately owned networks around the world. Joining networks together into larger networks so that users on different networks can communicate and share data creates an *internetwork*. Today's Internet joins together networks of over 500 million computers, or *Internet hosts*, to create the world's largest internetwork, supporting over 1.5 billion users (see Figure 4.2).[1] To fully understand the Internet, you must examine its origins.

FIGURE 4.2 • The Internet

The Internet provides high-speed information and communication thoroughfares between individuals and organizations around the globe.

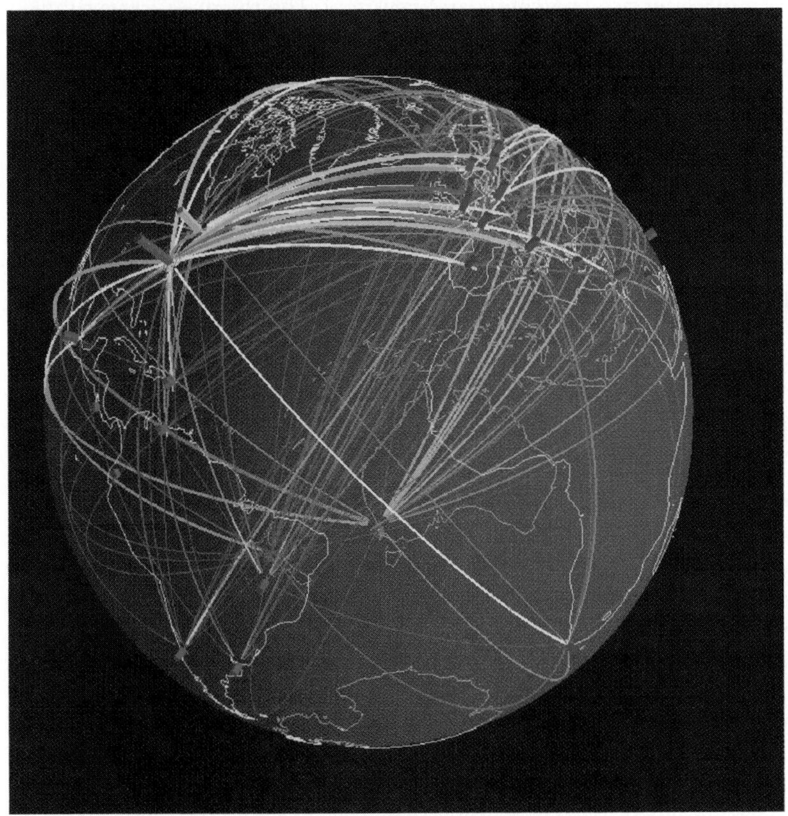

In 1957, computing was done primarily on large mainframe computers accessed from within an organization through a network of terminals. Government agencies, universities, businesses, and other large organizations all used this type of networking environment. In that same year, the USSR surprised the world by launching Sputnik, the first artificial earth satellite. The United States viewed the launch as a challenge. The following year President Eisenhower reacted by forming two government agencies under the Department of Defense (DoD) to advance space technologies, weapons, and communication systems: the Advanced Research Projects Agency (ARPA) and the National Aeronautics and Space Administration (NASA). Many amazing achievements were to come from these organizations, but among those that had the most social impact were placing the first man on the moon and establishing the Internet.

In 1969, ARPA commissioned ARPANET for research into networking. Its initial goal was to establish closer communications for research by connecting the computer networks of four research institutions: the University of California at Los Angeles, Stanford, the University of California at Santa Barbara, and the University of Utah. The goal was accomplished within the year. Once the groundwork was laid for successful communications between networks, ARPANET began growing exponentially. Table 4.1 summarizes the early milestones in the development of the Internet that led to the introduction of the World Wide Web at the end of 1993.

With the birth of the Web, the Internet exploded, with a 341,634 percent annual growth rate in Internet hosts in following years. Internet service providers began sprouting up all over the world to provide Internet service to businesses and

TABLE 4.1 • Pre-Web Internet development milestones[2]

Year	Internet hosts	Internet milestones
1970	13	The first cross-country link was installed by AT&T to connect networks across the country.
1973	35	ARPANET went international as it expanded overseas to University College in London, England, and the Royal Radar Establishment in Norway.
1983	562	ARPANET was divided into two subnetworks: MILNET, for military needs, and ARPANET, for research.
1990	313,000	The ARPANET project was officially concluded, and "the Internet" was turned over to the public, to be managed by the Internet Society (ISOC).
1991	617,000	The Commercial Internet Exchange (CIX) Association was established to allow businesses to connect to the Internet.
1993	2,056,000	The first Web browser, Mosaic, was released to Internet users to an unprecedented enthusiastic reception.

homes. With increasing numbers of consumers flocking to the Web, businesses recognized it as a powerful new marketing and sales tool. The Internet's focus shifted from supporting solely academic and government interests to supporting public and commercial interests. Today there are over 1.5 billion Internet users—over 23 percent of the world's population (see *www.internetworldstats.com/stats.htm* for the most current statistics). Among those that are not connected are populations that cannot afford computers and connections. This important social issue is referred to as the *digital divide*. There are also cultures and individuals who resist technology because of personal or religious philosophies.

The Internet is a combination of hardware, protocols, and software. The hardware provides the physical cables and devices that control and carry Internet data. *Protocols* are the rules that are implemented in network software and hardware to establish connections between two or more computers to allow them to communicate. Software allows users to interact with the Internet to access information and services. The following sections provide detailed explanations of the Internet's hardware, protocols, and software.

Internet Hardware. The hardware over which Internet traffic flows includes the Internet backbone, routers, and the computers that request and serve up information and services. The **Internet backbone**, the main Internet pathways and connections, is made up of the many national and international communication networks that are owned by major telecom companies, such as AT&T, British Telecom, and Sprint—the same companies and networks that provide telephone service. These companies agreed to connect their networks so that users on all the networks could share information over the Internet. The cables, switching stations, communication towers, and satellites that make up these telecommunication networks provide the hardware over which Internet traffic travels. These large telecom companies are called *network service providers* (*NSPs*). The combined backbones of these and other NSPs make up today's Internet backbone. The complexity of mapping the Internet's physical connections has become a daunting task. Some researchers use visualization software tools such as Walrus (*www.caida.org/tools/visualization/walrus/*) to create graphical representations of the Internet based on statistical data (see Figure 4.3).

FIGURE 4.3 • Visualizing the Internet

Using visualization tools, scientists are able to create theoretical 3D models of the complex linked connections that make up the Internet.

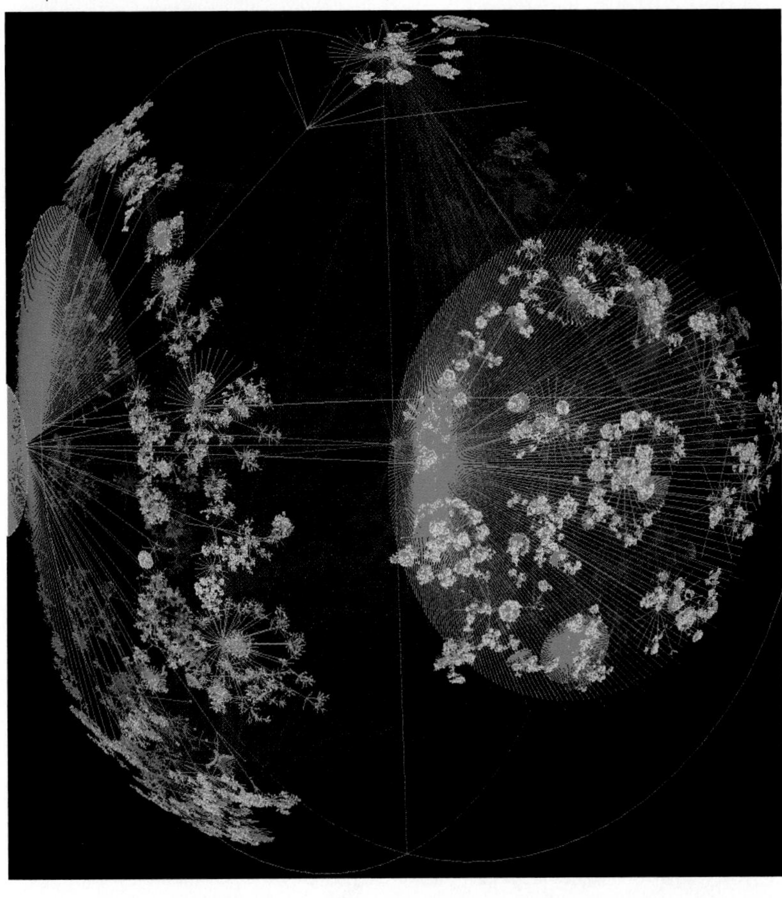

Network service providers enable Internet users to connect to their networks through utility stations called *points of presence (POPs)*. The visualization of the Internet shown in Figure 4.3 illustrates the hub-and-spokes nature of the Internet. The POPs act as the hubs, and the connections they provide, the spokes. The POPs are connected by the Internet backbone. Points of presence include networking hardware that allows individuals, companies, and service providers such as Comcast and America Online to connect to the Internet backbone. Large telecom companies, such as AT&T and Verizon, have tens of thousands of POPs throughout North America, Europe, and the Pacific Rim, each facilitating millions of user connections.

Companies that provide users with access to the Internet through NSP POPs are called **Internet service providers (ISPs)** (Figure 4.4). There are hundreds of ISPs from local to international levels. ISPs work as liaisons between Internet users and the telecommunications companies that own the backbones. They charge a monthly fee to Internet users and provide devices by which the user can connect to the Internet. Many companies, organizations, and institutions work directly with the network service providers to connect their own organizations' networks directly to a POP.

FIGURE 4.4 • Connecting to the Internet

Users connect to the Internet through an Internet service provider (ISP), which connects to the network service provider (NSP) through a point of presence (POP).

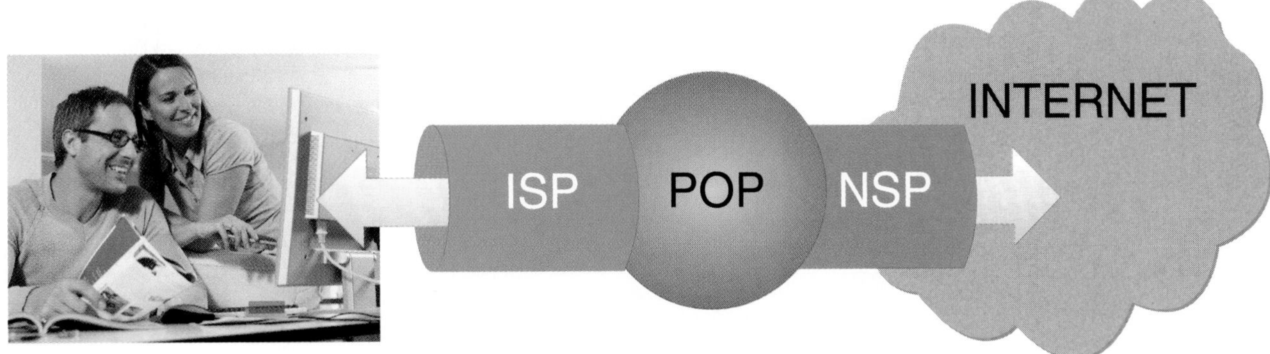

The Internet uses routers to make sure that information sent is directed to the intended recipient. **Routers** are special-purpose computing devices—typically small to large units with network ports—that manage network traffic by evaluating messages and routing them over the fastest path to their destination. Routers are typically located at network junctions, where one network is joined to another network. An e-mail message sent from New York to Los Angeles passes from router to router until it reaches its destination. Such an e-mail message might pass through as many as 20 routers along the way but would reach its destination within a fraction of a second. Figure 4.5 shows the path of a data packet traveling across the Internet from Florida State University to Google through 29 routers, across 7,244 miles, in 2.3 seconds.

FIGURE 4.5 • Internet routers in action

A visual trace route tool from *yougetsignal.com* shows the routes that data packets travel through routers on the Internet to get their destination.

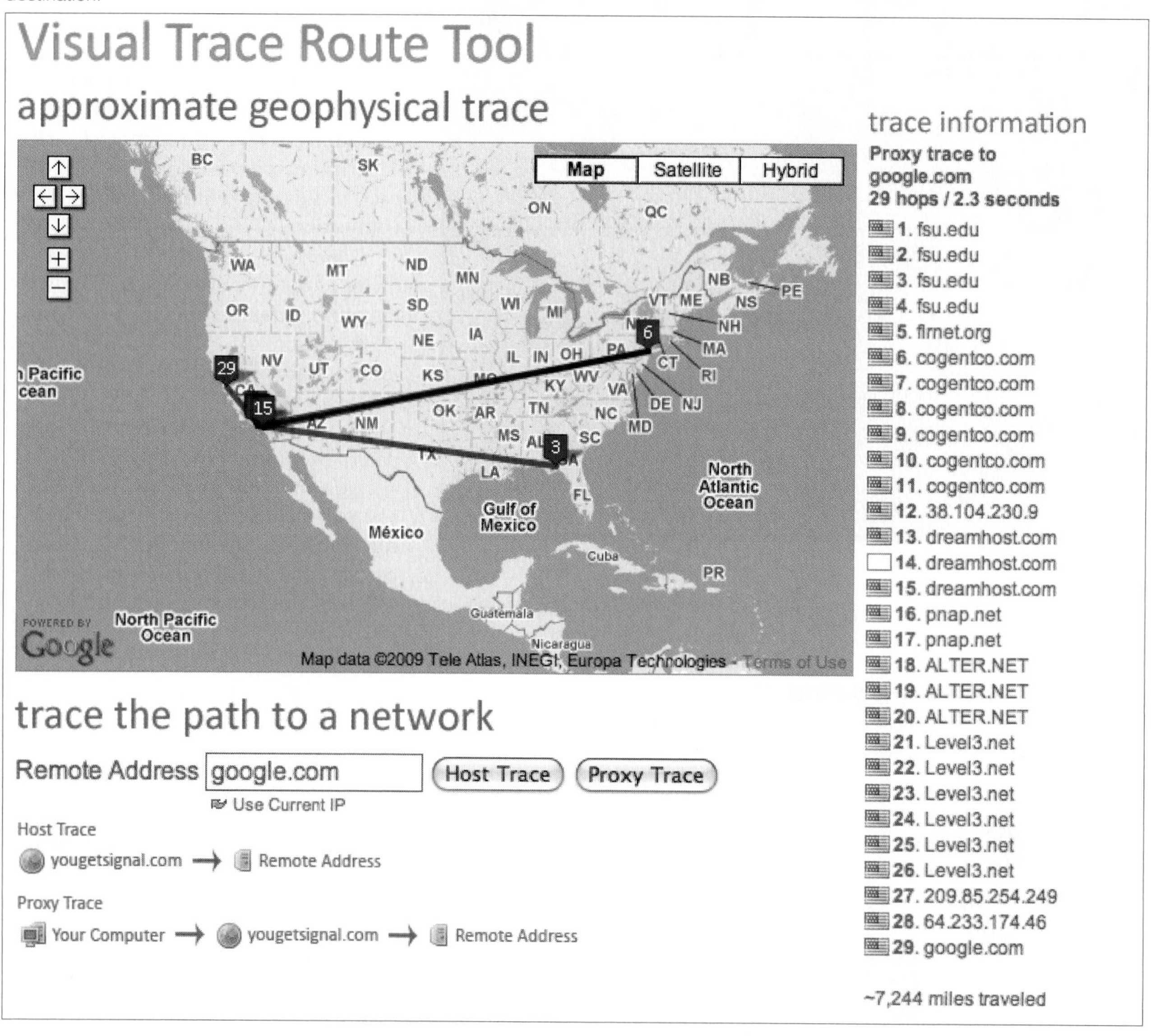

Accessing the Internet. Businesses, organizations, and individuals purchase access to the Internet from ISPs. Large businesses and institutions such as your college purchase industrial-strength connections to the Internet from telecom companies to connect their existing computer network to the Internet. Individuals and small businesses have several options for connecting to the Internet including a dial-up connection, cellular network, cable, DSL (digital subscriber line), and digital satellite service.

EXPAND YOUR KNOWLEDGE

To learn more about connecting to the Internet, go to www.cengage.com/computerconcepts/np/swt4. Click the link "Expand Your Knowledge" and then complete the lab entitled "Connecting to the Internet."

A **dial-up connection** is a low-speed Internet service that utilizes the customer's phone line for data transfer rates as high as 56 kilobits per second (Kbps), provided by any one of hundreds of Internet service providers. Customers are typically provided with a local or toll-free phone number along with a username and password. The computer's modem dials the number, establishes a connection to the ISP, and logs on. Dial-up connections tie up the phone line during use and cannot be used simultaneously with voice communications. Dial-up connections are used mainly where inexpensive high-speed connections are not yet available.

A **cable modem connection** is a high-speed Internet service provided by cable television service providers. Service plans range from economy plans for around $25 per month supporting up to 1 Mbps download rates, to premium plans for around $100 per month supporting up to 50 Mbps rates.

With a cable service, the Internet signal is carried along the same cable as the television signals. A cable TV receiver receives the frequencies reserved for television, and a cable modem receives the frequencies used for Internet. A cable splitter is used for customers who use the cable for both television and the Internet. The cable modem connects to a computer using its Ethernet connection and can be connected to several computers using a router or switch. Cable modems can be installed by professionals or by users with existing cable service who purchase a self-installation kit.

Cable modem network lines are shared by neighbors, so if many neighbors access the Internet simultaneously, they might experience slower throughput. Some concerns have been raised over the ability of the cable to support the Internet needs of everyone in a given neighborhood.

A **DSL (digital subscriber line) connection** uses the customer's phone line, but there is no dialing up and users can use the Internet and talk on the phone simultaneously. DSL provides high-speed Internet access through companies that utilize standard phone lines. Service plans range from standard plans for around $20 per month supporting up to 1 Mbps download rates, to premium plans for around $35 per month supporting up to 6 Mbps. DSL service is similar to a cable modem, except that here your telephone line is split to carry signals to both a DSL modem and your telephone. Like a cable modem, and unlike a dial-up connection, a DSL line provides an *always-on connection*. As with a cable modem, a DSL modem is connected to a computer through an Ethernet card or to a router to share the signal between multiple computers. DSL is slower than cable service, but because it is a dedicated line rather than a shared line, you don't compete with neighbors for bandwidth.

A *digital satellite service (DSS)* connection is a wireless high-speed Internet service provided to your home by companies such as EarthLink and HughesNet. Service plans range from standard plans for around $60 per month supporting up to 1 Mbps download rates, to premium plans for around $350 per month supporting up to 5 Mbps. Because satellite service is more expensive than cable and DSL service, it is typically not used in areas where either DSL or cable is available. Satellite Internet is installed by professionals in much the same manner as cable modems and DSL. Satellite is the only service with substantial setup and equipment costs; users may be charged as much as $400 up front for equipment and installation. DSL and cable typically have promotions that provide free installation and setup. Although DSS offers an always-on connection, users may lose their signal during stormy weather.

Most cell phone companies now support and promote Internet access over cellular networks. Service plans range from standard plans for around $60 per month supporting up to 1 Mbps download rates, to premium plans for around $70 per month supporting up to 6 Mbps. Some premium plans are available only in select cities that have been upgraded to 4G networks using technologies such as WiMAX or LTE (covered in the next chapter). A laptop connect card (Figure 4.6) is an expansion card for your notebook PC that can connect directly to the cell phone network without the need for a cell phone. Some users purchase a second line from the cell phone carrier for their laptop connect card. Table 4.2 compares Internet services and fees.

FIGURE 4.6 • Laptop connect card

By purchasing a laptop connect card, an additional line from your cell phone carrier, and data service, you can connect your notebook to the Internet anywhere you have cell phone coverage.

TABLE 4.2 • Internet service fees and speeds (2009–2010)

Service	Download speed/monthly cost standard plan	Download speed/monthly cost premium plan
Cable	15 Mbps/$42.95	50 Mpbs/$99.95
DSL	1 Mbps/$19.95	6 Mbps/$35
Satellite	1 Mbps/$59.99	5 Mbps/$349.99
Cellular	1 Mbps/$59.99	6 Mbps/$69.99
Dial-up	56 Kbps/$12.50	N/A
*Prices based on 2009 quotes from Comcast, Sprint, AT&T, and HughesNet		

Other forms of Internet access are emerging as efforts continue to provide access to everyone, anywhere, anytime. Although not yet widely offered, the power companies of the world are experimenting with broadband Internet over the power grids through technology called *broadband over power lines* or *BPL*. The advantage of BPL is that the power grid is the most pervasive network in the world, reaching many places where telephone and cable lines do not. Connecting a computer to the Internet would be as easy as plugging a BPL modem into a wall outlet. BPL access will be provided at speeds of up to 1 Mbps. BPL is being offered to U.S. residents in Manassas, Virginia; East Springfield, Massachusetts; Freeport, New York; and many other cities. The state of California has approved a rollout of BPL for its cities. BPL is also being deployed in South Africa, Portugal, Australia, Romania, Hungary, Saudi Arabia, and other countries.

Selecting an Internet Service Provider

Most colleges offer free Internet access to students. Upon graduating, students often find that monthly Internet access is a considerable expense; sometimes more costly than phone, cable TV, and other utilities. It pays to understand your options and to make sure you are paying only for services that you need.

This chapter provides general information on speed and cost of different types of services. Not all services are available in all locations. There are several Web sites that provide information on which services are available in your area based on your phone number and address. One such service is available at *http://reviews.cnet.com* under "Internet access."

Once you are aware of your options, you should consider the ways that you use the Internet. If you plan to use your Internet connection for accessing media such as video, music, and video games, or if you would like to use a Web cam for video conferencing, you will appreciate a connection faster than 2 Mbps, which means either cable or DSL. If all you plan on doing is checking your e-mail, you might be satisfied with a bargain-basement $9.00 per month dial-up connection.

Varying services offer different features. For example, commercial information services such as MSN and AOL provide software packages that include common tools for Internet use such as chat, instant messaging, Web browsing, shopping, news, e-mail, and more. Other Internet service providers provide only an Internet connection, relying on users to install their own Internet utilities such as a Web browser and instant messaging client. The difference in these types of services can be as much as $15 per month. Some of the more common features to be considered when selecting a service are the following:

- Price & data rate
- Download limits
- Mobility
- Security features
- Tech support
- Server storage
- E-mail
- Web hosting

Choosing an ISP is a matter of balancing your budget against your requirements. The advice of friends can be very helpful. Be cautious of signing up for lengthy contracts, and take advantage of promotions that allow you to try a service for free.

The Internet is becoming increasingly available in locations away from work and home through pay-as-needed services. Many bookstores, coffee shops, airports, and hotels offer Internet access for free or at a per-hour service charge. For example, Starbucks coffee shops offer Internet access through the T-mobile HotSpot service for $6 for the first hour and 10 cents per minute thereafter. Many hotels charge $10–$20 per day for guest access to the Internet. Boingo (*www.boingo.com*) is a service that provides wireless Internet access from thousands of locations around the world for a monthly or daily fee. Many airlines are rolling out in-flight wireless Internet service for passengers.

In summary, the physical building blocks of the Internet include the high-speed telecommunications networks that make up the Internet backbone, the network access points at which they connect, the routers that manage the traffic traveling over the Internet, and the cable, DSL, dial-up, or other modems or devices that connect to individual computers. The Internet could not exist without this hardware. Equally important are the rules that govern the format of Internet traffic, which are called the protocols.

Internet Protocols. Whether negotiating peace between nations at war, merging corporate infrastructures, or attempting to connect different types of networks, you must begin by striking common ground and establishing policies and procedures. In networking, policies and procedures for finding common ground for communications between two devices are defined by protocols. The protocols for the Internet are the *Transmission Control Protocol* (TCP) and *Internet Protocol* (IP). Together these two protocols are commonly referred to as **TCP/IP**.

Data is transported over the Internet in packets. A data *packet* is a small group of bytes that includes the data being sent and a header containing information about the data, such as its destination, origin, size, and identification number (see Figure 4.7). The Internet is a *packet-switching* network. Internet applications, such as e-mail, divide up information, such as an e-mail message, into small packets in order to make efficient use of the network. Upon arriving at their destination, the packets are reconstructed into the original message.

FIGURE 4.7 • Data packets

E-mail, Web pages, and all Internet data is broken up into consistent-sized data packets for efficient travel over the Internet.

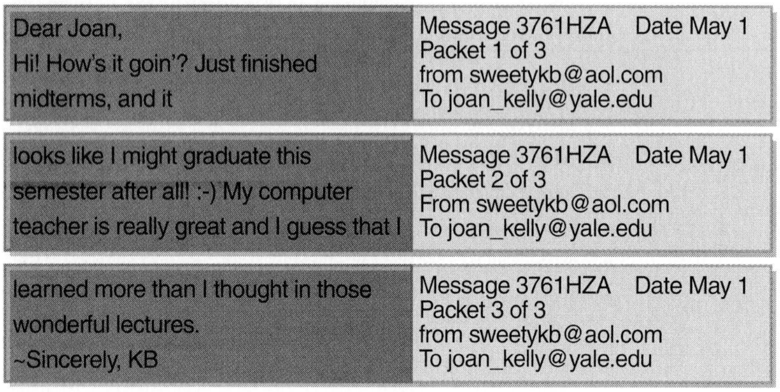

Dear Joan, Hi! How's it goin'? Just finished midterms, and it	Message 3761HZA Date May 1 Packet 1 of 3 from sweetykb@aol.com To joan_kelly@yale.edu
looks like I might graduate this semester after all! :-) My computer teacher is really great and I guess that I	Message 3761HZA Date May 1 Packet 2 of 3 From sweetykb@aol.com To joan_kelly@yale.edu
learned more than I thought in those wonderful lectures. ~Sincerely, KB	Message 3761HZA Date May 1 Packet 3 of 3 from sweetykb@aol.com To joan_kelly@yale.edu

The Internet Protocol (the IP in TCP/IP) defines the format and addressing scheme used for the packets. Routers on the Internet use the information in the packet header to direct the packet to its destination. The Transmission Control Protocol (the TCP in TCP/IP) enables two hosts to establish a connection and exchange streams of data. TCP guarantees delivery of data and also guarantees that packets are delivered in the same order in which they were sent.

The Internet Protocol requires that all devices connected to the Internet have a unique IP address. An **IP address** is a unique 32-bit identifier for Internet hosts. Read as decimal numbers, an IP address consists of four numbers (0 to 255) separated by periods, such as 64.233.161.104. IP addresses can be *static*, permanently assigned to a particular computer, or *dynamic*, assigned to computers as needed. Computers that provide services, such as *www.yahoo.com,* use static addresses, while IP addresses for user's computers are often dynamic and temporarily assigned to computers as needed. The over 500 million Internet hosts cited earlier is actually the number of assigned IP addresses. By using dynamic IP addresses, and with users sharing Internet hosts, the Internet can serve over 1.5 billion users.

The current IP addressing scheme can support only around 4 billion addresses. With individuals increasingly using multiple IP addresses to support multiple Internet-connected devices such as laptops, cell phones, game consoles, desktop PCs, and more, it is feared that we might soon run out of addresses. For this reason and others, a new version of the IP, version 6, is being rolled out. IPv6 utilizes 128 bits for IP addresses, a significant increase over the current 32-bit address format. The new address scheme will support over a nonillion addresses—3×10^{32} to be precise.

Because people are more comfortable dealing with names than numbers, IP addresses are assigned associated English names called *domain names*. For example, 64.233.161.104 is also known as *www.google.com*. Domain names and IP addresses are managed by the Internet Corporation for Assigned Names and Numbers (ICANN) and can be purchased from accredited registrars (*www.icann.org/registrars/accredited-list.html*). You can visit a registrar such as *www.enames.org* to find out if a particular name is available (you might find it interesting to see if your own name is registered), and for a small yearly fee you can claim an unregistered name for your own. Registering a domain name does not provide you with your own Web site, only with ownership of the name. You can associate the name with a Web site you have created and stored on a Web server with an assigned IP address.

The Internet uses the *Domain Name System (DNS)* to translate domain names into IP addresses. A database of addresses and names is stored on DNS servers. Internet services such as e-mail and the Web access DNS servers to translate the domain names to numeric IP addresses.

Many protocols are used on the Internet. Each service offered on the Internet—e-mail, the Web, instant messaging—has its own governing protocol. These protocols govern Internet communications and work much like TCP/IP does. Although you don't see these protocols at work, they are essential in all Internet communications.

Internet Software. Most computers on the Internet communicate using client/server relationships. **Client/server** describes a relationship between two computer programs in which one program, the *client*, makes a service request from another program, the *server*, which provides the service (see Figure 4.8). A Web browser such as Internet Explorer, for example, is a client that requests a Web page from a Web server, such as *www.monster.com*. An e-mail program, such as Outlook, Thunderbird, or Eudora, is a client that connects to an e-mail server to retrieve e-mail messages. Instant messaging (IM) clients connect to IM servers to connect and communicate with other users on the Internet, just as Chat clients connect to Chat servers for the same purpose.

FIGURE 4.8 • Client/server networking

Client/server technology is the basis of Internet services such as e-mail and the Web and uses server computers to distribute data to client applications such as Internet Explorer.

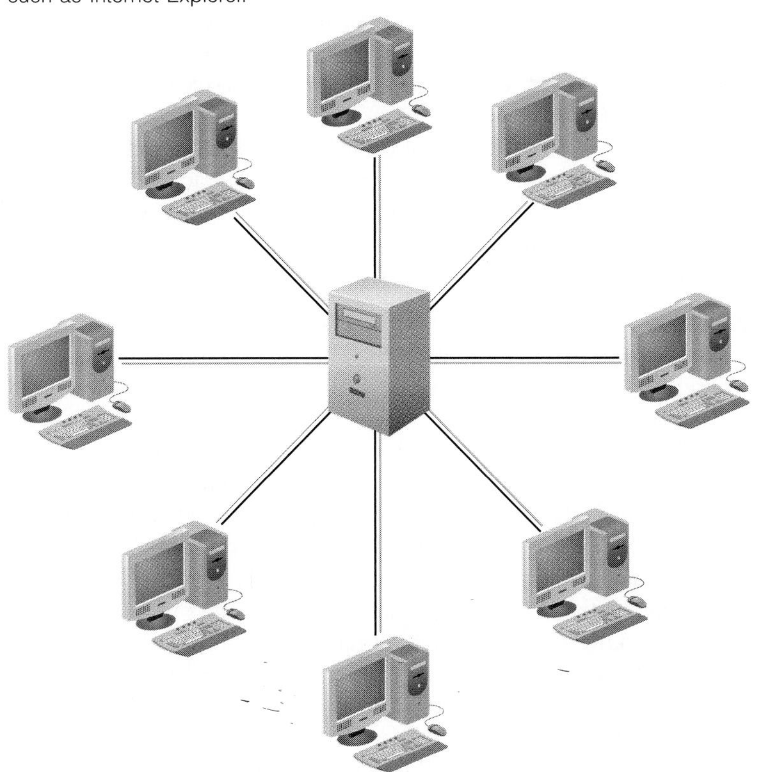

Server computers are typically powerful computers that can accommodate many simultaneous user requests. They run 24 hours a day, seven days a week to provide Internet services such as Web pages and e-mail service. The service performed by the server is defined by the type of server software it runs. A server running Web server software replies to Web page requests, and a server running e-mail server software governs the distribution of e-mail to and from the network. Different types of server software respond to requests that arrive at different ports on the server computer. In the client/server context, a **port** is a numeric address used by clients and servers that is associated with a specific service. For example, a server receives Web page requests on port 80 and domain name system requests on port 53; LimeWire, the popular file-sharing application, uses port 1214. The client application requesting the service includes the correct port number in the outgoing packet headers. The server software accepting requests on that port number can be assured of the nature of the request.

Some colleges are able to keep students from using controversial file-sharing software by closing off access to specific ports on the campus network. Likewise, a user's network activity can be tracked by checking the username for an IP address at a given time, and the port activity associated with that address. Recently, the Recording Industry Association of America has applied pressure to get Internet service providers to supply just such information as evidence to use in court in file-sharing copyright infringement cases.

In some cases a computer may act as both a client and a server, as happens in P2P networking. **Peer-to-peer (P2P)** networks do not utilize a central server but facilitate communications directly between clients (see Figure 4.9). Participants running P2P software make a portion of their file system available to other participants to access directly. In this relationship, an Internet user's personal computer acts as both server (as other users access files) and client (as the user accesses others' files). The Gnutella file-sharing system, which is at the heart of music-sharing services such as LimeWire, makes use of P2P networking.

FIGURE 4.9 • Peer-to-peer (P2P) networking

P2P networking allows users to link their computers over the Internet without using a server.

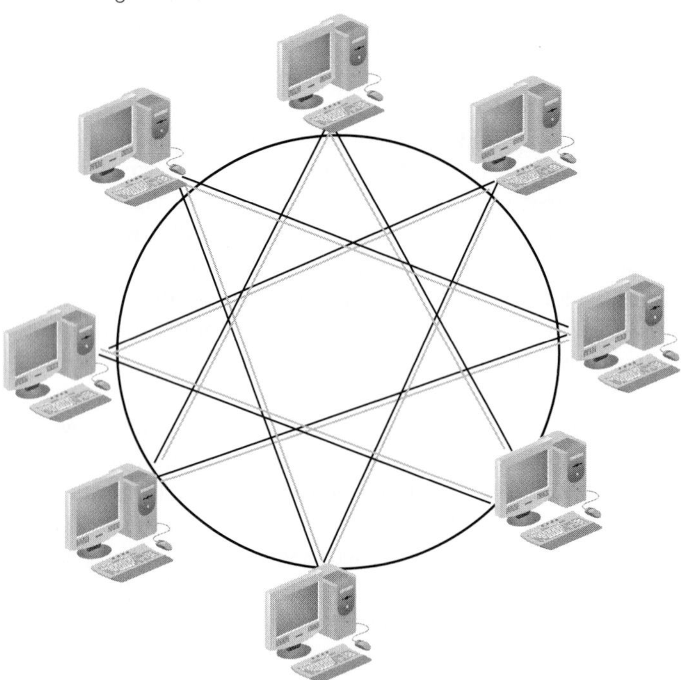

BitTorrent is a peer-to-peer file-sharing protocol that allows users to share files by downloading pieces of a file from multiple sources. *Torrenting* involves browsing the Web to find a file of interest, and then employing a BitTorrent client to download the file. As with most P2P services, the vast majority of music, movies, and software available as torrents are provided in violation of copyright.

The original Napster used a client/server system, which left the company liable for illegal file-sharing activities. Since P2P does not use a central server, it makes it more difficult to hold the software company liable for what users do with the software. However, by connecting directly without a central server, users sacrifice speed and some level of security. Providing access to your hard drive to thousands of strangers presents opportunities to hackers, viruses, and spyware that they would ordinarily not have. Also, since the files being swapped through these systems are unchecked and unregulated, many have been found to contain viruses and other security threats.

A Layered System. The Internet can be viewed conceptually as a multilayer system. You've examined three layers that involve hardware, protocols, and software. Experts refer to the software portion of the Internet as the *application layer.* The protocol portion of the Internet, where client software communicates requests to servers using the packet-switching rules of TCP/IP, is called the *transport layer.* The hardware associated with the Internet is referred to as the *physical layer.* This general three-layer conceptual view of Internet technology is illustrated in Figure 4.10. Network specialists find it useful to use a more detailed, seven-layer model called the *Open System Interconnection (OSI) model.* The OSI model provides network technicians and administrators with a deeper understanding of networking technology for designing and troubleshooting networks. For those just interested in using networks, however, the more general view provided here is enough to assist you in practical issues, such as selecting an Internet service provider, working with Internet applications, protecting yourself from hackers, and other issues that will be discussed as you progress through this book.

FIGURE 4.10 • Conceptual layers of the Internet

The Internet can be viewed conceptually as a multilayer system.

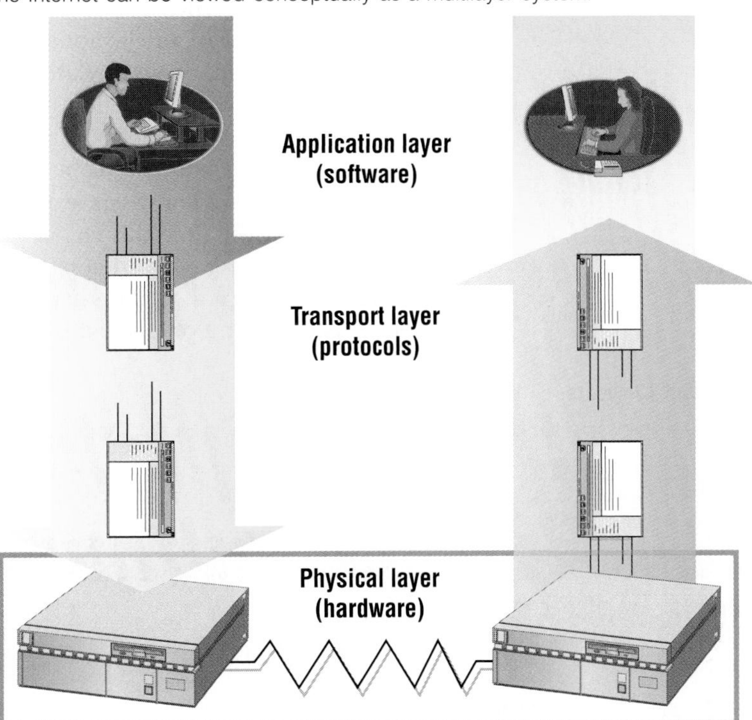

WEB TECHNOLOGY

The World Wide Web was developed by Tim Berners-Lee between 1989 and 1991 in his research at CERN, the European Organization for Nuclear Research (in French, *La Conseil Européan pour la Recherche Nucléaire*) in Geneva, and was released to the public in the form of the Mosaic Web browser in 1993. What he originally conceived of as an organizational tool to help keep track of his own personal documents has grown into an organizational tool that helps hundreds of millions of users share and access information on the Internet using an easy-to-use graphical interface. Recall that the Web is defined as an Internet service that provides convenient access to information through hyperlinks.

The process of "linking together" documents from diverse sources requires three components:

1. A defined system for linking the documents
2. Protocols that allow different computers to communicate
3. Tools to assist in creating the documents and the links between them

Tim Berners-Lee came up with all three: hyperlinks for linking documents, the Hypertext Transfer Protocol (HTTP) along with server and client software to manage communications between different computers, and HTML, a language for creating and linking documents.

Over the past decade many new technologies have been developed that work with Berners-Lee's original Web technologies to deliver richer Web content—animation, video, 3D views of objects and locations, music, and computer programs. This section covers the Web from the basics to state-of-the-art technologies.

Web Basics

The cornerstone of Tim Berners-Lee's World Wide Web is the hyperlink. A **hyperlink** is an element in an electronic document—a word, phrase, or image—that, when clicked, opens a related document. By relating documents to each other using hyperlinks, you form a web of interrelated information that is logically arranged and easy to explore. Some differentiate between *hypertext*, text that acts as a link, and *hypermedia*, pictures or other media that act as links.

There are dozens of Web browsers available free for download. Figure 4.11 shows the top five. At the time this chapter was most recently updated, Microsoft Internet Explorer claimed approximately 68 percent of the market, Mozilla Firefox, 22.5 percent, Apple Safari, 4 percent, Google Chrome 2.6 percent, Opera, 2 percent, and others divided the remainder.

FIGURE 4.11 • Web browsers

The most popular Web browsers are Microsoft Internet Explorer, Mozilla Firefox, Apple Safari, Google Chrome, and Opera.

FIGURE 4.12 • The handheld Web

Many Web publishers offer handheld versions of their sites.

The top browsers include many common features such as navigation tools, bookmarks, and tabbed browsing. While some features differentiate them, most users select a browser based on the speed with which it loads pages and applications, and its level of security. Ironically, the most popular browser, Internet Explorer, is currently ranked the slowest and the most targeted by hackers. Since it comes preinstalled on Windows PCs, most users are content to use it despite its shortcomings.

The protocol of the Web is called HTTP. The **Hypertext Transfer Protocol (HTTP)** controls communication between Web clients and servers. A Web client, commonly called a **Web browser**, takes the form of software such as Internet Explorer, Safari, and Firefox, and is used to request Web pages from Web servers. A **Web server** stores and delivers Web pages and other Web resources such as interactive Web content.

Web browsers are available for many different computing platforms. Desktop computers, notebook computers, and smart phones all include Web browsers. Many of the most popular Web sites are providing content in a stripped-down form for convenient navigating on a small smart phone display (see Figure 4.12). The Web is also available on televisions by using special Internet-connected set-top boxes. In the world of pervasive computing, Web interfaces are cropping up on all kinds of objects from refrigerators to automobiles.

All Web pages are identified and accessed using a URL. A **Uniform Resource Locator**, more commonly called a **URL,** acts as a Web page address, incorporating the domain name of the Web server and the location of the Web page file on the server. Figure 4.13 identifies the different components of a URL.

FIGURE 4.13 • Components of a URL

The URL http://www.cengage.com/cca/ch1/index.html consists of several components.

Protocol	Web server	Domain name	Location on server	Requested file
http://	www.	cengage.com/	cca/ch1/	index.html

The final portion of the domain name, .com, .edu, and so on, is called the *top-level domain* (*TLD*). Top-level domains classify Internet locations by type or, in the case of international Web sites, by location. There are hundreds of TLDs; the most common include .com and .biz for businesses, .edu for education, and .org for non-profit organizations. TLDs can also be country codes such as .uk for the United Kingdom. A complete list can be found at *www.iana.org/domains/root/db*.

Web Markup Languages

A *markup language* is used to describe how information is to be displayed. It typically combines the information, such as text and images, along with additional instructions for formatting. The primary markup language that is used to specify the formatting of a Web page is called **Hypertext Markup Language (HTML)**. Web pages are sometimes called HTML documents. HTML uses tags to describe the formatting of a page; an *HTML tag* is a specific command inside angle brackets (< >) that tells a Web browser how to display items on a page. Figure 4.14 illustrates HTML code and how the browser interprets it. Note that there are opening and closing versions of HTML tags. The closing tag is indicated by a forward slash. HTML commands operate on whatever is between the opening and closing tags. Thus, <b>HTML</b> tells the browser to display the letters *HTML* in a bold font. Viewing the figure, can you guess what effect the <em> command has?

FIGURE 4.14 • Hypertext Markup Language (HTML)

The HTML code at the top is read by a Web browser, which displays the content on the bottom.

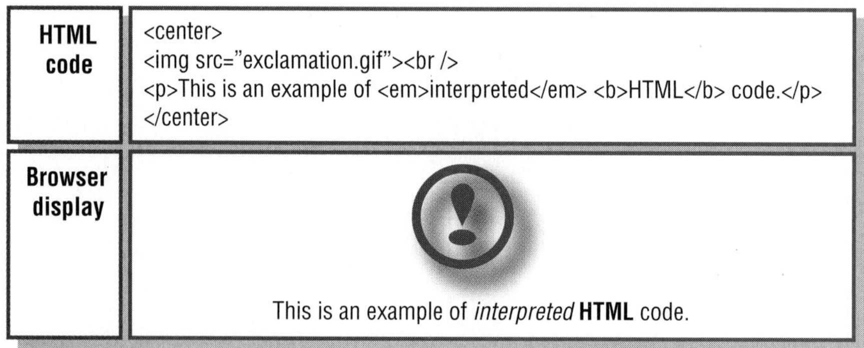

HTML code
<center>
<img src="exclamation.gif">
<p>This is an example of <em>interpreted</em> <b>HTML</b> code.</p>
</center>
Browser display
This is an example of *interpreted* **HTML** code.

A number of newer Web markup languages are increasing in popularity. One that is changing the landscape of the Web and other aspects of computing is the **Extensible Markup Language (XML)**. Although HTML provides a method of describing the format of a Web page, XML provides a method for describing and classifying the content of data in a Web page. Compare the HTML code and XML code in Figure 4.15. Although the XML code is simplified for the purpose of this example, it clearly illustrates how data is classified in XML code. In contrast, the HTML code says only how the data should look, and says nothing about the purpose of the data.

FIGURE 4.15 • XML

XML provides a method of describing or classifying data in a Web page.

Web content	HTML code	XML code
Reebok® Classic Ace Tennis Shoe **$49.95** Soft leather tennis shoe. Lightweight EVA molded midsole. Rubber outsole. China.	<strong><font face="Verdana, Arial, Helvetica, sans-serif">Reebok® Classic Ace Tennis Shoe </font></strong> <strong>$49.95</strong> <table width="100%" border="1"><tr><td>Soft leather tennis shoe. Lightweight EVA molded midsole. Rubber outsole. China. </td></tr></table>	**<product type="shoes">** **<name>** Reebok Classic Ace Tennis Shoe **</name>** **<price>$49.95</price>** **<description>** Soft leather tennis shoe. Lightweight EVA molded midsole. Rubber outsole. China. **</description>** **</product>**

XML provides several advantages to both Web content publishers and viewers. Publishers are able to use XML to separate data from Web page formatting. This is possible because XML Web content is implemented using several files: one that defines the structure of the data (product, name, price, and description), another that provides the actual data (Reebok, $49.95, and so on), and a third that defines the format of the presentation of the data in a Web browser. This method of organization offers great convenience to organizations that may change the content of a Web page frequently. For example, a news organization can use the same layout for their Web page, but change the data from day to day to reflect the latest news.

The structured data approach of XML provides convenience for Web browsing as well. Web searches become much easier when Web site content is classified and defined using XML tags. Imagine that the HTML and XML code in Figure 4.15 included descriptions of many tennis shoes. It would be much easier for a search engine to find a match for "price < $60" in the XML code than in the HTML code.

A slightly more structured version of HTML, called **XHTML**, is designed to integrate with XML code. After becoming well established as an HTML replacement, XHTML could be headed for retirement because a new, more powerful version of HTML (v5) has received the endorsement of the W3C and developers.[3] The differences between HTML and XHTML are slight, and the transition back to HTML should be smooth. HTML v5 fixes many of the problems inherent in previous HTML versions, and adds robust support for media.

EXPAND YOUR KNOWLEDGE

To learn more about how to create Web pages, go to www.cengage.com/computerconcepts/np/swt4. Click the link "Expand Your Knowledge" and then complete the lab entitled "Creating Web Pages."

In order to provide a consistent design and appearance across multiple pages in a Web site, Web designers use a technology called cascading style sheets. **Cascading style sheets**, or **CSS,** use special HTML tags to globally define font characteristics for a variety of page elements as well as how those elements are laid out on the Web page. So, rather than having to specify a font in each occurrence throughout a document, formatting can be specified once and applied to all occurrences. CSS styles are often defined in a separate file and applied to many pages in a Web site.

Just as XML extracts the data from an HTML file into a separate file, CSS extracts the formatting from the HTML file. Encapsulating the elements of a Web page, data, and style in separate files allows developers to do more with less coding. A minor change to one CSS file can affect (cascade across) hundreds of associated HTML files. XHTML files are used to pull together information from the XML and CSS files to create professional-looking Web documents (see Figure 4.16).

FIGURE 4.16 • XML, CSS, and XHTML

In most professional Web pages, the data is stored separately in an XML file, and the visual style is stored in a separate CSS file. Data and style are combined in the XHTML file and delivered to Web browsers.

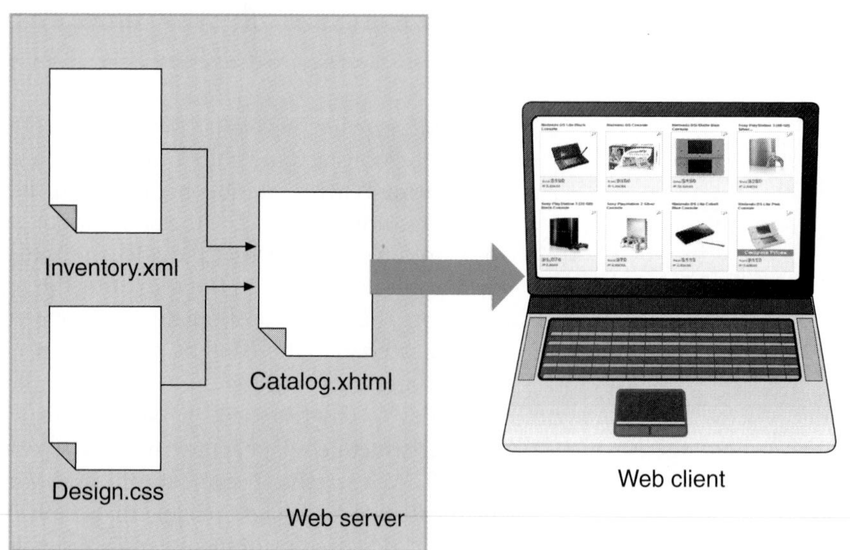

XML has been adopted by Microsoft in its Office suite to standardize data descriptions across applications. Because data is described the same with XML in Word, Excel, Access, and PowerPoint, as well as other Microsoft applications, it can be easily shared among those applications and published to the Web. Microsoft has replaced its proprietary file formats (.doc, .xls, .mdb, and .ppt) with standardized compressed .xml files (.docx, .xlsx, .mdbx, and .pptx). Because many software vendors support the XML standard of data representation, data can now easily be shared across software from different vendors, and even across a variety of computing platforms. A global standard for data representation is the first step to taking control of information.

EXPAND YOUR KNOWLEDGE

To learn more about designing Web pages, go to www.cengage.com/computerconcepts/np/swt4/. Click the link "Expand Your Knowledge" and then complete the lab entitled "Web Design Principles."

Web-Authoring Software

When the Web was new, creating Web sites was the domain of techies who took the time to learn HTML, and those who hired them. Today, anyone who can use a word processor can create professional-quality Web sites with little time and effort. All it takes is something worth writing about, a good sense of visual design, and some Web-authoring software. **Web-authoring software** is similar to a word processor and allows you to create HTML documents. Rather than having to type out HTML tags to create Web page formatting, the author defines the formatting using standard menu commands in a what-you-see-is-what-you-get (WYSIWYG) editor (Figure 4.17). *WYSIWYG* (pronounced wizzie-wig) implies that the Web page you design with the Web-authoring software will look the same when published on the Web. When you save your Web page, the software creates the HTML file with the appropriate tags.

FIGURE 4.17 • Web-authoring software

Web-authoring software allows the developer to create Web pages using HTML code and a WYSIWYG editor.

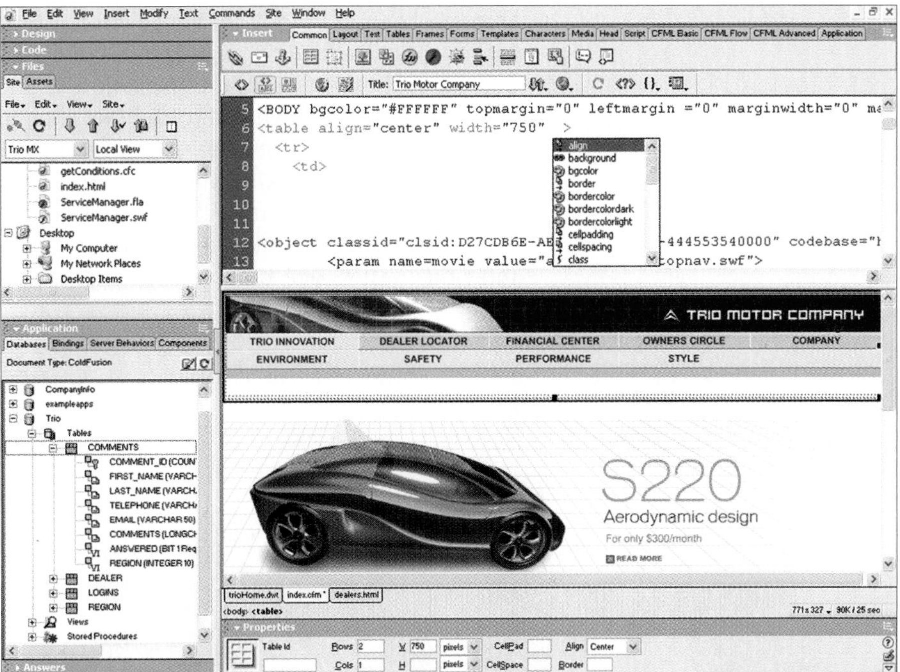

WYSIWYG editors are a great convenience for quickly creating Web pages. However, these editors fall somewhat short of automating all processes involved in Web production. Understanding HTML tags is still a valuable skill to possess in Web development.

Although most people who use the Web do not have their own Web site, it is likely that the percentage of people who do publish to the Web will continue to increase. Many nontechnical employees are now responsible for creating or maintaining content on professional Web sites. Outside of work, the Web is an ideal way to share files with friends, family, and strangers. You can use your Web site to share photos with family and friends, share your corporate mission statement with customers, or share your political philosophies with the world.

Programming the Web

While creating *static* Web pages, those that simply present unchanging information, has become easy, today's professional-quality Web sites have evolved well beyond these basics. Today's most popular Web sites are *dynamic*, providing users with an interactive experience tailored to the individual.

Have you ever had a Web page greet you by name? Many of today's commercial Web sites are created on-the-fly when the user accesses them. For example, if you have made purchases at Amazon.com you may notice that each time you visit Amazon.com you are greeted by name and presented with advertisements for products similar to those you have purchased before. Amazon custom-creates a Web page just for you. But, how does the Amazon server know who you are, and what you like? The answer involves cookies.

Today's Web browsers allow Web servers to store small text files called **cookies** on your computer. When you revisit a Web site, even though your computer may have a different IP address than the last time you visited, the Web site can recognize you by reading its associated cookie file from your PC (see Figure 4.18). Cookie files can contain data or perhaps a unique identifier that can be used to look up your personal profile in a database on the server. Information accessed through the use of cookies can include your name, address, and other personal information such as credit card numbers, items you've previously purchased at the Web site, items you've viewed on the Web site, and the amount of time spent viewing each item. This information is obtained through tracking your activities at the Web site and through the forms you filled out and submitted at the site. By collecting this information over time, a detailed customer profile can be developed and used to cater to your individual tastes each time you visit the Web site.

FIGURE 4.18 • Dynamic Web pages

Dynamic Web Pages are created on the fly, by identifying the user through a cookie ID and accessing user information from a database.

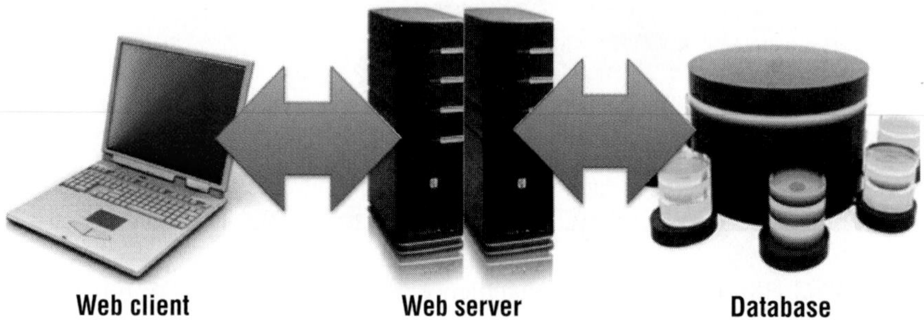

Some people worry that cookies may be a threat to security and privacy. Today's browsers provide means with which to heighten security and restrict the use of cookies. Users also have the power to delete cookie files from their systems. These files are so common, however, that nearly every commercial Web site uses them, and most users accept them as a fact of Internet life.

Besides markup language like HTML and XML, the Web also makes use of software technologies to manipulate user-provided information and provide a wide variety of services. The software typically runs on the server, using information collected from Web-based forms and mouse clicks as input. Some Web software is designed to run independently on the client computer. Whether on the server side or the client side, Web software plays a large role in how you use the Web today:

- Search engines use software to query databases with user-provided keywords.
- Shopping on the Web involves shopping cart software and software that manages the transaction.

In an effort to create a more open and transparent government, the White House under President Obama has created data.gov and USAspending.gov. Both Web sites are designed to allow U.S. citizens and businesses to access important budget and spending data directly from the White House, to manipulate and analyze as they choose.

Data.gov provides access to machine-readable data from dozens of federal agencies, including the Centers for Disease Control and Prevention, Department of Defense, Department of Homeland Security, Department of State, Department of the Treasury, Environmental Protection Agency, NASA, National Science Foundation, National Weather Service, U.S. Census, and the White House. Categories include Energy and Utilities, Fed Finance, Geography and Environment, Health and Nutrition, International Statistics, Population, Science and Technology, and others. Hundreds of predefined reports are available to view and download into a spreadsheet or database. Businesses and researchers can also access the data directly to design reports created by their own systems.

USASpending.gov has the slogan "Where Americans Can See Where Their Money Goes." For example, it shows that the federal government budgeted $9.6 billion for Department of Defense IT spending in 2009. The data is presented using meaningful charts, and can be downloaded into a spreadsheet or database. The site will be expanded to include all types of federal spending over time.

Data.gov and USASpending.gov are excellent examples of how the Web can act as a conduit to access data in a database. Besides providing access to government data that was previously difficult or impossible to view, the White House under President Obama has utilized the Web to collect the views of citizens, to hold online town hall meetings, and for a president's blog that provides access to presidential speeches on YouTube.

Questions

1. How has the White House utilized the Web to provide services to U.S. citizens?
2. What Web technologies has the U.S. government employed in its data.gov and USASpending.gov Web sites?
3. Is there any down side to the White House's efforts to use the Web to better communicate with U.S. citizens?

Sources

1. *Eaton, Kit, "White House Unveils USASpending.gov to Track IT Spending," FastCompany, June 30, 2009, www.fastcompany.com.*
2. *Jackson, Joab, "Visualization tools improve transparency by making sense of raw data," Government Computer News, August 24, 2009, http://gcn.com.*
3. *Masnick, Michael, "Is The Federal Government The Most Interesting Tech Startup For 2009?", TechDirt, August 17, 2009, www.techdirt.com.*
4. *Federal Data Web site, accessed August 26, 2009, http://data.gov.*
5. *Fed Spending Web site, accessed August 26, 2009, http://usaspending.gov/.*

- Software manages Web cookies and creates dynamic Web pages custom designed to the visitor.
- Online services such as online dating, games, animated cartoons, special-purpose calculators, local weather, and many others make use of Web-driven software.
- Social networking sites like Facebook and MySpace use software to manage user interaction.
- Software is used to filter out inappropriate photos on Flickr and copy-protected videos on YouTube.
- Increasingly, standard software applications like word processing are being delivered over the Web.

The four most prevalent programming languages used to implement this type of interactivity are Java, JavaScript, ActiveX, and Ajax. *Java* is an object-oriented programming language that allows software engineers to create programs that run on any computer platform. *JavaScript* is similar to Java in that it provides functionality in Web pages through programming code that is embedded in an HTML document. However, the two languages are very different. Java is a full-fledged programming language for all computing environments, but JavaScript was developed specifically for the Web and is more limited in nature. Microsoft has created an alternative to JavaScript for use in Internet Explorer called *ActiveX*. ActiveX controls are included with some Web pages to provide interactivity or animation. *Ajax*, which stands for *Asynchronous JavaScript and XML*, is a popular new set of technologies used to create many of the more recent programs delivered over the Web, such as Google Docs and Flickr's Photo Editor (see Figure 4.19). It allows the user to interact with the program without the need for frequent reloading of the Web page.

FIGURE 4.19 • Ajax Web-delivered software

Many of today's popular Web applications, like the photo editor in flickr, are created using Ajax technologies.

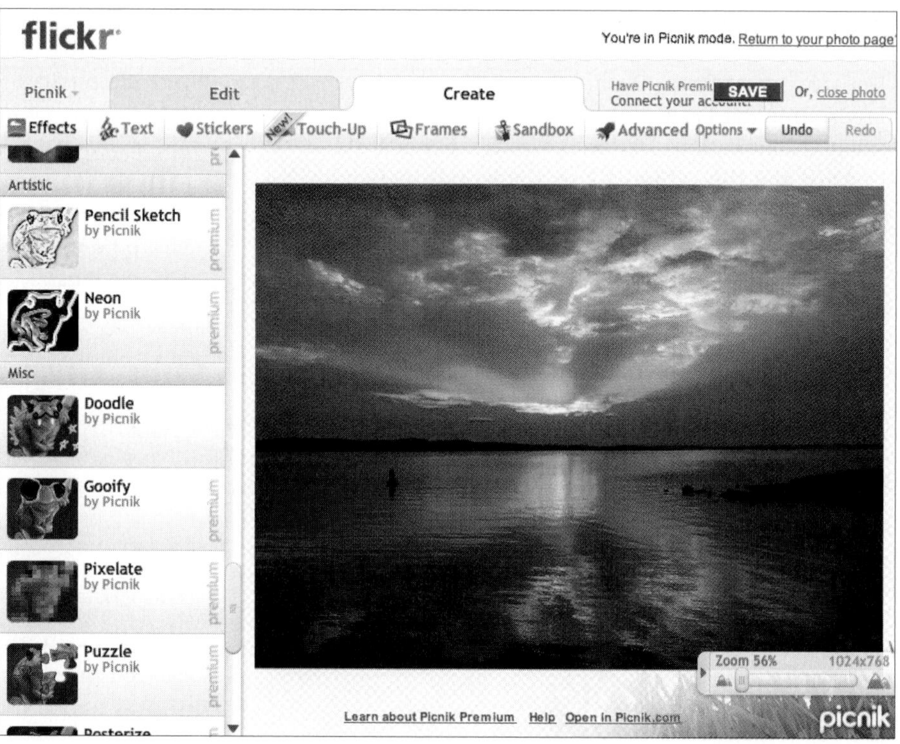

Web Browser Plug-Ins

Some software companies have developed software to extend the capabilities of HTML and Web browsers. HTML files can store only ASCII text. Binary data such as images, sound, and video must be stored in separate files. Web browsers support viewing some image formats and playing some basic sounds and animation. To employ more advanced Web content, or what some in the industry call *rich content*, such as video and interactive media, a helper application called a plug-in is required. A **plug-in** works with a Web browser to offer extended services such as audio players, video, animation, 3D graphics viewers, and interactive media. When a Web page contains content that requires a plug-in, you are typically provided with the opportunity to download and install the necessary tool at no cost, if you don't already have it. Adobe *Flash* is a popular plug-in; Flash enables users to view animations and videos and to interact with games and other multimedia content created with the Flash program (see Figure 4.20). Microsoft has developed a similar technology called Silverlight that is in some ways more powerful than Adobe Flash, but has yet to gain traction in the market.

FIGURE 4.20 • Flash animation

This Flash game provided at the Mini Cooper Web site attracts customers to the site and helps them have fun while they are shopping for a new vehicle.

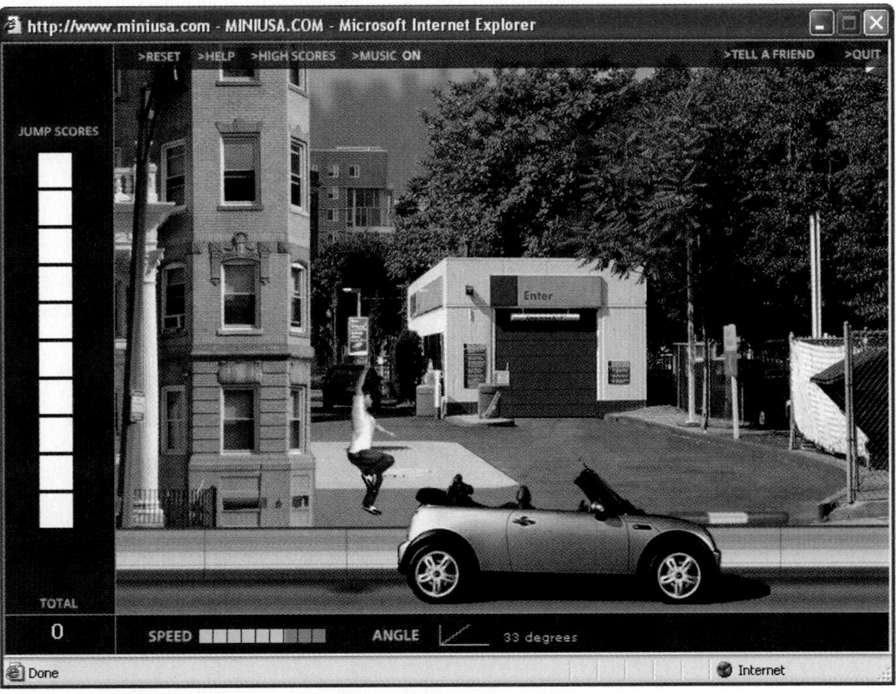

Many plug-ins available today address the issue of transferring large media files over the Web. The traditional method of viewing Web content is to request a file from a Web server by typing a URL or clicking a link, waiting while the file downloads to your computer, and then viewing the file in the Web browser window. The large size of audio and video files would leave users waiting for minutes, even hours, after they clicked a link before they could view the file. Some systems are able to reduce the wait by compressing the files to smaller sizes and storing the multimedia content in a more efficient manner. Another technique to deliver multimedia without the wait is called content streaming. With **content streaming**, sometimes called streaming media, streaming video, or streaming audio, the media begins playing while the file is being delivered. Problems arise with this technique only when the speed of play outpaces your Internet connection's speed of delivery.

INTERNET AND WEB APPLICATIONS

EXPAND YOUR KNOWLEDGE

To learn more about designing Internet applications, go to www.cengage.com/computerconcepts/np/swt4. Click the link "Expand Your Knowledge" and then complete the lab entitled "Getting the Most Out of the Internet."

The Internet has provided information services to researchers and scholars since 1970. The early Internet introduced a then-new and powerful messaging tool called e-mail that quickly became the most popular Internet application. An Internet tool called FTP (for file transfer protocol) was used to share files. Other tools were developed to catalog all of the files available on the Internet. For the first 23 years the Internet was a text-based medium accessed using a network command line. Because relatively few people had the ability to access and use a network command line, the Internet remained relatively obscure.

The birth of the World Wide Web in 1993 changed all of that. The World Wide Web and the Web browser provided a graphical user interface to Internet resources that opened the Internet up to the general public. Individuals, groups, organizations, and businesses began publishing information to the Internet for the general public to access using a Web browser. The Web quickly became the main gate for public access to resources on the Internet.

Everything on the Web exists on the Internet; however, the reverse is not true. Many people access e-mail without using a Web browser. Businesses and organizations pass private information over the Internet. Some users still make use of the old command line for using traditional Internet services. Figure 4.21 illustrates the relationship between the Web, the Internet, and Internet applications. The Web exists as an application on the Internet, and services such as communication, e-commerce, and information distribution exist both on the Internet and on the Web.

FIGURE 4.21 • The Web and the Internet

The Web exists as an application on the Internet and supports many Internet services.

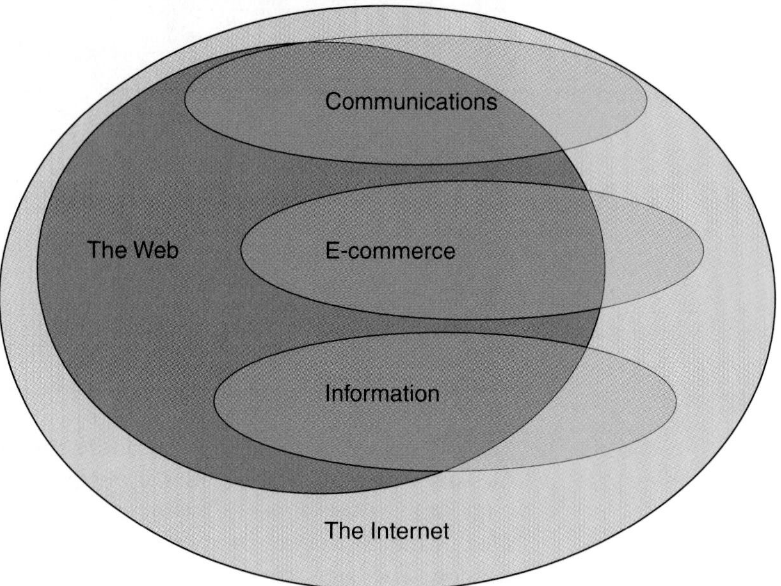

The Web is the ideal tool for sharing and organizing information for the general public. The Web contains millions of Web sites. Each Web site is unique, and most can be classified under one of the following categories:

- Information gathering
- Communication, collaboration, and social networking
- News
- Education and training
- E-commerce
- Travel
- Employment and careers
- Multimedia and entertainment
- Research

This section explores each of these Web applications as well as other Internet applications and how they can benefit you personally and professionally.

Information Gathering

The fundamental purpose of the Web is to make it easier to find related documents from diverse Internet sources by following hyperlinks. However, the Web has become so large that many complain of *information overload*, or the inability to find the information you need due to the overabundance of unrelated information. In order to relieve the strain of information overload, Web developers have provided powerful tools to assist in organizing and cataloging Web content.

A **search engine** is a valuable tool that enables you to find information on the Web by specifying words that are key to a topic of interest—*keywords*. Operators can also be employed for more precise search results. Table 4.3 provides examples of the use of operators in Google searches as listed on Google's help page (*www.google.com/help/cheatsheet.html*).

TABLE 4.3 • Using operators in Web searches

Keywords and operator typed	Search engine interpretation
vacation hawaii	The words *vacation* and *Hawaii*
Maui OR Hawaii	Either the word *Maui* or the word *Hawaii*
"To each his own"	The exact phrase *to each his own*
virus -computer	The word *virus*, but *not* the word *computer*
Star Wars Episode +I	This movie title, including the roman numeral *I*
~auto loan	Loan info for both the word *auto* and its synonyms: *truck*, *car*, etc.
define:computer	Definitions of the word *computer* from around the Web
red * blue	The words *red* and *blue* separated by one or more words

Search engines scour the Web with *bots* (automated programs) called *spiders* that follow all Web links in an attempt to catalog every Web page by topic. The process is called Web *crawling*, and due to the ever-changing nature of the Web, it is a job that never ends. Google maintains billions of indexed Web pages on hundreds of thousands of servers storing petabytes of data.

One of the challenges of Web crawling is determining which of the words on any given Web page describe its topic. Different search engines use different methods. Methods include counting word occurrences within the Web page, evaluating nouns and verbs in the page's title and subtitle, using keywords provided by the page's author in the HTML code, and evaluating the words used in links to the page from other pages. Once the search engine has a reasonable idea of a page's topic, it records the URL, page title, and associated information and keywords in a database.

After building the search database, the next challenge facing a search engine is to determine which of the hundreds or thousands of Web pages associated with a particular keyword are most useful. The method of ranking Web pages from most relevant to least differs from search engine to search engine. Google uses a popularity

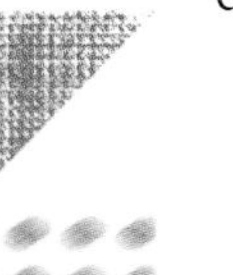

TechEdge

A FASTER, GREENER SEARCH

Every single time you search the Internet, you generate between 0.2 and 7 grams of carbon dioxide, a gas that is wreaking havoc on our climate. The problem is not just your computer, it's all the servers and data centers that need to be cooled to process your request. Feeling guilty yet? Well, soon, you might not have to. University of Glasgow researchers have created search engine processors that are 20 times faster than the standard processors used today. And that should shrink your carbon footprint significantly.

Faster searches key to a greener web
University of Glasgow: University News
August 31, 2009
http://www.gla.ac.uk/news/headline_128603_en.html

contest approach. Web pages that are referenced from other Web pages are ranked higher than those that are not. Each reference is considered a vote for the referenced page. The more votes a Web page gets, the higher its rank. References from higher-ranked pages weigh more heavily than those from lower-ranked pages.

A keyword search at a search engine isn't a search of the Web but rather a search of a database that stores information about Web pages. The database is continuously checked and refreshed so that it is an accurate reflection of the current status of the Web. The methods used by search engines to determine and display search results are referred to as a search algorithm. Those in the business invest heavily in refining and perfecting their search algorithm to provide the best search results.

Today's heated competition in the search engine market is pressing the big players to expand their services. Table 4.4 lists some specialized search engine services that are available from Google.

TABLE 4.4 • Google's specialized search applications

Service	What it does
Alerts	Get e-mail updates on the topics of your choice
Blog Search	Find blogs on your favorite topics
Book Search	Search the full text of books
Custom Search	Create a customized search experience for your community
Desktop	Search and personalize your computer
Directory	Search the Web, organized by topic or category
Images	Search for images on the Web
Maps	View maps and search for businesses in specific locations
News	Search online news stories
Patent Search	Search the full text of U.S. patents
Product Search	Search for stuff to buy
Scholar	Search scholarly papers
Videos	Search for videos on the Web

The Web search business has become very profitable due to the revenue earned from online advertising. While Google holds the lion's share of the search market (65 percent), Microsoft has been increasing its piece of the pie with the 2009 introduction of its Bing search engine that produces results that it claims are more useful than Google search results (see Figure 4.22). Microsoft calls Bing a decision engine, since its search results are engineered to assist people in making decisions. Shortly after the release of Bing, Microsoft partnered with Yahoo! to take on Google. The deal allows Yahoo! to use Bing as its search engine, and combines the companies' advertising departments, which are managed by Yahoo! The partnership of Microsoft and Yahoo! increased their combined market share to 23 percent.[4]

The Web is exploding with information-gathering applications, with new ones being introduced every day. Sometimes Web applications can be integrated

FIGURE 4.22 • Microsoft Bing

The Microsoft Bing "decision engine" formats search results in a manner that is useful for decision making.

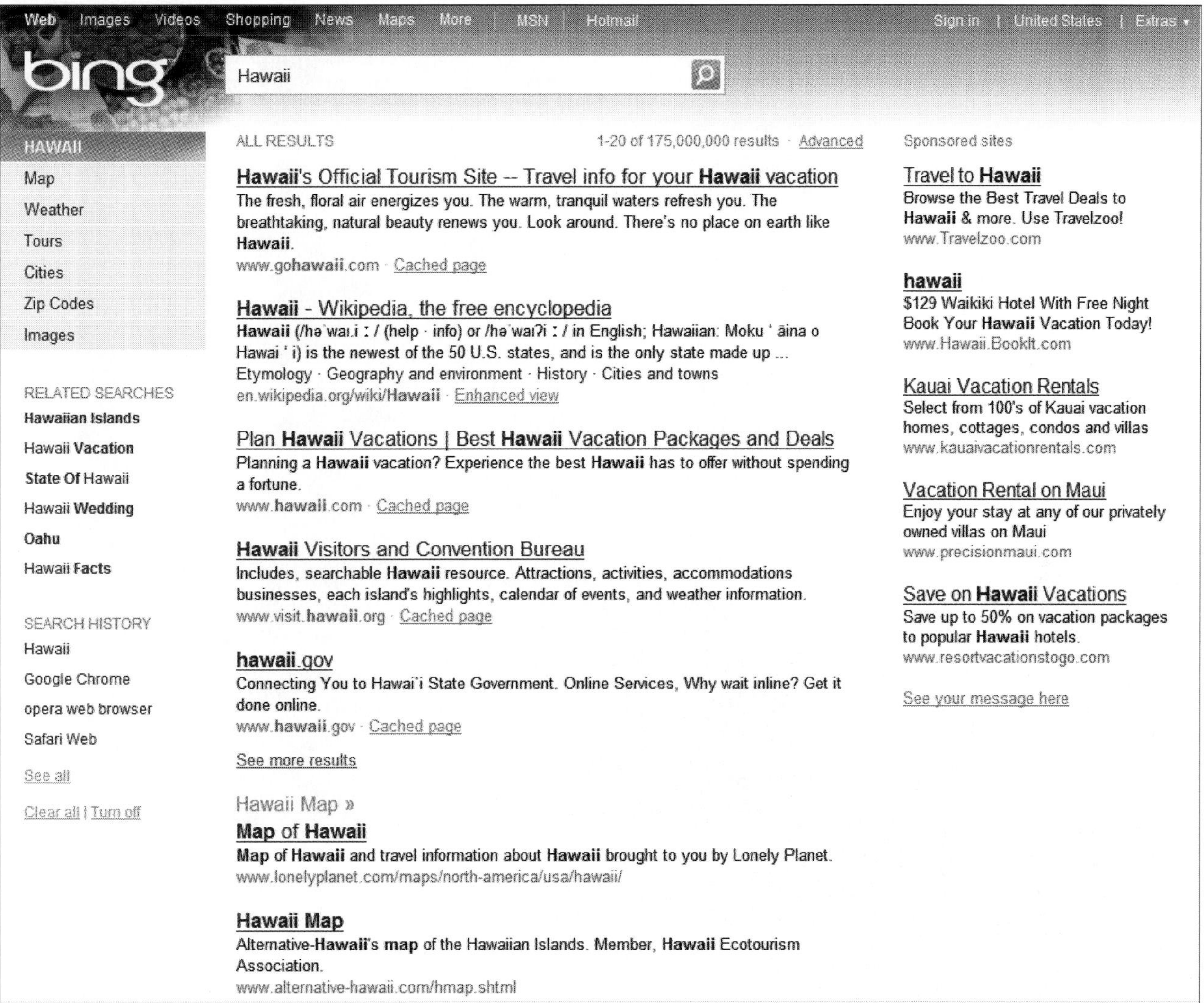

into a *mashup*, a single application that combines different Web applications (see Figure 4.23), to offer a greater value to users. For example, Google Maps provides views of street maps and directions between locations. Google has increased the value of Google Maps by mashing it up with Google Search by Location and a consumer opinion application. The result is a program that allows you to find your way around an unfamiliar city, locate a specific business, and read customer opinions about the business. Google Maps has been mashed up by private businesses to perform package tracking, weather forecasting, earthquake tracking, and traffic alerts. Many such mashups are occurring in search applications and in social network applications to the benefit of the Web community.

FIGURE 4.23 • Google Maps mashup

Google Maps is used in many mashups. Here it is shown integrating a street map application, a satellite image application, a "street view" application, and a traffic report application for San Francisco near the Golden Gate Bridge.

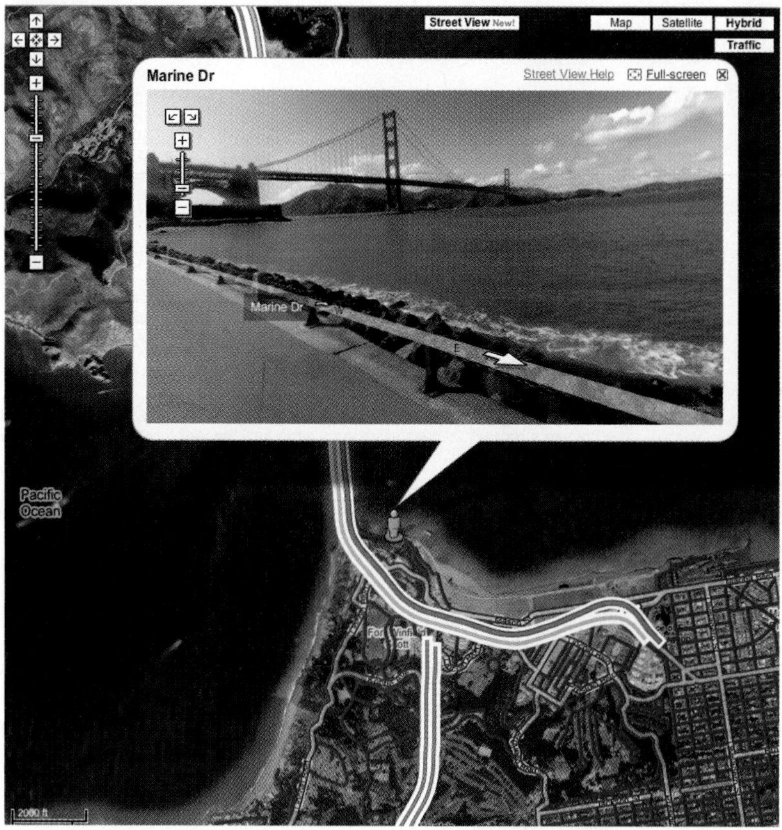

A *meta search engine* allows you to run keyword searches on several search engines at once. For example, a search run from *www.dogpile.com* returns results from Ask.com, FAST, FindWhat, Google, LookSmart, Overture, and other search engines.

A *subject directory* is a catalog of sites collected and organized by people rather than automated crawlers. Yahoo! provides a directory at *http://dir.yahoo.com* that divides Web topics into 14 general categories with many subcategories and levels of subcategories under each. Subject directories are often called subject trees because they start with relatively few main categories and then branch out into many subcategories, topics, and subtopics. Subject directories contain only a small percentage of all existing Web pages, but because they are created and maintained by people—not bots—they are more likely to contain relevant information.

Subject directories aren't the only human-powered resource on the Web. A number of companies are harnessing the skills of Web users to provide useful services on the Web. Internet start-up Mahalo, which is Hawaiian for "thank you," pays human experts to create search results pages that provide valuable information and references. Running a search on the name Barack Obama at *www.mahalo.com* generates impressive results (see Figure 4.24). Fast facts about President Obama are listed, including his birthday, birthplace, educational history, family information, and landmark dates in his political career, while the search results provide links to the top seven Web sites about the president, along with many photos of the president and videos of recent speeches. The results go on to categorize other links having to do with President Obama, including News and Articles, Photos, Videos, and Biographies. All of this is provided on one page; there's no need to filter through the 76,400,000 results provided by the same search at Google.

FIGURE 4.24 • Human-powered search: Mahalo

Mahalo provides search results created by human experts, reducing information overload and cutting to the important facts and references.

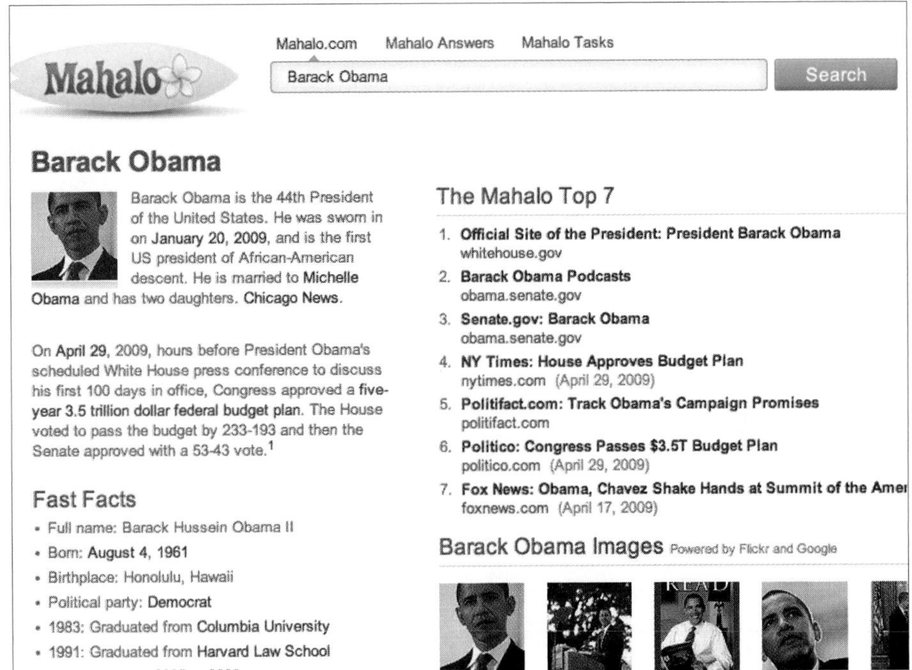

Another human-powered online resource is Cha Cha. Cha Cha is a free service that pays an online workforce to research and answer questions posed by visitors to *www.chacha.com*. Users can even submit questions via cell phone text messages to 242242 (cha cha) and have a response texted back within minutes.

Amazon's Mechanical Turk is yet another human-powered online service. Located at *www.mturk.com*, Mechanical Turk allows you to earn money doing activities that are difficult for computers. The service provides you with human intelligence tasks, or HITs, that companies are willing to pay you to do. For example, one HIT has people finding the most interesting people on MySpace. This is something that is easy for a human but difficult to automate in artificial intelligence. Mechanical Turk and other similar services are taking advantage of the fact that big jobs can be accomplished by breaking them into thousands of small ones and distributing them to willing workers interested in making a few bucks.

Finally, perhaps the most well known human-powered online resource is Wikipedia. A **wiki** is a Web site designed to allow users to add, remove, and edit content. Wiki is Hawaiian for "fast." The most popular wiki is Wikipedia, the "free encyclopedia that anyone can edit." For wikis to be most effective, it helps to have professionals reviewing new entries for accuracy. Wikipedia has tens of thousands of contributors, of whom over 1000 have earned a trustworthy reputation and have volunteered to monitor various subject areas. Wiki software has been used to create thousands of online wikis for many different purposes. Businesses like Nokia and Kodak use wikis for project management and cross-company collaboration.

Web portals are Web pages that are designed to act as entry points to the Web—the first page you open when you begin browsing the Web. They typically include a search engine, a subject directory, daily headlines, and other items of interest. They can be general or topic-specific in nature. Yahoo.com, lycos.com, aol.com, and msn.com are examples of horizontal Web portals; *horizontal* refers to the fact that they cover a wide range of topics. Some horizontal portals provide customization features. For example, iGoogle at *www.google.com/ig* allows users to build custom portals by selecting from hundreds of special-purpose widgets and arranging them on pages. Widgets include news feeds, feeds from Facebook, Twitter, and other social networks, e-mail, chat, calendar, photos, weather reports and maps, cartoons, games, and many other applications (see Figure 4.25). Vertical Web portals focus on special-interest groups. For example, the iVillage.com portal focuses on items of interest to women, and askmen.com is a vertical portal for men.

FIGURE 4.25 • Custom portal: iGoogle

iGoogle allows users to select from hundreds of widgets to create custom gateways to the Web.

Many businesses provide corporate Web portals for employees to access at work. Corporate portals include communication tools like bulletin boards and chat, access to corporate databases, corporate news, and other applications that support work-related activities. Corporate portals are sometimes used to limit employees' access to non-work-related online resources that serve as distractions.

Communication and Collaboration

Earlier, you learned how the digital revolution is ushering in the age of pervasive computing where anyone can have access to information anywhere. Equally important and influential is the birth of *pervasive communications*, the ability to communicate with anyone through a variety of formats from anywhere at anytime. Pervasive communications are the result of advances in wireless communications and Internet communications. This technology is fundamentally altering the ways in which personal and professional relationships are created and nurtured.

Prior to the Internet, forms of two-way communication were limited to face-to-face, telephone (wired), or printed word (as in mailing a letter). The Internet has broadened our communications options considerably. Today you can phone, e-mail, meet in person, instant message, blog, video chat, podcast, send a letter, post a message, update your status, tweet, geo-locate, and otherwise communicate with anyone, anytime, from any location. It is useful to consider your communication options and the strengths and weaknesses they exhibit.

There are two forms of communication: synchronous and asynchronous. In **synchronous communication**, people communicate in real time, exchanging thoughts in a flowing conversation. Synchronous communication is not always possible, as it requires all participants to be engaged in communication at the same time. Face-to-face conversations, telephone conversations, online chat, and instant messaging are examples of synchronous communication. **Asynchronous communication** allows participants to leave messages for each other to be read, heard, or watched, and responded to at the recipient's convenience. Answering machines, voice mail, and e-mail are tools for asynchronous communication.

Although it is sometimes more convenient, asynchronous communication is generally considered a weaker form of communication because the time lapse between thought exchanges can stifle the emergence of new ideas. For example, consider brainstorming sessions. The term *brainstorming session* refers to synchronous communication where participants bounce ideas off each other in order to arrive at optimal solutions. The synchronicity of such communication allows multiple minds to join together and act as one. Often a combined effort produces ideas better than any individual could produce; the group thought process is worth more than the sum of its parts. Such a phenomenon is severely inhibited if conducted asynchronously through e-mail. Asynchronous e-mail is perfect, however, for communications that require time for ponderance, and day-to-day communication such as "I'll pick you up at 8:00," "I agree to the terms of this contract," or "Did you hear about Chuck and Grace?"

Each form of communication should be evaluated in terms of quality, convenience, and time/delay. Typically you find that the quality and speed of communications compare inversely with the level of convenience (see Figure 4.26). Several forms of communication are discussed in the following sections.

FIGURE 4.26 • Evaluating forms of communication

Synchronous forms of communication that require individuals to be present and engaged simultaneously are less convenient but more powerful.

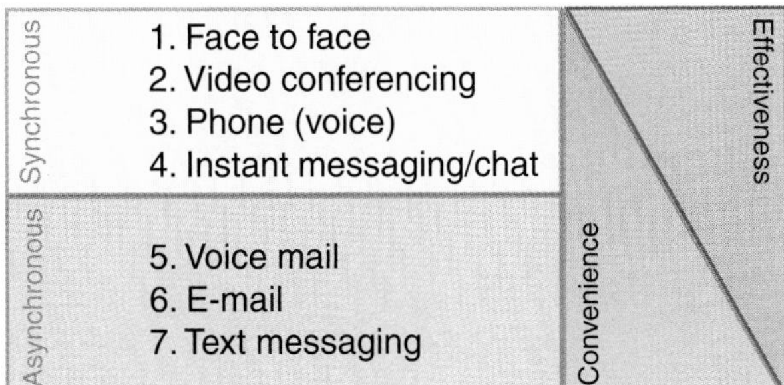

Text Communications. Internet text communications take many forms. Available in both synchronous and asynchronous formats, text communication allows participants to communicate via typed characters. The benefits of communicating electronically by text are that it is cheap and fast and the recipient receives what you type within a fraction of a second. The downside of text communication is that it communicates only words and lacks the information provided by nonverbal cues, such as voice inflection and facial expression. For this reason, text communication is notorious for creating misunderstandings.

To compensate for the lack of nonverbal cues, a method of conveying underlying sentiment has evolved using emoticons. *Emoticons* (smiley faces) combine keyboard characters to create a sideways facial expression. Table 4.5 shows some examples of commonly used emoticons and what they mean.

Today, many of the traditionally text-based forms of communication are accessed through graphic interfaces. Many e-mail and instant messaging interfaces provide small animated smiles that can be inserted into messages, like the one next to this paragraph.

TABLE 4.5 • Emoticons

Emoticon	Meaning
:-)	Happy or smiling
:- D	Really happy!
:-}	Embarrassed
:-?	Confused
;-)	Winking

TABLE 4.6 • Internet acronyms

Acronym	Meaning
L8R	Later
FYI	For your information
LOL	Laughing out loud
ROFL	Rolling on floor laughing
TTFN	Ta ta for now

Text communication can also be more time-consuming than the spoken word; just how time-consuming depends on your typing skills. To minimize the inconvenience of typing, people substitute a number of acronyms for commonly used phrases (see Table 4.6; also search the Web for "Internet acronyms".

A word of caution regarding the use of emoticons and acronyms. Most people regard the use of emoticons in business and formal communications to be inappropriate. Also, acronyms can confuse people who are unfamiliar with the vernacular. It is best to save these tools for friends with whom you are comfortable.

E-mail. **E-mail** (electronic mail) involves the transmission of messages over a computer network to support asynchronous text-based communication. E-mail is still the number-one Internet application. Many people are so dependent on e-mail that they must check it on an hourly basis lest they miss an urgent message. E-mail can be accessed from all types of computers. People are accessing e-mail anytime, anywhere, on their smart phones. Many business travelers depend on their smart phone to stay in constant e-mail contact with business associates.

EXPAND YOUR KNOWLEDGE

To learn how to compose and reply to e-mail messages, print e-mail, and more, go to www.cengage.com/computerconcepts/np/swt4. Click the link "Expand Your Knowledge" and then complete the lab entitled "E-Mail."

Like most Internet applications, e-mail uses client/server technology. E-mail clients communicate with e-mail servers to send and receive e-mail messages. E-mail messages, like the packets that carry them, include a header and a body. Sometimes e-mail messages can include an attached file (see Figure 4.27). The *e-mail header* contains technical information about the message: destination address, source address, subject, date and time, and other information required by the server. The *e-mail body* is an *ASCII text* message written by the sender to the recipient. The e-mail body may be presented as a text message or as an HTML document (a Web page). An e-mail message body cannot contain *binary data*—data that is encoded for a processor to process. An **e-mail attachment** is typically a binary file, such as an image file, Word document, music file, or spreadsheet, that travels along with an e-mail message but is not part of the e-mail ASCII text message itself.

FIGURE 4.27 • E-mail components

E-mail messages include a header and body and sometimes an attached file.

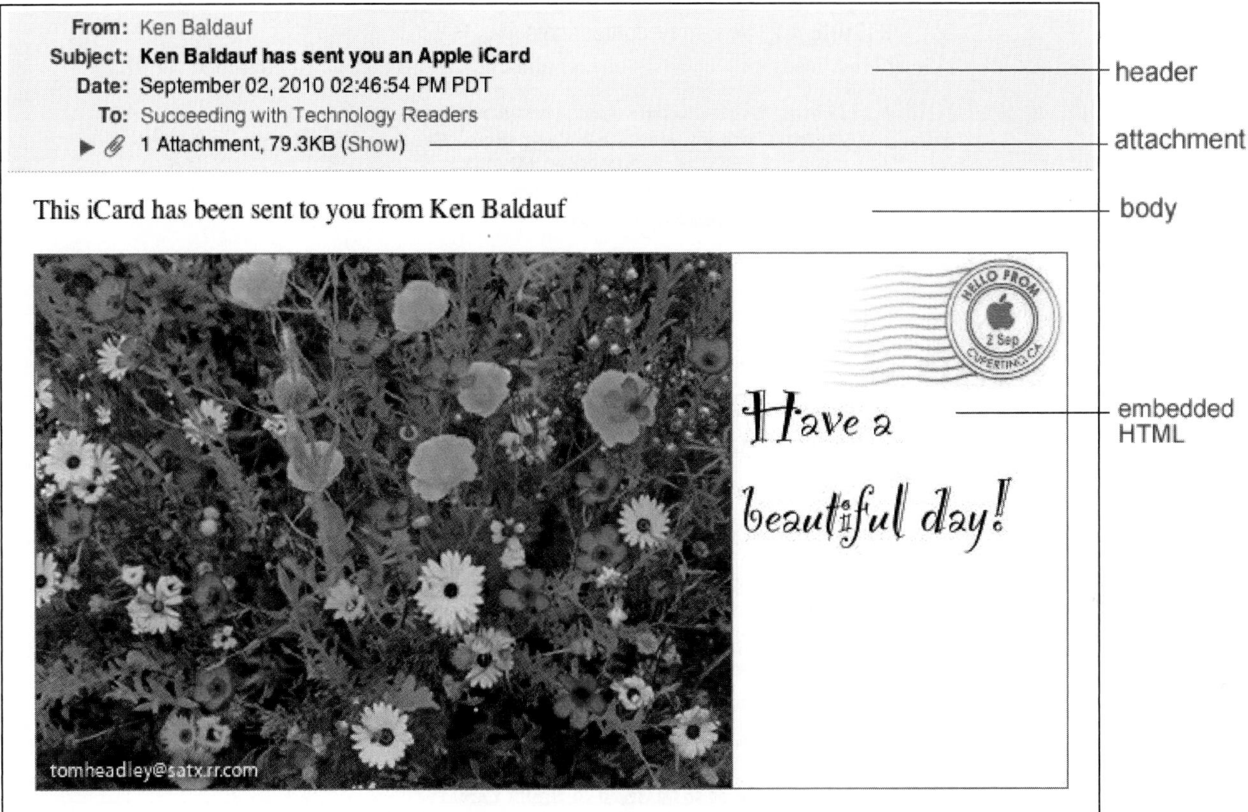

E-mail can be accessed on the Web through free services such as Gmail, Hotmail, and Yahoo! Mail, or through an e-mail client program such as Microsoft Outlook. Web-based e-mail is convenient for users who like to access their e-mail from any Internet-connected computer. E-mail client software usually provides additional capabilities, such as a calendar, a to-do list, and an address book. Microsoft Outlook is the most popular e-mail client and is included with most versions of Microsoft Office.

A number of services provide e-mail users with information about their favorite topics. Special-interest groups, called *listservs*, create online communities for discussing topic-related issues via e-mail. E-mail sent to the listserv is forwarded to all members. Another form of broadcast e-mail is subscription-based *newsletters*. For example, you can subscribe to *The New York Times* newsletter (*www.nytimes.com*) and receive the daily news in your e-mail inbox each morning (see Figure 4.28).

FIGURE 4.28 • E-mail components

E-mail messages include a header and body and sometimes an attached file.

From: NYTimes.com <nytdirect@nytimes.com>
Subject: **Today's Headlines: C.I.A. Abuse Cases Detailed in Report on Detainees**
Date: August 25, 2009 6:08:20 AM EDT
To: jjohnstonian@bedrock.com
Reply-To: nytdirect@nytimes.com

If you have trouble reading this e-mail, go to http://www.nytimes.com/todaysheadlines

The New York Times
Tuesday, August 25, 2009
Compiled 2 AM E.T.
Today's Headlines

In This E-Mail:

World | U.S. | Politics | Business | Technology | Sports | Arts | New York/Region | Science | Health | Editorials | Op-Ed |

Customize Today's Headlines | Search

TOP STORIES

C.I.A. Abuse Cases Detailed in Report on Detainees
By MARK MAZZETTI and SCOTT SHANE
Attorney General Eric H. Holder Jr. named a federal prosecutor to examine abuse of prisoners held by the C.I.A., as officials released a 2004 report detailing abuses inside C.I.A.-run prisons overseas.

Advertisement

4 Youth Prisons in New York Used Excessive Force
By NICHOLAS CONFESSORE
An investigation that found routine use of excessive physical force raised the possibility of a federal takeover of the state's youth detention system.

Calm, but Moved to Be Heard on Health Care
By KEVIN SACK
In the health care discussion, the respectful questioners like Bob Collier — those expressing discomfiting fears and legitimate concerns — may have the most impact.

• NYTimes.com Homepage Back to Top

Instant Messaging and Chat. **Instant messaging (IM)** is synchronous one-to-one text-based communication over the Internet. With instant messaging, participants build *buddy lists* or contact lists that allow them to keep track of which people are currently logged on to the Internet. You can send messages to one of your online buddies, which opens up a small dialog box on your buddy's computer or portable device and allows the two of you to chat via the keyboard (see Figure 4.29). While chat is typically one to one, and typically text based, more advanced forms of chat are emerging. Today's instant messaging software supports the following services:

- Instant messages: Send notes back and forth with a friend who is online.
- Chat: Create your own custom chat room to communicate with multiple friends or coworkers.
- Nudges, animated winks, and graphics: Use these to help get someone's attention or emphasize your point, or to create a personalized wallpaper and icons.
- Web links: Share links to your favorite Web sites.
- Images: Look at an image stored on your friend's computer.
- Sounds: Play sounds for your friends.

- Files: Share files by sending them directly to your friends.
- Talk: Use the Internet instead of a phone to orally speak with friends.
- Streaming content: Look at real-time or near-real-time stock quotes and news.

FIGURE 4.29 • Instant messaging

IM provides a way to stay in constant contact with online friends.

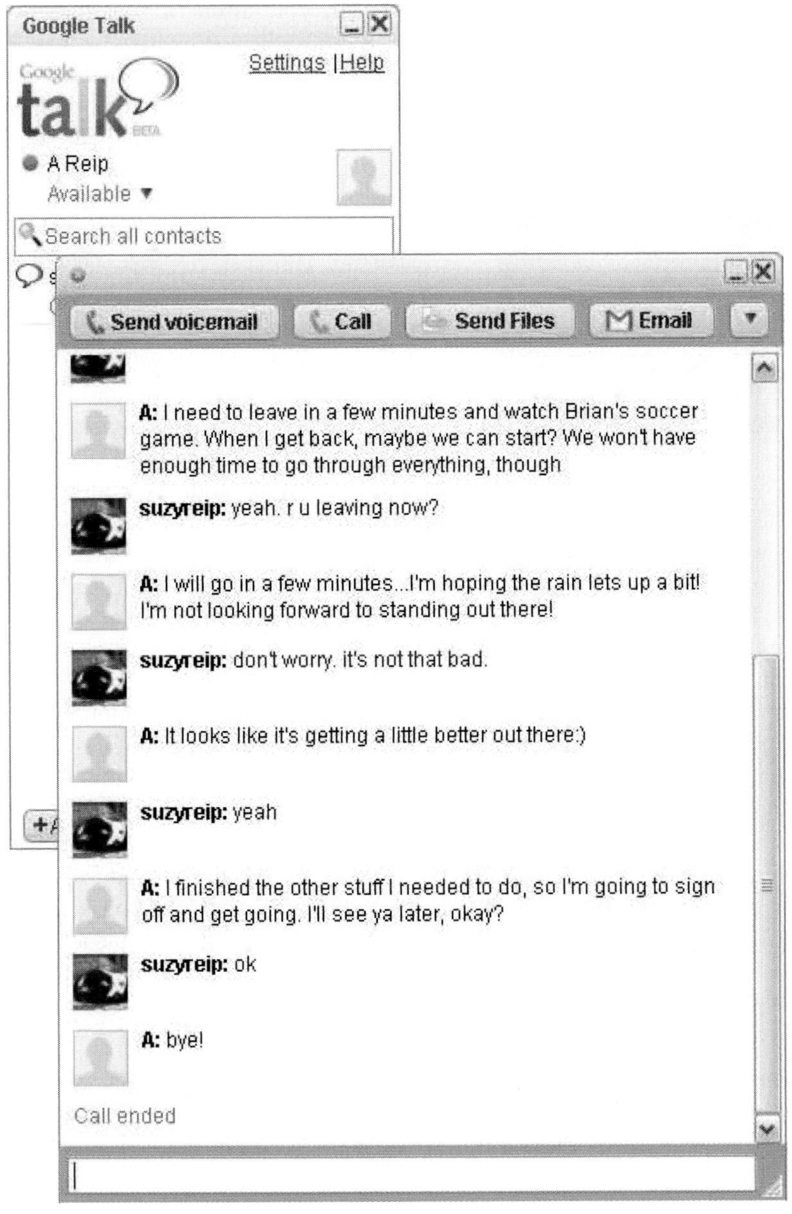

Popular instant messaging services include America Online Instant Messenger (AIM), MSN Messenger, ICQ (another AOL company), Google Talk, and Yahoo! Messenger. All are free to Internet users and provide client software that you can download online. The downside is that each of these products is *proprietary*—they do not communicate with each other. So, if you use AOL Instant Messenger, you can chat only with others using AOL Instant Messenger, not people using ICQ, MSN, or Yahoo!. Although some software tools have been developed to allow users to combine IM services, they are hampered by the services' unwillingness to use one standard platform.

Instant messaging started out as a fun communication tool for personal use, but it is becoming a serious business tool. Business users have discovered that instant messaging improves productivity and saves money by allowing employees to participate in virtual conferences and collaborate on projects from any location.

Internet **chat** involves synchronous text messaging between two or more participants. Participants log on to a chat server and send each other text messages in real time. As with most forms of group messaging, chat forums are organized by topics. Some services call the various topic-related forums *channels;* others call them *chat rooms*. The most popular public chat utility is called Internet Relay Chat (IRC). IRC has thousands of channels. Any IRC participant can create a channel. At any given time there can be hundreds of thousands of users logged on to IRC. Each channel has a moderator empowered to control the dialogue and even kick users out if they get unruly. Other than moderators, chat and many forms of Internet communication are uncensored. If the Internet had a rating system, many chat rooms would be rated for adult use only. Instant messaging and chat have been integrated into today's most popular social networking sites like Facebook and Twitter. While the older IM and chat services are still doing a big business, many users have migrated to social networks to stay in contact with online friends.

FIGURE 4.30 • Second Life

Chat participants navigate their avatars through a virtual world, chatting and interacting with other participants and their avatars.

Virtual Chat. *Virtual chat* provides a virtual world for you to enter and chat and interact with others. Software from worlds.com and secondlife.com can be downloaded and installed on your PC for free. When run, the software presents a 3D virtual world that can be explored by your *avatar*, a 3D representation of yourself in the virtual world. The software communicates with a Web server that allows you to see, chat with, and interact with other participants in the virtual world (see Figure 4.30). Avatars are fully articulated so that they move as real people would in the virtual space—they can even fly! Virtual worlds extend for miles and contain environments to suit every taste.

Second Life has impacted business, research, and education. Thousands of businesses have a virtual presence in Second Life where they answer customer questions, sell real products, and hold corporate meetings. Schools have a presence in Second Life as well, with many online classes taking place in the virtual environment. Teachers hold office hours in Second Life, and can present PowerPoint presentations and host discussion groups. Designers and architects use Second Life as an environment in which to experiment with new 3D designs for buildings, landscapes, floor plans, clothing, and other physical products. AI experts have used Second Life as a home for computer-controlled avatars, testing out the ability of AI computers to interact with humans without being detected. Sociologists and psychologists study Second Life to learn how people interact in virtual worlds, and how that applies to life in the real world.

Second Life even has its own currency (Linden dollars) and economy. Users purchase Linden dollars with real credit cards. The virtual money can be used to purchase virtual products and build virtual homes and businesses. A virtual business can make profits that can be exchanged back into real dollars. Some people actually earn a living buying and selling virtual products and services in Second Life. With millions of residents trading nearly $35 million worth of virtual property each month, this virtual world is definitly impacting the real world.

Text Messaging. Short Message Service (SMS), more commonly known as **text messaging** or *texting*, is a method of sending short messages, no longer than 160 characters, between cell phones. Using the keypad of the cell phone, users enter a short message and send it to a friend's cell phone. Once a message is sent, it is received by a Short Message Service Center (SMSC), which must then get it to the appropriate mobile device. If the intended recipient is offline or out of range, the SMSC holds the message and delivers it when the recipient returns. Some services allow messages to be sent from the Web to a cell phone and from cell phones to e-mail addresses. Texting is discussed more in the next chapter along with other cell phone services.

Blogs. *Web logs*, more commonly known as **blogs**, are Web sites created to express one or more individuals' views on a given topic. Originally blogs took the form of online journals, presenting a person's view on some aspect of life. As privately published blogs became more mainstream, tools were developed to assist anyone in creating a blog. Some blogs allow visitors to post comments. Such blogs can function as discussion boards on a particular topic as interested parties repeatedly check for new comments and leave their own messages in an ongoing dialogue. Bloggers may be famous thinkers, journalists, and authors such as Noam Chomsky and Thomas Friedman, or everyday folks. Some blogs make use of video, such as President Obama's blog at *www.whitehouse.gov.blog*. Blogs exemplify the power of the Internet to level the playing field and give everyone a voice. Blogs exist on nearly every topic and express most points of view. You can find many blog listings, such as the one at *www.bigeye.com/blogs.htm,* by searching the Web for "blog index".

FIGURE 4.31 • Blogs

Blogs exist on nearly every topic and present wide-ranging views, such as this news-focused blog, The Huffington Post.

There are thousands of blogs on the Internet, and it is a challenge to find a particular topic of interest. A number of blog search engines have been developed to assist in finding blog postings on particular topics. Technorati.com, bloglines.com, and rojo.com are three popular blog search engines. Google and Microsoft Bing also provide blog search tools.

Once you find blogs that interest you, it can become a burden trying to keep up with them as new articles are posted. A blog distribution system called *feeds* has been developed to help deliver and organize your blogs. Using a technology such as *RSS* (Really Simple Syndication), subscribers can have the daily updates of their favorite blogs delivered to their desktop. RSS uses XML to deliver Web content that changes on a regular basis. It is ideal for keeping up with blogs and news. Programs called aggregators or RSS readers can be downloaded from the Web (see *www.download.com*) and used to subscribe to blogs. Google users will find Google Reader an easy-to-use tool for subscribing to blogs.

Web sites that support RSS feeds are often marked by a small orange rectangular icon showing XML or RSS, like the one next to this paragraph. Web sites that support RSS feeds include *The New York Times*, Google News, Quotes of the Day, CNET News, *Scientific American*, and thousands of other popular and obscure sources. Table 4.7 lists some popular blogs to which people subscribed when this chapter was written. Check for the latest popular blogs at *www.technorati.com/pop/blogs/*.

TABLE 4.7 • Popular blogs

Blog	Description
BoingBoing (*www.boingboing.com*)	A Directory of Wonderful Things: Assorted articles on news, curiosities, technology
Engadget (*www.engadget.com*)	Cool new technologies explored
Gizmodo (*www.gizmodo.com*)	the Gadget Guide
Techcrunch (*www.techcrunch.com*)	Internet products review
The Huffington Post (*www.huffingtonpost.com*)	Breaking news and opinions
Lifehacker (*http://lifehacker.com*)	Productivity and software guide
Ars Technica (*http://arstechnica.com*)	The Art of Technology: News, analysis, and in-depth coverage of technology
Mashable (*http://mashable.com*)	Leading tech blog focused on Web 2.0 and social networking
The Official Google Blog (*http://googleblog.blogspot.com*)	Updates on Google research and business
TMZ.com (*www.tmz.com*)	Celebrity news and photos

Web 2.0 and Social Networking. A revolution is changing the way we use the Web, and it has been labeled Web 2.0. **Web 2.0** refers to Web resources that allow average users to collaborate and contribute to Web content. The Web 2.0 wave was inspired by the growing popularity of blogs. Through blogs, the Web community discovered that the Web was not something just to observe, but rather something in which to participate. There are many features and technologies associated with Web 2.0 (see Figure 4.32) and experts often disagree on which are most defining. But, in general terms, and at its minimum, Web 2.0 includes any Web site dedicated to user-created content. Besides blogs and wikis, which have already been discussed, these include social networking sites, media-sharing sites, and social bookmarking sites.

FIGURE 4.32 • Web 2.0

This cloud map illustrates the concepts and technologies behind Web 2.0 with larger words having greater importance.

Social networking Web sites provide Web-based tools for users to share information about themselves with others on the Web, and find, meet, and converse with other members. The most popular social networking sites are Facebook, MySpace, and LinkedIn. MySpace began as a listing service for musicians, and grew into a social network for the world. Facebook began as a social network for colleges, and later opened up to everyone. LinkedIn is different in that it is designed specifically as a social network for professionals wishing to make professional connections and discover job opportunities. Of the three, Facebook is the most popular with over 250 million users worldwide.[5] Many people use both Facebook (or MySpace) and LinkedIn: one for friends and the other for business.

Social networks provide members with their own personal Web page and allow them to post photos and information about themselves (see Figure 4.33). Social networking sites allow members to send messages to each other and post comments on each other's pages. Members accumulate friends through an invitation process. Special-interest groups can be created and joined as well. Tools are provided to search for others with similar interests. Social network access has extended to cell phone handsets as well.[6] Many users keep tabs on their social network throughout the day, seeing what their friends are up to by reading their latest posts.

SENSING SENTIMENT—ONLINE

You're lacing up your new shoes on your way out the door. But one of the holes is too small and you can't get that stupid lace through. It takes forever! You decide to vent your frustrations on Twitter. Now, new sentiment-analysis software might just pick up your complaint and let the shoe company know they have made you unhappy. The software gathers data from hundreds of thousands of sources, including blogs, news sites, and social media, and uses an algorithm to evaluate how people are feeling about a company or a product. It's a new way for companies to improve their bottom line by being more responsive to customers—like you.

Mining the Web for Feelings, Not Facts
Alex Wright
The New York Times
August 23, 2009
http://www.nytimes.com/2009/08/24/technology/internet/24emotion.html?_r=1

FIGURE 4.33 • Facebook

Facebook is a social networking site that provides members with personal Web pages and the ability to connect with others online.

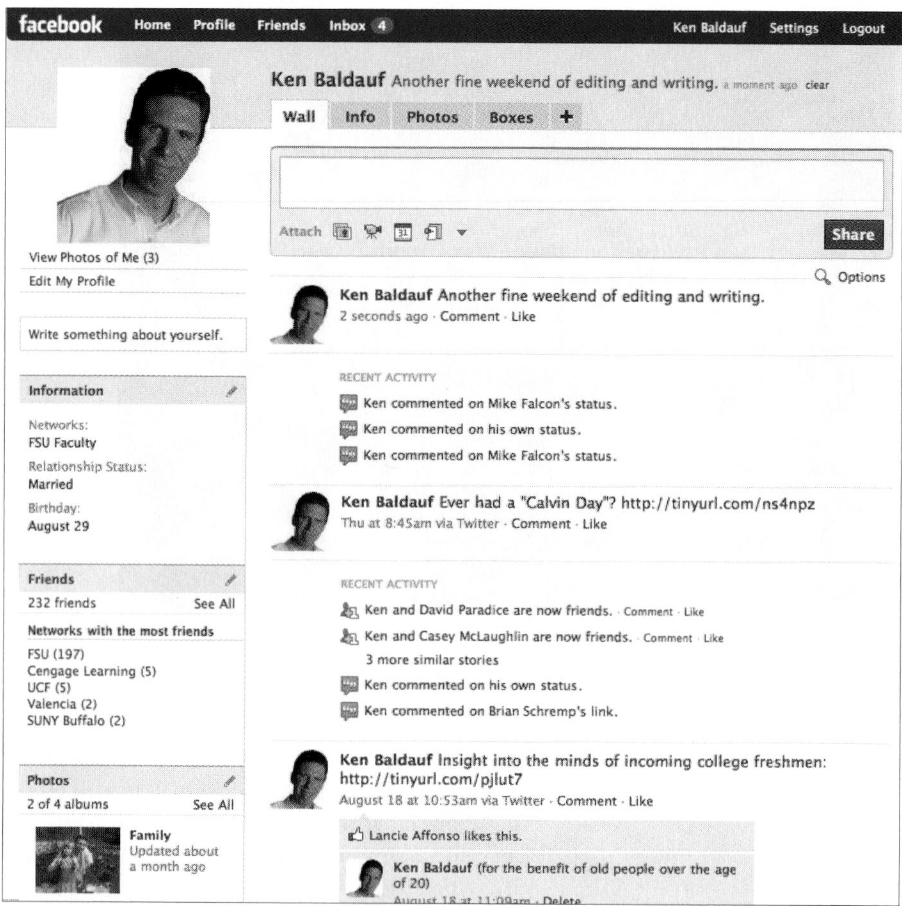

Facebook provides an application development platform so that tech-savvy members can create applications to run within Facebook. This has led to thousands of tools that Facebook users can add to their pages. For example, there are tools to connect to others with similar music tastes, to see your daily horoscope, to share videos, to find "Mr. or Ms. Right," to express your mood, to play games, and many, many more.

Another social networking site called Twitter (*www.twitter.com*) allows members to report on what they are doing throughout the day. Referred to as a microblogging service, Twitter allows users to send short text updates (up to 140 characters long), called tweets, from cell phones or the Internet to their Twitter page to let others know what they are up to. Twitter updates can be forwarded to MySpace or Facebook Web sites.

Online social networks have created an altogether new and different way for people to communicate and share. They have led to more open lifestyles where many individuals are sharing details of their lives with the world. Just as with other social environments, users of social networks should be aware of etiquette and safety (see the next Home Technology box).

Care should be taken when meeting people on social networking sites. While such sites have become very popular with individuals of all ages and backgrounds, they have also become popular with criminals looking for victims. Hackers are targeting social networking sites like Facebook to scam users into providing information that can be used in identity theft. Sex offenders have also

Etiquette for Social Networks

What you share on a social network presents the world with an impression of the type of person you are. While you may use a social network to communicate with your friends, you should be aware that very probably, others are watching, including family, present and future employers, teachers, marketers and advertisers, law enforcement officers, and criminals.

Here are some tips to help you make the best and safest use of social networks:

- Set privacy settings within the social network to allow your information to be viewable by only those you trust.
- Choose your friends wisely. Establish guidelines for who you will accept as a friend. Do not accept friend requests from strangers. Those that you do not wish to friend can simply be ignored.
- Limit what you share online. Posting every detail about your day may drive your friends away. Before posting to your social network, ask yourself if it contributes anything to the community.
- Keep private affairs off your social network. There are better methods of sharing private information with your dearest friends without including the rest of the world.
- Use discretion when publishing photos. Ask yourself two questions: Could this photo be embarrassing if my boss or family see it? and Does this photo provide any private information about me, such as where I live, that could be used by criminals? Posting photos of drinking and drug use are definitely unwise.
- Don't spam your friends with ads about products and applications to which you subscribe in the Social Net.
- Don't embarrass or anger your friends by posting photos or information about them without their consent.
- If you are in a relationship with someone, update your relationship status as a mutual decision. Don't break up with someone by changing your relationship status. Talk it through in person.
- Don't use your social network as a therapist. Life's hardships are too heavy and deep to share with those that aren't your closest friends and family.
- Keep confidential business information and sentiment off your social net. Employees have been fired for leaking classified information and bad-mouthing their employer on social networks.
- Demonstrate good communication skills. Think through what you write to make sure that it makes you appear intelligent.

Remember that most businesses do a thorough investigation of potential employees that includes researching social networks. Make sure your social network content provides an accurate reflection of you at your best. Once you get that dream job, make sure that social networks don't distract you from doing your work.

---

used social networks to lure victims. In some states, convicted sex offenders are outlawed from using social networks.[7]

Media-sharing Web sites, like YouTube for video sharing, and Flickr for photo sharing, provide methods for members to store and share digital media files on the Web. YouTube allows members to post homemade video content in categories such as comedy, entertainment, film and animation, how-to, news, people, pets, sports, and travel. Flickr allows its members to upload photos to their own personal online photo album and choose photos to share with chosen friends, family, or community.

What brings these media-sharing Web sites under the umbrella of Web 2.0 is their community aspect. Both Flickr and YouTube provide means by which members can comment on the media. YouTube allows visitors to e-mail links to favorite video clips to friends. Both sites provide methods for visitors to view the most popular media or search on a particular topic.

Flickr introduced a methodology of organizing content called a *folksonomy* or *collaborative tagging*. Collaborative tagging allows users to associate descriptive tags with photos. So a photo of your pet Weimaraner at the beach might be tagged with "Dog," "Pet," "Weimaraner," and "Beach." Using associated tags, Flickr can easily group common photos together and gather information on what types of photos are most abundant. Flickr uses this information to create a *tag cloud*—a diagram of keyword links with the size of each word representing the number of photos that use that tag. Tag clouds are another tool that Web 2.0 applications have embraced to show the importance of certain items over others. Figure 4.32 uses a tag cloud to show the importance of certain terms to the concept of Web 2.0. Tagging makes it easy for users to search for specific items. For example, Figure 4.34 shows the results of a search on "Weimaraner Beach" at Flickr. Tags have become popular organizational tools for blog entries, videos on YouTube, and Web pages on social bookmarking sites.

FIGURE 4.34 • Flickr's tag search

A search of photos tagged with Weimaraner and Beach at Flickr.

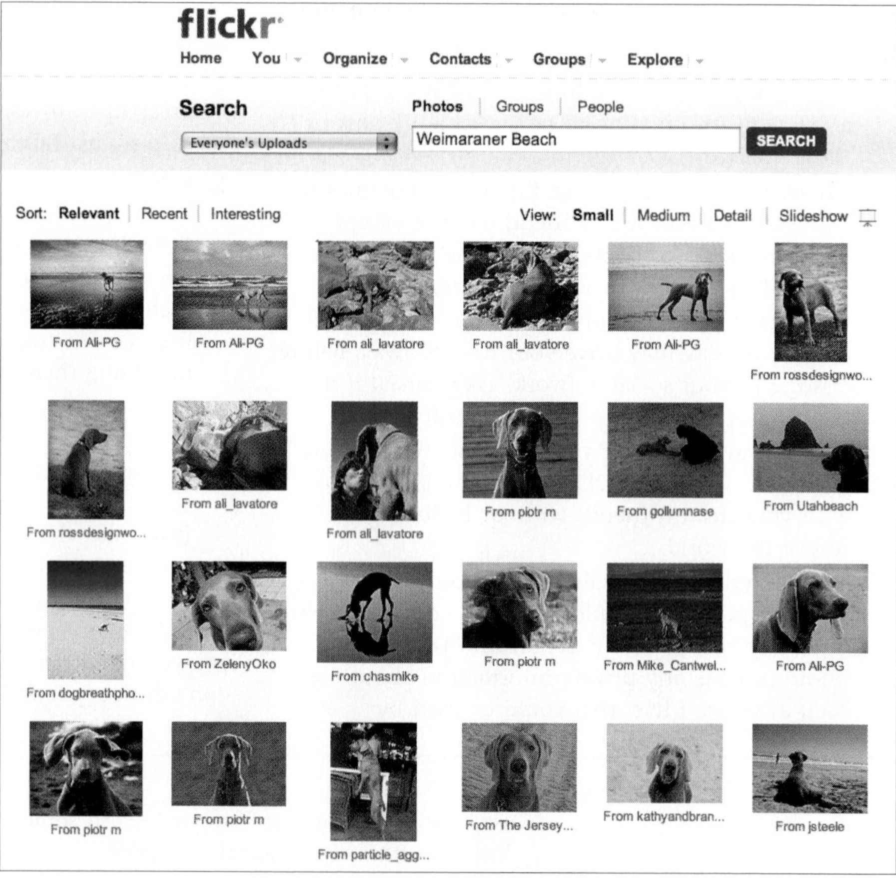

Another example of Web 2.0 can be found in social bookmarking sites. **Social bookmarking** sites provide a way for Web users to store, classify, share, and search Web bookmarks, also referred to as favorites. The main purpose of social bookmarking sites is typically to provide a view of the most popular Web sites, videos, blog articles, or other Web content at any given moment. Often social bookmarking sites provide Web browser add-ons (extensions) that provide a button on the toolbar for recommending Web content. For example, *del.icio.us* is a social bookmarking Web site that shows "what's hot right now." When you sign up for del.icio.us you can download software to install on your computer that provides two buttons on your browser toolbar (see Figure 4.35). When you find a page you wish to bookmark, just click the Tag button on your toolbar and the link is stored in your personal bookmark list on *http://del.icio.us*. Pages you bookmark are tallied with other users' bookmarks to determine the most popular pages on the Web at any given moment.

FIGURE 4.35 • Social bookmarking

Members of the del.icio.us social bookmarking Web site can use icons on their Web browser toolbar that allow them to quickly add Web pages to their bookmark lists.

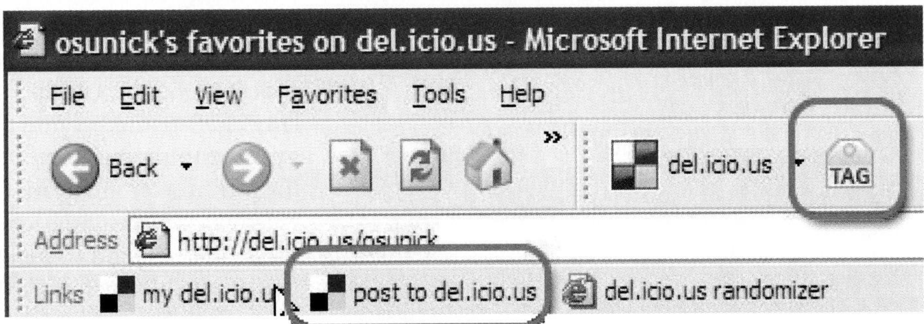

Digg is another very popular social bookmarking site dedicated to news. Many online news services provide "Digg this" buttons on articles so that readers can bookmark the article. At *www.digg.com* you can see the most popular news articles of the moment listed sequentially with the articles that accumulated the most "digs" listed first. Digg also provides links to the most popular videos and podcasts. Table 4.8 lists popular social bookmarking Web sites and other Web 2.0 sites. All Web 2.0 sites listed here are free for use but typically require you to become a member to enjoy a personalized experience.

Voice and Video Communications. Most telephone companies are implementing Internet technologies in their phone networks. The move is designed to lead to a wide range of improved services for consumers, such as online voice mail management. As voice communications are converted to digital services, the services offered by telephone systems and the Internet intermingle. Already, it is possible to access voice mail from your computer and e-mail on your phone. Google Voice is a service that allows users to manage incoming calls and voice mail online. Calls can be screened based on the caller ID, or forwarded to other numbers. Voice mail can be transcribed and retrieved from your inbox at the Google Voice site.[8] Soon we will no longer think in terms of phones and computers but rather in terms of communication devices that support voice, text, and video communications in both synchronous and asynchronous modes.

Voice over Internet Protocol (*VoIP*) is the first major step in this direction. *VoIP* is a popular technology that allows phone conversations to travel over the Internet or other data networks. Businesses and residential customers use VoIP to merge voice and data networks into one system in order to save money and enjoy additional conveniences made possible by merging Internet and voice communications. Businesses can save large amounts of money by not having to install a phone network.

BIG BROTHER IS WATCHING YOU ... SNEEZE

Got the sniffles? Health officials want you to blog about it. Health officials currently track the flu and other diseases through doctor reports. Although this system is reliable, it takes a week or more for this information to reach officials. Google's Flu Trends, by contrast, can report results in real time. Google keeps track of what queries are being entered and how often, and it not only provides early warning but also tracks people who aren't going to the doctor. Of course, Internet surveillance raises privacy concerns. Still, the Internet may well launch a whole new approach to disease prevention.

Flu Trackers Encourage Patients to Blog About It
Michael E. Ruane
The Washington Post
September 2, 2009

TABLE 4.8 • Popular Web 2.0 sites

- Social networking
  - *www.myspace.com*
  - *www.facebook.com*
  - *www.bebo.com*
  - *www.hi5.com*
  - *www.orkut.com*
- Microblogging
  - *www.twitter.com*
  - *www.jaiku.com*
- Media sharing
  - *www.youtube.com*
  - *www.flickr.com*
  - *www.photobucket.com*
- Social bookmarking
  - *www.digg.com*
  - *http://del.icio.us*
  - *http://reddit.com*
  - *http://slashdot.org*
  - *www.newsvine.com*
  - *www.technorati.com*
  - *www.stumbleupon.com*

Employees can use special VoIP handsets that connect to the data network to support standard voice communications and phone conferencing. Some high-end handsets have displays and cameras for video conferencing. VoIP business users can also make use of special software that allows them to check their e-mail and voice mail from any phone or Internet-connected computer.

Video communications are becoming more prevalent as technology advances to support it. Although video phones have been anticipated since the 1950s, the computer industry and high-speed Internet access are finally making the concept a reality. Digital video communications are particularly challenging because of the large quantities of bytes required to produce the video. To work around this limitation, video communications make use of small (3- to 4-inch) video windows, slower rates of frames per second (typically 15 fps or less), and sometimes fewer colors or monochrome images. Such sacrifices in video size and quality have made video communications a reality today. Video communications can take place over a stand-alone video phone, a TV-based video phone, or a PC-based video phone. Many Internet users connect inexpensive webcams to their home PCs for free video chats with friends and family (see Figure 4.36), and many new laptops come with built-in webcams.

FIGURE 4.36 • Video chat with Skype

Skype is a popular free application for Internet-based video chat.

FIGURE 4.37 • IP video phone

VoIP provides powerful communications systems within businesses and offers money-saving, feature-packed services for home users.

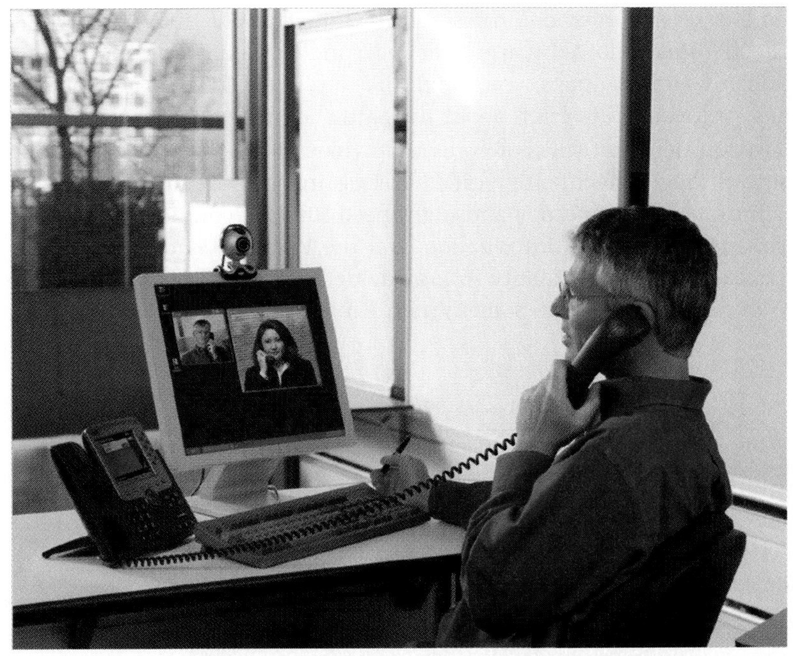

Video conferencing is a technology that combines video and phone call capabilities along with shared data and document access. It is replacing the need for travel in many industries. Through high-speed Internet and private network connections, individuals are able to communicate with associates around the world in "face-to-face" electronic meetings (see Figure 4.37). Several products that support this technology over the Web—called *Web conferencing*—are on the market. They include WebEx, GoToMeeting, Microsoft Office Live Meeting, and many others. Using Web conferencing, groups can see, hear, text chat, present, and share information in a collaborative manner.

Increasing numbers of professionals are using the power of Internet communications to work from home. *Telecommuting* is working from locations away from the office by using telecommunication technologies. Because most business documents are now digital, and most business communications can be accomplished electronically, there is less need for employees to be physically present in the office. Using technologies that allow employees to securely access corporate networks from home or anywhere else with Internet access, many of today's employees find it easier to be more productive working away from the office.

There are good and bad aspects to telecommuting. Working at home offers benefits to employees; those who have home obligations may find that telecommuting is the only solution to covering both work and home duties. Telecommuting reduces commute time and expenses, allowing employees to make better use of their time while reducing traffic and pollution. Telecommuters may also save on wardrobe and babysitters. Employers experience benefits as well. One study showed that an average home worker is able to produce seven hours of productive time per day, while in-office workers are productive for only six. Telecommuters also require no corporate office space and furniture.

The down side of telecommuting involves the elimination of what is known as "face time." The lack of face-to-face contact with coworkers can lead to a feeling of isolation and being out of the loop. It is difficult to train and keep an eye on new telecommuting employees. It is also more difficult for telecommuters to gain attention and be noticed when not sharing space with coworkers and the boss. For these reasons, telecommuting works better for some careers than others.

News

The Web is a powerful tool for keeping informed about local, state, national, and global news. It allows the public to actively research issues and become more knowledgeable about current events. Traditional news media deliver the news through television, radio, and newspapers. These media provide only the news that they consider of interest to the general public. Items of special or unique interest may be bumped and replaced with more general stories. In contrast, the Web has an abundance of special-interest coverage. It also provides the capacity to go deeper into the subject matter. For example, during the war in Iraq, online news services provided news articles in text, audio, and video coverage. Clicking links allowed you to *drill down* and find out more about geographic regions by viewing maps; you could link to historical coverage of U.S./ Iraqi relations, and you could learn about the battle equipment being deployed.

Most television news networks are providing video clips of news events from their Web sites through a technology called Webcasting. A *Webcast* takes advantage of streaming video technology and high-speed Internet connections to provide television-style delivery of information over the Web (see Figure 4.38). Webcasting expands the Web's ability to provide detailed news coverage and can transform Web news services into something resembling interactive TV.

FIGURE 4.38 • Webcasting

Some television news networks provide video clips of news events from their Web sites through a technology called Webcasting.

Many city newspapers are turning to the Web to save themselves from bankruptcy as increasing numbers of subscribers are giving up hard copy newspaper subscriptions for online news sources. Major national news agencies, such as Reuters and the Associated Press, also have a Web presence. You can get international news not only from U.S. news sources but also from other countries, providing a wide variety of perspectives on the news.

Web sites like *http://news.google.com*, *http://news.yahoo.com*, and *www.newsvine.com* provide the most popular or interesting news stories from a variety of news sources. Reuters (*www.reuters.com*), the Associated Press (*www.ap.org*), and the BBC (*www.bbc.com*) provide news from sources around the world. No Internet user can complain of being uninformed.

Some online newspapers available only through subscriptions, such as *The Wall Street Journal Online, LexisNexis, Consumer Reports,* and *Forrester Research,* are making individual articles available to the general public for small fees. Google and Yahoo! are working with news providers to develop a business model for à la carte news articles. The news publishers provide the search engines access to "deep Web" articles that were previously off limits. An abstract of the article is provided and for a few dollars the user can purchase the entire article.

There are countless special-interest news sources that provide industry-specific news and information. Table 4.9 lists a small segment of the wide variety of industry-specific news services available.

TABLE 4.9 • News services on the Web

Industry	News Web site
Biotechnology and pharmaceutical	*www.biospace.com*
Airline, airport, and aviation	*http://news.airwise.com*
Restaurant	*www.nrn.com*
Audio/visual communications	*www.infocomm.org*
Hospitality	*www.hotelnewsresource.com*
Customer relations management	*www.crmdaily.com*
Oil industry	*www.oilonline.com/news*
Realty	*www.realtor.org*
Textile, apparel, footwear	*www.just-style.com*
Information technology	*www.computerworld.com*

Other Web sites provide a wide survey of industry-specific news from the major news sources. For example, Yahoo! provides a categorized menu for industry news at *http://biz.yahoo.com/industry/.*

In a trend some refer to as *social journalism,* ordinary citizens are more involved in reporting the news than ever before. Through online tools such as blogs, podcasts, videocasts, discussion groups, and social networks, the online community is taking journalism into its own hands and reporting the news from individual perspectives. While social journalism provides important news we might not otherwise get, its sources may not be as reliable as mainstream media sources. As we hear the news from nonprofessional journalists, reporting without the strict guidelines of formal news agencies, it is important to remember that the information may be biased, misrepresented, mistaken, or perhaps even deliberately misleading.

Education and Training

Educational institutions of all types and sizes are using the Web to enhance classroom education or extend it to individuals who are unable to attend.

Primary schools use the Web to inform parents of school schedules and activities. Teachers give elementary school students research exercises in the classroom and at home that utilize Web resources. To make browsing safe for young users, *parental control* (also called *content-filtering*) software, such as Net Nanny, filters out adult content. By high school, students have integrated the Web into daily study habits. Teachers manage class Web pages that contain information and links for students to use in homework exercises.

eTextbooks

Big changes are brewing in the textbook and academic publishing industries. Both are on the cusp of going all-out digital.

Dozens of pilot programs are taking place in schools across the country, analyzing the benefits and drawbacks of replacing bound textbooks with digital e-texts. While there may be benefits to students in reduced cost and backpack bulk, *The Wall Street Journal* found that e-books are getting mixed reviews from students. A study at Northwest Missouri State provided 200 students with e-texts on Sony's e-book reader. Many of the students were won over by the technology, but dozens dropped out of the program, finding the e-texts awkward and inconvenient. Northwest Missouri State's students may not be isolated in their reactions to e-texts. One poll showed that as many as 75 percent of college students prefer print to digital texts.

Although some students may not be ready for e-texts, the move from paper to bits and bytes may be inevitable. The Amazon Kindle and other e-book readers are leading the charge, but it is likely that the Web will end up the victor. Textbook publishers are analyzing the market, weighing their options, and developing pricing models. Thousands of textbooks are being formatted for the Kindle, as well as online e-book services like CourseSmart. Harvard University Press announced that it will publish 1,000 of its books on Scribd—the largest online social publishing company in the world.

While we may be on the cusp of a new era in textbook publishing, some companies are looking ahead and wondering if e-texts will satisfy the needs of the next generation of college students. Today's grade school and middle school students are being raised with digital media, Internet video, and gaming in 3D virtual environments, and are likely to find current ebook technologies incredibly uninteresting. To meet the needs and tastes of a rapidly evolving student body, textbook companies must become innovative and nimble in order to serve up effective textbook lessons utilizing the latest technologies.

Questions

1. What are the benefits of eTextbooks to students and publishers?
2. What are the drawbacks of eTextbooks to students and publishers?
3. Are you in favor of eTextbooks? Why or why not?

Sources

1. *Knutson, Ryan and Fowler, Geoffrey, "Book Smarts? E-Texts Receive Mixed Reviews From Students,"* The Wall Street Journal, *July 20, 2009, http://online.wsj.com.*
2. *Stokes, Jon, "The future of scholarship? Harvard goes digital with Scribd," Ars Technica, July 17, 2009, www.arstechnica.com.*
3. *Trachtenberg, Jeff and Fowler, Geoffrey, "Publisher Delays E-Book Amid Debate on Pricing,"* The Wall Street Journal, *July 13, 2009, http://online.wsj.com.*
4. *Timmer, John, "Print, beware! Publishers are 'on the road' to pure digital," Ars Technica, August 13, 2009, www.arstechnica.com, Home Technology (p. 227–228).*

Increasing numbers of college-level courses rely on the Web to enhance learning. A 2009 study sponsored by the U.S. Department of Education found that contrary to popular opinion, "on average, students in online learning conditions performed better than those receiving face-to-face instruction."[9] Educational support products, such as Blackboard, provide an integrated Web environment that includes virtual chat for class members; a discussion group for posting questions and comments; access to the class syllabus and agenda, student grades, and class announcements; and links to class-related material. Some course Web sites even deliver filmed lectures using Webcasting technology. Such environments are used to complement the traditional classroom experience or as the sole method of course delivery.

Conducting classes over the Web with no physical class meetings is called *distance education*. Many colleges and universities offer distance education classes, which offer a convenient method for nontraditional students to attend college. Nontraditional students include older students who have job or family obligations that might otherwise prohibit them from attending college. Distance education offers them a way of working through class material on a flexible schedule. Some schools offer entire degree programs online through distance education. At *www.directoryofschools.com* you can find a listing of over 9000 accredited online degree programs.

In a program it calls OpenCourseWare, the Massachusetts Institute of Technology (MIT) is offering all of its courses free online. Students who take courses via OpenCourseWare will not earn credit toward a degree or have access to teachers. MIT has rolled out the program to provide educational options for those who are unable to afford them.

Increasing numbers of textbooks and academic publications are going digital. Amazon's Kindle and other e-book devices and Web services make it possible to reduce a heavy backpack full of textbooks to a device that weighs mere ounces. Rather than waiting in line to purchase textbooks for hundreds of dollars, and selling them back at the end of the semester, students may soon download their textbooks in a matter of minutes, and pay a reduced rental fee for their use over the period of the semester.

Kevin Callahan of Seattle (see Figure 4.39) makes use of video conferencing technology to offer guitar lessons online. Seeking to provide his students with an experience as close as possible to an in-person experience, he equipped his Power Mac G5 with Apple's iChat videoconferencing software, iSight camera and microphone package, GarageBand music mixer, and carefully selected lighting equipment. From his studio in Seattle, Kevin teaches students in Florida, California, Massachusetts, and Spain.

Beyond traditional education, corporations such as Skillsoft offer professional job-skills training over the Web (see Figure 4.40). Job seekers often use these services to acquire specialized business or technical training. Some of the training leads to certification. Certification verifies a person's skill and understanding in a particular area. It has become very important, especially for some technical skill sets, to assure an employer that a job applicant truly has the skills claimed. Some corporations and organizations contract with Skillsoft to provide on-the-job training for current employees to expand their skills.

FIGURE 4.39 • Distance guitar lessons

Using videoconferencing technologies, a guitar teacher can teach students around the world.

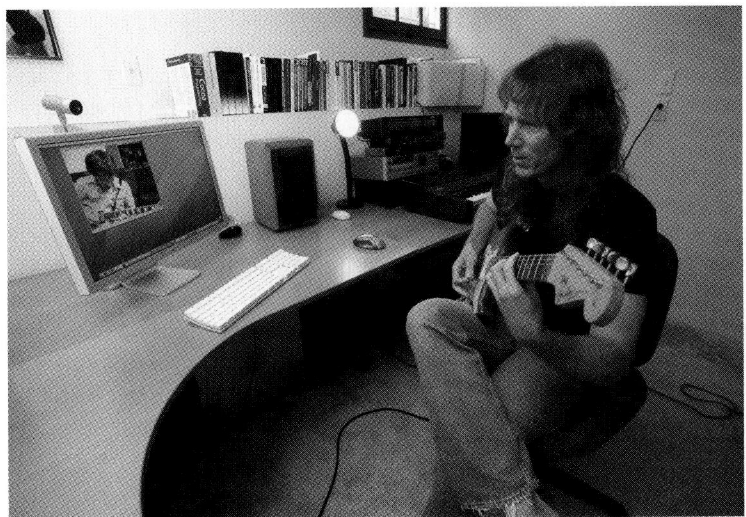

FIGURE 4.40 • Skillsoft

The Skillsoft lesson player delivers video lessons and quizzes students on what they have learned.

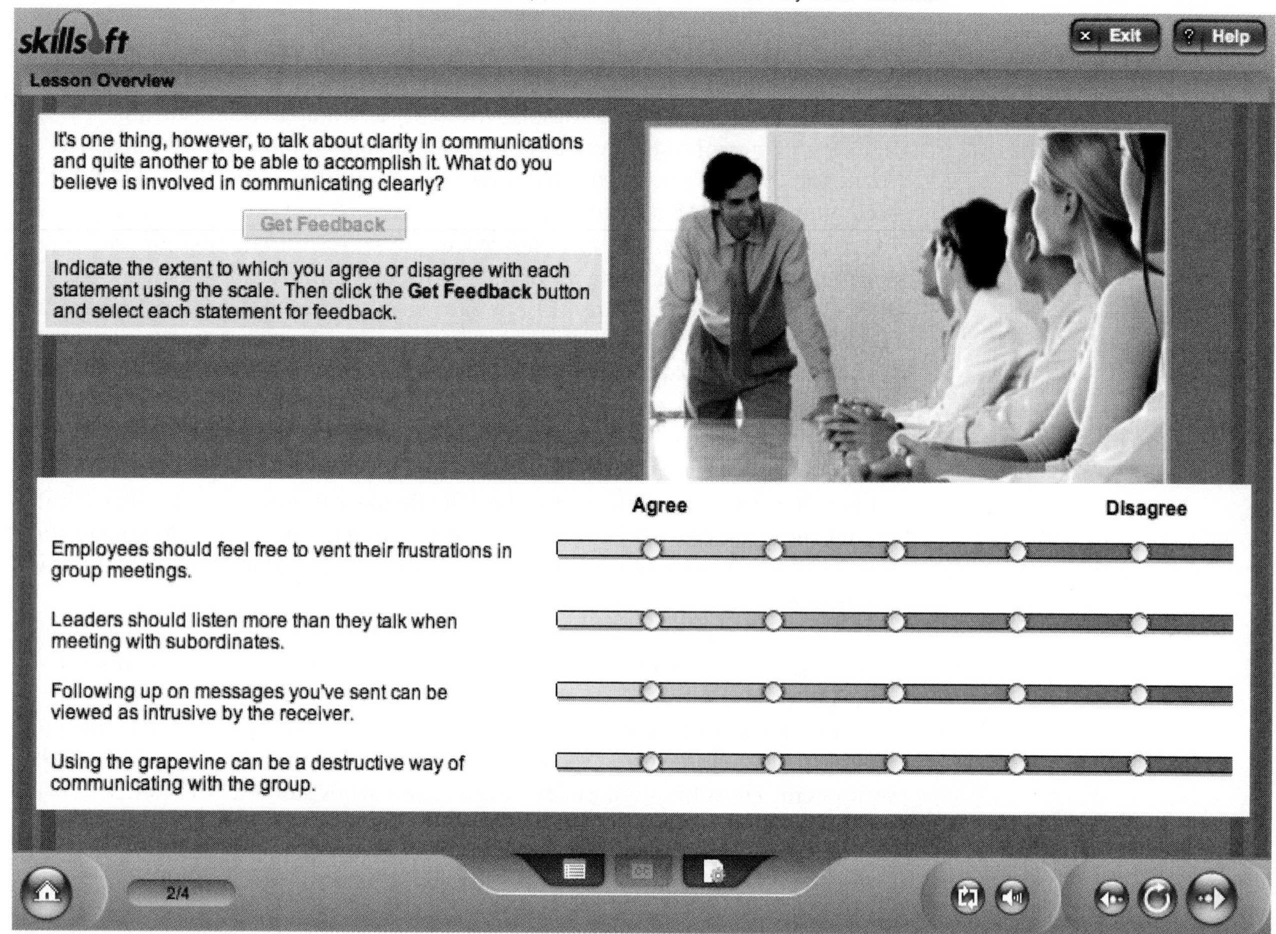

E-Commerce

The Web is an integral part of most business information infrastructures. It provides corporate information to employees, shareholders, the media, and the public. It can be and often is used as a primary interface to the corporate database. Its convenience and universal acceptance make it the ideal platform for communications. It helps support communication among the links in an organization's value chain—the string of companies working together to produce and deliver a product. A value chain typically consists of the suppliers of the raw materials that are used to create a product, the manufacturing unit, transportation and storage providers, marketing, sales, and customer support. The Web acts as the glue that holds all of these units together by providing a central point of access to corporate information. The Web provides a convenient platform for marketing and selling products and is very helpful in collecting marketing data. The Web strengthens communications with customers and improves overall customer satisfaction.

Travel

The Web has had a profound effect on the travel industry and the way you plan and prepare for trips. From getting assistance with short trips across town to planning summer-long holidays abroad, travelers are turning to the Web to save time and money and overcome much of the risk involved in visiting unknown places.

Many of the success stories of the Web come from the travel industry. Web sites become successful when they uniquely fill a public need. Mapquest.com, Microsoft Bing Maps, and Google Maps certainly performed that function. Offering free street maps for cities around the world, these tools assist travelers in finding their way around town and between towns. Provide your departure location and destination, and they produce a map that displays the fastest route.

Google Maps includes the ability to alter map directions incrementally. For example, if you want to take a trip from Orlando to visit your grandmother in Atlanta, and you decide that you want to visit friends in Charleston along the way, you can take the map generated for Orlando to Atlanta and click and drag the path to Charleston; Google Maps will provide the best route that includes your side trip. As mentioned earlier, Google Maps also provides extensive location-specific business information, satellite imagery, up-to-the-minute traffic reports, and Street View. What's Street View? Google employees drive the streets of cities around the world in vehicles equipped with high-tech camera gear, taking 360-degree images. These images are integrated into Google Maps to allow users to get a "street view" of an area that can be manipulated as if you are actually walking down the street looking around.

Mapping software packages from Google and Microsoft overlay road maps onto high-resolution satellite images of Earth to produce a zoomable view of the planet. You can view the planet from a mile out in space or zoom in to view a country or state, and then zoom in further to view roads and buildings. Using Microsoft Bing Maps' birds-eye view, it is possible to zoom in beyond satellite resolution to view photos taken from aircraft (see Figure 4.41). You can zoom in to view natural marvels such as the Grand Canyon and Niagara Falls. Type in an address, and not only view travel directions but visually fly over the roads to your destination. The satellite photographs used for these services were taken sometime within the last year. Imagine a time in the future when such images are delivered in real time—when you can stand in your backyard and wave to friends on the other side of the country or world and your image is relayed via satellite and Internet!

FIGURE 4.41 • Microsoft Bing Maps

Microsoft Bing Maps provides close-range aerial photography of locations like the beach at Miami Beach.

Web applications are becoming increasingly aware of user geographic location (geolocation). Gathered from GPS technologies, and the ability to calculate user location from Internet access points, Web applications are able to use the location of users' smart phones, notebooks, and desktop PCs to provide new services.

Geotagging is the process of adding location identification to online communications and content. Photos uploaded to media-sharing sites like Flickr can include the location where the photo was taken. Twitter uses geotagging so that users can include it with each tweet.[10] Several applications, such as Loopt and Google Latitude, allow users to keep track of their friends' current locations as blips on a map. As GPS becomes embedded in more cell phones, cameras, and other devices, geotagging and maps will become important tools in serving up useful information and services.

Travel Web sites such as travelocity.com, expedia.com, and priceline.com assist travelers in finding the best deals on flights, hotels, car rentals, vacation packages, and cruises. Provided with dates and locations of travel, most travel Web sites display the available flights and prices on which you can base your choice. Priceline.com offers a slightly different approach. It allows shoppers to name their own price and then works to find an airline that can meet that price. Once flights have been reserved, travelers can use these Web sites to book hotels and a rental car, often at discounted prices.

There are many special-purpose travel Web sites that assist individuals with particular needs. Some categories listed at Yahoo! include romantic, family, adventure, kids, singles, budget, and historic, to name a few.

Employment and Careers

Web sites provide useful tools for people seeking employment and for companies seeking employees. Web sites such as careerbuilder.com and monster.com provide resources for choosing a career and finding a job. Most colleges have career and job placement services that make use of the Web to connect graduating students with employers. Consider the Web's role in the job-hunting strategy provided in Table 4.10.

While searching for a way to make a living, don't be taken in by the many get-rich-quick scams that proliferate on the Web and through e-mail. Although there are many "work at home" offers on the Web, only a few offer legitimate means to make a living. You can get information about scams posing as business opportunities in the United States from the Federal Trade Commission (*www.ftc.gov/bcp/index.shtml*). In addition, the Internet Fraud Complaint Center, sponsored by the Federal Bureau of Investigation (FBI) and the National White Collar Crime Center (NW3C), provides information on how to spot Internet fraud and an online form for reporting Internet fraud (*www.ic3.gov*).

TABLE 4.10 • Job-hunting strategies: Using the Web to find a career and job

Step	Tips
Select a career	Use online references such as those at *www.jobweb.com* to discover your personal strengths and weaknesses and map them to your ideal job.
Discover who the players are in your chosen career	Search the Web on a given career and industry title and see what companies are represented. Discover online trade journals, and learn as much as you can.
Learn about the companies that interest you	Where better to start than the company's Web site? Many companies list career opportunities and provide you with information on how to apply.
Network with others in the field	There are many online industry-specific discussion groups and forums. Seek them out to make valuable contacts. You can start at *www.hotjobs.com/htdocs/client/splash/communities*.
View job listings at general employment Web sites	Web sites such as *www.hotjobs.yahoo.com*, *www.monster.com*, and *www.careerbuilder.com* have large databases of job openings where you can search by profession or keywords. A complete list of the best of these sites can be found at *www.quintcareers.com*.
View job listings at industry-specific employment Web sites	There are hundreds of specialized job Web sites, from employment recruiters of all types to specialized job databank sites that focus on a specific industry.
Create an impressive Web site to represent yourself	Consider purchasing your own domain name—for example, *www.janelle_johnson.com*. Include an attractive welcome page with links to your resume and other details regarding your experience and skills. Employers want hard-copy resumes to be brief. At the bottom of your resume, you can add "Please visit *www.janelle_johnson.com* for more information." Make sure that your Web site is professional in appearance and content. Also, make sure that nothing embarrassing comes up about you when you Google your name or view your pages on social networks. Employers typically do thorough online research on potential employees to see what kind of lifestyle they lead.

Multimedia and Entertainment

Faster Internet connections and advances in streaming technology have brought a wide range of media and gaming applications to the Web. The Web has had a dramatic impact on the music and motion picture industries, causing unprecedented changes in marketing and distribution approaches. Many in the software industry are betting that online gaming will increase in its appeal across gender and age markets. As home entertainment equipment begins to merge with home computing equipment, the Web is anticipating the call to deliver entertainment.

Music. *Internet radio* is similar to local AM and FM radio except that it is digitally delivered to your computer over the Internet, and there are a lot more choices of stations. For example, live365.com provides access to hundreds of radio stations in dozens of musical genre categories. All that is required to listen to Internet radio is a media player such as iTunes, Real media player, or Microsoft Windows Media Player. Some stations charge a subscription fee, but most do not. Pandora (*www.pandora.com*) offers a free music service that allows you to build your own radio station. You select artists and songs, and Pandora offers similar artists and songs for your station (see Figure 4.42).

FIGURE 4.42 • Internet radio: Pandora

Pandora allows you to create customized radio stations based on an artist or combination of artists.

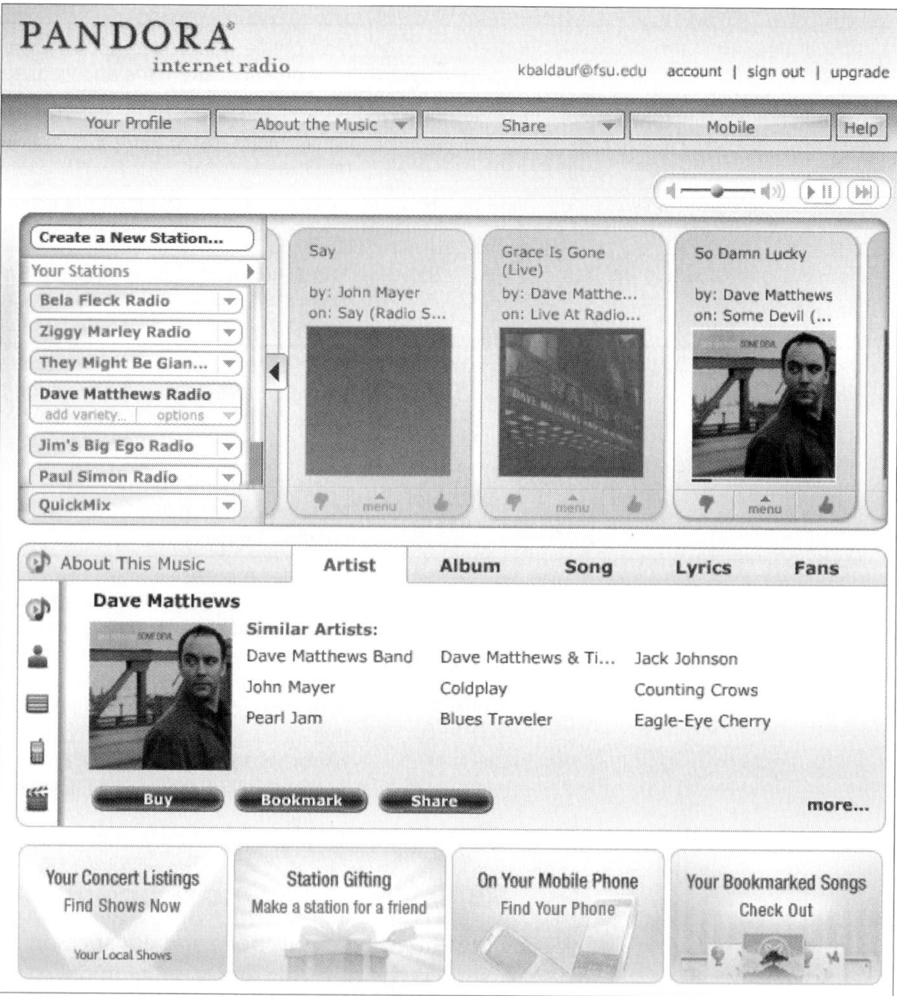

Compressed music formats such as MP3 have made music swapping over the Internet a convenient and popular activity. File-sharing software such as KaZaA and Limewire provide a means by which some music fans copy and distribute music, often without consideration to copyright law. The result is a popular music distribution system that is largely illegal and impossible to control, and it cuts deeply into the recording industry's profits. In addition, it is not always safe to swap files with strangers. One study discovered that 6 percent of all the music files downloaded from KaZaA are actually viruses renamed to look like MP3 files. Music industry giants have pulled together to win back customers by offering legal and safe alternatives to electronic music distribution that provide services and perks not offered by file-sharing networks—and at a reasonable price.

Popular music services include iTunes, Yahoo! Music Jukebox, Napster, Rhapsody, and AOL's MusicNet. These music services offer access to the catalog of the big five labels—Universal Music, Sony Music, Warner Music, BMG, and EMI, as well as minor labels and independent artists.

Television and Movies. The television and movie industry is also making the move to Internet distribution. The large size of video files has so far held video back from being as popular to swap on the Internet as music. However, with the increasing number of broadband connections, movie swapping is becoming increasingly popular. Most big movies are pirated and available on file-sharing networks within weeks or days of release in theaters. Either an inside source steals them or someone sneaks a digital camcorder into a theater and records the film off the screen. The Motion Picture Industry of America is so concerned about movie pirating that it has deployed metal detectors and night-vision goggles in some movie theaters.

Like the recording industry, the motion picture industry is undertaking both defensive and offensive tactics to thwart the trend toward illegal file sharing. One tactic is to develop a legitimate Internet distribution system. Netflix and Blockbuster provide movie rentals by Internet download or by delivering DVDs through the mail. They include thousands of titles, free delivery, no late fees, and prepaid return envelopes for a monthly subscription fee.

Apple's iTunes software allows people to buy and download movie and television programming. Popular television series like *The Office, Lost, Grey's Anatomy*, and *Stargate SG-1* sell for $1.99 per episode. Feature films like *Pirates of the Carribean* and *The Italian Job* sell for $9.99 or $14.99. You can watch the videos using iTunes on your computer or video iPod, or if you purchase an Apple TV, you can wirelessly stream the video from your PC to your TV.

Other Internet-driven software is attempting to turn your PC into a television set. Web sites like Joost (*www.joost.com*), Hulu (*www.hulu.com*), and Democracy Player (*www.getdemocracy.com*) offer hundreds of on-demand television shows and motion pictures to watch on your Internet-connected PC. Joost offers television programming from Comedy Central, MTV, National Geographic, and many other sources. Joost also provides Web 2.0 functionality by allowing viewers to comment and chat about the programming (see Figure 4.43). Joost is supported through sponsors and advertisements. Democracy Player is an open-source Internet TV platform that provides over 1000 free channels plus access to YouTube videos and supports high-definition, full-screen video. Democracy Player is supported through private donations. Hulu provides the largest collections of movies and TV shows, including popular series from Fox, NBC, ABC, Comedy Central—nearly 170 leading content companies in all.

FIGURE 4.43 • Internet TV - Joost

Joost provides movies and television programs in an online community format.

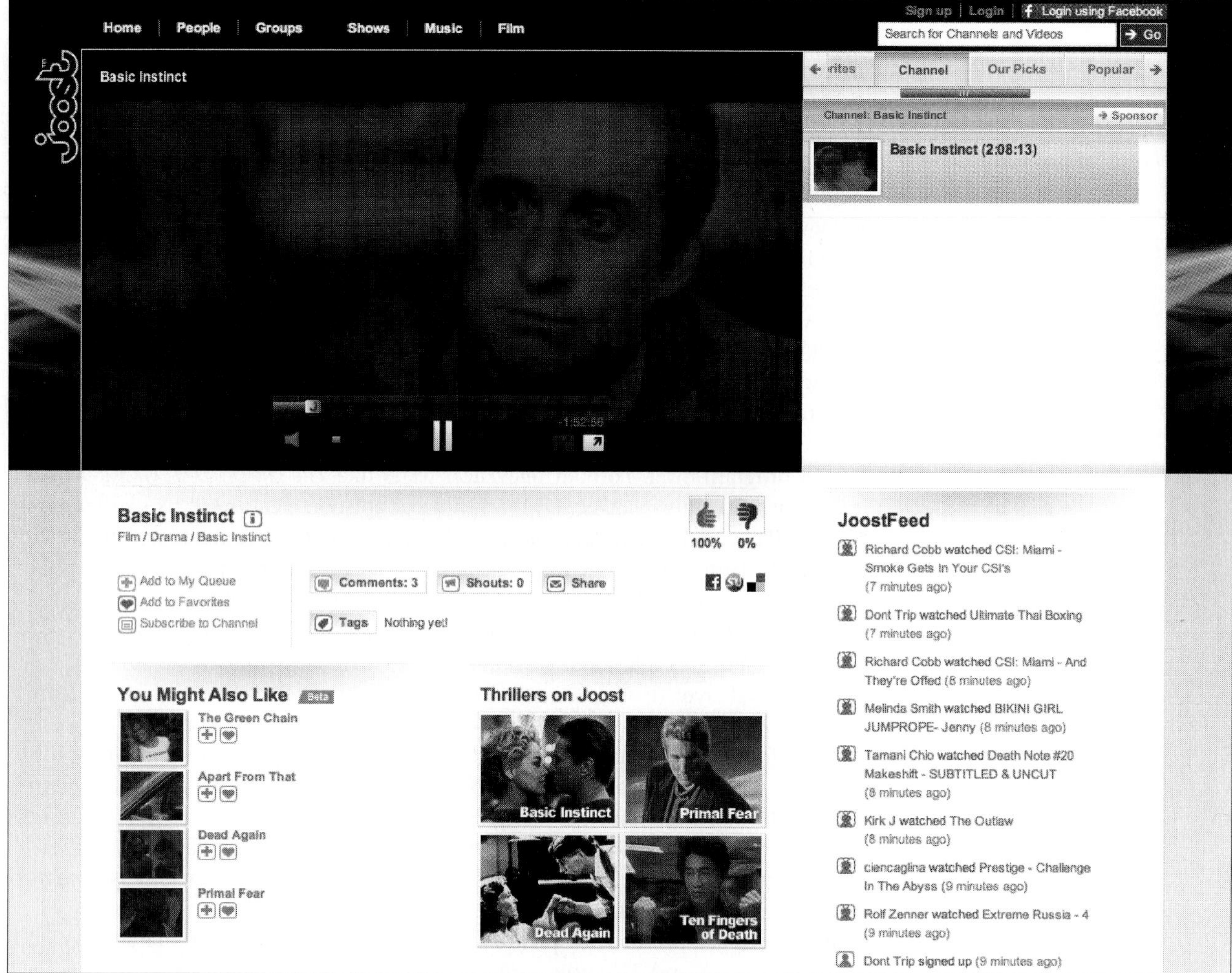

Games. The Web offers a multitude of games for individuals of all ages. From solitaire to massively multiplayer online role-playing games (MMORPG), there is a wide variety of offerings to suit every taste. Of course, the Web provides a medium for downloading single-player games to your desktop, notebook, handheld, or cell phone device (check *www.download.cnet.com*), but the power of the Web is most apparent with multiplayer games.

Multiplayer games allow you to interact with other users online using a variety of types and platforms. Multiplayer games support from two to thousands of players at a time. The game can be as simple as an online game of checkers. At the time of this writing, of the 165,627 people playing games at *http://zone.msn.com/*, 506 of them are playing checkers—253 simultaneous games. Meanwhile, at the Ferion game network (another online gaming site at *www.ferion.com*), hundreds of the 372,000 members are creating empires in space and exploring the virtual galaxy.

World of Warcraft is the most popular MMORPG and is set in the virtual Warcraft universe (see Figure 4.44). Players assume the roles of Warcraft heroes as they explore, adventure, and quest across a vast world. It is not unusual to find thousands of players interacting in the Warcraft universe at any given time. Players may adventure together or fight against each other in epic battles. Players form friendships, forge alliances, and compete with enemies for power and glory.

FIGURE 4.44 • World of Warcraft

Multiplayer games connect Internet users and allow them to interact in a virtual world.

Multiplayer online games can be categorized into the following genres:

- Action: Fast-paced games requiring accuracy and quick reflexes
- Board: Games involving play on a virtual game board
- Card: Games that involve the use of a virtual deck of cards
- Flight simulation: Games that involve taking on the role of a pilot in a WWI biplane or a futuristic starship
- Multiuser dimension or multiuser dungeon (MUD): Text-based games that make up for their lack of graphics with diverse and immersive game play
- Role-playing games (RPG): Games in which you take on the persona of a game character
- Sims (simulations): Games in which you create your own character that lives in a simulated environment
- Sports: Games involving sports
- Strategy: Games that require planning, tactics, and diplomacy
- Trivia/puzzle: Games that require a good memory or problem-solving skills

Although most multiplayer games are free, some of the best have fees associated with them. You may need to purchase software or pay monthly, yearly, or per-play subscription fees. For example, *World of Warcraft* (WoW) software costs $20, and membership (to play the game) costs $15 per month.

Game consoles such as Xbox 360, the Wii, and PlayStation3 provide multiplayer options for online gaming over the Internet. Subscribers can play with or against others who are logged on in 3D virtual environments. They can even talk to each other using a microphone headset. Microsoft Xbox Live provides features that allow users to keep track of their buddies online and match up with other players of the same skill level.

Research

The Web has become the most popular medium for distributing and accessing information. A study by comScore Networks found that "Consumers are increasingly reliant upon online resources to ease and inform major life events." Such events include planning a wedding, buying a home, changing jobs, and having a baby. The Web has become the first place people turn to when faced with a challenge or question.

Besides supporting practical decision making, the Web provides a wealth of information for curious minds. The connected world of the Web has, more than anything else, provided conveniently accessible answers to our questions. Life is full of wonder. Throughout the course of the day, you might wonder about a number of experiences or observations. In days past, you might have gone home and searched for explanations in the family encyclopedia or made a trip to the library. More likely than not, however, you would have found that researching the question wasn't worth the bother, or the question would simply have passed from your mind. But today, you're connected to the world's largest encyclopedia, with many people cracking it open every day. When you go online to check e-mail, you can take a moment to quickly run a search on something you were curious about during the day. As the Web moves to cell phones and other handheld devices, people are able to look up information at the moment a thought or question strikes. This form of research is known as *curiosity-driven research.* Curiosity-driven research is responsible for most of the world's great inventions.

In another form of research, *assigned research,* you are given a topic to explore for the purpose of education. This type of research is common in college and is often left open-ended. You are left to choose a topic, typically in a given subject area. The Web supports both forms of research at a number of levels. The following sections provide an overview of research techniques for the Internet.

FIGURE 4.45 • The Yahoo! subject directory
Online subject directories are a great place to explore research topics.

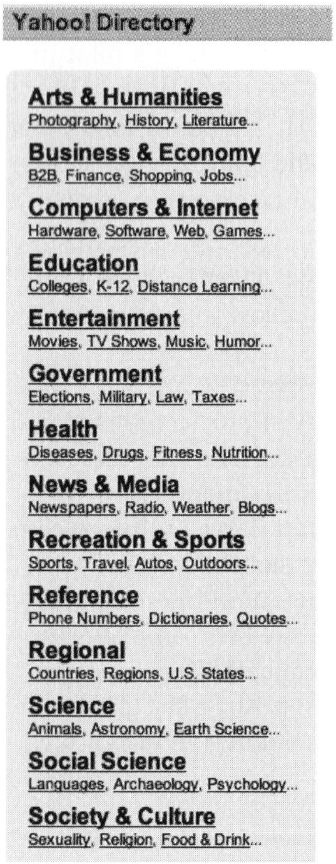

Yahoo! Directory

Arts & Humanities
Photography, History, Literature...

Business & Economy
B2B, Finance, Shopping, Jobs...

Computers & Internet
Hardware, Software, Web, Games...

Education
Colleges, K-12, Distance Learning...

Entertainment
Movies, TV Shows, Music, Humor...

Government
Elections, Military, Law, Taxes...

Health
Diseases, Drugs, Fitness, Nutrition...

News & Media
Newspapers, Radio, Weather, Blogs...

Recreation & Sports
Sports, Travel, Autos, Outdoors...

Reference
Phone Numbers, Dictionaries, Quotes...

Regional
Countries, Regions, U.S. States...

Science
Animals, Astronomy, Earth Science...

Social Science
Languages, Archaeology, Psychology...

Society & Culture
Sexuality, Religion, Food & Drink...

Selecting and Refining a Research Topic. Selecting a research topic generally goes through many stages of refinement. For example, you can begin by asking yourself the question "What in the universe would I like to explore?" Recall the subject directories found at Web portals such as Yahoo! that were noted earlier in the chapter. These Web portals are good places to begin exploring. For example, the subject directory at *http://dir.yahoo.com* contains the top-level topics shown in Figure 4.45.

If you were to select the Society & Culture listings, you would discover a list of at least 25 subcategories. From this list you might choose Issues and Causes to view yet another list of subcategories in greater detail. With each choice you make in the subcategories, you further refine your topic. At certain points in your research you may choose to back up and take a different path.

Although subject directories may not provide deep information on specific topics, the type required for college-level research, they do provide an overview of a wide breadth of information. Such an overview is useful in exploring and discovering new areas of interest and learning the basics on most topics.

Sources of Information. College-level research typically requires students to cite their sources. Research citations typically include information about the source from which you obtained information, including author, title, publisher, and date of publication. There are several citation styles, each used for different types of publications. Each has its own rules for what to include in a citation, depending on the type of source, and how to format your list of citations. Direct quotes from any publication must always be cited. Many papers also cite general sources from which information was used but not directly quoted.

Using information from some other source in a paper without a citation is called *plagiarism.* When you fail to recognize sources through formal citations, you present someone else's work as your own, which is considered theft of intellectual property. It is a great temptation for college students to plagiarize, considering the heavy workload of most students and the abundant amount of information conveniently available on the Web. There are plenty of Web sites that help students plagiarize. There are also strong tools that help teachers catch plagiarists. As increasing numbers of assignments are submitted electronically, it is becoming easier to electronically check assignment submissions for plagiarism, which is leading to more students getting busted. Penalties for plagiarism at most universities are severe, ranging from zero credit for the assignment, to zero credit for the course, to expulsion.

There are many electronic sources of information from which to draw. In addition to the information available through subject directories, Web search engines can point you to additional Web sites on a chosen topic. As you turn to Web search engines, you should do so with increased caution. With Web content, things aren't always what they seem. A Web page posted by the Freedom of Choice Coalition (FCC) condemning plans for government-sponsored health insurance may actually be sponsored by insurance companies trying to protect their own businesses. In the arena of Web research, you must follow up and check sources for validity and impartiality.

In judging information provided on the Web, always consider the source. Anonymous postings cannot be trusted. You must identify the provider of the information. If that person or organization is unfamiliar to you, search the Web for information on the provider. Providers of valid and trustworthy information on the Web typically go out of their way to include references to well-known and highly regarded authorities. For example, Wikipedia encourages all contributors to include links that support research on any topic. While it may not be appropriate to cite a Wikipedia article as a source, often you can find an acceptable source in the links provided in the Wikipedia article. On the Web, it is better to consider information inaccurate until proven valid rather than the other way around.

The most reliable sources of information can be found at your college library's Web site. The books, reference materials, journals, and other periodicals that are housed in your college or local library have undergone quality control evaluation to earn the right to sit on those shelves and Web pages. Books and periodicals considered fundamental to any given field are typically stocked in the library, and sometimes digitally on the library's Web site. Library resources are professionally analyzed and categorized in a logical manner that is easy to navigate. Best of all, the most knowledgeable of researchers, librarians, are available to assist you with your project. Most libraries have online card catalogs that allow you to search for books and journal articles from the comfort of your home.

Besides online card catalogs, libraries typically provide links to public and sometimes private research databases on the Web. Online research databases allow visitors to search for information in thousands of journal, magazine, and newspaper articles. Information database services are valuable because they offer the best in quality and convenience. They provide full-text articles from reputable sources conveniently over the Web. College and public libraries typically subscribe to many databases to support research. One of the most popular private databases is LexisNexis Academic Universe. LexisNexis provides access to full-text documents from over 5900 news, business, legal, medical, and reference publications, and you can access the information through a standard keyword search engine (see Figure 4.46). The sources from which LexisNexis draws include:

- National and regional newspapers, wire services, broadcast transcripts, international news sources, and non-English language sources
- U.S. federal and state case law, codes, regulations, legal news, law reviews, and international legal information

- *Shepard's Citations* for all U.S. Supreme Court cases back to 1789
- Business news journals, company financial information, SEC filings and reports, and industry and market news

FIGURE 4.46 • LexisNexis

A search at LexisNexis on "Health Care Reform" yields hundreds of full-text articles.

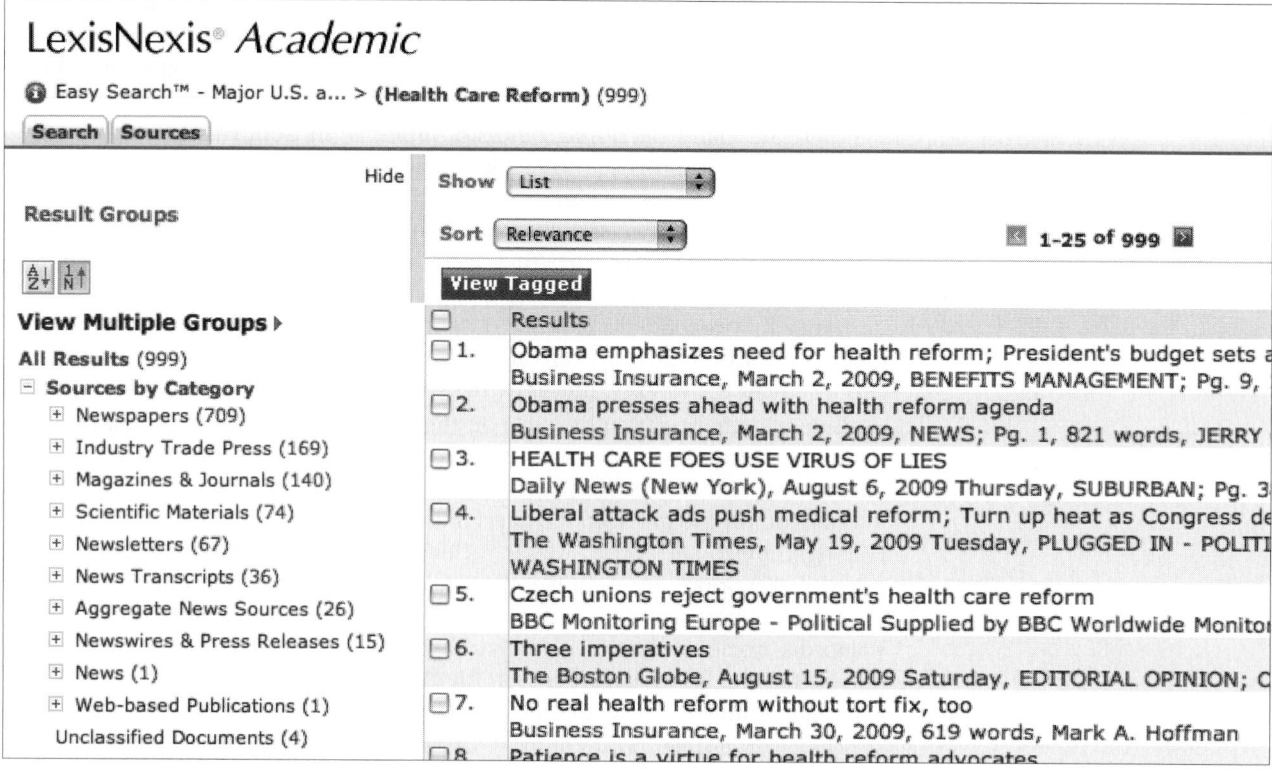

THE FUTURE INTERNET AND WEB

The Internet and Web are continuously evolving. Their basis in open standards has provided a fertile environment for innovative development. Anyone is free to design and implement new applications for use on the Internet and Web. This chapter has included many examples of the way Internet and Web technologies are being used today. This section provides a glimpse at how they might be used in the future.

Internet2 and Beyond

Significant efforts are under way to expand the capabilities of the Internet to support increasing numbers of users and applications at higher speeds. New technologies are being explored by scientists and network engineers to develop the next-generation Internet. *Internet2* is a research and development consortium led by over 200 U.S. universities and supported by partnerships with industry and government to develop and deploy advanced network applications and technologies for tomorrow's Internet. The stated goals of the organization are the following:

- Create a leading-edge network capability for the national research community.
- Enable revolutionary Internet applications.
- Ensure the rapid transfer of new network services and applications to the broader Internet community.

Internet2 is not a new Internet but rather a group developing new ways to improve the management and performance of the existing Internet. It includes dozens of research groups developing a variety of network applications in health sciences, arts and humanities, science and engineering, and education.

An offshoot of Internet2 that some call Internet3, which is officially named the *National LambdaRail* (NLR), is a cross-country, high-speed, fiber-optic network dedicated to research in high-speed networking applications (Figure 4.47). The NLR provides a unique national networking infrastructure to foster the advancement of networking research and next-generation network-based applications in science, engineering, and medicine. This new high-speed fiber-optic network will support the ever-increasing need of scientists to gather, transfer, and analyze massive amounts of scientific data.

FIGURE 4.47 • National LambdaRail (NLR)

NLR will, for the first time, provide the research community with direct control over a nationwide fiber-optic infrastructure.

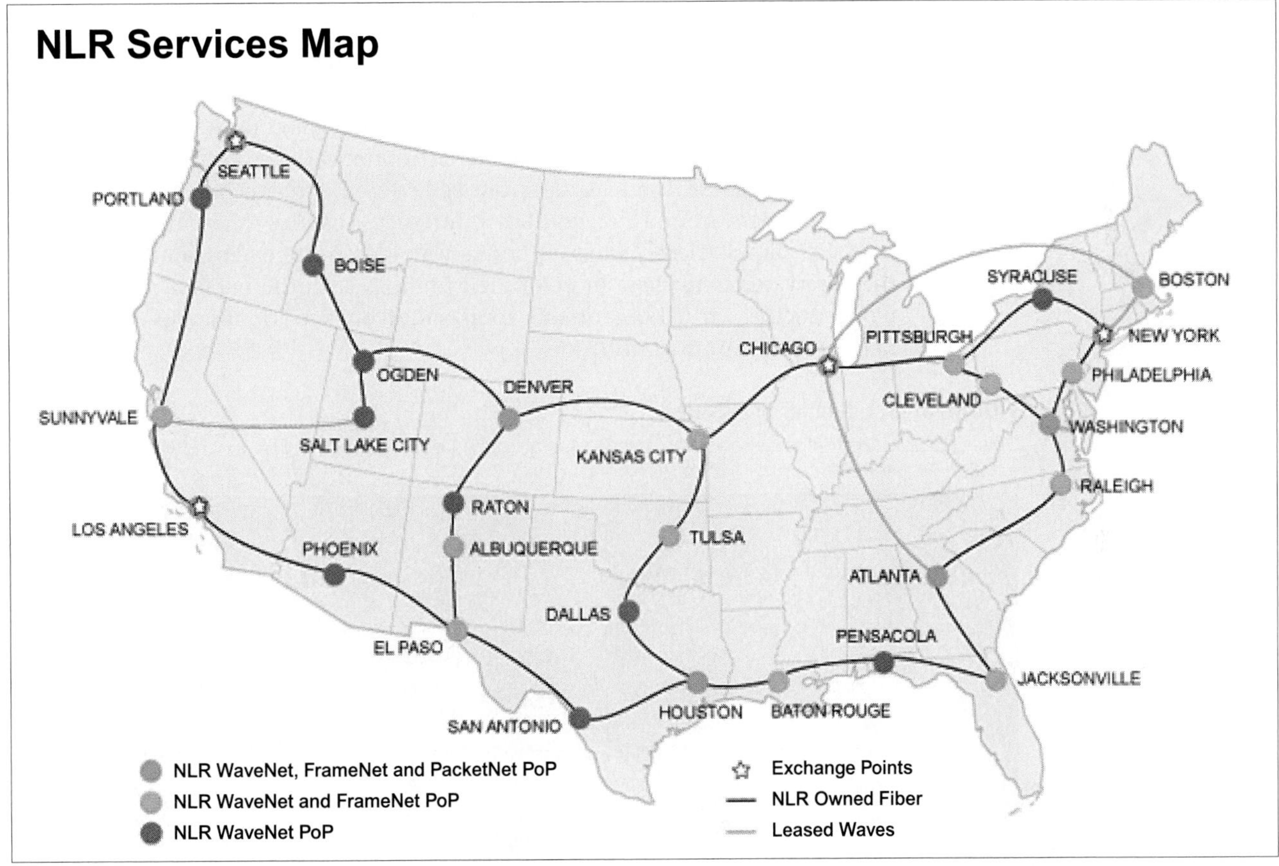

High-Speed Internet Applications

The new and exciting applications being explored on these super-speed networks fall under four categories:

- Interactive collaboration
- Real-time access to remote resources
- Large-scale, multisite computation and data mining
- Shared virtual reality

Some specific examples of these research areas follow.

Interactive Collaboration. Through new research in high-speed video and audio networking, individuals are able to collaborate from various locations in a common virtual environment. For example, technology named the Access Grid (*www.accessgrid.org*) uses large-format multimedia displays to create remote visualization environments. The Access Grid provides "designed spaces" that support the high-end audio/video technology needed to provide a compelling virtual collaborative experience that can be used for large-scale distributed meetings, seminars, lectures, tutorials, and training.

A similar technology, called the telecubicle, uses two office cubicle wall panels as display screens to produce an effect of participants seated around a table, even though they may be continents apart. With Internet2, interactive collaboration is the next best thing to being there.

Internet2 and interactive collaboration is finding a home in the arts as well. Hillary Herndon, master violist at the New World Symphony, is able to coach viola student Anna Simeone in the Conservatory of Music in Pisa, Italy, halfway around the world using video/audio connections over Internet2. The Manhattan School of Music offers group instrumental lessons and custom telementoring sessions with famous musicians on the faculty through the high-fidelity, broadcast-quality streaming audio and video available over Internet2.

Real-Time Access to Remote Resources. Internet2 is providing researchers, students, and audiences with access to remote equipment and environments. For example, the Gemini observatories (*www.gemini.edu*) are the result of a multinational project to build twin 8.1-meter astronomical telescopes in Hawaii and Chile (Figure 4.48). The telescopes can be accessed and controlled in real time by astronomers around the world over Internet2. The high-performance connection also allows scientists to collaborate via video conferencing and will enable the observatories to share more of their findings with the public through techniques such as virtual observatory tours and live video to museums, planetariums, and classrooms worldwide.

FIGURE 4.48 • Gemini observatory

Scientists can control the astronomical telescopes at Gemini observatories in Hawaii and Chile from any location on Internet2.

Visitors at Connecticut's Mystic Aquarium immerse themselves in an underwater world 3000 miles away by remotely controlling underwater cameras in California. Using interactive consoles at the Mystic Aquarium's Immersion Institute, visitors control three video cameras on an underwater submersible in Monterey Bay, the largest U.S. marine sanctuary. The live video is encoded and sent at an average rate of 6 megabits per second (Mbps) to the University of California, Santa Cruz, where it travels across Internet2 high-performance networks to the University of Connecticut and on to the Mystic Aquarium.

Large-Scale, Multisite Computation and Data Mining. New high-speed network technologies are providing powerful computing solutions for researchers who deal with enormous amounts of data. The National Scalable Cluster Project (NSCP) has pioneered an application that joins computers at various points on Internet2 to analyze data in terabyte-sized databases, faster than has ever before been possible.

Shared Virtual Reality. Shared virtual reality provides immersive virtual environments over a network to be shared by participants in different locales. For example, Virtual Harlem is a virtual reality environment originally developed in collaboration with the University of Missouri–Columbia to supplement African-American literature courses at Central Missouri State University. Students are able to step through a virtual "portal" to the 1925–1935 New York Harlem Renaissance to navigate the city streets, interact with key figures, and listen to music written and popularized during the era.

Shared virtual reality is a natural extension to today's massively multiplayer interactive games. Synthetic worlds may be an inevitable part of our future as people live increasing amounts of their lives online. It is only natural that efforts would be made to make our online experience more like the real world.

As these examples illustrate, a faster global Internet will provide opportunities to travel without leaving home. The future Internet will forge new professional and personal relationships to increase the interaction and collaboration between people from all walks of life with varying worldviews and experiences. The effects of such a ramping up of communications and information sharing is bound to have profound effects on our civilization.

Web 3.0

Web 2.0 changed the world's basic assumptions about how the Web could be used. Such radical change is often referred to as a paradigm shift. Technologies and services that combined to create what became known as Web 2.0 changed our perception of the Web from a system that delivered information (like a television), to a platform for collaboration and sharing.

The tremendous impact that Web 2.0 has had on society has many wondering what major change in Web technology—what paradigm shift—will occur next. What will constitute Web 3.0?

Some think we are seeing the beginning of Web 3.0 in cloud computing. Recall that cloud computing stores applications and data on Internet servers—in the "cloud"—and delivers them to Internet-connected devices as needed. With cloud computing, no software is installed on computers, nor is data stored locally. It's all in the cloud. Google Docs is a simple example of cloud computing. Large business systems like customer relationship management (CRM) software from salesforce.com are a larger more complex example.

While cloud computing is a growing trend in software delivery, it is doubtful that it alone will provide a paradigm shift like the one created by Web 2.0. More likely, *Web 3.0* will involve a combination of technologies that make "anywhere, anytime" information access effortless. Today, it may take 10 minutes to go online, touch base with your friends, find a movie, purchase tickets, check what bands are playing around town, and make reservations at your favorite restaurant. Web 3.0 might make it possible to do all these things within seconds or less. A combination of technologies might make this version of Web 3.0 a reality: intelligent agents, the semantic Web, a much faster, more pervasive Internet, cloud computing, and new, convenient forms of user interfaces.

An intelligent agent is a software program designed to autonomously perform specific tasks for a person (see Figure 4.49). Research is in progress to develop intelligent agents that study a person's behavior over time to learn the individual's tastes and habits. Combining the knowledge of a person's tastes and habits with information about the time of day and the person's location, an intelligent agent could make suggestions that assist the person even before the person thinks to ask! For example, knowing that the user enjoys an afternoon cup of coffee, an intelligent agent might point out a nearby Starbucks at 3:00 PM Or the intelligent agent might fetch a list of bands performing that evening based on the user's musical tastes and budget. Once approved, the agent could contact the user's friends to invite them to a concert—and perhaps communicate with their intelligent agents to find out if they are free.

FIGURE 4.49 • Intelligent agent

Soon your own digital personal assistant may be handling your online research and tasks.

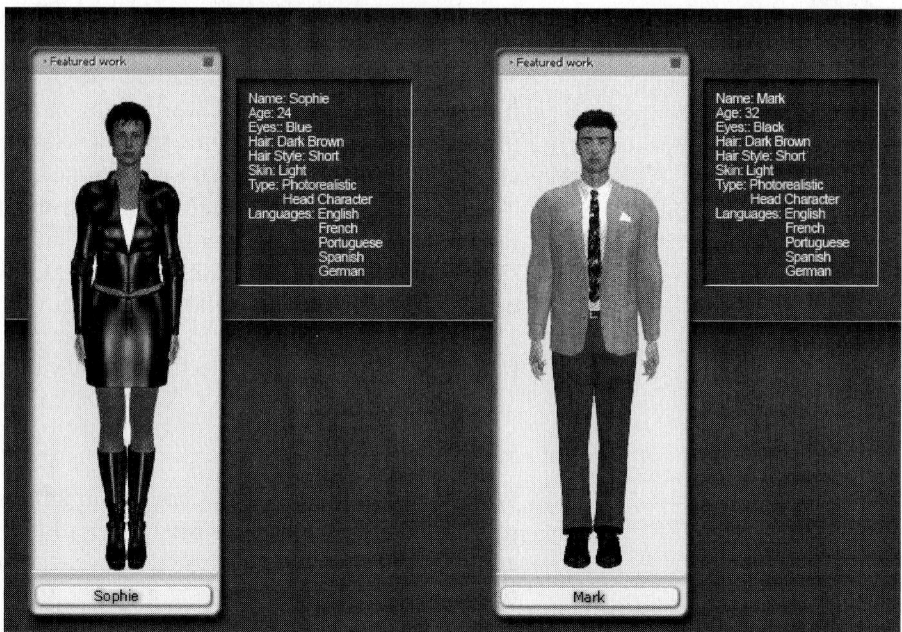

The *semantic Web* is a version of the Web where Web content is organized in a manner that makes it easier to identify and manage. Semantics refers to the study of meaning, in this case the meaning of information and services on the Web. Today's Web is designed for human navigation. We find information on the Web by entering key terms that will yield the best results from search engines. It is time consuming and often frustrating. The W3C and others are exploring alternative methods of classifying or tagging information on the Web that can allow the Web to act more like a database. Rather than having to search for key terms in Web page content, each Web page could be formatted in a manner that provides descriptive information. There are a number of technologies being explored to create the semantic Web.[11] Once created, the semantic Web will make it easy to automate processes of finding information for both humans and their intelligent agents.

In order to enjoy Web 3.0 services, high-speed wireless Internet access will need to be pervasive and abundant. Also, hands-free access to information would be more convenient. Wearable devices such as earbuds and microphones, combined with head-mounted displays, may provide one solution. Researchers are working on embedding a computer display in a contact lens (Figure 4.50),[12] as well as a variety of implant technologies that might assist in providing a continuous flow of useful and timely information wherever you roam.

It is possible that Web 3.0 may never occur. Technological advances may not combine to dramatically alter life over a short period. Our access to information may simply gradually improve over time, until someday in the future, we will look back and wonder at how things have changed. According to the principle of the technological singularity (the theoretical time when computers exceed human intelligence), that is more likely to be sooner than later.

FIGURE 4.50 • Contact lens display

Researchers at the University of Washington have taken the first steps toward embedding a computer display in a contact lens.

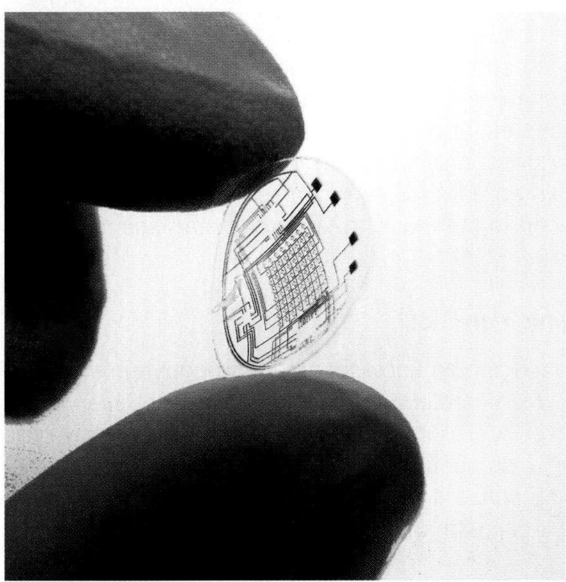

ACTION PLAN

Remember Josh Greene, who is disenchanted with the Web and feeling left out among his group of friends? Here are answers to his questions.

1. What enriching online activities can Josh use to improve his quality of life?

Josh can become more in touch with his friends, and make new friends by participating in social networks like Facebook and Twitter. Josh can pick up a new cell phone and service that supports online social networking so that he can text with his friends. He can involve himself in music and video clubs and multiplayer gaming. Josh can keep up with the latest news from online news services, and use technology news services to find out what's new on the Internet and Web. Josh might decide to broaden his knowledge or skills in a given area by using online training. He might even work toward certification in order to gain an edge when it comes time to look for a job. In fact, in today's competitive job market, it is never too soon to start looking. Josh can start scanning the job sites to help decide on a career and see what is out there.

2. What online activities are legal and safe, and which are not?

When accessing music and movies on the Web, Josh should know that ignoring copyrights can have serious consequences. Josh should also use caution when meeting new people online; not everyone is who they appear to be. Josh shouldn't travel solo to meet someone in person that he has met only online. When using material from the Web in his research paper, Josh should be sure to cite his sources and never submit someone else's work as his own. Using common sense and caution, and being aware of laws regarding intellectual property rights, Josh will find more legitimate and legal online activities and services than he has time to pursue.

3. How should Josh conduct research on his computer?

Josh could start looking for a topic at an online subject directory. Once he has selected a topic, he can research it using keyword searches at his school library's Web site, in the card catalog, and in online databases. He can refine his topic and search as he learns more about it. Finally, he can use Web search engines to access public knowledge on the topic, being careful to consider the source.

Summary

LEARNING OBJECTIVE 1

Describe how the Internet developed and how hardware, protocols, and software work together to create the Internet.

The Internet is the largest publicly owned network of networks. It was established in 1969 as the ARPANET under a U.S. government project named ARPA with a goal of connecting the computer networks of four universities. In 1990, it was turned over to the public to be managed by the Internet Society. The birth of the Web in 1993 led to an explosion in the Internet growth rate to the point that it connects millions of computers today.

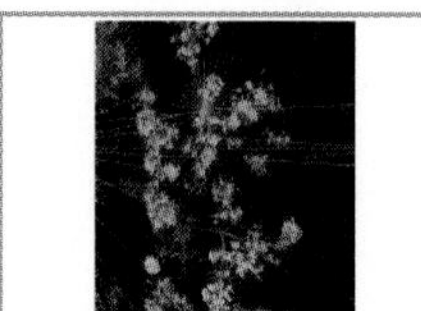

Figure 4.3—p. 199

The Internet combines hardware, protocols, and software to serve its users. Internet hardware consists of network backbones provided by the major telecommunication networks, routers that route packets of data to their destinations, and the computers that request and provide information and services. Internet service providers provide connections to points of presence on the Internet backbone for personal and professional use. The Internet is a packet-switching network that makes use of rules, called protocols, to pass packets of data between computers. Users connect to the Internet either through private networks at work or school that are connected to the Internet, or at home through high-speed cable modem or DSL connections, or slower dial-up connections.

The main protocols of the Internet are TCP/IP. The Internet Protocol (IP) defines the format and addressing scheme used for the packets. Transaction Control Protocol (TCP) enables two hosts to establish a connection and exchange streams of data. The Internet uses IP addresses to identify hosts. Domain names are English representations of IP addresses. The Internet makes use of client/server software to supply users with the information and services they request. Server computers use port numbers to segregate the various types of service requests. Peer-to-peer networks do not use a central server, but rather allow Internet users to create connections directly between their computers.

LEARNING OBJECTIVE 2

Explain the underlying structure of the Web and the technologies that support it.

The Web makes use of the Internet's client/server technology to provide a medium for users to conveniently publish, view, and find information on the Internet. It uses Hypertext Transfer Protocol (HTTP) to allow Web browsers (clients) to access Hypertext Markup Language (HTML) documents, called Web pages, stored on Web servers. HTML documents use hyperlinks to connect to other HTML documents. HTML tags specify the document format and other commands from within HTML documents. Uniform Resource Locators (URLs) are Web page addresses that allow you to access a specific Web page on a server. XML and XHTML are Web standards that allow for the storage and manipulation of structured data on the Web.

Figure 4.12—p. 209

Web plug-ins work with Web browsers to offer extended services—typically the ability to view audio, animations, or video. Java, JavaScript, ActiveX, and Ajax are programming languages and technologies that allow programs to be included in Web pages, allowing users to interact with Web content. Plug-ins work with a Web browser to offer extended media and other services.

Sometimes Web servers store a cookie, or a small text file, on your computer so that it can recognize you upon your next visit to a Web page. Cookies help Web pages present customized information to users. Web pages that are custom created on-the-fly are called dynamic Web pages. Others that are the same for every visitor are called static Web pages.

Portals are Web pages that provide an entry point to the Web. They typically include headline news and information, along with a search engine and subject directory to help you find information on the Web.

Web-authoring software allows you to create HTML documents in a WYSIWYG editor that works just like a word processor. With Web-authoring software, you can generate attractive Web pages without having to know HTML.

LEARNING OBJECTIVE 3

Define the categories of information and services that the Internet and Web provide and the forms of communication they support.

The Web provides a wide range of helpful applications. Search engines, subject directories, and portals assist in organizing and finding information on the Web. These applications provide communication and collaboration platforms that allow users to keep in touch, work together, and meet others with similar interests.

Figure 4.44—p. 251

Internet and Web communications provide synchronous or asynchronous forms of communication that can be text based, voice based, or video based. Forms of text communications include e-mail, discussion boards, chat, instant messaging, and text messaging. Because of the lack of nonverbal cues, e-mail is notorious for creating misunderstandings. Chat involves synchronous text messaging between two or more participants. Virtual Chat takes place in a virtual environment using avatars. Instant messaging is the most recent form of chat and allows users to build buddy lists to keep track of and communicate with friends online. Text messaging, or texting, is a technology that allows cell phone users to send short text messages to each other. Web logs, more commonly known as blogs, are Web sites created to express one or more individuals' views on a given topic. Web 2.0 refers to Web resources that allow average users to collaborate and contribute to Web content. Besides blogs, there are currently four popular manifestations of Web 2.0: social networking sites, media-sharing sites, wikis, and social bookmarking sites. Digital voice communication is creating a merger between Internet and telephone communications. This is particularly apparent in new cell phone technology and the emergence of video phone services.

The Internet and Web provide local, state, national, and international news on a level equal to if not better than traditional media. Educators and trainers use the Web to support and extend traditional learning environments or for distance education. Businesses rely on the Web to act as a central location for corporate information. The Web is one of the first places people turn to when planning a trip or looking for employment, and it plays an integral role in most job-hunting strategies. The Web supplies all forms of entertainment, including music, video, and gaming. It is also used as the primary tool for research, providing access to online library catalogs, databases, and public opinion.

LEARNING OBJECTIVE 4

Explain what Internet2 and Web 3.0 are and the types of applications they will provide in the future.

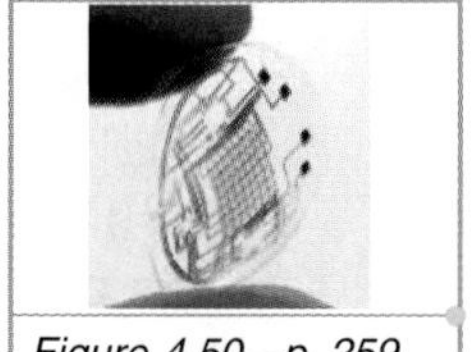

Figure 4.50—p. 259

Internet2 is a research and development consortium led by over 200 U.S. universities and supported by partnerships with industry and government to develop and deploy advanced network applications and technologies for tomorrow's Internet. The National LambdaRail (NLR) is a cross-country, high-speed, fiber-optic network dedicated to research in high-speed networking applications. New high-speed Internet applications emerging from research on Internet2 include interactive communication: video conferencing with individuals around the world; real-time access to remote resources such as scientific equipment or far-away events; large-scale, multisite computation; and shared virtual reality. Web 3.0 is the name given to the next paradigm shift in Internet and Web use, which will likely involve a combination of technologies that make "anywhere, anytime" information access effortless.

Test Yourself

LEARNING OBJECTIVE 1: Describe how the Internet developed and how hardware, protocols, and software work together to create the Internet.

1. The Internet ________________ is made up of a combination of many national and international communication networks.
   a. router
   b. protocol
   c. backbone
   d. server
2. True or False: HTTP is the main protocol of the Internet.
3. Internet applications such as e-mail divide up information, such as an e-mail message, into small ________________ in order to make efficient use of the network.

LEARNING OBJECTIVE 2: Explain the underlying structure of the Web and the technologies that support it.

4. True or False: The Web is simply another name for the Internet.
5. The design and style of a Web site is usually defined using ________________ .
   a. XHTML
   b. CSS
   c. XML
   d. Java
6. ________________ are small files of data that are stored and retrieved from your computer by a Web server each time you visit.
   a. Cookies
   b. JavaScripts
   c. ActiveX Controls
   d. Portals
7. True or False: Content streaming allows you to listen to or view content while it is being downloaded.

LEARNING OBJECTIVE 3: Define the categories of information and services that the Internet and Web provide and the forms of communication they support.

8. E-mail, voice mail, and SMS Texting are all examples of ________________ communication.
9. Social networking sites, media-sharing sites, blogs, and social bookmarking sites are all examples of ________________ .
   a. blogging
   b. Web 2.0
   c. Internet2
   d. synchronous communication
10. Digg.com is an example of a(n) ________________ Web site.
11. True or False: Serious business e-mail requires emoticons in order to avoid misunderstandings.
12. Web sites created to express one or more individuals' views on a given topic are called ________________ .
   a. portals
   b. search engines
   c. buddy lists
   d. blogs
13. The process of working from locations away from the office by using telecommunication technologies is called ________________ .

LEARNING OBJECTIVE 4: Explain what Internet2 and Web 3.0 are and the types of applications they will provide in the future.

14. True or False: Internet2 is a separate network from the original Internet.
15. The National LambdaRail (NLR) is a cross-country, high-speed, ________________ network dedicated to research in high-speed networking applications.
   a. fiber-optic
   b. cable
   c. wireless
   d. satellite
16. True or False: Most experts believe that cloud computing is Web 3.0.

Test Yourself Solutions **1.** c. backbone, **2.** False, **3.** packets, **4.** False, **5.** b. CSS, **6.** a. Cookies, **7.** True, **8.** asynchronous, **9.** Web 2.0, **10.** social bookmarking, **11.** False, **12.** d. blogs, **13.** telecommuting, **14.** False, **15.** a. fiber-optic, **16.** False.

Key Terms

Key Term	Page	Definition
asynchronous communication	225	Communication in which participants leave messages for each other to be read, heard, or watched, and responded to at the recipient's convenience
BitTorrent	206	A peer-to-peer file sharing protocol that allows users to share files by downloading pieces of a file from multiple sources
blog	230	Web sites created to express one or more individuals' views on a given topic
cable modem connection	201	High-speed Internet service, with data transfer rates as high as 8 Mbps, provided by cable television service providers
cascading style sheets (CSS)	212	A Web development technology that uses special HTML tags to globally define font characteristics for a variety of page elements as well as how those elements are laid out on the Web page
chat	229	Synchronous text messaging between two or more participants
client/server	205	A relationship between two computer programs in which one program, the *client*, makes a service request from another program, the *server*, which provides the service
content streaming	217	Sometimes called streaming media, streaming video, or streaming audio, a technique in which the media begins playing while the file is being delivered
cookies	214	Small text files stored on a computer by a Web server in order to recognize a user who revisits the Web site
dial-up connection	201	A low-speed Internet service that utilizes the customer's phone line for data transfer rates as high as 56 kilobits per second (Kbps)
DSL (digital subscriber line) connection	201	Uses the customer's phone line, but there is no dialing up and users can use the Internet and talk on the phone simultaneously
e-mail	226	The transmission of messages over a computer network to support asynchronous text-based communication
e-mail attachment	226	Typically a binary file, such as an image file, Word document, music file, or spreadsheet, that travels along with an e-mail message but is not part of the e-mail ASCII text message itself
Extensible Markup Language (XML)	210	A markup language that provides a method for describing and classifying the content of data in a Web page
hyperlink	208	An element in an electronic document—a word, phrase, or image—that when clicked, opens a related document
Hypertext Markup Language (HTML)	210	The primary markup language that is used to specify the formatting of a Web page; HTML v5 is the latest version
Hypertext Transfer Protocol (HTTP)	209	The protocol of the Web that controls communication between Web clients and servers
instant messaging (IM)	228	Synchronous one-to-one text-based communication over the Internet
Internet backbone	198	The main Internet pathways and connections made up of the many national and international communication networks that are owned by major telecom companies
Internet service provider (ISP)	199	Company that provides users with access to the Internet through network service providers' (NSPs') points of presence (POPs)
IP address	204	A unique 32-bit identifier for Internet hosts (all devices connected to the Internet)

Key Term	Page	Definition
peer-to-peer (P2P)	206	A network architecture that does not utilize a central server, but facilitates communications directly between clients
plug-in	216	Works with a Web browser to offer extended services such as audio players, video, animation, 3D graphics viewers, and interactive media
port	205	A logical address used by clients and servers that is associated with a specific service
router	199	Special-purpose computing device—typically a small to large unit with network ports—that manages network traffic by evaluating messages and routing them over the fastest path to their destination
search engine	219	A valuable tool that enables you to find information on the Web by specifying words that are key to a topic of interest (keywords)
social bookmarking	236	Web sites that provide a way for Web users to store, classify, share, and search Web bookmarks; also referred to as favorites
social networking	233	Sites that provide Web-based tools for users to share information about themselves with others on the Web and find, meet, and converse with other members
synchronous communication	225	Communication in which people exchange thoughts in real time in a flowing conversation
TCP/IP	204	The protocols for the Internet; *Transmission Control Protocol* (TCP) and *Internet Protocol* (IP)
text messaging	230	Method of sending short text messages, no longer than 160 characters, between cell phones
Uniform Resource Locator (URL)	209	A Web page address, incorporating the domain name of the Web server and the location of the Web page file on the server
video conferencing	239	Technology that combines video and phone call capabilities along with shared data and document access
Web 2.0	232	Web resources that allow average users to collaborate and contribute to Web content
Web-authoring software	213	Software like a word processor that allows you to create HTML documents
Web browser	209	Software such as Internet Explorer used to request Web pages from Web servers
Web server	209	Software that stores and delivers Web pages and other Web resources such as interactive Web content
wiki	223	Web site designed to allow users to add, remove, and edit content
XHTML	211	Markup language that uses most of the same tags as HTML but is more strict in what is allowed and not allowed, so it is more compliant with XML

Questions

Review Questions

1. What was the motivation behind the creation of the Internet?
2. What three components combined make up today's Web?
3. What is the Internet backbone, and who provides it?
4. What is the role of an ISP?
5. What Internet connection type offers the fastest connection speed?

6. What are the responsibilities of a router?
7. How does P2P networking differ from client/server?
8. What is the difference between synchronous and asynchronous communication?
9. What is the number one use of the Internet?
10. Why was P2P selected as the network architecture for today's file-sharing networks?
11. What is SMS text messaging, and how is it used?
12. What type of Web 2.0 application is Twitter?
13. Why is video conferencing so valuable?
14. What is the primary markup language and protocol of the Web?
15. What value do social bookmarking sites offer to the Web community?
16. What is meant by distance education?
17. What information and services can be found on the Web?
18. What are three common sources of information for research?

Discussion Questions

19. Describe how an e-mail message gets from your computer to your friend's computer.
20. Why are IP addresses important to Internet technology?
21. How have blogs changed the way that news is delivered?
22. What are the benefits and drawbacks of client/server architecture?
23. What are the benefits and drawbacks of P2P architecture?
24. Why might P2P networks be more hazardous, in terms of viruses and hackers, than client/server architectures?
25. What are the benefits and drawbacks of synchronous communication?
26. What are the benefits and drawbacks of asynchronous communication?
27. What is a common problem with communicating through e-mail? What can be done to help alleviate this problem?
28. What are binary files, and why can't they be sent as e-mail?
29. How will the semantic Web change the nature of the Web?
30. Why are plug-ins necessary for some Web sites?
31. What are the pros and cons of cookie technology?
32. How do search engines and subject directories differ? What types of scenarios does each support?
33. What is WYSIWYG, and why is it important to Web authors?
34. What is a concern of primary and secondary teachers when it comes to student Web use, and how can this concern be eased?
35. How is the Web used in job hunting?
36. Compare and contrast the pros and cons of library, database, and Web research.
37. Why is it important to cite sources on research papers?
38. What type of Internet Service Provider provides the most bang (speed) for the buck?

Exercises

Try It Yourself

1. Visit *www.secondlife.com*, join, and download the software. Log in to Second Life, and use your arrow keys to explore the virtual landscape, taking advantage of tutorials as they become available. Write a paper providing a summary of your experience in Second Life and your thoughts on the usefulness of the software.
2. Use your favorite Web search engine to find several online travel services. Evaluate each of the services; then, using a word processor, write a summary of your impressions. Which service do you think is most helpful? Why?
3. Do a search on *plagiarism* at your favorite search engine. Study the search results and find answers to the following questions:
   a. How prevalent is plagiarism on college campuses?
   b. In what ways does the Web support plagiarism?
   c. What are colleges doing to fight plagiarism?

   Write the results of your study using a word processor.
4. Visit *www.yougetsignal.com/tools/visual-tracert/*. This Web site provides access to a program called Traceroute that allows you to view the path of a packet across the Internet. Traceroute returns the name of each router that the packet encounters on its journey. Use this tool to trace the route of a packet from Brea, CA (the location of this Web server) to Google using the Host Trace option. The resulting list is the routers that your packet encountered on the way to Google. Zoom in on the map to view the details of the trip. Now try a Proxy Trace to louve.fr. This will show you the Internet path from your current Web server to Brea, CA, to The Louvre Museum in Paris, France. How many routers (hops) did your packet visit? How long did it take? What can you discern from the router information? Can you guess who owns any of the routers and where they are located?
5. Visit *http://youtube.com* and view the three most popular videos. Write a review of the videos and conclude with your impression of YouTube and the value it provides the Web community.
6. Search the Web for a biography on Tim Berners-Lee and use it to write a summary of his professional life.

Virtual Classroom Activities

For the following exercises, do not use face-to-face or telephone communications with your group members. Use only Internet communications.

7. Have each group member use a different search engine with the goal of finding the least expensive roundtrip airfare for a week in Jamaica. The flight can depart from any airport within 100 miles of your present location. Define the departure and return dates of the trip. The person with the lowest fare is the winner and gets to delegate the work of writing the team results.
8. Have group members sign up on Twitter at *www.twitter.com*. Each member should follow each other in Twitter so you can see what all group members tweet. Group members should use Twitter to log their hourly activities over the course of the week. At the end of the week, each member should submit a short paper on what they learned about the people in the group through using Twitter and provide an overall impression of the tool.

9. Have group members sign up on flickr.com. Create a group on Flickr and use it to share your favorite photos. Use the commenting feature to vote for the group's favorite photo from the photos submitted by group members. Write a review of Flickr, including interesting insights you gained from the exercise.

Teamwork

10. Each team member should use a word processor to write a specific description of the e-mail service(s) that he or she uses to access e-mail and the level of satisfaction with the service. Team members should e-mail their papers to each other as attachments. As a group, determine which members are using appropriate e-mail services and which should switch. Write up the results of your discussion.
11. Each team member should use Google Maps to route a round trip that visits four cities (the group can decide on which cities). Everyone should use the same cities. After you are finished, compare the time and miles of each team member's trip. Are they all the same? If not, why are they different? Who has the shortest trip? Why? Write up your results.
12. Have each group member go online in search of employment in his or her chosen field (if you don't have a chosen field, choose something of interest). Find a job posting in your field that lists the pay scale and job description. As a group, decide who found the best-paying job and whose job sounds most satisfying. Write up your results.

Endnotes

1 CIA World Fact Book, accessed August 20, 2009, https://www.cia.gov/library/publications/the-world-factbook/rankorder/2184rank.html.

2 Zakon, Robert H., Hobbes' Internet Timeline, v. 8.2, accessed September 9, 2009, http://www.zakon.org/robert/internet/timeline/.

3 Krill, Paul, "XHTML 2 language dumped in favor of HTML 5," *InfoWorld*, July 2, 2009, www.infoworld.com.

4 Staff, "Bing continues to gain search engine market-share," *Brafton Industry News*, August 18, 2009, www.brafton.com.

5 Gage, Deborah, "Facebook Claims 250 Million Users," *InformationWeek*, July 16, 2009, www.informationweek.com.

6 Long, Mark, "Tweet! New Handsets Designed for Twitter and Facebook," *NewsFactor*, August 4, 2009, www.newsfactor.com.

7 Gaudin, Sharon, "Illinois outlaws sex offenders from using Facebook, MySpace," *Computerworld*, August 14, 2009, www.computerworld.com.

8 Cheng, Jacqui, "Google Voice and you: what it is and how you use it," *Ars Technica*, August 10, 2009, www.arstechnica.com.

9 Lohr, Steve, "Study Finds That Online Education Beats the Classroom," *The New York Times*, August 19, 2009, www.nytimes.com.

10 Perez, Juan Carlos, "Update: Geolocation coming to Twitter and its external applications," *Computerworld*, August 20, 2009, www.computerworld.com.

11 Krill, Paul, "Semantic Web set for critical mass," *Computerworld*, June 17, 1009, www.computerworld.com.

12 Hanlon, Mike, "Electronic Contact Lens promises bionic capabilities for everyone," *gizmag*, January 21, 2008, www.gizmag.com.

TELECOMMUNICATIONS, WIRELESS TECHNOLOGIES, AND COMPUTER NETWORKS

Amanda Jackson is a news correspondent recently hired by National Public Radio (NPR). In her previous position with her small-town newspaper, she had a desk and PC at which she did most of her work. Her new job entails traveling the world reporting on stories where they occur. Amanda has been given a startup budget to purchase the reporting equipment she requires. She needs tools for taking notes and recording audio interviews. She needs telephone service wherever she travels so that she can supply on-location live reports. She also needs the ability to research facts on the Internet and the NPR archives located on the organization's private network.

Amanda is somewhat concerned about the complexities of the technology with which she'll be working. How will she transfer her notes between devices? How will her devices connect to the Internet and the private NPR network? Is it possible for a cell phone to work on international networks?

As you read through the chapter, consider the following questions:

1. What types of mobile device(s) will best suit Amanda's journalistic needs?
2. What types of notebook computer, networking media, devices, and software should Amanda use to connect to the Internet and the NPR network?
3. What networking technologies can Amanda use to transfer files between her devices?

Check out Amanda's *Action Plan* at the conclusion of this chapter.

5

LEARNING OBJECTIVES

1. Understand the fundamentals of data communications and the criteria for choosing a communications medium.
2. Explain how networking media, devices, and software work together to provide data-networking services, and describe the benefits of various types of media.
3. List and describe the most popular forms of wireless telecommunications technologies.
4. List the different classifications of computer networks and their defining characteristics, and understand the basics of wireless home networking.

CHAPTER CONTENT

Introduction

A network is fundamentally a communication system; it empowers individuals and groups to interact and access resources that would otherwise be more difficult or impossible to access. At home, networks allow household members to share documents, music, photos, and other media among home computers, as well as to access a world of resources on the Internet. In an organization, networks act as the circulatory system, providing a flow of information between group members. For organizations, teamwork is synonymous with success. The better the flow of information among group members, the more productive the group becomes. To reach goals more efficiently and effectively, an organization needs to ensure that its network can properly support its information and communication needs.

In selecting the components of a network, you must consider the speed and capacity of the medium that carries the communication signal. The communications medium works in conjunction with communication devices and software to provide a data communications network. There are numerous types of networks, each supporting the unique needs of its environment. Wireless mobile technologies are making it increasingly common to access networks anywhere, anytime. This chapter examines a variety of network types and their components to provide an understanding of how networks help us be connected and more productive in business, at home, and while traveling.

Today's telecommunications networks play a vital role in our daily activities. From the global telecom networks that make up the Internet to short-range wireless technologies that pass data back and forth between a cell phone and headset, telecommunications technologies keep us connected. In the first part of this chapter, you will learn the basics about telecommunications systems, how they work, and how their performance is measured. Next, you learn about the components that make up telecommunications systems: media, devices, and software. Section three of this chapter delves into wireless networking technologies, including cell phones, GPS, Wi-Fi, WiMAX, Bluetooth, and radio frequency ID (RFID). The chapter then turns its focus to the different types of computer networks and examines home networking technologies and applications.

FUNDAMENTALS OF TELECOMMUNICATIONS

Communications can be defined as the transmission of a signal from a sender to a receiver by way of a medium such as wires or radio waves. The signal can contain a message composed of data and information. It is important to note two characteristics of communications. First, the message is not communicated directly; rather, it is communicated by way of a *signal*. Second, the signal itself goes through a *communications medium*, which is anything that carries a signal between a sender and receiver.

You can easily recognize these aspects of communications if you consider what happens when humans communicate (see Figure 5.1). When you talk to someone face to face, you send messages to each other. One person may be the sender at one moment in time and the receiver a few seconds later. The same entity, a person in this case, can be a sender, a receiver, or both. This is typical of two-way synchronous communication. Some of the signals you use to convey these messages are the sound waves that represent our spoken words. Other signals are nonverbal, such as gestures and expressions. For communication to be effective, both sender and receiver must understand the signals and agree on what they mean. For example, if the sender in Figure 5.1 is speaking in a language the receiver does not understand, or if the sender believes a particular word or gesture has one meaning and the receiver believes it has some other meaning, effective communication cannot occur. Although these facts may seem obvious, they are important building blocks in understanding more complicated forms of electronic communications.

When you talk to someone, the transmission medium is the air. When you read, the transmission medium is the printed page. The traditional telephone converts a signal carried by the medium of air (sound waves) into an electronic signal carried over wires (another medium). A cell phone converts the sound waves created by your voice into a radio signal carried over air and received by a base station that transfers the signal to wires, and then perhaps to another cell phone over a radio signal, and finally to electronic impulses that vibrate the speaker diaphragm in the receiver handset.

As you consider the structure of telecommunications systems, keep these fundamental communications concepts in mind. For example, establishing a communication link between two digital devices requires that they "speak the same language" using protocols, and that software interprets the information being transmitted. And, as discussed later in this chapter, the characteristics of the medium—in particular, the speed at which it can carry a signal—is an important consideration.

FIGURE 5.1 • Face-to-face voice communications

In face-to-face voice communications, the transmission medium is the air, and the signal is the sound wave.

Telecommunications and Data Communications

Computing devices communicate with each other via telecommunications and data communications systems. **Telecommunications** refers to the electronic transmission and reception of signals for communications. Some telecommunications devices with which you interact daily include phones, radios, televisions, and networked computers. *Data communications*, a specialized subset of telecommunications, refers to the electronic transmission and reception of digital data, typically between computer systems. A *telecommunications network* connects communications and computing devices. A *computer network* is a specific type of telecommunications network that connects computers and computer systems for data communications. This chapter investigates popular uses of telecommunications networks.

There are three components of telecommunications networks: networking media, networking hardware, and networking software. **Networking media** is anything that carries a signal and creates an interface between a sending device and a receiving device. Networking hardware (or *networking devices*) and *networking software* work together to enable and control communications signals between communications and computer devices. As computers, cell phones, televisions, and other devices are connected to a network, they become part of the network infrastructure. Figure 5.2 shows a general model of telecommunications. The model starts with a sending unit, such as a PC, cell phone, or other device that originates the message. The sending unit transmits a signal to a networking device. The networking device can perform a number of functions, including changing or manipulating the signal. The networking device then sends the signal over a medium. The signal is received by another networking device that is connected to the receiving unit, which is a computer system, PC, cell phone, or other device that receives the message. The process can then be reversed, and another message can go back from the receiving unit to the original sending unit.

FIGURE 5.2 • General model of telecommunications

Sending and receiving units, such as computers or cell phones, use networking devices and media to communicate.

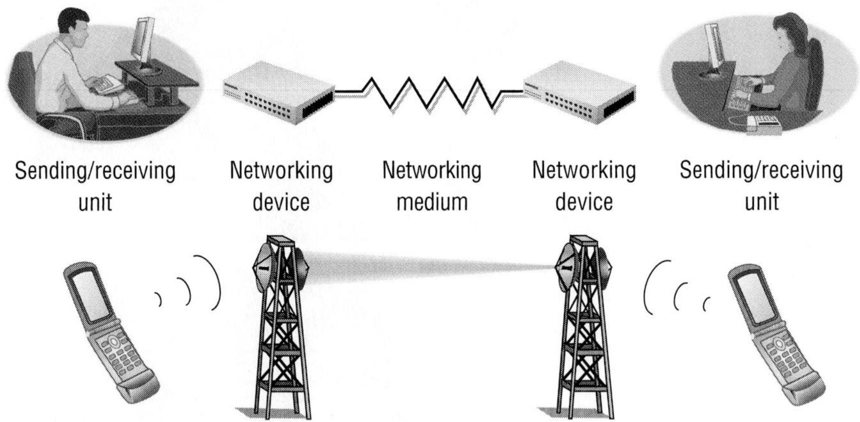

Characteristics of Telecommunications

The characteristics of telecommunications components can be analyzed in terms of speed, quality, and convenience. Telecommunications can allow people to be more productive. For example, being able to access and respond to e-mail during an hour-long daily commute on the bus or train frees up an hour later in the day for going to the gym or some other productive activity. Construction companies have found that investing in a wireless phone system boosts productivity by allowing job superintendents to communicate via phone or notebook computer, sharing problems and solutions, even transferring job site photos to the home office. Telecommunications allows one teacher in the Cleveland County school district to teach advanced placement courses at several high schools remotely and simultaneously.[1] Telecommunications technologies gave customer service provider Working Solutions a way to hire more call center agents in the United States, without having to outsource jobs overseas, by allowing the agents to work from home.[2] Telecommunications provides the backbone of communications for countless businesses with differing needs.

Types of Signals. If you were to measure the voltage on a telephone wire during a phone conversation, you would see fluctuations in voltages similar to those shown in Figure 5.3a. Such fluctuations occur thousands of times per second in varying intensities that mirror the sound waves of your voice. This type of signal is called an **analog signal**, and it fluctuates continuously.

In contrast, if you measured the voltage on cables used to connect PCs, you would probably see something comparable to Figure 5.3b. The signal in Figure 5.3b at any given time is either high or low. This type of discrete voltage state—either high or low—is called a **digital signal**. The two states are used to represent the state of a bit, high for 1, and low for 0.

Transmission Capacities. Some uses of telecommunications require very fast transmission speeds. For example, when the salesperson swipes your credit card at the checkout counter of a major department store, your purchase information joins that of thousands of others being routed to the credit card company for approval. Such networks must handle high-volume traffic very quickly so as not to keep customers waiting. Other signals, such as those used in a small office or home network, do not require as much transmission capacity and speed.

FIGURE 5.3 • Analog and digital signals

An analog signal continuously changes over time. A digital signal has a discrete state—either high or low.

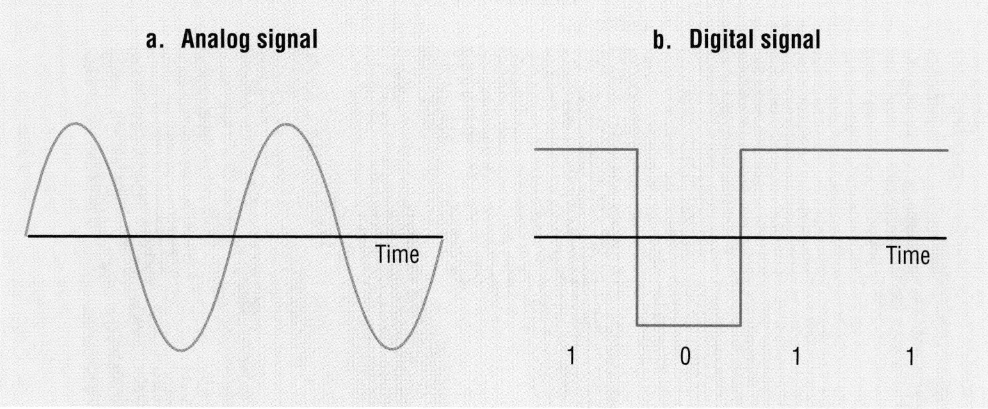

The speed at which an electronic communications signal can change from high to low is called the signal *frequency* (see Figure 5.4). A faster frequency means a faster data transmission rate. Signal frequency is measured in *hertz (Hz)*, or cycles per second. In computer networks, the data transmission rate is also referred to as the **bandwidth** and is measured in *bits per second (bps)*. Today's bandwidth options fall into one of two categories: narrowband or broadband.

FIGURE 5.4 • Frequency

The speed at which a signal changes from high to low, the signal frequency, dictates the rate of speed at which data is delivered, which is called the bandwidth.

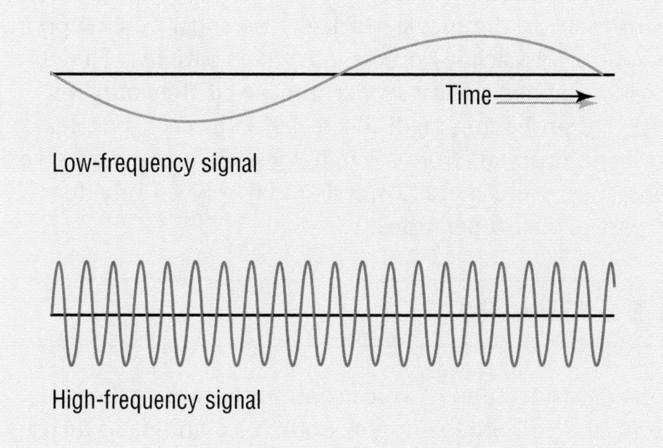

Broadband media are those advertised by Internet service providers as "high-speed." In everyday use, the terms **broadband** or *high-speed Internet* refer to a connection that is always on or active, such as cable or DSL. These connections are significantly faster than dial-up telephone connections. DSL and cable claim maximum download speeds of 6 Mbps and 50 Mbps, respectively. The minimum speed for a medium to be considered broadband is hotly debated. The FCC has defined broadband as faster than 200 Kbps. Almost everyone today would consider 200 Kbps to be an extremely slow connection. As the FCC and telecom service providers haggle over what data transfer rate constitutes broadband, many in the industry prefer to think of broadband as capabilities rather than bits per second. Broadband connections should enable users to access all Internet and Web content at speeds that are reasonable.[3] *Narrowband* would then be considered any medium with a speed less than 200 Kbps, or perhaps any speed that restricts a user from accessing Internet content at a reasonable speed.

Not long ago, broadband data transfer speeds were available only at a premium price to businesses and organizations to support high-traffic data communications. Today, inexpensive broadband access is available for homes and small businesses and has become the norm. Sixty percent of U.S. homes have access to broadband Internet. Some countries have a much higher percentage of broadband penetration. South Korea is at 95 percent, Singapore at 88 percent, and the Netherlands at 85 percent. The United States falls twentieth in the list of household broadband coverage.[4] The U.S. government has stepped up

FIGURE 5.5 • Digital hospitals require broadband networks

The huge array of digital records maintained by modern hospitals, including patient records and digital images from X-rays, MRIs, and other medical procedures, requires broadband networks to transfer records between locations.

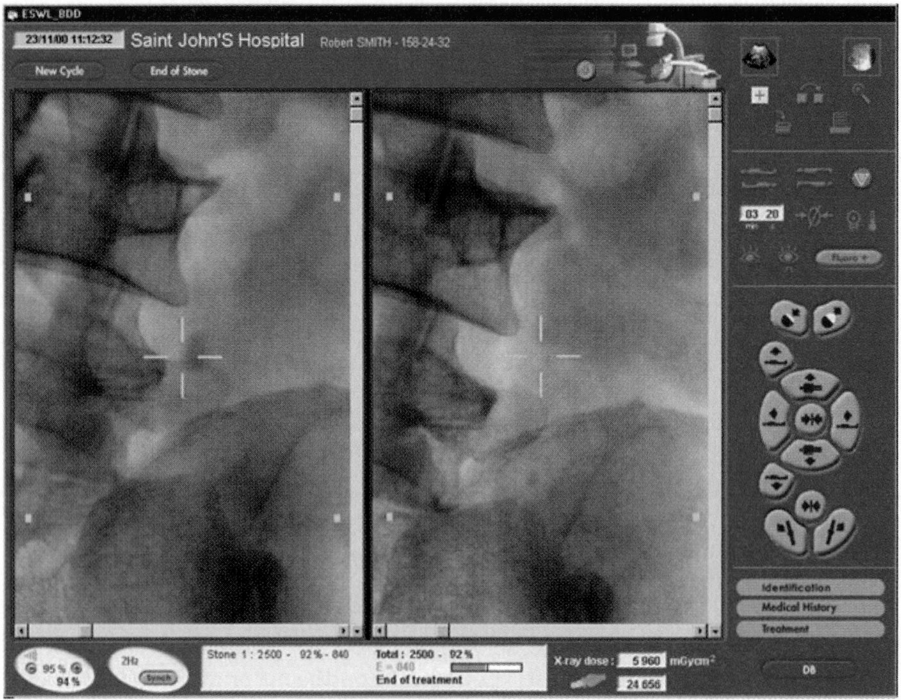

efforts to deliver broadband to everyone who wants it.[5]

The availability of broadband data communications is empowering professionals to become more effective in their careers. Consider Cambridge Health Alliance, a nationally recognized health-care system in Massachusetts that operates several hospitals and medical centers serving residents of Cambridge, Somerville, and Boston's Metro-North region. In the early 2000s, Cambridge Health began converting many of its paper-based and film-based systems to digital records. It needed a new broadband communications system that could handle the high-bandwidth demands of the newer systems that managed and transferred health records and digital images, such as X-rays and MRIs, across its many locations (see Figure 5.5). Cambridge Health hired Nortel Networks to install broadband networking media, devices, and software to support important network services for physicians, nurses, and their patients. The new broadband network provided higher-quality service and saved the company money. For example, rather than having medical specialists in each hospital, one specialist could service all the hospitals from a single location using high-speed network communications.[6] More and more hospitals today rely on broadband networks as an integral part of their operations.

NETWORKING MEDIA, DEVICES, AND SOFTWARE

EXPAND YOUR KNOWLEDGE

To learn more about networks, go to www.cengage.com/computerconcepts/np/swt4. Click the link "Expand Your Knowledge" and then complete the lab entitled "Networking Basics."

Some telecommunications networks support voice communications, others support data communications, and still others support both voice and data. Increasingly, both types of networks send information as bits, using the packet-switching technology of the Internet. No matter what the type, the communications that take place on these networks require networking media, hardware, and software. To understand the practical benefits of various network technologies, you must learn the strengths and weaknesses of their components. This section compares and contrasts different types of network media, and the devices and software that support them.

Networking Media

Various types of media are used for telecommunications networks. Each type of medium has its own characteristics, including transmission capacity, speed, convenience, and security. In developing a network, the selection of media depends on the environment and use of the network. Media should support the needs of the network users, in the given environment at the least cost, taking into account possible future needs of the network. For example, computer users in a rental apartment would probably not be allowed to run network cables through walls and attic spaces. In this situation, a wireless network setup would be more appropriate. A government security agency may opt for a wired network over a wireless network in order to provide the highest level of security for its data. A business traveler might purchase a wireless cell phone headset to avoid the inconvenience of tangled wires while rushing through airports. AT&T might decide to send a satellite into orbit, rather than run miles of cable, to provide faster service to a remote location for the lowest cost.

These examples illustrate the many environments and situations in which media considerations come into play. Not only are cost, quality, and speed important considerations, but also one must consider the future. For example, when a business invests in a network, it selects a network that will accommodate a reasonable amount of growth in both workforce and business needs without overestimating these requirements and wasting money.

Different communications media connect systems in different ways. Some media send signals along physical connections like cables, but others send signals through the air using radio waves.

Physical Cables. Different physical cables offer a range in bandwidth from narrowband to broadband. Cables have an advantage over wireless options because some cables support much higher data transfer rates than wireless technologies and are considered by some to be more secure. The disadvantage of cables is their physical presence. Cables need to be installed, typically in an inconspicuous manner: they are run underground, undersea, and through utility tunnels; strung from pole to pole, through attics and basements, and above ceiling tiles and pulled down inside walls, through walls, and around the interior of a room. Depending on the environment, laying cable can take a considerable amount of time and effort. Three types of transmission cables are typically used to connect data communications devices: twisted pair copper cable, coaxial cable, and fiber-optic cable.

Twisted pair copper cable consists of pairs of twisted wires covered with an insulating layer (see Figure 5.6a). Twisted pair is the type of cable that brings telephone service to your home and is used for dial-up modem connections. It is also used in most wire-based computer networks. Twisted pair comes in varying qualities and categories (Cats) that support a wide range of bandwidths. For example, Cat 1 and Cat 2 are used for home phone systems supporting 1 Mbps for voice communication. Cat 5 and Cat 6 are used in many private computer networks to support 100 Mbps to 1 Gbps for data communications. Cat 7 is used for heavy-traffic networks and supports 10 Gbps. Twisted pair is the least expensive cable option.

Figure 5.6b shows a typical coaxial cable. You may recognize this as the type of cable provided by cable television services that connects to your cable box. A **coaxial cable** consists of an inner conductor wire surrounded by insulation, a conductive shield (usually a layer of foil or metal braiding), and a cover. Coaxial cable is much faster than Cat 1 and 2 twisted pair copper cables, and at one time it was the preferred cable for computer networks. However, since the development of faster, less expensive Cat 5 twisted pair copper cables, coaxial is mostly used just for cable television and radio networks.

Twisted pair and coaxial cables transmit electrical signals over copper or other metal wires. In contrast, **fiber-optic cable**, which consists of extremely thin strands of glass or plastic bound together in a sheathing (a jacket), transmits signals with light beams (see Figure 5.6c). These high-intensity light beams are generated by lasers and are conducted along the transparent fibers. These fibers have a thin coating, called *cladding*, which effectively works like a mirror, preventing the light from leaking out of the fiber.

FIGURE 5.6 • Networking cables

Twisted pair (a), coaxial (b), and fiber-optic (c) networking cables provide support for a variety of bandwidth needs from 1 Mbps to 10 Tbps.

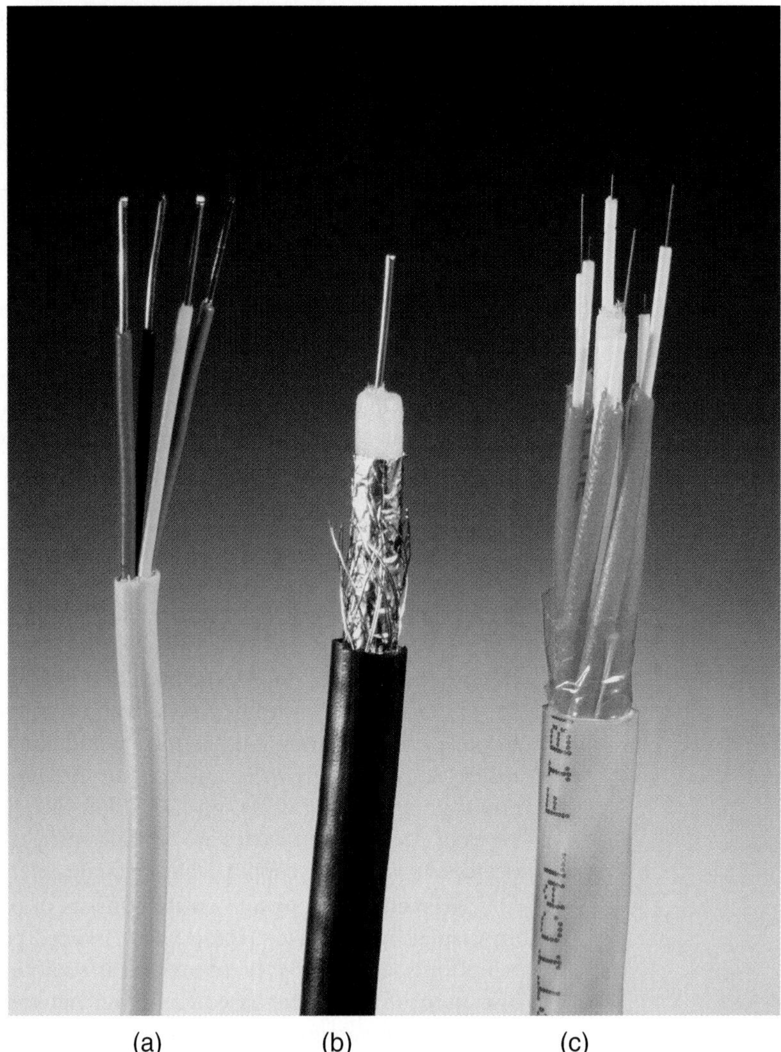

Fiber-optic cable has several advantages over traditional copper cable:

- Speed: Fiber-optic cables support data transfer rates of 1.6 terabits per second (Tbps) and have performed as fast as 10 Tbps in lab experiments.
- Size: Fiber-optic strands are much smaller in diameter than many copper wires. More strands can be bundled together in smaller cables than with copper.
- Clarity: Fiber-optic cables do not allow signals to bleed from one strand to another, unlike copper wire that often suffers from such interference.
- Security: Copper wires are easy to tap, but the same is not true for fiber-optic cable.

Fiber-optic cable suffers from one major disadvantage: price. It is much more expensive than copper; it is not financially feasible to run it to every household in a neighborhood. Once installed, though, fiber-optic cable is less expensive to maintain than copper cable.

Radio Signals and Light. Telecommunications signals can travel through air using radio waves and light. A *radio wave* is an electromagnetic wave transmitted through an antenna at different frequencies. The U.S. Federal Communications Commission assigns different frequencies for different uses in the United States. For example, FM radio, cell phones, baby monitors, and garage door openers all operate at different frequencies. Figure 5.7 illustrates some of the uses of frequencies over the radio spectrum. To show all frequency assignments would take a chart several feet tall (available at *www.fcc.gov/oet/spectrum*).

FIGURE 5.7 • The radio spectrum

The FCC assigns different frequencies of the radio spectrum for different uses in the United States. The spectrum is divided into eight bands: Very Low, Low, Medium, High, Very High, Ultra High, Super High, and Extremely High Frequencies.

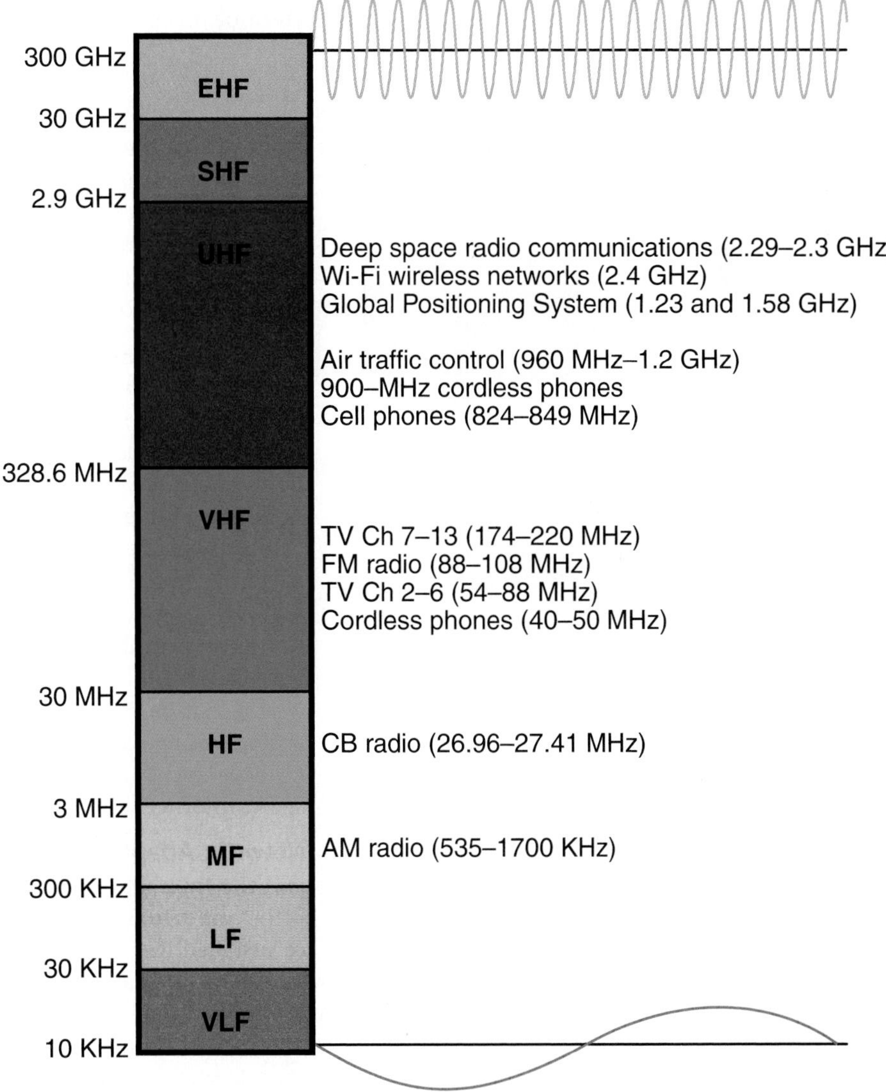

There are thousands of radio waves passing through the air and your body as you read this. AM and FM radio waves, television, wireless phone conversations, wireless computer networks, global positioning systems, ham radios, CB radios, police and emergency communications, satellite communications, and wireless clock systems all make use of radio waves. All it takes to receive the information being transmitted on a specific frequency is a device with an antenna that allows you to tune in to that frequency. For example, when you tune your car radio to 98.9 FM, you are selecting the signal being broadcast at 98.9 MHz, and your receiver translates the fluctuations of the radio waves it receives into sound.

Waves sent at the high end of the radio spectrum, between 1 and 300 GHz, are called *microwaves*. These high-frequency waves have numerous uses. As you may have guessed, microwave ovens use microwaves (2.45 GHz) to cook food. Microwave signals are also used for high-speed, high-capacity communication links and satellite communications.

Above microwaves in the radio spectrum come infrared light and then visible light. Infrared light is also used to carry telecommunications signals, as you'll learn later in the chapter.

Because of the convenience of wireless communications, advances in wireless technologies are occurring at a rapid pace and impacting all of our lives. For this reason, an entire section of this chapter is devoted to wireless technologies.

Networking Devices

Not long ago networking devices were of interest only to network technicians. Today, the increase in home networking and wireless networks has provided a reason for everyone to acquire a basic understanding of the most common networking devices such as modems, network adapters, access points, and other network control devices.

Modems. A **modem** modulates and demodulates signals from one form to another, typically for the purpose of connecting to the Internet. A modem can be either an internal or an external device. All methods of connecting to the Internet require some type of modem. Dial-up modems are standard on many PCs and support narrowband Internet connections over phone lines.

Other special-purpose modems support connections to high-speed networks. A *cable modem* provides Internet access to PCs and computer networks over a cable television network (see Figure 5.8). A cable modem is typically an external device that has two connections: one to the cable wall outlet and the other to a computer or computer network device. A *DSL modem* is similar to a cable modem and provides high-speed Internet service over telephone lines.

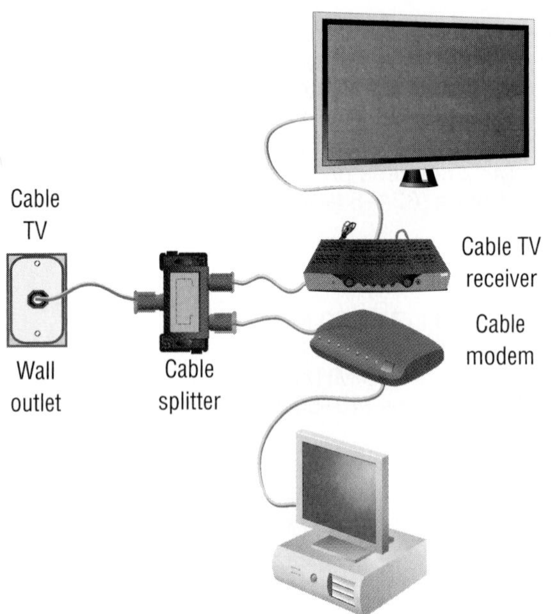

FIGURE 5.8 • Cable modem

A cable modem shares the cable TV connection to provide Internet access at data transmission rates much faster than a traditional dial-up connection.

Network Adapters. Computers can connect to networks and the Internet either by modem, network adapter, or a combination of both. A **network adapter** is a computer circuit board, PC card, or USB device installed in a computer so that the computer can be connected to a network. Network adapters come in two basic varieties: network interface cards and wireless adapters. A *network interface card (NIC)* is a circuit board or PC card that, when installed, provides a port for the device to connect to a wired network with traditional network cables. A *wireless adapter* can be a circuit board, PC card, or an external device that connects through a USB port (see Figure 5.9) that provides an external antenna to send and receive network radio signals. In addition to connecting devices to computer networks, network adapters are used to connect devices to cable modems and DSL modems.

FIGURE 5.9 • Wireless adapter

This wireless adapter connects to a PC or notebook computer via a USB port.

Network Control Devices. For multiple computers to communicate, special devices are required to control the flow of bits over the network medium and to ensure that information that is sent reaches its destination quickly and securely (see Figure 5.10). A number of different network control devices handle this responsibility. Table 5.1 provides brief descriptions of those that are most commonly used.

FIGURE 5.10 • Network control devices

A variety of special-purpose network control devices have been designed to control the movement of data over networks.

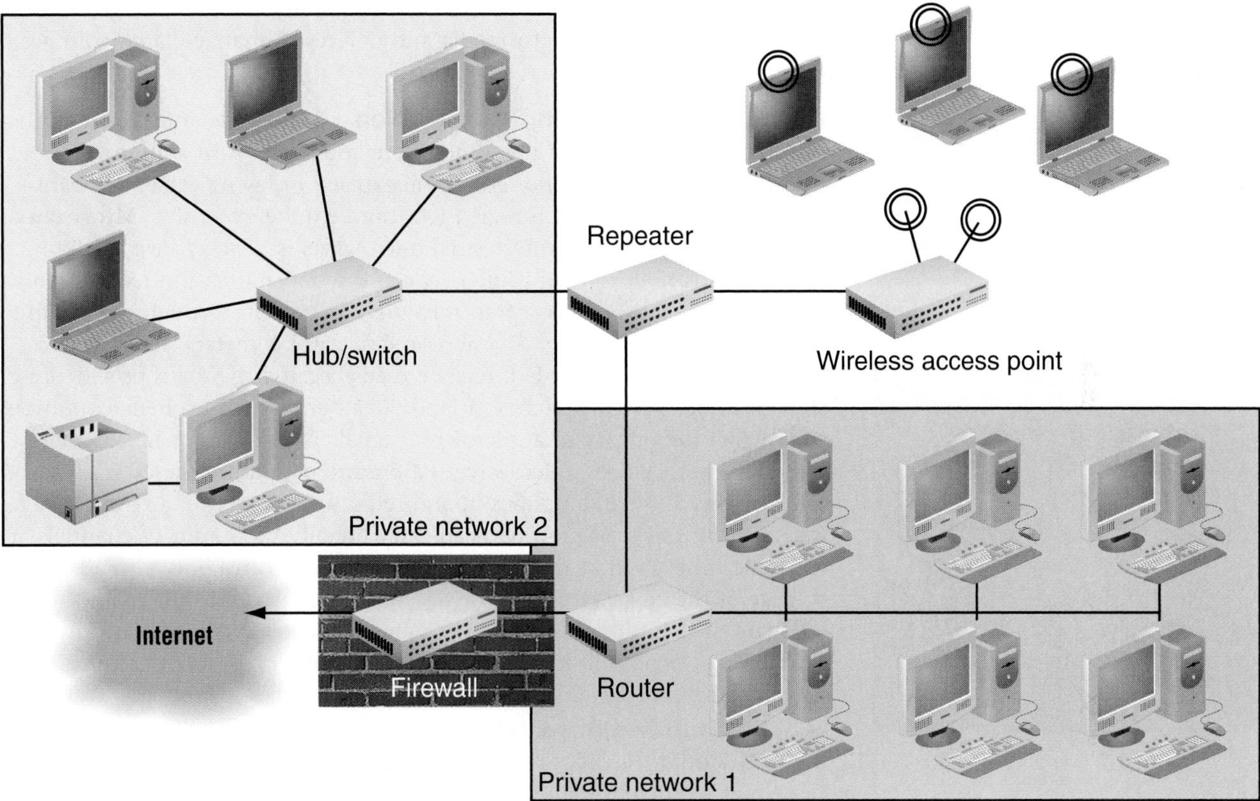

TABLE 5.1 • Network control devices

Network device	Purpose
Hub	A small electronic box that is used as a central point for connecting a series of computers; a hub sends the signal from each computer to all the other computers on the network.
Switch	A fundamental part of most networks; a switch makes it possible for several users to send information over a network at the same time without slowing each other down. Hubs and switches are often combined, and the terms are often used interchangeably.
Repeater	Connects multiple network segments; it listens to each segment and repeats the signal heard on one segment onto every other segment connected to the repeater. Repeaters are also helpful in situations where a weak signal requires a boost to continue on the medium.
Bridge	Connects two or more network segments, as a repeater does; a bridge also helps to regulate traffic.
Gateway	Network point that acts as an entrance to another network.
Router	Determines the best path for passing a data packet between networks to its destination.
Wireless access point	Connects to a wired network and receives and transmits data to wireless adapters installed in computers; it allows wireless devices to connect to a network.
Firewall	Device or software that filters the information coming onto a network; it protects the network computers from hackers, viruses, and other unwanted network traffic.

Sometimes network control devices can be combined in a single unit. For example, a home computer network might incorporate a device that includes a router to create a high-speed connection to the Internet, a switch to share Internet access over a wired network and connect computers, a wireless access point to connect wireless devices, and a firewall to protect the network from intruders.

Industrial Telecommunications Media and Devices

So far, you have learned about devices that most computer users encounter at some point while working with or setting up computer networks. Larger organizations require industrial-strength media and devices to manage large volumes of network traffic.

FIGURE 5.11 • Microwave towers

Microwave towers often support both microwave and cellular communications.

Microwave and Satellite Transmission. Microwave and satellite transmissions are sent through the atmosphere and space. Although using these transmission media does not entail the expense of laying cable, the transmission devices needed to utilize them can be quite expensive. **Microwave transmission**, also called terrestrial microwave, is a *line-of-sight* medium, which means that a straight line between the transmitter and receiver must be unobstructed. Microwave transmissions can be sent through the air up to distances of approximately 31 miles or about 50 kilometers. You often see microwave towers alongside interstate roads because the roads provide long, straight unobstructed stretches of land. Weather and atmospheric conditions can impact the quality of a microwave signal. Typically, to achieve longer transmission distances, microwave stations are placed in a series—one station receives a signal, amplifies it, and retransmits it to the next microwave transmission tower. Microwaves can carry literally thousands of channels at the same time. Even at that, a microwave link can carry only a small percentage of the capacity of a single fiber-optic strand. Once the main thoroughfare of the phone networks, today microwave towers support only a fraction of telecommunications traffic and often serve a more useful function as cell phone antenna towers (see Figure 5.11).

A **communications satellite** is basically a microwave station placed in the Earth's orbit. Satellites receive a signal from one point on Earth and then rebroadcast it at a different frequency to a different location (see Figure 5.12). The advantage of satellite communication is that it can transmit data quickly over long distances. This is important for companies that require high-speed transmission over large geographic regions. Problems such as the curvature of the Earth, mountains, and other structures that block line-of-sight terrestrial microwave transmission make satellites an attractive, albeit expensive, alternative.

Most of today's satellites are owned by telecommunications companies that rent or lease them to other companies. However, several large companies are now using their own satellites. Some large retail chains, like Wal-Mart, use satellite transmission to connect their main offices to retail stores and warehouses throughout the country or the world. Holiday Inn uses satellites to improve customer service by sending the latest room and rate information to reservation desks throughout Europe and the United States.

In addition to standard satellite stations, there are small mobile satellite systems that allow people and businesses to communicate. These portable systems have a dish a few feet in diameter that can operate on battery power anywhere in the world. This is important for news organizations that require the ability to transmit news stories from remote locations.

Exxon and Mobil gas stations offer a speedy way to pay for gas and merchandise. Wave a Speedpass key fob over the checkout keypad and within two seconds your credit is authorized and you are on your way. Speedpass utilizes two types of wireless networking technologies: (1) radio waves are sent from the key fob to the reader, relaying your credit card information and preferences, and (2) credit is quickly checked using high-speed satellite communications.

FIGURE 5.12 • Satellite transmission

Communications satellites are relay stations that receive signals from one Earth station and rebroadcast them to another.

Industrial Hardware. Large companies often lease dedicated lines from telecommunications companies to maintain long-distance connections. Unlike a *switched line* that maintains a connection only as long as the receiver is "off the hook," a *dedicated line* leaves the connection open continuously to support a data network connection.

To handle large quantities of data, businesses may lease a T1 line. A *T1 line* supports high data transmission rates by carrying 24 signals (64 Kbps) on one line. *T3 lines* carry 672 signals on one line and are used by telecommunications companies; some act as the Internet's backbone.

Managing industrial-level network traffic takes a considerable amount of orchestration. Signals sent over these high-speed lines must be processed in a manner that takes full advantage of the medium. Table 5.2 describes three devices that are commonly used to control and protect industrial-level telecommunications.

TABLE 5.2 • Industrial network control devices

Industrial network device	Purpose
Multiplexer	A multiplexer sends multiple signals or streams of information over a medium at the same time in the form of a single, complex signal. A demultiplexer at the receiving end recovers the separate signals. Often a multiplexer and demultiplexer are combined into one device.
Communications processor	Sometimes called a front-end processor, this device is devoted to managing communications to and from a large computer network
Encryption device	An encryption device is installed at the sending computer to alter outgoing communications according to an encoding scheme that makes the communications unintelligible during transport; a decryption device is installed at the receiving computer to decode incoming data and return it to its original state

Networking Software

As you have learned in previous chapters, hardware is useless without the software necessary to drive it, and so it is with networks. Networking software performs a number of important functions in a computer network. It monitors the load, or amount of traffic, on the network to ensure that users' needs are being met. It provides error checking and message formatting. In some cases, when there is a problem, the software can indicate what is wrong and suggest possible solutions. Networking software can also provide data security and privacy. Because networking software's main purpose is to support the functioning of the network, it is considered utility software. In its role as a utility, networking software runs mostly unnoticed by network users—with the exception of the network administrator.

A *network administrator*, sometimes called a *system administrator*, is a person responsible for setting up and maintaining the network, implementing network policies, and assigning user access permissions. A large organization might employ dozens of network administrators. With the increasing popularity of home networks, many nontechnical computer users are finding themselves in the role of network administrator. For example, a mother may find herself setting up a home network in a manner that filters out adult Web content from her children's computers. This section discusses a variety of commonly used network utilities.

Network Operating Systems. In Chapter 3, you learned that all computers have operating systems that control many functions. When an application program requires data from a disk drive, it goes through the operating system. Consider a scenario where many computers are accessing resources such as disk drives, printers, and other devices over a network. How does an application program request data from a disk drive on the network? The answer: through the network operating system.

A *network operating system (NOS)* performs the same types of functions for the network as operating system software performs for a computer, such as memory and task management and coordination of hardware. When network equipment such as printers and disk drives are required, the network operating system makes sure that these resources are correctly used. Network operating systems come preinstalled on midrange and mainframe servers. All of today's personal computer operating systems, including Windows, Mac, and Linux, can function as NOSs as well.

Network Management Software. In addition to network operating systems, there are a number of useful software tools and utilities for managing networks (see Figure 5.13). With network management software, a manager on a networked desktop can monitor the use of individual computers and shared hardware (such as printers), scan for viruses, and ensure compliance with software licenses. Network management software also simplifies the process of updating files and programs on computers on the network. Changes can be made through a communications server instead of on each individual computer. Some of the many benefits of network management software include fewer hours spent on routine tasks (such as installing new software), faster response to problems, and greater overall network control.

FIGURE 5.13 • Monitoring network usage

This network traffic monitor displays levels of incoming and outgoing packets over several Internet gateways at FSU over the course of 24 hours.

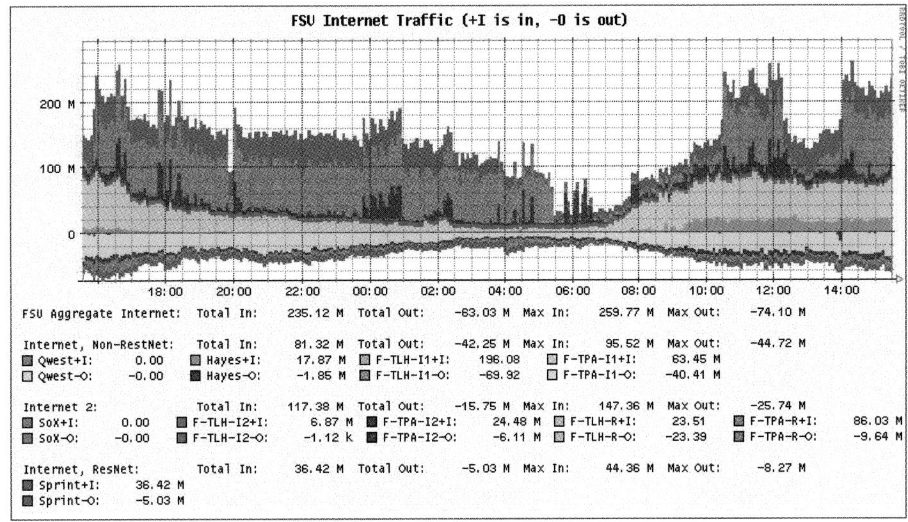

Network Device Software. Routers, switches, firewalls, modems, and other network control devices include software interfaces that allow you to change device settings. Once the device is connected to the network, its software interface can be accessed from a network computer. A wireless access point's software can be accessed to change security settings so that unauthorized users cannot access the network. A router's software can be used to divide a physical network into multiple virtual networks. A firewall's software can be used to specify what data packets to allow in and which to keep out. Software for a dial-up modem might allow you to enable or disable call waiting.

Communications Protocols and Standards. In Chapter 4, you learned that a *protocol* is an agreed-upon format for transmitting data between two devices. In Chapter 2, you learned that a *standard* is an agreed-upon way of doing something within an industry. In the world of networking, protocols and standards are essential for enabling devices to communicate with each other. Protocols define the format of the communications between devices, and standards provide the physical specifications of devices and how they interconnect. In Chapter 4, you also learned that the Internet uses the TCP and IP protocols. TCP/IP is the default protocol for many private networks as well.

Ethernet is the most widely used network standard for private networks. This standard defines the types of network interface cards, control devices, cables, and software required to create an Ethernet network. Other network standards, such as *token ring*, use unique hardware and software that are not compatible with Ethernet. Special devices, such as routers or gateways, are required to connect networks that use different standards.

WIRELESS TELECOMMUNICATIONS TECHNOLOGIES

Wireless communications and computing are sweeping the globe. Six out of every ten people in the world subscribe to a cell phone service—that's 4.1 billion people in all. Most of the current growth in cellular communications is coming from developing countries as they join the digital economy.[7] Wireless technologies support today's mobile workforce and have led us into the era of communications and computing that can occur anywhere, at anytime. In the previous chapter, you were introduced to the many communications options available over wireless networks, such as voice, e-mail, and text messaging. Beyond communications, today's wireless technologies allow you to connect to public and private networks; access television, music, and games; find your current location on a map; and access numerous information services. Wireless technologies put the world at your fingertips on cell phones, notebook computers, and other mobile devices, wherever you may travel.

Cell Phone Technologies

Today's cell phone services are founded on and also limited by cellular network technology. A **cellular network** is a radio network in which a geographic area is divided into cells with a transceiver antenna (tower) and station at the center of each cell, to support mobile communications. If a cell phone user travels from one cell to another, the system judges the cell phone's location based on its signal strength and passes the phone connection from one cell tower to the next. The signals from the cells are transmitted to a receiver and integrated into the regular phone system (see Figure 5.14).

Each cell tower has a transmission and receiving range of 3–15 miles (about 5–24 kilometers) depending on geography and environment. Because it is not economically feasible to cover the entire planet with towers every few miles, cell phone usage is limited to a network's coverage areas. The inability to provide 100 percent coverage and the limitations of working with wireless signals that are prone to interference make for less-than-perfect quality of service for cell phone users. A 2009 *Consumer Reports* survey found that "sixty percent of readers were completely or very satisfied with their service."[8] Dropped calls and coverage limitations are the biggest annoyances to cell phone users. Such issues cause many users to switch carriers, making for a very dynamic and volatile industry, with carriers falling in and out of favor each year.

WIRELESS CHECKUPS

Already, there are millions of mobile "telehealth" devices that physicians use to monitor the health of patients with chronic illnesses such as high blood pressure and diabetes. But that number will double in about two years. Wireless "telehealth" is increasing access and ease of home health monitoring. As health care workers and systems keep closer track of daily vital signs, they help patients avoid crises that land them in the emergency room. The result is fewer emergency room visits and improved patient care.

How emerging wireless techs are transforming healthcare
Brad Reed
Network World
September 8, 2009
http://www.networkworld.com/news/2009/090809-healthcare-wireless.html

FIGURE 5.14 • Cellular transmission

If a cell phone user moves from one cell to another, the system judges the cell phone's location based on its signal strength and passes the phone connection from one cell tower to the next.

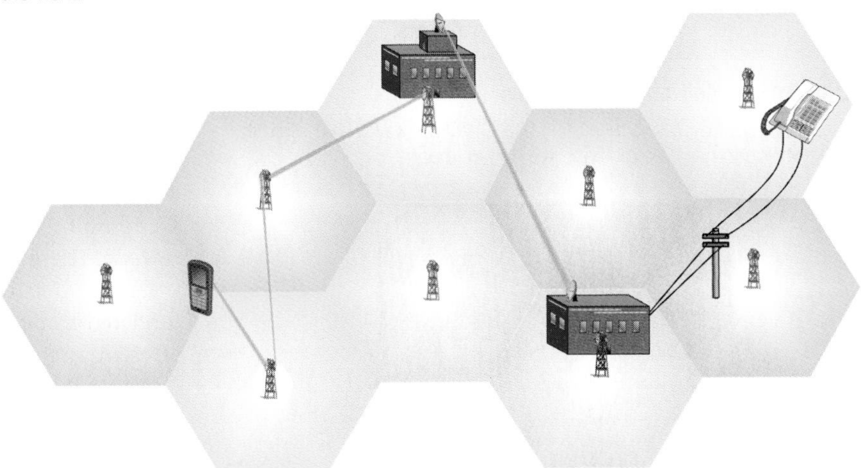

Cell phones provide more than voice communications. Today's cell phone users can choose to subscribe to dozens of communications, information, and entertainment services. Many in the telecommunications industry believe that the cell phone will become an individual's remote control to the world. For example, companies are deploying technologies that allow cell phone users to "point and click" at a cash register to pay a bill, at a billboard to order tickets to the concert advertised, or at a tag on a coat in a store to find out if they can get it for a better price elsewhere. Cell phones are able to plot your location on a map and, given that location, direct you to the nearest coffee shop. You can use your cell phone to access files from your home PC or e-mail from your Yahoo! account. Cell phones are becoming a primary information access device.

The technologies behind third-generation (3G) cell phones are providing the power necessary for many new and useful services (see Table 5.3 for information on cell phone generations). Current *3G cellular technology* is bringing wireless broadband data services to your mobile phone. Boasting speeds that compete with DSL and cable, 3G networks let you speed through Web pages, enjoy streaming music, watch on-demand video programming, download and play 3D games, and videoconference. Many favorite activities that people enjoy over high-speed Internet at home can now be taken on the road. The only limitation, which is substantial, is the tiny cell phone display.

TABLE 5.3 • Cell phone generations

1G–first generation	The original analog cell phone network
2G–second generation	Digital cell phone service
3G–third generation	Broadband Internet services over cellular network (today's networks)
4G–fourth generation	Very high-speed access, anywhere, anytime, to anything digital—audio, video, text, etc. (future networks)

Many of today's smart phones seek to minimize the limitation of display size by providing a display nearly as large as the device itself and a touch screen or slide-out keyboard (see Figure 5.15). Some smart phones allow you to zoom in and out of images, making it possible to navigate full-size Web pages and other documents.

FIGURE 5.15 • Cell phone keyboards

The Verizon/Nokia Twist swivels to reveal a QWERTY keyboard, while the T-Mobile MyTouch has a touch-sensitive soft keyboard.

Deciding on a cell phone service is no small task. The variables involved in the decision are many and complex. When you choose a cell phone service, there are three primary decisions to make: choose a carrier, choose a plan, and choose the phone, features, and services you want. These decisions are interdependent. Each carrier offers different phones, and services are related to phone capabilities. There are two different strategies for deciding on a mobile phone service. You can choose a phone first, and then find out which carriers support it, or you can choose a carrier first, and then choose one of the phones that the carrier supports. If you know of a phone that you simply must have, then the first strategy is for you. If you have a strong inclination for a specific carrier—for example, the carrier that *Consumer Reports* rates number one, or that your friends all use, or that you know has excellent coverage where you will be using the service—then the second strategy is for you.

Cellular Networks and Carriers. A **cellular carrier** is a company that builds and maintains a cellular network and provides cell phone service to the public. There are many carriers providing cell phone service worldwide. The most popular U.S. carriers are Verizon, T-Mobile, AT&T, and Sprint. Different carriers offer different cell phones, features, coverage areas, and services. It is important to take your time when selecting, as your carrier will define your cell phone experience. It is typically costly and inconvenient to change your carrier once you've signed on.

Today's cell phone networks are nearly all digital. The areas of coverage that still use the old analog network technology are being rapidly updated to digital technology. The predominant digital networking standards for cell phone networks are GSM and CDMA. *GSM* is the most popular international standard for mobile phones, used by over a billion people across more than 200 countries. The *CDMA* networking standard is predominantly used in the United States, where it is in equal competition with GSM. Verizon and Sprint are among the cell phone networks based on CDMA, while AT&T, T-Mobile, and others use GSM (see Figure 5.16). The two standards are not cross compatible. That is, handsets designed for CDMA networks cannot be used on a GSM network, and vice versa.

FIGURE 5.16 • GSM and CDMA

Today's cell phone carriers and handsets utilize either GSM or CDMA standards.

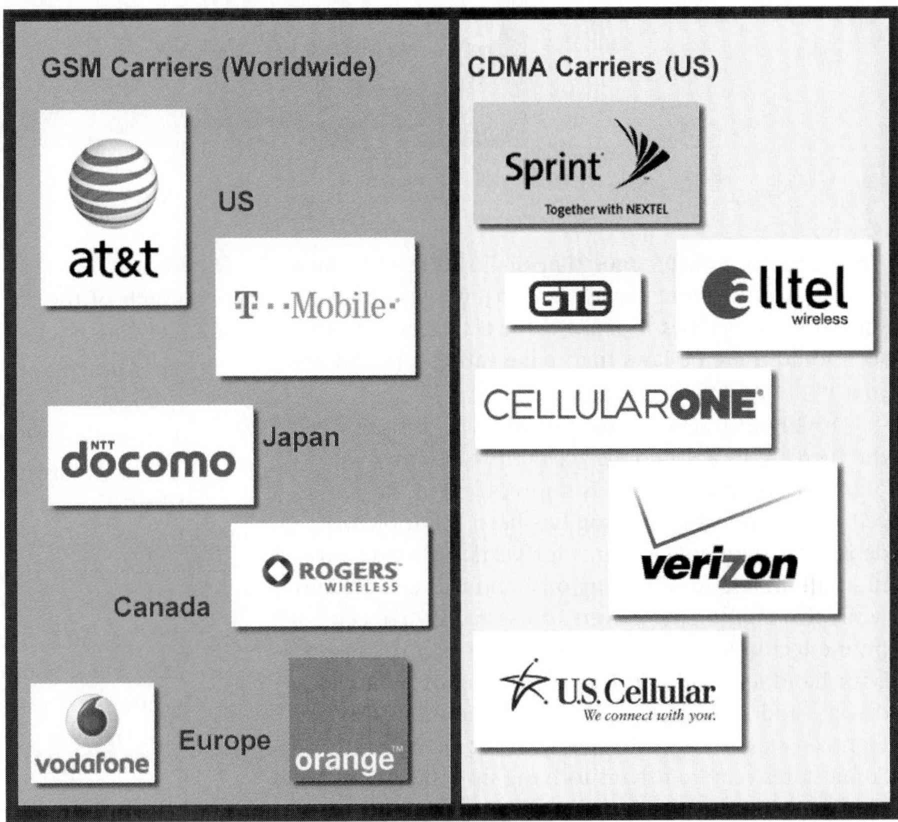

When choosing a carrier, it is useful to consult user survey data, such as that provided by *www.consumerreports.com*, as well as the opinions of friends. Check the coverage maps provided by the carrier's Web site to make sure that there is coverage in the areas you will be using your phone. Finally compare the carriers' networks (GSM or CDMA), phones, rates, and plans to find which best suits your needs.

Cellular Service Plans. Cell phone carriers offer service plans for every type of phone user. The trick is in determining your usage habits and needs. Do you plan to use your cell phone locally, regionally, nationally, or internationally? What time of day and days of the week will you use your phone? How many minutes during working days each week will you use your cell phone? Will you use your phone for data communications (Web access, e-mail, and so forth) as well as voice communications? These questions need to be addressed before selecting a plan.

Most carriers provide a choice of a "pay-as-you-go" plan without a contract, or a two-year subscription plan with a contract. Pay-as-you-go is a prepay system in which you buy minutes up front that must be used in a given time frame, such as 130 minutes for $25, which must be used in 90 days. Some pay-as-you-go plans charge daily rates for unlimited calls on the days that you use your phone. Users who opt to sign a two-year contract typically get a significant discount on their phone. Table 5.4 provides descriptions of common cell phone service options and specifications.

Driving Distractions

No one can seriously argue that dialing a cell phone or text messaging while driving isn't dangerous. But should there be laws to make these activities illegal? If so, should there be laws that make eating a burger and fries while driving illegal as well?

Driving distractions come in many forms; however, the increase in automobile accidents caused by cell phone use in recent years is unprecedented. Banning cell phone use while driving has been the topic of debate for state governments for years. Six states prohibit all drivers from talking on handheld cell phones while driving, forcing drivers to use hands-free cell phone technologies. Twenty-one states ban the use of both handheld and hands-free cell phones by novice drivers, and 17 states ban both for school bus drivers. Eighteen states ban text messaging for all drivers. Some states require drivers to hang up cell phones when entering school zones. A number of states have enacted laws against distracting activities in which cell phone use is included.

The U.S. federal government is considering putting pressure on states to ban text messaging while driving. A bill making its way through the Senate would impel states to draft texting laws or face a 25 percent reduction in federal highway funding. Sound severe? More than 46 countries around the world have completely banned cell phone use for drivers.

Questions

1. Which of the following do you support?
   a. Ban all cell phone use for drivers
   b. Allow hands-free cell phone use only
   c. Ban text messaging
   d. Some combination of the above
   e. None of the above

   Why?
2. Do you think it is wise to ban the use of cell phones while driving for novice drivers and/or school bus drivers?
3. Why would a state ban cell phone use in school zones but not elsewhere?
4. During what other activities might cell phone use be distracting and even deadly?

Sources

1. *Conneally, Tim, "New bill could make texting while driving illegal nationwide,"* BetaNews, *July 29, 2009, www.betanews.com.*
2. *"Cell Phone Driving Laws," Governors Highway Safety Association Web site, September 2009, http://www.ghsa.org/html/stateinfo/laws/cellphone_laws.html.*
3. *"Countries that ban cell phones while driving," Cellular-News, June 2009, www.cellular-news.com/car_bans/.*
4. *Vess, Jessica, "Drivers to hang up cell phones near schools," KVUE News, September 14, www.kvue.com.*

TABLE 5.4 • Cell phone options and specifications

Service option/specification	Description
Whenever, or anytime, minutes	The number of minutes per month, at any time of the day, that can be used for phone calls
Weeknight minutes	Typically Monday through Friday, 9:00 PM to 5:59 AM or 6:59 AM.
Weekend minutes	Typically Saturday 12:00 AM to Sunday 11:59 PM.
Rollover	A feature that allows you to apply unused minutes from one month to the next; because carriers charge you by the minute for any time used over your monthly allotment, rollover makes it possible to avoid those charges
"Mobile to mobile," "IN calling," or "in network"	Phone calls to other users of the same carrier; typically provided for free or at a steep discount
Additional minutes fees	Penalty for going over your allotted minutes for the month, typically charged by the minute
Roaming fees	Incurred when you use your phone outside your carrier's coverage area

If two plans from different carriers seem roughly comparable in terms of features, you should view the coverage map of both carriers (see Figure 5.17) and examine their phones and services. You should also find out which carrier your friends and family use, as phoning within the network typically saves you money.

FIGURE 5.17 • Cellular coverage

Cellular carriers provide coverage maps that illustrate signal strength in specific geographic areas.

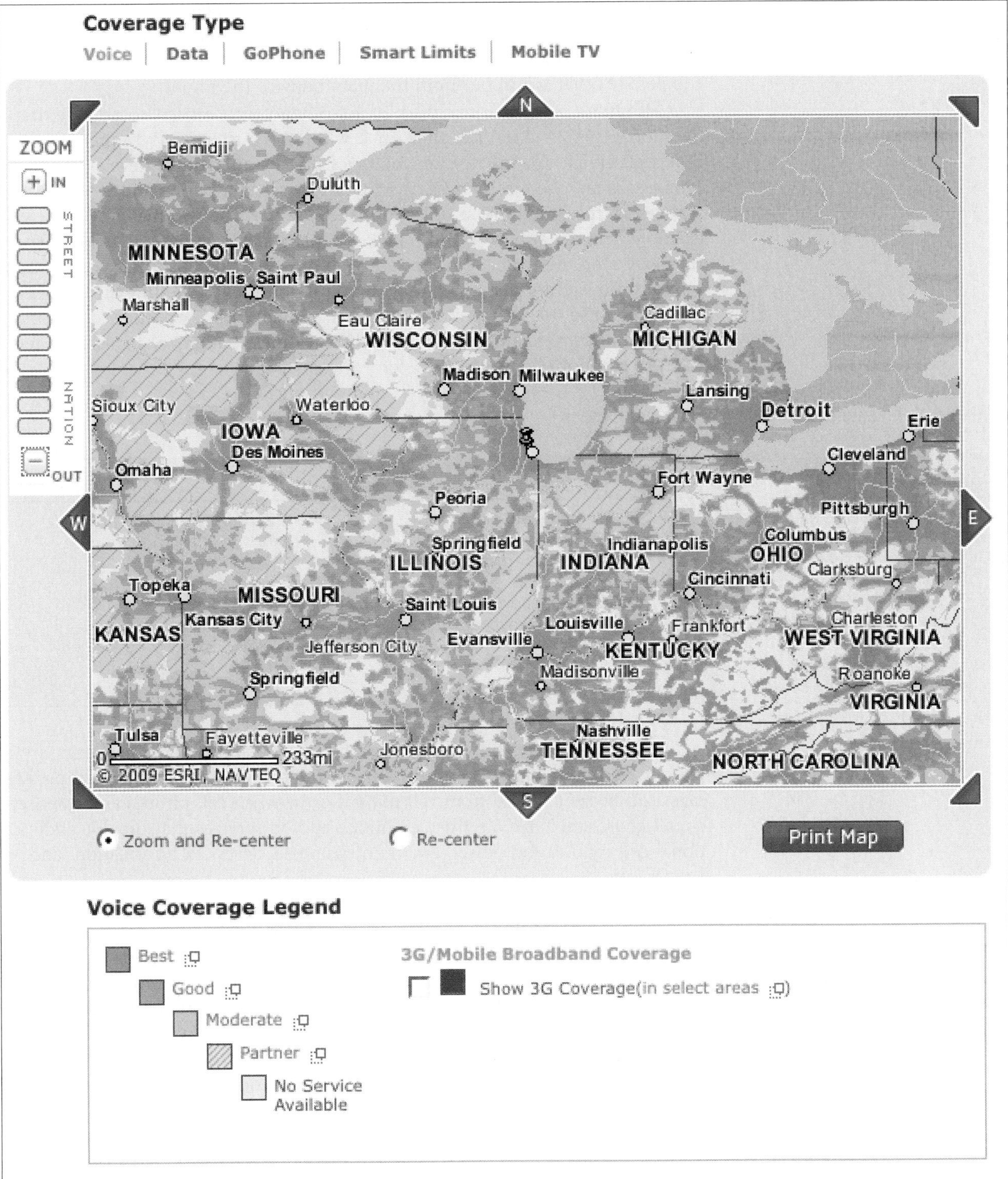

Cellular Handsets, Features, and Services. Advances in cell phone handsets have been fast and furious in recent years, with manufacturers such as Nokia, Samsung, Motorola, Audiovox, Kyocera, LG, Sony, HTC, and, Apple competing intensely to gain an edge in the largest technology market. Cell phone handsets range in price from free (with service subscription), to over $500 for the latest and greatest smart phones. There are several styles of cell phone: *Clamshell phones* consist of two halves hinged to open and close like a clam shell. *Bar phones* are a solid monolith leaving the display and buttons unprotected. *Flip phones* are bar phones with a cover that flips over the display and buttons. A *slide phone* has components, typically a keyboard, that slide out of the phone body. *Swivel phones* have components that swivel out from the main body of the phone.

Cell phone manufacturers work hand-in-hand with carriers to provide the functionality for the services they offer, while the carriers work to provide support and services for the new technologies that manufacturers develop. Because phones are matched to services, users typically select a phone and subscribe to services at the same time in order to make sure that the two match. For example, you wouldn't want to purchase a plan that includes a data plan but then buy a phone that doesn't have a Web browser. Note also that you are not typically allowed to take a phone with you if you move to a different carrier (unless you use tricks to "unlock" your cell phone); this is another reason to choose your carrier carefully. Table 5.5 lists features that are available on some of today's cell phones, and the list is growing.

TABLE 5.5 • Features available on some cell phones

Cell phone features		
• Bluetooth wireless technology • Camera • Changeable face plate • Color display • External caller ID • External display (clamshell phone) • GPS • Infrared and USB • Internet ready, PDA	• Memory card slot • MP3 player • MP3 player control buttons • Push to talk • Quad band world phone • QWERTY keyboard • Ruggedized • Speakerphone • Stereo headset	• Synchronization with PC • Text to speech • Touch screen • Vibrate mode • Video camera • Video player • Voice dialing • Wi-Fi

Cell phone carriers provide features that can be added on to monthly service plans at additional cost. The most popular add-on service is text messaging. Messages can be sent to and from cell phones or between cell phones and Internet e-mail addresses. Table 5.6 lists cell phone add-on services that provide additional communication power, entertaining media, access to information, and even safety.

Carriers are increasingly supporting Internet-delivered services. Map applications like Google Maps can be very useful for finding your way around a strange town. They become even more powerful if the cell phone is equipped with GPS so the map application can determine your current location automatically. YouTube is another Internet-delivered service provided as entertainment from a number of carriers. Weather forecasts are also a popular service. Social networks such as Facebook have applications that run on many different types of handsets; in fact, some handset manufacturers are designing handsets to facilitate social networking.[9] Microsoft has stepped up its efforts to bring Microsoft Office to more handsets as well.[10]

TABLE 5.6 • Cell phone add-on features and services

Feature	Description
Text messaging	Send text between phones or e-mail addresses
Data plans	Access Internet services, including Web browsing and e-mail
Picture and video messaging	Send images and videos phone to phone, or phone to e-mail
Instant messaging	Send messages to friends on AIM, ICQ, MSN Messenger, or Yahoo! Messenger
Push to talk	Connect using a walkie-talkie style interface
E-mail	Use carrier's e-mail service or your own corporate server
Airfone	Transfer your calls to the Airfone located in aircraft
Personalized ringtones	Hear music or sound clips when your phone rings
Caller tunes, ringback tones	Have your friends hear music or sound clips when they call you rather than the usual ringtone
Music ring tones	Hear tunes as recorded by original artists when your phone rings
Wallpaper	Customize the look of your display
Games	Play video games on your phone
Video on demand	Enjoy streaming video over broadband on your phone
Basic text info	Access news, weather, sports, horoscope, movie listings, and so on from leading providers such as CNN and ESPN
411 directory information	Have live operators answer your questions
Alerts	Schedule news to be delivered, such as news, sports scores, stock alerts, and so on
Roadside assistance	Get free jump starts, tire changes, refuels, lockout assistance, and towing from wherever you stall
Phone insurance	Have your phone replaced for free if it is lost, stolen, or damaged

FIGURE 5.18 • Hands-free phoning

Cell phone headsets provide for hands-free phoning, which is especially useful when driving.

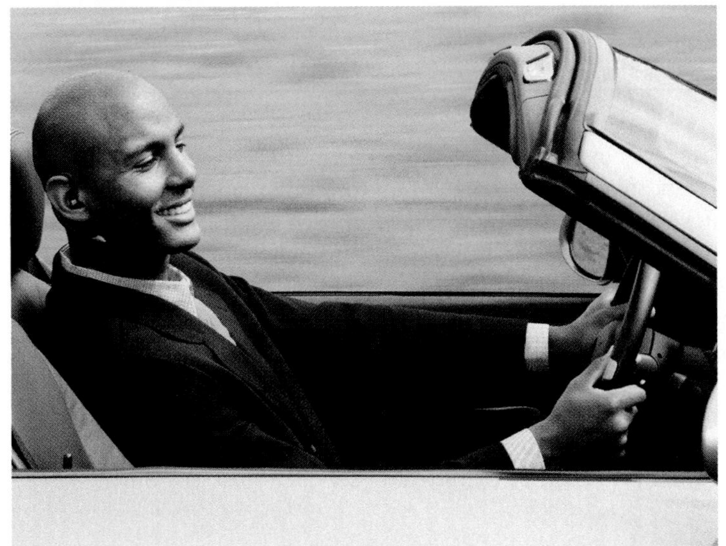

After selecting a carrier, plan, phone, and add-on services, you can also select cell phone accessories, such as a case or car charger, or a headset or earbud for hands-free phoning (see Figure 5.18). Some U.S. states are making headsets a requirement for using cell phones while driving (see the Community Technology box). If your cell phone plays digital music or other media, you may wish to purchase stereo headphones and an additional memory module for storing music and movies. Tiny memory modules based on a format developed by the SanDisk (SD) company called miniSD or microSD cards can add gigabytes of memory to your cell phone.

Pagers

Pagers are small, lightweight devices that receive signals from transmitters. Different pagers have varying levels of functionality. The most basic pager simply beeps, flashes, or vibrates to get the attention of the user. More sophisticated pagers accept numeric or text messages. Some pagers allow the owner to listen to voice messages, or send messages as well as receive them.

There are different types of paging systems. National and regional systems set up transmission towers, much like cell phone networks, to cover large geographic

Wireless E-Book Delivery

Competition in the e-book market is heating up. Looking at the competitors and their products, you can see that there are three components to a successful e-book platform: (1) an e-book reader (either a dedicated device or software for computers and mobile devices), (2) an extensive e-book catalog, and (3) wireless e-book delivery.

Amazon's e-book reader, the Kindle™, provides access to a library of more than 350,000 books that can be downloaded wirelessly over Whispernet, a cellular data network provided by Sprint. Sony's latest Reader™ provides access to a library of around 600,000 titles over a cellular data network provided by AT&T, and Sony has partnered with Google to gain access to over a million free public domain titles in Google's digital library via Internet download.

Barnes & Noble has partnered with e-book reader manufacturer Plastic Logic and wireless provider AT&T to provide wireless access to the "World's Largest eBookstore" of 700,000 titles. Barnes & Noble has the added advantage of owning brick-and-mortar book stores, where customers can hang out, drink coffee, and utilize free Wi-Fi to peruse and download e-books. Digital delivery of e-books seems to be a strong contributor to expanding wireless coverage.

Questions

1. Based on the information provided here, which of these e-book companies would you choose? Why?
2. An alternative to a dedicated e-book reader is delivery over the Web to your computer. Would you prefer reading books on a dedicated device or on your notebook computer? Why?
3. Why do you think publishers prefer utilizing dedicated e-book readers over Web delivery?

Sources

1. *Fallon, Sean, "Barnes and Noble Announces 'World's Largest eBookstore,' Upcoming eReader,"* Gizmodo, *July 20, 2009, http://gizmodo.com.*
2. *Ganapati, Priya, "Plastic Logic E-Book Reader to Use AT&T Wireless,"* Wired, *July 22, 2009, www.wired.com.*
3. *Guevin, Jennifer, "Google deal brings classic books to Sony Reader,"* Cnet News, *March 19, 2009, http://news.cnet.com.*
4. *McCracken, Harry, "Sony's E-Reader Finally Goes Wireless,"* EthioPlanet, *September 13, 2009, www.ethioplanet.com.*
5. *Hamblen, Matt, "Barnes & Noble to offer free Wi-Fi,"* Computerworld, *July 29, 2009, www.computerworld.com.*

areas. On-site paging systems use small desktop transmitters to send pages over a small wireless network that covers a range of up to 2 miles (about 3 kilometers).

On-site paging systems are finding a variety of uses in businesses and organizations. Pagers are being used in businesses to assist in customer service. For instance, in restaurants, emergency rooms, and golf courses, pagers can be given to customers and used to indicate when a table, doctor, or tee time is available. Pagers can also be used to call servers when food is ready to be served, or to call store managers to a checkout counter for a price check or check validation. Pagers can eliminate the need for invasive and annoying public address announcements, while supporting finely tuned orchestration between staff members and the provision of high-quality service to the customer.

Global Positioning Systems

A **global positioning system (GPS)** uses satellites to pinpoint the location of objects on Earth. Using a GPS receiver and a network of 24 satellites, the GPS can tell you the exact location of the receiver on the Earth's surface. The GPS satellites orbit the Earth in such a way that at any given time and location on Earth, four satellites are visible to a GPS receiver. By measuring the distance from the receiver to each satellite, and calculating those distances with the known position of each satellite, the receiver is able to determine its location on Earth. Like the Internet, GPS was originally developed for national security and later extended for public use.

FIGURE 5.19 • Cell phone with GPS

Cell phones with GPS have the capacity to provide turn-by-turn navigation.

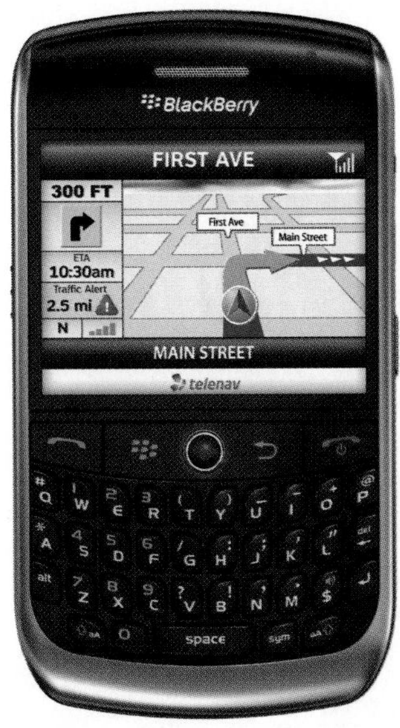

Early GPS receivers were expensive and used only in environments where determining your location was a matter of life and death, such as in far-traveling ships. Now, you can purchase a GPS receiver for under $130, and they are becoming increasingly popular in a variety of applications. Available as small handheld devices, add-ons for handheld computers and cell phones (see Figure 5.19), and as in-dashboard devices for automobiles, GPS receivers are primarily used to assist travelers in getting from one place to another. GPS software can display a traveler's location on a city map and give suggestions for the shortest routes to destinations.

Many car rental companies provide GPS units in order to assist customers from out of town with navigating in an unfamiliar city. The Hertz company developed a GPS service they call Never Lost (*http://hertzneverlost.com*). The GPS receiver in the vehicle is programmed with the desired destination, and the system acts as a navigator providing specific instructions along the way.

GPS has also been used to map the planet's surface. For example, a GPS receiver was taken to the peak of Mount Everest in 1999 to determine the exact height of the mountain. It was measured to be 29,035 feet above sea level, 7 feet taller than the previously accepted height calculated in the 1954 Survey of India. The GPS also revealed that Mount Everest is moving northeast at approximately 2.4 inches a year.

Software such as Loopt and Google Latitude (Figure 5.20), available for PCs and smart phones, allows friends to network in a new way. Using GPS technologies, friends are able to ping each other to view current locations on a map. You can even discover nearby business and restaurants that your friends have identified as favorites.

FIGURE 5.20 • Google Latitude

Google Latitude uses GPS to discover friends' current locations.

The GPS provides convenience and safety; however, as with all technology that accesses personal data (such as a person's location at a given time), the use of GPS technology may infringe on an individual's right to privacy. Consider, for instance, the possibility of someone stashing a GPS locator in your car or backpack in order to track your movements.

Wireless Fidelity

Wireless fidelity (Wi-Fi) is wireless networking technology that makes use of access points to wirelessly connect users to networks within a range of 120–600 feet (32–190 meters). The Wi-Fi standards, also known as the *802.11* family of standards, were developed by the Institute of Electrical and Electronics Engineers (IEEE) to support wireless computer networking within a limited range at broadband speeds. Table 5.7 shows the data rates and frequency bands of the most popular 802.11 standards. Currently, 802.11n is the fastest and most popular Wi-Fi standard.

Wi-Fi technology uses wireless *access points* that wirelessly send and receive data using radio frequencies to and from computers and other digital devices equipped with Wi-Fi cards or adapters. Access points are connected to networks (via network cable) that are typically connected to the Internet (see Figure 5.21). So, when connecting to an access point, a wireless user also connects to a local area network and the Internet. Wi-Fi has a maximum range of about 600 feet (190 meters) in open areas and 120 to 240 feet (32 to 64 meters) in closed areas. Areas around access points where users can connect to the Internet are often called

EXPAND YOUR KNOWLEDGE

To learn more about wireless networks, go to www.cengage.com/computerconcepts/np/swt4. Click the link "Expand Your Knowledge" and then complete the lab entitled "Wireless Networking."

hotspots. By positioning wireless access points at strategic locations throughout a building, campus, or city, Wi-Fi users can be continuously connected to the network and Internet, no matter where they roam on the premises. Wi-Fi has become increasingly popular for home networks. It provides an affordable and simple way to connect home computers without the need to run cables throughout the house.

FIGURE 5.21 • Wi-Fi access points

Wi-Fi access points are distributed around a geographic area to provide a network connection wherever you roam.

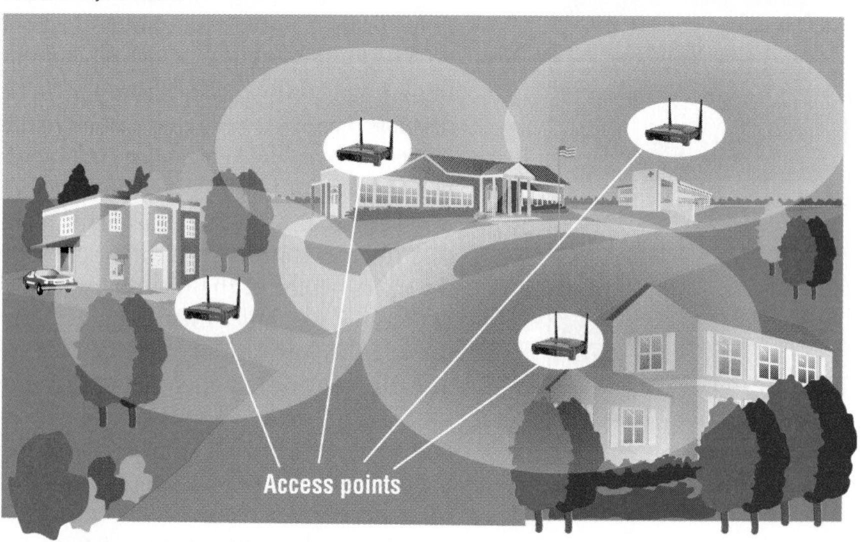

An increasing number of digital devices are incorporating Wi-Fi technology into their design. Most new notebook computers include Wi-Fi capability; however, most new desktop computers do not. Some printers have built-in Wi-Fi so that you needn't connect them to any single PC, but can print to them from any PC on the network. Wi-Fi capabilities can be easily added to a printer or computer by connecting a Wi-Fi adapter to the device's USB port. Game consoles like the Xbox 360 and PS3, and media devices like TiVo and Apple TV use Wi-Fi to connect home entertainment systems to home PCs and the Internet. Wi-Fi technology is even moving to automobiles. Autonet (*www.autonetmobile.com*) provides a mobile Wi-Fi hotspot for use in cars. The hotspot connects to the Internet over 3G cellular networks and disperses the wireless connection to passengers in the car.

TABLE 5.7 • Popular IEEE Wi-Fi standards

Wi-Fi standard	Maximum speed	Frequency band	Notes
802.11a	54 Mbps	5 GHz	Less potential for RF interference than 802.11b and 802.11g; relatively shorter range
802.11b	11 Mbps	2.4 GHz	Not interoperable with 802.11a; relatively larger range (fewer access points required) than 802.11a
802.11g	54 Mbps	2.4 GHz	Better security features and faster data rate than 802.11b; not interoperable with 802.11a
802.11n	600 Mbps	2.4 GHz and/or 5 GHz	Interoperates with 802.11 a, b, and g, but for maximum performance all devices should be 802.11n

An increasing number of cell phones are incorporating Wi-Fi to automatically switch over from the cell network to a faster Wi-Fi network where available for data and sometimes voice communications. The iPhone and other smart phones have the ability to connect to an access point for data communications such as e-mail and Web browsing, but not for voice. T-Mobile offers Unlimited Hotspot Calling that uses Wi-Fi for both data and voice communications where available. The service even provides a complimentary access point for use at home (high-speed Internet connection required), so that users are assured a good connection in their home. Using Wi-Fi for cell phones has the added benefit of saving the cell phone user the cost of minutes of connect time on the cell network.

Having a Wi-Fi-equipped device is useless, however, unless you have an access point to connect to. Access points are popping up in many locations where people tend to congregate. Internet cafés and even some McDonald's restaurants provide hotspots for their customers. Your school may offer hotspots on campus for wireless network and Internet access. If you do a lot of traveling you might want to look into Boingo. Boingo is a subscription service that for around $22 per month provides access to around 6000 hotspots in airports, hotels, cafes, coffee shops, and other public locations around the United States. Boingo Global provides service from over 100,000 hotspots worldwide.

Some cities, states, and even countries are providing free public hotspots. St. Cloud, Florida, and Mountain View, California, offer free Wi-Fi to residents and visitors. A number of cities such as Corpus Christi, Texas, and Tempe, Arizona, provide Wi-Fi Internet access for a small fee. Seattle, San Francisco, Austin, Portland, and Atlanta all rank high in providing their residents with wireless Internet. Overall though, U.S. cities lag behind other world cities in providing wireless Internet access. In Seoul, South Korea, Internet cafés and gaming parlors that offer free Wi-Fi, which South Koreans call "PC baang," are available on every street corner. Taipei, Taiwan, has installed 20,000 access points to service 90 percent of its population. Tokyo, Hong Kong, Singapore, and Stockholm all serve up inexpensive Wi-Fi to very large populations.[11]

In order to provide coverage throughout large geographic areas, many cities are incorporating *wireless mesh networks* that allow wireless routers to pass data over the network without being physically connected through wires. Wireless mesh technology saves a city from having to run cable to each of its access points.

A new type of voice communications technology that takes advantage of Wi-Fi network and VoIP (Voice over Internet Protocol) technologies is offered by Vocera Communications. The Vocera Communications system uses lightweight communications devices similar to the original Star Trek communicator, clipped to a lapel or pocket, or worn on a lanyard around the neck (see Figure 5.22).

FIGURE 5.22 • The Vocera Communications badge

Using Wi-Fi and VoIP, this hands-free device allows users to communicate with and locate others on the premises.

The Vocera device (which Vocera calls a badge) uses speech recognition to support hands-free communications. It is activated when you speak a command word. For instance, to initiate a conversation with Jim and Mary, the user says "Vocera, get me Jim and Mary." Jim's and Mary's badges alert them to your page and create a three-way connection for hands-free, wireless voice communications. The system allows users to be tracked geographically around a site and supports text messaging. The device is being marketed in several industries, including hospitals, where immediate communication among the staff can mean the difference between life and death.

4G Wireless Technologies

The race to get wireless broadband Internet connections to mobile users over large areas has begun. While Wi-Fi satisfies the need in small areas, it requires hundreds if not thousands of access points to cover a city. Cell phone technologies cover cities and large areas, but do not yet have the bandwidth to support high-speed Internet. Two technologies, WiMAX and Long Term Evolution (LTE), have emerged as fourth-generation (4G) solutions to offer Internet access over large areas with speeds that rival or surpass cable and DSL. Soon it may be possible to receive high-speed Internet at home, at work, in your car, on the street, in any restaurant or business, and everywhere you travel over one wireless network (see Figure 5.23).

FIGURE 5.23 • 4G networks

The WiMAX network card on this tablet computer allows it to connect to the Internet on the go.

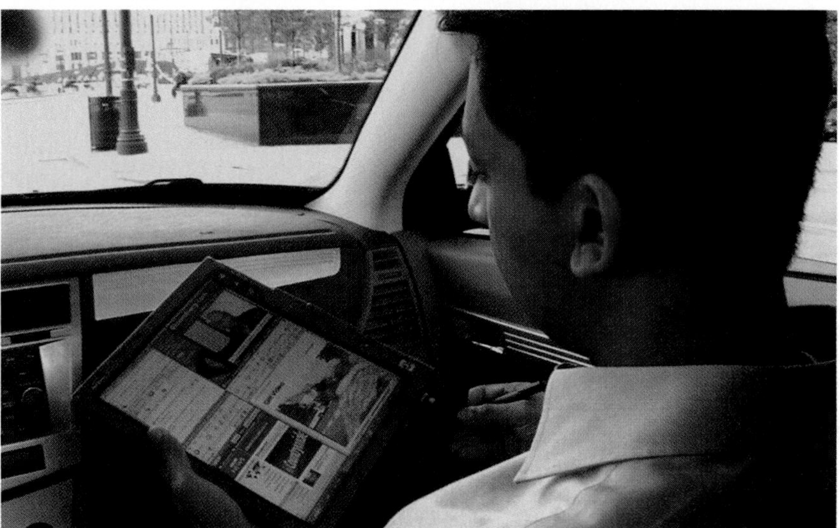

4G wireless technologies may provide a solution to the "last mile" problem. The *last mile* refers to the part of a telecommunications network that connects to residences and businesses. The problem with this portion of the network is that there are many residences and businesses and it is too expensive to deploy the fastest network components, such as fiber-optic cables, to so many end points. Using 4G would saturate citywide areas with high-speed Internet access, reducing, if not eliminating, the last mile problem.

WiMAX, which stands for Worldwide Interoperability for Microwave Access, also known as IEEE 802.16, is a next-generation wireless broadband technology that is both faster and has a longer range than Wi-Fi. WiMAX is built on Wi-Fi standards and is able to interoperate with Wi-Fi networks. A WiMAX access point has a

31-mile (50-kilometer) range and is a perfect technology to provide citywide high-speed Internet access (see Figure 5.24). Such networks are referred to as municipal wireless networks or muniwireless. Cities such as Chicago, San Francisco, and St. Louis have found the costs of Wi-Fi to outweigh its benefits. WiMAX can provide a better cost-benefit balance and bring muniwireless to many more cities. In fact, Seattle's famous Space Needle has become home to a WiMAX antenna that is providing high-speed Internet access to local subscribers that is comparable to premium cable modem service.

FIGURE 5.24 • WiMAX antenna

A WiMAX antenna can send a high-speed Internet signal up to 31 miles (50 kilometers).

Clearwire provides WiMAX high-speed Internet service in dozens of U.S. cities. Sprint offers WiMAX service called XOHM in Chicago, Baltimore, Washington, Boston, Philadelphia, and Dallas, with plans to expand to the rest of the country. WiMAX also has industry support from big companies such as Intel and Comcast.

Long Term Evolution (LTE) is a 4G wireless broadband technology that allows GSM cellular technology to provide very high-speed Internet access. LTE is being promoted by GSM cellular carriers such as AT&T and T-Mobile. LTE promises to bring wireless Internet connection speeds that are dozens of times faster than today's home connections. LTE is an extension of GSM, so only GSM carriers will be able to use it. However, Verizon announced that it will be pursuing LTE, indicating that its network will be gradually moved from CDMA to GSM.

LTE has the support of the big GSM network providers, and most international carriers, and it is currently considerably faster than WiMAX. Ultimately, LTE may be a large part of our 4G future, but it will face a number of obstacles. The biggest obstacle is the fact that WiMAX has a big head start. It remains to be seen if WiMAX, LTE, or some other newer technology will define the next generation of wireless networking.

Bluetooth

Bluetooth technology is becoming quite well known. Go shopping for a new cell phone or notebook computer, and there is a good chance that you will find Bluetooth listed among the specifications. The Bluetooth specification was developed by the Bluetooth Special Interest Group (BSIG), a trade organization composed of leaders of the telecommunications, computing, and network industries, such as 3Com, Agere, Ericsson, IBM, Intel, Microsoft, Motorola, Nokia, and Toshiba. **Bluetooth** (named after a tenth-century Danish king) enables a wide assortment of digital devices to communicate directly with each other wirelessly over short distances. Table 5.8 lists some Bluetooth-enabled devices.

TABLE 5.8 • Bluetooth-enabled devices

Some Bluetooth-enabled devices		
Personal computers Printers Keyboard and mouse	Mobile phones Handheld computers (PDAs) Digital cameras Portable MP3 players Headphones and headsets Speakers	Automobiles Microwave ovens Refrigerators Washers and dryers

Bluetooth-enabled devices communicate directly with each other in pairs. Up to seven devices can be paired simultaneously. The pairings may be created automatically or manually. For example, you might use a wireless headset to chat on a cell phone stored in your backpack. Your smart phone might be set to automatically synchronize with your personal computer when within range. The Lexus is among several cars that can pair with a cell phone to provide hands-free phone use (Figure 5.25). When the car is started, it automatically connects with your cell phone and displays your call info on an LCD display in the dash. The in-dash touch screen can be used to scroll through your address book, make calls, and check messages. The car utilizes a microphone and speaker on the driver's side for phone conversations. BMW, DaimlerChrysler, and Ford offer some form of Bluetooth connectivity in all or most of their cars in the United States. GM, Honda, Toyota, Lexus, and Volkswagen/Audi each offer at least one car with integrated Bluetooth.

FIGURE 5.25 • Lexus and Bluetooth

Once the Lexus pairs with your Bluetooth-enabled cell phone, you can make calls using the touch screen shown here, controls on the steering wheel, or voice commands.

There are three classes of Bluetooth with varying ranges and data rates. The most widely used version, Class 2, has a data rate of 3 Mbps and a range of

33 feet (10 meters). Bluetooth can also be used to connect devices to a computer network using access points, like Wi-Fi. Bluetooth and Wi-Fi compete in some areas but have unique qualities. Manufacturers are installing Bluetooth chips in a wide variety of communications and computer appliances to allow device-to-device connections. For example, six participants sitting around a conference table could exchange notes or business cards among their notebook computers or smart phones. In contrast, Wi-Fi is generally used to connect devices to a network and the Internet.

Infrared Transmission

Another type of wireless transmission, called *infrared transmission*, involves sending signals through the air via light waves. As mentioned earlier, these light waves are longer than the visible spectrum but shorter than radio waves. Infrared transmission requires a direct line-of-sight connection and operates at short distances. For example, your television remote control uses infrared to send signals to your TV, but it must be relatively close and have an unobstructed line-of-sight to the TV. Many notebook and handheld computers support the infrared data communications standard from the IrDA (Infrared Data Association) and include infrared ports called *IrDA ports*. External IrDA devices can be purchased and connected to desktop computers and printers. To transfer data between devices, you simply line up the infrared ports of the two devices within a couple feet of each other to create the connection. Once a connection is established, the operating system provides instructions or a wizard to allow you to share files.

Although infrared is slower than both Bluetooth and Wi-Fi, it has an advantage in that it uses light rather than broadcast technology. This makes it ideal for secure data transmissions that you do not want to have intercepted by spying devices. For instance, transferring credit card information to a cash register could be performed with infrared because the signal is directed to a specific device and is less likely to be hacked. ZOOP (*www.mzoop.com*), a South Korean company, provides a universal mobile payment system for cell phone users in South Korea and Japan. The system stores credit card information on the user's cell phone that can be transferred to cash registers, vending machines, and mass transit vehicles to pay for merchandise and services with a push of a button and an infrared signal.

Radio Frequency Identification (RFID)

Radio frequency identification (RFID) uses tiny transponders in tags that can be attached to merchandise or other objects and read wirelessly using an RFID reader. There are two important uses for RFID technology in today's marketplaces: embedded in products for identification and tracking purposes, and embedded in credit cards, cell phones, and other devices for enabling wireless transactions at checkout counters and vending machines.

For tracking merchandise, RFID tags are attached to products, and/or crates and pallets so inventory can be tracked from

RFID GUIDE DOGS?

Central Michigan University professor Kumar Yelamarthi and his engineering undergraduates are designing RFID products for people with disabilities. Their first prototype is a cane with a messenger bag for the blind. An RFID reader located in the bag helps the system determine the person's position along a preprogrammed route while an ultrasonic sensor in the cane detects obstacles. A speaker in the strap of the bag then communicates directions. Yelamarthi and his students are now hoping to turn the cane into a "canine" and develop the first RFID-enabled robotic seeing-eye dog.

Michigan Students to Develop RFID-enabled Robotic Guide Dog
Mary Catherine O'Connor
RFID Journal
September 14, 2009
http://www.rfidjournal.com/article/view/5214/1

the manufacturer to the retail store checkout counter. RFID tags consist of a transponder as small as a grain of sand, with an antenna embedded on a paper tag (see Figure 5.26). Readers may take the form of handheld devices, or devices mounted in the doorways of loading docks or in conveyor belt systems. It is anticipated that RFID will eventually replace the bar code as the primary identification system for merchandise since it is much more convenient and powerful. RFID systems are typically connected to central databases where inventory information is stored. As a tagged item progresses from manufacturing to warehouse to retail vendor to checkout counter, its database record is updated, providing up-to-the-minute information. This enables companies to gain better control over inventory, getting products to locations where they are needed just in time. Wal-Mart has required its suppliers to include RFID tags on all shipping crates and pallets.

FIGURE 5.26 • Radio frequency ID

RFID tags save time for Wal-Mart's distribution system. Automatic RFID scanning makes it unnecessary to open a box to find out what is inside.

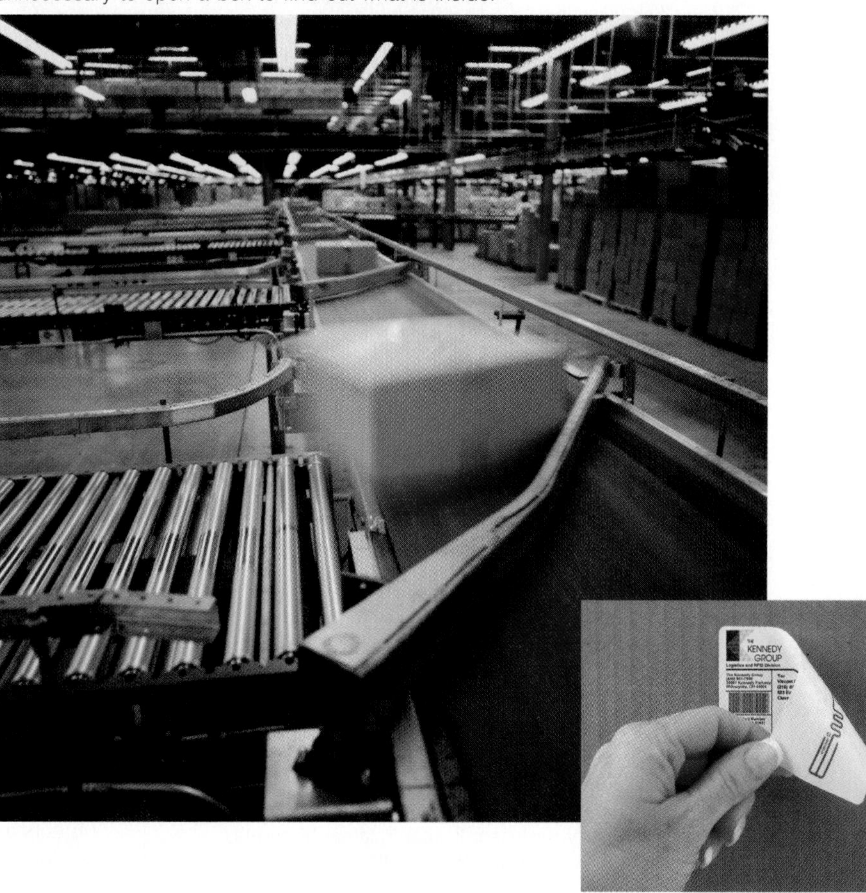

With the backing of huge retailers like Wal-Mart, it is clear that RFID technology for tagging merchandise is poised to take off. There are three issues that might slow the development of this technology: the inability of manufacturers to produce tags fast enough to cover individual merchandise items, the cost of tags for manufacturers, and concerns over privacy rights. Privacy advocates are concerned that if all merchandise contains RFID tags, it would become impossible to maintain privacy regarding one's own belongings.

RFID chips are being embedded in some credit cards to provide convience at the checkout counter. Rather than paying with cash or check, or having to swipe a credit card and provide a signature, RFID technology allows users to pay for merchandise by simply waving the credit card over a pad. *Contactless payment systems* make use of an RFID chip embedded in a credit card, ID card, and other device to wirelessly send data to an RFID reader installed in cash registers, vending machines, toll booths, and anywhere transactions take place (Figure 5.27).

FIGURE 5.27 • MasterCard PayPass

Just tap your card on the MasterCard PayPass reader, and you've paid.

Contactless payment systems are already in place in many businesses. For example, Boston commuters can make use of RFID-powered CharlieCards to electronically store and deliver subway fares. With lighter rules and restrictions governing credit card transactions that no longer require signatures and receipts for small purchases, it is expected that contactless payment will soon become the default payment method.

The obvious concern with contactless payment systems is security. If your credit card is transmitting private information through the air using radio signals, what's to stop a thief with a card reader from swiping that information? The credit card companies assure those concerned that they have a system in place to protect the private information, but some security experts remain skeptical.

Besides its use in retail inventory control and contactless payment systems, RFID is being used in a number of other areas where automatic identification is useful. Hospitals like the Jacobi Medical Center in New York City employ RFID patient wristbands to enhance patient care and staff working conditions, and to save on money and mistakes. Delta and other airlines are integrating RFID in their baggage-handling systems to more efficiently track the location of passenger baggage. Here are some other examples:

- A Spanish strawberry grower uses RFID to monitor the temperature of strawberries at the processing facility and as they are transported to buyers.[12]
- A Swiss art museum utilizes RFID and biometric technologies to analyze how patrons emotionally respond to various works of art.[13]
- RFID is used in safety devices that turn off the engine when a driver has fallen off a snowmobile.[14]
- The Shedd Aquarium in Chicago embeds RFID tags in aquatic objects in a simulated ocean floor to assist in educating children.[15]
- In Australia, RFID tags are used to identify the owners of trash receptacles and recycling bins.[16]

These are just a few of the thousands of applications of RFID. Other uses of RFID are more controversial due to issues of privacy. RFID chips have been embedded in the passports of international travelers. There is talk of embedding RFID tags in all automobile license plates, driver licenses, and even currency. RFID tags injected under the skin are used to track ex-convicts and employees in high-security facilities. Privacy advocates are concerned that RFID could be used in ways that infringe on privacy and civil liberties.

Near Field Communication (NFC)

Near field communication (NFC) technology is a wireless technology designed for short distances (up to 20 centimeters), aimed at utilizing cell phones for secure wireless payments. Nokia and mobile telecom carriers are using NFC to embed credit card information in a cell phone. The goal is to create a cashless and walletless culture where all you need to carry is your cell phone. With embedded NFC technology, you simply wave your cell phone over a cash register pad to pay. More expensive purchases might require keying in a four-digit authentication code. MasterCard has experimented with a cell phone version of its Tap N Go mobile payment system in New York City (see Figure 5.28).

FIGURE 5.28 • Paying with your phone

Near field communication (NFC) technology is being rolled out in the United States, enabling consumers to pay for products by waving their cell phone over a pad.

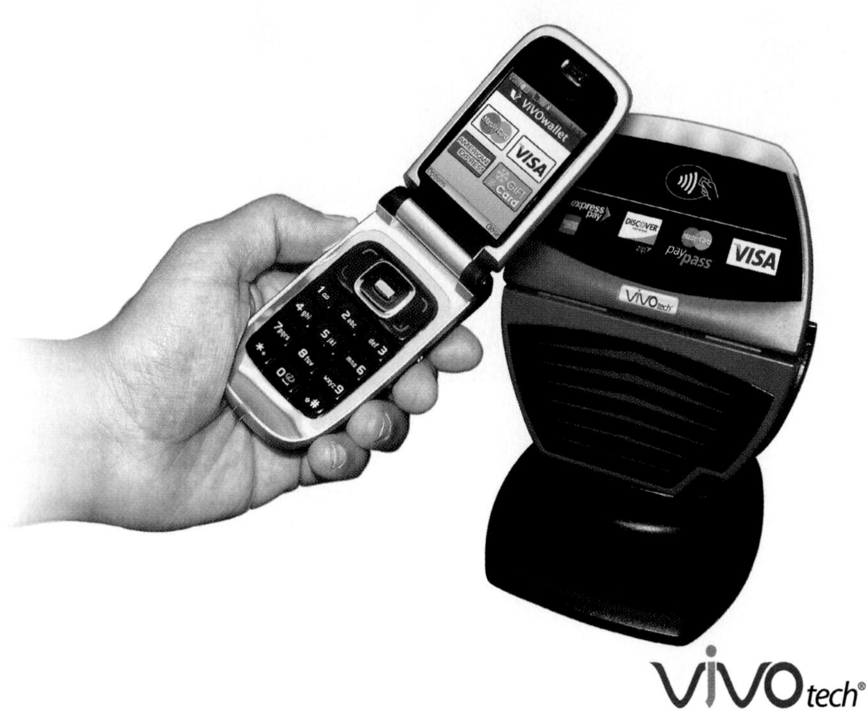

NETWORKS AND DISTRIBUTED COMPUTING

Most people are familiar with the benefits of sharing information between computers from their experience with the Internet and Web. Information sharing is just one of the benefits of networking.

Within a private network, computing resources are shared in order to maximize computing power and organizational effectiveness. You have learned that a computer includes devices for input, processing, storage, and output. These components can be distributed throughout a computer network. For instance, you may do your work on a terminal that connects you to a server shared by all employees in the organization. In such a scenario the input and output devices are on your desk, but the processing and storage may be handled at some other location. You may store your files on a network drive that exists on a file server and send your print jobs to a printer in a shared area of your office. A computing system may be distributed over components in one small business building, or around the world on a network operated by a global corporation (see Figure 5.29).

FIGURE 5.29 • Distributed network

As you sit at your desk at corporate headquarters, you may be accessing data from data centers around the world, and applications supplied by a server located across the country.

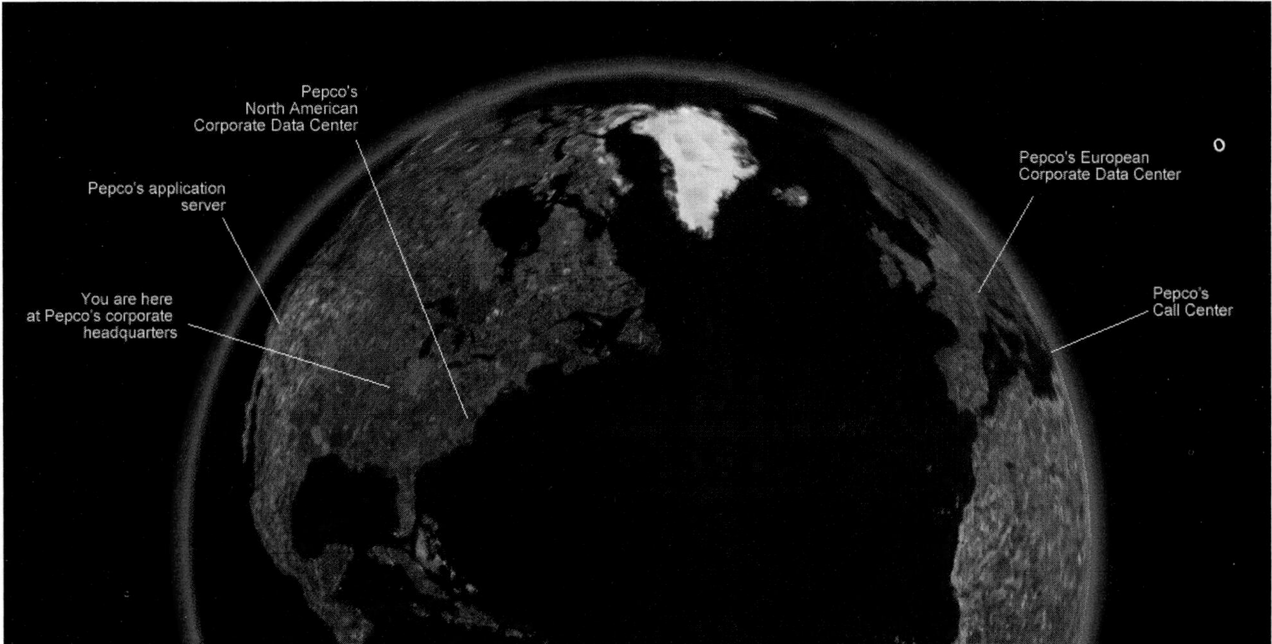

Computer Networking Concepts

Devices attached to a network are called *nodes*. Personal computers attached to a network are often called *workstations*. Workstations typically have access to two types of resources: local and network resources. *Local* resources are the files, drives, and perhaps a printer or other peripheral device that are connected directly to the workstation and accessible on or off the network. *Network* resources, also called *remote* resources, are resources that the workstation accesses over the network.

Network resources are often installed on a workstation in a manner that makes it difficult to tell which resources are local and which are on the network. For example, you might save a document on the F: drive. This drive could exist on your own workstation or on a server on the network. When you click the Adobe Illustrator icon to start the program, that program might be loaded from the local hard drive or from some other computer on the network. Hiding the underlying network structure from the user makes it invisible, or transparent, and uncomplicated to use. *Transparency* provides a more intuitive and user-friendly computing environment by hiding the complexities of the underlying system from the user. Rather than feeling like you are working on a 100-node network, you get the sense of working on one very powerful computer.

Distributed Computing. *Distributed computing* refers to computing that involves multiple remote computers that work together to solve a computation problem or perform information processing. Large businesses and organizations, sometimes called *enterprises*, make extensive use of distributed computing. In enterprises, distributed computing generally has meant putting various steps of business processes at the most efficient places in a network of computers. The user interface processing is done on the PC at the user's location, business processing is done on a remote computer, and database access and processing is done on another computer that provides centralized access for many business processes. Typically, this kind of distributed computing uses the client/server network model.

In Chapter 4, you learned that the Internet uses servers to serve up Internet resources, such as Web pages and e-mail, and it uses clients, such as Internet Explorer, to access those resources. Private networks also make use of client/server systems. *Database servers* store organizational databases and respond to user queries with requested information. *File servers* store organizational and user files, delivering them to workstations on request. *Application servers* store programs such as word processors and spreadsheets and deliver them to workstations to run when users click the program icon.

Hewlett-Packard (HP), IBM, and other enterprises provide a form of distributed computing through a technology called *blade computing*. Blade computing takes advantage of the fact that, of the many PCs installed in an enterprise, typically around 30 percent are not being used at any given time. In an organization with 1000 PCs, 300 of those PCs are not being used at any moment. Rather than removing 300 PCs from employees' desks and asking employees to share, the organization may replace the PCs with stripped-down network PCs called *thin clients* that cost less than half as much as a full-blown PC. A thin client includes a keyboard, a mouse, a display, and a small system unit that supplies only enough computing power to connect the device to a server over the network. Thin clients connect to clusters of blade servers. *Blade servers* are like PC motherboards that are rack-mounted together in groups of up to 20 to a case (see Figure 5.30). When an employee sits down to work at a workstation, the thin client connects with one of the available blade servers to provide a typical PC work environment. The result is a significant savings in equipment cost and energy.

FIGURE 5.30 • Blade server and thin client

HP's blade server includes many separate circuit boards that handle the processing for each thin client workstation.

Another technology that is creating savings for companies and the environment is virtual server technology. Similar to virtual machine technology, *virtual server* technology makes it possible to run multiple server operating systems on one server machine. Since servers are typically underused, the machines on which they run are capable of supporting many more operations. Virtual server technology allows each server to be used more economically, reducing the size of data centers and the related costs of electricity for servers and cooling systems.

Cloud Computing. A relatively recent networking trend that takes distributed computing to a new level is cloud computing. **Cloud computing** utilizes Internet-based service providers to deliver information and computing services, including software, business systems, and data storage, for business and personal use. The term "cloud computing" is derived from the use of clouds to represent the Internet in schematic figures (see Figure 5.31).

FIGURE 5.31 • Cloud computing

Cloud computing utilizes online service providers to deliver computing information and data storage services to individuals and businesses.

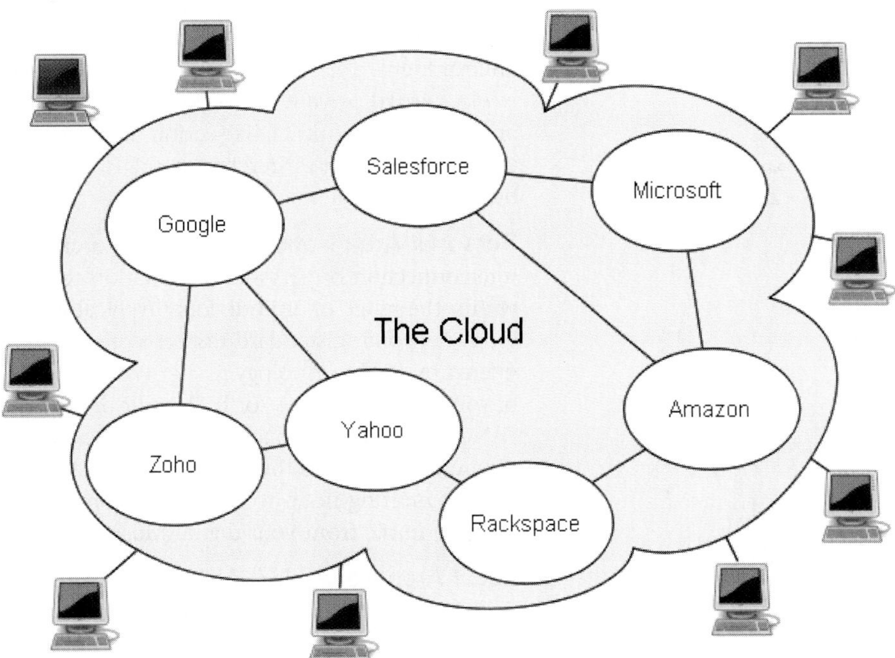

Cloud computing provides a valuable service to businesses and individuals because service providers shoulder the responsibility of managing computing resources. For example, users of Google Docs and Google Spreadsheet never have to worry about installing software or updates. They needn't worry about the software becoming corrupt from viruses. Nor do they have to worry about losing files due to hard disk failure. Google takes on all of that responsibility. The same holds true for businesses that utilize CRM cloud services from Salesforce.com. All their customer data and analytics are stored and managed by software and servers provided and maintained by Salesforce.com and delivered over the Internet via a Web interface.

The benefits of cloud computing are tempered by some risks. To place valuable data in the hands of a cloud computing service takes a lot of trust. Users must trust that their Internet service remains uninterrupted—the inability to connect to the Internet would mean the inability to work. Also, users must trust that the service provider backs up data reliably and handles data in a secure and private manner.

As Internet service becomes more robust and widespread, cloud computing is poised to take off. If successful, cloud computing can dramatically alter the manner in which individuals and businesses use computers. Computers would most likely transform from powerful computing devices with gigabytes of storage to simple, inexpensive Internet access devices designed to connect to the servers that deliver data and services. Giant data centers would spring up around the world to manage cloud computing's heavy computation and storage requirements, and service providers would become ever more important, shouldering a huge amount of responsibility and raking in a lot of money.

Network Types

Networks are classified by size in terms of the number of users they serve and the geographic area they cover. From a network that links two personal devices that serve an individual user, to international enterprise networks that serve large corporations, to the Internet, which serves the entire world, different types of networks are uniquely designed to accommodate the specific needs of their environment. Types of networks include personal area networks, local area networks, virtual private networks, metropolitan area networks, wide area networks, and global networks. This section also discusses home networking technologies and electronic data interchange (EDI), a network technology that provides links between businesses.

Personal Area Network (PAN). A **personal area network (PAN)** is the interconnection of personal information technology devices, typically wirelessly, within the range of an individual (typically around 33 feet or 10 meters). The Bluetooth networking standard discussed earlier brought attention to the conveniences offered by PAN technology. Using PAN technology you might be able to use one set of wireless headphones for both your digital music player and your cell phone. A PAN allows your notebook computer to automatically communicate with your cell phone to connect to the Internet. Your PAN could interact with other PANs to transfer meeting notes to others at a committee meeting or to allow your friends to listen to music from your digital music player on their headphones.

Local Area Network (LAN). A network that connects computer systems and devices within the same building or local geographical area is a **local area network (LAN)**. Figure 5.32 illustrates a LAN for a college campus. There are more local area networks than any other network type. LANs are used in homes, businesses, and other institutions and organizations.

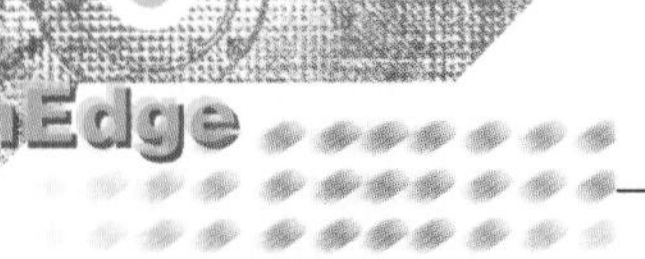

C-2-SHINING-C

You may think you should be pressing on the gas pedal, but sorry, your car just doesn't agree. It's been chatting with the SUV ahead of you, and they agree that you have a lead foot. Your car begins braking and saves you from a potential accident. That scenario may be a few years away, but European agencies and car makers are already working to create standards for car-to-car (C2C) communication, and to secure the data transmitted among these innovative wireless networks. The search for secure systems will hopefully prevent hackers from interfering in C2C communications and causing traffic jams or accidents.

On the road to secure car-to-car communications
ICT Results
September 14, 2009
http://cordis.europa.eu/ictresults/index.cfm?section=news&tpl=article&BrowsingType=Features&ID=90862

FIGURE 5.32 • Local area network

This local area network provides access to students and employees in campus buildings. The red lines represent fiber-optic cable, and the dots are nodes.

Local area networks can include personal computers, servers, printers, and other network-capable devices. Devices connect to LANs through network interface cards or wireless network adapters. Larger networks make use of servers to store databases, files, and programs. When a person on the network uses a program or data stored on the server, the server transfers the necessary programs or data to the user's computer. While servers are typically large multiuser computers, a server can be a computer of any size, even a personal computer. Any computer that serves up information or services to others on the network can be a server.

Since the rise in popularity of the Internet and Web, many LANs are incorporating familiar Internet technologies to create intranets. An **intranet** uses the protocols of the Internet and the Web—TCP/IP and HTTP, along with Internet services such as Web browsers—within the confines of a private network (see Figure 5.33). In an intranet, employees might access confidential documents using a Web browser, while those same documents remain secure from the outside world.

FIGURE 5.33 • Intranet

In an intranet, a Web server provides confidential data to LAN users, while keeping the data safe from those outside the organization through the use of a firewall.

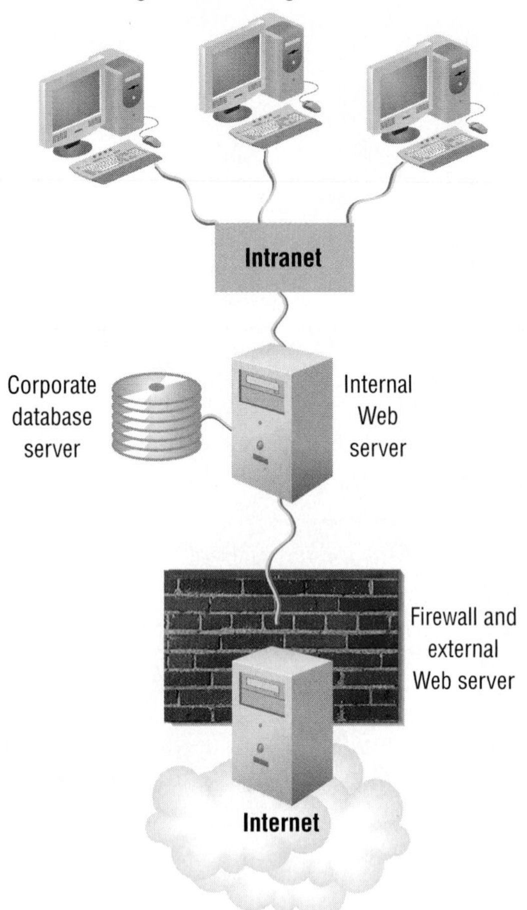

Enterprises typically allow users within their intranet to access the public Internet through firewalls that screen messages to maintain the security of the private network. An intranet may be extended beyond the confines of the LAN to connect with other networks to create a virtual private network. A **virtual private network (VPN)** uses a technique called *tunneling* to securely send private network data over the Internet. A VPN may be used to connect an organization's networks dispersed around the world into one large intranet.

Intranet content can be extended to specific individuals outside the network, such as customers, partners, or suppliers, in an arrangement called an *extranet.* Extranets are sometimes implemented through a simple login procedure on a Web server. For example, Wal-Mart provides key suppliers with access to its intranet so that they can see what products are selling fastest and ramp up production to meet the demand.

VPNs can also be used to allow employees access to the corporate intranet from home and while on the road. A large business or organization might hire an *enterprise service provider (ESP)* to set up a *network access server (NAS).* Users are provided with software that connects to the NAS, VPN, and ultimately the corporate intranet. Some services are set up so that if you have access to the Internet, then you also have secure access to your private intranet.

Metropolitan Area Network (MAN). A **metropolitan area network (MAN)** connects networks within a city or metropolitan-size area into a larger high-speed network. Many cities supply local businesses with access to a MAN to improve local commerce and communications. Often a MAN acts as a stepping stone to larger networks, such as the Internet. The WiMAX wireless high-speed technology introduced earlier is perfect for setting up a MAN, as it has a range to cover a city. The city of Corpus Christi, Texas, boasts a 147-square-mile Wi-Fi network designed to support public works and public safety departments. The city saves a significant amount of money with its ability to read meters digitally over the network, and police officers are able to perform more effectively given instant access to criminal records and mug shots.

Wide Area Network (WAN). A **wide area network (WAN)** connects LANs and MANs between cities, across country, and around the world using microwave and satellite transmission or telephone lines. A LAN becomes a WAN when it extends beyond one geographic location to another geographic location (see Figure 5.34). When you make a long-distance phone call, you are using a wide area network. AT&T, Verizon, Sprint, and other telecommunications companies are examples of companies that offer WAN services to the public. Companies, organizations, and government agencies also design and implement WANs for private use. These WANs usually consist of privately owned LANs connected over a dedicated line provided by a telecommunications company. For example, your college may maintain a LAN that covers the campus. The college network engineers may have laid fiber-optic cable across campus and connected it to networks in each building to provide high-speed networking to students, faculty, and staff. This network is owned and controlled by the college. If your college should decide to open a branch campus across the state, administrators may decide to join the LAN of the main campus with the LAN of the branch campus. Using a dedicated line leased from the phone company, your college creates a WAN by joining the two LANs.

FIGURE 5.34 • Wide area network (WAN)

A WAN connects LANs between cities, across country, and around the world using microwave and satellite transmission or telephone lines.

Global Networks. A WAN that crosses an international border is considered a global or international network. The Internet is the most obvious global network, but as an increasing number of businesses are entering global markets, private global networks are becoming more prevalent.

Creating and maintaining a global network has its challenges. In addition to requiring sophisticated equipment and software, global networks must meet specific national and international laws regulating the electronic flow of data across international boundaries, often called *transborder data flow.* Some countries have strict laws restricting the use of telecommunications and databases, making normal business transactions, such as payroll, costly, slow, or even impossible. Other countries have few laws restricting the use of telecommunications or databases. Other governments and companies can avoid their own country's laws by processing data within the boundaries of other countries, sometimes called *data havens*, that have few restrictions on telecommunications or databases. For example, the popular file-sharing service KaZaA was able to escape prosecution for many years by maintaining servers in Denmark, registering its domain in Australia, and running its software from the South Pacific island nation of Vanuatu, a well-known data haven.

Despite the obstacles, there are numerous private and public international networks. United Parcel Service (UPS), for example, covers over 200 countries with its international UPSnet network. UPS drivers use handheld computers

FIGURE 5.35 • UPS DIAD

A poster child for wireless networking, the latest version of the UPS DIAD is equipped with a bar code scanner, GPS receiver, Bluetooth, and Wi-Fi to assist drivers in organizing and delivering packages.

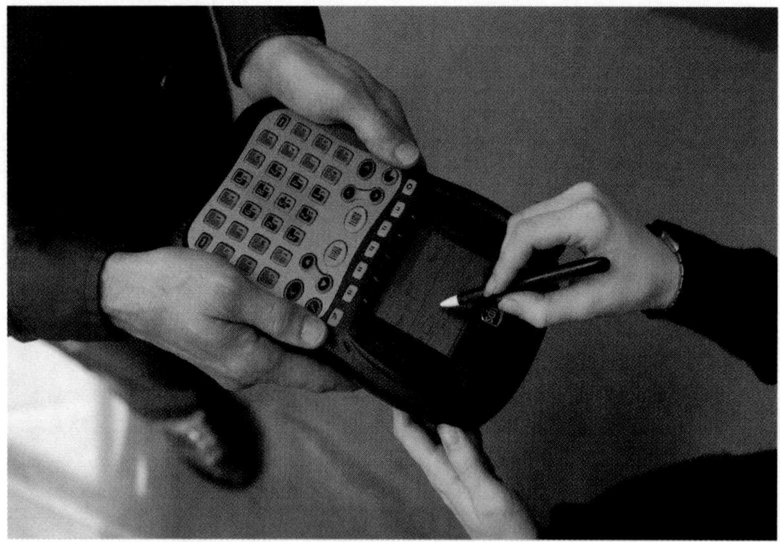

called DIADs (delivery information access devices) to send real-time information about pickups and deliveries to central data centers via UPSnet (see Figure 5.35). The GPS integrated into the system notifies drivers if they are about to deliver a package to the wrong location. In addition to the 81,000 DIADs for drivers, UPSnet uses 15 mainframes, 2342 mid-range computers, 8973 servers, 149,000 workstations, several satellite dishes, and enough fiber-optic cable to wrap around the Earth 25 times.[17] The huge network allows customers to retrieve data to track packages and the company to use data for faster billing, better fleet planning, and improved customer service.

Electronic Data Interchange (EDI). Connecting corporate computer systems among organizations is the idea behind *electronic data interchange (EDI).* EDI uses network systems and follows standards and procedures that allow output from one system to be processed directly as input to other systems, without human participation. With EDI, the computers of customers, retailers, manufacturers, and suppliers can be linked, typically utilizing the Internet. For example, as the cashier scans the bar code of the new blue jeans that you are purchasing, the inventory count of that item is decreased by one. The effect of the decrease may bring the total inventory amount for that item below a set threshold, indicating that more jeans need to be ordered. Because the retail store's computer system is connected to the supplier's computer system, the order for more jeans can be made automatically. The supplier's computer system receives the order and places the order in the queue to be processed. The supplier's computer system may be connected to its suppliers' computer systems. So as it begins running low on indigo dye, for example, an order for more is automatically generated and delivered to the dye producer.

For some industries, EDI is becoming a necessity. For many large companies, including General Motors and Dow Chemical, computer input often originates as output from another computer system. Some companies do business only with suppliers and vendors using compatible EDI systems, regardless of the expense or the effort involved. As more industries demand that businesses have this ability to stay competitive, EDI will cause massive changes in the firms' work activities. Companies will have to change the way they deal with processes as simple as billing and ordering, while new industries will emerge to help build the networks needed to support EDI.

Home Networks

Like televisions, telephones, and automobiles, personal computers have become such an integral part of many people's lives that many households have more than one. As PC prices continue to decrease, it is increasingly common to find one or more PCs per individual in a household. Whether the individuals are

Setting Up a Wireless Home Network

To set up a wireless home network you need a high-speed Internet connection, a wireless access point/router, and wireless network adapters for all devices that will connect to the network (see Figure 5.36).

Access points and network adapters come with software that is easy to install, and it works with your operating system to automatically configure your network. By following simple instructions, you can have your home network set up within an hour.

Because the range on access points is limited, it is best to find a location for the access point that is central to the area in which you will use the network. If your cable modem or DSL modem is not located in a central location, you need to move it by either switching it to another connector or running a length of cable to a central location. Make sure that the location you select for your access point is not near any electronic equipment that may interfere with the signal, such as stereo speakers or power transformers.

Connect the access point to the modem, and power it up. Read the instructions for installing the wireless network adapter to your PC. Once it is installed, you can access the setup software on the access point and configure your network settings. Wireless network adapters can be installed on all PCs in the residence. You can also use wireless network adapters for printers, televisions, and stereos.

Once your computers are communicating with each other over the network, users must determine what resources to make available to others on the network. Today's operating systems provide methods for specifying which drives, folders, directories, files, and printers you wish to share over the network. How you share and access network resources varies from operating system to operating system.

A primary concern about wireless networks, and perhaps their only drawback, is security. By default, Wi-Fi networks are set with no security in place. Once set up, they broadcast their existence to anyone within range, inviting them to join the network. With a click of the mouse, you, your neighbors, or someone passing on the street can all join the network. This makes it convenient to set up the network and get it working, but additional steps are required to secure it so only intended individuals may use it. Read your access point documentation to find out how to lock down your home network.

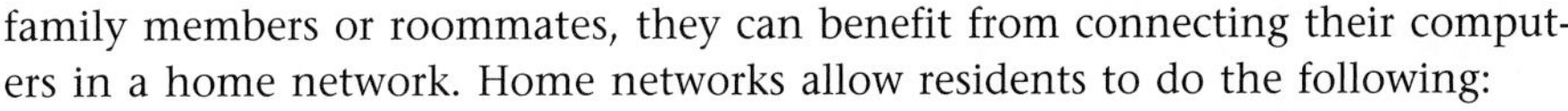

family members or roommates, they can benefit from connecting their computers in a home network. Home networks allow residents to do the following:

- Share a single Internet connection
- Share a single printer between computers
- Share files such as images, music, and programs
- Back up copies of important files to another PC for safekeeping
- Participate in multiplayer games
- Share output from devices such as a DVD player or Web cam
- Distribute media such as movies and music around a household

In the past, setting up a home network was an intimidating challenge. The computer industry has recognized home networking as one of the most important and lucrative markets of this century and has made available many new technologies that vastly improve the ease with which a home network can be installed.

Home Networking Technologies. Many of the technologies discussed in this chapter are applicable to home networks, which are typically based on Ethernet standards and can be wired or wireless. Some technically inclined people may

FIGURE 5.36 • Wireless home network

A typical wireless home network uses a wireless access point/router to connect the network to an ISP. Wireless adapters connected to each computer communicate with the access point.

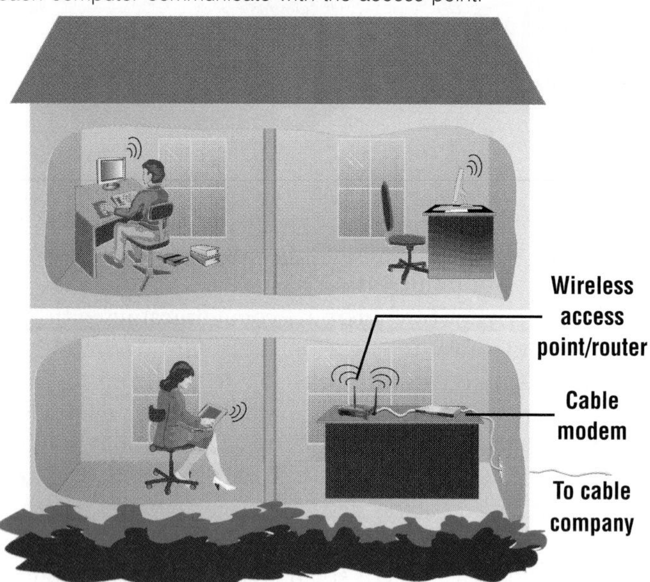

FIGURE 5.37 • Wireless home stereo

Systems from Linksys and others allow music to be shared wirelessly around the house.

opt to run twisted pair copper cable through the walls and attic space of their homes to set up a business-quality network. Other options take advantage of existing wires in the home. Phone-line networking, also called *HomePNA*, links computers through a home's phone wires, and power-line networking, or *Home PLC*, links computers through the power lines in the house. Most home users, however, take advantage of the convenience and power of Wi-Fi wireless technology for their home network.

Home Network Applications. The rapid rise in wireless home networks is spurring the development of new technologies that use Wi-Fi networks to provide useful residential services. Two of the most prevalent are technologies that assist in (1) data storage and access and (2) wireless media distribution throughout the home.

Like businesses, families are beginning to find a need for centralized file servers. For example, family members may take hundreds of digital photos that they would like to catalog and share. Rather than trying to remember whose computer holds which photos, it makes sense to store them all in one central location. Over a home network this can be accomplished by setting up a file server, connecting it to the router/access point, and naming it with a common drive letter on all network PCs. So, for instance, if you save your photos to the P: drive on any computer in the house, it is stored on one central location on the network.

In addition to storing and backing up data and files, home networking technologies can be used to distribute media files throughout your home. The SoundBlaster wireless music system allows you to transmit your MP3 music from your computer to any stereo or powered speaker system in your home over a Wi-Fi network (Figure 5.37). Connect the system to your stereo using standard stereo cables, install the software on your PC, and control the music using a remote control. The remote control lets you browse through your song lists to select the music you want to hear. For Apple users, the AirPort Express can be used to share music from your Apple computer with other computers or stereo systems in the house. Apple TV provides a similar service that streams video from iTunes on your PC to your TV. Other companies such as Linksys and Gateway also have Wi-Fi devices that play either audio files or both audio and video files, and sometimes streaming media from the Internet. Other technology allows you to send television signals from TV to TV in order to share a cable or satellite connection without wires.

A product from Microsoft called Windows Home Server is designed to do all of the above. It backs up important data files on network PCs, provides a central location for storing shared documents, and streams media between networked devices.

ACTION PLAN

Remember Amanda Jackson from the beginning of this chapter? She is the NPR news correspondent shopping for field equipment. Here are answers to the questions about Amanda's situation.

1. **What types of mobile devices best suit Amanda's journalistic needs?**

   Some of today's high-end smart phones include voice recording, note taking with a stylus or QWERTY keyboard, and cell phone capabilities. Amanda will want to choose a Quad band world phone that works on a variety of international networks. Because GSM networks are an international standard, she should probably look to GSM carriers such as AT&T and T-Mobile. When choosing a cellular service plan, she should invest in one that supports global travel. Because her cell phone will be her lifeline, she probably wants to include several add-on features and services. Certainly a GPS navigation system will be of great use when visiting foreign cities. A phone with a camera may be of use when gathering facts for her stories. She may also want to use her phone for relaxation by storing MP3s and accessing streaming video—and don't forget stereo headphones!

2. **What type of notebook computer, networking media, devices, and software should Amanda use to connect to the Internet and the NPR private network?**

   Whatever notebook Amanda chooses, it will likely include Wi-Fi, and there is a good chance Amanda can find an access point wherever she travels. As a backup she should make sure that her notebook includes an Ethernet cable port. Amanda might consider subscribing to the Boingo service that provides access to 100,000 hotspots worldwide. Amanda could also add broadband Internet access to her cell phone service and connect to the Internet through her phone. Amanda might want to choose a notebook that includes a Web cam so that she can use video conferencing over the Internet. Amanda may need to install VPN software on her notebook in order to connect to the NPR private network over her Internet connection.

3. **What networking technologies can Amanda use to transfer files between her devices?**

   Amanda might consider getting a Bluetooth-capable cell phone and a Bluetooth adapter for her notebook. This allows for a wireless connection between the devices to transfer data and to connect to the Internet. Smart phones typically come with a desktop cradle that can be used to transfer data to a notebook via the USB port. Another option is to store her notes, photos, and videos using cloud computing services that can be accessed from any of Amanda's devices.

Summary

LEARNING OBJECTIVE 1

Understand the fundamentals of data communications and the criteria for choosing a communications medium.

Communication takes place between sender and receiver by way of a signal that travels through a communications medium. Telecommunications refers to the electronic transmission of signals for communication. Data communications is a type of telecommunications that involves sending and receiving bits and bytes that represent data. A computer network connects computers for data communications.

Figure 5.2—p. 274

Telecommunications involves three components: networking media, devices, and software. A data-bearing signal travels over the media between devices that act as relay points. Network software controls the devices to manage telecommunications signals in an economical and efficient manner.

Telecommunications networks manipulate both analog and digital signals. The transmission speed of a given medium is dictated by the signal frequency, measured in hertz (Hz) and described in terms of the number of bits per second (bps) that the medium can deliver. The range of frequencies that can be sent over a given medium is known as its bandwidth.

LEARNING OBJECTIVE 2

Explain how networking media, devices, and software work together to provide data networking services, and describe the benefits of various types of media.

Network media include cables and wireless signals. The most common types of cables used in telecommunications are twisted pair copper cables, coaxial cable, and fiber-optic cable. Fiber-optic cable is the fastest cable medium. Wireless communications media include radio waves and infrared light. The U.S. Federal Communications Commission assigns different frequencies of radio waves for different uses. High-frequency signals are called microwaves.

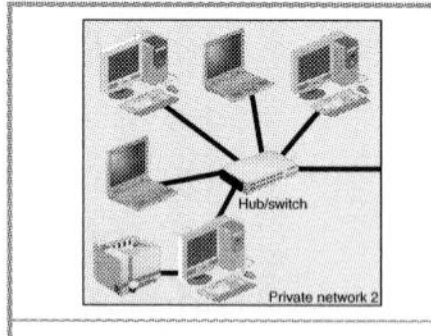

Figure 5.10—p. 281

Networking devices include modems, network adapters, and network control devices. Modems connect computers to various types of communication media. Network adapters are circuit boards, PC cards, or external devices that allow a computer to connect to a computer network. Hubs, switches, repeaters, bridges, gateways, and routers are used to control computer network traffic. A wireless access point connects wireless devices to a Wi-Fi network. A firewall can be either a device or software that filters the information coming onto a network to protect network computers from hackers, viruses, and other unwanted network traffic.

Microwave transmission sends signals through the air from tower to tower across the land or up to satellites that retransmit the signal to another location on Earth. Several other communications devices and media are designed for industrial use. T1 and T3 carrier lines support high-demand network traffic. Multiplexers and communications processors assist in managing the flow of information in networks with large quantities of network traffic. Encryption devices secure network traffic by encrypting data on the network so that it is unintelligible to all but intended receivers.

A network administrator is a person responsible for setting up and maintaining the network, implementing network policies, and assigning user access permissions. A network operating system (NOS) is installed on network servers and workstations, and it controls the computer systems and devices on a network, enabling them to communicate with each other. Ethernet is the most widely used network standard for private networks.

LEARNING OBJECTIVE 3

List and describe the most popular forms of wireless telecommunications technologies.

A cellular network is a radio network in which a geographic area is divided into cells, with a transceiver antenna (tower) and station at the center of each cell to support mobile communications. When you choose a cell phone service, there are three primary decisions to make: choose a carrier, choose a plan, and then choose a phone with particular features and services. A cellular carrier is a company that builds and maintains a cellular network and provides cell phone service to the public. The predominant digital networking standards used for cell phone networks are GSM and CDMA. GSM is the most popular global standard for mobile phones and is used by over a

Figure 5.17—p. 291

billion people across more than 200 countries. The CDMA networking standard is predominantly used in the United States, where it is in competition with GSM. Different carriers offer different cell phones, features, coverage areas, and services.

Pagers are small, lightweight devices that receive signals from transmitters. Global positioning systems (GPSs) use a constellation of satellites to pinpoint the location of a GPS receiver on Earth. Wireless fidelity (Wi-Fi) uses radio signals to connect computers to a network, which is typically connected to the Internet. WiMAX and LTE are next-generation (4G) wireless broadband technologies that are both faster and have longer ranges than Wi-Fi. Bluetooth-enabled devices use radio signals to communicate between personal and mobile devices. Infrared transmission uses infrared light to transfer data between devices at close range without wires. A radio frequency identification (RFID) device is a tiny microprocessor combined with an antenna that is able to broadcast identifying information to an RFID reader. RFID and near field communication (NFC) technologies are used to enable contactless payment systems.

LEARNING OBJECTIVE 4

List the different classifications of computer networks and their defining characteristics, and understand the basics of wireless home networking.

Distributed computing refers to computing that involves multiple remote computers that work together to solve a computation problem or perform information processing. Cloud computing utilizes Internet-based service providers to deliver information and computing services, including software, business systems, and data storage. Many large businesses and organizations use the client/server network architecture. Server computers are used to distribute data, files, and programs to users, or clients, on the network. Computers connected to a network are called workstations or nodes. A workstation has access to the local resources and the network, or remote resources.

Networks are classified based on size. From smallest to largest, they are PAN, LAN, MAN, WAN, and global networks. A personal area network (PAN) is the interconnection of information technology devices within the range of an individual. A network that connects computer systems and devices within the same geographical area is a local area network (LAN). A metropolitan area network (MAN) connects networks within a city or metropolitan-size area into a larger high-speed network. Wide area networks (WANs) tie together geographically dispersed LANs. WANs that cross international borders are called global networks. An intranet is a private network, set up in an organization and based on Internet protocols. When an intranet includes specific outside parties, it becomes an extranet. Intranets sometimes use the Internet to connect geographically dispersed networks in a virtual private network (VPN) using tunneling technology.

Figure 5.32—p. 309

Through electronic data interchange, or EDI, networks owned by different organizations can be joined and programmed to communicate so that the output of one system is processed as input by the other. EDI allows organizations to automate many time-consuming tasks.

Home networks are used to share hardware, files, and a common Internet connection. A modem, which provides the link between the ISP and the home computer, can be connected to a single computer or all computers within the home network. Home network technologies include phone-line networks (HomePNA), power-line networks (Home PLC), and wireless networks. Wireless home networks typically require a wireless access point and a wireless adapter for each computer on the network. Wireless networks require additional setup to ensure that the signals sent and received are secure and not accessible to others outside the network.

Test Yourself

LEARNING OBJECTIVE 1: Understand the fundamentals of data communications and the criteria for choosing a communications medium.

1. Telecommunications signals travel over telecommunications ________________ .
2. In computer networks, the data transmission rate is also referred to as ________________ and is measured in bits per second (bps).hertz
   a. frequency
   b. bandwidth
   c. broadband
3. True or False: A DSL modem delivers broadband performance.

LEARNING OBJECTIVE 2: Explain how networking media, devices, and software work together to provide data-networking services, and describe the benefits of various types of media.

4. True or False: For exceptionally high data transmission rates one should look to fiber-optic cabling.
5. A network ________________ is a computer circuit board, PC card, or USB device installed in a computing device so that it can be connected to a network.
6. A network ________________ is a person responsible for setting up and maintaining the network, implementing network policies, and assigning user access permissions.
   a. technician
   b. supervisor
   c. engineer
   d. administrator
7. True or False: Cable modems provide the fastest connection speeds for residential use where they are available.

LEARNING OBJECTIVE 3: List and describe the most popular forms of wireless telecommunications technologies.

8. True or False: Some cell phones provide voice communications over a Wi-Fi network.
9. GSM phones include a(n) ________________ card that stores subscriber information and personal data and can be transferred to other GSM phones.
   a. USB
   b. SMS
   c. SIM
   d. GPS
10. ________________ computing utilizes Internet-based service providers to supply computing services and data storage for individuals and businesses.
11. ________________ enables a wide assortment of digital devices to communicate wirelessly over short distances.
    a. Bluetooth
    b. Wi-Fi
    c. Fiber optics
    d. Microwave transmission

LEARNING OBJECTIVE 4: List the different classifications of computer networks and their defining characteristics, and understand the basics of wireless home networking.

12. True or False: A LAN is the most prevalent type of network.
13. A(n) ________________ is often used by enterprises to allow employees to access the corporate intranet from home and while on the road.
    a. virtual private network (VPN)
    b. extranet
    c. metropolitan area network (MAN)
    d. router
14. True or False: EDI uses network systems and follows standards and procedures that allow output from one system to be processed directly as input to other systems, without human intervention.
15. The ease of installation of a(n) ________________ network makes it the obvious choice for most home networks.
16. True or False: Access points are designed to be secure right out of the box.

Test Yourself Solutions **1.** media, **2.** c. bandwidth, **3.** True, **4.** True, **5.** adapter, **6.** d. administrator, **7.** True, **8.** True, **9.** c. SIM, **10.** Cloud, **11.** a. Bluetooth, **12.** True, **13.** a. virtual private network (VPN), **14.** True, **15.** Wi-Fi wireless, **16.** False.

Key Terms

Key Term	Page	Definition
analog signal	274	A signal of varying intensity that fluctuates continuously
bandwidth	275	The data transmission rate measured in bits per second (bps)
Bluetooth	299	Specification that enables a wide range of digital devices to communicate wirelessly over short distances
broadband	275	A high-speed Internet connection that is always on or active, such as cable or DSL
cellular carrier	288	A company that builds and maintains a cellular network and provides cell phone service to the public
cellular network	286	A radio network in which a geographic area is divided into cells with a transceiver antenna (tower) and station at the center of each cell, to support mobile communications
cloud computing	307	Utilizing Internet-based service providers to deliver information and computing services, including software, business systems, and data storage, for business and personal use
coaxial cable	277	A cable consisting of an inner conductor wire surrounded by insulation, a conductive shield (usually a layer of foil or metal braiding), and a cover
communications satellite	282	Essentially a microwave station placed in outer space that receives a signal from one point on Earth and then rebroadcasts it at a different frequency to a different location
digital signal	274	A signal with two discrete voltage states, high or low
Ethernet	285	The most widely used network standard for private networks
fiber-optic cable	277	A cable, consisting of thousands of extremely thin strands of glass or plastic bound together in a sheathing (a jacket), that transmits signals with light beams
global positioning system (GPS)	294	System that uses satellite and mobile communications to pintpoint exact locations
intranet	309	A networking technique that uses the protocols of the Internet and the Web—TCP/IP and HTTP, along with Internet services such as Web browsers—within the confines of a private network
local area network (LAN)	308	A network that connects computer systems and devices within the same building or local geographical area
Long Term Evolution (LTE)	299	A 4G wireless broadland technology that allows GSM cellular technology to provide very high-speed Internet access
metropolitan area network (MAN)	310	Connects networks within a city or metropolitan-size area into a larger high-speed network
microwave transmission	282	Sending line-of-sight high-fequency radio signals through the air
modem	280	Device that converts analog and digital signals from one form to the other
near field communication (NFC)	304	A wireless technology designed for short distances (up to 20 centimeters), aimed at utilizing cell phones for secure wireless payments
network adapter	280	A computer circuit board, PC card, or USB device installed in a computer so that the computer can be connected to a network
networking media	273	Anything that carries a signal and creates an interface between a sending device and a receiving device

Key Term	Page	Definition
personal area network (PAN)	308	The interconnection of personal information technology devices, typically wirelessly, within the range of an individual
radio frequency identification (RFID)	301	Uses tiny transponders in tags that can be attached to objects and read wirelessly using an RFID reader
telecommunications	273	The electronic transmission and reception of signals for communications
twisted pair copper cable	277	A cable consisting of pairs of twisted wires covered with an insulating layer
virtual private network (VPN)	310	Uses a technique called *tunneling* to securely send private network data over the Internet
wide area network (WAN)	310	Connects LANs and MANs between cities, across country, and around the world using microwave and satellite transmission or telephone lines
WiMAX	298	Worldwide Interoperability for Microwave Access, also known as IEEE 802.16; the next-generation wireless broadband technology that is both faster and has a longer range than Wi-Fi
wireless fidelity (Wi-Fi)	295	Wireless networking technology that makes use of access points to wirelessly connect users to networks within a range of 250–1000 feet (75–300 meters)

Questions

Review Questions

1. What four components enable communication to take place?
2. How do analog and digital signals differ?
3. What do you need to keep in mind when deciding on a networking medium?
4. List the three types of cables discussed in this chapter in order of lowest to highest bandwidth.
5. Name three advantages and one disadvantage of using fiber-optic cable as compared to coaxial and twisted pair.
6. Under what conditions might a company consider using a telecommunications satellite instead of microwave towers?
7. What are the fundamental differences between Wi-Fi and Bluetooth technologies?
8. Name two personal computer devices that are used to connect to networks.
9. What are the two primary uses of RFID technology?
10. What concerns do privacy advocates have about RFID?
11. What is the purpose of a firewall?
12. What is the difference between distributed computing and cloud computing?
13. What is the primary purpose of near field communication (NFC)?
14. What is the difference between local resources and remote resources on a network workstation?
15. What are three decisions required when purchasing cell phone service?
16. List network types in order of size.
17. What constitutes a personnel area network (PAN)?
18. How does an intranet differ from the Internet?
19. What unique concerns are associated with global networks?
20. What equipment is required to set up a wireless home network?
21. List six add-on cell phone services.

Discussion Questions

22. What are some negative effects of insufficient bandwidth for residential networks and professional business networks?

23. What personal and professional benefits are afforded by Bluetooth technology? What effect can Bluetooth have on the life of a person in your future profession?
24. What services are offered by smart phones such as the iPhone? In your opinion, does the value of the services justify the cost of the handset and monthly data plan for your needs?
25. How does a client/server network system assist in managing information in a large organization?
26. Envision yourself in your future career. What role might telecommuting play in your weekly activities? Will you be able to do some or all of your work from a home office? How?
27. What are the concerns over systems like MasterCard's PayPass? Would you use the technology? Why or why not?
28. What role does teamwork play in your career area? How can a computer network assist team members in their work?
29. What conditions, both in telecommunications infrastructure and service-provider procedures and policies, must exist to allow cloud computing to really take off?

Exercises

Try It Yourself

1. Sit down at a network computer on campus. Use a file management utility (such as the Computer or My Computer tool in Microsoft Windows) to determine which disk drives are local resources and which are network resources. What other local and network resources are available on the computer? Printers? Scanners? If you are unsure, ask a computer lab assistant or network administrator. Use a word processor to create a document that lists the location of the computer lab that you used and who manages the network (either a group or person). Include a two-column table listing local resources in the left column and network resources in the right. Use proper column headings and make your document look like an official report.
2. Find the Web page of the organization that provides your campus network. Find the network usage policy or agreement for your campus network. Use a word processor to list the five most interesting activities *not* allowed on your campus network and your rationale for why these rules might exist. Why is a network usage policy necessary?
3. Compare and contrast plans, phones, features, and services of two major cell phone carriers. Create a report, using a word processor, to tell which carrier best meets your needs, and explain why.
4. Visit the iPhone Web site and learn about its features. Visit *www.phonescoop.com* and view the latest cell phones. Write a two-page paper describing how you think the Apple iPhone has changed our view of the cell phone and how that has impacted cell phone designs by the competition.
5. Visit the Web site of the department of your major (or intended major). Create a document that lists the computing environment provided to you by the department. Does your department have its own computer lab, or are students expected to use campus labs? Why do you think this is? Does your field require special computing or networking hardware or software?
6. Use a spreadsheet and the Web to determine the costs of setting up a wireless network. Your wireless network should include an 802.11n wireless access point and three 802.11n wireless network adapters (USB). You might start your research at *www.cdw.com.* Calculate a subtotal, then add a wireless printer and media player, such as the Linksys Conductor Wireless-N Digital Music Center. Calculate the total.
7. Conduct a Web search on *Bluetooth*. Research several informative pages on the topic with at least one positive and one negative perspective. Write a two-page paper on how Bluetooth is being used, along with a summary of positive and negative comments about it.

Virtual Classroom Activities

For the following exercises, do not use face-to-face or telephone communications with your group members. Use only Internet communications.

8. Select a U.S. college, other than your own, and visit the college's Web site. Find information about computer access provided by the college. Does the college provide public computer labs? Does it provide wireless Internet access? If so, where? Are the dorms networked? How can notebook computers be connected to the campus network? Use a word processor to list interesting statistics, such as how many computer labs are available, how many computers are in each lab, what types of computers, and so on. Include anything that you find interesting and unique about the college's network setup. Each group member should distribute his or her findings to the group. Then, hold a group discussion and vote to determine which college has the best setup.
9. Have group members research the pros and cons of contactless payment systems on the Web. Conduct a discussion and come to a consensus stance on whether your group supports or does not support contactless payment systems. Provide notes on your discussion to the instructor for grading.
10. If you have set up or if you maintain a home computer network, create a document that lists the networking difficulties that you have experienced along with the benefits that the network has provided. Include in your document a detailed description of the type of network you have and the equipment you use. If you have no experience with home networking, interview someone who does, and write up his or her comments. Swap stories with other group members, and write a summary of shared experiences.

Teamwork

11. Scour the Web in search of the least expensive 802.11n wireless network setup. The wireless setup should include the components discussed in this chapter (see the "Setting Up a Wireless Home Network" section), it must accommodate two desktop PCs and two notebook computers, and it should connect all network users to a cable modem Internet connection. The team member who comes up with the cheapest network that meets the requirements wins! Make sure to include shipping costs.
12. The team should place itself in the role of system administrators of a corporate network. Each team member should work independently to design a network usage policy that restricts employees from wasting time on the corporate network for personal needs, while not overly restricting them. You should address issues such as personal e-mail, personal Web browsing, access to the network from home, and so on. After listing individual ideas for important issues and policies, team members should get together and share their ideas. Work to merge everyone's policies into one cohesive corporate network usage policy. Do not include policies that do not have full team support, but rather list those separately for further discussion in class.

Endnotes

[1] Cisco Staff, "K-12 School District Offers AP Classes in More Schools," Cisco Case Studies, accessed September 8, 2009, www.cisco.com.

[2] AT&T Staff, "Agents Meet the Toughest Challenges Without Ever Leaving Home," AT&T Case Study, accessed September 8, 2009, www.business.att.com/enterprise/resource_item/Insights/Case_Study/working_solutions/.

[3] Lasar, Matthew, "Big cable to FCC: don't define broadband by its actual speed," *Ars Technica*, September 2, 2009, www.arstechnica.com.

[4] Anderson, Nate, "US 20th in broadband penetration, trails S. Korea, Estonia," *Ars Technica*, June 19, 2009, www.arstechnica.com.

[5] Gross, Grant, "U.S. receives 2,200 applications for broadband funding," *Computerworld*, August 27, 2009, www.computerworld.com.

[6] Nortel staff, "IT: A critical component of cutting-edge healthcare," Nortel Case Study, accessed September 8, 2009, www.nortel.com.

[7] Jordans, Frank, "World's poor drive growth in global cellphone use," *USA Today*, March 2, 2009, www.usatoday.com.

[8] Consumer Reports Staff, "Best cell phone service," *Consumer Reports*, January 2009, www.consumerreports.org.

[9] Mukherjee, Pradipta, "Handset makers jump on to social networking bandwagon," *Business Standard,* September 3, 2009, www.business-standard.com.

[10] Fried, Ina, "Microsoft, Nokia ink mobile Office deal," *Cnet,* August 12, 2009, www.cnet.com.

[11] Woyke, Elizabeth, "The World's Most Wired Countries," *Forbes,* June 26, 2008, www.forbes.com.

[12] Swedberg, Claire, "Strawberry Grower Deploys RFID to Fix Temperature Troubles," *RFID Journal,* Sept 9, 2009, www.rfidjournal.com.

[13] Neely, Brett, RFID and Sensors Illustrate Art's Impact on People," *RFID Journal,* August 31, 2009, ww.rfidjournal.com.

[14] O'Connor, Mary Catherine, "RFID Stops a Snowmobile in Its Tracks," *RFID Journal,* August 27, 2009, www.rfidjournal.com.

[15] Swedberg, Claire, Aquarium Puts RFID on Its Ocean Floor," *RFID Journal,* August 17, 2009, www.rfidjournal.com.

[16] Friedlos, Dave, "Australian Waste-collection Businesses Tag Trash Bins," *RFID Journal,* August 18, 2009, www.rfidjournal.com.

[17] UPS Technology Facts Web page, www.ups.com/content/hn/en/about/facts/technology.html, accessed September 11, 2009.

DIGITAL MEDIA FOR WORK AND LEISURE

Ana Arguello is in her first semester of college. Away from home, on her own for the first time, she has a real sense of freedom—along with a bit of apprehension. Most of her friends have chosen a major and know what they want to do in life. Ana enjoys so many different things that she is having trouble choosing just one area to focus on. She has always been an expressive, artistic person. She has a good sense of style and real artistic talent. Besides sketching and painting, she has developed skills in using Photoshop and enjoys creating interesting digital images. She also plays the piano; she has taken lessons since she was in elementary school, and over the years she has developed an enthusiasm for music. She even received an award in the talent show during her senior year in high school. Over the years, Ana has built a large and impressive music collection on her notebook computer.

Computers have been very much a part of Ana's life. Her mom and dad work as computer consultants, and her older twin brothers always seem to be playing video games. By the time Ana went to college, her computer skills surpassed those of almost all of her friends. She enjoys the challenge of computer games and has mastered most of the major titles. She has a personal digital photo collection—photos that she has taken on her cell phone and digital camera—that easily numbers in the thousands. She has taken and edited digital video and loves going to the movies or watching movies on her iPhone. Ana has thought about majoring in a computer-related field, but wonders if she wouldn't be happier majoring in art or music.

As you read through the chapter, consider the following questions:

1. What careers and majors might Ana consider in digital media?
2. How can Ana use digital media software and services to manage her media collections?
3. How might Ana enjoy digital media as a hobby and as entertainment?

Check out Ana's *Action Plan* at the conclusion of this chapter.

6

LEARNING OBJECTIVES

1. Understand the uses of digital audio and today's digital music technologies.
2. Describe the many uses of 2D and 3D digital graphics and the technologies behind them.
3. Explain the technologies available to acquire, edit, distribute, and print digital photos, and list new advances in video technologies and distribution.
4. Discuss how interactive media is used to educate and entertain.

CHAPTER CONTENT

Digital Music and Audio

Digital Graphics

Digital Photography and Video

Interactive Media

Introduction

Digital technology and information systems are tremendously useful in many practical ways. Digital media brings these systems to life with stunning and vivid imagery, powerful sound and music, and realistic, interactive, animated 3D environments. If technology were alive, digital media might be considered its heart and soul. Digital media provides a technical venue for people to express themselves through audio and visual output. This chapter provides an overview of all areas of digital media, including digital music and audio, 2D and 3D digital graphics and animation, digital photography and video, and interactive media such as video games and interactive TV. This chapter examines state-of-the-art media technologies and how they affect us in our personal and professional lives.

You don't need to be artistically or musically inclined to use and appreciate digital media. The term *digital media* has different interpretations in different environments. For the purpose of this discussion, **digital media** encompasses digital technologies of all kinds that serve and support digital music, video, and graphics (see Figure 6.1). Desktop, notebook, and handheld computers, digital music players, digital cameras, video game consoles, DVD, Blu-ray, and CD players, and cell phones are all devices that serve up digital media. MP3 music, DVD movies, digital photos and artwork, cell phone ringtones and wallpaper, screen savers, motion picture special effects, animated television, and movies are examples of digital media. Media player software such as iTunes, Windows Media Player, and RealPlayer; paint and drawing software; photo- and video-editing software; and voice and music recording software are examples of digital media software. A combination of different digital media types, such as animation or video and audio, is called *multimedia* or sometimes *rich media*. Digital media that can be controlled, manipulated, or in some way interacted with is called *interactive media*.

Digital media is transforming the manner in which we access entertainment. Studies have revealed that adults prefer the Internet over television for information, news, and entertainment. Today's consumers have a preference for on-demand media. *On-demand media* refers to the ability to view or listen to programming or music at any time rather than at a time dictated by television and radio schedules. On-demand media is made possible by broadband Internet access at home and by cell phone, digital video recorders, portable digital music and video players, CDs and DVDs, and of course, the Web.

FIGURE 6.1 • Digital media

Digital media impacts our daily lives in many ways.

Digital media is fundamental to today's entertainment industry and key to many professions. Designers, engineers, and architects make use of digital graphics software to design 3D products and projects. Desktop publishers and Web designers use digital graphics software to develop attractive 2D print and Web pages. Manufacturers and retailers use digital media to sell products and support their customers. Scientists use digital media to simulate and interact with inaccessible objects and environments. Almost everyone uses or is affected by digital media in one manner or another.

An important aspect of today's digital media is that they are empowering ordinary people. Digital technologies have made it easy to capture professional-quality images and video, to create music and audio recordings, and most important, to share them over the Internet. No longer is media production solely for professionals. By posting a video to YouTube, a podcast to iTunes, or a collection of photos to Flickr, everyone can use digital technologies and the Internet as a means of self-expression. Throughout this chapter you will see examples of ways that you can express yourself through digital media.

Thousands of digital media software applications are available for both professional and personal use. This chapter discusses four general categories of digital media: digital music and audio, digital graphics, digital photography and video, and interactive media.

DIGITAL MUSIC AND AUDIO

EXPAND YOUR KNOWLEDGE

To learn more about working with audio, go to www.cengage.com/computerconcepts/np/swt4. Click the link "Expand Your Knowledge" and then complete the lab entitled "Working with Audio."

Digital audio is any type of sound, including voice, music, and sound effects, recorded and stored digitally as a series of 1s and 0s. **Digital music** is a subcategory of digital audio that involves recording and storing music.

The ability to digitize sound has dramatically altered our phone networks, radio, television, and the entertainment and music industries. Digital phone networks digitize speech and send it as bits over cables or through the air. The radio industry is being transformed by satellite and Internet-delivered digital radio services. Digital audio in the form of voice, sound effects, and music is embedded in television programs, motion pictures, animated media, and computer games to provide high-quality and sometimes dramatic realism. The digitization of music has fundamentally altered the production and distribution mechanisms within the music industry, providing musicians with powerfully creative tools, improving the quality of recorded music, and providing listeners with more convenient access. The digitization of music and audio has also created new challenges to the creative and intellectual property rights of artists and production companies.

Digitizing Music and Audio

In the natural world, sound is the displacement of air particles caused by vibration and sensed by the eardrum. One way to quantify sound is by measuring the amount of air particle displacement and charting it over time to create a graph, called an *analog sound wave*. The term *analog* refers to signals that vary continuously. An analog sound wave can be transmitted electrically using varying voltages of electricity, as over traditional telephone networks, or varying a radio signal, as in AM/FM radio. Another more recent way of quantifying sound is to represent sound waves with numbers, digitally, through a process called *analog to digital conversion (ADC)*.

ADC uses a technology called *sampling* to encode a sound wave as binary numbers (see Figure 6.2). When you digitize, or sample, a sound wave, you measure and record its amplitude (height) at regular time intervals called the sampling rate; the shorter the time interval, the higher the sampling rate and more accurate the reproduction of the sound. For example, the sampling rate for audio CDs is 44,100 samples per second, whereas the sampling rate of your voice on a digital cell phone is only 8000 times per second.

FIGURE 6.2 • Analog to digital conversion

A sound wave is sampled by measuring its amplitude at consistent time intervals and storing the amplitude values as a list of binary numbers.

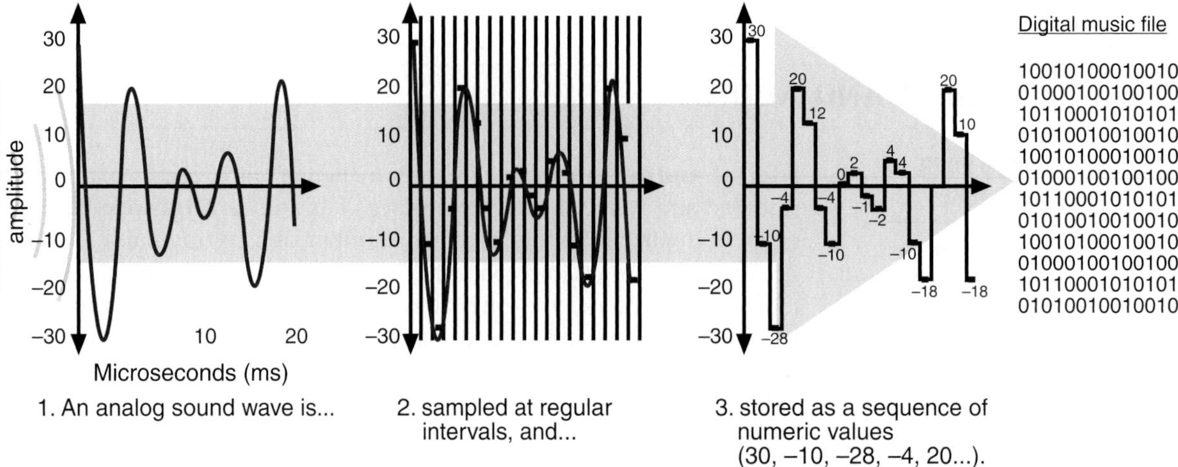

Digitized sound is transformed back into its analog form in a process called *digital to analog conversion*. Although the re-created sound wave is not an exact duplicate of the original live sound, a sampling rate of 44,100 times per second is close enough to the original sound to satisfy our less-than-perfect ears.

Digitized sound has tremendous advantages over analog sound in a number of ways. It can be easily duplicated and transmitted without any degeneration. It has a relatively limitless life span. It is easy to manipulate and process and can be encrypted for secure communications. Digital phones and media recorders/players include *analog-to-digital converters* and *digital-to-analog converters* to translate sound and music back and forth between analog and digital representation.

Digital Sound for Professionals

A number of nonentertainment professionals make use of digital sound technology in their work. Digital sound devices can help professionals who must rely on their ears to do their work more thoroughly and precisely.

Digital Voice Recorders. Professionals in many fields use portable *digital voice recorders* (see Figure 6.3) to capture dialog for future reference. Journalists, lawyers, investigators, and others whose work involves interviewing people rely on digital voice recorders to keep their facts straight. Doctors and other professionals use digital voice recorders to record notes for future transcription.

FIGURE 6.3 • Digital voice recorder

Portable digital voice recorders can store hours of interviews or oral notes for future transcription.

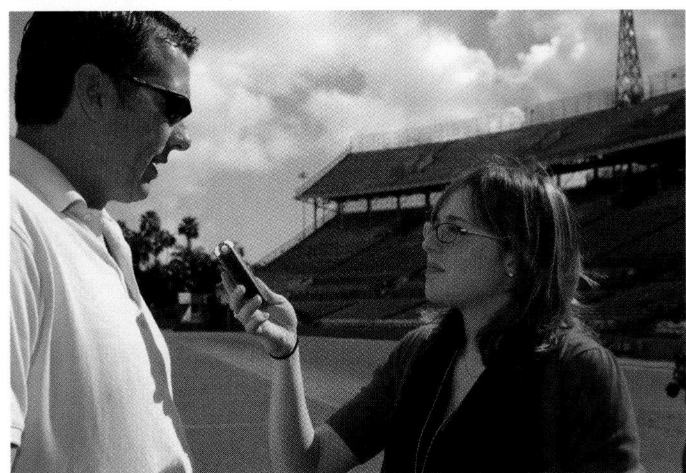

Digital voice recorders store recordings in standard digital sound formats that can be transferred to a computer for transcription or editing. Sound files can be edited for broadcast, played back and transcribed to text documents for print or Web publishing, or filed away for future reference.

Digital Sound in Scientific Research. Scientists have used digital audio to study various natural phenomena. The Australian Marine Mammal Research Centre used digital recordings to study whale songs off the east coast of Australia. Using three underwater microphones called *hydrophones* placed at different locations, the researchers were able to track the songs of individual whales as they migrated. Using sophisticated digital processing equipment, the researchers discovered that male whale song "is highly structured, and, at any one time, all the males in the population sing the same song using the same sounds arranged in the same pattern. Over time, however, this pattern changes, but all the singers make the same changes to their songs. After a few years the song may be quite different, but all the singers are still singing the same new song."[1] In almost all scientific and medical professions, researchers use digital sound technologies to help decipher the mysteries of the universe.

Digital Sound in Law Enforcement. Digital sound plays an important role in law enforcement. *Forensic audio* uses digital processing to denoise (remove nonessential sounds and audio interference), enhance, edit, and detect sounds to assist in criminal investigations. Among the many tools available to forensic audio specialists, the spectrographic sonogram is perhaps the most valuable. A spectrographic sonogram provides a visual fingerprint for various sounds in a recording. For instance, when a tape head engages the tape, it leaves a distinct impression (fingerprint) that can be used to determine if a tape was tampered with. Gunshots, car engines, and voices all have a unique pattern when viewed as a spectrographic sonogram. Figure 6.4 shows the spectrographic sonogram of a human voice. The process of identifying a recorded human voice is known as voice-print identification. The technique is considered highly reliable and has been used as evidence in more than 7000 criminal cases.

FIGURE 6.4 • Spectrographic sonogram of a human voice

Gunshots, car engines, and voices all have a unique pattern when viewed as a spectrographic sonogram.

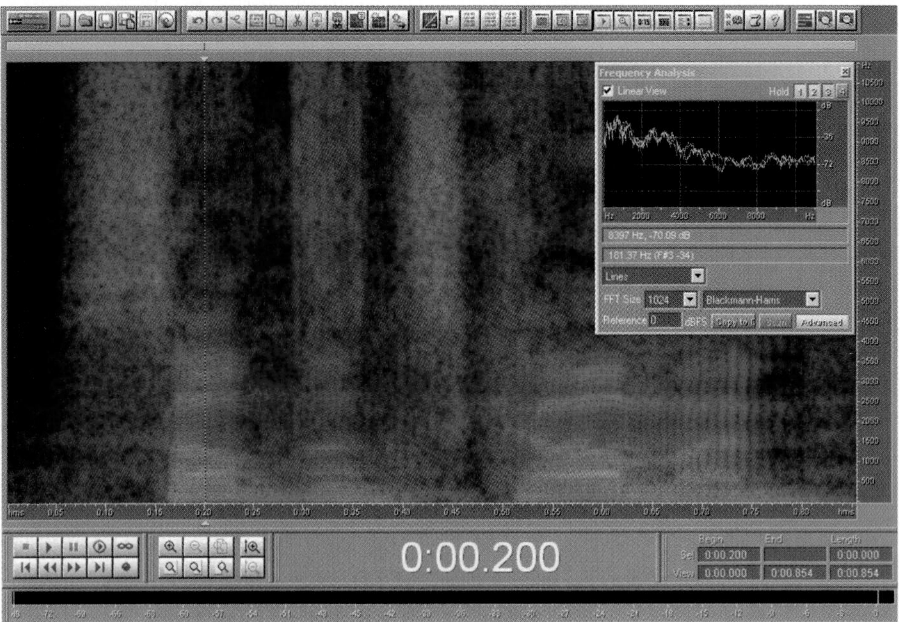

Digital Sound in Entertainment and Communication. The professional production and editing of digital audio takes place in sound production studios. A *sound production studio* uses a wide variety of audio hardware and software to record and manipulate music and sound recordings. Today's sound production studios typically record sound to digital media such as tapes or disks and then use digital sound-editing equipment to perfect what has been recorded. Figure 6.5 shows a top-notch Hollywood professional sound studio. Many professionals make their living in such studios working as digital sound engineers.

FIGURE 6.5 • Sound production studio

Sound production studios use a wide variety of audio hardware and software to record and manipulate music and sound recordings.

Digital Music and Audio Production

Although digital audio processing has many industrial and professional applications, it is most strongly connected with the music industry. Today's recording studios are high-tech digital processing centers. Even the most "unplugged"-sounding acoustic music recordings utilize digital sound-processing techniques to enrich and purify the sound so that it seems as though you are sitting right there with the musicians.

Professional Music Production. Today's recording studios use analog-to-digital converters to transform the recorded sound of voices, violins, horns, and other acoustic instruments to digital signals that can then be manipulated. Studios record music using multitrack recording devices. *Multitrack recording* devices treat each instrument or microphone as a separate input, or track. The engineer uses a *mixing board* (the large panel with many dials, buttons, and sliders in Figure 6.5) to adjust the sound quality of each instrument separately. Multitrack recording allows the instruments to be recorded either all at once or separately. For example, a jazz quintet might decide to record the rhythm section—bass, guitar, and drums—first. After the rhythm section tracks are recorded ("laid down"), the solo instruments and vocals can be added one at a time. Using multitrack recorders, studio engineers are able to mix many separate instrument tracks together to create the finished product. Using digital signal processing, the engineer can mold the sound of each instrument, adjusting the tone quality and adding effects. In what is called the "final mix," after all tracks have been recorded, the engineer plays the recording and applies changes to the volume levels of each track to balance the sound of the instruments and bring listeners' attention to specific instruments at specific times. As the engineer "mixes" the song, the computer stores the settings. The final product is then transferred to CD or some other storage medium.

Musicians, sound technicians, and engineers have many tools available for creating and manipulating sound. Table 6.1 lists the most popular ones. Synthesizers, samplers, drum machines, and sequencers are only a few examples of the many devices available for creating digital music. Most music production studios have large racks of interconnected digital audio devices, called *outboard devices*, to process digital music and audio signals.

TABLE 6.1 • Digital tools for musicians and sound engineers

Digital music device	Description
Synthesizer	Produces sounds designed to be similar to the sounds of real instruments; can also produce new sounds unlike any that a traditional instrument could produce
Sampler	Digitally records real musical instrument sounds and allows them to be played back at various pitches using an electronic keyboard
Drum machine	Records drum beat patterns tapped on pressure-sensitive buttons or pads to produce sampled drum sounds that can be played back in a looping pattern
Sequencer	Manages multitrack recording

The **musical instrument digital interface (MIDI)** protocol was implemented in 1983 to provide a standard language for digital music devices to use in communicating with each other. MIDI commands include basic control commands such as "Note on," "Note off," "Program change" (to change instrument sounds), and others. Using MIDI, a musician can connect and control many devices from a single synthesizer keyboard (Figure 6.6) or computer. MIDI is used in computers to control the *onboard synthesizer* that is housed on most computers' sound cards. You may have seen audio files with a .mid filename extension. These files contain the instructions that cause a MIDI synthesizer to play music on your computer.

FIGURE 6.6 • Synthesizer keyboard

This Yamaha synthesizer keyboard includes hundreds of digitally sampled instrument sounds and synthesized sounds.

Home Recording Studios. Digital technologies have transformed the process of music recording and made it possible for amateurs to afford, understand, and use recording equipment to create professional-sounding recordings. An *integrated digital studio* packages many digital recording devices in one unit for convenient home recording. For example, the Yamaha AW2400 includes a 16-channel mixing board, a 40 GB hard drive on which to record, an analog-to-digital converter, sequencing and sampling software, a CD burner, and many other technical features to take music from home performance to a distribution CD. A musician could purchase this device for about the same price as the cost of one day in a professional studio.

All of the digital music devices described in this section—drum machines, sequencers, samplers, and synthesizers—are available as personal computer software. The software interacts with the computer's onboard synthesizer to provide sound studio capabilities. Using sequencing software, such as Apple's Logic Studio shown in Figure 6.7, a personal computer can become a self-contained recording studio.

LOOK OUT NIRVANA! HERE COMES THE CYBRAPHON!

The Cybraphon is a robot band created by Scottish artists that changes its tune based on its online popularity. The mechanized acoustic instruments, which include an organ, cymbals, and an Indian instrument called a Shruti box, respond to the number of hits its Web site receives, playing slow dreary music when it receives little online attention and upbeat melodies as the hits increase. Its emotions, ranging from desolation to delirium, can be accessed via a Twitter feed.

Robot Band Plays Music, Obsesses About its Online Followers
Priya Ganapati
Wired
July 31, 2009
http://www.wired.com/gadgetlab/2009/07/cybraphon/

FIGURE 6.7 • Sequencing software

Sequencing software, such as Apple's Logic Studio, allows a personal computer to become a self-contained recording studio.

Grammy-award winning T-Pain uses Logic Studio to create his unique sound and style. He started creating music on his Mac using the user-friendly but powerful GarageBand music-editing software. After "messing with it" for 40 minutes he had created an interesting beat, which after another 40 minutes turned into his hit song "I'm N Luv." T-Pain progressed to Logic Studio, which gave him more control over his music and the ability to create unique signature sounds.[2]

Many musicians are taking control of their careers by connecting their PCs to home recording equipment to create their own professional-grade home recordings. Web sites like GarageBand.com (*http://garageband.com*) provide a distribution channel for independent artists to get their homegrown music to the masses.

Podcasting. Even nonmusicians are turning to PC-based home recording in the digital broadcast phenomenon called *podcasting*. A **podcast** is an audio file the contains a recorded broadcast distributed over the Internet. Podcasting gets its name from the Apple iPod, but the technology can be used on any media player that supports the MP3 format. Podcasts can contain news and information, interviews with celebrities, commercial radio programs or talk shows, music, comedy, instructional training, self-guided walking tours, academic presentations, personal discussions and commentaries, and more. Increasingly, novices who want to share their views, humor, talents, or musical taste with the world are using podcasting as a medium. Table 6.2 provides examples of popular podcasts available for free in the iTunes Store.

Tens of thousands of free podcasts are available on the Web. Most are regular publications with new releases available daily, weekly, or monthly. While iTunes is the most popular podcast directory, there are other good sources such as Podcast Alley (*www.podcastalley.com*), Podcast.com, and the Podcast Directory (*www.podcast.net*). Figure 6.8 shows the podcast page in iTunes.

TABLE 6.2 • A variety of free podcasts offered at the iTunes Store

Title	Description
Bandana Blues with Beardo and Spinner	Wry commentary and blues music played by unsigned artists or submitted with label/artist consent
This American Life	First-person stories and short fiction pieces that are touching, funny, and surprising
Coffee Break Spanish	Language-learning with your latte! (aimed at total beginners)
Joel Osteen Audio Podcast	The pastor of the largest and fastest-growing congregation in America speaks out
PodRunner	Energetic music for workouts from DJ Steve Boyett
ESPN Radio Daily	A daily offering of the best from ESPN Radio's *Mike and Mike in the Morning*
The Economist	Audio content from *The Economist* magazine

FIGURE 6.8 • Podcasts in iTunes

There are thousands of free podcasts in many categories available on the Web.

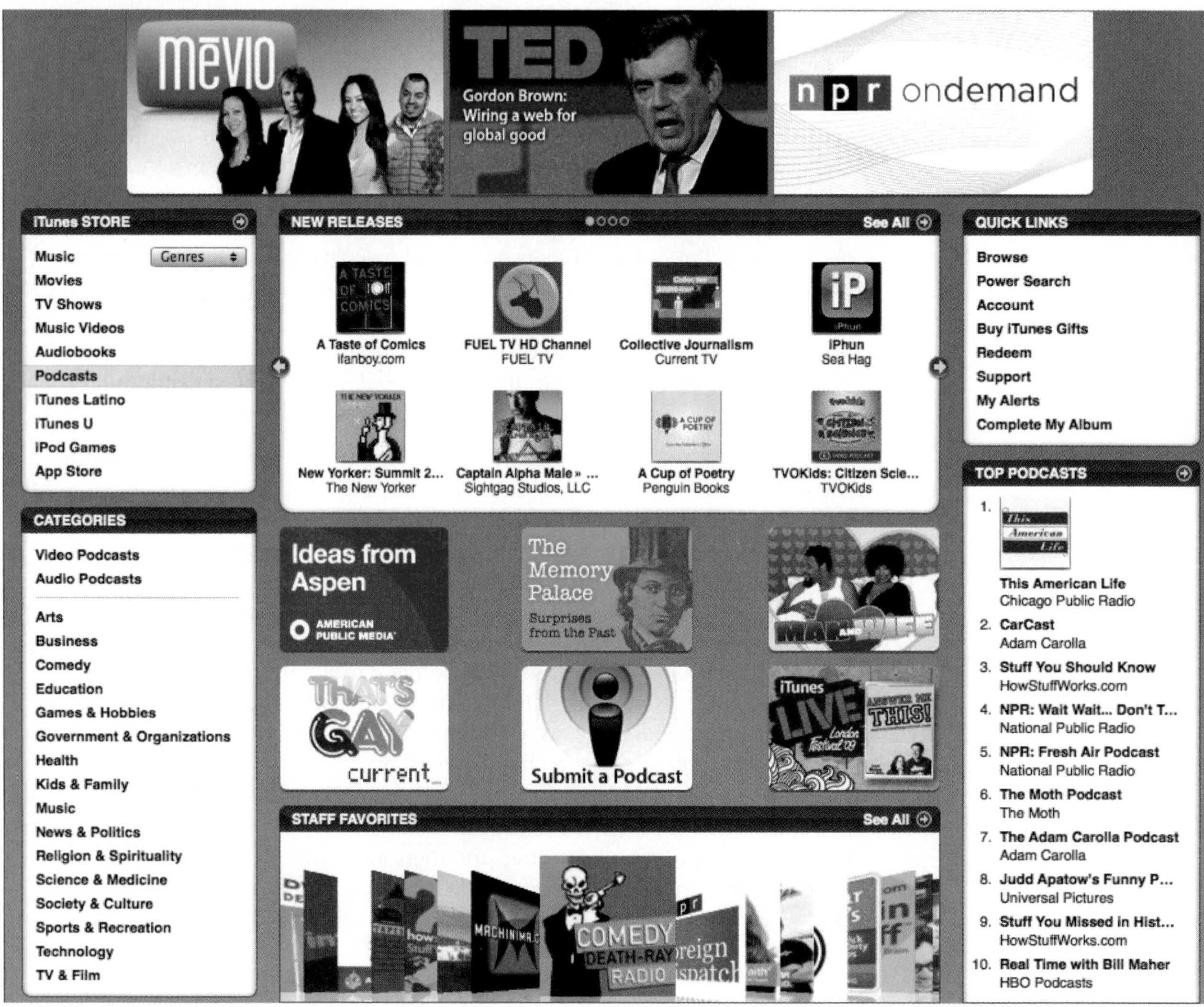

A podcast can be downloaded from a Web site and played using a PC media player, or transferred to a portable music player. Podcasts are also distributed using RSS technology. RSS, described in Chapter 5, is the technology used to subscribe to blogs. Software called a *podcast aggregator* or *podcast manager* uses RSS to allow you to subscribe to your favorite podcasts from one application. When you subscribe to a podcast, new episodes are automatically downloaded to your player as they are released. Apple iTunes is the most popular and easy-to-use podcast manager. Other podcast managers include Juice (*http://juicereceiver.sourceforge.net*) and Doppler (*www.dopplerradio.net*).

Podcasting is another example of how digital media is empowering individuals (see Figure 6.9). Rather than having to wait for a given time to listen to your favorite programming, podcasts allow you to listen at your convenience. Also, since podcasts are easy to produce and distribute (see the first Home Technology box), podcasts are giving voice to many individuals who might not otherwise have one.

FIGURE 6.9 • Podcaster Leo Laporte

Laporte is an award-winning podcaster of tech news and info.

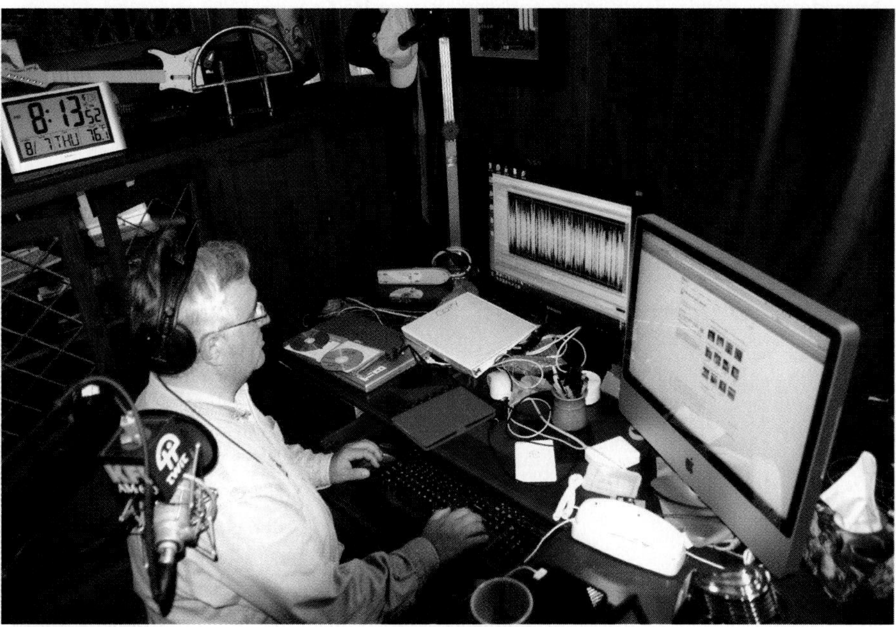

Digital Music: Audio Formats, Storage Media, Players, and Software

Producing, distributing, and enjoying digital music and audio involve several technology components: standardized media file formats, digital rights management (DRM) technology, software that interprets the format and DRM, storage media on which to store the files, and player devices. This section examines the digital music technologies that support music, podcasts, and other forms of digital audio.

Digital Music and Audio File Formats. Today, music is most often distributed on CDs, with an increasing trend toward distribution over the Internet. CDs made up 85 percent of album sales in 2008, even though digital download giant Apple iTunes overcame Wal-Mart to become the world's largest music retailer.[3] Digital music is burned to CD in a special format called pulse-code modulation or PCM. PCM stores the bits of the digitally sampled audio recording. These files are sometimes said to be in *native format* since it is the

Producing Your Own Podcasts

A podcast can be created by anyone with the desire to do so and the right equipment. When you visit a podcast directory, you find hundreds of podcasts created by amateurs who wish to share their unique perspectives with the world. To create professional-quality podcasts you need a headset with a noise-canceling microphone. Most PCs have ports that accommodate these devices. Digital recording software is required to record a podcast. Software such as Audacity (*http://audacity.sourceforge.net*) for Windows and GarageBand for Apple meets the basic needs for podcasting. Serious podcasters should invest in software specifically designed for podcasting, such as Propaganda (*www.makepropaganda.com*) or ePodcast Producer (*www.industrialaudiosoftware.com*). These packages allow you not only to record your voice but also to add music, sound effects, and other audio in real time. They also provide the tools to take your podcast online for others to access.

Once a podcast has been recorded, the MP3 file must be made available for users to access over podcast aggregators. Online services such as FeedBurner (*www.feedburner.com*) and Ourmedia.org provide wizards that allow you to put your podcast online for free. Some fee-based sites, such as Audioblog.com and Liberated Syndication (*www.libsyn.com*) charge monthly fees starting at $5.

Keep in mind that it is illegal to include any copyrighted music, graphic, audio, or other content in your podcasts.

pure digitized representation of the sound. Compact disc audio (.cda) files are used by CD players and computer media players to locate the beginning and end of tracks on the CD. Other music file formats are specifically designed for use on a computer. For example, the beeps and bells that are a standard part of the Windows interface are stored in .wav files; Apple computers use the .aiff music file format. These file formats are also considered native.

Larger audio files, such as a typical three-minute song, a voice recording, or a half-hour radio program, require a large amount of computer storage if stored in their native format. Three typical audio CDs' worth of music by your favorite artist would take up more than 1 GB of space on your hard drive if stored in their native format. Compression technologies are applied to audio files to greatly reduce their size with little or no loss to audible sound quality. *Digital audio compression* uses a technique called psychoacoustic modeling to remove frequencies from audio files that people are unable to perceive, reducing the size of the file. The most recognized compressed digital audio file format is MP3. The **MP3** file format compresses PCM music files to less than 10 percent of their original size. With MP3 compression, you could fit 30 CDs' worth of music rather than only 3 into 1 GB of space.

The new era of legal Internet music distribution has developed into something of a war of audio formats. The traditionally popular MP3 format is still preferred by many people who have most of their digital music stored in this format. Microsoft primarily supports the WMA (Windows Media Audio) format (.wma) in the services provided by Windows Media Player and Zune. Apple iTunes, the most popular music download service, uses the AAC (Advanced Audio Coding) format (.m4a and .m4p). WMA and AAC formats provide better

The Music Industry Changes Strategies

The battle between the Recording Industry Association of America, which represents the major record labels, and music fans may be drawing to a close, and it appears that the fans have won—for the most part.

The RIAA has invested in a two-pronged approach to keep music fans from illegally downloading music:

1. Hobble legally purchased digital music with DRM so that it cannot be copied and shared.
2. Hunt down and sue as many illegal downloaders as it can find—the vast majority of which have been college students.

The market has shown that DRM is a failure, at least in the music industry. Music fans hate it because it limits where they can listen to legally purchased music. All of the major online music distributers and record companies have dropped DRM from legally purchased music. Score one for music fans!

The RIAA has recently announced that it will abandon its strategy of mass lawsuits. Between September 2003 and February 2009, the RIAA sued 17,587 people. Most individuals sued settled out of court, paying an average of about $5000. The strategy did not have the sweeping effect the RIAA had hoped for; it enraged fans instead of discouraging them from file sharing. The RIAA has switched to a strategy of working with governments and Internet service providers to cut off Internet access to users who are habitual music-sharers.

Even with the change in strategy, RIAA court battles continue at a lesser rate as the RIAA clears its backlog. One headline-making case in 2009 resulted in a single mother being fined $1.92 million for sharing 24 songs. Shortly after that, a Boston University student was fined $675,000 for sharing 30 songs.

Questions

1. Why do you think the RIAA's strategy failed?
2. What caused the RIAA to change its strategy?
3. How might the RIAA still succeed in reducing the amount of illegal music-sharing?

Sources

1. *Gonsalves, Antone, "RIAA Spokesman Denies Saying 'DRM Is Dead'," InformationWeek, July 20, 2009, http://www.informationweek.com.*
2. *McBride, Sarah, "Music Industry to Abandon Mass Suits," The Wall Street Journal, December 18, 2008, online.wsj.com.*
3. *Saltzman, Jonathan, "BU student ordered to pay $675,000 in downloading case," The Boston Globe, July 31, 2009, http://www.boston.com.*
4. *RIAA Watch Web site, accessed August 2, 2009, http://sharenomore.blogspot.com/.*

sound quality than the MP3 format because they use more advanced compression technology. Users who collect music from varying sources will find themselves with a collection of music files in a variety of formats. Unfortunately, there are very few media players that support all three formats. The primary reason for this has to do with digital rights management.

Digital Rights Management (DRM). **Digital rights management**, or **DRM**, is technology that protects intellectual property by restricting the number of devices and applications on which a file can be opened, and the number of times that the file can be copied and burned to disc. DRM is applied to digital music, audiobooks, digital movies and e-books, and other forms of intellectual property.

Microsoft WMA and Apple's AAC file formats include DRM technology. DRM-protected AAC files use the .m4p file extension. Users who purchase songs from iTunes, Zune, Urge, and other online services may receive a file with DRM. While DRM was standard in the early days of digital music distribution, the public backlash against it due to the inconveniences it causes has led the music industry to begin phasing it out[4] (see the Community Technology box). When purchasing music online, it is wise to check if the songs you wish to download include DRM. Most popular online music stores have given up on DRM. DRM is still strong in other forms of digital media. Digital movies downloaded from Netflix, digital TV from Hulu, audiobooks from Audible, e-books for the Kindle, and PDF documents all make use of DRM to lock down intellectual property and prevent users from making copies (Figure 6.10).

FIGURE 6.10 • DRM at Audible.com

The audiobooks available for purchase at Audible.com use DRM to prevent users from sharing them with others.

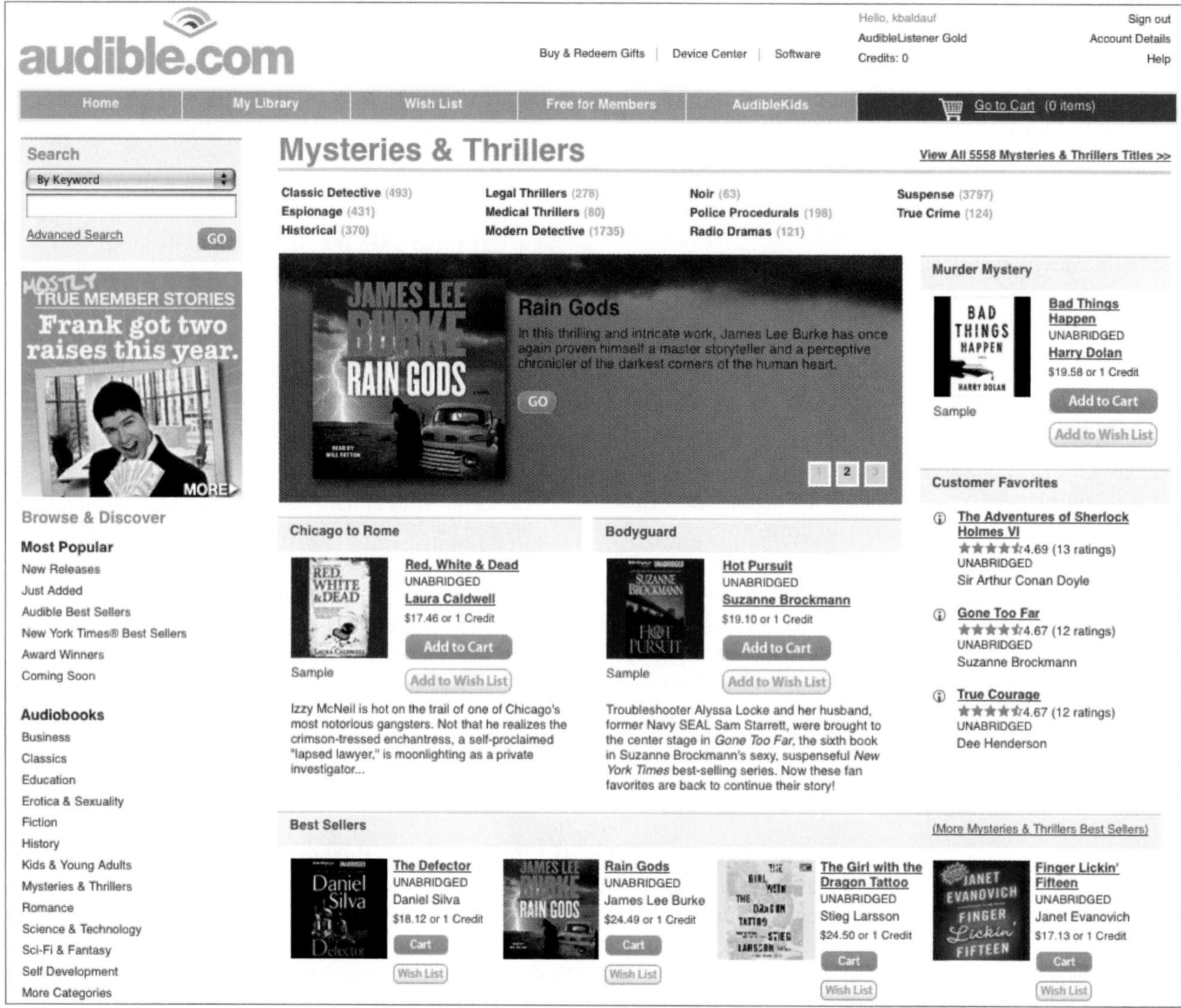

Digital Music and Audio Storage Media. There are three primary forms of audio storage media: CDs, hard drives, and flash memory. Because most music is available on CD, the CD player remains the most popular digital music player. In many media players, the ability to play music from CD is only one of many media-playing capabilities (see Figure 6.11).

Music fans can create their own mix of artists and songs on a CD-R (recordable CD) or CD-RW (rewritable CD), and are no longer bound by song sequences on store-bought CDs. Acquiring digital music from various sources, arranging the songs into personally appealing playlists, and recording the playlists to a CD-R has become a common activity and is yet another method of enjoying on-demand media.

FIGURE 6.11 • Mobile media center

The Alpine IVA-D106 plays CDs, DVD videos, satellite, local, and Internet radio; it also plays iPod/iPhone content and even includes a GPS receiver.

Some music lovers are doing away with the need for CDs and are storing their favorite music directly on their computer hard drive. Once on the computer, music tracks can be played on the PC or sent over a network to a home entertainment center, transferred to a portable digital music player, or burned to a CD to listen to while away from the computer. Today's high-capacity portable digital music players, like the iPod, make use of small microdrives to store gigabytes of music, room enough for hundreds, even thousands, of songs. Less-expensive digital music players, like the iPod Nano, make use of flash memory. Flash memory digital music players come in various sizes to accommodate up to several gigabytes of music.

Digital Music Players. There are hundreds of portable digital music players on the market, such as the Creative Zen X-Fi shown in Figure 6.12.

The first consideration in purchasing a player is the music formats that it supports. Table 6.3 lists the formats supported by three popular players. Shoppers need to make sure that the player they select can play the format of the music files they own.

FIGURE 6.12 • Portable players

The Zen X-Fi is a popular portable player from Creative. Other popular players are the Apple iPod/iTouch and Microsoft Zune.

Notice that only the iPod supports the iTunes Store format (.m4p), and only the Zune supports the Zune store format. There are many players that support the format and DRM used by Napster and Rhapsody, but the iPod and Zune do not. In this manner, players are directly linked to a particular format, DRM, and online music store. Since many online stores have moved to a DRM-free MP3 format, this issue has become somewhat less problematic. But, if you wish to use proprietary formats for higher-quality sound, you still need to be cautious about compatibility.

The second consideration when selecting a player, after compatible formats, is storage capacity. Smart shoppers first determine how they will be using the player, and how much music they wish to store. An iPod

TABLE 6.3 • Players and the formats they support

	wav	aiff	mp3	aac (m4a)	aac (m4p) *iTunes*	wma	wma (drm 9.0) Napster, Rhapsody, etc.	wma (drm 9.1) *Zune*
iPod	X	X	X	X	X			
Zen	X		X			X	X	
Zune			X	X		X		X

with a 60 GB hard drive could store your entire music (and photo) collection with ease (see Figure 6.13). To put this in perspective, if you completely filled up the iPod's 60 GB hard drive with digital music and listened to every song in order, it would take more than 41 days before the last song finished. Perhaps you don't need to have your entire collection with you everywhere you go. If you do, you will certainly want to maintain a backup copy in case you lose your iPod or it becomes damaged. Many people prefer to keep their entire collection on a PC and transfer only a portion of their music to their portable player. As wireless connection speeds continue to increase, some experts predict that you will soon be able to store and manage your personal digital music collection on the Internet and access it from anywhere wirelessly. In such an environment, storage capacity of portable players would not be an issue.

FIGURE 6.13 • Size matters

Larger-capacity players can store your entire music collection but are heavier and more cumbersome.

In order to save users from having to carry a digital music player and a cell phone, many of the latest cell phones double as digital music players. Cell phones like LG's Rhythm (see Figure 6.14), Sony Ericsson's W760a, Samsung's Trance, Nokia's 5800 Xpress Music, and of course the Apple iPhone, provide high-quality music features as well as cell phone and smart phone features. Music phones typically incorporate music player control buttons on the outside of a flip phone or side of a bar phone where they are easy to access. Special stereo headphones can be used that include a microphone and switch in the headphone cable near your mouth. When a call comes in, click the switch on the cable; your music pauses while you speak on the phone. Just click again to hang up and return to the music, all without having to take your phone out of your pocket.

FIGURE 6.14 • Music phone: LG Rhythm

High-quality music features are available in this smart phone.

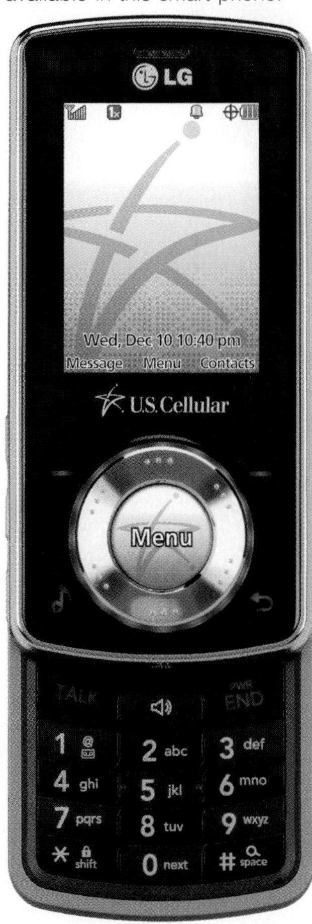

Music phones typically allow you to transfer music from your PC over a USB cable. For example, the iPhone synchronizes with iTunes on your PC to transfer music and video from your iTunes collection. In addition, cell phone carriers are providing music download services over the cell network. For example, Verizon offers V CAST—a library of over 1.9 million songs, most of which sell for between $.99 and $1.99 for direct download to your phone. Verizon users also have access to millions of songs from Rhapsody's online music store at similar prices. AT&T supports music on its phones by setting you up with subscription services from Napster and emusic.com on your computer, and allowing the music to be transferred from your PC to your phone. Some handsets provide a service that identifies music being played in the environment. Say you are listening to the radio and hear a song that you like and want to purchase but you don't know the title or artist. Press a few menu options on your phone, hold your phone up to the radio speaker, and the software will identify the song and artist and prompt you to purchase it.

Digital music can be enjoyed around the house, at the office, or in the car without the need for headphones. There are speaker systems designed for digital music players. For example, you can simply plug your iPod into a dock and the music is played through larger stereo speakers. You can use adapters in the car as well to connect your iPod to the car stereo system. Some phones and music players include an FM transmitter that transmits your music to an FM frequency where it can be tuned in on your car or home radio system.

Some digital music enthusiasts use their home PC as their primary home stereo, utilizing a wireless home network. Systems like Sonos (*www.sonos.com*) and Apple AirTunes allow you to send music from your PC to powered speakers anywhere in your house using your home Wi-Fi network. Sonos provides a handheld remote that is used to program music selections on your PC from any location on your wireless network. Powered speakers are connected to Sonos zone players placed around the home. You could play relaxing music in the living room for your roommate while you listen to salsa music in the kitchen as you prepare dinner—all from the same PC over your home wireless network.

A device called a *Wi-Fi radio* is a home stereo that accesses music and programs from Internet radio and music services with or without a PC, using your home wireless network. The Phillips Streamium and Logitech Squeezebox are popular Wi-Fi radios.

Digital Music Software. **Media player software**, such as iTunes, Windows Media Player, Zune, and RealPlayer, allows users to organize and play digital music, audio, and video files on PCs and media devices (Figure 6.15). Media player software can search for all music files on a PC and sort and arrange them by artist, genre, or album title. It also allows users to create custom playlists that can be transferred to a CD-R or portable player. Most popular media players provide a music download service so that users can conveniently build their digital music collections.

FIGURE 6.15 • Media player software

Windows Media Player and Apple iTunes are used to organize, manage, and play digital music and video.

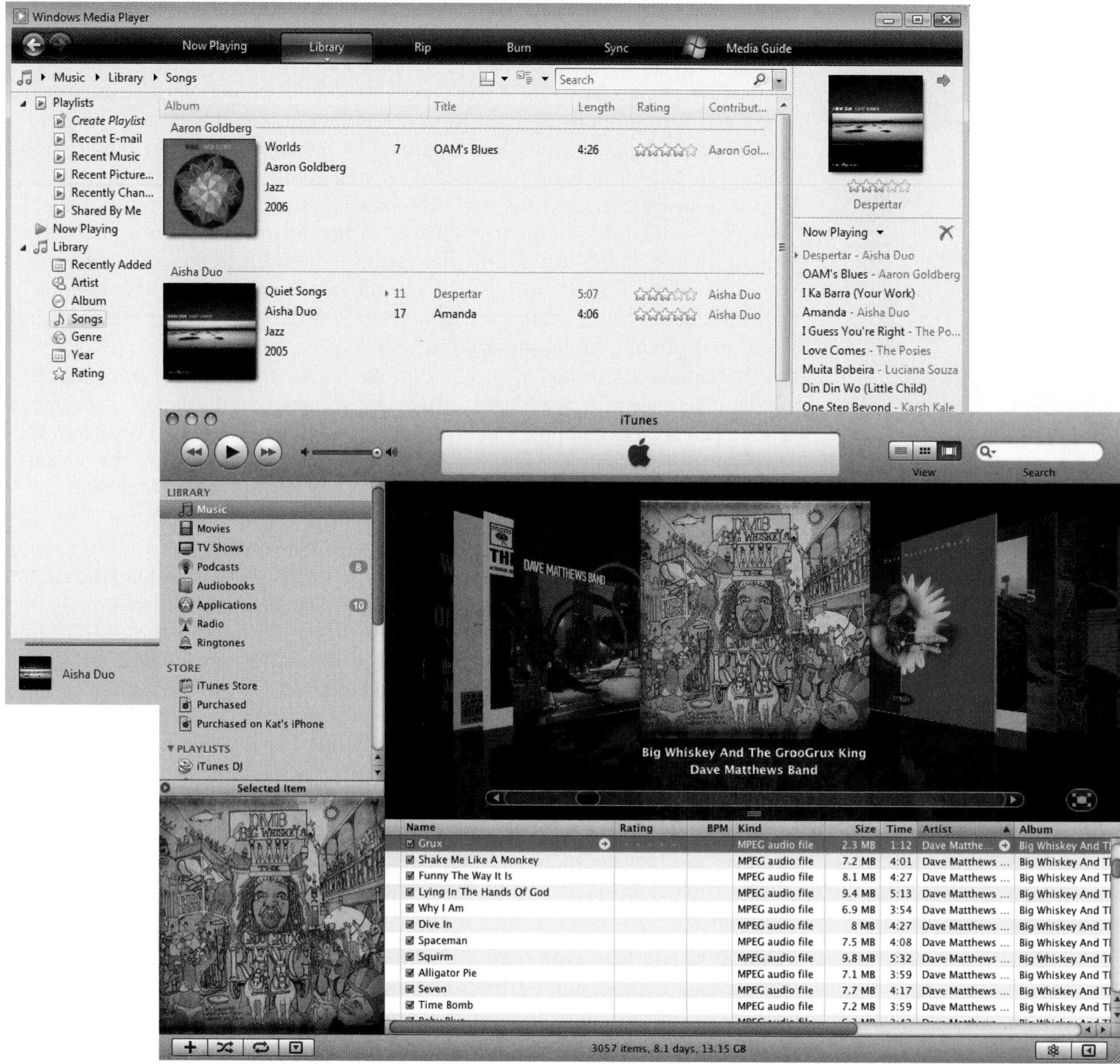

Media software typically allows you to synchronize, or sync, music with a portable music player through the USB port. Options allow you to either automatically sync user-defined playlists or manually sync playlists and songs. When you automatically sync your music, any new songs added to your PC or to specific playlists will automatically be transferred to your device the next time you connect. For example, if you subscribe to podcasts, automatic syncing will make sure that the latest editions of podcasts are transferred to your portable player.

There are numerous software utilities available for working with digital music files, many of which are built into popular media players. *Jukebox software* allows computer users to categorize and organize their digital music files for easy access. The process of transferring music from CD to MP3 or other digital audio format is called *ripping* a CD. *Ripper software* can be used to translate your favorite music CDs to MP3 files on your hard drive. Digital music files can be transferred from one format to another using *encoder software*.

Selecting a Digital Music Service

When selecting a legal digital music service, you need to consider many options and decide which are valuable to you. Subscription services often provide a free month for users to evaluate the service before having to pay. The following is a list of some of the options currently made available by today's most popular services.

- **Downloads**: All services provide the ability to purchase and download songs. The typical rate is $0.99 to $1.29. Visitors can listen to 30-second snippets of tunes to decide whether they wish to purchase them. Some purchased music may be constrained from being illegally copied with digital rights management (DRM) technology.
- **DRM-free downloads**: While most online stores sell tunes without DRM, the restrictive technology still exists in various music services. It is smart to confirm that the music you are downloading is DRM-free.
- **Subscriptions**: Monthly subscription services allow members to listen to full versions of millions of songs provided by the most popular recording labels. Songs are available to you only while you remain a subscriber. Subscription services typically use DRM and proprietary players to control the use of their libraries. They also offer the ability to purchase, download, and own music without DRM.
- **Music videos**: Some subscription services offer a library of music videos.
- **Music-to-go service**: Some subscription services also offer a higher-priced monthly subscription service that allows users to download and listen to music on select portable devices—as long as they continue membership.
- **Proprietary software**: Most subscription services require the use of their software to manage and play music. Purchased music can be listened to on software and devices that support the DRM used by the service.
- **Selection**: The top services advertise access to millions of songs.
- **Internet radio**: The most popular services provide free access to streamed Internet radio while connected.
- **Podcasts**: Some services provide free access to thousands of downloadable podcasts.
- **Tools**: All services provide tools that assist in organizing music and finding new music based on your tastes and preferences. Subscription services may also allow users to share playlists with other users.

Digital Music and Audio Distribution

Today music distribution and acquisition are at a crossroad. The application of digital compression to digital music brought us MP3 music files and the rise of file-sharing services like KaZaA and Limewire. Because the vast majority of commercial music in the United States is protected as intellectual property under copyright, people were placed in an untenable situation; one study found that in 2008, 95 percent of all music downloaded, 40 billion songs, was acquired illegally. Illegal downloading and copying is said to have contributed to the decline of legitimate music sales since 1999 when Napster originally introduced file-sharing technologies. In 2008, music sales declined another 18 percent, as online downloads continued to increase.[5] Such a contradiction between popular habit, law, and industry certainly could not exist for long.

To resolve the contradiction between law and social practice, and to protect its legal rights, the Record Industry Association of America (RIAA) has sued thousands of individuals involved in illegal MP3 file sharing while simultaneously developing new distribution models for digital music.

In 2004 the music industry finally caught up with the Internet generation and developed means for people to legally download music. Apple's iTunes was the first service to capture the attention of music downloaders, soon to be followed by several similar services. The number of people legally downloading music grew by 75 percent within the year following the introduction of iTunes. The number of legal song downloads from iTunes surpassed 6 billion in 2009, proving that increasing numbers of people are willing to pay for music once again.

Online Music Services. Online music services work with the recording industry to distribute music legally over the Internet. There are two types of online music services: download and subscription. Some of the more popular online music services include Apple's iTunes, Microsoft Zune, Napster, and Real's Rhapsody (see Figure 6.16). All four services offer 99-cents-per-song downloads. Napster and Rhapsody offer subscription services that provide additional features.

FIGURE 6.16 • Rhapsody music service

Rhapsody provides two options: a free online music store and a monthly fee-based subscription service.

All of the popular legitimate digital music services provide the option of paying for and owning music, typically for $.99 to $1.29 per tune. Subscription services like Napster and Rhapsody charge a monthly fee to provide the additional benefit of having free access to millions of songs that you can listen to during the time that you are a member. When and if your membership expires, you lose access to the library of songs but can keep any songs that you purchased.

Satellite Radio. **Satellite radio** is a form of digital radio that receives broadcast signals via a communications satellite. Unlike traditional AM and FM radio, so long as there is no major obstruction between the receiver and the satellite, the user can listen to available channels from any location in range—which could cover entire hemispheres of the planet.

FIGURE 6.17 • Satellite radio

A satellite radio receiver can be stationary, mobile, or a combination of both, such as this Delphi XM receiver that can be connected to powered speakers at home, in the car, or in the boat.

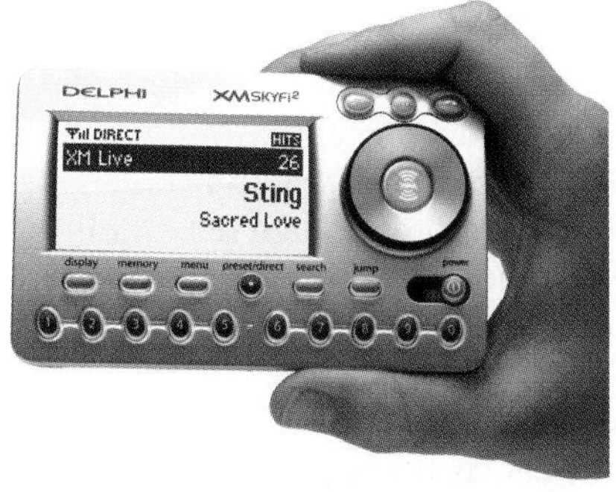

Satellite radio services charge a monthly subscription fee and offer stations featuring commercial-free music, comedy, news, talk, sports programming, and specialty channels providing music or features not typically available on commercial radio. The two most popular satellite radio services in the United States, XM and Sirius, have recently merged.

There are several options for satellite radio receivers: in-home, in-car, and mobile. Some systems have been designed to plug into a car unit and a home unit, so that you can take the receiver with you and use it in multiple environments (see Figure 6.17). Many new cars and rental cars come equipped with satellite receivers built into the car stereo system. Satellite radio can also be accessed by subscribers over the Internet and on smart phones.

Evaluating Music Options. This section has provided information on many ways to acquire and listen to music. Perhaps the only technologies not mentioned so far are AM/FM radio, digital local radio (sometimes called HD radio), and music over cable TV. Table 6.4 lists the music services/technologies available today.

TABLE 6.4 • Methods of acquiring music

Method
Buying music on CD
Buying music online for around 99 cents a song
Subscribing to an online service for access to millions of songs
Downloading music to your cell phone
Listening to free podcasts
Listening to free Internet radio
Subscribing to satellite radio
Listening to AM/FM radio
Listening to HD radio
Subscribing to cable TV music stations
Illegally sharing music over file-sharing networks
Illegally burning CDs for friends

Each type of music service and technology has certain benefits and drawbacks. For example, storing music on your PC hard drive is convenient in some respects, but if your hard drive crashes, you lose all of your music. Ripping CDs and sharing music with friends is easy and fun, but it's against the law. Downloading music to your cell phone is convenient, but it's difficult to play for your friends. Here are some considerations for evaluating and choosing music services and technologies:

- Is it legal, and if not, is it worth the risk?
- How much does it cost?
- Do you have to be connected to the Internet to listen?
- Do you own the music and, if so, can you play it anywhere, anytime, on any device?
- Is it accessible at home, at work, in your car, and walking about?
- Do you have control over the songs you hear (on demand) or is the playlist dictated by a DJ?
- Can you listen to it with your friends?

Even with all the options available, most people feel that there isn't one ideal, convenient, flexible, and inexpensive method for acquiring, organizing, and listening to music. Most of us rely on several methods. It is likely that once the turmoil in the industry subsides, there will be a service that provides the music you want to hear whenever and wherever you may be for a reasonable price that allows musicians to earn a good living. Through digital technologies, music and musicians are likely to thrive as never before.

DIGITAL GRAPHICS

Digital graphics refers to computer-based media applications that support creating, editing, and viewing 2D and 3D images and animation. At first glance, digital graphics might appear to be the exclusive domain of artists. In reality, many people, artistic and nonartistic alike, are finding themselves called upon or

EXPAND YOUR KNOWLEDGE

To learn more about working with digital graphics, go to www.cengage.com/computerconcepts/np/swt4. Click the link "Expand Your Knowledge" and then complete the lab entitled "Working with Graphics."

inspired to create digital artwork for personal and professional use. This section begins by explaining the technology behind digital graphics and then explores several ways in which digital graphics may be useful to you. A section is devoted to each of the primary types of digital graphics: vector graphics, 3D modeling, and animation. Digital photography and video are addressed in the next section.

Digitizing Graphics

The simple fact that graphic images can be represented digitally with binary numbers has brought us flatbed scanners, digital cameras, digital camcorders, digital cable TV, the DVD movie, and digital video recorders, high definition (HD) movies, and Blu-ray, not to mention phenomenal advances in movie production techniques. The fundamental technology behind all of these technologies rests on a small point of light or dot of ink called a pixel.

Digital images are made up of a grid of small points called **pixels** (short for picture element). *Pixel* is a good term to remember, as it has practical value when used to determine the quality of displays, printers, scanners, and digital cameras. Representing an image using bytes is simply a matter of storing the color of each pixel used in the image. Images stored in this manner are called **bit-mapped graphics** or *raster graphics*.

In bit-mapped graphics, colors are expressed using numbers that represent combinations of intensities of red, green, and blue (called the RGB color palette). One or more bytes may be used to express the intensity of each of red, green, and blue. For example, 0, 0, 255 would imply no red, no green, and full intensity of blue, and the resulting color is blue. See Figure 6.18 for more examples. Whenever all three bytes are set to the same values, the resulting color is a shade of gray. Often the hexadecimal number system is used to represent colors. Hexadecimal uses 16 digits: 0 through 9, and then A through F. (F is the highest value.) Artists use two hexadecimal digits for each of red, green, and blue to express colors. So 00FF00 would indicate no red, full green, no blue, and the resulting color is green.

FIGURE 6.18 • RGB color palette

In the RGB color palette, decimal or hexadecimal numbers represent the intensities of red, green, and blue used to create the colors for digital graphics.

	RGB Decimal	RGB Hex
	255, 000, 000	#FF0000
	255, 255, 000	#FFFF00
	000, 255, 000	#00FF00
	000, 255, 255	#00FFFF
	000, 000, 255	#0000FF
	255, 000, 255	#FF00FF
	000, 102, 000	#006600
	000, 000, 102	#000066
	000, 000, 000	#000000
	102, 102, 102	#666666
	255, 255, 255	#FFFFFF

Bit-mapped graphics are ideal for representing photo-realistic images, as they are able to capture minute details in an image. They do have some drawbacks, however, in that they are difficult to edit and enlarge. *Pixilation*, or fuzziness, occurs when bit-mapped images are made larger than the size at which they are captured.

Simpler images, such as those used in clip art, can be represented using vector graphics. **Vector graphics** use bytes to store geometric descriptions that define all the shapes in the image. Although vector graphics are impractical for representing photo-quality images, they are preferred for creating and storing drawings (see Figure 6.19). Vector graphics are easier to edit and manipulate than bit-mapped graphics and use far fewer bytes to store an image.

FIGURE 6.19 • Bit-mapped vs. vector graphics

Bit-mapped graphics (top) store images by specifying the color of each pixel and lose their clarity as they are enlarged; vector graphics (bottom) store pictures as defined shapes and retain clarity when enlarged.

Animation and video (moving pictures) are stored in the computer as a series of images called *frames*. When shown in quick succession, the frames create the illusion of movement. Television uses a rate of 30 frames per second (fps).

Graphics File Formats

There are many graphics file formats, most of which are proprietary; that is, they depend on the software with which they were created. For example, if you work on a photo in Adobe Photoshop, the file is saved by default as a .psd file that can be opened and manipulated only with Adobe products. Table 6.5 lists a few graphics file formats that have become standards across the industry.

Some graphics file formats support different types of file compression to reduce the file size. There are two types of compression: *lossless compression* allows the original data to be reconstructed without loss, while *lossy compression*

TABLE 6.5 • Common graphics file formats

Format	Description
Windows Bitmap (.bmp)	Used by the Windows operating system and recognized by most graphics software; not, however, recommended for use in generating images for the Web because not all browsers recognize it as a valid Web format
Graphics Interchange Format (.gif)	The standard for the Web; typically used for vector graphics and limited in that it supports only 255 colors
Joint Photographic Experts Group (.jpg or .jpeg)	The other standard for the Web and the default format on most digital cameras; JPG (pronounced jay-peg) is typically used for bit-mapped graphics and includes compression technology that allows images to be stored in less space
Portable Network Graphics (.png)	Developed to replace GIF on the Web; supports more colors than GIF and has other benefits as well
Tagged Image File Format (.tiff or .tif)	An industrial-strength format used by many professional photographers and graphic artists

accepts some loss of data to achieve higher rates of compression. The savings in file size can be considerable and is essential for fast-loading Web pages. For example, a 7 MB .tif file can be reduced to a 605 KB compressed .jpg file with little noticeable loss in quality.

File sizes and image quality can also be controlled by adjusting the color depth. Figure 6.20 provides an example of varying levels of color depth.

Uses of Digital Graphics

Digital graphics provides personal and professional benefits in several ways. It is used as a form of creative expression, as a means of visually presenting information, as a means to communicate and explore ideas, as a form of entertainment, as a tool to assist in the design of real-world objects, and as a method of documenting life.

Creative Expression. *Digital art* is a relatively new form of expression that uses computer software as the brush and the computer display as the canvas (check the digital art museum at *www.dam.org* and *http://digitalart.org*). Digital art can employ real or abstract images. The image shown in Figure 6.21 illustrates digital art depicting a surrealistic world in a superrealistic style. Other artists are taking advantage of aspects of computers that are not available to traditional visual artists. For example, the Database of Virtual Art (*www.virtualart.at*) catalogs many immersive, interactive, telematic, and genetic art projects that mix technology with visual art to create an interactive experience for the participant/viewer. The site includes videos of the artists' installations and exhibits.

FIGURE 6.20 • Color depth

This progression of images shows color depth progressing from 2 colors (1 bit), to 4 colors (2 bits), to 8 colors (3 bits), to 64 colors (6 bits), to 128 colors (7 bits), to millions of colors (24 bits), with file sizes progressing from 56 KB to 9.5 MB.

FIGURE 6.21 • Digital art

Digital art can employ real or abstract images.

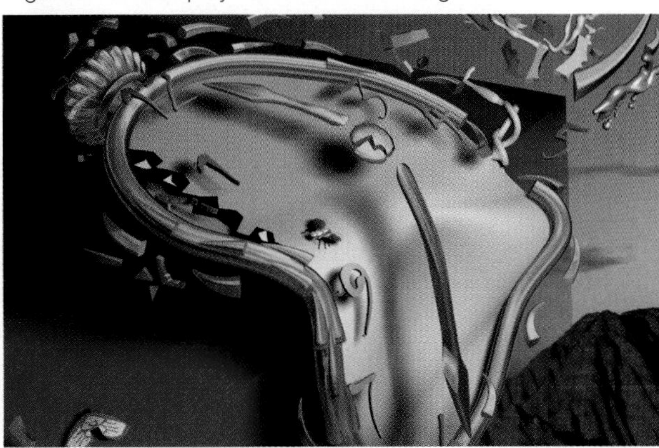

Photographers and videographers use digital graphics software to edit digital images for the purpose of creative expression. Artists of all genres are using computers in some aspect of their work. Sculptors use computer models to assist in planning their projects. Artists use the Internet as a platform for collaborating, publishing, and selling artwork of all kinds.

Amateurs as well as professionals enjoy using their computers to create artwork for the home and for friends. It is increasingly common to receive greeting cards made on a PC that incorporate personalized messages and photos. Digital photography makes it easy and inexpensive for nonprofessionals to experiment and to have fun taking pictures and enhancing them with special effects.

Presenting Information. Commercial graphics designers depend on graphics software to create visually appealing designs. Web designers are specialists in creating attractive Web page designs. They use graphics software to design buttons, backgrounds, and other stylistic elements that combine to make an appealing Web page. Desktop publishers use *desktop publishing* software to design page layouts for magazines, newspapers, books, and other publications (see Figure 6.22). Other graphics designers use computers to design company logos, product packaging, television and printed advertisements, billboards, and artwork for other commercial needs.

FIGURE 6.22 • Desktop publishing: Adobe Acrobat

Desktop publishing and design software provides powerful tools for publishing to paper or Web.

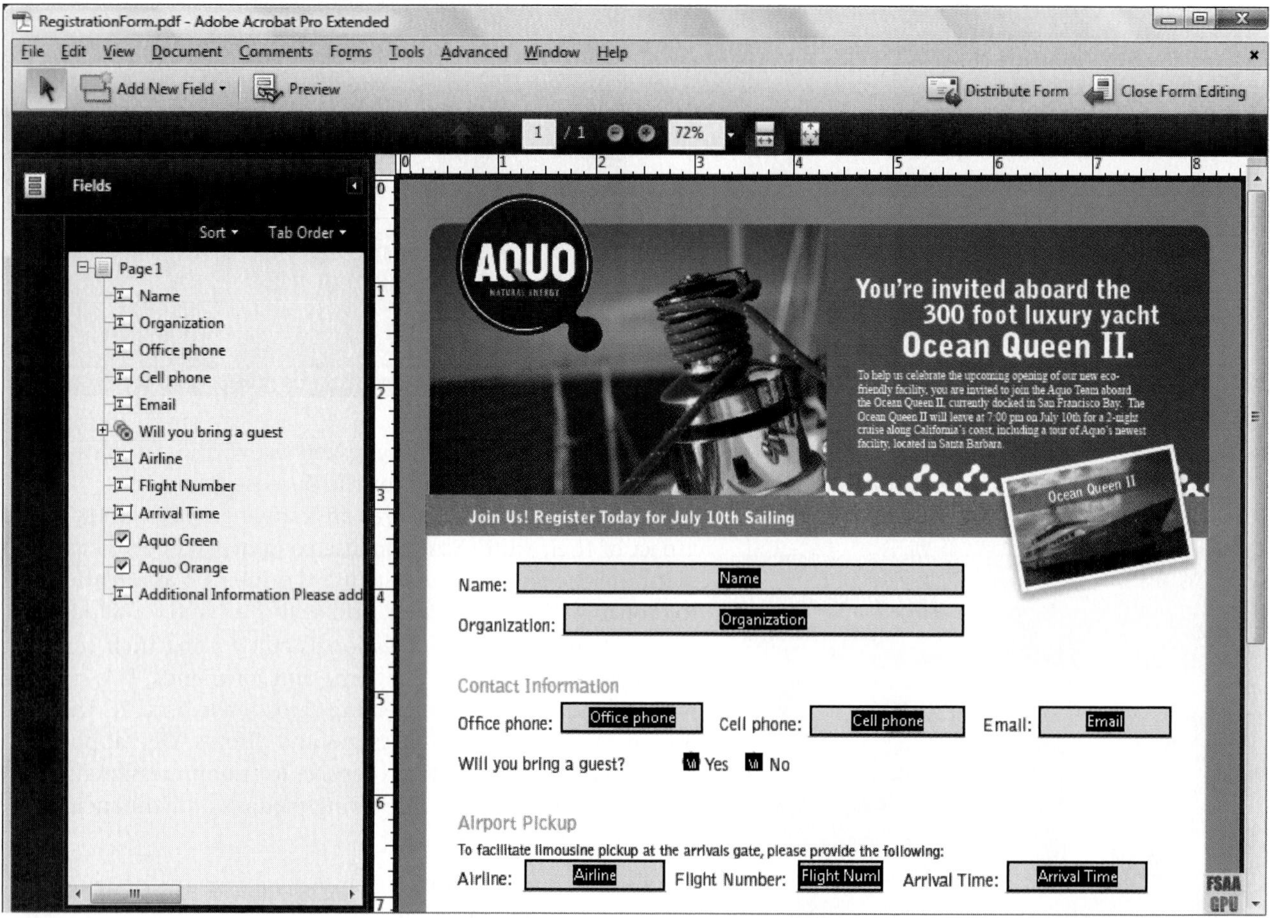

Digital video is becoming increasingly popular for presenting information and ideas. News organizations use video on their Web sites, and a wide variety of videos from useful to useless can be found on YouTube.

Communicating Ideas. Pictures, photographs, illustrations, graphs, animation, and video can communicate ideas in a more powerful manner than the printed or spoken word alone. Political cartoons might be the best example of this point. With biting wit, they quickly and concisely illustrate ideas in a manner that would be difficult to accomplish with words alone. Professionals from nearly every career area use graphics to make a point. Teachers and others who give educational presentations may use graphics presentation software to provide visual accompaniment to their presentations. Educators may incorporate video or animated simulations during presentations.

Illustrators use graphics software to illustrate children's stories in order to assist in developing a child's imagination. Technical artists illustrate instruction manuals and draw product specifications so customers can more easily assemble products and understand their workings. All of these professionals use computer-generated graphics to communicate ideas.

Some ideas can be described only in graphic form. Maps are created to graphically represent our world and are available on the Internet for nearly every location on earth. GPS (Global Positioning System) technology is used to accurately represent distances and elevations to the inch. Digital topography takes measurements and elevations as input and produces maps, even 3D maps, from the data.

Exploring New Ideas. **Scientific visualization** uses computer graphics to provide visual representations that improve our understanding of some phenomenon. There is a wide range of applications of scientific visualization, everything from presenting football team statistics to predicting the winner of the Super Bowl to studying the interaction of subatomic particles. Scientific visualization can be used to represent quantities of raw data as pictures. Meteorologists use visualization to study weather patterns such as the movement of air and pressure around and within tornadoes and hurricanes. Cardiologists use it to study irregular patterns in heartbeats. Scientific visualization can at times turn into beautiful imagery, as shown in Figure 6.23. This picture, from a large gallery of visualization graphics available at *www.ericjhellergallery.com,* illustrates the flow of electrons through a nanowire.

FIGURE 6.23 • Scientific visualization: electrons in a nanowire

This scientific visualization shows electrons flowing in a microscopic nanowire by assigning varying colors to the crests and troughs of the electron waves injected into the wire at the bright spot.

Entertainment. Artists in a variety of entertainment industries make use of digital graphics to create products for the enjoyment of their audiences. Cartoonists and comic book artists can produce their products much more quickly using graphics software than they can by sketching and coloring. Animators no longer need to work with markers on transparent sheets, drawing hundreds of individual pictures that take only a matter of seconds to play on the screen. Now animators draw cartoon characters on a computer and program them to move across the screen.

The motion picture industry is capitalizing on the power of computing to create effects that are not possible in the real world. Gradually, the motion picture industry is moving toward digital cinema, which will do away with outdated motion picture projection methods in favor of digital projection.

Designing Real-World Objects. **Computer-assisted design (CAD) software** assists designers, engineers, and architects in designing three-dimensional objects, from the gear mechanism in a watch to suspension bridges. CAD software provides tools to construct 3D objects on the computer screen, examine them from all angles, and test their properties (see Figure 6.24). CAD is able to turn designs on the computer into blueprint specifications for manufacturing. CAD output can also be used to directly control the manufacturing of products and parts. Using Z Corporation's ZPrinter 450, a 3D printer, engineers can take a CAD drawing and turn it into a 3D model or prototype. Urban and regional planners use CAD to design neighborhoods, shopping malls, and other large-scale construction.

FIGURE 6.24 • Computer-assisted design (CAD)

CAD is able to turn designs on the computer into blueprint specifications to bring ideas from your imagination to reality.

Interior designers and architects use CAD to visualize 3D room layouts. Professionals in the textile industry rely on computers to help design the graphic patterns for material. Computer systems are also used to apply those designs to the fabric.

Documenting Life. Photos and home movies preserve visual memories and act as a witness to special moments in our lives. Photojournalists as well as amateurs are moving to digital cameras and image processing for collecting, managing, and manipulating photographs and films for historical and sentimental value. Once digitized, these images are easily copied and shared with others over the Internet.

Vector Graphics Software

Vector graphics software, sometimes called *drawing software,* provides tools to create, arrange, and layer graphical objects on the screen. Vector graphics uses an object-oriented approach that recognizes pictures as being made up of layers of multiple objects, some in the foreground, some in the background, and some in between. Objects in a vector graphics image can be layered and grouped into larger objects. Each object's properties such as color and transparency can be altered. Figure 6.25 shows a restaurant menu created with Adobe Illustrator, a popular vector graphics software package. The menu is made up of many individual objects layered one upon another. Each can be moved, edited, and positioned anywhere on the page, making it easy to change the content and design.

FIGURE 6.25 • Vector graphics

This menu is made up of dozens of graphic objects that can be edited, layered, and arranged on the page.

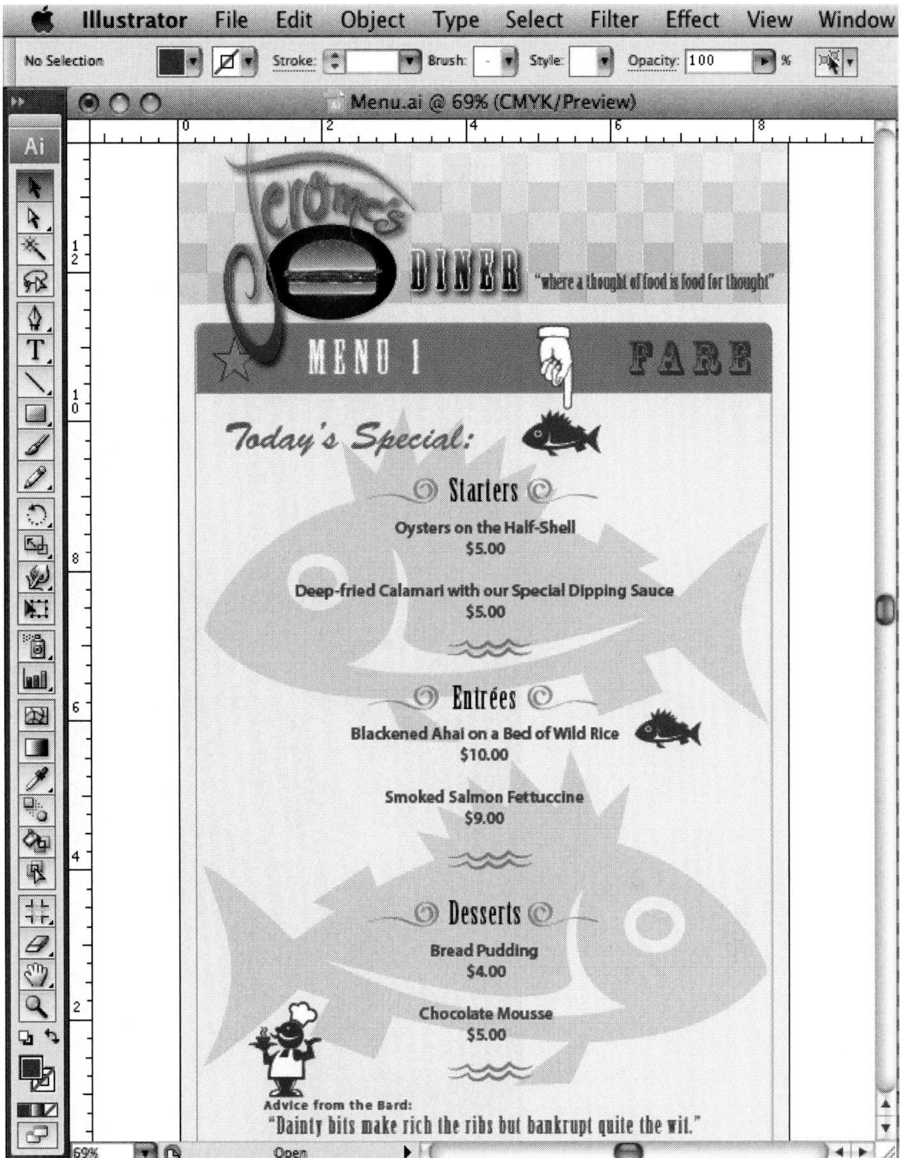

Vector graphics software like Adobe Illustrator and Corel Draw provides tools to create and manipulate vector graphics. Filter tools allow you to adjust the color of an object by altering the levels of brightness, contrast, hue, and saturation. Effects tools range from subtle effects, such as changing the sharpness or blurriness of edges within a drawing, to dramatic effects, such as changing a picture so that it looks as though you are viewing it through a glass block. When finished, vector graphics images can be exported as GIF, BMP, PNG, or other types of graphics files.

Three-Dimensional Modeling Software

The latest **3D modeling software** provides graphics tools that allow artists to create pictures of realistic 3D models. Three-dimensional modeling takes the object-oriented approach of vector graphics to the next level. The process of changing two-dimensional objects such as those created with vector graphics applications into 3D models involves adding shadows and light. Three-dimensional modeling is often referred to as *ray tracing* because the software must trace rays of light as it would interact with the models in the real world. Three-dimensional modeling also requires that surface textures be defined for models. Surface textures are an important element in the interaction between light and a model. Consider the way light interacts with the model in Figure 6.26. Although this figure looks a lot like a photograph, it is actually a computer drawing by digital artist Liam Kemp (*www.liamkemp.com*).

FIGURE 6.26 • Ray tracing

Ray tracing uses the software's ability to calculate how light interacts with models in the real world. Notice the detail, shadows, and reflections in this computer-generated image from digital artist Liam Kemp.

Creating 3D digital art takes place in a scene on a 3D stage (see Figure 6.27). The artist starts by defining a light source: the position of the light in the scene, the style of lighting—natural, spotlight, fluorescent, candle, table lamp, and so on—and the intensity of the light. Models are inserted into the scene by selecting from a library of predesigned 3D models, by creating the model from scratch through a process of manipulating virtual wire frames, or by using 3D scanners to import images of real models into the computer. The artist selects surface textures for each model and positions the models on the stage. Finally, the artist selects a background for the scene, and the software renders the scene. *Rendering* is the process of calculating the light interaction with the virtual 3D models in the scene and presenting the final drawing in two dimensions to be viewed on the screen or printed.

FIGURE 6.27 • Three-dimensional rendering

Producing 3D digital art takes place in a scene on a 3D stage. The artist defines a light source, places objects on the stage, and renders the image to observe the effect.

Three-dimensional graphics acts as a foundation for other technologies. For example, CAD software uses 3D graphics to design and view manufactured products. Virtual reality applications use 3D graphics to build virtual worlds in which users can interact with the 3D models. The fundamental component in computer-generated animation for video games and motion pictures is 3D graphics. Popular 3D graphics development software includes Blender, Maya, and LightWave.

Computer Animation

Digital graphics animation involves displaying digital images in rapid succession to provide the illusion of motion. Graphics animations can be as simple as a stick man jumping rope or as complex as major motion pictures such as *Ratatouille, UP,* and *Monsters vs. Aliens*—all of which were completely computer generated (Figure 6.28). Animated graphics employs either 2D or 3D objects, with 3D animations requiring the most advanced graphics software and processing power to create.

FIGURE 6.28 • Disney-Pixar's *UP*

The digitally animated motion picture *UP*, from Disney-Pixar, was created completely within the confines of a computer system.

Two-Dimensional Computer Animation. You may have seen simple animations on the Web, simple drawings that repeat the same motion over and over, endlessly. This is the most basic form of animation, called an *animated GIF* (pronounced *jiff*). Animated GIFs are created with simple tools that allow the artist to draw several images that, when played in succession, create the illusion of motion. The images are stored in one .gif file, and when viewed in a Web page, they are played sequentially to present the animation. The artist can set the animated GIF to loop endlessly, and he or she can control the speed of the sequence. The animated GIF format allows for as many images as are required for the animation; however, the more images loaded into the GIF file, the larger the file becomes and the longer it takes to load.

For more complex Web animations, artists must turn to programming languages such as Java or Web animation development platforms such as Adobe Flash or Microsoft Silverlight. Because most animators are not computer programmers, Flash has become the most popular tool for creating animated Web content. Flash provides a timeline tool that is used to cue movement in the animation (see Figure 6.29). Unlike animated GIF tools, Flash automates the frame production process. For example, a picture of a hula dancer can be placed in the upper-left corner of the Flash workspace at time unit 1; at time unit 10, the rocket can be placed at the right side of the workspace. Flash will "fill in" the movement from left to right evenly over the time between 1 and 10 according to your instructions; for example, you might instruct Flash to move the dancer in an *S* pattern.

FIGURE 6.29 • Adobe Flash

Adobe Flash provides a timeline tool that is used to cue movement in the animation. In this image, the hula dancer dances across the screen over the duration of the timeline.

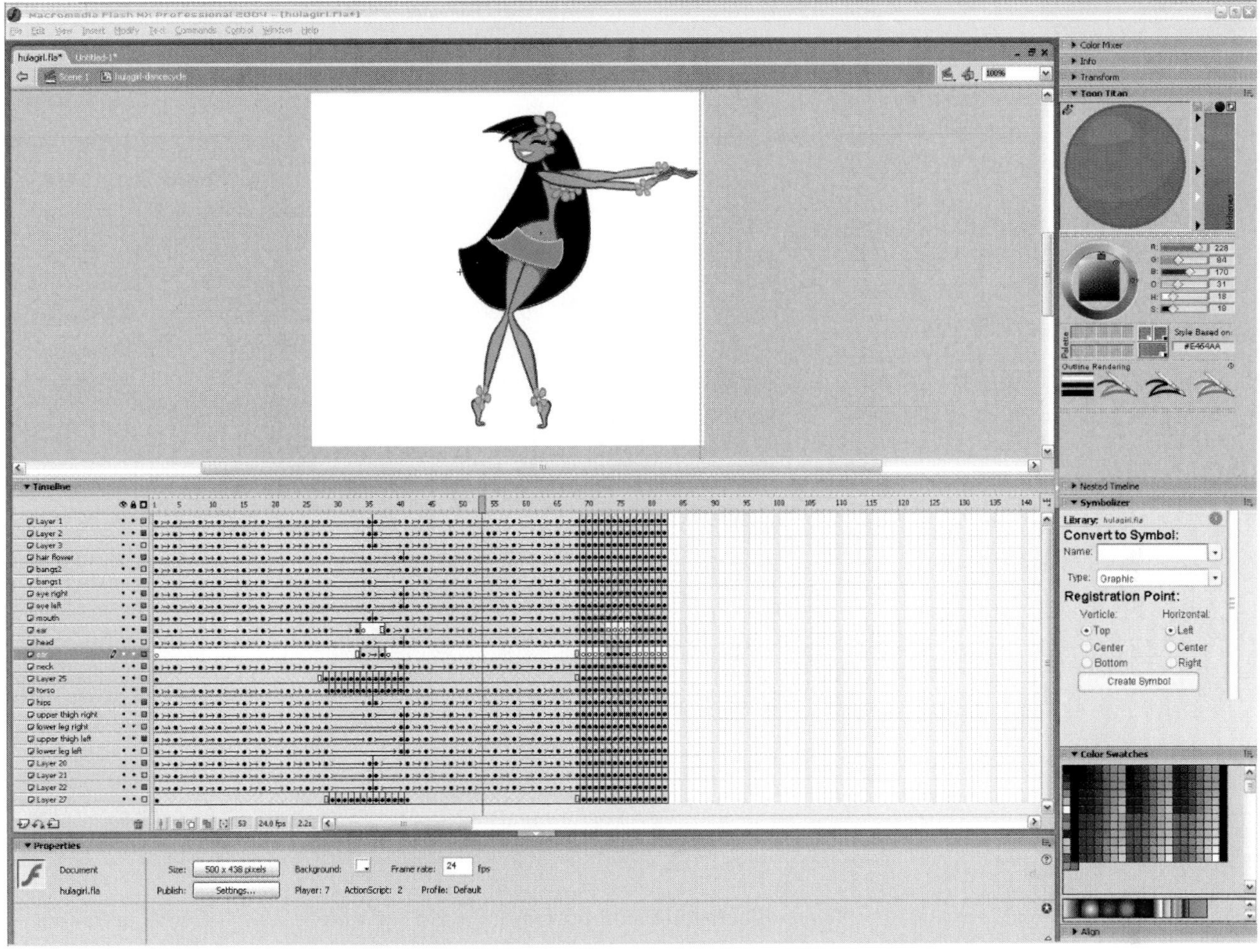

Flash can be used for simple or advanced Web animations and applications. Full-blown animated films can be produced, as well as interactive games. Flash includes its own scripting language—ActionScript—for more advanced applications. Besides Flash and Silverlight, other tools used to create animations on the Web include Adobe Director and Apple QuickTime.

Three-Dimensional Computer Animation. Three-dimensional computer animation is much more complex than the 2D form. *Three-dimensional computer animation* includes all of the complexity of 3D graphics rendering, multiplied by the necessity to render 24 3D images per second to create the illusion of movement. Three-dimensional animation software is typically packaged with 3D modeling software. These animation programs, such as LightWave from NewTek and Mental Ray from SoftImage, are used by professionals to create popular animated television shows, commercials, and movies; they range in price from $1595 to $13,000 and include a very steep learning curve.

Three-dimensional models of people, animals, and other moving objects created with the modeling software are provided with the ability to move by using avars. *Avars* are points on the object that are designed to bend or pivot at specific angles. They are used at joints in the model's skeleton to provide articulation—movement at the joints. Avars are also used for muscular movement in the skin; they are used to depict facial expressions of characters in animated films. Avars are controlled either by special input devices manipulated by the artists or through software. Figure 6.30 shows an avar placed on the eyelid of a virtual frog. A character in an animated feature film may have over 100 avars in the face alone.

FIGURE 6.30 • Animated 3D objects

An avar placed on the eyelid of this frog allows for a blinking motion.

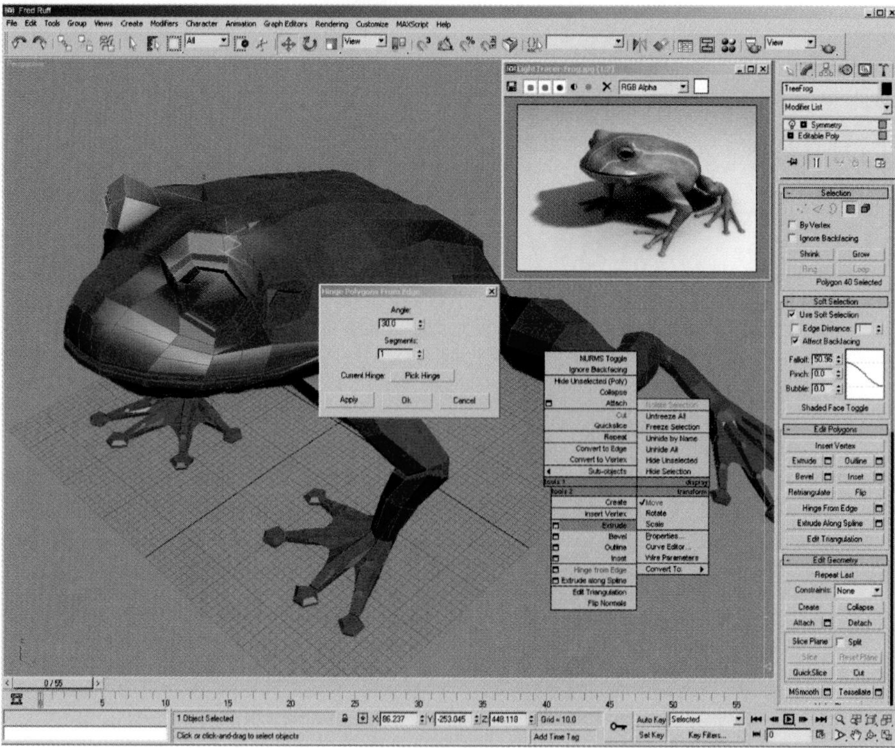

Three-dimensional computer animation software is able to move animated characters according to the direction of the artist and director. Rather than drawing and painting individual frames, animators are more like puppeteers who direct the animated characters around the set. After the action is recorded, rendering computers apply the 3D effects and lighting to each frame. Even with powerful computers, the high-quality rendering used for major animated motion pictures takes hours per frame.

Pixar, the company that brought *Toy Story, A Bug's Life, Monsters, Inc., Finding Nemo, The Incredibles, Cars, Ratatouille,* and *UP* to the screen, uses a powerful computer system called the RenderFarm. Pixar's RenderFarm has supercomputing power consisting of 1024 Intel Xeon processors housed in eight BladeRack supercomputing clusters running Pixar's own RenderMan software. The RenderFarm features two terabytes of memory and 60 terabytes of disk space.

DIGITAL PHOTOGRAPHY AND VIDEO

So far this chapter has covered only vector graphics and the method of creating and editing artwork, graphics, and animation by manipulating objects. Another method of working with photographic images and video is *digital imaging.* Instead of using vector graphics, digital imaging uses bit-mapped, or raster, images. Recall from earlier in the chapter that bit-mapped images store the color code for each individual pixel in the image. When you work with bit-mapped images, you lose the capacity to work with objects. While working with vector graphics is a lot like arranging cutouts to create an image, editing bit-mapped images is more like coloring with markers than arranging cutouts.

Digital Photography

Digital photography has become very popular primarily because inexpensive digital cameras and camera phones are widely available. Nearly everyone is taking digital photos and enjoying the instant gratification of viewing the image as soon as it is taken—something that previously was not possible. Gradually, photo albums are transforming from dusty bound volumes on bookshelves to volumes stored on hard drives and online services. The number of photos being generated is the highest ever, and hundreds of new devices, software titles, and services are rapidly being introduced to the market in support of the digital photo fever. This section surveys the latest technologies for creating, editing, sharing, and printing digital photos.

Creating Digital Photos. Digital photos are created, or acquired, using a digital camera or scanner and are saved as bit-mapped images. Digital cameras are ranked by the number of *megapixels* they can capture (1 megapixel = 1 million pixels) and the features they include. A good entry-level camera like the HP PhotoSmart (see Figure 6.31) costs around $100 and provides 6-megapixel images, but it has very few features. A midrange camera like the Sony Cyber-shot costs around $300, provides 8-megapixel images, and includes lots of features to assist in producing good-looking photos. A digital SLR (single lens reflex) camera like the Nikon D80x uses the same mirror and lens principles as professional-grade 35mm cameras to produce professional images typically over 10 megapixels. SLR cameras are expensive but are gradually coming down to the $1000 range. Table 6.6 lists digital camera specifications to consider.

FIGURE 6.31 • Digital cameras

As you progress from a basic digital camera like the HP Photosmart (left) to a midrange camera like the Sony Cyber-shot (middle) to a digital SLR camera like the Nikon D80x (right), the photos produced show marked improvements in quality.

Memory cards that come with digital cameras often have limited capacity, so it is usually a good idea to purchase a higher-capacity card. A 64 MB card can store over 100 medium-resolution photos, or 50 high-resolution photos. Even with a higher-capacity card, travelers often take along a laptop computer to download photos over the course of long trips, so they can clear and reuse the camera's memory card. An alternative is to bring your digital camera to a photo-processing service or kiosk to have your photos printed or transferred to CD or DVD.

TABLE 6.6 • Digital camera features and considerations

Feature	Considerations
Resolution	Three megapixels or more is best for recreational use, higher than 6 megapixels for serious hobbyists, and higher than 10 for professionals
Price	$100 to $300 for most recreational-grade cameras, $300 to $1000 for serious hobbyists, thousands of dollars for professional-grade cameras
Camera size	While some very small cameras can produce very good quality, the largest digital cameras (SLRs) offer the best quality
Display size and quality	Since digital photography uses an LCD display to line up the shot, it's important that you get one that is large enough to see and bright enough to see in direct sunlight
Lens type	Most people insist on a zoom lens with a range encompassing at least 38mm to 114mm
Storage media	Flash memory card with a lot of capacity; about 1 MB per photo
Photo file format	JPEG for recreational use, TIFF for professionals
Interfaces	USB, NTSC/PAL television connection for off-loading and viewing photos
Exposure controls	Automatic, programmed scene modes, exposure compensation (for tweaking the automatic exposure)
Focus controls	Automatic for recreational use; pros will want to include manual control as well
Flash modes	Automatic, fill, red-eye reduction
Software	Photo editor, photo stitching (combining photos into panoramas), photo album creator, slide show
Multimedia	VGA (640 x 480), 30 fps video-clip recording
Other useful features	Ultracompact design, webcam capabilities, voice recording, wireless transfer, large LCD picture display
Battery	Rechargeable or disposable battery models

Editing Digital Photos. **Photo-editing software**, such as Adobe Photoshop and Photoshop Elements, Apple iPhoto, Windows Live Photo Gallery, and online editors like Photoshop Express, Picnik, Flickr, and Picassa, include special tools and effects that you can use to improve or manipulate bit-mapped photographic images. Photo-editing software allows you to do the following:

- Alter the hue and saturation of the colors in the photograph to give skin tones a healthy glow, or enrich colors in a landscape
- Smooth surfaces or remove flaws in surfaces
- Remove "red-eye" (the effect of the camera flash on the eyes of subjects, which causes eyes to appear red in a photograph)
- Smooth edges and sharpen focus
- Crop and realign photos

Photo-editing tools also include special effects, such as the ability to transform photos into watercolor paintings. Or you can use edge detection to remove an object from one photo and insert it in another (see Figure 6.32). The ability to combine photo images to create fictitious photos has made it difficult to trust any photograph at face value.

A WHOLE NEW WAY OF SEEING

You've just met someone at a party and you cross into serious conversation. "Careful," she warns you. "The walls have eyes and ears!" Is she paranoid, or for real? Soon, she might just be right about the eyes! Researchers from MIT have created a fiber that can replace a camera lens. The fiber consists of a semiconductor that detects light electrodes that send signals to a microprocessor. Visualization software processes the data and creates an image. The polymer covering makes the fiber durable enough to be sewn into a shirt—or woven into wallpaper.

Futuristic Fibers Could Replace Camera Lenses
Phil Berardelli
ScienceNOW
July 10, 2009
http://cacm.acm.org/news/33930-futuristic-fibers-could-replace-camera-lenses/fulltext

FIGURE 6.32 • Photo editing

Here the author doctors a photo of the Incredible Hulk, placing his own head on the Hulk's body.

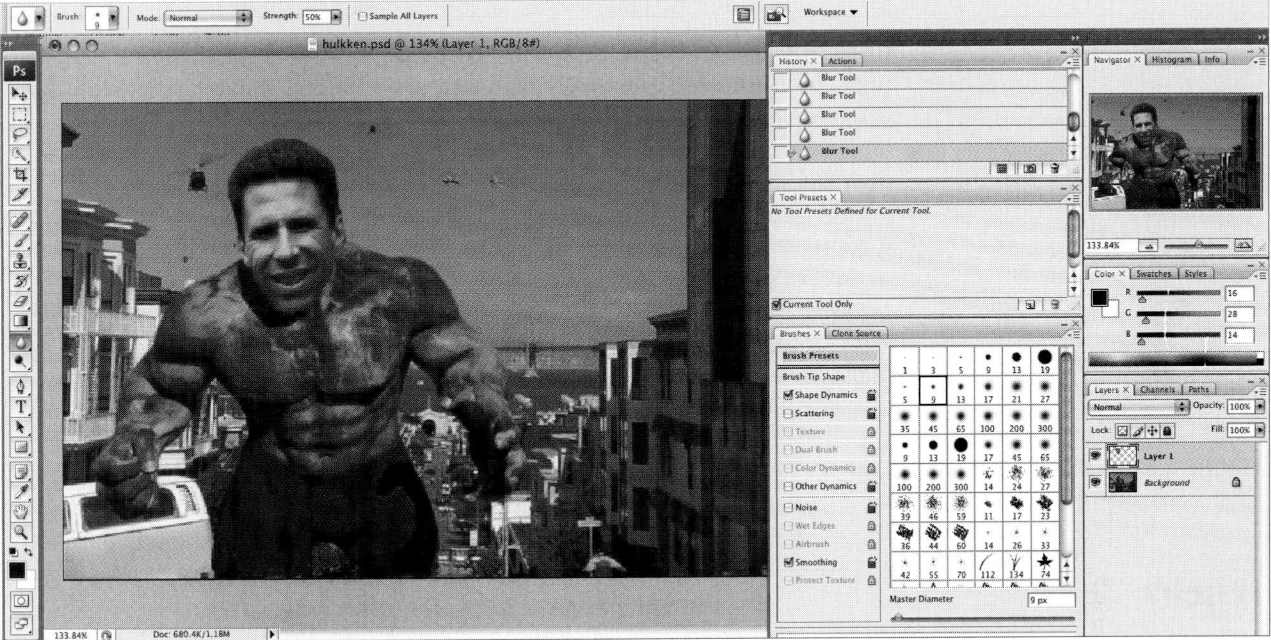

Most digital cameras come with photo-editing software designed for personal use, providing easy-to-use tools for cleaning up photos and integrating them into frames, greeting cards, calendars, and other popular printed forms. This software often includes wizards that walk the user through the photo-editing process. Professional-grade photo-editing software, such as Adobe Photoshop, provides many tools for retouching and editing photographs to professional standards.

Viewing and Sharing Digital Photos. There are several ways to view digital images and share them with friends. It is not always convenient to have everyone gather around the computer to view photos. However, there are systems designed to display photographs to groups. Many of today's cameras provide ways to display the images on a television as a slide show. As PCs become more integrated with entertainment systems, it will become increasingly common to gather around the television, or media display, to view family photos. There are even digital picture frames. The Ceiva Digital Photo Receiver (*www.ceiva.com*) looks like a regular desktop picture frame but is in reality an Internet-connected digital photo display. The picture frame connects to the Internet via a phone line. Each night it automatically dials up the Ceiva system and downloads to the picture frame new photos that have been sent to you by friends and family. Photos are sent to the picture frame using Web-based software or directly from camera phones. Other digital picture frames read photos directly from media cards.

Perhaps the most convenient way to share photos is over the Internet. E-mailing photos is problematic because photo files are typically large and can dramatically slow down e-mail delivery. It is much more practical and considerate to post photos on the Web and an e-mail link to your online photo album. Many companies offer such services, such as Flickr (*www.flickr.com*), Google's Picasa (*http://picasa.google.com*), and Kodak Gallery (*www.kodakgallery.com*).

Some services also offer the ability to upload and view photos from cell phones. For example, Yahoo! Go provides cell phone software that allows you to upload photos from cell phones directly to your Flickr account. This is quite valuable, as it is often difficult to transfer photos from a cell phone to a PC. There is no charge for the service and no limit to the number of photos that can be transferred.

Printing Digital Photos. As with most aspects of the rapidly expanding digital photo industry, options for printing photos are bountiful. Today many printers are designed specifically for printing photos, but many people prefer to have their digital photos printed by a professional service due to the low price, convenience, and high quality of such services. It is often difficult and time-consuming to match the quality provided by professional printing, and the price of paper, toner, and time invested in doing it yourself is often more expensive than paying the professionals.

Yahoo!'s Flickr photo service has partnered with Target stores to offer photo pickup service. Digital photos uploaded to Flickr can be sent to your local Target store for printing within one hour (Figure 6.33). Costco (*www.costco.com*), Walgreens (*http://photo.walgreens.com*), and Wal-Mart (*www.walmart.com*) also allow you to upload your photos for processing at your local store within an hour.

Photo kiosks are another popular option for printing digital photos. There are over 121,000 photo kiosks in the United States. Photo kiosks read photos from CDs or any of the popular media cards, allow you to crop and edit each image, and then print your photos—perhaps while you do a little shopping. Kiosks are popular for their ease of use, print quality, speed, and the amount of control they offer the user. Home photo printer manufacturers have designed several home printers that function in much the same manner as photo kiosks in an attempt to provide consumers with the conveniences they desire.

FIGURE 6.33 • Flickr/Target prints

Flickr and Target have teamed up to provide digital photo services from uploading to storing, printing, and picking up photos.

EXPAND YOUR KNOWLEDGE

To learn more about digital video, go to www.cengage.com/computerconcepts/np/swt4. Click the link "Expand Your Knowledge" and then complete the lab entitled "Working with Video."

Digital Video

Advances in digital technologies and broadband communications and information systems are having a profound effect on the creation, distribution, and enjoyment of video. Digital video is becoming increasingly accessible for personal enjoyment as well as professional use.

Both digital photography and digital video are used in a variety of research and other professional areas. *Forensic graphics* is used to create animations and exhibits to use in courts of law to explain theories and present evidence. Figure 6.34 shows a forensic graphics storyboard used to reconstruct the spread of an industrial fire. Forensic graphics experts also study photos and videotaped evidence in an effort to solve crimes. For example, a forensic graphics expert might study video of a convenience store robbery to ascertain the identity of the thieves. Video cameras mounted at intersections are increasingly being used to catch drivers who run red lights; they record the license number of the vehicle in the video image.

FIGURE 6.34 • Forensic graphics

Forensic graphics storyboards are used to reconstruct the spread of an industrial fire.

By studying digital video, athletes and trainers can review the movement of the athletes and determine how to perfect their abilities. Digital video is used to study pedestrian and traffic patterns. Scientists also use it to study the activity of microbes and other organisms.

Digital video is also finding a home in the hearts of consumers as a primary form of entertainment. Taking in a movie has become a favorite pastime for all ages. Digital cable networks, on-demand television, and DVDs have brought popular motion pictures to home television. Large high-definition displays and surround sound systems are providing theater-quality experiences at home. Broadband Internet and service providers are bringing motion pictures, television programming, and other video services to PCs and cell phones. Digital camcorders allow you to capture the important moments of your life in motion.

From 35mm Film to Digital Cinema

Digital cinema utilizes digital technologies to capture, store, and project motion pictures. You might think that motion pictures would have been digitized long ago, with the advent of the DVD. But going digital is no easy undertaking for such a huge industry. Cameras, distribution methods, and projection systems require upgrading. A typical digital projector costs $60,000.

Roughly 18,000 theaters out of around 110,000 theaters in the world have transitioned to digital technology. By 2012 it is expected that 20 percent will have made the change. The recent trend toward 3D films that require digital projectors is prompting many cinemas to upgrade even during economic hardship.

Recently AMC theaters closed a $315 million deal with Sony to upgrade all of its 2,000 projectors to digital by 2012. The UK Film Council announced that it will invest $1.9 million to bring digital cinema to rural areas in the United Kingdom. Film & Kino, the Norwegian interest organization for cinemas, launched an initiative being hailed as the world's first noncommercial, complete national digital rollout to upgrade all cinemas in Norway.

Digital cinema has several benefits and a few drawbacks. Going digital will massively improve film distribution. Rather than having to ship expensive reels of film around the world, digital films can be distributed on hard drive or downloaded over the Internet. This last fact has those in the business concerned over the possibility of rampant piracy. Going digital provides the opportunity to broadcast live events to cinemas over satellite or the Internet. For example, the Metropolitan Opera broadcasts its performances to a number of movie theaters. Digital motion pictures also have a slightly different appearance that fans and producers either like or dislike. But no one can argue that working with digital film doesn't provide numerous conveniences and advantages over working with 35mm film.

Questions

1. What benefits will digital cinema bring to consumers?
2. What benefits will digital cinema bring to the motion picture industry?
3. What challenges does the transition to digital cinema present for the industry?

Sources

1. *Staff, "Betting on cinemas in troubled times,"* Film Journal International, *July 13, 2009, http://www.filmjournal.com.*
2. *Stensland, Jorgan, "World's First Non-Commercial National Digital Cinema Roll-Out,"* DCinema Today, *Jun 24, 2009, http://www.dcinematoday.com.*

Creating Digital Video. Digital video cameras, called digital camcorders, are available in a wide range of prices with wide-ranging capabilities. At the low end of the spectrum are disposable camcorders that sell at local pharmacies for under $30. At the opposite end of the spectrum are high-definition camcorders selling for over $3000.

Camcorder prices have dropped significantly in recent years. For example, a pocket hi-def camcorder costs less than $180 (see Figure 6.35). Hi-def camcorders can record at 1080p, the native resolution of most hi-def televisions. Most camcorders can also capture still images, but not at the same high resolution as a good digital camera. (And good digital cameras are typically able to capture video but at very low resolution.) So, unfortunately, if you want to capture both high-quality photos and high-quality videos, you'll need two devices. No doubt that will change over time and the two functions will be integrated into one unit.

FIGURE 6.35 • Pocket hi-def camcorder

For a relatively small amount of money, pocket camcorders put major video capture power in an amazingly small device.

Editing Digital Video. With the increase in popularity of digital camcorders, increasing numbers of home PC users are finding it useful to edit their digital videos on their home PCs. Much of the footage captured on videotape is often not worth saving. **Video-editing software** allows professional and amateur videographers to edit out bad footage and rearrange the good footage to produce a professional-style video production. Popular video-editing software packages include Studio Moviebox for Windows from Pinnacle Systems; Adobe products such as Premier, Video Collection, and After Effects available for both Windows and Apple computers; Windows Movie Maker; and iDVD and Final Cut Pro for Apple. Many of today's camcorders include the ability to edit video directly on the camera. This provides the considerable convenience of not needing to download and edit on a PC. The tools provided are simple to use but not as powerful as video-editing software.

Digital video can be transferred to a computer directly from a camcorder or it can be read from a DVD. Video takes up a significant amount of space on the hard drive—roughly a gigabyte for one hour of video. For this reason most home users do not store many videos on their PC, but copy them to CD or DVD after they finish editing.

Video-editing software uses a *storyline* on which to build a video production. A storyline allows the videographer to arrange video scenes sequentially and specify the transition effects between each scene. Figure 6.36 illustrates the video-editing process. The videographer can add still images, background music, and text to the storyline along with video scenes. When the storyline is complete, it is saved to one of many possible video formats on a hard drive and published to the Web or burned to DVD to be viewed on TV.

FIGURE 6.36 • Video-editing storyline

Using video-editing software, a videographer arranges scenes and transitions between scenes on a storyline to create a video production.

The increase in home video production has led to a new form of expression on the Web called vlogs. *Vlog* is short for *video log*, and it is the video version of a blog. Just as podcasts might be considered a form of audio blog, a vlog presents a person's ideas or tells a story through video. Sometimes vlogs are called video podcasts. A search at your favorite search engine on *vlog* is sure to turn up interesting sites.

The birth of YouTube has energized the home video industry even more than the TV show *America's Funniest Home Videos*. Now anyone can share home-recorded videos with the world, and millions are. Hundreds of thousands of new videos are uploaded to YouTube daily in categories that include Autos & Vehicles, Comedy, Entertainment, Film & Animation, Howto & DIY, Music, News & Politics, People & Blogs, Pets & Animals, Sports, and Travel & Places. YouTube is increasingly being used for education and training. Many universities have their own YouTube channels where they broadcast lectures for their students and the rest of the world to view (see Figure 6.37).

FIGURE 6.37 • MIT on YouTube

MIT's YouTube channel provides lectures from a wide assortment of MIT classes.

Digital movies, which might otherwise require hundreds of gigabytes or even terabytes of storage space, are compressed down to less than 10 GB in order to fit onto a DVD. Digital video compression involves analyzing each frame of the video and storing only the pixels that change from frame to frame. Consider a nightly news show. Such video typically has little or no change to the background behind the news reporter. So, when compressed, the bits that make up the background need to be stored only once for the frames in which they remain unchanged. A video frame might display a million pixels but have only 1000 pixels that change from the previous frame, reducing the storage requirements one thousand times.

Digital Video, Television, and Movie Services. Besides the traditional forms of taking in movies—theater and television—many new forms of digital video delivery are becoming available. In earlier chapters you learned about Internet companies that provide motion picture download and DVD rental services, and cell phone services that provide video downloads (see Figure 6.38).

FIGURE 6.38 • TV on a smart phone

Television programming and movies are increasingly available anywhere, anytime: at home, in the car, on your PC, or on your phone.

It is clear that just as digital technologies are transforming the music industry, they are transforming the movie and video industries as well.

The rapid adoption of high-speed Internet connections makes trading pirated copies of movies online easier and more widespread. Still, sharing movies is not as widespread as sharing music because of the size of movie files: it can take an hour or more to download one DVD-quality movie. Major motion picture studios are scrambling to develop an online distribution model and invent strong incentives to offer consumers convenient legal options for accessing movies online, and many have digitized hundreds of movie titles in preparation for online sales.

Mobile television services are also on the rise. The Microsoft video download service provides daily television programming, entertainment clips, and other digital content for viewing on mobile Windows-based devices. The service can also be used to view shows recorded on a TiVo digital video recorder using a service called TiVoToGo. The new iPod can store 150 hours of video supplied by the iTunes service through cooperation with several movie and television companies.

Not to be left out of the race to digital convergence, cell phone companies are offering video and television programming over 3G networks. For example, Verizon's V CAST service provides video entertainment, news, weather, and sports from major media outlets for $15 per month.

Online services like Hulu, Joost, and Miro stream movies and television programming to users over the Internet, merging the Web with television. Apple introduced its Apple TV set-top box to allow those who purchase video content from iTunes to stream their movies to their television over a home wireless network. The Slingbox allows users to control and view their television from their computer, and through the home wireless network and the Internet on their iPhone, BlackBerry, or other smart phone (see Figure 6.39).

THE CABLE INDUSTRY FIGHTS BACK

As cable TV providers watched the music industry slowly sink, scuttled by the Internet, they knew it was only a matter of time. With increasing bandwidth, suddenly YouTube was licensing deals with content providers and Hulu was offering free TV over the Internet. The mass migration from cable to Internet had begun. So, in 2009, cable giants Comcast and Time Warner announced a push for TV everywhere—and began providing "on-demand online services." The only catch is that the user needs to be a cable customer—a condition they hope will keep providers' heads above water.

"Comcast, Time Warner Push 'TV Everywhere' — for a Price"
E-commerce Times
Renay San Miguel
June 24, 2009
http://www.ecommercetimes.com/story/67424.html

FIGURE 6.39 • SlingPlayer

Control and view your home TV from your PC and smart phone.

All of these examples point to the rapid integration and convergence taking place between computing, television, and communications networks. People are watching television at home, in the car, in an airplane, or in the park on a notebook or a cell phone display. Video programming is being delivered by television providers, phone providers, and Internet providers. Increasingly, service providers are bundling all three services, such as Comcast's Triple Play cable TV, phone, and Internet package. Through partnerships, takeovers, and mergers, competition in these areas is boiling down to only a handful of companies competing to provide all of our digital electronics connections.

INTERACTIVE MEDIA

Interactive media refers to digital media that involves user interaction for education, training, or entertainment. Interactive media is unique in that the audience is not passively observing the media; it is created specifically for the audience to take part in the creative or educational process. Interactive media typically combines digital audio and digital video.

When interactive media incorporates 3D graphic animation, the result is *virtual reality*. Virtual reality produces a simulated environment in which the human participant can move and manipulate objects. Adding surround sound makes the interactive experience more realistic.

Video games make up a large portion of the interactive media market (Figure 6.40). Other forms of interactive media provide computer-based tutorials and training, and still others are commercial applications that support the sales of products and provide customer support. Interactive media is becoming increasingly important as technology advances are able to support its large demands for processing speed, storage, and bandwidth. New development tools also better support interactive media over the Internet and Web. This section provides an overview of interactive media and its value in our lives.

FIGURE 6.40 • 3D interactive game environments

NBA Street Homecourt for the Xbox 360 is as realistic as it gets, providing the player with near superhuman strength and abilities in a variety of environments.

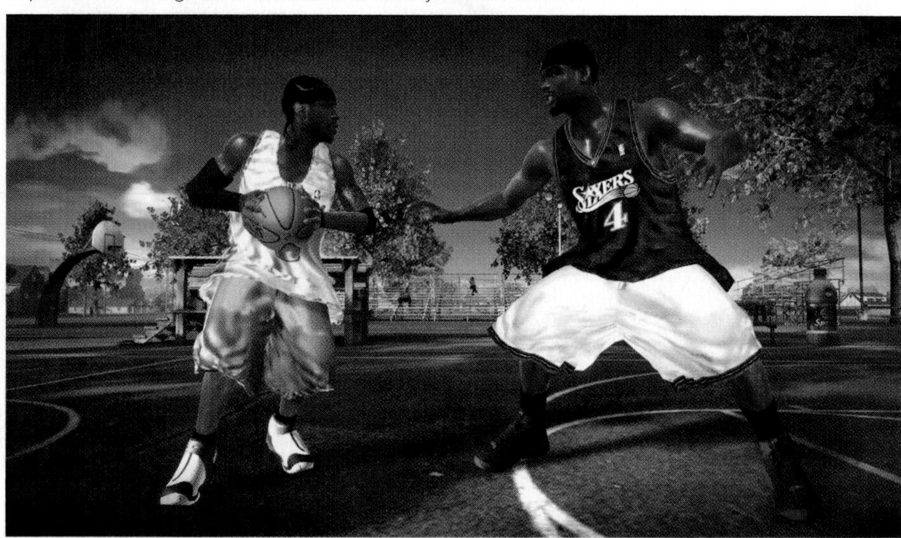

Education and Training

Research shows that most individuals are able to comprehend complex ideas more thoroughly and quickly when they are able to interact with them using digital media. For example, engineering professors at the University of Missouri turned to interactive media to assist students who were having difficulty understanding the theories behind stress transformation—the internal stresses and forces that loads place on building materials. They developed an interactive media tool that allowed students to witness the effects of stress on different materials and the associated stress transformation equations. By visually associating the stress placed on virtual objects with the equations, students could more easily understand how abstract concepts relate to the real world. Results from the study showed that when lecture, interactive media, and textbook reading are compared, students felt that they learned best in lectures and preferred interactive media over textbook reading. Educational research also shows that everyone learns differently. For this reason many curricula are including digital media and interactive multimedia components.

Many teachers are finding the simulated worlds of virtual reality games a fertile environment for learning. The Muzzy Lane Software Company develops gaming software for the classroom to help high school and college students learn about history and develop thinking skills. *Making History* is a multiplayer simulation that puts players in control of European governments before, during, and after World War II. The game integrates learning into the software through player experience rather than traditional methods that preach to the player.

The hand-eye coordination developed through the use of video games can be translated to skills in various professions. Dr. James Rosser, Jr., a top surgeon and director of the Advanced Medical Technologies Institute at Beth Israel Medical Center in New York, uses video games to help train laparoscopic surgeons. Surgeons who play video games three hours a week have 37 percent fewer errors and accomplish tasks 27 percent faster, he says, basing his observation on results of tests using the video game *Super Monkey Ball*.

Microsoft *Flight Simulator* is used by professional and amateur pilots to learn how to fly a variety of aircraft (see Figure 6.41). One of the most demanding programs for PCs, *Flight Simulator* renders landscapes on the fly at 24 frames per second as you pilot between virtual representations of actual airports. Real flight consoles and controls are incorporated into the virtual renditions of the planes to give the pilot a feeling of flying the actual plane. You can even flip on the Fasten Seatbelt sign for your passengers when you experience some turbulence.

FIGURE 6.41 • Microsoft Flight Simulator X

Flight Simulator X allows you to pilot any one of hundreds of different types of aircraft through a variety of weather conditions, between virtual renderings of real airports.

Video games are being adopted by corporations to assist with training employees. The Cold Stone Creamery ice cream corporation uses a video game to assist new employees in learning how to serve ice cream quickly with minimal waste. Video games are used by Cisco Systems, Canon, and other big corporations to train service staff, technicians, and management. IBM has developed "Serious Game," a business simulation game that trains corporate managers how to optimize costs, mitigate risks, and work in the global market. One study predicts that by 2012, one quarter of Global Fortune 500 companies will adopt gaming for learning and training.[6]

Video games and simulations can help train professionals before they go into dangerous situations. STATCare lets medics bandage wounds, apply tourniquets, administer intravenous fluids, inject medications, and make all of the other assessments that would be required of them on an actual battlefield. *HazMat: Hotzone* teaches firefighters how to respond to a chemical-weapons attack. *FXTrader* shows financiers the ins and outs of currency trading, and college administrators use *Virtual U* to practice management techniques such as dealing with faculty salaries, student parking, and the board of trustees.

Interactive media is being used in many education environments:

- In the traditional classroom setting, it helps students learn difficult concepts.
- In distance learning, it sometimes takes the place of lecture demonstrations.

- In museums, it allows the public to interact with virtual objects and environments that are not possible to interact with in real life.
- In skills training, interactive multimedia simulations are used to train pilots and others in a host of skills-based occupations.

Interactive lessons can be presented on PCs or public kiosks. They allow learners to work at their own pace and often in their own environment. Often multimedia permits interaction that is not feasible or convenient in real life.

Commercial Applications of Interactive Media

Companies have jumped on interactive media to offer customers additional services and benefits. Interactive media plays a large role in Web-based e-commerce. It provides the fundamental technology for 3D product viewing, which allows online customers to thoroughly examine products. Travelers can take virtual tours of resort destinations prior to booking a room (see Figure 6.42); furniture buyers can "try out" different fabrics on a sofa, and hairstylists can show you "the new you" before snipping. Web marketers even use interactive games to get users to click banner ads.

FIGURE 6.42 • Interactive virtual tours

Many resorts provide virtual tours that allow you to stroll around their property prior to making reservations.

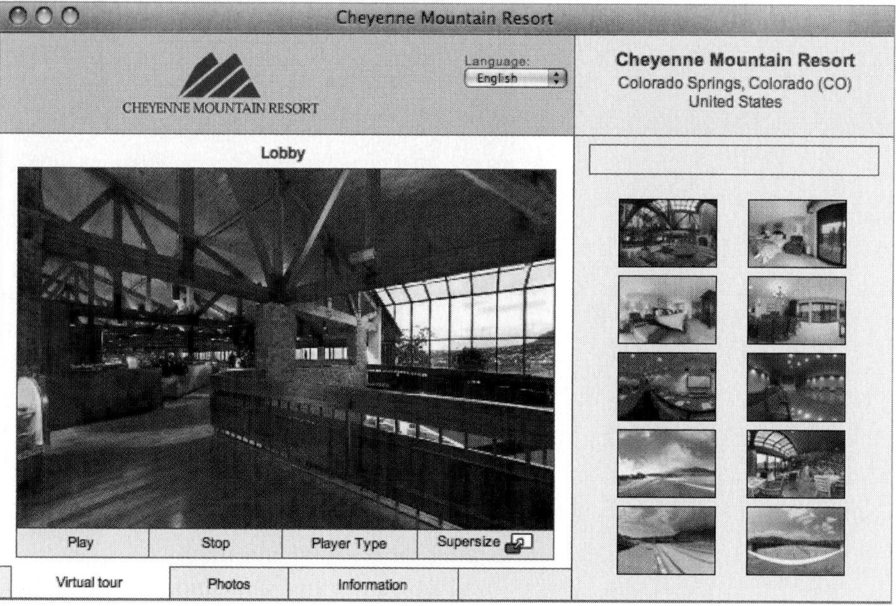

Interactive media is also used to provide product support and customer training. For example, Mercedes provides its customers with interactive media on CD that allows them to explore the parts and features of their new automobile. In the construction industry, electronic blueprints provide a 3D view of a home. The owner can click an option to view the home's electrical system and rotate the image to determine how and where to add an additional wall outlet. Interactive 3D is used in interior design to place objects within a virtual home and determine what looks best.

Interactive multimedia is playing a large role in attracting customers to Web sites, and once they are there, it plays a role in keeping them. The Web site for the Honda Civic Hybrid uses interactive multimedia in nearly every conceivable way, short of taking an actual test drive. It includes 360-degree interior and exterior views of the car, educational animations that explain the unique gas-electric hybrid engine design, and a wizard that allows you to custom design your own model.

Interactive Video Games

In the area of interactive multimedia entertainment, the computer video game reigns supreme. Video games employ nearly every aspect of digital media discussed in this chapter. Gaming takes place on computers or special-purpose gaming devices. **Video game consoles**, such as the Nintendo Wii, the Sony PlayStation 3 (PS3), and Microsoft Xbox 360, are high-powered multiprocessor computers designed to support 3D interactive multimedia. They come equipped with a fast microprocessor that works in conjunction with a graphics coprocessor to support fast-paced gaming action. The microprocessor is specially designed to handle the high demands of live-action 3D rendering. These units also include memory, storage similar to a PC, and an optional Internet connection to connect with gamers in other locations.

FIGURE 6.43 • Nintendo Wii

The Nintendo Wii and its motion-sensitive controller get players off the couch.

The Nintendo Wii broke new ground for game consoles by introducing a wireless, motion-sensitive game controller (Figure 6.43). The motion-sensitive controller allows players to swing and move the controller to roll bowling balls; swing tennis rackets, golf clubs, or swords; or otherwise control objects in the virtual space presented on the television display.

The quality of the video gaming experience has dramatically increased over the past few years. From thunderstorms rolling over panoramic landscapes to the minute detail of grass blades rustling in a soft breeze, today's video games use powerful algorithms to match the physics of the real world. Now that designers are achieving realism in virtual worlds, they are taking the next step by creating games that defy the laws of physics. For example, the Lucasarts game *Thrillville*, subtitled "Off the Rails," allows gamers to create theme park rides that go far beyond any ride ever created. Roller-coaster cars leave the rails, fly through the air, shoot through tubes, and parachute to the ground. Players in fantasy games fly through virtual space. Players in sports games can jump higher and run faster than humanly possible. Today's computer games are allowing players to experience life as it might be in dreams but not in reality.

Gaming is becoming an increasingly popular mobile activity due to new next-generation handheld game devices such as the Sony PlayStation Portable and PSP.go and Nintendo DSi and DS Lite. The Sony PSP brings PlayStation-quality 3D graphics to a handheld device that doubles as a music and movie player (see Figure 6.44). Movies are available for the PSP from Sony, Disney, and Buena Vista Home Entertainment.

FIGURE 6.44 • PSP.go

The PSP.go brings high-quality 3D graphics to a slick handheld design.

In Japan, Nintendo has established over 1000 Wi-Fi hotspots where owners of its DS portable game machines can play games with others online for free.

Cell phones are bringing the gaming world to increasing numbers of adults. Short, uncomplicated games like Tetris, Solitaire, and PacMan allow users to pass the time between appointments without needing to invest a lot of time and effort. Smart phones like the iPhone support gaming action at the level of a PSP or DS. Many game developers are moving to the iPhone as a primary gaming platform since so many iPhones are in use. There are over 6,000 games available for the iPhone, far surpassing any gaming console or handheld device.

Video game development requires a team effort from specialists in a variety of areas: game designers, artists, sound designers, programmers, and testers. Putting a new game on the market requires a large financial investment and is a big risk—a risk that many developers are willing to take in pursuit of the rewards that come with having a hit. A successful game must engage the user by allowing progress through the game at just the right pace, with action sequences timed at just the right intervals. Successful video games are easy to learn but difficult to master.

In efforts to engage teen and older gamers, games have progressively moved to more violent themes (Figure 6.45). The popular but controversial *Grand Theft Auto* is all the more popular for the stir it creates over its use of extreme violence, and has experienced record sales, maintaining the game's number one position over many editions. Some people have become concerned about the effects of prolonged exposure to violence on game users.

FIGURE 6.45 • Video game violence

With the popularity of games such as *Grand Theft Auto*, many people wonder how prolonged exposure to violence might be affecting the young people who play it.

This screenshot taken from Grand Theft Auto IV: The Lost and Damned - the exclusive new episode available only on Xbox LIVE®. Coming February 17, 2009.

Interactive TV

Interactive TV has been touted as "the next big thing" in interactive multimedia entertainment. Various features of interactive TV are available to cable subscribers in select areas. **Interactive TV** is a digital television service that includes one or more of the following: video on demand, personal video recorder, local information on TV, purchase over TV, Internet access over TV, and video games over TV. *Video on demand (VoD)* allows digital cable customers to select from hundreds of movies and programs to watch anytime they choose. The movie or program may be stored using a set-top box and can be paused, rewound, and treated as a DVD. *Personal video recorders* (PVR), such as TiVo and Replay TV, provide large hard-drive storage to record dozens of movies and programs to be watched at your leisure. Comcast has partnered with TiVo to design a set-top box for its customers that is available in most cities. *Local information on TV* provides local community news and information. *Purchase over TV*, sometimes called *t-commerce*, allows viewers to make purchases over their cable TV connection much as computer users make purchases on the Web. *Internet access over TV*, through services like WebTV, allows viewers to navigate the Web on their television sets. Cable TV services provide access to video games through *video games over TV*.

As with the Web, interactive TV has the potential to provide individual targeted marketing. Cable providers are considering ways they can collect customer information in order to provide customers with television commercials that are targeted to individuals' interests. Using *behavioral profiling*, cable TV providers can observe customers' viewing patterns in order to develop an understanding of their interests. Imagine watching television and being shown only commercials for products and services that interest you. Some cable providers consider targeted marketing to be a core business advantage of interactive television.

The form that interactive TV takes, and who will be providing it, have yet to be decided. It could be provided by cable companies over TV, or by Internet service providers to your PC, or by telecom companies to cell phones. Most likely, it will be provided by all three, merging Internet, Web, communications, and TV into a single streaming service to large household entertainment/information centers, office computers, and mobile devices of many sizes.

ACTION PLAN

Remember Ana Arguello from the beginning of this chapter? She was the college freshman considering how to merge her artistic talent and computer skills into a college degree and fulfilling career. Here are answers to the questions about Ana's situation.

1. **What careers and majors might Ana consider in digital media?**

   Enjoying computers does not necessarily imply that you enjoy programming computers. Ana might try a beginning computer programming class to see if she likes it, but it sounds as though her creative talents and interests in the arts may overshadow her interest in the workings of a computer. Artists, musicians, photographers, videographers, and designers all rely heavily on computers. No matter what Ana chooses, she will continue working closely with computers; in fact, her considerable computer skills give her an advantage over others in whatever major she chooses. Ana's experience and interests lend themselves to working in graphic design, music production, music composition, motion pictures, art, and photography. There are many professions that make use of the combination of Ana's skills to develop Web sites, video games, movies, and all sorts of popular media products.

2. **How can Ana use digital media software and services to manage her media collections?**

   Ana can make use of online music services to access her favorite music and develop playlists to match her every mood. Ana might also find other musicians online with whom she could collaborate. She can download free software to manage her digital photo collection and make photo albums to share with her friends and family online. Ana can make use of online movie services to download and enjoy her favorite movies and to discover new favorites.

3. **How might Ana enjoy digital media as a hobby and as entertainment?**

   Ana can make use of powerful tools to create and edit digital music, graphics, photos, and video for professional-grade results. Ana can enjoy music, pictures, and movies produced by others through online services that provide media to her notebook computer, television, and cell phone.

Summary

LEARNING OBJECTIVE 1

Understand the uses of digital audio and today's digital music technologies.

Digital audio includes both digital music and digital sound. A sound wave can be represented with numbers, digitally, through a process called analog-to-digital conversion (ADC). ADC uses a technology called sampling to encode a sound wave as binary numbers in Pulse Code Modulation (PCM) format. Digital sound is useful in professions including scientific research, law enforcement, entertainment, and communication. The professional production and editing of digital audio takes place in sound production studios. Sound production is an important part of music, movies, radio, television, video games, and the Internet.

Figure 6.12—p. 339

Digital technology is applied to all aspects of the music industry: creation, production, and distribution. Digital instruments such as synthesizer keyboards, samplers, and drum machines are used in the creation of digital music. A recording studio employs many digital sound production tools, such as sequencers and outboard devices, to record and manipulate digital music. The MIDI (Musical Instrument Digital Interface) protocol provides a standard language for digital music devices to use in communicating with each other. Many people are taking advantage of digital audio production at home to create home recordings and podcasts.

A wide array of digital music software and devices is available today to provide users with more control over their music-listening experience. The production, distribution, and enjoyment of digital music and audio depend on four technology components: standardized media file formats, storage media on which to store the files, players, and software that can read and manipulate the files from the media. Online music services work with the recording industry to distribute music legally over the Internet using technologies like DRM. Satellite radio and other digital music distribution systems are providing the public with many options for enjoying digital music.

LEARNING OBJECTIVE 2

Describe the many uses of 2D and 3D digital graphics and the technologies behind them.

Digital graphics refers to computer-based media applications that support creating, editing, and viewing 2D and 3D images and animation. Graphics can be digitized by storing the color of each pixel used in the image as a combination of intensities of red, green, and blue, as is done in bit-mapped graphics, or storing a description of the shapes that compose the image, as in vector graphics. Digital graphics is used as a form of creative expression, as a means of presenting information in a visually pleasing fashion, as a means to communicate and explore ideas, as a form of entertainment, as a tool to assist in the design of real-world objects, and as a method of documenting life. Vector graphics software, sometimes called drawing software, provides tools to create, arrange, and layer graphical objects on the screen to create pictures. Vector graphics software also provides filtering and effects tools to further manipulate objects in the picture. Three-dimensional modeling software provides graphics tools that allow artists to create pictures of realistic 3D models. Ray tracing involves calculating how light interacts with surfaces in a picture to create shadows and reflections. Digital graphics animation involves displaying digital images in rapid succession to provide the illusion of motion. Three-dimensional computer animation includes all of the complexity of 3D graphic rendering, multiplied by the necessity to render 24 3D images per second to create the illusion of movement.

Figure 6.26—p. 354

LEARNING OBJECTIVE 3

Explain the technologies available to acquire, edit, distribute, and print digital photos, and list new advances in video technologies and distribution.

Digital photos are acquired from a digital camera or scanner. There are many factors to consider when choosing a digital camera. Photo-editing software provides editing tools for manipulating, enhancing, and repairing digital photographs. Photo editing also includes special effects, such as the ability to remove an object from one photo and insert it in another. Personal photo-editing software provides easy-to-use tools for cleaning up photos and integrating them into frames, greeting cards, calendars, and other popular printed forms. Digital photos can be stored and shared with others using free Web services. Digital photos can be printed at home on a standard printer or a specially designed photo printer. Many Web-based services and photo kiosks are available for convenient photo printing.

Figure 6.36—p. 366

Digital video is acquired using a digital camcorder. Video-editing software uses a storyline on which to build a video production. The videographer cuts scenes out of the video footage and drags the scenes to a position on the storyline. After cutting and pasting scenes onto the storyline, the videographer defines the transitions between scenes to create a professional-looking video production. There are many new services that provide access to motion pictures, video clips, and television programming on the Web that enable people to view video almost anywhere.

LEARNING OBJECTIVE 4

Discuss how interactive media is used to educate and entertain.

Interactive media refers to multimedia presentations that involve user interaction for education, training, or entertainment. Interactive media is unique because it empowers the audience to take part in the creative or educational process. Companies use interactive media to offer customers additional services and benefits.

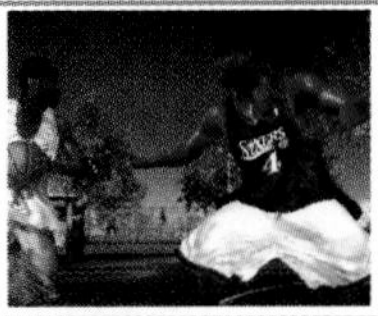

Computer video games make up a large portion of the interactive media market. Most gaming takes place on game consoles wired to television sets, rather than on computers. The three big gaming consoles on the market today are Nintendo Wii, Sony PlayStation 3 (PS3), and Microsoft Xbox 360. Today's gaming consoles are high-powered multiprocessor computers designed to support 3D interactive multimedia. Video game development requires a team effort from specialists in game design, art, sound design, programming, and testing. Interactive TV is likely to be the next big thing in interactive multimedia. Interactive TV includes digital services such as video on demand, personal video recorder (PVR), purchase over TV, Web TV, and video games over TV.

Figure 6.40—p. 370

Test Yourself

LEARNING OBJECTIVE 1: Understand the uses of digital audio and today's digital music technologies.

1. Digitizing sound uses a technology called ________________ that measures a sound wave at regular time intervals, typically thousands of times per second.
2. The ________________ protocol was implemented in 1983 to provide a standard language for digital music devices to use in communicating with each other.
   a. Integrated Digital Studio (IDS)
   b. Digital Music Media (DMM)
   c. Musical Instrument Digital Interface (MIDI)
   d. Compact Disc Audio (CDA)
3. True or False: Sharing copies of copyright-protected music is legal.
4. The ________________ music format compresses CD music files to less than 10 percent of their original size.
5. When you "rip" a CD you are ________________ .
   a. stealing it or its content
   b. encoding music to a CD-R
   c. obtaining music files from a file-sharing network
   d. transferring music from CD to your computer
6. A(n) ________________ is an audio file that contains a recorded broadcast distributed over the Internet.

LEARNING OBJECTIVE 2: Describe the many uses of 2D and 3D digital graphics and the technologies behind them.

7. ________________ graphics images are a collection of geometric objects that can be layered and postioned to create the image.

8. ________________ is the process of calculating the light interaction with the virtual 3D models in a scene and presenting the final drawing in two dimensions to be viewed on the screen or printed.
   a. Rendering
   b. Animating
   c. Compiling
   d. Light tracing
9. True or False: Bitmapped graphics are easier to edit than vector graphics.
10. ________________ software is able to turn designs on the computer into blueprint specifications for manufacturing.
11. Most photographs are stored as ________________ graphics, storing the color of each pixel in the photo.
   a. bit-mapped
   b. 3D
   c. animated
   d. vector

LEARNING OBJECTIVE 3: Explain the technologies available to acquire, edit, distribute, and print digital photos, and list new advances in video technologies and distribution.

12. Digital cameras are ranked by the amount of ________________ they can capture.
   a. photos
   b. light
   c. pixels
   d. color
13. True or False: Digital photography makes it easy to detect when a photograph has been tampered with.
14. A digital ________________ is used to acquire digital video and is available in standard-def and high-def.
15. True or False: Printing your own photos can save you a lot of money.

LEARNING OBJECTIVE 4: Discuss how interactive media is used to educate and entertain.

16. The Nintendo Wii is a ________________ .
   a. video game console
   b. home entertainment system
   c. digital cell phone
   d. handheld computer
17. True or False: Some video games have practical uses.

Test Yourself Solutions: 1. sampling, 2. c. Musical Instrument Digital Interface (MIDI), 3. False, 4. MP3, 5. d. transferring music from CD to your computer, 6. podcast, 7. Vector, 8. a. Rendering, 9. False, 10. CAD, 11. d. vector, 12. c. pixels, 13. False, 14. camcorder, 15. False, 16. a. video game console, 17. True.

Key Terms

Key Term	Page	Definition
3D modeling software	353	Provides graphics tools that allow artists to create pictures of realistic 3D models
bit-mapped graphics	346	Represents an image by using bytes to store the color of each pixel used in the image
computer-assisted design (CAD) software	352	Assists designers, engineers, and architects in designing three-dimensional objects, from the gear mechanism in a watch to suspension bridges
digital audio	327	Any type of sound, including voice, music, and sound effects, recorded and stored digitally as a series of 1s and 0s
digital graphics	345	Computer-based media applications that support creating, editing, and viewing 2D and 3D images and animation

Key Term	Page	Definition
digital media	326	Digital technologies of all kinds that serve and support digital music, video, and graphics
digital music	327	A subcategory of digital audio that involves recording and storing music
digital rights management (DRM)	337	Technology that protects intellectual property by restricting the number of devices and applications on which a file can be opened, and the number of times that the file can be copied and burned to disk
interactive media	369	Digital media that involves user interaction for education, training, or entertainment
interactive TV	375	Digital television service that includes one or more of the following: video on demand, personal video recorder, local information on TV, purchase over TV, Internet access over TV, and video games over TV
media player software	341	Allows users to organize and play digital music, audio, and video files on PCs and media devices
MP3	336	File format that compresses PCM music files to less than 10 percent of their original size
musical instrument digital interface (MIDI)	331	Protocol used to provide a standard language for digital music devices to use in communicating with each other
photo-editing software	360	Programs with special tools and effects designed for improving or manipulating digital photos
pixels	346	Small points or dots of light that make up digital images
podcast	333	An audio file that contains a recorded broadcast distributed over the Internet
satellite radio	344	A form of digital radio that receives broadcast signals via a communications satellite
scientific visualization	351	Uses computer graphics to provide visual representations that improve our understanding of some phenomenon
vector graphics	346	A technique that uses bytes to store geometric descriptions that define all the shapes in the image
video game consoles	373	High-powered multiprocessor computers designed to support 3D interactive multimedia
video-editing software	365	Allows professional and amateur videographers to edit out bad footage and rearrange the good footage to produce a professional-style video production

Questions

Review Questions

1. Name and define the subcategories of digital media.
2. Define digital audio.
3. What is the purpose of MIDI?
4. What is the purpose of sequencing software?
5. Provide one example of a career, outside of the entertainment industry, that depends on digital sound.
6. Who produces podcasts?
7. Name three methods of transferring music to your computer.
8. What is DRM and why is it used?

9. What types of professionals make use of CAD software?
10. How do vector graphics differ from bit-mapped graphics?
11. What does it mean to render 3D models?
12. What are animated GIFs, and where do you usually find them?
13. What benefits does Adobe Flash offer for Web content?
14. What are avars and how do they give life to 3D animations?
15. Name four forms of interactive media.
16. What are some commercial and business uses of interactive media?
17. What are the three most popular models and manufacturers of video game consoles?
18. Provide three examples of digital convergence in digital media.
19. What types of specialists are typically involved in video game production?
20. Name five services associated with interactive TV.
21. What are the benefits and drawbacks of satellite radio?

Discussion Questions

22. How is forensic audio used to catch criminals?
23. How is music digitized?
24. How has digital music empowered musicians?
25. How has digital music empowered music fans?
26. What is MP3 and how did it change the face of music distribution?
27. How are colors represented in digital graphics?
28. What is the difference between Napster and iTunes, and how do they provide music to users?
29. What is scientific visualization, and how is it used?
30. Why did the recording industry eventually give in to pressure to sell music online without DRM?
31. What is digital cinema, and how will it affect the motion picture industry?
32. Why is vector graphics considered to be object oriented?
33. Why is the process of 3D modeling sometimes called ray tracing?
34. How do you and will you interact with digital audio in your personal and professional lives?
35. How do you and will you interact with digital graphics and photography applications in your personal and professional lives?

Exercises

Try It Yourself

1. Digital Sound Factory sells sampled and synthesized instrument sound packages that can be downloaded to synthesizers for performance and recording. Listen to some of the samples at digitalsoundfactory.com. Listen to both real instrument sounds like those in the orchestral and World sections, and synthesized sounds like those in the Dance/Electronica and HipHop/Urban sections. Write your impressions in a few paragraphs and submit them to your instructor.
2. Visit *www.irtc.org* and *www.digitalart.org* and view the digital artwork that you find there. Write a few paragraphs on which piece most affects you or interests you from each site and why. If none interests you, explain why not.
3. Visit *www.rhapsody.com* and try out the free version of Rhapsody. Consider the benefits of having access to millions of songs on the Internet. Read the details about Rhapsody's subscription service. Do you think it would be worth the $12.99 per month subscription price? Write up your review and opinion of the service.
4. Visit *www.pixar.com* and view the link that explains Pixar's animation and movie-making process. Summarize the steps of the animation process in a word-processing document and submit it to your instructor.

Virtual Classroom Activities

For the following exercises, do not use face-to-face or telephone communications with your group members. Use only Internet communications.

5. Have the group members answer the following questions:
   a. What methods and services do you use to acquire music?
   b. What are the benefits and drawbacks of each method you use to acquire music?
   c. What method of digital music distribution would you propose that would allow musicians and the music industry to prosper and provide music fans with affordable music?

   Write up your findings and share them with your teacher and class.

6. Using a virtual classroom application or other chat utility, as a group, visit *www.worth1000.com*—the Web site of faked and creative photos. Explore the galleries you find there, and decide which image everyone in the group enjoys most. Share it with your instructor.

Teamwork

7. Try or view a demonstration of the video game *Grand Theft Auto* by visiting a video game retail store or accessing it in some other way. Learn the goals in the game and the details of the challenges. Have a group debate to decide whether or not the game desensitizes users to violence. After everyone has a chance to express an opinion, take a vote and submit the results to the instructor.

8. Use a group member's digital camera (or borrow one from a friend) to take a group photo. Distribute the photo electronically to all group members and, using photo-editing software, have a contest to see who can edit the photo in the most interesting way. Submit all entries to the instructor.

9. Assign various legal music download services to group members: Napster, Rhapsody, iTunes, MSN Music. Have group members write critiques of their assigned service, share your findings, and summarize the group results in charts and slides.

10. All team members should set up an account on Flickr. The team leader should create a Flickr group to allow group members to share photos. Have a campus photo contest. Have each group member submit a photo taken on campus, and have each member vote for their favorite photo using the commenting feature in Flickr.

Endnotes

[1] Whale Dreams Web site, accessed Aug 2, 2009, http://www.abc.net.au/oceans/whale/song.htm.

[2] Driver, Dustin, "T-Pain: Sprung," Logic Studio in Action, accessed Aug 2, 2009, http://www.apple.com/logicstudio/in-action/tpain/.

[3] Staff, "IFPI publishes Digital Music Report 2009," IFPI, January 16, 2009, http://www.ifpi.org/content/section_resources/dmr2009.html.

[4] Gibbs, Mark, "DRM Is Sorta, Kinda, Maybe Dead," *PCWorld*, Jul 31, 2009, http://www.pcworld.com/article/169439/drm_is_sorta_kinda_maybe_dead.html.

[5] "2008 Year-End Shipment Statistics," RIAA, http://www.riaa.com.

[6] IBM Staff, "IBM 'Serious Game' Provides Training to Tackle Global Business Challenges," IBM Press Release, February 19, 2009, http://www-03.ibm.com/press/us/en/pressrelease/26734.wss.

DATABASE SYSTEMS

When Mary Bolger found her grandfather's recipes in a small box in the attic, she never thought those few papers would turn into money. It all started when she shared Grandpa's special butter-cheese spread at a get-together with friends. Her friends loved it and begged to know where they could buy it. The spread became an annual holiday present that her friends expected from her each year. Before long, Mary had an arrangement to sell her spread through some of the local grocery stores in Waukesha, Wisconsin. After college, Mary got a job working for an upscale retail store, but she still sold her Wisconsin's-Best brand of cheese spread as a side business. Now she is thinking of quitting her job and going full-time with her own business. She would use more of Grandpa's recipes to create a product line of gourmet spreads. In order to start her own business, Mary would have to get organized. She needs a way to keep track of her inventory, customers, and future employees. From her experience working in retail, she knows a database is the best tool for her needs, but she has never used one herself. Mary currently has a personal computer with Microsoft Office Professional.

As you read through the chapter, consider the following questions:

1. How can Mary use a database to keep track of the different cheeses, butters, spices, crocks, and other supplies she needs?
2. If she starts a small business, how will she be able to pay her employees, pay her bills, and keep track of other business transactions?

Check out Mary's *Action Plan* at the conclusion of this chapter.

7

LEARNING OBJECTIVES

1. Understand basic data management concepts.
2. Describe database models and characteristics.
3. Discuss the different types of database management systems and their design and use by individuals and organizations.
4. Describe how organizations use database systems to perform routine processing and provide information and decision support, and how they use data warehouses, marts, and mining.
5. Discuss additional database systems, including distributed systems, data centers, and Web-based systems.
6. Describe the role of the database administrator (DBA) and database policies and security practices.

CHAPTER CONTENT

Introduction

People and organizations need a way to store data and to convert that data into important information. Databases serve this function, and without them, today's businesses could not survive. Databases are also used in medicine, science, engineering, the military, and most other fields. They are useful to individuals for keeping track of items in an apartment, tracks in a music collection, and expenses used to prepare a budget and complete a tax return. Databases are also a key ingredient of today's most popular Internet services, and the backbone of our information-driven economy. To manage information wisely and make the best use of the information systems on which we depend, it is useful to understand basic data management concepts.

BASIC DATA MANAGEMENT CONCEPTS

Recall that data consists of raw facts, like sales or weather statistics. For data to be transformed into useful information, such as quarterly profits or hurricane predictions, it must first be organized in some meaningful way. As you learned in Chapter 1, a *database* is a collection of data organized to meet users' needs. Throughout your career, you will directly or indirectly access a variety of databases ranging from a simple list of music in your collection to a fully integrated database at work.

A database can help individuals and organizations maximize data as a valuable resource. Databases also help individuals and organizations achieve their goals. UPS, the world's largest shipping company, uses a database to process, track, and deliver 15.5 million packages a day to 7.9 million customers in over 200 countries and territories around the world (see Figure 7.1).[1] When you shop online, you access the merchants' inventory databases that store thousands of products. Database software has also been used to help save endangered species and track terrorists.

FIGURE 7.1 • Accessing the UPS database online

UPS provides convenient online tracking that accesses the UPS database to show customers where their package is in the shipping process.

The FBI depends on a huge database and powerful data analysis tools in its fight against terrorists. The FBI's Counterterrorism database contains millions of records, which include information on suspected terrorists, communications, and financial transactions. The database was developed from more than 50 government agency sources in an effort to "connect the dots," that is, to find related data from different sources and create new useful information. Sharing attributes and data items can be a critical factor in coordinating responses across diverse functional areas of an organization.

Access to private information has also raised social issues about the use of databases. Some people feel their privacy rights and even civil rights could be violated by governments and other institutions that collect information about them. For example, in the United Kingdom, the government is developing a database that some citizens feel infringes on their privacy. It contains personal information on all citizens, including airline bookings, advance passenger information, financial, telephone, tax, health, passport and biometric records, and phone and Internet communications.[2]

Databases are typically accessed using software called a **database management system (DBMS)**. A DBMS consists of a group of programs that manipulate the database and provide an interface between the database and the user or the database and application programs. For example, the previously mentioned FBI database is accessed by 13,000 agents and analysts through a DBMS that allows them to search the database using key terms. A search on key terms "Mohammad Atta" (one of the hijackers of the September 11, 2001, bombings) and "flight training" turns up 250 database articles. DBMSs are available for many sizes and types of computers, and are covered in more detail later in the chapter.

A database, a DBMS, and the application programs that utilize the data in the database make up a *database system* or database environment. Some of the functions of a DBMS include:

- Storing important data for individuals, groups, and organizations, including numbers, text, visual images, audio signals, and so on
- Performing routine tasks, such as helping an individual prepare income tax forms or helping an organization produce paychecks for its employees
- Providing information to help people, groups, and organizations make better decisions by asking questions of the database and creating reports
- Ensuring that the data is protected and safe from attacks and unauthorized access

Data Management for Individuals and Organizations

Individuals use personal databases to store addresses and contact information, keep track of important dates, keep track of valuables for possible insurance claims, catalogue music and book collections, and store and manage other large lists of personal data. We all interact with databases over the Internet. For example, our e-mail is stored and organized in databases; search engines are based on database technologies; iTunes, Pandora, Napster, and other online music services use databases to organize music and provide suggestions of music that you might enjoy; eBay uses a database to keep track of items and bids; Facebook and MySpace use databases to keep track of friends; YouTube manages videos with databases; and Flickr stores photos in databases. In fact, the Web itself could be viewed as the world's largest DBMS.

Without data and the ability to process it, an organization would not be able to successfully engage in business activities. It would not be able to generate reports to support knowledge workers and decision makers to help achieve organizational goals. Businesses would find it difficult to pay employees, send out bills, and order new inventory. Databases have made it possible to map the structure of DNA and to share scientists' research (see Figure 7.2); without databases, the human genome project would not be possible.

FIGURE 7.2 • Accessing the human genome database

Through the use of extensive research databases, scientists all over the world have access to the most up-to-date data available relating to the human genome and mouse genome projects.

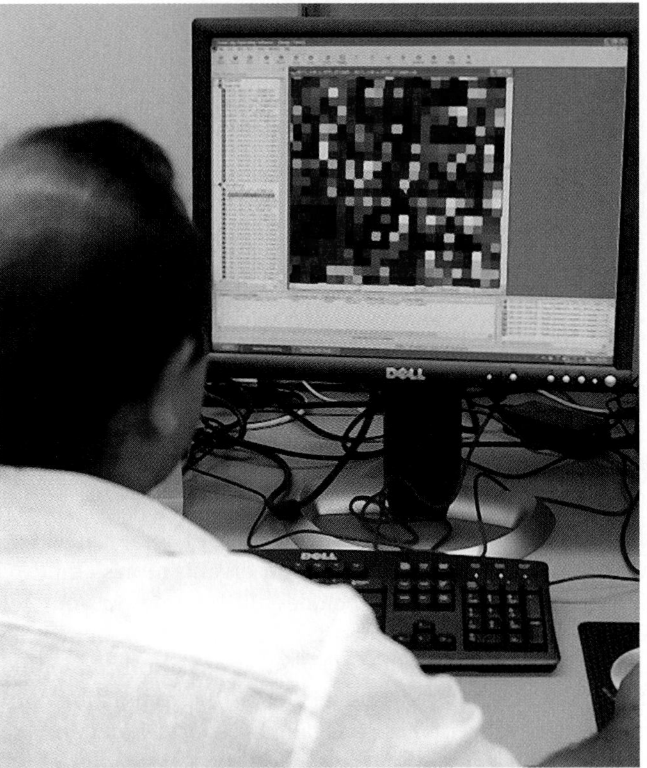

The Hierarchy of Data

Recall that in a computer, a byte is used to represent a character, which is the basic building block of information. Characters can be uppercase or lowercase letters (A, a, B, b, C, c,...Z), numeric digits (0, 1, 2,...9), or special symbols (.![+][-]/€¥...).

In a database, characters are put together to form a field, the smallest practical unit in most databases. A **field** is typically a name, number, or combination of characters that in some way describes an aspect of an object (an individual, a song in a music library, an item in inventory, a photograph in an album) or activity (a business transaction, an interaction). Every field has a *field name* and can have either a fixed or variable length. For example, EmployeeNumber might be a field that is a fixed eight characters long. PartDescription might be a field where the length of the description can vary, depending on the part. Database syntax typically requires that field names not include any spaces. So a field that contains the "employee identification number" might be named "EmployeeNumber" or "employee_ID".

A collection of related fields that describe some object or activity is a **record**. You can create a more complete description of an object or activity by combining fields that represent various characteristics of objects or activities into records. For instance, a database record for music in the iTunes Store combines fields for Name, Time, Artist, Price, Release Date, Track #, and others to fully describe the track (see Figure 7.3).

FIGURE 7.3 • Database records and fields in iTunes

A database record for music in the iTunes store includes fields for Name, Time, Artist, Album, Price, Release Date, and Track #.

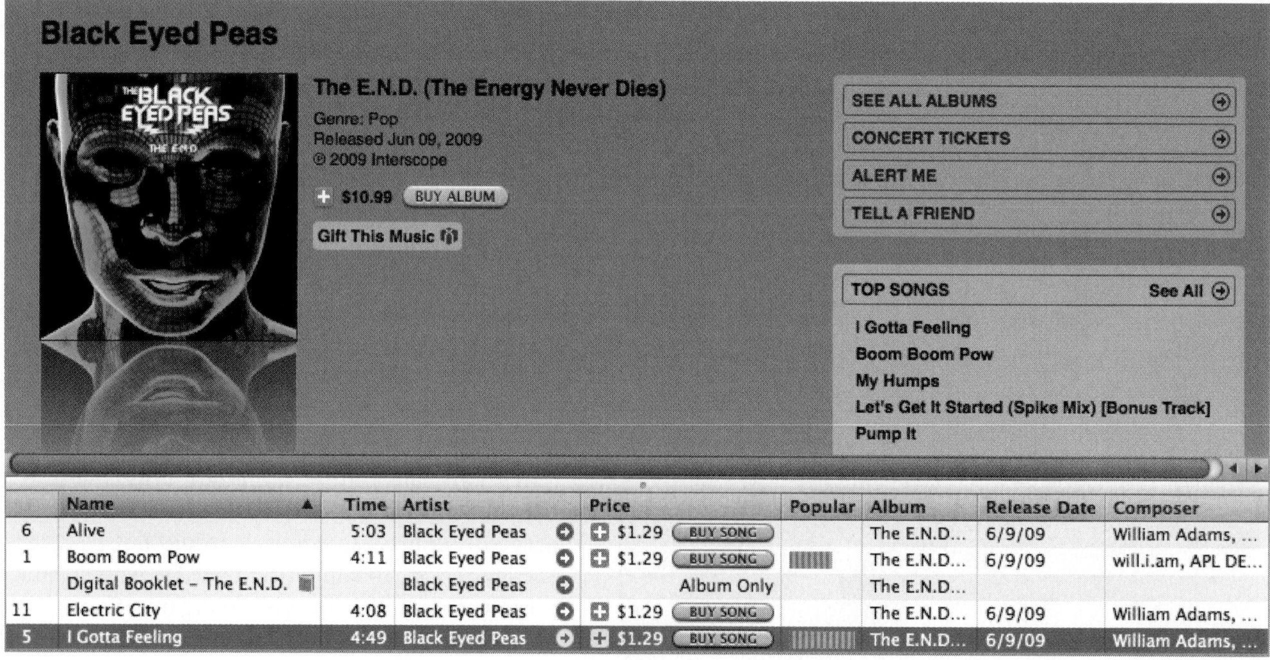

A collection of related records is a **file**, also called a *table* in some databases. For example, an employee file is a collection of all of an organization's employee records. Likewise, an iTunes music library that includes all the songs in your collection is a database file. These types of database files are examples of *master files*, permanent files that are updated over time. Organizations also have temporary files that hold data that needs to be processed, such as the transactions of paying employees or taking sales orders. These are called *transaction files* and are temporary files that contain data representing transactions or actions that must be taken. A file containing the number of hours employees worked last week or the sales orders from yesterday are examples of transaction files. They must be processed to pay employees or fill orders. Transaction files often cause changes to master files. An inventory master file containing the current amount of an inventory item has to be adjusted (reduced in this case) to reflect new sales of the inventory item contained in the order transaction file. If a customer orders five cookbooks from an online bookstore, the online bookstore must subtract five cookbooks from its inventory master file to keep the master file current and accurate.

At the highest level of this hierarchy is a database, a collection of integrated and related files or tables. For example, iTunes may store music data in one database file, movie data in another, TV show data in another, and podcast data in yet another. The combination of these files is the complete iTunes database.

Together, characters, fields, records, files, and databases form the data hierarchy (see Figure 7.4). The **data hierarchy** refers to the manner in which data in a database is organized into sequential levels of detail. Characters are combined to make a field, fields are combined to make a record, records are combined to make a file, and files are combined to make a database. It is important to remember that a database houses not only all of these levels of data but the relationships among them.

FIGURE 7.4 • The data hierarchy

The data hierarchy represents the idea that characters are combined to make a field, fields are combined to make a record, records are combined to make a file, and files are combined to make a database.

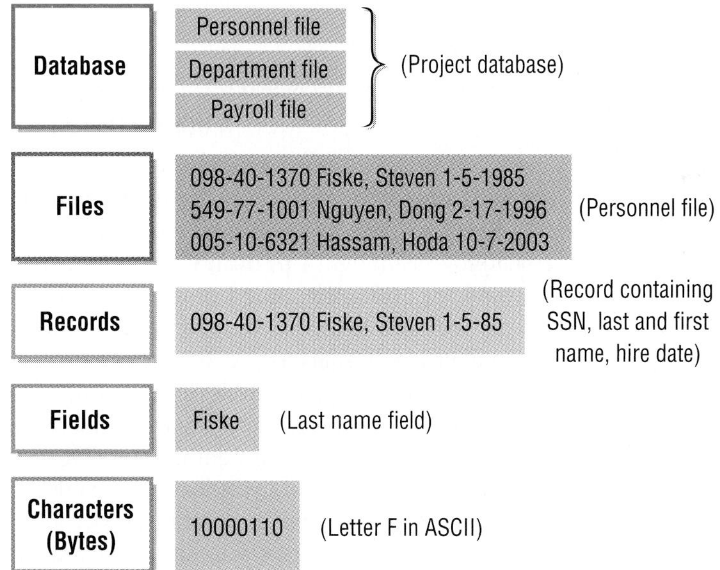

Data Entities, Attributes, and Keys

Databases use entities, attributes, and keys to store data and information. An *entity* is a generalized class of people, places, or things (objects) for which data is collected, stored, and maintained. Examples of entities include music CDs, the contents of an apartment, employees, inventory, and customers. Most organizations store data about entities; which are represented as records in a database.

An *attribute* is a characteristic of an entity. For example, employee number, last name, first name, hire date, and department number are attributes for an employee (see Figure 7.5). Inventory number, description, number of units on hand, and location of the inventory item in the warehouse are examples of attributes for items in inventory; customer number, name, address, phone number, credit rating, and contact person are examples of attributes for customers. Attributes are usually selected to capture the relevant characteristics of entities such as employees or customers. The specific value of an attribute, called a *data item*, can be found in the fields of the record describing an entity. Federal databases, for example, often include the results of DNA tests as an attribute in databases of convicted criminals.

FIGURE 7.5 • Entities, attributes, and keys

The attributes of these entities include employee number, last name, first name, hire date, and department number. Employee number is the primary key because it uniquely identifies each entity.

Employee number	Last name	First name	Hire date	Dept. number
005-10-6321	Hassam	Hoda	10-7-2003	257
549-77-1001	Nguyen	Dong	2-17-1996	650
098-40-1370	Fiske	Steven	1-5-1985	598

Entities (records)

Primary key field

Attributes (fields)

As discussed, a collection of fields about a specific entity is a record. A *key* is a field in a record that is used to identify the record, for example, EmployeeNumber. A **primary key** uniquely identifies the record. No other record can have the same primary key. The primary key distinguishes records so that they can be accessed, organized, and manipulated. In Figure 7.5, Employee Number is a primary key.

Primary keys are essential to DBMS functioning. In its database, eBay uses the item number as the primary key to uniquely identify every item that is sold and up for sale (see Figure 7.6). If item numbers were not unique, the wrong item might be shipped to a customer. Credit card companies use the customer's credit card number. The U.S. Internal Revenue Service and businesses use the Social Security number as the primary key to ensure that tax information and payments are correctly routed. However, for privacy reasons, schools are switching from student Social Security numbers to a unique assigned student ID number as primary key.

FIGURE 7.6 • Primary key

Online auction site eBay uses the item number as the primary key in its database to uniquely identify every item it sells.

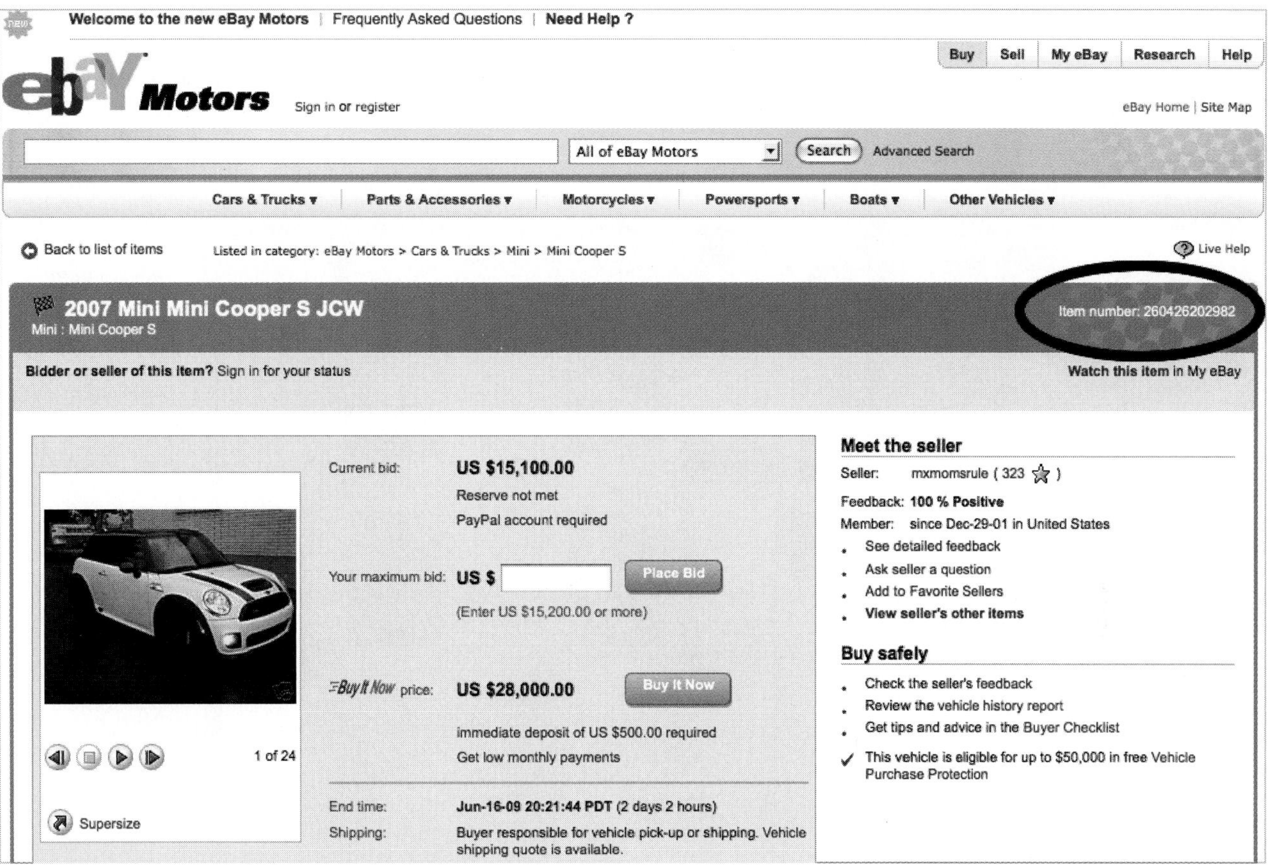

In some cases, multiple fields may be combined as a primary key. For example, what would iTunes use as a primary key for its music files? The artist field may tempt you, but each artist has many tracks. The artist field is not unique for each database record. The track title is another option, since each database record represents a unique track. But the best songs are often recorded by multiple artists, so the track title may not be unique to each database record. One solution is to use the combination of artist and track title to create the primary key. This way Joni Mitchell's *Big Yellow Taxi* can be uniquely identified from Counting Crows & Vanessa Carlton's *Big Yellow Taxi*. However, if Joni Mitchell has more than one recording of *Big Yellow Taxi*, problems will arise. Often database designers get around these challenges by assigning each record a unique ID number that acts as a primary key.

Simple Approaches to Data Management

There are a number of simple ways to manage data. For example, simple data management software packages are easy to use and update. You can use personal information managers (PIMs) to keep track of phone numbers, addresses, Web sites, and e-mail addresses (see Figure 7.7). PIMs are often accessed from personal computers and smart phones. A PIM also contains a calendar, in which you can enter appointments. A home budget software package is another example of a simple data management system. You can enter expense items, and the software computes totals and compares your actual expenses to your budget. Although these data management systems are simple to use, their structure can be very difficult or impossible to change. For example, the home budget program might limit you to a certain number of income and expense categories.

FIGURE 7.7 • A simple calendar database

Personal information management (PIM) makes use of simple databases to store appointments, contact information, and to-do lists.

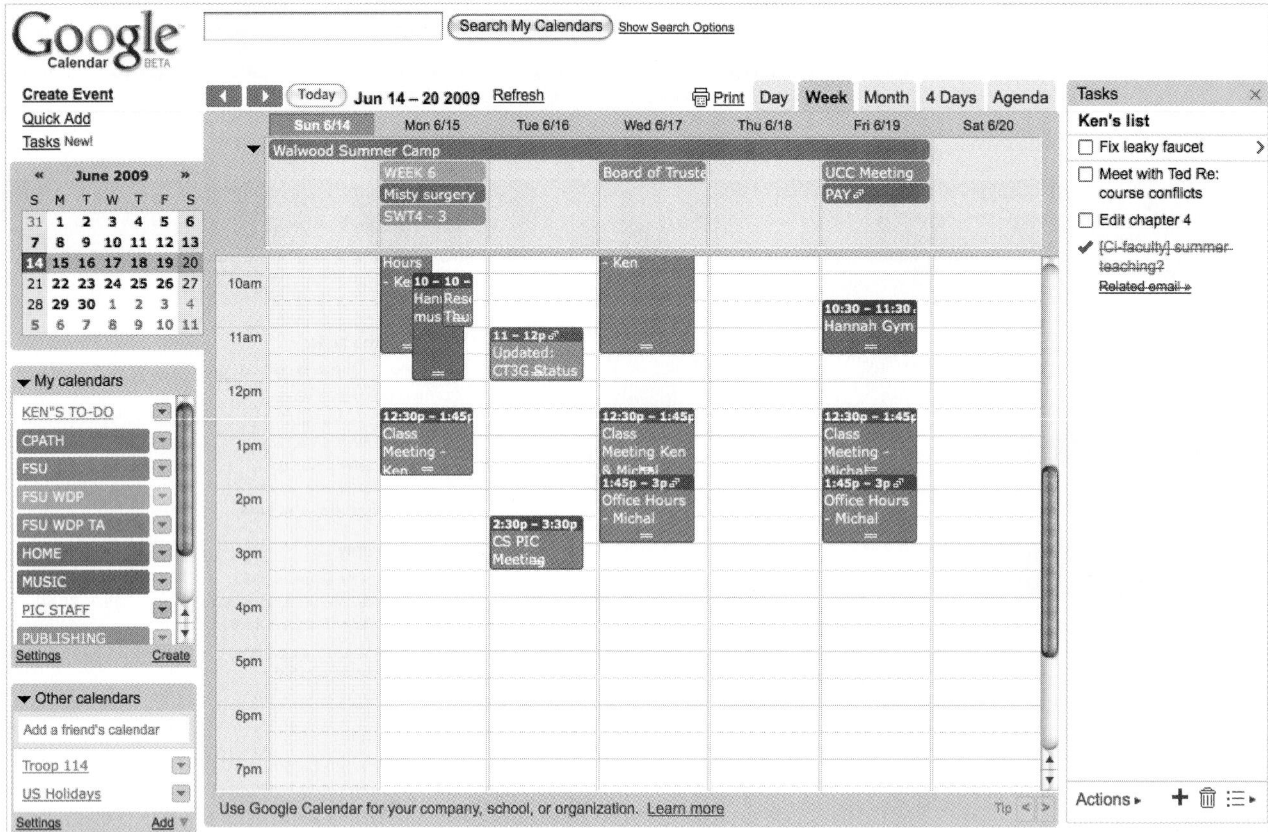

The Database Approach to Data Management

In a *centralized database approach* to data management, multiple application programs share a pool of related data. Rather than each application having its own separate data files, each shares a collection of data files that are maintained in a database stored in a central location sometimes called a data center. A grocery store chain, for example, can use the centralized database approach to allow multiple applications to run from a common database system. The approach allows the grocer to obtain and analyze customer receipts from hundreds of stores in a digital format. Storing data in one centralized database is more efficient and less prone to errors.

Using the centralized database approach to data management requires a database management system (DBMS). Recall that a DBMS consists of a group of programs that can be used as an interface between a database and the user of the database and application programs. Typically, this software acts as a buffer between the application programs and the database itself. Figure 7.8 illustrates the database approach, where a centralized database system contains all the data for the organization or individual. The DBMS interacts directly with the database and passes data to various applications. A centralized database approach also reduces *data redundancy*. Data redundancy occurs when data is copied, stored, and used from different locations. Redundant data is difficult to manage because any required change must be applied to all copies of the data, but a copy is often overlooked and becomes inaccurate. Data that is inaccurate can be more dangerous to an organization or individual than no data at all. Because a centralized database managed by a DBMS stores data only once, the problem of data redundancy is solved. Reducing copies of data also means that less storage space is required.

FIGURE 7.8 • The centralized database approach to data management

In the centralized database approach, one database contains all the data for the organization or individual. The DBMS interacts directly with the database and passes data to various applications.

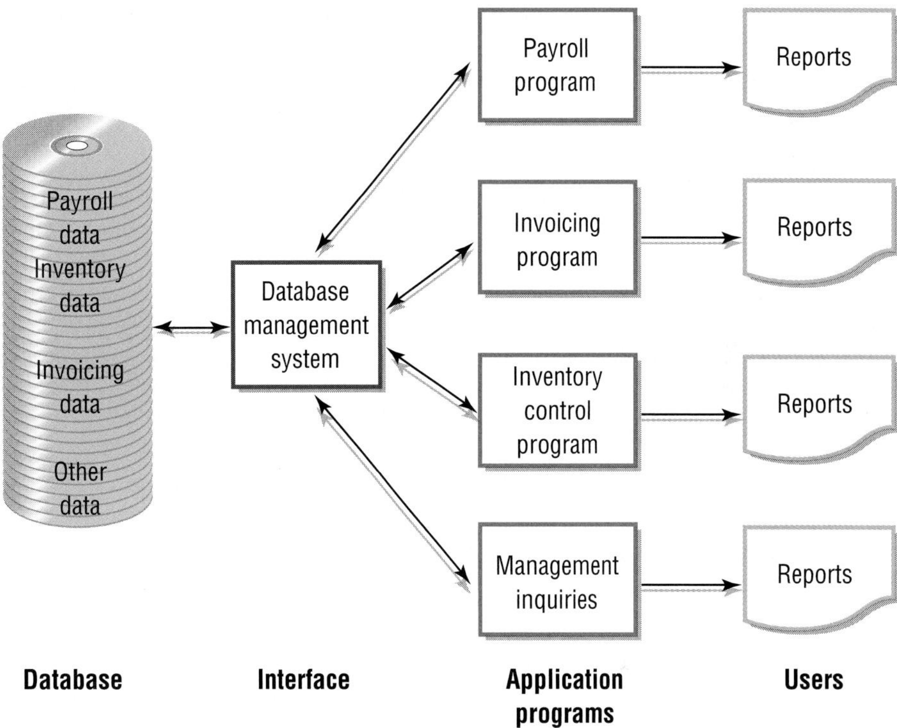

Many modern databases are organization-wide, encompassing much of the data of the entire organization. Table 7.1 lists some of the primary advantages of the centralized database approach. While databases and data centers can be costly to set up and maintain, companies and organizations find that the advantages more than justify the costs.

TABLE 7.1 • Advantages of the centralized database approach

Advantage	Explanation
Reduced data redundancy	Data redundancy can be reduced or eliminated because data is organized by the DBMS and stored in only one location; this results in more efficient utilization of system storage space.
Improved data integrity	Because there are no separate files that contain copies of the same piece of data, it no longer happens that changes sometimes are not reflected in all copies.
Easier modification and updating	The DBMS coordinates updates and data modifications; programmers and users do not have to know where data is physically stored. Modification and updating of data happens in only one step because the data is stored at only one location in most cases.
Data and program independence	The DBMS organizes the data independently of the application program. The application program is not affected by the location or type of data. Introduction of new types of data not relevant to a particular application does not require the rewriting of that application to maintain compatibility with the data file.
Better access to data and information	Most DBMSs have software that makes it easy to store and retrieve data from a database. In most cases, simple information commands can be given to get important information. Relationships between records can be more easily investigated and exploited, and applications can be more easily combined.
Standardization of data access	Database access is standardized and uniform; this means that all application programs use the same overall procedures to retrieve data and information.
Better overall protection of the data	The use of and access to centrally located data is easier to monitor and control; security codes and passwords can ensure privacy by allowing only authorized people to have access to particular data and information in the database.
Shared data and information resources	The cost of hardware, software, and personnel can be spread over a large number of applications and users.

ORGANIZING DATA IN A DATABASE

Because many of today's organizations are large and complex, it is critical to keep data organized so that it can be effectively utilized. A museum, for example, needs to organize its database to make sure it can catalog and retrieve all of its items or pieces. Without a well-organized database, it would be difficult or impossible for the museum to know exactly what items were part of its collection and where each item was located. This type of information could be critical if the museum has a break-in and an insurance company needs to determine what was stolen. It is also critical during audits of the museum's assets.

A database should be designed to store all data relevant to the organization and provide quick access and easy modification. In building a database, careful consideration must be given to these questions:

- Content: What data is to be collected and at what cost?
- Access: What data is to be provided to which users when appropriate?
- Security: How will the data be kept safe from unauthorized access?
- Logical structure: How is the data to be arranged so that it makes sense to users?
- Physical organization: Where is the data to be physically located?
- Management and coordination: Who is responsible for maintaining an accurate database system, including the development of data modeling?

The Relational Database Model

The structure of the relationships in most databases follows a logical model. Many types of database models have been used over the years, including hierarchical, network, relational, object-oriented, and object-relational. The object-oriented model encapsulates data and database functionality together in software objects. Object-relational databases combine features of the object-oriented model with the relational model. The model that is by far most popular is the relational model.

The overall purpose of the relational model is to describe data using a standard tabular format. In a database structured according to the **relational model**, all data elements are placed in two-dimensional tables called *relations* that are the logical equivalent of files. The tables in relational databases organize data in rows and columns, simplifying data access and manipulation (see Figure 7.9). Notice in the figure that the tables are "related" by a common element, Dept. number. Having tables related by common elements allows them to be linked to produce useful information.

FIGURE 7.9 • The relational database model

In the relational model, all data elements are placed in two-dimensional tables. As long as they share at least one common element, these tables can be linked to produce useful information.

Data Table 1: Project Table

Project number	Description	Dept. number
155	Payroll	257
498	Widgets	632
226	Sales Manual	598

Data Table 2: Department Table

Dept. number	Dept. name	Manager SSN
257	Accounting	421-55-9993
632	Manufacturing	765-00-3192
598	Marketing	098-40-1370

Data Table 3: Manager Table

SSN	Last name	First name	Hire date	Dept. number
005-10-6321	Hassam	Hoda	10-7-2003	257
549-77-1001	Nguyen	Dong	2-17-1996	650
098-40-1370	Fiske	Steven	1-5-1985	598

Once data has been placed into a relational database, data inquiries and manipulations can be made. Two common data manipulations are selecting data and joining tables. *Selecting* involves choosing data based on certain criteria. Suppose a Project table contains the project number, description, and department number for all projects being performed by an organization, as seen in Figure 7.9. The president of the company might want to find the department number for Project 226, which is a sales manual project. Using selection, the president can see only the data for number 226 and determine that the department number for the department completing the sales manual project is 598.

Joining involves combining two or more tables. For example, you could combine the Project table and the Department table to get a new table with the project number, project description, department number, department name, and the Social Security number for the manager in charge of the project.

Being able to relate tables to each other through common data elements is one of the keys to the flexibility and power of relational databases. Suppose that the president of a company wants to find out the name of the manager of the sales manual project and how long the manager has been with the company (see Figure 7.10). The president would make the inquiry to the database, perhaps via a desktop personal computer. The DBMS starts with the project description and searches the Project table to find out the project's department number. It then uses the department number to search the Department table for the department manager's Social Security number. The department number is also in the Department table and is the common element that allows the Project table and the Department table to be related. The DBMS then uses the manager's Social Security number to search the Manager table for the manager's hire date. The final result: the manager's name and hire date are presented to the president as a response to the inquiry. Creating relationships between tables is especially useful when information is needed from multiple tables, as in this example.

FIGURE 7.10 • Relating data tables to answer an inquiry

In finding the name and hiring date of the manager working on the sales manual project, the president needs three tables: Project, Department, and Manager. The project description (Sales Manual) leads to the department number (598) in the Project table, which leads to the manager's SSN (098-40-1370) in the Department table, which leads to the manager's name (Fiske) and hiring date (1-5-1985) in the Manager table.

Project Table

Project number	Description	Dept. number
155	Payroll	257
498	Widgets	632
226	Sales Manual	598

Department Table

Dept. number	Dept. name	Manager SSN
257	Accounting	421-55-9993
632	Manufacturing	765-00-3192
598	Marketing	098-40-1370

Manager Table

SSN	Last name	First name	Hire date	Dept. number
005-10-6321	Hassam	Hoda	10-7-2003	257
549-77-1001	Nguyen	Dong	2-17-1996	650
098-40-1370	Fiske	Steven	1-5-1985	598

Relationships. The ability to connect data in different tables through a common field is sometimes referred to as a *relationship*. Relationships between tables can be illustrated through an *entity relationship diagram*. Study the entity relationship diagram for an online auction database provided in Figure 7.11. Notice that there are four tables in this database, one that contains information about sellers, another with information about buyers, a third with information about all items up for auction, and a fourth that stores all the bids made on items up for auction. The fields included in each table are listed in the boxes.

FIGURE 7.11 • Entity relationship diagram for an online auction

An online auction Web site might depend on four database tables: one for seller info, one for buyer info, one for auction item info, and one for bids, all related by common fields.

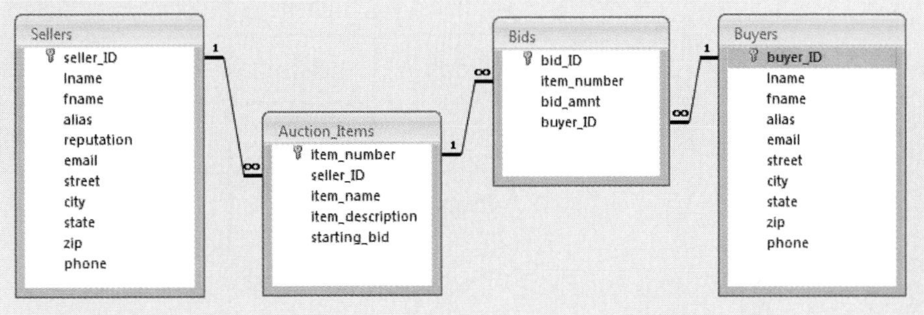

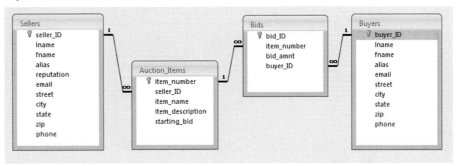

Notice the lines connecting the tables in Figure 7.11. These represent the relationships between the tables and indicate which fields in the tables hold common information. For example, the seller_ID field is used to connect the Sellers table to the Auction_Items table, the item_number field is used to connect the Auction_Items table to the Bids table, and the buyer_ID field is used to connect the Bids table to the Buyers table.

Also notice the 1 and infinity symbols used on the relationship lines. These indicate a special kind of relationship called a *one-to-many relationship*. For example, the relationship between the Sellers table and the Auction_Items table has a 1 on the Sellers side. This is because there is only one record for every seller_ID in the Sellers table because seller_ID is the primary key. However, there is an infinity sign over the Auction_Items side of the relationship since each seller can have more than one item up for auction—the seller_ID is not a primary key in the Auction_Items table. There can also exist one-to-one and many-to-many relationships, depending on whether the field used is a primary key or not.

You may be asking yourself, "Is all this complexity necessary? Why not just put all the data in one large table?" Databases are best designed using small, logically interconnected tables to reduce data redundancy. If the tables in the database shown in Figure 7.11 were joined into one big table, each of the presumably millions of bids would have to include all item specifications, all seller specifications, and all of the buyer specifications. So, for example, the seller's name, address, and phone number would be stored and listed with every bid made on every item the seller was selling. The database would be thousands of times larger than if it used multiple smaller, but related, tables. Designing a database to be efficient and logical is the most challenging task of database designers.

Data Analysis. Having the ability to create relationships between tables becomes very important when trying to ensure that the content of a database is "good." Good data should be nonredundant, flexible, simple, and adaptable to a number of different applications. The purpose of data analysis is to develop data with these characteristics. **Data analysis** is a process that involves evaluating data to identify problems with the content of a database. Consider a database for a fitness center that contains the customer's name, phone number, gender, dues paid, and date paid (see Figure 7.12). As the records in Figure 7.12 show, Brown and Thomas paid their dues in September. Thomas has paid his dues in two installments. Note that no primary key uniquely identifies each record, which in this case will lead to problems for Thomas, S.

FIGURE 7.12 • Database anomaly

In this fitness center dues table, there are two records for Thomas, S. with two different phone numbers. Are these two different people or one person with two phones?

Name	Phone	Gender	Dues Paid	Date Paid
Brown, A.	468-3342	Female	$50	September 15th
Thomas, S.	468-8788	Male	$25	September 15th
Thomas, S.	468-5238	Male	$25	September 15th

This database was designed to keep track of the dues that fitness center members paid in September. Because Thomas has paid dues twice, the data in the database is now redundant. The name, phone number, and gender for Thomas are repeated in two records. Notice that the data in the database is also inconsistent: Thomas has changed his phone number, but only one of the records reflects this change. Further reducing this database's reliability is the fact that no primary key exists to uniquely identify Thomas's record. The first Thomas could be Sam Thomas, but the second might be Steve Thomas. These problems and irregularities in data are called *anomalies*. Data anomalies often result in incorrect information, causing database users to be misinformed about actual conditions. These anomalies and others must be corrected.

To solve these problems, you can add a primary key, called Member number, and put the data into two tables: a Fitness Center Members table with gender, phone number, and related information, and a Dues Paid table with dues paid and date paid. As you can see in Figure 7.13, both tables include the Member number field that can be used to create a relationship between the two.

With the relations in Figure 7.13, the redundancy has been reduced and the potential problem of having two different phone numbers for the member has been eliminated. Also note that the member number gives each record in the Fitness Center Members table a primary key. Because there are two dues paid ($25 each) with the same member number (SN656), you know this is the same person, not two different people.

The process of correcting data problems or anomalies is called *normalization*. It ensures that the database contains "good data." Normalization normally involves breaking one table into two or more tables in order to correct a data problem or anomaly, as in Figure 7.13. Normalization is a very important technique in database management and is yet another advantage of using a relational database. The details of normalization, however, are beyond the scope of this text.

FIGURE 7.13 • Database normalization

To solve data problems, add a primary key, called Member number, and put the data into two tables: a Fitness Center Members table with gender, phone number, and related information; and a Dues Paid table with dues paid and date paid.

Fitness Center Members Table

Member number	Name	Phone	Gender
SN123	Brown, A.	468-3342	Female
SN656	Thomas, S.	468-5238	Male

Fitness Center Dues Paid Table

Member number	Dues paid	Date paid
SN123	$50	September 15th
SN656	$25	September 15th
SN656	$25	September 15th

Database Characteristics

The information needs of individuals or organizations have an impact on what type of data is collected and what type of database model is used. Important characteristics of databases include the amount of data, the volatility of the data, and how immediately the data needs to be updated.

- The database size or *amount* depends on the number of records or files in the database. The size determines the overall storage requirement for the database.
- *Volatility* of data is a measure of the changes, such as additions, deletions, or modifications, typically required in a given period of time.
- *Immediacy* is a measure of how rapidly changes must be made to data. Some applications, such as providing concert ticket reservations, require immediate updating and processing so that two customers are not booked for the same seat. Other applications, such as payroll, can be done once a week or less frequently and do not require immediate processing. If an application demands immediacy, it also demands rapid recovery facilities in the event the computer system shuts down temporarily.

The preceding characteristics are important for any individual or organization. They determine the requirements of the database and the type of database system that is needed for the amount of data, the volatility of the data, and the possible need for rapid changes. These characteristics are important in selecting and designing a database management system.

DATABASE MANAGEMENT SYSTEMS

EXPAND YOUR KNOWLEDGE

To learn more about database systems, go to www.cengage.com/computerconcepts/np/swt4. Click the link "Expand Your Knowledge" and then complete the lab entitled "Advanced Databases."

Creating and implementing the right database system ensures that the database can support individual and organizational goals. For example, an effective database management system can help doctors provide better patient care—a key goal of any hospital. A DBMS can also help streamline paperwork.

Creating and implementing the right database system involves determining how data is stored and retrieved, how people will see and use the database, how the database will be created and maintained, and how reports and documents will be generated. But how do you actually create, implement, use, and update a database? What type of database is needed?

Overview of Database Types

Database management systems can range from small, inexpensive software packages to sophisticated systems costing hundreds of thousands of dollars. A few popular alternatives include flat file, single-user, multiuser, and general-purpose and special-purpose systems. Open-source databases are also available.

Flat File. A *flat file database* stores database records in a plain text file. Flat file databases don't use any of the database models discussed earlier. This method of data storage typically stores each record as a line of text, and uses commas, tabs, or other indicators within the line to separate the fields within the record. The most common type of flat file format is called *CSV* for *comma-separated values*. The contents of a file named addressbook.csv might look something like this when viewed with a text editor:

```
Smith,Jon,1881 Mango Ct,Atlanta,GA,31123
Peters,Linda,2991 Montrose,Chicago,IL,60645
```

Databases and even spreadsheet software can read a .csv file, using the line breaks and commas to interpret the data as a table. Some Web-based software uses flat files to store data in an organized manner without the need to set up a complicated database. Flat files can also delineate fields by using fixed-width columns rather than commas, as follows:

```
Smith  Jon   1881 Mango Ct Atlanta GA 31123
Peters Linda 2991 Montrose Chicago IL 60645
```

Flat files are standardized and understood by many different database and spreadsheet applications, so they are handy for sharing data between different types of software (see Figure 7.14).

MAKING THE SCIENTIFIC METHOD OBSOLETE?

Since the Newtonian revolution, scientific inquiry has been defined by the formation of hypotheses tested by experimentation. Today, however, with the creation of massive repositories of scientific data, such as the University of Texas' *Corral*, a new type of exploration, called *data-driven science*, is emerging. This line of inquiry applies mathematical analysis and statistics to large amounts of data to interpret the relationship between natural phenomena, perhaps making the hypothesis—obsolete.

Managing the Data Deluge
By Aaron Dubrow and Faith Singer-Villalobos
Texas Advanced Computing Center
June 5, 2009
http://www.tacc.utexas.edu/research/users/features/dynamic.php?m_b_c=corral

FIGURE 7.14 • Accessing data from different applications

Storing or exporting data to a standard and broadly recognized format such as a flat file (.csv file) allows users to operate on data using different applications and platforms. Here an Access database table has been exported and opened in Excel.

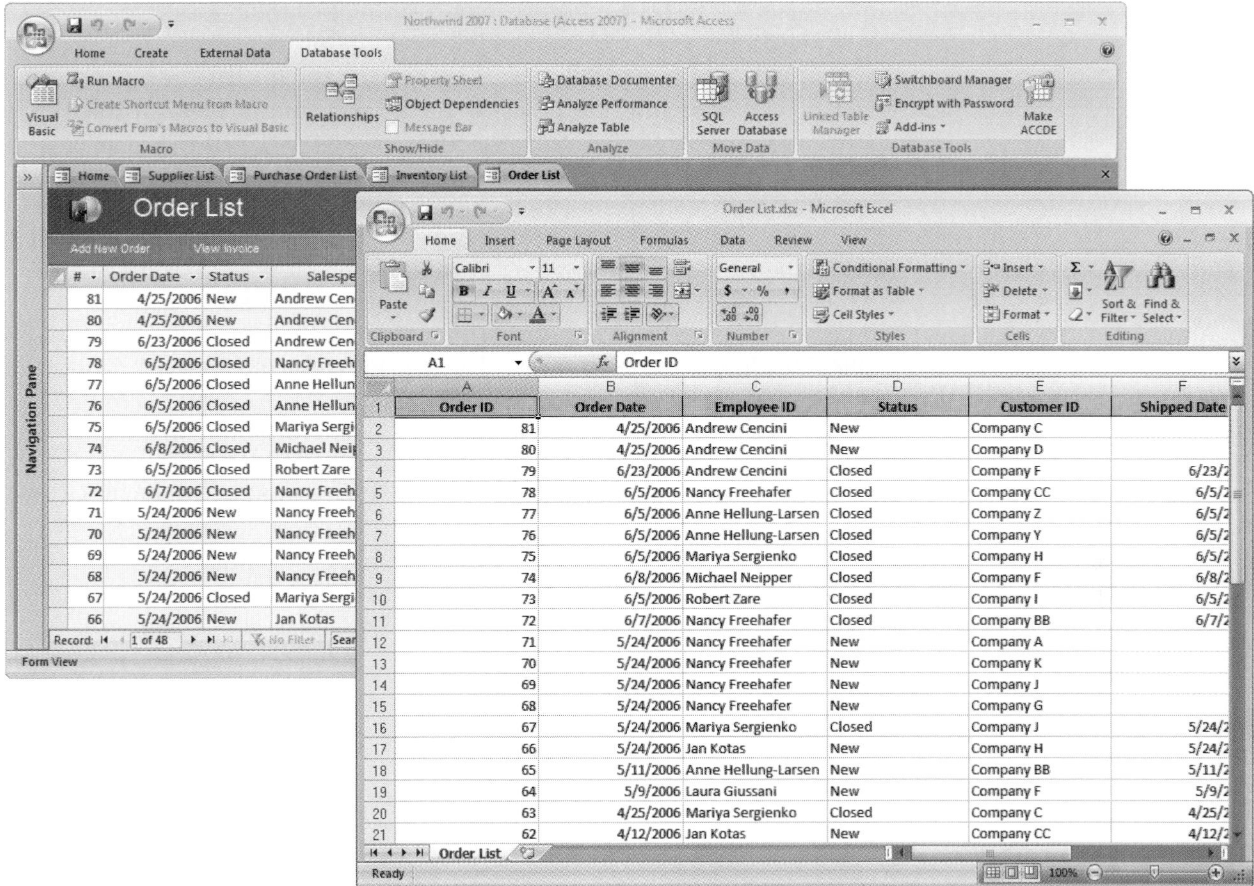

Single User. Databases for personal computers are most often designed for a single user. Only one person can use the database at any time. Microsoft Outlook and Quicken are examples of popular single-user DBMSs used to store and manipulate personal data. Outlook organizes contacts, address lists, e-mail, and to-do lists, and Quicken is used for financial data. Microsoft InfoPath is another example of a single-user database. Infopath is part of the Microsoft Office suite and helps people collect and organize information from a variety of sources. InfoPath has built-in forms that can be used to enter expense information, time-sheet data, and a variety of other information. Oracle has developed Database Lite 11*g* for laptop computers and other mobile or wireless devices. Database Lite is designed to give professionals access to corporate data while on the road and disconnected from corporate servers. OpenOffice.org Base is an open-source single-user database available for free download.

Multiuser. Most small, medium, and large businesses require multiuser DBMSs that allow multiple employees to access and edit data simultaneously. These are typically referred to as *database development platforms* since they allow you to create a database and a DBMS for accessing and manipulating data in the database. Multiuser DBMSs make use of a unique manner of reading and writing data to allow users simultaneous access to a shared database.

Most PC software, like spreadsheet software, is designed for use by one individual at a time. When you open a spreadsheet, the entire spreadsheet file is loaded into the memory of your computer and the file on disk is locked from anyone else who might attempt to access it over a network. When you edit the spreadsheet, changes are made to the copy of the spreadsheet stored in memory on your PC. Those changes are not made to the file on disk until you save the file. In this manner, the data in the spreadsheet can be manipulated by only one user at a time. This keeps users from overwriting each other's work.

When a multiuser database file is opened, the DBMS is loaded into the memory of your computer, which allows you to view the data in the file on the hard drive. When you edit data in the database, the changes are made to the actual data on disk, not in memory. In this manner, different cells may be edited in the same database on disk simultaneously by multiple users. You may be changing the address for customer William Shatner while someone in the next office is editing William Shatner's phone number—both in the same database at the same moment. Since everyone working on the database sees changes as they are made, no one's work is overwritten. That is, except in the rare instance when two or more individuals are editing the same cell at the exact same time. In such a case, the last change made is the one that remains.

Microsoft Access is one of the smaller database development platforms available for use by individuals and small businesses and organizations. Large, industrial-strength databases such as IBM DB2, Microsoft SQL Server, and Oracle are much more powerful, and expensive, and they allow dozens, hundreds, even thousands of people to access the same database system at the same time.

For example, the U.S. federal government has developed a Web-based DBMS that provides access to 100,000 federal data sources to U.S. citizens at *www.data.gov* (see Figure 7.15). This effort toward more open government requires a powerful DBMS and many multiuser databases.[3]

FIGURE 7.15 • Multiuser database: data.gov

Data.gov provides Web-based access to over 100,000 federal datasets to U.S. citizens.

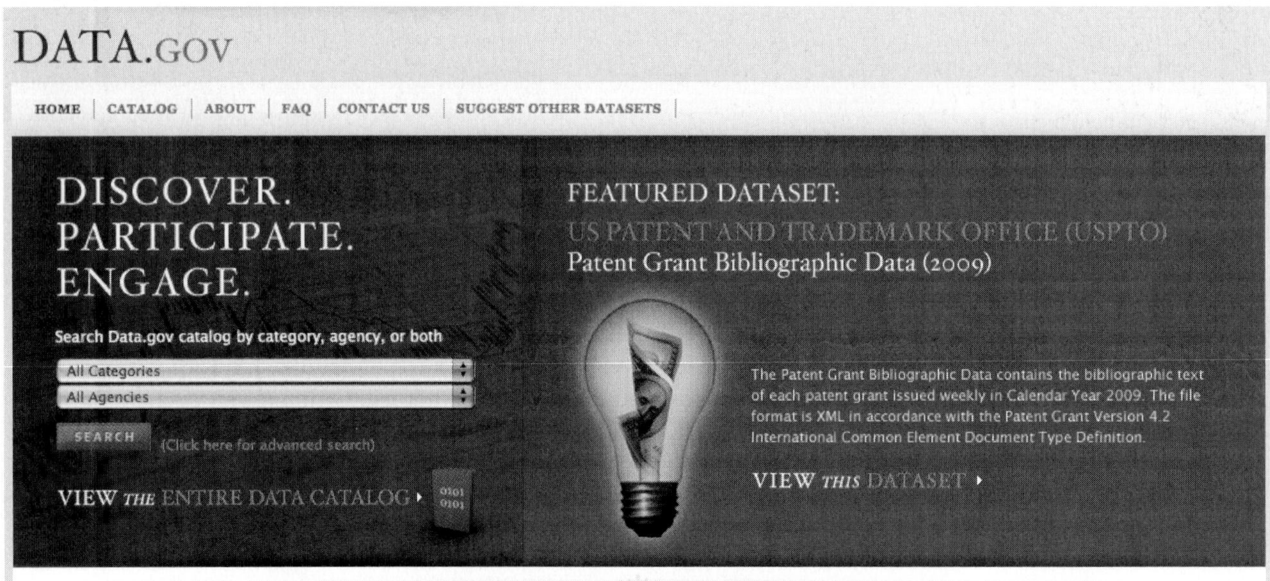

General-Purpose and Special-Purpose Databases. A *general-purpose database* can be used for a large number of applications. Oracle, Sybase, and IBM databases are examples of general-purpose database software that can be used by businesses, the military, charitable organizations, scientific researchers, and most other organizations for many different types of applications. Oracle is currently the market leader in general-purpose databases, with about 44.1 percent of the \$18.6 billion global database market.[4]

In contrast, a *special-purpose database* is designed for one purpose or a limited number of applications. The Israeli Holocaust Database (*www.yadvashem.org*) is a special-purpose database available through the Internet and contains information on about 3 million people in 14 languages.

Another example of a special-purpose database is QuickBooks, an accounting program for small businesses. In many cases, the overall structure of the database and the reports that can be generated are already developed for easy use. MindManager is a special-purpose database used to organize projects and people's thoughts and ideas (see Figure 7.16).

FIGURE 7.16 • MindManager

MindManager is a special-purpose database used to organize projects and people's thoughts and ideas.

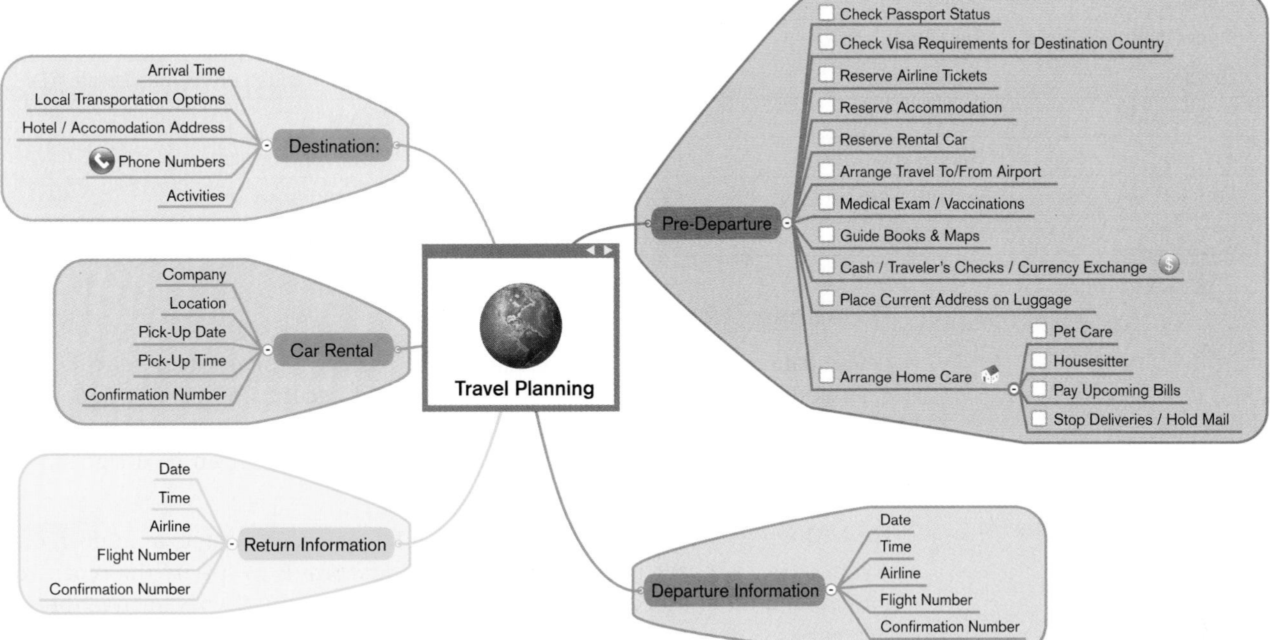

Open-Source Database Systems. As in other software areas, open-source DBMSs, including MySQL, PostgreSQL, and Ingres, are increasing in popularity. Open-source DBMSs are used by travel agencies, manufacturing companies, and other companies. One study found that the open-source DMBS MySQL is deployed 30 percent more frequently that Oracle, SQL Server, or DB2.[5]

Open-source database management systems offer the same advantages as all open-source software: there is strong community support, they are completely customizable, and they are free. The popular online service craigslist uses open-source MySQL to store and serve up tens of millions of classified ads and user comments to hundreds of millions of users per day.[6] Also, the world's oldest and largest news agency, the Associated Press, uses MySQL to distribute news stories to news outlets like *The New York Times* and CNN.[7]

Table 7.2 lists some popular DBMSs from various vendors.

TABLE 7.2 • Popular database management systems

DBMS	Vendor	Database model	Computer type
Access	Microsoft Corp.	Relational	PC, server, PDA
Approach	Lotus Development Corp.	Relational	PC, server
DB2	IBM Corp.	Object-relational	PC, midrange server, mainframe
FileMaker	FileMaker, Inc.	Relational	PC, server, PDA
Informix	IBM Corp.	Relational	PC, midrange server, mainframe
Ingres	Computer Associates International, Inc.	Relational	PC, midrange server, mainframe
MySQL	MySQL AB	Relational; open source	PC, midrange server, mainframe
OpenOffice.org Base	Sun, Open source	Relational	PC, server
Oracle	Oracle Corp.	Object-relational	PC, midrange server, mainframe, PDA
SQL Server	Microsoft Corp.	Relational	Server
Sybase	Sybase Inc.	Relational	PC, midrange server, PDA
Versant	Versant Corp.	Object-oriented	PC, midrange server
Visual FoxPro	Microsoft Corp.	Relational	PC, server

Database Design

Before data can be stored, manipulated, and retrieved, the database must be logically designed. At a minimum, this requires field, record, and table design. All database management systems have the ability to perform these important design functions. In addition, other aspects of the database can be designed, including the input and output interfaces.

Field Design. As mentioned earlier, a field is typically a name, a number, or a combination of characters. The purpose of *field design* is to specify the type, size, format, and other aspects of each field. Some popular field types include the following:

- Numeric: A *numeric field* contains numbers that can be used in making calculations, such as inventory_amt.
- Alphanumeric: *Alphanumeric* or character data includes characters or numbers that cannot be manipulated or used in calculations, such as street_address.
- Date: Databases allow you to enter dates, such as 06/12/10, into the database.
- Logical: A *logical field* contains items such as *yes* or *no*.
- Computed: A *computed field*, also called a calculated field, is calculated from other fields instead of being entered into the database, such as (target_level – available_inventory); see Figure 7.17.

FIGURE 7.17 • Field data types

This table from a food distributor includes an alphanumeric field (Product), several numeric fields needed for calculations, and three calculated fields: Available Inventory, Combined Total, and Qty To Reorder.

Inventory List

Add Product | Home

Product	Total Inventory	Allocated Inventory	Available Inventory	Inventory Due from Supplier	Combined Total	Target Level	Qty To Reorder	Purchase from Supplier
Northwind Traders Chai	25	25	0	41	41	40	0	Purchase
Northwind Traders Syrup	50	0	50	50	100	100	0	Purchase
Northwind Traders Cajun Seasonin	0	0	0	40	40	40	0	Purchase
Northwind Traders Olive Oil	15	0	15	0	15	40	25	Purchase
Northwind Traders Boysenberry Sp	0	0	0	10	10	100	90	Purchase
Northwind Traders Dried Pears	0	0	0	0	0	40	40	Purchase
Northwind Traders Curry Sauce	0	0	0	0	0	40	40	Purchase
Northwind Traders Walnuts	40	0	40	0	40	40	0	Purchase
Northwind Traders Fruit Cocktail	0	0	0	0	0	40	40	Purchase
Northwind Traders Chocolate Biscu	0	0	0	20	20	20	0	Purchase

Figure 7.17 illustrates a table that uses several different data types. The Product field holds alphanumeric data. Total Inventory, Allocated Inventory, Inventory Due from Supplier, and Target Level hold numeric data. The remaining fields are calculated fields: Available Inventory subtracts Allocated Inventory from Total Inventory, Combined Total adds Available Inventory to Inventory Due from Supplier, and Qty To Reorder subtracts Combined Total from Target Level. Red text is used when Available Inventory reaches zero, or when Combined Total is less than Target Level.

Record and Table Design. Recall that a record is a collection of related fields, and a table (or file) is a collection of related records. In any database, you must identify the exact fields that are contained in each record, and the types of records that may be included in each table. For example, you might want to develop a database for your DVD movie collection. Suitable fields might be ID_Number, Title, Year, Category, Actors, and Rating. Similar record designs can be specified for a database of the members in a volunteer group that builds homes, a list of items in your apartment for insurance purposes in case of a fire or theft, the results of a scientific experiment in your nutrition class, and the required courses you must complete to graduate.

Database tables can contain a few or millions of records and fields. Tables can be organized in a variety of ways, and different tables can be related, as discussed earlier in the section on relational databases. You can sort on one or more fields to help organize a table. For a table containing the first and last names of members of a student group, you could sort on last name as the first sorting key and on the first name as the secondary sorting key. Adams would be sorted before Brill, and Crystal Adams would appear before Jake Adams. As mentioned before, tables can also be selected and joined.

Input and Output Interface Design. Designing effective interfaces is a convenient and powerful database design feature in most database management systems. Designers can create easy-to-understand forms that users can fill out for each record (see Figure 7.18), and after users completely enter data into a field, the database automatically goes to the next field, without requiring the user to press Enter for each field.

FIGURE 7.18 • Input and output design

Database designers can create forms that are easy for users to fill out and reports that present useful information in a clear and attractive format.

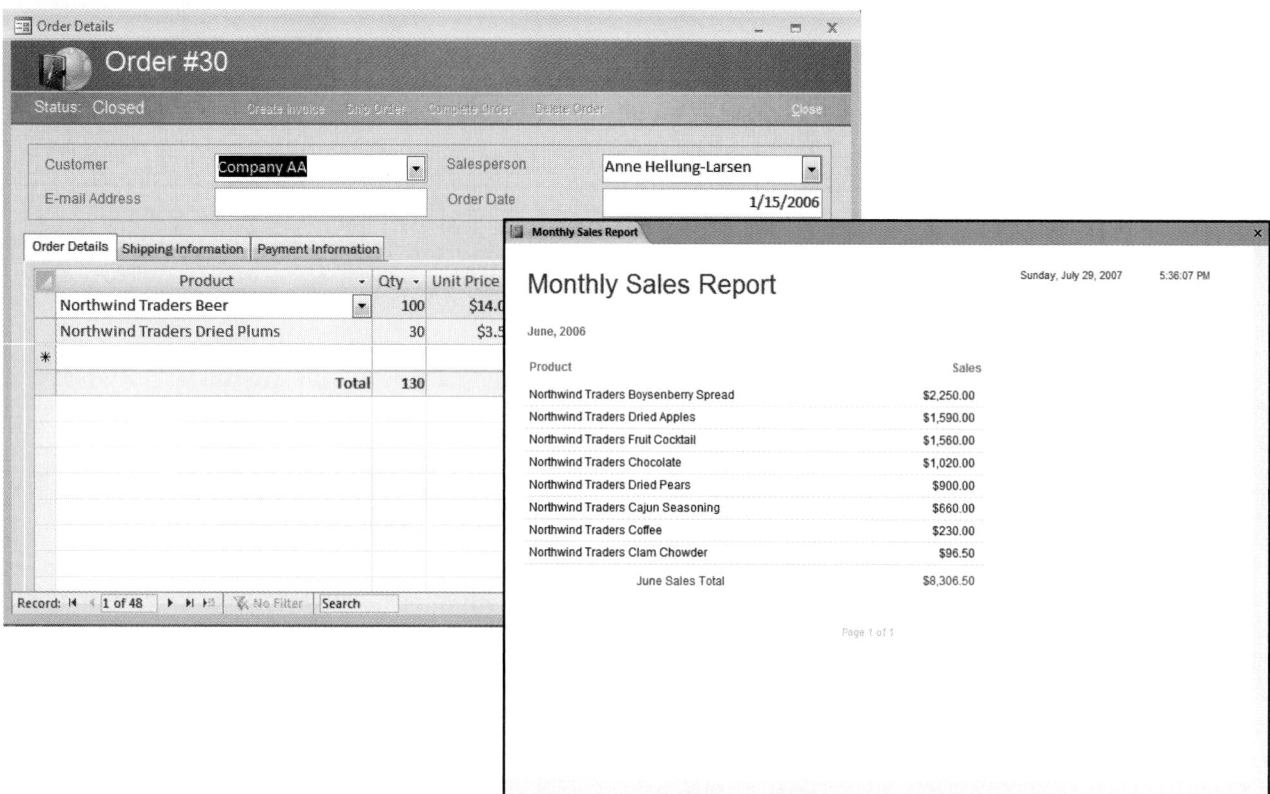

Reports and other outputs from the database can also be designed to be powerful and packed with useful information. A university can have a report that lists only those students who haven't paid their fees; a civil engineering firm could design a report that lists stress points in an old bridge; and a medical blood test report could be designed to include a column with all tests that are outside of normal ranges. These types of reports are an important aspect of providing information support to administrators, military generals, engineers, doctors, and corporate executives.

Using Databases with Other Software

Database management systems are often used in conjunction with other software packages or the Internet. A database management system can act as a front-end application or a back-end application. A *front-end application* is one that directly interacts with users. A *back-end application* interacts with other programs and databases; it interacts only indirectly with users. For example, if you bank online, your bank's Web site acts as the system's front-end application, the part with which customers interact. The back-end applications are those that interact with the database on the server to provide you with banking services (see Figure 7.19).

FIGURE 7.19 • Databases with other software

Databases often supply data to custom-designed software on back-end systems, which deliver services to the user who interacts with front-end applications.

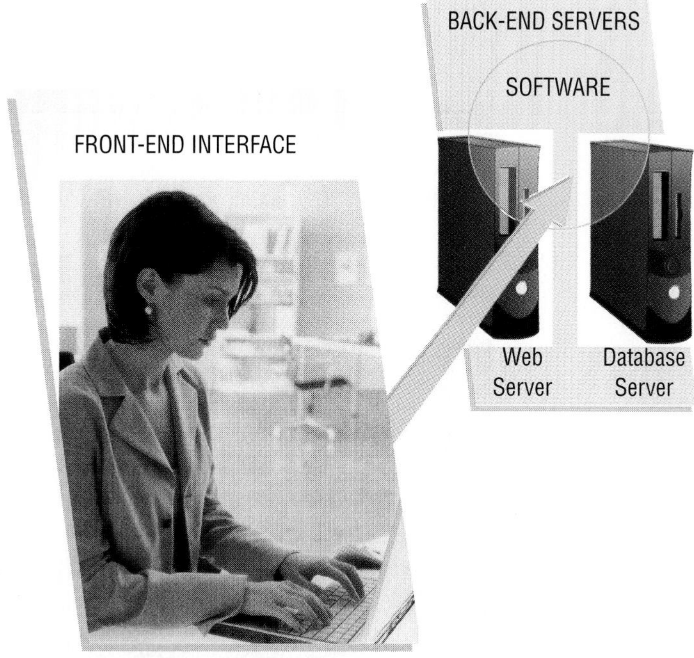

System designers are increasingly using the Web as the front end to database systems. The Web page *www.google.com* acts as the front end to the huge Google database that resides at the back end of the system. On corporate intranets, a Web browser serves as the perfect front end to private database systems because employees are already comfortable with using Web browsers and require little training to use the system.

Databases are written following open standards that allow programmers to easily integrate the database with all kinds of software functionality. Whenever you submit a form on a Web page, custom-designed software on the server accepts your form data as input and performs some processing, typically with the assistance of a database.

Data Accuracy and Integrity

As first discussed in Chapter 1, to be of value, data must be accurate. **Data integrity** means that data stored in the database is accurate and up to date. There are many possibilities for inaccuracies in today's information-rich society. Many people have been unable to get credit cards, car loans, or home mortgages because data about them stored by credit bureaus was wrong. In a manufacturing company, a clerk might enter the hours an employee worked as 4 hours instead of 40 hours. In some cases, a retail store may report that someone didn't pay his or her bills, when the bills were paid in full. These types of errors are caused by entering inaccurate data into a database. The results are inaccurate output. This is sometimes referred to as **garbage in, garbage out (GIGO)**. Computer systems are often blamed for such errors, but in reality, the errors are more often human.

In other cases, data is simply old and no longer valid. Managers have made multimillion-dollar decisions based on out-of-date information. A manager might decide to build a new manufacturing plant based on old sales data that was much higher than current numbers. A nurse may give the wrong drugs to a patient because the prescribed treatment reflected the patient's past situation.

In other cases, people intentionally enter wrong data for their own gain. In the corporate scandals of the early 2000s, a number of executives and accountants falsified records to inflate profits or hide expenses to get higher bonuses based on the company's stock performance (see Figure 7.20). In an effort to get more articles published and gain tenure, a promotion, or salary increase, some medical researchers have falsified research results.

FIGURE 7.20 • Damaging data integrity

In the corporate scandals of the early 2000s, a number of executives and accountants falsified records to inflate profits or hide expenses to get higher bonuses based on the company's stock performance. Many of the people involved had to testify in court and some were imprisoned.

Database management systems must be programmed to detect and eliminate data inaccuracies whenever possible. For example, if the combined expenses of various departments or branches are greater than the total expenses reported on a company's income statement, something is probably wrong. If everyone in a department was reported to have worked only four hours last week, a clerical error has probably been made. Although it is not possible to eliminate all data inaccuracies, good database design and development requires setting up checks and balances to detect and eliminate errors.

Creating and Modifying a Database

One of the first steps in creating a database is to outline the logical and physical structure of the data and relationships among the data in the database. This description is called a **schema** (as in schematic diagram). A schema can be part of the database or a separate schema file. The DBMS can reference a schema to find where to access the requested data in relation to another piece of data. Schemas are entered into the DBMS (usually by database personnel) via a data definition language. A *data definition language (DDL)* is a collection of instructions and commands used to define and describe data and data relationships in a specific database.

Another important step in creating a database is to establish a **data dictionary**, a detailed description of all data used in the database. The data dictionary includes information such as the name of the data item, who prepared the data, who approved the data, the date, a description, other names, the range of values for the data, the data type (numeric or alphanumeric), and the number of positions or space needed for the data. A data dictionary provides standard definitions of terms and data elements that can be referenced by programmers, database administrators, and users to maintain data integrity. Figure 7.21 shows a typical data dictionary entry.

FIGURE 7.21 • A typical data dictionary entry

The data dictionary includes information such as the name of the data item, who prepared the data, who approved the data, the date, a description, other names, the range of values for the data, the data type (numeric or alphanumeric), and the number of positions or space needed for the data.

```
          NORTHWESTERN
          MANUFACTURING
PREPARED BY:         D. BORDWELL
DATE:                04 AUGUST
APPORVED BY:         J. EDWARDS       DATE: 13 OCTOBER
DATE:                13 OCTOBER
VERSION:             3.1
PAGE:                1 OF 1

DATA ELEMENT NAME:   PARTNO
DESCRIPTION:         INVENTORY PART NUMBER
OTHER NAMES:         PTNO
VALUE RANGE:         100 TO 5000
DATA TYPE:           NUMERIC
POSITONS:            4 POSITIONS OF COLUMNS
```

Updating a Database

Databases are updated by adding, modifying, and deleting records. A paleontologist looking for dinosaur bones can add records to her database at each new dig. A university can modify your student records to include courses you just completed last semester along with your new GPA. A company can delete customers who paid their bills completely from its accounts receivable table, which lists all customers who still owe the company money from past sales. Continual database updating is absolutely essential to maintain a high degree of data accuracy and integrity. As mentioned earlier, a front-end application can be used to enter the changes, which are then transferred to the database. A unique Web-based DBMS for biologists called Morphbank (*www.morphbank.net*) allows researchers from around the world to update and build a huge library of biological images to share with the scientific community and public (see Figure 7.22).

FIGURE 7.22 • Morphbank database

The Web-based Morphbank database allows scientists from around the world to upload and share biological and microscopic photographs and descriptions that support research in many areas.

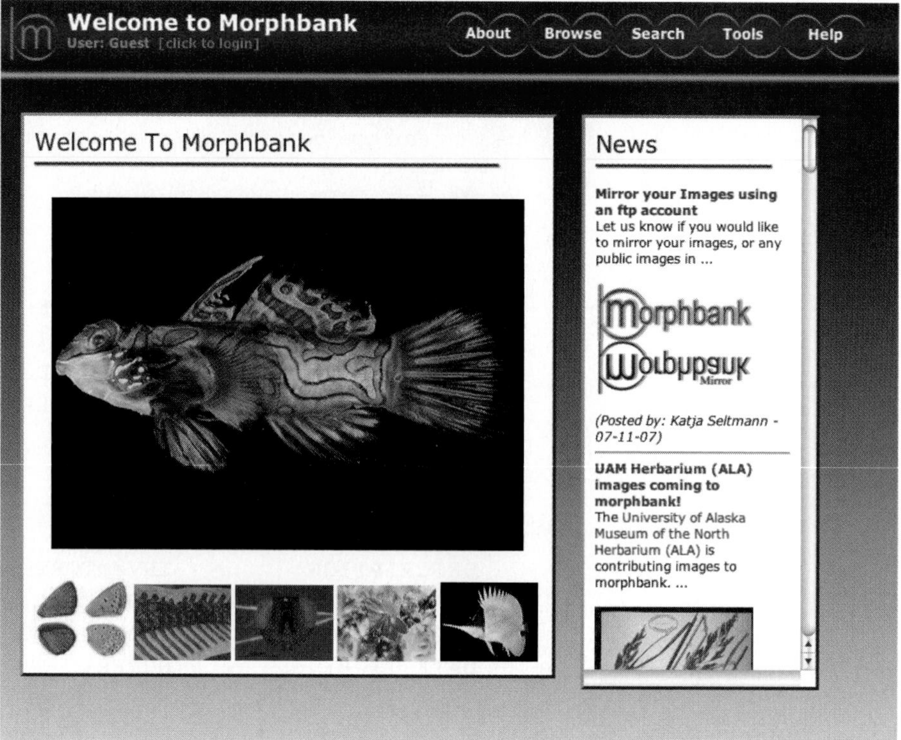

Manipulating Data and Generating Reports

Once a DBMS has been installed and a database and tables are created, the system can be used via specific commands in various programming languages or queried using a data manipulation language. In general, a *data manipulation language* (*DML*) is a specific language provided with the DBMS that allows people and other database users to access, modify, and make queries about data contained in the database and to generate reports. Many databases use *query by example* (*QBE*) to give you ideas and examples of how queries can be made. QBE is a very visual approach to making queries or getting answers to questions by entering names, values, and other items into a window (see Figure 7.23). As you can see, QBE makes manipulating databases much easier and faster than learning formal DMLs such as SQL, which is discussed next.

In the 1970s, D. D. Chamberlain and others at the IBM Research Laboratory in San Jose, California, developed a standardized data manipulation language called **Structured Query Language (SQL)**, pronounced "sequel." In 1986, the American National Standards Institute (ANSI) adopted SQL as the standard query language for relational databases. Today, SQL is an integral part of popular databases on both mainframe and personal computers. The following query is written in SQL:

```
SELECT * FROM EMPLOYEE WHERE JOB_CLASSIFICATION = 'C2'
```

This query tells the DBMS to select all (*) columns from the EMPLOYEE table for which the JOB_CLASSIFICATION value is equal to C2.

SQL is actually a programming language, but it is easy for nonprogrammers to understand and use; note the English-like commands. Programmers can use

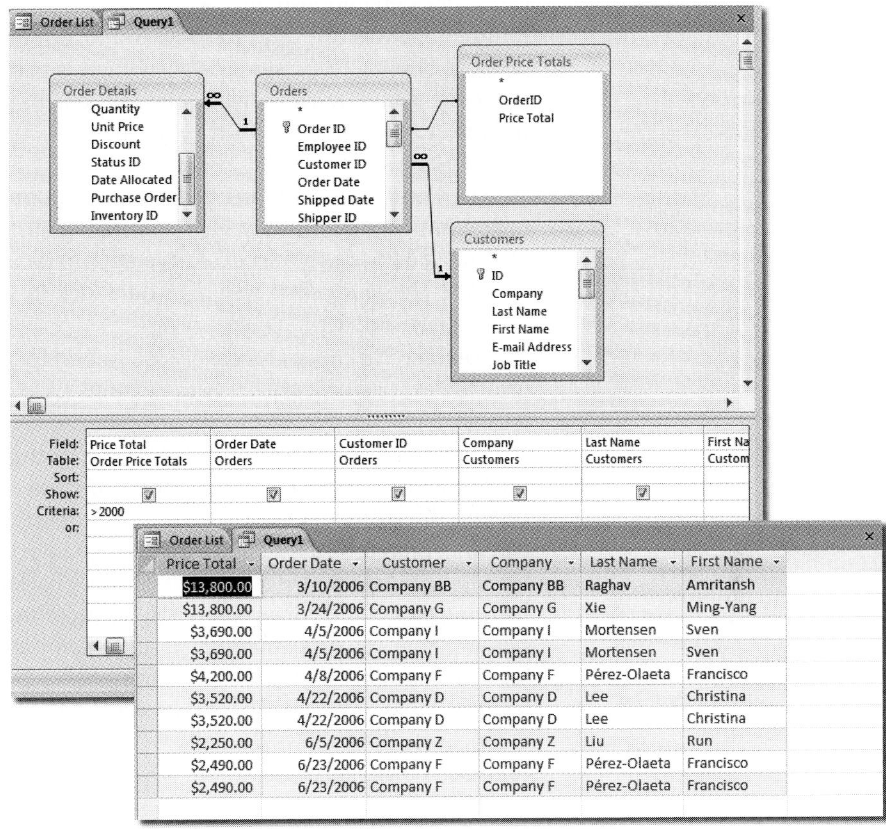

FIGURE 7.23 • Query by example

Microsoft Access calls QBE a simple query: select the tables to include, specify criteria, and click Run. In this case the query lists customers who purchased more than $2000 of products.

SQL on systems ranging from PCs to the largest mainframe computers. SQL statements also can be embedded in many programming languages, such as the widely used language Java. Table 7.3 contains examples of SQL commands.

TABLE 7.3 • Examples of SQL commands

SQL command	Description

`SELECT ClientName, Debt`
`FROM Client`
`WHERE Debt > 1000`
	This query displays all clients (ClientName) and the amount they owe the company (Debt) from a database table called Client for clients that owe the company more than $1000 (WHERE Debt > 1000).

`SELECT ClientName, ClientNum, OrderNum`
`FROM Client, Order`
`WHERE Client.ClientNum = Order.ClientNum`
	This command is an example of a join command that combines data from two tables—the client table and the order table (FROM Client, Order). The command creates a new table with the client name, client number, and order number (SELECT ClientName, ClientNum, OrderNum). Both tables include the customer number, which allows them to be joined. This is indicated in the WHERE clause that states that the client number in the client table is the same (equal to) the client number in the order table (WHERE Client.ClientNum = Order.ClientNum).

`GRANT INSERT ON Client to BGuthrie`	This command is an example of a security command; it allows "Bob Guthrie" to insert new values or rows into the Client table.

Database Backup and Recovery

When databases and information systems fail, businesses and organizations can suffer tremendously unless the systems can be brought back online within minutes. Providing a plan for how to bring systems back online after an emergency is known as *disaster recovery*, which is part of a larger process called *business continuity planning*. Those who maintain databases and IT systems around or near the hurricane-prone U.S. Gulf Coast are certainly familiar with this concept. The city of Gainesville, Florida, has built a cement fortress to house its data and DBMS servers. Continuity planning is especially important to government agencies that maintain information on which national security depends. The U.S. Department of Homeland Security has extensive backup data centers in Mississippi and Virginia. The redundant systems would kick in should the main systems in Washington suffer problems.[8]

Database backup and recovery are important functions of any DBMS. Some database experts believe that organizations have an obligation to provide secure and reliable databases by using adequate database backup procedures. A *database backup* is a copy of all or part of the database. For example, if you have a database containing the items in your apartment, you can create a database backup by making a copy of the entire database on a second storage device. It is also possible to make a partial backup of only the data that has changed since the last backup. Database backup software can automate the database backup process. Some backup software makes copies of a database every day or more frequently. Database backup hardware can also be used. Some individuals and organizations purchase special hard disks for data backup. Other larger organizations, such as the Department of Homeland Security, build large redundant data centers to serve as backups. Microsoft has a product called Windows Home Server that automatically backs up all data on all computers connected to a home or small business network.

Database recovery is the process of returning the database to its original, correct condition if the database has crashed or been corrupted. If the database containing the items in your apartment crashes or becomes unusable, you can recover by using the backup copy. Most database backup software and hardware have excellent recovery capabilities to restore the database if something goes wrong. In some cases, it is possible to give one command or push a button to restore a damaged database. Some organizations use *redundant array of independent disks (RAID)* to store duplicate data on multiple disks or a *storage area network (SAN)* to connect multiple storage devices on high-speed networks to make recovering from a database failure faster and more efficient.

USING DATABASE SYSTEMS IN ORGANIZATIONS

You have explored a number of database applications in this chapter, from an individual entering a list of video DVDs to large corporations keeping track of business operations. This section takes a closer look at how databases are used in organizations, including transaction processing, information and decision support, and a variety of other areas.

Routine Processing

All organizations need to process routine transactions. Organizations of all sizes have to pay their employees. A small business needs to send out bills quickly to maintain a healthy cash flow, and a religious organization might want to send out a monthly newsletter. A manufacturing company needs to pay its suppliers for parts and raw materials. These are all routine processing activities that can be implemented with a database system.

Life Fitness Corporation, a global leader in the fitness equipment industry, uses an Oracle database to access routine corporate data on a minute-by-minute basis. The electronic reports generated by the database allow Life Fitness managers to schedule shipments, identify product issues, and guide future product design.[9]

Information and Decision Support

Database systems are a valuable tool for producing information that supports decision making for people and organizations. A database by Intellifit can help shoppers make better decisions and get clothes that fit when shopping online. The database contains true sizes of apparel from various clothing companies that do business on the Web. The process starts when a customer's body is scanned into a database at one of the company's locations, typically in a shopping mall (see Figure 7.24). About 200,000 measurements are taken to construct a 3D image of the person's body shape. The database then compares the actual body dimensions with sizes given by Web-based clothing stores to get an excellent fit. The Intellifit company claims a 90 percent rate of accuracy when it comes to finding sizes and the styles and the brands that fit best.

FIGURE 7.24 • Intellifit: Decision support for clothes shopping

A whole-body scanner inputs your precise measurements, compares them to a database of clothing, sizes, and styles, and makes suggestions for apparel that will fit just right.

Manipulating the data in a database into valuable information has helped many people achieve their goals. A hotel chain achieves better customer satisfaction using a database system to customize service. This type of database system can provide detailed information about customers. A hotel receptionist in New York, for example, might apologize to a customer for not having her room cleaned up as desired during a recent stay at one of the chain's hotels in Orlando. The receptionist at the New York hotel might offer the customer a special rate or provide additional service as a result of the data about the customer's Orlando stay in the hotel's database (see Figure 7.25).

FIGURE 7.25 • Hilton's OnQ

Hotels in the Hilton family of brands use proprietary OnQ technology to understand and deliver on guest preferences. Customers opt in to provide profile information, which is combined with history from past stays. The information is encoded on tags that can be read at check-in and used by hotel team members to enhance the guest's stay.

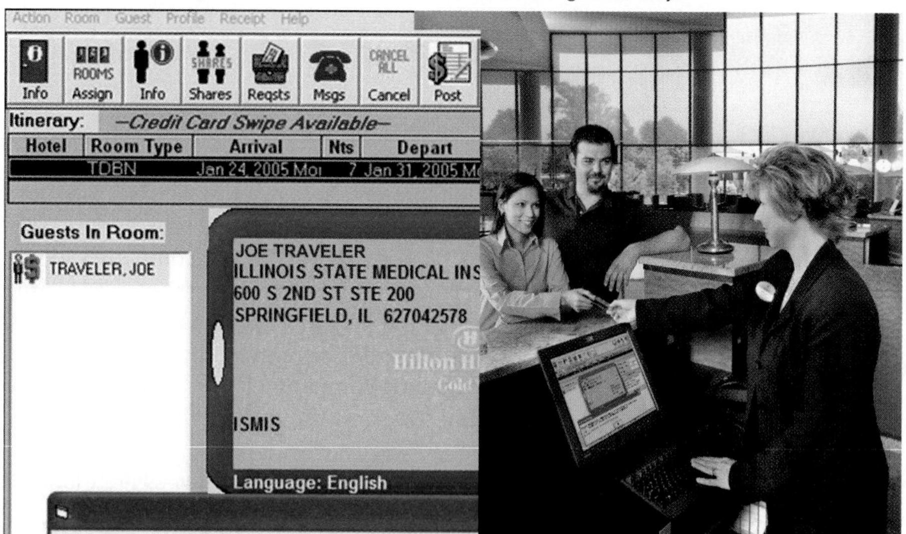

Data Warehouses, Data Marts, and Data Mining

To realize the potential of databases to provide information and decision support, a number of technologies have been developed. A **data warehouse** is a typically large database that holds important information from a variety of sources. It is usually a subset of multiple databases maintained by an organization or individual. The first data warehouses were developed at PacTel Cellular, Aetna Casualty, and Blue Cross/Blue Shield in the 1980s. Today, data warehouses are used by many companies and organizations. A hardware store, for example, can use a data warehouse to analyze pricing trends. This can help the store determine what inventory to carry and what price to charge. As a result, the store might lower the price of wheelbarrows and sell twice as many each year. With a data warehouse, all you have to do is ask where a certain product is selling well and a colorful table showing sales performance by region, product type, and time frame pops up on the screen.

China's Yangtze Power Company, a huge energy company that is responsible for the Three Gorges Dam project, utilizes a data warehouse to analyze its enterprise-wide performance each day. The data warehouse collects data from numerous branch offices and combines it into a single coherent database. Each morning, high-level executives analyze the previous day's critical activities that guide their business decisions. The huge data warehouse maintains data over a three-year period, making it easy to discover trends and anomalies over time.[10]

A *data mart* is a small data warehouse, often developed for a specific person or purpose. It can be generated from a data warehouse using a database management

Databases in the Cloud

The latest trend in databases and data warehouses is "floating in the cloud." Google, Greenplum, and other database service providers are applying cloud computing principles to database technologies. Cloud computing refers to accessing data and information services from the Internet (the cloud) utilizing a standard Web-based interface. Cloud computing promises to move many computing resources from PCs and business servers to Internet servers created and maintained by information service companies.

Google has announced a new online database called Fusion Tables that takes a new approach to database management. Fusion Tables stores data on Google servers, which allows users from multiple locations convenient access to the data and powerful tools for data manipulation. Fusion Tables utilizes a technology called data spaces that eliminates the problems inherent with working with different data types and formats. Some analysts believe that this technology will make conventional databases as obsolete as the rotary phone.

Greenplum, a data warehousing vendor, has developed an Enterprise Data Cloud (EDC) Initiative to provide self-service data warehousing and data mining. Greenplum's EDC approach allows companies to create data warehouses from numerous data sources and mine the data utilizing Web-based tools.

Questions

1. What are the benefits of cloud computing for databases and data warehouses?
2. What are some possible concerns for companies that utilize the cloud to store and deliver important corporate information?
3. What do you think Google has to gain from venturing into the cloud database business?

Sources

1. *Perez, Juan Carlos, "Watch out, Oracle: Google tests cloud-based database,"* Computerworld, *June 11, 2009, www.computerworld.com.*
2. *Kanaracus, Chris, "Greenplum rolls out self-service data warehousing in the cloud,"* Computerworld, *June 8, 2009, www.computerworld.com.*
3. *Greenplum Web site, accessed June 12, 2009, www.greenplum.com.*
4. *Google Fusion Tables Web site, accessed June 12, 2009, http://tables.googlelabs.com.*

system (see Figure 7.26). **Data mining** is the process of extracting information from a data warehouse or a data mart. The DBMS can be used to generate a variety of reports that assist people and organizations to make decisions and achieve their goals. Data mining has been used in the airline-passenger profiling system used to block suspected terrorists from flying. Data mining is also used by the Terrorism Information Awareness Program, which attempts to detect patterns of terrorist activity. The U.S. Centers for Disease Control and Prevention relies on the data mining of data marts created by international disease-surveillance systems to track, report, and confirm the spread of diseases like the H1N1 (swine flu) virus. The information mined allows the organization to respond quickly to reduce the possibility of a pandemic.[11]

FIGURE 7.26 • Generating business intelligence from data warehouses and data marts

Data warehouses are generated from a database and other sources; a data mart is a small data warehouse, often developed for a specific person or purpose. Data mining can be used to generate business intelligence.

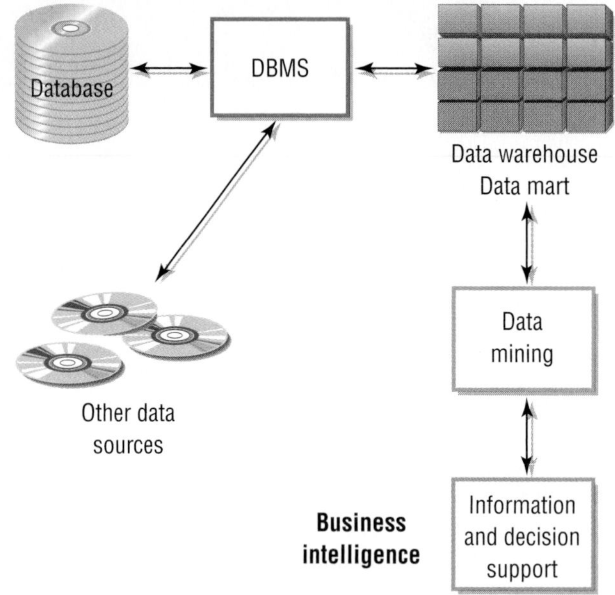

In a business setting, data mining can yield outstanding results. Often called **business intelligence**, a term first coined by a consultant at Gartner Group, the business use of data mining can help increase efficiency, reduce costs, or increase profits. The business-intelligence approach was first used by Procter & Gamble in 1985 to analyze data from checkout scanners. Today, a number of companies use business intelligence. Hundreds of hotels use business-intelligence software to get valuable customer information used to develop marketing programs. Companies like Ben & Jerry's store and process huge amounts of data. The company collects data on all 190,000 pints of ice cream it produces in its factories each day, with all the data being shipped to the company's headquarters in Burlington, Vermont. In the marketing department, the massive amount of data is analyzed. Using business-intelligence software, the company is able to cut costs and improve customer satisfaction (see Figure 7.27). The software allows Ben & Jerry's to match over 200 calls and e-mails received each week with ice cream products and supplies. Today, the company can quickly determine if there was a bad batch of milk or eggs. The company can also determine if sales of Chocolate Chip Cookie Dough are gaining on the No. 1 seller, Cherry Garcia.

FIGURE 7.27 • Business-intelligence software

BI "dashboards" help executives quickly receive statistics and trends in a mostly graphic format.

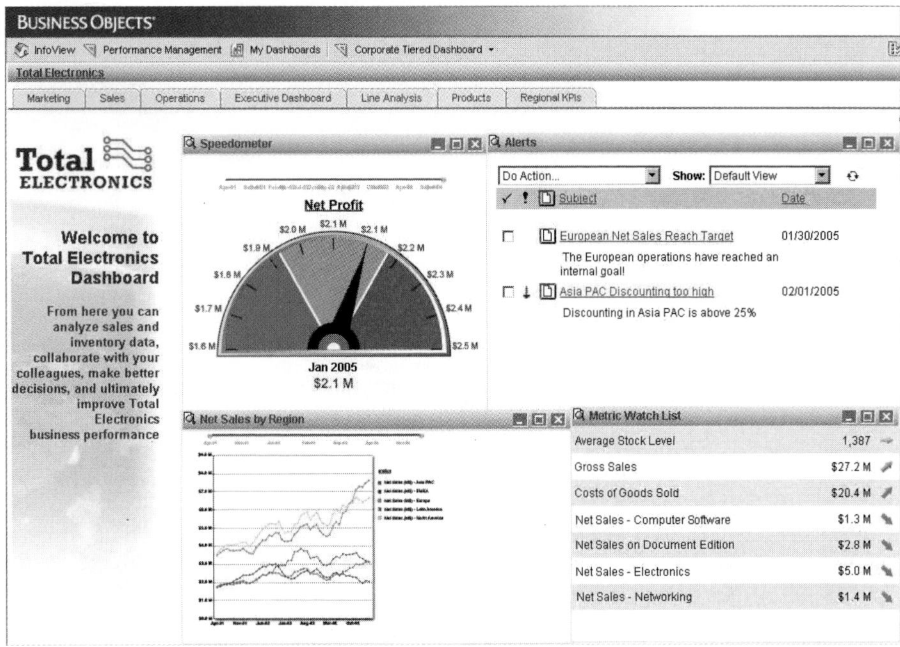

DATABASE TRENDS

The types of data and information that people and organizations need can change. A number of trends in the development and use of databases and database management systems will meet these changing needs. For example, more and more organizations are finding they need to coordinate databases at different locations, create secure locations for mission-critical data and services, and access databases through the Internet. Some people and organizations need to store audio and video files in an organized database. These trends are explored in this section.

Distributed Databases

With a **distributed database**, also called a *virtualized database,* the actual data may be spread across several databases at different locations. To users, the distributed databases appear to be a single, unified database. Distributed databases connect data at different locations via telecommunications. A user in the Milwaukee branch of a shoe manufacturer, for example, might make a request for data that is physically located at corporate headquarters in Milan, Italy. The user does not have to know where the data is physically stored. He or she makes a request for data, and the DBMS determines where the data is physically located and retrieves it (see Figure 7.28).

FIGURE 7.28 • A distributed database

For a shoe manufacturer, computers may be located at corporate headquarters, in the research and development center, at the warehouse, and in a company-owned retail store. Telecommunications systems link the computers so that users at all locations can access the same distributed database no matter where the data is actually stored.

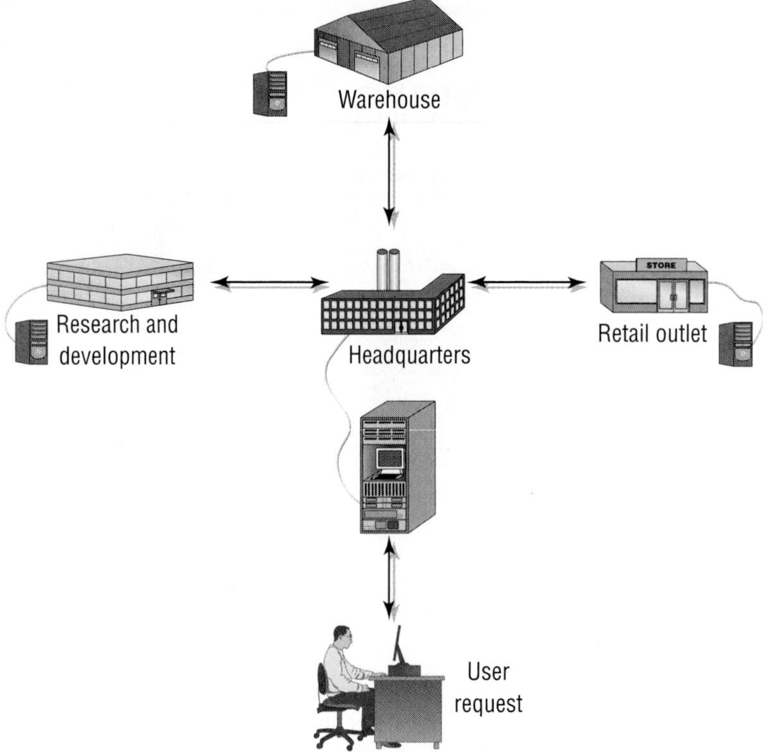

A distributed database creates additional challenges in maintaining data security, accuracy, timeliness, and conformance to standards. Distributed databases allow more users direct access at different user sites; thus, controlling who accesses and changes data is sometimes difficult. Also, because distributed databases rely on telecommunications to transport data, access to data can be slower. To reduce the demand on telecommunications media, some organizations build a replicated database. A *replicated database* is a database that holds a duplicate set of frequently used data. At the beginning of the day, an organization sends a copy of important data to each distributed processing location. At the end of the day, the different sites send the changed data back to be stored in the main database.

GUESS WHOO'S BUILDING A COOP?

Who? Yahoo! The company is building a new data center called "Yahoo Computing Coop" that won't use chillers. Chillers provide refrigerated water to keep the computers cool, but they use up lots of energy. Instead, Yahoo has designed the center to use five prefabricated metal coops that pull in cold air from the outside—very energy efficient, but they make the center look a lot like a place where—well—a chicken might live.

Yahoo's 'Chicken Coop' Data Center Design
Rich Miller
Data Center Knowledge
June 30, 2009
http://www.datacenterknowledge.com/archives/2009/06/30/yahoos-fresh-air-computing-coop/

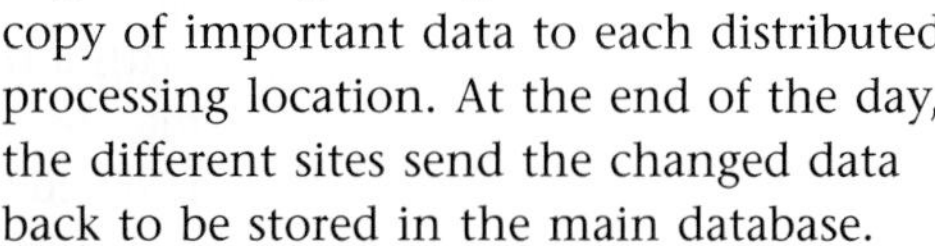

Data Centers

Corporate databases and database management systems are typically housed in facilities called data centers. A **data center** is a climate-controlled building or set of buildings that house the servers that store and deliver mission-critical information and services. Data centers of large organizations are often distributed over several locations, as described, but a recent trend has many organizations consolidating their many

Green Data Centers

The high cost of keeping large data centers cool concerns both environmentalists and business owners. Nearly all large businesses are looking to new technologies to decrease energy expenses, help protect the environment, and improve their reputations. Lowering energy costs is difficult, especially with the growing demand for larger data centers to store increasing amounts of data.

Highmark Inc., a regional health insurance company, was voted the year's greenest IT company by *Computerworld* magazine for upgrades it made to its large data center. Highmark spent roughly $45,000 each month to meet the energy needs of its 24,000-square-foot data center in Pennsylvania. The company scrapped its old data center and built a new 86,000-square-foot facility utilizing all recycled building materials. By using the latest technologies such as server virtualization and next-generation cooling equipment, the company was able to triple its data center capacity while maintaining the same $45,000 utility bill each month.

Highmark isn't alone in its effort. Around the world companies are investing in server virtualization to reduce the number of servers needed to store and deliver information. They are also making wiser choices in data center location, with some companies creating floating, water-cooled data centers at sea, and others selecting cooler land environments. Oracle is building a green data center in Utah, where the air is dry and cooling is cheaper. Other companies are building data centers underground and in caves. Still others are looking to solar and hydropower sources to lessen the environmental impact.

Questions

1. How does "going green" with data centers benefit businesses?
2. Why has power consumption in data centers become an important issue?
3. What technologies can assist a company in reducing the power demands of its data centers?

Sources

1. *King, Julia, "Top 12 Green-IT Users: No. 1 Highmark Inc,"* Computerworld, *February 15, 2008, www.computerworld.com.*
2. *Lawson, Stephen, "Oracle looks to Utah for green data center,"* Computerworld, *August 17, 2008, www.computerworld.com.*
3. *Fanning, Ellen, "The Top Green-IT Organizations find fertile ground for innovation,"* Computerworld, *April 20, 2009, www.computerworld.com.*

data centers into just a few large facilities. For example, the U.S. federal government believes that it can save billions of dollars by consolidating its data into a few large data centers. The state of Texas has consolidated 31 data centers into two facilities in San Angelo and Austin. Microsoft is building a 44-acre data center in San Antonio at a cost of $550 million. Google is putting up $600 million for a mega-data center in Lenoir, North Carolina, and $750 million for another in Goose Creek, South Carolina. Clearly, storing and managing data is serious business.

While a company's data sits in large super-cooled data centers, the people accessing that data are typically in offices spread across the country or around the world. In fact, the expectation of data center specialists is that in the near future the only personnel on duty at data centers will be security guards. Data centers are approaching the point of automation where they can run and manage themselves while being monitored remotely. This is referred to as a "lights out" environment.

The high cost of cooling data centers has become a growing concern to environmentalists and business owners. For a large data center such as those owned by Microsoft and Google, the cost of keeping servers cool is equal to that of the energy used to cool a city. For this reason there have been strong efforts to reduce the heat output of processors, and to utilize environments that minimize cooling expenses. Reducing costs of cooling data centers has become a major component of green computing efforts.

Database Systems, the Internet, and Networks

Anyone who has even limited experience with the Internet knows that a vast amount of raw data and important information is available on the Web. In most cases, a traditional database, such as a relational database, is used to store and organize that information. As mentioned before, the database is often the back-end application. From a user's perspective, the traditional database is invisible and behind the scenes. The Web is then used as the front end. All requests made to the database go through the Internet (see Figure 7.29).

FIGURE 7.29 • Database access through the Internet

This online shopping site uses the Web as the front end to a database of thousands of products and reviews. From a user's perspective, the back-end database is invisible and behind the scenes.

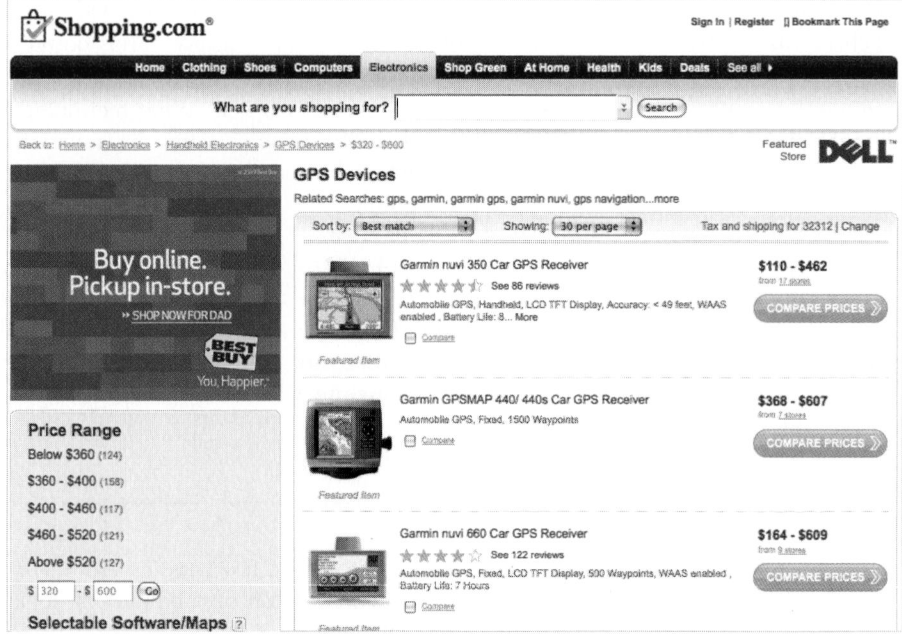

A number of Internet development tools can be used to interact with a traditional database. Most of these tools were introduced in Chapter 4. HTML, XML, and other Web development tools can all be used to develop a Web site to be a front-end interface to a traditional database system. For example, most colleges provide students access to databases that allow them to find and register for classes.

Some people, however, are concerned about the accuracy and privacy of the information in databases that are accessible from the Web or linked to other private networks. Some security experts believe that up to 40 percent of Web sites that connect to corporate databases are susceptible to letting hackers take complete control of the database. By typing certain characters in a form on some Web sites, a hacker is able to give SQL commands to control the corporate database.

Visual, Audio, Unstructured, and Other Database Systems

In addition to text and numbers, organizations increasingly need to store large amounts of visual and audio data in an organized fashion (see Figure 7.30). Music companies, for example, need to store and manipulate sound from recording studios. Drug companies often need to analyze a large number of visual images from laboratories. Other visual databases allow petroleum engineers to analyze geographic information to help them determine where to drill for oil and gas. A visual-fingerprint database can be used to solve a cold-case murder that has gone unsolved for decades.

FIGURE 7.30 • Visual database

Visual databases of fingerprints have become an essential tool for law enforcement and crime investigations.

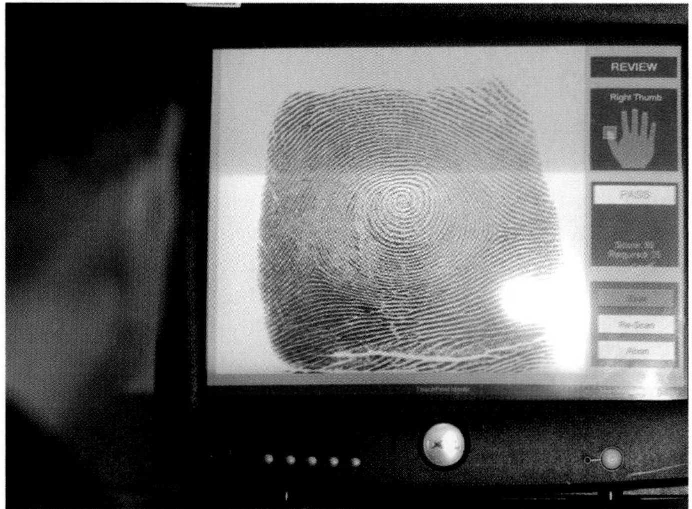

An *unstructured database* contains data that is difficult or impossible to place in a traditional database system. The data can include notes, drawings, fingerprints, medical abstracts, sound recordings, and other data. OneNote by Microsoft is an example of a database that can store and retrieve unstructured data. EverNote is a free database that can store notes and other pieces of information. In the future, you will see more databases that can handle unstructured data.

MANAGING DATABASES

Managing a database is complex and requires great skill. Hiring a good database administrator (DBA), concentrating on important and strategic aspects of databases, training database users, and developing good security procedures are all important.

Database Administration

Databases and database management systems are typically installed and coordinated by an individual or group responsible for managing one of the most valuable resources of any organization: its data. These **database administrators (DBAs)** are skilled and trained computer professionals who direct all activities related to an organization's database, including providing security from intruders. DBAs must work well with both programmers and nonprogrammer users of the database. Most database administrators are responsible for the following areas:

- Overall design and coordination of the database
- Development and maintenance of schemas
- Development and maintenance of the data dictionary
- Implementation of the DBMS
- System and user documentation

BIOMETRIC ID GOES BEYOND YOUR HANDS AND FACE

You may have seen it on TV—that particularly gruesome crime where the victim's head and fingers are severed from the body to prevent identification. But now the University of Michigan has developed a new database of soft biometrics—scars, tattoos, and other marks. The database will allow law enforcement officials to identify and track down victims and suspects using an automatic system that uses image features such as color, shape, and texture to retrieve possible matches.

Scars, marks, and tattoos: a soft biometric for identifying suspects and victims
Anil Jain and Jung- Eun Lee
SPIE Newsroom
June 15, 2009
http://spie.org/x35455.xml?highlight=x2412&ArticleID=x35455

- User support and training
- Overall operation of the DBMS
- Testing and maintaining the DBMS
- Establishing emergency or failure-recovery procedures
- Ensuring data security

Many large businesses outsource database and data center operations to an outside technology company. San Francisco–based Gap, Inc., which includes Gap stores, Banana Republic, and Old Navy, decided to hand over management of its databases and IT systems to IBM. The hope is that the move will streamline operations and reduce costs. The 10-year contract is estimated to be worth $1.1 billion.

Database Use, Policies, and Security

With the proliferation of low-cost hardware and off-the-shelf database and other software packages, traditional end users are now developing computer systems to solve their own problems. *End-user computing* can be broadly defined as the development and use of application programs and computer systems by users who are not computer systems professionals. Concerns with end-user computing are generally related to issues of training and control. As you've seen, data contained within an organization's databases is usually critical to the basic functioning of the organization. It is often proprietary in nature, confidential, and of strategic importance. Therefore, the following end-user computing issues must be addressed in terms of database policies and use:

- What data can users read, update, or write in a database?
- Under what circumstances can data be transferred from a personal computer or small computer system to the large corporate system?
- Under what circumstances can data be transferred from the large mainframe or server system to personal computers or small computer systems?
- What procedures are needed to guarantee proper database use and security?

Because there are so many users of any one database, potential data security and invasion-of-privacy problems have become increasingly important.

ACTION PLAN

Remember Mary from the beginning of the chapter? Mary wants to go into business for herself selling Wisconsin's-Best cheese spreads. She wants to learn how to use a database to help run her business. Here are answers to her questions.

1. **How can Mary use a database to keep track of the different cheeses, butters, spices, crocks, and other supplies she needs?**

   Mary could use the database or flat file capabilities of a spreadsheet or word-processing program. She could also use a general database system designed for a personal computer or a specialized database system for small businesses to keep track of this information. Because Mary is thinking about starting a small business, a specialized database system would likely be the best option for her.

2. **If she starts a small business, how will she be able to pay her employees, pay her bills, and keep track of other business transactions?**

   Starting a small business requires more than the database capabilities of a spreadsheet or word-processing program. Mary could develop everything she needs for a small business using a general database program, like Microsoft Access or FileMaker Pro, but she should also consider a specialized database system for small businesses, such as QuickBooks. Mary will need to organize her business data into related tables. Typically, tables for inventory, customers, and transactions are required. Primary keys will need to be established for each table and relationships created between the tables.

Summary

LEARNING OBJECTIVE 1

Understand basic data management concepts.

Data is one of the most valuable resources an organization possesses. Data is organized into a hierarchy that builds from the smallest element to the largest. The smallest element is the byte, which represents a character. A group of characters, such as a name or number, is called a field. A collection of related fields is a record; a collection of related records is called a file. The database, at the top of the hierarchy, is an integrated collection of files.

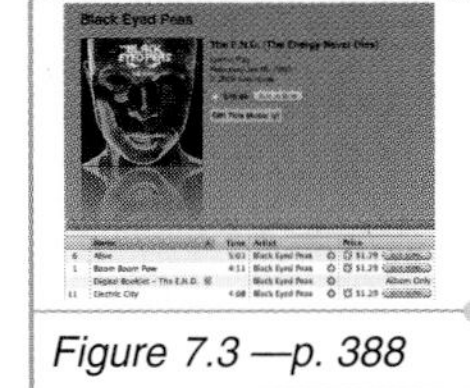
Figure 7.3 —p. 388

An entity is a generalized class of objects for which data is collected, stored, and maintained. An attribute is a characteristic of an entity. Specific values of attributes, called data items, can be found in the fields of the record describing an entity. A primary key uniquely identifies a record.

The database approach has a number of benefits, including reduced data redundancy, improved data consistency and integrity, easier modification and updating, data and program independence, standardization of data access, and more efficient program development. A DBMS consists of a group of programs that manipulate the database and provide an interface between the database and user or the database and application programs.

LEARNING OBJECTIVE 2

Describe database models and characteristics.

Database designers can use a data model to show the relationships among data. One of the most flexible database models is the relational model. Data is set up in two-dimensional tables. Tables can be linked by common data elements, which are used to access data when the database is queried. Each row represents a record. Columns of the tables are called attributes, and allowable values for these attributes are called the domain. Basic data manipulations include selecting and joining.

Data Table 1: Project Table

Project number	Description	Dept. number
155	Payroll	257
498	Widgets	632
226	Sales Manual	598

Figure 7.9 —p. 395

Databases are best designed using small, logically interconnected tables to reduce data redundancy. The ability to connect data in different tables through a common field is referred to as a relationship. Relationships between tables can be defined as one-to-many, one-to-one, or many-to-many.

Data analysis is used to uncover problems with the content of the database. Problems and irregularities in data are called anomalies. The process of correcting anomalies is called normalization. Normalization involves breaking one file into two or more tables in order to reduce redundancy and inconsistency in the data.

LEARNING OBJECTIVE 3

Discuss the different types of database management systems and their design and use by individuals and organizations.

A DBMS is a group of programs used as an interface between a database and application programs. Database types include flat file, single-user, multiuser, general-purpose, and special-purpose databases. Open-source databases are becoming very popular.

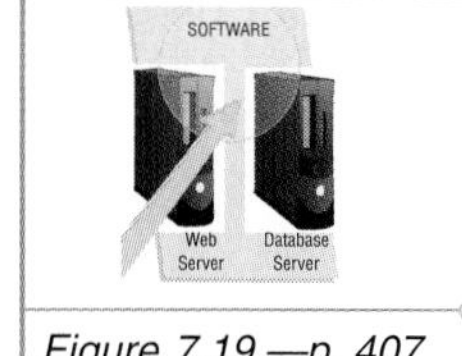

Figure 7.19 —p. 407

Schemas are used to describe the entire database, its record types, and their relationships to the DBMS. Schemas are entered into the computer via a data definition language (DDL), which describes the data and relationships in a specific database. Another tool used in database management is the data dictionary, which contains detailed descriptions of all data in the database.

Once a DBMS has been installed, the database may be accessed, modified, and queried via a data manipulation language (DML). A more specialized DML is the query language; the most common are query by example (QBE) and Structured Query Language (SQL). QBE and SQL are used in several popular database packages.

When databases and information systems fail, businesses and organizations can suffer tremendously unless the systems can be brought back online within minutes. Providing a plan for how to bring systems back online after an emergency is known as disaster recovery. Disaster recovery is part of a larger process called business continuity planning.

LEARNING OBJECTIVE 4

Describe how organizations use database systems to perform routine processing and provide information and decision support, and how they use data warehouses, marts, and mining.

Most organizations use a database system to send out bills, pay suppliers, print paychecks, and perform other routine transaction-processing activities.

Perhaps the biggest potential of a database system is to provide information and decision support. The data contained in a database can be filtered and manipulated to provide critical information to a wide range of organizations.

Information is usually obtained and decision support is usually provided using data warehouses, data marts, and data mining. A data warehouse is a database that holds important information from a variety of sources. A data warehouse normally contains a subset of the data stored in the database system. A data mart is a small data warehouse. Data mining is the process of extracting information from data warehouses and data marts.

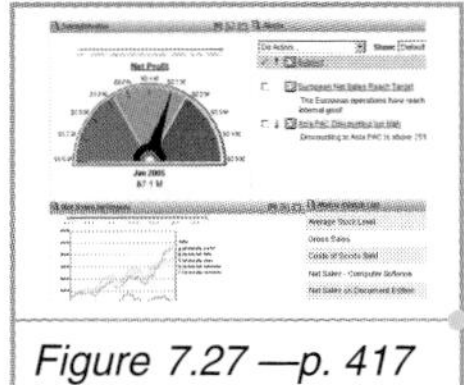

Figure 7.27 —p. 417

LEARNING OBJECTIVE 5

Discuss additional database systems, including distributed systems, data centers, and Web-based systems.

A distributed database allows data to be spread across several databases at different locations. Corporate databases and database management systems are typically housed in facilities called data centers. A data center is a climate-controlled building, or set of buildings, that house the servers that store and deliver mission-critical information and services. Corporations are making efforts to utilize new technologies to reduce the high costs of cooling data centers as a move toward green computing.

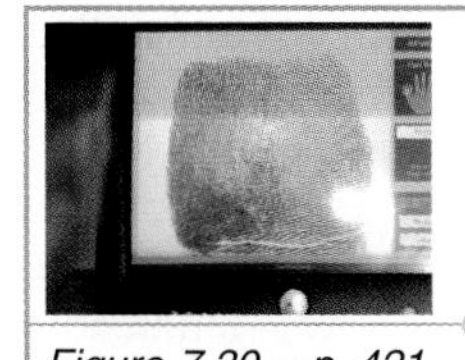

Figure 7.30 —p. 421

Database systems are often used in conjunction with the Internet and networks. In many cases, the Internet or network is used as the front end, where requests for information and data orginate. The database management system is the back end, providing the needed information and data.

An increasing amount of the data used by organizations is in the form of visual images, which can be stored in image databases. Audio databases are used to store audio data, including voice and music. Some organizations are using virtual databases that can integrate separate databases into a unified system that acts like a single database.

LEARNING OBJECTIVE 6

Describe the role of the database administrator (DBA) and database policies and security practices.

Management of the database is part of database administration. Database administrators (DBAs) are responsible for database use, policies, and security. They help control DBMS design, implementation, and maintenance. They also establish security and control measures, monitor and tune the database, and perform many other aspects of database use and control.

Test Yourself

LEARNING OBJECTIVE 1: Understand basic data management concepts.

1. A(n) ________________ consists of a group of programs that perform the actual manipulation of data in the database.
2. In the data hierarchy, fields combine to create a ________________ .
   a. file
   b. character
   c. record
   d. database
3. True or False: Records are the equivalent of attributes, and fields are the equivalent of entries.
4. True or False: A primary key uniquely identifies a record.

LEARNING OBJECTIVE 2: Describe database models and characteristics.

5. A(n) ________________ diagram illustrates the relationships between tables in a relational database.
6. The ________________ model places data in two-dimensional tables.
7. ________________ is a process that involves evaluating data to identify problems with the content of a database.
   a. joining
   b. selecting
   c. normalizing
   d. data analysis
8. True or False: A one-to-many relationship links tables through a field that is a primary key in both tables.

LEARNING OBJECTIVE 3: Discuss the different types of database management systems and their design and use by individuals and organizations.

9. True or False: A database that can be used to store and manipulate a single table in a spreadsheet or word-processing program is called a single-user database.
10. A situation where inaccurate input causes inaccurate output in a database is often called ________________ .
11. True or False: Oracle is an example of a special-purpose database.
12. A ________________ utilizes commands used to change a database.
    a. data definition language
    b. physical access language
    c. data manipulation language
    d. logical access language

LEARNING OBJECTIVE 4: Describe how organizations use database systems to perform routine processing and provide information and decision support, and how they use data warehouses, marts, and mining.

13. A(n) _______________ is a collection of data from sources across an entire enterprise.
14. True or False: Data mining often yields business intelligence.
15. What is the process of extracting information from a data warehouse or data mart?
    a. Logical access
    b. Physical access
    c. Decision support
    d. Data mining

LEARNING OBJECTIVE 5: Discuss additional database systems, including distributed systems, data centers, and Web-based systems.

16. With a(n) _______________ the actual data may be spread across several databases at different locations.
17. True or False: Power consumption in data centers is a primary concern in green computing.
18. A(n) _______________ contains data that is difficult to place in a traditional database system, such as drawings, fingerprints, and sound recordings.
    a. entity relationship diagram
    b. object-oriented database
    c. unstructured database
    d. data mart

LEARNING OBJECTIVE 6: Describe the role of the database administrator (DBA) and database policies and security practices.

19. True or False: Database systems are typically installed and coordinated by the chief information officer.
20. _______________ computing is a cause of concern for data security due to issues of training and control.

Test Yourself Solutions: **1.** database management system, **2.** c. record, **3.** False, **4.** True, **5.** entity relationship, **6.** relational, **7.** d. data analysis, **8.** False, **9.** False, **10.** garbage in, garbage out (GIGO), **11.** False, **12.** c. data manipulation language, **13.** data warehouse, **14.** True, **15.** d. Data mining, **16.** distributed database, **17.** True, **18.** unstructured database, **19.** False, **20.** End-user.

Key Terms

Key Term	Page	Definition
data analysis	398	A process that involves evaluating data to identify problems with the content of a database.
data center	418	A climate-controlled building or set of buildings. that house the servers that store and deliver mission-critical information and services.
data dictionary	408	A detailed description of all data used in the database.
data hierarchy	389	The manner in which data in a database is organized into sequential levels of detail.
data integrity	407	The situation when data stored in the database is accurate and up to date.
data mining	415	The process of extracting information from a data warehouse or a data mart.
data warehouse	414	A typically large database that holds important information from a variety of sources.
database administrator (DBA)	421	A skilled and trained computer professional who directs all activities related to an organization's database, including providing security from intruders.

Key Term	Page	Definition
database management system (DBMS)	387	A group of programs that manipulate the database and provide an interface between the database and the user or the database and application programs.
distributed database	417	A database where data is spread across several databases at different locations.
field	388	The components of a database record, which may be a name, number, or combination of characters that in some way describes an aspect of an object.
file	388	A collection of related records, sometimes called a table.
garbage in, garbage out (GIGO)	407	A situation where inaccurate input causes inaccurate output in a database.
primary key	390	A field that uniquely identifies each record in a database file.
record	388	A collection of related fields that describe some object or activity.
relational model	395	A database model in which all data elements are placed in two-dimensional tables called *relations* that are the logical equivalent of files.
schema	408	An outline of the logical and physical structure of the data and relationships among the data in the database.
Structured Query Language (SQL)	410	A popular standardized data manipulation language.

Questions

Review Questions

1. What is a database management system?
2. What is a field? What is a record?
3. What are entities and attributes? What is a key?
4. What is a primary key?
5. Describe simple approaches to data management.
6. What are the advantages of a centralized database approach?
7. Describe the relational model.
8. Describe the characteristics of a relational database model.
9. How does single-user software manage data differently than a multiuser database system?
10. Why is it better to store data in multiple related tables, rather than one big table?
11. What is a flat file? What is a single-user database?
12. What is the purpose of a data definition language (DDL)? A data dictionary?
13. What is query by example? What is SQL?
14. Describe at least three widely used open-source database systems.
15. How are databases used in organizations?
16. What is a data warehouse? What is a data mart?
17. How are databases used to create business intelligence?
18. What is a distributed database system?
19. What role does a data center play in an organization?
20. List and describe the newer types of database systems. What types of data might they house?
21. Explain the responsibilities of a database administrator.

Discussion Questions

22. Why is a database a necessary component of a computer system? Why is the selection of DBMS software so important to organizations?
23. In what way do database systems apply to your personal life?
24. What databases on your campus contain your name? Off campus? What is your primary key on campus?
25. What is a data model?
26. What role is a DBMS likely to play in your future career?

Exercises

Try It Yourself

1. Using the database of your choice, create a database of the top 10 jobs you would like to have. Your database should include the company or organization, possible salary, location, and similar attributes. Sort your database according to salary.
2. A university needs to design and implement a relational database to maintain records for students and student organizations. The student table will include fields for student ID number, name, major, and GPA. The student organization table will include fields for organization ID number, name, president, and membership amount. Using an entity relationship diagram (refer to Figure 7.11), show the logical structure of the relational tables for this proposed database. In your design, include any table names, field names, primary keys, and relationships. Once your design is complete, create the database using Microsoft Access or similar database software.
3. A movie rental store is using a relational database to store the following information on movie rentals to answer customer questions: movie ID number, movie title, year made, movie type (comedy, drama, horror, science fiction, or western), rating (G, PG, PG-13, R, or X), and quantity on hand. Develop a database table to store this information for 20 movies. Develop a report that lists all horror movies.
4. Based upon the database design from exercise 3, design a data-entry screen that could be used to enter information into this database. Also include some examples of typical queries the salespeople would use to respond to customers' requests.

Virtual Classroom Activities

For the following exercises, do not use face-to-face or telephone communications with your group members. Use only Internet communications.

5. With distance learning, students from around the world can be classmates in the same course. It is also possible to have several different instructors located around the world. With your group, develop a brief report that describes how several instructors at different locations could integrate their databases of assignments, tests, and student grades.
6. On the Internet, research one database system that you could use, such as Access, MindManager, or Quicken. Write a paper describing the features of each database system. Using a spreadsheet program, summarize the costs of each database system. All group members should participate in developing the paper and spreadsheet without any face-to-face meetings.
7. With your team, develop a report that compares two traditional databases, like Oracle, with two open-source databases. Include descriptions, advantages, and disadvantages of each database.

Teamwork

8. In a team of three or four classmates, interview three users, programmers, or system analysts from different organizations that use DBMSs. Determine what DBMSs they are using. How did these people choose the DBMSs that they are using? What do they like about their DBMSs and what could be improved? Considering the information obtained from these people, select one DBMS and briefly present your selection and the rationale for your selection to the class.
9. Using the Internet or your school library, research object-oriented databases. Use a database system to summarize your findings. At a minimum, your database should have columns on the database name, the cost to purchase or lease, and a brief description.

Endnotes

[1] Staff, UPS Fact Sheet, accessed June 10, 2009, http://www.pressroom.ups.com/mediakits/factsheet/0,2305,866,00.html?mkname=companyinfo.

[2] Maclean, William. "UK must pry on data to block threats: ex-spy boss," Reuters, March 25, 2009, www.reuters.com.

[3] Thibodeau, Patric, "White House set to unleash 100,000 federal data sources via data.gov," *Computerworld*, June 4, 2009, www.computerworld.com.

[4] Babcock, Charles, "In Database Market, Oracle Gets Bigger, Others Hang On," *InformationWeek*, April 25, 2008, www.informationweek.com.

[5] Staff, "MySQL Market Share," MySQL Web site, accessed June 12, 2009, www.mysql.com/why-mysql/marketshare.

[6] Staff, "craigslist Relies on MySQL to Serve Millions of Classified Ads," *Behind the Scenes with MySQL*, accessed June 12, 2009, http://www.mysql.com/why-mysql/case-studies/mysql-craigslist-casestudy.pdf.

[7] Staff, "MySQL Powers Transaction-Heavy News Delivery System for the Associated Press," *Behind the Scenes with MySQL*, accessed June 12, 2009, http://www.mysql.com/why-mysql/case-studies/mysql-ap-casestudy.pdf.

[8] Hoover, Nicholas, "DHS Disaster Recovery Plans Lacking, Report Finds," *InformationWeek*, May 14, 2009, www.informationweek.com.

[9] Staff, "Life Fitness Improves Product Insight and Decision Making with Dashboard-Based Business Intelligence," *Oracle Customer Snapshot*, accessed June 12, 2009, http://www.oracle.com/customers/snapshots/life-fitness-bi-snapshot.pdf.

[10] Staff, "Yangtze Power Improves Business Intelligence with Integrated Database and Analysis Tools," Oracle Customer Case Study, accessed June 12, 2009, http://www.oracle.com/customers/snapshots/yangtze-power-case-study.pdf.

[11] Mearian, Lucas, "E-health data collection key to tracking swine flu spread," *Computerworld*, April 29, 2009, www. computerworld.com.

E-COMMERCE

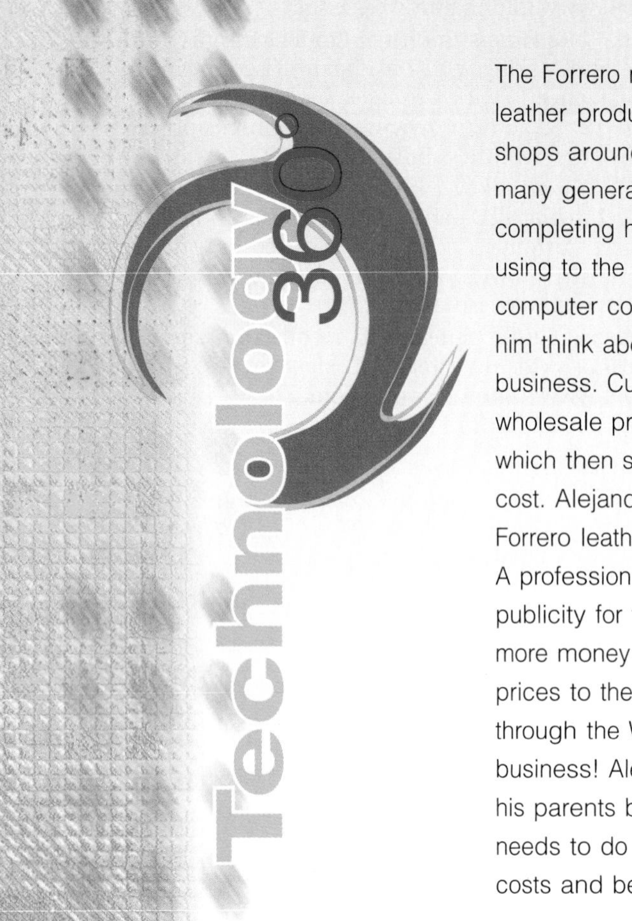

The Forrero name is well known as a maker of fine handcrafted leather products. You can find Forrero products in many gift shops around the country. Alejandro Forrero is the youngest in many generations of leather artisans and is currently completing his college education, which he plans on using to the benefit of the family business. The computer course that Alejandro is taking has made him think about new possibilities for the family business. Currently, Forrero products are marketed at wholesale prices only to retail clothing and gift shops, which then sell them to consumers at twice the wholesale cost. Alejandro is considering the possibility of selling Forrero leather products directly to consumers on the Web. A professionally designed Web site would provide great publicity for the company, the family would be able to make more money per sale, and they would be able to offer better prices to their customers. Selling directly to consumers through the Web could dramatically change the family business! Alejandro is excited about sharing the idea with his parents but wants to do it right and make them proud. He needs to do some research and write a proposal that provides details on the costs and benefits of taking the family business online.

As you read through the chapter, consider the following questions:

1. What will it take to put the Forrero family business online?
2. What benefits might the Forrero family enjoy from an online presence? Do these benefits outweigh the costs?
3. Besides taking the business online, in what other ways might e-commerce assist the Forrero family business?

Check out Alejandro's *Action Plan* at the conclusion of this chapter.

8

LEARNING OBJECTIVES

1. Define e-commerce, and understand its role as a transaction processing system.
2. List the three types of e-commerce, and explain how e-commerce supports the stages of the buying process and methods of marketing and selling.
3. Discuss several examples of e-commerce applications and services.
4. Define m-commerce, and describe several m-commerce services.
5. List the components of an e-commerce system, and explain how they function together to provide e-commerce services.

CHAPTER CONTENT

The Roots of E-Commerce

Overview of Electronic Commerce

E-Commerce Applications

Mobile Commerce

E-Commerce Implementation

Introduction

E-commerce has provided a fresh platform for business that has changed the way businesses and consumers think about buying and selling. Increasingly, buyers and sellers are turning to their computers to make transactions and are enjoying the benefits. Conducting business online offers convenience and savings to both buyers and sellers. It also empowers consumers to find the best deals and service, placing additional pressure on businesses to cater to consumer needs. This chapter explores the impact of e-commerce and m-commerce on consumers and businesses, what it takes to set up a successful e-commerce Web site, and the challenges and issues faced by e-commerce participants.

E-commerce or **electronic commerce** refers to systems that support electronically executed business transactions. E-commerce has changed the world and continues to do so in very dramatic ways. The residents of the remote Alaskan villages of Arctic Village and Nulato existed in relative isolation until recently when, through a relationship with Philadelphia University researchers, they opened an online store. The e-commerce Web site ArcticWays.com allows shoppers from around the world to acquire rarely seen, handmade items from these small villages in bush Alaska.

An increasing percentage of commerce is migrating online. While gradeschool kids' favorite meeting places used to be the playground or the mall, today thousands are meeting, playing, and spending money online at Club Penguin (see Figure 8.1). Club Penguin was developed by the Canadian company New Horizon Interactive as a safe, monitored, online community for kids ages 6 to 14. Over its first two years, the site grew to accommodate more than 12 million registered users (penguins), with hundreds of thousands paying $5.95 per month for the benefit of membership.

Club Penguin isn't alone in capturing the imagination and dollars of today's youth. Neopets, Habbo Hotel, and Webkinz have been similary successful. Mattel's virtual world BarbiGirls signed up 3.5 million users in its first three months.[1] Hundreds of kid-targeted virtual worlds are launching to take advantage of this growing market. For today's kids, and many others who lead online lifestyles, e-commerce is becoming a way of life. In reality, e-commerce makes up a relatively small but rapidly growing percentage of all commerce.

FIGURE 8.1 • E-commerce Club Penguin style

Providing kids with a safe environment to "Waddle around and meet new friends" earned this online company more than 12 million active registered users.

The widespread movement from commerce to e-commerce can be traced back to the early 1990s and the birth of the first Web browser, Mosaic. By 1997, it was clear that the future of commerce was electronic. In that year the White House released a report called "A Framework for Global E-Commerce," which set forth principles for a worldwide free-trade zone on the Internet. The framework seems to be working, judging from the 15 percent annual rate of growth in online sales illustrated in Figure 8.2.[2]

There are many influences that have propelled e-commerce. Table 8.1 lists 12 major influences on e-commerce over the last decade. However, the roots of e-commerce go back more than a decade, even earlier than 1991 and the first Web browser.

FIGURE 8.2 • E-commerce growth

The percentage of overall sales in manufacturing and retail conducted online has grown steadily even through tough economic times.

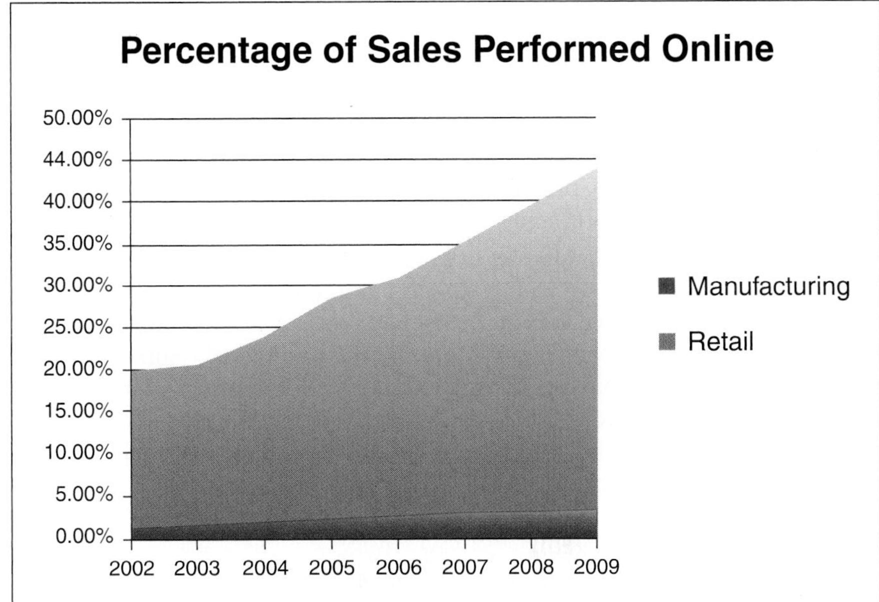

TABLE 8.1 • Major e-commerce developments of the last decade

Development	Description
Google	Search engine used by more than 30 percent of the Internet population
Broadband	High-speed access used by more than 50 percent of Internet users, making it much more convenient to shop
eBay	Web site that introduced the masses to the power and benefits of e-commerce
Amazon	Pioneer of e-commerce that sets the standard for online transactions
Google AdWords	Today's biggest online advertising vehicle that generated over $21 billion for Google in 2008
Open standards	Standards such as HTML and XML that provide opportunities for everyone, not just a select few
Wi-Fi	Wireless technology that helped move e-commerce from desktops to mobile devices
User-generated content	Contributions to the online community by anyone and everyone via Web sites like Facebook and YouTube
iTunes	Application that legitimized music distribution over the Internet
BlackBerry	Smart phone that helped to create a new mobile business culture
iPhone	Created a market for online mobile applications and services
GPS (global postitioning system)	Leading the way to next-generation location-aware products and services

THE ROOTS OF E-COMMERCE

Even though the Internet and the Web were responsible for the boom in electronic commerce, note that the words *Internet* and *Web* are not part of the definition of e-commerce. Although most consumers with Internet access purchase products over the Internet, these purchases are only a small percentage of the electronic business transactions that take place. Many electronically executed transactions take place off the Internet, on private networks. In fact, electronically executing business transactions predates the Internet.

E-Commerce History

In the 1960s, banks began to use computers and magnetic ink recognition to automate check processing, a step that significantly reduced staffing needs and increased efficiency and accuracy. Soon a variety of industries began to use computers to keep accounting ledgers, administer payroll, create management reports, and schedule production. Computer-based information systems became an accepted part of streamlining business processes.

In the 1970s and 1980s, businesses extended their computer-based information systems beyond their corporate walls to connect with other companies' systems using **electronic data interchange (EDI)**. EDI uses private communications networks called *value-added networks* (*VANs*) to transmit standardized transaction data between business partners and suppliers (see Figure 8.3). Automating transactions using EDI drastically reduced the amount of paperwork and the need for human intervention. This was the true beginning of e-commerce, even if it would take another 20 years for the term to be coined.

FIGURE 8.3 • Electronic data interchange (EDI)

EDI uses private communications networks called value-added networks (VANs) to transmit standardized transaction data between business partners and suppliers.

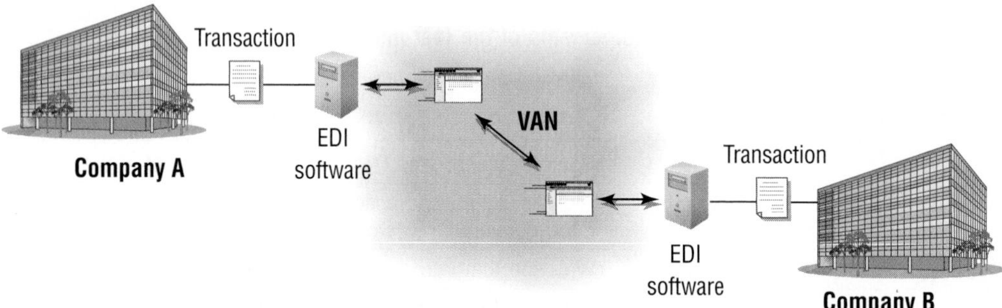

Even though it improved transactions between businesses, EDI had some problems and was costly. Only businesses that paid for a VAN connection could participate. For e-commerce to really take off, businesses and people needed an inexpensive universal network to which everyone could connect. The Internet provided the ideal platform for conducting EDI transactions as well as other forms of transaction processing between businesses. The invention of the Web provided the first opportunity for businesses to conduct transactions with consumers over a computer network. Businesses and consumers alike embraced doing business online. The far-reaching implications of the Web as a tool for executing business transactions soon became clear.

To fully understand the benefits of e-commerce, you need to examine its fundamental purpose: to execute transactions.

Transaction Processing

A *transaction* is an exchange involving goods or services, such as buying medical supplies for a hospital or purchasing and downloading music on the Internet. E-commerce is a form of transaction processing system. A *transaction processing system (TPS)* is an information system used to support and record transactions such as paying for products or paying an employee. The transaction information collected by the TPS is fundamental to the operation of other information systems that support important decision making. For example, the company contracted to provide food services for your campus uses a TPS to collect sales information from the cashier's point-of-sale terminal in the school cafeteria (see Figure 8.4). That sales information is then processed by another information system, such as a management information system (MIS), to determine which food items are selling best. Items that don't sell may be discontinued and replaced with new items. Through this approach, the food service provider can use the transaction information to continuously improve its service to customers.

FIGURE 8.4 • The value of transaction processing

The transaction data collected through point-of-sale terminals can be used to assess which products are selling well and which are not.

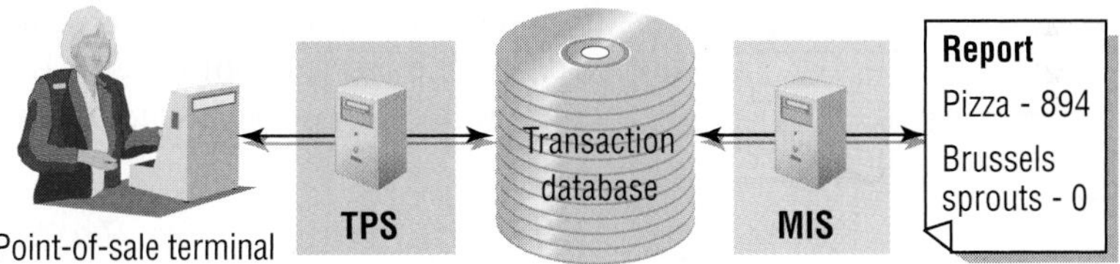

Transaction processing takes place in many different environments, and the systems that support it must be created to suit the environment. The electronic checkout system at Amazon.com is a TPS, as is the checkout system at your local bookstore. The payroll system that calculates an employee's pay and cuts a check is also a TPS. The ATM at your bank is a TPS, as is the keypad on a gas station filling pump. Transaction processing includes capturing input data, making calculations, storing information in a database, and producing various forms of output such as receipts and purchase orders.

There are two methods of processing transactions: batch and online. In *batch processing*, transactions are collected over time and processed together in batches. Batch processing is useful in situations where transactions take place away from the computer system, or when processing would slow down the collection of transaction data. For example, a sales representative operating from a booth at a trade show might record orders on a laptop computer and enter the orders into the main system in a batch upon returning to the home office and connecting to the corporate network.

With *online transaction processing* the processing takes place at the point of sale. For example, as you pay for your concert ticket, the seat you choose is marked as reserved in the concert hall database and your payment is recorded in the day's earnings. Online transaction processing is critical to time-sensitive transactions such as selling concert tickets and making flight reservations, as well as for college class registration systems. If the transaction isn't processed immediately, seats could become double-booked or classes filled beyond capacity.

FIGURE 8.5 • The transaction processing cycle

Data-processing activities of a transaction processing system

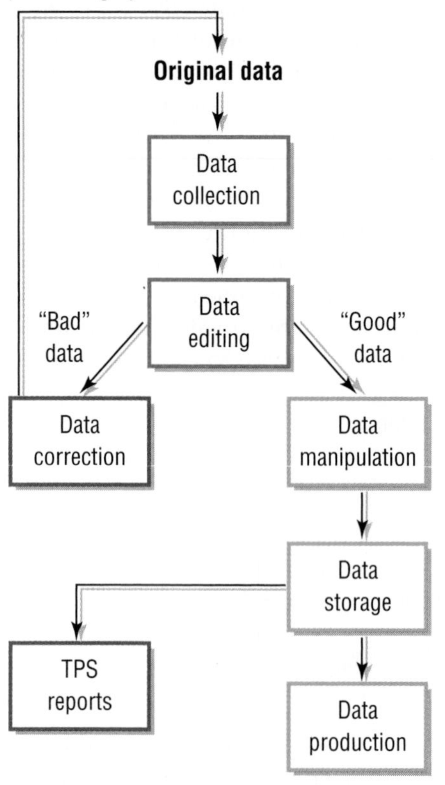

The Transaction Processing Cycle

E-commerce and all other transaction processing systems share a common set of activities called the *transaction processing cycle*. The stages of the transaction processing cycle are shown in Figure 8.5. They include the following:

1. Data collection: Capture transaction-related data such as item number, quantity, and payment method.
2. Data editing: Check validity of the data entered, such as whether item number and credit card number are valid.
3. Data correction: Request correction if data editing reveals invalid data.
4. Data manipulation: Process the transaction data, calculate totals, tax, shipping, and so on.
5. Data storage: Store transaction-related data in the transaction database.
6. Data output: Output receipts, picking lists for the warehouse, or other documents.

To conclude the transaction, documents may be produced or displayed. For example, after making an online purchase, verification is displayed on the screen, an electronic receipt is sent to your e-mail address, and a document called a picking list is produced in the warehouse to tell the workers what to pack and where to ship it.

Different Transaction Processing for Different Needs

There are a variety of transaction processing systems and subsystems that serve many functions within an organization. The two primary categories of TPS are order processing systems and purchasing systems. An *order processing system* supports the sales of goods or services to customers and arranges for shipment of products. A *purchasing system* supports the purchase of goods and raw materials from suppliers for the manufacturing of products. Each of these systems is composed of subsystems that interact to address the needs of an organization. Figure 8.6 illustrates how the TPSs interact within an organization to address the needs of the organization. Notice how the inventory control system acts to connect the order processing system and purchasing system.

In each step of the process and in each subsystem, vendors strive to carry out the action in a streamlined manner with the least amount of effort and cost and the highest amount of speed and quality. In this way, transaction processing systems can assist a business in gaining an edge over the competition.

FIGURE 8.6 • Transaction processing system interaction

Transaction processing typically makes use of many interconnected systems and subsystems.

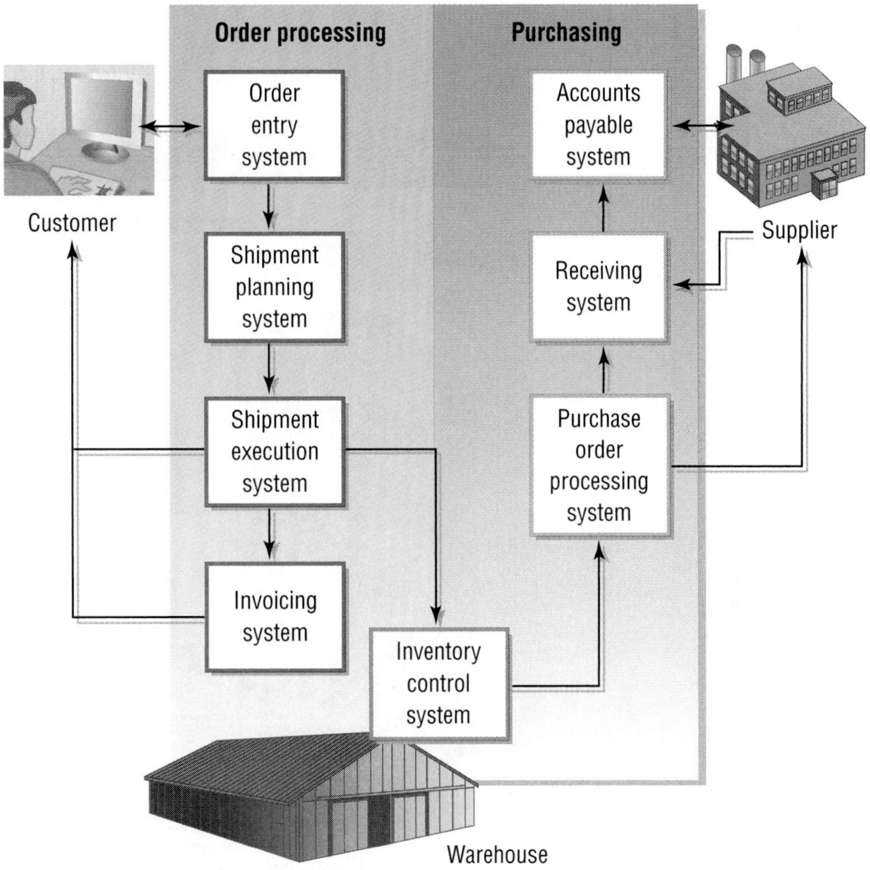

OVERVIEW OF ELECTRONIC COMMERCE

EXPAND YOUR KNOWLEDGE

To learn more about e-commerce transactions, e-commerce security, and other aspects of e-commerce, go to www.cengage.com/computerconcepts/np/swt4. Click the link "Expand Your Knowledge" and then complete the lab entitled "Electronic Commerce."

Just as there are different types of transaction processing systems, there are also different types of e-commerce: business-to-consumer, business-to-business, and consumer-to-consumer. This section provides a view of e-commerce from the buyer's and seller's perspectives, including the benefits and challenges of effectively conducting e-commerce.

Types of E-Commerce

When most of us think of e-commerce, we think of companies like Amazon.com, the longest-running e-commerce success story. Founded on a great idea—selling books online—and a deep understanding of both technology and business, Amazon.com has succeeded where thousands of others have failed. With annual net sales that surpass those of traditional retailers such as Sears, Amazon.com has expanded into dozens of retail arenas and is proof that success can be found in doing business on the Web.

Amazon.com is an example of business-to-consumer e-commerce. **Business-to-consumer e-commerce**, or **B2C e-commerce**, makes use of the Web to connect individual consumers directly with sellers to purchase products. B2C e-commerce is sometimes called *e-tailing*, a takeoff on the term *retailing*, as it is the electronic equivalent of a *brick-and-mortar* retail store (see Figure 8.7).

FIGURE 8.7 • Business-to-consumer e-commerce—Lands' End

Lands' End provides B2C e-commerce that strives for a brick-and-mortar retail experience, complete with an online dressing room and a virtual model on which to try on clothes.

Although B2C is the most visible form of e-commerce, consumers' online purchasing power pales in comparison to the amount of merchandise and services that businesses purchase online. **Business-to-business e-commerce**, or **B2B e-commerce**, supports transactions between businesses across private networks, the Internet, and the Web. Because businesses conduct frequent and high-volume transactions, B2B e-commerce is especially valuable.

B2C and B2B are terms used to categorize all forms of commerce, not just e-commerce. Three useful facts to know about B2C and B2B commerce are that:

- Overall, B2B and B2C sales (e-commerce and otherwise) in the United States are roughly equal. In 2007, there was a total $11,088 billion in B2B sales (manufacturing and wholesale) and $10,759 billion in B2C sales (retail and selected services), according to the U.S. Census.[3]
- Of these roughly equal sales amounts, e-commerce makes up a much greater percentage of B2B sales than B2C sales. E-commerce makes up roughly 28 percent of B2B sales and only 2.3 percent of B2C sales.
- The percentage of e-commerce sales is growing at a steady rate in both B2B and B2C. At current growth rates, e-commerce sales will soon make up more than half of B2B sales and one-tenth of retail sales and double in amount from 2009 to 2012 up to $335 billion.[4]

The graph in Figure 8.8, taken from the U.S. Census Bureau's E-commerce Multi-sector report (published in 2009), illustrates the dramatic difference between B2C and B2B sales between 2002 and 2007—shown here in billions of dollars. The report classifies manufacturing and wholesale (the tall bars on the graph) as B2B, and retail and selected services (the short bars) as B2C.

The fact that businesses have adopted e-commerce for purchasing merchandise more rapidly than consumers is easy to understand. E-commerce saves businesses money and provides competitive advantages. Businesses use B2B e-commerce for these purchases:

- Raw materials for production of products
- Tools, parts, and machinery for the production line
- Office furnishings, equipment, and products
- Transportation and shipping services

FIGURE 8.8 • B2C vs. B2B

B2B (manufacturing and wholesale) makes up a much larger percentage of e-commerce than B2C (retail and services) with both growing at approximately 15 percent annually.

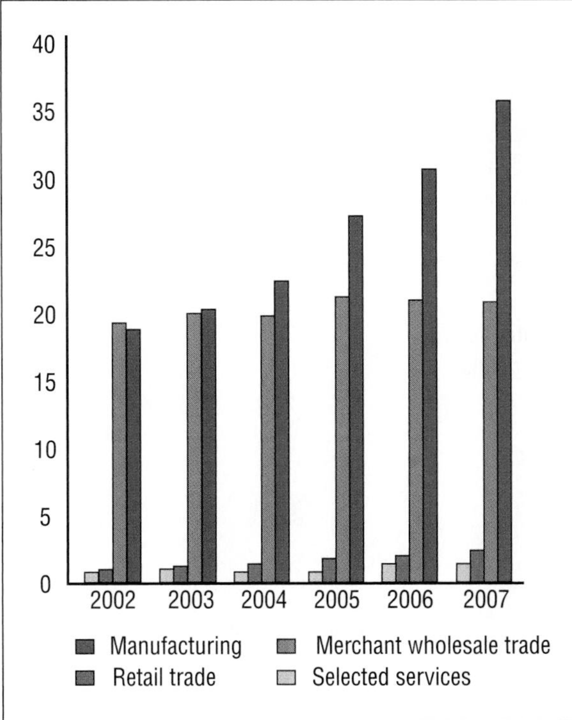

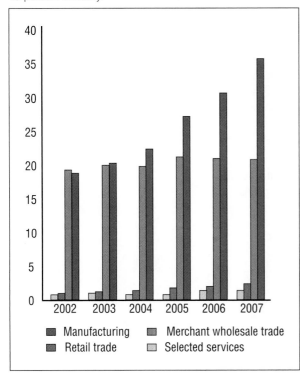

Many B2B transactions take place over EDI networks. As mentioned earlier, there is a growing trend for EDI transactions to take place over the Internet, rather than over private networks. Wal-Mart has requested that its more than 10,000 suppliers implement Internet-based EDI—changing from the previously used private network. The suppliers were given one year to comply. EDI allows Wal-Mart to place product orders directly to suppliers' information systems without human intervention. In some cases, these orders can be automatically placed by software that recognizes when inventory becomes low. The convenience of automating B2B transactions saves buyers and sellers significant time and money.

The third form of e-commerce is epitomized by the popular trend of consumers selling their own belongings on eBay. **Consumer-to-consumer e-commerce**, or **C2C**, uses the Web to connect individuals who wish to sell their personal belongings with people shopping for used items. Although eBay supports all forms of e-commerce, many credit it with being the first C2C e-commerce Web site. Since C2C does not create revenue for businesses, it is not included in most economic studies such as the one cited earlier by the U.S. Census Bureau. However, when you consider that \$60 billion of merchandise was sold on eBay in 2007, compared to \$138 billion in B2C the same year, it is easy to see that people and companies are very invested in buying and selling things online.[5]

E-Commerce from the Buyer's Perspective

The process of buying or acquiring goods or services takes place in six distinct stages (see Figure 8.9). E-commerce can assist buyers with each of these stages of buying. Consider the following scenario.

1. Realizing a need: You spy an ad on the Web for a smart phone that doubles as a GPS navigation system. That is something you simply must have.
2. Researching a product: Running a Web search on *GPS phone*, you learn that smart phones with GPS capabilities are relatively new. While most can approximate your location, few can provide turn-by-turn navigation while driving. You read several user reviews and consult a friend who has just purchased a phone with GPS capabilities.

3. Selecting a vendor: You search the Web for handsets and service providers offering the best price with the best reputation. Fortunately, the company offering the lowest price also has a good reputation and is highly recommended by the 574 customers who have ranked its service.
4. Providing payment: You proceed to the cellular provider's Web site and, finding that there are units in stock that can be shipped immediately, you place the item in your electronic shopping cart and proceed to checkout. You give the cellular provider your shipping information and credit card number using the secure electronic checkout form, and the transaction is approved and completed.
5. Accepting delivery: Three days later, a package arrives at your doorstep. After reviewing the manual and setting up service, you are enjoying your new handset.
6. Using product support: Should your new smart phone break down while under warranty, or if you have questions about setting it up, you can visit the manufacturer's Web site to gather information or arrange an exchange.

FIGURE 8.9 • The six stages of buying goods

E-commerce can assist consumers with each of the six stages of the buying process.

Consider the benefits that e-commerce provided you in this scenario, compared with traditional forms of shopping. Without the Web, you might or might not have heard about GPS phones. Without the Web, you would have had to rely on trade magazines or store salespeople as resources for information about the product.

Perhaps the biggest advantage offered by the Web is the ability to comparison shop and read customer reviews. The Web provides consumers a platform to express disappointment or satisfaction with their purchases. Through Web sites like Epinions.com and ConsumerReports.org, and customer review tools on large e-commerce sites like Amazon.com, consumers are able to learn from other customers' experiences prior to making purchases (see Figure 8.10).

FIGURE 8.10 • Consumer reviews—Epinions.com

Consumer review Web sites like Epinions.com help shoppers avoid purchasing mistakes and pressure manufacturers to produce better products.

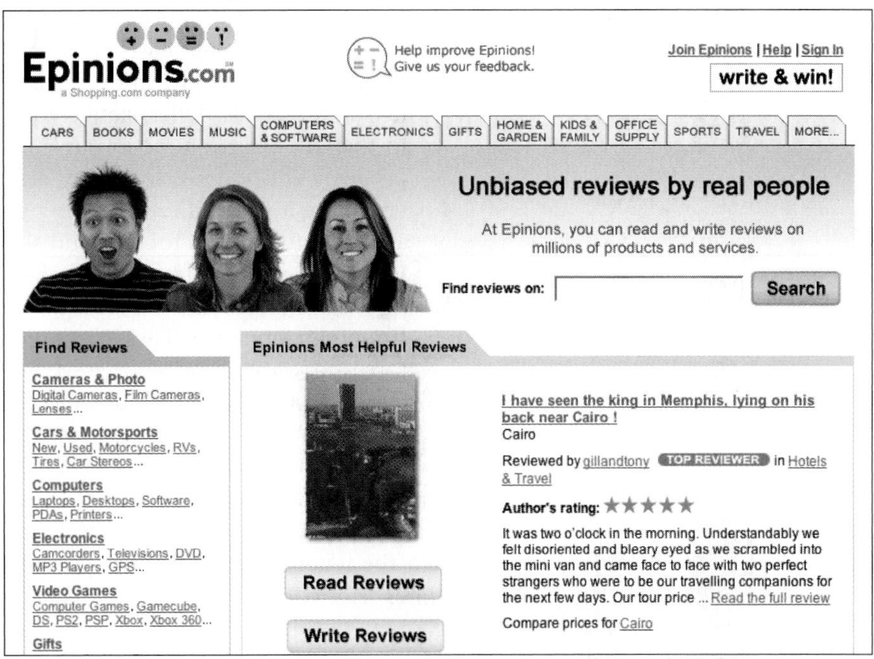

Manufacturers also use customer reviews to gain insight that can be used to improve their products. For example, Rubbermaid has produced a popular line of garden sheds that are advertised to "assemble in under an hour." Reading customer reviews of the shed at Epinions.com, you will find that all who have bought it were ultimately happy with the shed but warn that it takes several hours and a lot of muscle power to assemble. Customers point out several misleading steps in the instructions and provide tips to make the most difficult steps easier. In their reviews, customers also complained about security issues due to a plastic lock hasp. A Rubbermaid representative posted to the Epinions board that Rubbermaid has changed the lock hasp to a metal one after reading about concerns posted in customer reviews.

On the other hand, shopping locally provides the advantage of taking possession of the product at the point of purchase. Local retailers may also offer benefits that are difficult to duplicate over the Web such as demonstrations, installation, and the ability to exchange a faulty product for a new one without shipping delays. One of the challenges of e-commerce is to offer online shoppers all the benefits found with local merchants along with the added convenience of shopping from home.

E-Commerce from the Seller's Perspective

Sellers strive to influence and support the stages of the buying process using the following business practices. Note how e-commerce assists the seller in meeting objectives.

1. Market research to identify customer needs: Sellers may monitor the flow of Web traffic and solicit customer opinions using Web-based forms in order to conduct market research.
2. Manufacturing products or supplying services that meet customer needs: B2B e-commerce is used to acquire raw materials for the manufacturing

of products. Often the products sold or services provided are complemented by or even dependent on Web technology. For example, software, e-books, digital music, and movies can all be delivered via the Internet. Airlines, shipping companies, and banks provide free and valuable services to their customers on the Web.

3. Marketing and advertising to make customers aware of available products and services: Sellers actively use the Web for advertising, as you saw in the GPS smart phone example, in order to make customers aware of products and services they may desire.
4. Providing a method for acquiring payments: Banks provide merchant accounts to e-tailers for safe and secure credit card transactions over the Web (more on this later in the chapter).
5. Making arrangements for delivery of the product: E-tailers work with shipping companies like UPS to provide several shipping options to customers at varying price levels. As noted earlier, some services and products can be delivered via download over the Internet.
6. Providing after-sales support: E-tailers and manufacturers may provide product support on their Web site, or through telephone, e-mail, or online chat. Manufacturers' warranties are typically the same for items purchased online and in a local store.

From the seller's perspective, the process of producing and selling goods is sometimes referred to as *supply chain management (SCM)*. Supply chain management involves three areas of focus: demand planning, supply planning, and demand fulfillment (see Figure 8.11). *Demand planning* involves analyzing buying patterns and forecasting customer demand. *Supply planning* involves producing and making logistical arrangements to ensure that you are able to meet the forecasted demand. *Demand fulfillment* is the process of getting the product or service to the customer. E-commerce is ideally suited for streamlining these processes, saving sellers time and money while providing more accurate information.

FIGURE 8.11 • Supply chain management

Supply chain management involves three areas of focus: demand planning, supply planning, and demand fulfillment.

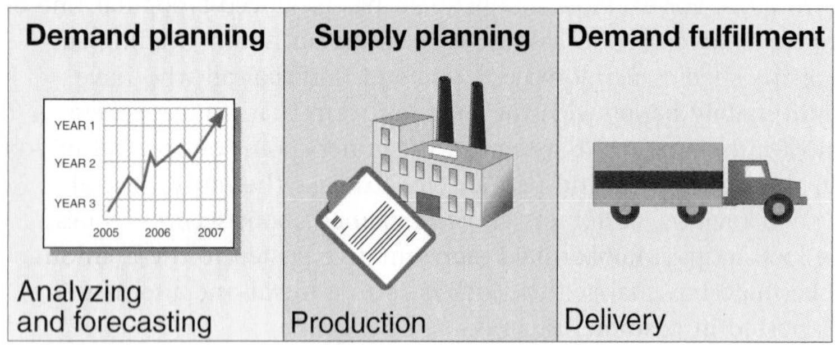

Benefits and Challenges of E-Commerce

E-commerce offers advantages to both buyers and sellers. Buyers enjoy the convenience of shopping from their desktop, or in the case of B2B, fully automated order placement. Sellers value e-commerce because it dramatically extends their markets. Farmyard Nurseries provides a striking example. Prior to e-commerce, this small nursery that grows a wide variety of specialty plants in Llandysul, West Wales, did the majority of its business (90 percent) with local residents. A year after expanding to the Web, Farmyard Nurseries found that the majority of its business now came from the rest of Wales (36 percent) and the United Kingdom (37 percent), with distribution beginning to extend around the world (see Figure 8.12). By expanding its operations to the Web, Farmyard retained the same amount of local business, and increased its overall customer base by 900 percent.

B2C e-commerce levels the playing field between large and small businesses, making it much easier for new companies to enter a market and for small businesses to gain market share from large businesses. The Web is an equalizer in that it allows businesses to win over customers with high-quality services and low prices,

FIGURE 8.12 • E-commerce can dramatically extend a business's market

Farmyard Nurseries' customers consisted of mostly local residents before e-commerce, but expanded to include customers from all over the world after implementing e-commerce.

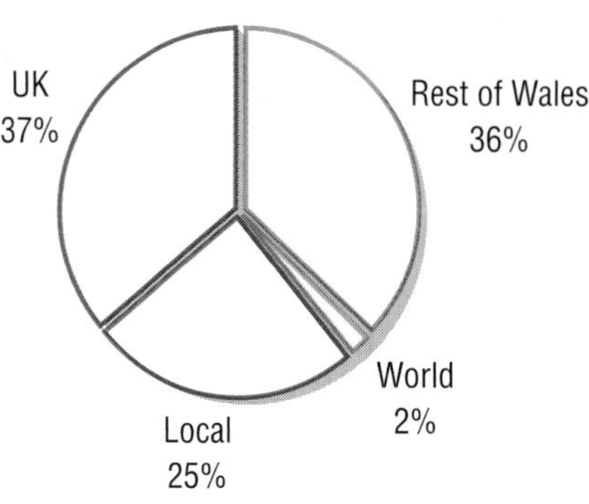

rather than through size and monopoly power. Consider, for instance, a young entrepreneur who decides to open a small hardware store. What chance for success would you give such a business, considering that local competition consists of the two largest superwarehouse home improvement chains in the world? Could the small private business compete with the superstores' discount prices and wide selection? What if the young entrepreneur specialized in unique and hard-to-find items on a professionally managed e-commerce site? This would expand the potential customer base for this business from people in the local community to the entire Internet population. Certainly, the chances for this small business would improve in the online environment.

In some cases, e-commerce has extended a lifeline to businesses selling products or services that were made obsolete by technology. For example, realizing that photographic film and regular cameras are gradually being replaced by memory sticks and digital cameras, Kodak worked to change its image from that of a film company to that of a picture company. It put its efforts and investments into digital camera

NO-STOP SHOPPING GETS EVEN BETTER

Feet too tired to meet up with your friends at the mall? No problem. FriendShopper.com has come out with the first social shopping platform. You can chat, shop, and check out products together in real-time online. Just drop the FriendShopper bookmarklet into your browser toolbar, and when you come across an interesting product on a vendor's site, you can save it and share it with your friends—in just one click!

Shop Alone No Longer: FriendShopper.com Brings the Live Shopping Experience to E-Commerce
PR Newsire
July 7, 2009
http://news.prnewswire.com/ViewContent.aspx?ACCT=109&STORY=/www/story/07-072009/0005056026&EDATE=

technology and an online presence, where it provides products and tools for digital photographers (see Figure 8.13). Apple saw an opportunity for online music distribution and developed iTunes, offering a lifeline to a music industry losing the battle against online music piracy. Network TV is gradually moving its content online in order to survive against strong competition from online video sources such as YouTube and Boxee. Newspapers have been hard hit by online competition as well, and in some cases are phasing out their print publications and reinventing the newspaper online (see the Job Technology box).

FIGURE 8.13 • Kodak adapts to digital photography and e-commerce

Kodak changed its image from that of a film company to that of a picture company by investing in digital camera technology and an online presence, where it provides products and tools for digital photographers.

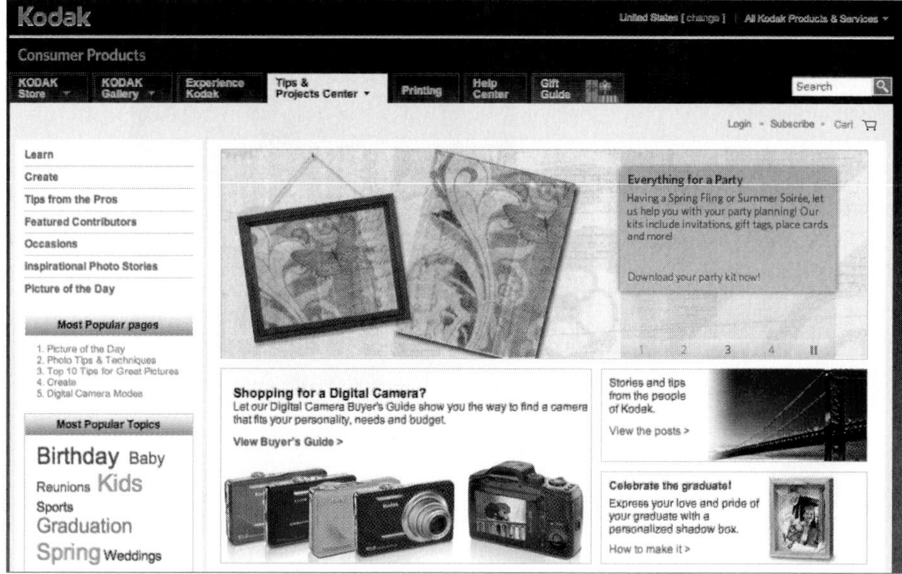

Although there are numerous advantages to e-commerce, there are also some challenges. Established businesses that wish to expand to the Internet need to alter systems and business practices to accommodate the new method of transaction processing that e-commerce requires. The larger and more established the business, the more costly this change can be. Consider the changes that must have been required at Farmyard Nurseries (Figure 8.12) when the business shifted from serving local customers to serving the world. Now consider an equal upheaval in a business with 15,000 employees.

There are also issues of security, privacy, and reliability. E-commerce can survive only if those involved can trust the system. Scams, identity theft, and fraud are a prevalent and real concern for all involved in e-commerce.

Finally, there are social concerns. Not everyone has equal access to the technology of e-commerce. People with low incomes and people living in less developed countries often don't have computers, mobile telephones, and Internet access. Many people in the United States and European Union do not have high-speed, broadband Internet access. The differences between those who have access to technology and those who do not are deepened with the increased use of e-commerce—those without access to the Internet are denied the benefits of e-commerce technology. In addition, accessibility advocates warn that as society uses increasingly smaller devices for day-to-day business, accommodations must be made for individuals who are unable to manipulate such small devices due to old age, poor vision, or other physical limitations.

JOB TECHNOLOGY

Redefining Newspapers Online

The migration of information and entertainment from traditional media such as paper, television, and radio to the Web has deeply impacted many industries. It has provided unparalleled opportunities for new, nimble, and inventive businesses while seriously challenging large, traditional media companies. Faced with extinction, a number of traditional businesses are reinventing themselves in order to survive. The newspaper industry is a prime example.

Newspapers are in crisis as they compete with rapidly growing online news sources. Advertisers are abandoning print and moving online, dramatically affecting traditional newspapers' ability to make a profit. The *San Francisco Chronicle* experienced a 15 percent decrease in advertising in 2008, resulting in a loss of more than $50 million in revenue. The *Seattle Post-Intelligencer* and other well-known newspapers have closed, or are considering closing, their print editions in favor of online publication.

Frank Bennack, chief executive of the Hearst Corporation and owner of the *Seattle Post-Intelligencer*, said, "Our goal now is to turn *seattlepi.com* into the leading news and information portal in the region." Hearst does not intend to simply create an online newspaper. The company intends to create a "new type of digital business" that provides a community-focused news and online information service.

The *Denver Times* has taken a similar approach. Its new online incarnation, *indenvertimes.com*, focuses on local news and features interactive chats, mobile feeds, and Web 2.0 technologies. The online news service hopes to sign up over 50,000 subscribers in its first two months.

Questions:

1. Why are print newspapers having a hard time staying in business?
2. Would you rather read the news online or on paper? Why?
3. How do you think the move to the Web will impact professional journalists and their industry?

Sources

1. Keating, Gina, "Hearst prints final Seattle PI as newspapers dwindle," Reuters, March 16, 2009, www.reuters.com.
2. DeBruin, Lynn, "Rocky Mountain News to close, publish final edition Friday," Rocky Mountain News, February 26, 2009, www.rockymountainnews.com.
3. InDenver Times Web site, accessed July 1, 2009, www.indenvertimes.com.

E-COMMERCE APPLICATIONS

E-commerce is playing an increasingly important role in our personal and professional lives. It allows us to discover new and interesting products that may not be available in our own community. For items that are available locally, it allows us to find better deals. We use e-commerce to monitor our bank accounts and transfer electronic funds. Businesses use e-commerce to streamline transaction processes and reach new customers. This section provides a categorical and comprehensive view of e-commerce and applications from both the buyer's and seller's perspectives.

Retail E-Commerce: Shopping Online

As previously discussed, e-tailing has dramatically influenced the way people shop by providing customers with product information and the ability to comparison shop for most products. Price battles continually rage on the Web to the benefit of consumers. Web sites such as mySimon.com, DealTime.com, PriceSCAN.com, PriceGrabber.com, bizrate.com, and NexTag.com provide product price quotations from numerous e-tailers to help you to find the best deal (see Figure 8.14). It may happen that the best deal is found at your local warehouse store. In such a case, shopping online provides the assurance that you really are getting the best deal. In some cases, consumers can use prices found online to negotiate a better price with a local dealer. E-commerce can empower consumers.

FIGURE 8.14 • Comparison shopping at DealTime

The DealTime site provides product price quotations from numerous e-tailers to help you find the best deal on many different products.

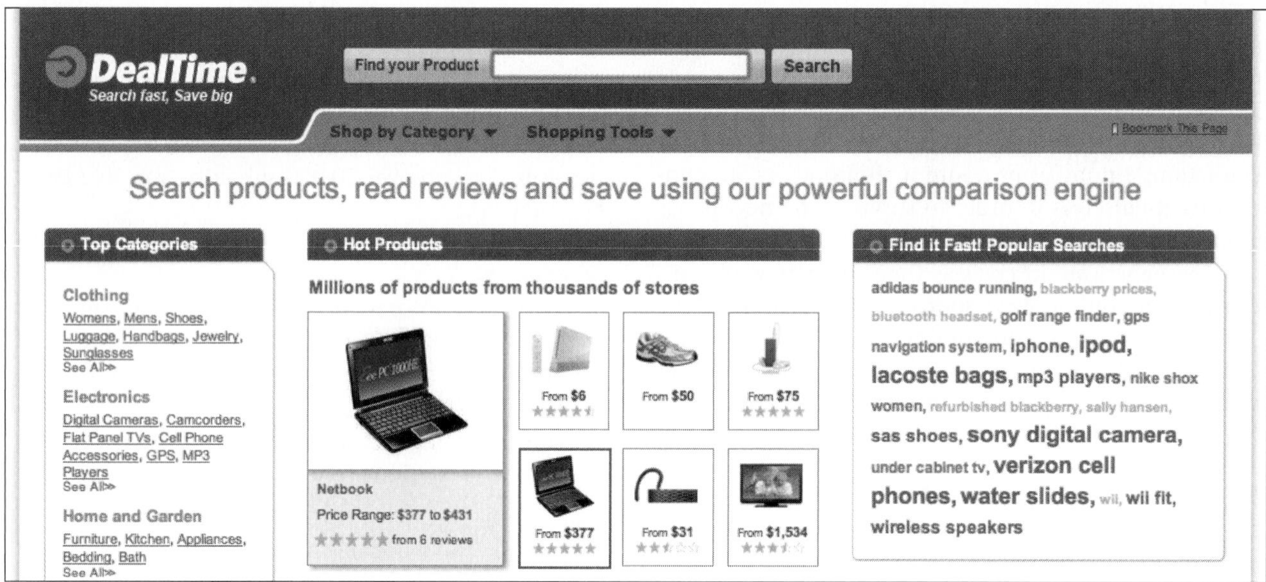

Some items are easier to sell online than others. Some purchases are determined not by holding a product in your hands, but by the description or demonstration of the product. Such is the case with books, digital music, computer software, and games—items that sell easily on the Web. Tangibles, such as DVD players, blue jeans, and automobiles, are more difficult to sell online. However, examining tangible items online has become significantly easier with the development of 3D virtual imagery. Three-dimensional virtual imagery allows a Web user to rotate objects on the screen and view them from every angle. This technology has been a tremendous help to businesses selling tangible products online.

There are several approaches to e-tailing. A business can set up its own electronic storefront, such as *www.landsend.com* or *www.bestbuy.com*, and provide visitors access to an electronic catalog of products, an electronic shopping cart for items they wish to purchase, and an electronic checkout procedure. Another e-tailing option is to lease space in a cybermall. A *cybermall* is a Web site that allows visitors to browse through a wide variety of products from varying e-tailers (see Figure 8.15). Cybermalls are typically aligned with popular Web portals and include Yahoo!'s *http://shopping.yahoo.com*, Google's *www.google.com/products*, and MSN's *http://shopping.msn.com*.

FIGURE 8.15 • Cybermall

Cybermalls like Yahoo! Shopping provide merchandise from thousands of stores at one Web location.

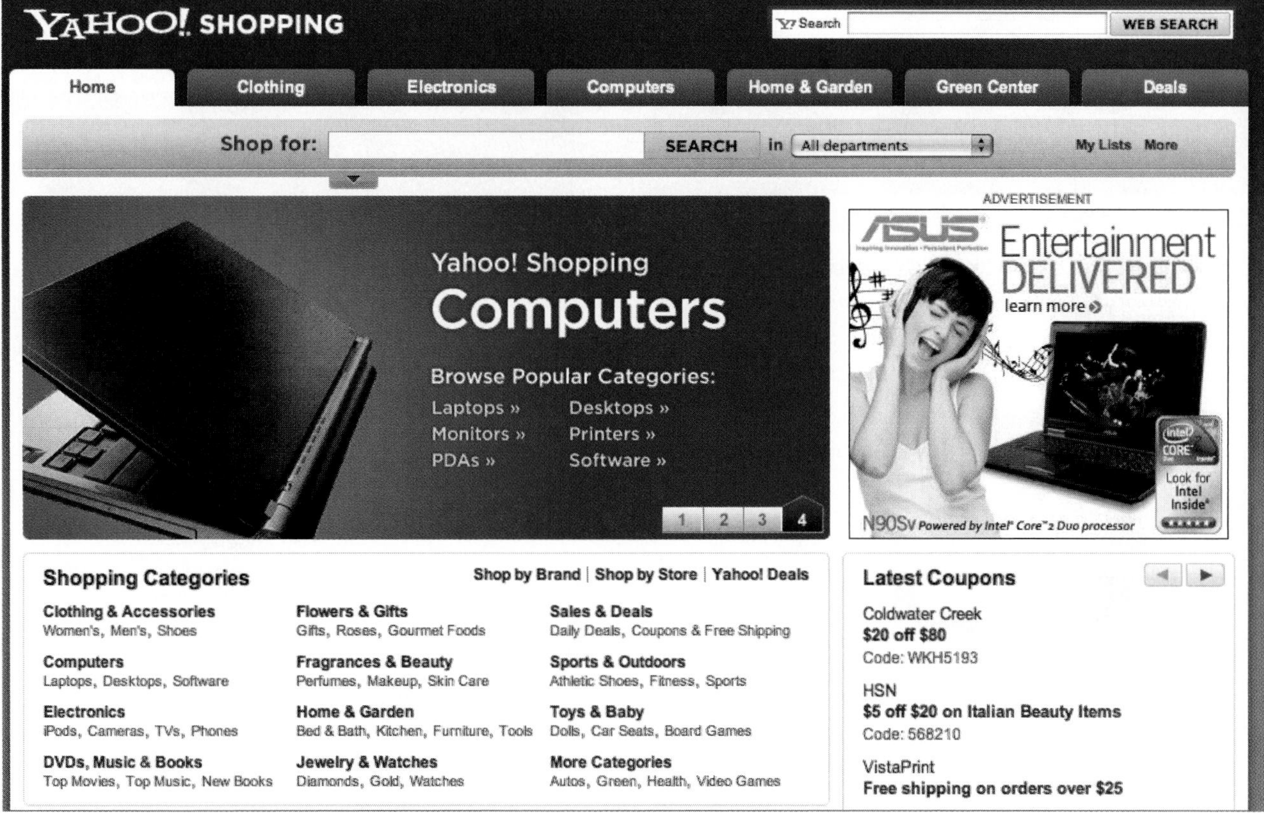

Online Clearinghouses, Web Auctions, and Marketplaces

Online clearinghouses, Web auctions, and *marketplaces* provide a platform for businesses and individuals to sell their products and belongings. Online clearinghouses such as *uBid.com* provide a method for manufacturers to liquidate stock and consumers to find a good deal. Outdated or overstocked items are put on the virtual auction block for customers to bid on. Users place bids on the objects, and the highest bidder(s), when the auction closes, get the merchandise—often for less than 50 percent of the advertised retail price. Credit card numbers are collected at the time that bids are placed. Figure 8.16 shows information on an item up for bid on uBid. A good rule to keep in mind is not to place a bid on an item unless you are prepared to buy it.

The most popular auction/marketplace is eBay.com, which provides a public platform for global trading where practically anyone can buy, sell, or trade practically anything.[6] The site offers a wide variety of features and services that enable members to buy and sell on eBay quickly and conveniently. Buyers have the option to purchase items in auction-style format, or they can purchase items at a fixed price. On any given day, millions of items are listed on eBay across thousands of categories.

Auction houses such as eBay accept limited liability for problems that buyers or sellers may experience in their transactions; deals that make use of eBay's PayPal service are protected, but others may be risky. Participants should be aware that the possibility of fraud is very real in any such Internet dealings.

FIGURE 8.16 • uBid auction item

Information about auction items on uBid includes item details, Quantity Available, Bid to Beat, Bid Increment, how much time is left in the auction, and the current highest bids.

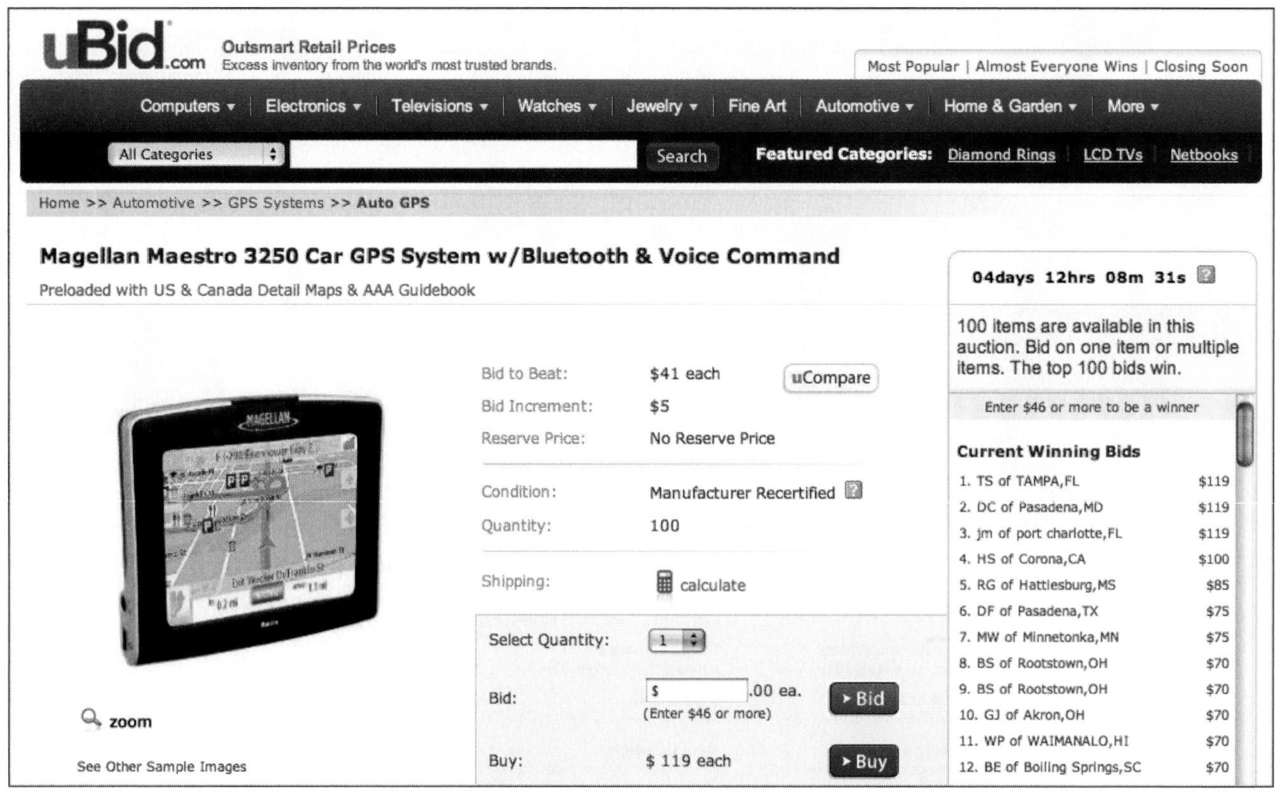

B2B Global Supply Management and Electronic Exchanges

By now you know that the Internet serves as an ideal way for businesses to connect. The real challenge lies in organizing relationships between businesses. For example, imagine that you have a great idea for a new product, such as a new lightweight, motorized campus scooter. You have test-marketed the product, which students on campus greeted with great enthusiasm; you've done all the necessary background work and preparation; you've found a wealthy investor; and you are ready to go into production. You have a list of parts required for the manufacturing of your scooter. But how do you go about finding suppliers that are both reputable and inexpensive? The solution for your scooter-manufacturing business is the same as for any business: global supply management.

Global supply management (*GSM*) provides methods for businesses to find the best deals on the global market for raw materials and supplies needed to manufacture their products. Many GSM products and services available on the Web promise to lower a business's costs by providing connections to a wide variety of reputable suppliers along with negotiation tools that allow a business to be assured that it is getting the best deal. Ariba (*www.ariba.com*), a GSM company, advertises that its services and software can cut total supply costs by 45 percent.

Some businesses join together with others in their industry to pool resources in Web-based electronic exchanges. An *electronic exchange* is an industry-specific Web resource created to provide a convenient centralized platform for B2B e-commerce among manufacturers, suppliers, and customers. Electronic exchanges promote cooperation between competing companies for greater industry-wide efficiency and effectiveness. Through an electronic exchange, a manufacturer has access to a wide variety of industry-specific suppliers and services. Once business relationships are established between members, the electronic exchange provides the framework for fast and efficient transactions.

Covisint (*www.covisint.com*) is an electronic exchange for automotive manufacturers. Founded by DaimlerChrysler AG, Ford Motor Company, General Motors, Nissan, and Renault, Covisint has created alliances between automotive manufacturers and suppliers and contracted with several of the largest technology providers to create "the most successful business-to-business electronic exchange the world has ever seen."[7] Covisint members have access to online catalogs and auctions, tools that assist in quality management and problem solving, and an industry portal (see Figure 8.17). The industry portal is software installed on a member's computer system that provides secure access to the electronic exchange's services. Covisint has been so successful in the automotive industry that it has expanded to provide similar services in the health-care industry.

FIGURE 8.17 • Covisint

The Covisint portal provides convenient access to valuable automotive industry resources.

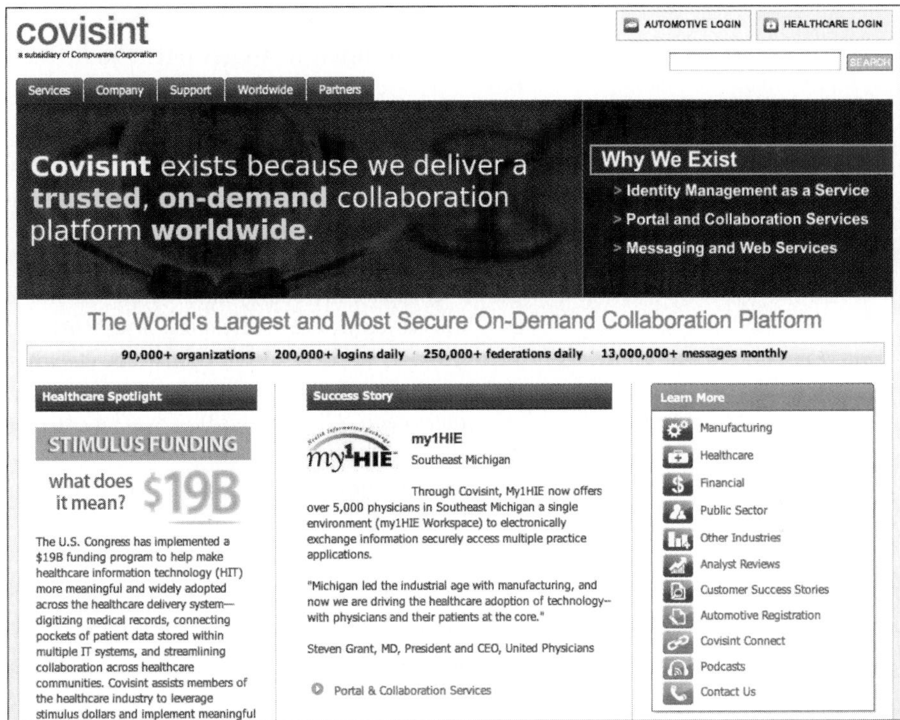

Marketing

Internet users are well aware of marketing on the Internet. Banner ads, pop-up ads, and now video ads threaten to crowd out Web content, and e-mail inboxes brim with spam. Although some Internet marketing is intrusive, there are many benefits provided to both consumers and corporations through e-commerce applications of marketing. For example, advertisements make it possible for services such as Google and Yahoo! to be available free of charge. Online margeting techniques also make it possible to match ads to a user's specific interests, providing valuable sevice to consumers.

E-commerce has affected the marketing process perhaps more than any other area of business. The Web is used for the following:

- Unsolicited advertising to make buyers aware of products
- Access to product information (solicited advertising) through business Web sites, which allow buyers to find information about products they are actively pursuing
- Market research, to find out what consumers want

The focus of marketing in many organizations is shifting from television and print media to the Internet, Web, cell phone networks, electronic games, and even software. Microsoft is experimenting with the use of ads in its Microsoft Works software.[8] Since people are increasingly turning to the Web and their cell phones for information and entertainment, it makes sense that advertiser dollars will follow.

The migration of news, information, and entertainment to digital devices isn't the only force that is transforming marketing approaches. Our on-demand culture is losing patience with mass-marketing approaches that force the viewer to listen to ads that are of little or no interest. Nor do we want to give up precious time to listen to a sales pitch. So marketers are using new tactics to target buyers in a less obtrusive manner. This section explores the manner in which e-commerce and marketing interact.

Access to Product Information. The ability to get better deals and make informed decisions is turning many people into Web researchers. In some cases, Web-based product research leads to e-commerce purchases; in others, it leads to more traditional-style purchases. For example, when shopping for a car, many people compare and contrast a variety of makes and models on Web sites such as Edmunds.com, CarSmart.com, and Motortrend.com; on auto manufacturers' Web sites; or on ConsumerReports.org (see Figure 8.18). Upon deciding on a make and model, the purchaser might get some price quotes on the Web (*www.pricequotes.com*). Ultimately, however, most buyers will visit an auto dealer to test drive and purchase a vehicle.

Whether they deal with an auto salesperson, a mechanic, a loan officer, a financial advisor, or any number of professionals, the Web can empower consumers with knowledge in areas previously reserved for professionals. The Web can better equip people to ask intelligent questions and confront those who might otherwise take advantage of uninformed consumers.

Market Research. Traditional marketing researchers observe what products customers purchase or desire and interview customers to find out how they feel about specific products. Interviews may take place on the street, by phone, by mail, or with paid focus-group participants who try a product and provide their opinions. Through *market segmentation,* customer opinions are divided into demographic variables such as race, gender, income, education, and age to determine which segment a product appeals to most. Although this method of market research is useful, it has some significant shortcomings. For one, it is expensive for those doing the research and inconvenient for those being interviewed. These restrictions make it difficult for market researchers to obtain the views of a representative cross section of the population. Another problem is that market segmentation caters to a majority and may exclude individuals who think differently than their peers.

E-commerce allows market segmentation to take place at the level of each individual consumer. E-commerce tools make it possible to follow a visitor around a Web site, monitor which areas and products draw the visitor's attention, and monitor how much time the visitor spends in each area. This data is

FIGURE 8.18 • Consumer Reports

Consumer Reports advertises unbiased product testing and reviews. Many consumers find it worth the subscription fee to access its vehicle ratings.

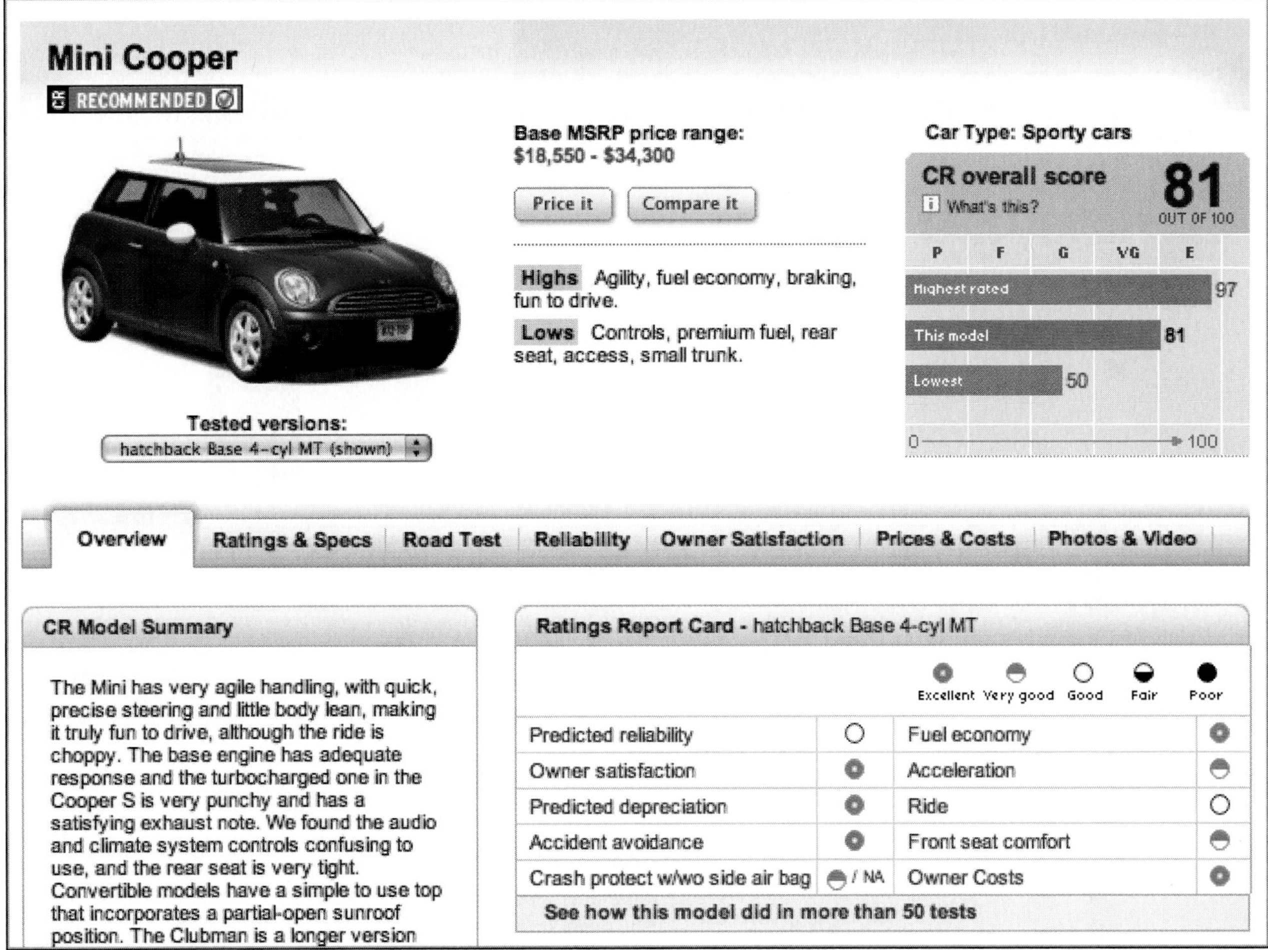

often collected without the customer's knowledge—so it is in no way an inconvenience and requires very little investment on the e-tailer's part. With the use of cookies (data files placed on the user's computer by a Web server), an e-tailer can maintain a history of customer preferences and highlight products that have proven historically to best hold the customer's interest (see Figure 8.19). This is referred to as *personalized* or *one-to-one marketing.*

It is also possible to develop a customer profile based on broader Internet browsing patterns. Marketing companies such as DoubleClick provide advertising servers that display ads on client Web sites. Many free online services hire DoubleClick to handle Web advertisements. Each time you visit these sites, DoubleClick inserts an advertisement from a sponsor into space provided on the Web site. Often, a different ad will be in the banner each time you visit.

Web advertising and marketing companies collect large amounts of data that can be mined to determine buying patterns and trends. This provides significantly more detailed market research than traditional methods. It also provides fuel for privacy groups who consider the practice to be invasive (see the Community Technology box).

Advertising. Some advertising campaigns don't require much in the way of market analysis; the products, such as the latest Hollywood blockbuster, are designed to be enjoyed across a wide range of demographics. In such cases, large amounts of

FIGURE 8.19 • Personalized Amazon.com

Amazon.com custom-creates its Web page for each visitor, providing items it thinks will interest you based on a customer profile stored in its database.

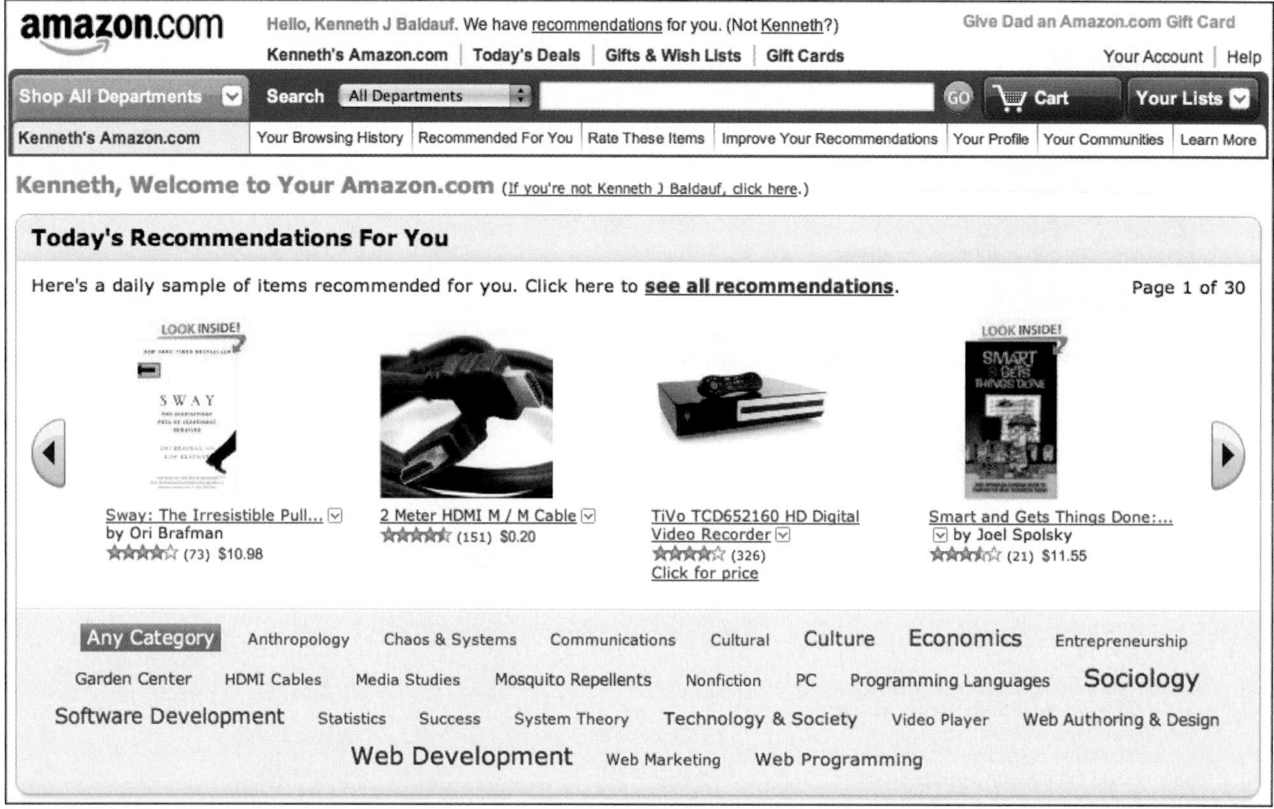

money are invested in placing advertisements everywhere. Most products, however, benefit by targeting a particular demographic. For example, you are more likely to find ads for IBM mainframe servers on technology-related Web sites; just as you are probably more likely to find commercials for masculine products aired during the Super Bowl. If you are a woman who enjoys football, you probably find this offensive, and rightfully so. Traditional market segmentation approaches are based on stereotypes. They are useful for businesses advertising on mass-market media such as television, radio, and newspapers, and provide the best return on investment.

The Web, however, is a different type of mass-market medium. For one thing, users do not typically share their computer screen with others, so ads can be personalized. Also, the Web supports communication in two directions, so through market research techniques discussed in the previous section, advertisers can learn about your personal interests. For these reasons, as technology becomes smarter, and as people spend more time on the Web filling databases with more precise profiling information, Web content and ads will become more personally targeted. Imagine a television channel that provides only television programs that you like, and includes commercials only for products and services that interest you. That is what is most likely in store as the Web continues to evolve.

Advertisements over the Web take many forms; Table 8.2 lists the most popular. *Rich media,* used in many of today's Web ads, refers to ads that use animation, video, sound, and sometimes interactive components. Many rich media ads are animations developed with Adobe Flash. These ads are effective in calling attention to themselves but are considered distracting and intrusive by some consumers. Some rich media ads are played above the Web page content as the page is loaded, and they block access to the content for a limited amount of time.

Interest-Based Advertising vs. User Privacy

The primary business model emerging for Web-based services appears to be "ad-supported and free." Web giants like Google, Facebook, and Yahoo! depend on sponsored advertisements for their income. The more effective the ad, the more online companies can charge sponsors. The more information about each individual user that online companies can collect to pass along to ad agencies, the more effective the advertisements can become.

Anne Toth, head of privacy for Yahoo! Inc., calls it interest-based advertising. Others call it one-to-one marketing, or personalized marketing. Whatever you call it, it requires detailed data collection on users gathered over time, to provide an accurate profile of the interests and activities of online users that can be referenced to provide effective advertisements.

Representative Joe Barton of Texas thinks "it's a big deal if someone tracks where you go and what you look at without your personal approval. We wouldn't like that in the non-Internet world and I personally don't like it in the Internet world." Political leaders around the world have been struggling to design baseline protections for Internet users with regard to information collected about their online activities.

Most companies collect user information in a manner that is invisible to users. The U.S. House of Representatives is working to pass a law that requires Web companies to inform users of what information is being collected and shared with online marketers. There is much debate on whether online information collection should be assumed, with an opportunity for users to "opt out," or if no information collection should be assumed, with an opportunity for users to "opt in." Many Web companies prefer the former, while privacy advocates support the latter.

Questions:

1. What benefits to both consumers and online marketers does interest-based advertising provide?
2. Why are privacy activists so concerned about the practice of invisible online information collection? Does it concern you? How much?
3. Do you feel that information gathering on Web sites like Facebook should be "opt in" or "opt out"? Why?

Sources

1. *Schatz, Amy, "Lawmakers Blast Internet Data Collection,"* The Wall Street Journal, *June 19, 2009, http://online.wsj.com.*
2. *Walters, Chris, "Facebook's New Terms of Service: 'We Can Do Anything We Want With Your Content. Forever.',"* The Consumerist, *February 15, 2009, http://consumerist.com.*

TABLE 8.2 • Methods of Web advertising

Type of ad	Description
Banner	A rectangular area embedded in the Web page content for advertising, often across the top of the page
Floating	An ad that floats across the screen above the Web page content
Pop-up	A new window that opens above the current one to display an advertisement
Pop-under	A new window that opens behind the current one with an advertisement that isn't noticed until the front window is closed
Interstitial	A full-page advertisement displayed prior to progressing to the requested content
Expanding	An ad that changes size and may cover up or alter the Web page content
Trick banner	A banner ad that looks like a Windows dialog box and tricks you into clicking it
Video ad	A banner ad that incorporates video clips

One reason Google has become so popular is its use of nonintrusive, text-only ads called *AdWords*. Ironically, Google's subtle form of Web advertisement seems to be more effective than the more intrusive ads and is responsible for much of Google's prosperity. Google's patented method of placing contextual ads in online content has earned it billions of dollars. *Contextual ads* are ads specifically selected and placed to match the content of a Web page—and hopefully the interests of the person viewing the page.

In addition to Web page advertisements, marketers are using other digital media. Advertisements are being distributed through e-mail, instant messaging, and SMS texting. As phones become increasingly used for Web access, the advertising methods used on the Web will be modified to accommodate the small display of cell phones. Google has adapted AdWords for use in mobile Web browsers and perhaps other applications in its Android smart phone operating system.[9] Advertisers are also placing ads in video games (see Figure 8.20). For example, in the 2008 U.S. presidential election, gamers driving through virtual raceways in Burnout Paradise on the Xbox 360 flew by ads for Barack Obama on large virtual billboards.[10]

FIGURE 8.20 • Ads in video games

Advertisements are being placed in video games, such as Burnout Paradise shown here, on the XBox 360 and other Internet-connected gaming systems.

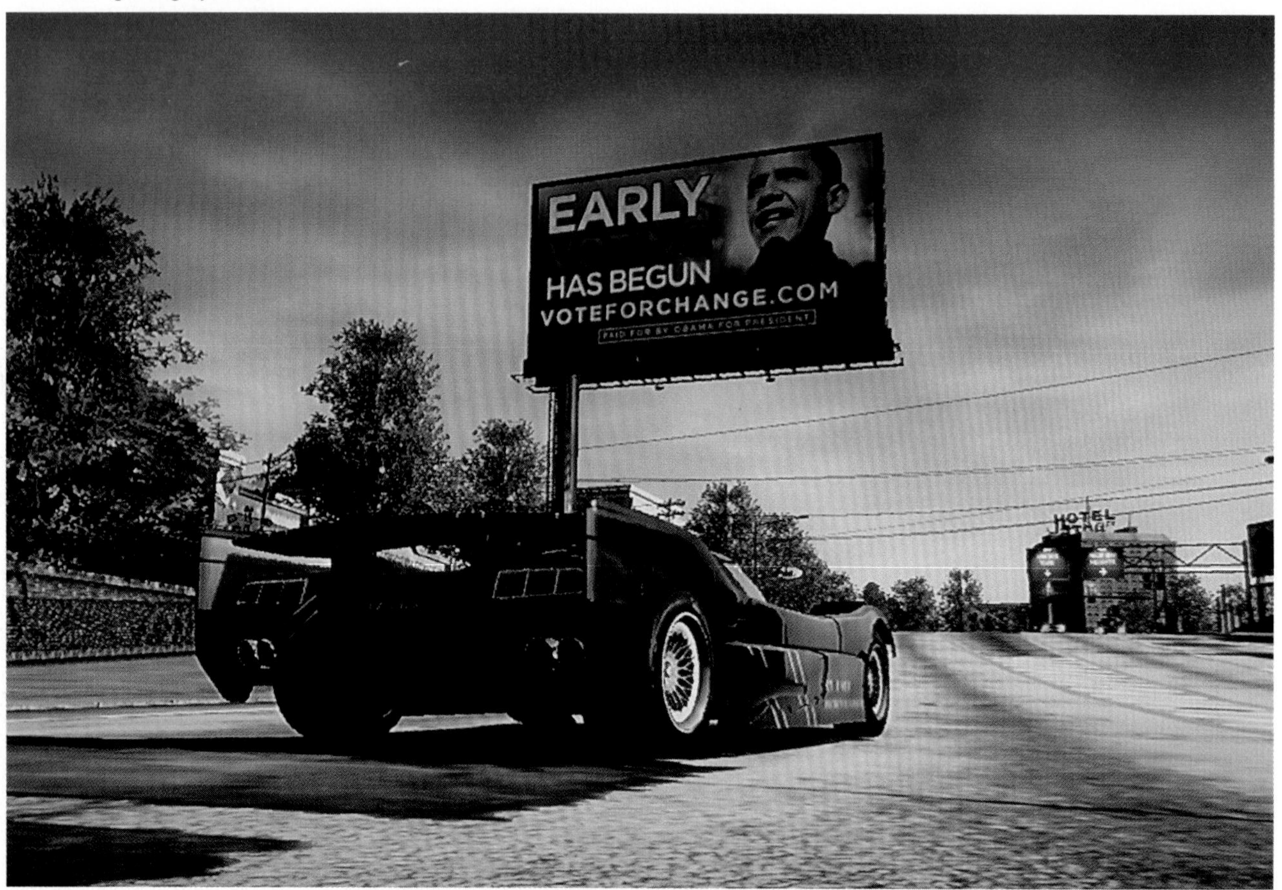

Banking, Finance, and Investment

Since banks have moved online, managing money has never been easier. Online banking provides convenient access to bank balance information and the ability to transfer funds, pay bills, and obtain account histories. Most bank Web sites provide a way to link your online financial records with financial software, such as Quicken, on your home PC in order to make use of advanced tools that assist with financial management.

Electronic funds transfer has become popular for paying bills and receiving paychecks. Electronic bill payments save companies so much money that many are considering requiring it of their customers. British Telecommunications (BT) is encouraging its customers to pay bills online after learning that it would save 45 cents per bill. If BT could get 90 percent of its more than 21 million customers signed up and paying bills online, it could save close to $110 million annually.

BT and others promoting online billing and payments emphasize the environmental savings and often market the practice as a greener alternative to traditional billing. E-billing reduces carbon emissions by eliminating the need to transport bills and payments, and also saves trees. Most banks include an automatic bill payment service that can be configured from the bank's Web site. You can also set up automatic payments at the Web sites of companies to which you are making payments or through third-party services that perform the transfers for you for a small monthly fee.

Investing activities have also moved to the Web in a big way. Online brokerages offer low-cost stock trades and tools to assist you in making investment decisions (see Figure 8.21).

FIGURE 8.21 • Ameritrade's Command Center software

Online trading companies like Ameritrade offer powerful market analysis tools.

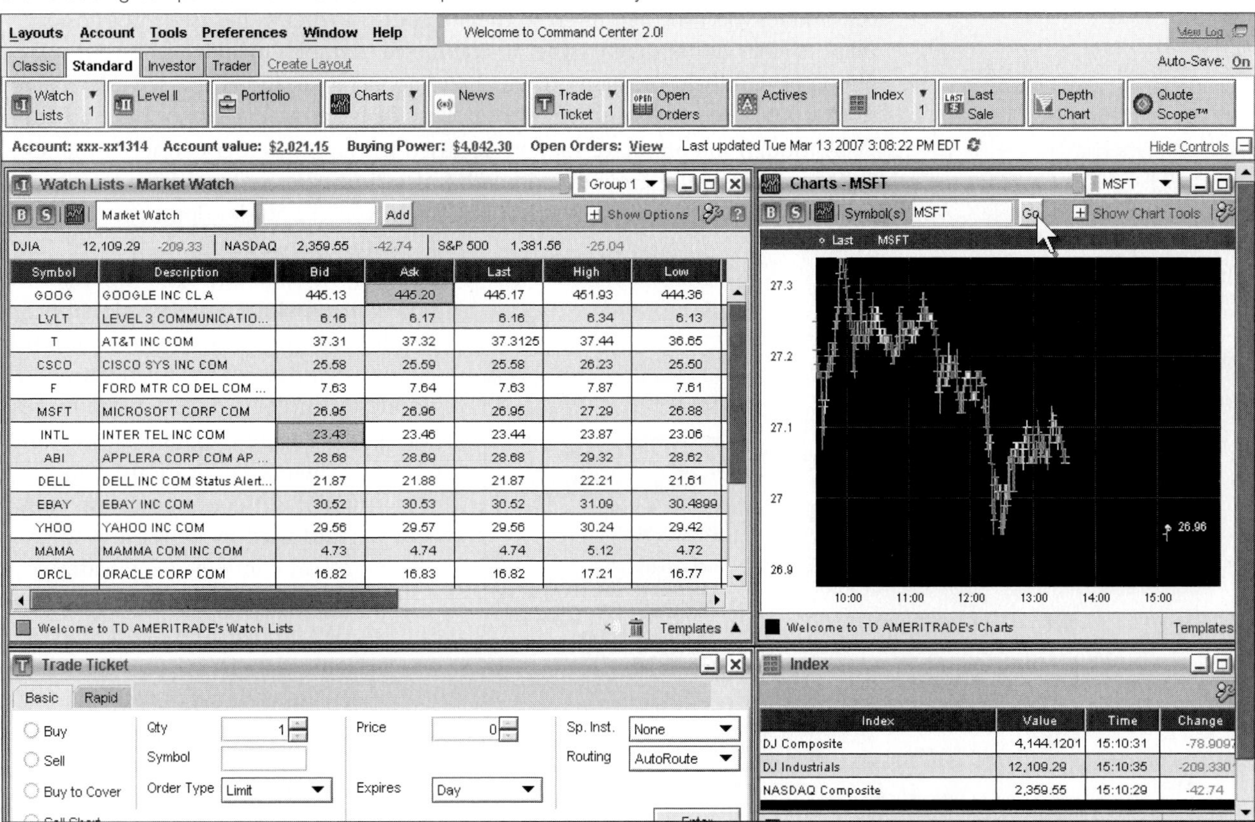

Online brokerages are able to execute trades fast, within seconds, allowing customers to buy or sell at the moment of opportunity. Most services offer helpful software that provides free quotes and streaming news for a first look at the stories that shape the market. Market research tools are available to help in the decision-making process. For example, Ameritrade provides over 20 software tools for computers and smart phones that support fast decision making and transactions from anywhere you have an Internet connection.

Popular online brokerages include Ameritrade (*www.ameritrade.com*), Ing Direct's ShareBuilder (*www.sharebuilder.com*), and E*Trade (*http://us.etrade.com*). For more information about online trading, visit *www.investingonline.org*. You can also find information about various online brokers at The Motley Fool (*www.fool.com*).

MOBILE COMMERCE

M-commerce, or **mobile commerce**, is a form of e-commerce that takes place over wireless mobile devices such as handheld computers and cell phones as well as emerging technologies such as *dashtop computers* embedded in automobile dashboards. Although most of the principles and practices of e-commerce extend to m-commerce, m-commerce presents unique opportunities and challenges. This section examines the technologies on which m-commerce is built and provides examples of how m-commerce is used.

M-Commerce Technology

M-commerce depends on the proliferation of mobile communications and computing devices. Through m-commerce, you can purchase and download songs to your cell phone; you can then listen to them through a wireless headset and transfer them to your home stereo. Other m-commerce examples include using your cell phone or handheld computer to purchase mobile applications and services, trade stocks, purchase concert tickets, have flowers delivered, call a cab, or book a flight.

Although m-commerce may be accessed through Internet-connected handheld computers, the growing popularity of cell phones and advances in cell phone technology are driving m-commerce research and development. The next generation of cell phones, referred to as *smart phones*, include the computational power, bandwidth, and functionality required for m-commerce. In addition to taking advantage of next-generation cell phone technology, m-commerce makes use of other technologies and standards:

- Wireless Application Protocol (WAP): A communication standard used by developers to create m-commerce applications
- Wireless Markup Language (WML): A part of WAP that is similar to HTML and is used to create Web pages designed to fit on the small displays of mobile devices (see Figure 8.22)
- Near Field Communications (NFC), RFID, infrared, and Bluetooth wireless networking technology: Technology that enables wireless, private, close-range, device-to-device communications

FIGURE 8.22 • M-commerce from Verizon

Verizon offers many products and services through its handsets.

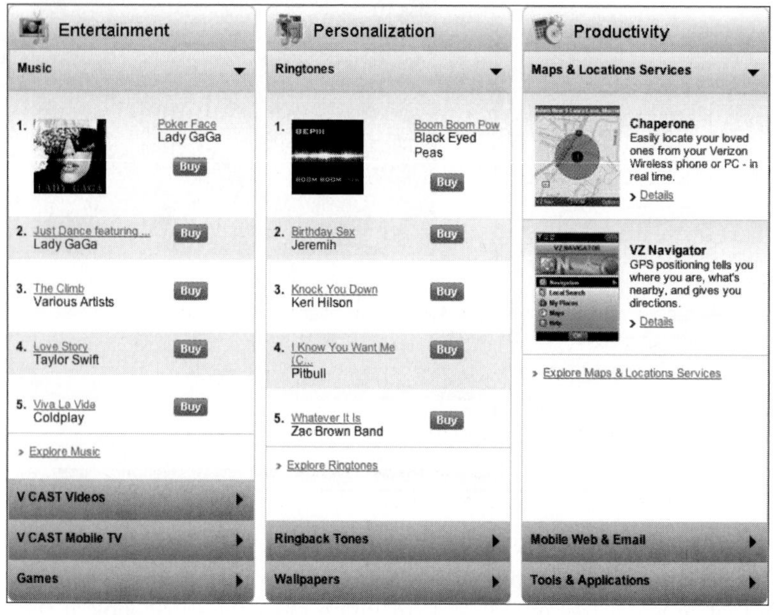

M-commerce technology received a big boost when industry leaders set aside competitive attitudes to join together in support of the open standards on which m-commerce is built. The *Open Mobile Alliance (OMA)* (*www.openmobilealliance.org*) comprises hundreds of the world's leading mobile operators, device and network suppliers, information technology companies, and content providers, which have joined together to create standards and ensure interoperability between mobile devices.

Types of M-Commerce and Applications

There are four methods at present for delivering m-commerce services to cell phones and other portable devices:

- Directly from cell phone service providers
- Via mobile Internet or Web applications
- Using Short Message Service (SMS) text messaging or Multimedia Messaging Service (MMS)
- Over short-range wireless data communications

Through Cell Phone Service Providers. Any cell phone user is aware that cell phone service providers sell a lot more than just the ability to communicate with others. Cell phone service providers make a lot of money from text, picture, and video messaging. Ring tones, wallpaper, games, and news alerts provide additional revenues for the phone company as well as the companies providing the service or product. These inexpensive services represent the beginnings of m-commerce. The introduction of handsets with broadband capabilities is bringing m-commerce into its next phase—media! Almost all cell phone service providers now offer services that allow customers to access streamed music and video clips from such media companies as Sony, Fox, Disney, ESPN, and CNN.

The birth of the iPhone brought a new mobile product: mobile applications (see Figure 8.23). The iPhone App Store provides access to tens of thousands of iPhone applications in categories that include games, business, education, finance, health care, navigation, and social networking. Apps range in price from free to hundreds of dollars. Impressed by Apple's success with its App Store, many other companies, including Palm and Google, are working on their own mobile app stores.

FIGURE 8.23 • iPhone m-commerce applications

The Amazon iPhone application allows users to browse and purchase products conveniently from the Amazon catalog.

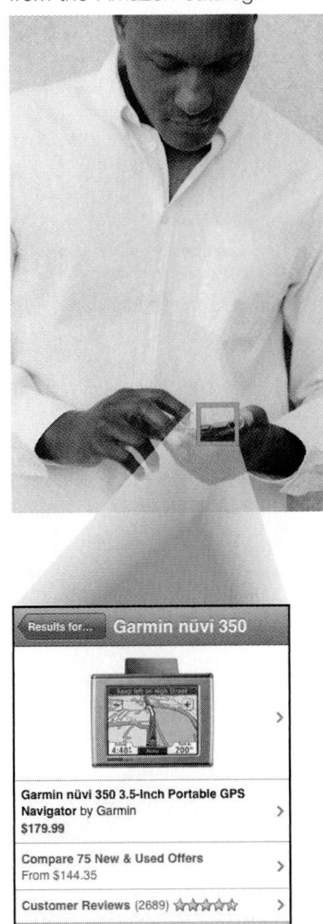

Over the Mobile Web. Web-based and application-based m-commerce allow the mobile user to interact with a seller's e-commerce system over the Internet or Web. Because smart phones can run Java applications, users can download m-commerce applications to their cell phones and use them to purchase products or services.

Many m-commerce applications can be accessed through your mobile Web browser, in much the same way that you access e-commerce applications through regular Web browsers. Web developers use WML to create small Web pages designed to fit the mobile display and provide easy navigation of the mobile device interface. M-commerce Web sites typically focus on delivering services that are useful to users on the go, such as news, stock tickers, local weather, maps, traffic information, flight schedules and delays, even mobile banking and auctions.

Location-based m-commerce applications make use of the global positioning system (GPS) or the cell network to track your current location in order to provide location-related services. These services include weather reports, road maps, lists of nearby merchants, lists of nearby friends, and traffic reports. For example, for a small monthly fee, the MyTraffic service from Traffic.com delivers updated traffic information by text to a cell phone or other wireless device.

Through SMS Text Messaging. Cell phone text messaging, or texting, can be used to order merchandise or services, or it can be used for advertisements. Spam over SMS texting is raising concerns in the United Kingdom, where texting has been in use longer than in the United States. It is estimated that more than half of British firms are using text messaging as a marketing tool. U.S. firms are likely to follow suit. In the United Kingdom, text messaging service charges are picked up by the sender. In the United States, however, many services require the receiver to pick up the bill, making mobile spam all the more disconcerting. Consumers can use SMS technology to purchase tickets to events and have them delivered electronically to their cell phone. Simply present your cell phone at the turnstile to enter the event.

Through Short-Range Wireless Data Communications. Short-range wireless technology enables some interesting m-commerce applications. The concept of a cashless society has been a dream of the technology industry for quite some time. In such a society, no one would need to carry wallets or money, and transactions would take place through automatic debits and credits to consumer and merchant accounts. Today these transactions can indeed take place using a small device like a cell phone and short-range wireless data transmission, such as that provided by infrared and NFC. While infrared is being used for short-range communications in Korea and Japan, the United States is leaning toward the use of near field communications (NFC) technologies. Referred to as a *proximity payment system,* devices such as Vivo, shown in Figure 8.24, allow customers to transfer funds wirelessly between their mobile device and a point-of-sale terminal.

FIGURE 8.24 • Proximity payment system

Proximity payment systems such as Vivo store credit card information on your cell phone and transfer funds wirelessly to point-of-sale terminals.

E-commerce and m-commerce applications are limited only by imagination. Although each application is suited to a unique service or product, all applications provide extended service to buyers and increased revenues to sellers.

E-COMMERCE IMPLEMENTATION

Implementing e-commerce systems requires a significant amount of investment and expertise. When a company decides to invest in e-commerce, it places itself at considerable risk. Because e-commerce is highly visible to the public, executing it poorly could tarnish the reputation of an otherwise well-respected company. E-commerce requires not only significant hardware and networking capabilities to accommodate heavy traffic, but also expertise in system administration, software development, Web design, and graphics design. Anything less than a professional approach in any of these areas could mean embarrassment for the company. For this reason, companies typically either hire specialists in these areas or contract the work out to professional e-commerce hosting companies.

An **e-commerce host** is a company that takes on some or all of the responsibility of setting up and maintaining an e-commerce system for a business or organization. Hosting services range in price from $7.95 per month to thousands of dollars per month, depending on the size of the business and the services offered by the host. Companies like ValueWeb provide everything needed for a simple e-commerce online business—online catalog, shopping cart, and transaction processing—for about $49.95 per month. For more money, you can get more storage space, a higher data transfer amount, and additional services.

Very large companies with more complicated systems might contract with IBM or Sprint to cooperate with them in developing Web e-commerce solutions at a considerably higher cost. For example, Office Depot contracted with IBM to design and implement a Web-based system that would accommodate transactions with customers and businesses (see Figure 8.25).

FIGURE 8.25 • Office Depot: A large e-commerce system

Office Depot contracted with IBM to design this e-commerce system to support both B2C and B2B transactions.

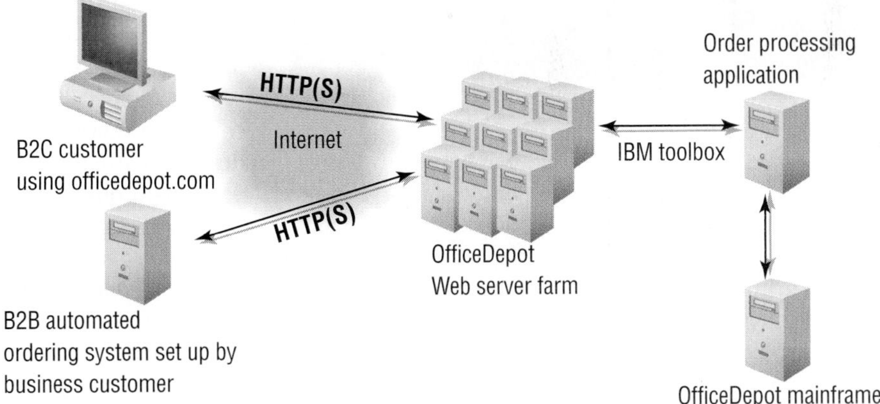

Whether you are creating and implementing your own e-commerce Web site or contracting the work out to a professional e-commerce hosting company, you need to understand the basics of e-commerce infrastructure, hardware and networking, and software issues. You also need to have a grasp of how to build Web site traffic, electronic payment systems, and international markets, as well as the security and privacy issues involved.

Infrastructure

E-commerce typically requires significant changes in an organization's infrastructure. Organizations expanding to the Web find that all areas of the business are affected to some degree; manufacturing, financial departments, sales, and customer service all need to adapt procedures to support doing business online. Consider the effect of e-commerce on television broadcasting and advertising. NSC and News Corp. recognized the threat that Internet video and online piracy posed to their businesses. The companies partnered to establish their own online television service: Hulu.com. Entirely new methods of programming and advertising had to be invented to utilize the new medium while not detracting from the companies' traditional television programming.[11] Similar transformations are occurring in most industries as businesses adjust to take advantage of e-commerce. A large part of Amazon.com's success arose from its ability to develop new business models that took advantage of e-commerce benefits before traditional retailers were aware of the opportunity (see Figure 8.26).

FIGURE 8.26 • Amazon's distribution center

Amazon.com developed new methods of packing and shipping products based on its revolutionary new e-commerce model.

A business that uses e-commerce needs to employ people who are technically savvy and able to understand how technology can assist in meeting the goals of the organization. Knowledge of the technology is necessary even for a small business using an e-commerce hosting company to maintain a Web site. An e-commerce hosting company is responsible only for providing the tools of e-commerce, not for the success of the business. Owners and managers of large businesses benefit as well, but they usually enhance their knowledge through a team of experts assigned to support e-commerce operations.

B2C e-commerce often connects manufacturers directly with consumers, cutting out the middleman. This usually means drastic changes in manufacturing, storage, and shipping. Rather than shipping bulk products to retailers, B2C e-commerce requires shipping individual products directly to consumers. This may result in minor changes to manufacturing processes and major changes in shipping and storage practices. An extreme example can be found in Izumiya Co. Ltd. of Japan. Izumiya, a retail chain offering food, clothing, books, furniture, and housewares, provides an amazing service (see Figure 8.27). If you're in Hakone, Japan, and you realize that you don't have enough sushi to accommodate your dinner guests, you can log on to *www.izumiya.co.jp* and order sushi or any other item in Izumiya's inventory to be on your doorstep within an hour. Such a service requires significant support from inventory management systems, storage facilities, distribution networks, and support staff. To handle online orders, an entirely new system is often needed, one that works in harmony with the existing system that services in-store customers.

Hardware and Networking

Web-based e-commerce requires enough computing power and network bandwidth to support the Web traffic your site generates. Underestimating the amount of Web traffic leads to network stalls and long wait times that leave visitors frustrated. A typical e-commerce Web site employs one or more server computers and a high-speed Internet connection. Businesses that choose to outsource to a Web hosting company are typically guaranteed operation 24 hours a day, 7 days a week, accommodating a specific number or volume of users. Such hosting companies typically

FIGURE 8.27 • B2C e-commerce

Trends in e-commerce extend around the world. Izumiya provides Web-based one-hour grocery delivery service to residents' doorsteps in Japan.

use *load balancing* among servers so that if one goes down, the others pick up the slack. They also have backup power sources, such as an uninterruptible power supply backed up by a diesel generator, to keep the system up and running in case of power failure.

Software

Several categories of software are associated with e-commerce, from the low-level software that controls the functioning of the Web server to high-level software used to design Web pages and graphics. To succeed at e-commerce, you need to understand Web server software and utility programs, e-commerce software, Web site design tools, graphics applications, and Web site development tools.

Web Server Software. The primary purpose of *Web server software* is to fulfill requests for Web pages from browsers. For e-commerce applications, Web servers also provide security by encrypting sensitive transaction data such as credit card information. Web servers work with custom-designed programs and databases to provide e-commerce functionality. The two most popular Web server applications are Apache, which owns 47 percent of market share, and Microsoft Internet Information Services (IIS), which owns 25 percent.[12] Other Web server platforms include qq.com, Google, nginx, and Sun.

Web Server Utility Programs. *Web server utility programs,* sometimes called *Web analytics*, provide statistical information about server usage and Web site traffic patterns (see Figure 8.28). This information can be used to gauge the success of a Web site, its products, and its services, and to build profiles of individual Web site visitors based on their usage of the Web site.

FIGURE 8.28 • Web analytics from Google

Google Analytics provides useful information about Web page visitors such as traffic over time, site usage, vistor location, traffic sources, and browsers.

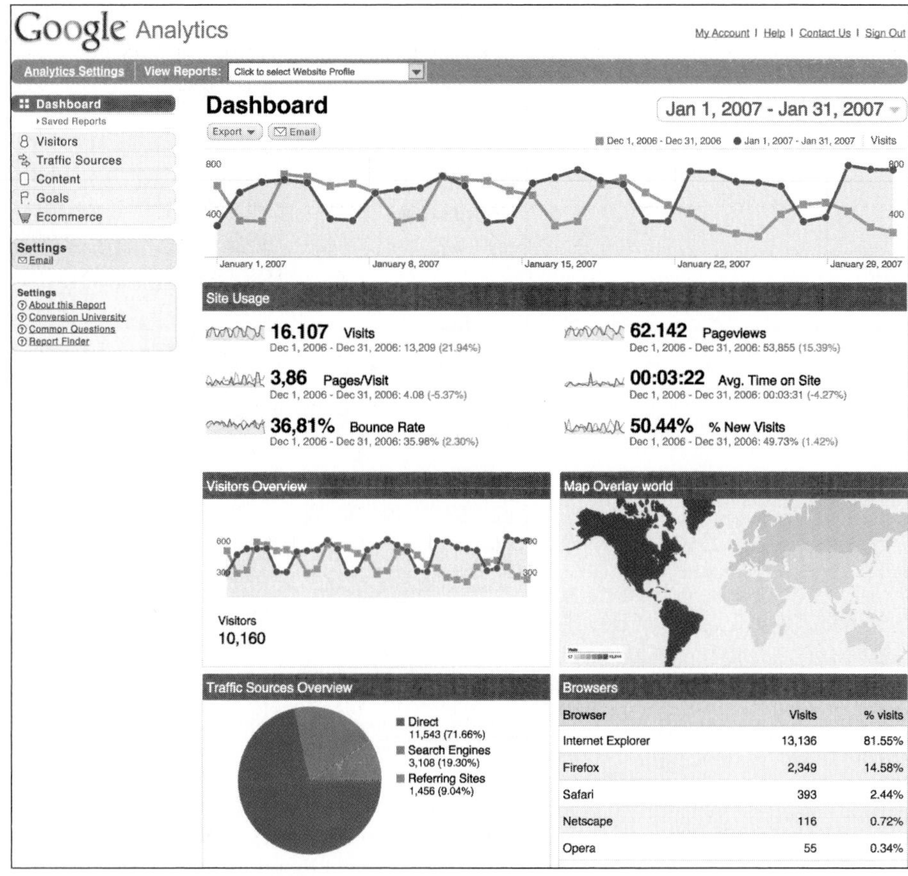

E-Commerce Software. *E-commerce software* is designed specifically to support e-commerce activities. It includes the following:

- Catalog management software: Used for organizing a product line into a convenient format for Web navigation
- Electronic shopping cart software: Allows visitors to collect items to purchase
- Payment software: Facilitates payment for the selected merchandise and arranges shipping

Web Site Design Tools. Web site design tools are typically what-you-see-is-what-you-get (WYSIWYG) applications or wizards that make it simple to graphically lay out a Web page design. Popular Web design software includes Adobe Dreamweaver and Mozilla Nvu. It is highly desirable for a Web site to have a consistent look and feel. Typically, design tools allow you to develop a standard template to be used in creating all Web site pages within a site.

Graphics Applications. Graphics applications are particularly important in Web site design. Graphics applications, such as Adobe Photoshop, Illustrator, and Fireworks, allow the Web developer to design and create the graphic elements that give a Web site its style and overall appearance. Menus, menu buttons, corporate logos, backgrounds, and other graphic elements combine to give a Web site a professional look. Businesses are wise to hire professional Web graphic designers to come up with the initial design of a Web site.

Web Site Development Tools. Web site development tools include *application programming interfaces (APIs)* that allow software engineers to develop Web-driven programs. Using programming languages such as Java, Ajax, PHP, or Perl, software engineers develop applications that allow Web pages to be custom created and delivered as users call up a URL. *Dynamic Web pages* are assembled as they are requested, often pulling custom data from database servers.

Building Traffic

The expression "If you build it, they will come" does not hold true in e-commerce. A new e-commerce Web site is just one among billions of Web sites and will remain undiscovered unless brought to the attention of the online community. Once a Web site gains attention, it must provide content that keeps users coming back, because a stagnant Web site will quickly lose visitors. E-commerce companies use several approaches to build traffic to their Web sites. These include the 3Cs approach, keywords and search engines, partnerships, and marketing to build Web site traffic.

The 3Cs Approach. Many B2C e-commerce businesses use the *3Cs approach* for capturing the interest of the online community: Content, Community, and Commerce. The underlying assumption of this approach is that people prefer Web sites that offer free and useful information and services over those that offer only a sales pitch. A 3Cs Web site provides useful content to the public. For example, a Web site sponsored by a health food company might offer valuable suggestions for good health, references on medical research, and a calculator that allows visitors to calculate daily caloric needs. The Web site might be updated weekly to encourage return visits. As the Web site builds traffic, an online, health-minded community is formed. This community can be nurtured by providing a free membership option. Members provide you with information to receive e-mail news bulletins and gain access to other special members-only privileges. Web 2.0 features are being used by many businesses to build community on their e-commerce sites. Finally, in addition to the content and community being provided, the sponsor can offer its visitors a catalog of products to assist them in meeting their health objectives. The General Nutrition Center Web site (*www.gnc.com*) in Figure 8.29 provides a good example of the 3Cs approach and other traffic-building tactics.

Keywords and Search Engines. People discover many Web sites by using search engines. There are steps that business owners can take to better ensure that their company's Web site appears in search results. First, a business should choose its name and its product names in a manner that best describes its purpose and features. A hair salon with the name Quality Hair Stylings would be recognized by a search engine for what it is much more easily than one with the name Haute Headz.

Second, a business should select a descriptive domain name; if possible, it should be a name that is the same or similar to the business name—*www.qualityhairstylings.com*. Domain names can be acquired from one of the accredited registrars listed at *www.icann.org/registrars/accredited-list.html*.

Third, business-related keywords can be listed in the HTML code of a Web page in a meta tag. *Meta tags* are read by search engines and Web servers, but are not displayed on the page by a Web browser. Here is the meta tag from *www.hersheys.com* (see it yourself by visiting the site and choosing View Source from your browser menus):

```
<meta name="keywords" content="HERSHEY'S, chocolate, candy
bars, gum, mints, gifts, promotions, products, recipes,
KISSES, REESE'S, ICE BREAKERS"/>
```

FIGURE 8.29 • GNC: Building Web site traffic

Consider portions of the GNC Web page that utilize the 3Cs approach to traffic-building.

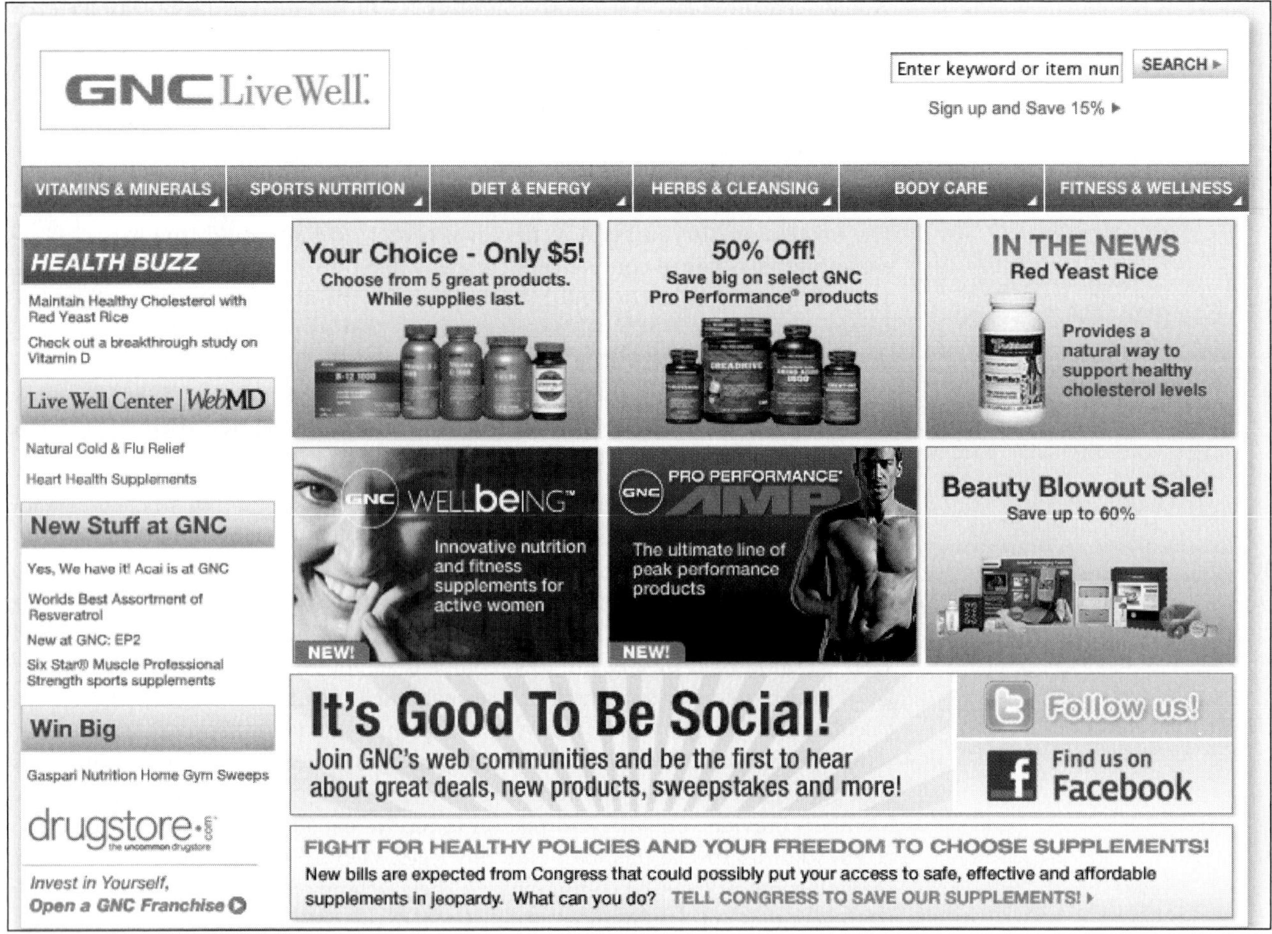

Some search engines rely on meta tags to define the important keywords on the Web page. Web page URLs are stored in the search engine database according to the terms listed in the meta tag. Searches run on keywords such as *Kisses* or any of the other keywords listed in the hersheys.com meta tag would return the Hershey URL.

Most search engines use a combination of techniques and information, which include the title tag and meta tags, to classify Web sites, as discussed in Chapter 4. To ensure that your site is listed in a search engine or directory, you can use a link at the site that allows you to submit your URL. For example, you can use *http://google.com/addurl/* to get your Web site noticed by Google. Also, if other Web sites have links to your site, you are more likely to rank higher in search results.

Getting noticed by search engines has become a full-time job for some professionals. The specialized skill is referred to as *search engine optimization (SEO)*, and many corporations hire IT staff members or consultants to work in this area.

Marketing. If a business is unable to generate traffic to its Web site using free methods, such as search engines and partnerships, it often invests in advertising. Marketing companies can be hired to advertise a Web site online using banner ads, pop-up ads, and e-mail. Search engines such as Google and Yahoo! offer paid advertising services (described earlier) that make your Web site more likely to be noticed than the hundreds of other links that are displayed as the result of a search. Web sites are also advertised offline using traditional advertising media such as magazines, newspapers, radio, and television.

Electronic Payment Systems

In most e-commerce transactions, the customer typically pays with either a credit card number (B2C) or a merchant account number (B2B). Using a secure encrypted connection, the buyer enters the account information in a Web form and submits it. The merchant's Web server passes the information along to the payment processing system, which checks the validity of the account number and balance on the account. If the credit card checks out, the transaction is processed (see Figure 8.30). The only difference between online credit card processing and in-store processing is that laws require online retailers to wait until they ship the product to deduct funds from the credit card account. Because of this, e-tailers put a hold on the funds until the product is shipped, at which time the funds are transferred.

FIGURE 8.30 • Online credit card transaction

Online vendors use payment processing systems to check credit and arrange for the transfer of funds.

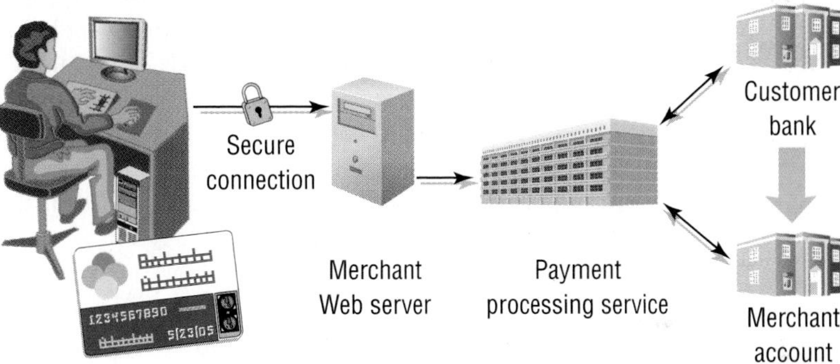

For individuals who do not have a credit card or do not wish to provide their credit card information to merchants online, or in the case of C2C, where the seller does not have the ability to process credit card transactions, there is electronic cash. **Electronic cash** or **e-cash** is a Web service that provides a private and secure method of transferring funds from a bank account or credit card to online vendors or individuals. PayPal is the best-known e-cash provider. Owned by eBay, PayPal allows members (membership is free) to transfer funds into their PayPal account from a bank account or credit card (see Figure 8.31). You can use the funds in your PayPal account for purchases from online vendors or purchases made on eBay. You can also e-mail PayPal e-cash to individuals. Google has an e-cash system called Google Checkout. Google Checkout is somewhat simpler to use than PayPal, but has fewer options. For example, Google Checkout supports payments only from credit or debit cards and not directly from a bank account.

INSTANT CASH

Forgot someone's birthday? Want to send cash? Now you won't have to wait the extra couple of days for a check to arrive in the mail. CashEdge has developed a new application called "Pay Other People" money, or POPmoney, that allows people to send cash through e-mail or text messaging. You can electronically transfer money simply by texting the recipient's phone number, e-mail address, or account number to your bank through POPmoney.

Dad, Can You Text Me $200?
Jonnelle Marte
The Wall Street Journal
June 23, 2009
http://www.cashedge.com/news-events-news-20090623.php

FIGURE 8.31 • Payment options

E-commerce systems provide many secure options for payment, sometimes including e-cash systems like PayPal and Google Checkout.

An e-cash system has two fundamental benefits:

- It protects privacy by hiding your account information from vendors; the e-cash provider is the only one that knows this information.
- It provides a method for making e-commerce transactions in circumstances where the seller cannot process a credit card or the buyer does not own a credit card.

Although many large online vendors do not support PayPal, there are indications that the service is gaining more widespread acceptance. Bango, a mobile content provider, contracted with PayPal to support purchases from mobile phones. Users can pay for games, ringtones, videos, and wallpaper using their PayPal accounts.

Several software vendors have created electronic wallet applications to make online transactions more convenient. An *electronic wallet*, or *e-wallet*, is an application that encrypts and stores your credit card information, e-cash information, bank account information, name, address—essentially, all the personal information required for e-commerce transactions—securely on your computer. The convenience provided by e-wallets is significant; rather than having to fill out forms for each online purchase, you simply click a button that withdraws the funds from your e-wallet. However, in the several years that e-wallet applications have been available, there has been no agreed-upon standard for the technology, so online merchants have been unwilling to support it.

Smart cards are credit cards or ID cards with embedded microchips that can store and process data. Smart cards can be used as electronic wallets, storing account information and balances and calculating new balances after being used for purchases. Smart cards are used in MasterCard's PayPass service, Visa's payWave service, and the ExpressPay service of American Express to enable contactless payments. Simply wave your smart card near the reader to make a payment.

International Markets

Taking a business online automatically turns your business into a global enterprise. Internet users of all nationalities will have access to your products and may wish to purchase them. Business owners need to determine if and how to market their products in the global market. Recent trends have indicated that business outside the United States can be lucrative. For example, Amazon.com's international sales are greater than its U.S. sales.

The first consideration of a global e-commerce strategy is to make sure that visitors of all nationalities and cultures feel at home and comfortable while viewing your Web content. Although English is widely spoken and understood around the world, and some browsers are even able to translate Web page content to different languages, local references and colloquialisms may confuse and alienate international visitors.

A more costly approach is to create multiple versions of your Web site, each in a different language and catering to a different cultural bias (see Figure 8.32). Lands' End, for example, has launched separate Web sites in the United Kingdom, Japan, and Germany. This process, called *localization*, requires hiring international Web developers to assist with translation and cultural issues. Each time the Web site is updated, this may require editing all of the associated international Web sites.

Localization can be applied to smaller areas such as a region, city, or zip code. Consider the various versions of The Weather Channel and its associated Web site that are created to focus on different areas of the United States as well as different countries in the world.

Once an international market is courted and won over, the e-tailer must be able to carry out transactions in foreign currency, including pricing items properly, applying the correct national taxes, and accommodating the possibly complex

FIGURE 8.32 • Localization

Some e-businesses create multiple versions of their Web site, each in a different language and catering to a different cultural bias.

issues of international shipping. E-commerce hosting companies can assist with some of the transaction details. Shipping companies also assist e-businesses with the complications of international shipping. FedEx, for example, provides a free service called FedEx Global Trade Manager. The application helps shippers understand global trade regulations and prepare the appropriate import or export forms based on the commodity being shipped and the countries of origin and destination.

E-Commerce Security Issues

Figure 8.33 displays a typical Web form used to submit bank account information to PayPal. Would you feel comfortable filling out and submitting this form? If you were to submit this form, would it be possible for a hacker to intercept your account information on its way to PayPal? Are you certain that the Web server is really owned and protected by PayPal? How can PayPal tell that the account information you are providing is really yours? There are significant and legitimate concerns regarding e-commerce privacy and security. Security concerns arise from the dangers of carrying out electronic funds transfers over a public network without buyer and seller identity verification. In addition, e-businesses are vulnerable to hacker attacks that can put them temporarily or permanently out of business. Identity verification, securing data in transit, and business resumption planning are discussed next.

Identity Verification. Because e-commerce transactions occur electronically, and at times automatically, it is important that the identities of the two or more participants in a transaction are positively verified. Consumers need to make sure that they are giving their credit card number to a legitimate and trustworthy business, and businesses need to confirm that the customer is the owner of the credit card being used. Transaction data must be accessed only by intended

FIGURE 8.33 • Web form for submitting bank account information

Is it safe to provide your bank information using this form?

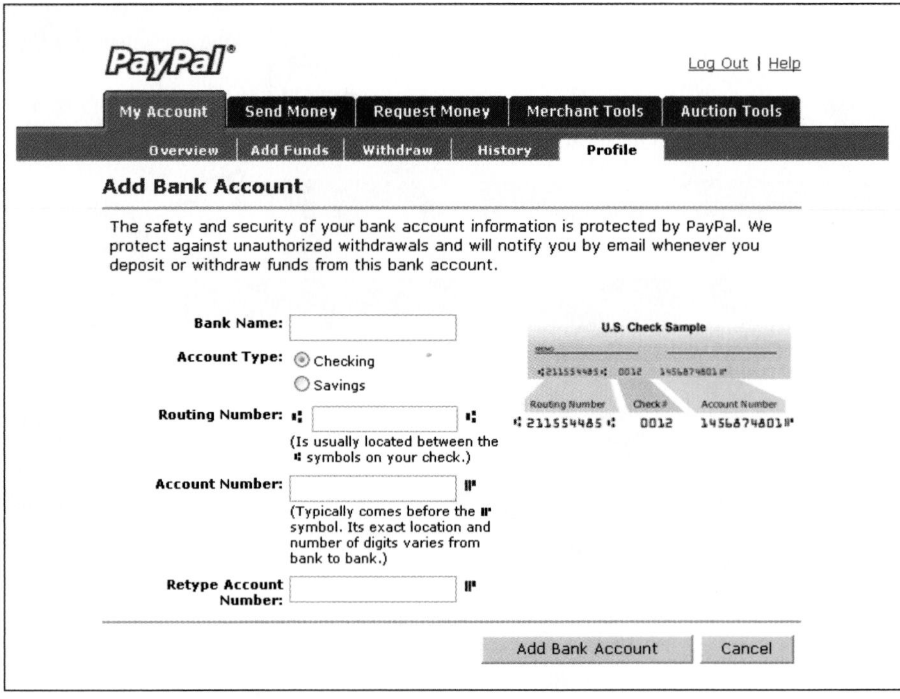

PayPal®

Log Out | Help

My Account | Send Money | Request Money | Merchant Tools | Auction Tools

Overview | Add Funds | Withdraw | History | Profile

Add Bank Account

The safety and security of your bank account information is protected by PayPal. We protect against unauthorized withdrawals and will notify you by email whenever you deposit or withdraw funds from this bank account.

Bank Name:

Account Type: Checking / Savings

Routing Number: (Is usually located between the ⑆ symbols on your check.)

Account Number: (Typically comes before the ⑈ symbol. Its exact location and number of digits varies from bank to bank.)

Retype Account Number:

U.S. Check Sample

Routing Number ⑆ 211554485 ⑆ | Check # 0012 | Account Number 1456874801⑈

Add Bank Account | Cancel

parties, and must not be intercepted by outsiders. A variety of technologies are available to assist individuals and businesses in meeting these goals, including digital certificates and encryption.

A **digital certificate** is a type of electronic business card that is attached to Internet transaction data to verify the sender of the data. Digital certificates are provided by *certification authorities* such as VeriSign (*www.verisign.com*) and Thawte (*www.thawte.com*). They can be used to verify the sender of e-mail and other forms of Internet communication. Digital certificates for use in encrypting Web communications and credit card transactions cost the provider between $350 and $1400, depending on the level of security and type of communications. Certificates cost more for e-commerce than for nonbusiness use. Digital certificates for personal e-mail are provided by Thawte for free.

A digital certificate contains the owner's name, a serial number, an expiration date, and a public key. The public key is used in encrypting messages and digital certificates. **Encryption** uses high-level mathematical functions and computer algorithms to encode data so that it is unintelligible to all but the intended recipient. Through the use of a public key (a large number) and a private key (kept by the certification authority), an encrypted message can be decrypted back into its original state.

Securing Data in Transit. Digital certificates combined with *Secure Sockets Layer* (*SSL*) and a more recent version of SSL

MORE THAN TOKEN SECURITY

You're used to looking for that little padlock at the bottom of a Web page—showing the Web page has SSL and TSL encryption. That means your financial data is safe, right? Not necessarily. Increasingly, data is stolen not during the transaction, but after it. But now tokenization can keep prying eyes away. This encryption technology converts your 16-digit credit card number into a token so that the token, and not your card number, is passed along as your order is processed in the vendor's computer system.

Keeping Credit Card Numbers Well-Cloaked: Q&A with Fingerhut's Mark Lieberg
Renay San Miguel
E-Commerce Times
June 11, 2009
http://www.ecommercetimes.com/story/67302.html

called *Transport Layer Security* (*TLS*) technologies allow for encrypted communications to occur between Web browser and Web server (see Figure 8.34). This combination of technology is what is used to secure usernames, passwords, and credit card information when they are typed into a Web form and sent to a Web server. The presence of an SSL connection is usually indicated by a URL that uses *https://* rather than *http://*. Also, a closed lock icon appears in the address bar or at the bottom of the browser window when the connection is secure. You can click the icon to view the digital certificate. The many threats to e-commerce are further discussed in Chapter 11.

FIGURE 8.34 • Secure Sockets Layer (SSL)

SSL encrypts data sent over the Web and verifies the identity of the Web server.

Business Continuity Planning. Transaction processing systems, especially order processing systems, are so important to a business that great pains are taken to ensure that they stay up and running. Web businesses are particularly vulnerable because every minute that the Web site is out of commission could mean losses of thousands of dollars. **Business continuity planning (BCP)** guards against every conceivable disaster that could negatively impact the system and provides courses of action to minimize their effects. Through the use of backup power systems, backup computer systems, and security software, BCP takes into account natural disasters such as flood, fire, and earthquake, and man-made disasters such as employee strikes and accidental or intentional sabotage. The goal of business continuity planning is to protect data and keep key systems operational until order is resumed. Business continuity planning was discussed in the previous chapter on databases. It is an important aspect of all electronic business systems.

ACTION PLAN

Remember Alejandro from the beginning of the chapter? He wants to add an online presence to his family's business. Here are answers to his questions.

1. **What will it take to put the Forrero family business online?**

   The Forreros need to make changes in infrastructure to support direct sales to consumers in addition to bulk sales to retailers. This will most likely require additional personnel. After he graduates, Alejandro can act as the director of e-commerce operations and can implement needed changes in the manufacturing, storage, and shipment procedures.

   The Forreros can outsource the setup and maintenance of the Web site to an e-commerce hosting company at a cost of under $100 per month. They may need to contract with a graphic artist and Web designer to design a Web site that has a professional appearance. The Forreros may also wish to invest in advertisements for their new Web site.

2. **What benefits might the Forrero family enjoy from an online presence? Do these benefits outweigh the costs?**

   By taking their business online, the Forreros will acquire greatly increased international exposure for their business. Online sales will represent a new source of revenue, and these sales can be used to fund their overall e-commerce investment. The Forrero Web site will increase the Forrero brand-name recognition, improving sales in retail gift shops on which the business depends. Although these benefits seem significant, it will take time to build traffic to the Web site and reap the associated rewards. If the Forreros take it slowly, investing minimally at first and reinvesting the revenues into the system, an e-commerce venture should pay off.

3. **Besides taking the business online, in what other ways might e-commerce assist the Forrero family business?**

   The Forreros can streamline transactions and save time and money by using the e-commerce systems of their suppliers, and by implementing an e-commerce system with their retail buyers. Retailers will appreciate efforts to streamline the ordering process, giving Forrero a competitive advantage.

Summary

LEARNING OBJECTIVE 1

Define e-commerce, and understand its role as a transaction processing system.

E-commerce refers to systems that support electronically executed transactions over the Internet, Web, or a private network. Prior to the Internet, e-commerce took place using electronic data interchange (EDI) over private value-added networks (VANs). Today e-commerce takes place mostly over the Internet and Web. E-commerce is a form of transaction processing system. A transaction processing system (TPS) supports and records transactions and is at the heart of most businesses. All transaction processing systems share a common set of

Figure 8.4—p. 437

activities called the transaction processing cycle. This includes data collection, data editing, data correction, data manipulation, data storage, and document and report production. There are different TPSs for different needs. An order processing system supports the sales of goods or services to customers and arranges for shipment of products. A purchasing system supports the purchasing of goods and raw materials from suppliers for the manufacturing of products.

LEARNING OBJECTIVE 2

List the three types of e-commerce, and explain how e-commerce supports the stages of the buying process and methods of marketing and selling.

The three main types of e-commerce are business-to-consumer (B2C), business-to-business (B2B), and consumer-to-consumer (C2C). B2C, sometimes called e-tailing, involves retailers selling products to consumers. B2B services often take place privately between manufacturers and suppliers. C2C Web sites allow consumers to sell items and trade items with each other. Of these three types of e-commerce, B2B involves the greatest number of business transactions.

Figure 8.9—p. 442

E-commerce supports the six stages of buying a product: (1) realizing a need, (2) researching a product, (3) selecting a vendor, (4) providing payment, (5) accepting delivery of the product, and (6) taking advantage of product support. It also supports the seller's efforts to facilitate these stages. The seller's considerations are sometimes referred to as supply chain management, which involves three areas of focus: demand planning, supply planning, and demand fulfillment.

LEARNING OBJECTIVE 3

Discuss several examples of e-commerce applications and services.

Retail Web sites allow consumers to comparison shop to find the best deals. Wholesale Web sites provide a way for suppliers to do business with manufacturers and retailers. Clearinghouses provide good deals to consumers on overstocked or outdated items and assist businesses in clearing their inventory. Web auctions sell merchandise to the highest bidders, and online marketplaces provide a method for consumers to sell their own possessions.

Figure 8.13—p. 446

Manufacturers join together in global supply management services and industry-specific electronic exchanges to more easily connect with suppliers. E-commerce has made market research much easier and less intrusive, but somewhat worrisome to privacy advocates. E-commerce brings convenience to banking and investing by allowing people to monitor their finances and make investments online.

LEARNING OBJECTIVE 4

Define m-commerce, and describe several types of m-commerce services.

Mobile commerce, or m-commerce, is a form of e-commerce that takes place over wireless mobile devices such as smart phones. M-commerce uses a mobile device's Internet capabilities for commerce. Through text messaging, Web applications, and short-range wireless networking, smart phones can access m-commerce services. M-commerce developers use special protocols and languages such as the Wireless Application Protocol (WAP) and Wireless Markup Language (WML) to create m-commerce applications that can run on smart phones and other small handheld displays.

Figure 8.24—p. 460

Four methods are currently being pursued for m-commerce service delivery. The first takes advantage of the connection between cell phone and cell phone service provider. The second utilizes the cell phone's ability to run applications and access the Internet and Web services. The third uses a cell phone's Short Message Service (SMS) text messaging and Multimedia Messaging Service (MMS). The last uses short-range wireless technology, such as Near Field Communications (NFC), and a portable device's ability to use it to communicate with other devices such as cash registers.

LEARNING OBJECTIVE 5

List the components of an e-commerce system, and explain how they function together to provide e-commerce services.

E-commerce requires investment in networking, hardware, and a wide variety of software. It requires changes in infrastructure and can include hiring of specialists such as system administrators, Web designers, and graphic artists. Many firms decide to outsource their e-commerce operations to e-commerce hosting businesses.

Hardware and networking services for e-commerce must be robust and trustworthy so that service is never interrupted. Software required for e-commerce includes Web server software to deliver Web pages and services; Web server utilities to provide statistical information about Web traffic; e-commerce software to provide a merchandise catalog, shopping cart, and checkout services; and the software used to design Web pages, graphics, and Web applications.

Businesses use a variety of techniques to build traffic to a Web site. Providing interesting content, building community, and providing commerce (the 3Cs) is one technique. Choosing appropriate names for a business, products, and domain helps search engines recognize a Web site for what it is. Keywords can be included in a Web page's meta tags, which are visible to search engines but not to people viewing the Web page. E-tailers can also profit from forming alliances with others on the Web and promoting each other's Web sites.

E-commerce electronic payment systems typically handle credit card transactions. E-cash supports financial transactions over the Web without the need for credit cards; an electronic wallet stores transaction information in an encrypted file on your PC. Smart cards store financial information in a microprocessor embedded in a credit card and provide a more secure and convenient method of carrying out e-commerce transactions.

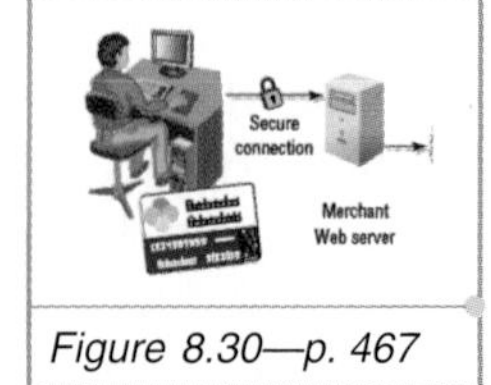

Figure 8.30—p. 467

E-commerce sites that participate in the global market must provide Web sites that cater to the needs of various cultures. Consumers and e-tailers should be aware of security issues associated with e-commerce, including identity verification and methods of securing transaction data transmitted over the Internet. Business continuity planning takes into account every conceivable disaster that could have a negative impact on the system and provides courses of action to minimize their effects.

Test Yourself

LEARNING OBJECTIVE 1: Define e-commerce, and understand its role as a transaction processing system.

1. ________________ refers to systems that support electronically executed transactions over the Internet, Web, or a private network.

2. Prior to the Internet, electronic transactions between businesses were often carried out using ________________ over a value-added network.
   a. an order processing system
   b. electronic data interchange (EDI)
   c. business resumption planning
   d. source data automation

3. True or False: An airline's flight reservation system is likely to use the batch processing method of transaction processing.

4. The transaction processing cycle includes all of the following except ________________ .
   a. data collection
   b. data storage
   c. data transaction
   d. data manipulation

LEARNING OBJECTIVE 2: List the three types of e-commerce, and explain how e-commerce supports the stages of the buying process and methods of marketing and selling.

5. ________________ has the highest dollar amount of transactions of all the types of e-commerce.
   a. B2C
   b. B2B
   c. C2C
   d. C2B

6. True or False: Retail e-commerce transactions make up more than 10 percent of all transactions in the United States.

7. If you were to sell your textbook to someone on Amazon.com, you would be utilizing a type of e-commerce called ________________ .

LEARNING OBJECTIVE 3: Discuss several examples of e-commerce applications and services.

8. A(n) ________________ is a Web site that allows visitors to browse through a wide variety of products from varying e-tailers.

9. An industry-specific Web resource created to provide a convenient centralized platform for B2B e-commerce between manufacturers, suppliers, and customers is called a(n) ________________ .
   a. Web portal
   b. Web auction
   c. electronic exchange
   d. online marketplace

10. True or False: E-commerce supports a more detailed level of market segmentation than traditional market research.

LEARNING OBJECTIVE 4: Define m-commerce, and describe several types of m-commerce services.

11. ________________ is a form of e-commerce that takes place over wireless mobile devices such as smart phones.

12. A(n) ________________ payment system uses Near Field Communications or infrared to beam credit card information from a cell phone.
    a. e-wallet
    b. e-cash
    c. proximity
    d. smart card

13. What new type of m-commerce product did the iPhone make popular?
    a. mobile applications
    b. music
    c. wallpaper
    d. online news reports

LEARNING OBJECTIVE 5: List the components of an e-commerce system, and explain how they function together to provide e-commerce services.

14. A(n) ________________ is a company that takes on some or all of the responsibility of setting up and maintaining an e-commerce system for a business or organization.

15. E-commerce Web sites use ________________ to attract customers.
    a. smart cards
    b. electronic exchanges
    c. Web-driven programs
    d. the 3C approach

16. True or False: E-cash is most useful for C2C e-commerce.

17. ________________ provides an encrypted connection between Web client and server for secure data transfer.

Test Yourself Solutions 1. E-commerce, 2. b. EDI, 3. False, 4. c. data transaction, 5. b. B2B, 6. False, 7. C2C, 8. cybermall, 9. c. electronic exchange, 10. True, 11. m-commerce, 12. c. proximity, 13. a. mobile applications, 14. e-commerce host, 15. d. the 3C approach, 16. True, 17. HTTPS or SSL (Secure Sockets Layer) or TLS (Transport Layer Security).

Key Terms

Key Term	Page	Definition
business continuity planning (BCP)	471	Reviewing every conceivable disaster that could impact a transaction processing system, and providing courses of action to minimize the effects of such events
business-to-business e-commerce (B2B)	440	The type of e-commerce that supports transactions between businesses across private networks, the Internet, and the Web
business-to-consumer e-commerce (B2C)	439	The type of e-commerce that makes use of the Web to connect individual consumers directly with sellers to purchase products
consumer-to-consumer e-commerce (C2C)	441	The type of e-commerce that uses the Web to connect individuals who wish to sell their personal belongings with people shopping for used items
digital certificate	470	A type of electronic business card that is attached to Internet transaction data to verify the sender of the data
e-commerce (electronic commerce)	434	Systems that support electronically executed business transactions
e-commerce host	461	A company that takes on some or all of the responsibility of setting up and maintaining an e-commerce system for a business or organization
electronic cash (e-cash)	467	Web service that provides a private and secure method of transferring funds from a bank account or credit card to online vendors or individuals
electronic data interchange (EDI)	436	Networking technology that uses private communications networks called value-added networks (VANs) to transmit standardized transaction data between business partners and suppliers
encryption	470	A security technology that uses high-level mathematical functions and computer algorithms to encode data so that it is unintelligible to all but the intended recipient
m-commerce (mobile commerce)	458	A form of e-commerce that takes place over wireless mobile devices such as handheld computers and cell phones as well as emerging technologies such as dashtop computers embedded in automobile dashboards
smart cards	468	Credit cards or ID cards with embedded microchips that can store and process data; can be used as electronic wallets, storing account information and balances and calculating new balances after being used for purchases

Questions

Review Questions

1. When did e-commerce originate?
2. What is the purpose of EDI?
3. What types of transactions benefit from batch processing?
4. What types of transactions benefit from online processing?
5. What are the two primary categories of TPS?
6. List the steps of the transaction processing cycle.
7. What takes place in the data editing stage of the transaction processing cycle?
8. List three examples of TPS online and in stores.
9. What is the difference between e-commerce and m-commerce?
10. Name the three types of e-commerce, and provide examples of each.
11. What are the six stages of buying?
12. What are the three areas of supply chain management?
13. What device is closely associated with m-commerce? What next-generation features of this device are used in m-commerce?
14. List five methods of selling items on the Web.

15. What are the three methods of providing m-commerce services?
16. What is a problematic application of m-commerce?
17. List the types of software associated with implementing e-commerce.
18. What is a primary hardware and network concern of an e-commerce vendor?
19. List four methods of building traffic to a Web site.
20. List two benefits and one drawback of e-cash.
21. How does SSL make shopping on the Web more secure?
22. What are the goals of business resumption planning?

Discussion Questions

23. Describe benefits that e-commerce provides for buyers and sellers.
24. Describe challenges that e-commerce faces.
25. List five types of e-commerce applications, and provide examples of each.
26. What are the benefits for both suppliers and manufacturers of joining an electronic exchange?
27. What are the pros and cons of online marketing?
28. How can e-commerce affect the infrastructure of an organization?
29. What are the security risks for buyers who participate in e-commerce?
30. What are the security risks for sellers who participate in e-commerce?

Exercises

Try It Yourself

1. Write a proposal for a new e-commerce Web site to sell a product or service of your choosing.
   a. Select a business name that is creative and descriptive.
   b. Use *www.enameco.com* (or any of the accredited registrars at *www.icann.org/en/registrars/accredited-list.html*) to find an available domain name for your Web site that is logical and descriptive.
   c. Describe the product you intend to sell and why you think that it will sell well on the Web.
   d. Describe the type of content (one of the 3Cs) that you will provide to visitors to keep them coming back to your Web site.
   e. Describe what tools you will make available to build community (another of the 3Cs).
   f. List other types of online businesses that sell complementary products and would make good partners for your business.
   g. List 12 keywords that you would want search engines to associate with your product Web site.
2. Surf the Web to find two Web sites (other than *www.gnc.com*) that follow the 3Cs approach to Web development. Use a word-processing program to describe what elements of each Web site contribute to content, community, and commerce. Provide your opinion on which Web site does a better job of making you want to visit again, and why.
3. Use a paint program to design a logo and Web page template for an imaginary e-commerce Web site. Include a Web site menu for navigation around the Web site.
4. Search the Web on the keywords *contactless payment*. Write a description of contactless payment systems available today, and the benefits and drawbacks of using such systems.
5. Consider an electronics device that you might like to purchase over the next year (for example, a smart phone, digital camera, MP3 player, and so on). Use *www.mysimon.com* to learn more about the product and determine your preferred vendor. Write a couple of paragraphs explaining your logic for choosing the device and vendor. Include the features of the particular product that you found attractive and why, out of all the vendors selling this product, you decided on the one you did.
6. Consider an electronics device that you might like to purchase over the next year (for example, a smart phone, digital camera, MP3 player, and so on). Use *www.ubid.com* and *www.ebay.com* to shop for the item. After finding a good deal, search for the same item (using manufacturer and product name along with model number) on

the Web using a standard search engine or *www.mysimon.com*. Were you able to find the same item? If so, was the deal you found at eBay or uBid as good as you originally thought? Write a summary of your findings.

Virtual Classroom Activities

For the following exercises, do not use face-to-face or telephone communications with your group members. Use only Internet communications.

7. Each group member should select an object that he or she is interested in shopping for online. Be very specific in regard to the item's specifications (for example, a 10-megapixel digital camera, a pair of black leather moccasins with beads, and so on). Compile everyone's choices into a list and conduct a Web scavenger hunt. The person who finds the most items at the lowest total cost is the winner.
8. List the group members alphabetically and assign member numbers according to the ordering. Each group member should use *www.paypal.com* to e-mail the next group member $1. The last group member should e-mail the first group member. You need to set up a PayPal account and add funds to it from your checking account or credit card prior to sending the e-cash. After collecting each other's dollar, each group member should write a review of the PayPal service. You can delete your account information on PayPal after this experiment if you so desire.
9. Each group member should visit the App Store in iTunes (*www.apple.com/itunes*). Decide on 10 favorite applications. How much is your total bill? Share your lists with your group. Have the group vote on the 10 most valuable applications found between members.
10. Each group member should visit the Web site of his or her favorite "brick-and-mortar" retail store. Write a review of the site, including how the online shopping experience compares to shopping in the brick-and-mortar store. Also include how the Web site makes use of the 3Cs approach to attracting visitors. Collect reviews of all group members and decide which of the sites is the best. Write up the results.

Teamwork

11. Team members should each set out on the Web to find the best monthly price on e-commerce hosting. You can start at *www.cnet.com* and look under Reviews, then Web Hosting, and then E-commerce Hosting. Follow links and view advertised prices and specifications. The service should include e-commerce software (for example, Miva), a merchant account, a payment gateway service, 500 MB of space, a 30 GB data transfer rate, 24-hour technical support, and data backup services.
12. Each team member should share a favorite online place to shop with the group. Compile a list of all Web sites and have all team members explore and rank the list of Web sites in order from best to worst. Each team member should create a document listing the Web sites in order of preference with a paragraph explaining what aspects of the favored Web site sold him or her on the site. Include comments on the 3Cs.

Endnotes

1 Cai, Michael, "Virtual Worlds: And the Children Shall Lead," *Linux Insider*, July 1, 2008, www.linuxinsider.com.

2 Staff, "E-Stats – Measuring the Electronic Economy," *U.S. Census Bureau*, accessed June 20, 2009, www.census.gov/eos/www/ebusiness614.htm.

3 *ibid.*

4 *ibid.*

5 Staff, "eBay Inc: A Short History," eBay Web site, accessed June 20, 2009, http://news.ebay.com/about.cfm.

6 Covisint Web site, accessed June 21, 2009, www.covisint.com/about/alliances.

7 Fried, Ina, "Microsoft quietly offering ad-funded Works," *cnet news*, April 18, 2008, news.cnet.com.

8 Perez, Marin, "Google Tweaks AdWords for Android G1, iPhone," *InformationWeek*, December 9, 2008, www.informationweek.com.

9 Staff, "Obama Ads Invade Video Games," *Fox News*, October 15, 2008, www.foxnews.com.

10 Meisner, Jeff, "Rear-View Mirror: 5 Bold, Brilliant Tech Gambits, Part 1," *Ecommerce Times*, November 24, 2008, www.ecommercetimes.com/story/65257.html.

11 Staff, "June 2009 Web Server Survey," *Netcraft*, http://news.netcraft.com/archives/web_server_survey.html.

Information, Decision Support, and Special-Purpose Systems

Maurice Duchane is entering his senior year at Tulane University, where he will soon complete his Bachelor of Science in Management degree. While Maurice finds his studies interesting, he has an equal enthusiasm for football and works part-time as an assistant on the offensive coaching staff of the Green Wave, Tulane's football team.

Maurice's responsibilities include cataloging game tapes and managing the computer systems that store and deliver strategic information like the offensive plays, statistics on teams and players, and coaches' notes. Needless to say, Maurice has earned a lot of responsibility over the three years he has worked on the staff. The coaches are impressed by Maurice's enthusiasm for the team and his organizational skills, which complement his command of technology.

With training for the new season in full swing, the head coach of the team, Bob Toledo, has been putting pressure on the coaching staff to become more creative with its plays and take better advantage of opponents' weaknesses. The information system on which the coaching staff depends is becoming outdated. Football teams are constantly upgrading and improving their information systems to get the right information to the right coach at the right time to call the perfect play.

Maurice believes that he can help in this regard. After his years of study, he knows information management, and he is more familiar with the team's information system than just about anyone else. He has ideas for improving the team's information system to manage data more efficiently and effectively and to deliver key information to coaches when they need it. He also has ideas for a system that could streamline the process of accessing information—a system that can guess what information a coach needs in a given scenario and provide intelligent suggestions. Maurice hopes that he has earned enough trust and respect that the coaches will give him a shot at trying out his ideas.

As you read through this chapter, consider the following questions:

1. What type of information system could help a football team's coaching staff organize its data and retrieve valuable information quickly and efficiently? How would it work?
2. What type of information system could anticipate the information required in a given scenario and provide intelligent suggestions?
3. What components will Maurice require to build his systems so that they can deliver information in real time during a game?

Check out Maurice's *Action Plan* at the conclusion of this chapter.

9

LEARNING OBJECTIVES

1. Define the stages of decision making and problem solving.
2. Discuss the use of management information systems in providing reports to help solve structured problems.
3. Describe how decision support systems are used to solve nonprogrammed and unstructured problems.
4. Explain how a group decision support system can help people and organizations collaborate on team projects.
5. Discuss the uses of hybrid and special-purpose systems.

CHAPTER CONTENT

Introduction

Decisions lie at the heart of just about everything you do. You can't get through a day without making many decisions—some large, some small. In our careers, some decisions can have great significance and affect many other people. A doctor who makes the right diagnosis and prescribes the right treatment can improve lives and sometimes save them. The decisions made by scientists, engineers, and technicians at NASA have life-or-death consequences for astronauts. Management information and decision support systems can provide a wealth of information to help people make better decisions. Business executives, engineers, environmental specialists, military personnel, music producers, scientists, librarians—people in most careers—can benefit from getting better reports and decision support from computer systems.

Increasingly, people work in small teams. Meetings can be either a big waste of time or a productive tool to accomplish organizational objectives. Group decision support systems can help people work effectively in groups, avoiding the pitfalls of negative group behavior while taking advantage of working in teams. Knowing a little about what these systems can do and how they function can help you use them more effectively.

Although people use computer systems to perform tasks more efficiently and less expensively, the true potential of computer systems is in providing information to help people and organizations make smarter decisions to achieve their goals more quickly. Police and investigators use computer systems to help solve crimes; engineers use computer systems to design better electric circuits and safer buildings and bridges. In business, computer systems help sales representatives target customers with the greatest potential. In this chapter, you explore how computer systems can provide a wealth of information and decision support to individuals and organizations, regardless of their field. To understand how computer systems can provide decision support, you first need a basic understanding of decision making and problem solving.

DECISION MAKING AND PROBLEM SOLVING

One of the highest compliments is to be recognized by your friends and coworkers as a "real problem solver." In general, problem solving is the most critical activity an individual or organization undertakes (see Figure 9.1). It makes the difference between success and failure, profit and loss.

FIGURE 9.1 • Decision making and problem solving

Decision making and problem solving are critical activities for individuals and organizations.

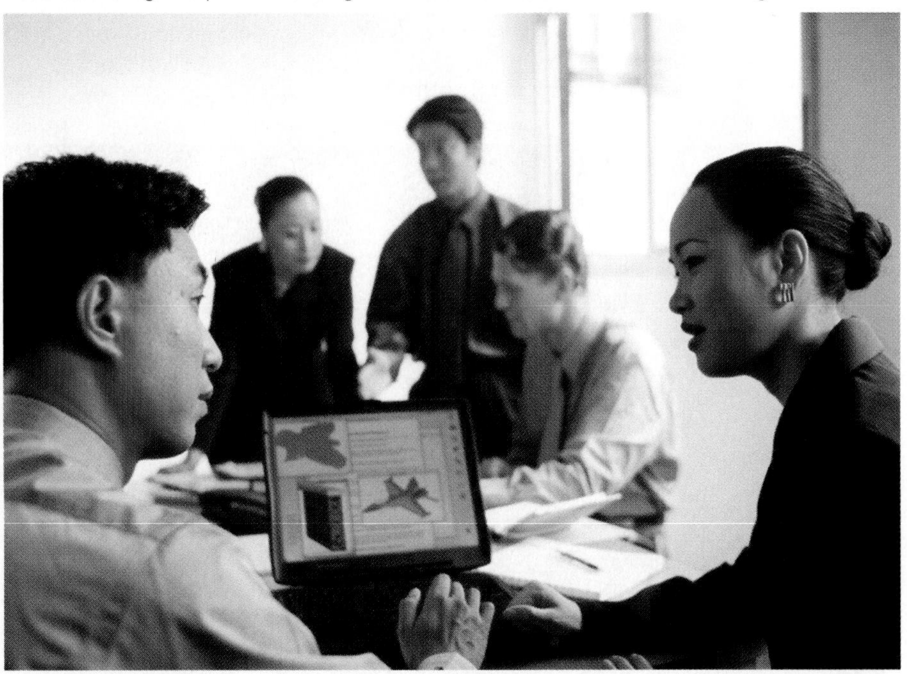

Problem solving begins with decision making. **Decision making** is a process that takes place in three stages: intelligence, design, and choice. **Problem solving** includes and goes beyond decision making to include implementation and monitoring (see Figure 9.2). Here is a brief description of the problem-solving process:

FIGURE 9.2 • The problem-solving process

Decision making is the first part of problem solving.

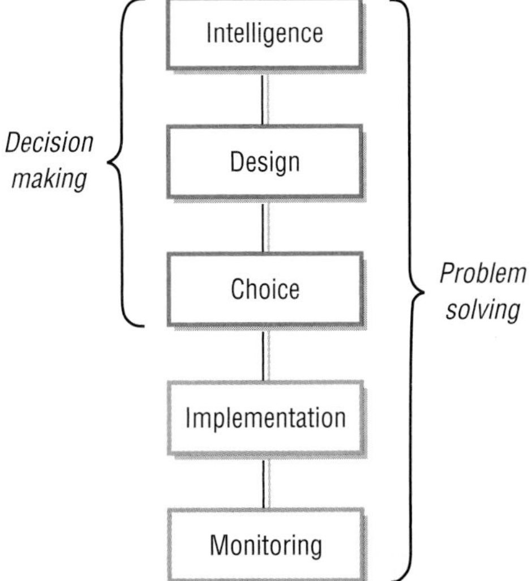

- Intelligence stage: Problems and opportunities are identified and defined. Information on the cause and scope of the problem or opportunity is gathered. The problem or opportunity environment is investigated, and things that might constrain the solution are identified.
- Design stage: Alternative solutions to the problem are developed. In addition, the feasibility and implications of these alternatives are evaluated.
- Choice stage: A course of action is selected.
- Implementation stage: Action is taken to put the solution into effect.
- Monitoring stage: The decision makers evaluate the implementation of the solution to determine whether the anticipated results were achieved and to modify the process in light of new information learned during the implementation stage. The monitoring stage involves a feedback and adjustment process.

Individuals and organizations can use a reactive or a proactive approach to problem solving. With a *reactive problem-solving approach*, the problem solver waits until a problem surfaces or becomes apparent before taking any action. With a *proactive problem-solving approach*, the problem solver seeks out potential problems before they become serious. For example, an FBI agent could predict a future terrorist attack using credible intelligence information, which could save thousands of lives and millions or even billions of dollars in damage (Figure 9.3). Both reactive and proactive problem solvers can turn problems into opportunities, but taking a proactive approach means you can identify opportunities earlier and exploit them faster. In reality, most organizations and individuals use a combination of reactive and proactive problem-solving approaches.

FIGURE 9.3 • Proactive problem solving at the FBI

The FBI collects and analyzes many different types of data to help predict, prepare for, and avoid possible security threats.

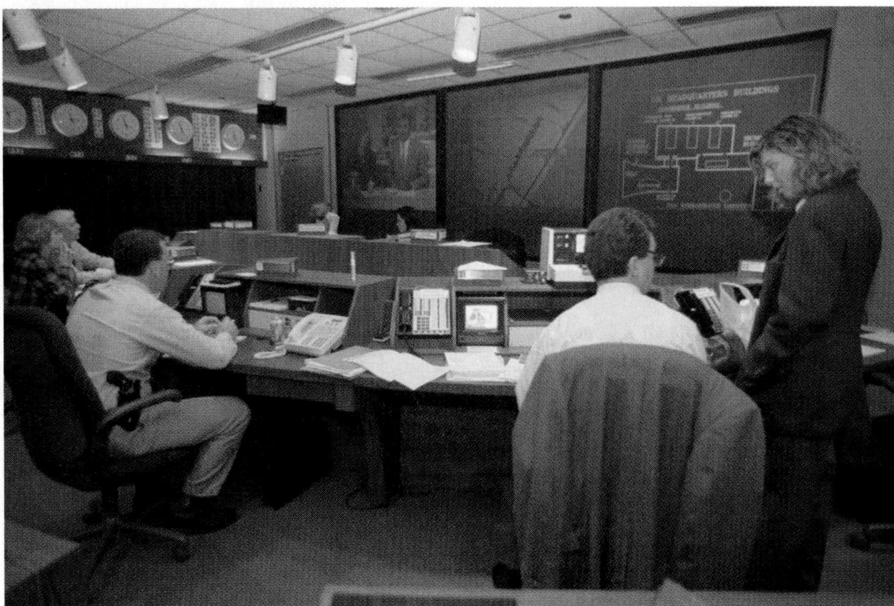

Programmed vs Nonprogrammed Decisions

In the choice stage, a number of factors influence the decision maker's selection of a solution. One factor is whether or not the decision can be programmed. **Programmed decisions** are ones that are made using a rule, procedure, or quantitative method. They are easy to automate using traditional computer systems (see Figure 9.4). It is simple, for example, for a music store to program a computer to order more CDs of a popular artist when inventory levels fall to 10 or fewer units. Information systems are often used to support programmed decisions by providing reports on problems that are routine and that have well-defined relationships; these types of problems are called *structured problems*.

FIGURE 9.4 • Programmed and nonprogrammed decisions

Inventory management is easily accomplished through programmed decisions based on quantities. Selecting the right person for a job based on a resume and interview is a nonprogrammed decision.

Nonprogrammed decisions, however, deal with unusual or exceptional situations. In many cases, these decisions are difficult to represent as a rule, procedure, or quantitative method (see Figure 9.4). Determining what research projects a genetics company should fund and pursue is an example of a nonprogrammed decision. Determining the appropriate training program for a new employee, deciding whether to buy a townhouse or rent an apartment, and weighing the benefits and disadvantages of various diets are additional examples of nonprogrammed decisions. Each of these decisions involves many unique characteristics for which the application of rules or procedures is not so obvious. Nonprogrammed decisions require human knowledge or software that has human knowledge embedded in it. Today, *decision support systems* and *expert systems* are being used to solve a variety of nonprogrammed decisions in which the problem is not routine and rules and relationships are not well defined. These are called *unstructured problems*.

Optimization and Heuristic Approaches

Optimization and heuristic approaches are popular problem-solving methods used in decision support systems. An **optimization model** finds the best solution, usually the one that will best help individuals or organizations meet their goals. For example, an optimization model can find the best way to schedule nurses at a hospital or the appropriate number of products an organization should produce to meet a profit goal, given certain conditions and assumptions. Optimization is used by airlines to create flight schedules that provide the best return on investment (see Figure 9.5). Optimization models utilize problem constraints. A limit on the number of available work hours in a manufacturing facility is an example of a problem constraint.

FIGURE 9.5 • Optimization

Airlines use sophisticated information systems to analyze information about aircraft, flight crews, airport locations, and customer demand to create optimal schedules to serve customers and create profit.

Heuristics, often referred to as "rules of thumb" (commonly accepted guidelines or procedures that usually find a good solution, but not necessarily the optimal solution), are often used in the decision-making process. An example of a heuristic rule in the military is to "get there first with the most firepower." A heuristic procedure used by baseball team managers is to place those batters most likely to get on base at the top of the lineup, followed by the "power hitters" who will drive the leadoff batters in to score. An example of a heuristic used in business is to order a four months' supply of inventory for a particular item when the inventory level drops to 20 or fewer units. Even

UPS Optimizes Routes, Saves Money and the Environment

There is a popular exercise performed by most computer science students that teaches computational approaches to optimization. It is commonly referred to as the "traveling salesman problem." A traveling salesman needs to figure out the shortest route to visit a number of cities, given the distances between each city. Needless to say, the problem gets more complicated as the number of cities increases. This becomes more than just an exercise for businesses like UPS that have saved millions of dollars each year through efficient routing of delivery trucks and aircraft.

UPS is obsessive about delivering packages in the shortest amount of time at the lowest cost. Once packages arrive at the UPS Worldport in Louisville, Kentucky, they make their way through 110 miles of conveyor belts to a truck or plane waiting to take them to their destinations. In peak holiday season, the belt system processes about 2.5 million packages every 3.5 hours. The information system that coordinates traffic at UPS Worldport has optimization scheduling routines programmed to minimize the amount of time that trucks and planes are idling. The system is also optimized to route packages by using the shortest path through UPS hubs and airports around the world.

UPS also has their delivery trucks wired to the max. Each truck and delivery is tracked using GPS and cell phone technology. Over 200 components of each UPS truck are networked to provide UPS mechanics exact information about oil pressure, seat belts, cargo doors, reverse gears, number of times the starter is engaged, how many miles per gallon each truck is getting, and how often the brake is applied.

Utilizing this information, UPS optimization software is able to choose the most efficient routes based on traffic, distance, and package volume for maximum deliveries using the time and fuel; find the best parking locations; advise drivers on driving techniques that can save fuel and time; and appropriately schedule vehicle maintenance.

Questions

1. What benefits has UPS enjoyed through the use of optimization software?
2. What other savings might be created through the use of truck data wirelessly fed into UPS information systems?
3. What type of pressure does optimization place on UPS drivers? How would you cope as a UPS driver?

Sources

1. *Murphy, Chris, "UPS: Positioned for the Long Haul,"* InformationWeek, *January 19, 2009, www.informationweek.com.*
2. *Rose, Coral, "Route Optimization Saves UPS 3 Million Gallons of Gas,"* Sustainable Action Leadership, *September 10, 2008, http://coralrose.typepad.com/my_weblog/2008/09/route-optimizat.html.*

though this heuristic may not minimize total inventory costs, it may be a very good rule of thumb that avoids stockouts without amassing too much inventory. Trend Micro, a provider of enterprise-level security software, uses heuristics to protect information systems from viruses, scams, and hackers, and to reduce spam by 90 percent.[1]

MANAGEMENT INFORMATION SYSTEMS

A **management information system (MIS)** is often used to support programmed decisions made in response to structured problems. The primary purpose of an MIS is to help individuals and organizations achieve their goals by providing reports and information used to make better decisions. An individual, for example, might want to get a doctor's report on the results of a routine physical exam, or a report comparing features and prices of a particular make and model of car at auto dealers within 100 miles of home. A swimming coach at a university might want a report showing all swimmers who have grades below a certain GPA. Filtering and analyzing highly detailed data can produce these reports.

Inputs to a Management Information System

An MIS is fueled by databases. It pulls data from one or more databases, sorts and sifts the data based on specific criteria, and produces reports of useful information. The primary source of input for the MIS of a business is its transaction database. Transaction processing systems record data in a database for every transaction within a business—credits and debits. An MIS can mine transaction data for interesting trends and important statistics. For example, Best Western may find that occupancy at its hotels that provide free wireless Internet access is 8 percent higher than in locations where there is a fee for Internet access.

Organizations typically have many internal databases that keep track of various aspects of the business. Wherever there is a database, there is an MIS seeking new insight and intelligence hidden in the data. A database containing research results on new drugs, for example, can be used by a pharmaceutical company to produce a variety of reports about which drugs seem to be working as expected.

An MIS sometimes depends on external data as well. External data may be stored on databases within the organization or in an external database. For example, a supplier may use an MIS that connects to a database of its customers in order to monitor inventory levels and deliver products just in time. New U.S. federal regulations from the IRS on how public and private organizations report their activities is another example of an external source of information. Figure 9.6 shows the inputs and outputs of an MIS. Outputs are discussed next.

FIGURE 9.6 • Inputs and outputs of an MIS

An MIS usues Internal and external data to produce reports that support decision making.

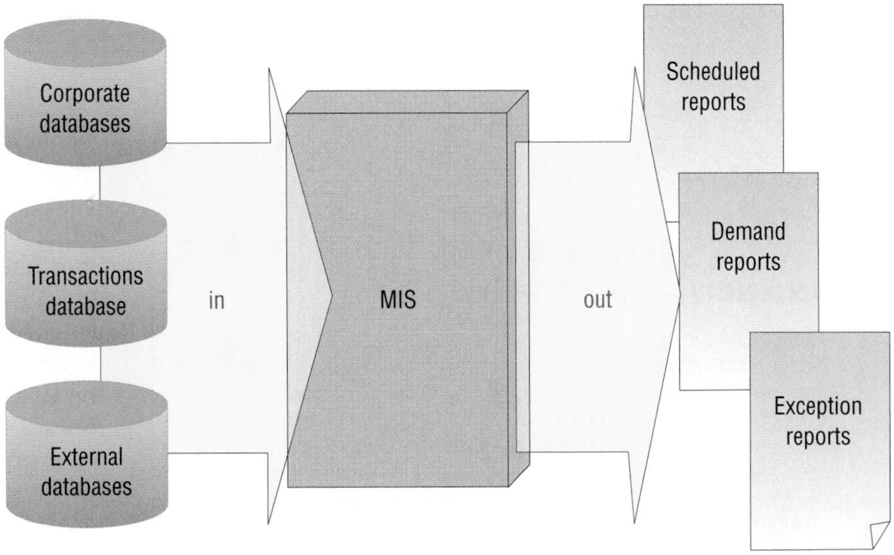

Outputs of a Management Information System

The output of most management information systems is a collection of reports, as shown in Figure 9.6. These reports can be produced on paper or, increasingly, distributed and viewed electronically. In what is commonly called an *executive dashboard* (see Figure 9.7), management information systems from providers like Cognos, SAS, IBM, and Oracle provide real-time reporting that allows decision makers to stay connected to dynamic changes in the business. For example, the University of Minnesota uses an executive dashboard from IBM to allow deans to monitor enrollment. The system also allows the university to understand how tutition is generated and the corresponding costs of instruction, by closely observing the supply and demand of courses.[2]

FIGURE 9.7 • An executive dashboard

This MIS reporting system puts many kinds of real-time information at managers' fingertips to aid decision making.

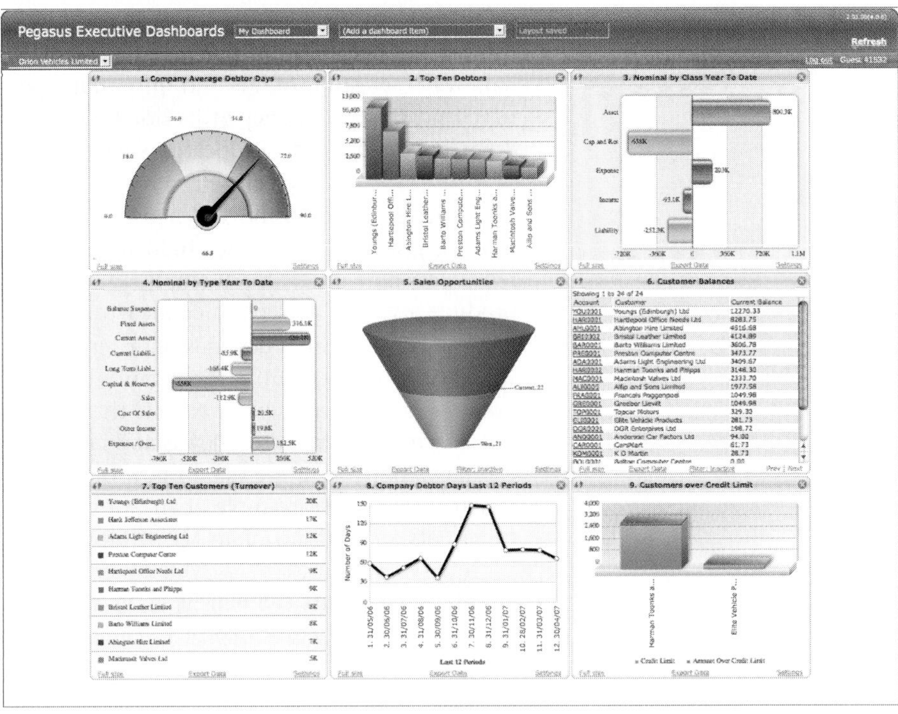

AND NOW—SMART GRIDS?

That's right. Smart electric grids can increase energy efficiency by letting customers know how they can reduce both their costs and their carbon footprint. Leading business software company SAP has developed AMI Integration for Utilities software that energy companies can integrate into their ERP systems. Consumer Energy reported that residential customer use has increased by 8 percent over the last decade. By linking AMI to their billing and customer relations systems, the company can give each consumer data that will help bring that number back down.

Consumers Energy Becomes First Utility to Purchase Smart Metering Software for Utilities from SAP
SAP Global
July 16, 2009
http://www.sap.com/solutions/business-suite/erp/newsevents/press.epx?pressid=10902

The information produced in MIS reports is commonly referred to as business intelligence. **Business intelligence (BI)** refers to technologies that are used to gather and report information that supports intelligent business decision making. BI is a contemporary term for an MIS designed for specific business needs. It has become a buzzword in business because of the ability of BI to propel a company forward—good business intelligence makes for smarter decision making, giving a company a strong competitive advantage. Many corporations have adopted the term business intelligence to label their MIS systems. For example, Oracle has a division called Oracle Business Intelligence, Microsoft has SQL Server Business Intelligence, and IBM has Data Warehousing and Business Intelligence.

Law Enforcement Uses BI to Accomplish More with Less

As with most businesses in a struggling economy, law enforcement agencies are being asked to do more with less. Many are turning to sophisticated information systems to help make officers more efficient and effective. Such is the case with the police department in Erlanger, Kentucky.

Officials in Erlanger have spent years preparing for advanced business intelligence tools to assist officers. They have built up a large database full of crime statistics just waiting to be mined by a system that could deliver helpful information to officers on patrol. Two problems prevented them from going forward: neighboring districts did not maintain similar crime data, and there was no available tool that provided the services that Erlanger needed.

After months of research, the Erlanger Police Department commissioned two information systems companies to collaborate to create a custom solution. The resulting system combines a geographic information system that displays crime data on a map, a search utility that allows officers to find crime information quickly, and business intelligence tools that provide crime reports that assist patrol sergeants in managing the officers to effectively curb crime.

Using its new Web-based Law Enforcement Analytics system, patrol sergeants arriving on duty are now able to review an analysis of calls that arrived over the past 24 hours and make appropriate decisions on where to send officers. Officers are able to access the system in squad cars through a wireless cellular connection. They can use the search function to run searches on a license number to view past records related to the number. They can view crime activity in progress on the map. Officers and sergeants can view reports of criminal activity over time, identifying common areas of violence on the map.

With the successful launch of the new system, the Erlanger PD has been able to inspire its neighbors to invest in the system and share their data. Over time, it is hoped that the network will grow to cover larger surrounding areas, allowing officers to be more effective without the addition of new officers to the force.

Questions

1. How does the Law Enforcement Analytics system allow police officers in Erlanger, Kentucky, to be more effective with fewer officers?
2. What type of information would you request from business intelligence tools in order to be more effective at law enforcement?
3. Why is it useful for similar BI tools to be used by neighboring law enforcement agencies?

Sources

1. *Havenstein, Heather, "Better BI: Erlanger (KY) Police Department," Computerworld, September 1, 2008, www.computerworld.com.*
2. *WebFOCUS Web site, accessed June 24, 2009, www.informationbuilders.com/products/webfocus.*

The main types of reports produced by an MIS are scheduled reports, demand reports, and exception reports.

Scheduled Reports. **Scheduled reports** are produced periodically or on a schedule, such as daily, weekly, or monthly. An investor can receive monthly statements summarizing the performance of his or her stock and bond holdings (see Figure 9.8). A university student receives a report at the end of each semester or quarter summarizing his or her grades.

FIGURE 9.8 • Schedule reports

A schedule report can summerize stock and bond positions every month.

MONTHLY PORTFOLIO PERFORMANCE

Name	Symbol	Quote	Shares	Current market value	Previous market value
Fiserve Inc.	FISV	$28.86	8	$230.88	$245.21
The Sports Authority	TSA	$25.23	11	$277.53	$251.55
Oracle	ORCL	$12.19	15	$182.85	$176.20
Total				$691.26	$685.55

FIGURE 9.9 • Inventory demand report

An executive might look at this inventory demand report to learn the inventory level for Green Trek Antelope 800 bicycles with a 20-inch frame.

INVENTORY DEMAND REPORT

Model	Size	Color	Quantity in stock
Antelope 800	20-inch frame	Green	4

FIGURE 9.10 • Exception report

This exception report from a medical lab shows only blood test results that are out of normal range.

EXCEPTION REPORT

Facility: Dallas Primary Care
Physician: Welch
Patient: Ben Bechtold

Test Name	Units	Results	Range	Flag (H–high; L–low)
Sodium	mEq/L	133	(135–146)	L
Cholesterol	mg/dL	265	(140–200)	H

A *key-indicator report,* a special type of scheduled report, summarizes the previous day's critical activities and is typically available at the beginning of each workday. The president of the United States, for example, receives daily reports in the morning on national security, terrorism, the economy, and many other areas. Key-indicator reports can summarize inventory levels, production activity, sales volume, and the like. Key-indicator reports allow people to take quick, corrective action when it is most needed.

Demand Reports. **Demand reports** are developed to give certain information at a person's request. In other words, these reports are produced on demand. An executive, for example, may want to know the inventory level for a particular item, such as the number of Antelope 800 Trek bicycles with a 20-inch frame that are in stock (see Figure 9.9). A demand report can be generated to give the requested information. You can view your credit report online on demand. Finding the right classes and professors can be critical for college students. Today, students can get demand reports on both. Other examples of demand reports include reports requested by executives to show the hours worked by a particular employee, total sales for a product for the year, and so on.

Exception Reports. **Exception reports** are reports that are automatically produced when a situation is unusual or requires action. For example, a patient will get an exception report from a clinic only if a blood test shows a possible problem (Figure 9.10). A manager might set a parameter that generates a report of all inventory items with fewer than 50 units on hand. The exception report generated by this parameter would contain only those items with fewer than 50 units in inventory. A bank can use exception reports to get a list of customer inquiries that have been open for a period of time without some progress or closure. As with key-indicator reports, exception reports are most often used to monitor aspects critical to an organization's success. In general, when an exception report is produced, an appropriate individual or executive takes action.

Exception reports are also used to help fight terrorism. Airline passenger lists are checked against the U.S. federal government's "no-fly list" and "Secondary Security Screening Selection," generating an exception report of passengers who could be a threat, so authorities can remove the suspected passengers before the plane takes off. The system has been controversial due to the numerous false positives it has generated, which have inconenienced some law-abiding citizens.

Functional Aspects of Management Information Systems

Management information systems are often designed to meet specific needs within an organization. For example, Oracle's Business Intelligence (BI) products include Financial Analytics, Human Resources Analytics, Supply Chain Analytics, Order Management and Fulfillment Analytics, Sales Analytics, and Marketing Analytics. These are typical categories for MISs. These BI products designed for specific functional aspects of a business incorporate state-of-the-art business-analysis tools. They provide each department within a business a foundation on which to manage effectively. For example, *supply chain management (SCM) systems* have become a necessity for businesses looking to streamline production, and *customer relationship management (CRM) systems* are used by many businesses for gauging customer satisfaction and responding to customer issues. Table 9.1 lists the various types of reports associated with the various functional units of a business. This illustrates that MFSs are integrated with all areas of an oganization's operations.

REVOLUTION IN BASEBALL STATISTICS

Oh, you can keep talking about RBIs and strikeout-to-walk ratios, but baseball has moved way beyond that. Cameras and a new software system have made it possible to measure an outfielder's arm strength and accuracy, how fast a base runner travels from first to third, and which shortstops catch those up-the-middle grounders. The system also provides hundreds of other new statistics. It will not only rate players more accurately, but it should also make the game even more exciting.

Digital Eyes Will Chart Baseball's Unseen Skills
Alan Schwarz
New York Times
July 10, 2009
http://www.nytimes.com/2009/07/10/sports/baseball/10cameras.html?_r=1

TABLE 9.1 • MIS reports in different areas of a business

Area	Reports
Financial	• Payables • Receivables • General ledger • Profitability
Human Resources (HR)	• Compensation • HR performance • Retention • Workforce profile and compliance
Order Management and Fulfillment	• Business performance • Billing • Order fulfillment
Supply Chain	• Procurement and spending • Supplier performance • Inventory
Sales	• Profits by product • Profits by customer • Competition analysis
Service	• Service effectiveness • Employee effectiveness • Customer insight
Contact Center	• Customer service • Agent performance • Service and delivery cost • Contact center sales
Marketing	• Marketing planning • Campaign performance • Customer insight

Enterprise Resource Planning

You have seen how management information systems are integrated into the functional aspects of an organization. As information systems and technologies developed, many businesses haphazardly adopted the latest and greatest technologies and eventually found themselves with overly complex systems that were expensive, difficult to maintain, and complicated to use. Many businesses were dependent on several different MISs designed for various business units by different vendors with a variety of compatibility issues.

One solution to such complexity is an enterprise resource planning system. An **enterprise resource planning (ERP) system** integrates all data processing in a corporation (enterprise) into one unified system that draws from a common set of databases (see Figure 9.11). An ERP for a large business would include components for manufacturing, supply chain management, financials, project management, human resources, customer relationship management, and data warehousing applications. All of these systems would share data, would have a standardized user interface, and would be centrally administered and maintained.

FIGURE 9.11 • An enterprise resource planning system

An ERP unifies all information systems serving various functional units of an enterprise into one comprehensive system.

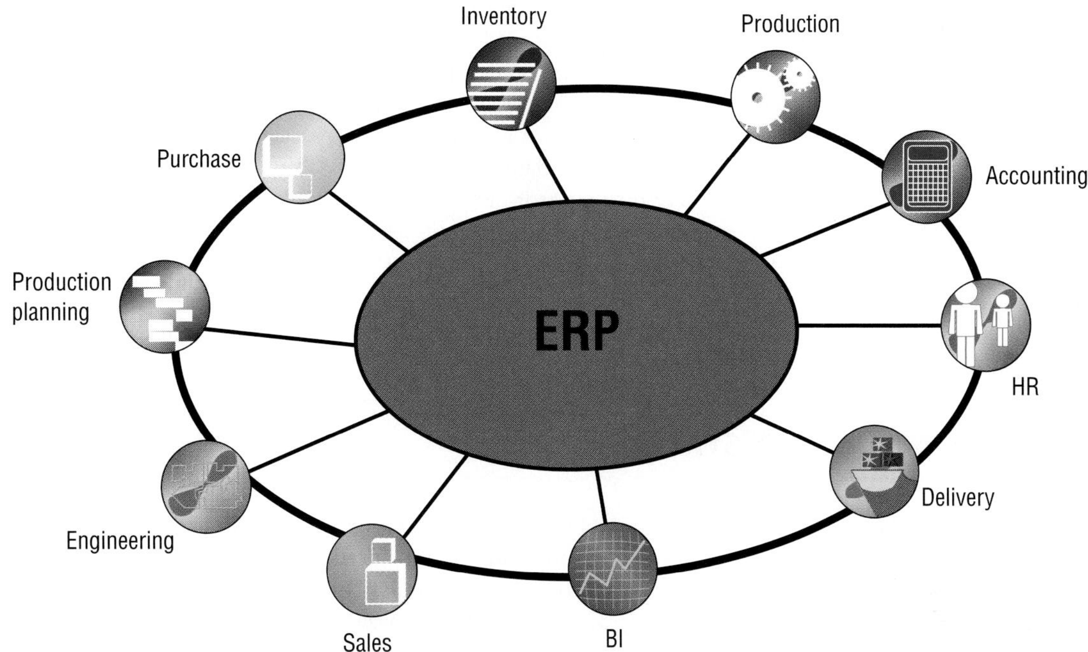

Over the past decade, many corporations have implemented ERP systems with dramatic results. As you might imagine, adopting an ERP system is a major undertaking. Every information system in the organization is studied and redesigned. Old systems are gradually retired while the new systems are activated. For a large business, the process takes years and millions of dollars. Typically, a corporation contracts a professional ERP vendor to manage the design and installation of the system. Vendors include Oracle, Microsoft, IBM, SAS, and SAP. When the transition to an ERP is complete, employees find that they are able to accomplish much more in less time. No longer are they limited to viewing only the portion of corporate information accessible to their functional unit. If it is deemed safe and beneficial, an employee could access any information that exists anywhere in the system. Table 9.2 provides a list of benefits and drawbacks of implementing an ERP.

TABLE 9.2 • Benefits and drawbacks of ERP

Benefits	Drawbacks
• Improved access to data throughout the enterprise with less redundancy • Elimination of outdated disparate systems • Streamlined work processes • Simplified maintenance and upgrades on unified system • Improved communication between functional areas • Better corporate performance offering a competitive advantage	• Expense in time and money • Learning curve and employees' resistance to change • Dependence on one vendor • Risk! Failure is not an option—it typically means the collapse of the business

Telecom giant Verizon Communications provides an excellent example of a large global business that survived and flourished after adoption of an ERP system. Verizon Communications formed as a merger between three telecom companies: Bell Atlantic, GTE, and NYNEX. The complexity of combining the many information systems that made up these three companies could only be solved through the massive undertaking of an ERP. Verizon hired ERP vendor SAP to combine all of the varied systems into a "data universe that can be accessed via the Web to analyze pivotal business data.[3] The resulting system provides information to Verizon construction supervisors and engineers, managers in finance, personnel, and other business units, as well as top VPs and decision-makers.

However, a company doesn't need to be a huge global enterprise to take advantage of the benefits of ERP. The Buncombe County government in North Carolina used the same SAP ERP system to streamline its business processes and improve constituent services.[4]

DECISION SUPPORT SYSTEMS

As discussed in Chapter 1, a decision support system (DSS) is an information system used to support problem-specific decision making. Unlike an MIS, which supports decisions related to structured problems through database queries, the focus of a DSS is on decision-making effectiveness when faced with unstructured or semistructured problems. A DSS often uses mathematical models and calculations designed to solve a specific problem. For a TV producer, it could mean better ratings through a more comprehensive analysis of viewer desires. For a business, it could mean higher profits, lower costs, and better products and services.

Overall, a decision support system should assist people and organizations with all aspects of decision making. Moreover, the DSS approach emphasizes that people, not machines, make decisions. DSS technology is used primarily to support making decisions that can solve problems and help achieve individual and organizational goals. For example, ePocrates is a clinical information and decision support system used by over 750,000 healthcare professionals worldwide to find answers quickly, improve patient care, reduce medical errors, and increase productivity (see Figure 9.12).

FIGURE 9.12 • ePocrates

Products like ePocrates offer doctors instant access to medical information, aid in the treatment and diagnosis of patients, and provide improved patient care and safety.

Characteristics of a Decision Support System

Decision support systems have a number of characteristics. In general, a decision support system can perform the functions described in the following sections.

Handle a Range of Data from Small Amounts to Large Amounts. For instance, advanced database management systems have allowed people to search databases of any size for information when using a DSS. As futures and options trading is becoming totally electronic, many trading firms are using DSS software to perform sophisticated analysis on huge amounts of financial data in order to make intelligent buys and sells and earn substantial profits for traders and investors. Some DSS trading software is programmed to place buy and sell orders automatically without a trader manually entering a trade, based on parameters set by the trader. See Figure 9.13.

FIGURE 9.13 • Trading DSS

Brokers and traders use a DSS to decide when to buy and sell.

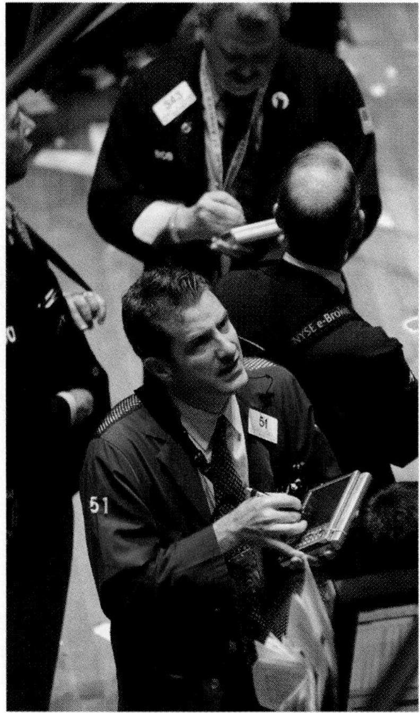

Obtain and Process Data from Different Sources. Some data sources may reside in databases on personal computers; others could be located on different mainframe systems or networks. DSSs can access data external to the organization and integrate this data with internal data.

Provide Report and Presentation Flexibility. One of the reasons for developing DSSs was that TPSs and MISs were not flexible enough to meet the full variety of decision makers' problem or information needs. Whereas other information systems produce primarily fixed-format reports, DSSs have more widely varied formats. People can get the information they want, presented in a format that suits their needs, such as textual or graphical.

Perform Complex, Sophisticated Analysis and Comparisons Using Advanced Software Packages. Marketing research surveys, for example, can be analyzed in a variety of ways using analysis programs that are part of a DSS. Many of the analytical programs associated with a DSS are actually stand-alone programs. The DSS provides a means of bringing these together. For example, retailers use decision support systems to intelligently decide what products to carry and what product prices to mark down for special sales. A retail DSS incorporates revenue optimization software, merchandise planning software, and merchandise forecasting software.

Support Optimization and Heuristic Approaches. For smaller problems, decision support systems have the capability to find the best (optimal) solution. For more complex problems, heuristics are used. With heuristics, the computer system can determine a very good—but not necessarily the optimal—solution. For example, a state that settles a drug case can, by using heuristics, order drug companies to distribute scarce drugs worth hundreds of millions of dollars to hospitals and clinics. By supporting all types of decision-making approaches, a DSS gives the decision maker a great deal of flexibility in getting computer support for decision-making activities.

Perform "What-If" and Goal-Seeking Analysis. **What-if analysis** is the process of making hypothetical changes to problem data and observing the impact on the results. Consider an emergency disaster plan. What-if analysis could determine the consequences of a hurricane slamming into New Orleans with heavy flooding or the consequences of the hurricane hitting the Florida coast instead. With what-if analysis, a person can make changes to problem data (where the hurricane hits) and immediately see the impact on the results (the damage done and the lives lost). See Figure 9.14. **Goal-seeking analysis** is the process of determining what problem data is required for a given result. For example, suppose a financial manager has a goal to earn a return of 9 percent on any investment, and she is considering an investment with a certain monthly net income. Goal seeking allows the manager to determine what monthly net income (problem data) is needed to have a return of 9 percent (problem result).

FIGURE 9.14 • The value of what-if analysis

What-if analysis could determine the consequences of a hurricane slamming into the Florida coast.

Perform Simulation. With *simulation*, the DSS attempts to mimic an event that could happen in the future. Simulation uses chance or probability. For example, there is a certain chance, or probability, that it will rain tomorrow or during the next several months. Sometimes a problem is so complex that a normal decision support system is just too difficult to develop. One popular alternative is to develop a computer simulation that allows people to analyze various possibilities and scenarios. Corporate executives and military commanders often use computer simulations to try different strategies in different situations. Corporate executives, for example, can try different marketing decisions in various market conditions. Military commanders often use computer war games to fine-tune their military strategies in different war conditions. Air traffic controllers can hone their skills and emergency responses in various scenarios. See Figure 9.15.

PREDICTING WAR

What if you could accurately predict whether another country was going to attack or develop a dangerous weapon? Political scientist Bruce Bueno de Mesquita has developed a computer model that uses game theory to do just that with 90 percent certainty. Experts generally evaluate who has how much influence and what their preferences are. But experts can only keep track of a handful of relevant players. The computer program can model interactions between large numbers of players—and so the program gets it right, even when the experts get it wrong.

Mathematical Fortune-Telling: How well can game theory solve business and political disputes?
Julie Rehmeyer
Science News
Feb 8, 2009
http://blog.sciencenews.org/view/generic/id/9041/title/Math_Trek__Mathematical_Fortune-Telling

FIGURE 9.15 • Simulation

Air traffic controllers use simulation to learn and practice skills and emergency responses without endangering anyone.

Of course, not all DSSs work the same or have all of the characteristics summarized in Table 9.3. Some are small in scope and take advantage of only some of the characteristics in Table 9.3. An agricultural department for a state university, for example, can develop a DSS based on an Excel spreadsheet to help farmers decide what to plant to maximize their revenues. Other small-scale DSSs can provide patients and their families with important medical records and reports, which can be critical to patient involvement and recovery from disease.

TABLE 9.3 • Characteristics of decision support systems

DSS characteristics
Large amounts of data
Different data sources
Report and presentation flexibility
Orientation toward individual decision-making styles
Modular format
Sophisticated analysis
Graphical orientation
Optimization and heuristic approach
What-if and goal-seeking analysis
Simulation

As you can see from the list of DSS characteristics, a DSS is "smarter" than an MIS. It is smarter in that it applies mathematical models to data in order to reach conclusions, such as "moving operations to Austin will provide higher revenues over five years than moving to Boston." An MIS does little in the way of modeling, but instead provides the information from corporate databases that decision makers can then use as they see fit.

For a system to be more intelligent than a DSS, artificial intelligence (AI) techniques would have to be leveraged to give the system the ability to reach conclusions and offer advice, even with insufficient information on which to base a decision. Such systems are called expert systems and are used to support specialized tasks for businesses, organizations, and individuals. Expert systems were discussed in Chapter 3.

Figure 9.16 illustrates the level of complexity, intelligence, and workload of the primary computer-based information systems discussed. Note that as you ascend the pyramid, each system builds and relies on the underlying systems. For example, an MIS uses data produced by the TPS, a DSS often requires the database queries of an MIS to calculate its results, and an ES extends the functionality of a DSS by implementing AI techniques.

FIGURE 9.16 • Information system relationships

Information systems range in complexity and programmed intelligence, with TPS being the least intelligent but busiest, and expert systems being the most intelligent and least commonly used.

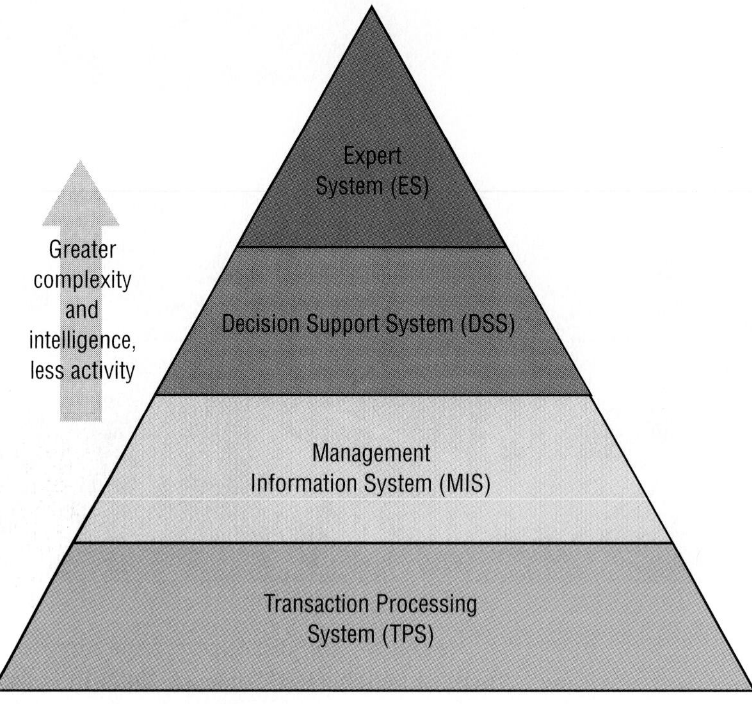

THE GROUP DECISION SUPPORT SYSTEM

The DSS approach has resulted in better decision making for all kinds of individual users. However, many DSS approaches and techniques are not suitable for a group decision-making environment. Although not everyone is involved in committee meetings and group decision-making sessions, many people spend more than half of their decision-making time in a group setting. Such people need effective approaches to assist with group decision making, such as a formal decision room (see Figure 9.17). A **group decision support system (GDSS)**, also called a *computerized collaborative work system*, consists of the hardware, software, people, databases, and procedures needed to provide effective support in group decision-making settings, a process sometimes referred to as computer supported cooperative work. A group of petroleum engineers located around the world, for example, might be collaborating on a new refinery. A GDSS can be used to help the engineers design the new refinery by providing a means to communicate with each other and share design ideas.

FIGURE 9.17 • Group decision support system

High-tech rooms like the one shown here create a group dynamic that allows people to come together to explore solutions to complex problems.

Characteristics of a GDSS

A GDSS has a number of characteristics that go beyond the traditional DSS. These systems try to build on the advantages of individual support systems while responding to the fact that new and additional approaches are needed in a group decision-making environment. Some GDSSs allow the exchange of information and expertise among people without meetings or direct face-to-face interaction, sometimes utilizing wiki and blog technologies. The characteristics of a typical GDSS include the following:

- Flexibility
- Support for anonymous input
- Reduction of negative group behavior
- Support of positive group behavior

GDSS Software or Groupware

GDSS software, often called **groupware**, helps with joint workgroup scheduling, communication, and management. One popular groupware package, Lotus Notes, can capture, store, manipulate, and distribute memos and communications that are developed during group projects. By using groupware, all group members can share information to accomplish joint work, even when group members are located around the globe. Furniture manufacturer Steelcase utilizes Microsoft Groove groupware to support collaboration between its employees in France, Germany, Italy, and Japan.[5] Increasingly, groupware is being used on the Internet. WebEx (*www.webex.com*), Genesys Meeting Center (*www.genesys.com*), and GoToMeeting Corporate (*www.gotomeeting.com*) are examples of groupware products available on the Web. Using groupware gives every employee rapid access to a vast source of information.

Microsoft SharePoint has emerged as a popular GDSS that supports group interaction in a number of ways. Available as a Web-based tool or installed on corporate intranets, SharePoint includes collaboration functions, process management modules, a document-management platform, and communication features such as wikis and blogs. CocaCola Enterprises uses Microsoft SharePoint Online to provide an effective method of collaboration in a workforce that is mostly mobile. Utilizing SharePoint, Coca-Cola was able to reduce the number of internal meetings, providing the sales force with more time to increase sales.[6]

HYBRID SYSTEMS AND SPECIAL-PURPOSE SYSTEMS

The four most common types of information systems, TPS, MIS, DSS, and ES, are common in all industries and professions. However, there are many other types of systems that are important for professionals. Often, multiple systems are merged into multifunction hybrid systems that support a variety of activities. Other information systems have more specialized purposes, such as knowledge management or manipulating and displaying geographic information.

Hybrid Systems

It is useful to understand the functions of the primary types of information systems. However, in day-to-day work, users do not address their systems as TPSs, MISs, or DSSs, but rather by whatever functional name is provided for the product. For example, at Florida State University, faculty and staff in all business areas—including departmental staff, the registrar's office, financial office, and human resources—all log on to the OMNI (online management of networked information) system to access information systems that draw from the university database. The OMNI system is an ERP system developed over several years for FSU by PeopleSoft Corporation at a cost of hundreds of thousands of dollars. The system includes TPSs, MISs, and DSSs that support every business operation at the university. People who use the system know it simply as OMNI, and the majority of the staff couldn't function without it.

A *hybrid system* contains multiple types of information systems accessed through one central interface. Hybrid systems allow organizations to streamline and simplify their information systems. The interface used to access hybrid systems is often referred to as a *corporate portal* that gives easy access to commonly used information and tools. Portals are typically customized to meet the needs of individual users. Figure 9.18 shows a corporate services portal designed by DBS Corporation for Tourism New Zealand (TNZ). The portal is used by marketing and operations teams around the world working with TNZ to manage budgets, forecasts, and campaign finances.[7] The corporate portal provides convenient access to powerful and varied information systems provided by the SAP Corporation.

FIGURE 9.18 • Corporate services portal

This portal is used by Tourism New Zealand employees and partners to enter and access data in corporate information systems and databases.

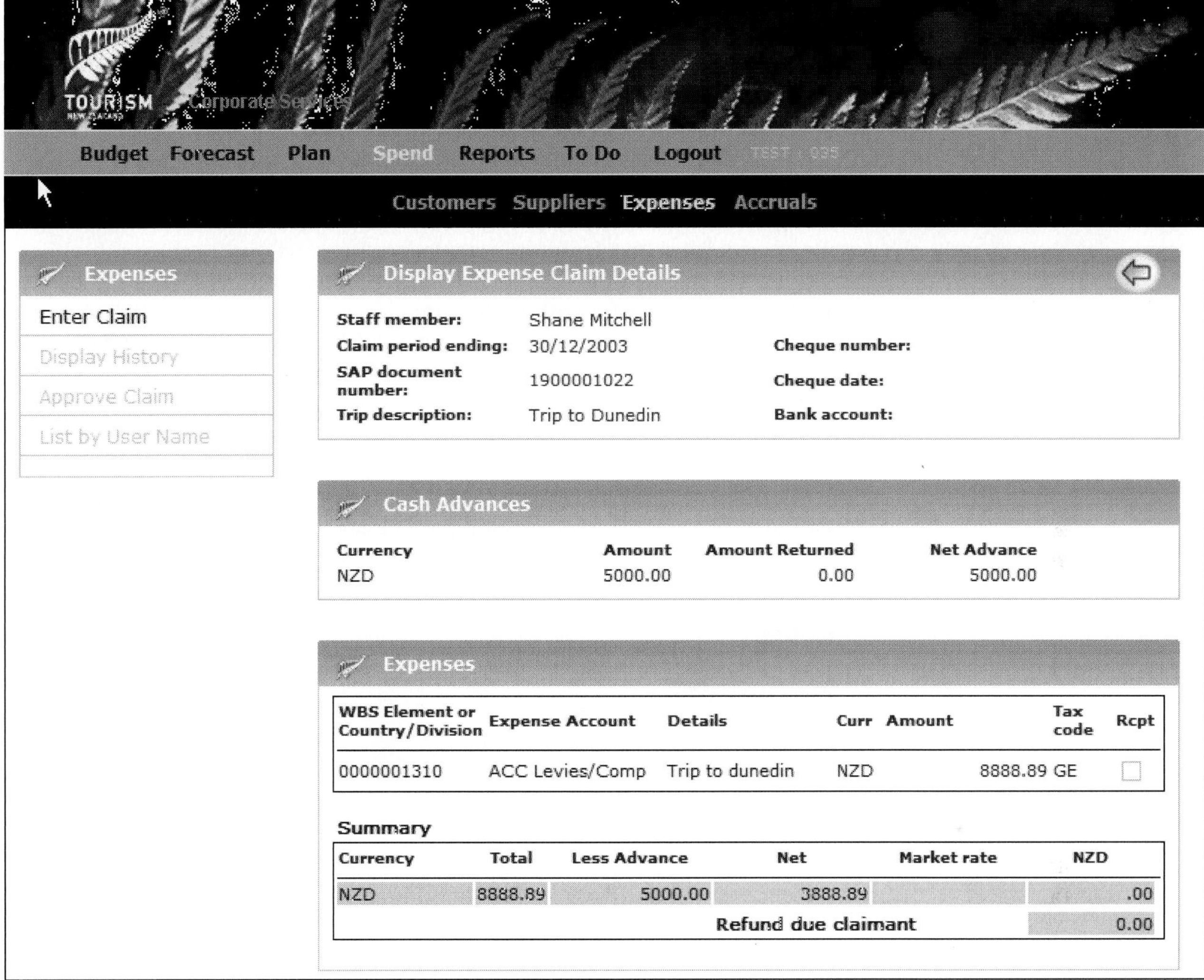

Portals are often created as Web pages and make use of the Internet or an intranet to communicate with servers. Portals can include an executive dashboard that graphically presents current business statistics. Many information systems vendors, like IBM, Sun, SAP, SAS, and Oracle, custom design portal applications to interconnect with information systems for businesses and organizations. Custom-designed hybrid systems and corporate portals are what most users interact with when using TPSs, MISs, and DSSs.

Knowledge Management Systems

A **knowledge management (KM) system** assists an organization in capturing, storing, and distributing knowledge for use and reuse by the organization and sometimes by its partners and customers. In the mid-1990s, it was recognized that organizational knowledge existed primarily in the minds of employees, and that there was a need to record and dispense this knowledge in a way that benefited the organization. Thus, knowledge management systems were born. When individuals in an organization share their insight, it allows others with less experience or skill to learn and become more valuable to the organization. This is especially important when an employee leaves an organization—companies don't want to lose corporate knowledge with the employee. Also, the ability to share knowledge with partners and customers makes for good communication and relationships. Although there are nontechnological approaches to knowledge management, technology has become key to collecting and distributing knowledge and to providing communications channels between knowledge holders and knowledge seekers. The term knowledge worker originated in the field of knowledge management.

Knowledge management systems are diverse. All information systems assist in the management of knowledge, but some are more directly focused on dispersing knowledge. For example, Citrix Systems Corporation is a networking software company that found its help-desk call centers overflowing with phone calls. It hired Jive Software Corporation to develop an online knowledge base and discussion forum for customers to quickly access solutions for themselves (Figure 9.19). The ability to search a knowledge base of documents and discussions in the forum reduced calls to the call centers by 30 percent within the first month.[8] This is just one example of a knowledge management issue resolved through information systems.

FIGURE 9.19 • Knowledge management

Citrix and many other technology companies provide searchable online knowledge bases to assist customers and employees with questions and problems.

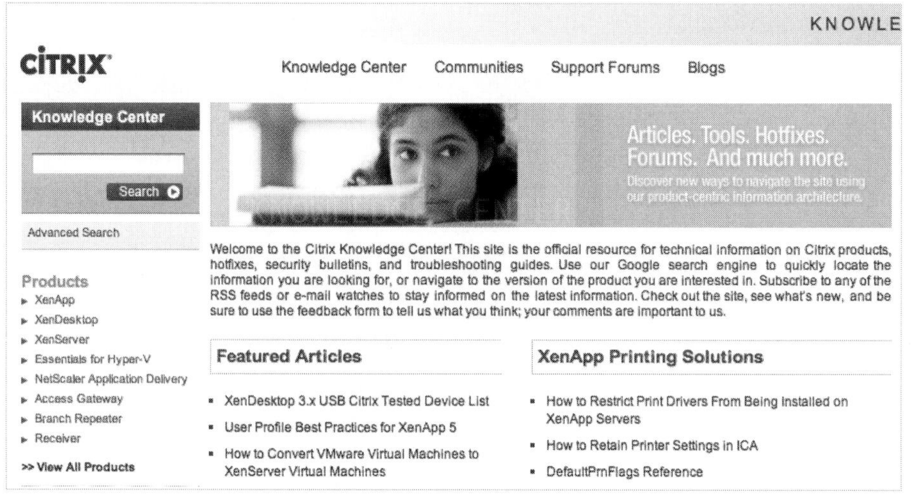

Geographic Information Systems

A **geographic information system (GIS)** is capable of storing, manipulating, and displaying geographic or special information, including maps of locations or regions around the world (see Figure 9.20). A 911 operator can use a GIS to quickly determine the specific location of a caller with an emergency. The GIS converts the caller's phone number to the specific address of the caller and the directions for the police or an ambulance to get to the caller in a minimum amount of time. A business can use a GIS to display sales information for a specific region of the country. Higher sales can be displayed in red, and lower sales can be displayed in green or blue. This can give sales representatives a visual image of where to find sales opportunities and target their efforts. The military can use a GIS to target enemy forces on a battlefield. Using a GIS, along with other GPSs (global positioning systems), a tank group can quickly identify enemy positions and equipment in a constantly and rapidly changing battle situation. This helps a military force devastate an enemy position while avoiding friendly fire casualties. GPSs were first used by the military. The technology uses satellites to determine one's location. GISs are also used in urban planning, social work, criminology and law enforcement, and a variety of other fields.

FIGURE 9.20 • Geographic information system

Google Earth overlays traffic, weather, and other local information on its 3D maps.

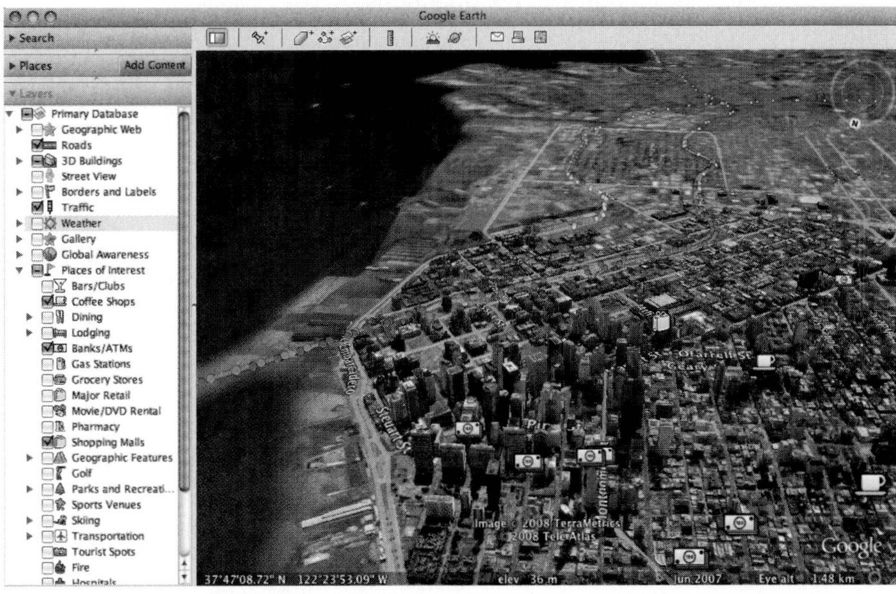

Other Specialized Systems

In addition to the preceding applications, there are a number of other exciting special-purpose systems. **Informatics** combines traditional disciplines, like science and medicine, with computer systems and technology. *Bioinformatics,* for example, combines biology and computer science. Also called computational biology, bioinformatics has been used to help map the human genome and conduct research on biological organisms. Using sophisticated databases and artificial intelligence, bioinformatics is being used to help unlock the secrets of the human genome, which could eventually prevent diseases and save lives. Stanford University has a course on bioinformatics and offers a bioinformatics certification. *Medical informatics* combines traditional medical research with computer science. Journals such as *Healthcare Informatics* report research on ways to reduce medical errors and improve health care delivery by using computer systems and technology in medicine. The University of Edinburgh in Scotland has a School of Informatics offering courses in the structure, behavior, and interactions of natural and artificial computational systems. The program combines artificial intelligence, computer science, engineering, and science.

Just as a wide array of informatics systems have been developed for specific medical and biological professions, there are information systems designed for every industry, and every activity within every industry. Information systems are pervasive in organizations, and without them, business activities and technology advances would come to a virtual standstill.

ACTION PLAN

Remember Maurice Duchane from the beginning of the chapter? Maurice hopes to develop an information system to help Tulane's football coaches. Here are answers to his questions.

1. **What type of information system could help a football team's coaching staff organize its data and retrieve valuable information quickly and efficiently? How would it work?**

   A management information system (MIS) could be used to provide detailed reports to coaches that include statistics about players and teams. The MIS would be fueled by data stored in a secure team database. Reports could be custom-designed to answer specific questions that coaches find important and might supply unique information that other teams don't have, thereby giving Maurice's team an advantage. A knowledge management system could also be implemented to assist coaches and players with looking up plays and other necessary organizational knowledge. A portal and/or dashboard could be a simple interface to the MIS and knowledge management system, making all information available from one central application.

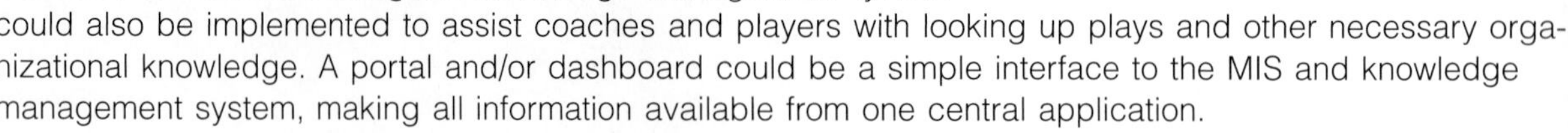

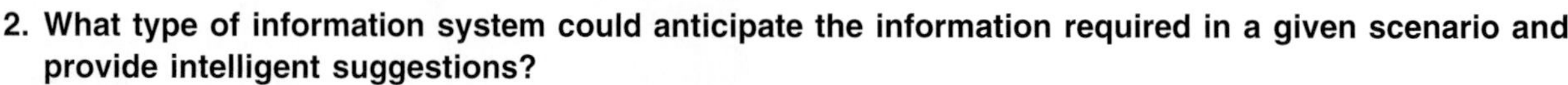

2. **What type of information system could anticipate the information required in a given scenario and provide intelligent suggestions?**

   Decision support systems (DSSs) could be designed to support problem-specific tasks such as selecting a starting offensive and defensive line, and selecting plays that might be effective against a particular team. The DSSs would use models to perform the calculations necessary to make informed suggestions. For instance, a DSS that assisted in choosing the starting lineups would need to evaluate the characteristics of each player on both the home team and visiting team to determine strengths and weaknesses and choose players accordingly. DSSs could be included on the portal interface used with the MIS.

3. **What components will Maurice require to build his systems so that they can deliver information in real time during a game?**

   The portal used to access team systems could be designed specifically for small, rugged tablet PCs that coaches could carry like notebooks. The tablets could transfer data back and forth to an application server wirelessly over a secure virtual private network (VPN).

Summary

LEARNING OBJECTIVE 1

Define the stages of decision making and problem solving.

The true potential of computer systems is in providing information to help people and organizations make better decisions. Decision making is divided into three phases: intelligence, design, and choice. Problem solving takes decision making a step further and involves taking action by implementing the choice made by the decision maker and monitoring the effects of the decision.

Figure 9.1—p. 482

The types of decisions made by an organization can range from structured, programmed decisions to unstructured, nonprogrammed decisions. In some instances, when the optimal solution to a problem must be determined, optimization models assist in finding the best solution. In other cases, a solution that meets a basic set of criteria may be acceptable, although not optimal. This heuristic approach is often used because it is more cost-effective than the optimization approach. In addition, individuals and organizations can use a reactive or proactive approach to problem solving. With a reactive problem-solving approach, the problem solver waits until a problem surfaces or becomes apparent before taking any action. With a proactive problem-solving approach, the problem solver seeks out potential problems before they become serious.

LEARNING OBJECTIVE 2

Discuss the use of management information systems in providing reports to help solve structured problems.

A management information system (MIS) is a computer-based information system that provides managers and decision makers with information to help achieve organizational goals. An MIS draws information from internal and external databases. An MIS can help an organization achieve its goals by providing managers with insight into the regular operations of the organization so that they can control, organize, and plan more effectively and efficiently. The output of most management information systems is a collection of reports that are distributed to managers. These reports include scheduled reports, demand reports, and exception reports. Scheduled reports are produced periodically or on a schedule, such as daily, weekly, or monthly. A key-indicator report is a special type of scheduled report that summarizes the previous day's critical activities. Demand reports are developed to give certain information at a manager's request. Exception reports are reports that are automatically produced when a situation is unusual or requires management action.

Business intelligence (BI) refers to technologies that are used to gather and report information that supports intelligent business decision making. Many information system corporations have adopted the term business intelligence to label their MIS systems. Management information systems are often designed for special needs within an organization like supply chain management (SCM) and customer relationship management (CRM). An enterprise resource planning (ERP) system integrates all data processing in a corporation (enterprise) into one unified system that draws from a common database system.

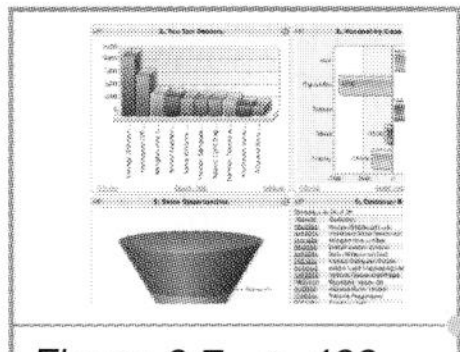

Figure 9.7—p. 488

LEARNING OBJECTIVE 3

Describe how decision support systems are used to solve nonprogrammed and unstructured problems.

A decision support system (DSS) is a computer-based information system that works to support managerial decision making. DSSs provide assistance through all phases of the decision-making process. Decision support systems can handle a large amount of data, and obtain and process data from different sources; provide report and presentation flexibility, with both textual and graphical orientation; and perform complex and sophisticated analysis, support optimization and heuristic approaches, and perform what-if and goal-seeking analysis. A DSS is more intelligent than an MIS because it includes models and calculations necessary to provide solutions. A DSS, however, does not use AI, so it is not as intelligent as an expert system.

Figure 9.14—p. 496

LEARNING OBJECTIVE 4

Explain how a group decision support system can help people and organizations collaborate on team projects.

A group decision support system (GDSS), also called a computerized collaborative work system, consists of hardware, software, people, databases, and procedures needed to provide effective support in group decision-making settings. GDSSs are typically easy to learn and use and can offer specific or general decision-making support.

A GDSS also has some unique components, such as compound documents, groupware, and telecommunications links. Groupware is specially designed software that helps generate lists of decision alternatives and performs data analysis. These packages let people work on joint documents and files over a network. The characteristics of a GDSS include special design, ease of use, flexibility, anonymous input, reduced negative behavior, and support of positive group behavior.

Figure 9.17—p. 499

LEARNING OBJECTIVE 5

Discuss the uses of hybrid and special-purpose systems.

A hybrid system contains multiple types of information systems accessed through one central interface. Hybrid systems allow organizations to streamline and simplify information systems. The interface used to access hybrid systems is often referred to as a corporate portal and includes easy access to commonly used information and tools. A knowledge management (KM) system assists an organization in capturing, storing, and distributing knowledge for use and reuse by the organization and sometimes its partners and customers.

There are a number of special-purpose systems. Geographic information systems and informatics are two examples. A geographic information system is capable of storing, manipulating, and displaying geographic information, including maps of locations or regions around the world. Informatics combines traditional disciplines, like science and medicine, with computer systems and technology.

Figure 9.20—p. 503

Test Yourself

LEARNING OBJECTIVE 1: Define the stages of decision making and problem solving.

1. ________________ involves three stages: intelligence, design, and choice.
2. True or False: Nonprogrammed decisions are easier to make than programmed decisions.
3. ________________ decision makers believe in addressing problems as they arise.
   a. Reactive
   b. Proactive
   c. Heuristic
   d. Goal seeking
4. The final stage of the problem-solving process is ________________ .
5. True or False: Optimized decisions are typically more cost-effective than relying on heuristics.
6. What is commonly referred to as a "rule of thumb"?
   a. heuristic
   b. optimization
   c. goal seeking
   d. nonprogrammed decision

LEARNING OBJECTIVE 2: Discuss the use of management information systems in providing reports to help solve structured problems.

7. True or False: The primary form of output from an MIS takes the form of a report.
8. What types of reports are produced periodically?
   a. demand
   b. scheduled
   c. heuristic
   d. optimization
9. ________________, a contemporary term for an MIS, refers to technologies that are used to gather and report information that supports intelligent business decision making.
10. True or False: An MIS is a costly enterprise-wide system that integrates all data processing in a corporation into one unified system that draws from a common database system.

LEARNING OBJECTIVE 3: Describe how decision support systems are used to solve nonprogrammed and unstructured problems.

11. A(n) ________________ is used when people or organizations face unstructured or semistructured problems.
12. What is the process of determining the problem data required for a given result?
    a. heuristic
    b. optimizing
    c. goal-seeking
    d. simulation
13. True or False: One characteristic of a DSS is that it utilizes AI techniques to suggest a plan of action.
14. Which is the proper ordering of information systems from simplest to most intelligent?
    a. MIS, TPS, DSS, ES
    b. TPS, DSS, MIS, ES
    c. TPS, MIS, DSS, ES
    d. ES, DSS, MIS, TPS
15. ________________ is the process of making hypothetical changes to problem data and observing the impact on the results.

LEARNING OBJECTIVE 4: Explain how a group decision support system can help people and organizations collaborate on team projects.

16. What type of software is used to allow two or more individuals to work together effectively in a group?
    a. groupware
    b. decisionware
    c. cooperative software
    d. teamware
17. True or False: Many knowledge workers make most business decisions in groups.

LEARNING OBJECTIVE 5: Discuss the uses of hybrid and special-purpose systems.

18. A(n) ________________ system contains multiple types of information systems accessed through one central interface.
19. The searchable knowledge base that assists users with finding solutions to problems at Microsoft's online Help Center is considered what type of system?
    a. management information system
    b. decision support system
    c. enterprise resource planning system
    d. knowledge management system
20. True or False: Google Earth is considered a geographic information system (GIS).

Test Yourself Answers **1.** Decision making, **2.** False, **3.** a. Reactive, **4.** monitoring, **5.** False, **6.** a. heuristic, **7.** True, **8.** b. scheduled, **9.** BI, **10.** False, **11.** decision support system, **12.** c. goal-seeking, **13.** False, **14.** c. TPS, MIS, DSS, ES **15.** What-if analysis, **16.** a. groupware, **17.** True, **18.** hybrid, **19.** d. knowledge management system, **20.** True.

Key Terms

Term	Page	Definition
business intelligence (BI)	488	Technologies that are used to gather and report information that supports intelligent business decision making
decision making	482	A process that takes place in three stages: intelligence, design, and choice
demand report	490	An MIS report developed to give certain information at a person's request
enterprise resource planning (ERP) system	492	An information system that integrates all data processing in a corporation (enterprise) into one unified system that draws from a common database system
exception report	490	An MIS report that is automatically produced when a situation is unusual or requires action
geographic information system (GIS)	502	An information system capable of storing, manipulating, and displaying geographic or special information, including maps of locations or regions around the world
goal-seeking analysis	495	The process of determining what problem data is required for a given result
group decision support system (GDSS)	498	The hardware, software, people, databases, and procedures needed to provide effective support in group decision-making settings; also called a computerized collaborative work system
groupware	499	Software that helps with joint work group scheduling, communication, and management
heuristics	485	Often referred to as "rules of thumb" (commonly accepted guidelines or procedures that usually find a good solution, but not necessarily the optimal solution); often used in the decision-making process
informatics	503	Combines traditional disciplines, like science and medicine, with computer systems and technology
knowledge management (KM) system	501	System that assists an organization in capturing, storing, and distributing knowledge for use and reuse by the organization, and sometimes its partners and customers
management information system (MIS)	486	An information system that helps individuals and organizations achieve their goals by providing reports and information to make better decisions
nonprogrammed decision	484	Decision that deals with unusual or exceptional situations; difficult to represent as a rule, procedure, or quantitative method
optimization model	485	Conceptualization that finds the best solution, usually the one that will best help individuals or organizations meet their goals
problem solving	482	A process that includes five stages: intelligence, design, choice, implementation, and monitoring
programmed decision	484	Decision that is made using a rule, procedure, or quantitative method
scheduled report	489	An MIS report produced periodically or on a schedule, such as daily, weekly, or monthly
what-if analysis	495	The process of making hypothetical changes to problem data and observing the impact on the results

Questions

Review Questions

1. Describe the stages of decision making.
2. What is the overall purpose of the design stage of decision making?
3. Describe the stages of problem solving.
4. What is a programmed decision?
5. What is the heuristic approach?
6. What is a management information system (MIS)?
7. What are the inputs to an MIS?
8. Describe the outputs of management information systems.
9. What is business intelligence?
10. How does a customer relationship management (CRM) system help an organization?
11. What is the difference between a scheduled report and a demand report?
12. What is a key-indicator report?
13. Define a decision support system. What are its characteristics?
14. Describe what-if analysis.
15. How can goal-seeking analysis be used?
16. Describe the overall approach of simulation.
17. What is a group decision support system (GDSS)?
18. List five characteristics of a GDSS.
19. Which is more intelligent, an MIS or a DSS? Why?
20. What is the least intelligent, but typically the busiest, information system in business?
21. What is common to all forms of informatics?
22. Describe the use of groupware.
23. Why is it common to find hybrid systems in today's businesses?
24. Why is knowledge management important to an organization?
25. What is a geographic information system?

Discussion Questions

26. Think of an important decision you made in the last few years. Describe the results of decision-making and problem-solving steps you used.
27. When might a business want to consider implementing an ERP system?
28. Discuss the difference between scheduled, demand, and exception reports.
29. Provide examples of two heuristics that you use in everyday decision making.
30. What functions do decision support systems (DSS) support in organizations?
31. List one or two career areas that interest you. Describe how a DSS might be used to help you achieve your career goals.
32. How is decision making in a group environment different from individual decision making, and why are information systems that assist in the group environment different? What are the advantages and disadvantages of making decisions as a group?
33. How might knowledge management assist a company that has a high rate of employee turnover?

Exercises

Try It Yourself

1. You have been asked to set up some reports to help your school better plan course offerings. Your school's registration system collects data not only on what classes students have enrolled in, but also on what classes students tried to enroll in but were denied enrollment because the class was full. Using the data in the following table, create two reports: (1) an exception report listing all courses that more than three students couldn't get into because the class was full, and (2) a scheduled report listing the students who are enrolled in each class (a class roster). This scheduled report will be printed every day during registration and can also be used on demand after registration is over.

Course#	StudentID	Status	Date	Reason
370	5987	Enroll	10/13/10	
370	9237	Enroll	10/15/10	
567	1629	Enroll	10/14/10	
567	2863	Denied	10/15/10	Full
567	4631	Enroll	10/14/10	
567	4731	Denied	10/15/10	Full
567	5987	Enroll	10/13/10	
567	9237	Denied	10/15/10	Full
567	9832	Enroll	10/13/10	
963	3958	Denied	10/13/10	Full
963	5678	Denied	10/13/10	Full
963	9832	Denied	10/13/10	Full

2. Search for home mortgage calculators on the Web. Use one to discover what type of home loan you could afford if you were able to pay $1,200 per month. See if you can build your own home mortgage calculator in a speedsheet utilizing formulas found on the Web. Use goal seeking to quickly determine the loan amount that would meet your $1,200 per month budget. Using a word processor, write what you have learned about decision support systems in this exercise, and submit the document with your spreadsheet.
3. Run an Internet search on the keywords *business intelligence*. Find five companies that provide BI tools. Visit their Web sites and write up a short paragraph for each company's BI tool that describes how it can benefit an organization.
4. Visit *www.computerworld.com* and run a search on *ERP*. Find an article that provides an example of a business that benefited from an ERP implementation and write a summary of the article.

Virtual Classroom Activities

For the following exercises, do not use face-to-face or telephone communications with your group members. Use only Internet communications.

5. As discussed in the chapter, a nonprogrammed decision can involve unusual or exceptional situations. Your virtual classroom group should first list three nonprogrammed decisions that a freshman in college might encounter. For each nonprogrammed decision, develop a brief description of the factors to consider during the intelligence and design phases of decision making to help the freshman make the best decision.
6. Groupware is often used to help make business decisions. Visit *www.gotomeeting.com* and set up a free trial account. Arrange a meeting with members of your group. Explore the features of the collaborative tool. The members of your virtual classroom group should summarize the features, advantages, and disadvantages of the groupware product.

Teamwork

7. Your team is to design an information system for a local bookstore chain. Currently, there is a system installed to process sales transactions, but an integrated information system does not exist. Andy Masters, owner of the local bookstore, is planning on expanding from four stores to ten within the next year. To manage this growth, and to keep track of the regular operations of the business, he wants to have a management information system that links together all stores. Prepare a brief memo to Andy explaining five different reports that the information system should produce. Include at least one demand and exception report. Your group should create a layout of the bookstore's new management information system using presentation graphics software.
8. Your team should develop a spreadsheet to be used to estimate the expenses to move off campus next year. The model must allow input of a variety of rent amounts, food costs, transportation costs, and so on, as well as tuition and books. Each team member should put in his or her current estimated costs. Assume that tuition and books are fixed at this year's amounts. After finding an average of the group members' current costs, perform two what-if scenarios. For the first, assume no change in costs except for 2 percent inflation. For the second, assume 5 percent inflation. Do the projection for a year. Create a word-processed document to explain your model to a novice student who might use it to guide decision making for next year.
9. Your team should brainstorm at least three ideas for decision support systems that would be useful on campus. Try to develop models and calculations that you might use to make decisions (say, to choose classes for a semester).

Endnotes

[1] Staff, "Enterprise Solutions," *Trend Microsystems*, accessed June 23, 2009, http://us.trendmicro.com/us/products/enterprise/interscan-messaging-hosted-security/frequently-asked-questions.

[2] Staff, "Customer success in education," IBM Cognos Software, accessed June 23, 2009, http://www.cognos.com/solutions/success/index.html.

[3] Staff, "Verizon Standardizes Reporting Tools and Cuts Report Product Times by 99%," *SAP Business Objects Success Stories*, accessed June 24, 2009, www.sap.com.

[4] Staff, "Buncombe County: Efficient Government Services with SAP® BusinessObjects™ Software," *SAP Business Objects Success Stories*, accessed June 24, 2009, www.sap.com.

[5] Staff, "Global Furniture Manufacturer Cuts Costs, Improves Productivity with Collaboration Tool," *Microsoft Case Studies*, accessed June 24, 2009, www.microsoft.com/casestudies.

[6] Microsoft SharePoint Case Studies, accessed July 3, 2009, http://sharepoint.microsoft.com/case-studies/Pages/default.aspx.

[7] Staff, "Tourism New Zealand corporate services portal," *DBS Track Record*, accessed June 24, 2009, www.dbsys.co.nz/trackrecord.

[8] "Citrix case study," *Jive Software Case Studies*, accessed June 24, 2009, www.jivesoftware.com/customers/case-studies/citrix.

SYSTEMS DEVELOPMENT

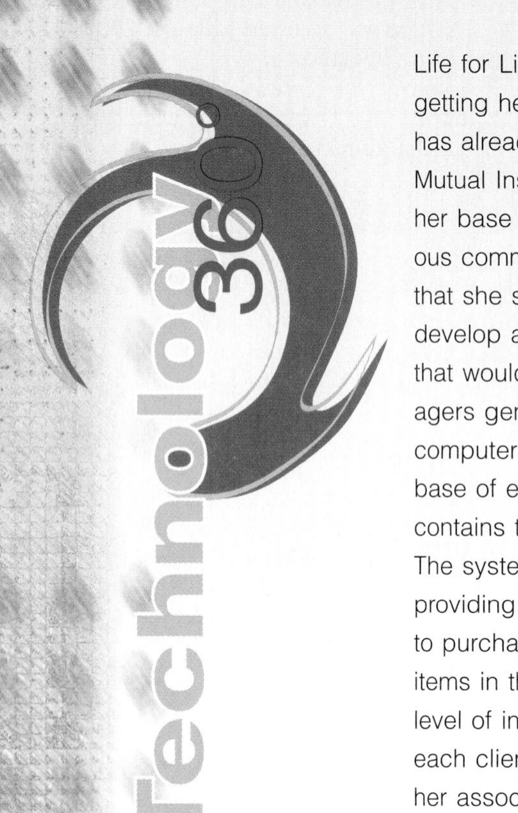

Life for Linda Perez has been good. Two years after getting her undergraduate degree in business, she has already been promoted to account manager at Mutual Insurance in Tampa, Florida. In addition to her base salary, Mutual is offering Linda a generous commission for each new insurance customer that she signs. Linda would like the company to develop an insurance and risk analysis program that would help her and other account managers generate even more business. The new computer system would draw from a database of existing and potential customers that contains their information and insurance needs. The system would generate a monthly report providing a list of individuals who might be likely to purchase or upgrade an insurance policy. The items in the report would be listed in order of the level of insurance required for the amount of risk each client posed. Such a report would be valuable in allowing Linda and her associates to concentrate their efforts on the most valuable clients. Linda recently met James Jones, a systems analyst with the company, at a party. When she discussed her ideas for the program with him, he was very excited about it and gave her more ideas for how she could also use the program to improve customer service. Now she wants to present her ideas to the company.

As you read through this chapter, consider the following questions:

1. How should Linda approach her company to get the new program developed?
2. If the company decides to develop the new program, how should Linda be involved in the process?
3. What role would James and people like him play in developing the new program?

Check out Linda's *Action Plan* at the end of this chapter.

10

LEARNING OBJECTIVES

1. Describe the systems development life cycle, who participates in it, and why it is important.
2. Discuss systems development tools.
3. Understand how systems development projects are investigated.
4. Describe how an existing system can be evaluated.
5. Discuss what is involved in planning a new system.
6. List the steps to implement a new or modified system.
7. Describe the importance of updating and monitoring a system.

CHAPTER CONTENT

Introduction

Throughout this book, you have seen how computer and information systems have helped people and organizations in a variety of settings: engineering, science, the arts, business, library studies, sociology, criminology, architecture, music, the military, and many other fields. But how are these systems acquired or developed? And how can the people and organizations that use these systems make sure those systems truly help them achieve their goals? The answer is a process called *systems development.*

This chapter introduces the systems development process, including systems investigation, analysis, design, implementation, maintenance, and review. In this chapter, you will see how you can be involved in systems development to advance your career and help your company or organization. You will also see how IT professionals, including systems analysts and computer programmers, work together to develop effective computer and information systems. In addition, the chapter discusses how to use the systems development process to obtain the systems and software you need. In the pages that follow, you will see how systems development can be used to realize the true potential of computer systems in almost every field or discipline.

Systems development is the activity of creating new computer-based information systems or modifying existing ones to meet individual or organizational goals. It refers to all aspects of the process—from identifying problems to be solved or opportunities to be exploited to evaluating and possibly refining the chosen solution. Throughout this book, you have seen the results of systems development in numerous examples. All of these uses of computer systems are a direct result of the systems development process discussed in this chapter.

AN OVERVIEW OF SYSTEMS DEVELOPMENT

Systems development efforts can range from a small project, such as purchasing an inexpensive computer program, to a major undertaking, such as installing a huge system that includes hardware, software, communications systems, and databases, and requires new computer systems personnel. Some systems development projects can involve millions of dollars. For example, the U.S. federal government budgeted $38.6 billion for information system development in 2009.[1] The Justice Department itself averages $125 million per IT project. The State Department averages $64 million; NASA, $56 million; and the Smithsonian Institution, $55 million.[2] Businesses invest heavily in systems development as well. While they invest heavily, they also expect a swift return on investment (ROI). Other systems development focuses on humanitarian needs. Table 10.1 summarizes some recent humanitarian systems development projects.

TABLE 10.1 • Successful humanitarian systems development projects

Organization	Description
Deaf Link, Inc.	Developed a system that allows deaf and hard-of-hearing citizens in the United States to receive sign language services remotely over Internet video, saving hospitals and other facilities as much as 60 percent on yearly interpreting costs and providing better accessibility to those in need.
One Hen, Inc.	Developed online interactive games and stories for kids that introduce them to entrepreneurship concepts, helping them become "financially responsible, global citizens."
UNICEF	Mandated by the United Nations General Assembly to advocate for the protection of children's rights, UNICEF developed a system called Fly-Away VSAT and Enterprise Management System, which provides an "office in a box" that can be deployed in under four hours to provide Internet communications via satellite anywhere in the world.
The University of Texas M. D. Anderson Cancer Center	Developed ClinicStation, the first electronic medical record system that seamlessly integrates clinical and research information for physicians working in the nation's top-rated hospital for cancer care.
Source: Computerworld's *2008 and 2009 Honors Program at www.cwhonors.org*	

Organizations have used different approaches to developing computer and information systems. In some cases, these approaches are formalized and captured in volumes of documents. In other cases, less formal approaches are used. The steps of systems development vary from one organization to the next, but most approaches have five common phases: investigation, analysis, design, implementation, and maintenance and review.

The systems development process is an ongoing and cyclic activity. Once a system is developed, it is reviewed and, over time, often revised and improved. The **systems development life cycle (SDLC)** is the ongoing activity associated with

FIGURE 10.1 • The systems development life cycle (SDLC)

The systems development life cycle (SDLC) involves working through a number of steps to go from the initial idea to a finished system. Sometimes information learned in a particular phase requires cycling back to a previous phase.

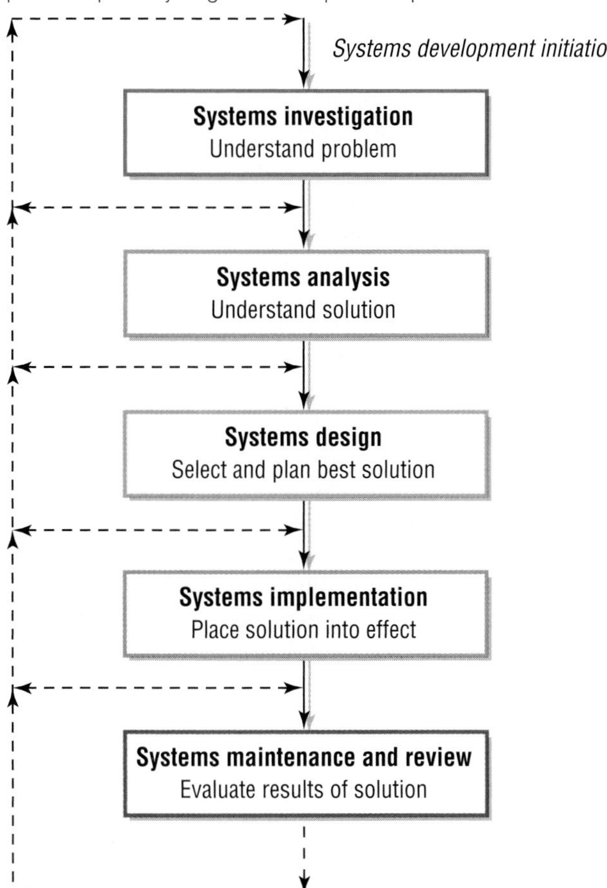

the systems development process, including investigation, analysis, design, implementation, and maintenance and review, as shown in Figure 10.1. Systems investigation and analysis look at the existing system and determine if the existing system can and should be improved. Systems design and implementation involve modifying an existing system or developing a new one and placing it into operation. Finally, maintenance and review make sure that the new or modified system is operating as intended.

As each system is being built, the project has timelines and deadlines, until at last the system is installed and accepted. The life of the system continues as it is maintained and reviewed. If the system needs significant improvement beyond the scope of maintenance—if it needs to be replaced due to a new generation of technology, or if there is a major change in the organization's requirements—a new systems development project is initiated, and the cycle starts over.

As Figure 10.1 shows, a particular system under development may move from one phase of the SDLC to the next, and then back to a previous phase, and so on. In an ideal world, it is unnecessary to return to a previous phase to correct errors or make adjustments. In reality, activities in a later phase of the SDLC may uncover a need to change the results of previous steps. For example, a medical researcher might realize during implementation of a new software system that the current computers are too slow. This might require upgrades to hardware and software, which could restart the systems design phase. Thus, although it is described as a series of steps, the SDLC is more likely to cycle back and forth between steps to continuously rebuild and refine a system. At each step, there are checkpoints to determine if the step has been successfully completed, if additional work is needed, and if the systems development process should continue.

Even if they use the preceding steps, many systems development efforts fail to achieve their goals. Organizations have lost hundreds of millions of dollars on failed systems development efforts. In addition, an organization's clients or customers can also suffer losses. In one classic case, a major stock exchange tried to implement a new computerized trading system. Companies and individuals that interacted with the new system had to spend money to change their systems to work with the new trading system. When the new trading system didn't work and was never implemented, the companies and individuals that interacted with the stock exchange had to change back to their old systems, wasting a tremendous amount of time and money.

The percentage of information systems (IS) development projects that fail is high. A 2009 study found that over a one-year period only 32 percent of IT projects were considered successful, 24 percent of projects failed (were cancelled before completion), and 44 percent were considered challenged (completed late and/or over budget).[3] In recent years, IT project failure rates have climbed due to economic hardships and insufficient resources. While proper resources are important to the success of IT projects, most systems analysts will tell you that good communication between system developers, management, and users is essential to successful IS implementation. Other problems that might bring down a project are insufficient resource planning (running out of money) and unrealistic deadlines. For new systems to be developed successfully, it is important for all participants to be well informed and participate in the development process.

Participants in Systems Development

Effective systems development requires a team effort. The team usually consists of system stakeholders, users, managers, systems development specialists, and various support personnel. This team, called the development team, is responsible for determining the objectives of the system and delivering to the organization a system that meets these objectives. **System stakeholders** are individuals who will ultimately benefit from the systems development project, either directly or through the organization they represent.

Users are a specific type of stakeholder. Users are individuals who will be interacting with the system on a regular basis. They can be employees, managers, customers, suppliers, vendors, and others. Physicians, for example, can be actively involved in developing a 3D system for surgery that allows surgeons to practice on simulations of a patient's internal organs before actually performing the surgery, thus preventing mistakes and saving lives (see Figure 10.2).

FIGURE 10.2 • A surgical training system

Doctors can use this virtual reality training system to practice new techniques.

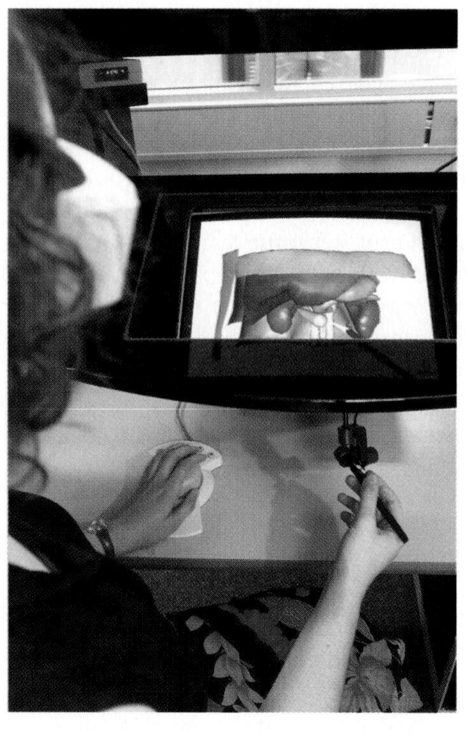

Managers are people within an organization most capable of initiating and maintaining change. For large-scale systems development projects, where the investment in and value of a system can be quite high, it is common to have senior-level managers as part of the development team. The director of a World War II museum, for example, may be involved in developing a new museum database system that contains data and information on all of the World War II exhibits and artifacts stored in the museum.

Systems development specialists typically are IT personnel. Depending on the nature of the systems project, the development team might include the project leader, systems analyst, and software engineer, among others. A *project leader* is the individual in charge of the systems development effort. This person coordinates all aspects of the systems development effort and is responsible for its success. A **systems analyst** is a professional who specializes in analyzing and designing systems. Systems analysts play important roles while interacting with the system stakeholders and users, management, software engineers, and other IT support personnel (see Figure 10.3). Like an architect developing blueprints for a new building, a systems analyst develops detailed plans for the new or modified system. The *software engineer*, sometimes called a computer programmer, is responsible for modifying existing programs or developing new programs to satisfy user requirements. Like a contractor constructing a new building or renovating an existing one, the programmer takes the plans from the systems analyst and builds or modifies the necessary software.

FIGURE 10.3 • Participants in systems development

The systems development process typically involves communication between many people within and outside an organinzation, with the systems analyst acting as the central coordinator.

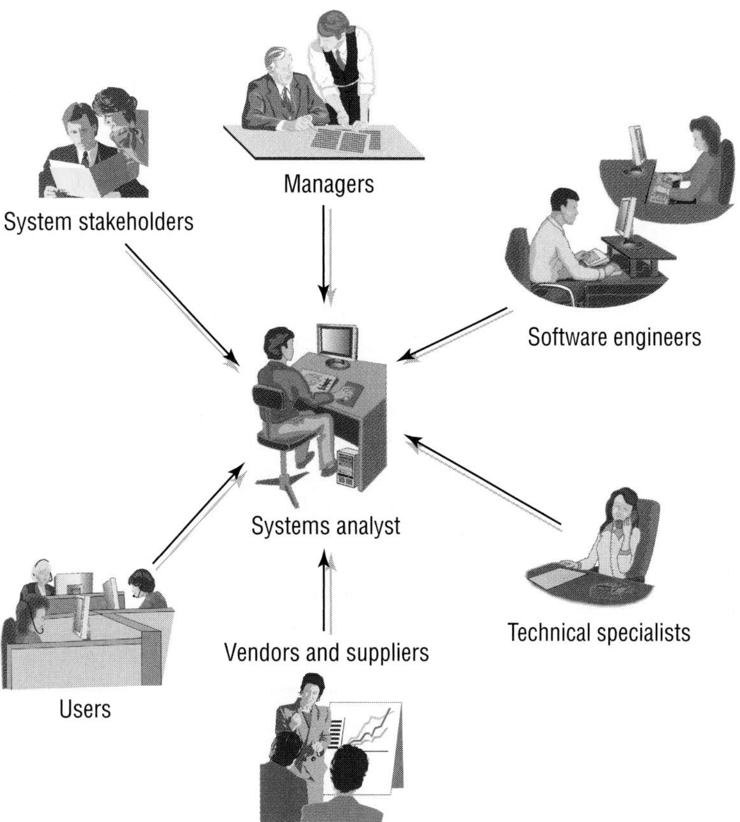

The other support personnel on the development team are mostly technical specialists, either IT department employees or outside consultants, including database and telecommunications experts, knowledge engineers, and other personnel such as vendor or supplier representatives. Some specialize in building new systems, and others might specialize in implementing systems or testing them. Depending on the magnitude of the systems development project and the number of systems development specialists on the team, the group may also include one or more computer systems managers. *Computer systems management* can include the chief information officer (CIO) and other computer and information systems executives.

A NEW OS FOR NETBOOKS

Think about it. The operating system (OS) you're using on your computer was designed years ago—before the advent of the Web. Does it really make sense that you should have to boot your computer and open the browser to access e-mail? Not according to Google, which developed the Chrome OS, especially designed for netbooks, whose primary purpose is to perform Web-based tasks. Chrome is designed to be fast, unobtrusive, and virus resistant.

Google to Release OS Aimed at Netbooks
Joab Jackson
Application Development Trends
July 8, 2009
http://adtmag.com/articles/2009/07/08/google-to-release-os-aimed-at-netbooks.aspx

Why Start a Systems Development Project?

Organizations can start a systems development project for many reasons, including problems with the existing system, mergers, competition, and even pressure from government agencies. In the wake of financial scandals, for example, the U.S. government instituted corporate financial reporting rules under the Sarbanes-Oxley Act. These reporting regulations caused many U.S. companies to initiate systems development efforts to comply with the regulations.

Many systems are developed simply because someone in the organization comes up with a good idea. In most cases, information systems are developed to allow an organization to become more efficient. For example, aircraft manufacturer Embraer developed an information system that allowed it to test new aircraft to meet certification standards more thoroughly in less time.[4]

Many organizations initiate systems development projects that they expect will provide a competitive advantage. Software companies are always exploring ways to make new products that people will flock to. Most companies want to maximize their profits. Figuring out how to gain a competitive advantage usually requires creative and critical analysis. Becoming environmentally responsible while cutting costs has become yet another motivation for systems development. Many companies are redesigning enterprise-wide systems to employ less processing power, use fewer servers, and reduce energy consumption.

Creative analysis involves seeking new approaches to existing problems. For example, Google Voice is a service that allows users to manage their phone lines in a whole new way (see Figure 10.4). Using a Google Voice phone number, the system routes your phone calls to any one of multiple phone numbers, providing advanced filtering features along the way.[5] By looking at problems in new or different ways and by introducing innovative methods to solve them, many organizations have gained significant competitive advantage.

FIGURE 10.4 • Competing creatively – Google Voice

Google Voice offers a new type of telephone system that routes phone calls through its feature-rich, Internet-based switchboard.

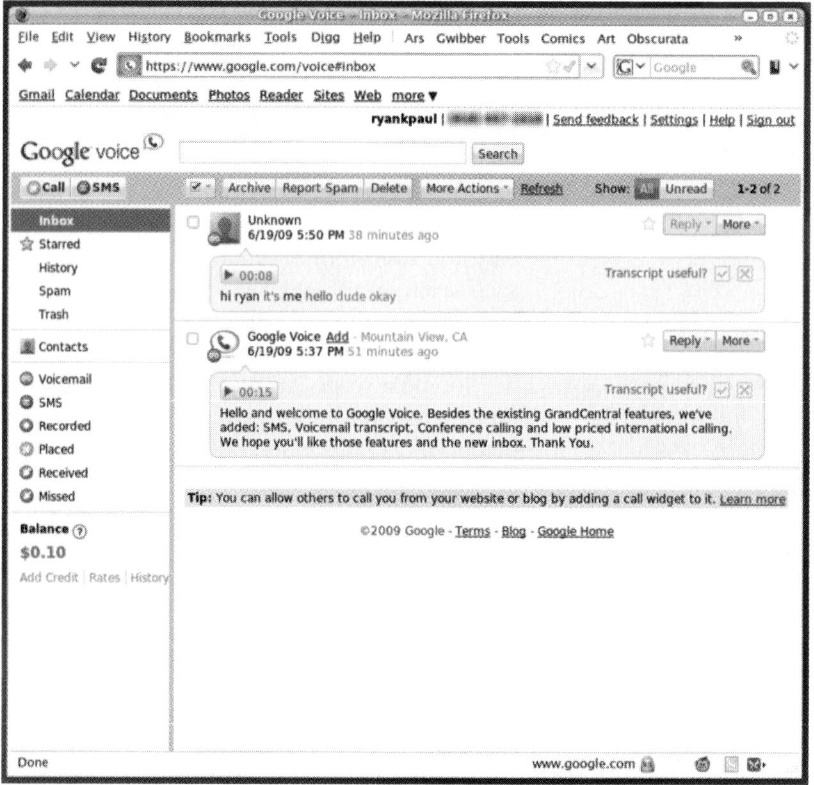

Critical analysis means being skeptical and doubtful, and requires questioning whether the current system is still effective and efficient. Critical analysis can result in finding better ways of doing things or ways of doing business that give a competitive advantage. An airline company, for example, can use critical analysis and decide that providing wireless Internet on many of its flights would attract more business customers and generate additional revenue.[6]

The systems development process often begins with gathering information on users' needs. Questioning users about their needs and being skeptical and doubtful about initial responses can result in better systems and more accurate predictions of how those systems will work. Too often, system stakeholders and users specify certain system requirements because they assume the only way to meet their needs is through those requirements. But often, their needs might best be met through an alternate approach. For example, a movie producer might decide to hire a team of stuntmen for an action scene because this is how she has done it for decades. However, a new computerized imaging system might be able to digitally generate the scenes she wants at less expense. All too often, solutions are selected before a complete understanding of the nature of the problem itself is obtained. The understanding can come from systems development planning.

Systems Development Planning

Systems development planning is the translation of organizational or individual goals into systems development initiatives. For example, an organization may identify organizational goals of doubling sales revenue within five years, reducing administrative expenses by 20 percent over three years, acquiring at least two competing companies within a year, or attaining market leadership in a given product category. An individual might identify a personal goal of being able to develop beautiful videos or photos. These goals are translated into specific systems development goals. For example, the Cleveland Metroparks Zoo's mission is to influence and educate people to "positively impact wildlife and wild places through their caring, decision making, and actions." The zoo's administration wanted to extend its influence to individuals unable to visit the zoo. To do so, they developed a Distance Learning Program that incorporates real-time interactive video access to animal exhibits (see Figure 10.5).[7]

FIGURE 10.5 • Systems development at the Cleveland Metroparks Zoo

Not satisfied with educating only zoo vistors, administrators developed a new system to distribute interactive educational video and lessons over the Internet.

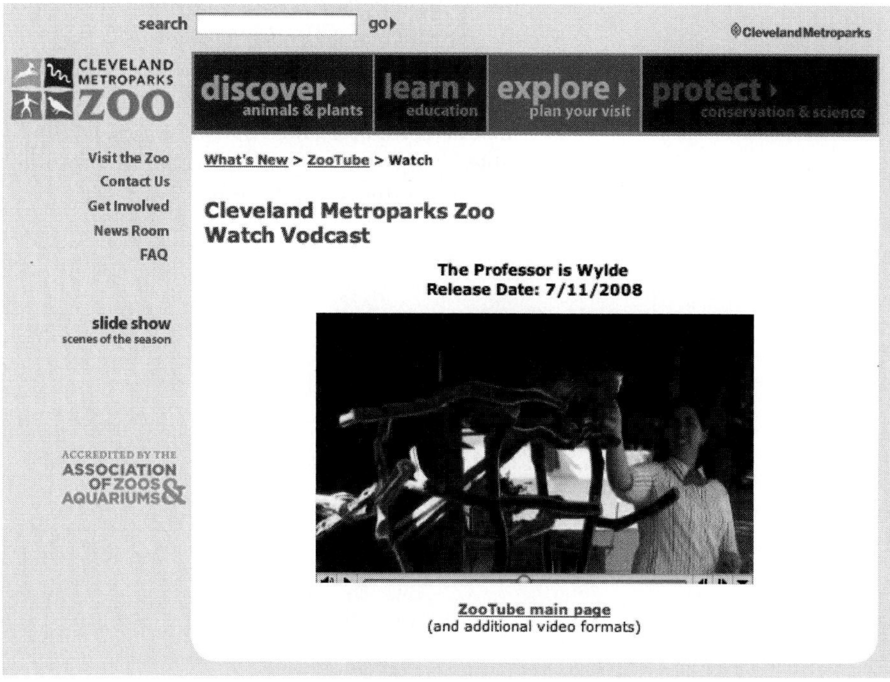

End-User Systems Development

End-user systems development is the development of information systems by individuals outside of the formal information systems planning and departmental structure. With the increased availability and use of general-purpose information technology and the flexibility of many packaged software programs, employees outside of the IT department can independently develop information systems that meet their needs. These employees feel that by bypassing the formal requisitioning of developmental resources from the IT department, they can develop systems more quickly. In addition, these individuals often feel that they have better insight into their own needs and can develop systems better suited to their purposes. Adobe, for example, has an end-user systems development tool called Contribute that is designed to make it easy for people to develop and edit Web pages. Such a Web development tool can be used to let designated people and groups edit specified Web sites. In addition, many end users are increasingly developing computer systems or solving computer-related problems for others. It should be noted, however, that not all organizations encourage or allow end-user systems development.

Systems developed by end users range from the very small (a software routine to merge data with form letters) to those of significant organizational value (such as customer contact databases). Like all projects, some systems developed by end users fail and others are successful. Initially, IT professionals discounted the value of these projects and basically ignored them. As the number and magnitude of these projects increased, however, IT professionals began to realize that for the good of the entire organization, their involvement with these projects needed to increase. Rather than ignoring these initiatives, astute IT professionals encourage them by offering guidance and support. Technical assistance, communication of standards, and the sharing of best practices throughout the organization are just some of the ways IT professionals work with motivated managers and employees undertaking their own systems development. IT professionals can also help end users apply systems development tools.

TOOLS AND TECHNIQUES FOR SYSTEMS DEVELOPMENT

Just as hammers, screwdrivers, and other tools can be used to make home repairs easier, *systems development tools* can greatly simplify the systems development process. In the strictest sense, a tool can be almost any instrument, from a pencil to a large, complex machine. Systems development tools most often used include computer-aided software engineering (CASE) tools, flowcharts, decision tables, project management software, prototyping, outsourcing, and object-oriented systems development.

iPhone Systems Development

Systems development projects often originate because new technologies provide new opportunities. One such "new technology" that has inspired both novice and experienced developers is the iPhone.

The iPhone software development kit (SDK) is freely available for download to anyone who wants to develop an iPhone app, and many are taking advantage of it. There are tens of thousands of iPhone apps available in the iPhone App Store, ranging from the silly to the serious. Amateurs are developing apps for the iPhone, inspired by simple apps that made their developers wealthy. However, most are finding that such windfalls are few and far between. Serious corporate systems developers are also focusing on the iPhone, seeking to extend access to corporate systems to more users in more environments.

Travis Warren, CIO of WhippleHill Communications, began developing for the iPhone to satisfy his customers' desires. WhippleHill develops software that delivers online services for private schools. It provides Web access to school records, including attendance, contacts, schedules, and progress reports, to teachers, administrators, coaches, parents, and students. Many of WhippleHill's customers expressed a desire to access those records from their iPhones as well.

WhippleHill developers ran the numbers and determined that the iPhone software would be too expensive to generate in house. They contacted software development firms in India but discovered that those firms were not yet familiar with developing iPhone apps. The company ended up hiring TerriblyClever, a company that a group of students from Stanford formed around a successful iPhone app that they had created.

After six months and a lot of coding both for the iPhone and on the backend system at WhippleHill, TerriblyClever delivered an iPhone app for customers to download at $2 a copy that provided access to student records using the iPhone's small touch screen.

In the end, the development of the app cost WhippleHill nothing. An agreement was struck with the Stanford students to split the profits generated by the app 50/50. Travis Warren and many other CIOs believe that the future of systems development relies heavily on developing robust backend systems that are accessible from all types of mobile devices.

Questions

1. Why did WhippleHill decide to take on an iPhone system development project? What benefits did it hope to gain?
2. Why did WhippleHill outsource the project? What benefits and drawbacks were involved?
3. Why is there a rush to develop for the iPhone?

Sources

1. *Kaneshige, Tom, "Racing Toward an iPhone App,"* Computerworld, *June 4, 2009, www.computerworld.com.*
2. *Claburn, Thomas, "Apple iPhone Developers Mostly Don't Make Much Money,"* InformationWeek, *June 12, 2009, www.informationweek.com.*
3. *Chen, Brian, "iPhone Fart App Rakes in $10,000 a Day,"* Wired, *December 24, 2008, www.wired.com.*

Computer-Aided Software Engineering

One type of systems development tool consists of software programs that help automate various aspects of the systems development process. *Software engineering*, a formal way of conducting systems development, typically employs systems development software commonly referred to as CASE tools. **Computer-aided software engineering (CASE) tools** automate many of the tasks required in a systems development effort (Figure 10.6).

FIGURE 10.6 • CASE tools

CASE tools can be used to diagram and develop new computer and information systems.

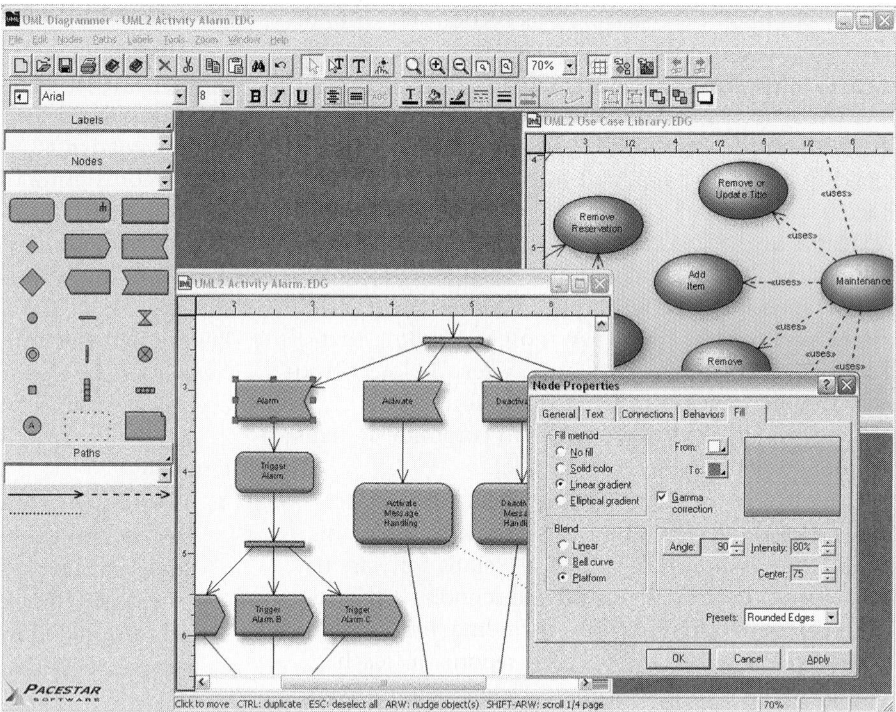

As with any team, coordinating the efforts of members of a systems development team can be challenging. To help address coordination problems, CASE tools allow more than one person to work on the same system at the same time via a multiuser interface, which coordinates and integrates the work of all team members. With this facility, one person working on one aspect of systems development can automatically share results with someone working on another aspect of the same system.

Flowcharts

Like a road map, a **flowchart** is a system design diagram that charts the path from a starting point to the final goal of a system. Flowcharts can display various amounts of detail. Using symbols, they show the logical relationships between system components. Like other systems development tools, flowcharts can be useful in areas other than program design and development. For example, they can be used to display and understand what courses are needed to complete a college or university degree and what activities must be completed to finish a project at work.

When developing a system, a flowchart is used to describe the overall purpose and structure of the system. This is usually called the system flowchart or application flowchart. An *application flowchart* for a simplified payroll application is shown in Figure 10.7. Inputs include an employee file that contains an employee's pay rate and a time file that contains the hours the employee worked during the week. The payroll program multiplies the pay rate times the hours worked and subtracts any deductions to compute the paycheck for the employee. More detailed flowcharts, called *program flowcharts*, are needed to reveal how each software program is to be developed.

FIGURE 10.7 • Flowchart of a simplified payroll application

Circles in this application flowchart show that inputs include an employee file and a time file. The process square labeled "Payroll program" represents the operations of multiplying the pay rate times the hours worked and subtracting deductions to compute the employee's paycheck.

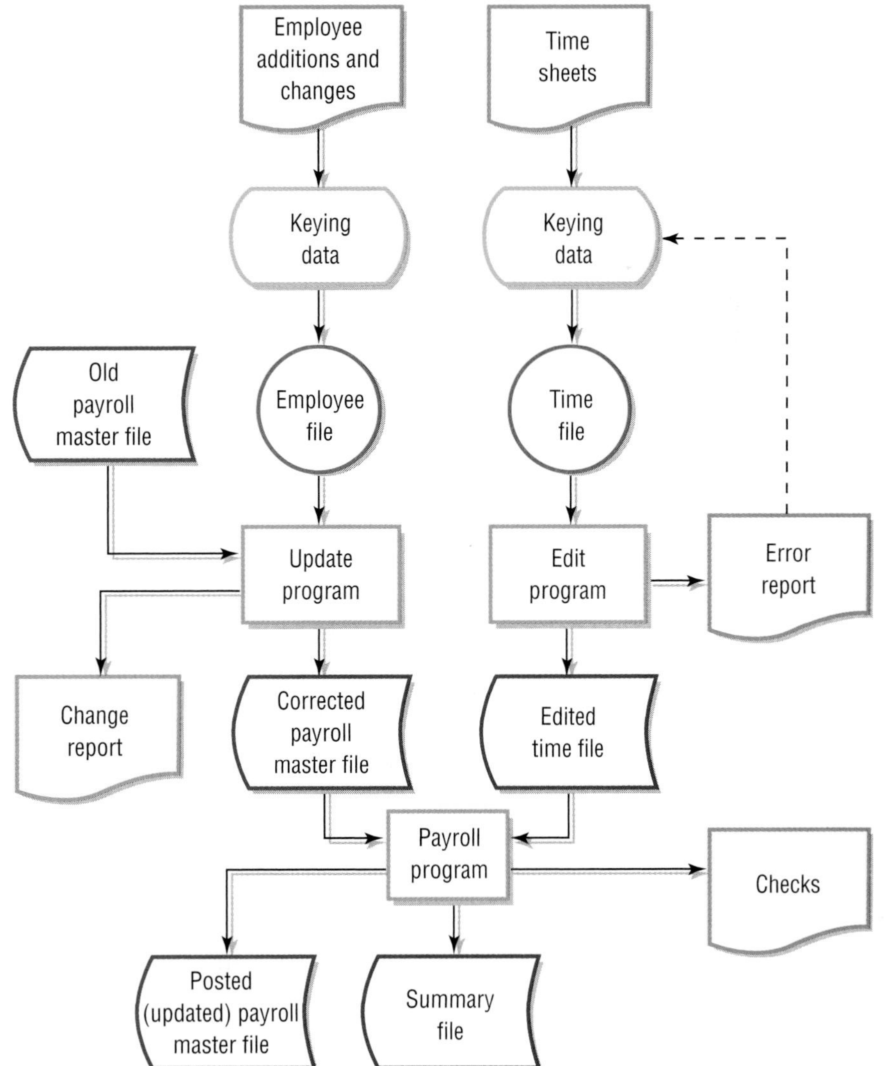

Flowcharts have a number of limitations. They were originally developed to help programmers and analysts design and document computer and information systems and programs. As programs became larger, flowcharts became more difficult to implement. You can imagine how difficult it would be to develop a detailed flowchart for a program containing more than 50,000 program statements. As a result, many organizations are reducing the amount of flowcharting they use. Some rely more on techniques such as computer-aided software engineering (CASE) tools.

Decision Tables

A **decision table** is a systems development tool that displays the various conditions that could exist in a system and the different actions that the computer should take as a result of these conditions. A decision table can be used as an alternative to or in conjunction with flowcharts. When there are a large number of branches or paths within a software program, decision tables are particularly useful; in fact, in these cases, decision tables are preferable to flowcharts. A decision table that aids decisions regarding airline reservations is shown in Figure 10.8.

Figure 10.8 • A decision table for an airline reservation application

A decision table displays the various conditions that can exist and the different actions the computer should take as a result of any one condition.

	Airline reservation application	Rule number				
Name of decision table		1	2	3	4	**Rule numbers**
	Condition statements					
	First-class requested	Y	Y	N	N	
Condition statement	First-class available	Y	N	N	N	**Actual conditions**
	Tourist-class requested	N	N	Y	Y	
	Tourist-class available	N	N	Y	N	
	Actions taken					
	First-class ticket issued	X				
Action statement	Tourist-class ticket issued			X		**Action taken**
	First-class wait listed		X			
	Tourist-class wait listed				X	

Project Management Tools

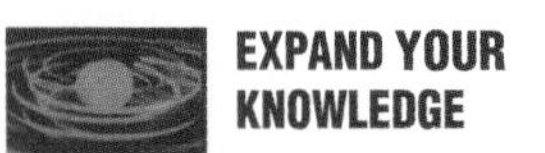

EXPAND YOUR KNOWLEDGE

To learn more about project management tools, go to www.cengage.com/computerconcepts/np/swt4. Click the link "Expand Your Knowledge" and then complete the lab entitled "Project Management."

Although the steps of systems development seem straightforward, larger projects can become complex, requiring literally hundreds or thousands of separate activities. For these types of systems development efforts, project management becomes essential. The overall purpose of **project management** is to plan, monitor, and control necessary development activities.

Two techniques frequently used in project management are program evaluation and review technique (PERT) and Gantt charting. *PERT* is a formalized approach to project management that involves creating three time estimates for an activity: the shortest possible time, the most likely time, and the longest possible time. A formula is then applied to come up with a single PERT time estimate. A *Gant chart* is a graphical tool used for planning, monitoring, and coordinating projects. A Gantt chart is essentially a grid that lists activities and deadlines. Each time a task is completed, a darkened line is placed in the proper grid cell to indicate completion of a task (see Figure 10.9).

Both PERT and Gantt techniques can be automated using project management software, such as Microsoft Project and Open Workbench. This type of software monitors all project activities and determines if activities and the entire project are on time and within budget. It also has workgroup capabilities, handling multiple projects and enabling a team of people to interact with the same software. Project management software helps people determine the best way to reduce project completion time at the least cost. Reducing project completion time is called *project crashing*. This project management software feature can be very useful if a project starts to fall behind schedule or becomes more expensive than originally planned.

FIGURE 10.9 • Project management software

Project management software, like Microsoft Project and the open-source OpenProj, helps people determine the best way to reduce project completion time at the least cost, utilizing database and spreadsheet functionality and displaying a project overview using a Gantt chart.

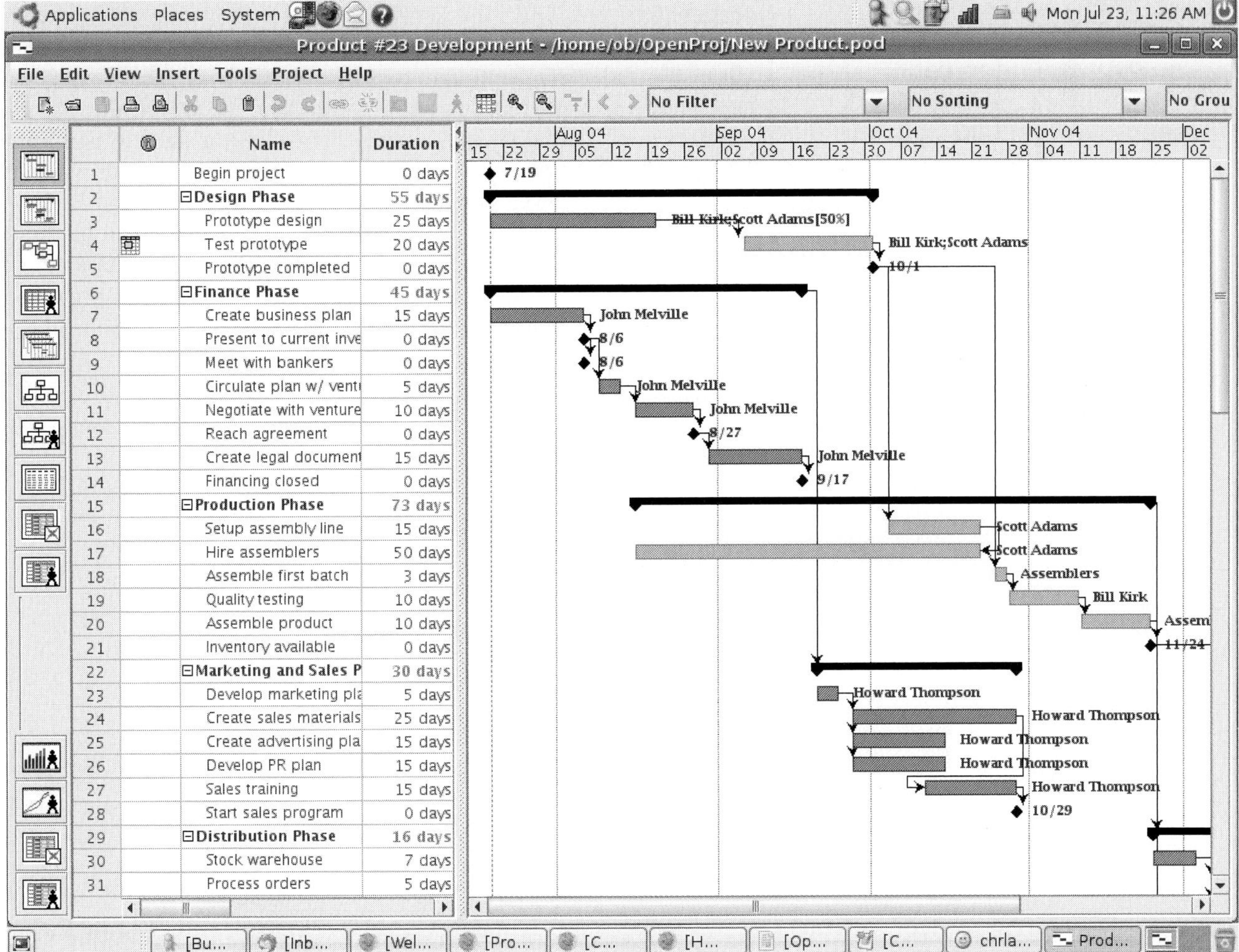

Prototyping

A different technique for systems development uses a phased or *iterative approach*. With the iterative approach to systems development, each phase of the

SDLC is repeated several times (iterated). During each iteration, requirements and alternative solutions to the problem are analyzed, solutions are designed, and some portion of the system is implemented and subjected to a user review (see Figure 10.10).

FIGURE 10.10 • An iterative approach to systems development

Using an iterative approach, each phase of the SDLC is repeated several times. System requirements and alternate solutions to the problem are analyzed, solutions are designed, and some portion of the system is implemented and subjected to a user review.

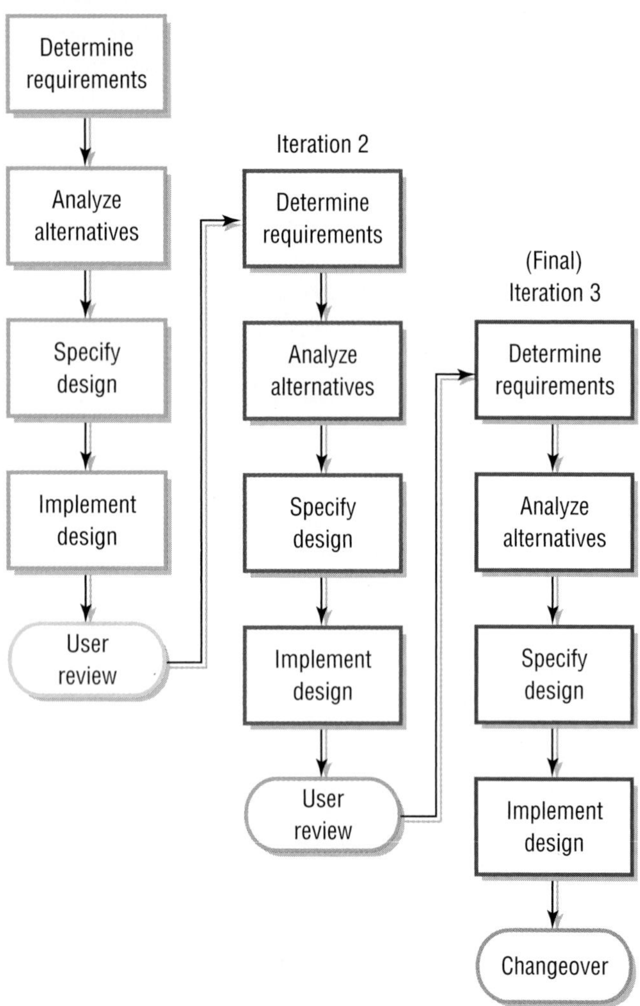

A prominent example of an iterative technique for systems development is prototyping. **Prototyping** typically involves creating a preliminary model or version of a major subsystem, or a small or scaled-down version of the entire system. For example, a prototype might be developed to show sample report formats and input screens using a graphics program. Once developed and refined, the prototype reports and input screens developed in the graphics program are used as models for the actual system, which may be developed using a programming language. In many cases, prototyping continues until the complete system is developed.

Outsourcing

Outsourcing occurs when a business uses an outside company to take over portions of its workload. Many organizations hire an outside consulting firm that specializes in systems development to perform some or all of its computer and information systems development activities. Accenture, IBM, and EDS are examples of consulting companies that can be hired to take over some or all computer-related tasks for an organization. Outsourcing is gaining in popularity (see Figure 10.11).

FIGURE 10.11 • Outsourcing – India call center

Services such as tech support and call centers are often cheaper when outsourced to developing countries.

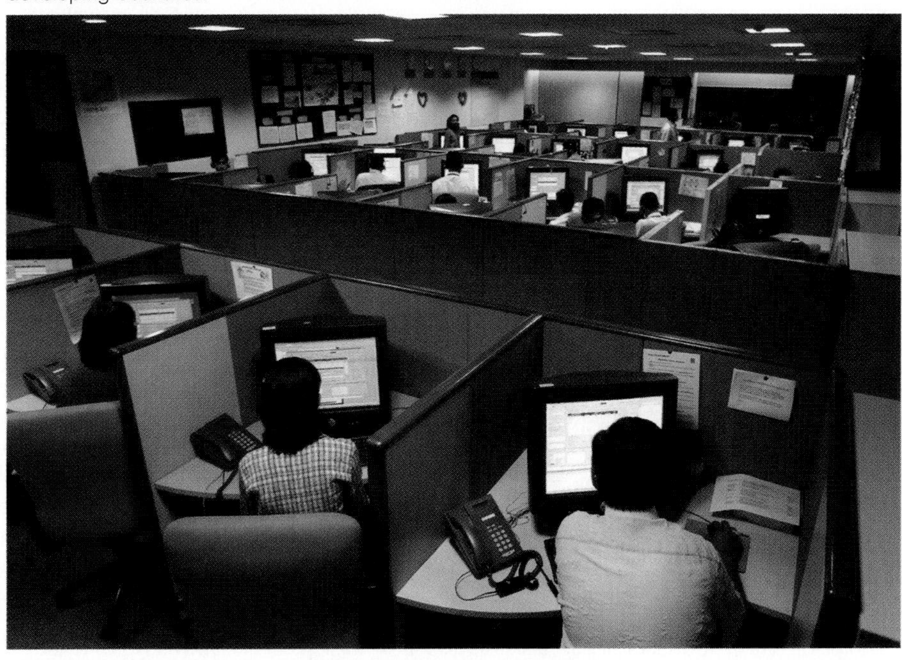

Outsourcing has also become an important economic and political issue in today's economy for companies that outsource overseas. Groups and organizations have formed to try to appease those who fear job loss in the United States resulting from outsourcing. Companies can spend millions or even billions of dollars to hire other companies to manage Web sites, network servers, data storage devices, and help-desk operations. Much of U.S. outsourcing is being provided from developing countries where the work can be done less expensively.

Reducing costs, obtaining state-of-the-art technology, eliminating staffing and personnel problems, and increasing technological flexibility are reasons that organizations have used outsourcing. One American computer company, for example, estimated that a programmer with three to five years of experience in China would cost $12.50 per hour, while a programmer with similar experience in the United States would cost $56 per hour. As work within an organization becomes increasingly distributed, projects become more challenging to manage. Communication can be challenging as well when a project is divided between different countries and cultures. Outsourcing can involve a large number of countries and companies in bringing new products and services to market. The idea for a new computer server can originate in Singapore and be approved in Houston, designed in India, engineered in Taiwan, and assembled in Australia. The chain of events can be complex.

There are other challenges and disadvantages to outsourcing. Internal expertise

LOOKING TO THE CROWD FOR DEVELOPMENT

You've heard of outsourcing. You've heard of insourcing. Well, now there's *crowdsourcing*. And it's hot for some very good reasons. Rather than hire programmers, a company holds a competition for the best code. In 2009, for example, Netflix ended a $1 million competition to improve their movie recommendation software by 10 percent. The frontrunner was a team of seven programmers from companies like AT&T and Yahoo!. This new employment model, which like Wikipedia is powered by people's need to share their talents and ideas, spurs innovation in product development and R&D.

The Crowd Is Wise (When It's Focused)
Steve Lohr
The New York Times
July 18, 2009
http://www.nytimes.com/2009/07/19/technology/internet/19unboxed.html

and loyalty can suffer under an outsourcing arrangement. People who lose their jobs to outsourcing can become very upset. When an organization uses outsourcing, key IT personnel with expertise in technical and organizational functions are no longer needed. Once these IT employees leave, the organization loses their experience with the organization and their expertise in computer systems. For other companies, it can be difficult to achieve a competitive advantage when competitors are using the same outsourcing company. It has been estimated that about 80 percent of U.S. companies outsource critical activities to India, Russia, Pakistan, and China, which could jeopardize security. How will important data and trade secrets be guarded?

FIGURE 10.12 • Use case diagram for a college

This basic use case diagram illustrates the actors and use case interactions in college system.

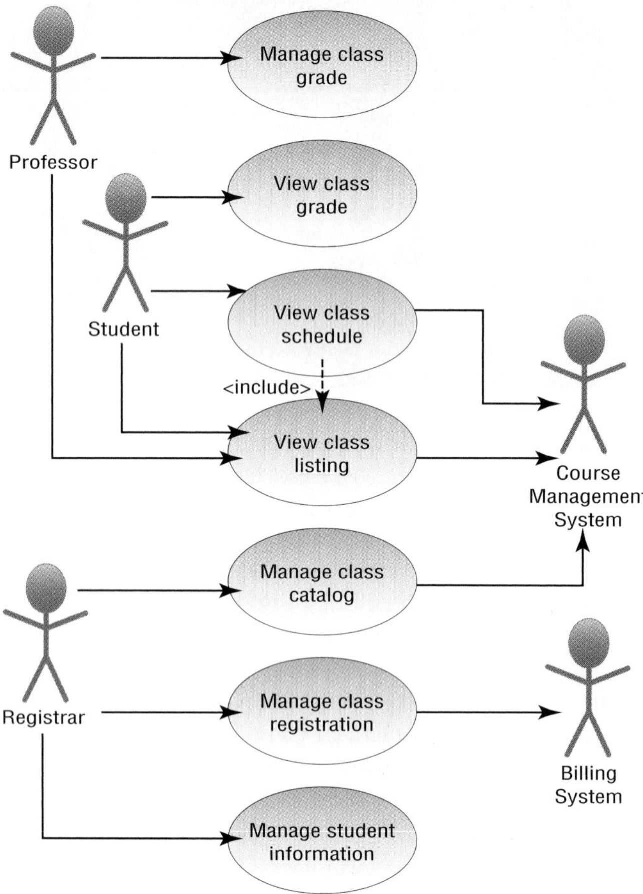

Object-Oriented Systems Development

Object-oriented (OO) systems development is an extension of object-oriented programming. OO development follows a defined system development life cycle, much like the SDLC. The life cycle phases can be, and usually are, completed with numerous iterations.

The object-oriented approach can be used during all phases of systems development, from investigation to maintenance and review. This approach views components of an information system as objects, each object with attributes (characteristics) and methods (actions). By defining the interactions between objects, a system is developed that is modular and easily customized.

Use cases—how people interact with the system—are often examined to define the objects in a system. Consider Figure 10.12, which provides a use case diagram for a college. A use case diagram illustrates how people, referred to as actors, interact with functions, referred to as use cases, of a system. Defining all the actors and use cases in a system allows the systems developer to understand the interaction of objects in object-oriented systems development.

SYSTEMS INVESTIGATION

Systems investigation is usually the first step in the development of a new or modified information system. The overall purpose of **systems investigation** is to determine whether or not the objectives met by the existing system are satisfying the goals of the organization. In systems investigation, potential problems and opportunities are identified. Investigation attempts to reveal the cause and scope of the problem or opportunity. In general, systems investigation attempts to uncover answers to the following types of questions:

- What primary problems might a new or enhanced system solve?
- What opportunities might a new or enhanced system provide?

- What new hardware, software, databases, telecommunications, personnel, or procedures will improve an existing system, or are required in a new system?
- What are the potential costs?
- What are the associated risks?

Conducting a feasibility study is usually an important part of the systems investigation phase.

Feasibility Analysis

A key part of the systems investigation phase is **feasibility analysis**, which investigates the problem to be solved or opportunity to be met. Feasibility analysis involves an investigation into technical, economic, legal, operational, and schedule feasibility. Table 10.2 describes each type of feasibility.

TABLE 10.2 • Types of feasibility

Type of feasibility	Description
Technical feasibility	Determines whether or not hardware, software, and other system components can be acquired or developed
Economic feasibility	Determines if the project makes financial sense
Legal feasibility	Determines whether laws or regulations may prevent or limit a systems development project
Operational feasibility	Measures whether or not the project can be put into action or operation
Schedule feasibility	Determines if the project can be completed in a reasonable amount of time

If a systems development project is determined to be worthwhile and feasible, systems analysis formally begins.

SYSTEMS ANALYSIS

After a project has been approved for further study during systems investigation, the next step is to perform a detailed analysis of the existing system, whether or not it is currently computer based. **Systems analysis** attempts to understand how the existing system helps solve the problem identified in systems investigation and answers the question "What must the information system do to solve the problem?" The process involves understanding the broader aspects of the system that would be required to solve the problem and the limitations of the existing system as identified in systems investigation. The overall emphasis of analysis is to gather data on the existing system and the requirements for the new system, and to consider alternative solutions to the problem within these constraints and the feasibility of these solutions. The primary result of systems analysis is a list of systems requirements and priorities.

General Analysis Considerations

Systems analysis starts by clarifying the overall goals of the individual or organization and determining how the existing or proposed information system helps meet these goals. A university, for example, might want to develop a fundraising database that contains information on all of the people, trusts, and organizations that have made financial contributions or donations to the university. This goal can be translated into one or more informational needs. One need might be to create and maintain an accurate list of all projects funded by donations made to the university. Another need might be to produce a list of all donors who contributed more than $1000 over the last year. The list can be used to generate personalized thank-you letters.

Analysis of a small organization's information system can be fairly straightforward. On the other hand, evaluating an existing information system for a large organization can be a long, tedious process. As a result, large organizations evaluating a major information system normally follow a formalized analysis procedure by first collecting appropriate data, then analyzing the data, and finally determining new system requirements and project priorities.

Collecting Data

The purpose of data collection is to seek additional information about the problems or needs identified during systems investigation. In many cases, the strengths and weaknesses of the existing system are uncovered.

Data collection involves identifying and locating the various sources of data. In general, there are both internal sources and external sources (see Table 10.3).

TABLE 10.3 • Internal and external sources of data for systems analysis

Internal sources	External sources
Users, stakeholders, and managers	Customers
Organizational charts	Suppliers
Forms and documents, including input documents from accounting and other transactions	Stockholders
Procedure manuals and written policies	Local, state, and federal government agencies
Financial reports	Competitors
Computer documents, including information systems manuals	Outside organizations, such as environmental associations
Other measures of existing processes	Trade journals, books, and periodicals related to the organization
	External consultants and other commercial groups

FIGURE 10.13 • The steps in data collection

After data sources have been identified, data is collected. Often, it is necessary to clarify what the data means.

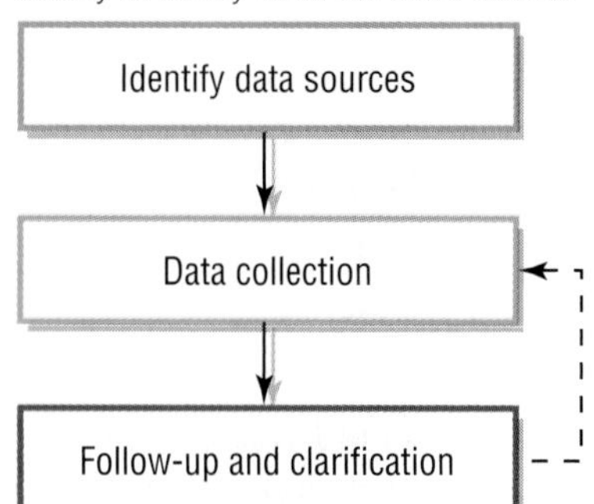

Once data collection sources have been identified, data collection begins. Figure 10.13 shows the steps involved.

Data collection may require a number of tools and techniques, such as the following:

- Interviews: In a *structured interview*, questions are written in advance. In an *unstructured interview*, the questions are not written in advance; the interviewer relies on experience in asking the best questions to uncover the inherent problems and weaknesses of the existing system.
- Direct observation: One or more members of the analysis team directly observe the existing system in action.
- Outputs: Outputs from the existing system, both manual and computerized, are obtained during data collection. See Figure 10.14.

- Questionnaires: When many data sources are spread over a wide geographic area, questionnaires may be the best approach. Like interviews, questionnaires can be either structured or unstructured.
- Other data collection methods: Telephone calls, simulations of actual events and activities, and random samples of data are other data collection techniques.

FIGURE 10.14 • Outputs from existing systems

This output from a university course look-up system would be valuable data to systems developers looking to improve the system.

Course Number	Sect.	Course Ref #	Title	Instructor	Seats	Seats Left	Bldg	Room	Days	Begin	End
LIS3784	01	02224	INFO ORG AND COMM	Currim, Sabah A	72	0	HCB	0315	T R	02:00 PM	03:15 PM
Comments: INTRODUCTORY COURSE / PREREQUISITES: LIS3353, LIS3267, DATABASE CONCEPTS											
LIS3793	01	02225	INFO ARCHITECTURE	Lustria, Mia A	40	16	HCB	0308	T R	02:00 PM	03:15 PM
Comments: Service Learning required ( ). INFO ORG & COMM TRACK ELECTIVE / RECOMMENDED PREREQ: LIS4264											
LIS4264	01	02226	SYS APPRCH INFO ENV	Miner, David R	40	1	HCB	0309	T R	02:00 PM	03:15 PM
Comments: INFO SYSTEMS & SERVICES TRACK ELECTIVE / PREREQS: LIS3353, LIS3267											
LIS4277	01	02227	USABILITY INFO SYS	Douglas, Ian W	40	2	HCB	0309	T R	09:30 AM	10:45 AM
Comments: INFO ORG & COMM TRACK ELECTIVE											
LIS4365	01	02229	ADV WEB APPLICATIONS	Riccardi, Gregory A	40	17	HCB	0309	M W F	12:20 PM	01:10 PM
Comments: CROSS-TRACK ELECTIVE											

Data Analysis

Data collected in its raw form is usually not adequate to determine either the effectiveness and efficiency of an existing system or the requirements for a new system. The next step is to use data analysis to put the collected data into a form that is usable by the members of the development team participating in systems analysis. Two commonly used data analysis tools are application flowcharts and CASE tools, which were discussed earlier.

Requirements Analysis

The overall purpose of **requirements analysis** is to determine user, stakeholder, and organizational needs. For an accounts payable application, the stakeholders could include suppliers and members of the purchasing department. Questions that should be asked during requirements analysis include the following: "Are these stakeholders satisfied with the current accounts payable application?" and "What improvements could be made to satisfy suppliers and help the purchasing department?"

Numerous tools and techniques can be used to capture systems requirements. Some of the most common are described in Table 10.4.

TABLE 10.4 • Methods of capturing systems requirements

Method	Description
Direct questions	Some or all users and stakeholders are asked what they want and expect from a new or modified system.
Critical success factors	Users and stakeholders are asked to list only those factors or items that are critical to the success of their area or the organization.
Joint application development (JAD)	JAD involves group meetings in which users, stakeholders, and information systems professionals work together to analyze existing systems, propose possible solutions, and define the requirements of a new or modified system (see Figure 10.15).
Rapid application development (RAD)	RAD involves a process in which a developer first builds a working model, or prototype, of the system to help a group of stakeholders, users, or managers identify how well the system meets their requirements; the prototypes are then refined to more closely align with stated requirements.

FIGURE 10.15 • Joint application development

Joint application development includes a group leader for the meetings, people who will use the system, and one or more individuals who act as secretaries and clerks to record what is accomplished and to provide general support for the sessions.

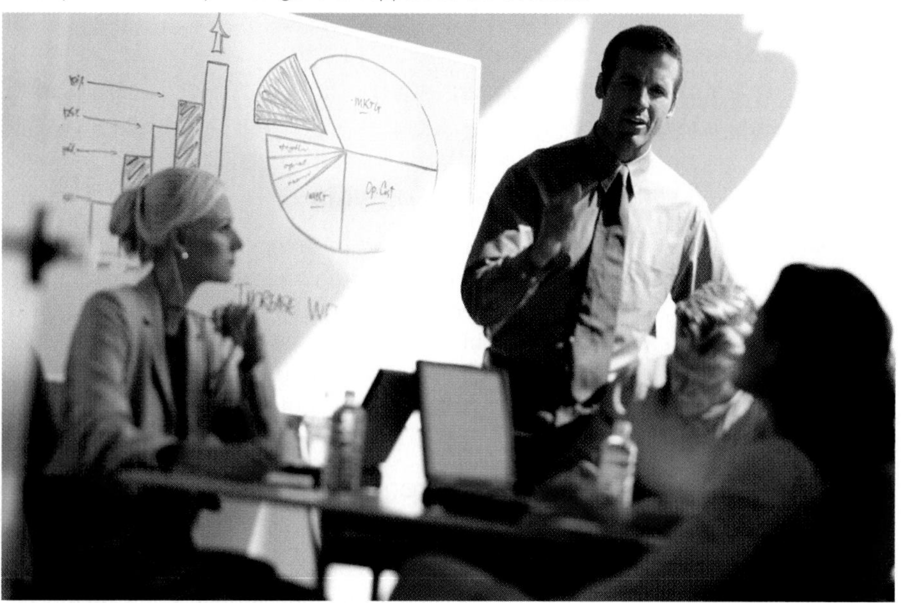

SYSTEMS DESIGN

The purpose of **systems design** is to select and plan a system that meets the requirements defined in the requirements analysis. This can often involve outside companies and vendors, especially if additional hardware and software are needed. Systems design results in a new or modified system, and thus results in change. If the problems are minor, only small modifications are required. On the other hand, major changes may be suggested by systems analysis. In these cases, major investments in additional hardware, software, and personnel may be necessary. The first step of systems design is to generate systems design alternatives.

Generating Systems Design Alternatives

The first step of design is to investigate the various alternatives for all components of the new system; this can include hardware, software, databases, telecommunications, personnel, and more. When additional hardware is not required, alternative designs are often generated without input from vendors. A *vendor* is a company that provides computer hardware, equipment, supplies, and a variety of services. Vendors include hardware companies, such as IBM and Dell; software companies, such as Microsoft; database companies, such as Oracle; and a variety of other companies.

A museum might not need a vendor if it wants to modify one of its databases to include the estimated value of each item in the museum and where each item is located. This modification likely requires someone on the museum staff working with the database management system without the need for input from outside vendors. However, if the new system is a complex one, the original development team may want to involve additional personnel in generating alternative designs. If new hardware and software are to be acquired from an outside vendor, various requests can be made of the vendor.

A *request for information* (*RFI*) asks an IT vendor to provide information about its products or services, and a *request for quotes* (*RFQ*) asks the vendor to give prices for its products or services. The **request for proposal (RFP)** is generated during systems development when an organization wants an IT vendor to submit a bid for a new or modified system. It often results in a formal bid that is used to determine who gets a contract for new or modified systems. The RFP specifies, in detail, required resources such as hardware and software. It communicates these needs to one or more vendors, and it provides a way to evaluate whether or not the vendor has delivered what was expected. In some cases, the RFP is made a part of the vendor contract. The table of contents of a typical RFP is shown in Figure 10.16.

FIGURE 10.16 • A typical table of contents for a request for proposal (RFP)

The RFP specifies required resources such as hardware and software. It communicates these needs to one or more vendors, and it provides a way to evaluate whether or not the vendor has delivered what was expected.

JOHNSON & FLORIN, INC.
REQUEST FOR PROPOSAL

Table of Contents

Cover page (with company name and contact person)
Brief description of the company
Overview of the existing computer system
Summary of computer-related needs and/or problems
Objectives of the project
Description of what is needed
Hardware requirements
Software requirements
Personnel requirements
Communications requirements
Procedures to be developed
Training requirements
Maintenance requirements
Evaluation procedures (how vendors will be judged)
Proposal format (description of how vendors should respond)
Important dates (when tasks are to be completed)
Summary

Evaluating and Selecting a Systems Design

The next step in systems design is to evaluate the various design alternatives and select the design that offers the best solution supporting organizational goals. For a simple design, such as a new graphics program for a commercial artist, one person can complete the system design. A moderate design project can involve a number of people inside the organization. To modify a database or an existing software program at a tax preparation company, programmers from inside the organization can be used.

After the final presentations and demonstrations have been given, the organization makes the final evaluation and selection. Cost comparisons, hardware performance, delivery dates, price, modularity, backup facilities, available software training, and maintenance factors are considered. Although it is good to compare computer speeds, storage capacities, and other similar characteristics, it is also necessary to carefully analyze whether the characteristics of the proposed systems meet the objectives set for the system and how they will help the organization solve problems and reach goals.

The Contract

When large information systems are purchased, the hardware vendor often requires a contract. Most computer vendors provide standard contracts; however, these contracts are designed to protect the vendor, not necessarily the organization buying the computer equipment. Developing a good contract can be one of the most important steps in systems design if new computer facilities are to be acquired.

More and more organizations are developing their own contracts, stipulating exactly what they expect from the system vendor and what interaction will occur between the vendor and the organization. All equipment specifications, software, training, installation, maintenance, and so on are clearly stated. Furthermore, deadlines for the various stages or milestones of installation and implementation are stipulated, as well as actions to be taken by the vendor in case of delays or problems. Some organizations include penalty clauses in the contract, in case the vendor is unable to meet its obligation by the specified date. Typically, the request for proposal (RFP) becomes part of the contract. This saves a considerable amount of time in developing the contract, because the RFP specifies in detail what is expected from the system vendor or vendors.

SYSTEMS IMPLEMENTATION

After the information system has been designed, a number of tasks must be completed before the system is installed and ready to operate. This process, called **systems implementation**, includes hardware acquisition, software acquisition or development, user preparation, hiring and training of personnel, site and data preparation, installation, testing, start-up, and user acceptance. The typical sequence of these systems implementation activities is shown in Figure 10.17. In many cases, some of the steps of systems implementation can be performed at the same time. For example, while hardware is being acquired, software can be developed and new computer personnel can be hired.

FIGURE 10.17 • Typical steps in systems implementation

To realize the full potential of new or modified systems, organizations must carefully analyze the trade-offs at each step in the implementation process.

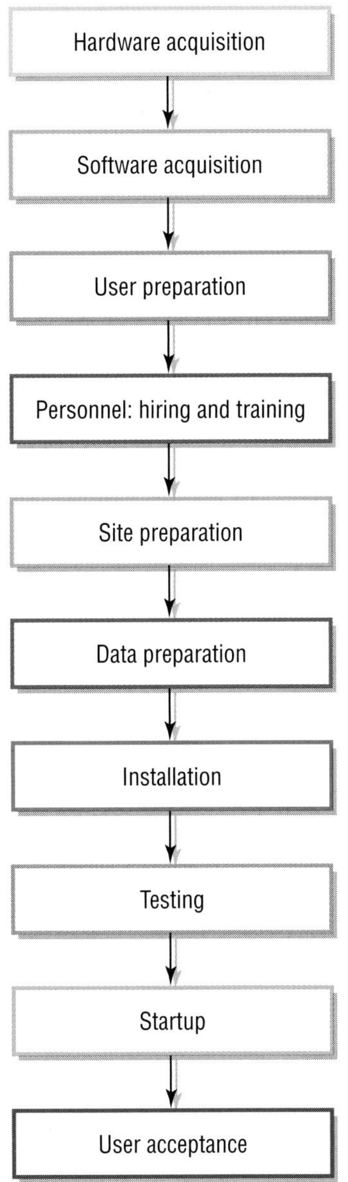

At each step shown in Figure 10.17, there are choices and trade-offs to be made that involve analyzing the benefits of the various choices. Unfortunately, many organizations do not take full advantage of these steps or carefully analyze the trade-offs, and hence never realize the full potential of new or modified systems. The carelessness that often causes these steps to be overlooked must be avoided if organizations are to achieve their objectives and get the most from the new or modified computer system.

Acquiring Hardware

Although you can build your own computer using commonly available hardware components or have someone build a computer for you, most people and organizations acquire hardware and computers by purchasing, leasing, or renting computer resources from a computer systems vendor.

In addition to buying, leasing, or renting computer hardware, it is also possible for an organization to pay only for the computing that it uses. Called "pay as you go computing" or "utility computing," this approach means that an organization pays only for the computer power it uses. This is similar to paying only for the electricity you use. Many companies, like IBM, offer this service. Hewlett-Packard has a "capacity-on-demand" approach, where organizations pay according to the computer resources actually used, including processors, storage devices, and network facilities. Another option is to utilize software as a service (SaaS), or cloud computing, where software services are provided over the Internet delivered from hardware owned and maintained by the software vendor. Hardware is expensive, and it can become error prone and technologically obsolete over time. As a result, some organizations include hardware replacement costs in their annual budgets.

Selecting and Acquiring Software: Make, Buy, or Rent

Like hardware, software can be acquired in several ways. As previously discussed, software can be purchased from external developers or developed in house. Global companies doing business around the world often select a standardized, global software package, such as SAP, a popular enterprise resource planning (ERP) package.

Sometimes developing software in house produces the most effective result. NASA developed a software program called DAC for space exploration to analyze how a spacecraft enters distant environments and atmospheres (see Figure 10.18). This award-winning software has been used for the Mars Global Surveyor and the Mars Odyssey missions.

FIGURE 10.18 • NASA DAC software

NASA's award-winning DAC software is used to analyze how a spacecraft enters distant environments and atmospheres.

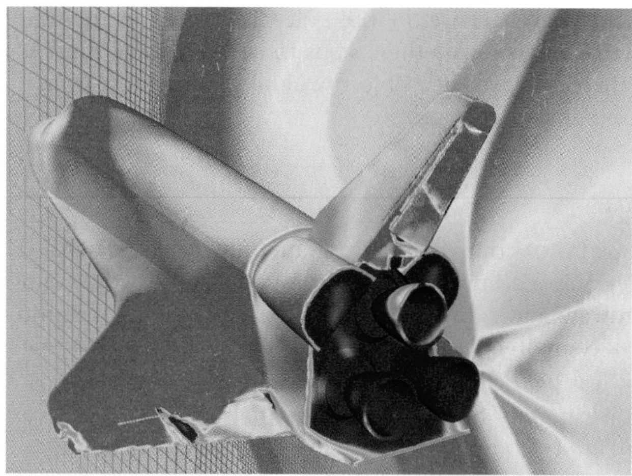

Software engineers, or programmers, are responsible for developing the software that drives the larger information system. The process of developing software involves a series of activities, similar to the systems development life cycle, called the *program development life cycle*. Programmers are provided with a description of what the software must accomplish, called the *program specification*. From the program specification, they use programming logic to develop an *algorithm*, a step-by-step sequence of computer instructions, that when given specified input, yields the desired results. The algorithm is then translated into a program language to create the executable programs that will control the system.

Software is tested thoroughly with every possible input in order to uncover possible *bugs*, errors in the program code that cause the software to malfunction. Bugs can be caused by *syntax errors* (errors in the use of the programming language syntax) or by *logic errors* (errors in the programming logic that governs the action of the software). Once released, software, like systems, is continuously evaluated and periodically revamped and improved with the release of new editions.

In some cases, organizations use a blend of external and internal software development. That is, proprietary software or open-source programs are modified or customized by in-house personnel. Some of the reasons that an organization might purchase or lease externally developed software include lower costs, less risk regarding the features and performance of the package, and ease of installation. The development effort is usually less when programmers use or modify a purchased software product rather than write all of the program code themselves.

As mentioned, software as a service (SaaS) is a model of software application delivery in which the software resides on the vendor's servers. The vendor, sometimes called an *application service provider* (*ASP*), develops, maintains, and stores the software and makes it available to customers over the Internet. Using SaaS can be faster and less expensive than developing software, but it can be more difficult to get the necessary features or to make software changes when needed. Still, with software gradually moving to a Web-delivered model, the SaaS market is growing rapidly.

Acquiring Database and Telecommunications Systems

Acquiring or upgrading database systems can be one of the most important parts of a systems development effort. Acquiring a database system can be closely linked to the systems development process, since many systems development projects involve a new or modified database system. Because databases are a blend of hardware and software, many of the approaches discussed for acquiring hardware and software also apply to database systems. For example, an upgraded inventory control system may require database capabilities, including more hard disk storage or a new DBMS. Additional storage hardware would have to be acquired from a computer systems vendor. New or upgraded software could be purchased or developed in house.

Telecommunications is one of the fastest-growing applications for today's businesses and individuals. The NASDAQ Stock Market, for example, has invested millions of dollars in a network system to streamline operations and cut costs. Like database systems, telecommunications systems require a blend of hardware and software.

As you learned in Chapter 6, telecommunications hardware for personal computer systems usually includes some type of modem, plus a router or perhaps wireless equipment. For larger client/server systems, the hardware can include multiplexers, concentrators, communications processors, and a variety of network equipment (Figure 10.19). Communications software also has to be acquired from a software company or developed in house. You acquire telecommunications hardware and software in much the same way you acquire computer system hardware and software.

FIGURE 10.19 • Telecommunications and database equipment

Database servers and telecommunications hardware fill large rooms of most corporations.

User Preparation

User preparation is the process of readying managers and decision makers, employees, and other users and stakeholders for the new or modified system. System developers need to provide users with the proper preparation and training to make sure they use the system correctly, efficiently, and effectively. User preparation can include marketing, training, documentation, and support.

Without question, training users is an essential part of user preparation, whether they are trained by internal training personnel or by external training firms. In some cases, companies that provide software also provide user training at no charge or at a reasonable price. Training can be negotiated during the selection of new software. Some companies conduct user training throughout the systems development process to eliminate fears and apprehensions about the new system. Old and new employees should be acquainted with the system's capabilities and limitations (see Figure 10.20).

FIGURE 10.20 • User preparation

User preparation is the process of readying managers and decision makers, employees, users, and stakeholders for the new system.

IT Personnel: Hiring and Training

Depending on the size of the new system, a number of IT personnel may have to be hired and, in some cases, trained. A systems manager, computer programmers, data-entry operators, and similar personnel may be needed for the new system. As with users, the eventual success of any system depends on how it is used by the IT personnel within the organization. This cannot be overemphasized. Training programs should be conducted for the IT personnel who will be using or dealing with the computer system. These programs will be similar to those for the users, although they may be more detailed in terms of technical aspects of the systems. Effective training helps personnel use the new system to perform their jobs and helps them provide support to the other users in the organization.

Site Preparation

The actual location of the new system needs to be prepared in a process called *site preparation*. For a small system, this may simply mean rearranging the furniture in an office to make room for a personal computer. For a larger system, this process is not so easy. It may require additional furniture, special wiring and air conditioning, and complete renovations of one or two rooms. A special floor may have to be built, under which the cables connecting the various computer components are placed, and a new security system may have to be installed to protect the equipment. Larger systems may also require additional electrical circuits. In extreme cases, it might be necessary to construct multimillion-dollar data centers like those owned by Google, Microsoft, and other large tech companies. See Figure 10.21.

FIGURE 10.21 • Google's data center

Today's largest businesses use massive data centers that draw huge amounts of electricity for operations and cooling.

Data Preparation

If an organization is about to turn to digital systems, all its nondigital files, such as information on paper in file folders, must be converted into computer files in a process called *data preparation*. For old computerized files, *data conversion* may be required to transform existing computerized files into the proper format for the new system. All of the permanent data must be placed on a permanent storage device, such as magnetic tape or disk. Usually the organization hires some temporary, part-time data-entry operators or a service company to convert manual data. Once the information has been converted into computer files, the data-entry operators or the service company are no longer needed. A computerized database system or other software is used to maintain and update these computer files.

Installation

Installation is the process of physically placing the computer equipment on the site and making it operational. For a small systems development project, this might require making room on top of a desk for a new PC, plugging it into a wall outlet, and following the manufacturer's instructions to turn it on. For a larger project with a mainframe computer system, installation usually involves the hardware manufacturer. Although it is normally the responsibility of the manufacturer to install the computer equipment for larger systems development projects, someone from the organization—usually the chief information officer (CIO) or the IT manager—should oversee this process, making sure that all of the equipment specified in the contract is installed at the proper location. After the system is installed, the manufacturer performs several tests to ensure that the equipment is operating as it should. See Figure 10.22.

FIGURE 10.22 • Installation

Installation involves placing the computer equipment on the site and making it operational.

Testing

Testing involves the entire computer system and requires several approaches, outlined in Table 10.5. Millions of dollars or even individual lives can be lost because of inadequate testing. It is always difficult to determine how much testing is needed before a new or modified system is placed into operation.

TABLE 10.5 • Methods of testing new systems

Method	Description
Unit testing	Uses test data that forces the computer to execute every statement in the program and tests each program with abnormal data to determine how it handles problems with bad data
System testing	Tests all of the programs together and ensures that connections work when one program's output feeds into another program
Volume testing	Makes sure that the entire system can handle a large amount of data under normal operating conditions
Integration testing	Ensures that the new program(s) can interact with other major applications and that data flows efficiently and without error to other applications
Acceptance testing	Makes sure that the objectives of the new or modified system are being met

Startup

Startup begins with the final tested computer system. When startup is finished, the system is fully operational. Different startup approaches include direct conversion, phase-in and parallel conversion, and pilot conversion (see Figure 10.23).

SYSTEMS DEVELOPMENT MOVES INTO THE CLOUD

And why not? Cloud computing provides highly scalable virtual IT resources over the Internet. Companies can rent virtual servers and software on an as-needed basis, and individuals from almost anywhere can log in and collaborate. Systems development is project-based and yet it monopolizes 30 to 50 percent of infrastructure resources. So, after two years of research, IBM has released its first line of products for small and large businesses, allowing them to test and develop in the cloud.

IBM preps cloud services; Targets software development and testing
Zdnet
Larry Dignan
June 15, 2009
http://blogs.zdnet.com/BTL/?p=19731

Direct conversion involves stopping the old system and starting the new system on a given date. This is usually the least desirable approach because of the potential for problems and errors when the old system is completely shut off and the new system is turned on at the same instant.

The **phase-in approach** is a popular technique preferred by many organizations. In this approach, the new system is slowly phased in while the old one is slowly phased out. During this process, parts of the old system and new system are running at the same time, in parallel. This is called a *parallel conversion*. When everyone is confident that the new system is performing as expected, the old system is completely phased out. This process is repeated for each application until the new system is running every application.

Pilot conversion involves running a pilot or small version of the new system along with the old. After the pilot runs without errors or problems, the old system is stopped and the new system is fully operational. With pilot conversion, small pilots can be introduced until the complete new system is operational. For example, a state prison system with a number of correctional facilities throughout the state could use the pilot approach and install a new computerized security system at one of the facilities. When this pilot program at the pilot facility runs without errors or problems, the new security system can be implemented at other prisons throughout the state.

FIGURE 10.23 • Startup approaches

Startup begins with the final tested computer system. When startup is finished, the system is fully operational.

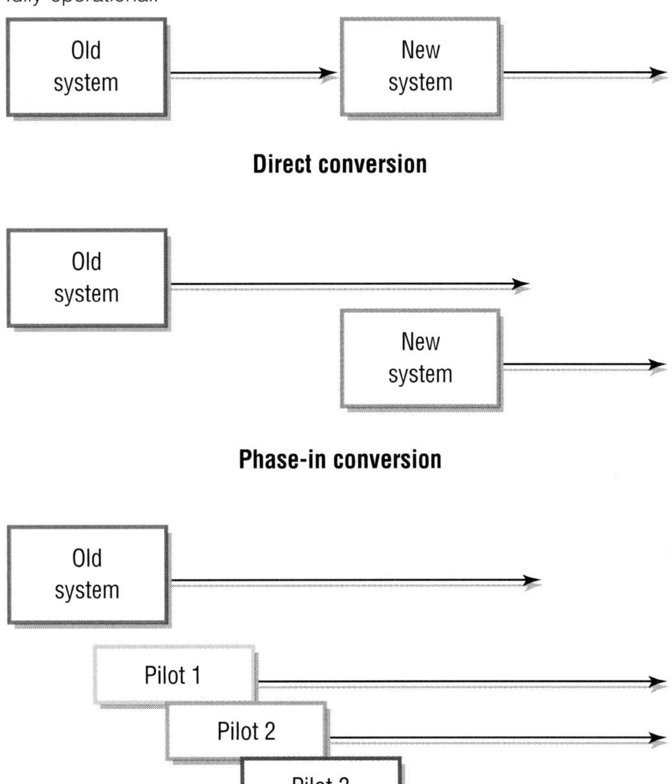

User Acceptance and Documentation

User acceptance and documentation is usually done for larger systems development projects that require new computers or servers. Smaller systems development projects, such as a musician's new software to blend several music tracks into a finished song, usually don't require user acceptance and documentation.

A **user acceptance document** is a formal agreement signed by the user that approves a phase of the installation or the complete system. This is a legal document that usually removes or reduces the vendor's liability or responsibility for problems that occur after the user acceptance document has been signed. Because this document is so important, many organizations get legal assistance before they sign the acceptance document. Stakeholders may also be involved in acceptance to make sure that the benefits to them are indeed realized.

The system should also be fully documented. *Documentation* includes all flowcharts, diagrams, and other written materials that describe the new or modified system. In general, there are two types of documentation. *Systems documentation* describes the technical aspects of the new or modified system. It can be used by the chief information officer (CIO), systems analysts, programmers, and other computer-related staff. *User documentation* describes how the system can be used by noncomputer personnel. A manual on how to use a spreadsheet program or an operating system is an example of user documentation.

SYSTEMS MAINTENANCE AND REVIEW

The final steps of systems development are systems maintenance and review. **Systems maintenance** involves checking, changing, and enhancing the system to make it more useful in achieving user and organizational goals. In some cases, an organization encounters major problems that involve recycling through the entire systems development process. In other situations, minor modifications are sufficient.

Reasons for Maintenance

Maintenance can involve all aspects of the system, including hardware, software, databases, telecommunications, personnel, and other system components. Older hardware, for example, may be too slow and lack enough storage capacity. Older software can also require maintenance. Once a program is written, it should ideally require little or no maintenance, but old programs require maintenance to make them faster or enhance their capabilities. In addition, new federal regulations or new computer technology may require that computer programs be modified. Experience shows that frequent, minor maintenance to a program, if properly done, can prevent major system failures later on. Today, the maintenance function is becoming more automated. A large home improvement chain, for example, can use new maintenance tools and software that allow the large chain to maintain and upgrade software centrally.

The following are some of the major reasons for systems maintenance:

- New requests from stakeholders, users, and managers
- Bugs or errors in the program
- Technical and hardware problems
- Corporate mergers and acquisitions
- Governmental regulations that require changes in programs

Developing Systems that Respect Users' Privacy

Business system development efforts are often sparked by new government regulations. Government regulations are typically enacted due to pressure from the public. Lately, the public has been very concerned about its privacy. As people spend increasing amounts of time online, protecting the privacy of their online activities has become important to them. Businesses anxious to learn about consumer behavior have been intensively watching and recording what people do online in order to create consumer profiles that can be used to effectively pitch products, a practice called behavioral advertising. Much of this profiling has been done without the public's knowledge and consent, which when discovered led to pressure on the U.S. government to regulate online data collection.

In order to head off government regulation, Internet marketers are making efforts to self-regulate. A coalition of advertising industry trade organizations set forth seven privacy protection principles that it wants all its members to follow. The "Self-Regulatory Principles for Online Behavioral Advertising" are presented in a 48-page document, and are generally stated in the document's summary as follows:

1. The Education Principle calls for entities to participate in efforts to educate consumers and businesses about online behavioral advertising.
2. The Transparency Principle requires the deployment of multiple mechanisms for clearly disclosing and informing consumers about data collection and use practices associated with online behavioral advertising.
3. The Consumer Control Principle enables Web site users to choose whether data is collected, used, or transferred for purposes of online behavioral advertising.
4. The Data Security Principle requires entities to provide reasonable security for, and limited retention of, data collected and used for online behavioral advertising purposes.
5. The Material Changes Principle directs entities to obtain consent before applying any change to their online behavioral advertising data collection and use policy that is less restrictive to data collected prior to such material change.
6. The Sensitive Data Principle recognizes that certain data collected and used for online behavioral advertising purposes merits different treatment.
7. The Accountability Principle calls upon entities representing the wide range of actors in the online behavioral advertising ecosystem to develop and implement policies and programs to further adherence to these principles.

Whether government regulated or self regulated, these principles will generate systems development projects and adaptation across all online advertising companies, and the many Web sites that depend on the money made from sponsored ads.

Questions

1. What social issues might prompt governments to regulate a business and impact what it does with information systems?
2. How specifically would this set of regulatory principles impact information systems of a Web site like Facebook, which makes its money from behavioral advertising?
3. What is the difference between the effectiveness of government regulation and self-regulation in this particular case?

Sources

1. *Claburn, Thomas, "Ad Industry Sets Seven Privacy Protection Principles,"* InformationWeek, *July 2, 2009, www.informationweek.com.*
2. *"Self-Regulatory Prinicples for Online Behavioral Advertising,"* The Interactive Advertising Bureau (IAB), *July 2009, www.iab.net/media/file/ven-principles-07-01-09.pdf.*

When it comes to making necessary changes, most organizations modify their existing programs instead of developing new ones. That is, as new systems needs are identified, most often the burden of fulfilling these needs falls upon the existing system. Old programs are repeatedly modified to meet ever-changing needs, but over time, these modifications tend to interfere with the system's overall structure, reducing its efficiency and making further modifications more burdensome.

The Financial Implications of Maintenance

The cost of maintenance—including hardware, software, databases, telecommunications, and other computer components—is staggering. For older software developed in house, for example, the total cost of maintenance can be up to five times greater than the total cost of development. In other words, a program that originally cost $50,000 to develop may cost $250,000 to maintain over its lifetime. The average programmer can spend from 50 percent to over 75 percent of his or her time maintaining existing programs as opposed to developing new ones. Furthermore, as programs get older, total maintenance expenditures in time and money increase, as illustrated in Figure 10.24. With the use of newer programming languages and approaches, including object-oriented programming, maintenance costs are expected to decline. Even so, many organizations have literally millions of dollars invested in applications written in older languages, such as COBOL, that are both expensive and time-consuming to maintain.

FIGURE 10.24 • Maintenance costs as a function of age

As programs get older, total maintenance expenditures in time and money increase.

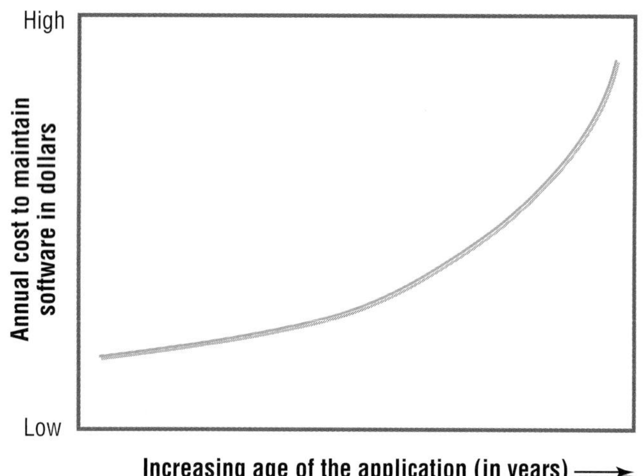

The financial implications of maintenance make it important to keep track of why systems are maintained, in addition to tracking the cost. For this reason, documentation of maintenance tasks is crucial. A determining factor in the decision to replace a system is the point at which it is costing more to fix it than to enhance or replace it.

Systems Review

Systems review, the final phase of the systems development life cycle, is the process of analyzing systems to make sure that they are operating as intended. All aspects of the system are reviewed, including hardware, software, database systems, networks and Internet, people, and procedures. Systems review often involves comparing the expected performance and benefits of the system as it was designed with the actual performance and benefits of the system in operation. Increasingly, organizations are using software and the Internet to review existing systems.

There are two types of review procedures: event driven and time driven. An *event-driven review* is one that is triggered or caused by a problem or opportunity such as an error, a corporate merger, or a new government regulation. In some cases, an individual or organization will wait until a large or important problem or opportunity occurs before making a change. In this case, minor problems may be ignored. Today, some organizations use a *continuous improvement* approach to systems development. With this approach, an organization makes changes to a system when even small problems or opportunities occur. Although this approach can keep the system current and responsive, doing the repeated design and implementation can be time-consuming and expensive. A *time-driven review* is one that is started after a specified amount of time. Many application programs are reviewed every six months to a year. With this approach, an existing system is monitored on a schedule. If problems or opportunities are uncovered, a new systems development cycle may be initiated. A computer-assisted bicycle design program may be reviewed once a year to make sure that it is still operating as expected; if not, changes are made.

Many organizations use both approaches. A computerized program to choreograph new dance routines for a theater production company, for example, might be reviewed once a year for opportunities to display new dance moves. This is a time-driven approach. In addition, the dance program might be redone if errors or program crashes make the software difficult to use. This is an event-driven approach.

ACTION PLAN

Remember Linda from the beginning of the chapter? Linda had an idea for a new system that would help increase her productivity and win her company more clients. Here are answers to her questions.

1. **How should Linda approach her company to get the new program developed?**

   Linda should follow corporate procedures, if they exist. She should demonstrate how such a program can help the company achieve its goals of getting new insurance customers and servicing existing ones.

2. **If the company decides to develop a new insurance program, how should Linda be involved in the process?**

   If the company decides to undertake systems development to create a new computer program, Linda's involvement is critical. She needs to help the people in the computer systems department determine exactly what reports and output can help her and other insurance agents. Linda should also be involved during the process to make sure that her needs are satisfied by the new system.

3. **What role would James and people like him play in developing a new insurance program?**

   As a systems analyst, James could help in developing plans and documents for a new sales program, including CASE documents, flowcharts, and so on. If he is involved in the project, he might even work with Linda in determining her needs and desires for the new program. He would also work with programmers. Working with users and programmers is the classic role of the systems analyst.

Summary

LEARNING OBJECTIVE 1

Describe the systems development life cycle, who participates in it, and why it is important.

The systems development process is called a systems development life cycle (SDLC) because the activities associated with it are ongoing. The five phases of the SDLC are investigation, analysis, design, implementation, and maintenance and review.

The systems development team consists of stakeholders, users, managers, systems development specialists, and various support personnel. The development team is responsible for determining the objectives of the information system and delivering to the organization a system that meets its objectives.

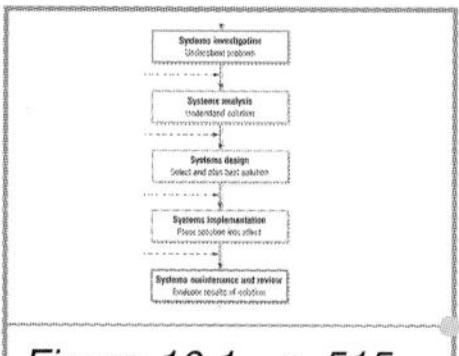
Figure 10.1—p. 515

Many organizations initiate systems development projects to gain a competitive advantage. This usually requires creative and critical analysis. Creative analysis involves the investigation of new approaches to existing problems. Critical analysis means being skeptical and doubtful, and requires questioning whether or not the existing system is effective and efficient.

End-user systems development is a term that was originally used to describe the development of computer systems by individuals outside of the formal computer systems planning and departmental structure. The proliferation of general-purpose information technology and the flexibility of many packaged software programs have allowed employees outside of the IT department to independently develop computer and information systems that meet their needs.

LEARNING OBJECTIVE 2

Discuss systems development tools.

Some common tools and techniques for systems development include CASE tools, flowcharts, decision tables, project management tools, prototyping, outsourcing, and object-oriented systems development. Some formalized systems development approaches have come to be called software engineering. These approaches typically employ the use of software-based systems development tools called computer-aided software engineering (CASE) tools that automate many of the tasks required in a systems development effort. Like a road map, a flowchart reveals the path from a starting point to the final destination. A decision table can be used as an alternative to or in conjunction with flowcharts. When there are a large number of branches or paths within a software program, decision tables are preferable to flowcharts. The overall purpose of project management is to plan, monitor, and control necessary development activities. A prominent technique for systems development is prototyping, which typically involves the creation of some preliminary models or versions of major subsystems or scaled-down versions of the entire system. Many organizations hire an outside consulting firm that specializes in systems development to take over some or all of its computer and information systems development activities. This approach is called outsourcing. Object-oriented (OO) systems development combines a modular approach to structured systems development with the power of object-oriented modeling and programming. OO development follows a defined system development life cycle, much like the SDLC.

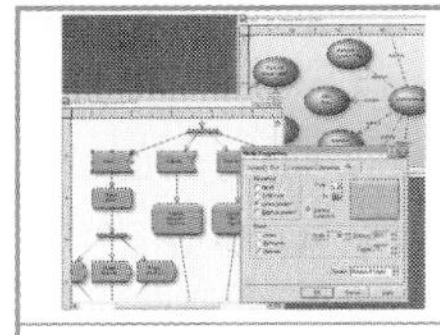

Figure 10.6—p. 522

LEARNING OBJECTIVE 3

Understand how systems development projects are investigated.

Systems investigation is usually the first step in the development of a new or modified information system. The overall purpose of systems investigation is to determine whether or not the objectives met by the existing system are satisfying the goals of the individual or organization. Systems investigation is designed to assess the feasibility of implementing systems solutions, including technical, economic, legal, operational, and schedule feasibility.

LEARNING OBJECTIVE 4

Describe how an existing system can be evaluated.

Systems analysis is the examination of existing systems. This step is undertaken once approval for further study is received. The additional study of a selected system attempts to further understand the system's weaknesses and potential improvement areas. Data collection methods include observation, interviews, and questionnaires. Data analysis manipulates the data collected. The analysis includes flowcharts, CASE tools, and other approaches. The overall purpose of requirements analysis is to determine user and organizational needs. Asking directly or using critical success factors are two ways to complete requirements analysis. Joint application development (JAD) can be used in place of traditional data collection and requirements analysis procedures. Another efficient approach to determine and define systems requirements from a group is called rapid application development. Rapid application development (RAD) combines JAD, prototyping, and other structured techniques in order to quickly and accurately determine the requirements of the system.

Figure 10.5—p. 519

LEARNING OBJECTIVE 5

Discuss what is involved in planning a new system.

The purpose of systems design is to prepare the detailed design needs for a new system or modifications to the existing system. Organizations often develop a request for information (RFI) to get information from vendors. If new hardware or software will be purchased from a vendor, a formal request for proposal (RFP) is needed. The RFP outlines the company's needs; in response, the vendor provides a written reply. The final phase of system design is evaluation and selection of alternatives. Although most vendors provide standard contracts for new hardware, software, and systems, organizations today are increasingly developing their own contracts.

LEARNING OBJECTIVE 6

List the steps to implement a new or modified system.

Systems implementation includes hardware acquisition, software acquisition or development, user preparation, hiring and training of personnel, site and data preparation, installation, testing, startup, and user acceptance. Hardware acquisition requires purchasing, leasing, or renting computer resources from a vendor. Types of vendors include small and general computer manufacturers, peripheral equipment manufacturers, leasing companies, time-sharing companies, software companies, dealers, distributors, service companies, and others. Software can be purchased from external vendors or developed in house. User preparation involves readying managers, employees, and other users for the new system. New IT personnel may need to be hired, and users must be well trained in the system's functions. Preparation of the physical site of the system must be done, and any existing data to be used in the new system requires conversion to the new format. Hardware installation is done during the implementation step, as is testing. Testing includes program (unit) testing, systems testing, volume testing, integration testing, and acceptance testing. Startup begins with the final tested computer system. Startup approaches include direct conversion, phase-in, and pilot. Direct conversion involves stopping the old system and starting the new system on a given date. The phase-in approach involves gradually phasing the old system out and the new system in. Pilot conversion involves running a pilot or small version of the new software along with the old. Users typically perform an acceptance test to be sure that the capabilities promised were actually delivered.

Figure 10.22—p. 540

LEARNING OBJECTIVE 7

Describe the importance of updating and monitoring a system.

Systems maintenance involves checking, changing, and enhancing the system to make it more useful in achieving user and organizational goals. Maintenance is critical for the continued smooth operation of the system. The costs of performing maintenance can well exceed the original cost of acquiring the system. Maintenance can vary from a small change to a large one.

Systems review is the process of analyzing systems to make sure that they are operating as intended. The two types of review procedures are event-driven review and time-driven review. An event-driven review is one that is triggered or caused by a problem or opportunity. A time-driven review is one that is started after a specified amount of time.

Test Yourself

LEARNING OBJECTIVE 1: Describe the systems development life cycle, who participates in it, and why it is important.

1. True or False: The systems analyst is the individual who ultimately benefits from systems development.
2. Who interacts with the users and others to develop detailed plans for the new or modified systems, like an architect developing blueprints for a new building?
   a. systems analyst
   b. programmer
   c. stakeholder
   d. chief information officer
3. The ________________ is the ongoing activity associated with the system development process, including investigation, analysis, design, implementation, and maintenance and review.

LEARNING OBJECTIVE 2: Discuss systems development tools.

4. True or False: CASE tools are used by one person at a time to make sure the results are consistent and accurate.
5. A ________________ may be used to show the logical relationships between system components and how information flows through the system.
6. What systems development tool is appropriate for programs that have a large number of branches or paths?
   a. flowchart
   b. PERT diagram
   c. decision table
   d. Gantt chart
7. Use-case diagrams are often used with ________________ .
   a. flowcharts
   b. object-oriented systems development
   c. PERT
   d. Gantt

LEARNING OBJECTIVE 3: Understand how systems development projects are investigated

8. ________________ feasibility is concerned with whether or not hardware, software, and other systems components can be acquired or developed to solve the problem.
9. True or False: Operational feasibility determines whether the project can be completed in a reasonable amount of time.

LEARNING OBJECTIVE 4: Describe how an existing system can be evaluated.

10. The purpose of ________________ analysis is to determine user, stakeholder, and organizational needs.
11. What technique was developed by IBM and uses group meetings in which users, stakeholders, and computer systems personnel work together to analyze the existing system?
    a. joint application development
    b. rapid application development
    c. critical success factors
    d. prototyping

LEARNING OBJECTIVE 5: Discuss what is involved in planning a new system.

12. True or False: A request for proposal (RFP) specifies required resources such as hardware, telecommunications, and software.
13. The purpose of ________________ is to select and plan a system that meets defined requirements.
    a. systems investigation
    b. systems analysis
    c. systems design
    d. systems implementation
14. Cost comparisons, hardware performance, delivery dates, price, modularity, backup facilities, available software training, and maintenance factors are considered during ________________ .
15. True or False: More and more organizations are developing their own contracts, stipulating exactly what they expect from the system vendor and what interaction will occur between the vendor and the organization.

LEARNING OBJECTIVE 6: List the steps to implement a new or modified system.

16. ________________ includes hardware acquisition, software acquisition or development, user preparation, hiring and training of personnel, site and data preparation, installation, testing, start-up, and user acceptance.
17. True or False: Site preparation is the process of physically placing the computer equipment on the site and making it operational.
18. What requires the testing of all of the programs together?
    a. unit testing
    b. system testing
    c. integration testing
    d. acceptance testing

LEARNING OBJECTIVE 7: Describe the importance of updating and monitoring a system.

19. ________________ involves checking, changing, and enhancing the system to make it more useful in achieving user and organizational goals.
20. True or False: Systems review can include an event-driven review and a time-driven review.

Test Yourself Solutions: **1.** False, **2.** a. systems analyst, **3.** Systems Development Life Cycle, **4.** False, **5.** flowchart, **6.** c. decision table, **7.** b. object-oriented systems development, **8.** Technical, **9.** False, **10.** requirements, **11.** a. joint application development, **12.** True, **13.** c. systems design, **14.** selection and final evaluation, **15.** True, **16.** Systems implementation, **17.** False, **18.** b. system testing, **19.** Systems maintenance, **20.** True.

Key Terms

Key Term	Page	Definition
computer-aided software engineering (CASE) tools	522	Software tools that automate many of the tasks required in a systems development effort
decision table	524	A systems development tool that displays the various conditions that could exist in a system and the different actions that the computer should take as a result of these conditions
direct conversion	541	A system startup approach that stops the old system and starts the new system on a given date
feasibility analysis	529	A key part of the systems investigation phase that investigates the problem to be solved or opportunity to be met in terms of technical, economic, legal, operational, and schedule feasibility
flowchart	523	A system design diagram that charts the path from a starting point to the final goal of a system
object-oriented (OO) systems development	528	An extension of object-oriented programming that follows a defined system development life cycle, much like the SDLC
outsourcing	526	The use of an outside company to take over portions of a business's workload
phase-in approach	541	A system startup approach in which the new system is slowly phased in while the old one is slowly phased out
pilot conversion	541	A system startup approach that involves running a pilot or small version of the new system along with the old
project management	524	The process of planning, monitoring, and controlling necessary systems development activities.
prototyping	526	Creating a preliminary model or version of a major subsystem, or a small or scaled-down version of the entire system
request for proposal (RFP)	533	A document generated during systems development when an organization wants a computer systems vendor to submit a bid for a new or modified system

Key Term	Page	Definition
requirements analysis	531	Determines user, stakeholder, and organizational needs
system stakeholder	516	Individual who will ultimately benefit from the systems development project, either directly or through the organization he or she represents
systems analysis	529	The second stage of the systems development life cycle that attempts to understand how the existing system helps solve the problem identified in systems investigation and answers the question "What must the computer system do to solve the problem?"
systems analyst	516	A professional who specializes in analyzing and designing systems
systems design	532	The third stage of the systems development life cycle, with the purpose of selecting and planning a system that meets the requirements defined in the requirements analysis
systems development	514	The activity of creating new systems or modifying existing ones
systems development life cycle (SDLC)	514	The ongoing activities associated with the system development process including investigation, analysis, design, implementation, and maintenance and review
systems implementation	534	A fourth stage of the systems development life cycle that includes hardware acquisition, software acquisition or development, user preparation, hiring and training of personnel, site and data preparation, installation, testing, startup, and user acceptance
systems investigation	528	The first stage of the systems development life cycle with the purpose of determining whether or not the objectives met by the existing system are satisfying the goals of the organization
systems maintenance	542	A part of the last stage of the systems development life cycle with the purpose of checking, changing, and enhancing the system to make it more useful in achieving user and organizational goals
systems review	544	A part of the last stage of the systems development life cycle with the purpose of analyzing systems to make sure that they are operating as intended
user acceptance document	542	A formal agreement signed by the user to approve a phase of the installation or the complete system

Questions

Review Questions

1. What are the phases of the systems development life cycle? What tasks are performed in each phase?
2. Who are the participants in systems development?
3. What is the role of a systems analyst?
4. List three reasons a systems development project might be launched.
5. Give an example of how an organization can use systems development to achieve a competitive advantage.
6. What is end-user systems development?
7. What is an application flowchart?
8. What is the purpose of a Gantt chart?
9. Describe when a decision table should be used.
10. What is prototyping? What are the steps involved in developing a prototype?
11. What are the benefits of using an iterative approach to systems development?
12. What is the purpose of systems investigation?
13. What is technical feasibility? What is economic feasibility?
14. What is the difference between operational and schedule feasibility?

15. What is systems analysis? What steps are included in systems analysis?
16. What tools and techniques are used for data collection and analysis?
17. What are joint application development and rapid application development?
18. What is the purpose of systems design?
19. What is the difference between a request for information and a request for proposal? Give an example of each.
20. What are the preliminary and final evaluation steps in systems design?
21. What is systems implementation?
22. List the types of information systems vendors.
23. What steps are involved in testing the information system?
24. What are some of the reasons for program maintenance?
25. What is systems review, and what are the two types of review procedures?
26. Describe the different types of feasibility. Give an example of each.
27. Describe the various methods used to perform requirements analysis and when each should be used.

Discussion Questions

28. Why is the term *systems development life cycle* used to describe the process of systems development?
29. For what types of system development projects might prototyping be especially useful? What might be some of the characteristics of a system developed with a prototyping technique?
30. Describe how you could use systems development tools, such as flowcharts and decision tables, in diagramming tasks and activities you must perform for one of your classes.
31. Why is outsourcing an attractive systems development alternative for many organizations? What are the potential negative aspects of outsourcing? How would you prioritize worker attitudes, the feelings of remaining workers, the lower price for products and services, and other factors in making a decision to outsource systems development projects to other countries?
32. Your company is developing a new Web site to sell clothes online. The Web site interacts with other programs and several databases. What types of testing are needed? How much testing should be performed before the new Web site is made operational?
33. Assume that you are responsible for the site preparation of the building where a new computer system will be installed. What are some of the equipment, improvement, and other considerations that you would have during this process?
34. You have been put in charge of reviewing the new computer system at your organization. What factors would you consider, and how might you evaluate these factors?
35. Why might an organization decide to phase in a new system rather than use a direct conversion?

Exercises

Try It Yourself

1. You are developing a new information system for The Fitness Center, a company that has five fitness centers in your metropolitan area, with about 650 members and 30 employees in each location. Both members and fitness consultants will use the system to keep track of participation in various fitness activities, such as free weights, volleyball, swimming, stair climbers, and aerobic classes. Prepare a brief memo detailing the required participants in the development team for this systems development project. Describe in your memo how you would determine the requirements for the new system.
2. Using the Internet, investigate several organizations that have launched large systems development initiatives lately. Develop a presentation on what you found, using presentation software such as PowerPoint.
3. Using the Internet, search for movie rental services. Describe the different types of services you find. Using your word-processing program, write a brief report describing what you learned about how computer and information services are

likely to be used by these services. What types of systems development tools would be useful for them?

4. If you haven't previously tried it, join Facebook.com. Explore and evaluate the Applications available to Facebook users. Write a review on the quality and usefulness of the applications. How much do the applications contribute to the Facebook experience?

5. Use flowchart symbols available in PowerPoint and other graphics software to illustrate the process that occurs in the self-serve system that allows customers to access and pay for gasoline at a gas station.

6. Create a decision table that illustrates the possible actions of an automated telephone system designed to connect customers to either a sales representative, a tech support agent, or a specific person via an extension number.

Virtual Classroom

For the following exercises, do not use face-to-face or telephone communications with your group members. Use only Internet communications.

7. Pick a career area or field that is of interest to your group. Develop a report that describes how an information system that offers a new and unique service not currently available could be developed for this career area or field. Each group member should develop a separate part of the report.

8. Describe a new or modified computer system that can make life easier for students at your college or university. Develop a plan to implement the new system utilizing a Gantt chart.

9. Your virtual team should investigate three business or organizations that have recently used systems development successfully. Create a one-page report that describes the costs and benefits associated with the systems development project.

Teamwork

10. Effective systems development requires a team effort. The team usually consists of system stakeholders and users, managers, system development specialists, and various support personnel. This team, called the development team, is responsible for determining the objectives of the computer system and delivering to the organization a system that meets these objectives. Have each team member choose a different role to play: chief information officer, systems analyst, senior-level management, or system stakeholder or user. Someone from this group should also be chosen as project leader. Having created the team, develop a profile of the "organization" for which you will develop a system. What is the name of the organization? How many employees does it have? Where is it located? What are its main activities? What are its products or services? Who are its customers and members? Using a word-processing program, create a document that can give someone who knows nothing about this organization an understanding of the nature of the organization.

11. Using the organization you created in exercise 10, go through the steps of design for a new computer system.

12. Describe how the organization should implement and maintain the new system.

Endnotes

[1] Claburn, Thomas, "Federal CIO Launches IT Spending Site Built for Sharing," *Information Week*, July 1, 2009, www.informationweek.com.

[2] Evans, Bob, "How U.S. Government Spends $200M Daily on IT," *Information Week*, July 1, 2009, www.informationweek.com.

[3] Levinson, Meredith, "Recession Causes Rising IT Project Failure Rates," *Computerworld*, June 18, 2009, www.computerworld.com.

[4] Embraer Staff, "Computerworld Honors Program: In-Flight Test Engineering Database," *Computerworld*, 2008, www.cwhonors.org.

[5] Anhalt, Robert, "Google Voice plans to be the Gmail for phones," *Examiner.com*, July 2, 2009, www.examiner.com.

[6] Sharkey, Joe, "The Race to Provide Wi-Fi at 30,000 Feet," *The New York Times*, May 18, 2009, www.nytimes.com.

[7] Cleveland Metroparks Zoo Staff, "Computerworld Honors Program: Interactive Distance Learning with Cleveland Metroparks Zoo," 2008, www.cwhonors.org.

Computer Crime and Information Security

Technology 360°

It was 4:35 p.m. on a Monday when Jan Minski received the call. A polite, business-like woman inquired whether Jan had recently traveled to Montreal, Canada. "What is this about?" Jan asked. The woman explained that recently an unusually large number of purchases had been made on her credit card in Montreal, and because the credit card company found this suspicious, it was phoning to investigate.

It so happened that Jan had not been traveling, but someone had been traveling under her identity. She panicked when she found out that $2900 had been charged over a 24-hour period. Fortunately, the credit card company insured its customers against identity theft and Jan got off with only a small service fee.

During the investigation of the crime, the company noted that Jan had used her credit card on several occasions to make online purchases and suggested that perhaps Jan's credit card information had been stolen from her PC. Jan's PC is connected to the campus network, which is in turn connected to the Internet. She has no idea how someone could steal information from her PC or how to prevent it from happening again.

As you read through this chapter, consider the following:

1. What are the first steps Jan should take in her crime scene investigation to find out if indeed her computer was broken into?
2. What possible methods could a hacker have used to steal Jan's credit card information?
3. What precautions can Jan take to make sure this doesn't happen again?

Check out Jan's *Action Plan* at the conclusion of this chapter.

LEARNING OBJECTIVES

1. Describe the types of information that must be kept secure and the types of threats against them.
2. Describe methods of keeping a PC safe and secure.
3. Discuss the threats and defenses unique to multiuser networks.
4. Discuss the threats and defenses unique to wireless networks.
5. Describe the threats faced by Internet users, and the methods of defending against them.

CHAPTER CONTENT

Introduction

The global information economy depends on computer and information systems to reliably store, process, and transfer information. Threats to system reliability and information integrity undermine our economy and security. Information is money, and thieves are working to divert the flow of information and money to their own pockets, leaving many innocent victims in their wake. In this chapter, you will learn about the value of information, the threats to information security, and ways that you can secure information for yourself, your employer, your country, and the world.

You check your e-mail, and discover a happy greeting informing you that an old friend has sent you a virtual postcard with the message, "Click here to access your card." Upon clicking the link, you arrive at the virtual postcard Web site and are asked to enter the claim number provided by the e-mail and then click the Continue button. After doing so, an error message is displayed saying that the claim number is not valid. After several tries you give up and go back to checking your other e-mail, soon forgetting the incident. In the next few days, you notice that your computer isn't behaving as it should. It is sluggish, confusing error messages occasionally pop up, and sometimes the computer locks up or turns itself off.

Chances are that your computer has contracted a virus. Not only is the virus affecting your computer's performance and irritating you, but it may also be allowing someone on the Internet to access your PC, your files, and personal information. Another real possibility is that your computer has been enslaved and forced to deliver spam or viruses to others on the Internet. Although such news is bound to be disconcerting, you can take some comfort in knowing that you are not alone. Billions of individuals worldwide are dealing with the same problem (see Figure 11.1).

FIGURE 11.1 • Virus infection

On this map from McAfee, areas in dark red had over a billion computers infected by computer viruses in a 30-day period.

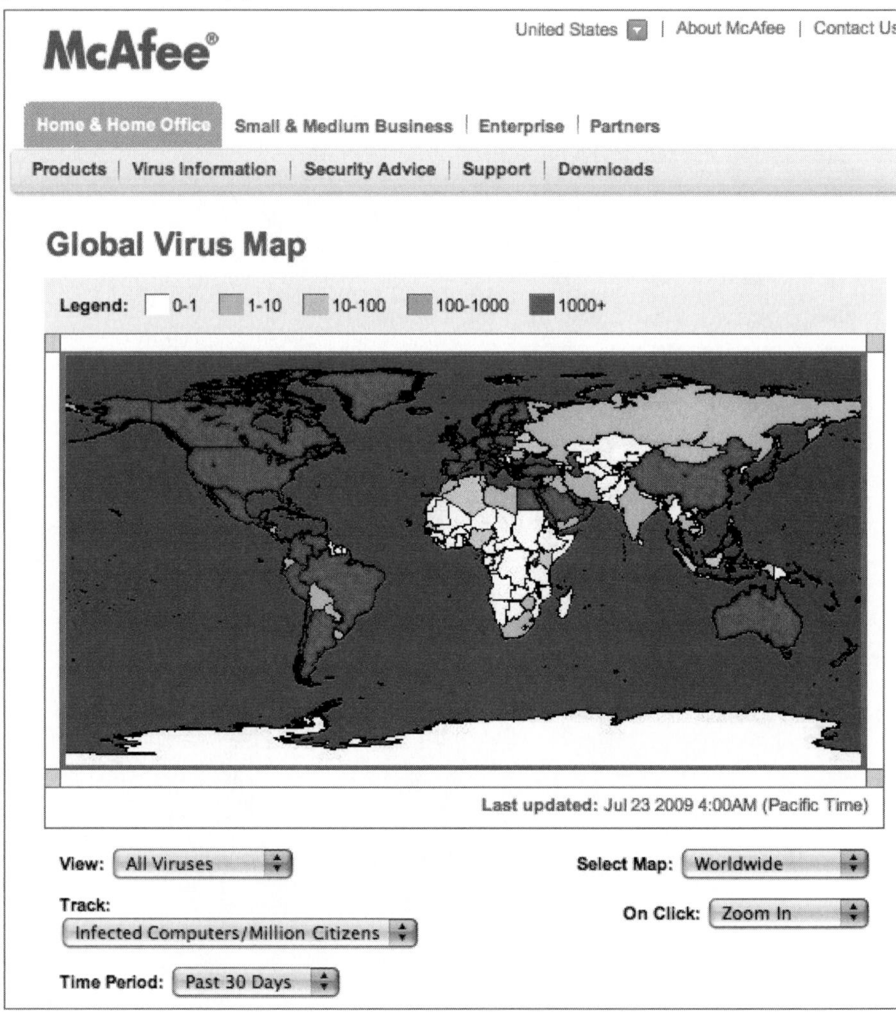

Viruses are one example of the many types of attacks on computer systems that take place every day. Consider the following recent news headlines:

- "NYSE, Nasdaq Sites Targeted by 'Cyber Attack'," *The Wall Street Journal*[1]
- "North Korea Blamed for Cyberattacks on U.S., South Korea," *CIO Today*[2]
- "U.K. Web hoster, customers scramble after attack deletes 100,000 sites," *Computerworld*[3]?
- "ATM malware spreading around the world, researcher says," *Computerworld*[4]?
- "Pentagon Plans New Arm to Wage Cyberspace Wars," *The New York Times*[5]?
- "Hackers launch phishing attack on Facebook users," *Reuters*[6]
- "Botnet master hits the kill switch, takes down 100,000 PCs," *Ars Technica*[7]
- "Analyst: cyberwarfare arms race with China imminent," *Ars Technica*[8]
- "Update: 160,000 accounts breached at UC Berkeley," *Computerworld*[9]
- "Air Traffic Systems Vulnerable to Attack," *NewsFactor*[10]

These are representative of hundreds of similar stories reported by news services every month. If these reports give the impression that a war is being waged, it is for good reason. Corporate and government networks and home computers are under attack, and the Internet is the battlefield. The 2008 Computer Security Institute's Computer Crime and Security survey found that 49 percent of businesses experience computer virus infestations, 27 percent suffer targeted attacks from hackers, and 12 percent suffer from electronic financial fraud, costing on average nearly $500,000.[11]

The victims in this war include individuals, businesses, and governments. There are billions of dollars in losses each year due to identity theft, financial fraud, and other forms of theft and destruction wrought through the manipulation of computer resources. Two hundred and sixty-four million dollars were reported lost to Internet fraud in 2008 in the United States alone.[12] Prisoners in this war include hackers like Jeffrey Lee Parson, a 19-year-old who served time for releasing a version of the Blaster Internet worm that attacked the Microsoft Web site and corrupted an estimated 48,000 computers, and Dmitriy Guzner, who launched cyberattacks against the Church of Scientology and faces 10 years in prison (Figure 11.2).

FIGURE 11.2 • Going too far

Ninteen-year-old New Jersey native Dmitriy Guzner faces 10 years in jail for his cybercrimes against the Church of Scientology.

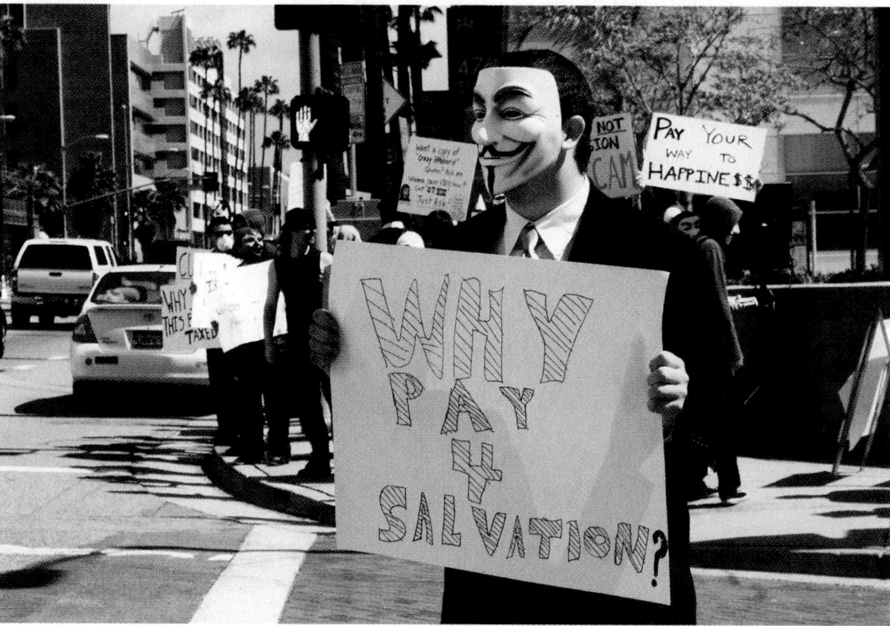

Many believe the battle will only get more intense. Viruses and security attacks have increased consistently each year. Today's virus scanners are programmed to detect hundreds of thousands of different viruses, worms, Trojan horses, and other potentially unwanted applications.

In Chapter 1, information security was defined as being concerned with three main areas:

- Confidentiality: Information should be available only to those who rightfully have access to it.
- Integrity: Information should be modified only by those who are authorized to do so.
- Availability: Information should be accessible to those who need it when they need it.

This chapter discusses all aspects of information security as it relates to personal computers, organizational systems, and the Internet. It discusses what is at stake, how our computer systems are vulnerable, and how to keep them as safe as possible. The material in this chapter is organized to address the multiple layers of computer security that combine to provide total information security (see Figure 11.3).

FIGURE 11.3 • Layers of information security

Computer users are at the heart of information security and are targeted through their use of computers connected to networks connected to the Internet.

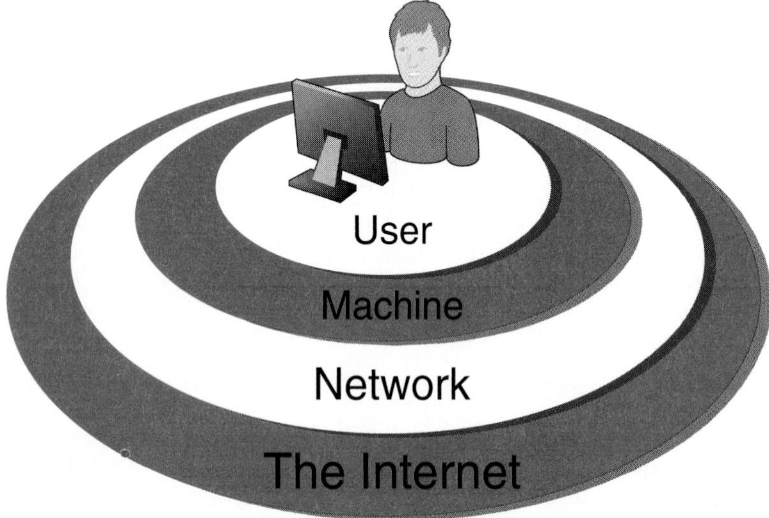

Total information security refers to securing all components of the global digital information infrastructure—from cell phones to PCs, to business and government networks, to Internet routers and communications satellites. You, the computer user, are at the heart of the total information security effort. Your cognizance of security risks and the actions you take to secure the systems with which you interact are the most important component of total information security. It is the user who suffers from the results of attacks against computer systems and who is responsible for safeguarding systems against those attacks. As a computer user, you must learn about security risks at three levels: the machine level, the network level (including wireless networks), and the Internet level. As you move from one level to the next, you face increasing exposure and risks.

INFORMATION SECURITY AND VULNERABILITY

It is clear that information security is an important issue today. To understand its importance, you need to consider exactly what is at stake and the sources of the danger.

What Is at Stake?

The concept of information security is built on the assumption that the information you create, store, maintain, and transfer is valuable, confidential, and worth protecting. This section examines the value of digital information from personal, organizational, national, and international perspectives and the consequences if that information is stolen or made inaccessible.

Personal Information. What would concern you most if a person who wished to do you harm had full control of your personal computer? Unfortunately, this is an all-too-real possibility. Through any one of many methods discussed later in the chapter, intruders can gain control of home PCs through Internet connections and have a field day with what they find. While at their own computer, intruders can view and manipulate your computer system just as if they were sitting with your computer in their lap. The intruder could be in the apartment next door or on the other side of the world. The intruder could steal your Internet access and e-mail passwords, any information that your operating system has stored about you, your Web browser history and cache, your e-mail, and your computer files. If you bank and pay your bills online, it is possible that a hacker could steal your account numbers.

Using key pieces of personal information stolen from an individual's personal computer, a business's database, or even discarded paper documents, a thief can steal your identity. **Identity theft** is the criminal act of using stolen information about a person to assume that person's identity, typically for financial gain. The U.S. Federal Trade Commission (FTC) breaks down identity theft into several subcategories of fraud based on how the stolen identity is used. Credit card fraud is the most common, making up 20 percent of ID theft cases, then there is government documents/benefits fraud (15 percent), employment fraud (15 percent), phone or utilities fraud (13 percent), bank fraud (11 percent), and loan fraud (4 percent). In 2008, the FTC received over 1.2 million consumer fraud and identity theft complaints. U.S. consumers reported losses from fraud of more than $1.8 billion, up from $1.3 billion in 2007. Individuals between the ages of 20 and 29 are hardest hit by ID theft (see Figure 11.4).[13] Given a person's Social Security number, birth date, or other personal identifiers, identity thieves can apply for a new credit card in the victim's name and have it delivered to a post office box. A crime ring in California, for example, unsuccessfully tried to apply for a credit card using the personal information of one of the authors of this book. Identity thieves can make purchases on stolen credit card numbers, make bank withdrawals, apply for loans, or buy a car. The damage caused can be quite serious. An identity thief can also do damage to a victim's reputation by perpetrating crimes under the victim's identity.

FIGURE 11.4 • Identity theft

Individuals between the ages of 20 and 29 are most affected by identity theft.

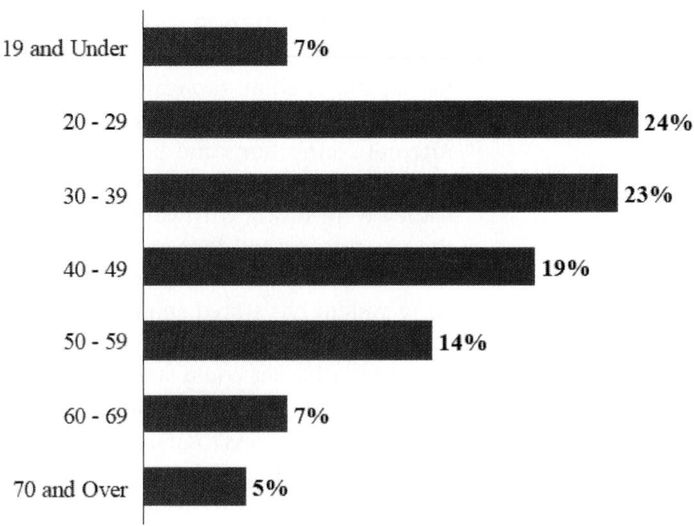

Based on "Consumer Fraud and Identity Theft Complaint Data, 2008" accessed at www.consumer.gov/sentinel/.

Not only can attackers steal information from your PC, and in some cases steal your identity, but in many instances an attacker or virus can corrupt your system so that you no longer have access to your computer or the data it stores. For many victims, this can be as damaging as having information stolen. Many people collect irreplaceable information on their computers of both practical and sentimental value—personal writing, correspondence, music, photos, professional documents, financial records, and much more. To lose computer documents can be like losing a part of your life. The hours and days invested in creating your collection of files are wasted. Moments of your life preserved in bits may be lost forever.

Intellectual Property. **Intellectual property** refers to a product of the mind or intellect over which the owner holds legal entitlement. Intellectual property includes ideas and intangible objects such as poetry, stories, music, and new ways of doing things or making things (see Figure 11.5). Like tangible objects, intellectual property has value and is owned by an individual or organization. Each time you use software, listen to music, read a book or newspaper article, or see a movie, you are enjoying someone else's intellectual property. The most valuable intellectual properties are typically the result of years invested in study and training. The sale of that intellectual property provides an income for the creator and a return on his or her investment.

FIGURE 11.5 • Intellectual property

Intellectual property such as music, software, movies, TV shows, books, and product designs is typically protected by law from illegal copying and distribution in order to allow those who create intellectual property to earn a living.

A respect for the value of intellectual property makes it possible for individuals who create intangible products such as music and software to earn a living. The digitization of many forms of intellectual property, including books, movies, artwork, and music, has transformed tangible products into intangible products. Unfortunately, people don't always respect the value of these forms of intellectual property as they do physical property. Consider, for example, the explosion in sales of portable digital music players like the iPod. While millions of people have purchased iPods, paying up to $250, many of those same people do not feel obligated to pay a penny for the music they listen to on the player. Which is more valuable, the player or the music?

Because software, audio and music recordings, movies, television and other video products, books, and other writings are stored as bits, it is easy and convenient to copy and distribute them, sometimes without consideration to the creator. This, in the view of the creators of the intellectual property, is as much a theft as if you steal an iPod from someone's backpack. When intellectual property is copied and distributed by the public, rather than by the legal distributor, it dramatically impacts the amount of money earned by the owner of the intellectual property. Rather than selling thousands of copies, for thousands of dollars, to thousands of fans, an artist might be able to sell only hundreds of copies for hundreds of dollars to hundreds of fans who then make thousands of copies for their friends. When those who produce intellectual property can no longer earn a living, they will turn to some other career.

Digitization, the Internet, and a general failure to protect intellectual property have combined to create serious issues for the software, music, movie, and publishing industries. An important component of total information security is the protection of intellectual property rights.

Intellectual property rights concern the ownership and use of intellectual property such as software, music, movies, data, and information. Protection of intellectual property can take many forms, including copyrights, trademarks, trade secrets, and patents. See Table 11.1.

TABLE 11.1 • Protecting intellectual property rights

There are a number of ways to protect intellectual property, including copyrights, trademarks, trade secrets, and patents.

Protection	Description
Copyright	Protects words, music, and other expressions for the life of the copyright holder plus 70 years; the *fair use doctrine* describes when and how copyrighted material can be legally used. The *Digital Millennium Copyright Act* provides global copyright protection.
Trademark	Protects a unique symbol or word used by a business to identify a product or service
Trade secret	Protects secrets or proprietary information of individuals and organizations as long as the trade secret is adequately protected
Patent	Protects an invention by giving the patent holder a monopoly on the use of the invention for 20 years after the patent application has been applied

Organizational Information. For a business or nonprofit organization, the information it processes is often highly valuable and key to its success. To have that information compromised can result in a loss of market share and in some cases total business failure. For example, in 2009, Twitter's corporate network was hacked into and the thief made off with over 300 confidential documents. Several sensitive documents were made public on TechCrunch.com and included confidential dealings between Twitter and Google, Microsoft, and others. Making these documents public was an embarrassment to Twitter, and provided valuable information that competitors could use to gain an advantage over Twitter.[14] This example illustrates why businesses and organizations take information security very seriously.

Because businesses typically hold the most valuable information, they are the targets of the most attacks. Table 11.2 lists the types of attacks against businesses and the percentage of businesses that experience them.

TABLE 11.2 • Cyber attacks against businesses and percentages of businesses affected in 2008

Percentage affected	Type of attack or threat
50%	Virus
44%	Insider abuse
42%	Laptop theft
29%	Unauthorized access
21%	Instant messaging abuse
21%	Denial of service
20%	Bots
17%	Theft/loss of customer data
14%	Abuse of wireless network
13%	System penetration
12%	Financial fraud
11%	Misuse of Web application
9%	Theft/loss of proprietary information
9%	Password sniffing
8%	DNS attacks
6%	Web site defacement
5%	Telecom fraud
2%	Sabotage

Source: Computer Security Institute 2008 Security Survey, www.gocsi.com.

Business intelligence is the process of gathering and analyzing information in the pursuit of business advantage. Companies are continuously gathering and analyzing information about economic indicators, industry statistics, marketing research, public opinion, and anything that can assist in creating a product or service that bests their competition with the lowest amount of investment. *Competitive intelligence* is a form of business intelligence concerned with information about competitors. Sometimes, gathering competitive intelligence can become unlawful. For instance, one satellite service vendor paid hackers to break the encryption code of a rival service provider.[15] *Counterintelligence* is a form of business intelligence concerned with protecting your own information from access by your competitors. Many businesses employ strict policies and procedures to keep valuable data from wandering off. For example, it is not uncommon for a business to prohibit the use of USB storage devices. Some businesses store all data on servers and do not allow data to be stored on a PC's local hard drive. Many businesses keep track of which users are logged on to which workstations at every moment of the day to more easily track errors or thefts. The techniques of information security discussed in this chapter provide valuable tools for counterintelligence.

Besides protecting its own proprietary information, a business also has a responsibility to its customers to safeguard their private information. Until recently, businesses had little accountability for what they did with customer information. Customer data collected by one company has often been sold to other companies for profit. New laws have been proposed to hold companies responsible for maintaining the privacy of their customers' information. Some politicians would like to require entities that collect sensitive information such as Social Security numbers to secure the data physically and technologically and to notify consumers nationwide when data is compromised. In other words, companies would be responsible for storing sensitive data in a manner that withstands intruder attacks either over the network or by cooperation with insiders. Besides protecting personal identifiers such as Social Security numbers, the protection of medical and health information has also become a great concern to lawmakers (see Figure 11.6).

FIGURE 11.6 • HIPAA

The Health Insurance Portability and Accountability Act (HIPAA) privacy requirements have those in the medical profession taking patient privacy very seriously.

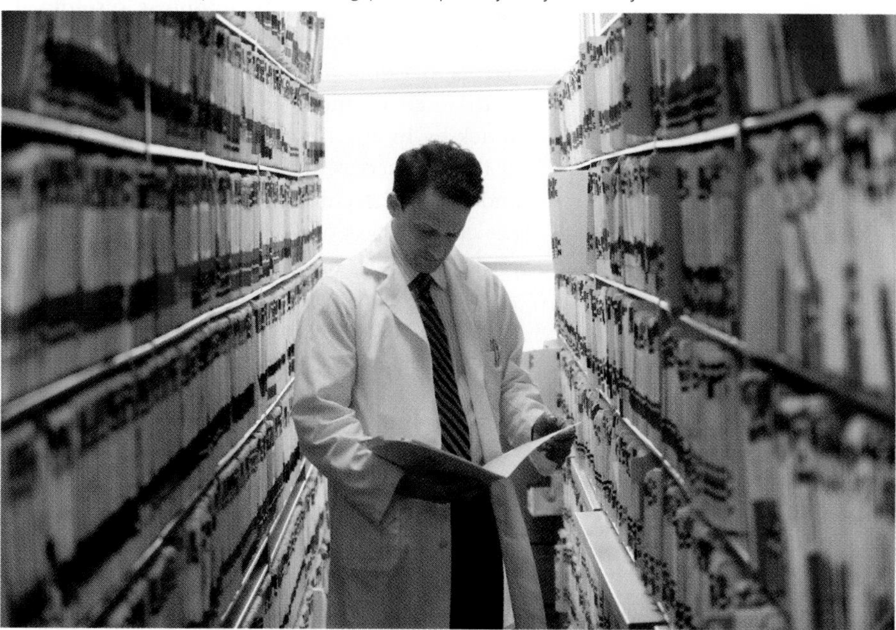

Table 11.3 lists several U.S. laws that require companies and other entities to take information security very seriously. Table 11.3 clearly indicates that businesses and other organizations that maintain databases of customer information are under pressure to manage that information responsibly by making sure there is no unauthorized access and that the information is not shared without the customer's knowledge. State laws have an equally strong effect on businesses that operate over the Internet. For example, California has nearly a dozen privacy laws that must be followed by organizations, wherever they may be located, if they wish to do business with California residents.

Some industries are creating standards of their own to support responsible data management. For example, MasterCard and Visa have developed data-protection procedures that are required of companies using the popular credit cards. The Payment Card Industry Data Security Standard has a set of protection rules and procedures, including encryption, logging of credit activities, user access, and monitoring, that merchants and others using MasterCard and Visa credit cards must implement. A certified assessor performs annual tests of compliance.

TABLE 11.3 • U.S. laws that protect information and privacy

Law	Description
Health Insurance Portability and Accountability Act (HIPAA) of 1996	Requires those in the health industry to protect the privacy of health information and provides policies and procedures for doing so
Consumer Internet Privacy Protection Act of 1997	Requires data collectors to alert people that their personal information is being shared with other organizations
Gramm-Leach-Bliley Act (GLBA) of 1999	Requires banks and financial institutions to alert customers to their policies and practices in disclosing customer information
The Children's Online Privacy Protection Act of 1998	Gives parents control over what information is collected from their children online and how such information may be used
Sarbanes-Oxley Act ("Sarbox") of 2002	Fights corporate corruption by imposing stringent reporting requirements and internal controls on electronic financial records and transactions

National and Global Security. Just as businesses benefit from digital technologies and the Internet, so do governments and government agencies all over the world. Government computing systems, databases, and networks process, store, and transfer confidential government information, citizen records, state secrets, national defense strategies, and many other classified documents. Many of these government networks are connected to the Internet and can be open to attack by international hackers. Consider U.K. citizen Gary McKinnon, accused of illegally accessing 98 U.S. Department of Defense computers. He deleted files and accessed secure military information and military computers at a time when the country was on high alert. McKinnon awaits extradition to the United States for trial.[16]

Today's national economies and security depend strongly on technology and the Internet. Technology and the Internet have become tools to protect nations, as well as points of vulnerability (see Figure 11.7). Threats to the Internet and the national information infrastructure that it supports are serious threats to the nation. **Cyberterrorism** is a form of terrorism that uses attacks over the Internet to intimidate and harm a population. The United States Computer Emergency Readiness Team (US-CERT) was established to monitor the security of U.S. networks and the Internet and respond to episodes of cyberterrorism. US-CERT is part of the National Cyber Security Division of the U.S. Department of Homeland Security. The US-CERT Web site, *www.us-cert.gov*, gives network administrators and computer users up-to-date information on security threats and defenses. US-CERT is also responsible for supporting and implementing the National Strategy to Secure Cyberspace, introduced in Chapter 1. The strategic objectives of the National Strategy to Secure Cyberspace are to accomplish the following:

- Prevent cyberattacks against America's critical infrastructures.
- Reduce national vulnerability to cyberattacks.
- Minimize damage and recovery time from cyberattacks that do occur.

CYBERTERRORISTS MAY GO NUCLEAR

Sirens blare. The radar screen in the control room shows eight incoming nuclear missiles, estimated impact in six minutes. Do you retaliate before it's too late? If you do, you might be playing into the hands of cyberterrorists. A new study shows that while the odds of hackers gaining direct access to the nuclear launch system are slim, they could feed false data to officials and the information system. Cyberterrorists may find it easier, the report said, to trick a government into launching a nuclear counterstrike than to acquire a weapon themselves.

Terrorists could use internet to launch nuclear attack: report
Bobbie Johnson
The Guardian
July 24, 2009
http://www.guardian.co.uk/technology/2009/jul/24/internet-cyber-attack-terrorists

FIGURE 11.7 • Homeland security

The National Operations Center for U.S. Homeland Security protects the country's borders in real space and cyberspace.

Cybersecurity became a priority under President Obama's administration. In 2009, President Obama created a new senior-level position in the White House to oversee cybersecurity across all areas of government and national infrastructure.[17] Also in 2009, the Pentagon created a new command dedicated to securing the nation's networks from cyberattack, especially from China and Russia.[18]

In recent years, international cyberattacks against U.S. government networks have dramatically increased. US-CERT reported 5,488 cases of unauthorized access of government computers in 2008, up 40 percent from 2007, a trend that continued through 2009. Joel Brenner, counterintelligence chief in the U.S. Office of the Director of National Intelligence, stated that "Government systems are under constant attack."[19]

Many cyberattacks originate overseas. Russia has a reputation of being home to prolific hacker activity. The weakness of the Russian economy combined with the criminal opportunities provided by the Internet and the failure of the Russian government to prosecute hackers have inspired many technically savvy Russians to turn to hacking.

Besides attacks from independent hackers, governments themselves have become involved in cyberespionage and attacks. There is a suspicion that the Chinese government has had its hand in cyberattacks on the United States and elsewhere.[20] It is often difficult to trace attacks to an individual person or organization.

Cyberattacks have become a key component in military strategy. Hackers have the ability to take down important communications and information networks. There is concern that the networks and computers that control the U.S. power grid are vulnerable,[21] as are systems used in air traffic control.[22] A cyberattack on these important national infrastructures could certainly do damage, and aid a physical attack. The United States and most other world powers are heavily invested in both cyberdefense and attacks.

Defending against international attacks is particularly difficult because there are currently no global cybercrime laws. The laws of one country cannot be enforced in another without the cooperation of both governments. A computer attack may be designed by hackers in country A and launched in country B in order to attack computers in country C. Increasingly, botnets (infected computers under autonomous control) are used in cyberattacks. A botnet may consist of tens or hundreds of thousands of computers spread around the world. Some countries are discussing the establishment of a global cybercrime task force, similar to the Interpol international police network. One step in that direction was the Council of Europe's (Figure 11.8) convention on cybercrime. The convention on cybercrime produced a treaty signed in November 2001 that calls on countries to work together to create international laws that address cybercrime.[23]

FIGURE 11.8 • The Council of Europe

The Council of Europe promotes democracy and human rights as well as developing standards in international cooperation for information security.

Threats to Information Security

To achieve total information security, many diverse threats must be addressed. From the inherent flaws in software, to intentional or unintended acts by law-abiding citizens, to attacks by those wishing to do serious damage, to government-sponsored attacks, the threats are abundant and complex. This section examines common sources of information security threats: software and network vulnerabilities, user negligence, pirates and plagiarists, and attackers.

Software and Network Vulnerabilities. Perfect software would be impossible to hack. If Microsoft Windows and other operating systems, as well as Web browsers and all Internet software, were perfectly designed, no one would be able to access someone else's private computer and data. The fact is that people are not perfect, and their creations such as software are bound to include imperfections.

Some argue that the software industry could do a better job of securing software and computer systems. Some in the software industry argue that the complexity of today's software makes it impossible to guarantee any software to be

100 percent secure. No matter which position is correct, it is clear that the software and systems that hold and control our data are vulnerable. Security vulnerabilities or **security holes** are software bugs that allow violations of information security.

Recognizing that information security is a major concern, software and hardware companies have made it a priority in their development efforts (Figure 11.9). The Microsoft *Trustworthy Computing* initiative is "a long-term, collaborative effort to provide more secure, private, and reliable computing experiences for everyone."[24] Microsoft claims that Trustworthy Computing is a core company tenet that guides virtually everything they do. Microsoft categorizes Trustworthy Computing into four "pillars": security, privacy, and reliability in their software, services, and products, and integrity in their business practices. One example of Microsoft efforts to implement security is Windows Update, a service that allows patches to be applied to security holes as they are discovered. **Software patches** are corrections to the software bugs that cause security holes. Microsoft releases monthly updates that include patches for minor software flaws as well as critical patches to repair flaws that allow for serious breaches of security. Microsoft provides dozens of critical patches through Windows Update every year.

FIGURE 11.9 • Cybersecurity is a priority

Cisco Systems Chairman and CEO John Chambers delivers a keynote address at a 2009 security conference.

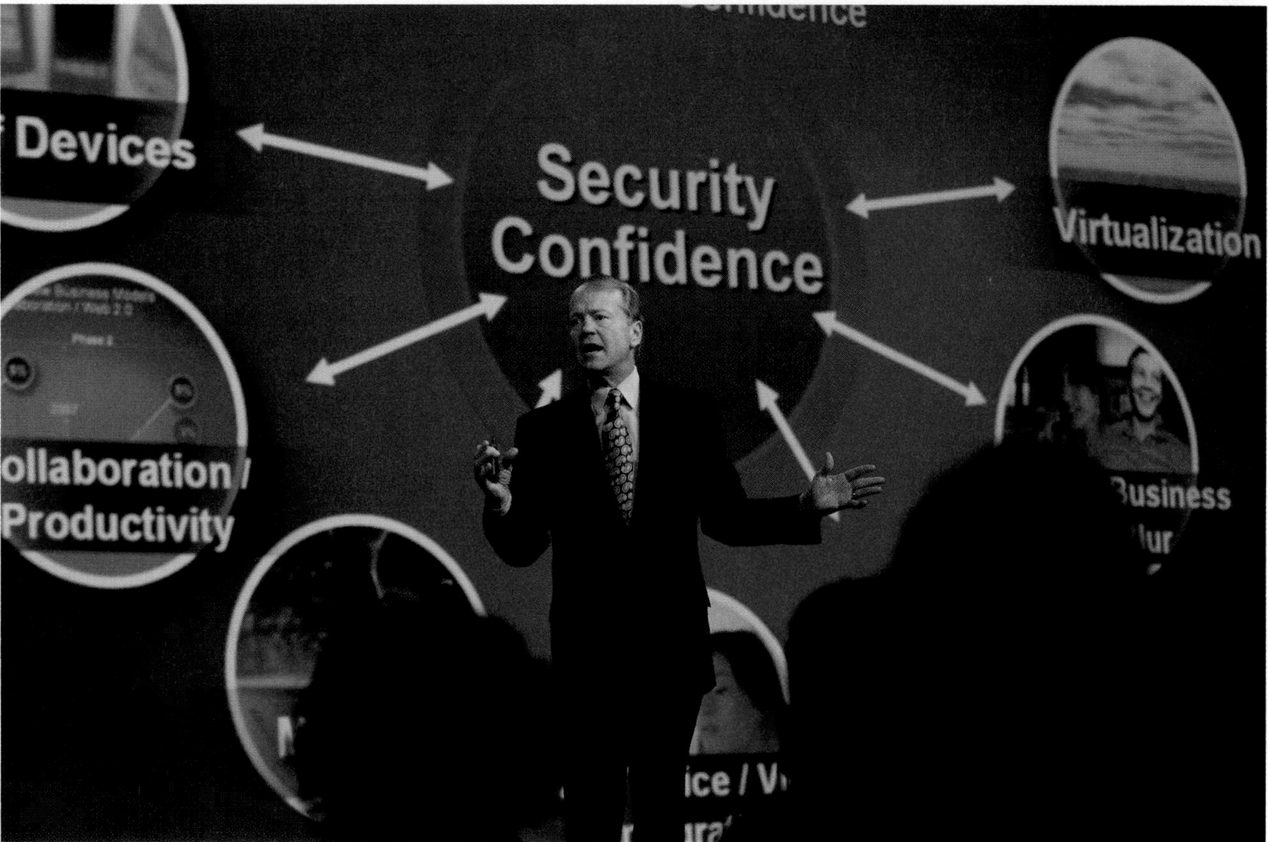

FIGURE 11.10 • Oops!

User mistakes are common and range in severity from accidentally deleting a file to multimillion-dollar errors in recordkeeping.

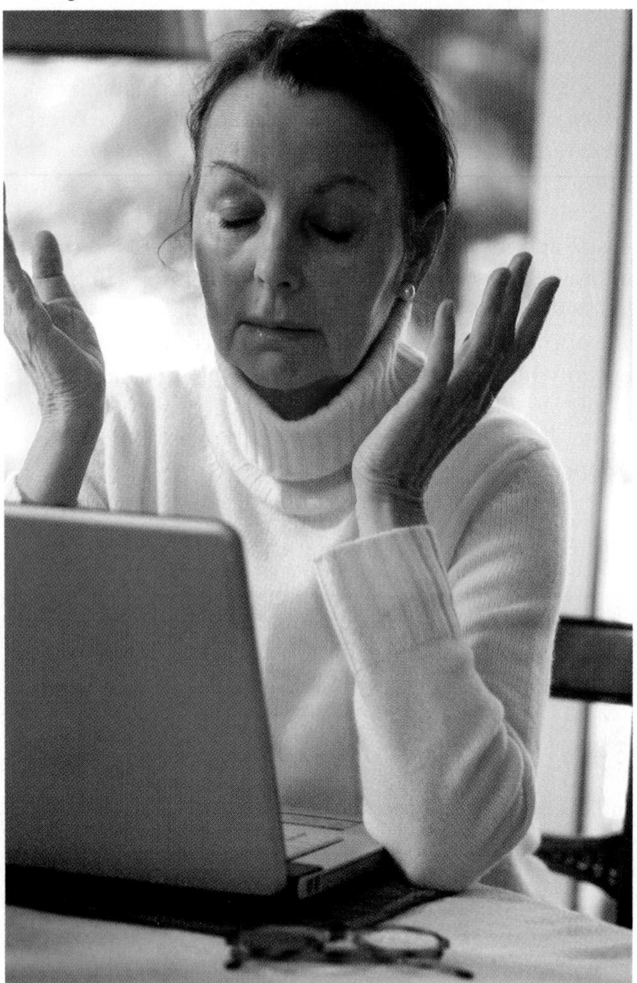

One negative effect of the Microsoft monthly patch announcements is that in addition to informing the general public of security holes, they also serve to inform attackers. Many attackers use the Microsoft monthly announcements to reverse-engineer hacking tools that take advantage of the newly found bugs. In many cases, code that exploits the security hole is available to hackers on the Web within days of the Microsoft announcement. It becomes a race between hackers who exploit the bug and users applying patches to protect themselves. Microsoft encourages its users to use the automatic update option that applies patches as soon as they are released over the Internet.

User Negligence. There are many situations where innocent human mistakes result in monumental problems. Take, for example, the Taiwan stock trader who mistakenly bought $251 million worth of shares due to a typing error, causing her company a paper loss of more than $12 million. In another type of mistake, the U.S. Defense Department, Internal Revenue Service (IRS), and Justice Department have misplaced hundreds of government notebook computers, many of which contain classified government documents. In a more common act of negligence, many users provide hackers with easy access to computer systems by using passwords that are easy to guess, or storing passwords and other private information where others can access them (see Figure 11.10).

People's mistakes can lead to problems with security, accuracy, or reliability of computer systems and information. The major types of human errors include those shown in Table 11.4.

A number of actions can be taken by individuals and organizations to prevent computer-related mistakes. Smart businesses and organizations automate data entry whenever possible to cut down on typing errors. Database management systems and spreadsheets can be programmed to allow only reasonable figures to be entered. Businesses typically have data backup policies and procedures, as well as backup power supplies and surge protection, to assure the safety of computer systems against mechanical failure, natural disaster, and human mistakes. Businesses also employ technology experts to set up and maintain computer systems so that both the hardware and software are safe and secure. It is not uncommon for a business to adopt policies that outline how employees are to use information systems and handle data in soft and hard copy. For example, a business may have a policy that calls for employees to shred all documents that contain private information. Just as today's best businesses employ smart and thorough information security practices, individuals should do the same in managing their own personal computers and information.

TABLE 11.4 • Types of user negligence

Type of mistake	Example
Data-entry errors	A military commander might enter the wrong GPS coordinates for enemy troops into the computer; this data-entry error might cause friendly troops to be killed.
Errors in computer programs	A payroll program might multiply a person's pay rate by 2 for overtime instead of 1.5; this programming error results in a higher paycheck than the employee should receive for overtime work.
Improper installation and setup of computer systems	A person may neglect to properly set the necessary security settings to secure a home wireless network.
Mishandling of computer output	A medical office might send lab results to the wrong person; the person receiving the results has access to another person's private medical information.
Inadequate planning for and control of equipment malfunctions	An individual's hard drive might fail; if the person has not backed up important files recently, he or she will lose access to important information and have to redo work.
Inadequate planning for and control of electrical problems, humidity problems, and other environmental difficulties	A power outage in an area could shut down an organization's computer system; without a backup power supply and protection from electrical surges, information and data might be lost and equipment might be ruined.

Pirates and Plagiarists. Pirates and plagiarists are two classifications of individuals who violate the laws regarding intellectual property rights. **Piracy** involves the illegal copying, use, and distribution of digital intellectual property such as software, music, and movies. **Plagiarism** involves taking credit for someone else's intellectual property, typically a written idea, by claiming it as your own.

Pirated software, music, and videos can be accessed through file-sharing networks or from others on flash drives or homemade CDs and DVDs. Because technology allows media files to be copied, many otherwise law-abiding citizens feel as though it must be okay. Organizations such as the Recording Industry Association of America (RIAA), the Motion Picture Association of America (MPAA), and the Software & Information Industry Association are making it known that piracy is not okay. The RIAA has sued thousands of individuals involved in illegal MP3 file sharing for significant financial settlements. One case lasted several years and finally cost the defendant, Jammie Thomas, $1.92 million in fines for sharing 24 songs.[25] The RIAA and associates have been successful in closing down most file-sharing businesses, starting with the original Napster in 2001, followed by Limewire and Kazaa, and others. In 2009, founders of the popular file-sharing site The Pirate Bay were arrested, sentenced to a year in prison, and fined $4.5 million.[26] Even so, as one file-sharing avenue closes, several others open.

Recently, the RIAA has changed strategies from suing music fans to having them cut off from the Internet. The RIAA and MPAA are coordinating with governments and Internet service providers to cut Internet service to users who illegally share intellectual property over the Internet. Some U.S. ISPs are experimenting with the RIAA's "three-strikes and you're out" plan, sending out notices to users found in violation of the law, warning that they will be severed from the Internet if they infringe again. Similar efforts are underway in Ireland, France, the United Kingdom, South Korea, Australia, New Zealand, and elsewhere.[27]

International commercial piracy is of great concern to those in the music, motion picture, and software industries. The vast majority of motion pictures sold in Russia and Romania are pirated (see Figure 11.11). In Vietnam, China, and Ukraine, most software in use is pirated. Around half the digital music in the United States is pirated.

FIGURE 11.11 • International piracy

In countries such as Romania, street vendors sell pirated copies of software, music, and motion pictures without any fear of legal recrimination.

Plagiarism has been an issue of legal and social concern for as long as people have produced intellectual property. Stealing the ideas and thoughts of others and presenting them as your own is a serious breach of ethics matched by serious penalties if you are caught. A student caught submitting the work of another for a grade may face expulsion. A professional journalist, author, or researcher could face an expensive lawsuit and loss of a career. (Social and ethical concerns are discussed in more depth in Chapter 12.)

While plagiarism has been a social issue for a long time, the digitization of the written word, the Internet, and cut-and-paste methods of writing have made it all the more common. Some Web sites provide students with free research papers for class projects. Submitting papers from such Web sites is considered plagiarism and is subject to strict and severe penalties by colleges. Software such as Turnitin (*www.turnitin.com*), and iThenticate (*www.ithenticate.com*) is used by many high school and college teachers to find instances of plagiarism in electronically submitted homework files, with a high rate of success (see Figure 11.12).

FIGURE 11.12 • Turnitin report

Many instructors use software from turnitin.com that works within online systems like Blackboard to find instances of plagiarism in student work. This Turnitin report indicates that the paper is 55 percent plagiarized and provides links to the original source of the material on the Web.

TurnitinUK Originality Report ◂previous next▸ print save refresh prefs **help** turnitinUK

Human Genome Project by Paste Ncut

Processed on [illegible] ID: 106256 Word Count: 700

Overall Similarity Index: 56% exclude quoted exclude bibliography mode: show highest matches together

In July 2001, the Wellcome Trust announced a 5-year investment in Ensembl of more than F8.8 million for automatic annotation of human genome data, including recognition of genes and other biologically important sequence features. [3]

A 2.91-billion base pair (bp) consensus sequence of the euchromatic portion of the human genome was generated by the whole-genome shotgun sequencing method. [1]

Two assembly strategieswere used,

combining sequence data from Celera and the publicly funded genome effort. [1]

Without including biases inherent in the cloning and assembly procedure used by [1]

the publicly funded group, the public data were shredded [1]

1. 27% match (internet) http://www.sciencemag.org
2. 14% match (internet) http://shgc-www.stanford.edu
3. 10% match (internet) http://www.ornl.gov
4. 7% match (Proquest) A physical map of the human genome, Nature Vol 409, Iss 6822, Feb 15, 2001
5. 2% match (internet) http://www.biomedcentral.com
6. 2% match (internet) http://www.cop.ufl.edu
7. 2% match (internet) http://cyberdocuments.rero.ch

RUSSIAN CYBERROGUES TOPPLE TWITTER

For over two hours in the summer of 2009, cybersocialites clicked in frustration as Facebook traffic slowed almost to a halt and Twitter was kicked entirely offline. Many North Americans drinking their coffee that morning had never heard of the breakaway Republic of Ossetia or the Russian invasion of Georgia. Yet it was a Russian denial of service attack on a pro-Georgian blogger's social networking sites that was the cause of their frustration. The attack is part of an emerging trend toward waging political and military battles in both the real world and cyberspace.

Twitter Attack Looks Politically Motivated
Thomas Claburn
InformationWeek
August 7, 2009
http://www.informationweek.com/news/security/attacks/showArticle.jhtml?articleID=219100463

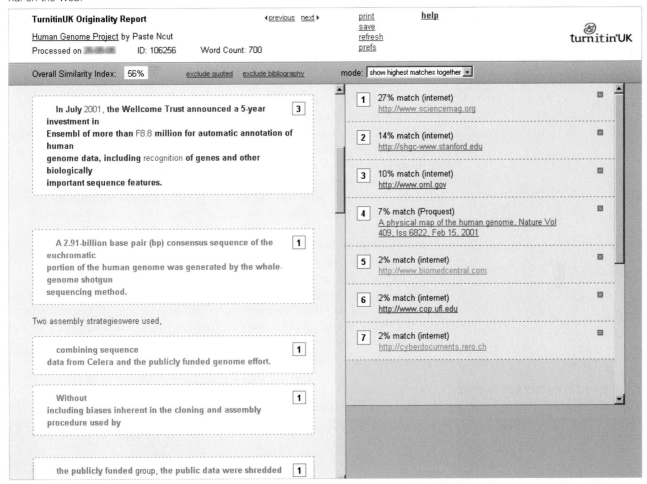

Hackers, Crackers, Intruders, and Attackers. Chapter 1 defined a *hacker* as an individual who subverts computer security without authorization. Security professionals refer to this as *system penetration*. Many names are used to label those who unlawfully hack into secure computers and networks; the news media generally uses the term *hacker*. Hackers and others who wish to differentiate between lawbreakers and innocent techies use the term *cracker*, for criminal hacker, claiming that hackers do not necessarily break laws. Those in the information security industry tend to prefer the labels *attacker* and *intruder*.

There are several labels associated with different forms of hacking. Some of the most common include the following:

- Black-hat hacker: Hacker who takes advantage of security vulnerabilities to gain unlawful access to private networks for the purpose of private advantage
- White-hat hacker: Individual who considers it working for the common good to hack into networks in order to call attention to flaws in security so that they can be fixed
- Gray-hat hacker: A hacker of questionable ethics
- Script kiddie: A person with little technical knowledge who follows the instructions of others to hack networks

Notice that there are ranges of ethics embraced by varying types of hackers. Not all hackers are considered unethical. Some, such as white-hat hackers, consider themselves to have altruistic motivation—even though they do break the letter of the law. Microsoft has, in the past, extended a hand to the hacking community, hoping to get white-hat hackers on its side. Microsoft sponsors an annual conference named BlueHat Security Briefings (the Microsoft corporate color is blue). Microsoft is hoping that meeting with altruistic hackers can help to make Windows and other Microsoft products more bulletproof.

Many hackers belong to groups and assist each other with new methods for hacking systems, often using Web sites, wikis, and online forums to communicate. *The Hacker Quarterly* (*www.2600.com*) is a favored hacker publication (online and in print) that also sponsors monthly meetings in hundreds of cities around the world on the first Friday of every month (*www.2600.com/meetings*). The Black Hat Briefings is the biggest annual information security conference for hackers and computer security professionals (Figure 11.13).

FIGURE 11.13 • Black Hat Briefings

The Black Hat Briefings is the largest annual conference for hackers and computer security professionals.

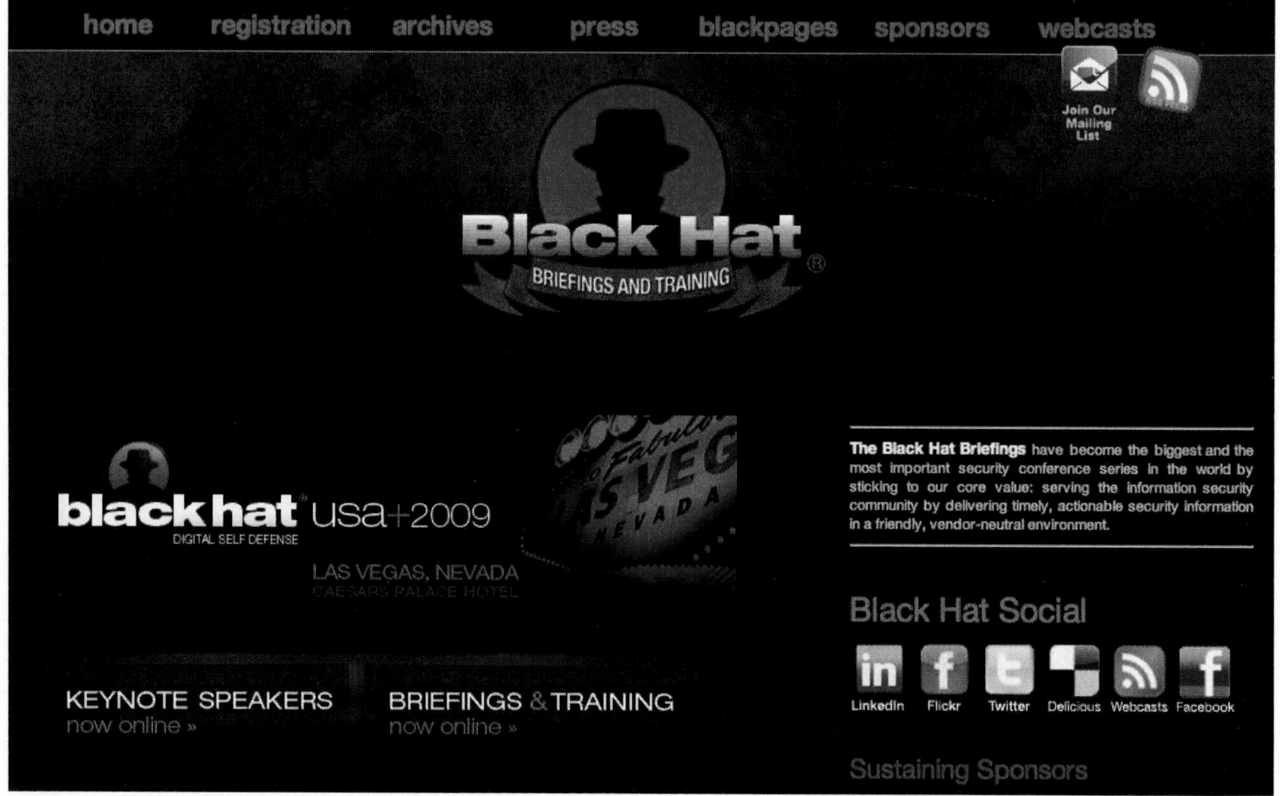

Law enforcement agencies invest significant amounts of money in tracking criminal hackers and keeping tabs on the hacker population. An important area of law enforcement is computer forensics, also referred to as *digital forensics*. **Computer forensics** is the process of examining computing equipment to determine if it has been used for illegal, unauthorized, or unusual activities. This area of research has become formalized and well respected. Many educational institutions offer degrees or certification in computer forensics.

MACHINE-LEVEL SECURITY

At the beginning of this chapter, you learned that information security is implemented in layers: the machine layer, the network layer, and the Internet layer. This section examines security from the perspective of the individual machine and discusses security precautions for personal computers that may or may not be connected to a network or the Internet. By learning how to protect standalone PCs, you also learn about the first line of defense for the networks to which those PCs may be connected.

FIGURE 11.14 • Authentication

User authentication can be based on something you know, something you carry with you, or some unique personal physical trait.

Access to today's PCs is typically guarded with a username and password. In security terms, this is called *authentication*, a method by which to confirm the identity of a user (see Figure 11.14). There are three common forms of authentication:

- Something you know: A password or personal identification number (PIN), for example
- Something you have: ID cards, smartcards, badges, keys, and other items designed to be used to authorize access to secure areas and systems
- Something about you: Unique physical characteristics such as fingerprints, voice quality, retinal patterns, and facial features that can be examined and used for authentication

This discussion of PC security begins with methods of authentication, then presents ways to protect the data on your PC, followed by some tips for keeping your PC running smoothly and safely.

Passwords

A **username** identifies a user to the computer system. Varying levels of computer access and environmental preferences are associated with a username. For example, the username adkins may be associated with a system administrator who is granted access to the entire system and uses a *Star Wars* wallpaper, while user johnson has access to only his own files and six programs, and uses a plain blue wallpaper. Different operating systems provide differing levels of access and customization features.

While usernames can act as a form of authentication, they are not very secure. Most systems do not allow access without a valid username, but at the same time, a valid username is typically easy to guess. For example, usernames are often all or part of an e-mail address. For this reason, computers require passwords to be provided with usernames.

A **password** is a combination of characters known only to the user that is used for authentication. Passwords can be an effective form of authentication if they are difficult to guess, kept confidential, and

FIGURE 11.15 • Passwords, weakest to strongest

Strong passwords use words that are unrelated to your interests and include uppercase and lowercase letters, numbers, and symbols.

weakest
john
kelley
JohnnieD
yankees#1
HeresJohnnie
NYcoolboy
Hypertree
nyKOOLB@Y (ideal)
Hyper#tree9 (ideal)
re@Lpharm# (ideal)
92Tpo5#cCw
strongest

changed regularly. However, passwords are considered the weakest form of authentication because they can be used by others to access systems without your knowledge. For this reason it is important to create passwords that are strong—that is, difficult to guess.

The strongest passwords are a minimum of eight characters in length and do not include any known words or names, especially ones that are related to you or your interests. Strong passwords include uppercase and lowercase letters, numbers, and symbols. For example, sk3&KxD$ would be difficult for anyone to guess. Unfortunately, it is also very difficult for the user to remember. The most effective passwords are ones that are difficult for others to guess but easy for you to remember. For this reason, some people combine words they can remember with numbers and symbols, such as bluedoor*45. Another trick is to fabricate words from symbols, numbers, and characters, such as L@@K4me or 2gud2btru. This gives the appearance of randomness while providing personal meaning so you can remember them. Figure 11.15 illustrates passwords created by John Driesdale from New York, across a spectrum from weak to strong. Notice that the most effective passwords are those that include multiple words not closely associated with John or his interests; are a mix of letters, numbers, and symbols; and are relatively easy to remember.

It is not uncommon to have to remember several passwords for several different systems: a password for your home PC, a password for your school account, another for your e-mail, and several others for Web sites. How can you possibly remember that many complex passwords? The easiest solution, and the most dangerous, is to use the same password for all accounts. This is dangerous because if a hacker discovers your password on one account, all your accounts are vulnerable. A scary statistic from a study performed by security firm Sophos showed that 40 percent of Internet users use one common password for all their online accounts.[28] Such was the case with the previously mentioned Twitter attack. Posing as a Twitter executive, the hacker successfully answered the security questions provided by gmail, to change the executive's gmail password. Using this password, the hacker was able to access sensitive corporate documents stored in Twitter's Google Apps Web site.

One smart password strategy is to use different passwords for different resources depending on the level of security required. For example, 80 percent of the passwords you maintain may be for unimportant low-security resources such as online news and information sources. There's no reason why you shouldn't use one common, easy-to-remember password for all of these services. As you move up to resources that include personal accountability, financial access, and access to private information, passwords should become increasingly strong and unique. Table 11.5 illustrates this point.

TABLE 11.5 • Passwords

The strength and uniqueness of passwords should be based on the level of importance of the resource being accessed.

Security level	Examples	Password use
High: Resources that include access to finances and private information	• Home PC • School account • E-mail • Bank account • Financial services such as PayPal • E-commerce Web sites that store credit card information for express checkout	Use a unique and strong password for each resource.
Medium: Resources that do not contain private or financial data but impact your reputation or require personal accountability	• Online blogs, chat, and discussion • Online support Web sites • Online auctions like eBay	Choose password strength based on level of accountability; do not use any passwords that are used for high-security resources.
Low: Resources that do not contain private or financial data and do not impact your reputation in any way	• Free online news sources such as *The New York Times* • Other free information and services provided on the Web	Use one common, easy-to-remember password for all; make sure the password is different from any password used for medium- and high-security resources.

Besides choosing passwords wisely and making sure that passwords are unique for important resources, users should also change passwords regularly—typically once or twice a year. It is possible that a hacker could be accessing your account without your knowledge. By changing your password, you can re-secure your account.

This discussion about passwords illustrates an important point that will be confirmed throughout this chapter: total information security is inconvenient and difficult. Security and convenience are often diametrically opposed. To achieve total information security, users must be convinced of its importance, and at the same time, security must be made as convenient as possible.

In the case of passwords, there are some very useful tools to help make password management more convenient. Programs such as Password Agent from Moon Software (*www.moonsoftware.com*) act as a secure database for storing passwords. Using Password Agent, you need only remember one password, the one that opens the Password Agent software. Once in the software, you can store and retrieve passwords used for all your accounts. This software stores your passwords in an encrypted database, making them impossible for others to read unless they have the one password that accesses the software and database file. Storing passwords in a regular unencrypted file is a big security risk.

Software from Billeo (*www.billeo.com*) also uses encryption to secure password information. Billeo's Password Manager Plus also fills in usernames, passwords, and other data automatically in Web forms. Billeo suggests storing the software on a USB drive so that you can take your usernames and passwords with you everywhere you go. Because the software is password protected, you needn't worry about losing your USB drive and having your database of passwords stolen. Similar products have been designed for use on handheld computers and smart phones.

There are many other password-management software applications available. Operating systems and Web browsers can also be used to securely store and automatically fill in passwords. Caution should be used, however, to make sure that no one else accesses PCs running this software, and that full reliance is not placed on such systems. If your system fails, you should maintain access to your passwords.

ID Devices and Biometrics

A number of devices are used in corporations and organizations to identify users and provide access to restricted areas and computer systems. These technologies make use of the "something you have" form of authentication. Sometimes they are combined with a password to increase the security level. The most popular of these devices are ID cards and tokens that sometimes take the form of a key-chain fob. ID cards may contain forms of identification in a magnetic strip or in a microchip, as is found in a smart card. Tokens contain microchips that hold ID information. Cards with magnetic strips are swiped in card readers, and smart cards may be swiped or simply waved in front of a card reader. ID tokens can also be used with proximity readers or read by silicon key readers, as is shown in Figure 11.16.

FIGURE 11.16 • Security ID

This security ID token contains a microchip that holds authentication data and is read by pressing the tip of the token into the recessed area of the reader.

Although ID cards and tokens are primarily used in businesses today, they are making their way into the home as well. The U.S. federal government is requiring banks to beef up security for Internet customers, and bank Web sites are implementing two-factor authentication to access account services. Some banks have their customers use the traditional username and password, and some form of hardware token that provides a continuously changing numeric access code. Other banks are placing an electronic token on the customer's PC. The PC provides a numeric code that must be entered along with the username and password; this system prohibits access from any PC other than the registered PC. Banks may also turn to biometrics or smart cards to positively identify Internet customers.

Biometrics is the science and technology of authentication by scanning and measuring a person's unique physical features such as fingerprints, retinal patterns, and facial characteristics. Fingerprints have been used in areas of security and law enforcement for decades. The digitization of biometric traits and the computer's ability to quickly scan and interpret the data have led to rapid growth in the biometrics field.

Law enforcement agencies and airport security agents are using facial pattern recognition in efforts to catch criminals and terrorists. *Facial pattern recognition* uses a mathematical technique to measure the distances between 128 points on the face (see Figure 11.17). Taking a weighted sum of these measurements, software can quickly scan a database of known faces and come up with a match if one exists. Cameras posted at airport security gates and on city streets can continuously scan for faces of known criminals. Oki Electric Corporation (*www.oki.com*) is marketing face recognition software for camera phones. Once installed, the phone is trained to recognize your face (using the phone's camera), and from that point on will operate only for you—or perhaps your identical twin. Another form of biometrics is the retinal scan. *Retinal scanning* analyzes the pattern of blood vessels at the back of the eye.

FIGURE 11.17 • Facial recognition

By taking measurements of facial features and matching them to the measurements of known faces, biometric software can help identify people.

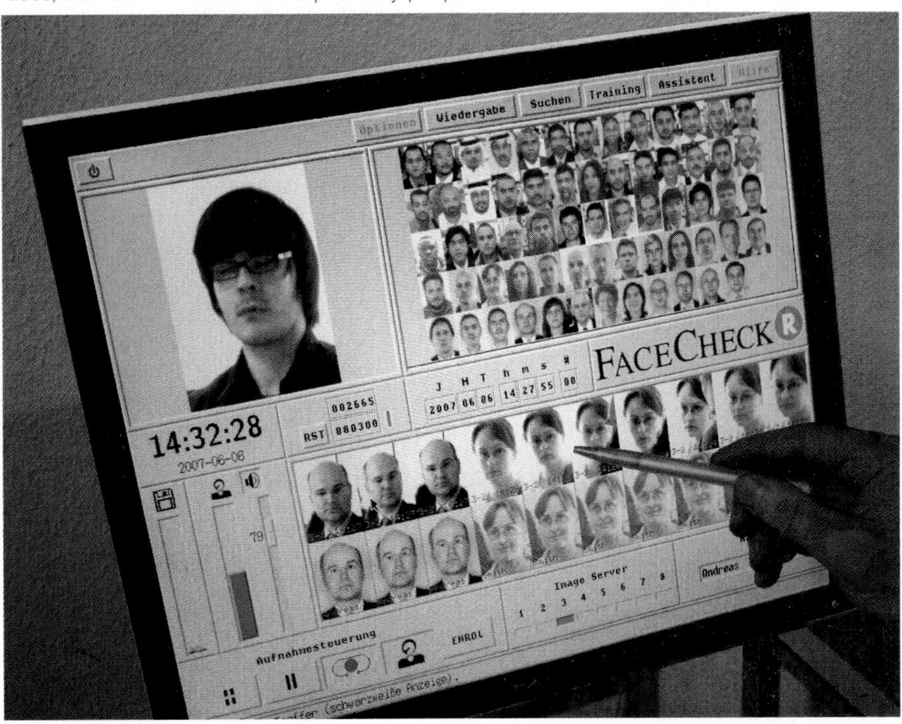

FIGURE 11.18 • Fingerprint ID

Using a USB fingerprint identity device, you simply press your finger to the device every time you are asked for a password.

Perhaps the easiest form of biometrics is the *fingerprint scan.* Fingerprint scans are an increasingly common method of authentication for access to secure areas, for validating credit card purchases, and for logging on to computers. Using a USB device (see Figure 11.18) or a built-in fingerprint scanner, a computer user can log in without having to enter a username and password. These devices can also be used to enter your usernames and passwords on Web and other login screens by simply pressing your index finger on the device.

User authentication can also be based on a person's voice. Voice recognition, also called speaker authentication, identifies a user by the sound of his or her voice. Unlike speech recognition, voice recognition is not concerned with determining what words are being spoken, but with who is speaking them. For example, a cell phone may incorporate a system that requires the owner to speak a word or phrase into the handset to activate the phone. Others speaking the word or phrase would not be provided access, since the system analyzes the sound wave to confirm it belongs to the owner. Voice recognition is sometimes classified as behaviormetrics rather than biometrics, since the analysis is based on the study of the manner in which a person speaks, which is a behavior rather than a physical trait.

Encrypting Stored Data

With the increase in use of mobile computers such as notebooks, tablets, and handhelds, the possibility of losing a computer or having it stolen is very real. In fact, Los Angeles International Airport reported that on average, 1,200 laptops per week are lost on its premises.[29] Sometimes the data stored on a portable PC is more valuable than the computer itself. For this reason, many businesses have employees store data files on the corporate network servers rather than on their notebook computers. Once in a thief's possession, the hard drive can be removed from a notebook and the files accessed without the need for a username or password. For this reason and others, it is a good idea to encrypt any confidential files stored on a computer.

Encryption has been defined as a security technique that uses high-level mathematical functions and computer algorithms to encode data so that it is unintelligible to all but the intended recipient. Today's Apple and Windows PCs include security tools that can encrypt files stored on disks and flash drives. This is useful in situations where the information you are storing is confidential or valuable, and there is a possibility that your computer can be accessed by others, lost, or stolen.

Files can be encrypted "on the fly" as they are being saved, and decrypted as they are opened. To open encrypted files, you must enter a password. Encryption and decryption does tend to slow a computer down slightly when opening and saving files, so encryption is not typically turned on by default. Instead, the user manually selects the files or folders that contain confidential information and marks them for encryption.

Mac OS X uses a system it calls FileVault for file encryption. FileVault uses the latest U.S. government security standard, AES-128 encryption, to safeguard confidential documents. Microsoft Windows Vista and Windows 7 provide BitLocker Drive Encryption, which is machine-level data encryption that can secure the entire hard drive, protecting the data even if the PC is stolen (see Figure 11.19).

FIGURE 11.19 • Windows security—BitLocker

Windows Vista and Windows 7 include many security features including BitLocker to encrypt the hard drive.

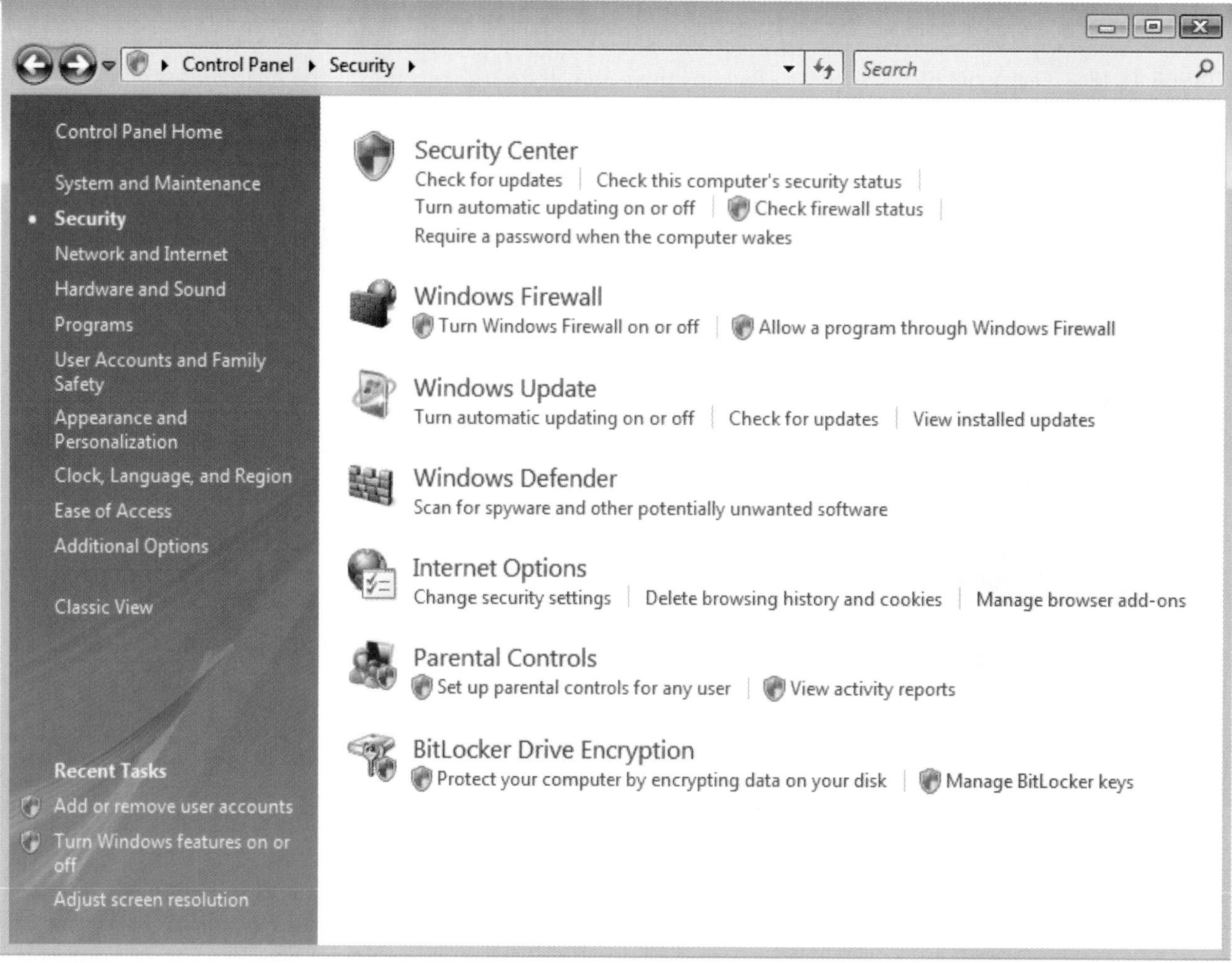

Some Windows PCs include an embedded security subsystem that stores passwords and encryption keys on a dedicated security chip on the motherboard. Storing security information in a dedicated chip rather than in a file on the hard drive offers perhaps the strongest method of personal computer security.

Backing Up Data and Systems

The most common cause of data loss, according to engineers at data recovery vendor Ontrack (*www.ontrack.com*), is hardware failure (56 percent), followed by human error (26 percent), software corruption (9 percent), viruses (4 percent), and natural disasters (2 percent). The only method that provides 100 percent protection for data against all of these disasters is to back it up! Still it is amazing that less than half of computer users have a regular backup procedure in place. Today's backup technologies make backing up important data and system files an effortless task.

System Backup and Restore. When the files that make up an operating system become corrupted, either due to mechanical failure of the hard drive or a virus, your computer may simply not start. To safeguard against operating system failure, operating systems and security software provide a means to create a rescue disk. A *rescue disk* is created while a system is operational and backs up important operating systems files. For example, if the hard drive fails, essential operating system files can be loaded from the rescue disk, which allows you or a computer technician to repair the damage done to the system.

Windows PC users who find their system damaged but are still able to start the computer can benefit from the System Restore utility. Periodically, Windows creates backups of the state of the operating system at what it calls "restore points." If the computer contracts a virus, or newly installed software causes system problems, the system can be "taken back in time" to when the computer was without problems. Data files are left intact, but software and the operating system are reconfigured to match the state they were in at the restore point. So, for example, if you recall that your computer was working just fine last week, you can select the restore point created last week to take your system back to its state at that time. Apple Mac OS X Leopard provides a similar tool called Time Machine (see Figure 11.20). Time Machine backs up not only your system files, but also your data files; if you accidentally delete a file, you can go back in time and retrieve it.

FIGURE 11.20 • Mac OS X Time Machine

The Time Machine utility in Mac OS X Leopard allows you to go back in time and retrieve files from the past that may no longer be on your Mac.

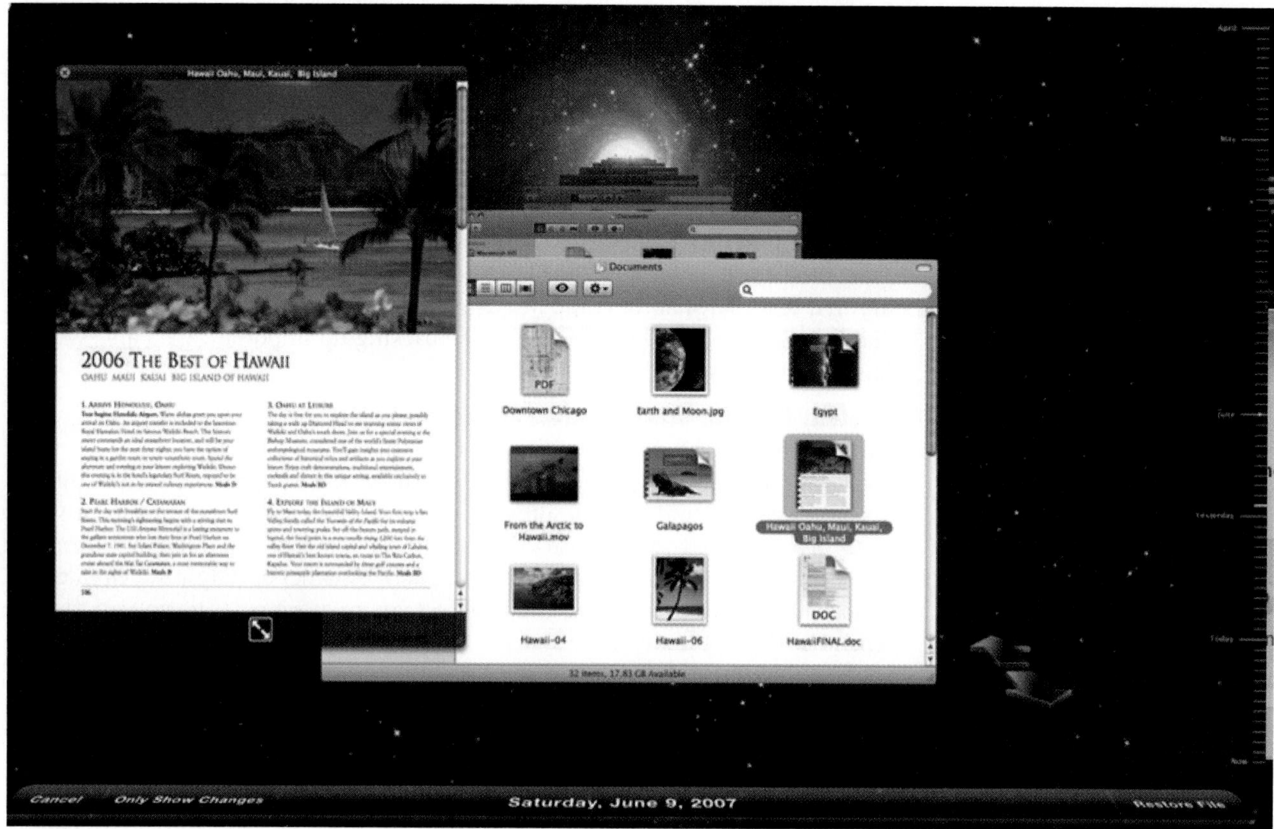

Backing up Data Files. Most businesses have regular backup procedures that back up corporate data to disk drives, tape, or online storage media. Individuals typically back up their personal data files to CD, DVD, USB drive, or a network drive located on another computer and accessed over a network (Figure 11.21). Operating systems usually provide a backup utility that can be used to back up data files; both Apple and Microsoft Windows provide utilities called Backup. Typical backup software collects the files you wish to back up into a compressed file called an archive. Some backup software provides the ability to encrypt the archive and password-protect it. Backup software typically provides the following options:

- Select the files and folders you wish to back up.
- Choose the location to store the archive file.
- Choose whether to back up all files (a *full backup*), or just those that have changed since the last backup (an *incremental backup*).

Most backup utilities also provide a scheduling option that allows you to automatically run backup routines at specified dates and times. For example, you might set a backup routine to back up only files on your system that have changed since the last backup and schedule it to run every day at 4:00 a.m.

FIGURE 11.21 • USB drive

External drives like this one from Seagate provide hundreds of gigabytes of capacity for convenient scheduled or one-click backups.

FreeAgent | Go™
The ultimate portable storage solution with the world's first hard drive docking station for easy access to all your stuff. Sleek, ultra-thin design that's as stylish as it is striking.
Perfect For
Store photos, music, and other files
Carry your data anywhere you want
Sync data between computers
Back up files using the optional dock
Color
Capacity 500 GB
Interface USB 2.0
Model ST905003FLA2E1-RK | Sky Blue | USB 2.0 | 500 GB
Clear All Selections

Some users prefer to have exact copies of their data files on a backup disk rather than building a compressed archive file. Exact copies are useful if you need to occasionally access individual files from the backup. An archive file would not allow this, making you first restore the entire archive. However, an archive file takes up much less space than storing an exact copy of a file system. Creating an exact copy of a system or portion of a system is called *mirroring*.

Remote Data Backup. Internet-based backup services are becoming increasingly popular as more users connect to the Internet through high-speed connections. For example, Mozy (*http://mozy.com*) provides automated backup of your data every night over your Internet connection for an inexpensive monthly fee (see Figure 11.22). Carbonite (*www.carbonite.com*) offers a similar service that backs up files continuously whenever the computer is connected to the Internet. An important feature of remote data backup is that it allows you to back up your data off-site in a location away from your computer. It is smart to keep backups off-site, as keeping them on-site may expose them to the same destructive forces that wipe out the original data: fire, flood, power surge, and so on. With remote data backups, changes to your hard drive are collected, compressed, encrypted, and transmitted via your Internet connection to remote data centers.

FIGURE 11.22 • Remote backup

Backing up files to a remote server over the Internet can be a cost-effective option.

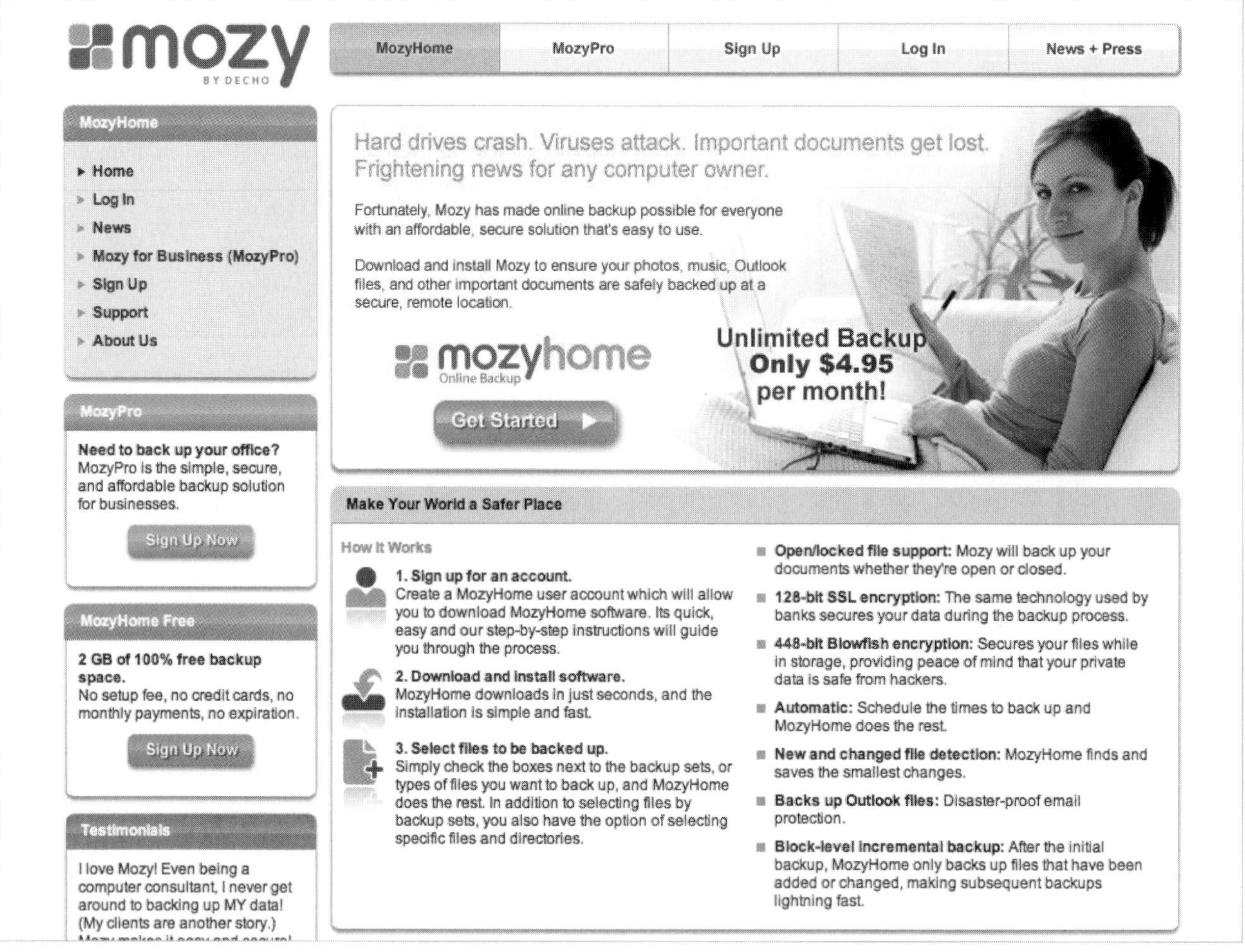

System Maintenance

In addition to the smart use and management of passwords, encrypting confidential files, and backing up data and systems, there are other steps that can be taken to secure a PC and the data it stores.

System and Software Updates. Most software has an update feature that applies patches to bugs discovered in the software after release. Some updates, such as Windows Update (discussed earlier), can be set to download and install automatically when they are available. Other updates require the user to check periodically at the vendor's Web site or click a Check for Updates option in the software's Help menu. Recall that about 9 percent of data loss is attributed to software corruption. Keeping your operating system and software up to date is the best way to avoid problems caused by faulty software. Users also benefit from additional features that are sometimes provided free of charge in software updates.

Computer Housecleaning. *Computer housecleaning* involves organizing the data files and software on your computer. Housecleaning can include these activities:

- Deleting unneeded data files
- Organizing the remaining data files logically into folders and subfolders
- Emptying the Recycle Bin (Windows) or trash can (Mac)
- Deleting unneeded saved e-mail messages
- Cleaning out Web cookie files, and other temporary Internet files
- Uninstalling software that is no longer needed
- Cleaning and reorganizing the computer desktop for quick access to items you use most often
- Organizing Web browser favorites

Your operating system may include a utility that hunts down unnecessary files on your system and allows you to mark them for deletion. After completing your housekeeping, don't be surprised to find several gigabytes of additional space on your hard drive.

While deleting software and files from your system, the remaining files on your hard drive will become fragmented; that is, they will be scattered about the disk in nonadjacent clusters, creating slower access times. A *defragmentation utility* provided with your operating system or purchased separately can be used to defragment your hard drive, aligning your files in adjacent clusters and improving your computer's performance. Mac PCs include a disk utility that provides a "Verify Disk" command to repair any hard drive issues.

Windows Cleaners. After a while, Microsoft Windows users may notice problems with system performance: the system may drag, or perhaps error messages will pop up during system startup. Although this may indicate the presence of a computer virus or spyware, it may also be that the Windows Registry has become cluttered with data left by low-quality software that has been installed and perhaps uninstalled. Recall that the Windows Registry is a system database file that stores data about the system configuration and the configuration of software running on the system. Utility software referred to as *Windows cleaners*, or *Windows Registry cleaners*, such as CleanMyPC and Registry Mechanic (see Figure 11.23), scan the Windows Registry, correcting incorrect or obsolete information. Some Windows cleaners are available free on the Web, for example, at *www.pcpitstop.com*. As the Registry is very important to the proper functioning of Windows, the utmost care must be taken when working with it. Windows cleaners should include a backup/restore function that lets you back up the Registry prior to cleaning so you can restore the Registry to its previous state should you encounter problems.

FIGURE 11.23 • Windows cleaner

Windows cleaners maintain the Windows Registry and other system files to boost the performance of a Windows PC.

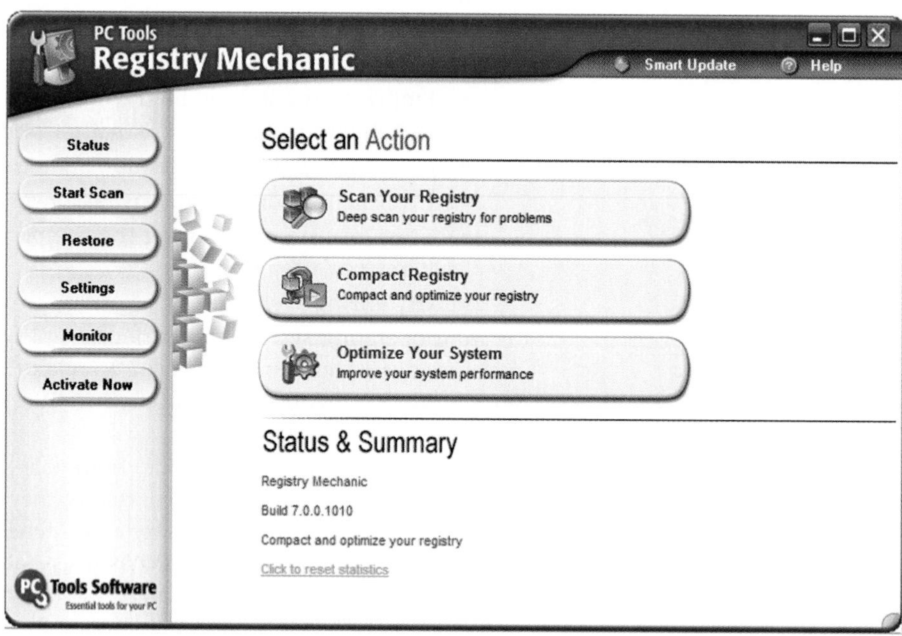

NETWORK SECURITY

When a computer is connected to a network, security risks increase a hundredfold. Connecting to the Internet increases risks a million times that of a stand-alone computer. In fact, for information of highest security, government agencies use computers that are not connected to agency networks or the Internet. So long as there is a network connection, there is danger of unauthorized access from a remote connection.

This section discusses threats, considerations, and security for networked computers in general. A later section deals specifically with security measures for computers connected to the Internet. Networked computers may be in a government agency; a large, medium-sized, or small business; a college campus or campus housing; an apartment building; or a home. The considerations are the same in any of these environments, although the value of the information may vary.

Multiuser System Considerations

A *multiuser system* is a computer system, such as a computer network, where multiple users share access to resources such as file systems (see Figure 11.24). When sharing resources, users are naturally concerned about the privacy and protection of their data files. System administrators are concerned with protecting the system from intentional or unintentional damage. If a corporation owns the network, corporate management is concerned about the security and privacy of corporate information. This section deals with the issue of restricting the access of network users.

FIGURE 11.24 • Multiuser systems

Multiuser systems require special software mechanisms that control user access to shared resources.

User Permissions. *User permissions* refer to the access privileges afforded to each network user. Network operating systems such as Windows Vista, Apple OS X, Linux, NetWare, and UNIX provide methods for associating user permissions with each user account. As each user logs on to a workstation connected to the network, the permission policies are applied, and the user can access only the resources defined by those policies.

To control user access to system resources such as files, folders, and disk drives, access policies must be defined for both the resources and the users. For example, a user may be restricted to have access only to files that he or she created. Files and folders on the system must carry information that identifies their creator. This is referred to as *file ownership*. Users are the owners of the files they create.

To facilitate sharing files between users on the network, user groups can be established by the system administrator. For example, you and some of your classmates might be working on a project utilizing the campus network. You might be able to ask the system administrator to create a network group named comp1 that you can use for sharing files with your group. Each user would then be identified as a comp1 member by the system and would be able to access files and folders marked as being accessible to the group. This is referred to as *group ownership*. System resources can also be set so that they are available to everyone on the network. This is sometimes referred to as *world ownership*.

The system administrator is responsible for setting the access rights of users and for setting the permissions on system resources. Users have the power to set permission settings of the files they own. The system administrator is typically the only user who has full access to the system. Figure 11.25 illustrates the effect of user permissions on file access.

FIGURE 11.25 • User permissions control access to system resources

User A can access the files he owns, 1 and 2, and the files shared by his group, files 3 and 4. User B can access her own files, 5, 6, and 7, and the group's files 3 and 4. The system administrator can access everything.

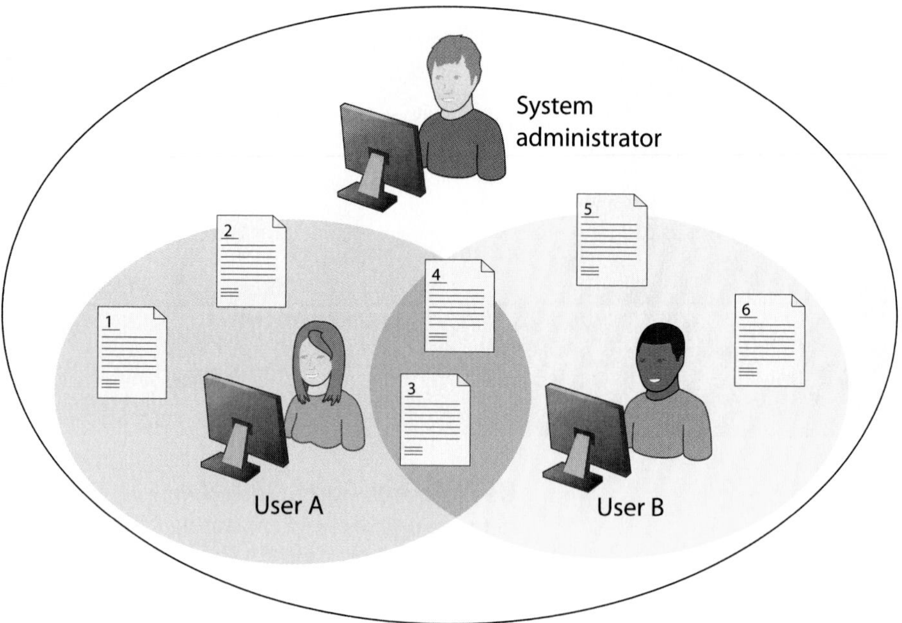

The system administrator can also define the type of access allowed. Access to files and folders can be classified as read or write. For example, in Figure 11.25, User A may have read and write permissions for file 3, so he can view and edit the file, but User B may have only read permission so that she can view but not edit the file.

The ability to carry out various system commands can also be restricted through user permissions. For example, Microsoft Windows Vista uses three classifications for user accounts: Administrator, Standard, and Guest. Those with Standard access can change only their own account password and associated icon. They cannot access system settings in the Control Panel or install or uninstall hardware and software. A Guest account is for someone who does not have a permanent account and needs to temporarily access computer or network resources. Guests cannot change settings, install hardware or software, or create passwords. The Guest account is turned off by default. An Administrator has full access to system commands and resources. Users shouldn't perform day-to-day operations logged in as an administrator, since it opens up the entire system to viruses and corruption. It is best to use administrator accounts only when system settings need to be changed and use standard access for everyday use.

FIGURE 11.26 • Ownership and permissions in Mac OS X

By viewing file properties, Mac users can set files to share with others on the network.

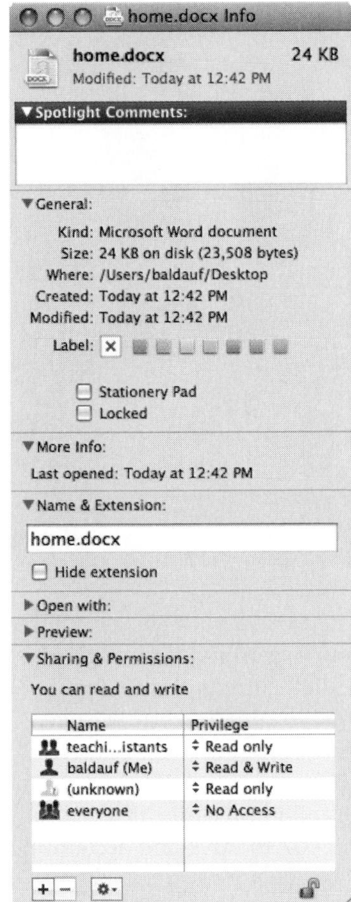

Home users can set permissions on their own files so that others on the network can access them or not (see Figure 11.26). By default, the personal files and folders on both Windows Vista and Mac OS X computers are off limits to others on a network. You can adjust file permissions for a specific file or folder by accessing the file properties (right-click and choose Properties in Windows) or info (on Macs). These tools lead you to settings for file permissions.

User permissions provide a second layer of security for computer networks. Usernames and passwords and the login process are the primary way of keeping unregistered users out of the system. User permissions provide registered users with access to the files they need, while restricting access to private resources.

Interior Threats

Threats from within a private network are often referred to as *interior threats*. Interior threats can be intentional or unintentional. Unintentional threats can occur when users make mistakes or exceed their authorization. Intentional threats come from registered users who desire to do the system harm or steal information.

Threats to System Health and Stability. Earlier in this chapter, Table 11.4 listed user mistakes that can lead to system instability and data corruption. There are two other common problems that occur on networks, both stemming from allowing network users to introduce software and data files from outside the network.

On most business networks, users are not allowed to install software without the network administrator's authorization. Although such a policy creates inconvenience for users, it is supported by a very good rationale (once again, security at the cost of convenience). There are thousands of software applications available, and many are unstable and dangerous. Although you may be willing to risk the stability of your own PC for the sake of free software, system administrators would be remiss in their duties if they allowed you to jeopardize the entire network. Also, system administrators are responsible for ensuring that all software installed on the network is properly licensed.

In addition, software and data files brought in from outside could contain viruses or spyware. Many viruses are designed to take advantage of network connections and spread to all connected computers. This is the reason that so many college campus computer labs and dorms act as breeding grounds for computer viruses (Figure 11.27), and why you should heed the advice provided in this chapter.

FIGURE 11.27 • Computer labs are fertile ground for viruses

College and student housing computer labs act as breeding grounds for computer viruses as they spread from one computer to the next over the network.

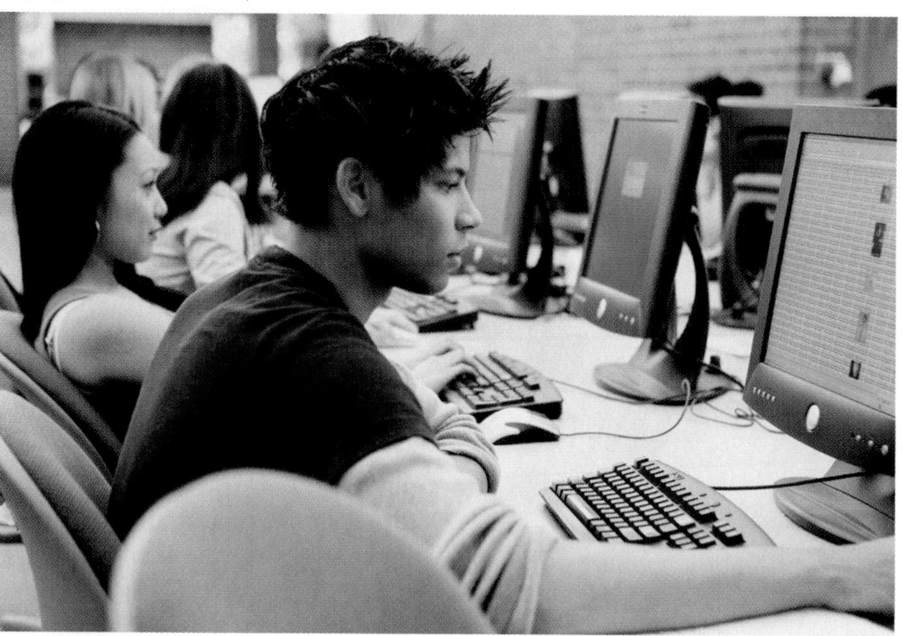

Information Theft. Many instances of identity theft occur with the assistance of insiders with corporate network access. For example, personal information, Social Security numbers, and e-mail addresses of 65,000 current and former Aetna employees were most likely stolen by someone logging in as a registered user.[30] In a number of instances, data has mysteriously gone missing. LexisNexis experienced a similar incident affecting 32,000 of its customers.[31] The Identity Theft Resource Center (ITRC) reported a total of 36 million records breached in 2008 with incidents of insider theft doubling from 2007 to 2008 and accounting for more than 15 percent of breaches.[32]

Businesses are well aware of the rising rate of information theft and many are taking action against it. Companies are further restricting access to physical locations, systems, and databases. Many companies supply their employees with PCs that do not have any external drives or USB ports so that employees are unable to copy data to portable storage media and devices. Even iPods are being scrutinized. A report from the Gartner analyst group suggests that companies should consider banning iPods and other portable devices that can be attached to computer systems, in order to protect the corporate network from malicious software.

Security and Usage Policies

To safeguard against threats to a network's health and stability and to prevent information theft, businesses and organizations often implement security and network usage policies. A security and network usage policy is a document, agreement, or contract that defines acceptable and unacceptable uses of computer and network resources. New users are often asked to agree to the conditions of the policy prior to receiving a network account. Users are held liable for upholding the policies and can lose their network account or job if they violate the rules.

Employers are not legally responsible for notifying employees of network usage policies. If policies are not provided at the time of receiving network privileges, it is wise for the new user to ask what is and isn't allowed on the network. Private network administrators have the right to listen in on network communications, read employee e-mail, and electronically monitor employees' Web activities without giving notice to the employee. Employees enjoy very little legal protection in regard to privacy when using employer-owned networks. People have lost their jobs over activities that they thought were okay, but their employer thought were wrong.

Network usage policies typically warn against using the network for illegal activities. They also cover issues that may not be as obvious. For example, some college networks do not allow students to use their network account to run a business. Some businesses do not allow employees to use their business e-mail account for personal correspondence. Table 11.6 lists some corporate security and usage policies and examples.

TABLE 11.6 • Examples of corporate network policies

Corporate policies often address issues regarding the network, e-mail, and Web use.

Policy type	Examples taken from actual company policies
Network and computer use	• Users are responsible for maintaining the security of their passwords. • Users are responsible for using the network facilities in a manner that is ethical, legal, and not to the detriment of others. • It is against federal law and corporate policy to violate the copyrights or patents on computer software. • Users must request permission of system administration for the installation of software and provide proof of the ownership of the software license.
E-mail use	• Employees shall use corporate e-mail systems only for corporate business purposes. • E-mail systems shall not be used for transmission or storage of information that promotes discrimination. • Employees must use judgment on the type of information sent through e-mail. • The use of network systems to send and forward chain letters and other inappropriate messages is prohibited. • The office may access an employee's e-mail media.
Internet use	• The use of Internet access and the Web should be restricted to corporate business purposes. • Users shall request the permission of system administration prior to the installation of Web plug-in applications. • The use of peer-to-peer networks and file-sharing software is strictly forbidden.

WIRELESS NETWORK SECURITY

Wireless networks provide wonderful convenience, but as is usually the case, with convenience come security risks. With wireless technologies, an attacker no longer has to establish a wired connection to a network. Attackers located within the range of the wireless signal, perhaps on the floor above, or in a car parked outside, can attack a wireless network to gain access.

Today the most popular wireless protocol is Wi-Fi. Wi-Fi networks have popped up in offices and homes, on city streets, in airports, coffee shops, and even McDonald's (see Figure 11.28). To make Wi-Fi easy to set up, manufacturers sometimes disable all forms of security in new Wi-Fi access points. Several steps are required to secure a Wi-Fi network. Researchers estimate that only 20 percent of Wi-Fi users and network administrators take those steps. For this reason, such networks have become a playground for hackers.

FIGURE 11.28 • Wi-Fi network

Wi-Fi networks at McDonald's and other public places provide additional opportunities for hackers.

Wi-Fi doesn't necessarily have to mean "come and get it" for hackers. Strong security tools are available. This section will examine the threats to Wi-Fi networks and the means with which to thwart them.

Threats to Wireless Networks

Recall that most Wi-Fi networks are centered around a device called an *access point*. The access point sends and receives signals to and from computers on the wireless local area network or *WLAN* (pronounced *W-lan*). By default, access points are set to broadcast their presence. So, for instance, if you open up your notebook computer in a coffee shop, a message may pop up on your display letting you know that the Starnet wireless network is within range and asking you if you would like to connect. Starnet is the SSID (service set identifier) of the wireless network. Clicking the Connect icon establishes your wireless connection with the access point. In the case of commercial providers, you may then be asked for a credit card number to pay for the service.

If an access point has no security enabled, clicking the Connect icon puts you on the network, no questions asked. Consider the user in a small apartment who decides to set up a Wi-Fi network. Once the access point is set up, a dialog box appears on the owner's computer with the message "Network available, would you like to connect?" Easy, right? At the same time, the wireless-enabled computers of neighbors on either side and upstairs and downstairs get a similar message. Now there are five users connected to the "private" home Wi-Fi network without the owner's knowledge. This is the fundamental problem of Wi-Fi networks.

Neighbors may find it hard to resist free wireless network access when a pop-up message offers it. But there are other intruders who go out looking for open wireless networks. *War driving* is the act of driving through neighborhoods with a wireless notebook or handheld computer and looking for unsecured Wi-Fi networks (see Figure 11.29). Homemade war-driving kits include high-powered antennae attached to the vehicle roof, a long-lasting power supply for the computer, software such as NetStumbler that probes and scans for networks, and sometimes a GPS receiver to mark coordinates that can be shared with others over services on the Web. The legality of war driving is questionable. Some feel that if wireless networks are left open, the owner either wishes for others to share the network or takes responsibility for any problems that ensue.

FIGURE 11.29 • War driving

Armed with a notebook, a Wi-Fi antenna, and a power supply, war drivers cruise neighborhoods looking for accessible Wi-Fi networks.

As wireless networking becomes more established and new wireless technologies emerge, hackers adapt. For example, war nibbling is the activity of hacking into Bluetooth networks. Recall that Bluetooth is the technology behind personal area networks that allows personal digital devices, like cell phones and headsets, to communicate wirelessly at short distances. It is almost guaranteed that whatever the new technology, somewhere there is a hacker working out plans to alter or attack it.

Securing a Wireless Network

So, how can Wi-Fi network owners keep neighbors and war drivers off their private networks? Access points provide several settings that can all but bulletproof a wireless network. The access point configuration settings are accessed using a Web browser on a network-connected computer (see Figure 11.30). The Web address and the password are provided in the owner's manual.

FIGURE 11.30 • Wi-Fi access point configuration settings

Wi-Fi access points are configured using a Web browser on a network-connected PC using the Web address and a password.

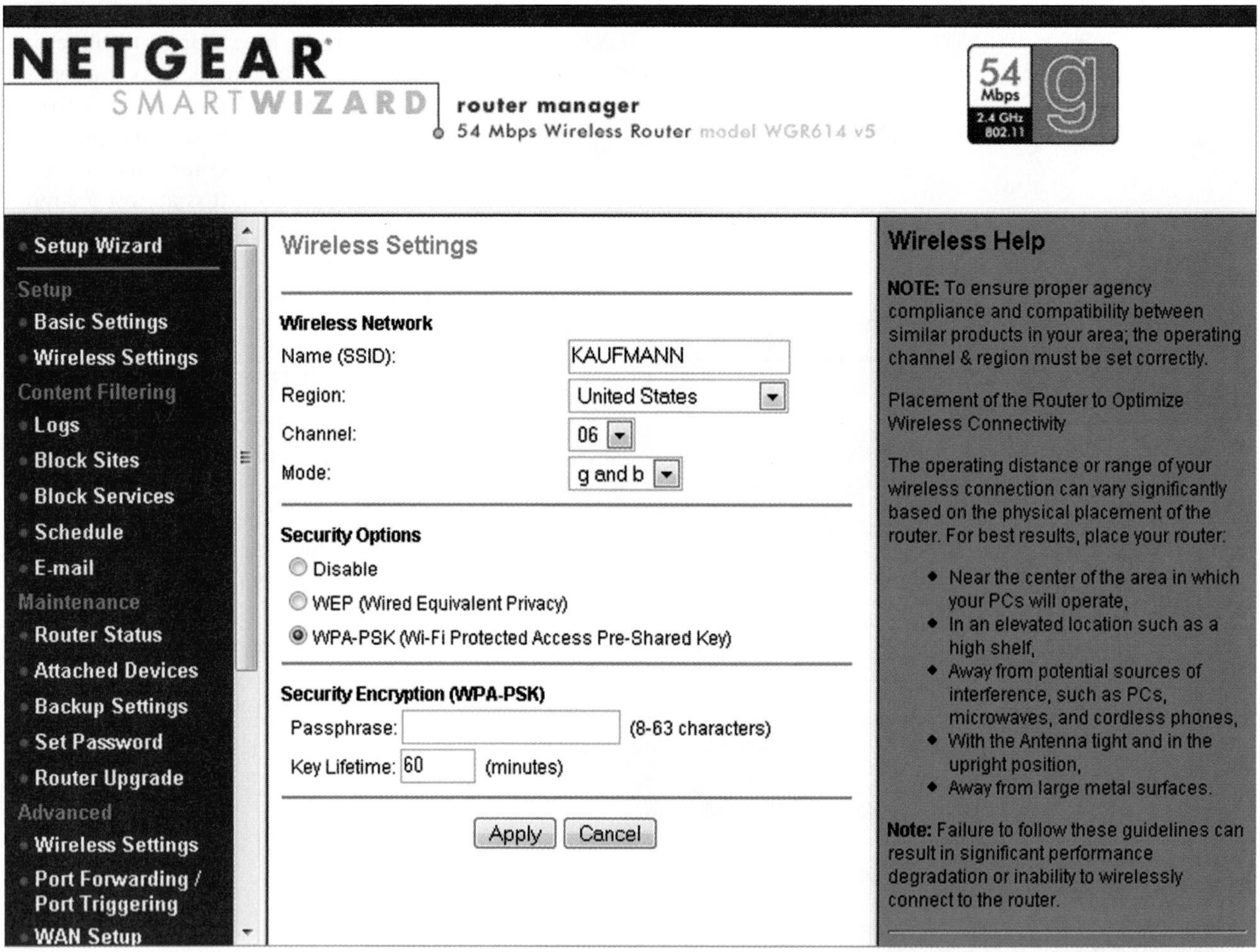

Making a Wireless Network Invisible. Options within the configuration software allow you to disable the access point's broadcasting of the network ID, the SSID. By shutting down the broadcast, neighbors and attackers no longer see a message pop up on their display asking if they want to connect.

Keeping Unwanted Computers Off a Wireless Network. Just because the SSID broadcast is disabled doesn't mean that someone who knows the SSID can't still connect. Two other steps are necessary to keep others from connecting to a wireless network.

First, it is very important that you change the password used to connect to the access point. This is easily done using the configuration settings of the access point. The default password is supplied in the owner's manual—and every war driver knows it. You don't want to give attackers the opportunity to log in to your access point and change the settings.

Second, the access point can be set to allow only certain computers to connect. Every Wi-Fi adapter, the hardware used by computers to connect to Wi-Fi networks, has a unique *MAC* (Media Access Control) *address* that is usually printed on the adapter. Notebook computers that come equipped with Wi-Fi capability have a sticker on the bottom of the notebook with the adapter's MAC address. MAC address filtering can be enabled in the access point so that it allows only specified MAC addresses to connect to the network.

Encrypting Data. The preceding steps are sufficient for keeping others off a WLAN. However, attackers may still listen in on the wireless communications. To minimize this possibility, wireless communications can be encrypted by using one of several wireless encryption protocols. *Wired Equivalent Privacy* (*WEP*) and *Wi-Fi Protected Access* (*WPA*) are the two most popular. WPA2 is the most recent version. WPA is far more difficult to crack than WEP. Encryption tends to slow down communication, and the better the encryption the slower the communication. Encryption needs to be enabled at both the access point and on all computers using the WLAN.

These steps take only a short time and very little effort, but the impact on wireless network security is the difference between zero and nearly 100 percent. Detailed instructions for securing a wireless network are typically provided by the manufacturer of the networking equipment. For example, Linksys, a popular vendor, provides a thorough explanation of locking down a wireless network at its Web site (*www.linksys.com*).

INTERNET SECURITY

Expanding from a local area network to the Internet is akin to moving from a small rural village to downtown Manhattan. While your access to information is dramatically increased, so is your exposure to risk. When a computer is connected to the Internet, it becomes visible to billions of Internet users, and a target to millions of various attacks (Figure 11.31).

Connections to the Internet are not a one-way street. Just as you can request information and services from servers, so, too, can intruders attempt to access information and services from your computer. On the Internet everyone is just a number—an Internet (IP) address. An address such as 128.186.88.100 could be a Web server, an e-mail server, or your PC. While you may be anonymous, your computer's IP address is registered and known to others.

Attacks against Internet-connected computers can come in the form of direct attacks by hackers (system penetration), or through viruses, worms, or spyware obtained though e-mail, the Web, or downloaded files. Internet users are also at risk of being manipulated through scams and hoaxes. This section addresses all of these risks and more, and offers practical advice for protecting Internet-connected computers and networks.

FIGURE 11.31 • Global exposure

When connected to the Internet, your computer becomes a target to tens of thousands of hackers around the world.

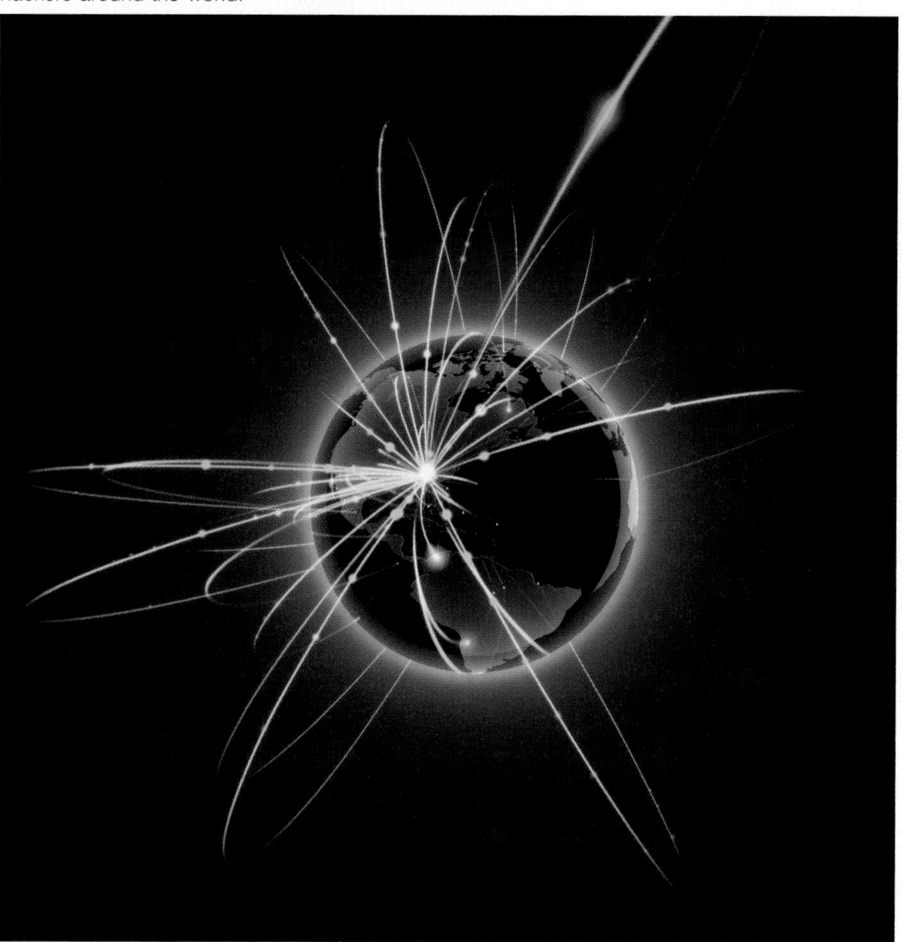

Hackers on the Internet

Earlier in this chapter, you were introduced to hackers, crackers, attackers, and intruders. This section examines the methods and motivations of these individuals as well as ways to defend against their attacks.

Methods of Attack. Different hacking tools and techniques are used to accomplish different goals. For example, a hacker can remotely install *key-logging software* on a computer to record all keystrokes and commands. The recording is later collected from a remote computer over the Internet and played back in order to spy on the user's actions and sometimes to steal usernames and passwords.

Hackers also use *packet-sniffing software* to steal private data being transported over a network. Packet-sniffing software captures and analyzes all packets flowing over a network or the Internet. It can be programmed to look for personal information such as passwords and credit card numbers.

In a targeted attack, an attacker must first find out the IP address of the target computer. Obtaining IP addresses of Web pages is a simple matter using commonly known Internet commands. Once the IP address is discovered, the attacker can attempt attacks based on known software security flaws. The attacker can also scan for open ports on the victim's computer. Recall that a *port* is a logical address used by clients and servers that is associated with a specific service. For example, port 80 sends and receives Web page requests. Ports can act as entry points for attackers. By sending messages to all the ports on a computer, a hacker can establish which ports are open and use known techniques to command the computer through messages to the open port.

For random attacks, an attacker may employ *port-scanning software* to search random IP addresses for open ports (see Figure 11.32). Port-scanning software is allowed to run for several hours, after which the attacker can collect a list of IP addresses waiting to be hacked.

FIGURE 11.32 • Port-scanning software

Port-scanning software such as Nmap from Insecure.org can be used by hackers to probe Internet computers for security holes.

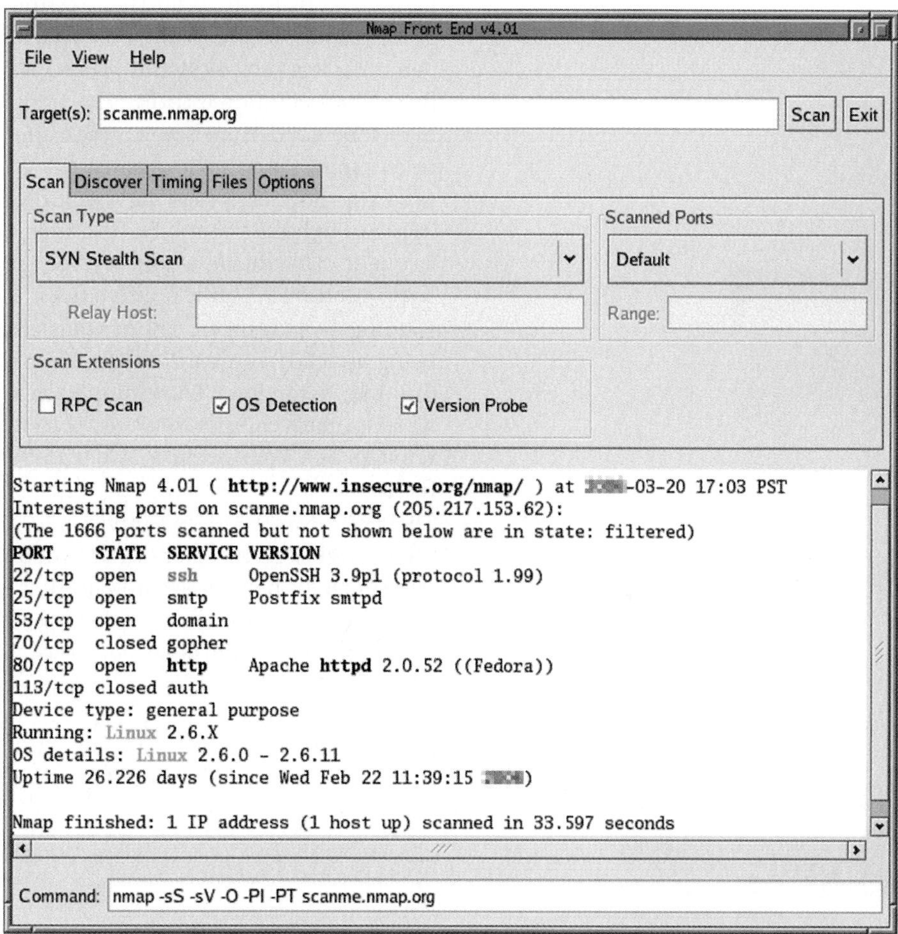

Hackers may gain access to corporate databases by taking advantage of security holes in the user interface. For example, a Web form designed to gather customer information provides a direct line from the user interface to the database. A hacker could type in database commands, typically SQL commands, rather than customer information, to take control of the database. This type of attack is referred to as *SQL injection*. If the company has taken the proper precautions, utilizing known defenses to filter out SQL commands from user input, the database can remain safe. However, hackers have been successful in using this popular exploit to steal user identities and millions of dollars.

Hackers also apply social engineering to acquire private information. *Social engineering* exploits the natural human tendency to trust others. For example, a social engineer might phone a person and pretend to be a system administrator in order to get that person to provide a password. A social engineer may even go *dumpster diving*; that is, rummaging through trash to steal credit card numbers or other personal information.

Attacks may also be automated in the form of viruses, worms, and spyware. These topics, discussed later, can achieve many of the goals of common attacks without the need for directly manipulating a system.

Motivation and Goals for Attacks. Just as there are many different types of Internet attacks, there are many different motivations. A person or organization may be targeted by an attacker or selected at random. The purpose of the attack may to vandalize, steal, or spy. Here are some common motivations:

- Hobby and challenge: Many hackers hack for the technical challenge of it. They want to show off their technical prowess by accessing data that is supposedly secure. Being able to access important secure information demonstrates their skill and power. The fact that there is legal risk may provide an additional thrill.
- Malicious vandalism: Some attacks are motivated by hate and resentment. Resentment against the establishment and those with economic or political power has been the cause of many protests and uprisings throughout history. For example, ethnic Russian hackers launched frequent cyberattacks against former Soviet republics like Georgia and Kyrgyzstan over political differences.[33]
- Gaining a platform for anonymous attacks: Increasingly, computers are being attacked and controlled to be used as a platform to launch attacks on other computers. For example, in *distributed denial-of-service (DDoS) attacks*, many computers are used to launch simultaneous repeated requests at a Web server in order to overwhelm it so that it is unable to function.[34]
- Theft of information and services: In recent years, hackers have become increasingly organized and more professional (see Figure 11.33). A higher percentage of hackers are now in it "for the money." Many hire themselves out to businesses that pay them to "take out the competition," steal confidential information, distribute spam, or spy on users. For example, Max Ray Butler, known as "Iceman," faces 40 years in prison and a $1.5 million fine for hacking into numerous financial institutions and card-processing networks and stealing the credit card data and personal information of hundreds of thousands of people.[35]

THE GREAT 7-ELEVEN HEIST

What? You don't think robbing a convenience store is a memorable historical event? Well, it just happens to be part of the largest identity theft scheme in U.S. history. Former Secret Service informant Albert Gonzalez lead a group of hackers who broke into the computer systems of 7-Eleven and three other national retailers and stole over 130 debit and credit card numbers. Although Gonzalez may face 35 years in prison, SQL injection attacks, like those Gonzalez carried out, are now the top cyberattack technique.

TJX Hacker Charged with Heartland, Hannaford Breaches
Kim Zetter
Wired
August 17, 2009
http://www.wired.com/threatlevel/2009/08/tjx-hacker-charged-with-heartland/

FIGURE 11.33 • Hacker Kevin Mitnick now and then

Kevin Mitnick hacked to steal software and expose security holes. After serving nearly five years in U.S. federal prison, Mitnick now has his own information security consulting business.

- Spying: Through key loggers, packet sniffers, and access to e-mail, Web logs, and file systems, hackers can create a detailed log of everything you do on your computer. Such logs can be very revealing about financial transactions and other private information. An intruder may spy on someone for professional or personal reasons.

Defending Against Hackers. As mentioned earlier, keeping up to date with operating system and software patches is an important step to protect against intruders. An equally important tool for blocking out hackers is a firewall. A **firewall** is network hardware or software that examines all incoming packets and filters out packets that are potentially dangerous. A firewall protects all the ports of a network or PC from intruders and guards against known methods of attack. Figure 11.34 shows details of many attacks on one PC over the course of a day. Details of the attack are provided at the bottom of the window. Chances are, if your PC is connected to the Internet, it is attacked daily.

Encrypting confidential data that is stored and transmitted over a wireless data over the Web, make sure the browser is using a secure connection, indicated by the https:// in the address bar and the closed lock icon at the bottom of the browser screen. Also make sure that any other Internet software that you use applies encryption to sensitive data. For example, traditional FTP (file transfer protocol) software does not use encryption. Newer SFTP (secure FTP) software does. Many colleges now insist that students use SFTP. E-mail servers and client software can also be set to encrypt e-mail, and to use digital certificates to prove your identity in electronic transactions.

FIGURE 11.34 • McAfee firewall

A look at McAfee firewall's event log indicates that there have been many attacks on this PC over the course of one day.

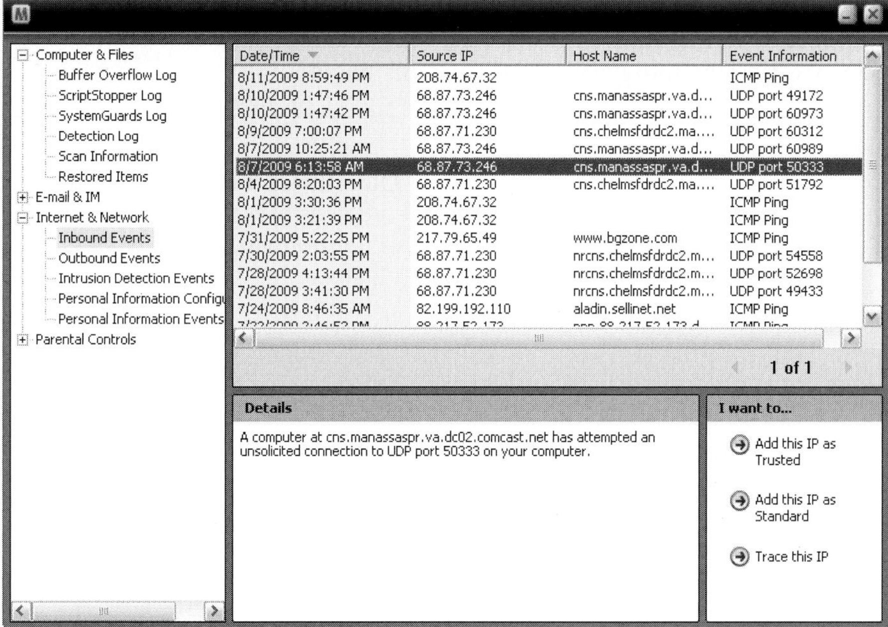

Help Wanted: Experienced Hackers

What happens to hackers when they grow up? Often they become security experts. Criminal hacking is risky work with high stakes, and is by no means encouraged. However, sometimes individuals who start out as teen hackers land great jobs and establish respectable careers as information security experts. Consider perhaps the most famous hacker, Kevin Mitnick (Figure 11.33), who made headlines in the mid-1990s for hacking into software companies and telephone companies. He spent five years in prison, and now runs a successful cybersecurity consulting service.

Admittedly, Kevin paid the price for his crimes, and suffered for his eventual reward. But some of today's young hackers are getting off scot-free and winning lucrative careers. Consider 17-year-old "Mikeyy" Mooney who engineered a computer worm that attacked Twitter, causing the company embarrassment and financial loss. Upon claiming responsibility for the attacks, Mikeyy wasn't arrested—no, he received two job offers. Another 17-year-old who was the first to hack the iPhone was offered three locked iPhones and a Nissan 350Z in exchange for the unlocked iPhone. A 15-year-old who was the subject of a *Wall Street Journal* story entitled, "How I Spent My Summer: Hacking Into iPhones with Friends," found himself inundated with job offers from around the world. Who says crime doesn't pay?

Even the U.S. federal government is getting in on the action. A recent ad posted by the Department of Homeland Security stated that it is looking for someone who can "think like the bad guy," understand hacker's tools and tactics, analyze Internet traffic, and identify vulnerabilities in federal systems. The Pentagon plans to increase the number of cyberexperts it trains each year from 80 to 250 by 2011.

Questions

1. Why do you think the demand for computer hackers in legitimate businesses is so high?
2. Why is the federal government interested in increasing its cyberprotection by 300 percent?
3. What lesson can be found here for today's youth?

Sources

1. *Heussner, Ki Mae, "Hacking Their Way to a Job," ABC News, April 17, 2009, http://abcnews.go.com.*
2. *Baldor, Lolita (AP), "Wanted: Computer hackers ...to help government," PhysOrg.com, April 19, 2009, www.physorg.com.*
3. *Kane, Yukari, "How I Spent My Summer: Hacking Into iPhones With Friends,"* The Wall Street Journal, *July 7, 2009, http://online.wsj.com.*

Figure 11.35 shows the security setup options in Microsoft Outlook 2007. Additional methods of blocking intruders and their tricks are provided in the following sections on viruses and worms, spyware, and other Internet scams, frauds, and hoaxes.

FIGURE 11.35 • Microsoft Outlook security options

E-mail clients, like Microsoft Outlook 2007, provide options for securing e-mail communications.

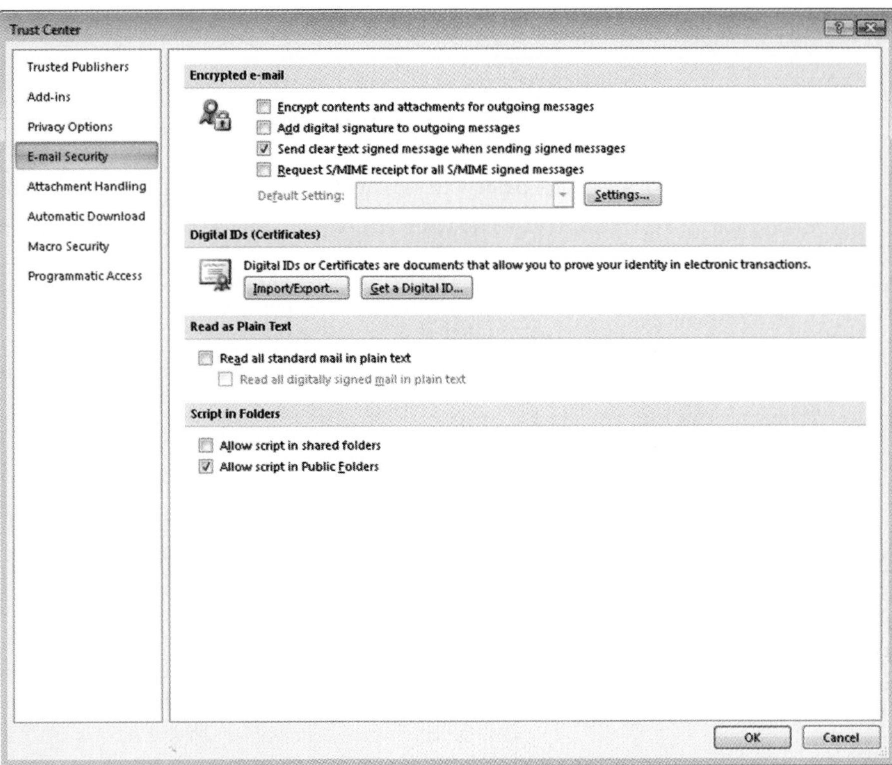

EXPAND YOUR KNOWLEDGE

To learn more about computer viruses, go to www.cengage.com/computerconcepts/np/swt4. Click the link "Expand Your Knowledge" and then complete the lab entitled "Keeping Your Computer Virus-Free."

Viruses and Worms

Cyberattacks can take the form of software that is distributed and executed on a computer without the user's knowledge for the purpose of corrupting or disrupting systems. The most common of these types of programs are viruses and worms, which due to their malicious nature are sometimes referred to as *malware*.

A **virus** is a program that attaches itself to a file, spreads to other files, and delivers a destructive action called a *payload*. The payload could be the corruption of computer data files or system files resulting in the loss of data or a malfunctioning computer. A worst-case scenario for damage would be the total loss of data and software. Recovery would involve wiping the hard drive of all files to remove all infection, reinstalling the operating system and all software, and restoring data files from backup. So far, viruses have not been known to damage hardware components of a computer system. Table 11.7 provides an overview of some common types of viruses.

Many current viruses leave no indications or symptoms of their presence so that the computer may be remotely controlled without the owner's knowledge. Viruses may allow back-door access to a hacker who can then share system resources and use the infected computer to launch attacks. Viruses are sometimes delivered through a technique called a Trojan horse, or just a Trojan. Like

TABLE 11.7 • Varieties of viruses

Numerous viruses have been designed to infect systems in different ways and avoid detection.

Virus	Description
Boot virus	Infects a computer's startup program so that the virus becomes active as soon as the computer starts up
Direct action virus	Drops payload and spreads when defined conditions are met; can usually be removed without damage to infected files using antivirus software
Directory virus	Changes the paths that indicate the location of file on the computer system
Encrypted virus	Encrypts itself so as to be hidden from scans; decrypts itself before performing its task
File virus	Attaches to other software so that the virus instructions are processed along with the software instructions
Logic bomb	Delivers its payload when certain system conditions have been met, for example, the absence of an employee's name from the corporate database
Macro virus	Infects macros embedded in data files created with other software; infects and spreads to other files viewed by that software
Multipartite virus	Creates multiple types of infections using several techniques, making the virus difficult to detect and remove
Overwrite virus	Deletes information contained in the files that it infects, rendering them partially or totally useless
Polymorphic virus	Encrypts itself in a different way every time it infects a system, making it very difficult to detect
Resident virus	Hides permanently in the system's memory, controlling and intercepting all system operations
Time bomb	Delivers its payload when the system date and clock reach a specified time and date

the Trojan horse in Greek mythology, these *Trojan horses* appear to be harmless programs, but when they run, they install other programs on the computer that can be harmful. A *backdoor Trojan* opens up ports (back doors) on the computer to allow access to intruders.

A recent trend called *ransomware* uses a Trojan to hold the user's data files captive. For example, Ransom-A was one of the first ransomware Trojans, appearing in 2006. It encrypted all of the user's data files and demanded $10.95 to be paid through Western Union. It threatened to delete a file every 30 minutes until the ransom was received. Zippo, another ransomware, demanded $300, while Archiveus demanded that the victim buy goods from an online drugstore.

A **worm** does not attach itself to other programs but rather acts as a free agent, replicating itself numerous times in an effort to overwhelm systems. For example, within 10 minutes of its introduction, the Slammer worm had attacked more than 75,000 computers. Thirty minutes later, some believe the worm had disrupted one in five data packets sent over the Internet.

How Viruses and Worms Spread. Worms may spread through Web pages, P2P networks, and e-mail, but, like viruses, can infect your PC from many sources (see Figure 11.36). Consider this abridged description of the action of the medium-risk Netsky worm from McAfee's virus database:

1. A variant of W32/Netsky@MM has been received that spreads through e-mail and P2P networks.
2. When run, the worm copies itself to the Windows directory as FVProtect.exe along with six other files.
3. The worm adds itself to the Windows Registry file.
4. The worm sends itself via e-mail—constructing messages using its own e-mail engine.
5. The worm spoofs the From field in the e-mail header and fills it with an address from the infected system.

6. The mailing component harvests addresses from the infected system.
7. The worm copies itself into the folders of file-sharing software on the infected system, adopting a name of a media file such as Harry Potter 5.mpg.exe to spread over P2P systems.

FIGURE 11.36 • Worm and virus sources

Worms and viruses can infect your PC from Web pages, P2P file-sharing networks, a local area network, e-mail, instant messages, or portable devices like a flash drive.

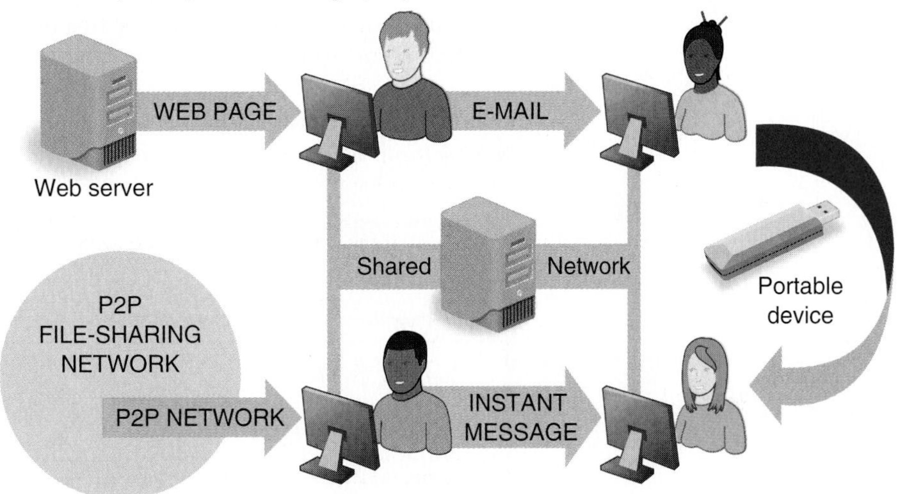

There are a few important items to note in this description of an active worm. This worm, like most other worms and viruses, attacks computers running Microsoft Windows but not Mac or UNIX/Linux machines. There are a few theories on why worms and viruses target Windows computers. One is that hackers and virus authors hate Microsoft. Another is that hackers and virus writers target the dominant platform in order to do the most damage to the most people. The third is that Microsoft Windows has more security holes than other operating systems and is easier to attack. Perhaps all three theories are correct in part.

Also note that this worm, and most other recent worms, propagates through e-mail by creating e-mail messages and sending them to every address found on the infected system—in your address book, in your in-box, or in deleted messages. The worm selects one of these addresses and places it in the From field. This means that when you receive a worm through e-mail, it most likely did not come from the person it indicates but rather from someone that person knows and has corresponded with. Worms also can include personal data found on the infected PC in the distributed e-mail.

Worms can also propagate through P2P networks. The worm masquerades as a media file in the shared folder of P2P users. It uses a filename with a double extension such as Harry Potter 5.mpg.exe, taking advantage of the fact that Windows, by default, hides file extensions. On most Windows machines this file appears as "Harry Potter 5.mpg," a harmless-looking video file. But when you play it—surprise!—the cycle begins all over from another infected PC.

Viruses and worms also spread through *Web scripts* (small programs that run on Web pages). An attack called a *drive-by download* places enticing links on Web pages that when clicked run a Web script that infects the visitor's PC. This has become one of the most popular ways to spread viruses, especially through social networks like Facebook.

Viruses and worms have found a new home in instant messaging and chat programs. Just like e-mail, instant messages can contain binary attachments, which in turn can hide viruses and worms. There have also been isolated cases of viruses spreading through cell phones.

Computers can also become infected through downloaded software files. Viruses are sometimes hidden in browser plug-in applications. A Web page may inform you that you need a particular viewer in order to view the contents of the Web site and ask you to click OK to download. Your browser may ask you to confirm before installing downloaded software (Figure 11.37). If the Web site is of questionable origin, chances are the plug-in contains a virus. Viruses also may be included in software available for free on the Web. Typically, if you find a deal that seems too good to be true, there is some hidden agenda at work.

FIGURE 11.37 • Watch out for warnings

Many viruses and worms infect PCs through Web plug-ins. If you get a warning such as this one, consider the source of the Web site carefully before proceeding with the installation.

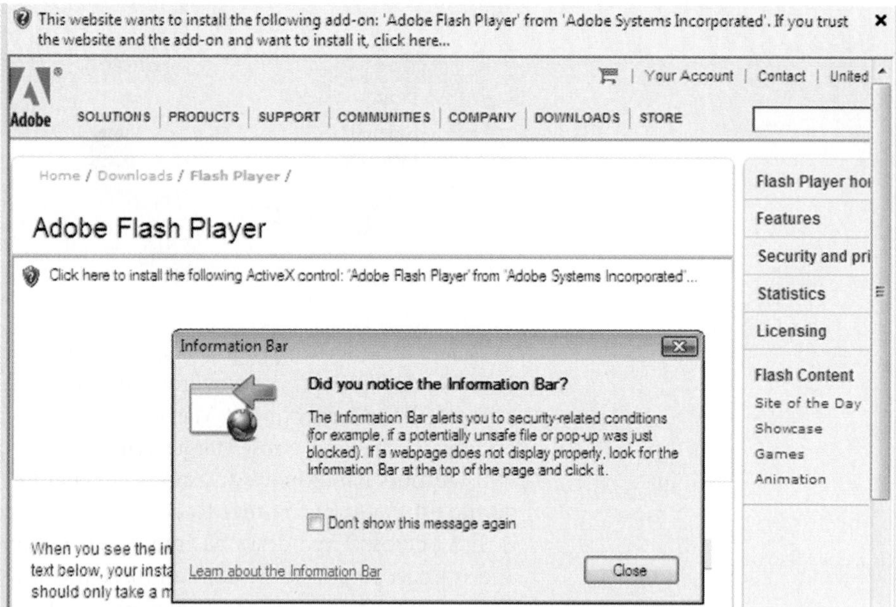

Defending Against Viruses and Worms. The number one tool against viruses and worms is antivirus software. **Antivirus software**, also known as virus-scan software, uses several techniques to find viruses on a computer system, remove them if possible, and keep additional viruses from infecting the system. Antivirus software is effective only if it is updated as new virus information becomes known. For this reason, Internet subscription services such as Microsoft Security Essentials, Norton AntiVirus, and McAfee VirusScan, all of which update automatically when necessary, are preferred (see Figure 11.38). Antivirus software is often packaged with firewall software for robust Internet security.

FIGURE 11.38 • Microsoft Security Essentials

Microsoft Security Essentials is an all-in-one security suite that includes antivirus software, anti-spyware, a firewall, a phishing filter, a performance-enhancing utility, and backup software.

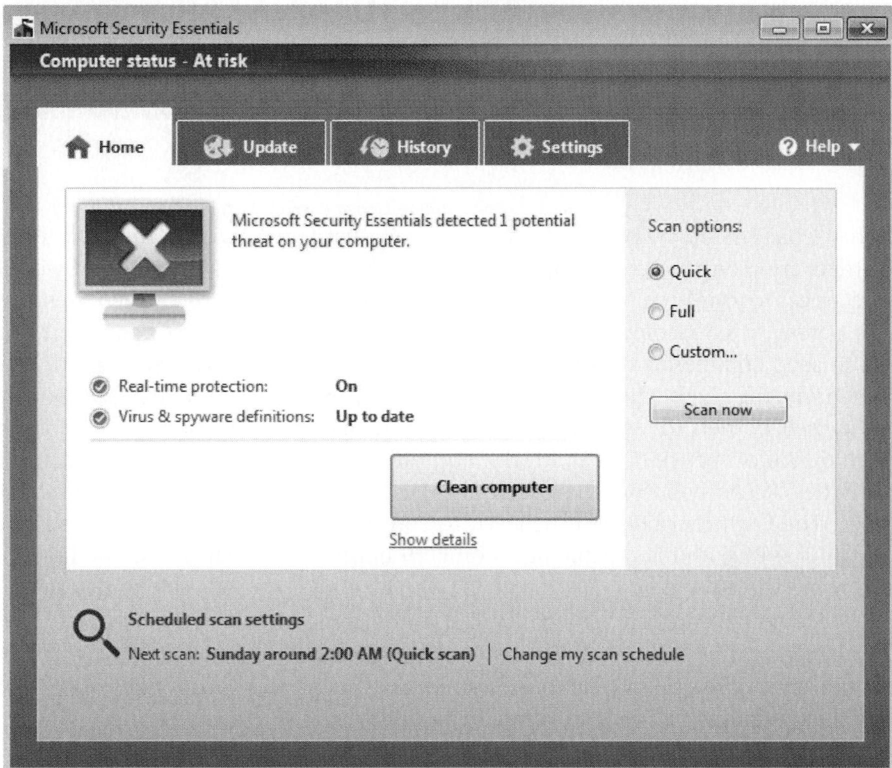

Knowledge and caution play a big part in protecting PCs against viruses and worms:

- Don't open e-mail or IM attachments that come from friends or strangers unless they are expected and inspected by antivirus software.
- Keep up with software patches for your operating system, your Web browser, your e-mail, and IM software.
- Use caution when exploring Web sites created and maintained by unknown parties.
- Use extreme caution when asked to install a plug-in or software to view Web content. Avoid software from untrusted sources.
- Stay away from file-sharing networks; they do not protect users from dangerous files that are being swapped.

Spyware, Adware, and Zombies

Spyware is software installed on a computer without the user's knowledge to either monitor the user or allow an outside party to control the computer. Spyware is so prolific that any unprotected computer that spends time on the Web has probably contracted it. Spyware differs from viruses and worms in that it does not self-replicate. Spyware is often used for commercial gain by displaying pop-up ads, stealing credit card numbers, distributing spam, monitoring Web activity and delivering it to businesses for marketing purposes, and hijacking the Web browser to show advertising sites. *Adware* is spyware that displays advertisements.

Elusive Attackers Hide Behind Botnets

Today's hackers utilize botnets to do their dirty work. Botnets are groups of compromised computers that a hacker can control remotely. A hacker, referred to as a bot herder, utilizes command and control (C&C) servers to send commands to computers in the botnet, synchronizing their actions like an army. Bot herders lease their botnets for sending spam, launching distributed denial of service (DDoS) attacks, and other illegal activities. Recently botnets have become alarmingly large. The Conficker botnet is believed to control over 10 million PCs, and is capable of sending 10 billion spam messages per day.

Since botnets are remotely controlled, finding the bot herder can be difficult if not impossible. The commands controlling botnet computers utilize sophisticated encryption that makes it difficult to discover where the command and control server is located. Also, botnets have the ability to change the IP address and location of command and control servers frequently. If one server is found and put out of commission, there could be many other backup servers ready to take over.

The July 4, 2009 DDoS attacks on high-visibility Web sites in the United States and South Korea provide a good example of the complexities of finding the perpetrators of botnet attacks. The initial investigators of the attack assumed that it must have originated in North Korea since it is well known that North Korea is vexed with both South Korea and the United States. Upon investigation, it was discovered that the attacks on more than a dozen Web servers were the result of 166,000 zombie computers located in 74 countries. It was further discovered that those 166,000 zombie computers made up six different botnets. Vietnam's Computer Emergency Response Team was able to gain control of two of the command and control botnet servers. Upon analyzing the logs on the servers, it was discovered that they were in turn controlled by a master server in the United Kingdom. The British company that owned the server was able to determine that the server was operating under instructions provided from a PC in Miami, Florida connected to the server through a VPN connection. It is still not known who was operating that PC.

Questions

1. How were the July 4th attackers able to hide their tracks?
2. What points of weakness in user behavior, software, and policies made this DDoS attack possible?
3. What actions might you take to ensure that your computer is not operating in a botnet?

Sources

1. *Gorman/Ramstad, "Cyber Blitz Hits U.S., Korea,"* The Wall Street Journal, *July 9, 2009, http://online.wsj.com.*
2. *Zetter, Kim, "Cyber Attacks Traced to the U.S., Britain,"* Wired, *July 14, 2009, www.wired.com.*

Spyware is distributed by deceiving the user into installing it by hiding it in shareware, Web plug-ins, and other software acting as a Trojan horse. Viruses are often used as a delivery mechanism for spyware. Spyware can also enter a system through security holes exploited by software on the Web. Once on a system, spyware runs in the background, unknown to the user, carrying out the wishes of its creator. Spyware can communicate with its creator over the Internet.

A computer that carries out actions (often malicious) under the remote control of a hacker either directly or through spyware or a virus is called a **zombie computer**. Experts say hundreds of thousands of computers are added to the ranks of zombies each week. Zombie computers can join together to form botnets. **Botnets** apply the power of many PCs to overwhelm Web sites with distributed denial-of-service (DDOS) attacks, to crack complicated security codes, or to generate huge batches of spam. It has been estimated that 80 to 90 percent of spam originates from zombie computers.[36] Botnets can also be used for blackmail. In one such case, a small British online payment-processing company, Protx, was shut down after being bombarded in a DDoS attack and warned that problems would continue unless a $10,000 payment was made.

Defending Against Spyware. Most spyware has so far been directed at Windows PCs, so defenses have also been focused on Windows. **Antispyware** is software that searches a computer for spyware and other software that may violate a user's privacy, allows the user to remove it, and provides continuing protection against future attacks. Antispyware is now incorporated into most security suites such as Norton Internet Security, Microsoft Security Essentials, and McAfee SecurityCenter. Spyware that is found by these tools is typically ranked in terms of threat level. For example, low-threat spyware includes commercial software that has the facility to automatically check for updates over the Internet. While this type of spyware provides a service—the automatic update of your software—it may be doing so without your knowledge, and it might be sending information about your computer usage. High-threat spyware is spyware that is known to be carrying out illegal activities.

Scams, Spam, Fraud, and Hoaxes

There are many ways in which shysters attempt to take advantage of Internet users and make off with their money. Perhaps you have received e-mail that begins something like this:

- "My name is dr.david konbuna, the manager, credit and foreign bills of bank of africa (boa). I am writing in respect of a foreign customer of my bank with account number 14-255-1004/boa/t who perished in a plane crash with the whole passengers aboard..."
- "This letter may come to you as a surprise due to the fact that we have not yet met. My name is VIJAY SINGH, a merchant in Dubai, in the U.A.E. I have been diagnosed with prostate and esophageal Cancer that was discovered very late due to my laxity in caring for my health. It has defiled all form of medicine and right now, I have only about a few months to live according to medical experts..."

If you ever receive such an e-mail, take it for what it really is, a scam, and do not provide the sender with your bank account information or credit card number as requested.

Internet fraud is the crime of deliberately deceiving a person over the Internet in order to cause damage and to unjustly obtain property or services from the victim. Many instances of Internet fraud occur through e-mail, though most are not as obvious as the above examples.

Phishing and Pharming. A **phishing** scam combines both spoofed e-mail and a spoofed Web site in order to trick a person into providing private information. Recall that *spoofing* is the act of assuming the identity of another. In a phishing scam the hacker sends out mass e-mailings (sometimes using zombie networks) that appear to come from a legitimate company such as PayPal, a credit card company, or a bank (see Figure 11.39). The e-mail warns of some trouble with your account and provides a link that you should click to address the problem. The link, such as *https://www.paypal.com/customer-service,* may look safe, but a click takes you to a different Web address that looks just like the real PayPal login page, so you don't notice a slightly different URL in the address box. The page looks like the PayPal page because the hacker copied the page exactly from PayPal to his own Web server.

FIGURE 11.39 • Phishing

Phishing scams use official-looking e-mail and Web pages to con people into giving private information.

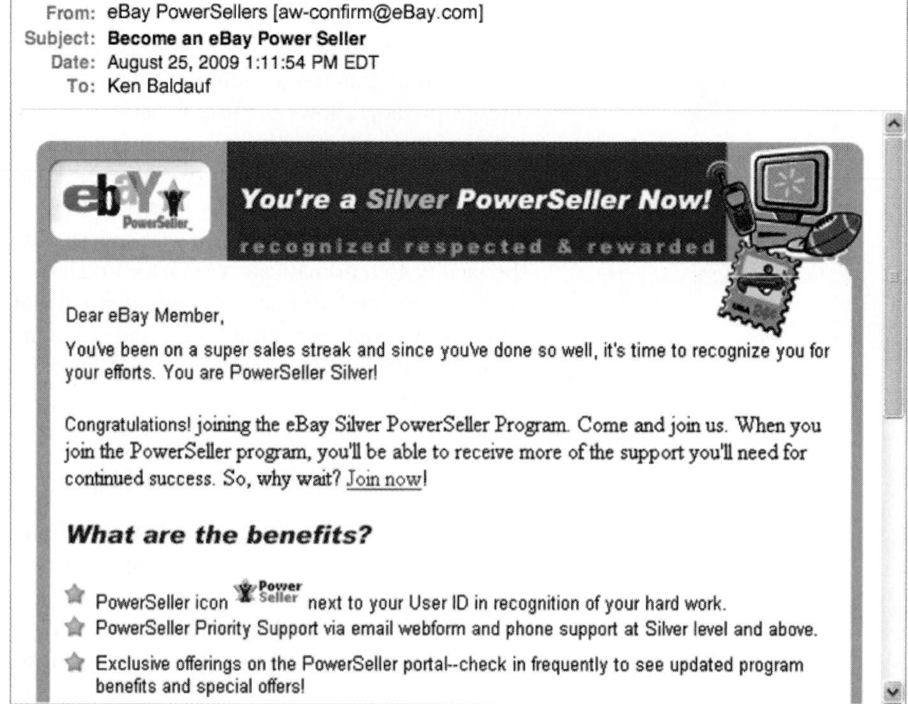

From this point in the phishing scam a number of things can occur. Most commonly the user logs in as requested; the hacker has then obtained his goal of stealing the user's login information. Next, the user gets a message like "Incorrect Password. Click here to try again." When the user clicks to try again, the software may send the user to the real login screen, where the user is able to log in without any trouble. The victim is totally unaware of the fraud or identity theft that has occurred.

In addition to stealing login information and perhaps more, depending on how long the user can be strung along, phishing pages can also install spyware on a computer. The Web site *www.antiphishing.org* receives around 2500 phishing reports each month. Some politicians are pushing to tighten regulations, and impose stiff penalties on those that participate in phishing scams and spyware.

Phishing tactics are getting more sophisticated. In an attack called *spear phishing*, private or personal information is used to target a specific individual. The fraudulent e-mail received is so convincing that it is impossible to guess that it isn't a legitimate request.

In the criminal act of *pharming*, hackers hijack a domain name service (DNS) server to automatically redirect users from legitimate Web sites to spoofed Web sites in the effort to steal personal information. In pharming, a user may type *www.PayPal.com* into the Web browser address bar, but when the request is received at the DNS server, rather than routing the packets to the PayPal server, they are hijacked to the hacker's Web site. Pharming strikes a serious blow to the underlying architecture of the Web as it is nearly impossible to detect. The ability of hackers to corrupt DNS computers could undermine the public's faith in e-commerce and the Internet altogether.

Spam. Spam has been discussed throughout this book. It is the unsolicited junk mail that makes up more than the vast majority of today's e-mail. There are laws against spam in many states and countries but they have not had much effect on the volume of spam. Because spammers have gone into partnership with hackers they are often well protected behind botnets and virus-infected computers (Figure 11.40).

FIGURE 11.40 • Spam

Spam is often tied up with other forms of computer crime such as fraud and spyware.

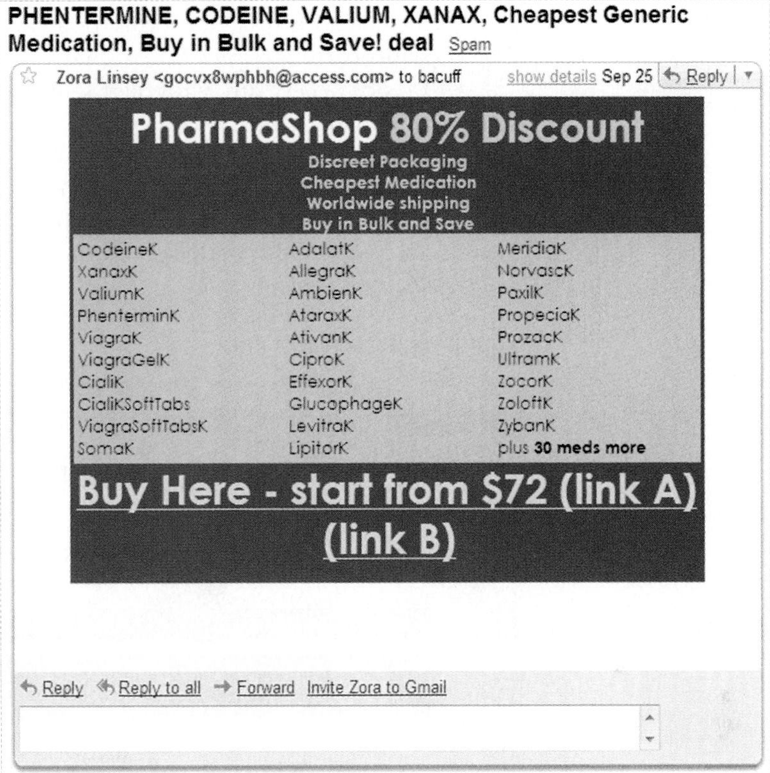

The U.S. Federal Trade Commission has begun shutting down Web hosts suspected of controlling botnets. The closure of Pricewert ISP in 2009 reduced U.S. spam by 15 percent.[37] Unfortunately, such retaliation is only temporary, as hackers find other Web hosts over time.

Leaders in the tech industry have teamed up to develop solutions to spam that include these:

- Bayesian filters that learn to identify spam and filter it to a spam folder
- Simple authentication technology that verifies the sender of a message
- "Trusted sender" technology to identify e-mail senders who can be trusted
- Reputation systems to allow everyone on the Internet to cooperate in identifying good and bad e-mail senders
- Interfaces for client-side tools to allow end users to report spam

The frustration caused by spam presents another threat to the growth of the Internet. It is hoped that a two-pronged approach that attacks spam from technical and legal perspectives can provide a solution that works.

Virus Hoaxes. A **virus hoax** is an e-mail that warns of a virus that doesn't exist. In some cases, a virus hoax is just an inconvenience or nuisance. In other cases, it can cause serious problems. If the hoax tells you to delete a "virus" file that is actually an uninfected and important system file and you delete it, you may not be able to run your computer.

Defending Against Scams, Spam, Fraud, and Hoaxes. The main defenses against scams, spam, fraud, and hoaxes are awareness and common sense. If something seems too good to be true, it probably isn't true. Other important safeguards include the following:

- Do not click links received in e-mails. Instead, type URLs directly into your Web browser.
- Examine Web addresses closely to make sure that they are legitimate and include an https:// for forms, or a closed lock icon in the address or status bar.
- Do not believe any virus alert sent through e-mail unless it comes from a verifiable source.

There are many spam filters that can dramatically reduce the amount of spam in your inbox (Figure 11.41). If you use Web e-mail such as Hotmail, your only option is to use the spam filter of the service provider. If you use an e-mail client such as Microsoft Outlook, you can use a plug-in filter such as Spam Bayes (*http://spambayes.sourceforge.net*).

FIGURE 11.41 • E-mail filter

Web-based e-mail services often offer tools for reporting spam to improve filtering.

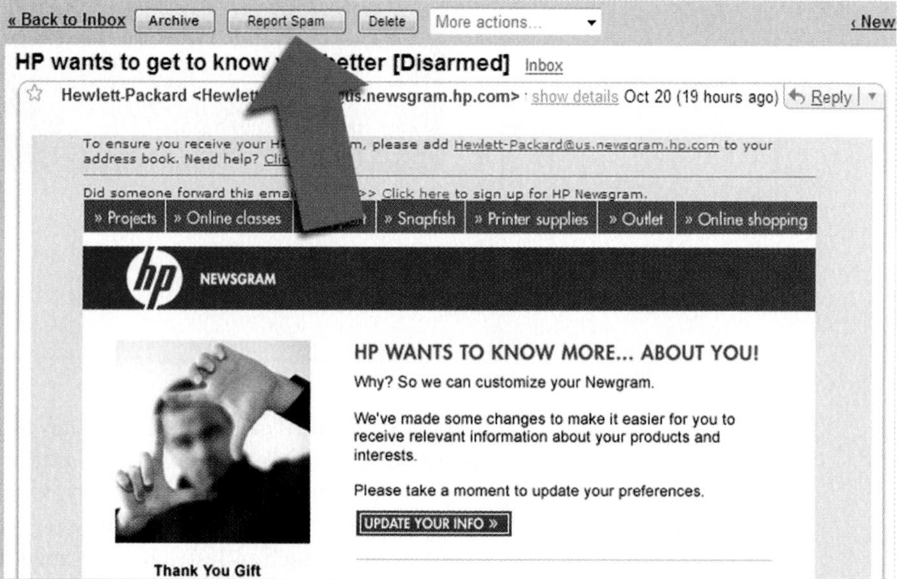

As mentioned at the beginning of this chapter, to achieve total information security, efforts must be made at multiple levels. Individuals, businesses, organizations, and governments must work together to secure independent computers, private and public networks, and the Internet. Each individual wears different security hats depending on the computing environment. In your personal life you must be on guard to protect your own personal information and systems. When accessing business or organization networks at work and in your day-to-day life, you must be on guard to protect those networks and the sensitive and private information they may contain. You must also be aware of the impact of information security on your country and the world.

Information security is often inconvenient. It requires time and effort that most of us would prefer not to invest. However, as this chapter has underscored, your efforts are essential to support this goal.

A PC Security Checklist

Keeping your computer and the information it holds safe and secure requires a two-pronged approach: applying software security tools and maintaining safe, vigilant behavior. Throughout this chapter you have been provided with a lot of advice; so much that you may not remember it all. The checklists here are provided to make personal information security as simple and straightforward as possible. The items are ordered by level of importance, the most important items first. Many of the items at the top of these lists are of equal importance.

Applying Software Security Tools

- Windows users should set Windows to update automatically.
- Install and use antivirus software.
- Install and use firewall software.
- Install and use antispyware software.
- Make sure that all security, antivirus, firewall, and antispyware software is set to update automatically.
- Use backup software to back up important data files automatically on a regular schedule.
- Windows users can consider using Windows cleaner software to maintain the Windows Registry.
- Use a security suite such as Windows Live OneCare, which manages all of the above.
- Install Web browser security updates as soon as they are released.
- Use encryption for private files stored on your computer, to secure Web transactions, and to secure wireless networks.
- When connected to a network, make sure that user permissions are set to share only the files you wish to share.
- If you use a home wireless network, disable SSID broadcasting on the access point, change passwords on the access point, and enable security features (set it to connect with only specific MAC addresses).
- Use spam filters on your e-mail.

Maintaining Safe and Vigilant Behaviors

- Select passwords carefully and change them regularly.
- Do not open attachments unless they are expected and scanned for viruses.
- Do not click links received in e-mails.
- Examine Web addresses closely to make sure that they are legitimate and include an https:// for forms.
- Avoid P2P file-sharing networks.
- Avoid installing plug-ins, viewers, and software offered by questionable Web sites.
- Keep your computer system well organized and up to date using the housecleaning tips provided in this chapter.
- Do not forward e-mail virus alerts.

ACTION PLAN

Remember Jan Minski from the beginning of this chapter? She is the student whose credit card information was stolen. Here are answers to the questions about Jan's situation.

1. **What are the first steps Jan should take in her crime scene investigation to find out if indeed her computer was broken into?**

   Jan should scan her computer for viruses, worms, and spyware using antivirus software and antispyware. She should also check her data files to see if she has credit card information stored anywhere on her computer where it might be stolen.

2. **What possible methods could a hacker have used to steal Jan's credit card information?**

   A hacker may have a virus or spyware installed on Jan's computer to record her activities. During her last online credit card purchase the illicit software may have recorded her credit card number, expiration date, and code. If Jan stored her credit card info in a data file on her computer, say in her budget spreadsheet, an intruder may have stolen the file to access her info. Other possibilities are that Jan was tricked by a phishing scam to supply her credit card information to a fraudulent Web site or her credit card information was sniffed off the Internet if she supplied it for a purchase over an unsecured Internet connection. Finally, the credit card number could have been stolen from the transaction databases on the servers of merchants either by insiders within the company or by hackers outside the company.

3. **What precautions can Jan take to make sure this doesn't happen again?**

   Jan should make sure that her operating system and Web browser are patched and up to date. She should install antivirus software, antispyware, and firewall software, or a security suite. She should encrypt her private data files on her computer and be cautious when supplying credit card information online.

Summary

LEARNING OBJECTIVE 1

Describe the types of information that must be kept secure and the types of threats against them.

Total information security refers to securing all components of the global digital information infrastructure, from cell phones to PCs, to business and government networks, to Internet routers and communications satellites. As a computer user, you must learn about security risks at three levels: the machine level; the network level, including wireless networks; and the Internet level. As you move from one level to the next, you face increasing exposure and risks. Personal, organizational, national, and international information is all at risk. Identity theft refers to the criminal act of using stolen information about a person to assume that person's identity. Intellectual property is also the target of crimes. Intellectual property refers to a product of the mind or intellect over which the owner holds legal entitlement. Intellectual property rights concern the ownership and use of intellectual property such as software, music, movies, data, and information. For a business or nonprofit organization, the information it processes is often highly valued and key to its

Figure 11.2 —p. 557

success. For this reason, businesses and organizations take information security very seriously. Besides protecting its own proprietary information, a business also has a responsibility to its customers to safeguard their private information against unauthorized access. New laws are holding companies responsible for maintaining the privacy of their customers' private information. Just as businesses benefit from digital technologies and the Internet, so do governments and government agencies all over the world. Cyberterrorism is a form of terrorism that makes use of attacks over the Internet to intimidate and harm a population. Increasingly, governments are involved in cybersecurity, cyberespionage, and cyberattacks against other government.

To achieve total information security, many diverse threats must be addressed. Security vulnerabilities or security holes are software bugs that allow deliberate violations to information security. Software patches are corrections to the software bugs that cause security holes. There are many situations where innocent human mistakes result in monumental problems. Pirates and plagiarists are two classifications of individuals who violate the laws regarding intellectual property rights. A hacker, cracker, attacker, or intruder is an individual who subverts computer security without authorization. Hackers often belong to groups and assist each other with new methods for hacking systems. Computer forensics is the process of examining computing equipment to determine if it has been used for illegal, unauthorized, or unusual activities.

LEARNING OBJECTIVE 2

Describe methods of keeping a PC safe and secure.

The most basic and fundamental security is implemented at the individual machine level, the point of entry to computers, computer networks, and the Internet. Access to today's PCs is typically guarded with a username and password. In security terms, this is regarded as authentication, a way with which to confirm the identity of a user. Passwords can be an effective form of authentication if they are difficult to guess, kept confidential, and changed regularly. A number of devices are used in corporations and organizations to provide access to restricted areas and computer systems. The most popular of these devices are ID cards and keychain ID fobs. Biometrics is the science and technology of authentication by scanning and measuring a person's unique physical features such as fingerprints, retinal patterns, and facial characteristics. Today's Apple and Windows PCs include security tools that can encrypt files stored on disks and flash drives. This is useful in situations where the information stored is confidential or valuable, and there is a possibility that your computer can be accessed by others, lost, or stolen. The most effective way to protect data and information is to back it up. Software updates, computer housekeeping, and Windows cleaners are other ways to keep a personal computer running smoothly and securely.

Figure 11.18 —p. 577

LEARNING OBJECTIVE 3

Discuss the threats and defenses unique to multiuser networks.

When a computer is connected to a network, security risks increase. A multiuser system is a computer system, such as a computer network, in which multiple users share access to resources such as file systems. User permissions are the defined access privileges afforded to each network user. Interior threats, those that come from registered users, can be intentional or unintentional. Many instances of identity theft occur with the assistance of insiders with corporate network access. To safeguard against threats to a network's health and stability and against information theft, businesses and organizations often design security and network usage policies.

Figure 11.27 —p. 588

LEARNING OBJECTIVE 4

Discuss the threats and defenses unique to wireless networks.

With wireless technologies, an attacker no longer has to establish a wired connection to a network. Attackers located within the range of the wireless signal, perhaps on the floor above or in a car parked outside, can gain access to an unsecured wireless network. To make Wi-Fi easy to set up, manufacturers disable all forms of security in new Wi-Fi access points. Several steps are required to secure a Wi-Fi network. Options within the configuration software allow you to disable the broadcasting of the SSID (network ID). Access points can be set to allow only certain computers to connect. Several encryption protocols exist for wireless communications. Wired Equivalent Privacy (WEP) and Wi-Fi Protected Access (WPA and WPA2) are the most popular. War driving is the act of driving through neighborhoods with a wireless notebook or handheld computer looking for unsecured Wi-Fi networks.

Figure 11.31 —p. 594

LEARNING OBJECTIVE 5

Describe the threats faced by Internet users, and the methods of defending against them.

Attacks against Internet-connected computers may come in the form of direct attacks by hackers (system penetration), or through viruses, worms, or spyware obtained though e-mail, the Web, or downloaded files. Internet users are also at risk of being manipulated through scams and hoaxes. A hacker can remotely install key-logging software on a computer to record all keystrokes and commands. For random attacks an attacker may employ port-scanning software to search IP addresses for ports open to attack. Hackers also apply social engineering to acquire private information. A firewall is network hardware or software that examines all incoming packets and filters out packets that are potentially dangerous. Encrypting confidential data that is stored and transmitted over a network greatly adds to your protection. A virus is a program that attaches itself to a file, spreads to other files, and delivers a destructive action called a payload. A worm does not attach itself to other programs but rather acts as a free agent, replicating itself numerous times in an effort to overwhelm systems. Antivirus software uses several techniques to find viruses on a computer system, remove them if possible, and keep additional viruses from infecting the system. Spyware is software installed on a computer without the user's knowledge to either monitor the user or to allow an outside party to control the computer. Antispyware is software that searches a computer for spyware and any software that may violate a user's privacy, allows the user to remove it, and provides continuing protection against future attacks. Internet fraud is the crime of deliberately deceiving a person over the Internet in order to cause damage and to obtain property or services. A phishing scam can be a spoofed e-mail or Web site that tricks a person into providing private information. A virus hoax is e-mail sent to people warning them of a virus that doesn't exist.

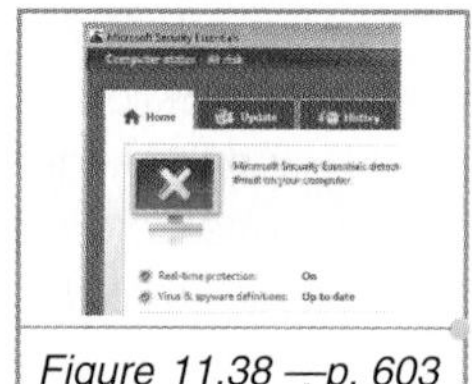

Figure 11.38 —p. 603

Test Yourself

LEARNING OBJECTIVE 1: Describe the types of information that must be kept secure and the types of threats against them.

1. ________________ refers to the criminal act of using stolen information about a person to assume that person's identity.
2. Illegally copying and distributing music is an issue related to ________________.
   a. cyberterrorism
   b. intellectual property rights
   c. plagiarism
   d. identity theft
3. True or False: Businesses are fairly unrestricted in their use of customers' information.
4. ________________ utilizes attacks over the Internet to intimidate and harm a population.

LEARNING OBJECTIVE 2: Describe methods of keeping a PC safe and secure.

5. ________________ can be an effective form of authentication if they are difficult to guess, kept confidential, and changed regularly.
6. ________________ is a form of biometrics being used for personal computing.
   a. Facial recognition
   b. Retinal scan
   c. Usernames and passwords
   d. Fingerprint scan
7. True or False: Most data files on PCs are automatically encrypted when they are saved to disk.
8. Which of the following protects a computer from hackers, viruses, and hard disk failure?
   a. hard drive backup
   b. virus detection
   c. firewall
   d. encryption

LEARNING OBJECTIVE 3: Discuss the threats and defenses unique to multiuser networks.

9. ________________ threats originate from users that already have legal access to a computer system.
   a. Interior
   b. Hacker
   c. Virus
   d. Security
10. True or False: Most business networks do not allow users to install software without the network administrator's authorization.
11. True or False: Employers are legally responsible for notifying employees of network usage policies.

LEARNING OBJECTIVE 4: Discuss the threats and defenses unique to wireless networks.

12. By default, Wi-Fi ________________ are set to broadcast their presence.
    a. adapters
    b. access points
    c. routers
    d. computers
13. A mobile technique used by hackers to locate and hack Wi-Fi networks is called ________________.
14. True or False: Wireless networks are more difficult to hack than wired networks.
15. Which of the following is not a method used to secure a wireless network?
    a. disable SSID broadcasting
    b. encrypt your files
    c. set access point to connect to specific MAC addresses
    d. place access point in a secure location

LEARNING OBJECTIVE 5: Describe the threats faced by Internet users, and the methods of defending against them.

16. Hackers often enter a computer through an unprotected ________________ .
    a. user account
    b. port
    c. ISP
    d. firewall
17. True or False: Hackers always have illegal or unethical motivations.
18. A ________________ attack uses many computers to launch simultaneous repeated requests at a Web server in order to overwhelm it so that it is unable to function.
19. A ________________ combines the resources of thousands of compromised PCs to launch DDoS attacks or distribute spam.
20. A ________________ is a program that attaches itself to a file, spreads to other files, and delivers a destructive action called a payload.
    a. virus
    b. worm
    c. Trojan horse
    d. spyware
21. A ________________ scam combines spoofed e-mail and a spoofed Web site in order to trick a person into providing private information.

Test Yourself Solutions: 1. Identity theft, 2. b. intellectual property rights, 3. False, 4. Cyberterrorism, 5. Passwords, 6. d. Fingerprint scan, 7. False, 8. a. hard drive backup, 9. Interior, 10. True, 11. False, 12. b. access points, 13. war driving, 14. False, 15. d. place access point in a secure location, 16. b. port, 17. False, 18. distributed denial-of-service (DDoS), 19. botnet, 20. a. virus, 21. phishing.

Key Terms

Term	Page	Definition
antispyware	605	Software that searches a computer for spyware and other software that may violate a user's privacy, allows the user to remove it, and provides continuing protection against future attacks
antivirus software	602	Uses several techniques to find viruses on a computer system, remove them if possible, and keep additional viruses from infecting the system
biometrics	576	The science and technology of authentication by scanning and measuring a person's unique physical features such as fingerprints, retinal patterns, and facial characteristics
botnet	604	A group of computers under the remote control of a hacker for purposes of implementing denial-of-service attacks, cracking security codes, or generating huge batches of spam
computer forensics	573	The process of examining computing equipment to determine if it has been used for illegal, unauthorized, or unusual activities
cyberterrorism	564	A form of terrorism that uses attacks over the Internet to intimidate and harm a population
firewall	597	Network hardware or software that examines all incoming packets and filters out packets that are potentially dangerous
identity theft	559	The criminal act of using stolen information about a person to assume that person's identity
intellectual property	560	A product of the mind or intellect over which the owner holds legal entitlement
intellectual property rights	561	Rights relative to the ownership and use of intellectual property such as software, music, movies, data, and information

Term	Page	Definition
Internet fraud	605	The crime of deliberately deceiving a person over the Internet in order to cause damage and to unjustly obtain property or services from the victim
password	573	A combination of characters known only to the user that is used for authentication
phishing	605	Scam that combines spoofed e-mail and a spoofed Web site in order to trick a person into providing private information
piracy	569	The illegal copying, use, and distribution of digital intellectual property such as software, music, and movies
plagiarism	569	Taking credit for someone else's intellectual property, typically a written idea, by claiming it as your own
security holes	567	Software bugs that allow violations of information security
software patches	567	Corrections to the software bugs that cause security holes
spyware	603	Software installed on a computer without the user's knowledge to either monitor the user or allow an outside party to control the computer
username	573	Identifies a user to the computer system
virus	599	A program that attaches itself to a file, spreads to other files, and delivers a destructive action called a payload
virus hoax	607	An e-mail that warns of a virus that doesn't exist
worm	600	A program that does not attach itself to other programs but rather acts as a free agent, replicating itself numerous times in an effort to overwhelm systems
zombie computer	604	A computer that carries out actions (often malicious) under the remote control of a hacker either directly or through spyware or a virus

Questions

Review Questions

1. Information security is concerned with what three main areas?
2. What is "total information security"?
3. What information is typically stolen in cases of identity theft?
4. What is competitive intelligence, and how does it differ from counterintelligence?
5. In what ways is cyberterrorism a threat?
6. What is a software patch used for?
7. What is computer forensics?
8. What are three common forms of authentication?
9. Provide some good advice about choosing a password.
10. What is biometrics, and how is it used for information security?
11. What is an incremental backup?
12. Why is the U.S. government concerned about cybersecurity?
13. What service does user permissions provide?
14. What software tool is the best defense against hackers?
15. How do viruses and worms differ?
16. In what ways can spyware be acquired?
17. List four actions that can protect a wireless network.
18. What are the best ways to avoid phishing scams?
19. What is a virus hoax?
20. What is a botnet?

Discussion Questions

21. Could anything less than "total information security" provide society with complete security? Why or why not?
22. What can you do to protect yourself against identity theft?
23. Is sharing your favorite music with friends, by giving them a copy of the CD, legal? Is it ethical? Why or why not?
24. What national infrastructures are threatened by cyberattacks?
25. What is business intelligence, and how is it concerned with information security?
26. Considering the cost to businesses that is passed on to customers, do you think it is necessary to have so many laws about information use and privacy? Why or why not?
27. Who shares the blame for information insecurity?
28. How do piracy and plagiarism differ? What do they have in common?
29. Is there such a thing as an ethical hacker? Why or why not?
30. Explain three ways that encryption can be used to secure information on PCs, networks, and the Internet.
31. What are the risks, costs, and benefits of remote data backup?
32. List several methods of maintaining a personal computer so that it runs smoothly and safely.
33. What are the concerns of users, system administrators, and business managers regarding multiuser systems?
34. What issues are addressed in a typical security and network usage policy?
35. Do you think war driving is ethically wrong? Why or why not?

Exercises

Try It Yourself

1. Use a word-processing application to create a checklist for yourself based on the PC Security Checklist provided in the Home Technology box near the end of the chapter. Check off the items that you feel you have covered adequately. Form a list of areas in which you can improve.
2. If you use Windows, download and install free antispyware software from the Internet (such as from *www.safer-networking.org/en/index.html* or *http://free.avg.com*) and run the software. Take a screen shot of the results page (Ctrl+PrtSc) and paste it into a word-processing document.
3. Create a practice spreadsheet file—it can be empty. Save the file on your computer, and then encrypt the file (use the Help feature on your operating system to find out how). Open the encrypted file to witness the password protection.
4. Visit the McAfee Threat Center (*www.mcafee.com/us/threat_center*) and read the details about the top three current malware threats. Write up a summary describing how the each type of malware infects its victims, what symptoms it shows, what it does to the computer, and how to get rid of it.

Virtual Classroom Activities

For the following exercises, do not use face-to-face or telephone communications with your group members. Use only Internet communications.

5. Have an online chat about what each group member feels is the most valuable information stored on his or her computer. Group the items as being either financially or sentimentally valuable, and decide as a group what items are most valuable.
6. Use a discussion board to post your worst computer nightmares—unfortunate events, user mistakes, attacks, and accidents that have occurred on or to your computer that brought loss, embarrassment, or destruction of information. If you've never had an unfortunate event, you can share stories you've heard from others.
7. Have a group scavenger hunt to find the usage policies governing your school network. The first one to find it online provides the URL and wins a prize (you determine what it is). Discuss each of the issues on the usage policy and their purpose as well as your feelings about them.

Teamwork

8. Evaluate the top (ranked by CNET and users) free antivirus, firewall, monitoring, and spyware software listed at *http://download.cnet.com* and decide as a group which is best. Divide up the research among group members and present your findings in a report.
9. Evaluate Norton and McAfee security software suites, and compare and contrast them with the software evaluated in the previous task. Do you feel that there is significant quality improvement for the paid subscription services over the free services? Divide up the research and present your results in a report.
10. Perform an Internet search on privacy laws for your state and country. Compile a list of the state and federal privacy laws that you find, along with a short explanation of each.

Endnotes

[1] Bunge, Jacob, "NYSE, Nasdaq Sites Targeted by 'Cyber Attack'," *The Wall Street Journal*, July 8, 2009, http://online.wsj.com.

[2] Resende, Patricia, "North Korea Blamed for Cyberattacks on U.S., South Korea," *CIO Today*, July 8, 2009, www.cio-today.com.

[3] Vijayan, Jaikumar, "U.K. Web hoster, customers scramble after attack deletes 100,000 sites," *Computerworld*, June 10, 2009, www.computerworld.com.

[4] Kirk, Jeremy, "ATM malware spreading around the world, researcher says," *Computerworld*, June 5, 2009, www.computerworld.com.

[5] Sanger, David, "Pentagon Plans New Arm to Wage Cyberspace Wars," *The New York Times*, May 28, 2009, www.nytimes.com.

[6] Finkle, Jim, "Hackers launch phishing attack on Facebook users," *Reuters*, May 15, 2009, www. reuters.com.

[7] Cheng, Jacque, "Botnet master hits the kill switch, takes down 100,000 PCs," *Ars Technica*, May 8, 2009, www.arstechnica.com.

[8] Paul, Ryan, "Analyst: cyberwarfare arms race with China imminent," *Ars Technica*, May 14, 2009, www.arstechnica.com.

[9] Vijayan, Jaikumar, "Update: 160,000 accounts breached at UC Berkeley," *Computerworld*, May 8, 2009, www.computerworld.com.

[10] Baldor, Lolita, "Air Traffic Systems Vulnerable to Attack," *NewsFactor*, May 8, 2009, www.newsfactor.com.

[11] CSI Staff, "CSI 2008 Security Survey," Computer Security Institute, www.gocsi.com/forms/csi_survey.jhtml.

[12] IC3 2008 Annual Report on Internet Crime, http://www.ic3.gov/media/annualreport/2008_IC3Report.pdf.

[13] "Consumer Sentinel Network Data Book for January – December 2008," Federal Trade Commission, February 2009, http://www.ftc.gov/sentinel/reports/sentinel-annual-reports/sentinel-cy2008.pdf.

[14] Schonfeld, Erick, "Twitter's Internal Strategy Laid Bare: To Be 'The Pulse Of The Planet'," *Tech Crunch*, July 16, 2009, www.techcrunch.com.

[15] Vijayan, Jaikumar, "Satellite vendor charged with conspiracy to hack Dish Network," *Computerworld*, July 15, 2009, www.computerworld.com.

[16] Shipman, Tim, "So why is the U.S. so eager to lock up Gary McKinnon, the Asperger's Syndrome hacker?", MailOnline, July 3, 2009, www.dailymail. co.uk.

[17] Gross, Grant, "Obama's Cybersecurity Initiative Wins Praise," *PCWorld*, May 29, 2009, www.pcworld.com.

[18] Gorman/Dreazen, "Military Command Is Created for Cyber Security," *The Wall Street Journal*, June 24, 2009, http://online.wsj.com.

[19] UPI Staff, "Cyberattacks on U.S. gov't seen rising," UPI, Feb 17, 2009, www.upi.com.

[20] Worthen Ben, "Wide Cyber Attack Linked to China," *The Wall Street Journal*, March 30, 2009, www.wsjonline.com.

[21] McMillan, Robert, "Power grid is found susceptible to cyberattack," *NetworkWorld*, March 21, 2009, www.networkworld.com.

[22] Kirk, Jeremy, "Study: U.S. air traffic control vulnerable to cyberattack," *NetworkWorld*, May 7, 2009, www.networkworld.com.

[23] "Convention on Cybercrime," Council of Europe, accessed July 24, 2009, http://conventions.coe.int/Treaty/EN/Treaties/Html/185.htm.

[24] Microsoft's Trustworthy Computing Web site, accessed July 24, 2009, www.microsoft.com/mscorp/twc.

[25] Jennings, Richi, "RIAA $1.92 mil. award 'not excessive' sez Obama's DoJ," *Computerworld*, August 17, 2009, www.computerworld.com.

[26] BBC Staff, "Court jails Pirate Bay founders," BBC, April 17, 2009, http://news.bbc.co.uk.

[27] Liza, Porteus Viana, "Three Strikes and You're Offline: Music Industry, ISPs May Cut Internet Access for File-Sharers," Fox News, March 26, 2009, www.foxnews.com.

[28] Cain Miller, Claire, "Twitter Hack Raises Flags on Security," *The New York Times*, July 15, 2009, www.nytimes.com.

[29] Mikulan, Steven, "Airport Surprise: 1,200 Laptops a Week Lost at LAX," *LAWeekly*, July 7, 2009, http://blogs.laweekly.com.

[30] Kirk, Jeremy, "Aetna warns 65,000 about Web site data breach," *Computerworld*, May 28, 2009, www.computerworld.com.

[31] Westfeldt, Amy, "LexisNexis Warns 32,000 People About Data Breach," *NewsFactor*, May 5, 2009, www.newsfactor.com.

[32] Staff, "Data Breaches Skyrocketed in 2008," *NewsFactor*, May 6, 2009, www.newsfactor.com.

[33] Keizer, Gregg, "Russian hackers knock Kyrgyzstan offline," *TechWorld*, January 29, 2009, www.techworld.com.

[34] Newman, Jared, "Twitter Temporarily Knocked Offline: Service Now Restored," *PCWorld*, August 20, 2009, www.pcworld.com.

[35] Vjayan, Jaikumar, "'Iceman' pleads guilty to massive computer hacking," *Computerworld*, June 30, 2009, www.computerworld.com.

[36] Cheng, Jacqui, "Report: botnets sent over 80% of all June spam," *Ars Technica*, June 29, 2009, www.arstechnica.com.

[37] Ngo, Dong, "Spam reduced following Pricewert shutdown," *ZDNet*, June 10, 2009, http://news.zdnet.com.

Digital Society, Ethics, and Globalization

John Toh considers himself a naturalist. He has one year to go to finish his degree in Civil and Environmental Engineering. John worries about technology's impact on society and the natural order of the world. He is concerned that people are losing touch with their natural environment and even with each other because of the increasing time everyone spends on computers and cell phones.

John is also concerned that large corporations and government might use technology in ways that negatively impact the environment and citizens' civil rights. He wonders if people might lose their souls and unique identities to technology and become just a list of numbers in a spreadsheet. He also worries about all the people being displaced from their jobs by the advance of technology. He can envision a bleak future where the Earth is devoid of nature; where computers, or perhaps tyrants empowered by computers, run the planet, and people are forced to do their bidding.

As you read through the chapter, consider the following questions:

1. Are computers alienating people from each other and the natural environment?
2. Are computers putting power and control into the hands of a few at the expense of freedom of the many?
3. Are computers reducing the need for a human workforce and overshadowing basic human needs?

Check out John's *Action Plan* at the conclusion of this chapter.

12

LEARNING OBJECTIVES

1. Describe how technology is affecting the definition of community, and list some physical, mental, and environmental health dangers associated with excessive computer use.
2. Describe the negative and positive impact of technology on freedom of speech, and list forms of speech and expression that are censored on the Web.
3. Explain the ways in which technology is used to invade personal privacy, and provide examples of laws that protect citizens from privacy invasion.
4. List ethical issues related to digital technology that confront individuals in personal and professional life, businesses, and governments.
5. Explain what globalization is, what forces are behind it, and how it is affecting the United States and other nations.

CHAPTER CONTENT

Living Online

Freedom of Speech

Privacy Issues

Ethics and Social Responsibility

Globalization

Introduction

Digital technologies have had a profound impact on most aspects of human life. The rapid pace of technological development has given the current generation one of the most fascinating eras in which to live. Technological advances are leading to life-changing scientific breakthroughs, new business management paradigms, and a more inclusive and connected global society. The application of digital technologies to accomplish more with fewer resources is turning lives upside down in both negative and positive ways. The social impact of these technologies seems to occur with little or no forethought by those responsible for developing and applying the technology. Governments are scrambling to establish laws to minimize negative impacts, while ethicists struggle to apply traditional ethical standards to brand-new modes of human interaction. This chapter examines the impact of digital technologies on our sense of community, freedom of speech, privacy, ethics, and globalization.

Think about some of the ways that digital technologies have changed an average individual's life over the past 25 years (see Figure 12.1). To make this a manageable task, consider these changes in the areas of communication, information access, commerce, professions, and leisure. Though many examples of the effects of technology have been provided throughout this book, this chapter focuses on the effects of technology from a quality-of-life perspective—what has been lost, and what has been gained.

Popular forms of communications have undergone dramatic changes over the past 25 years. Wireless technologies allow communication with friends and business associates at any time from nearly any place, whether from across town or the other side of the world. Twenty-five years ago, you would need to be at home, at work, or at a pay phone to chat with a friend or confer with a business associate at some other location. Back then, an executive might dictate a letter to be mailed to an overseas partner. The fax machine was just making its debut as a modern marvel. People spent a lot more time meeting and talking with others around them than with those in other locations. Today you can communicate via text, voice, or video, while sharing data and information in any format, instantaneously around the world, making it possible to befriend, communicate with, and collaborate with individuals almost as though they were sitting next to you.

FIGURE 12.1 • Communication then and now

An individual from the 1980s would be astounded by today's pervasive communications.

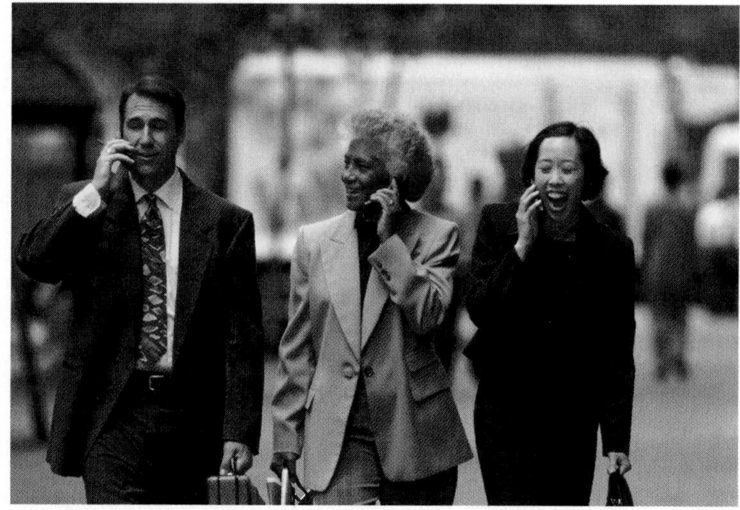

Your access to information and the amount of information available to you have vastly expanded over the past 25 years. In the 1980s, your primary resources in education were books, journals, textbooks, encyclopedias, and other library reference books. People received their daily news from journalists and reporters through television, radio, and newspapers. Today, in addition to these traditional forms of media and information, you can access an ever-increasing store of public knowledge and opinion on the Internet and Web. Rather than obtaining news and information from the small percentage of the population who are professional journalists, authors, and reporters, you are able to access the news and views from anyone connected to the Internet. More and more news stories are delivered directly from the individuals involved. The Web is a jumble of opinion, information, and misinformation. Blogs, discussion groups, and podcasts have provided mouthpieces for anyone with something to say, bringing to light both hidden genius and stupidity.

In the area of commerce, technologies have provided access to vast quantities of merchandise and merchants. No longer confined to dealing with local merchants, consumers can use the Web to find the lowest price in the world. Managing money and transferring funds has never been so easy. Nor has there ever been a time when private consumer information was handled by so many individuals in business and stored in so many databases. This creates more opportunities for identity theft and abuses of civil liberties.

Work environments have been greatly impacted by technologies as well. Many low-level jobs have been automated or outsourced to lower-cost workers in developing countries. Certain unskilled and uneducated workers are finding it increasingly difficult to find work in the United States and elsewhere, while developing countries such as India are experiencing an economic boom. The increased competition in the global market is placing pressure on businesses to innovate as never before. Never have a college education and computer skills been so highly valued.

Leisure activities have also been affected by technology over the past 25 years. More leisure activities are "plugged in," providing people with virtual worlds as their playgrounds. A third grader is more likely to be found designing virtual cities or battling aliens than playing on the backyard swing set. Consider the leisure activities that you enjoy and the role that technology plays in delivering those activities.

The power of technology to change individual lives is considerable. Its impact is magnified when you consider its uses in businesses, organizations, and governments. Competition in the marketplace is fierce, and technology is the primary tool for gaining an edge. Businesses are continuously redesigning themselves to take advantage of the latest technological advances. Technology supports an increasingly distributed workforce, where portions of product development may be accomplished in different parts of the world (see Figure 12.2). The goal is always to produce the most attractive product at the lowest possible cost.

FIGURE 12.2 • Telepresence

Through products like HP Halo, team members from around the world can virtually gather around a table using high-speed Internet connections and video links.

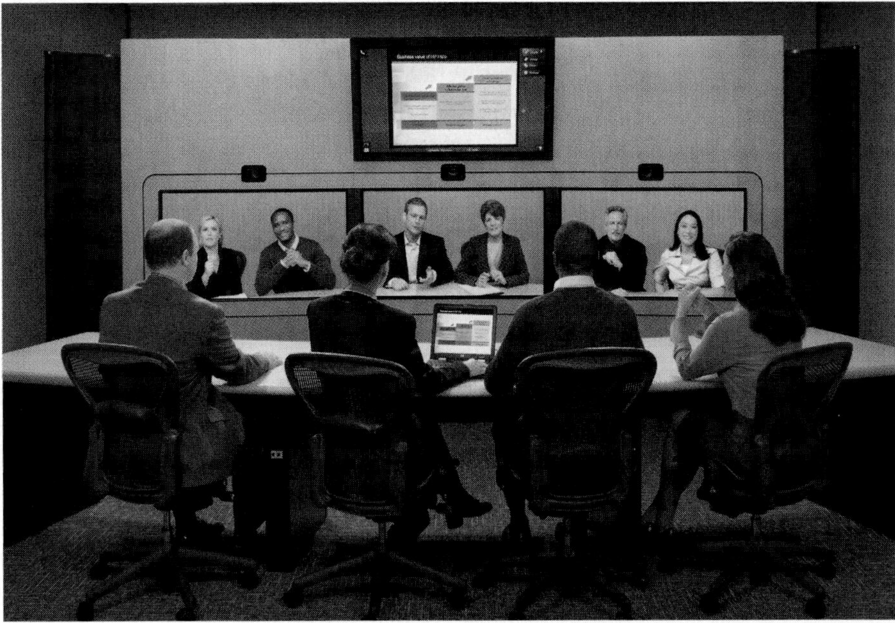

Most social change caused by the application of technologies has both benefits and costs. A student benefits from the ability to talk with a friend on a cell phone at the conclusion of class but may miss out on an opportunity to meet someone new sitting in a neighboring seat. Citizens benefit from the use of technologies in law enforcement by living in safer conditions but might pay a price in terms of personal privacy. Big businesses benefit from outsourcing labor at the expense of the job market at home. The benefits and costs range from personal to global. Balancing benefits against costs and determining which outweighs the other is highly personal and subjective. This chapter examines the ways that technology affects people's lives on many levels so that you can decide for yourself the benefits and costs of technology in your life.

LIVING ONLINE

As people spend increasing amounts of time engaged in virtual space rather than real space, changes occur in social structures and mechanisms. *Virtual space* may be loosely defined as an environment that exists in the mind rather than in physical space. People find virtual space in a daydream, in a book, in a movie, on a cell phone, on the Internet, or when participating in any activity that takes their minds and attentions away from their present physical surroundings. When absorbed in these activities, the here and now of the physical world can become overshadowed by involvement in virtual space. While books, movies, and daydreams have provided private virtual space for the imagination for decades, today's networking technologies have provided a platform for building virtual space that can be shared by many. Cell phones let you connect with others and, in a manner of speaking, leave the here and now. Other forms of electronic and Internet communications allow you to build virtual communities that foster relationships through electronic communications. The Internet opens an entire virtual world of information, people, and groups, in which you can literally lose yourself.

Computers and Community

On June 3, 2003, more than 100 people converged upon the ninth floor of Macy's New York City department store and gathered around a very expensive rug. When asked by sales assistants what they were doing, each individual answered that they lived together in a warehouse on the outskirts of town and were shopping for a rug. The group dispersed as quickly as it arrived. Later, over 200 people flooded the lobby of the New York Hyatt, applauded for 15 seconds, and then disappeared. In both cases, the reality of the matter was that most of the participants had never even met. These episodes marked the beginning of a new fad called flash mobs.

A *flash mob* is a group of people who assemble suddenly in a public place, do something unusual, and then disperse (see Figure 12.3). Flash mobs organize through cell phone text messaging and e-mail. Participants are given precise instructions on where to meet, how to act, and what to say if questioned. Since 2003, many flash mobs have appeared around the world, confused the general public, and disappeared. There have been numerous flash mob pranks in the UK and Europe, Asia, Latin America, and Australia. In India, a large group gathered in a shopping center, talked loudly about stock prices, danced for a few minutes, and dispersed. In Bucharest, Romania, a flash mob assembled to protest censorship in the news media. Flash mobs serve as an interesting example of the impact of digital technologies on the concept of community.

FIGURE 12.3 • Pillow fight flash mob

On a peaceful night, hundreds of people arrived seemingly out of nowhere to claim the street for a pillow fight.

Increasing amounts of correspondence between friends and acquaintances take place electronically through text messaging, cell phones, e-mail, and other Internet communications. Many of today's relationships are maintained more through electronic communications than face to face. People collaborate on projects, carry out complicated business transactions, meet, and even fall in love in virtual space without ever physically meeting. Communities are increasingly defined by online social networks like MySpace, Facebook, and Twitter, and less by those with whom physical space is shared.

Virtual communities and "anywhere, anytime" communications are also affecting traditional social mechanisms. The new cell phone generation is less concerned with making formal social plans and tends to be more spontaneous than previous generations. Meeting times and locations can change en route. The days of being stranded or stood up due to miscommunication are all but over: just pick up your phone and get an update.

The use of cell phones in public places sometimes offends traditional courtesy and etiquette. Table 12.1 lists some common dos and don'ts of cell phone etiquette. Bear in mind that notions of courtesy and etiquette are likely to change as digital technologies become even more important and invasive.

Meeting people has never been easier. Rather than finding friends through chance encounters, you can meet and get to know many individuals with similar interests through the Internet. The entire framework of the medium is designed to create connections between people. Social networking sites, blogs, and other Internet forums make it easy to find others with similar interests, while Internet communications make it quick and easy to meet and get to know friends of friends of friends. If you are looking for romance, you'll find no shortage of online services designed to find Mr. or Ms. Right.

TABLE 12.1 • Cell phone etiquette

Ten common courtesies show respect to those you speak to on the phone as well as those with whom you share physical space.

Topic	Courtesy tip
1. Safety	Do not dial your cell phone while driving or performing other dangerous tasks that require your full attention.
2. Volume	Speak softly, at a volume that cannot be overheard by others. Unlike traditional phones, cell phones do not allow you to hear the volume of your own voice on the line. People often speak louder than they need to on cell phones in an effort to be heard.
3. Proximity	Do not intrude on others' personal space; 10 feet (3 m) is the minimum distance that should be maintained between you and others while on the phone.
4. Content	Keep your business private. Typically, people do not wish to hear about the details of your life and find it offensive to have to listen to them. Others who may be interested in your private affairs should cause you concern.
5. Tone	Keep a civil and pleasant tone. Never lose your temper while on a cell phone in a public place; it does not reflect well on you.
6. Location	Know when to make and accept calls based on your strength of signal. Do not engage in important conversations in areas where the signal is weak. Losing a signal during a conversation can be construed as an insult to the person you phoned.
7. Timing	There is a time and place for cell phone conversations. Most people feel that restaurants, classrooms, concerts, churches, and other public places where personal space is tight are not among them. Turn off cell phone ringers in any such location.
8. Multitasking	Concentrate on one thing at a time; those you speak to on the phone appreciate your undivided attention, while those sharing your public space also deserve your undivided attention.
9. Courtesy	Do not interrupt a face-to-face conversation to take a cell phone call; make sure that your phone call does not inconvenience those around you.
10. Information	Inform those you call or who phone you that you are on a cell phone and where you are, so they can anticipate distractions or disconnections.

Health Issues: Keeping a Balance

Spending more time in virtual communities and in virtual space has its benefits and costs. The benefits have been emphasized throughout this book. There are a number of psychological and physical health concerns that can arise due to the amount of time people spend in contact with computers and other devices, and in virtual space. It should be noted that the health problems created by the use of technology pale in comparison to the health solutions that technology provides.

Physical Health Concerns. Working and living with computers and digital technologies can lead to potential physical health problems. As people increasingly use computers at work and at home, more people are suffering from computer-related health problems. Insurance claims relating to repetitive motion disorder, which can be caused by working with computer keyboards and other equipment, have increased greatly in recent years. *Repetitive stress injury (RSI)* is an injury such as tendinitis and tennis elbow, caused by a repetitive motion. The most common RSI for computer users is carpal tunnel syndrome. **Carpal tunnel syndrome (CTS)** is the aggravation of the pathway for nerves that travel through the wrist (the carpal tunnel), typically caused by long hours at the computer keyboard with wrists cocked and fingers typing. CTS can cause wrist pain, a feeling of tingling and numbness, and difficulty in grasping and holding objects. CTS can be difficult to correct; use of a wrist brace is typically prescribed, and sometimes surgery is needed. Some owners of smart phones who type a lot with their thumbs develop RSI in their thumbs, making it painful to type (see Figure 12.4). The injury is common enough to have its own name: "BlackBerry Thumb."

FIGURE 12.4 • Thumb typing RSI

Using thumbs for typing for long stretches of time can lead to a repetitive stress injury that makes it painful to use your thumbs.

Working long hours staring at a computer screen without proper light can cause a variety of vision problems. In some cases, your eyes get tired, itch, or even burn. In more severe cases, double or blurred vision can result, making it unpleasant to work and reducing your efficiency. In addition to problems with wrists and eyes, you can get a sore back, sore arms, and headaches from long hours working on a computer without adequate breaks.

Mental Health and Related Problems. In addition to physical health concerns, computer use can cause a variety of mental health issues and related problems.

The use of the Internet can be addictive. Some people spend most of their time connected to the Internet staring at the computer screen. When this behavior becomes compulsive, it can interfere with normal daily activities, including work, relationships, and other activities. Often, Internet addiction means that a person is isolated and doesn't interact with other people, unless they are also online. **Internet addiction** may exist if people are online for long periods of time, cannot control their online usage, jeopardize their career or family life from excessive Internet usage, and lie to family, friends, and coworkers about excessive Internet usage. Scientists studying Internet addiction categorize several different types: pornography, gambling, multiplayer online gaming, e-shopping, and social networking addictions.

The abundance of free pornography on the Web has caused some individuals to become addicted. It has been estimated that 12 percent of Internet content is pornography.[1] Viewing and sharing pornography in large quantities can alter an individual's perception of what is socially acceptable and normal. Also, in efforts to supply increasingly outlandish pornography, some have crossed the line into unhealthy and illegal practices. Many individuals from a variety of backgrounds have sought professional help in dealing with Internet-based pornography and sexual addictions.

Compulsive gambling is a problem for some people using the Internet. Compulsive gamblers find using the Internet much easier than driving to a gambling casino. Although Internet gambling is illegal in the United States, it is not illegal in other countries. As a result, Web sites have surfaced in foreign countries that permit gambling on the Internet and have combined to build a $20 billion market, one of the largest businesses on the Internet.[2] In 2006, President Bush signed the Unlawful Internet Gambling Enforcement Act, which makes it illegal for U.S. citizens to gamble on the Internet no matter where the online casino is located. This bill, however, has had little impact since it is difficult for law enforcement to know which online transactions are gambling related. Some Internet users become addicted to massively multiplayer online role-playing games (MMORPGs). Some gamers find the virtual worlds of online games more interesting and rewarding than real life and spend increasing amounts of time in virtual worlds (see Figure 12.5).[3] Others are addicted to online shopping and online social networks. While these activities are not unhealthy in reasonable quantity, spending more time online than offline can become problematic.

FIGURE 12.5 • Video game addiction

Obsessive gaming can create real-life problems.

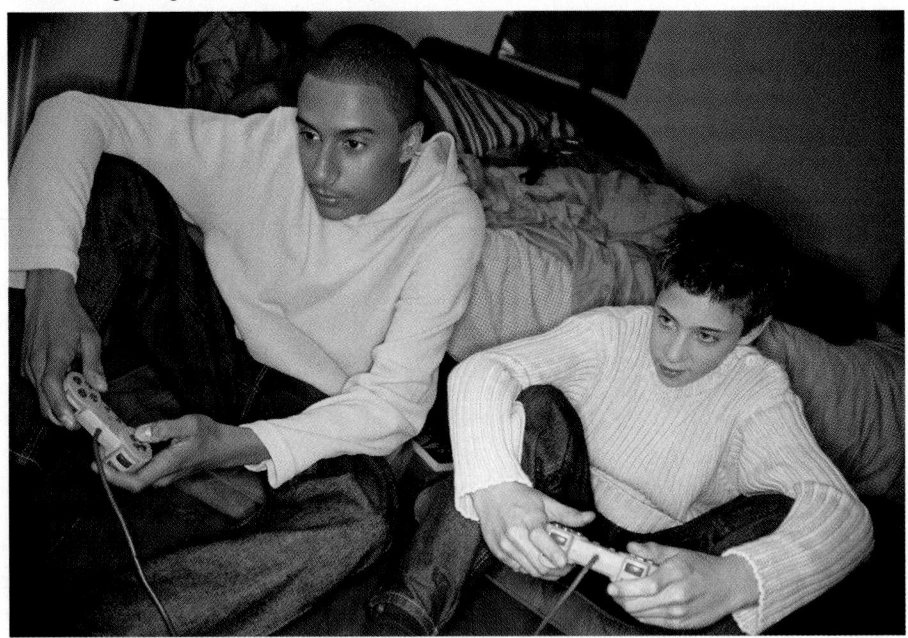

For some people, working with computers can cause occupational stress or information overload. Feelings of job insecurity, loss of control, incompetence, and demotion are just a few of the fears people might experience. These fears could become a serious problem for some employees. Some experts believe this fear might cause threatened workers to sabotage computer systems and equipment. If a manager determines that an employee has this type of fear, training and counseling can often help the employee and avoid potential problems.

Avoiding Health Problems. Many computer-related physical health problems are minor and are caused by a poorly designed work environment. The computer screen may be hard to read, with the problems of glare and poor contrast. Desks and chairs may be uncomfortable. Keyboards and computer screens may be fixed and difficult or impossible to move. The hazardous activities associated with these types of unfavorable conditions are collectively referred to as *work stressors*. Although these problems may not be of major concern to casual users of computer systems, continued stressors such as repetitive motion, awkward posture, and eyestrain can cause more serious and long-term injuries. If nothing else, these problems can limit productivity and performance.

The study of designing and positioning work environment and computer equipment in a healthy manner, called **ergonomics**, has suggested a number of approaches to reducing these health problems. The slope of the keyboard, the position and design of display screens, and the placement and design of computer tables and chairs have been carefully studied (see Figure 12.6). Flexibility is a major component of ergonomics and an important feature of computer devices. People of differing sizes and tastes require different positioning of equipment for best results. Some people, for example, want to have the keyboard in their laps; others prefer to place the keyboard on a solid table. The increased use of notebook PCs has led to new forms of ergonomic study. Notebooks are not designed for ergonomic comfort. When working for long stretches of time, it is useful to attach an exernal display. Some people prefer to attach an external mouse as well. Because of these individual differences, computer designers are attempting to develop systems that provide a great deal of flexibility.

FIGURE 12.6 • Ergonomics

People who use computers for long stretches of time should be mindful of good ergonomic practices.

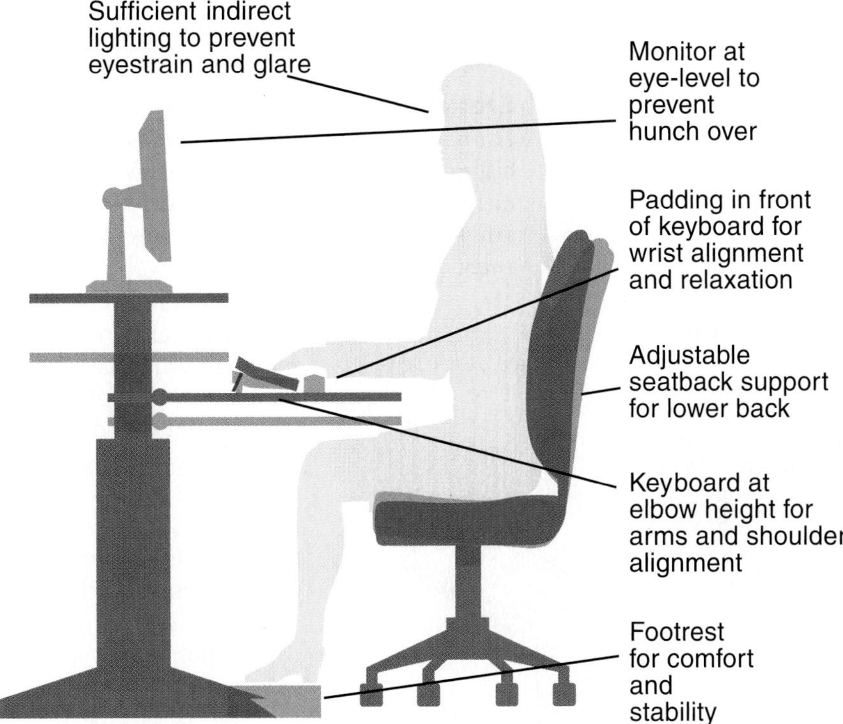

Many feel that the best way to avoid or recover from any computer-related health issue, physical or mental, is to live a balanced life. A balanced life includes technology time and time away from technology; time alone and time enjoying the company of others; time on the phone and time in face-to-face interaction; time indoors and time with nature. Some psychologists feel that many young people suffer from nature deficit disorder.[4] They believe that people tend to stay healthier when they stay in touch with nature. The more balance you provide in your life, the more balanced your mental and physical health and development will be. If you feel that you suffer from any of the above-mentioned physical or mental health problems, you should seek help from a physician or counselor as soon as possible before the condition worsens.

Green Computing

The serious reality of global warming has given many of us a heightened awareness of our natural environment and the dangers it faces. Individuals, organizations, and governments are making efforts to reduce our carbon footprint—the amount of greenhouse gasses we produce—and to manufacture and use computing resources in an environmentally conscientious manner.

The Intergovernmental Panel on Climate Change (*www.ipcc.ch*) has determined that the buildup of greenhouse gases resulting from human activity, such as the burning of fossil fuels and deforestation, is primarily responsible for recent trends in global warming. Digital technologies contribute to global warming through the large amounts of energy they require, causing power plants to generate increasing amounts of electricity and carbon emissions.

In an effort to improve the world, and perhaps their reputations in the process, tech companies and companies that use technology are going to great lengths to implement green computing initiatives. **Green computing** refers to the efforts of individuals, businesses, and governments to utilize practices both in the manufacturing and the use of digital technologies that are environmentally conscientious. Green computing initiatives generally fall into one of two categories: energy efficiency or ecology.

Energy Efficiency. The energy used in manufacturing and using computers can be reduced in many ways. Most companies that manufacture computers are beginning to utilize reusable energy sources for a portion of their energy requirements rather than traditional coal-burning energy plants. They are also streamlining the manufacturing processes themselves to be more efficient and less energy demanding (Figure 12.7).

FIGURE 12.7 • Data centers at sea

Google's patent request describes a data center powered and cooled by sea water.

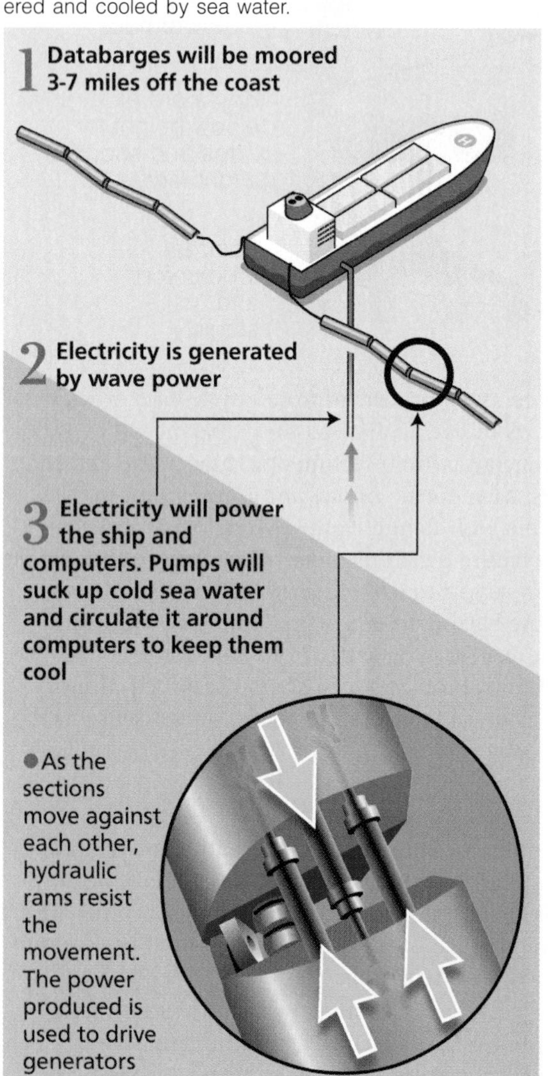

1 Databarges will be moored 3-7 miles off the coast
2 Electricity is generated by wave power
3 Electricity will power the ship and computers. Pumps will suck up cold sea water and circulate it around computers to keep them cool
As the sections move against each other, hydraulic rams resist the movement. The power produced is used to drive generators

Computing technologies are being invented that use less energy. For example, the light-emitting diodes (LEDs) used in some newer displays reduce energy use by 80 percent over standard LCD displays. Solid state drives (SSD) are poised to replace hard disk drives, providing faster data access and dramatic energy savings. One report states that if SSDs were used in the world's data centers, the savings would be enough to power an entire country.[5] Finally, processor manufacturers, such as Intel, are working hard to create more powerful processors that require less energy.

It's not only hardware that impacts a computer's power consumption; software also has a big impact. Software can be written in a manner that requires fewer processor cycles to carry out tasks. Operating systems are very influential on a computer's power consumption. Also, the energy-saving features in an operating system, used to power down a computer when not in use, are valuable in conserving energy.

The Energy Star program was created in 1992 by the U.S. Environmental Protection Agency in order to inspire energy conservation in electronics products. Computers that are Energy Star certified save 20–30 percent on energy consumption on average. The ENERGY STAR 5 requirements for computers went into effect July 1, 2009 and have the strictest energy requirements to date.

The power consumption of an individual PC is a drop in the bucket compared to that of corporate data centers. Some data centers have power requirements equal to that of medium-sized cities. Data centers require massive amounts of power for processing and especially for cooling. Most companies are working to reduce the energy requirements of their data centers by making more efficient use of servers. Many companies are replacing old power-wasting servers with new models designed to be more efficient. Virtual servers are being used as well, to maximize the amount of work that can be managed by a single server. Virtual servers allow a single physical server to behave like several servers.

Ecology. Computer technologies have not traditionally been very ecologically friendly. Dangerous compounds and chemicals are used in manufacturing some computing equipment, and recycling programs for digital electronics components have been far from robust.

The rapid growth in digital devices from computers to cell phones to digital cameras has many concerned about e-waste. **E-waste** refers to discarded digital electronics devices and components. The Environmental Protection Agency estimates that 400,000 tons of e-waste are sent to recycling services each year. Much of that waste contains dangerous contaminants such as lead, cadmium, beryllium, polyvinyl chloride (PVC), and brominated flame retardants (BFRs). There is a general concern about digital electronics being discarded at rates that will soon overfill our landfills. There is also a concern about recycling practices that are hazardous to those involved and the environment. Roughly 80 percent of recycled e-waste is shipped (oftentimes illegally) to developing areas of the world, such as Guiyu, China and Lagos, Nigeria. Working for pennies an hour, workers dismantle, burn, or give acid baths to circuit boards, wires, microprocessors, displays, and other components to salvage valuable metals such as copper and gold, at the cost of their health, and the health of their environment (Figure 12.8). Children are exposed to dioxins, soil is poisoned with lead, chromium, tin, and other heavy metals, and the water becomes undrinkable.

FIGURE 12.8 • E-waste mountains in Guiyu, China

Guiyu citizens have built their lives around salvaging every ounce of valuable metal from recycled digital electronics with disregard to serious health and environmental hazards.

Computer manufacturers are working hard to reduce the amount of dangerous contaminants in computing products, and implementing take-back programs to assist customers with recycling.

Table 12.2 provides some examples of green initiatives by companies that manufacture and use digital devices.

TABLE 12.2 • Sample green computing initiatives

Nokia	• Eliminated PVC, brominated and chlorinated compounds, and antimony trioxide from the manufacturing of new cell phones • Has comprehensive voluntary take-back (recycle) program in 84 countries • Reduced CO_2 emissions in manufacturing by 10 percent • Use of renewable energy sources for 50 percent of operations • Number 1 ranked tech company in Greenpeace's *Guide to Greener Electronics* in 2008 and 2009[6]
Apple's Mac Mini	• Eliminated BFRs and PVC from all components • Utilizes highly recyclable aluminum and polycarbonate in its tiny case • Reduced packaging material by 31 percent • Energy-efficient hardware and operating systems use as much as 45 percent less power when idle • Meets ENERGY STAR 5.0 requirements • Earned highest rating of EPEAT Gold[7]
Cell phone manufacturers	• Apple, LG, Motorola, NEC, Nokia, Qualcomm, RIM, Samsung, Sony Ericsson, and Texas Instruments agreed to use a standardized mobile phone charger in order to reduce e-waste and improve energy efficiency[8]
IBM	• Consolidated server use, reducing energy consumption by 6.1 percent, saving $32.3 million • Utilized renewable energy, reducing CO2 emissions by 1.6 percent • Reduced the use of dangerous perfluorocompounds in its semiconductor manufacturing by 30.4 percent • Recycled and reused 99.4 percent of e-waste[9]
Marriott	• Purchases Energy-Star-compliant equipment • Utilized EPEAT to purchase equipment from green manufacturers • Uses HP's technology take-back program for toner cartridges • Recycles e-waste through environmentally conscious recycling programs[10]

FREEDOM OF SPEECH

The First Amendment to the U.S. Constitution guarantees citizens the right to free speech. The Internet and Web have allowed people to communicate their views to a greater extent and with a broader reach than has ever before been possible, and many are taking full advantage of this freedom. There are Web sites, blogs, online communications, forums, and podcasts devoted to every conceivable topic and point of view. The Internet is used to espouse the views and beliefs of every religious and political group. Web sites may include points of view that many find offensive and even dangerous, such as Web sites that support or promote suicide or terrorism. This section examines the social implications of freedom of speech on the Internet and how varying societies deal with controlling what is expressed.

Challenging the Establishment and Traditional Institutions

The Internet has been grasped as a tool to empower those who have traditionally been without a public voice. Consider Web sites such as Complaints.com and the Rip-off Report sponsored by the Bad Business Bureau (*www.badbusinessbureau.com*). Customers who feel they have been ripped off by a business post complaints that act as warnings to others. This Web service stores the complaints registered to create a working history of a particular business and identify habitual bad business practices. Visitors can run searches to see all complaints against a particular business.

Bloggers are becoming an increasingly important component in journalism. Blogswarms—news stories that attract massive amounts of blogger attention—have been responsible for correcting errors made by mainstream news sources. For example, Dan Rather quit his job as news anchor for CBS after being criticized by bloggers for running a news story that was based on inaccurate information. CNN's chief news executive Eason Jordan was forced to resign under similar circumstances.

News-reporting bloggers are sometimes referred to as *citizen journalists*. Mainstream media—the traditional news organizations—discredit much of citizen journalism as the work of amateurs without credentials who operate without proper journalistic mechanisms such as reliable sources, proper quality control, and editing. Others consider citizen journalism a healthy democratic counterbalance to mainstream media, forcing more transparency and honesty in news reporting. A new form of journalism is emerging that blends the old and the new. Many popular Web sites that orginated as blogs are producing Internet-delivered news and information (see Figure 12.9) and are improving in journalistic integrity. Instead of depending on a few network television stations for news, you can now find dozens of video news sources online.

FIGURE 12.9 • Mainstream journalism vs. Internet journalism

New forms of journalism have sprung from Internet blogs such as BoingBoing, threatening traditional forms of journalism.

The proliferation of digital cameras and camera phones and the ability to easily transfer digital photos has led to many amateur photographers having their photos published. More and more amateur photos are gracing the front pages of newspapers, because a member of the public with a digital camera is often at the scene of a breaking story before the press. A passerby is often able to get shots that professionals can't, simply by being in the right place at the right time.

The role of the public in capturing and reporting news, called *consumer-generated media* (*CGM*) or *user-generated content* (*UGC*), has vastly increased over the past 10 years. Some are embracing CGM as the way of the future. "Current" is a television network that uses CGM (Figure 12.10). Viewers contribute a portion of the network's content over the Internet in two- to seven-minute *vlogs*—video logs—that are woven together into programs. Vlogs, called *pods* by the network, cover topics such as travel, current events, jobs, and technology. Shows can be viewed on television or on the Web site *www.current.tv*. Visitors to the Web site decide which of the submitted vlogs is broadcast. One of Current's programs is based on whatever is the most popular Google search of the day.

FIGURE 12.10 • Current TV

Current TV empowers the public to create television programming over the Internet to be broadcast on its cable TV network.

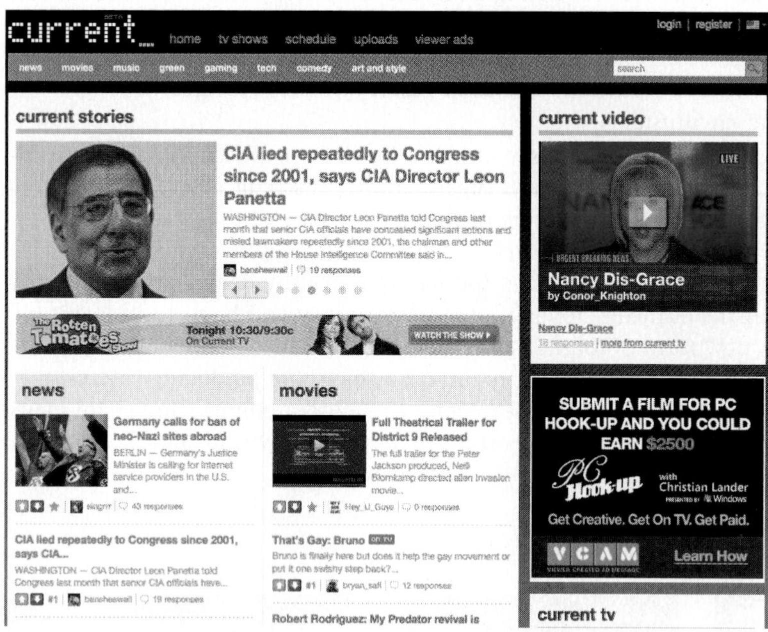

Laws and Censorship

While the First Amendment protects free speech in the United States, there is some restriction placed on speech. *Libel* is the deliberate act of defamation of character by making false statements about a person. Libel and direct, specific threats are not protected under the First Amendment. Consider the Wisconsin woman convicted of criminal libel for anonymously e-mailing a teacher's supervisor, claiming the teacher was involved in sexual misconduct. After the teacher was suspended and an investigation was performed, it was discovered that the accusations were lies, and the accuser was dating the teacher's ex-boyfriend. The lie cost the accuser a $10,000 fine.[11]

Of course, laws regarding speech vary from country to country. When a government or authority controls speech and other forms of expression, it is called **censorship**. Various forms of censorship exist around the world.

Political Freedom. Freedom of speech and Internet technologies are most threatening to oppressive governments whose citizens lack political and social freedom. Burma has banned the use of the Internet and the creation of Web pages deemed harmful to the government's policies. Vietnam uses Internet filtering technology to block anticommunist communications. The Chinese government channels all Internet traffic through a small number of monitored gateways in order to more easily control what is sent into and out of the country (Figure 12.11).

CYBERACTIVISTS BATTLE FOR FREEDOM

By the end of June 2009, the streets of Iran were quiet. The government had quelled protests and banned journalists from reporting on post-election dissent. But in cyberspace, hactivists around the world teamed up to defend freedom of speech. They launched attacks on state news agency and government sites. They wrote code to help Iranians access government-blocked sites. They helped create proxy sites to make it difficult for the government to discover the identity and location of those who chose to speak out and organize—online.

'Hacktivists' take up Iran fight as streets quiet
Shaya Tayefe Mohajer
Associated Press
June 27, 2009
http://news.yahoo.com/s/ap/20090627/ap_on_re_mi_ea/ml_iran_hack_backlash_1

FIGURE 12.11 • Internet censorship in China

Chinese police are stationed in public Internet cafés to monitor what information is accessed.

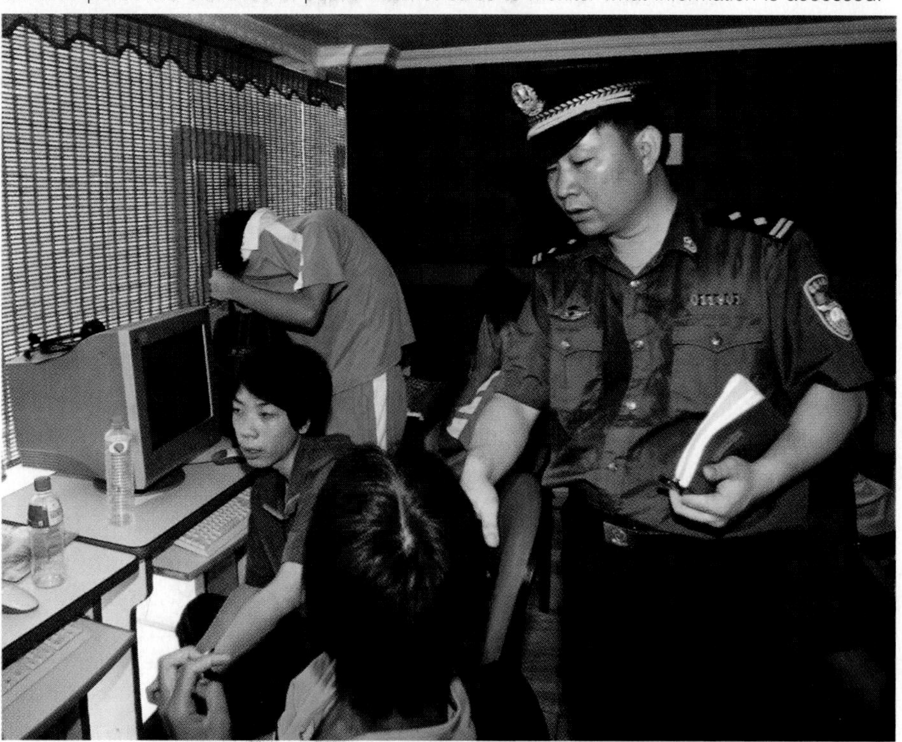

It is difficult to control the flow of information over the Internet. Individuals can set up their own satellite dishes to bypass government monitoring. For this reason, some governments make it illegal to have a satellite dish.

Pornography and Issues of Decency. Most countries support the Internet's ability to empower their citizens but struggle with issues regarding the perceived negative aspects. One major concern is keeping indecent content from minors. Because the Internet does not have a rating system like motion pictures and television, anyone who can connect to the Internet can theoretically view any content there. With increasing numbers of very young children making the Internet a part of their daily lives, it is natural for parents and governments to wish to protect them from viewing content that is inappropriate and dangerous.

Australia has a commonwealth law that holds Internet service providers and Internet content hosts responsible for deleting content from their servers that is deemed "objectionable" or "unsuitable for minors" on receipt of a take-down notice from the government regulator, the Australian Broadcasting Authority.[12] Some Australians feel that the law has failed to reduce the availability of pornography as it is still readily available from other countries.

The U.S. government has made similar attempts to eliminate indecent content from the Web with its 1996 Communications Decency Act. The law was struck down by the U.S. Supreme Court due to the government's inability to define terms such as *indecent, obscene,* and *lewd,* on which the law was based. One person's obscenity may be another person's work of art. During its brief enactment, the law had a serious effect on legitimate and useful Web sites that may have been considered indecent under the terms of the law. Family planning Web sites, medical Web sites, and art and literature Web sites pulled their content in fear of prosecution. For example, it was difficult to find information regarding breast cancer on the Web while the law was in effect.

Beijing Curbs Internet Access

The Chinese Health Ministry is tightening the belt around Internet access. In what it calls its antipornography campaign, the Ministry has required Google to develop technologies to keep links to pornography from coming up in Google searches from China. It has also required all new computers imported into China to include preinstalled Internet-filtering software. In order to keep a foothold in China's expanding economy, Google and U.S. PC manufacturers have scrambled to comply.

So, you might ask, what is wrong with China cracking down on pornography? Well, beyond the fact that pornography lies in the eye of the beholder, and a government agency might not be the best authority on defining what is decent and what is not, many might argue that there is nothing wrong with China's efforts in this regard. However, look a little deeper and you will find that it isn't only pornography that China's Health Ministry is looking to filter. Google is also filtering search results that contain information about antigovernment Chinese factions, government-banned spiritual movements, and information surrounding the 1989 killings in Tiananmen Square.

Many experts see China's antipornography campaign as "a harbinger of a broader crackdown on freedom and dissent." Requiring filtering software on all PCs and the most popular Web search engine leaves Chinese citizens with only news and information that its government finds acceptable. Perhaps, not-so-coincidentally, at the same time China cracked down on Internet pornography, it also imprisoned well-known online dissidents, and refused to renew licenses of lawyers representing prisoners in human rights cases.

Questions

1. Why is there concern about the Chinese government filtering pornography delivered over the Internet to its citizens?
2. Australia's government has similar rules about Internet pornography, and a filtering mechanism in place (*http://www.efa.org.au/Issues/Censor/cens1.html*). How does the situation differ in the two countries? Is either approach acceptable in your opinion?
3. Should the U.S. government be doing more to control online pornography in the U.S.?

Sources

1. *Bradsher, Keith, "Beijing Adds Curbs on Access to Internet,"* The New York Times, *June 25, 2009, http://www.nytimes.com/2009/06/26/world/asia/26china.html?ref=technology.*
2. *Fletcher, Owen, "China's Web Porn Arrests Include Tech-savvy Site Owners,"* PCWorld, *July 13, 2009, www.pcworld.com.*
3. *Cheng, Jacqui, "China/Google drama persists, sexual health sites soon barred,"* Ars Technica, June 25, 2009, *http://www.arstechnica.com/.*

The challenge of censorship is in keeping certain content (perhaps pornography) from a subset of the population (minors), without encroaching upon the freedom of adults. One solution is content-filtering software. **Content-filtering software** works with the Web browser to check each Web site for indecent materials (defined by the installer of the software) and allows only "decent" Web pages to be displayed (see Figure 12.12).

FIGURE 12.12 • Content-filtering software

Software such as Net Nanny allows parents and administrators to filter out objectionable Web content.

Child pornography goes beyond being indecent and is unlawful in most countries. Many criminals have gone to jail for producing, publishing, and viewing child pornography. British Telecommunications (BT) has applied content-filtering software to the entire British Internet infrastructure to block access to child pornography Web sites.

Content-filtering software is ideal for situations where one person is responsible for setting the rules and defining what is allowable and not. For example, at home, parents may use filtering to block what they consider inappropriate for their children. In the workplace, management may use such software to filter out non-business-related Web sites. Such software becomes problematic in larger democratic situations where definitions of decency may vary. For example, the 2000 Children's Internet Protection Act requires schools and libraries that receive federal funding for technology to implement content filtering. The law created a stir in the public library system when it was discovered that filters block access to many valuable nonpornographic Web sites such as these:

- Sites about Middlesex University in London and the University of Essex
- The court decision about the Communications Decency Act
- Student organizations at Carnegie Mellon University
- A Robert Frost poem that includes the phrase "My little horse must think it queer to stop without a farmhouse near."
- The home page of Yale University's Biology Department
- A map of Disney World
- The Heritage Foundation (a conservative think tank)

Libraries bound to their own Library Bill of Rights, which opposes restrictions based on age, were forced to find creative strategies to meet the letter of the law while providing the maximum amount of access to adults.

Dangerous Information. Some information is censored because it is deemed to be dangerous to the public. For example, it is illegal in the United States to make certain encryption technologies available to certain foreign governments. This is in an effort to keep potentially dangerous foreign governments from using U.S. technologies to decrypt national secrets.

After the shootings at Columbine High School in Littleton, Colorado, the U.S. Congress passed a law mandating 20 years in prison for anyone distributing bomb-making information with the intent to cause violence. Because explosives have numerous industrial uses, there remain many Web sites that contain bomb-making instructions. The Internet is not the only method for obtaining such information, however. The Encyclopedia Britannica includes bomb-making instructions, as does a booklet published by the U.S. Department of Agriculture. The same types of explosives used by farmers to remove tree stumps were used in the Oklahoma City bombing in which 168 people lost their lives. Once again, this law illustrates the difficulty of censoring information that is valuable for both legal and illegal purposes.

Censorship is a hot topic in the scientific research community as an increasing number of scientific publications are being censored on the grounds that they are a threat to national security. The National Academy of Sciences suspended the publication of an article in its journal that described the risk of terrorists poisoning the nation's milk supply using botulinum toxin. The U.S. Department of Health and Human Services warned that information in the article could be used by terrorists. The purpose of the article was to better inform those in the dairy industry of the threat so that they could take precautions. While suspending the publication may have kept that information out of the hands of terrorists, it also kept the information away from the people who could prevent the poisoning from taking place.

These examples illustrate the difficulty in censoring public speech. Censorship typically includes an infringement on an individual's rights in exchange for a perceived greater public good. Because concepts such as decency differ in definition from person to person, any government that attempts to define these terms for its citizens risks alienating a percentage of the population. Censorship often contradicts the basic tenets of societies that value freedom and individual rights. Censorship could backfire if stemming the flow of information impedes people's ability to design effective solutions.

PRIVACY ISSUES

EXPAND YOUR KNOWLEDGE

To learn more about protecting your privacy, go to www.cengage.com/computersconcepts/np/swt4. Click the link "Expand Your Knowledge" and then complete the lab entitled "Protecting Your Privacy Online."

Computer technology provides us with the ability to collect, maintain, process, and transfer much more information than has ever before been possible. This power has given rise to a seemingly endless number of public and private databases that include details about many individuals' private matters. Together, these databases could tell a person's life story in terms of daily activities, personal interests, and health. This aggregation of personal information, combined with surveillance technologies that include the increasing use of cameras in public places (see Figure 12.13), have given rise to legitimate concerns over the invasion of privacy in the digital era.

FIGURE 12.13 • Video surveillance

Increasing numbers of video cameras in public places can make you feel as though you are always being watched.

Privacy issues that concern most people include freedom from intrusion (the right to be left alone), freedom from surveillance, and control over the information collected and kept about one's self. The previous chapter touched on this last issue of protecting individuals from identity theft. The point was made that security often comes at the cost of some level of convenience and privacy. This section looks at the extent to which your privacy may be sacrificed in order to provide conveniences offered by the digital world and to increase your personal safety and national security.

Personal Information Privacy

Much of the information-gathering about individuals is done without their knowledge. This invisible information-gathering takes many forms. For example, a person might join a discount club at a local grocery store to enjoy special deals on products and to facilitate a faster checkout process. That person might not be aware that the club membership card also allows the store to digitally track his or her buying patterns. The customer may receive special mailings providing information on products that he or she typically buys. Some customers find this a valuable service, while others consider it an invasion of privacy.

The Internet acts as a supercharged tool for invisible information-gathering. Through the use of cookies, Web companies can accumulate immense amounts of information about customers visiting their Web sites. This type of *computer profiling* is the primary service provided by private information service companies such as ChoicePoint (see Figure 12.14). ChoicePoint collects and combines information from the three big credit bureaus; public records of numerous local, state, and federal government agencies; telephone records; liens; deeds; and other sources to develop detailed information about individuals, companies, and organizations. Over the years ChoicePoint has purchased many other large personal information services, increasing their database to include drug test records, physician backgrounds, insurance fraud information, and a host of other specialized pieces of valuable personal information. Businesses and organizations contract with ChoicePoint to provide information on specific individuals for a variety of uses.

FIGURE 12.14 • ChoicePoint information services

Using ChoicePoint's powerful search capabilities, businesses and government agencies can search over 10 billion records on individuals and businesses.

ChoicePoint has more information about U.S. citizens than the government. As a matter of fact, it has a multimillion-dollar contract with the Justice Department and the IRS. FBI agents consult information supplied by ChoicePoint when involved in criminal investigations.

Privacy and Government

The previous chapter presented some of the laws that govern the privacy of consumer and medical records for businesses and health-care companies. Government agencies in the United States and many other democratic countries are regulated far more stringently than businesses and professionals in health care when it comes to the privacy of confidential records.

The Privacy Act of 1974 is the primary law controlling what many government agencies can and cannot do with the information they hold. The primary tenets of the law include the rights of citizens to know what information certain government agencies store about them, and to exercise control over the accuracy of that information and how it is used. Other laws that control the U.S. government's handling of information are listed in Table 12.3.

TABLE 12.3 • U.S. federal privacy laws

Law	Explanation
Family Educational Rights and Privacy Act of 2003	Restricts the collection of data by federally funded schools
USA PATRIOT Act of 2002	Provides the government with the power to view the customer records of Internet service providers and telephone companies without a court order in cases of terrorist investigations
Computer Matching and Privacy Protection Act of 1988	Regulates cross-references of data between federal agencies
Tax Reform Act of 1979	Controls the collection and use of certain information collected by the IRS
Right to Financial Privacy Act of 1978	Restricts the government's access to certain financial records maintained by financial institutions
Freedom of Information Act of 1970	Gives citizens the right to view their own personal records maintained by federal agencies

SELF-DESTRUCTING IN THREE...TWO...ONE

The ever-increasing amount of personal and business data stored on centralized machines or virtual servers in the cloud is becoming increasingly difficult to secure. That's why University of Washington computer scientists developed Vanish, software that enables electronic messages to automatically self-destruct after a certain period of time. Vanish uses an encryption key that is scattered across a peer-to-peer file-sharing system and gradually "erodes" over time until the message disappears.

New Technology to Make Digital Data Self-Destruct
John Markoff
The New York Times
July 20, 2009
http://www.nytimes.com/2009/07/21/science/21crypto.html

In cases of war, governments can set aside some restrictions over privacy in an effort to capture or defeat the enemy. Such has been the case since the attacks of September 11, 2001, and the beginning of the war on terrorism. The USA PATRIOT Act gave the federal government certain authorizations regarding access to private information and the treatment of suspected terrorists. It was designed to "deter and punish terrorist acts in the United States and around the world, to enhance law enforcement investigatory tools, and for other purposes."[13] It includes measures to "enhance surveillance procedures."

The easing of government regulations in time of war makes many privacy advocates nervous. They fear that in a state of panic, the government may sacrifice civil liberties and rights. The Fourth Amendment to the U.S. Constitution was created to guarantee a right to privacy: "The right of the people to be secure in their persons, houses, papers, and effects, against unreasonable searches and seizures, shall not be violated, and no Warrants shall issue, but upon probable cause, supported by Oath or affirmation, and particularly describing the place to be searched, and the persons or things to be seized."

FIGURE 12.15 • Total Information Awareness

The logo of the Total Information Awareness office presents an intimidating image of an all-seeing eye watching the world.

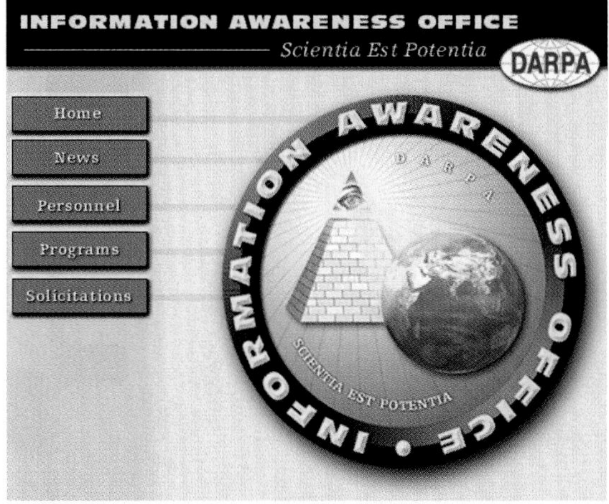

When DARPA's Information Awareness Office (Figure 12.15) proposed a new tracking information system called Total Information Awareness (TIA), privacy advocates complained loudly. Total Information Awareness was designed to capture the "information signature" of people so that the government could track potential terrorists and criminals. An information signature is any unique information stored about an individual, such as information about property, boats, address history, utility connections, bankruptcies, liens, and business filings, as well as a host of other information.[14] Data-mining techniques were to be applied to the database developed by the TIA system in order to "connect the dots" and detect potential terrorist activity.

What outraged privacy advocates was that this system could be used to track all citizens, not just those suspected of crimes. It was essentially a form of the "Big Brother" concept introduced by George Orwell in his book *1984* (see Figure 12.16). In this story, the government, Big Brother, watched over everyone in society by using information-gathering and video surveillance. In this Orwellian society, there was little in the way of crime, nor was there any privacy or freedom. It was like living in a prison. In the case of Total Information Awareness, the privacy advocates won out, the concept was dramatically rethought, and the name was changed from Total Information Awareness to Terrorism Information Awareness.

FIGURE 12.16 • Big Brother is watching you

Actor Edmond O'Brien portrays a citizen in the movie adaptation of George Orwell's book *1984*, which depicts a totalitarian society where government monitors citizens in all locations, even in their homes.

Following the fiasco with Total Information Awareness, in 2002 the U.S. government developed a system called Matrix (Multistate Anti-Terrorism Information Exchange). Matrix combined state records and data culled by Seisint, a database and information service provider, to give investigators fast access to information on crime and terrorism suspects. Seisint developed a scoring technology that evaluated each citizen and assigned a number used to rate that individual's "terrorist factor." Because the system included information on innocent people as well as known criminals, Matrix drew objections from liberal and conservative privacy groups. Many of the states participating in Matrix pulled out due to the controversy, and Matrix was abandoned at the federal level in 2005. However, a few states still use Matrix-like technologies on the state level for finding criminals.

Surveillance Technologies

The personal information stored in databases is just one of several privacy concerns. **Surveillance** is the close monitoring of behavior. Computer-controlled surveillance technologies combined with ubiquitous networks and powerful information-processing systems have made it possible to gather huge quantities of video, audio, and communications signals and process them to reveal personal information. While this is mostly done in an effort to curb crime and catch criminals, some people are concerned with the lack of oversight (see Figure 12.17). Who is monitoring those individuals doing the monitoring? The surveillance technologies that cause the most concern are wiretapping, video and audio surveillance, and certain uses of GPS and RFID.

FIGURE 12.17 • USA PATRIOT Act protest

Protestors fear that the USA PATRIOT Act gives government power at the expense of citizens' civil liberties.

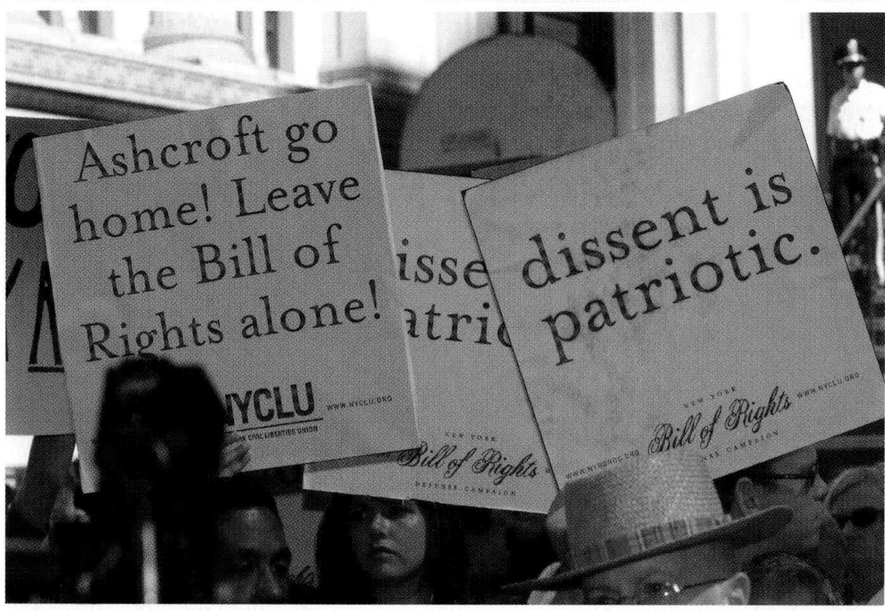

Wiretapping. Wiretapping has been around as long as there have been wires to tap, and now extends to wireless communications. With increased dependence on electronic communications, wiretapping has grown to be an important tool for law enforcement and a major concern for those interested in personal privacy. The act of wiretapping involves secretly listening in on conversations taking place over telecommunications networks, including telephone (wired and wireless), e-mail, instant messaging, VoIP, and other forms of Internet communications.

Federal laws governing wiretapping are generally the same for all forms of communication. The federal Wiretap Act, enacted in 1968 and expanded in 1986, sometimes referred to as Title III, sets procedures for court authorization of real-time surveillance of all kinds of electronic communications in criminal investigations. It normally requires a court order issued by a judge who must conclude, based on an affidavit submitted by the government, that there is probable cause to believe that a crime has been, is being, or is about to be committed. The Foreign Intelligence

STEP ASIDE BATMAN, HERE COMES GOOGLE

All around the world, Google cars drive through the streets of cities, towns, and villages taking photos to upload into the Google Street View mapping application. Enter an address and you can see a photo of houses, parks, vehicles, and even people on the street. To protect the privacy of individuals, Google blurs faces. But in March 2009, a teenager in the Netherlands recognized two figures in Street View—twin brothers who had mugged him six months earlier. Google, substantiating fears that its application could be used to spy on people, provided police with the original image, and the police identified and arrested the brothers.

Google Street View Solves Crime
Thomas Claburn
InformationWeek
June 19, 2009
http://www.informationweek.com/blog/main/archives/2009/06/google_street_v_2.html;jsessionid=F0VMDQZM2JNN4QSNDLPCKHSCJUNN2JVN?queryText=surveillance

Surveillance Act of 1978 allows wiretapping based on a finding of probable cause to believe that the target is a member of a foreign terrorist group or an agent of a foreign power. Both laws allow the government to carry out wiretaps without a court order in emergency situations involving risk of death or serious bodily injury and in national security cases.

With cooperation from Internet service providers, an FBI surveillance system called Carnivore has been used to monitor e-mail correspondence. The system has alarmed privacy advocates and some members of Congress because of the manner in which it surveys all e-mail on the system, not just e-mail of suspected criminals. Recently the FBI switched from Carnivore to its own proprietary system, of which little is known.

Wiretap laws govern the level to which colleges can snoop on student, staff, and faculty e-mail and electronic correspondence. Without a court order, a university cannot intercept the contents of electronic transmissions unless an exception applies.[15] Exceptions include the following:

- Situations where wiretapping is required to protect the university's rights and property
- Situations where an unauthorized person is using the network
- Monitoring network traffic for management purposes

Such laws do not regulate private business networks, however. Studies have found that most corporations with 1000 or more employees either employ or plan to hire workers to read outbound e-mail, due to growing concern over sensitive information leaving the enterprise through e-mail.

States also have wiretapping laws to control the use of wiretaps by government agencies. Some nonprofit groups have alleged that Google's Gmail service violates California's wiretapping laws. The problem is in the fact that Gmail provides context-sensitive advertising with each e-mail message it displays. Say, for instance, that a friend e-mailed you about his new Toyota Prius. Gmail might place a link to a Toyota dealership in the margin of the e-mail. Many Gmail users find this acceptable, if not useful. While Gmail users may agree to Gmail's "content extraction" system, those who send messages to Gmail users have not given their permission to have their e-mail scanned. Therefore, some feel that Gmail violates the privacy of those users.

FIGURE 12.18 • Operation Disruption

Chicago police control hundreds of cameras with microphones mounted on light posts citywide to focus on crime from squad cars or from a central operations center.

Video and Audio Surveillance. Increasingly, cities are turning to networked video surveillance to monitor their streets. Video cameras in public places are assisting in capturing criminals who may otherwise escape. For example, video surveillance cameras in London's King's Cross train station were used to identify suspects in the July 7, 2005, train bombings.

Perhaps the most advanced video surveillance system can be found in Chicago. The multimillion-dollar system dubbed Operation Disruption includes hundreds of street surveillance cameras in Chicago's most crime-ridden neighborhoods. The cameras include microphones that can detect gunshots, even when a silencer is being used. When a gunshot is detected, the camera is electronically triggered to swing around and focus in the direction of the shot. Cameras are perched in bulletproof boxes atop light poles (see Figure 12.18). Video from cameras is delivered wirelessly to squad cars and a central command center, where retired police officers monitor activity. The system has recently been upgraded to utilize artificial intelligence (AI) software from IBM that automates the process of recognizing suspicious behavior.[16] Chicago is not alone. Many other cities have installed or are planning to install similar surveillance technology.

Adding cameras to city streets doesn't necessarily reduce crime. The American Civil Liberties Union has released a report entitled "Under the Watchful Eye." The report cautions that video surveillance in California threatens the privacy of the citizens. The report states that 37 cities in California use video surveillance, 18 have significant surveillance, and 10 are considering expansive programs.[17] Even with all those cameras watching the streets, the report states that the cameras have had "next to zero impact on fighting crime." To make the situation even worse, California laws make it possible for anyone to access video surveillance tapes. Of course, this problem isn't confined to California. Most cities in developed countries are utilizing security cameras in public places. There has been a significant boost in the number of those cameras recently due to efforts to step up defenses against terrorism.

The increasing numbers of surveillance cameras used for crime detection and prevention by both cities and private businesses leave very few public spaces unmonitored in most cities. The recent addition of audio recording devices with cameras has some concerned about eavesdropping on private conversations. Once again, citizens are asking, "Who is monitoring the people doing the monitoring?"

High-resolution cameras attached to satellites and trained on the Earth are providing amazing new mapping technologies, as illustrated through satellite-mapping software (Figure 12.19). These same technologies are used by law enforcement to track criminals and by governments to spy on each other. Japan has launched 100 minisatellites designed to monitor natural disasters, traffic patterns, and other global events. Each satellite is the size of a school backpack and costs between $3 and $4 million.[18] China is in a push to launch 100 satellites by 2020. Thirty of the satellites will make up China's own GPS and the others are designed for a variety of other types of observation.[19]

FIGURE 12.19 • Satellite photos

Increasing numbers of high-resolution cameras are focused on Earth from satellites, capturing life on the planet, enemy movements, and well-known cities and monuments such as the Eiffel Tower shown here.

Video and audio digital technologies provide the tools for individuals to practice surveillance. Camera phones are now banned from some businesses, such as bars and health clubs, in order to provide privacy for patrons. Digital cameras are being used by unscrupulous photographers to capture others' private moments and post them on the Web.

Some cell phones can be used to bug a remote location. Left hidden in a room with the ringer turned off, the phone can be dialed up to listen in on nearby conversations. Some unscrupulous individuals have been known to use this trick to gain an advantage in negotiations. Leaving their cell phone on the conference table, they excuse themselves to use the restroom, and then listen to the conversation that takes place in their absence.

Video and audio technologies combine with networking technologies to provide the power of remote presence. As with most technology, such power can be used to the advantage of society or abused to invade an individual's privacy.

FIGURE 12.20 • RFID implants

RFID implants and tags have been considered for tracking prisoners around a prison, employees around secure facilities, and gradeschool students around schools.

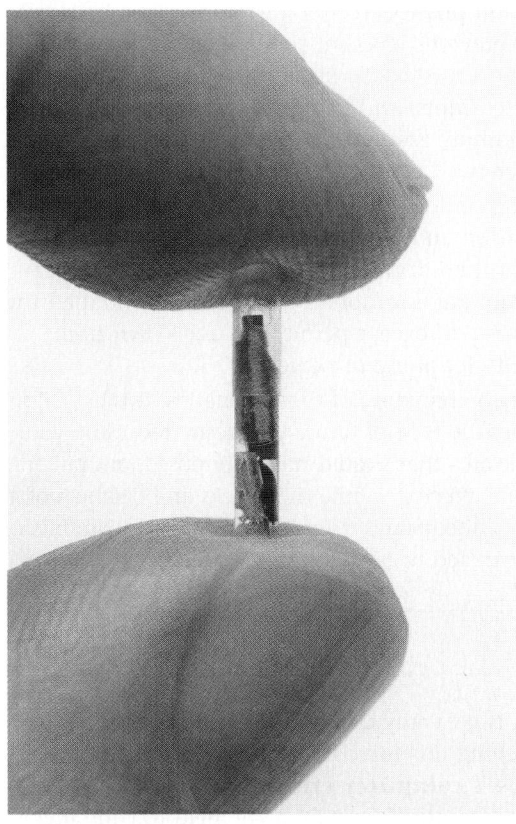

GPS and RFID Surveillance. Global Positioning System (GPS) and radio frequency identification (RFID) technologies are very useful, but they can also be used to invade privacy (Figure 12.20). Consider the case that was classified by police investigators as a true "twenty-first-century stalking." The case involved a man who taped a GPS tracking device to the undercarriage of his ex-girlfriend's car to monitor her movements. The man was picked up by police after his ex found him under her car changing the battery on the device. He's serving time in a California prison.

GPS devices are being considered by some states for tracking ex-cons. Some in law enforcement believe that GPS microchips should be implanted in former convicts on parole and probation, so that they can be monitored remotely. Florida, Missouri, Ohio, and Oklahoma all passed laws requiring lifetime GPS monitoring for some sex offenders, even if their sentences would normally have expired. Although this may prevent some ex-cons from backsliding, it also infringes on their privacy rights after they have paid their debt to society.

In a small community in California, parents of Brittan Elementary School students stood up for their children's rights to privacy when the school implemented a new student RFID inventory system. The grade school required seventh- and eighth-grade students to wear RFID badges that tracked their movement around campus. Some parents were outraged, fearing it would take away their children's privacy. The backlash from the failed policy has caused California lawmakers to push for a ban on such use of the technology throughout the state.

Malaysia, the United Kingdom, Japan, South Africa, and even some states in the United States have plans to tag cars with RFID-embedded license plates. Privacy advocates fear that monitoring vehicles electronically can lead to a database of information that can pinpoint the location of any vehicle at any time.

The combination of data mining, consumer and government databases, electronic eavesdropping, video and audio surveillance, satellite surveillance, and GPS and RFID location monitoring adds up to the possibility of serious invasion and abuse of basic privacy rights. Currently, at least in the United States, privacy laws and advocates keep government agencies in check over who can be monitored. A second deterrent to abuse of surveillance technologies by government is a lack of funding and personnel. It takes a considerable investment to monitor video from thousands of cameras. As technology improves and surveillance becomes increasingly automated, funding and personnel will become a nonissue—we may soon be able to entrust the monitoring of surveillance data to a powerful AI computer. Once again, this matter becomes a case of trust—can those monitoring society be trusted to use surveillance only in the best interest of the public without invading the privacy of law-abiding citizens?

Some experts believe that there are three scenarios regarding the relationship of technology, privacy, and society:

- Full privacy: Citizens should be assured of 100 percent privacy. They should have absolute control over what personal information is maintained in public and private databases, and there should be no surveillance of any kind for any purpose.
- Full trust: Citizens should trust governments to provide surveillance in a safe and secure manner that respects privacy rights.
- Full transparency: All surveillance and information should be accessible to every law-abiding citizen. Governments and law enforcement should not maintain exclusive control over surveillance. Citizens should have the ability to turn the cameras on authority to ensure that power is not being abused.

Some feel that it is too late for full privacy. Technology and its use have progressed past the point of regaining previous levels of privacy. If full privacy is not attainable, some feel it would be a mistake to fully trust those in power to manage privacy responsibly. Power corrupts, and being responsible for all private information of a population would imply absolute power. Such a scenario, some fear, could lead to an Orwellian society.

Full transparency is an intriguing notion. How would society change if everyone had equal access to all information and surveillance? No group would hold an advantage over others because of the information they controlled. Any person could view surveillance data from any location. Everyone would hold all the cards. While there would be little privacy, except perhaps in one's own home, there would also be little opportunity for abuse of power.

While fate will probably deal society a mixture of these scenarios, it is an important exercise for you to consider the type of future you desire regarding your personal rights to privacy. This is one area that should not be imposed, but rather decided thoughtfully by those that are affected. While the checks and balances of a democratic society may preserve the United States from becoming Orwellian, bits of freedom and privacy lost over time can add up to significantly affect people's lives.

ETHICS AND SOCIAL RESPONSIBILITY

The field of **ethics** deals with what is generally considered right or wrong. You can imagine how broad and far-reaching this topic is. This section focuses on ethical issues that deal with computer use—**computer ethics**. Most authorities on the subject define computer ethics differently. Many limit the field to computer professionals—those who develop and manage computer systems—and the ethical responsibilities that they shoulder. Rather than focus exclusively on the ethics of computer professionals, this section also discusses governmental computer ethics and personal computer ethics. All three areas involve ethical responsibility, and it is important and valuable to examine their different spheres of influence.

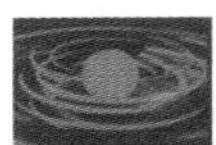

EXPAND YOUR KNOWLEDGE

To learn more about computer ethics, go to www.cengage.com/computerconcepts/np/swt4. Click the link "Expand Your Knowledge" and then complete the lab entitled "Computer Ethics."

Personal Ethical Considerations

Personal computer ethics involves the responsible use of computers outside of professional environments. Each person has his or her own sense of what is right and wrong regarding computer use and behavior. So, personal computer ethics is highly subjective except in issues of local, state, and federal law, where ethical issues are clearly defined. Using a computer to create destructive software such as viruses and worms, to steal credit card numbers, or to invade privacy with spyware is illegal, as you learned in Chapter 11. Copyright infringement (P2P file sharing) and plagiarism were covered in that chapter rather than here to emphasize the point that these are crimes and not just ethical points of view. Those who participate in such activities may pay the price in terms of jail time and fines (Figure 12.21).

FIGURE 12.21 • Pirate Bay founders

Gottfrid Svartholm and Fredrik Neij were fined $3.6 million and sentenced to a year in prison for running the world's most popular and mostly illegal file-sharing service.

However, when a significant portion of a population in a democratic society opposes a law, there arises substantial pressure on the government to change the law or change conditions in society. For example, the MP3 music standard and the availability of P2P file-sharing software and recordable CDs created a situation where many law-abiding individuals were actively violating copyright law. In this case, courts affirmed that owners of intellectual property deserve compensation. Through a lengthy process of court battles, technological solutions, and adjustments in the market, a slow but purposeful change is occurring in society's views on intellectual property and the manner in which music and other forms of intellectual property are distributed. It accommodates both the public's need for robust, easy, and inexpensive access and the creators' need to make a living.

This is how governance and law evolve—these institutions should not be rigid and unchanging but flexible and responsive to society. Good laws evaluate a situation from all perspectives and implement a solution that provides the greatest public good. If individuals are able to examine situations intelligently and unselfishly from all perspectives, then personal ethics would also serve the greatest public good.

Personal ethics regarding computer use typically combines what is legal, what is best for the public good, and what is best for the person in terms of mental and physical well-being. Fear of the law may keep an individual from hacking a computer network. A feeling of social responsibility may guide a computer user to treat others online with respect. A person's own sense of morality may keep that person from becoming involved with Web content that has a negative impact on one's self, friends and family, and community. Personal computer ethics requires examining one's own soul and weighing benefits against costs in terms of personal, social, and legal considerations.

Professional Ethical Considerations

Professional computer ethics involves the ethical issues faced by professionals in their use of computer systems as part of their jobs. This includes responsibilities toward customers, coworkers, employers, and all others with whom they interact and who are impacted in some way by their computer use on the job. It includes those who produce computers, software, and information systems as well as those who use them at work.

Law can also govern professional ethics. For example, legislation has been introduced in the U.S. Congress that would require businesses to secure sensitive data physically and technologically and to notify consumers nationwide when such data is compromised. The Children's Online Privacy Protection Act of 1998 prohibits businesses from collecting personal data online from children under the age of 13. The House Subcommittee on Communications, Technology and the Internet is crafting legislation to force Web sites and advertisers to implement online practices that respect users' privacy.[20] This illustrates how ethical behaviors are sometimes imposed upon a business by the government.

A number of organizations and associations go beyond what is required by law and establish their own codes of ethics. Codes of ethical conduct can foster ethical behavior in the organization and give confidence to people who interact with the organization, including clients and customers. Some organizations and associations that have developed a code of ethical conduct include the following:

- Computer Professionals for Social Responsibility (CPSR)
- Association of Information Technology Professionals (AITP)
- The Association for Computing Machinery (ACM)
- The Institute of Electrical and Electronics Engineers (IEEE)
- The British Computer Society (BCS)

The Code of Ethics used by the Association of Computing Machinery (ACM) is listed at *www.acm.org/constitution/code.html*. It includes statements such as "As an ACM member I will contribute to society and human well-being, be honest and trustworthy, respect the privacy of others, maintain professional competence," and many other ethical oaths. ACM membership consists of nearly

80,000 computing professionals from industry, academia, and government institutions around the world. Each of these individuals, regardless of his or her employer, is guided by these principles.

Governmental Ethical Considerations

Governments face many of the same ethical considerations as businesses in respect to their use of computers and information systems. Governments, however, have the added responsibility of guiding the influence of technology on their populations. They create laws that govern the use of technology so that citizens are protected from those who abuse others through the use of technology. Besides keeping information and people safe, government also has a responsibility to make sure that everyone has equal access to technology in order to enjoy the associated benefits.

FIGURE 12.22 • President Obama signs stimulus package into law

The stimulus package includes billions of dollars for extending high-speed Internet access to underserved areas of the country.

In Chapter 1, the *digital divide* was defined as the social and economic gap between those who have access to computers and the Internet and those who do not. This is an issue of access, and the difference in opportunities between the "haves" and "have-nots." Most agree that those without access to technology are seriously disenfranchised in today's digital world. The have-nots in this scenario may be unable to access technology due to physical disability, financial limitations, geographic isolation, or political or social repression. In developed countries, a higher-level divide has been identified based on the speed of an Internet connection. Those with access to high-speed Internet have services and opportunities not enjoyed by those with dial-up access (Figure 12.22). It should be noted that some cultures prefer to do without technology because of their religious or philosophical beliefs. For all but this last category of people, governments and nonprofit organizations can make, and have made, a big difference in broadening access to technology.

The term *digital divide* is used to label the study of technological imbalances among many social groups. There are digital divides based on sex, ethnicity, race, age, income, location, and disability. Any group that is not provided equal opportunities in computer use and access can refer to their disadvantage in relation to the rest of the world as a digital divide. This section focuses on digital divides for the disabled and those with socioeconomic disadvantages.

Accessible Computing. There is a growing body of laws and policies in many countries that address accessibility of information and communications technology (ICT), including the Internet and the Web. Laws differ from country to country. Some treat access to ICT as a human or civil right; others control only the purchase of

The Broadband Divide

For all its innovation and wealth, the United States does not rank well globally in providing high-speed Internet to its citizens. According to the Organization for Economic Cooperation and Development (*www.oecd.org*), and the International Telecommunications Union (*www.itu.int*), the United States isn't even in the top 10 in broadband Internet penetration. One of President Obama's campaign promises was to bring high-speed Internet access to underserved and rural areas of the country, and elevate broadband Internet penetration in the United States.

In the president's $787 billion economic stimulus package, $7.2 billion was dedicated to bolstering Internet access. The investment drew criticism from some who felt that taxpayer dollars should not fund Internet access for those who decide to live away from urban areas. The cost of building out broadband Internet to cover small towns in the wilderness is huge. The price per individual is hundreds of times higher for rural residents than for urban residents. Some urban residents don't feel they should have to foot the bill.

Others argue that broadband Internet access has become a necessity that no U.S. citizen should have to live without. Just as the United States decided years ago to extend power and phone lines to rural America, it is argued, now it is time to extend broadband Internet.

Like it or not, billions of dollars are being invested in bringing broadband to every U.S. home. Underserved areas are receiving the bulk of the dollars. Underserved is defined as areas where fewer than half of the residents are wired for broadband. Wireless long-distance technologies, such as Wi-MAX, are likely to play a big role. Building infrastructure, however, is only one component in expanding broadband use, and not necessarily the most important. A 2008 Pew study revealed that more common reasons for people not using broadband were lack of interest, cost or difficulty of using it, or the lack of a PC.

Questions

1. Why do some people think that it is a waste of money to provide broadband Internet to rural America? Do you agree or disagree? Why?
2. What types of telecommunications technologies are likely to be the most useful in covering large sparsely populated regions? Why?
3. Besides building out the country's telecommunications infrastructure, what other measures would you recommend for empowering more people with the benefits of high-speed Internet?

Sources

1. *Meckler, Laura, "Obama Signs Stimulus Into Law,"* The Wall Street Journal, *February 18, 2009, http://online.wsj.com.*
2. *Berkes, Howard, "Stimulus Stirs Debate Over Rural Broadband Access,"* National Public Radio, *February 16, 2009, www.npr.org.*
3. *Gabriel, Caroline, "Criteria for US broadband stimulus funds released,"* Rethink Wireless, *July 2, 2009, http://www.rethink-wireless.com/.*

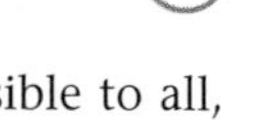

ICT by government, ensuring that government-controlled ICT is accessible to all, including the disabled; others specify that ICT sold in a given market must be accessible.

Section 255 of the U.S. Telecommunications Act of 1996 requires telecommunications manufacturers and service providers to make their products and services accessible to people with disabilities, if readily achievable. The World Wide Web Consortium (W3C) has developed Web Content Accessibility Guidelines for businesses and organizations to use in making their Web content accessible to users with disabilities, such as those who are unable to see, hear, or move.

The U.S. Department of Education has developed "Requirements for Accessible Software Design" in order to ensure that all software used in schools is accessible to all students, faculty, and staff. The Americans with Disabilities Act of 1990 requires businesses to provide equal access to individuals with disabilities, including Web content and services. Many countries have instituted similar laws and considerations for the disabled.[21]

In addition to the accessibility features built into popular operating systems, there are numerous software and hardware tools available to assist the disabled in using PCs (see Figure 12.23). Individuals may use screen-enlargement software to make computer screens easier to read and use. Screen-reader software such as JAWS allows blind users to interact with the computer by using text-to-speech technology to read whatever words are displayed on the screen. The user manipulates the software using predefined hotkeys, or shortcut keys. Some phone companies offer a service that uses a webcam attached to a deaf person's computer. When the person makes a call and uses sign language to communicate, an operator translates the hand signals to a hearing person at the other end of the line.

FIGURE 12.23 • Stephen Hawking

Computer systems can be liberating to great minds in disabled bodies or, if designed poorly, they can deny the disabled access to valuable information and services.

Accessibility issues extend beyond PCs to all types of digital devices. The mobile computing revolution has further complicated life for the disabled with tiny devices that are difficult to manipulate. The use of touchscreens as the primary interface, such as on the iPhone, eliminates tactile feedback that blind

FIGURE 12.24 • Jitterbug phone

The Jitterbug phone uses an uncomplicated design with large buttons and display characters. These features have proven accessible to older and visually-impaired users, as well as any user seeking a simple, straightforward cell phone.

individuals depend on. Some companies are designing cell phones to accommodate users with unique needs (Figure 12.24).

Socioeconomic Digital Divides. The economic digital divide in the United States, although of significant concern, has been shrinking since the turn of the millennium. The number of Internet users in the low-income range (earning less than $25,000/year) soared, making them the fastest-growing segment of Internet users. According to a U.S. Department of Commerce (USDC) study, more than half of the nation is now online, with two million new Internet users per month. Efforts to bring computers and Internet access to all public schools under the No Child Left Behind Act of 2001 have significantly narrowed the digital divide in computer usage rates between children from high- and low-income families.

Another contribution that is narrowing the digital divide is provided by public libraries. A study conducted by researchers at Florida State University found that nearly every library in the United States (98.9 percent) offers free public Internet access. Such service provides Internet access to citizens without the financial means to purchase their own computers. The study also found that a significant number of libraries offer wireless Internet access allowing individuals to connect using their own notebook PC, freeing up more desktop PCs for others who don't own a computer.

The *global* digital divide provides a greater social and ethical challenge. The World Economic Forum Web site (*www.weforum.org*) states that industrialized countries, with only 15 percent of the world's population, are home to 88 percent of all Internet users. Finland alone has more Internet users than the whole of Latin America. It has been estimated that fewer than 10 percent of the world's population has basic Internet access.

Computer engineers are working on new technologies that can bring computers and the Internet to those who cannot afford them or are in remote locations. A group of not-for-profit developers, called Ndiyo (Swahili for *yes*), has developed an ultrathin client system, which it says could make computing available to billions more people across the planet.[22]

An international consortium, including Indian and American companies as well as the World Bank, is building thousands of rural Internet centers in India. Each center connects to the Internet by either land lines or satellite links, and includes 5 to 10 inexpensive, thin client PCs to provide access to government, banking, and education services in isolated villages.

If humans are to utilize the Internet to build a global community, it is clear that the more affluent "neighborhoods" in this community cannot ignore the needs of the less fortunate. Those seeking to assist developing nations believe that societies must move from "divide" to "include" as the central organizing principle of their analysis and actions. Passing out PCs and providing Internet access is the first step, providing education is the next step, and inclusion in the information economy is an important last step.

FIGURE 12.25 • The digital divide

Urban poverty in Brazil provides a testbed for digital divide solutions developed by the World Economic Forum.

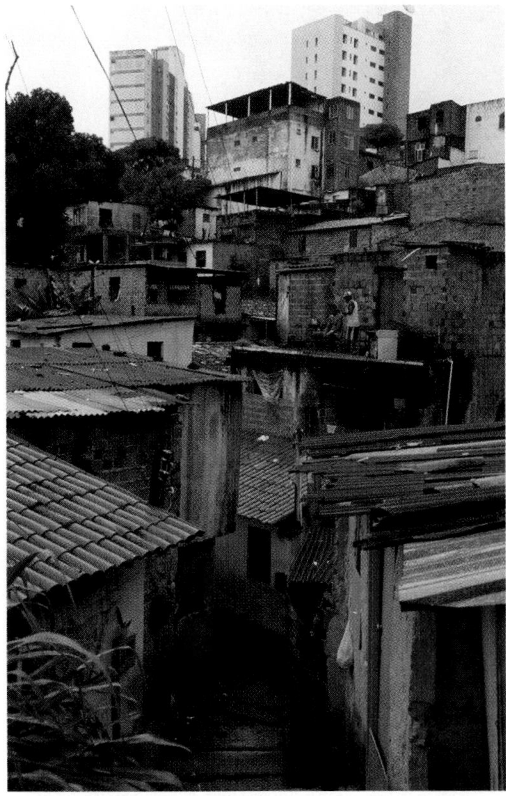

The World Economic Forum is working to provide all required components to bring developing nations into the digital fold. In 2004, the World Economic Forum launched the IT Access for Everyone (ITAFE) initiative to develop new models of collaboration to accelerate digital access and inclusion.[23] Brazil was selected as a pilot country for prototype solutions to be developed and tested (see Figure 12.25).

Bridging global digital divides requires extensive commitment and organization. Many feel that it is an important investment worth the expense and effort. Although the information and communication technology revolution offers genuine potential, if humans do not take a global perspective, there is a risk that a significant portion of the world will lose out. As technology reaches out to the world with fiber-optic, wireless, and high-speed connections, the rest of the world must be able to respond and participate. The Internet has created a seemingly smaller world and in so doing calls attention to social and economic problems. It is up to the more developed nations to recognize these problems and find solutions to help eliminate them. However, if countries adopt a self-serving, opportunistic approach to technology, then both the digital divide and global unrest will grow.

GLOBALIZATION

Globalization refers to changes in societies and the world economy resulting from dramatically increased international trade and cultural exchange. The largest contributors to globalization are computers, a global telecommunications infrastructure, and the Internet. High-speed fiber-optic global networks make it possible to communicate with, befriend, and collaborate with individuals around the globe as if they were sitting across the table from you. Breaking the traditional barriers of time and space has created a global community and economy (see Figure 12.26).

The technology bubble of the 1990s provided funding for installing transcontinental fiber-optic cables to connect the world in high-speed networks. The bursting of that bubble in the late 1990s dramatically reduced the price for using those connections because there was a huge supply of global bandwidth and a relative lack of demand. Early pioneers of globalization saw business opportunities in these global connections—specifically in the area of outsourcing.

FIGURE 12.26 • Starbucks in China's Forbidden City

The Starbucks in China's Forbidden City surrounding the Imperial Palace in Beijing is startling evidence of globalization.

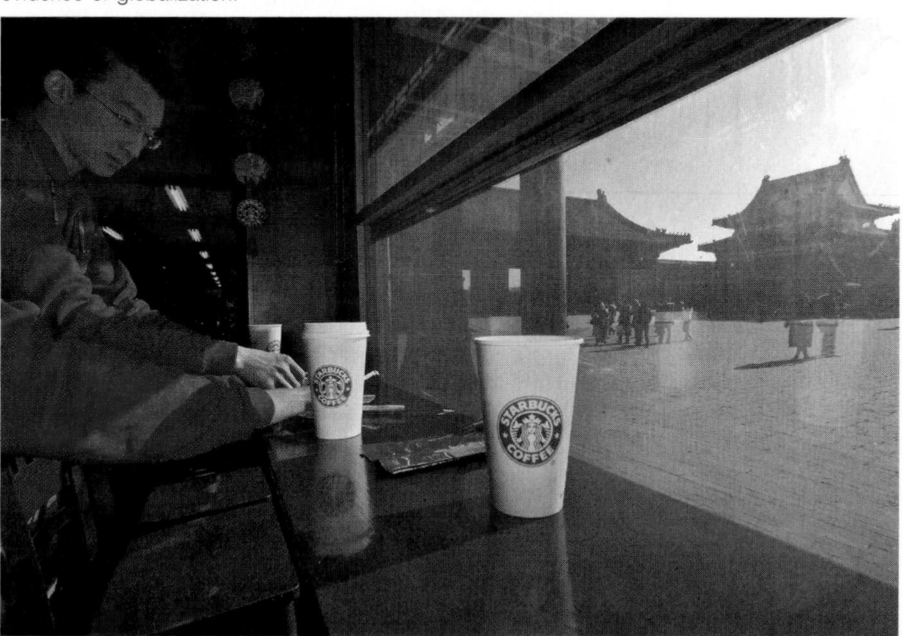

Outsourcing

Outsourcing was defined in Chapter 10 as a business's use of an outside company to take over portions of its workload. Have you heard of the Y2K bug? The Y2K bug was the problem faced at the end of the 20th century due to computer systems using only two digits to represent years. When the year switched from 1999 to the year 2000 (Y2K), most computer systems would assume that they had gone back to year zero (00). As a consequence of this error, many anticipated that electronic systems would fail in every industry, including vital areas such as banking, medical equipment, manufacturing, and transportation. Because there were not enough computer programmers available to prepare for Y2K, many companies outsourced their Y2K problems to India. When midnight of December 31, 1999, passed without any significant problems, many thought that the entire Y2K scare was all hype. It is more probable that the programmers in India were responsible for saving the day.

Indian programmers earned the respect of many large U.S. corporations, as well as corporations in other developed nations, through their participation in Y2K and other projects. Because Indian programmers worked for pennies on the dollar compared to workers in the United States and other developed nations, it wasn't long before most major companies called upon Indian programmers for many routine programming jobs. Communications lines between the United States and India became busy with IT business as teams in the two countries collaborated. Software to manage distributed project components became an urgent need, and software companies responded with sophisticated workflow packages. Workflow software empowered project managers to stay in touch with team members around the world and manage multiple project modules in simultaneous development. Team members dispersed around the world could communicate in real time through text, voice, or video, and could pass around project files as though they were sharing a conference table.

Bangalore has become known as the Silicon Valley of India. Many technology companies such as Microsoft, IBM, Texas Instruments, HP, GE, and others have built large corporate offices there (see Figure 12.27). Any service that can be digitized and handled by the Indian workforce is being outsourced. Call center operations, U.S. tax returns, medical imaging analysis, news reporting, publishing, you name it—India can do it cheaper than it can be done in developed countries. Although much of the work being outsourced is basic, low-skill services, as Indian education levels rise, higher levels of work are being outsourced. For example, Microsoft recently opened a major research facility in Bangalore.

FIGURE 12.27 • Technology companies in Bangalore

Many U.S. corporations have set up shop in Bangalore, the "Silicon Valley" of India.

Although India is the biggest destination of outsourced services, Russia, the Philippines, Ireland, Israel, China, and other countries provide outsourced services. In fact, most nations, including the United States, provide outsourced services. The difference is in the type of services being offered. The United States, with its advanced technology skills, provides many services and products whose quality and price cannot be matched elsewhere.

If you are starting to see the big picture of nations trading services and competing with each other in price and quality on a global scale, you are beginning to understand globalization. Enlarging the marketplace from local to global can have a profound effect on national and international economics and development. For example, outsourcing low-end tech jobs to India has provided a boom in India's economy, while thousands of U.S. workers who used to do the work being outsourced have been laid off. The prosperity in India increases the demand for U.S. products in India, which in turn provides growth in some U.S. industries and the need to hire more labor. India's population is more than three times larger than that of the United States, and presents a growing customer base for U.S. products as increasing numbers of Indians rise above poverty. In the United States, there is a general shift in employment from low-skill labor to higher-skill labor and pressure on U.S. companies to be creative innovators in order to remain leaders in the global economy.

Offshoring

Offshoring is somewhat different than outsourcing. With outsourcing, a portion of a work process is hired out. **Offshoring** is a business practice that relocates an entire production line to another location, typically in another country, in order to enjoy cheaper labor, lower taxes, and other forms of lower overhead. If Bangalore, India, is the current global center of outsourcing, then Beijing, China, is the global center of offshoring. At the end of 2001 when China joined the World Trade Organization and agreed to follow international trade laws, it opened a floodgate for trade and innovation. Corporations around the world sought to take advantage of China's large population, cheap labor, and high-quality production to save in manufacturing costs (see Figure 12.28). Textiles, furniture, consumer electronics, and a host of other products are manufactured for global distribution in China for a fraction of the cost of manufacturing in more developed countries.

FIGURE 12.28 • Offshore manufacturing in China

The abundant Chinese workforce eager to work for pennies on American dollars provides a low-cost manufacturing alternative for corporations striving to provide low prices to customers.

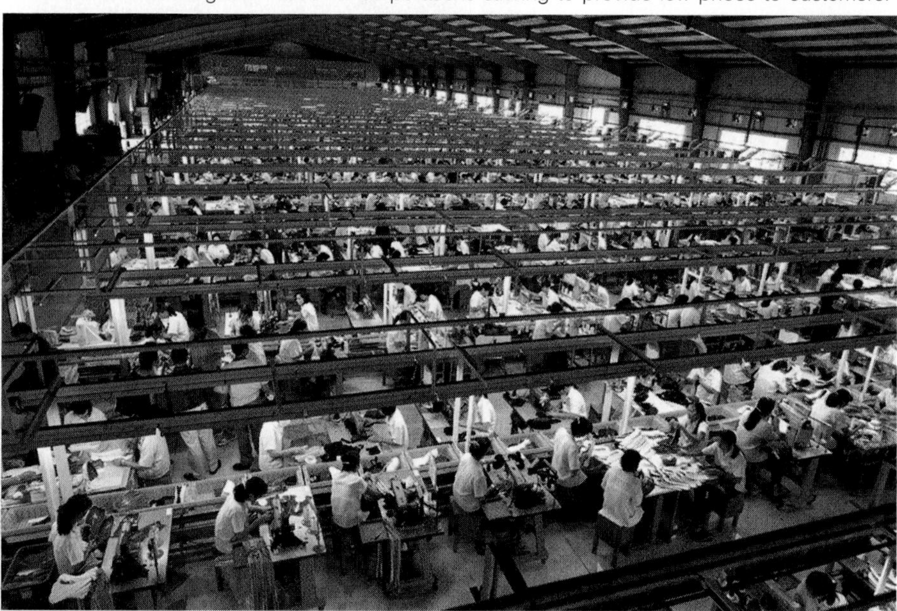

Companies that take advantage of the cost savings achieved by manufacturing in China and other low-cost manufacturing centers in Eastern Europe and elsewhere in the developing world gain a considerable advantage over competitors that don't. Many business consultants recommend that U.S. companies offshore labor-intensive operations in order to stay competitive. Businesses in other developed nations are following suit. As with outsourcing, offshoring has caused concerns for the labor markets in developed countries, especially in the United States. But as with outsourcing, offshoring is predominantly used for low-skill, labor-intensive manufacturing. Higher-level manufacturing still takes place in the United States. For example, General Motors may use some parts manufactured in China in vehicles assembled in Detroit.

As with India, a growing and prosperous China means increasing demand for U.S. products. China's population is more than four times that of the United States, and presents a growing customer base for U.S. products. Many U.S. companies have opened branches in China in order to have first crack at the huge market that is developing there. The United States remains the world's largest manufacturer, leading the world in aerospace, pharmaceuticals, automobiles, and other high-tech industries. Through globalization, the field of competition has broadened significantly. As with outsourcing, offshoring is forcing U.S. businesses to stay innovative and competitive.

Business Challenges in Globalization

There are a number of alternatives for how organizations participate in the global marketplace, depending on where the organization's operations are located and how they are managed. Table 12.4 summarizes these approaches.

TABLE 12.4 • Globalization approaches

Multinational and transnational organizations may enjoy financial benefits by moving some operations to other countries, but they also face significant challenges.

Globalization approach	Management of operations	Location of operations
Importer/exporter	In the home country	In the home country
Multinational	In the home country	In other countries
Transnational	In other countries	In other countries

With the benefits of outsourcing and offshoring come substantial challenges:

- Culture: Countries and regional areas have their own cultures and customs that can have a significant impact on individuals and organizations involved in global trade.
- Language: Language differences are another challenge. In some cases, it is difficult to translate exact meanings from one language to another. An exact translation of an advertising slogan, for example, might have a totally different meaning or even be offensive or disgusting to people in other countries. For example, Kentucky Fried Chicken's old slogan "finger lickin' good" translated into Chinese as "eat your fingers off." The Chevy Nova didn't sell too well in South America because "no va" means "it won't go" in Spanish.[24]
- Time and distance: Time and distance issues can be difficult to overcome for individuals and organizations involved with global trade in remote locations. In other cases, it can be an advantage. For example, outsourcing to India allows a company to work 24 hours a day because it is day in India when it is night in the United States.
- Infrastructure: People and organizations operating in developed countries expect an excellent infrastructure. In some countries, electricity may fluctuate in voltage, damaging machines and computers, or may be off for large periods of the day. Water may be dirty, and phone and Internet service might be problematic.
- Currency: The value of different currencies can vary significantly over time. Sometimes currencies can dramatically fluctuate in a few days or less.

- State, regional, and national laws: Every state, region, and country has a set of laws that must be obeyed by individuals and organizations operating in the country. These laws can deal with a variety of issues, including trade secrets, patents, copyrights, protection of personal data, protection of financial data, privacy, and much more.

Governments can be very helpful in encouraging global trade by implementing trade agreements with other nations. The North American Free Trade Agreement (NAFTA) and the Central America Free Trade Agreement (CAFTA) are examples. The overall objective of NAFTA is to eliminate trade barriers and to facilitate the movement of goods and services between Canada, the United States, and Mexico.[25] It also attempts to protect and enforce intellectual property rights. CAFTA extends the same free trade agreements between the United States and various countries in Central America (see Figure 12.29).[26]

FIGURE 12.29 • The European Council

The Council consists of European heads of state or government who define the general guidelines of the European Union to promote peace and encourage free trade.

The European Union (EU) is another example of countries with an international trade agreement.[27] The EU is a collection of mostly European countries that have joined together for peace and prosperity. The idea of the EU started in the early 1950s when several European countries signed a trade agreement involving coal and steel. In 1992, a far-reaching treaty formed the EU with a handful of countries. Today, the countries in the EU include Austria, Belgium, Denmark, Finland, France, Germany, Greece, Ireland, Italy, Spain, the United Kingdom, and many other countries. Most of the countries in the EU support the euro, a universal currency that simplifies the purchase and sale of products and services. Like other trade agreements, a primary purpose of the EU was to eliminate trade barriers and obstacles.

CONCLUSION

Throughout this book, you have seen how technology assists people to achieve their goals and succeed in life. The positive effects of technology on society can be huge. They include finding cures for deadly diseases, eroding the power of totalitarian governments and dictators, developing alternate environmentally friendly energy sources (see Figure 12.30), and reducing dependence on coal and oil, providing opportunities for developing countries and flattening global economics to spread wealth more evenly, providing people with more engaging and challenging professions, and in general improving the overall quality of life on Earth. There is little doubt that technology can be harnessed to improve life.

FIGURE 12.30 • Arklow Bank offshore wind power facility, Ireland

Positive uses of technology include GE's 30-story-high wind turbines, seven of which power 16,000 households across Ireland.

These last two chapters have focused on some of the challenges of living with digital technology. The negative effects of technology on society can be significant. Those who wish to oppress and benefit at the expense of others have found a powerful tool in technology. Criminals steal information and identities and cash them in for illegal gains; intellectual property is devalued, copied, and freely distributed at the expense of the creative minds that produced it; scam artists pilfer money from online victims; online vandals corrupt and destroy information systems for the pleasure of it; hate groups, terrorist organizations, and extremists of all kinds use the Web to further their causes and recruit new members (Figure 12.31); and governments could use surveillance and information systems to establish totalitarian rule and a police state that dissolves civil liberties.

FIGURE 12.31 • Hate group recruitment

The Web provides a platform for groups of all persuasions, including those that promote hate.

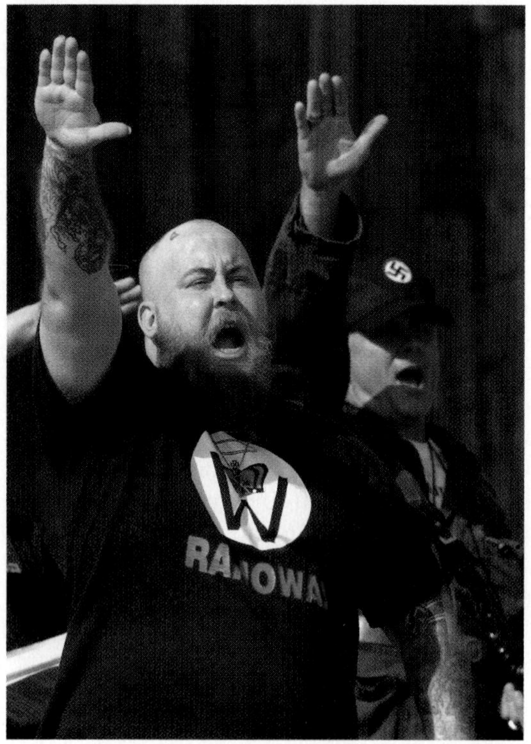

Technology can impact the world and society in major ways, both positive and negative. It impacts each of us on a daily basis in small ways too numerous to list. When you weigh the negative against the positive in your life, which way do the scales tip?

As you examine the uses of technology, you probably notice that it is a magnifier of human nature, increasing your power to do what is positive, negative, and indifferent. Your feelings toward technology should reflect your feelings about humankind in general. Are humans basically good, with occasional deviant behavior? Are people basically bad and doomed for destruction? Or, is humanity an equal balance of good and evil in continuous flux? Technology is only a tool to be wielded to obtain human goals.

So far, history shows that overall, technology has had a more positive than negative effect on the world. Equal access to information for all has undermined those who would otherwise monopolize information to take advantage of others. The Internet and wireless technologies have opened a pipeline of information that is flowing into isolated and oppressed societies to show them that there is a better life.

Political leaders, the news media, and corporate executives have been placed in the spotlight of public awareness and forced to do the right thing or face public humiliation. Widespread access to information is building a more transparent society where everyone who wishes can examine the current state of affairs and take an active role in changing the world for the better. People no longer need to place all their trust in authority because authority no longer has exclusive access to all the facts.

All of this sounds very empowering, but will the citizens of the world bother to take advantage of this power? It requires time and effort for people to seize ownership of their own lives. Consider the effort you are making to educate yourself in order to establish yourself in a career that will support your needs and desires. Taking ownership of your role in society and the world takes even more effort. You can spend the time to learn about your local, state, and federal governments and the laws they pass that affect your life. You can learn about international relations. You can examine the practices of big businesses and how they relate to government policies. You can learn about other cultures and other ways of thinking about things. You can follow the news, look deeply into issues online, discuss issues with others, and shape your own informed opinions. Never before has so much information been so readily available to absorb. And information is power.

The alternative to owning up to your own personal, social, and global responsibilities is to leave it to others to worry about. Those who decide to take this path have no room to complain if the world goes in a direction that they find objectionable.

Thus the torch is handed to you. The torch is technology. The torch is information. The torch is power, freedom, and responsibility (Figure 12.32). You may take up this torch to propel yourself forward to meet your personal and professional objectives, to achieve more than you ever thought possible, to impact those around you, your government, your culture, and the world. You may take up this torch to propagate negativity, hate, and dissonance. Or, you may leave this torch for someone else to pick up. The choice is yours.

FIGURE 12.32 • The torch of freedom and responsibility

Technology provides power, freedom, and responsibility.

ACTION PLAN

Remember John Toh, the naturalist from the beginning of this chapter? John was leery of technology's impact on society and the natural order of the world. Here are some answers to the questions about John's situation.

1. **Are computers alienating the population from each other and the natural environment?**

   Computers can alienate individuals if used excessively. As with any activity, moderation is the key. If used wisely, computers can create and foster healthy relationships between individuals and can place people in environments where they can interact with and impact far more people than they could without the use of technology. Computers and the Internet can be used to learn more about the natural environment and help to preserve it.

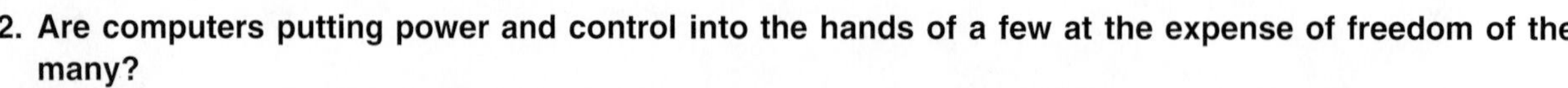

2. **Are computers putting power and control into the hands of a few at the expense of freedom of the many?**

   Information and surveillance technology can provide power and control to those who own them. The Internet is a leveling force in that it provides equal access to information for everyone, not just the wealthy and powerful. It is important that society keep an eye on those that are keeping an eye on them. It is also notable that the Internet has provided liberty to many people who were at one time oppressed.

3. **Are computers reducing the need for a human workforce and overshadowing basic human needs?**

   Technology is shifting work demands differently in different countries, and almost always elevating the level of work, knowledge, and skills required of the workforce. Developing countries are teaching their citizens the basics about technology in order to pull themselves out of poverty, while developed countries are challenged to innovate and take the global society to the next level, whatever that may be. Overall, technology's impact on our global society has been positive, increasing the level of the global economy and providing more people with a worthwhile existence.

Summary

LEARNING OBJECTIVE 1

Describe how technology is affecting the definition of community, and list some physical, mental, and environmental health dangers associated with excessive computer use.

The Internet provides an entire virtual world of information, people, and groups in which you can literally lose yourself. Virtual communities and "anywhere, anytime" communications are affecting traditional social mechanisms. The use of cell phones in public places sometimes offends traditional courtesy and etiquette. The Internet provides new means to meet and get to know individuals with similar interests, but might create a shift away from face-to-face interaction.

Figure 12.4—p. 627

A number of psychological and physical health concerns have arisen because of the amount of time people are spending on computers and in virtual space. Repetitive stress injuries (RSI) such as carpal tunnel syndrome (CTS) can be painful and debilitating. In addition to physical health concerns, the use of computer systems can cause a variety of mental health issues. Internet addictions are evidenced by individuals who allow use of the Internet to deteriorate their quality of life and feel powerless to control it. Such addictions include pornography, online multiplayer gaming, e-shopping, gambling, and social networking addictions. Use of the Internet and its technologies can also lead to information overload and increased workplace stress. The study of designing and positioning the work environment and computer equipment in a healthy manner, called ergonomics, has suggested a number of approaches to reducing these health problems. Many feel that the best way to avoid or recover from any computer-related health issue, physical or mental, is to live a balanced life.

Green computing refers to the efforts of individuals, businesses, and governments to utilize environmentally conscious practices in manufacturing digital products and the use of digital technologies.

LEARNING OBJECTIVE 2

Describe the negative and positive impact of technology on freedom of speech, and list forms of speech and expression that are censored on the Web.

The First Amendment to the U.S. Constitution guarantees citizens the right to free speech. The Internet and Web have been grasped as tools to extend the reach of communications and to empower those who have traditionally been without a public voice. Bloggers are becoming an increasingly important component in journalism, and the role of the public in capturing and reporting news, called consumer-generated media (CGM), has vastly increased over the past 10 years.

Figure 12.11—p. 635

Libel (the deliberate act of defamation of character by making false statements) and direct, specific threats are not protected under the First Amendment. When a government controls speech and other forms of expression, it is called censorship. Various forms of censorship exist around the world. Freedom of speech and Internet technologies are most threatening to oppressive governments whose citizens lack political and social freedom. Most countries support the Internet's ability to empower its citizens but struggle with issues regarding the perceived negative aspects. One major concern is keeping indecent content from minors. Content-filtering software works with the Web browser to check each Web site for indecent materials (defined by the installer of the software) and allows only "decent" Web pages to be displayed. Some information is censored due to its danger to the public.

LEARNING OBJECTIVE 3

Explain the ways in which technology is used to invade personal privacy, and provide examples of laws that protect citizens from privacy invasion.

Computer technology provides the ability to collect, maintain, process, and transfer much more information than has ever before been possible. This power has given rise to a seemingly endless number of public and private databases that include details about many individuals. Privacy issues that concern most people include being free from intrusion (the right to be left alone), freedom from surveillance, and control over the information collected and kept about one's self. Much of the information gathered about individuals is done without their knowledge. This invisible information-gathering takes many forms. Computer profiling is the primary service provided by private information service companies such as ChoicePoint.

Figure 12.17—p. 642

Government agencies in the United States and many other democratic countries are regulated far more stringently than businesses and professionals when it comes to the privacy of confidential records. The Privacy Act of 1974 is the primary law controlling what many U.S. government agencies can and cannot do with the information they hold. In cases of war, governments sometimes set aside some privacy restrictions in an effort to capture or defeat the enemy.

Computer-controlled surveillance combined with ubiquitous networks and powerful information-processing systems have made it possible to gather huge quantities of video, audio, and communications data and process them to reveal personal information. Although this is mostly done in an effort to curb crime and catch criminals, some people are concerned with the lack of oversight. Who is monitoring the individuals doing the monitoring? Wiretapping involves secretly listening in on conversations taking place over telecommunications networks, including telephone, e-mail, instant messaging, VoIP, and other forms of Internet communications. Many cities are using video surveillance to monitor their streets. GPS and RFID are location and tracking technologies that are very useful but can also be used in manners that invade an individual's privacy.

LEARNING OBJECTIVE 4

List ethical issues related to technology that confront individuals in personal and professional life, businesses, and governments.

The field of ethics deals with what is generally considered right or wrong. Computer ethics deals with ethical issues in regard to computer use. Personal computer ethics involves the responsible use of computers outside of the professional environment. Professional computer ethics involves the ethical issues faced by professionals in their use of computer systems as part of their jobs. This includes responsibilities toward customers, coworkers, employers, and all others with whom they interact and who are impacted in some way by their computer use. A number of organizations and associations go beyond what is required by law and establish their own codes of ethics.

Figure 12.21—p. 647

Governments face many of the same ethical considerations as businesses in respect to their use of information systems. Governments, however, have the added responsibility of guiding the influence of technology on their populations. The digital divide is the social and economic gap between those who have access to computers and the Internet and those who do not. There are digital divides based on sex, ethnicity, race, income, location, and disability. A growing body of national laws and policies in many countries addresses accessibility of information and communications technology (ICT) for users with disabilities such as those who have limited vision, hearing, or mobility.

LEARNING OBJECTIVE 5

Explain what globalization is, what forces are behind it, and how it is affecting the United States and other nations.

Globalization refers to changes in societies and the world economy resulting from dramatically increased international trade and cultural exchange. The largest contributors to globalization are computers, a global telecommunication infrastructure, and the Internet. Outsourcing refers to a business's use of an outside company to take over portions of its workload. Offshoring is somewhat different than outsourcing. With outsourcing, a portion of a work process is hired out. Offshoring relocates an entire production line to another location, typically in another country, in order to enjoy cheaper labor, lower taxes, and other forms of lower overhead. There are a number of alternatives for how an organization participates in the global marketplace, depending on where the organization's operations are located and how they are managed. Governments can be very helpful in encouraging global trade by implementing trade agreements with other nations.

Figure 12.26—p. 654

Test Yourself

LEARNING OBJECTIVE 1: Describe how technology is affecting our definition of community, and list some physical, mental, and environmental health dangers associated with excessive computer use.

1. A ________________ is a spontaneous gathering of a group of people organized through cell phones, text messaging, or e-mail.
2. Which of the following is *not* a type of Internet addiction ?
   a. video games
   b. stock market analysis
   c. gambling
   d. pornography
3. True or False: Most recycled computer parts end up polluting poorer developing nations.

LEARNING OBJECTIVE 2: Describe the negative and positive impact of technology on freedom of speech, and list forms of speech and expression that are censored on the Web.

4. The role of the public in capturing and reporting news is called ________________ .
   a. social journalism
   b. citizen journalism
   c. public discourse
   d. blogging
5. When a government controls speech and other forms of expression, it is called ________________ .
6. True or False: Content-filtering software has proven to be the ideal solution for libraries who wish to keep pornography off their computers.

LEARNING OBJECTIVE 3: Explain the ways in which technology is used to invade personal privacy, and provide examples of laws that protect citizens from privacy invasion.

7. The practice of using computers to cross-reference and pool electronic customer records into large customer profiles is referred to as ________________ .
   a. computer profiling
   b. customer profiling
   c. consumer profiling
   d. e-commerce
8. ________________ is the close monitoring of behavior.
9. True or False: China is well known for electronic surveillance of its citizens, but the democratic form of government prevents this from occurring in the United States.

LEARNING OBJECTIVE 4: List ethical issues related to digital technology that confront individuals in personal and professional life, businesses, and governments.

10. ________________ is a field of study that deals with what is generally considered right or wrong.
11. Any group that is not provided equal opportunities in computer use and access can refer to their disadvantage in relation to the rest of the world as a ________________ .
12. ________________ refers to designing software and hardware so that it is usable for all people, including those with disabilities.
    a. The digital divide
    b. Usable computing
    c. Interpreted computing
    d. Accessible computing

LEARNING OBJECTIVE 5: Explain what globalization is, what forces are behind it, and how it is affecting the United States and other nations.

13. ________________ refers to changes in societies and the world economy resulting from dramatically increased international trade and cultural exchange.
14. A business practice that relocates an entire production line to another location, typically in another country, in order to enjoy cheaper labor, lower taxes, and other forms of lower overhead is referred to as ________________ .
    a. offshoring
    b. outsourcing
    c. exporting
    d. globalization

15. True or False: Outsourcing and offshoring have a negative effect on the global economy.

Test Yourself Solutions: **1.** flash mob, **2.** b. stock market analysis, **3.** True, **4.** b. citizen journalism, **5.** censorship, **6.** False, **7.** a. computer profiling, **8.** Surveillance, **9.** False, **10.** Ethics, **11.** digital divide, **12.** d. Accessible computing, **13.** Globalization, **14.** a. offshoring, **15.** False.

Key Terms

Term	Page	Definition
carpal tunnel syndrome (CTS)	626	Aggravation of the pathway for nerves that travel through the wrist (the carpal tunnel), typically caused by long hours at the computer keyboard with wrists cocked and fingers typing
censorship	634	The act of a government or authority controlling speech and other forms of expression
computer ethics	646	Ethical issues that deal with computer use
content-filtering software	636	Software that works with the Web browser to check Web sites for indecent materials (defined by the installer of the software) and allows only "decent" Web pages to be displayed
ergonomics	628	The study of designing and positioning the work environment and computer equipment in a healthy manner
ethics	646	The study of what is generally considered right or wrong
e-waste	631	Discarded digital electronics devices and components
globalization	653	Changes in societies and the world economy resulting from dramatically increased international trade and cultural exchange
green computing	630	The efforts of individuals, businesses, and governments to utilize practices both in the manufacturing and the use of digital technologies that are environmentally conscientious
Internet addiction	627	Compulsive use of the Internet that interferes with normal daily life and relationships
offshoring	656	Business practice that relocates an entire production line to another location, typically in another country, in order to enjoy cheaper labor, lower taxes, and other forms of lower overhead
surveillance	641	The close monitoring of behavior

Questions

Review Questions

1. How have digital technologies changed society over the past 25 years in terms of communications, access to information, commerce, work environments, and leisure activities?
2. List three physical health concerns having to do with computer use, and how they can be prevented or treated.
3. List three mental health issues related to computer use.
4. List four types of Internet addiction.
5. What is the purpose of ergonomics?
6. What legal principle guarantees U.S. citizens the right to free speech?
7. What is the purpose of content-filtering software?

8. What is censorship?
9. What benefit does computer profiling provide for businesses?
10. List four forms of electronic surveillance, and provide examples of each.
11. What is computer ethics, and what are the three areas of computer ethics discussed in this chapter?
12. What are the goals of green computing initiatives from a corporate perspective?
13. Why do businesses outsource and offshore?

Discussion Questions

14. Provide an example of how the concept of flash mobs can be applied to a useful activity.
15. What is nature deficit disorder? Do you believe that it is an issue for yourself?
16. What is citizen journalism? Do you think it helps or hurts the public? Why or why not?
17. Do you feel that some form of government censorship is needed on the Web for content that is legal but may be dangerous or unhealthy for society? Why or why not?
18. Should content-filtering software be used in campus computer labs? Why or why not?
19. Some people debate whether Internet addictions should be classified as mental disorders. Do you think people can really get addicted to computer and game use? Why or why not?
20. What are the benefits and shortcomings of content-filtering software?
21. Should dangerous information, such as how to build a bomb, be allowed on the Web? Why or why not?
22. Should governments be allowed to use systems such as Total Information Awareness and Matrix in their efforts to catch terrorists? Why or why not?
23. What categories of Web content do you find most unhealthy for society? Should the government step in to filter such content? Why or why not?
24. Many personal ethical beliefs are not backed by laws. What are some behaviors, by individuals, businesses, or governments, that you have observed that you wish were prohibited by law?
25. Explain the differences between outsourcing and offshoring.
26. Describe the positive and negative aspects of globalization.
27. Understanding what you do about outsourcing and offshoring, what is the best career advice you could provide to a graduating high school student in the United States? Provide a rationale.
28. List several globalization challenges for businesses.
29. When it comes to privacy, which option would you vote for: full privacy for all, government-controlled surveilance only, or full transparency for all? Why?
30. When it comes to the variety of content that exists on the Web, do you feel your views are more conservative or more liberal than the sum of the Web community? What does this say about your ethics?

Exercises

Try It Yourself

1. Use a Web search engine to find online dating services. Visit the top six services and write a paragraph review of each. Conclude with a paragraph discussing whether or not you feel that such services are safe and valuable.
2. Do a Web search on *ergonomics*. Find a list of the most important measurements and angles representing the healthiest computing posture. Write a summary of your use of digital technologies, including desktop PC, notebook PC, and cell phone, noting how you could improve the ergonomics of your use.
3. Search for information on green computing and learn what the experts have to say on the topic. Write a short paper (at least 400 words) listing three companies that you feel are making earnest efforts toward green computing, and three companies that could try a lot harder. Include the business habits and activities that factored into your conclusions.

Virtual Classroom Activities

For the following exercises, do not use face-to-face or telephone communications with your group members. Use only Internet communications.

4. Divide the class into groups of three to five students. Each group should conduct an online chat providing group members with opportunities to sound off about cell phone etiquette. Use Table 12.1 as a basis for your discussion. Rank the 10 items in order of importance. Decide if any of these items are unrealistic. Summarize your conclusion and make a presentation to your instructor and class on the class discussion board.

5. Learn as much as you can about Google Earth by either downloading and installing free evaluation versions of the software and trying it out, or by reading about it at *http://earth.google.com*. Write a short paper (no less than 400 words) on how this technology affects national security. Conclude with your thoughts on whether such technology should be available to the public.

6. What accommodations does your school provide to assist disabled students in accessing and using computers on campus? Use your school's Web site to find out, and record your findings in a Word document to submit.

Teamwork

7. Have group members scour through your school's policies as listed in the general bulletin, code of conduct, class syllabus, network usage policies, and any other official policies you can find. See if you can find issues of censorship. Build a list of policies that can be considered censorship and vote on whether each is justifiable or not. Provide your results in a document to be submitted to the instructor and/or discussed with the class.

8. Have a surveillance camera scavenger hunt. Use a campus map to divide up the campus between team members. Find as many surveillance cameras as possible. Keep in mind the types of facilities that may use surveillance: entrances to student housing, ATMs, lecture halls, stores, and so on. Use an electronic version of the campus map (either found on your school Web site or scanned in by yourself) and graphics software to plot the locations of all cameras found on the map. Whoever finds the most cameras is the winner! Submit your map electronically for grading.

Endnotes

[1] Ropelato, Jerry, "Internet Pornography Statistics," TopTenReviews, accessed July 9, 2009, http://internet-filter-review.toptenreviews.com/internet-pornography-statistics.html.

[2] Abate, Tom, "EU and US at odds over Internet gambling," *Global Post*, June 25, 2009, www.globalpost.com.

[3] Hills, Richard, "The Internet: How much is too much?", *The Examiner*, June 24, 2009, www.examiner.com.

[4] Louv, Richard, "No More 'Nature-Deficit Disorder'," *Psychology Today*, January 29, 2009, www.psychologytoday.com.

[5] Oliver, Shawn, "iSuppli: SSD Energy Savings Could Power A Nation," *Hot Hardware*, May 8, 2009, hothardware.com.

[6] *GreenPeace Guide to Greener Electronics – 12*, accessed July 9, 2009, www.greenpeace.org/raw/content/usa/press-center/reports4/guide-to-greener-electronics-12.pdf.

[7] Apple Web site, accessed July 9, 2009, www.apple.com/macmini/environment.html.

[8] Marshall, Rosalie, "Apple Backs Energy-Saving Universal Phone Charger," *Greener Computing*, June 29, 2009, www.greenercomputing.com.

[9] GreenBiz Staff, "IBM Reports Progress Toward CSR Goals," *Greenbiz*, July 6, 2009, www.greenercomputing.com.

[10] Fister Gale, Sarah, "E-Waste: When Landfills Are Not an Option," *Greener Computing*, July 1, 2009, www.greenercomputing.com.

[11] Fredrickson, Samantha, "Wisconsin woman convicted of criminal libel," Reporters Committee for Freedom of the Press, October 31, 2008, www. rcfp.org.

[12] Internet censorship in Australia Web page, www.efa.org.au/Issues/Censor/cens1.html, accessed July 9, 2009.

[13] "The USA PATRIOT Act," www.epic.org/privacy/terrorism/hr3162.html, accessed July 9, 2009.

[14] Electronic Privacy Information Center Web site, www.epic.org/privacy/profiling/tia/#introduction, accessed July 9, 2009.

[15] Cal State San Bernardino Web site on Wiretap Laws, www.infosec.csusb.edu/policies/wiretap.html, accessed July 9, 2009.

[16] SecurityPark Staff, "IBM integrated network video monitoring systems for Navy Pier in Chicago," *SecurityPark*, February 7, 2009, www.securitypark.co.uk/security_article263264.html

[17] Schlosberg, Mark, Ozer , Nicole, "ACLU Issues Report on the Proliferation of Video Surveillance Systems in California," ACLU, accessed July 9, 2009, www.aclunc.org

[18] AP Staff, "Japan to build 100 mini-satellites," *China Daily*, April 17, 2009, www.chinadaily.com.cn .

[19] China Academy of Space Technology Web site, "Satellites will help predict distasters ," March 31, 2009, www.cast.cn/CastEn/show.asp?ArticleID =30801 ; Staff, "China launches second 'Compass' satellite for global navigation system, *xinhuanet* , April 15, 2009, http://news.xinhuanet.com .

[20] Singel , Ryan, "Online Privacy Law on the Way, Congressman Promises," Wired , April 23, 2009, www.wired.com/epicenter/2009/04/netonline-priva/.

[21] W3C Web Accessibility Initiative Web site, www.w3.org/WAI/Policy/, accessed July 9, 2009.

[22] The Ndiyo Project Web site, www.ndiyo.org, accessed July 9, 2009.

[23] Information Technology Access for Everyone Web site, www.weforum.org/en/initiatives/itafe, accessed July 9, 2009.

[24] Funny Translation Errors, accessed July 9, 2009, www.ojohaven.com/fun/translation.funnies.html

[25] NAFTA Secretariat Web page, www.nafta-sec-alena.org, accessed July 9, 2009.

[26] Public Citizen Web page, www.citizen.org/trade/cafta , accessed July 9, 2009, 2007 .

[27] European Union Web page, www.europa.eu., accessed July 9, 2009.

Glossary

Note: Terms in bold are Key Terms, found in the Key Terms sections at the end of each chapter. Terms in italic are important terms mentioned in the book, but not included in the Key Terms sections at the end of each chapter.

3Cs approach — Emphasizing content, community, and commerce on a B2C e-commerce Web site, a strategy for capturing the interest of the online community.

3D modeling software — Programs that provide graphic tools that allow artists to create pictures of 3D, realistic models.

3D printer — Printer that uses CAD blueprints as input, and outputs an actual 3D color scale prototype model.

3g cellular technology — Current wireless technology that is bringing wireless broadband data services to your mobile phone.

802.11 — Family of standards developed by the Institute of Electrical and Electronics Engineers (IEEE) to support wireless computer networking. See Table 5.7.

acceptance testing — Conducting tests required by the user, to make sure that the new or modified system is operating as intended.

access point — Wireless network site, also known as a hot spot, that broadcasts network traffic using radio frequencies to computers or other devices equipped with wireless fidelity (Wi-Fi) cards or adapters.

access time — The amount of time it takes for a request for data to be fulfilled by a storage device.

ActiveX — Microsoft alternative to the JavaScript Web programming language.

adware — Software placed on your computer system without your knowledge or consent, normally through the Internet, to secretly spy on you and collect information, especially for advertising purposes.

Ajax — Stands for *Asynchronous JavaScript and XML,* a popular technology used to create many interactive programs delivered over the Web, such as Google Maps.

algorithm — A step-by-step problem-solving process that arrives at a solution in a finite amount of time; sometimes called program logic; a detailed procedure or formula for solving a problem.

alphanumeric — In database fields, character-type data, including characters or numbers that will not be manipulated or used in calculations.

always-on connection — An Internet connection that is continuous, such as a DSL or cable modem connection. *Compare to* dial-up connection.

American Standard Code for Information Interchange (ASCII) — A code for representing keyboard text characters that the computer industry agreed upon in the early days of computing.

analog — Signals that vary continuously; the opposite of digital.

analog signal — A signal that continuously fluctuates over time between high and low voltage.

analog-to-digital converter — A device that translates sound and music to digital signals.

animated GIF — Simple drawings, created with simple software tools, that repeat the same motion over and over endlessly; the most basic form of animation.

anomalies — Problems and irregularities in data.

antispyware — Software that searches a computer for spyware and other software that may violate a user's privacy, allows the user to remove it, and provides continuing protection against future attacks.

antivirus software — Software that uses several techniques to find viruses on a computer system, remove them if possible, and keep additional viruses from infecting the system. Also known as virus-scan software.

application flowchart — A general flowchart used to describe the overall purpose and structure of a system; also known as the system flowchart.

application layer — The software portion of the three-layer Internet model, which also includes transport (protocol) and physical (hardware) layers.

application programming interface (API) — Web site development tool that allows software engineers to develop Web-driven programs.

application servers — Computers that store programs, such as word processors and spreadsheets, and deliver them to workstations to run when users click the program icon.

application service provider (ASP) — A company that provides software and support, such as computer personnel, to run the software.

application software — Programs that apply the power of computers to help perform tasks or solve problems for people, groups, and organizations; along with systems software, one of two basic types of software.

arithmetic logic unit (ALU) — One of three primary elements within a central processing unit (CPU), it contains the circuitry to carry out instructions, such as mathematical calculations and logical comparisons.

artificial creativity — A branch of AI that works to program computers to express themselves through art, music, poetry, and other expressive outlets.

artificial intelligence (AI) — An area of computer science that deals with simulating human thought and behavior in computers.

ASCII text — Text represented as ASCII code, rather than as binary data. *See* American Standard Code for Information Interchange (ASCII).

assigned research — A form of research in which the topic to explore is given, rather than prompted by curiosity, for the purpose of education.

asynchronous communication — A form of electronic communications that allows participants to leave messages for each other to be read, heard, watched, and responded to at the recipient's convenience, such as by using answering machines, voice mail, and e-mail.

attosecond — A billionth of a billionth of a second.

attribute — A characteristic of an entity; in the relational data model, a column of a table; an identifying characteristic, such as a variable, that is associated with an object in object-oriented design.

authentication — A manner in which to confirm the identity of a user. There are three common forms of authentication: something you know (such as a password or PIN), something you have (such as an ID card or badge), and something about you (a unique physical characteristic such as your fingerprint).

automation — Utilizing computers to control otherwise human actions and activities.

avars — Points on a computerized 3-D object that are designed to bend or pivot at specific angles.

avatar — A 3-D representation of a participant in a virtual world environment, which can be used to navigate through the virtual world.

B2B e-commerce — Business-to-business e-commerce, a system supporting transactions between businesses across private networks, the Internet, and the Web.

B2C e-commerce — Business-to-consumer e-commerce, the use of the Web to connect individual consumers directly with sellers to purchase products.

backdoor Trojan — A Trojan horse program that opens up ports (back doors) on the computer to allow access to intruders.

back-end application — Software that interacts with other programs or applications, and only indirectly with people or users.

backward compatibility — The ability of a newer version of software to automatically read files from an older version of the same software.

backward-compatible — Capable of supporting previous technology. For example, DVD drives are backward-compatible and thus can play CDs as well as DVDs.

bandwidth — The data transmission rate of a network medium measured in bits per second.

bar phone — A cell phone handset that is a solid monolith, leaving the display and buttons unprotected.

batch processing — A method of processing transactions by collecting them over time and processing them together in batches.

Bayesian network — A graphical model that represents a set of variables and their relationships and dependencies, sometimes called a belief network.

behavioral profiling — Observing customers' cable TV viewing patterns in order to develop an understanding of their interests.

behavior-based AI — Popular methodology in the programming of robots that simulates intelligence by combining many semiautonomous modules.

binary data — Encoded data that is intended for a processor to process.

binary digit — *See* bit.

binary number system — A number system that uses only two values, 0 and 1, and is used by computers and digital devices to represent and process numeric data.

bioinformatics — Also called computational biology, a combination of biology and computer science that has been used to help map the human genome and conduct research on biological organisms.

biometrics — The science and technology of authentication by scanning and measuring a person's physical features such as fingerprints, retinal patterns, and facial characteristics; the study of measurable biological characteristics.

bit — Short for binary digit, represents data using technologies that can be set to one of two states, such as on or off, or changed or not changed.

bit-mapped graphics — A representational method that uses bytes to store the color of each pixel in an image. Also known as raster graphics.

bits per second (bps) — A measurement of data transmission speed.

BitTorrent — A peer-to-peer file-sharing protocol that allows users to share files by downloading pieces of a file from multiple sources.

blade computing — A type of enterprise computing that uses stripped-down network PCs called thin clients connected to clusters of blade servers. This system, paired with a file server that stores user files, is significantly less costly than regular PCs for large enterprises, but offers identical services to users and convenience for system administrators.

blade server — PC motherboards that are rack-mounted together in groups of up to 20 to a case.

blog — Short for Web log, Web sites created to express one or more individual's views on a given topic.

Bluetooth — A low-cost, short-range wireless specification for connecting mobile products; Bluetooth technology enables a wide assortment of digital devices to communicate wirelessly over short distances.

Blu-ray DVD — Technology that uses the shorter wavelength of blue light to read and write pits on the optical disc surface for higher capacity. HD-DVD uses similar technology.

booting — The process of checking a computer's hardware components and loading its operating system.

boot process — When a computer is first turned on, this process is carried out to test the hardware components and load the operating system from storage to RAM.

bot — An automated program that scours the Web in an attempt to catalog every Web page by topic; also called a spider or crawler.

botnet — A group of compromised or zombie computers that a hacker can control remotely to distribute spam or launch denial-of-service or other malicious attacks.

brainstorming — A group decision-making approach that often consists of members offering ideas "off the top of their heads."

brick-and-mortar — A term used to refer to a traditional retail store.

bridge — Device that connects two or more network segments and helps regulate network traffic.

broadband — A high-speed Internet connection that is always on or active, such as cable or DSL.

Broadband over Power Lines (BPL) — A broadband Internet access, not yet widely offered, over the power grids; connecting a computer to the Internet would be as easy as plugging a power line modem into a wall outlet.

broadband phone — Residential VoIP service that utilizes a high-speed Internet connection to provide telephone services.

buddy list — Also known as a contact list, names of people who are frequent communication partners in chat rooms or via instant messaging.

buffer — Intermediate storage area between a microprocessor and other hardware or software.

bug — *See* software bug.

burning — The process of writing to an optical disk.

bus — A network topology consisting of one main cable or telecommunications line with devices attached to it.

business continuity planning (BCP) — The review of every conceivable disaster that could negatively impact a transaction processing system, and the provision of courses of action to minimize their effects.

business intelligence (BI) — The business use of data mining to help increase efficiency, reduce costs, or increase profits.

business-to-business (B2B) e-commerce — A system supporting transactions between businesses over private networks, the Internet, and the Web.

business-to-consumer (B2C) e-commerce — The use of the Web to connect individual consumers directly with sellers to purchase products; also known as e-tailing.

byte — A group of eight bits used to represent all types of useful data and information, such as characters, words, or sounds; the standard unit of storage in digital electronics.

C2C e-commerce — Consumer-to-consumer e-commerce, the use of the Web to connect individuals who wish to sell their personal belongings with people shopping for used items.

cable modem — A signal-conversion device that provides Internet access over a cable television network; it offers faster data transmission rates than a traditional dial-up connection.

cable modem connection — A broadband Internet service, with data transfer rates of up to 8 Mbps, provided by cable television providers.

cache memory — A type of high-speed memory that a processor can access more rapidly than RAM, allowing for quick retrieval of program instructions and data.

carpal tunnel syndrome (CTS) — An inflammation of the pathways for nerves that travel through the wrist (the carpal tunnel), that involves wrist pain, a feeling of tingling and numbness, and difficulty in grasping and holding objects; a condition sometimes associated with long hours at the computer keyboard.

cascading style sheets (CSS) — Technology that uses special HTML tags to globally define font characteristics for a variety of page elements as well as how those elements are laid out on the Web page.

case-based reasoning — Artificial intelligence (AI) approach in which AI software maintains a library of problem cases and solutions and, when confronted by a new problem, adjusts and applies a relevant previous solution to the new problem.

CD-RW — Compact disc-rewritable; a type of CD where the data can be written over many times.

CDMA — One of two predominant cell phone networking standards in the United States, the other being GSM. GSM is also used in Europe and Asia, though GSM is rapidly gaining ground in the United States as well.

cellular carrier — A company that builds and maintains a cellular network and provides cell phone service to the public.

cellular network — A radio network in which a geographic area is divided into cells with a transceiver antenna (tower) and station at the center of each cell to support mobile communications.

censorship — When a government or authority controls speech and other forms of expression.

central processing unit (CPU) — The group of integrated circuits that work together to perform any system processing, such as arithmetic calculations, logic comparisons, and data access.

centralized database approach — Data management technology that allows multiple applications to run from one common database system; reduces data redundancy and improves data integrity.

certification authorities — Businesses, such as VeriSign, that provide digital certificates.

channels — Also known as chat rooms, the various topic-related forums on the Internet for synchronous text messaging between two or more participants.

character recognition software — Software that when combined with a scanner can transform document images into editable word-processing documents.

chat — On the Internet, synchronous text messaging between two or more participants.

chat rooms — Also known as channels, the various topic-related forums on the Internet for synchronous text messaging between two or more participants.

chip — Another term for microprocessor.

chipset — Set of processors that tie together several bus systems in a computer, sending and receiving bytes from memory, input and output devices, storage, networks, and other motherboard components.

citizen journalists — News-reporting bloggers, not professional journalists.

cladding — Thin coating over fiber-optic cable that effectively works like a mirror, preventing the light from leaking out of the fiber.

clamshell phone — A cell phone handset that consists of two halves hinged to open and close like a clamshell.

client — The program, in a client/server relationship, that makes a service request.

client/server — A relationship between two computer programs in which one program, the client, makes a service request from another program, the server, which provides the service.

clock speed — The rate, typically measured in megahertz or gigahertz, at which a CPU's system clock produces a series of electronic pulses, which is a factor in overall system performance.

cloud computing — Utilizing Internet-based service providers to deliver information and computing services, including software, business systems, and data storage.

clustering — A technique that allows processors from different computers to work together over a network on complex problems. Also called grid computing.

CMOS memory — Short for complementary metal oxide semiconductor, it provides semi-permanent storage for system configuration information that may change.

coaxial cable — A type of cable consisting of an inner conductor wire surrounded by insulation, a conductive shield, and a cover; the type of cable provided by cable television services.

collaborative tagging — Methodology of ranking content that has become popular with many Web 2.0 sites. Also called folksonomy, it allows users to associate descriptive tags with photos, music, or other content. Using associated tags, it is easy to group common items together.

command prompt — A location on-screen where users can enter text-based commands, marked by a prompt symbol or symbols, such as C:\>:.

command-based user interface — Access to and command of a computer system by giving the computer text commands to perform basic activities.

communications medium — Anything that carries a signal between a sender and a receiver, such as wires or radio waves.

communications satellite — A microwave station placed in outer space that receives a signal from one point on Earth and then rebroadcasts it at a different frequency to a different location.

compact disc read-only memory (CD-ROM) — Commonly referred to as a CD, the first optical media to be mass-marketed to the general public. CDs are read-only—once data has been recorded on one, it cannot be modified.

competitive intelligence — A form of business intelligence concerned with information about competitors.

compiler — A language translator that coverts a complete program, such as a COBOL program, into a complete machine-language program.

computational intelligence — Artificial intelligence methodologies such as neural networks, fuzzy systems, and evolutionary computation that set up a system whereby the software can develop intelligence through an iterative process.

computational science — An area of computer science that applies the combined power of computer hardware and software to solving difficult problems in various scientific disciplines.

computed field — A field determined from other fields, instead of being entered into a database; also called a calculated field.

computer — A digital electronics device that combines hardware and software to accept the input of data, process and store the data, and produce some useful output.

computer ethics — Ethical issues that deal with computer use; also, the ethical responsibilities of those that work with and develop computer systems.

computer forensics — The process of examining computing equipment to determine if it has been used for illegal, unauthorized, or unusual activities.

computer housecleaning — Involves organizing the data files and software on your computer and removing unneeded files, thus improving computer performance and enhancing your use of the computer.

computer literacy — A working understanding of the fundamentals of computers and their uses.

computer network — A collection of computing devices connected together to share resources such as files, software, processors, storage, and printers; a specific type of telecommunications network that connects computers and computer systems for data communications.

computer platform — The combination of hardware configuration and system software for a particular computer system.

computer profiling — The use of cookies and other Web technologies to gather information about customers visiting Web sites. This information is then used for targeted marketing, and has raised concerns about privacy.

computer scientist — A person who uses computers to help with the software design process or conducts research into computing topics such as artificial intelligence, robotics, and electrical circuits.

computer system — Any device that supports the activities of input, processing, storage, and output; the hardware, software, the Internet, databases, telecommunications, people, and procedures that the computing experience comprises.

computer systems management — The team of managers that can include the chief information officer (CIO) and other computer systems executives.

computer vision — Combines hardware (cameras and scanners) and AI software that permit computers to capture, store, and interpret visual images and pictures.

computer-aided software engineering (CASE) — Software-based tools that automate many of the tasks required in a systems development effort.

computer-assisted design (CAD) software — Software that assists designers, engineers, and architects in designing three-dimensional objects.

computer-assisted manufacturing (CAM) — Software that assists in manufacturing physical objects/products.

computer-based information system (CBIS) — An information system that makes use of hardware and software, databases, telecommunications, people, and procedures to manage and distribute digital information.

computerized collaborative work system — The hardware, software, people, databases, and procedures needed to provide effective support in group decision-making settings; also called a group decision support system.

consumer-generated media (CGM) — News or other topical coverage that is captured or reported by nonprofessionals, that is, the general public.

consumer-to-consumer (C2C) e-commerce — The use of the Web to connect individuals who wish to sell their personal belongings with people shopping for used items.

contactless payment system — Makes use of an RFID chip embedded in a credit card, ID card, and other device to wirelessly send data to an RFID reader installed in a cash register, vending machine, toll booth, or other point of sale.

content-filtering software — "Parental control" software that works with the Web browser to check each Web site for indecent materials (defined by the installer of the software) and allow only "decent" Web pages to be displayed.

content streaming — Also known as streaming media, streaming video, or streaming audio, a technique to deliver multimedia without a wait, since the media begins playing while the file is still being delivered.

contextual ads — Ads specifically selected and placed to match the content of a Web page.

continuous improvement — An approach to systems development in which an organization makes changes to a system when even small problems or opportunities occur.

contract software — A specific software program developed for a particular company or organization.

control unit — One of three primary elements within a central processing unit (CPU), it sequentially accesses program instructions, decodes them, and also coordinates the flow of data in and out of various system components.

conventional AI — Artificial intelligence methodologies such as expert systems, case-based reasoning, Bayesian networks, and behavior-based AI that rely on the programmer to instill the software with logical functionality to solve problems.

convertible model tablet PC — Converts between notebook PC and tablet by allowing the display to be opened, rotated, and then closed so that the display is on the outside. *Compare to* slate model tablet PC.

cookie — A text file placed on your hard disk by a Web site you visit, for the purpose of storing information about you and your preferences.

coprocessor — Special-purpose processor, typically used in larger workstations, that speeds processing by executing specific types of instructions, while the CPU works on another processing activity.

copyright — Defines exclusive rights legally granted to the owner of a published work.

corporate portal — The interface used to access an organization's information systems, giving easy access to commonly used information and tools.

counterintelligence — A form of business intelligence concerned with protecting your own information from access by your competitors.

cracker — A criminal hacker, a computer-savvy person who attempts to gain unauthorized or illegal access to other computer systems to harm the system or to make money illegally.

cradle — *See* docking station.

crawling — The process of continually following all Web links in an attempt to catalog every Web page by topic.

creative analysis — The investigation of new approaches to existing problems.

Creative Commons license — Designed to allow the creators of intellectual property to specify the terms of the license in order to grant certain freedoms to users, while still providing the owner with some control of the property.

critical analysis — A skeptical and doubtful approach to problems, such as questioning whether or not the current computer system is still effective and efficient.

CSV (comma-separated values) — Flat-file data storage method that uses commas, tabs, or other indicators within the line to separate the fields within the record.

curiosity-driven research — A form of research based on seeking information prompted by a personal thought or question, rather than a topic being assigned, that is responsible for most of the world's great inventions.

customer relationship management (CRM) system — System used by many businesses to gauge customer satisfaction and respond to customer issues.

custom software — Programs built or developed by individuals and organizations to address specific needs.

cybermall — A Web site that allows visitors to browse through a wide variety of products from varying e-tailers.

cyberterrorism— A form of terrorism that uses attacks over the Internet to intimidate and harm a population.

dashtop computer — Computer embedded in an automobile dashboard.

data — Items stored on a digital electronics device, including numbers, characters, sound, music, graphics, anything that can be expressed and recorded.

data analysis — A process that involves developing good, nonredundant, adaptable data, and evaluating data to identify problems with the content of a database.

data center — A climate-controlled building, or set of buildings, that house the servers that store and deliver mission-critical information and services.

data communications — A specialized subset of telecommunications, referring to the electronic collection, processing, and distribution of data, typically between computer system hardware devices.

data conversion — The transformation of existing computerized files into the proper format to be used by a new system.

data definition language (DDL) — A collection of instructions and commands used to define and describe data and data relationships in a specific database.

data dictionary — A detailed description of all data used in a database, including information such as the name of the data item, who prepared the data, and the range of values for the data.

data haven — Country that has few restrictions on telecommunications or databases.

data hierarchy — The manner in which data in a database is combined and organized into sequential levels of detail.

data integrity — Ensuring that data stored in the database is accurate and up to date.

data item — The specific value of an attribute, found in the fields of the record describing an entity.

data manipulation language (DML) — A specific language provided with a database management system, that allows people and other database users to access, modify, and make queries about data contained in the database and to generate reports.

data mart — A small data warehouse, often developed for a specific person or purpose.

data mining — The process of extracting information from a data warehouse or a data mart; sifting through the combined information of any one customer or group of customers to recognize trends and tendencies — and ultimately pitch products and services specifically for that customer's interests.

data preparation — The process of converting manual files into computer files.

data redundancy — Duplication of data that occurs when data is copied, stored, and used from different locations.

data warehouse — A database that holds important information from a variety of sources.

database — A collection of integrated and related files; a collection of data organized to meet users' needs; an organized collection of facts and information.

database administrator (DBA) — A skilled and trained computer professional who directs all activities related to an organization's database, including providing security from intruders.

database backup — A copy of all or part of a database, usually made on a regularly scheduled basis.

database development platform — Multiuser database management systems (DBMSs) that allow multiple employees to access and edit data simultaneously.

database management software — Personal productivity software that can be used to store large tables of information and produce documents and reports.

database management system (DBMS) — A group of programs that manipulate a database and provide an interface between the database and the user or the database and application programs.

database recovery — The process of returning the database to its original, correct condition if the database has crashed or been corrupted.

database servers — Computers that store organizational databases, and respond to user queries with requested information.

database system — Everything that makes up the database environment, including a database, a database management system, and the application programs that utilize the data in the database.

decision making — A process that takes place in three stages: intelligence, design, and choice.

decision support system (DSS) — An information system used to support problem-specific decision making.

decision table — A systems development tool, often used as an alternative to or in conjunction with flowcharts, for displaying various conditions that could exist in a system and the different actions the computer should take as a result of these conditions.

dedicated line — A line that leaves the connection open continuously to support a data network connection.

default settings — In software installation, the settings chosen in advance for you as typical settings.

defragmentation utility — Program that rearranges files on a hard disk to increase the speed of executing programs and retrieving data on the hard disk.

demand fulfillment — The supply chain management process of getting the product or service to the customer.

demand planning — The supply chain management activity of analyzing buying patterns and forecasting customer demand.

demand report — Report developed to give certain information at a person's request.

desktop computer — One of the most popular types of personal computers, designed to sit on a desktop.

desktop publishing — Software to design page layouts for magazines, newspapers, books, and other publications.

device driver — Software that interfaces with an operating system to control an input or output device, such as a printer.

dial-up connection — A low-speed Internet service, with data transfer rates of up to 56 Kbps, provided by an Internet service provider (ISP).

digital — Broadly, technologies and devices based on numbers; in current use, based on signals that exist in one of two possible values; the opposite of analog.

digital art — A new form of art that uses computer software as the brush and the computer display as the canvas.

digital audio — Any type of sound, including voice, music, and sound effects, recorded and stored digitally as a series of 1s and 0s.

digital audio compression — Technology, such as the MP3 file format, that reduces the size of an audio file.

digital camcorder — Special-purpose computer device used to take full-length digital video that you can watch on your TV, download to your computer, or transfer to CD, DVD, or VCR tape.

digital camera — An optical recording device or special-purpose computer device that captures images through a lens and stores them digitally rather than on film.

digital certificate — A type of electronic business card that is attached to Internet transaction data to verify the sender of the data.

digital convergence — The trend to merge multiple digital services into one device.

digital divide — The social and economic gap between those who have access to computers and the Internet and those who do not.

digital electronics device — Any device that stores and processes bits electronically.

digital forensics — *See* computer forensics.

digital graphics — Computer-based media applications that support the creation, editing, and viewing of 2D and 3D images, animation, and video.

digital graphics animation — The display of digital images in rapid succession to provide the illusion of motion.

digital imaging — A method of working with photographic images and video using bit-mapped or raster images instead of vector graphics.

digital media — Digital technologies of all kinds that serve and support digital music, video, and graphics.

Digital Millennium Copyright Act — A U.S. law enacted in 1998 that provides global copyright protection.

digital music — A subcategory of digital audio that involves recording and storing music as a series of 1s and 0s.

digital rights management (DRM) — The technology invented to protect intellectual property in digital files.

digital satellite service (DSS) — A wireless broadband Internet service, with data transfer rates of up to 6 Mbps, provided by companies such as EarthLink and StarBand, typically used in situations where neither cable broadband nor DSL is available.

digital signal — A signal that at any given time is either high or low, in discrete voltage states.

digital-to-analog conversion — The process through which digitized sound is transformed back into an analog form.

digital-to-analog converter — A device that translates digital sound and music to analog signals.

digital video disc read-only memory (DVD-ROM) — An optical media that stores over 4.7 GB of data in a fashion similar to CDs except that DVDs are able to write and read much smaller pits on the disc surface.

digital voice recorder — A device that stores recordings in standard digital sound formats that can be transferred to a computer for transcription or editing.

digitization — The process of transforming nondigital information to bit representation.

direct access — A storage medium feature that allows a computer to go directly to a desired piece of data, by positioning the read-write head over the proper track of a revolving disk.

direct conversion — A start-up approach that involves stopping the old system and starting the new system on a given date.

disaster recovery — Providing a plan for how to bring systems back online after an emergency; part of business continuity planning.

display resolution — A measure, typically in terms of width and height, of the number of pixels on the screen, with a larger number of pixels per square inch considered a higher image resolution.

distance education — Conducting classes over the Web with no physical class meetings.

distributed computing — Computing that involves multiple remote computers that work together to solve a computation problem or to perform information processing.

distributed database — A database in which the actual data may be spread across several databases at different locations, connected via telecommunications devices. Also called a virtualized database.

distributed denial of service (DDoS) attack — A type of computer attack in which many computers are used to launch simultaneous repeated requests at a Web server in order to overwhelm it so that it is unable to function.

docking station — A small stand for a handheld device that is used to recharge its battery and to connect to a PC.

documentation — All flowcharts, diagrams, and other written materials that describe the new or modified system.

domain name — The English name associated with a numerical Internet Protocol (IP) address, such as www.fsu.edu.

Domain Name System (DNS) — Used on the Internet to translate domain names into IP addresses.

dot pitch — The measure of space between pixels. The lower the dot pitch, the better the image quality.

dots per inch (dpi) — A printer's output resolution; the greater the number of dots printed per inch, the higher the resolution.

drawing software — Programs that provide tools to create, arrange, and layer graphical objects on the screen to create pictures; also called vector graphics software.

drill down — Clicking links through a series of Web pages to find additional information.

drive-by download — A popular way of spreading viruses, especially through social networks like Facebook; an attack places enticing links on Web pages that infect the visitor's PC when clicked.

drum machines — Musical instruments that allow the musician to record drum beat patterns by tapping on pressure-sensitive buttons or pads to produce sampled drum sounds that can be played back in a looping pattern.

DSL (Digital Subscriber Line) connection — A broadband Internet access, with data transfer rates of around 1.5 Mbps, provided by the phone company, or Internet service providers working with the phone company.

DSL modem — Digital Subscriber Line modem, for connecting digital devices using a digital signal over telephone lines, for relatively inexpensive high-speed access to the Internet.

dual booting — A computer system that provides the user with the option of booting into one of two operating systems.

dual-core processor — A processor that uses two processors on one chip that work together to provide twice the speed of traditional single-core chips.

dual in-line memory module (DIMM) — A circuit board that holds a group of memory chips, or RAM.

dumpster diving — Rummaging through trash to steal credit card numbers or other personal information.

dynamic IP address — An Internet Protocol (IP) address that is assigned to computers as needed.

dynamic Web pages — Web pages that are custom created on-the-fly.

e-book — Digital versions of books and other text-based publications.

e-cash — Electronic cash, a Web service that provides a private and secure method of transferring funds from a bank account or credit card to online vendors or individuals for e-commerce transactions.

e-commerce (electronic commerce) — The process of conducting business or other transactions online, over the Internet, or using other telecommunications and network systems; systems that support electronically executed transactions.

e-commerce host — A company that takes on some or all of the responsibility of setting up and maintaining an e-commerce system for a business or organization.

e-commerce software — Software designed specifically to support e-commerce activities, including catalog management, shopping cart use, and payment.

economic feasibility — The determination of whether a project makes financial sense and whether predicted benefits offset the cost and time needed to obtain them.

electronic cash — A Web service that provides a private and secure method of transferring funds from a bank account or credit card to online vendors or individuals for e-commerce transactions; also known as e-cash.

electronic data interchange (EDI) — Networking systems technology, standards, and procedures that allow output from one system to be processed directly as input to other systems, without human intervention.

electronic exchange — An industry-specific Web resource created to provide a convenient centralized platform for B2B e-commerce among manufacturers, suppliers, and customers.

electronic funds transfer (EFT) — Moving money electronically from one institution to another.

electronic wallet — An application that encrypts and stores credit-card information, e-cash information, bank account information—all the personal information required for e-commerce transactions—securely on your computer; also known as e-wallet.

e-mail — Electronic mail; the transmission of messages over a network to support asynchronous text-based communications.

e-mail attachment — Typically a binary file or a formatted text file that travels along with an e-mail message but is not part of the e-mail ASCII text message itself.

e-mail body — The component of an e-mail transmission that contains an ASCII text message written by the sender to the recipient.

e-mail header — The component of an e-mail transmission that contains technical information about the message, such as the destination address, source address, subject, and date and time.

e-mail server — Server that handles sending and receiving e-mail messages.

embedded computer — A special-purpose computer that is embedded in and controls many electrical devices on which we depend.

embedded operating systems — Operating systems, like those for many small computers and special-purpose devices, that are embedded in a computer chip.

emoticon — Combination of keyboard characters to convey underlying sentiments, such as :-) to create a sideways facial expression meaning happy or smiling.

encoder software — Software used to transfer digital music files from one format to another.

encryption — The use of high-level mathematical functions and computer algorithms to encode data so that it is unintelligible to all but the intended recipient.

end-user computing — Development and use of application programs and computer systems by users who are not computer systems professionals.

end-user systems development — The development of computer systems by individuals outside of the formal computer systems planning and departmental structure.

enterprise resource planning (ERP) system — An information system that integrates all data processing in a corporation (enterprise) into one unified system that draws from a common database system.

enterprises — Large businesses and organizations, which make extensive use of distributed computing.

enterprise service provider (ESP) — A company that provides users, typically large businesses or organizations, server connections and software that allow employees to access a corporate Intranet from outside the office.

entity — A generalized class of people, places, or things (objects) for which data is collected, stored, and maintained.

entity relationship diagram — A graphical illustration of the relationships among database tables.

ergonomic keyboard — A set of keys designed so that the user can enter data in a manner that is comfortable and avoids strain on the hands or wrists.

ergonomics — The applied science of designing and arranging the things we work with, such as computer systems, in a manner that promotes health, especially the study of designing and positioning computer equipment to reduce health problems.

e-tailing — B2C e-commerce; a take-off on the term retailing, since it is the electronic equivalent of a brick-and-mortar retail store.

Ethernet — The most widely used network standard for private networks.

ethics — The study of what is generally considered right or wrong.

event-driven review — A systems review procedure that is triggered or caused by a problem or opportunity such as an error, a corporate merger, or a new government regulation.

evolutionary computation — Includes areas of AI that derive intelligence by attempting many solutions and throwing away the ones that don't work; a "survival of the fittest" approach.

e-wallet — *See* electronic wallet.

e-waste — Discarded digital electronics devices and components.

execution phase — Executing an instruction and storing the results; the second of the two phases of a typical computer's machine cycle, the first being the instruction phase.

executive dashboard — A management information system consisting of a collection of visually oriented reports, usually distributed and viewed electronically.

exception report — Report automatically produced when a situation is unusual or requires action.

expansion board — Also known as an expansion card, a circuit board often packaged with specialized peripheral devices for installation on a computer's motherboard.

expansion card — Same as expansion board.

expansion slots — Connecting sites on a computer motherboard where circuit boards can be inserted to add additional system capabilities.

expert system (ES) — A computerized system that acts or behaves like a human expert in a field or area; an information system that can make suggestions and reach conclusions in much the same way that a human expert can; a subfield of artificial intelligence.

Extensible Markup Language (XML) — *See* XML.

extension — An addition to a filename, placed after the filename following a period, which identifies the file type. For example, many word-processing files have a .doc or .docx extension.

extranet — An arrangement whereby Intranet content is extended to specific individuals outside the network, such as customers, partners, or suppliers.

facial pattern recognition — A method of identification that uses a mathematical technique to measure the distances between points on the face. Software can quickly compare these measurements to a database of known faces and come up with a match if one exists.

fair use doctrine — The legal principle that describes when and how copyrighted material can be legally used.

feasibility analysis — A key part of the systems development process that involves investigation into technical, economic, legal, operational, and schedule feasibility of a problem to be solved or an opportunity to be met.

feeds — A blog distribution system that uses RSS technology and XML to deliver Web content that changes on a regular basis.

fiber-optic cable — A type of cable that consists of thousands of extremely thin strands of glass or plastic bound together in sheathing; because it transmits signals via light rather than electricity, fiber-optic cable is extremely fast and reliable.

field — A name, number, or combination of characters that in some way describes an aspect of an object or activity.

field design — The specification of type, size, format, and other aspects of each field.

field name — An identifying label applied to a particular field.

file — A named collection of instructions or data stored in a computer or computer device; a collection of related records; also called a table in some databases.

file allocation table (FAT) — The file system used by MS-DOS and older Windows operating systems.

file ownership — An identification of the creator of a file or folder. In an operating system, users are the owners of the files they create.

file server — Computer that stores organizational and user files, delivering them to workstations on request.

file system — A way of organizing how data and files are physically stored and how they are logically manipulated; a function of the operating system.

fingerprint scan — A form of biometric authentication in which a user presses a finger on a scanning device to establish his or her identity.

firewall — Network hardware device or software that filters the information coming onto a network to protect the network computer from hackers, viruses, and other unwanted network traffic.

FireWire — A standard, and a type of expansion card, for fast video transfer from a camera to the computer; also known as IEEE 1394.

Flash — A popular Web browser plug-in that enables users to view animations and videos and to interact with games and other multimedia content created with the Adobe Flash program.

flash BIOS — A basic input/output system recorded on a flash memory chip rather than a ROM chip. Flash memory can store data permanently, like ROM, but can also be updated with revisions when they become available.

flash drive — A small flash memory module, about the size of your thumb or smaller, that plugs into the USB port of a PC or other digital electronics device to provide convenient, portable, high-capacity storage. Also called thumb drive or USB drive.

flash memory — A chip that, unlike RAM, is nonvolatile and keeps its memory when the power is shut off.

flash memory card — A small, easily modifiable and reprogrammable memory chip.

flash mob — A group of people who assemble suddenly in a public place, do something unusual, and then disperse. Flash mobs organize through cell phone text messaging or e-mail.

flat file database — A type of database in which there is no relationship between the records; often used to store and manipulate a single table or file.

flat panel display — A flat display that uses liquid crystals or plasma gas between two pieces of glass to form characters and graphic images on a screen; types are liquid crystal display (LCD) and plasma display.

flexible display — A form of e-paper that can be rolled, folded, or dropped with no damage to the flexible plastic material.

flip phone — Bar phone with a cover that flips over the display and buttons.

FLOPS — Floating-point operations per second, a more precise measure than MIPS of processor performance.

flowchart — A systems design diagram that charts the path from a starting point to the final goal of the system.

folksonomy — Methodology of ranking content that has become popular with many Web 2.0 sites. Also called collaborative tagging, it allows users to associate descriptive tags with photos, music, or other content. Using associated tags, it is easy to group common items together.

forensic audio — Digital processing to de-noise, enhance, edit, and detect sounds to assist in criminal investigations.

forensic graphics — Art used to create animations and demonstrative exhibits to use in courts of law in order to explain theories and present evidence.

frames — Series of bit-mapped images that when shown in quick succession create the illusion of movement.

free software — Term coined by Richard Stallman and the Free Software Foundation, implying that the software is both freeware and open source.

freeware — Software that has been placed in the public domain and is free to use.

frequency — The speed at which an electronic communications signal can change from high to low.

front-end application — Software that directly interacts with people or users.

front side bus (FSB) — The connecting path between the processor and other key components such as the memory controller hub; FSB speed is measured in GHz or MHz.

full backup — Backing up all files. *Compare to* incremental backup.

fuzzy control system — A system based on approximate, as opposed to precise, reasoning; typically used to control machines.

fuzzy logic — A specialty research area in computer science developed to deal with ambiguous criteria or probabilities and events that are not mutually exclusive; also known as fuzzy sets; a form of mathematical logic used in artificial intelligence systems.

game controller — A specialized input device used to control and manipulate game characters in a virtual world.

Gantt chart — A graphical tool used for planning, monitoring, and coordinating projects.

garbage in, garbage out (GIGO) — Inaccurate data being entered into a database, resulting in inaccurate output.

gateway — Network point that acts as an entrance to another network.

general-purpose computer — Computer that can be programmed and used for a wide variety of tasks or purposes, such as mobile and personal computers.

general-purpose database — A database that can be used for a large number of applications.

general-purpose I/O device — Input or output devices designed for a variety of computer environments, such as the standard keyboard and mouse.

genetic algorithm — An approach, based on the theory of evolution, to solving large, complex problems where a number of algorithms or models change and evolve until the best one emerges.

geographic information system (GIS) — An application capable of storing, manipulating, and displaying geographic or special information, including maps of locations or regions around the world.

geotagging — Adding location identification to online communications and content.

gigaflop — Billions of floating-point operations per second, a measurement for rating the speed of microprocessors.

gigahertz (GHz) — Billions of cycles per second, a measurement used to identify CPU clock speed; for example, a 500 GHz processor runs at 500 billion cycles per second.

global positioning system (GPS) — A sophisticated satellite networking system that is able to pinpoint exact objects and locations on Earth; a special-purpose computing device, typically installed in an automobile or boat, that uses satellite and mobile communications technology to pinpoint current location.

globalization — Changes in societies and the world economy resulting from dramatically increased international trade and cultural exchange.

global supply management (GSM) — A process that provides methods for businesses to find the best deals on the global market for raw materials and supplies needed to manufacture their products.

GNU General Public License (GPL) — A legal arrangement that makes software available for free to its users.

goal-seeking analysis — The process of determining what problem data is required for a given result.

graphical user interface (GUI) — Access to and command of a computer system by using pictures or icons on the screen and menus, which many people find easier to learn and use compared to a command-based user interface.

graphics card — Circuit board, also called a *video card*, that contains the graphics memory, GPU, and other graphics hardware and is plugged into the motherboard.

graphics memory — Sometimes called *video RAM* or *VRAM*, used to store image data for a computer display in order to speed the processing and display of video images.

graphics processing unit (GPU) — Integrated circuit board that processes graphics and takes the load off the CPU.

graphics tablets and pens — Input tools that allow you to draw with a penlike device on a tablet to create drawings on a display.

green computing — Efforts made by individuals, businesses, and governments to utilize environmentally conscientious practices in the manufacture and use of digital technology.

grid computing — *See* clustering.

group decision support system (GDSS) — The hardware, software, people, databases, and procedures needed to provide effective support in group decision-making settings; also called a computerized collaborative work system.

group ownership — Access to files and folders based on membership in groups established by the system administrator.

groupware — Group decision support system software that helps with joint work group scheduling, communication, and management; software that allows network users to collaborate over the network; also called workgroup software.

GSM — One of two predominant cell phone networking standards, the other being CDMA. GSM is also used in Europe and Asia.

hacker — A person who knows computer technology and spends time learning and using computer systems. More recently used to label individuals who subvert computer security without authorization.

handheld computer — A type of small, easy-to-use mobile computer.

handheld scanner — Compact data input scanning device that can convert pictures, forms, and text into bit-mapped images.

handwriting recognition — Uses artificial intelligence techniques in software that is able to translate handwritten characters or words into computer-readable data.

haptic output — Computer output that the user feels, such as vibration in a game controller as a race car rolls over gravel.

hard copy — Computer output printed to paper.

hardware — The tangible components of a computer system.

hardware independence — Having an OS layer that adapts to new and varied hardware, which allows software engineers to design many thousands of applications that can function on different types of hardware.

HD-DVD — Technology that uses the shorter wavelength of blue light to read and write smaller pits on the optical disc surface for higher capacity. Blu-ray DVD uses similar technology.

health care informatics — Research on ways to reduce medical errors and improve health care delivery through using computers and digital technology.

hertz (Hz) — A measurement of signal frequency, in cycles per second.

heuristics — A problem-solving method used in decision support systems, often referred to as "rules of thumb"—commonly accepted guidelines or procedures that usually find a good, though not optimal, solution.

high-definition TV (HDTV) — Television that uses a resolution that is twice that of traditional television displays for sharper, crisper images. HDTV uses a widescreen format, which means it uses the same height and width ratio used in movie theaters.

high-speed Internet — Refers to a connection that is always on or active, such as cable or DSL. *See* broadband.

Home PLC — Home power-line communication, networking that takes advantage of a home's existing power lines and electrical outlets to connect computers; also called power-line networking.

HomePNA — Home phone-line networking alliance, networking that takes advantage of existing phone wiring in a residence; also called phone-line networking.

horizontal portal — A Web portal that covers a wide range of topics.

hotspot — Area within the range of a Wi-Fi network or networks where users can connect to the Internet.

HTML tag — Hypertext Markup Language tag, a specific command indicated with angle brackets (< >) that tells a Web browser how to display items on a page.

hub — A small network device used as a central point for connecting a series of computers; sends the signal from each computer to all other computers on the network.

human-readable data — Data that a person can read and understand.

hybrid drive — Storage device that combines flash memory and magnetic storage. A hybrid drive boots very quickly and runs very quietly.

hybrid system — Contains multiple types of information systems accessed through one central interface.

hydrophone — Underwater microphone.

hyperlink — An element in an electronic document, such as a word, phrase, or an image, that when clicked opens a related document. Hyperlinks are a cornerstone of the World Wide Web.

hypermedia — Pictures or other media that act as a links to related documents.

hypertext — Text that acts as a link to a related document.

Hypertext Markup Language (HTML) — The primary markup language that is used to specify the formatting of a Web page.

Hypertext Transfer Protocol (HTTP) — The protocol used to control communication between Web clients and servers.

identity theft — The criminal act of using stolen information about a person to assume that person's identity.

immediacy — A database characteristic, referring to a measure of how rapidly changes must be made to data.

immersive virtual reality — A simulation in which the user becomes fully immersed in an artificial, three-dimensional world that is completely generated by a computer.

incremental backup — Backing up only the files that have changed since the last backup. *Compare to* full backup.

informatics — The combination of traditional disciplines, like science and medicine, with computer systems and technology.

information — Data organized and presented in a manner that has additional value beyond the value of the data itself.

information overload — The inability to find the information you need on the ever-growing Web due to an overabundance of unrelated information.

information security — The protection of information systems and the information they manage against unauthorized access, use, manipulation, or destruction, and against the denial of service to authorized users.

information system — A computer system that makes use of hardware, software, databases, telecommunications, people, and procedures to manage and distribute digital information.

information technology — Issues related to the components of a computer-based information system.

infrared transmission — Sending signals through the air via light waves, a type of wireless media.

ink-jet printer — A popular type of printer, providing economical but relatively low-print-quality black and white or color output.

input device — A device that helps to capture and enter raw data into a computer system, such as a keyboard, mouse, or touch screen.

installation — The process of physically placing computer equipment on the site and making it operational.

instant messaging (IM) — Synchronous one-to-one text-based communication over the Internet.

instruction phase — Involves fetching and decoding instructions; the first of two phases of the machine cycle in a typical computer, the other being the execution phase.

instruction set — The specific set of instructions that a processor is engineered to carry out.

integrated circuit — A module, or chip, consisting of multiple electronic components and used to store and process bits and bytes in today's computers.

integrated development environment (IDE) — Combines all the tools required for software engineering in one package. The majority of software used today is created using an IDE such as Microsoft Visual Studio.

integrated digital studio — High-tech electronic system that packages many digital recording devices in one unit for convenient home recording.

integrated software package — An application that contains several basic programs, such as word processing, spreadsheet, and calendar, offering a range of capabilities, but with less power and for less money than the standalone software included in software suites.

integration testing — Testing all related systems together, to ensure that the new program(s) can interact with other major applications.

intellectual property — A product of the mind or intellect over which the owner holds legal entitlement. Intellectual property includes ideas and intangible objects such as poetry, stories, music, and new ways of doing things or making things.

intellectual property rights — Rights associated with the ownership and use of software, music, movies, data, and information.

intelligent agent — An intelligent robot, or bot, consisting of programs and a knowledge base used to perform a specific task for a person, a process, or another program.

interactive media — Multimedia presentations that involve user interaction for education, training, or entertainment, typically by combining both digital audio and digital video for a full multimedia experience.

interactive TV — A digital television service that includes one or more of the following: video on demand, personal video recorder, local information on TV, purchase over TV, Internet access over TV, and video games over TV.

interior threats — Threats from within a private network that can be intentional or unintentional. Unintentional threats can occur when users make mistakes or exceed their authorization. Intentional threats come from registered users who desire to do the system harm or steal information.

Internet — The world's largest public computer network; a network of networks that provides a vast array of services to individuals, businesses, and organizations around the world.

Internet2 — A research and development consortium led by U.S. universities and supported by industry and government to develop and deploy advanced network applications and technologies for tomorrow's Internet.

Internet access over TV — Services, such as WebTV, that allow viewers to navigate the Web on their television sets.

Internet addiction — A condition that can exist when people are online for long periods of time, cannot control their online usage, jeopardize their career or family life from excessive Internet usage, and lie to family, friends, and coworkers about excessive Internet use.

Internet backbone — The collection of the many national and international communications networks owned by major telecommunication companies, such as Verizon and Sprint, that provides the hardware over which Internet traffic travels.

Internet fraud — The crime of deliberately deceiving a person over the Internet to cause damage or to unjustly obtain property or services.

Internet hosts — The more than 500 million computers joined together to create the Internet, the world's largest network.

Internet Protocol (IP) — Along with Transmission Control Protocol (TCP), one of the sets of policies, procedures, and standards used on the Internet to enable communications between two devices; defines the format and addressing scheme used for packets.

Internet radio — Radio programming that is similar to local AM and FM radio, except that it is digitally delivered to a computer over the Internet, and there are more choices of stations.

Internet service provider (ISP) — Company that provides users access to the Internet through network service providers' points of presence.

internetwork — Networks joined together to make larger networks, such as today's Internet, so that users on different networks can communicate and share data.

interpreter — A language translator that converts each statement in a programming language into a machine language and executes the statement.

intranet — A private network that uses the protocols of the Internet and the Web, TCP/IP and HTTP, along with Internet services such as Web browsers.

invisible information gathering — Collecting and storing information about individuals without their knowledge or explicit consent.

IP address — A unique Internet Protocol address consisting of a series of four numbers (0 to 255) separated by periods, assigned to all devices connected to the Internet.

IrDA port — Infrared Data Association port, for using infrared transmission to connect most handheld and notebook computers to desktop computers and other digital devices.

iterative approach — An approach to systems development in which each phase of the SDLC is repeated several times (iterated).

Java — An object-oriented programming language developed by Sun Microsystems that can be used to create programs that run on any operating system and on the Internet.

JavaScript — A programming language developed specifically for the Web and more limited in nature than Java and other high-level programming languages.

joining — A basic data manipulation that involves combining two or more tables.

joystick — A specialized input device, in the form of a swiveling stick, used to control and manipulate game characters in a virtual world.

jukebox software — Software that allows computer users to categorize and organize digital music files for easy access.

key — A field in a record that is used to identify the record.

key-indicator report — A special type of scheduled report that summarizes the previous day's critical activities, and is typically available at the beginning of each workday.

key-logging software — Software that is installed on a computer to record all keystrokes and commands. The recording is later collected from a remote computer over the Internet and played back in order to spy on the user's actions and sometimes to steal usernames and passwords.

keywords — Words that are specified to a search engine to find information on a topic of interest.

kiosk — Special-purpose computing station, often equipped with touch-sensitive screens, made available where the public can access location-relevant information.

knowledge management (KM) system — Information system that captures, stores, and distributes knowledge for use and reuse by an organization and sometimes by its partners and customers.

knowledge worker — A professional who makes use of information and knowledge as a significant part of his or her work.

laptop computer — Also called a notebook, a type of personal computer designed for portability.

laser printer — A popular type of printer that provides the cleanest output and is typically used when professional-quality documents are required.

LCD projector — Small, portable device used to project presentations from a computer onto a larger screen.

legal feasibility — The determination of whether laws or regulations may prevent or limit a systems development project.

libel — The deliberate act of defamation of character by making false statements about a person.

license agreement — A contract that software companies may require users to accept that specifies how the software can be used.

light-emitting diode (LED) display — Display technology that uses LEDs to provide the backlight in thin displays rather than the fluorescent light used in traditional LCDs.

line-of-sight — A medium in which the straight-line view between sender and receiver must be unobstructed.

Linux — An open-source, GUI-based operating system developed in 1991 by Linus Torvalds, which runs on computer systems ranging from small personal computers to large mainframe systems.

liquid crystal display (LCD) — A flat, space-saving panel display that uses liquid crystals between two pieces of glass to form characters and graphic images on a backlit screen; also known as flat panel display.

listservs — Special interest groups that create online communities for discussing topic-related issues via e-mail.

load balancing — Sharing system processing among servers so that if one goes down, the others pick up the slack.

local area network (LAN) — A network that connects computer systems and devices within the same geographical area.

local information on TV — A feature of interactive TV that provides local community news and information.

localization — The process of creating multiple versions of a Web site, each in a different language and catering to a different cultural bias.

local resource — Along with network, one of two types of resources that workstations typically have access to: the files, drives, and printers or other peripheral devices that are accessible to the workstation on or off the network.

location-based m-commerce — Making use of a global positioning system (GPS) or the cell network to track your current location in order to provide location-related services such as weather reports, road maps, lists of nearby merchants, lists of nearby friends, and traffic reports.

logical field — Database field limited to certain operators, such as "yes" or "no."

logical view — The way a programmer or user thinks about data. With a logical view, the programmer or user doesn't have to know where the data is physically stored in the computer system. *Compare to* physical view.

logic error — The result of a poor algorithm that contains a flaw in reasoning, causing a program to crash, behave in an unexpected fashion, or not effectively solve the problem for which it was designed.

Long Term Evolution (LTE) — A 4G wireless broadband technology that allows GSM devices to provide very high-speed Internet access.

lossless compression — A type of file compression that allows the original data to be reconstructed without loss.

lossy compression — A type of file compression that accepts some loss of data to achieve higher rates of compression. Savings in file size can be considerable and is essential for fast-loading Web pages.

MAC address — Media Access Control address, a unique hardware code printed by the manufacturer on network interface cards and wireless adapters, and is how the devices are identified on the network. Notebook computers with Wi-Fi capability have a sticker on the bottom with the adapter's MAC address. MAC address filtering can be enabled in routers and access points so that they allow only specified MAC addresses to connect to the network.

machine cycle — The combination of the instruction phase and the execution phase, which together are required to execute an instruction.

machine learning — The ability of a computer to learn with experience to become better at what it is designed to do.

machine-readable data — Data that can be read only by electronic devices.

Mac OS — The native operating system for Apple PCs.

magnetic disk — A thin steel platter (hard disk) or piece of Mylar film (floppy disk) used to store data, with widely varying capacity and portability.

magnetic ink character recognition (MICR) — Use of a special-purpose optical reading device to read magnetic-ink characters, such as those written on the bottom of a check.

magnetic storage — Technology that uses magnetic properties of iron oxide particles to store data more permanently than RAM.

magnetic tape — Mylar film coated with an iron oxide; used as a sequential access storage medium.

mainframe — Computer system typically used by universities and large organizations, which requires plenty of processing power and speed.

malware — Computer viruses and worms or other software with malicious intent.

management information system (MIS) — An information system used to provide useful information to decision makers, usually in the form of a report.

managers — The people within an organization who are most capable of initiating and maintaining change.

marketplace — E-commerce site where businesses and individuals can buy and sell their products and belongings.

market segmentation — A method of market research in which customer opinions are divided into categories of race, gender, and age to determine which segment a product appeals to most.

markup language — Used to describe how information is to be displayed on a Web browser. It typically combines the information, such as text and images, along with additional instructions for formatting. HTML is an example.

mashup — A single application that combines different Web applications. For example, Google Maps provides views of street maps and directions between locations.

massively parallel processing (MPP) — A form of multiprocessing, used in supercomputers, that works by linking a large number of powerful processors to operate together.

master file — Permanent file that is updated over time.

m-commerce (mobile commerce) — A form of e-commerce that takes place over wireless mobile devices such as handheld computers, cell phones, and dashtop computers.

media card — Flash memory card used in media devices such as digital cameras, camcorders, and portable MP3 players.

media player software — Media software programs that combine digital music functions with video support; popular media players such as Windows Media Player from Microsoft and QuickTime Player from Apple are free downloads.

media sharing — Service provided by Web sites like YouTube for videos and Flickr for photos that allows members to store and share digital media files.

medical informatics — Combining traditional medical research with computer systems and technology to reduce medical errors and improve health care delivery.

megahertz (MHz) — Millions of cycles per second, a measurement used to identify CPU clock speed; for example, a 500 MHz processor runs at 500 million cycles per second.

megapixel — 1 megapixel = 1 million pixels, a measure of picture resolution in digital cameras. An inexpensive digital camera can capture around 6 megapixels, and the best can capture over 10 megapixels.

memory — *See* primary storage.

meta search engine — A tool that allows you to run keyword searches on several search engines at once.

meta tags — Information tags, containing terms such as business-related keywords, that are read by search engines and Web servers, but not displayed on the page by a Web browser.

metropolitan area network (MAN) — A large, high-speed network connecting a series of smaller networks within a city or metropolitan size area.

microcontroller — Special-purpose computer (typically an entire computer on one chip) that is embedded in electrical and mechanical devices in order to control them. Also called embedded computer.

microdrive — Tiny hard drives that can store gigabytes of data on a disk one or two inches in size, usually found in handheld computers.

microprocessor — A single module, smaller than a fingernail, that holds all of a computer's central processing unit (CPU) circuits and performs system processing.

Microsoft Windows — The most popular operating system for personal computers.

microwaves — Waves at the high end of the radio spectrum, between 1 and 300 GHz, used for high-speed, high-capacity communication links and satellite communications.

microwave transmission — Also known as terrestrial microwave, the line-of-sight sending of high-frequency radio signals through the air.

midrange server — Also called minicomputer, computer system that is more powerful than personal computers and is used by small businesses and organizations to perform business functions, scientific research, and more.

MIPS — Millions of instructions per second, indicating the amount of time it takes a processor to execute an instruction, a measure of processor performance.

mirroring — Creating an exact copy of a system or portion of a system. Some software provides real-time mirroring, in which files are automatically updated in their primary storage space and the mirrored copy whenever they are created or changed.

mixing board — A large panel with many dials, buttons, and sliders that a sound engineer uses to adjust the sound quality of each instrument separately.

modem — An external or internal device that converts analog and digital signals from one form to the other, typically for the purpose of connecting to the Internet.

Moore's Law — A trend, first predicted by Intel cofounder Gordon Moore in 1965 and since proven true, that technological innovations would be capable of doubling the transistor densities in an integrated circuit every two years, resulting in increased processor speeds.

motherboard — Also called the system board, the main circuit board of the computer where many of the hardware components are placed, such as the central processing unit, memory, storage, and other supportive chips.

MP3 — A digital music file format that compresses music files to less than 10 percent of their original size.

MP3 player — Device that plays music stored in the digital MP3 format.

multicore technology — The latest technique in chip design, housing more than one processor on a chip.

multifunction printer — A printer that combines the functionality of a printer, fax machine, copy machine, and digital scanner in one device.

multimedia — Digital devices of all kinds that serve and support digital media such as music, video, and graphics; the computer's ability to present and manipulate visual and audio media such as graphics, animation, video, sound, and music.

multiprocessing — The simultaneous operation of more than one processing unit.

multitasking — Running more than one application at the same time.

multitrack recording — In digital music recording, treating each instrument or microphone as a separate input, or track.

multiuser system — A computer system, such as a computer network, where multiple users share access to resources such as file systems.

musical instrument digital interface (MIDI) — A protocol, implemented in 1983, that provides a standard language for digital music devices to use in communicating with each other; enables a musician to control many devices from a single synthesizer keyboard or computer.

narrowband — A category of bandwidth; narrowband is slower than broadband and is more restricted in its applications and uses.

National Lambda Rail (NLR) — A U.S. cross-country, high-speed, fiber-optic network dedicated to research in high-speed networking applications.

National Strategy to Secure Cyberspace — A framework for protecting cyberspace, which is recognized as essential to the U.S. economy, security, and way of life.

native format — The file format that an application normally reads and writes.

natural language processing — Often referred to as speech recognition, the AI technique that allows a computer to understand and react to statements and commands made in a "natural" language, such as English.

near field communication (NFC) — A wireless technology designed for short distances (up to 20 centimeters), aimed at utilizing cell phones for secure wireless payments.

netbook — A small, inexpensive ultraportable notebook designed primarily for Web applications and lightweight productivity applications.

nettop — PC models with touch-sensitive displays designed for casual home use; called nettops rather than desktops because their primary function is to access the Internet.

network — Interlinked system that can connect computers and computer equipment in a building, across the country, or around the world.

network access server (NAS) — A computer that large businesses or organizations use to access the corporate intranet.

network adapter — A computer circuit board, PC Card, or USB device installed in a computing device so that it can be connected to a network.

network administrator — Person responsible for setting up and maintaining a network, implementing policies, and assigning user access permissions. Also known as system administrator.

network interface card (NIC) — A circuit board or PC card that, when installed, provides a port for the device to connect to a wired network with traditional network cables.

network operating system (NOS) — Operating system software that controls the computer systems and devices on a network and allows them to communicate with each other; includes security and network management features. Almost all modern operating systems are network operating systems.

networking devices — Hardware components that together with networking software enable and control communications signals between communications and computer devices.

networking media — Anything that carries an electronic signal and creates an interface between a sending device and a receiving device.

networking software — Software components that work together with hardware components to enable and control communications signals between communications and computer devices.

network service provider (NSP) — Major telecom companies, such as Sprint and Verizon, that agree to connect their networks so that users on all the networks can share information over the Internet.

neural network — A computer system that can act like or simulate the functioning of a human brain, process many pieces of data at once, and learn to recognize patterns; a branch of artificial intelligence.

newsletter — Subscription-based broadcast e-mail communication, such as *The New York Times* newsletter.

node — Device attached to a network.

nonprogrammed decision — Decision that deals with unusual or exceptional situations that are difficult to look at as a matter of a rule, procedure, or quantitative method.

normalization — The process of correcting data problems or anomalies to ensure that the database contains accurate data.

notebook computer — Also called a laptop, a popular type of personal computer designed for its portability.

NTFS — New Technology File System, the default file system for newer and current Windows operating systems.

numeric field — A database field that contains numbers that can be used in making calculations.

object — An element of the object-oriented design approach that is composed of attributes and methods.

object code — The machine-language code necessary for a computer to execute programming instructions.

object-oriented programming — An approach to programming that derives the solution to the program specification from the interaction of objects.

object-oriented programming languages — High-level programming languages, such as Visual Basic .NET, C++, and Java, that group together data, instructions, and other programming procedures.

object-oriented (OO) systems development — A systems development process that follows a defined life cycle, much like the SDLC, and typically involves defining requirements, designing the system, implementation and programming, monitoring, evaluation, and review.

offshoring — A business practice that relocates an entire production line to another location, typically in another country, in order to enjoy cheaper labor, lower taxes, and other forms of lower overhead.

off-the-shelf software — An existing software program developed for the general market.

on-board synthesizers — Synthesizers located on most personal computers' sound cards that include all the standard synthesizer keyboard sounds.

on-demand media — The ability to view or listen to programming or music at any time rather than at a time dictated by television and radio schedules.

one-to-many relationship — In a database, a relationship between fields in different tables that specifies that one instance in one table can be related to many instances in another table. For example, one Student can take many Classes.

online clearinghouses — E-commerce sites that provide a method for manufacturers to liquidate stock and consumers to find a good deal.

online transaction processing — A method of processing transactions at the point of sale, which is critical for time-sensitive transactions such as making flight reservations.

Open Mobile Alliance (OMA) — An organization composed of hundreds of the world's leading mobile operators, device and network suppliers, information technology companies, and content providers, which have joined together to create standards and ensure interoperability between mobile devices.

open-source software — Software programs that make the source or machine code available to the public, allowing users to make changes to the software or develop new software that integrates with the open-source software.

Open System Interconnection (OSI) model — A detailed, seven-layer model for networks, such as the Internet, that provides network technicians and administrators with a deeper understanding of the technology to design and troubleshoot networks.

operating system (OS) — A set of computer programs that runs or controls the computer hardware, acts like a buffer between hardware and application software, and acts as an interface between application programs and users.

operational feasibility — The determination, affected by both physical and motivational considerations, of whether or not a project can be put into action or operation.

optical character recognition (OCR) — Use of a special-purpose reading device to read hand-printed characters.

optical mark recognition (OMR) — Use of a special-purpose reading device to read "bubbled-in" forms, such as those found on exams and ballots.

optical processor — Microprocessors that use light waves instead of electrical current. It has been estimated that optical processors have the potential of being 500 times faster than traditional electronic circuits.

optical storage — Technology that uses an optical laser to burn pits into the surface of a highly reflective disc, such as a CD, DVD, or Blu-ray to store data. Such discs hold significantly more data than a magnetic storage device.

optimization model — A popular problem-solving method, used in decision support systems, that identifies the best solution, usually the one that best helps individuals or organizations meet their goals.

order processing system — A type of transaction processing system that supports the sales of goods or services to customers and arranges for the shipment of products.

organic electronics — An area of research aimed at building electronics out of conductive polymers or plastics that have carbon-based molecules.

outboard devices — Large racks of interconnected digital audio devices used in sound recording studios to process digital music and audio signals.

output — The results of the processing produced in a manner that is discernable to human senses or used as input into another system.

output device — A piece of hardware that allows us to observe the results of computer processing with one or more of our senses, such as a display monitor or printer.

outsourcing — A business' use of an outside company to take over portions of its workload.

packet — Data transported over the Internet as a small group of bytes, which includes the data being sent as well as a header containing information about the data, such as its destination, origin, size, and identification number.

packet-sniffing software — Software that captures and analyzes all packets flowing over a network or the Internet, often used by criminals to steal private data such as passwords and credit card numbers.

packet switching — The dividing of information into small groups of bytes in order to make efficient use of the network.

pager — Small lightweight device that receives signals from transmitters.

page scanner — Data input scanning device that can convert pictures, forms, and text into bit-mapped images.

pages printed per minute (ppm) — A measurement used to compare the speed of printers.

parallel conversion — A process during the phase-in start-up approach in which parts of the old system and new system are running at the same time.

parallel processing — A form of multiprocessing that works by linking several microprocessors to operate at the same time, or in parallel.

parental controls — Applications, such as Net Nanny, that filter out adult content to make Web browsing safe for young users.

partitioning — Dividing a hard disk into two or more sections, usually to contain different operating systems.

password — A secret combination of characters, known only to the user, that is used for authentication.

payload — The destructive action of a computer virus, such as the corruption of computer data files or system files, resulting in the loss of data or a malfunctioning computer.

PC Card or PCMCIA card — Small expansion cards typically inserted into notebook computers to support network adapters, modems, and additional storage devices.

PCMCIA slot — The area on notebook computers where PCMCIA cards can be inserted.

PDA (personal digital assistant) — A type of small, easy-to-use mobile computer.

peer-to-peer (P2P) — A network architecture that does not utilize a central server, but facilitates communications directly between clients.

personal area network (PAN) — The interconnection of personal information technology devices, typically wirelessly, within the range of an individual, usually around 33 feet or 10 meters.

personal computer (PC) — A general-purpose computer designed to accommodate the needs of an individual, such as a desktop, notebook, tablet, or handheld computer.

personal information manager (PIM) — Software that individuals, groups, and organizations can use to store information, such as a list of tasks to complete or a list of names and addresses; a special-purpose database for storing personal information.

personalized or one-to-one marketing — Using cookies (data files placed on the user's computer by a Web server), an e-tailer can maintain a history of customer preferences and highlight products that have proven historically of interest to a customer.

personal video recorder (PVR) — Electronic device, such as TiVo and Replay TV, which provides large hard drive storage to record dozens of movies and programs to be watched at your leisure.

PERT — Program Evaluation and Review Technique, a formalized approach to project management that involves creating three time estimates for an activity: the shortest possible time, the most likely time, and the longest possible time.

pervasive communications — The ability to communicate with anyone, anywhere, anytime, through a variety of formats, resulting from advances in wireless and Internet communications.

pervasive computing — The growing spread of computer devices to the point where everything and anything can be used for input and output.

peta — A prefix that represents 2 to the 50th power (roughly a quadrillion, or a thousand million).

petaflop — Quadrillions of floating-point operations per second, a measurement for rating the speed of microprocessors.

pharming — A criminal act in which hackers hijack a domain name service (DNS) server to automatically redirect users from legitimate Web sites to spoofed Web sites in order to steal personal information.

phase-in approach — A popular start-up technique preferred by many organizations, in which the new system is slowly phased in, while the old one is slowly phased out.

phishing — A scam in which spoofed e-mail and Web sites are used to impersonate an authentic business in an effort to get unsuspecting customers to provide personal and private information.

photo-editing software — Programs with special tools and effects designed for improving or manipulating digital photograph images.

photo printer — Printer, often used in conjunction with digital cameras, that produces photo-quality images on special photo-quality paper.

physical layer — The hardware portion of the three-layer Internet model, which also includes application (software) and transport (protocol) layers.

physical view — A view of data which includes the specific location of the data in storage or memory and the techniques needed to access the data.

pico projector — A tiny LCD projector that can project images from smart phones, designed for ultraportability.

pilot conversion — A start-up approach that involves running a pilot or small version of the new system along with the old.

piracy — The illegal copying, use, and distribution of digital intellectual property such as software, music, and movies.

pixel — Short for picture elements, small points of light or dots of ink that make up digital images.

pixilation — Fuzziness that occurs when bit-mapped images are made larger than the size at which they are captured.

plagiarism — Taking credit for someone else's intellectual property, typically a written idea, by claiming it as your own.

plasma display — A flat panel display that uses plasma gas between two flat panels to excite phosphors and create light.

platform — A computer's type, processor, and operating system. Windows and Apple are the two most popular PC platforms.

plotter — Output device that produces hard copy for general design work, such as blueprints and schematics.

plug-in — An application, such as Adobe Flash, that works with a Web browser to offer extended services, such as the ability to view audio, animations, or video.

podcast — An MP3 audio file that contains a recorded broadcast distributed over the Internet.

podcast aggregator — Software that allows you to subscribe to your favorite podcasts; also called podcast manager.

podcasting — PC-based home recording that is distributed over the Internet.

point of presence (POP) — Utility station that enables Internet users to connect to network service providers, including networking hardware for dial-up connections.

point of sale (POS) device — Terminal or other I/O device connected to a larger system, with scanners that read codes on retail items and enter the item number into a computer system.

port — (1) A logical address used by clients and servers that is associated with a specific service; (2) a socket in a computer used to connect peripherals and other devices like digital cameras and MP3 players.

portable media center — Portable devices that play not only digital music, but also play digital movies and sometimes TV.

port-scanning software — Software that searches random IP addresses for open ports. The software is allowed to run for several hours, after which the attacker can collect a list of IP addresses waiting to be hacked.

Post Office Protocol (POP) — The standard used to transfer e-mails from an e-mail server to a PC.

presentation software — Personal productivity software programs, such as Microsoft PowerPoint, that enable people to create slideshow presentations using built-in features ranging from developing charts and drawings, to formatting text, to inserting movies and sound clips.

primary key — A database field that uniquely identifies a record.

primary storage— Another term for RAM or volatile computer memory.

print server — A server that manages the printing requests for a printer shared by multiple users on a network.

proactive problem-solving approach — An approach to solving problems in which the problem solver seeks out potential problems before they become serious. *Compare to* reactive problem-solving approach.

problem solving — A process that combines the three phases of decision making (intelligence, design, and choice) with implementation and monitoring.

processing — An action a computer takes to convert or transform data into useful outputs; the act of manipulating data in a manner defined by programmed instructions.

processor — *See* microprocessor.

processor number — Designation on Intel processors that represents performance specifications, such as QX6800 for the Intel Core2 Extreme processor.

productivity software — Software designed to help individuals be more productive, such as word processors, spreadsheets, database-management systems, presentation graphics software, and personal information management software.

program code — The set of instructions that signal the CPU to perform circuit-switching operations.

program development life cycle — A five-step sequence of activities for developing and maintaining programming code that includes problem analysis, program design, program implementation, testing and debugging, and maintenance.

program flowchart — Detailed chart that reveals how a software program in a system is to be developed.

program specification — A document, resulting from problem analysis, that defines the requirements of the program in terms of input, processing, and output.

programmed decisions — Decisions that are made using a rule, procedure, or quantitative method.

programming language — The primary tool of software engineers, provides English-like commands for writing software that is translated to the detailed step-by-step instructions executed by the processor.

project crashing — Reducing project development time.

project leader — The individual in charge of the systems development effort, who coordinates all aspects and is responsible for its success.

project management — The planning, monitoring, and controlling of necessary systems development activities.

proprietary — Services or products that are protected by exclusive legal rights and thus, for example, often do not communicate or easily interconnect with each other.

protocols — Rules that ensure that devices participating in a network are communicating in a uniform and manageable manner; an agreed-upon format for transmitting data between two or more devices.

prototyping — An iterative technique for systems development that typically involves the creation of some preliminary model or version of a major subsystem, or a small or "scaled-down" version of the entire system.

proximity payment system — A mobile commerce transaction method using devices that allow customers to transfer funds wirelessly between their mobile device and a point-of-sale terminal.

public domain — Software that is not protected by copyright laws and can be freely copied and used.

purchase over TV — A feature of interactive TV that allows viewers to make purchases over their cable TV connection, much as computer users make purchases on the Web; sometimes called t-commerce.

purchasing system — A type of transaction processing system that supports the purchase of goods and raw materials from suppliers for the manufacturing of products.

quad-core processor — A processor that uses four CPUs on one chip to provide four times the processing speed of a traditional single-core chip.

qubit — A quantum bit. A qubit displays properties in adherence to the laws of quantum mechanics, which differ radically from the laws of classical physics.

query by example (QBE) — An easy and fast way to make queries about data contained in a database; many databases use this approach to give users ideas and examples of how queries can be made.

radio frequency identification (RFID) — A tiny transponder or microprocessor combined with an antenna that is able to broadcast identifying information to an RFID reader, primarily used to track merchandise from supplier to retailer to customer.

radio wave — An electromagnetic wave transmitted through an antenna at different frequencies.

RAID — Redundant array of independent disks, a system of magnetic disks used to maintain a backup copy of the data stored on the primary disks. If the original drives or data become damaged, the secondary disks can take over with little loss of time or work.

random access memory (RAM) — Temporary, or volatile, memory that stores bytes of data and program instructions in addressed cells for the processor to access.

ransomware — A type of Trojan horse malware that holds the user's data files captive until a certain fee is paid or demand is met.

raster graphics — Bit-mapped graphics, in which bytes are used to store the color of each pixel in an image.

ray tracing — Creating computerized 3D models by adding shadows and light, which 3D modeling software does by tracing beams of light as they would interact with the models in the real world.

reactive problem-solving approach — An approach to solving problems in which the problem solver waits until a problem surfaces or becomes apparent before any action is taken. *Compare to* proactive problem-solving approach.

read-only memory (ROM) — Permanent storage for data and instructions that do not change, like programs and data from the computer manufacturer, including the boot process used to start the computer.

record — A collection of related fields that describe some object or activity.

redundant array of independent disks — *See* RAID.

register — One of three primary elements within a central processing unit (CPU), they hold the bytes that are currently being processed.

Registry — A database in Windows operating systems that stores important information on hardware devices, software settings, and user preferences.

relational model — A database model in which all data elements are placed in two-dimensional tables called relations that are the logical equivalent of files.

relations — Two-dimensional tables that are the logical equivalent of files.

relationship — In databases, the ability to connect data in different tables through a common field.

remote resource — Along with local, one of two types of resources that workstations typically have access to: those that the workstation can access only while connected to the network; also called network resources.

rendering — The process of calculating the light interaction with the virtual 3D models in a scene and presenting the final drawing in two dimensions to be viewed on the screen or printed.

repeater — Device that connects multiple network segments; it repeats the signal heard on one segment onto every other connected segment; also boosts weak signals.

repetitive stress injury (RSI) — A potentially computer-related health problem characterized by conditions such as tendinitis, tennis elbow, the inability to hold objects, and sharp pain in the fingers, caused by long hours at the computer keyboard; also known as repetitive motion disorder.

replicated database — A database that holds a duplicate set of frequently used data.

request for information (RFI) — A request directed to a computer systems vendor to provide information about its products or services.

request for proposal (RFP) — A request directed to a computer systems vendor to submit a bid for a new or modified system.

request for quotes (RFQ) — A request directed to a computer systems vendor to give prices for its products or services.

requirements analysis — The process of determining user, stakeholder, and organizational needs.

rescue disk — Software on a floppy disk, CD-ROM, or other disk used to start or boot your computer in case you can't start or boot your computer from your hard disk.

retinal scanning — A form of biometrics that analyzes the pattern of blood vessels at the back of the eye.

rich content — Web content that contains more than just text and simple images, such as video and interactive media.

rich Internet application (RIA) — Software delivered over a Web interface.

rich media — When different digital media types are combined, such as animation or video and audio, Also called multimedia.

ripper software — Programs that can be used to translate music CDs to MP3 files on your hard drive.

ripping — The process of transferring music from CD or DVD to an MP3 or other digital format.

robotics — The development of mechanical or computer devices to perform tasks that require a high degree of precision or that are tedious or hazardous for humans.

router — Special-purpose computing device, typically a small to large box with network ports, that manages network traffic by evaluating messages and routing them to their destination.

RSS — Really Simple Syndication, a Web technology that enables subscribers to receive daily or periodic updates of their favorite blogs. RSS uses XML to deliver Web content that changes on a regular basis.

sampling — Measuring a sound wave's amplitude at regular timed intervals by encoding the sound wave as binary numbers.

satellite radio — A form of digital radio that receives broadcast signals via a communications satellite. Satellite radio services charge a monthly subscription fee and offer stations featuring commercial-free music, comedy, news, talk, and sports programming.

schedule feasibility — The determination of whether a project can be completed in a reasonable amount of time.

scheduled report — Report produced periodically or on a schedule, such as daily, weekly, or monthly.

schema — A description or diagram of the logical and physical structure of the data and relationships among the data in a database; a description of the entire database.

scientific visualization — The use of computer graphics to provide visual representations that improve our understanding of some phenomenon.

search engine — A tool that enables a user to find information on the Web by specifying keywords.

search engine optimization (SEO) — Skill and practice of getting Web pages noticed by search engines.

secondary storage — Nonvolatile devices that are used to store data and programs more permanently than RAM, while the computer is turned off.

Secure Sockets Layer (SSL) — Technology that encrypts data sent over the Web and verifies the identity of the Web server; in combination with digital certificates it allows for encrypted communications between Web browser and Web server. A newer version is called Transport Layer Security (TLS).

security holes — Software bugs that allow violations of information security.

selecting — A basic data manipulation, involving choosing data according to certain criteria.

semantic Web — The seamless integration of traditional databases with the Internet, allowing people to more easily access and manipulate a number of traditional databases at the same time.

sequential access — A storage medium feature that makes a computer that needs to read data from, for example, the middle of a reel of magnetic tape, sequentially pass over all of the tape before reaching the desired piece of data. It is one disadvantage of magnetic tape.

server — A computer system with hardware and software operating over a network or the Internet, and often sharing common resources, such as disks and printers; in a client/server relationship, the program that receives a service request and provides the service.

shareware — Software, usually for personal computers, that is inexpensive and can often be tried before purchase from the software developer.

Short Message Service (SMS) — A method for sending short messages, no longer than 160 characters, between cell phones. Also called text messaging or texting.

signal — The communications element, containing a message composed of data and information, that is transmitted by way of a medium from a sender to a receiver.

simulation — Mimicking or modeling an event or situation that could happen in the future.

single in-line memory module (SIMM) — An older circuit board that holds a group of memory chips, or RAM. Dual in-line memory modules (DIMMs) are more recent.

single-user license — Permits the user to install the software on one computer, or sometimes two computers, used by one person.

site preparation — The process of preparing the actual location so it is ready for a new computer system, which may mean simply rearranging furniture in an office or may require installing special wiring and air conditioning.

slate model tablet PC — PC that does not have a keyboard, but uses a touch-sensitive display on which you can write and draw. *Compare to* convertible model tablet PC.

slide phone — Cell phone with components, typically a keyboard, that slide out of the phone body.

smart cards — Credit cards with embedded microchips, which are playing an increasing role in e-commerce payment methods.

smart home — Technology that allows residents to open and close curtains, turn on sprinkler systems, control media throughout the house, and adjust environmental controls from any Internet-connected computer or wall-mounted display.

smart phone — Handheld device that includes both cell phone and computer capabilities. A smart phone can offer the benefits of several digital devices in one: a PDA, a cell phone, a digital music player, and a portable video player.

social bookmarking — Web sites that provide a way for Web users to store, classify, share, and search Web bookmarks or favorites.

social engineering — A method used by hackers to acquire information such as usernames and passwords that will gain them access to a computer system or database. Social engineering exploits the natural human tendency to trust others to acquire private information.

social journalism — *See* citizen journalists.

social networking — Sites that provide Web-based tools for users to share information about themselves with others on the Web and find, meet, and converse with other members.

soft keyboard — A keyboard implemented via software on a touch-sensitive display.

software — Programs and instructions given to the computer to execute or run; computer programs that control the workings of the computer hardware.

software as a service (SaaS) — A model of software application delivery in which the software resides on the vendor's servers.

software bug — Error in coding or logic that prevent a program from working properly.

software development kit (SDK) — A programming environment designed to facilitate writing software for a particular platform.

software engineer — A software developer, an individual who designs and modifies software; sometimes called a computer programmer.

software engineering — Software development, the process of developing computer programs to address a specific need or problem.

software license — Defines the permissions, rights, and restrictions provided to the person who purchases a copy of the software.

software patch — Correction to software bugs that cause security holes.

software suite — A collection of application software bundled together into one package, often including word processors, spreadsheets, presentation graphics, and more.

Solaris — By Sun Microsystems, the most popular version of the UNIX operating system for industry.

solid-state disk (SSD) — Disk drive that uses flash technology. An SSD drive reads data 300 percent faster and writes data 150 percent faster than traditional magnetic hard drives.

solid-state notebook — A notebook computer with an SSD that contains no moving parts save for an optical drive.

solid-state storage — Device that stores data using transistors; can be volatile (as with RAM), or nonvolatile (as with flash memory).

sound production studios — Facilities that use a wide variety of audio hardware and software to record and produce music and sound recordings.

source code — The high-level program code that a language translator converts into object code.

source data automation — The process of automating the entry of data close to where it is created, thus ensuring accuracy and timeliness.

spear phishing — E-mail that uses private or personal information to target a specific individual in an attempt to perpetrate fraud or identity theft.

special-purpose computers — Computers developed and used for primarily one task or function, such as MP3 players for listening to digital music files.

special-purpose database — A database designed for one purpose or a limited number of applications.

special-purpose I/O device — Input or output device designed for a unique purpose, such as a pill-sized camera that can be swallowed to record images of the digestive system.

speech recognition software — Allows a computer to understand and react to spoken statements and commands.

spider — Automated search program that follows all Web links in an attempt to catalog every Web page by topic; also called a bot or crawler.

spoofing — A technique used to impersonate others on the Internet.

spreadsheet software — Personal productivity software that stores rows and columns of data and is used for making calculations, analyzing data, and generating graphs.

spyware — Software placed on your computer system without your knowledge or consent, normally through the Internet, to secretly spy on you and collect information.

SQL injection — An attack that occurs when a hacker takes control of a database using SQL database commands.

standard — An agreed-upon way of doing something within an industry.

start-up — The next-to-last step in systems implementation, beginning with the final tested computer system and finishing with the fully operational system.

static — When referring to an Internet Protocol (IP) address, one that is permanently assigned to a particular computer. When referring to a Web page, a page whose content does not change.

storage — The ability to maintain data within the system temporarily or permanently.

storage area network (SAN) — A technology that links together many storage devices over a network and treats them as one large disk; helps in recovery from database failure.

storage capacity — The maximum number of bytes a storage medium can hold.

storage device — The drive that reads, writes, and stores data.

storage media — Objects that hold data, such as disks.

storyline — A feature of video-editing software that allows the videographer to arrange video scenes sequentially and specify the transition effects between each scene.

streaming media — An Internet technology that plays audio or video files as they are in the process of being delivered.

structured interview — A data collection technique in which an interviewer relies on questions written in advance.

structured problem — A problem that is routine and where the relationships are well defined.

Structured Query Language (SQL) — A standardized data manipulation language; the standard query language for relational databases.

stylus — A short, penlike device, without ink, used to select items on a touch screen.

subject directory — A catalog of sites collected and organized by human beings, not automated crawlers, such as the directory found at Yahoo.com.

subscription model — A model for software distributions in which, instead of purchasing the software with a one-time fee, you pay an annual fee for as long as you wish to use the software.

supercomputer — The most powerful and advanced type of computer, often used for sophisticated and complex tasks and calculations.

supply chain management (SCM) — The process of producing and selling goods, involving demand planning, supply planning, and demand fulfillment.

supply planning — The supply chain management activity of producing and making logistical arrangements to ensure that a company is able to meet the forecasted demand.

surveillance — The close monitoring of behavior. Computer-controlled surveillance technologies combined with ubiquitous networks and powerful information-processing systems have made it possible to gather huge quantities of video, audio, and communications signals and process them to reveal personal information.

switch — A networking device that makes it possible for many users to send information over a network at the same time; a fundamental part of most networks.

switched line — A line that maintains a network connection only as long as the receiver is active.

swivel phone — A cell phone with components that swivel out from the main body of the phone.

synchronize or **sync** — To update the files shared between two digital devices so that both copies are up-to-date and identical.

synchronous communication — Along with asynchronous, one of two forms of electronic communications, allowing participants to communicate in real time as phrases are transmitted, whether spoken or typed, such as by using telephones, online chat, and instant messaging.

syntax — The set of rules each programming language has that dictates how the symbols should be combined into statements capable of conveying meaningful instructions to the CPU.

syntax error — An error in the form of a program's coding, such as a missing semicolon at the end of a command.

synthesizer — A digital music instrument that electronically produces sounds designed to be similar to real instruments or produces new sounds unlike any that a traditional instrument could produce.

system administrator — Person responsible for setting up and maintaining the network, implementing network policies, and assigning user access permissions; also called network administrator.

system clock — The CPU component that determines the speed at which the processor can carry out an instruction.

system penetration — Unlawful access obtained by hacking into computers and networks.

system requirements — The storage, processor, and memory requirements to run software.

system software — A collection of programs that interact with the computer hardware and application programs.

system stakeholders — The individuals who will ultimately benefit from a systems development project, either directly or through the organization they represent.

system storage — Storage that is used by a computer system for standard operations.

system testing — Testing an entire system of programs together, ensuring that all parts work as expected.

systems analysis — A process that attempts to understand how the existing system helps solve the problem identified in systems investigation and answer the question, "What must the computer system do to solve the problem?"

systems analyst — An IT professional who specializes in analyzing and designing computer systems.

systems design — The selection and planning of a system to meet the requirements outlined during systems analysis, which are needed to deliver a problem solution.

systems development — The activity or process of creating new or modifying existing computer systems.

systems development life cycle (SDLC) — The ongoing activities associated with the systems development process, including investigation, analysis, design, implementation, and maintenance and review.

systems development planning — The translation of organizational or individual goals into systems development initiatives.

systems development specialists — IT personnel who might include a project leader, systems analysts, and software programmers.

systems development tools — Instruments such as computer-aided software engineering tools, flowcharts, and decision tables that can greatly simplify the systems development process.

systems documentation — Written materials that describe the technical aspects of a new or modified system.

systems implementation — A process that includes hardware acquisition, software acquisition or development, user preparation, hiring and training of personnel, site and data preparation, installation, testing, start-up, and user acceptance, according to the systems design.

systems investigation — The first step in the development of a new or modified computer system, the purpose of which is to determine whether the objectives met by the existing system are satisfying the goals of the organization; the activity of exploring potential problems or opportunities in an existing system or situation.

systems maintenance — One of the final systems development steps, involving the checking, changing, and enhancing of the system to make it more useful in achieving user and organizational goals.

systems review — The process of analyzing systems to make sure that they are operating as intended, the final phase of the systems development life cycle.

T1 line — A network line that supports high data transmission rates by carrying 24 signals on one line.

T3 line — Network line that carries 672 signals on one line and is used by telecommunications companies; some act as the Internet's backbone.

table — A collection of related records; also called a file.

tablet PC — A type of small, easy-to-use mobile computer. Tablet PCs come in slate models that have a shape similar to a writing tablet or slate, and convertible models, which can convert from a slate style to a more standard laptop style, and include a keyboard.

tag cloud — A diagram of keyword links with the size of each word representing the number of items that use that tag.

t-commerce — Purchasing items or services over a TV interface.

TCP/IP — Transmission Control Protocol/Internet Protocol, the two primary Internet protocols.

technical feasibility — The determination of whether or not hardware, software, and other system components can be acquired or developed to solve a problem.

technological singularity — A term coined by Ray Kurzweil that refers to the time when computer intelligence exceeds human intelligence.

technology — Tools, materials, and processes that help solve human problems. Many of today's technologies fall under the classification of digital electronics.

telecommunications — The electronic transmission and reception of signals for communications.

telecommunications industry — Businesses that focus on electronic voice and data communications over national and international networks; also known as the telecom industry.

telecommunications network — A network that connects communications and computing devices.

telecommuting — The ability to work away from the office using network connections.

teraflop — Trillions of floating-point operations per second, a measurement for rating the speed of microprocessors.

terminal — Desktop computers with a keyboard and display but little else; used to connect to a mainframe and access data.

testing — Conducting tests on the entire computer system, including each of the individual programs, the entire system of programs, the application with a large amount of data, and all related systems together.

tethering — Sharing a cell phone Internet subscription with a notebook computer.

texting — *See* text messaging.

text messaging — A method of sending short messages, no longer than 160 characters, between cell phones, also called texting or SMS (Short Message Service).

thin client — Stripped-down network PCs, which include a keyboard, mouse, display, and a small system unit that supplies only enough computing power to connect the device to a server over the network.

third-generation (3G) cell phone — A cell phone that offers high-speed Internet access.

thumb drive — Same as USB drive.

time-driven review — A systems review procedure that is started after a specified amount of time.

time sharing — More than one person using a computer system at the same time.

token ring — A network standard using unique hardware and software that does not work with Ethernet.

top-level domain (TLD) — The final portion, such as .com or .edu, of a domain name, classifying Internet locations by type or, in the case of international Web sites, by location.

torrenting — Browsing the Web to find a media file of interest, and then employing a BitTorrent client to download the file.

total information security — The goal of securing all components of the global digital information infrastructure, including cell phones, PCs, business and government networks, Internet routers, and communications satellites.

touch pad — A touch-sensitive input pad below the spacebar on notebook computers that allows you to control the mouse cursor.

touch screen — An input device that allows users to select screen items by touching them on the display with a finger or stylus.

trackball — An input device that allows you to control the mouse pointer by rolling a stationary, mounted ball.

transaction — An exchange involving goods or services, such as buying medical supplies at a hospital or downloading music on the Internet.

transaction file — Temporary file that contains data representing transactions or actions that must be taken.

transaction processing cycle — The common set of activities, including the collection, editing, correction, manipulation, and storage of data, that e-commerce and all other forms of transaction processing systems share.

transaction processing system (TPS) — An information system used to support and record transactions.

transborder data flow — Specific national and international laws regulating the electronic flow of data across international boundaries.

transistor — An electronics component composed of semiconducting material, typically silicon, that opens or closes a circuit to alter the flow of electricity to store and manipulate bits.

Transmission Control Protocol (TCP) — Along with Internet Protocol (IP), one of the sets of policies, procedures, and standards used on the Internet to enable communications between two devices.

transparency — A feature of network management, in which the underlying network structure is hidden from the user, promoting ease of use.

transport layer — The protocol portion of the three-layer Internet model, which also includes application (software) and physical (hardware) layers.

Transport Layer Security (TLS) — A more recent implementation of Secure Sockets Layer (SSL).

Trojan horse — Program that appears to be useful but actually masks a destructive program.

Trustworthy Computing — A long-term Microsoft initiative to provide more reliable, secure, and private computing experiences for their users.

tunneling — A technology used by virtual private networks to securely send private network data over the Internet.

Turing Test — A proposal by British mathematician Alan Turing that says that a computer exhibits "intelligent" behavior if the responses from the computer are indistinguishable from responses from a human.

twisted pair cable — A cable consisting of pairs of insulated twisted copper wires bound together in a sheath; the type of cable that brings telephone service to homes and is used for dial-up modem connections.

ubiquitous computing — A vision of a future so completely saturated with computer technology that we no longer even notice it.

Uniform Resource Locator (URL) — The unique string of characters, such as http://www.course.com, that indicates where a particular Web page resides on the Internet; a Web address.

unit testing — Testing each of the individual programs in the computer system, which is accomplished by developing test data that will force the computer to execute every statement in the program.

Universal Product Code (UPC) — An identification code placed on products that can be read by scanners.

Universal Serial Bus (USB) — A standard that allows a wide array of devices to connect to a computer through a common port.

unstructured database — Database that contains data that is difficult to place in a traditional database system, such as notes, drawings, fingerprints, medical abstracts, or sound recordings.

unstructured interview — A data collection technique in which an interviewer relies on experience, rather than on questions written in advance, to formulate questions designed to uncover the inherent problems and weaknesses of an existing system.

unstructured problem — A problem that is not routine and does not have well-defined rules and relationships.

USB drive — Small flash memory module that plugs into the universal serial bus port found on many computers, digital cameras, and MP3 players. Also called a thumb drive or flash drive.

user — A specific type of stakeholder who will be interacting with the system on a regular basis; people who use computers to their benefit.

user acceptance document — A formal agreement signed by the user approving a phase of the installation or the complete system.

user documentation — Written materials that describe how the computer system can be used by noncomputer personnel.

user-generated content (UGC) — *See* consumer-generated media.

username — A name entered at a computer that identifies a user to the computer system.

user permissions — The access privileges afforded to each network user. Network operating systems such as Windows XP, Apple OS X, Linux, NetWare, and UNIX provide methods for associating user permissions with each user account.

user preparation — The process of readying managers and decision makers, employees, and other users and stakeholders for new or modified systems.

utility program — System software that is used to perform important routine tasks, such as to merge and sort sets of data or to keep track of computer jobs being run.

value-added network (VAN) — A private communications network used in electronic data interchange (EDI) to transmit standardized transaction data between business partners and suppliers.

value-added software vendor — A third-party software firm that develops or modifies a software program to meet the needs of a particular industry or company.

vector graphics — A representational method that uses bytes to store geometric formulas that define all the shapes in an image.

vector graphics software — Programs that provide tools to create, arrange, and layer graphical objects on the screen to create pictures; also called drawing software.

vendor — A company that provides computer hardware, equipment, supplies, and a variety of services.

video card — *See* graphics card.

video conferencing — Technology that combines video and phone call capabilities along with shared data and document access.

video-editing software — Programs that allow professional and amateur videographers to edit bad footage out of digital video and rearrange the good footage to produce a professional video production.

video game consoles — High-powered multiprocessor computers designed to support 3D interactive multimedia.

video games over TV — A feature of interactive TV that provides access to video games.

video on demand (VoD) — Technology that allows digital cable customers to select from hundreds of movies and programs to watch at anytime they choose.

video RAM (VRAM) — A buffer, sometimes referred to as a frame buffer, that stores image data after they are read from RAM and before they are written to the display.

virtual chat — Synchronous text messaging between two or more participants in a virtual environment using avatars.

virtual machine (VM) software — *See* virtualization software.

virtual memory — Also known as virtual storage, an operating system feature that allows users to store and retrieve more data without physically increasing the actual storage capacity of memory.

virtual private network (VPN) — A network technology that uses a technique called tunneling to securely send private network data over the Internet.

virtual reality — A computer-simulated environment or event that can be manipulated by a user.

virtual reality headset — A gogglelike device, with spatial sensors as input devices, that projects output in the form of three-dimensional color images.

virtual space — An environment that exists in the mind rather than in physical space.

virtual server — Running multiple server operating systems on one physical server, thereby creating savings for companies and for the environment.

virtual storage — Also known as virtual memory, an operating system feature that allows users to store and retrieve more data without physically increasing the actual storage capacity of memory.

virtualization software — Allows one operating system to run on top of another by creating a virtual machine on which the guest operating system can run; also called virtual machine (VM) software.

virtualized database — *See* distributed database.

virus — A program that attaches itself to a file, spreads to other files, and delivers a destructive action called a *payload.*

virus hoax — E-mail sent to people warning them of a virus that doesn't actually exist.

virus-scanning software — Programs that detect viruses and worms on a personal computer.

Visual Basic — By Microsoft, one of the first visual programming interfaces.

visual programming — A method of software development that uses a graphical or visual interface for programming, combined with text-based commands.

visual programming languages — Programming languages that use a graphical or visual interface, allowing programmers to "drag and drop" programming objects onto the computer screen.

vlog — Video log; similar to a blog, but using video, covering topics such as travel, current events, jobs, and technology.

Voice over Internet Protocol (VoIP) — A popular technology that allows phone conversations to travel over the Internet or other data networks.

voice recognition — A technology, similar to speech recognition, used by security systems to allow only authorized personnel into restricted areas.

volatile — A characteristic of primary memory storage, such that a loss of power to the computer means that the contents of memory is also lost or eliminated; temporary memory storage that is cleared each time the computer is shut down.

volatility — A database characteristic, referring to a measure of the changes, such as additions, deletions, or modifications, typically required in a given period of time.

volume testing — Testing an application with a large amount of data, to ensure that the entire system can handle it under normal operating conditions.

war driving — The act of driving through neighborhoods with a wireless notebook or handheld computer looking for unsecured Wi-Fi networks.

wearable PC — Small system units that can clip to a belt or fit in a pack, head-mounted displays that only partially obscure vision, and hands-free or one-handed input devices. They are used in industry for individuals who need to have access to data while doing physical work.

Web — Short for World Wide Web, an application that makes use of the Internet to deliver information and services through a convenient interface utilizing hyperlinks.

Web 2.0 — Web resources that allow average users to collaborate and contribute to Web content.

Web 3.0 — The next paradigm shift in Internet and Web use; likely to involve a combination of technologies that will make "anywhere, anytime" information access effortless.

Web analytics — Web server utility programs that provide statistical information about server usage and Web site traffic patterns.

Web auctions — E-commerce sites that provide a virtual auction block where users can place bids on items.

Web authoring software — Software that allows users to create HTML documents using word-processor-like programs.

Web browser — Web client software such as Internet Explorer and Firefox, that is used to request Web pages from Web servers.

Web-based operating system (WebOS) — Type of operating system currently being developed in which the operating system, software, and data files all reside on a Web server.

Webcam — Typically, a low-priced video camera, often used for video conferencing over the Internet.

Webcast — A means of providing television-style delivery of information over the Web; a videoclip of a news event or other event.

Web conferencing — Online video conferencing, allowing groups to see, hear, text chat, present, and share information in a collaborative manner.

Web-driven programs — Programs that allow users to interact with Web sites to access useful information and services.

Web log — *See* blog.

Web portals — Web pages that serve as entry points to the Web.

Web script — Small programs that run on Web pages. One avenue for the spread of viruses and worms.

Web server — Server that stores and delivers Web pages and other Web services such as interactive Web content.

Web server software — Software whose primary purpose is to respond to requests for Web pages from browsers.

Web server utility programs — Software programs that provide statistical information about server usage and Web site traffic patterns.

Web service — A software system that automates tasks by controlling communication between computers over the Internet.

what-if analysis — The process of making hypothetical changes to problem data and observing the impact on the results.

wide area network (WAN) — A network connecting local area networks between cities, cross country, and around the world using microwave and satellite transmission or telephone lines.

Wi-Fi — Short for wireless fidelity, a popular networking technology based on the IEEE 802.11 standards that connects computers wirelessly to other computers and to computer networks.

Wi-Fi Protected Access (WPA) — The most secure wireless encryption protocol available at present (WPA2), more secure than Wired Equivalent Privacy (WEP).

Wi-Fi radio — Mobile or home stereo device that accesses music and radio programs from the Internet, with or without connection to a PC.

wiki — Web site designed to allow users to add, remove, and edit content.

WiMAX — Also known as IEEE 802.16, the next-generation wireless broadband technology that is both faster and has a longer range than Wi-Fi. WiMAX is built on Wi-Fi standards and is able to interoperate with Wi-Fi networks. A WiMAX access point has a 31-mile (50-kilometer) range.

Windows cleaners — Utility software that scans the Windows Registry, correcting incorrect or obsolete information.

Wired Equivalent Privacy (WEP) — An early wireless encryption protocol, less secure than Wi-Fi Protected Access (WPA).

wireless access point — A site that is connected to a wired network and receives data from and transmits data to wireless adapters installed in computers.

wireless adapter — A circuit board, PC card, or an external USB device that provides an external antenna to send and receive network radio signals.

wireless fidelity (Wi-Fi) — Wireless networking technology that makes use of access points to wirelessly connect users to networks within a range of 120–600 feet (32–190 meters). The Wi-Fi standards, also known as the 802.11 family of standards, were developed by the Institute of Electrical and Electronics Engineers (IEEE).

wireless mesh network — Network technology that allows wireless routers to pass data over the network. Wireless mesh technology saves a city from having to run cable to each of its access points.

wireless networking — Uses radio signals or infrared rather than cables to connect computers and digital devices to computer networks and through those networks to the Internet.

WLAN — Wireless local area network, usually based on the IEEE 802.11 standards.

wordlength — The number of bits that a CPU can process at one time; the larger the wordlength, the more powerful the computer.

word-processing software — Text and document manipulation software, such as Microsoft Word, that is perhaps the most highly used application software for individuals.

workstation — A powerful desktop computer used to make sophisticated calculations or graphic manipulations; a personal computer attached to a network.

work stressors — Hazardous activities associated with unfavorable work conditions, such as hard-to-read computer screens, uncomfortable desks and chairs, and fixed keyboards, possibly leading to serious and long-term injuries.

world ownership — Files, folders, or other resources on a network that are available to all users.

World Wide Web — Also known as the Web, a client/server Internet application that links together related documents from diverse sources providing an easy navigation system with which to find information; an Internet-access application that uses a graphical interface to ease Internet navigation.

worm — A program that, rather than attaching itself to another program, acts as a free agent, placing copies of itself into other systems, destroying programs, and interrupting the operation of networks and computer systems.

WYSIWYG — Pronounced wizzie-wig, and short for "what you see is what you get." It is a feature of Web-site editing programs, such as Dreamweaver, that allows users to design Web pages that will look the same when published on the Web.

XHTML — A successor to Hypertext Markup Language that embodies the best of HTML and XML in one markup language.

XML — Extensible Markup Language, a markup language that provides a method for describing and classifying the content of data on a Web page, unlike HTML, which only describes the format.

zombie computer — Computer on the Internet that is either hacked into directly or under the influence of a virus or worm, and made to carry out Internet activities on the hacker's behalf. *See* botnet.

Subject Index

Note: **Boldfaced** page numbers indicate key term definitions.

B

E

G

P

Q

R

S

T

U

V

W

X

Y

Z

Career Index

Photo Credits

Chapter 1

Figure 1.1: Image copyright 2009, EdBockStock. Used under license from Shutterstock.com
Figure 1.2: AP Photo/CP, Chuck Stoody
Figure 1.4: Courtesy of Dell Inc.
Figure 1.5: © Ethan Miller/Getty Images
Figure 1.6: © XenLights/Alamy
Figure 1.7: AP Photo/Paul Sakuma
Figure 1.8a: AP Photo/Jae C. Hong
Figure 1.8b: AP Photo/Dan Steinberg
Figure 1.8c: Cathal McNaughton/PA Wire
Figure 1.9: Courtesy of Sun Microsystems, Inc.
Figure 1.10: Los Alamos National Laboratory
Figure 1.11: Courtesy of Amazon.com
Figure 1.12: Courtesy of Brookhaven National Laboratory
Figure 1.13: © Jupiterimages
Figure 1.16: © Steven Hunt/Getty Images
Figure 1.17: © Bananastock/Superstock
Figure 1.18: © CostinT/iStockphoto.com
Figure 1.19: Courtesy of Visual & Broadcast Communications Virginia Tech
Figure 1.20: Linnea Mullins/Sonoma State University
Figure 1.25: Courtesy of NASA
Figure 1.26: Courtesy ofIntel Corporation
Figure 1.27a,b,c: © Ryan McVay/Getty Images; Kim Steele/Getty Images; © Daniel Allen/Getty Images
Figure 1.28: NASA
Figure 1.29: © David Sailors/Corbis
Figure 1.30: Courtesy of Adobe Systems, Inc.
Figure 1.31: Courtesy of U.S. Census Bureau
Figure 1.32: © Reza Estakhrian/Getty Images
Figure 1.33: © Thinkstock/Getty Images
Figure 1.35: Courtesy of The Knot, Inc.
Figure 1.36: Courtesy of EHARMONY.COM, Inc.
Figure 1.38: © Marc Romanelli/Getty Images
Figure 1.39: © Pal Pillai/AFP/Getty Images

Chapter 2

Figure 2.1a,b,c: © Zsolt Nyulaszi/iStockphoto; © Leigh Schindler/iStockphoto; © Pamela Moore/iStockphoto
Figure 2.3a,b,c: © Travelpix Ltd/Getty Images; Courtesy of Apple; Courtesy of Hewlett-Packard Company
Figure 2.4: Courtesy of HTC Corporation
Figure 2.5: Courtesy of Dr. Nourine Hadjikhani
Figure 2.6: Courtesy of Microsoft Corporation
Figure 2.8: Courtesy of Intel Corporation
Figure 2.9: Courtesy of Intel Corporation
Figure 2.12: AP Photo/MTI/Imre Foeldi
Figure 2.13: Courtesy of NASA
Figure 2.14: Courtesy of Intel Corporation
Figure 2.15: © Eduard Andras/iStockphoto
Figure 2.17: Courtesy of AMD
Figure 2.18: Courtesy of National Energy Research Scientific Computing Center
Figure 2.19: © frenchmen77/iStockphoto.com
Figure 2.2: Courtesy of Toshiba
Figure 2.21: Courtesy of IBM Corporation
Figure 2.23: AP Photo/Paul Sakuma
Figure 2.24: Courtesy of SanDiskCorporation
Figure 2.25: Courtesy of Iomega
Figure 2.26: Courtesy of Sony Electronics, Inc.
Figure 2.27: Courtesy of Motorola
Figure 2.28: Courtesy of Microsoft Corporation
Figure 2.29: Courtesy of Wacom Technology Corp.
Figure 2.30: REUTERS/Mike Segar/Landov
Figure 2.31: Reuters/Landov
Figure 2.32: Courtesy of NEC Display Solutions
Figure 2.33: Courtesy of Plastic Logic Limited
Figure 2.34: Courtesy of Microvision, Inc.
Figure 2.35: Courtesy of Hewlett-Packard Company
Figure 2.36: Image taken in the Visual Computing Lab of ISTI-CNR, Pisa, Italy by ALoopingIcon
Figure 2.37: Courtesy of WetPC Pty Ltd.
Figure 2.38 a&b: © Lee Pettet/iStockphoto.com; © Daniel Gale/iStockphoto.com
Figure 2.39: Image copyright 2009, Olga Lipatova. Used under license from Shutterstock.com
Figure 2.40: Courtesy of Motorola

Chapter 3

Figure 3.4: Courtesy of Microsoft Corporation
Figure 3.10: © Tony Freeman/PhotoEdit
Figure 3.22: Courtesy of Microsoft Corporation
Figure 3.24: Courtesy of Microsoft Corporation
Figure 3.25: Courtesy of Apple
Figure 3.27: Courtesy of Fermilab Visual Media Services
Figure 3.29: Courtesy of NASA
Figure 3.4: Courtesy of Microsoft Corporation
Figure 3.41: Courtesy of Adobe Systems Inc.
Figure 3.42: AP Photo/George Widman
Figure 3.42-b: Screens from the TopCat catalogue management system, courtesy of Catalogue Solutions Ltd.
Figure 3.43: © Marc Romanelli/Getty Images

Figure 3.44: © Rick Friedman/Corbis
Figure 3.45: © 20th Century Fox/Courtesy Everett Collection
Figure 3.46: © John Allison/Peter Arnold Inc.
Figure 3.49: AP Photo/Neil Brake
Figure 3.51: Courtesy of WowWee Group Limited
Figure 3.52: Courtesy of AlanTuring.net; Courtesy of Paul Thompson, Professor of Neurology Lab of Neuro Imaging UCLA School of Medicine
Figure 3.55: AP Photo/Shizuo Kambayashi
Figure 3.56: © Peter Dazeley/Getty Images
Figure 3.57: Courtesy of Aurora Computer Services Ltd
Figure 3.59: Courtesy of Kurzweil CyberArt Technologies, Inc.
Figure 3.60: © Floris Leeuwenberg/The Cover Story/Corbis

Chapter 4
Figure 4.1: © Phlippe Galvez, Caltech VRVS Project at www.vrvs.org
Figure 4.2: Courtesy of Stephen G. Eick, SSS Research Inc.
Figure 4.3: Courtesy of William Decker/University of California San Diego
Figure 4.4: © Andreas Pollok/Getty Images
Figure 4.6: Courtesy of Damon Hart-Davis/DHD Multimedia Gallery (http://gallery.hd.org/)
Figure 4.12: AP Photo/Palm Inc., Achille Bigliardi/ho
Figure 4.17: Courtesy of Adobe Systems, Inc.
Figure 4.19: no credit
Figure 4.20: Courtesy of Mini USA
Figure 4.22: Courtesy of Microsoft Corporation
Figure 4.29: Courtesy of Google
Figure 4.30: Copyright 2007, Linden Research, Inc. All Rights Reserved.
Figure 4.32: Luca Cremonini Source: http://www.railsonwave.it/railsonwave/2007/1/2/web-2-0-map
Figure 4.36: Courtesy of Skype Limited
Figure 4.47: Courtesy of National LambdaRail
Figure 4.48: Courtesy of Gemini Observatory
Figure 4.50: Courtesy of Professor Babak Parviz/University of Washington

Chapter 5
Figure 5.1: © Powerstock/Superstock
Figure 5.5: Courtesy of TMS – TECHNOMED MEDICAL SYSTEMS TMS S.A.
Figure 5.6: © Phil Degginger/Getty Images
Figure 5.9: Courtesy of Linksys by Cisco
Figure 5.11: © Hoby Finn/Getty Images
Figure 5.12: © Max Dannenbaum/Getty Images
Figure 5.15: AP Photo/Eric Risberg; Courtesy of Nokia
Figure 5.18: Courtesy of Jabra
Figure 5.19: Courtesy of Telenav
Figure 5.20: Courtesy of Google
Figure 5.22: Courtesy of Vocera
Figure 5.23: Baden Copeland/The New York Times/Redux; Photo courtesy of Motorola © 2009
Figure 5.24: Courtesy of Intel Corporation
Figure 5.25: Courtesy of Toyota
Figure 5.26: © Jon Riley/Getty Images
Figure 5.27: Courtesy of MasterCard Worldwide
Figure 5.28: Courtesy of ViVOtech
Figure 5.29: Courtesy of NASA
Figure 5.30: Courtesy of Hewlett-Packard Company; Courtesy of Fujitsu-Siemens Computers
Figure 5.31a&b: Created by Sam Johnston using OminGroup's OmniGraffle and Inkscape
Figure 5.32: © Bill Grove/iStockphoto
Figure 5.34: Credit Provided by the SeaWiFS Project, NASA/Goddard Space Flight Center, and ORBIMAGE
Figure 5.35: Courtesy of UPS
Figure 5.37: Courtesy of Cisco Systems, Inc.

Chapter 6
Figure 6.1a, b, c: a. © Smith Collection/Getty Images; b. © imagebroker/Alamy; c. © Blend Images/Alamy
Figure 6.3: © Jeff Greenberg/Alamy
Figure 6.4: Courtesy of Creative Forensic Services
Figure 6.5: © Plush Studios/Getty Images
Figure 6.6: Yamaha Motif 6 ES Music Production Synthesizer Workstation courtesy of Yamaha Corporation of America
Figure 6.9: Courtesy of Leo Laporte
Figure 6.11: Courtesy of Alpine Electronics of America, Inc.
Figure 6.12a: Courtesy of Creative Technology Ltd.
Figure 6.13: Courtesy of Apple
Figure 6.14: Courtesy of LG Electronics Inc.
Figure 6.17: Courtesy of Delphi Corporation
Figure 6.21: Courtesy of Mindjet
Figure 6.22: Reprinted with permission of Quark, Inc., and its affiliates.
Figure 6.23: © Sharl Heller/Resonance Fine Art
Figure 6.24: Courtesy of IMSI/Design LLC
Figure 6.26: © Liam Kemp
Figure 6.28: © Walt Disney Co./courtesy Everett Collection
Figure 6.29: Courtesy of Adobe Systems, Inc.
Figure 6.31a,b,c: Courtesy of Hewlett-Packard Company; Courtesy of Sony Electronics, Inc.; Courtesy of Nikon Inc., Melville New York
Figure 6.34: Courtesy of AEC – Michael Bloomenfeld
Figure 6.35: © KAZUHIRO NOGI/AFP/Getty Images
Figure 6.38: © David Hancock/Alamy
Figure 6.39: Courtesy of Sling Media, Inc.
Figure 6.40: Courtesy of Electronic Arts, Inc.
Figure 6.41: Microsoft product screen shot(s) reprinted with permission from Microsoft Corporation
Figure 6.43: Courtesy of Nintendo Corporation
Figure 6.44: © Kevork Djansezian/Getty Images

Chapter 7
Figure 7.2: AP Photo/Bob Child
Figure 7.16: Courtesy of Microsoft Corporation
Figure 7.19: © iStockphoto
Figure 7.20: AP Photo/Dennis Cook
Figure 7.24: Courtesy of Intellifit
Figure 7.25: Courtesy of Hilton Hospitality, Inc.
Figure 7.29: Courtesy of Business Objects SA
Figure 7.30: AP Photo/Denis Poroy

Chapter 8
Figure 8.1: Courtesy of Club Penguin
Figure 8.12: © Frank Siteman/Getty Images
Figure 8.20: Courtesy of Electronic Arts
Figure 8.21: Courtesy of Ameritrade, Inc.
Figure 8.23: © PT Images/Getty Images
Figure 8.26: AP Photo/Scott Sady
Figure 8.28: Will Scully-Power, Managing Director – Datarati – http://willscullypower.files.wordpress.com/2008/10/google-analytics-dashboard1.jpg

Chapter 9
Figure 9.1: © PhotoAlto/Superstock
Figure 9.3: AP Photo/Bebeto Matthews
Figure 9.4a & b: © Alistair Berg/Getty Images; © Creatas Images/Jupiter Images
Figure 9.5: © Andy Caulfield/Getty Images

Figure 9.12: Courtesy of ePocrates, Inc.
Figure 9.13: © Mario Tama/Getty Images
Figure 9.14: AP Photo/Kevork Djansezian
Figure 9.15: AP Photo/The Oklahoman, Paul B. Southerland
Figure 9.17: Courtesy of Touchstone Consulting Group, Inc.
Figure 9.20: Courtesy of Google

Chapter 10
Figure 10.2: : Courtesy of Duncan Stevenson at CSIRO.AU
Figure 10.5: : Courtesy of Adobe Systems, Inc.
Figure 10.6: : Courtesy of Pacestar Software
Figure 10.11: SHERWIN CRASTO/ Reuters/Landov
Figure 10.15: © Steve Chenn/Corbis
Figure 10.18: Courtesy of NASA
Figure 10.19: © ColorBlind Images/ Getty Images
Figure 10.20: © Dennis MacDonald/ Alamy
Figure 10.21: © Getty Images
Figure 10.22: © Thinkstock/ Superstock

Chapter 11
Figure 11.1: Courtesy of McAfee
Figure 11.2: Courtesy of Jason Scragz
Figure 11.6: © Jose Luis Pelaez/Getty Images
Figure 11.7: National Operations Center, DHS Photo/Bahler
Figure 11.8: Vincent Kessler/Reuters /Landov
Figure 11.9: © Justin Sullivan/Getty Images
Figure 11.10: © Stephan Zabel/ iStockphoto.com
Figure 11.11: © Robyn Beck/AFP/Getty Images
Figure 11.12: Turnitin is a service of iParadigms, LLC.
Figure 11.14: Courtesy of International Barcode; Eric Miller/Getty Images
Figure 11.16: Courtesy of CS Technologies
Figure 11.17: © Jan-Peter Kasper/epa/ Corbis
Figure 11.18: Courtesy of Transcend Information, Inc.
Figure 11.20: Courtesy of Apple
Figure 11.23: Courtesy of PC Tools
Figure 11.24: © Yellow Dog Productions/Getty Images
Figure 11.27: © Blend Images/Alamy
Figure 11.28: © Getty Images
Figure 11.29: © Kenny@Hektik.org
Figure 11.31: Image copyright 2009, Oleg Yarko. Used under license from Shutterstock.com
Figure 11.33: © Getty Images
Figure 11.34: Courtesy of McAfee

Chapter 12
Figure 12.1a: © Anthony Redpath/ CORBIS
Figure 12.1b: © Gabe Palmer/Alamy
Figure 12.2: Courtesy of Hewlett-Packard Company
Figure 12.3: © Jeff Moore/Maxppp/ Landov
Figure 12.4: AP Photo/Bernadette Tuazon
Figure 12.5: © image100/Alamy
Figure 12.7: Copyright 2009 Times Newspapers Ltd.
Figure 12.8: © 2009 Basel Action Network (BAN).
Figure 12.9: Donna Svennevik/ © ABC/Courtesy: Everett Collection
Figure 12.11: Reuters/Landov
Figure 12.12: Courtesy of ContentWatch, Inc.
Figure 12.13: Courtesy of RG Networks
Figure 12.14: © Erik S. Lesser/Getty Images
Figure 12.16: © Columbia/The Kobal Collection
Figure 12.17: © Joseph Khakshouri/ Corbis
Figure 12.18: © Tim Boyle/Getty Images
Figure 12.19: © Digital Globe/ GettyImages
Figure 12.20: © Don Farrall/Getty Images
Figure 12.21: © AFP/Getty Images
Figure 12.22: AP Photo/David Zalubowski
Figure 12.23: © AFP/Getty Images
Figure 12.24: Courtesy of Samsung Telecommunications America and Jitterbug
Figure 12.25: © Dave G. Houser/ PostHouserstock/Corbis
Figure 12.26: © AFP/Getty Images
Figure 12.27: AP Photo/Gautam Singh
Figure 12.28: AP Photo/Richard Vogel
Figure 12.29: The Council of the European Union
Figure 12.30: Courtesy of General Electric
Figure 12.31: AP Photo/Carolyn Kaster
Figure 12.32: © Index Open